BARRON'S

HOW TO PREPARE FOR THE

SSAT/ ISEE

SECONDARY SCHOOL ADMISSIONS TEST/ INDEPENDENT SCHOOL ENTRANCE EXAM

9TH EDITION

Jerome Shostak
Former District Supervisor of Guidance
New York City Schools

Max Peters
Former Chairman, Mathematics Department
George W. Wingate High School, New York

All inquiries should be addressed to:
Barron's Educational Series, Inc.
250 Wireless Boulevard
Hauppauge, New York 11788
www.barronseduc.com

Library of Congress Catalog No. 2001025762

International Standard Book No. 0-7641-1380-1

Library of Congress Cataloging-in-Publication Data

Peters, Max, 1906-
How to prepare for the SSAT, ISEE high school entrance examinations / by Max Peters, Jerome Shostak.—9th ed.
p. cm.
ISBN 0-7641-1380-1
1. Secondary School Admission Test—Study guides—Juvenile literature. 2. Independent School Entrance Examination—Study guides—Juvenile literature. 3. High schools—United States—Entrance examinations—Study guides—Juvenile literature. [1. High schools—Entrance examinations—Study guides.] I. Shostak, Jerome. II. Title.

LB3060.24.P47 2001
373.126'2—dc 21

2001025762

PRINTED IN THE UNITED STATES OF AMERICA
9

Contents

DIGEST OF COMMUNICATION SKILLS 87

DIGEST OF MATHEMATICAL SKILLS 331

Test-Taking Tips

1. The best preparation for any test such as these is to have studied well in your classes at school, but even the best of students need to brush up on some things. Memory fades and skills diminish over time. This book is designed to give you ample opportunity to review and practice the skills needed to do well on these tests. You should allow yourself adequate time to make full use of this book—at least a month. Establish a schedule so that you will spend some time each day on the material in this book but not feel hurried or panicky.

2. Be well rested on test day. Get a good night's sleep, and eat a good breakfast; do not stray too far from your regular schedule. Try not to let other things intrude on your concentration. Don't plan on any other activities following the test. You will probably want to rest.

3. Be sure you understand what materials you may have with you during the test. Take advantage of every opportunity given to you, but do no more than what is permitted. An adequate supply of pencils of the appropriate type, an eraser, and your wits are the minimum to have with you.

4. Follow the directions of the people giving the test. Be sure you understand the bathroom rules. Plan to use the full time allotted.

5. All answers must be recorded accurately and clearly on the answer sheet. Be sure that you fill in the circle for each answer fully and darkly. If you temporarily skip a question, be doubly sure that later answers are recorded in the correct space. Don't make any stray marks or notes on the Answer Sheet; the scoring machine may read them as answers.

6. Do not spend too much time on any one question. Skip questions that you know will take you a long time to do; come back to them later.

7. In some math questions it might be more time-efficient to plug in possible answers to determine the correct response. Usually, performing the indicated operations is more efficient, but if the math is too difficult, you can eliminate some answers as being impossible and plug in the others until you find one that works.

8. DO NOT leave any answer blank. The machine that scores your test does not know whether you guessed or not. If at the end of the test, you find some questions that you just cannot answer, try to eliminate some responses as being impossible or unlikely, and GUESS. Keep an eye on the clock toward the end of the test, and use the last few minutes to be sure that every question has a response.

9. When time is called, stop immediately, and follow the directions given for handing in the test.

10. Celebrate having done the very best you can do.

Test Taker's Checklist on the Day of the Test

1. Check and recheck the date, time, and place of the exam. Avoid last-minute haste and anxiety.

2. Plan to arrive at the test center between 8:30 and 8:45 a.m. You will not be admitted if you arrive after the test has begun.

3. When you choose your clothing, remember that the temperature in the test room may be lower or higher than you are accustomed to working in. Be sure to dress accordingly. Layers of clothing, which can be retained or removed as needed, will enable you to adjust to the room temperature.

4. Be sure to have with you

   ___ your admission ticket or other authorization to take the test

   ___ 3 or 4 soft-leaded pencils (equivalent of U.S. No. 2)

   ___ a good eraser

   ___ a working pen if required

5. Do not plan to take any books, papers, notes, calculators, calculator watches, snacks, or beverages into the test room.

6. Before you start to answer any questions, clear your head. Don't clutter your mind with unrelated thoughts. You can cross only one bridge at a time!

7. Pace yourself. Work without haste, but as rapidly as you can without sacrificing accuracy.

8. Bear in mind that you don't have to answer every question. Many test takers leave some questions unanswered.

What You Need to Know About High School Entrance Examinations

The majority of students entering junior or senior high school are not required to take entrance examinations, because they will be attending general public high schools. However, each year thousands of students—and the numbers increase every year—are asked to take comprehensive entrance examinations when they apply to private secondary schools, to secondary schools affiliated with various religious faiths, and to specialized public junior and senior high schools (such as Hunter College High School and the science high schools of New York City). Examinations for admission to these schools are becoming as rigorous at their level as the college entrance examinations are at the college level.

Which High School Entrance Examination Should I Take?

The high school applied to, not the candidate or his or her parents, determines which local or nationwide examination is to be part of the candidate's admission record. After consultation with the principal or guidance counselor in the school now being attended, the student and parents usually begin the process by sending requests for applications for admission to the schools selected. Letter forms and school addresses can be supplied by the guidance office.

When the high school being applied to sends the forms to be filled out and the list of its application requirements, it may include a bulletin of information and an application for the specific examination required, or it will tell the candidate how to obtain this material. It is the student's responsibility to send the applications and fees to the proper testing authorities. The student must also advise the testing company of the schools that should receive test scores. Here, too, the school counselor can be of assistance in explaining procedures.

How Are Successful Candidates Selected?

Most counselors and admission officers review a number of criteria in evaluating the appropriateness of their school for a student. Among the factors likely to be considered are the following:

- curriculum followed
- grades
- teachers' recommendations
- personal recommendations
- extracurricular activities
- standardized test results
- writing sample
- interview

Most of these items give a picture of the candidate in relation to the other students currently attending the school. Only the standard test results—and the entrance examination scores are included among these—compare the student's record with the records of all the other candidates for admission. Entrance examination results, therefore, can play an important part in the selection process.

An Overview of the Most Popular Tests

GROUP ONE: STANDARDIZED TESTS

The tests in this group take, with time-outs included, approximately $2^1/_2$–4 hours to administer. The basic areas that they all cover are reading comprehension, computational skills, other mathematical skills, and vocabulary. Many also include the language arts (grammar, usage, sentence sense, etc.). A few tests require the writing of an essay; otherwise, the questions are of the multiple-choice variety.

The scores on these tests as they are sent to the schools and to the candidates do not represent the number of questions answered correctly. Rather, the results are given in the form of a ranking. In other words, the results indicate how the present candidates compare with all of the other students who have taken any form of the same test. A significant aspect of this type of scoring is that a school can compare the scores of present candidates with those of all of the students who have been successful or unsuccessful in that school. From the scores, the school can judge what a particular student's chances of success will be if he or she is admitted.

Of course, admissions officers rarely rely on only one aspect of the admissions process. The final decision is usually based on a weighting of all of the components of the student's school record: curriculum, grades, extracurricular activities, and teachers' recommendations. However, you can readily see how important standardized test results can be in a school's final decision about admitting a particular candidate.

Secondary School Admission Test (SSAT)

The SSAT, administered by the Educational Testing Bureau, has been used since 1957 by nonpublic schools to aid in the selection of students. Today more than 500 schools rely upon this five-part test to help them choose the best candidates from among the nearly 30,000 students who take the test annually.

Although the SSAT can be taken during any month, most candidates take the test in a local school test center on one of seven Saturday administrations planned during the school year. Special arrangements can be made to accommodate Sabbath observers, students living abroad, and, in special cases, walk-in applicants.

The SSAT has four sections, plus an experimental section, and all questions are multiple choice. Since each part has a 25-minute time limit, the test booklet scrambles the units. One candidate may be answering math questions while the person sitting in front or beside her is doing the verbal ability section.

The SSAT has two additional unusual aspects:

1. A right answer is given one credit. For each wrong answer $^1/_4$ point is subtracted from the total in order to discourage wild guessing.

2. The results on only four of the sections are included in the rating. The other section is considered as experimental. Since, however, the candidates do not know which is the experimental section, they have to do their best on all five!

Independent School Entrance Examination (ISEE)

The ISEE is a relatively new entrant into the field. The Educational Records Bureau (ERB) administers the test, which was developed for the ERB by the Educational Testing Bureau.

The ISEE has become the test of choice for the member schools of the Independent Schools Association of New York City. Many other schools now accept ISEE scores as an alternative to SSAT scores. If you are applying to a school that accepts either the ISEE or the SSAT, you and your parents should consult with your present guidance counselor or principal to find out which examination you should take. If you still find yourself in doubt, take the practice examinations in this book to find out which test will show your abilities to better advantage.

The ISEE consists of four multiple-choice sections and an essay section. The essay is sent unmarked, along with your score on the rest of the test, to the schools of your choice. The essay enables the admissions officers to make a comparative evaluation of your theme-writing ability and general language mastery.

Cooperative (COOP) Admissions Examination

The Cooperative Admissions Examination is available only to eighth graders applying for admission to specific Catholic high schools in New York City, Buffalo, and parts of Westchester, Nassau, and Suffolk counties. Candidates may take the examination, which is given on a designated day in November, once and once only. Students may send their test results to three high schools.

In order to evaluate both academic potential and achievement, the Coop test contains ten units. The items measuring potential resemble those found on IQ tests. The achievement items range from mathematical problems and conventional reading comprehension, spelling, and vocabulary questions to units on grammatical terms.

The companion book to this one—*Barron's How to Prepare for Catholic High School Entrance Examinations: COOP/HSPT*—contains a fuller discussion of the COOP test, as well as a diagnostic and two practice tests following the format of the actual test.

High School Placement Test (HSPT)

The HSPT, administered by the Scholastic Testing Service, is one of the most widely used high school tests; it is given in approximately 50% of Catholic high schools in various regions of the country. Used nationwide for both admission and placement, it is scored separately for cognitive skills (potential) and achievement in basic skills.

This test has a flexible schedule. It is administered at times set by the individual school, school district, or diocese.

The cognitive skills questions tend to resemble those found in IQ tests, while the achievement questions are in the traditional format.

The school may also administer three optional test sections: Science, Mechanical Aptitude, and Catholic Religion. The results on these sections are not included in the standardized score used for admission and placement.

The companion book to this one—*Barron's How to Prepare for Catholic High School Entrance Examinations: COOP/HSPT*—contains a fuller discussion of the High School Placement Test, as well as a diagnostic and two practice tests following the format of the actual test.

National Educational Development Test (NEDT)

The NEDT, published by CTB/Macmillan/McGraw-Hill, was designed primarily to assess the skills levels of ninth- and tenth-grade students. It is also used as a high school entrance exam.

The test is given twice a year during a two-week period in October and February. Each school or district selects its own date (within the two-week period) and its own time and place. Make-up testing for absentees is at the discretion of the school or district.

The test consists of five parts: English usage, mathematics usage (problems), natural science reading, social studies reading, and a fifth unit that covers verbal, numerical, reasoning, and spatial abilities. While taking any one part of the exam, a student is not permitted to look ahead or back at any other section of the test booklet.

Comprehensive Testing Program (CTP II)

The CTP II was planned cooperatively by the Educational Records Bureau (ERB) and the schools that administer it, primarily to compare the performances of students in similar schools. Level 4, which is designed to be used with students from the spring of sixth grade through the fall of the ninth year, has become an instrument for evaluating candidates for admission to the high schools enrolled in the ERB program. Because of the length of the examination (six hours), it is usually given in two sessions. See Outline of High School Entrance Exams for the subjects covered.

3R Placement and Counseling Test

The 3R Placement and Counseling Test, published by CTB/Macmillan/ McGraw-Hill, is part of an entire program designed for students in the fourth through the tenth grades. The testing program has forms for three levels of difficulty based on given age ranges. The entire program is used to evaluate student progress through the grades and to provide long-range career counseling.

The entire program involves a full day of testing annually. Most schools using the test for admission purposes require that the students take only the appropriate 3R portion of the test, which lasts about two hours.

The 3R Placement and Counseling Test is given on a flexible schedule set by the school or district to which the candidate applies for admission.

GROUP TWO: SPECIALIZED TESTS

In addition to the schools that require that candidates for admission take nationwide standardized tests, there are many high schools that have their own entrance examinations developed by the faculty to help in student selection. Too few students take any one of these tests for it to be standardized. As a result, the score achieved is based on the number of correct answers, and the highest rank is that of the student with the greatest number of right answers. For this reason, the abilities of current candidates cannot be compared with those of previous ones on the basis of this test.

Catholic High School Entrance Examination

The Catholic High School Entrance Examination is administered to graduating eighth-grade students applying for admission to the ninth grade in any one of the 13 high schools located within the Diocese of Rockville Centre in New York State. The examination is administered in each of these schools on the same day in November. (There is a make-up test held in December in two of the schools.)

The test, lasting for approximately three hours, measures both ability and achievement. All of the items, except writing, consist of multiple-choice questions.

The first section testing ability resembles an intelligence test. The achievement sections consist of items in reading, mathematics, and language, and a writing exercise.

The reading items consist of questions based on given paragraphs. The math items are mainly of the problem-solving type. The language items include spelling, vocabulary, capitalization, and punctuation. The writing section consists of straight copying and a brief composition on a given topic.

Because this test most closely resembles the Coop examination, the companion book to this one—*Barron's How to Prepare for Catholic High School Entrance Examinations: COOP/HSPT*—would be your best guide to maximum scores. The diagnostic and two practice tests for the Coop examination will reveal your weaknesses and the study guide will help you overcome them.

Hunter College High School Examination

Hunter College High School is one of the oldest schools established in our country for the intellectually gifted. Enrolled students must be residents of New York City from the seventh through the twelfth grade.

The entrance examination for Hunter College High School is usually given to sixth-grade New York City students, whose applications are processed through the principals of their schools. Approximately 3,000 students take the entrance examination in January of their sixth-grade year. Of these, 280 are admitted.

The examination consists of multiple-choice items in mathematics and English, and an essay question. The math items are of the problem-solving type. The English items include vocabulary, reading comprehension, and language usage. The English and mathematics parts are given equal weight. In addition, candidates are asked to write a short essay as evidence of their ability to express themselves effectively in standard written English.

New York City's Science High Schools

These three schools are Bronx High School of Science, Brooklyn Technical High School, and Stuyvesant High School. Only residents of New York City may apply for admission to these prestigious schools. Eighth- and ninth-grade students residing in the five boroughs of the city are eligible to take the two-hour test consisting of 115 multiple-choice questions.

The same examination is given for all three high schools, and students who qualify may attend whichever school they choose. Candidates take the exam at the schools of their choice. To be accepted, students must score above the established cut-off score, which may vary from school to school. Since the offerings and specializations of the three schools differ, it is imperative that student and parents discuss the choice of school before the exam is taken; a student who is accepted must attend the school that he or she has designated.

LOOKING AHEAD

See the Outline of High School Entrance Exams that follows for important information about the various tests: description/purpose, format, time allowed, and subtests. Also included, in the first column, is the address to which you should direct questions regarding each test. If any unanswered question remains, see your guidance counselor.

OUTLINE OF HIGH SCHOOL ENTRANCE EXAMS

Exam Title/ Administering Organization	Description/Purpose	Format of Exam	Total Time Allowed	Subtests (Subject, Number of Questions, Time)	Corresponding Section of This Book
SECONDARY SCHOOL ADMISSIONS TEST (SSAT) Educational Testing Service CN 6450 Princeton, NJ 08541-6450	The most popular of all the high school entrance and scholarship tests. Required by over 500 private, tuition-charging academies and prep schools. Two forms of the test—Lower Level and Upper Level—are given.	Multiple-choice questions; machine-scored answer sheet.	About $2^1/_2$ hours	**Quantitative Ability** Mathematics (25 questions, 25 minutes) Additional mathematics section (25 questions, 25 minutes)	Chapter 8
				Verbal Ability (25 questions total) Vocabulary—synonyms (30 questions) Vocabulary—analogies (30 questions)	Chapter 4
				Reading Comprehension (40 questions, 25 minutes)	Chapter 5
				Experimental Section (25 minutes)	
INDEPENDENT SCHOOL ENTRANCE EXAMINATION (ISEE) ISEE Operations Office 423 Morris Street Durham, NC 27701	To evaluate candidates for admission to high schools. Two forms of the test—Middle Level and Upper Level—are given.	Multiple-choice questions; machine-scored answer sheet; essay section.	About 3 hours	**Verbal Ability** (40 questions, 20 minutes) Synonyms Sentence completion	Chapter 4
				Quantitative Ability (40 questions, 35 minutes) Concepts/Understanding Application	Chapter 8
				Reading Comprehension (40 questions 35 minutes) Science passages Social Studies passages	Chapter 5
				Mathematics Achievement (50 questions, 40 minutes) Computation, Applications } Middle Level Arithmetic concepts, Algebraic concepts, Geometric concepts } Upper Level	Chapters 8–14
				Essay (30 minutes)	Chapter 7
COOPERATIVE ADMISSIONS EXAMINATION (Coop) Admissions Examination Office CTB 20 Ryan Ranch Road Monterey, CA 93940	Widely used by Catholic, parochial high schools, both parish and diocesan.	Multiple-choice questions; machine-scored answer sheet.	About 4 hours	**Sequences** (20 questions, 12 minutes)	*
				Analogies (20 questions, 7 minutes)	*
				Memory (20 questions, 20 minutes)	*
				Verbal Reasoning (20 questions, 12 minutes)	*
				Reading Vocabulary (40 questions, 18 minutes)	*
				Reading Comprehension (34 questions, 32 minutes)	*
				Mathematics Computation (30 questions, 25 minutes)	*

*Refer to *How to Prepare for the Cooperative Admissions Examination (Coop)/High School Placement Test (HSPT),* also published by Barron's.

				Mathematics Concepts and Applications (35 questions, 27 minutes)	*
				Language Mechanics (20 questions, 10 minutes)	*
				Language Expression (32 questions, 25 minutes)	*
HIGH SCHOOL PLACEMENT TEST (HSPT) Scholastic Testing Service 480 Meyer Road Bensenville, IL 60106-1617	Used for high school admissions, grade placement, and scholarship awards, predominantly by Catholic high schools.	Multiple-choice questions; machine-scored answer sheet	About $2^1/_2$ hours	**Verbal Skills** (60 questions, 16 minutes) Synonyms (15 questions) Antonyms (9 questions) Analogies (10 questions) Logic (10 questions) Verbal classifications (16 questions)	*
				Quantitative Skills (52 questions, 30 minutes) Numbers in series (18 questions) Geometric comparisons (9 questions) Nongeometric comparisons (8 questions) Number manipulations (17 questions)	*
				Reading (62 questions, 25 minutes) Comprehension (40 questions) Vocabulary (22 questions)	*
				Mathematics (64 questions, 45 minutes) Mathematical concepts (24 questions) Problem solving (40 questions)	*
				Language (60 questions, 25 minutes) Capitalization, punctuation, and usage (40 questions) Spelling (10 questions) Composition (10 questions)	*
CATHOLIC HIGH SCHOOL ENTRANCE EXAMINATION Catholic Secondary School Administrators P.O. Box 361 Mineola, NY 11501	To evaluate candidates for admission to 13 high schools located in the Diocese of Rockville Centre, New York	Multiple-choice questions; machine-scored answer sheet; essay and copying section.	About 3 hours	**Ability Test** about 80 questions, 45 minutes on four of the following: verbal analogies, diagrammed analogies, sequences, verbal reasoning, number relations, reasoning, number relationships, comparisons	Chapter 14
				Achievement Test:	
				Part I **Reading** (40 questions) 6 reading passages (40 minutes)	Chapter 5
				Part II **Word Study** (25 minutes)	
				Spelling (30 questions)	Chapter 6
				Vocabulary (20 questions)	Chapter 4
				Part III **Language** (50 questions, 30 minutes) capitalization, punctuation, usage, sentence sense	Chapter 6
				Part IV **Mathematical Problems** (40 items, 35 minutes)	Chapters 8–14
				Part V **Writing** (15 minutes) Straight copy of a short passage Brief written reaction to a statement	Chapter 7

OUTLINE OF HIGH SCHOOL ENTRANCE EXAMS

Exam Title/ Administering Organization	Description/Purpose	Format of Exam	Total Time Allowed	Subtests (Subject, Number of Questions, Time)	Corresponding Section of This Book
NATIONAL EDUCATIONAL TEST DEVELOPMENT (NEDT) Admissions Examination Office CTB/Macmillan/McGraw-Hill 20 Ryan Ranch Road Monterey, CA 93940	To test developed skill levels; to select students for admission.	Multiple-choice questions; machine-scored answer sheet.	About 3 hours	**English Usage** (50 questions, 30 minutes)	Chapters 4–6
				General usage (30 questions)	
				Sentence reconstruction (20 questions)	
				Mathematics Usage (56 questions, 40 minutes)	Chapters 8–14
				Number problems (40 questions)	
				Verbal problems (16 questions)	
				Natural Science Reading (32 questions, 30 minutes)	Chapter 5
				Social Studies Reading (32 questions, 30 minutes)	Chapter 5
				Educational Abilities	
				Part I (40 questions, 10 minutes)	
				Word groupings (10 questions)	
				Vocabulary (30 questions)	
				Part II (25 questions, 10 minutes)	
				Number series (4 questions)	
				Letter series (6 questions)	
				Spatial relations (15 questions)	
COMPREHENSIVE TESTING PROGRAM (CTP II) Educational Records Bureau 3 East 80th Street New York, NY 10021	To evaluate candidates for admission to high schools enrolled in the ERB program.	Multiple-choice questions; machine-scored answer sheet.	About 6 hours	**Analogies** (50 questions, 20 minutes)	Chapter 4
				Quantitative (50 questions, 20 minutes)	Chapter 14
				Vocabulary (35 questions, 20 minutes)	Chapter 4
				Reading Comprehension (45 questions, 45 minutes)	Chapter 5
				Spelling (20 questions, 10 minutes)	Chapter 6
				Capitalization (25 questions, 15 minutes)	Chapter 6
				Punctuation (35 questions, 20 minutes)	Chapter 6
				Grammar and Usage (50 questions, 40 minutes)	Chapter 6
				Mathematics Basic Concepts (50 questions, 40 minutes)	Chapter 8
				Mathematics Computation (60 questions, 40 minutes)	Chapter 8
3R PLACEMENT AND COUNSELING TEST CTB/Macmillan/McGraw-Hill 20 Ryan Ranch Road Monterey, CA 93940	To evaluate candidates for admission to high schools.	Multiple-choice questions; machine-scored answer sheet.	About 2 hours	**Reading**	Chapter 5
				Words in context (20 questions, 8 minutes)	
				Comprehension (28 questions, 22 minutes)	
				Mathematics	Chapters 8–14
				Arithmetic computation (22 questions, 18 minutes)	
				Concepts and problem solving (32 questions, 30 minutes)	

				Language Arts Sentence sense (16 questions, 8 minutes) Usage (21 questions, 10 minutes) Spelling (16 questions, 8 minutes)	Chapter 6
SCIENCE HIGH SCHOOLS ADMISSIONS TEST Brooklyn Technical High School 29 Fort Greene Place Brooklyn, NY 11217 Bronx High School of Science 75 West 205th Street Bronx, NY 10468 Stuyvesant High School 345 Chambers Street New York, NY 10280	To select students for the New York City public high schools for academically gifted students.	Multiple-choice questions; machine-scored answer sheet.	About $2^{1}/_{2}$ hours	**Verbal Ability** (55 questions, 70 minutes) Word Meaning (10 questions) Sentence Completion (10 questions) Logical Reasoning (10 questions) Reading Comprehension (25 questions on 5 passages) **Mathematics** (50 questions, 70 minutes) Greater of two quantities Word problems Computation	Chapter 4 Chapter 8
HUNTER COLLEGE HIGH SCHOOL ENTRANCE TEST Hunter College High School 71 East 94th Street New York, NY 10028	To select students for admission to Hunter College High School, a school for intellectually gifted students in grades 7–12. (The school is administered by the City University of New York, and students must be New York City residents.)	Multiple-choice questions; (machine-scored answer sheet); essay.	About 3 hours	**Language** (75 questions) Vocabulary Sentence Completion Grammar Reading Comprehension Spelling Punctuation **Mathematics** (25 questions) **Essay**	Chapters 4–6 Chapter 8 Chapter 7

Planning a Study Strategy

The book includes many features that will enable you to prepare thoroughly for virtually any academic high school entrance examination. It has been designed with a particular study strategy in mind, one that involves several distinct steps and can be used regardless of how much time you have to prepare for an exam. The six steps follow:

- Begin by looking at the Outline of High School Entrance Exams in this chapter to determine exactly what subject areas are covered in the test you plan to take. The Outline of High School Entrance Exams includes the most popular tests; however, if you are taking a test not listed, you will have to consult the literature on that particular test.
- Once you have determined what general subject areas will be covered, turn to Chapters 2 and 3 and take the corresponding Diagnostic Tests.
- Having taken the appropriate Diagnostic Tests, turn to the Answer Key and, based on the "Rating Your Results" charts, see how you have done on each test or each test subsection. Now you can make lists of tests or test subsections on which you rated (1) superior, (2) average, and (3) below average. Include on these lists the page references indicated in the rating charts.
- Next, set up a study schedule. The amount of time you spend preparing obviously will depend on how many days you have before the exam and how many hours each day you can devote to this purpose. You will benefit more by studying every day rather than trying to cram just before the exam. Also, plan to devote two thirds of your study time to the subject matter on your "below average" list.
- Once your study schedule is established, turn to the pages of this book that correspond to one of the subject areas on your "below average" list. Review the material and do the exercises, practice tests, and/or Mastery Exams. By the time you have finished working on a certain subject area, you should have a strong command of it. At that point, go on to another subject on your "below average" list. Continue in this manner, covering "below average" subjects, then "average" subjects, and finally "superior" subjects.
- If you plan to take the SSAT or the ISEE, do one final thing the day before the actual exam: take one or both of the appropriate practice exams in the final section of this book.

If you follow these steps, you will use your study time most efficiently and will gain confidence in your knowledge of the subjects you will be tested on.

If You Are Taking the Secondary School Admission Test (SSAT)

On seven Saturdays each year, the Secondary School Admission Test (SSAT) is administered at test centers in more than 250 cities and towns throughout the world. Special arrangements can be made for Sabbath observers, for applicants who live far from the scheduled test center, and for students with disabilities. Approximately 30,000 students in grades 5–11 take the test, seeking admission to the more than 500 schools that make up the Secondary School Admission Test Board.

The SSAT is given on two levels of difficulty. The Lower Level is for students in grades 5, 6, and 7; the Upper Level is for those in grades 8, 9, 10, and 11. Within each level, the questions vary in difficulty, and some of the same questions appear in both levels. Students in higher grades are expected to answer more questions correctly than students in lower grades. For example, students in grade 10 should have more correct answers than students in grade 9.

Frequently Asked Questions About the SSAT

How does the SSAT differ from other school tests?

Most of the tests students take are achievement tests that measure how much the student has learned and how well he or she can apply that information. The SSAT does not concentrate on memorized information; it measures ability with questions on reading comprehension, word recognition and comparison, and mathematical reasoning to assess how well the student will do in high school.

What does the SSAT consist of?

This multiple-choice test consists of five sections:

Section 1: Mathematics Computation
25 questions, 25 minutes

Section 2: Verbal Ability *25 minutes total*
Vocabulary—Synonyms *30 questions*
Vocabulary—Analogies *30 questions*

Section 3: Mathematics Concepts
25 questions, 25 minutes

Section 4: Reading Comprehension
40 questions, 25 minutes

Section 5: Experimental Section
This section may appear anywhere in the test. It may be similar in form or content to any one of the other sections but answers to questions in this section are not counted in test scores. An experimental section is not included in the practice tests.

How can I determine which is the experimental section?

Don't waste your time trying to identify this section. It may appear anywhere on the test. Do your best on all sections.

Should I leave troublesome questions unanswered?

The SSAT gives one point for each correct answer. One-quarter point is deducted for each incorrect answer. No deduction is made for answers left blank. Since wrong answers count against you, you can penalize yourself by guessing wildly.

Should I make an educated guess?

Yes, if you can shift the odds in your favor. If you can eliminate one or more of the choices as definitely wrong, then guessing is in order. But if you cannot eliminate any of the choices, leave the answer space blank.

How important is scratch work on the SSAT?

Your scratch work is done in the question booklet and is strictly to help you. The only thing the machine marks is your answer sheet. Make certain that you do not do any scratch work on the answer sheet. The scoring machine may mistake a stray mark for a second answer to a question and give you no credit for either answer.

How much mathematics is required for the SSAT?

The purpose of the SSAT is not to find out how much math you know. The test attempts to discover your ability to reason with mathematical symbols, to solve problems, and to interpret data. Since these questions are designed to test thinking power, you should expect to solve most problems by close inspection and reasoning rather than by complicated work.

How are the SSAT scores reported?

The raw score, the number of correct answers minus a fraction of a point for each wrong answer, is converted into a scaled score. The scale for the lower grades (grades 5, 6, and 7) ranges from 230 to 320. The scale for the upper grades (grades 8, 9, 10, and 11) ranges from 250 to 350. With no answer correct, a student in the lower grades still achieves 230; in the upper grades, 250. Since the score represents a comparison with other students taking the test, a test taker can achieve a top score even with some unanswered or incorrectly answered questions.

Separate scores are given for reading comprehension, verbal, and mathematical areas. However, only the verbal and mathematical scaled scores contribute to the total score. The total score does not represent the number right or wrong; it indicates how the candidate compares with the other candidates in verbal and mathematical abilities.

How are the tests scored?

The student's answers are read by a scanning machine that records them on computer tape. The computer then compares each answer with the correct response for that question.

What if I make a mistake on the answer sheet?

There are only two mistakes that can involve the computer, the answer sheet, and the candidate. If the candidate blocks out two letters on one line, the computer labels the answer incorrect. If the candidate fails to remove an erased answer completely, the machine then finds two answers on a line and again labels that question as incorrectly answered.

What if I think that the scoring was wrong?

For a fee, the Educational Testing Service will score your answer sheet by hand. See the bulletin you will receive with your score for the procedure, or discuss the problem with your school counselor.

What is meant by program percentiles?

The program percentiles do not represent the number of questions answered correctly. Rather they compare the candidate with all of the students who took the test in the past 3 years. A mark around the 50th percentile means that the student was in the middle of the group. A mark in the 25th percentile is below 75% of the group. A mark in the 75th percentile places the candidate in the top 25% of the group who took the test.

How important are SSAT scores?

When making their admission decisions, schools differ on the amount of weight they give to these scores. Most schools consider far more than the scores when evaluating candidates. They also look at school grades, extracurricular activities, teachers' recommendations, other objective test records, letters of recommendation, and interviews. However, the results of the SSAT do give a scientific way of comparing all candidates in regard to their abilities to do high school work. Because of the breadth of comparison, admissions officers realize that this examination affords equal opportunity to every one applying.

How can this chapter help me in preparing for the SSAT?

It will familiarize you with the kinds of questions that appear on the SSAT. Knowing what to expect when you take the test is important in preparing for the test and succeeding in it.

This chapter has been organized so that it parallels the sections of the SSAT. The Verbal Ability Section, the Mathematics Sections, and the Reading Comprehension Section have been treated separately. Each part of the chapter presents sample questions with answers, strategies for success, a Diagnostic Test with answers and explanations, and a study plan for the particular SSAT section being discussed. No time limits have been imposed on the Diagnostic Tests because their main purpose is to help you discover your weaknesses and strengths. After completing this chapter, you will know what steps are necessary in order to do your best on the SSAT.

The Verbal Ability Section

The two verbal subsections have a total of 60 questions: 30 synonyms and 30 analogies. You are allowed 25 minutes for the entire verbal ability section. Your high school success will be closely bound to your ability to understand the vocabulary used in the textbooks and classroom discussions that will be your primary sources for acquiring knowledge. Therefore, the SSAT tests knowledge of words found in formal written English rather than the words used in everyday speech.

Sample Synonym Questions

This subsection tests your vocabulary directly. You are given a word and then five choices of words or phrases from which you are to select the one closest in meaning to the given word. The directions and sample questions below are typical of those encountered on the synonym subsection of the SSAT.

DIRECTIONS: Select, from the lettered choices, the word or phrase closest in meaning to the word in capital letters.

1. MOW:
(A) pave smoothly (B) water daily (C) reseed swiftly (D) cut down (E) shave quickly

2. RASH:
(F) bruised (G) hasty (H) infected (J) bold (K) elevated in rank

3. VIVID:
(A) angry (B) clever (C) uncertain (D) certain (E) colorful

4. ADJACENT:
(F) dim (G) old and feeble (H) profitable (J) neighboring (K) noisy and quarrelsome

5. BEFUDDLE:
(A) contest (B) confuse (C) commit (D) counsel (E) confine

6. VANQUISH:
(F) subdue (G) cleanse (H) delay (J) revolt (K) disappear

7. ACCLIMATE:
(A) travel (B) repair (C) adjust (D) heal (E) winterize

8. PRATTLE:
(F) picket fence (G) teacher's lecture (H) sewing (J) idle chatter (K) careful selection

9. MARAUDER:
(A) sailor (B) raider (C) traveler (D) beggar (E) liar

10. FEUD:
(F) duty (G) enemy (H) uselessness (J) quarrel (K) act

Answers

1. **D**	3. **E**	5. **B**	7. **C**	9. **B**
2. **G**	4. **J**	6. **F**	8. **J**	10. **J**

STRATEGIES FOR SUCCESS

- If you have easy recognition of the given word, its definition or synonym will quickly come to your mind. You will painlessly identify the correct choice. To prevent carelessness, however, eliminate the other choices before marking the answer sheet.
- If all the choices for a given word seem to be wrong, don't suspect a misprint. Instead, realize that a less familiar use of the given word may be involved. Many words, such as *port, stern,* and *light,* have a variety of meanings.
- If a word does not slot easily, try to recall a phrase in which you have met it. Use the phrase to evaluate the choices. Do not skip any choice. The word *guile* may yield its meaning through a phrase like "trickster full of guile." The key to *incessant* could be "incessant complaining." The three strategies above should

give you a handle on more than 80% of the test words. How should you approach the others?

- ➤ Sometimes thinking of an antonym can help. What is the opposite of the given word? Use the opposite to evaluate the synonym choices. Possible clues may be found in antonyms like *prolong* and *shorten, legitimate* and *unlawful.* If this method is successful, make certain that you check all of the choices before selecting the best answer.
- ➤ When the word is one that you have met before, but none of the choices works, don't spend time agonizing. Circle the number of the given word in the test booklet, and plan to come back if time permits. Very often when you return for a second try, your mind has identified the word and the answer becomes clear.
- ➤ Even though words in the test supposedly are in order of increasing difficulty, don't give up because you find the words becoming unfamiliar. Go through the entire list! Some words that others find troublesome, you may find fairly simple.
- ➤ Should you guess? Again, if you are *totally* unfamiliar with the given word, the penalty for wrong answers outweighs the chances of guessing the right one. Only when you can eliminate one or more of the choices should you toss a mental coin.

Diagnostic Test Synonyms

The Diagnostic Test that follows will help you to evaluate your strengths and weaknesses in the type of verbal ability measured by the synonym subsection. No time limit is given. The results should help you to decide how much of your study time should be devoted to doing the exercises in Chapter 4, Vocabulary, beginning on page 89.

Only 30 items are included in the synonym section of the SSAT. To increase the predictive value of this synonym Diagnostic Test, the number of words tested has been increased to 50. This test is planned for those preparing for both the Lower and Upper forms of the test.

> DIRECTIONS: Select, from the lettered choices, the word or phrase closest in meaning to the word in capital letters. Fill in the circle that has the same letter as your answer choice.
>
> **SAMPLE QUESTION:**
>
> MENACE:
> (A) manage (B) hinder (C) defeat
> (D) control (E) threaten
>
> Ⓐ Ⓑ Ⓒ Ⓓ ●

1. ACQUIRE:
(A) ask (B) lend (C) retell
(D) concentrate (E) gain
Ⓐ Ⓑ Ⓒ Ⓓ Ⓔ

2. BLISS:
(F) joy (G) infant (H) praise
(J) blame (K) blunder
Ⓕ Ⓖ Ⓗ Ⓙ Ⓚ

3. BLEND:
(A) choose from (B) mix together
(C) grieve for (D) render sightless
(E) refuse admission
Ⓐ Ⓑ Ⓒ Ⓓ Ⓔ

4. DENT:
(F) point out (G) break (H) enrage
(J) depress (K) ignore
Ⓕ Ⓖ Ⓗ Ⓙ Ⓚ

5. MODERATE:
(A) soften (B) injure (C) conceal
(D) free (E) deserve
Ⓐ Ⓑ Ⓒ Ⓓ Ⓔ

6. PERIL:
(F) jewelry (G) surplus (H) danger (J) inspiration (K) disaster
Ⓕ Ⓖ Ⓗ Ⓙ Ⓚ

7. PEEVISH:
(A) heavy (B) fretful (C) insincere (D) gawky (E) athletic
Ⓐ Ⓑ Ⓒ Ⓓ Ⓔ

8 HUMILIATE:
(F) empower (G) ignore (H) ridicule (J) serve (K) embarrass
Ⓕ Ⓖ Ⓗ Ⓙ Ⓚ

9. HEEDLESS:
(A) disobedient (B) slow (C) insensitive (D) daring (E) senseless
Ⓐ Ⓑ Ⓒ Ⓓ Ⓔ

10. TRANSACTION:
(F) profit (G) participation (H) trade (J) gamble (K) partnership
Ⓕ Ⓖ Ⓗ Ⓙ Ⓚ

11. SURPLUS:
(A) military (B) useless (C) sanitary (D) excess (E) ordinary
Ⓐ Ⓑ Ⓒ Ⓓ Ⓔ

12. SOLITUDE:
(F) companion (G) isolation (H) fear (J) ambition (K) card game
Ⓕ Ⓖ Ⓗ Ⓙ Ⓚ

13. HAMPER:
(A) hold back (B) force forward (C) deposit in (D) make bold (E) hasten forward
Ⓐ Ⓑ Ⓒ Ⓓ Ⓔ

14. SPECIFIC:
(F) required (G) wrong (H) definite (J) exaggerated (K) legal
Ⓕ Ⓖ Ⓗ Ⓙ Ⓚ

15. VINDICTIVE:
(A) provable (B) vengeful (C) guilty (D) severe (E) successful
Ⓐ Ⓑ Ⓒ Ⓓ Ⓔ

16. TENACIOUS:
(F) well-knit (G) lacking experience (H) stuck up (J) displaying envy (K) holding fast
Ⓕ Ⓖ Ⓗ Ⓙ Ⓚ

17. TRESPASS:
(A) silence (B) seize (C) consolidate (D) invade (E) expire
Ⓐ Ⓑ Ⓒ Ⓓ Ⓔ

18. MALICIOUS:
(F) awkward (G) guilty (H) gainful (J) spiteful (K) playful
Ⓕ Ⓖ Ⓗ Ⓙ Ⓚ

19. IMPAIR:
(A) force (B) correct (C) damage (D) contest (E) double
Ⓐ Ⓑ Ⓒ Ⓓ Ⓔ

20. HAWSER:
(F) cable (G) carcass (H) ship (J) animal (K) cowboy
Ⓕ Ⓖ Ⓗ Ⓙ Ⓚ

21. WAVER:
(A) go on record (B) show doubt (C) agree with (D) let go (E) hold on high
Ⓐ Ⓑ Ⓒ Ⓓ Ⓔ

22. VIVACIOUS:
(F) silent (G) athletic (H) concerned (J) pathetic (K) lively
Ⓕ Ⓖ Ⓗ Ⓙ Ⓚ

23. INTERMISSION:
(A) play (B) rocket (C) interruption (D) contest (E) visit
Ⓐ Ⓑ Ⓒ Ⓓ Ⓔ

24. PARTICLE:
(F) picture (G) tiny part (H) slice (J) organization (K) inner circle
Ⓕ Ⓖ Ⓗ Ⓙ Ⓚ

25. DETACH:
(A) group (B) solder (C) destroy (D) untie (E) dispute
Ⓐ Ⓑ Ⓒ Ⓓ Ⓔ

26. PRODUCTIVE:
(F) fruitful (G) passive (H) pensive
(J) selective (K) sound
Ⓕ Ⓖ Ⓗ Ⓙ Ⓚ

27. HARASS:
(A) pester (B) soften (C) harness
(D) console (E) relieve
Ⓐ Ⓑ Ⓒ Ⓓ Ⓔ

28. AGGRESSIVE:
(F) agitated (G) jubilant (H) pushy
(J) agile (K) violent
Ⓕ Ⓖ Ⓗ Ⓙ Ⓚ

29. DONATOR:
(A) charity (B) relative (C) gift
(D) money (E) giver
Ⓐ Ⓑ Ⓒ Ⓓ Ⓔ

30. BLUNDER:
(F) err (G) track (H) overload
(J) enslave (K) judge hastily
Ⓕ Ⓖ Ⓗ Ⓙ Ⓚ

31. CLEAVE:
(A) catch (B) brighten (C) divide
(D) disdain (E) disturb
Ⓐ Ⓑ Ⓒ Ⓓ Ⓔ

32. LAMENT:
(F) paint (G) mourn (H) strengthen
(J) confer (K) glue together
Ⓕ Ⓖ Ⓗ Ⓙ Ⓚ

33. PLACID:
(A) watery (B) singular (C) childish
(D) peaceful (E) primitive
Ⓐ Ⓑ Ⓒ Ⓓ Ⓔ

34. SURPASS:
(F) leave behind (G) catch up with
(H) compete against
(J) be involved with
(K) join forces with
Ⓕ Ⓖ Ⓗ Ⓙ Ⓚ

35. POSSESS:
(A) please (B) radiate (C) injure
(D) condemn (E) dominate
Ⓐ Ⓑ Ⓒ Ⓓ Ⓔ

36. FOE:
(F) spy (G) enemy (H) fighter
(J) traitor (K) conspirator
Ⓕ Ⓖ Ⓗ Ⓙ Ⓚ

37. CONSOLE:
(A) preserve (B) hide (C) protect
(D) comfort (E) cooperate
Ⓐ Ⓑ Ⓒ Ⓓ Ⓔ

38. VILE:
(F) mean (G) total (H) bloody
(J) excessive (K) outstanding
Ⓕ Ⓖ Ⓗ Ⓙ Ⓚ

39. PLUMP:
(A) pretty (B) ordinary (C) chubby
(D) foolish (E) dark
Ⓐ Ⓑ Ⓒ Ⓓ Ⓔ

40. CURB:
(F) mix (G) check (H) deal
(J) center (K) pave
Ⓕ Ⓖ Ⓗ Ⓙ Ⓚ

41. GRATIS:
(A) with thanks (B) without care
(C) free of charge (D) under pressure
(E) at cost
Ⓐ Ⓑ Ⓒ Ⓓ Ⓔ

42. CURT:
(F) attractive (G) simple (H) abrupt
(J) witty (K) old-fashioned
Ⓕ Ⓖ Ⓗ Ⓙ Ⓚ

43. SOLACE:
(A) comfort (B) warmth (C) pity
(D) concern (E) sun deck
Ⓐ Ⓑ Ⓒ Ⓓ Ⓔ

44. HOLOCAUST:
(F) monument (G) destruction
(H) symbol (J) souvenir (K) cruelty
Ⓕ Ⓖ Ⓗ Ⓙ Ⓚ

45. ADAGE:
(A) leader (B) addition (C) link
(D) proverb (E) building
Ⓐ Ⓑ Ⓒ Ⓓ Ⓔ

46. DIGRESS:
(F) see (G) wander (H) explain
(J) lecture (K) hurry

Ⓕ Ⓖ Ⓗ Ⓙ Ⓚ

47. CORSAIR:
(A) pirate (B) guard (C) officer (D) ship
(E) prisoner

Ⓐ Ⓑ Ⓒ Ⓓ Ⓔ

48. OBESE:
(F) round (G) innocent
(H) without purpose
(J) inclined to be rash
(K) overweight

Ⓕ Ⓖ Ⓗ Ⓙ Ⓚ

49. LAUD:
(A) overload (B) praise (C) empower
(D) miss (E) pray

Ⓐ Ⓑ Ⓒ Ⓓ Ⓔ

50. PRELATE:
(F) judge (G) constituent
(H) clergyman (J) relative
(K) arbitrator

Ⓕ Ⓖ Ⓗ Ⓙ Ⓚ

Answers—Diagnostic Test Synonyms

1. **E**	11. **D**	21. **B**	31. **C**	41. **C**
2. **F**	12. **G**	22. **K**	32. **G**	42. **H**
3. **B**	13. **A**	23. **C**	33. **D**	43. **A**
4. **J**	14. **H**	24. **G**	34. **F**	44. **G**
5. **A**	15. **B**	25. **D**	35. **E**	45. **D**
6. **H**	16. **K**	26. **F**	36. **G**	46. **G**
7. **B**	17. **D**	27. **A**	37. **D**	47. **A**
8. **K**	18. **J**	28. **H**	38. **F**	48. **K**
9. **C**	19. **C**	29. **E**	39. **C**	49. **B**
10. **H**	20. **F**	30. **F**	40. **G**	50. **H**

Rating Your Results

If you are in grade 5,6, or 7 (Lower Level):

Superior	41–50 correct
Average	31–40 correct
Below average	30 or fewer correct

If you are in grade 8, 9, 10 or 11 (Upper Level):

Superior	44–50 correct
Average	37–43 correct
Below average	30 or fewer correct

Material to Review: Chapter 4

Sample Analogy Questions

The analogy question tests your understanding of logical relationships among words and ideas. You are given one pair, and you must select from the choices another pair that is related in the same way.

Example:

1. Hive is to bee as
(A) letter is to file
(B) zoo is to cage
(C) writer is to book
(D) den is to bear
(E) hunter is to hut

Analysis: Since bees live in hives and bears live in dens, the correct answer is (D).

Some analogy questions have three parts in the statement and only one in the choice. The following is an example of this form.

Example:

2. Shower is to tornado as pool is to
(F) beach
(G) mountainside
(H) lake
(J) teardrop
(K) ocean liner

Analysis: The answer is (H) since pool and lake have the same relationship of small to large as do shower and tornado.

Many relationships are possible. The two terms of the first pair can be:

1. Synonyms (words similar in meaning)
Solid is to *firm* as
2. Antonyms (words opposite in meaning)
Close is to *open* as
3. Member is to group or class
Salmon is to *fish* as
4. Part is to whole
Fret is to *guitar* as
5. Tool is to function
Hammer is to *drive* as

6. Noun is to adjective
Cow is to *bovine* as

7. Worker is to tool
Surgeon is to *clamp* as

8. Young is to adult
Cub is to *bear* as

9. Male is to female
Bull is to *cow* as

10. Form is to form
Triangle (two-dimensional) is to *cube* (three dimensional) as

11. Product is to material
Jacket is to *cloth* as

12. Cause is to effect
Cold is to *cough* as

13. Title is to specialty
Ornithologist is to *birds* as

14. Worker is to product
Composer is to *symphony* as

15. One is to many
Voter is to *electorate* as

The directions and sample questions below are typical of those encountered on the analogies subsection of the SSAT.

> DIRECTIONS: Each question gives two words that relate in a certain way. Determine this relationship, and choose the answer that best completes the meaning of the sentence.

1. Music is to hearing as
(A) seasoning is to feeling
(B) book is to touch
(C) step is to movement
(D) sketch is to sight
(E) humor is to taste

2. Play is to juvenile lead as
(F) plot is to scenery
(G) opera is to baritone
(H) skyscraper is to architect
(J) script is to director
(K) automobile is to mechanic

3. Scalpel is to doctor as
(A) dictionary is to writer
(B) vise is to plumber
(C) words are to poet
(D) textbook is to student
(E) saw is to carpenter

4. The sun is to a planet as the
(F) diameter is to a circle
(G) moon is to a star
(H) flower is to its stem
(J) trunk is to the tree
(K) hub is to the rim

5. Coward is to fearless as
(A) miser is to generous
(B) gambler is to lucky
(C) leader is to humble
(D) youth is to experience
(E) scholar is to wise

Answers and Analysis

1. **D** We hear music, and we see a painter's sketch.
2. **G** A juvenile lead portrays a character in a play; a baritone portrays a character in an opera.
3. **E** As a scalpel is a cutting tool of a surgeon, so the saw is the cutting tool of the carpenter.
4. **K** As the planets circle around the sun, so the rim of a wheel turns around its center, the hub.
5. **A** A coward is not fearless; a miser is not generous.

STRATEGIES FOR SUCCESS

➤ Concentrate your attention on uncovering the link or relationship between the first pair of words.

Skit is to play as
(Skit is a type of play.)
Dodo is to bird as
(A dodo is a bird no longer in existence.)
Window is to sill as
(The base of the frame for a window is a sill.)

➤ If the comparison is clear to you at first glance, blacken the letter of the correct choice. To prevent loss of credit through carelessness, eliminate the other four choices before marking the answer sheet.

➤ For all other test items, first eliminate the obviously wrong choices. If you have difficulty, do not dawdle over any one question. Circle the number of the question in the test booklet, and go on to the next. Plan to go back to the circled ones later—if you have time. When you go back, you will often find that your mind has been working on the question and the answer has become obvious.

Diagnostic Test Analogies

The Diagnostic Test that follows will help you to evaluate your strengths and weaknesses in the handling of verbal analogies. No time limit is given. The results should help you to decide how much of your study time should be devoted to doing the exercises on analogies beginning on page 96. This 30-item test is planned for those preparing for both the Lower and Upper forms of the test.

DIRECTIONS: Each question gives two words that relate in a certain way. Determine this relationship and choose the answer that best completes the meaning of the sentence. Fill in the circle that has the same letter as your answer choice.

SAMPLE QUESTION:

Goose is to gander as
(A) sparrow is to bird
(B) chick is to hen
(C) ewe is to ram
(D) kitten is to fawn
(E) bull is to cow

Ⓐ Ⓑ ● Ⓓ Ⓔ

Choice (C) is the best answer because a ewe and a ram are female and male, respectively as are a goose and a gander. There is no gender relationship in choices (A), (B), and (D), and the female/male relationship is reversed in choice (E).

1. Saw is to cut as
(A) drill is to bit
(B) ruler is to edge
(C) pliers are to hold
(D) screwdriver is to measure
(E) hammer is to straighten

Ⓐ Ⓑ Ⓒ Ⓓ Ⓔ

2. Rooster is to crow as
(F) lion is to hunt
(G) deer is to graze
(H) snake is to hiss
(J) tiger is to bellow
(K) bear is to squeeze

Ⓕ Ⓖ Ⓗ Ⓙ Ⓚ

3. Eggshell is to brittle as
(A) rubber is to inflexible
(B) concrete is to painted
(C) pottery is to waterproof
(D) iron is to heavy
(E) glass is to fragile

Ⓐ Ⓑ Ⓒ Ⓓ Ⓔ

4. Glance is to stare as
(F) mountain is to molehill
(G) aide is to friend
(H) mansion is to hut
(J) snack is to meal
(K) wave is to crest

Ⓕ Ⓖ Ⓗ Ⓙ Ⓚ

5. Greyhound is to swift as coyote is to
   (A) sly
   (B) stubborn
   (C) sluggish
   (D) cautious
   (E) timid

Ⓐ Ⓑ Ⓒ Ⓓ Ⓔ

6. Thermometer is to temperature as
   (F) barometer is to thickness
   (G) watch is to appointments
   (H) calendar is to numbers
   (J) schedule is to efficiency
   (K) ruler is to length

Ⓕ Ⓖ Ⓗ Ⓙ Ⓚ

7. Envy is to jealous as
   (A) love is to humble
   (B) admiration is to wealthy
   (C) cowardice is to fearful
   (D) bravery is to timid
   (E) scorn is to considerate

Ⓐ Ⓑ Ⓒ Ⓓ Ⓔ

8. Cupboard is to dishes as
   (F) library is to closet
   (G) warehouse is to sale
   (H) armory is to weapons
   (J) factory is to workers
   (K) tailor is to clothing

Ⓕ Ⓖ Ⓗ Ⓙ Ⓚ

9. Chick is to rooster as gosling is to
   (A) hen
   (B) goat
   (C) crown
   (D) gander
   (E) pig

Ⓐ Ⓑ Ⓒ Ⓓ Ⓔ

10. Amble is to walk as
   (F) slither is to graze
   (G) stride is to parade
   (H) race is to compete
   (J) waltz is to dance
   (K) strut is to follow

Ⓕ Ⓖ Ⓗ Ⓙ Ⓚ

11. Story is to character as
   (A) recipe is to ingredient
   (B) plot is to outcome
   (C) author is to royalty
   (D) building is to architect
   (E) school is to computer

Ⓐ Ⓑ Ⓒ Ⓓ Ⓔ

12. Lumber is to elephant as
   (F) acquit is to criminal
   (G) rein is to horse
   (H) roar is to lion
   (J) pitch is to salesman
   (K) waddle is to duck

Ⓕ Ⓖ Ⓗ Ⓙ Ⓚ

13. Page is to book as
   (A) poetry is to verse
   (B) Latin is to Spanish
   (C) comedy is to tragedy
   (D) Brazil is to South America
   (E) letter is to diagram

Ⓐ Ⓑ Ⓒ Ⓓ Ⓔ

14. Length is to feet as
   (F) height is to scale
   (G) weight is to pounds
   (H) unit is to cycle
   (J) wealth is to comfort
   (K) width is to tape measure

Ⓕ Ⓖ Ⓗ Ⓙ Ⓚ

15. Penny is to dime as
   (A) dime is to quarter
   (B) quarter is to dollar
   (C) dollar is to penny
   (D) nickel is to half-dollar
   (E) half-dollar is to quarter

Ⓐ Ⓑ Ⓒ Ⓓ Ⓔ

16. Rant is to anger as
   (F) display is to enthusiasm
   (G) proclaim is to confidence
   (H) whisper is to caution
   (J) lecture is to wisdom
   (K) confer is to self-reliance

Ⓕ Ⓖ Ⓗ Ⓙ Ⓚ

17. Attempt is to try as
(A) tussle is to drown
(B) avoid is to shun
(C) shriek is to pain
(D) scorch is to tan
(E) toil is to reward
Ⓐ Ⓑ Ⓒ Ⓓ Ⓔ

18. Deaf is to hearing as mute is to
(F) greed
(G) remorse
(H) joy
(J) understanding
(K) speech
Ⓕ Ⓖ Ⓗ Ⓙ Ⓚ

19. Therapist is to lisp as
(A) dentist is to fluoride
(B) dietitian is to menu
(C) social worker is to welfare
(D) surgeon is to malformation
(E) psychologist is to malpractice
Ⓐ Ⓑ Ⓒ Ⓓ Ⓔ

20. Hollow is to solidity as
(F) livable is to coziness
(G) liquid is to fluidity
(H) little is to immensity
(J) meek is to tolerance
(K) muscular is to brawn
Ⓕ Ⓖ Ⓗ Ⓙ Ⓚ

21. Glitter is to jewels as
(A) blurt is to orator
(B) gurgle is to ocean waves
(C) blare is to loud speaker
(D) twinkle is to moonlight
(E) glimmer is to sunlight
Ⓐ Ⓑ Ⓒ Ⓓ Ⓔ

22. Incautious is to reckless as
(F) supreme is to mediocre
(G) thoughtful is to thoughtless
(H) stylish is to modest
(J) slender is to skinny
(K) openhanded is to proud
Ⓕ Ⓖ Ⓗ Ⓙ Ⓚ

23. Honest is to principles as
(A) blunt is to trickery
(B) dependable is to vision
(C) faithful is to loyalty
(D) deceitful is to trust
(E) frank is to courage
Ⓐ Ⓑ Ⓒ Ⓓ Ⓔ

24. Seal is to aquarium as bird is to
(F) tree
(G) birdbath
(H) aviary
(J) garden
(K) forest
Ⓕ Ⓖ Ⓗ Ⓙ Ⓚ

25. Tourist is to motel as
(A) airplane is to garage
(B) racehorse is to arena
(C) wrestler is to grandstand
(D) boat is to marina
(E) clown is to air
Ⓐ Ⓑ Ⓒ Ⓓ Ⓔ

26. Crest is to wave as apex is to
(F) climax
(G) career
(H) failure
(J) tide
(K) aftermath
Ⓕ Ⓖ Ⓗ Ⓙ Ⓚ

27. Browse is to selectively as
(A) gulp is to carefully
(B) munch is to speedily
(C) gobble is to silently
(D) chomp is to hastily
(E) nibble is to slowly
Ⓐ Ⓑ Ⓒ Ⓓ Ⓔ

28. Glue is to separate as fire is to
(F) consume
(G) employ
(H) burn
(J) shoot at
(K) explode
Ⓕ Ⓖ Ⓗ Ⓙ Ⓚ

29. Town is to metropolis as
   (A) speedway is to highway
   (B) road is to shoulder
   (C) lane is to avenue
   (D) throughway is to turnpike
   (E) expressway is to main artery

Ⓐ Ⓑ Ⓒ Ⓓ Ⓔ

30. Retreat is to rout as
   (F) thrill is to boredom
   (G) bleach is to damage
   (H) acquaintance is to ignorance
   (J) setback is to defeat
   (K) encounter is to clash

Ⓕ Ⓖ Ⓗ Ⓙ Ⓚ

Answers—Diagnostic Test Analogies

1. **C**	7. **C**	13. **D**	19. **D**	25. **D**
2. **H**	8. **H**	14. **G**	20. **H**	26. **G**
3. **E**	9. **D**	15. **D**	21. **C**	27. **E**
4. **J**	10. **J**	16. **H**	22. **J**	28. **G**
5. **A**	11. **A**	17. **B**	23. **C**	29. **C**
6. **K**	12. **K**	18. **K**	24. **H**	30. **J**

Rating Your Results

If you are in grade 5,6, or 7 (Lower Level):

Superior	26–30 correct
Average	18–25 correct
Below average	17 or fewer correct

If you are in grade 8, 9, 10 or 11 (Upper Level):

Superior	28–30 correct
Average	23–27 correct
Below average	22 or fewer correct

Material to Review: Chapter 4

Explanations

1. **C** A saw is used to cut; a pair of pliers is used to clamp or hold.
2. **H** A rooster produces sound by crowing; a snake by hissing.
3. **E** Being brittle is a characteristic of an eggshell; being fragile is a characteristic of glass.
4. **J** A glance is a brief form of a stare; a snack is a brief form of a meal.
5. **A** Greyhounds are stereotyped as swift, as coyotes are labeled as crafty or sly.
6. **K** A thermometer measures temperature; a ruler is used to measure length.
7. **C** Envy causes a person to be jealous; cowardice causes a person to be fearful.
8. **H** A cupboard is used to store dishes; an armory is used to store weapons.
9. **D** A rooster is the male parent of a chick; a gander is the male parent of a gosling.
10. **J** To amble is to walk in a certain way; to waltz is to dance in a certain way.
11. **A** A character is one part of a story; an ingredient is one part of a recipe.
12. **K** When an elephant walks, it lumbers; when a duck walks, it waddles.
13. **D** A book is made up of pages; South America is made up countries such as Brazil.
14. **G** Length is measured in feet; weight is measured in pounds.
15. **D** A penny is $\frac{1}{10}$ of a dime; a nickel is $\frac{1}{10}$ of a half-dollar.
16. **H** Anger may cause one to rant; caution may cause one to whisper.
17. **B** To attempt means to try; to avoid means to shun.
18. **K** One who is deaf lacks hearing; one who is mute lacks speech.
19. **D** A therapist attempts to cure a lisp. A surgeon attempts to cure malformations.
20. **H** That which is hollow lacks solidity; that which is little lacks immensity.
21. **C** At their most intense jewels glitter and loudspeakers blare.
22. **J** Incautious is a synonym of reckless; slender is a synonym of skinny.
23. **C** Honesty is based on principles, while faith is based on loyalty.
24. **H** People display seals in aquariums and birds in aviaries.
25. **D** Motels are stopover places for tourist; marinas are stopover places for boats.
26. **G** Apex, like crest, is the highest or culminating point. The apex of a career is its moment of greatest success.
27. **E** Browsing involves eating selectively, choosing with care, while nibbling implies eating slowly.
28. **G** Gluing is doing the opposite of separating; firing a person is doing the opposite of employing someone.
29. **(C)** A town is a smaller version of a metropolis; a lane is a smaller (narrower) version of an avenue.

30. **J** A retreat lacks the intensity and inclusiveness of a rout; a setback lacks the intensity and completeness of a defeat.

STUDY PLAN FOR THE VERBAL ABILITY SECTION

The key to improving your score on the Verbal Ability Section is the amount of time you can spend on the lists, practice tests, and Mastery Exams in Chapter 4, Vocabulary, beginning on page 89.

Long-Term Program

1. Review the vocabulary used in Chapter 4, beginning on page 89. Check the words you are unfamiliar with, and study them four or five at a time. You will be pleasantly surprised at how quickly you will master them! A 10-minute session each day is the secret to success.
2. Do not skip the varied practice tests and Mastery Exams. They will reinforce your control of your growing vocabulary and increase your speed in handling the actual examination items.
3. Use the Practice SSATs beginning on page 510 as your final step in preparation.

Crash Program

1. Concentrate your study time on doing as many as you can of the practice tests and Mastery Exams in Chapter 4, Vocabulary beginning on page 89. Several short sessions are much more effective than one long one. The varied exercises will help you gain speed and accuracy in handling vocabulary questions.
2. Use the Practice SSATs beginning on page 510 as your final step.

The Mathematics Sections

WHAT YOU NEED TO KNOW

Of the four test sections that comprise the SSAT, two deal with mathematics. Each mathematics section consists of 25 questions to be answered in 25 minutes. In general the emphasis in the questions is on mathematical reasoning and mathematical applications as well as on computation. The best preparation for the test involves coverage of the wide range of basic arithmetic, algebra, and geometry. The outline below lists the areas to be covered. All of these areas are developed in this book with a considerable amount of practice material. To provide for efficient self-study, you are given the answers to all practice problems.

Here is what you need to know in mathematics if you are taking the SSAT:

1. Basic mathematical operations with whole numbers, fractions, decimals, and percents.
2. Common units of measure and operations with these measures.
3. The metric system.
4. Ratio and proportion.
5. Mathematical applications and problem solving:
   A. Using basic operations.
   B. Percentage problems.
   C. Profit and loss.
   D. Taxation.
   E. Commission.
   F. Discount.
   G. Interest.
   H. Averages.
6. Basic algebra:
   A. Algebraic representation.
   B. Exponents and evaluation of algebraic expressions.
   C. Evaluation of formulas.
   D. Solving equations.
   E. Solving problems by using equations.
   F. Solving inequalities.
7. Numbers and number systems:
   A. Sets.
   B. Numeration.
   C. Exponents and expanded form.
8. The set of natural numbers and the set of whole numbers:
   A. Factors and primes
   B. Divisibility.
   C. Symbols of inequality.
   D. Order in the set of integers.
9. The set of rational numbers.
10. The set of real numbers.
11. Laws of operation for real numbers.
12. Interpreting tables, maps, and graphs.
13. Geometry:
   A. The basics.
   B. Perimeter area and volume.
   C. Indirect measurement:
      – Pythagorean Theorem and square root.
      – Congruence and similarity.
      – Coordinate geometry.
14. Mathematical reasoning.
15. Interpretation of graphs.

Sample Questions

The topics listed above are used in solving such typical questions as the samples shown below. These samples are applicable to both levels of the SSAT.

EXAMPLE 1: If $6 + 8 + \square = 5 + 9 + 4$ then $\square =$

(A) 5 (B) 6 (C) 4 (D) 7 (E) 9

SOLUTION: Note that $6 + 8 = 14$ and $5 + 9 = 14$. Thus, the problem may be written as

$$14 + \square = 14 + 4$$
$$\text{and } \square = 4$$

The correct choice is (C).

This problem may also be solved by standard methods as follows:

$$6 + 8 + \square = 5 + 9 + 4$$
$$14 + \square = 18$$
$$\square = 18 - 14$$
$$\square = 4$$

EXAMPLE 2: Mr. Green has $(x + 4)$ more miles to travel to complete his motor trip. After he has covered 10 additional miles, how many more miles must he travel?

(F) $x + 14$ (G) $x + 10$ (H) $14 - x$
(J) $x - 10$ (K) $x - 6$

SOLUTION: To find the remaining mileage, we must subtract 10 from $x + 4$.

$$x + 4 - 10 = x - 6$$

The correct choice is (K).

EXAMPLE 3: The expense budget of the Evans family is shown on the graph. What fractional part of the budget is spent for expenses other than food and rent?

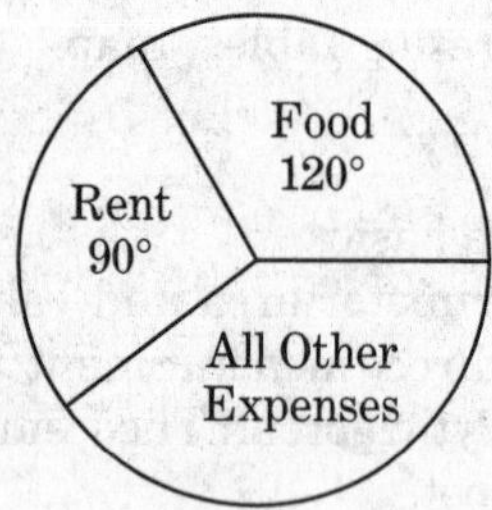

EXPENSE BUDGET

(A) $\frac{1}{3}$ (B) $\frac{5}{12}$ (C) $\frac{1}{4}$ (D) $\frac{3}{8}$ (E) $\frac{2}{9}$

SOLUTION: The sum of the measures of the angles around a point in a plane is 360°. Therefore the angle at the center representing all other expenses is $360 - 120 - 90 = 150°$.

$$\frac{150}{360} = \frac{5}{12}$$

The correct choice is (B).

EXAMPLE 4: On a high school football squad there were exactly three times as many linemen as backfield men. How many players could have been on the squad?

(F) 38 (G) 42 (H) 37 (J) 45
(K) none of these

SOLUTION: Let x = number of backfield men on the squad, and $3x$ = number of linemen on the squad. Total number of players = $x + 3x = 4x$.

Since x is a whole number, $4x$ is also a whole number and $4x$ is a multiple of 4.

Neither 38, 42, 37, or 45 is a multiple of 4.
Thus the correct choice is (K).

EXAMPLE 5: The population of a certain state is 3 million and the population of a town in that state is 15 thousand. The number of people living in the state is how many times the number of people living in the town?

(A) 20 (B) 2 (C) 200 (D) 2,000
(E) none of these

SOLUTION: We must find the quotient when 3,000,000 is divided by 15,000. When we perform the division, we note that $3{,}000{,}000 \div 15{,}000 = 200$.

The correct choice is (C).

EXAMPLE 6: Mr. Long bought 60 shares of VX Corporation at $18\frac{7}{8}$. Six months later he sold the stock at $22\frac{1}{4}$. How much was his profit before deducting commission and tax?

(F) \$20.25 (G) \$210.00 (H) \$198.50
(J) \$205.00 (K) \$202.50

SOLUTION: To find the profit on each share, we subtract $18\frac{7}{8}$ from $22\frac{1}{4}$.
$22\frac{1}{4} - 18\frac{7}{8} = 3\frac{3}{8}$

On 60 shares the profit is $3\frac{3}{8} \times 60 = \$202.50$.
The correct choice is (K).

EXAMPLE 7: On a cold winter day the temperature was 7° at noon and –5 ° at midnight. The change in temperature could be represented as

(A) 2° (B) –2° (C) 12° (D) –12°
(E) none of these

SOLUTION: In going from 7° to –5° the temperature first dropped from 7° to 0°, a drop of 7° (represented as –7°). The temperature then dropped another 5° (represented as –5°). The total drop in temperature was $(-7°) + (-5°) = -12°$.

The correct choice is (D)

EXAMPLE 8: For all real numbers a and b, $a/b = (a + b) - (a - b)$.

Then $\overline{8}/\overline{5}$ =

(F) 10 (G) 13 (H) 40 (J) 16 (K) 18

SOLUTION: $\bar{8}/\bar{5} = (8 + 5) - (8 - 5) = 13 - 3 = 10$
The correct choice is (F).

EXAMPLE 9: If $\frac{4}{7}$ of a number is 12 then $\frac{2}{3}$ of the number is

(A) 15 (B) 14 (C) 20 (D) 24 (E) 25

SOLUTION: Here is a quick way to solve this problem: If $\frac{4}{7}$ of a number is 12, then $\frac{1}{7}$ of the number is 3 and the number is $7 \times 3 = 21$.
$\frac{2}{3} \times 21 = 14$

The correct choice is (B).

The problem can also be solved algebraically as follows:

Let x = the number.
$\frac{4}{7}x = 12$
$4x = 7 \times 12 = 84$
$x = 84 \div 4 = 21$
$\frac{2}{3}x = \frac{2}{3} \times 21 = 14$

STRATEGIES FOR SUCCESS

The mathematics sections of the SSAT involve multiple-choice questions in arithmetic, simple algebra, and basic plane geometry. The emphasis is on mathematical reasoning ability and the understanding of mathematical concepts as well as on computational ability. The suggestions below are designed to help you to attain your best score.

➤ ***Tactic 1:*** Read each question carefully. Every word in a mathematical statement is precise and important.

➤ ***Tactic 2:*** Determine what information is given and exactly what must be found. This analysis will give you the gist of the problem.

➤ ***Tactic 3:*** Develop a plan for a solution. Such a plan will involve a link between the given information and what you must find.

➤ ***Tactic 4:*** Use your plan as a guide to complete the solution to the problem.

➤ ***Tactic 5:*** Check your answer.

➤ ***Tactic 6:*** Be sure that your answer is given in the units specified in the question.

➤ ***Tactic 7:*** Do not get upset if you cannot answer a question. You do not have to answer every question to get a good score. If you do not see an immediate approach to the solution of a problem, leave it and return to it later if time permits

➤ ***Tactic 8:*** Do not spend too much time on any one question. Since you have 25 minutes to answer 25 questions, you cannot afford to dwell on a troublesome problem.

➤ ***Tactic 9:*** Avoid random guessing. On this test, one quarter of the number of wrong answers will be deducted from the number of right answers. Since there is a penalty for guessing, you may lower your score appreciably by wild guessing. In general, you should not guess unless you can definitely eliminate one or two of the five choices given. If you are certain that one or more choices are incorrect, it is advisable to guess from among the remaining choices.

Diagnostic Test Mathematics

The purpose of the Diagnostic Test that follows is not to provide an exact equivalent of the real test but rather to pinpoint areas where you need additional learning. No time limit is given, and the questions may be slightly easier than those on sample tests in later chapters or on the actual test.

Only 25 items are included in each mathematics section of the SSAT. To increase the predictive value of this Diagnostic Test, the number of questions has been increased to 40.

After taking the test, be sure to use the "Material to Review" section on page 31 as a guide for further study.

DIRECTIONS: Five possible answers follow each question below. You may work out each problem in your head or use the margins of the test pages for scratch work. Decide which of the possible answers is best, and fill in the circle with the same letter as your answer choice.

SAMPLE PROBLEM:

$$\begin{array}{r} 8{,}652 \\ -\,3{,}914 \\ \hline \end{array}$$

(A) 4,728 (B) 4,748 (C) 4,738
(D) 5,738 (E) 4,838

1. If 100 + □ = 301 – 169, then □ =

(A) 132 (B) 232 (C) 30 (D) 32 (E) 332

Ⓐ Ⓑ Ⓒ Ⓓ Ⓔ

2. Which of the following is closest to 0.51×98?

(F) 2×50 (G) $\frac{1}{2} \times 100$ (H) $\frac{1}{4}$ of 150
(J) 2×51 (K) 50×100

Ⓕ Ⓖ Ⓗ Ⓙ Ⓚ

3. In the right triangle at the right what is the value of x?

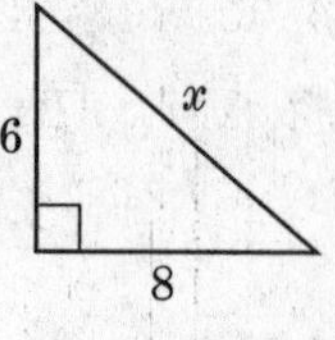

(A) 9 (B) 7 (C) 5
(D) 12 (E) 10

Ⓐ Ⓑ Ⓒ Ⓓ Ⓔ

4. If $12 > N > 1$ and N is a multiple of 5, then N =

(F) 10 (G) 9 (H) 6 (J) 4 (K) 3

Ⓕ Ⓖ Ⓗ Ⓙ Ⓚ

5. If $\frac{1}{3}$ of a number is less than 24, then the number must be

(A) less than 8 (B) less than 48
(C) more than 72 (D) less than 72
(E) more than 24

Ⓐ Ⓑ Ⓒ Ⓓ Ⓔ

6. If, in the sketch below, xz = 40 inches, yw = 40 inches, and yz = 15 inches, what is the length, in inches, of xw?

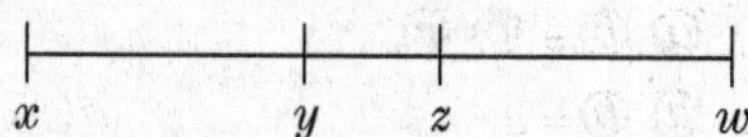

(F) 80 (G) 95 (H) 65 (J) 25 (K) 50

Ⓕ Ⓖ Ⓗ Ⓙ Ⓚ

7. What is the value of $6897 \times 25 + 6897 \times 75$? (Do NOT perform the indicated multiplications.)

(A) 68,970 (B) 689,700 (C) 689,725
(D) 689,000 (E) 689,070

Ⓐ Ⓑ Ⓒ Ⓓ Ⓔ

8. If a worker can turn out 84 machine parts in 15 hours, how many machine parts can he turn out in 20 hours?

(F) 63 (G) 89 (H) 96 (J) 100 (K) 112

Ⓕ Ⓖ Ⓗ Ⓙ Ⓚ

9. Ms. Johnson bought 120 shares of XYZ stock at $27\frac{5}{8}$. Nine months later she sold the stock at $30\frac{1}{4}$. What was her profit before deductions for commission and taxes?

(A) $360.00 (B) $315.00 (C) $345.00
(D) $380.00 (E) $375.00

Ⓐ Ⓑ Ⓒ Ⓓ Ⓔ

Questions 10–12 refer to the following definition:

For all real numbers a and b, ⓐ ⓑ = $(a - b) + ab$.

EXAMPLE: ⑥ ④ = $(6 - 4) + 6 \times 4 = 2 + 24 = 26$.

10. ⑨ ⑤ =

(F) 41 (G) 45 (H) 196 (J) 49 (K) 50

Ⓕ Ⓖ Ⓗ Ⓙ Ⓚ

11. If ⓧ④ = 31, then x =

(A) 6 (B) 7 (C) 8 (D) 9 (E) 10

Ⓐ Ⓑ Ⓒ Ⓓ Ⓔ

12. If a and b are numbers not equal to zero, which of the following must be true?

I. ⓐ ⓑ = ⓑ ⓐ
II. ⓐ ⓑ = a
III. ⓐ ⓑ + ⓑ ⓐ = $2ab$

(F) I only (G) I and II only
(H) I and III only (J) II and III only
(K) I, II, and III

Ⓕ Ⓖ Ⓗ Ⓙ Ⓚ

13. A library shelf contains only fiction and science books. If the shelf contains three times as many fiction books as science books, which could be the total number of books on the shelf?

(A) 82 (B) 79 (C) 65 (D) 84 (E) 75

Ⓐ Ⓑ Ⓒ Ⓓ Ⓔ

14. Bill has y dollars, and Jack has \$10 more than Bill. If Jack gives Bill \$4, how many dollars will Jack have left?

(F) 6 (G) $y + 6$ (H) 10 (J) $y - 4$ (K) $y + 4$

Ⓕ Ⓖ Ⓗ Ⓙ Ⓚ

15. Last year the ABC corporation's volume of business was \$7.4 billion. The preceding year the ABC corporation's volume of business was \$6.8 billion. The increase in volume of business was approximately

(A) 9.5% (B) 8.1% (C) 7.5% (D) 7.8%
(E) 8.8%

Ⓐ Ⓑ Ⓒ Ⓓ Ⓔ

16. A club collected \$300 by assessing each member the same whole number of dollars. Which of the following CANNOT be the amount each member was assessed?

(F) \$10 (G) \$12 (H) \$18 (J) \$20 (K) \$25

Ⓕ Ⓖ Ⓗ Ⓙ Ⓚ

17. How many square units of area are contained in the parallelogram below?

(A) 12
(B) 6
(C) 8
(D) 9
(E) 7

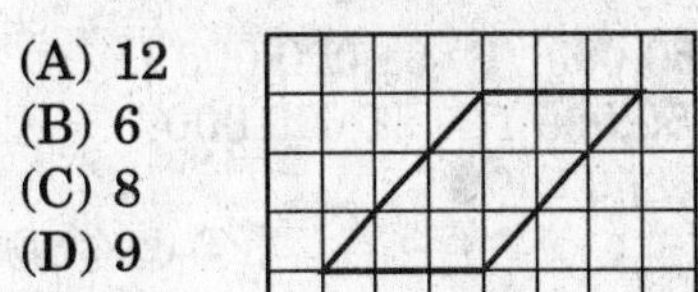

Ⓐ Ⓑ Ⓒ Ⓓ Ⓔ

18. If $\frac{7}{9} = \frac{\square}{36}$, the value of □ is

(F) 49 (G) 28 (H) 21 (J) 35 (K) 40

Ⓕ Ⓖ Ⓗ Ⓙ Ⓚ

19. If $3 \times 5 \times N = 0$, then N =

(A) $\frac{1}{5}$ (B) $\frac{1}{3}$ (C) 10 (D) 0 (F) 5

Ⓐ Ⓑ Ⓒ Ⓓ Ⓔ

20. If N is an odd number, then an even number is

(F) $N + 2$ (G) $N + 1$ (H) $3N$ (J) $2N - 1$
(K) $N + 4$

Ⓕ Ⓖ Ⓗ Ⓙ Ⓚ

21. All the following are less than $\frac{3}{4}$ except

(A) 0.72 (B) $\frac{5}{8}$ (C) $\frac{11}{15}$ (D) 80% (E) 69%

Ⓐ Ⓑ Ⓒ Ⓓ Ⓔ

22. The cost of a radio is \$26.50. This price includes a sales tax of 6%. What is the price of the radio without the tax?

(F) \$25.00 (G) \$24.41 (H) \$28.09
(J) \$1.50 (K) \$24.50

Ⓕ Ⓖ Ⓗ Ⓙ Ⓚ

23. To which of the following is 7.08 closest?

(A) 7.8 (B) 6.9 (C) 8.01 (D) 7.1 (E) 7

Ⓐ Ⓑ Ⓒ Ⓓ Ⓔ

24. When N is divided by 7, the quotient is 12 and the remainder is 6. $N =$

(F) 84 (G) 90 (H) 126 (J) 25 (K) 104

Ⓕ Ⓖ Ⓗ Ⓙ Ⓚ

25. The newspaper reports that next year's budget for a small town is 1.3 million dollars. This is \$350,000 more than the current budget. The current budget figure is

(A) \$1,950,000 (B) \$1,050,000 (C) \$950,000 (D) \$1,600,000 (E) \$850,000

Ⓐ Ⓑ Ⓒ Ⓓ Ⓔ

26. The graph below indicates the number of houses built by the Alpha Co. during a 5-year period. What was the average number of houses this company built in a single year during this period?

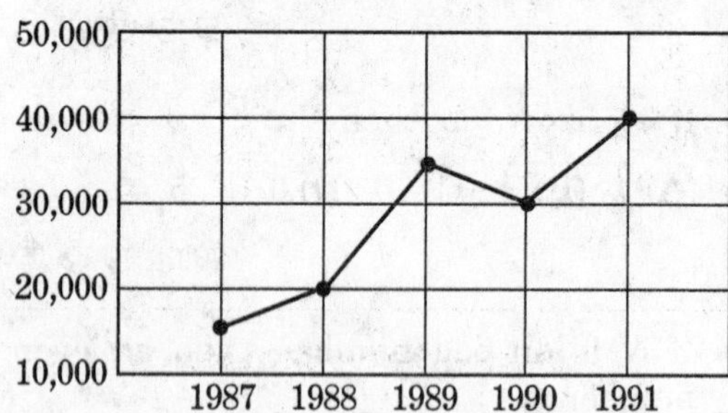

(F) 30,000 (G) 32,000 (H) 18,000 (J) 28,000 (K) 19,000

Ⓕ Ⓖ Ⓗ Ⓙ Ⓚ

27. An oil tank contains 540 gallons of heating oil. During the month of November, $\frac{1}{5}$ of the oil is consumed. In December, $\frac{1}{3}$ of the remaining oil is consumed. The number of gallons left in the tank is

(A) 388 (B) 288 (C) 308 (D) 252 (E) 200

Ⓐ Ⓑ Ⓒ Ⓓ Ⓔ

28. A garden plot is 120 feet long and 80 feet wide. The gardener wishes to divide the plot into squares 40 feet on a side. How many such squares will he obtain?

(F) 7 (G) 9 (H) 8 (J) 4 (K) 6

Ⓕ Ⓖ Ⓗ Ⓙ Ⓚ

29. In 1 day the Ace Supermarket sold twice as many apples as pears and 20 more oranges than pears. If 960 of these fruits were sold that day, how many were pears?

(A) 235 (B) 250 (C) 470 (D) 255 (E) 300

Ⓐ Ⓑ Ⓒ Ⓓ Ⓔ

30. A tank holds 60 gallons of a mixture of alcohol and water that is 20% alcohol. If 40 gallons of water are added, the percent of alcohol in the tank is

(F) 12% (G) 15% (H) 20% (J) 25% (K) 40%

Ⓕ Ⓖ Ⓗ Ⓙ Ⓚ

31. A piece of beef weighs 3 pounds 10 ounces. At \$2.48 per pound, what is the cost of this piece of beef?

(A) \$8.09 (B) \$8.99 (C) \$8.79 (D) \$9.99 (E) \$7.89

Ⓐ Ⓑ Ⓒ Ⓓ Ⓔ

32. The graph below shows the population of a certain county over a 6-year period. Between which 2 years was the growth in population the greatest?

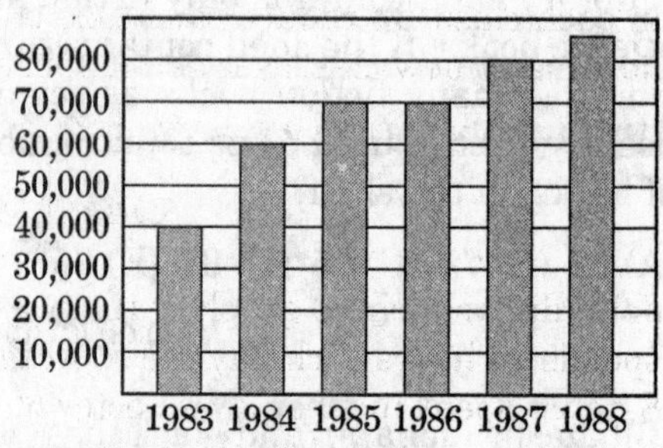

(F) 1983–1984 (G) 1984–1985 (H) 1985–1986 (J) 1986–1987 (K) 1987–1988

Ⓕ Ⓖ Ⓗ Ⓙ Ⓚ

33. The table below indicates times and distances covered on an airplane trip. If it is assumed that the plane travels at a steady rate, how many miles should be covered by 2:30 P.M.?

Time	Noon	1 P.M.	2 P.M.
Distance covered (in miles)	100	420	740

(A) 840 (B) 880 (C) 900 (D) 950 (E) 980

Ⓐ Ⓑ Ⓒ Ⓓ Ⓔ

34. Which of the following is NOT equal to the others?

(F) $2\frac{1}{2}\%$ (G) $\frac{25}{1,000}$ (H) 0.25 (J) 0.025 (K) 2.5%

Ⓕ Ⓖ Ⓗ Ⓙ Ⓚ

35. At a concert an auditorium is $\frac{3}{4}$ full. To fill the auditorium, 300 more seats would have to be occupied. How many seats does the auditorium have?

(A) 1,000 (B) 900 (C) 800 (D) 850 (E) 1,200

Ⓐ Ⓑ Ⓒ Ⓓ Ⓔ

36. A school has 30 classes with 32 students in each class. To reduce class size to 24, how many new classes must be formed?

(F) 10 (G) 8 (H) 12 (J) 6 (K) 9

Ⓕ Ⓖ Ⓗ Ⓙ Ⓚ

37. John draws a circle graph of the way he spends 24 hours each day. He represents 8 hours spent in sleep by a sector of the circle whose central angle measures

(A) 8° (B) 80° (C) 100° (D) 120° (E) 160°

Ⓐ Ⓑ Ⓒ Ⓓ Ⓔ

38. If $2x + 3 = 15$, then $x^2 - 2x =$

(F) 42 (G) 48 (H) 54 (J) 60 (K) 72

Ⓕ Ⓖ Ⓗ Ⓙ Ⓚ

39. Mrs. Brown bought a coat for $240 after it had been reduced by 25%. What was the original cost of the coat?

(A) $180 (B) $200 (C) $260 (D) $300 (E) $320

Ⓐ Ⓑ Ⓒ Ⓓ Ⓔ

40. If $3x + y = 50$ and $x = 3y$, then $y =$

(F) 5 (G) 10 (H) 6 (J) 12 (K) 20

Ⓕ Ⓖ Ⓗ Ⓙ Ⓚ

Answers—Diagnostic Test Mathematics

1. **D**	11. **B**	21. **D**	31. **B**
2. **G**	12. **J**	22. **F**	32. **F**
3. **E**	13. **D**	23. **D**	33. **C**
4. **F**	14. **G**	24. **G**	34. **H**
5. **D**	15. **E**	25. **C**	35. **E**
6. **H**	16. **H**	26. **J**	36. **F**
7. **B**	17. **D**	27. **B**	37. **D**
8. **K**	18. **G**	28. **K**	38. **G**
9. **B**	19. **D**	29. **A**	39. **E**
10. **J**	20. **G**	30. **F**	40. **F**

Rating Your Results

If you are in grade 5,6, or 7 (Lower Level):

Superior	32–40 correct
Average	22–31 correct
Below average	21 or fewer correct

If you are in grade 8, 9, 10 or 11 (Upper Level):

Superior	35–40 correct
Average	28–34 correct
Below average	27 or fewer correct

Material to Review:

If you missed these questions:	Review:
2, 8–9, 15–16, 18, 21, 23, 25, 27, 30–31, 34	**Chapter 8**
5, 35	**Chapter 9**
1, 4, 10–14, 19–20, 22, 24, 36, 38–40	**Chapter 10**
7	**Chapter 11**
26, 32, 33, 37	**Chapter 12**
3, 6, 17, 28	**Chapter 13**

Explanations

1. **D** 100+□ = 301 − 169. This is an equation with □ as the unknown.
□ = 301 − 169 − 100
□ = 301 − 269
□ = 32

2. **G** We note that 0.51 is slightly more that $\frac{1}{2}$ and 98 is slightly less than 100. Therefore, 0.51 × 98 is approximately equal to $\frac{1}{2} \times 100$.

3. **E** We use the Pythagorean Theorem in this right triangle to obtain this equation:
$$x^2 = 6^2 + 8^2$$
$$x^2 = 36 + 64 = 100$$
$$x = \sqrt{100} = 10$$

4. **F** The inequality $12 > N > 1$ tells us the N is greater than 1 and less than 12. Since N is a multiple of 5, N must be either 5 or 10. Since 5 is not offered as a choice, the correct selection is 10.

5. **D** Let x = the number.
Then $\frac{x}{3} < 24$.
If we multiply both sides of this inequality by 3, we have the result $x < 72$.

6. **H**
$$xw = xy + yz + zw$$
$$xy + yz = xz = 40$$
$$zw + yz = yw = 40$$
$$xy + yz + zw + yz = 40 + 40 = 80$$
$$xw + yz = 80$$
$$xw + 15 = 80$$
$$xw = 80 - 15 = 65$$

7. **B** According to the Distributive Property,
$6897 \times 25 + 6897 \times 75 = 6897\ (25 + 75)$
$= 6897(100)$
$= 689{,}700$

8. **K** Let x = number of machine parts turned out in 20 hours. We form the proportion
$$\frac{15}{84} = \frac{20}{x}$$
$$15x = 20(84) = 1{,}680$$
$$x = 1{,}680 \div 15 = 112$$

9. **(B)** $30\frac{1}{4} - 27\frac{5}{8} = 2\frac{5}{8}$ profit per share
$120 \times \frac{21}{8}$ = \$315.00, profit on 120 shares

10. **J** ⑨ ⑤ = 9 − 5 + 9(5) = 4 + 45 = 49

11. **B** ⓧ ④ $= x - 4 + 4x = 31$
$$5x - 4 = 31$$
$$5x = 31 + 4 = 35$$
$$x = 35 \div 5 = 7$$

12. **J** I. ⓐ ⓑ $= a - b + ab$, ⓑ ⓐ $= b - a + ba$ ⓐ ⓑ does not equal ⓑ ⓐ. This is untrue.
II. ⓐ ⓪ $= a - 0 + a \times 0 = a - 0 + 0 = a$. This statement is true.
III. ⓐ ⓑ $= a - b + ab$, ⓑ ⓐ $= b - a + ab = ab + ab = 2ab$. This statement is true.

13. **D** Let a = number of science books, and $3a$ = number of fiction books. Then $4a$ = total number of books. Thus, the total number of books must be a multiple of 4. Of the choices given, only 84 is a multiple of 4.

14. **G** Jack has $(y + 10)$ dollars. After Jack gives Bill 4 dollars, Jack has $y + 10 - 4 = (y + 6)$ dollars.

15. **E** 7.4 − 6.8 = 0.6 billion dollars of increase. Percent of increase = $\frac{0.6}{6.8} = \frac{6}{68}$ = 0.88, or 8.8%.

16. **H** 300 must be a multiple of any number of dollars paid by each member. Of the choices given, only 300 ÷ 18 does not yield a whole number.

17. **D** The area of a parallelogram = bh. In this case, b = 3 units and h = 3 units. Area = 3 × 3 = 9 square units.

18. **G** $\frac{7}{9} = \frac{\square}{36}$
$9 \times \square = 7 \times 36$
$\square = \frac{7 \times 36}{9} = 28$

19. **D** If the product of two or more numbers is 0, then one number of the product must be 0. Since neither 3 nor 5 is 0, N must be 0.

20. **G** If N is an odd number, then the next higher number is even. The next higher number is $N + 1$.

21. **D** $\frac{3}{4}$ = 0.75 = 75%
80% > 75%

22. **F** Let x = cost of radio.
$$x + 0.06x = 26.50$$
$$1.06x = 26.50$$
$$x = 26.50 \div 1.06 = \$25.00$$

23. **D** 7.08 = 7.1 to the nearest tenth

24. **G** $\frac{N}{7} = 12 + \frac{6}{7}$
If we multiply both sides of the equation by 7, we have $N = 12 \times 7 + 6$
$= 84 + 6 = 90$

25. **C** 1.3 million = 1,300,000
1,300,000 – 350,000 = $950,000

26. **J** We must find the average of 15,000, 20,000, 35,000, 30,000 and 40,000.
15,000 + 20,000 +
35,000 + 30,000 + 40,000 = 140,000
140,000 ÷ 5 = 28,000

27. **B** $540 \times \frac{1}{5} = 108$; $540 - 108 = 432$ gallons left after November
$432 \times \frac{1}{3} = 144$; $432 - 144 = 288$ gallons left after December

28. **K** The gardener can fit 3 squares along the length and 2 squares along the width. He will obtain $3 \times 2 = 6$ squares.

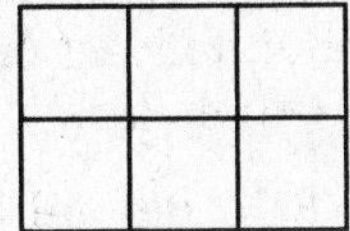

29. **A** Let x = number of pears,
$2x$ = number of apples,
and $x + 20$ = number of oranges.
$x + 2x + x + 20 = 960$
$4x + 20 = 960$
$4x = 960 - 20 = 940$
$x = 940 \div 4 = 235$

30. **F** 20% of 60 = $\frac{1}{5}(60) = 12$ gallons of alcohol in tank. To obtain the percent of alcohol in the tank, we set up the equation

$$\frac{\text{alcohol: } 12}{\text{mixture: } 60 + 40} = \frac{12}{100} = 12\%$$

31. **B** 3 pounds 10 ounces = $3\frac{10}{16}$ pounds
$3\frac{10}{16} = 3\frac{5}{8} = \frac{29}{8}$ pound
$\frac{29}{8}(2.48) = 29\,(0.31) = \$8.99$

32. **F** Study of the graph indicates that there was a 20,000 population growth from 1983 to 1984. This growth was larger than the growth in any other 2-year period.

33. **C** Study of the table indicates that the plane covers 320 miles per hour. By 2:30 P.M. the plane should cover $740 + \frac{1}{2}(320)$ miles. $740 + \frac{1}{2}(320) = 740 + 160 = 900$ miles.

34. **H** 0.25 = 25%, or $\frac{1}{4}$. All other numbers are equivalent to $2\frac{1}{2}$%.

35. **E** $\frac{1}{4}$ of the auditorium represents 300 seats. $\frac{4}{4}$, or the full auditorium, represents 4(300) = 1,200 seats.

36. **F** To reduce class size from 32 to 24, 8 students must be dropped from each class. In 30 classes, $30 \times 8 = 240$ students must be dropped. $240 \div 24 = 10$ new classes must be formed.

37. **D** John spends $\frac{8}{24}$, or $\frac{1}{3}$, of his day in sleep. The sum of the measures of the angles around a point in a plane is 360°. $\frac{1}{3}$ of 360° = 120°

38. **G** $2x + 3 = 15$
$2x = 15 - 3 = 12$
$x = 6$
$x^2 + 2x = (6)^2 + 2(6) = 36 + 12 = 48$

39. **E** Since the coat was reduced in price by 25%, Mrs. Brown paid 75% of the cost of the coat.
Let x = original price of the coat.
$0.75x = 240$
$75x = 24{,}000$
$x = 24{,}000 \div 75 = \$320$

40. **F** Since $x = 3y$ then $3x = 3(3y) = 9y$.
$9x + y = 50$
$10y = 50$
$y = 5$

STUDY PLAN FOR THE MATHEMATICS SECTIONS

The amount of time necessary for a thorough study program to prepare for the mathematics sections of the SSAT will vary greatly from individual to individual. It is not necessary to work through all the detailed exercise material given in the book. On any given topic it is suggested that you take one of the practice tests. If you can answer correctly at least 80% of the questions on the test, there is no need for you to linger; you may proceed to the next topic. Such a plan of procedure will enable you to concentrate on the areas in which you are weak. In general, there are three major areas to cover.

1. ***Basic arithmetic.*** This topic, which involves fundamental operations with whole numbers, fractions, decimals and percents, is covered completely in Chapter 8.

   It is recommended that you cover Chapter 9, "Application of Basic Mathematical Skills," in some detail. The emphasis in this chapter on verbal problems and special topics will be very helpful in developing problem-solving skills.

2. ***Algebra.*** The algebra content on the SSAT is limited and is thoroughly covered in Chapters 10 and 11. In preparing for the test, you are advised to study these chapters carefully. The exercise material is good preparation for the test.

   Chapter 12 on tables, maps, and graphs also anticipates likely test questions.

3. ***Geometry*** The geometry content required on the SSAT is also limited and is concisely covered in Chapter 13. This chapter should be studied in detail.

   Chapter 14, "Reasoning Skills," will help you develop resourcefulness in tackling a typical mathematical situation.

The Reading Comprehension Section

A basic key to academic success is skill in extracting information from the printed page. Even though many students now spend more time watching television than regarding printed matter, our schools are geared to using books as the primary communication medium. The SSAT, therefore, tests your ability to handle the many types of reading materials you will meet in high school.

The passages in the Reading Comprehension Section of the SSAT may be selected from the following content areas:

Narrative:	novels, short stories, essays
Humanities:	art, biographies, poetry
Social Studies:	history, economics, sociology
Science:	medicine, astronomy, chemistry, physics, anthropology, psychology
Argument:	the presentation of a clear, definite point of view on a subject

The test section consists of seven reading passages selected from varied reading matter—books, magazines, and newspapers. Each passage is followed by a series of questions, 40 in all. The questions are of seven basic types:

1. ***Main idea:*** These questions test your ability to recognize the main idea or basic subject matter (topic) of the passage.

EXAMPLE:
This selection deals mainly with (A)...(B)...etc.

2. ***Factual:*** These questions test your direct understanding of what is stated or not stated in the selection.

EXAMPLE:
The source of the money available for this project is (A)...(B)...etc.

3. ***Word meaning:*** These questions test your ability to recognize or to infer the most appropriate meaning of a word or phrase as it is used in the passage.

EXAMPLE:
The word ______________ as used in this selection means (A)...(B)...etc.

4. ***Writer's attitude toward the subject:*** These questions test your ability to identify the attitude, (e.g., objective, critical, approving) that the author reveals in discussing the subject matter of the paragraph.

EXAMPLE:
The attitude of the writer toward his subject is (A)...(B)...etc.

5. ***Mood or tone of the passage:*** These questions test your recognition of the dominant mood (e.g., optimistic, hopeless, skeptical) of the passage.

EXAMPLE:
The mood of the passage is (A)... (B)...etc.

6. ***Inferences and implications:*** These questions test your ability to draw inferences or conclusions from what is stated or implied in the passage.

EXAMPLES:
The author implies that (A)...(B)...etc.
The author would most likely agree that (A)...(B)...etc.

Which of the following can be inferred (A)...(B)...etc.

7. ***Style:*** These questions test your ability to recognize the techniques used by the author in writing the selection.

EXAMPLE:
The style of the passage is most like that in (A)...(B)...etc.

Sample Questions

The directions and sample questions below are typical of those encountered on the Reading Comprehension Section of the SSAT.

DIRECTIONS: Carefully read the passage below and the questions that follow. Select the choice which, on the basis of the passage, best answers the question.

The need for protection of snakes today is as great as was the need for protection of birds in the days of Audubon. No other animals are subject to as much needless destruction as snakes. Countless thousands are killed indiscriminately by those who encounter them. They are stoned, crushed, and shot by ignorant, careless, or frightened people. Many are mashed during the warmer months by trucks and cars on the highways. In farmlands, field machinery such as mowers not only kill off many but, at the same time, destroy the snakes' habitat and food supply. The bulldozer, the major tool for city and suburban development, is a great enemy of snakes.

Snakes are beneficial to humanity. None of them are vegetarians; they do not attack crops or plantings. Their major sources of food are the mice and rats that plague our communities. Many snakes are fast becoming endangered species!

1. Which of the following is not mentioned in the selection as a reason for protecting snakes?
   (A) They help protect our farm crops.
   (B) They do not attack our food supply.
   (C) They are in danger of disappearing forever.
   (D) They have the same right to be here as we do.
   (E) They are being killed in great numbers.

2. The destruction is needless because
   I. the killers sell the snakeskins
   II. the snakes would die anyway
   III. no one benefits from it
   IV. the environmentalist fights against it
   (F) I only
   (G) I, II, and IV only
   (H) II and III only
   (J) III only
   (K) II, III, and IV only

3. An example of a snake's habitat would be
   (A) its fangs
   (B) its venom
   (C) a hollow under a boulder
   (D) the zoo
   (E) a chicken coop

4. The author does not explain
   (F) how the snakes are destroyed
   (G) why they are destroyed
   (H) which groups of people are mainly responsible for the destruction
   (J) why the snakes need protection at the present time
   (K) why the snakes expose themselves to this destruction

Answers and Analysis

1. **D** (A) is wrong because snakes protect crops by eating mice and rats. (B) is wrong because "they do not attack crops or plantings." (C) is wrong because they are "becoming endangered species." (E) is wrong because "Countless thousands are killed..."
2. **J** Nothing is said in this passage about any benefit resulting from the snakes' death.
3. **C** Because field machinery destroys their habitat and food supply, some of their habitats must be in or near open fields.
4. **K** (F) is wrong because the article mentions that snakes are destroyed by stones, trucks and cars, bullets, mowers, and bulldozers; (G) is wrong because the article says that snakes are killed out of ignorance, carelessness, and fear; (H) is wrong because the article blames much of the destruction on thoughtless people and also on those who clear fields for development; and (J) is wrong because the fact that thousands of snakes are dying makes the need to protect them an urgent one.

STRATEGIES FOR SUCCESS

- Zero in on the paragraphs to be read. Clear your mind of everything else.
- Since this is a test of your ability to read, do not rely on your own knowledge as the basis of your answer. Each passage contains all the information you will need to answer the questions.
- Read the passage quickly to decide what it is about.
- Before you turn to the questions, read the passage a second time, sentence by sentence.
- Take the questions in order. Read all the choices before you select the best answer.
- Do not hesitate to turn back to the paragraph to verify your choices.
- Passages about familiar subjects or areas of your interest take less time than others. However, if you find a passage that seems too difficult, go on to the next; come back to it later if you have time. When you return to the passage, it may seem much easier to grasp.
- Often picking out the key sentence will organize your thinking about the selection.
- Some people find that looking at the questions first can point to the meaning of a difficult paragraph. Others find this approach very time-consuming; they prefer to get the main ideas in the selection before looking at the questions. While taking the practice tests, try both methods to see which one works better for you.
- Some people find underlining key phrases helpful. This process can slow your reading down too much. It may be better to concentrate on the sentence-by-sentence reading approach to find principal ideas, facts, and author's point of view.
- There is no substitute for practice. The more varied your reading, the better your score. Set aside some time each day for recreational reading and reading for information. The editorial page of the daily newspaper is an ideal source. And so are your textbooks!

Diagnostic Test Reading Comprehension

This test is planned for both the Upper and Lower forms of the test. When you take this Diagnostic Test, simulate examination conditions as closely as you can. Choose a quiet time of the day and a quiet room. Try to avoid interruptions. Concentrate on the test and give it your undivided attention.

DIRECTIONS: Carefully read each passage below and the questions that follow. Select the choice which, on the basis of the passage, best answers the question. Then fill in the circle with the same letter as your answer choice.

The battle between giants seems to have come to an end. In 1952, a team of British surveyors labeled Peak XV in the Himalayas as the highest mountain in the world. They changed its name to Mount Everest in honor of Sir George Everest, a British geophysicist. Mount Everest wore its majestic crown with proper dignity until 1954 when an American professor of astronomy, George Wallterstein, led an expedition that took the title away. The survey revealed that K-2, 800 miles northwest of Everest in northern Kashmir, was 36 feet higher.

The title remained with K-2 until 1987 when an Italian team, aided by satellites with advanced instruments on board, determined that Everest was really 29,108 feet above sea level, 840 feet higher than K-2. These measurements, made more difficult because of the heavy snow, were not made solely to keep the record straight. They were necessary preliminaries to exploration of the geologic depths of the Himalayas to determine the cause of these spectacular heights.

1. The "giants" in line 1 are identified as
   (A) Everest and Wallerstein
   (B) the satellites and Italy
   (C) the British and the Italians
   (D) the satellites and Peak K-2
   (E) Peaks XV and K-2

   Ⓐ Ⓑ Ⓒ Ⓓ Ⓔ

2. The battle came to an end because
   (F) the ice fields on top of Everest grew faster
   (G) the Himalayas are growing
   (H) more accurate measurements were possible
   (J) the English reached the top
   (K) the Americans were careful surveyors

   Ⓕ Ⓖ Ⓗ Ⓙ Ⓚ

3. The satellites referred to in the second paragraph were most likely
   (A) supplied by the American team of 1954
   (B) located at the base of Mount Everest
   (C) continuously circling the earth
   (D) developed by Italian astronomers
   (E) launched in Russia

   Ⓐ Ⓑ Ⓒ Ⓓ Ⓔ

4. The height of Mount Everest was difficult to measure because
   I. the snow was so deep around it
   II. the instruments were not up to the task
   III. the Himalayas are shifting
   IV. the natives objected to the process
   (F) I, II, and IV only
   (G) II and III only
   (H) I and II only
   (J) I and III only
   (K) II, III, and IV only

   Ⓕ Ⓖ Ⓗ Ⓙ Ⓚ

5. According to the passage all of the following statements are true EXCEPT:
   (A) For 33 years, K-2 was called the world's highest mountain.
   (B) An American team proved that Everest was highest.
   (C) George Everest did not establish his fame as a mountain climber.
   (D) Mount Everest has also been known as Peak XV.
   (E) Exact heights of mountains help to reveal the processes that create mountains.

   Ⓐ Ⓑ Ⓒ Ⓓ Ⓔ

6. The tone of the article reveals the author as
   (F) prejudiced
   (G) imaginative
   (H) argumentative
   (J) factual
   (K) joyous

   Ⓕ Ⓖ Ⓗ Ⓙ Ⓚ

Gerard Kremer, who lived in the sixteenth century, is better known by the Latin form of his name, Gerardus Mercator. His claim to fame is based on his attempts to develop a map of the surface of the earth in true proportions.

Equal distances apart on the globe, the parallels of latitude when copied on a flat surface like a map must be drawn with increasing separation as the distance from the equator increases. Thus the major disadvantage of the Mercator projection that Gerardus Mercator devised is that areas are exaggerated with increasing distance from the equator.

This type of projection gives an incorrect impression of the relative sizes of the countries of the world. As an example, Greenland shows up much larger than it really is—although its shape is preserved.

In present-day textbooks, the Mercator projections have been replaced by maps that give more accurate representations resulting from advances in computer studies.

7. This passage is primarily about
   (A) the general process of map making
   (B) the relationship between landmass size and distance from the equator
   (C) map making by computer
   (D) Mercator's success in making maps with true proportions
   (E) the misrepresentations in Mercator projections

   Ⓐ Ⓑ Ⓒ Ⓓ Ⓔ

8. Which of the following statements is (are) NOT true?
   I. The equator is distorted on Mercator's maps.
   II. A Mercator map can be identified by the size of Greenland.
   III. A projection map is a true representation of global dimensions.
   IV. Most modern maps are still Mercator projections.
   (F) I only
   (G) I and IV only
   (H) I, III, and IV
   (J) III and IV only
   (K) II and IV only

   Ⓕ Ⓖ Ⓗ Ⓙ Ⓚ

9. Which of the following statements is NOT true?
   (A) Mercator's maps were used by Columbus during his voyages of discovery.
   (B) Sailors could not navigate with Mercator's projections.
   (C) Present-day maps are better proportioned than were those made by Mercator.
   (D) Long-range compass directions were not distorted by Mercator.
   (E) Modern mapmakers have better instruments to work out the necessary proportions.

   Ⓐ Ⓑ Ⓒ Ⓓ Ⓔ

10. The tone of this selection is
    (F) angry
    (G) apologetic
    (H) accusative
    (J) humorous
    (K) objective

    Ⓕ Ⓖ Ⓗ Ⓙ Ⓚ

Fellow citizens! Before you cast your ballots and bring this crucial issue to the moment of decision, I ask you to pause and reflect while there is still time.

Unfortunately, during the recent debates and discussions, the heat of argument too frequently obscured the key facts available to us. We listened to persuasive speakers on each side. But we listened without complete awareness. We carried away only the beliefs that we had brought with us.

May I plead with you! This is the last moment for sifting for the truth, free from our likes and dislikes. For once, let us take a fresh view. Let us examine the issues from the most basic approach: Who will benefit now if this bill becomes law? Will voting yes mean that our children will have a better chance for the better life? Will voting yes mean that a small minority will no longer dictate our way of life? Will voting yes safeguard our liberties?

These are the only questions that must be asked. All others fade in significance before them! Let your minds and not your hearts make the decision for all of us!

11. The speaker most likely was
    I. outside the voting place
    II. a disappointed candidate
    III. in the midst of a debate
    IV. in favor of the bill
    (A) I, II, and IV only
    (B) I, II, and III only
    (C) III only
    (D) I and IV only
    (E) All of the above

Ⓐ Ⓑ Ⓒ Ⓓ Ⓔ

12. The issue is labeled "crucial" because
    (F) it is to be voted upon
    (G) the speaker says so
    (H) the speaker wrote the proposal
    (J) it involves important considerations
    (K) it is being considered

Ⓕ Ⓖ Ⓗ Ⓙ Ⓚ

13. The speaker does not tell the voters
    (A) that much is at stake in this vote
    (B) that they must exercise their democratic right to vote
    (C) that she is not concerned about how they vote but why they vote as they do
    (D) that the vote will affect the present and the future
    (E) that they must vote with their minds and not their feelings

Ⓐ Ⓑ Ⓒ Ⓓ Ⓔ

14. The speaker wants the voters to
    (F) tell their children how to vote
    (G) rebel against the leaders
    (H) vote for her party
    (J) disregard their prejudices
    (K) be proud of their right to vote

Ⓕ Ⓖ Ⓗ Ⓙ Ⓚ

15. The speaker did not feel that in the debates
    (A) the debaters were very skillful
    (B) the facts were clearly explained
    (C) the voters listened with closed minds
    (D) the voters knew what was really happening
    (E) the debaters were emotional

Ⓐ Ⓑ Ⓒ Ⓓ Ⓔ

16. The tone of the speaker's remarks is one of
    (F) annoyance
    (G) desperation
    (H) flattery
    (J) pessimism
    (K) resignation

Ⓕ Ⓖ Ⓗ Ⓙ Ⓚ

If I ever marry and have children, I am sure of one thing: as a father, I'll give my son a chance to explain before I decide what the punishment will be. Then again, I don't think I'll even punish him for doing something foolish, or childish, or thoughtless or rash or absurd, something that of course did harm to nobody. If he thinks it was the right thing to do, I'll back him up and tell everyone that he has a right to his own opinion—or mistakes.

I'll let his conscience handle the rewards and punishments. I'll let him learn at his own rate from his own experiences. I'll never give him a going-over or a what-for in front of others. Especially not before his friends.

And another thing: I'll never let anyone compare him with his sister. I wouldn't want him to grow up hating her because she does things more to please the adults in the family than to please her brother or herself.

Maybe I'll solve it all by never marrying. I haven't thought it all through, but right now things are getting too complicated, and I'll have to settle that later. Right now I think I'm getting a bit hungry. I'll see what's in the fridge.

17. The speaker is most likely
    (A) 20 years old
    (B) 13 years old
    (C) 6 years old
    (D) 18 years old
    (E) 24 years old

Ⓐ Ⓑ Ⓒ Ⓓ Ⓔ

18. The speaker makes clear
    (F) how the father felt about what the speaker had done
    (G) what the punishment was
    (H) where the speaker lives
    (J) what the speaker's name is
    (K) how his mother felt about what the speaker had done

Ⓕ Ⓖ Ⓗ Ⓙ Ⓚ

19. The speaker feels that his father was unfair because
    (A) his father punished him too severely
    (B) his sister went unpunished although she was just as guilty
    (C) his father never asked why the speaker had done what he had done
    (D) his father had lectured him too long
    (E) even the speaker's friends agreed that his father was unfair

Ⓐ Ⓑ Ⓒ Ⓓ Ⓔ

20. The speaker is angry with his sister because she
    (F) told her father what had happened
    (G) refused to listen to him
    (H) had teased him
    (J) avoids such scenes with their parents
    (K) was much older than he

Ⓕ Ⓖ Ⓗ Ⓙ Ⓚ

21. The speaker is talking to
    I. his best friend
    II. himself
    III. his mother
    IV. his parakeet
    (A) I, II, or IV
    (B) II only
    (C) I or II only
    (D) II or IV
    (E) I, II, III or IV

Ⓐ Ⓑ Ⓒ Ⓓ Ⓔ

One-eighth of the whole population were slaves, not distributed generally over the Union, but localized in the southern part of it. These slaves constituted a peculiar and powerful interest. All knew that this interest was, somehow, the cause of the war. To strengthen, perpetuate, and extend this interest was the object for which the insurgents would rend the Union, even by war; while the government claimed no right to do more than to restrict the territorial enlargement of it. Neither party expected for the war, the magnitude, the duration, which it had already attained. Neither anticipated that the original cause of the conflict—secession—might cease to be the issue when, or even before, the conflict itself should cease. Each looked for an easier triumph, and a result less fundamental and astounding.

22. This selection was most likely written
    (F) a few years before the Civil War began
    (G) just after the Civil War ended
    (H) during the first months of the Civil War
    (J) a year or two after it had begun
    (K) in the twentieth century

Ⓕ Ⓖ Ⓗ Ⓙ Ⓚ

23. The writer used the term "insurgents" (line 8) to describe the Southerners because
    (A) he wanted to show that he sympathized with the South
    (B) they were fighting against their government
    (C) they wanted to keep slavery
    (D) the North was winning
    (E) it was important to gain the sympathy of the Europeans

Ⓐ Ⓑ Ⓒ Ⓓ Ⓔ

24. When the war began both sides
    (F) fought hard enough to achieve victory
    (G) thought that victory was far away
    (H) anticipated many bloody battles
    (J) felt that there would be no compromise on slavery
    (K) felt that the main issue was the right to secede

Ⓕ Ⓖ Ⓗ Ⓙ Ⓚ

25. At the beginning of the war, the leaders in Washington
    (A) wanted to end slavery in the South
    (B) planned to end slavery gradually throughout the country
    (C) wanted to keep slavery out of new territories
    (D) wanted to end slavery immediately
    (E) stopped thinking about the slavery issue

Ⓐ Ⓑ Ⓒ Ⓓ Ⓔ

26. The author's attitude toward the Civil War may be best described as
    I. in favor of a Southern victory
    II. in favor of a Northern victory
    III. horrified by the idea of slavery
    IV. willing to compromise on slavery for the sake of unity
    (F) II and IV only
    (G) I and IV only
    (H) III only
    (J) IV only
    (K) none of the above

Ⓕ Ⓖ Ⓗ Ⓙ Ⓚ

Bonsai, as developed by the Japanese, are hardy trees and shrubs kept dwarfed and trained into interesting shapes. As with normal trees and shrubs, their year-round home is outdoors, in the open sun and air. They do poorly when moved into the confines of a house or indoor garden. Specimens that are naturally twisted or gnarled—the kinds we normally bypass—make the most interesting and beautiful bonsai.

The plants are dwarfed by hard pruning of the top as well as of the roots. The pruning is usually done gradually and only once or twice a year, to reduce the danger of shock. The shape of the plants is changed in small stages by gradually bending or guiding it with braces and heavy bonsai wire. Some tropical trees and shrubs—for example, the silk oak—have been successfully trained like bonsai for indoor living.

27. Bonsai in a garden
    I. are easy to identify
    II. look like young plants
    III. must be shaped by gardeners
    IV. are natural dwarfs
    (A) I only
    (B) II and IV only
    (C) I, II, and III
    (D) I, III, and IV
    (E) I and III only

Ⓐ Ⓑ Ⓒ Ⓓ Ⓔ

28. The pruning is done in small doses to prevent
    (F) mistakes
    (G) loss of water
    (H) a severe reaction
    (J) loss of beauty
    (K) leaves from growing too small

Ⓕ Ⓖ Ⓗ Ⓙ Ⓚ

29. Which of the following definitions is most appropriate for the word "confines" as used in line 6 of this selection?
    (A) experimental setting
    (B) cold temperatures
    (C) limitless scope
    (D) unfriendly atmosphere
    (E) artificial restraints

Ⓐ Ⓑ Ⓒ Ⓓ Ⓔ

30. Which of the following is the most appropriate title for this selection?
    (F) Cruelty to Nature
    (G) The Art of Bonsai
    (H) Interesting Shapes
    (J) An Unusual Hobby
    (K) Growing Trees and Shrubs

Ⓕ Ⓖ Ⓗ Ⓙ Ⓚ

31. The author's tone in this passage can best be described as
    (A) authoritative
    (B) admiring
    (C) questioning
    (D) cautious
    (E) unconcerned

Ⓐ Ⓑ Ⓒ Ⓓ Ⓔ

Roses for you
Embedded whites and yellows
Delicate pink or purple red
To dry and fade with grace,
And scent the air;
With varied low impatiens
And stately lilies
In clusters round the edges.

Flowers for you
Fragile companions
Reminders, soundless voices
Like you
Like you.

32. In the first stanza, the author describes a
(F) garden
(G) bed of flowers
(H) dream
(J) bouquet
(K) forest

Ⓕ Ⓖ Ⓗ Ⓙ Ⓚ

33. The flowers are "fragile companions" because
I. they are easily destroyed
II. their perfume is so delicate
III. they are symbols
IV. they are part of the author's reality

(A) I and IV only
(B) II and III only
(C) III and IV only
(D) I and II only
(E) I, III, and IV

Ⓐ Ⓑ Ⓒ Ⓓ Ⓔ

34. Which of the following could be the reason why the author selected only the most common varieties of flowers?
(F) They are easily available.
(G) The colors of these flowers are in harmony with each other
(H) They are part of our everyday existence.
(J) They look expensive.
(K) The choice was unintentional.

Ⓕ Ⓖ Ⓗ Ⓙ Ⓚ

35. Which of the following is the most appropriate title for this poem?
(A) A Lovely Bouquet
(B) Greetings on a Happy Occasion
(C) Lament for a Lost Love
(D) Living Flowers
(E) Anniversary Time

Ⓐ Ⓑ Ⓒ Ⓓ Ⓔ

The danger lies not in change but in the fear of change. Stagnation sets in quickly when the one major concern is to keep things as they are, to avoid everything that might upset the applecart or modify procedures or results.

Instead, we have to accept as basic to all our activities the realization that living means adjustment. Of course, this does not mean that the degree of change is constant. This is where our intellectual grasp and emotional stability take control and decide which and how much modification is required. As we must not refuse to alter when alteration is necessary, so we must not blindly accept all change as being mandated.

36. An example of a person who would not accept the conclusions in this selection is one who
I. joins the Navy to see the world
II. refuses to move to a better neighborhood because he is so used to the old
III. leaves a job because he is bored by doing the same routines
IV. goes to evening school to learn a new trade

(F) I only
(G) II only
(H) II and III only
(J) I and III only
(K) I, III, andIV

Ⓕ Ⓖ Ⓗ Ⓙ Ⓚ

37. Which of the following is an example of the type of stagnation referred to by the author?
    (A) the unmoving water in a swampy area
    (B) the state of mind of a person who is pleased with the way things are and hopes they won't change for the worse
    (C) the situation when a company's business falls to almost nothing
    (D) the failure of a school's team to win a game for three years
    (E) the mental state of someone who feels an intense need to be forever young and have the world and people around him remain ever the same

Ⓐ Ⓑ Ⓒ Ⓓ Ⓔ

38. According to the author, what are the various aspects of the best attitude toward change?
    I. So long as we live, we must expect change.
    II. The big decision is not whether to adjust but how much we are to adjust.
    III. There is some good in all change.
    IV. If we are strong enough, we can avoid change.

    (F) I and III only
    (G) II and III only
    (H) I and II only
    (J) I only
    (K) I, III, and IV

Ⓕ Ⓖ Ⓗ Ⓙ Ⓚ

39. Which of the following is a major weakness in the author's presentation?
    I. She repeats herself too often.
    II. She uses too many difficult words.
    III. She is too technical.
    IV. She presents no proof through examples.

    (A) I, II, and III
    (B) II and IV
    (C) III and IV
    (D) III only
    (E) IV only

Ⓐ Ⓑ Ⓒ Ⓓ Ⓔ

40. Which of the following best describes the tone of this selection?
    (F) emotional
    (G) sentimental
    (H) opinionated
    (J) condemnatory
    (K) cheerful

Ⓕ Ⓖ Ⓗ Ⓙ Ⓚ

Answers—Diagnostic Test Reading Comprehension

1. **E**	9. **A**	17. **B**	25. **C**	33. **E**
2. **H**	10. **K**	18. **F**	26. **K**	34. **H**
3. **C**	11. **E**	19. **C**	27. **E**	35. **C**
4. **H**	12. **J**	20. **J**	28. **H**	36. **G**
5. **B**	13. **B**	21. **E**	29. **E**	37. **E**
6. **J**	14. **J**	22. **J**	30. **G**	38. **H**
7. **E**	15. **D**	23. **B**	31. **A**	39. **E**
8. **H**	16. **G**	24. **K**	32. **J**	40. **H**

Rating Your Results

If you are in grade 5,6, or 7 (Lower Level):

Superior	34–40 correct
Average	26–34 correct
Below average	25 or fewer correct

If you are in grade 8, 9, 10 or 11 (Upper Level):

Superior	36–40 correct
Average	29–35 correct
Below average	28 or fewer correct

Material to Review: Chapter 5

Explanations

1. **E** Nothing in the selection is as gigantic as the peaks.

2. **H** "...an Italian team, aided by satellites..."

3. **C** Modern satellites carry instruments around the planet earth. Nothing in the passage supports the other choices.

4. **H** The natives and the shifting mountains are not mentioned.

5. **B** The American team did the reverse.

6. **J** The selection contains provable facts, not opinions.

7. **E** "This type of projection [Mercator's] gives an incorrect impression of the relative sizes of the countries of the world." Choice (A) is too general; choices (B) and (C) are minor points; and choice (D) is inaccurate.

8. **H** The oversized Greenland is the cue.

9. **A** Mercator lived in the sixteenth century; Columbus's voyage took place in 1492 (fifteenth century).

10. **K** Facts, not reactions to facts, are presented.

11. **E** All four choices are possible; a case could be made for any of them.

12. **J** Something that is labeled as crucial always involves important considerations.

13. **B** She does not urge them to vote.

14. **J** "...sifting for the truth free from our likes and dislikes..."

15 **D** "...the heat of argument...obscured the key facts."

16. **G** "May I plead with you...this is the last moment..."

17. **B** He sounds like a typical movie stereotype of a teenager.

18. **F** The mother is not mentioned.

19. **C** "I'll give my son a chance to explain..."

20. **J** "she does things more to please the adults..."

21. **E** The listener, if any, could be any one of the four.

22. **J** "Neither side expected for the war...the duration, which it had already attained."

23. **B** The Southerners fit the dictionary definition.

24. **K** Neither anticipated that the original cause—secession—might cease to be the issue.

25. **C** "While the government...restrict the territorial enlargement."

26. **K** The author expressed none of the ideas listed.

27. **E** They are old plants dwarfed into unusual shapes by periodic pruning.

28. **H** "The pruning is usually done...only once or twice a year, to reduce the danger of shock."

29. **E** The only definition that is appropriate is restraints. None of the other choices can be logically applied to a house or indoor garden.

30. **G** The only specific choice is (G). The others are too general; they give little or no indication of the subject matter.

31. **A** No statement is supported by proof. The author is the authority.

32. **J** Only the flower parts of the plants are mentioned.

33. **E** Perfume is not usually related to fragility.

34. **H** The person memorialized was the roses, impatiens, and lilies of the author's life—in other words, part of his "everyday existence."

35. **C** The poem expresses the writer's feeling of sorrow. Note the clues: "to dry and fade with grace"; "Fragile companions/Reminders, soundless voices/Like you."

36. **G** The author favors the realization that we must be ready for change.

37. **E** It is the stagnation of people who greatly fear change.

38. **H** We cannot prevent change, but we can decide how much the adjustment should be.

39. **E** There are no examples in the selection.

40. **H** The author says it is so because she says it is so.

STUDY PLAN

The key to raising your score in this area is the amount of time you can spend on the exercises, practice tests, and Mastery Exams in Chapter 5, Reading, beginning on page 140.

Long-Term Program

1. The pages on Work-Study Skills consist of exercises and techniques to improve your speed and comprehension. Typical examination questions are analyzed in the sections that follow. The Mastery Exams will assure increased ability and speed.
2. The lists of things to do and facts to master in Chapter 6 are long—and rewarding! All you have to do is to budget your time properly. Browse through the chapter and decide where to begin. Spend no more than 25 minutes on each practice session. Do not skip the varied exercises, practice tests, and Mastery Exams. They lead to confidence and speed in handling the actual SSAT.
3. Use the Practice SSATs beginning on page 510 as your final step in preparation.

Crash Program

1. Turn to Chapter 5, Reading, beginning on page 140. Do as many of the exercises, practice tests, and Mastery Exams as you can to gain speed and accuracy. Several short sessions are always more productive than one long haul.
2. Use the Practice SSATs beginning on page 510 as your final step.

If You Are Taking the Independent School Entrance Examination (ISEE)

The Independent School Entrance Examination (ISEE) has a flexible administration schedule; examination dates and locations vary from area to area. Your guidance counselor or the admissions officer of the school to which you apply will help find the best time and location for you.

The ISEE is given on two levels. The Middle Level is for candidates for grades 6, 7, and 8; the Upper Level, for candidates for grades 9 through 12. Within each level, the questions vary in difficulty, but some of the questions appear in both levels. Students in higher grades are expected to answer correctly more questions than students in middle grades. For example, students in grade 10 should have more correct answers than students in grade 9.

The ISEE measures major abilities that lead to academic success in high school. Through multiple-choice questions it tests verbal ability, quantitative ability, reading comprehension, and mathematics achievement. In addition, it includes the writing of an essay.

Frequently Asked Questions About the ISEE

When should candidates apply?

The completed registration form must be received by the Educational Records Bureau (ERB) Operations Office no later than three weeks before the scheduled test date. Late and walk-in registrations are possible for an additional fee.

How soon are scores reported to schools and parents?

The Individual Student Reports are sent to schools and parents within three days after receipt of the answer sheet and essay.

What does the ISEE consist of?

The test consists of five sections.

Verbal Ability
- Synonyms — 20 questions
- Sentence completions — 20 questions

Quantitative Ability — 40 questions
- Concepts/Understanding
- Application

Rereading Comprehension — 40 questions
- Science passages
- Social studies passages

Mathematics Achievement — 50 questions
- Middle Level
  - Computation
  - Applications
- Upper Level
  - Arithmetic concepts
  - Algebraic concepts
  - Geometric concepts

Essay

How many times may a candidate take the test?

A candidate may take the test only once within a 6-month period. Results of a second testing during any 6-month period will not be reported to the designated schools.

Should I leave troublesome questions unanswered?

The ISEE gives one point for each correct answer. No deduction is made for wrong answers or answers left blank. There is no penalty for guessing.

Should I make an educated guess?

Yes, but try first to shift the odds in your favor. If you can eliminate one or more of the choices as definitely wrong, you increase greatly your chance of guessing correctly. However, even if you cannot eliminate any of the choices, you still have a 25% chance of guessing correctly.

How important is scratch work on the ISEE?

Your scratch work is done in the question booklet and is strictly to help you. The only thing the machine marks is your answer sheet. Make certain that you do not do any scratch work on the answer sheet. The scoring machine may mistake a stray mark for a second answer to a question and give you no credit even if your intended answer is correct.

How much mathematics is required for the ISEE?

The purpose of the ISEE is not to find out how much math you know. Rather, the test attempts to discover your ability to reason with mathematical symbols, to solve problems, and to interpret data. Since these questions are designed to test thinking power, you should expect to solve most problems by close inspection and reasoning rather than by complicated work.

How are the ISEE scores reported?

The Individual Student Reports sent to schools and parents include test scores and diagnostic information showing how the candidate compares with the others who have applied for admission.

How are the tests scored?

Each answer is read by a scanning machine that records it on computer tape. The computer then compares the student's answers with the correct response for that question.

What if I make a mistake on the answer sheet?

There are only two mistakes that can involve the computer, the answer sheet, and the candidate. If the candidate blocks out two letters on one line, the computer labels the answer incorrect. If the candidate fails to remove an erased answer completely, the machine then finds two answers on a line and again labels that question incorrectly answered.

What if I think that the scoring was wrong?

For a fee, the ERB Operations Office will rescore your answer sheet by hand. If handscoring results in a change in score, the fee will be refunded. If the need to resort to this procedure arises, discuss the problem with your school counselor.

How important are ISEE scores?

When making their admission decisions, schools differ on the amount of weight they give to these scores. Most schools consider far more than the scores when evaluating candidates. They also look at school grades, extracurricular activities, teachers' recommendations, other objective test records, letters of recommendation, interviews, and the essay written as part of the ISEE battery. However, the results of the ISEE do provide a scientific way of comparing all candidates in regard to their abilities to do high school work. Because of the breadth of comparison, admissions officers realize that this examination affords equal opportunity to everyone applying.

To what extent does the essay affect the final decision of the admission officers?

The extent to which the essay helps in reaching the big decision varies from school to school. Although the essay cannot be given an objective grade, it reveals much about the candidate's training, readiness to enter middle or high school, and mastery of language skills. It can afford the admissions officer an opportunity to compare individual candidates from another angle of ability and achievement.

How can this chapter help me in preparing for the ISEE?

It will familiarize you with the kinds of questions that appear on the ISEE. Knowing what to expect when you take the test is important in preparing for the test and succeeding in it.

This chapter has been organized so that it parallels the sections of the ISEE. The Verbal Ability, Quantitative Ability, Reading Comprehension, and Mathematics Achievement sections are treated separately. Each part of the chapter presents sample questions with answers, strategies for success, a Diagnostic Test with answers and explanations, and a study plan for the particular ISEE section being discussed. No time limits have been imposed on the diagnostic tests because their main purpose is to help you discover your weaknesses and strengths. After completing this chapter, you will know what steps are necessary for you to do your best on the ISEE.

Verbal Ability

The two verbal subsections have a total of 40 questions: 20 synonyms and 20 sentence completions. On the ISEE, you are allowed 20 minutes for the entire verbal section. Your future middle or high school success will be closely bound to your ability to understand the vocabulary used in the textbooks and classroom discussions that will be your primary sources for acquiring knowledge. Therefore, the ISEE tests knowledge of words found in formal written English rather than the words used in everyday speech.

Sample Synonym Questions

This subsection tests your vocabulary directly. You are given a word and then four choices from which to select the one closest in meaning to a given word. The directions and sample questions below are typical of those encountered in the synonym subsection of the ISEE.

DIRECTIONS: Each question consists of a word in capital letters followed by four choices. Circle the letter of the word that is most nearly the same in meaning as the word in capital letters.

1. PRIOR:

   (A) pitiful (B) previous (C) trained (D) serious

2. APEX:

   (A) beginning (B) midpoint (C) peak (D) destination

3. SLACK:

   (A) sly (B) lost (C) deserted (D) loose

4. CHASTISE:

   (A) complain (B) purify (C) punish (D) overcome

5. PREVARICATE:

   (A) lie (B) prefer (C) proclaim (D) conceal

Answers

1. **B** 2. **C** 3. **D** 4. **C** 5. **A**

STRATEGIES FOR SUCCESS

- If you have easy recognition of the given word, its definition or synonym will come quickly to your mind. You will painlessly identify the correct choice. To prevent carelessness, however, eliminate the other choices before marking the answer sheet.
- If all the choices for a given word seem to be wrong, don't suspect a misprint. Instead, realize that a less familiar meaning of the given word may be involved. Many words, such as *port, stern,* and *light* have a variety of meanings.
- If a word does not slot easily, try to recall a phrase in which you have met it. Use the phrase to evaluate the choices. Do not skip any choice. The word *guile* may yield its meaning through a phrase like "trickster full of guile." The key to *incessant* could be "incessant complaining." The three strategies above should give you a handle on more than 80% of the test words. How should you approach the others?
- Sometimes thinking of an antonym can help. What is the opposite of a given word? Use the opposite to evaluate the synonym choices. Possible clues may be found in antonyms like *prolong* and *shorten, legitimate* and *unlawful.* If this method is successful, make certain that you check all of the choices before selecting the best answer.
- When the word is one that you have met before, but none of the choices works, don't spend time agonizing. Circle the number of the given word in the test booklet. Plan to come back to the circle if time permits. Very often when you return for a second try, your mind has identified the word and the answer becomes clear.

- Even though words in the test supposedly are in order of increasing difficulty, don't give up because you find the words becoming unfamiliar. Go through the entire list! Some words that others find troublesome, you may find fairly simple.
- Should you guess? Try to eliminate as many of the choices as you can. Since there is no penalty for guessing on this test, however, you should leave no blanks.

Diagnostic Test Synonyms

Only 20 items are included in the Verbal Ability Section of the ISEE. In order to increase the predictive value of this synonym Diagnostic Test, however, the number of words tested has been increased to 50. This test is planned for those preparing for both the Middle and Upper forms of the test.

DIRECTIONS: Each question consists of a word in capital letters followed by four choices. Select the word that is most nearly the same in meaning as the word in capital letters, and fill in the circle that has the same letter as your answer choice.

1. PLACID:
(A) watery (B) visual (C) calm (D) beautiful
Ⓐ Ⓑ Ⓒ Ⓓ

2. QUIVER:
(A) question (B) huddle (C) portfolio (D) receptacle
Ⓐ Ⓑ Ⓒ Ⓓ

3. ROBUST:
(A) wholesale (B) wholesome (C) dark (D) hardy
Ⓐ Ⓑ Ⓒ Ⓓ

4. TREAD:
(A) string (B) step (C) tire (D) imprint
Ⓐ Ⓑ Ⓒ Ⓓ

5. VIGILANT:
(A) wary (B) energetic (C) docile (D) troublesome
Ⓐ Ⓑ Ⓒ Ⓓ

6. HUMID:
(A) funny (B) damp (C) reheated (D) rainy
Ⓐ Ⓑ Ⓒ Ⓓ

7. GHASTLY:
(A) shocking (B) haphazard (C) dangerous (D) injured
Ⓐ Ⓑ Ⓒ Ⓓ

8. FATHOM:
(A) dig (B) mean (C) comprehend (D) row
Ⓐ Ⓑ Ⓒ Ⓓ

9. ENGROSS:
(A) preoccupy (B) profit (C) fatten (D) diet
Ⓐ Ⓑ Ⓒ Ⓓ

10. CONTROVERSY:
(A) dispute (B) opposition (C) refusal (D) temptation
Ⓐ Ⓑ Ⓒ Ⓓ

11. CONCUR:
(A) race (B) collide (C) discuss (D) agree
Ⓐ Ⓑ Ⓒ Ⓓ

12. ADHERE:
(A) cling (B) depart (C) arrive
(D) exaggerate
Ⓐ Ⓑ Ⓒ Ⓓ

13. BLEAK:
(A) sound (B) desolate (C) distorted
(D) eminent
Ⓐ Ⓑ Ⓒ Ⓓ

14. CONGENIAL:
(A) inherited (B) agreeable
(C) acquired (D) human
Ⓐ Ⓑ Ⓒ Ⓓ

15. FLOURISH:
(A) create (B) thrive (C) conquer
(D) console
Ⓐ Ⓑ Ⓒ Ⓓ

16. FEIGN:
(A) delegate (B) display (C) pretend
(D) prefer
Ⓐ Ⓑ Ⓒ Ⓓ

17. QUELL:
(A) quit (B) substitute (C) subdue
(D) modify
Ⓐ Ⓑ Ⓒ Ⓓ

18. REVISE:
(A) ridicule (B) restore (C) create
(D) modify
Ⓐ Ⓑ Ⓒ Ⓓ

19. INFAMOUS:
(A) wicked (B) ignorant
(C) inconsiderate (D) awkward
Ⓐ Ⓑ Ⓒ Ⓓ

20. STATUTE:
(A) sculptor (B) sculpture (C) law
(D) mold
Ⓐ Ⓑ Ⓒ Ⓓ

21. ACCLIMATE:
(A) accustom (B) freeze (C) defer
(D) imprison
Ⓐ Ⓑ Ⓒ Ⓓ

22. CHARY:
(A) cautious (B) noted (C) brave
(D) cowardly
Ⓐ Ⓑ Ⓒ Ⓓ

23. AVARICE:
(A) affection (B) jealousy (C) hatred
(D) greed
Ⓐ Ⓑ Ⓒ Ⓓ

24. PUGNACIOUS:
(A) aggressive (B) dogged
(C) pertinent (D) talkative
Ⓐ Ⓑ Ⓒ Ⓓ

25. WONT:
(A) desire (B) refusal (C) reluctance
(D) habit
Ⓐ Ⓑ Ⓒ Ⓓ

26. TANTALIZE:
(A) relate (B) tease (C) enlarge
(D) complicate
Ⓐ Ⓑ Ⓒ Ⓓ

27. SCRUPULOUS:
(A) conscientious (B) clear
(C) deferential (D) rash
Ⓐ Ⓑ Ⓒ Ⓓ

28. NOSTALGIA:
(A) illness (B) nightmare (C) fright
(D) homesickness
Ⓐ Ⓑ Ⓒ Ⓓ

29. OVERT:
(A) preventable (B) obvious
(C) seasoned (D) inevitable
Ⓐ Ⓑ Ⓒ Ⓓ

30. LAVISH:
(A) insolent (B) generous (C) lively
(D) decorative
Ⓐ Ⓑ Ⓒ Ⓓ

31. MOLEST:
(A) conquer (B) reveal (C) greet
(D) annoy
Ⓐ Ⓑ Ⓒ Ⓓ

32. PERSEVERANCE:
(A) torture (B) reward (C) separation
(D) persistence
Ⓐ Ⓑ Ⓒ Ⓓ

33. ONSLAUGHT:
(A) attack (B) murder (C) exploration
(D) negotiation
Ⓐ Ⓑ Ⓒ Ⓓ

34. GRATIS:
    (A) rough (B) expensive
    (C) inexpensive (D) free
    Ⓐ Ⓑ Ⓒ Ⓓ

35. LAUD:
    (A) praise (B) rule (C) veto
    (D) sing
    Ⓐ Ⓑ Ⓒ Ⓓ

36. PETRIFY:
    (A) abolish (B) consign (C) rout
    (D) terrify
    Ⓐ Ⓑ Ⓒ Ⓓ

37. STUPEFY:
    (A) polish (B) astound (C) defeat
    (D) punish
    Ⓐ Ⓑ Ⓒ Ⓓ

38. TITANIC:
    (A) gigantic (B) ancient (C) watery
    (D) indestructible
    Ⓐ Ⓑ Ⓒ Ⓓ

39. OBESE:
    (A) obstinate (B) hardly (C) irrelevant
    (D) fat
    Ⓐ Ⓑ Ⓒ Ⓓ

40. MORTIFY:
    (A) harden (B) slaughter
    (C) humiliate (D) console
    Ⓐ Ⓑ Ⓒ Ⓓ

41. PERT:
    (A) saucy (B) relevant (C) typical
    (D) bitter
    Ⓐ Ⓑ Ⓒ Ⓓ

42. OBSOLETE:
    (A) powerful (B) preoccupied
    (C) dying (D) outdated
    Ⓐ Ⓑ Ⓒ Ⓓ

43. VIVACIOUS:
    (A) lively (B) livelong (C) livable
    (D) lithe
    Ⓐ Ⓑ Ⓒ Ⓓ

44. ALLAY:
    (A) befriend (B) assail (C) govern
    (D) soothe
    Ⓐ Ⓑ Ⓒ Ⓓ

45. GALA:
    (A) feminine (B) ethnic (C) festive
    (D) religious
    Ⓐ Ⓑ Ⓒ Ⓓ

46. FREEBOOTER:
    (A) pirate (B) parasite (C) official
    (D) mule
    Ⓐ Ⓑ Ⓒ Ⓓ

47. HAVEN:
    (A) warehouse (B) city (C) shelter
    (D) mansion
    Ⓐ Ⓑ Ⓒ Ⓓ

48. GRIMY:
    (A) serious (B) childish (C) guilty
    (D) dirty
    Ⓐ Ⓑ Ⓒ Ⓓ

49. TEPID:
    (A) lukewarm (B) sheltering (C) heady
    (D) hoarse
    Ⓐ Ⓑ Ⓒ Ⓓ

50. SYNTHETIC:
    (A) rare (B) artificial (C) gemlike
    (D) dull
    Ⓐ Ⓑ Ⓒ Ⓓ

Answers—Diagnostic Test Synonyms

1. **C**	14. **B**	27. **A**	39. **D**
2. **D**	15. **B**	28. **D**	30. **C**
3. **D**	16. **C**	29. **B**	41. **A**
4. **B**	17. **C**	30. **B**	42. **D**
5. **A**	18. **D**	31. **D**	43. **A**
6. **B**	19. **A**	32. **D**	44. **D**
7. **A**	20. **C**	33. **A**	45. **C**
8. **C**	21. **A**	34. **D**	46. **A**
9. **A**	22. **A**	35. **A**	47. **C**
10. **A**	23. **D**	36. **D**	48. **D**
11. **D**	24. **A**	37. **B**	49. **A**
12. **A**	25. **D**	38. **A**	50. **B**
13. **B**	26. **B**		

Rating Your Results

If you are in grade 5, 6, or 7 (Middle Level):

Superior	41–50 correct
Average	31–40 correct
Below Average	30 or fewer correct

If you are in grade 8, 9, 10, or 11 (Upper Level):

Superior	44–50 correct
Average	37–43 correct
Below Average	30 or fewer correct

Material to Review: Chapter 4

Sample Completion Questions

This subsection tests your vocabulary in context. You are given a sentence with one or two blanks, followed by four choices of words to complete the sentence.

DIRECTIONS: Each question below consists of a sentence with one or two blanks. Circle the letter of the choice that will best complete the meaning of the sentence as a whole.

1. The statements of the prosecutor's witnesses were so vague that the judge felt compelled to _______ the accused.

   (A) sentence
   (B) punish
   (C) compliment
   (D) acquit

2. The mother patiently listened to the _______ demands of the overtired child.

   (A) petulant
   (B) predatory
   (C) concise
   (D) understated

3. The visiting head of state admired the costly decoration that set off the _______ feasts given in her honor.

   (A) length
   (B) superficial
   (C) sumptuous
   (D) substantiated

4. In the fall the _______ voices of the _______ noisy crickets filled the night air in the valley.

   (A) strident...countless
   (B) harmonious...indigenous
   (C) concertizing...joyous
   (D) irritating...occasional

5. The _______ vulture had _______ so much that it was unable to fly away when danger approached.

   (A) gigantic...wheedled
   (B) finicky...digested
   (C) wily...eaten
   (D) voracious...gorged

Answers

1. **D** 2. **A** 3. **C** 4. **A** 5. **D**

STRATEGIES FOR SUCCESS

➤ Begin by planning positively, looking among the choices for the word or words that logically complete the sentence. In sentence 1, the lack of detail from the prosecutor's witnesses leads to choice (D), *acquit.* To prevent careless errors, however, eliminate the other choices before marking the answer sheet.

➤ Sometimes the sentence will contain a definition or synonym of the correct choice. In sentence 4, *noisy* points directly toward *strident.*

➤ Given two blanks to be filled, don't fall into the trap in which one of the choices in a pair seems appropriate. Both must fit the context. In sentence 5, *eaten* could fit, but *wily* does not describe a vulture so gluttonous that it loses the ability to escape danger.

➤ Be patient. Test each choice before marking the answer sheet. Sentence completion questions take much more time and concentration than selecting synonyms.

➤ If you find that an answer isn't coming, use the process of elimination. Put a line through each choice that is obviously wrong: an inappropriate, difficult word, an antonym for the appropriate word, a word that makes the sentence meaningless. If none of this helps, don't dawdle. Go on to the next question and plan to come back to the puzzler, if you can, after you have completed the others. Very often, when you return for a second try, the answer becomes clear.

➤ Finally, leave no blanks.

Diagnostic Test Sentence Completion

Only 20 items are included in the sentence-completion section of the ISEE. In order to increase the predictive value of this sentence-completion Diagnostic Test, the number of items has been increased to 50. This test is planned for those preparing for both the Middle and Upper forms of the test.

DIRECTIONS: Each question below consists of a sentence with one or two blanks. Select the word or words that will best complete the meaning of the sentence, and fill in the circle that has the same letter as your answer choice.

1. We soon found that no commercial crop could grow in the _______ soil of this desertlike countryside.
(A) enriched (B) cultivated
(C) barren (D) lush
Ⓐ Ⓑ Ⓒ Ⓓ

2. These backward people are held in _______ not by chains but by their own ignorance and superstitions.
(A) awe (B) contempt (C) reverence
(D) bondage
Ⓐ Ⓑ Ⓒ Ⓓ

3. The parents tried in vain to _______ the child who had lost his dog.
(A) discipline (B) distress
(C) captivate (D) console
Ⓐ Ⓑ Ⓒ Ⓓ

4. Freedom of speech and religion are the very _______ of democracy.
(A) core (B) antithesis (C) enemies
(D) creations
Ⓐ Ⓑ Ⓒ Ⓓ

5. We will have to _______ our trip to the Caribbean until the hurricane season ends.
(A) revise (B) defer (C) advance
(D) hasten
Ⓐ Ⓑ Ⓒ Ⓓ

6. Because she blamed her friends for her failure, the _______ teenager felt that she could trust no one.
(A) jubilant (B) confident
(C) embittered (D) annihilated
Ⓐ Ⓑ Ⓒ Ⓓ

7. The young reporter telephoned his editor to tell her that the report of his death was _______ .
(A) explicit (B) erroneous
(C) coincidental (D) authentic
Ⓐ Ⓑ Ⓒ Ⓓ

8. The _______ faces of the released prisoners showed how poorly they had been cared for.
(A) grateful (B) well-groomed
(C) haggard (D) cheerful
Ⓐ Ⓑ Ⓒ Ⓓ

9. The rebels held the dictator's family _______ until all political prisoners were released.
   (A) entrap (B) diffused (C) entombed
   (D) hostage
   Ⓐ Ⓑ Ⓒ Ⓓ

10. Few animals are _______ enough to live in Antarctica with its extreme cold.
    (A) intellectual (B) conscientious
    (C) immature (D) hardy
    Ⓐ Ⓑ Ⓒ Ⓓ

11. To the optimist, nothing is _______ except death and taxes.
    (A) inevitable (B) perilous
    (C) self-defeating (D) avoidable
    Ⓐ Ⓑ Ⓒ Ⓓ

12. Because we had kept the secret well, Sarah had no _______ of the surprise party planned for her.
    (A) impression (B) vista (C) vestiges
    (D) inkling
    Ⓐ Ⓑ Ⓒ Ⓓ

13. The company was accused of selling milk that had been _______ by the addition of water.
    (A) condensed (B) improved
    (C) adulterated (D) endangered
    Ⓐ Ⓑ Ⓒ Ⓓ

14. The strongest weapon that the public has to _______ inefficient elected officials is the ballot.
    (A) honor (B) investigate (C) castigate
    (D) cajole
    Ⓐ Ⓑ Ⓒ Ⓓ

15. Our extravagant purchases soon _______ our bank balance.
    (A) completed (B) refilled
    (C) preceded (D) depleted
    Ⓐ Ⓑ Ⓒ Ⓓ

16. Susanna's _______ parents will never deny her anything that they can possibly get to fulfill her wishes.
    (A) dogmatic (B) doting (C) frugal
    (D) noncommittal
    Ⓐ Ⓑ Ⓒ Ⓓ

17. When it comes to ice cream, I admit I am a(n) _______ who can eat huge quantities without ever satisfying my appetite.
    (A) sage (B) felon (C) mendicant
    (D) glutton
    Ⓐ Ⓑ Ⓒ Ⓓ

18. My grandfather had the goodwill, wisdom, and strength to be able to _______ most of the serious quarrels in our village.
    (A) instigate (B) extol (C) mediate
    (D) ignore
    Ⓐ Ⓑ Ⓒ Ⓓ

19. Dressed in _______ black, the humorless assistant kept us quiet and completely depressed in spirit.
    (A) scintillating (B) startling
    (C) modern (D) somber
    Ⓐ Ⓑ Ⓒ Ⓓ

20. Because the governor disagreed with their purposes, he _______ three bills passed by the legislature.
    (A) approved (B) revised
    (C) disregarded (D) vetoed
    Ⓐ Ⓑ Ⓒ Ⓓ

21. Because Beth exercises so infrequently, she has a(n) _______ to gain weight quickly.
    (A) tendency (B) urgency (C) inability
    (D) reason
    Ⓐ Ⓑ Ⓒ Ⓓ

22. Baseball fans love to _______ the umpire when he makes a "wrong" decision.
    (A) extol (B) annihilate
    (C) taunt (D) overrule
    Ⓐ Ⓑ Ⓒ Ⓓ

23. Because of Brazil's ideal climate, its production of coffee _______ that of any other country in the world.
(A) equals (B) trifles (C) suppresses (D) surpasses
Ⓐ Ⓑ Ⓒ Ⓓ

24. Because we lost our major contract, we shall have to _______ your employment at the end of the week.
(A) reconstitute (B) refurbish (C) terminate (D) disengage
Ⓐ Ⓑ Ⓒ Ⓓ

25. With _______ dignity, the elderly couple danced the anniversary waltz to the applause of their guests.
(A) awkward (B) youthful (C) stately (D) ungainly
Ⓐ Ⓑ Ⓒ Ⓓ

26. After surviving incredible hardships, the _______ explorers planted a flag at the _______ of Mount Everest.
(A) fearful...base
(B) victorious...summit
(C) unconquerable...ridge
(D) dreaded...pinnacle
Ⓐ Ⓑ Ⓒ Ⓓ

27. Ability to speak several foreign languages _______ is _______ to success as a diplomat assigned to the United Nations.
(A) haltingly...equivalent
(B) occasionally...unrelated
(C) fluently...requisite
(D) briefly...essential
Ⓐ Ⓑ Ⓒ Ⓓ

28. The drunken driver was filled with _______ for having caused the _______ injuries to the child.
(A) remorse...fatal
(B) tension...self-inflicted
(C) excuses...senseless
(D) consternation...insensible
Ⓐ Ⓑ Ⓒ Ⓓ

29. Because of Eileen's sharp tongue and quick temper, it is _______ that her insulting remarks will _______ a fight.
(A) possible...prevent
(B) customary...end
(C) inevitable...provoke
(D) incidental...intensify
Ⓐ Ⓑ Ⓒ Ⓓ

30. The supervisor's benevolence and _______ toward his favorites made his crew _______ and bitter.
(A) indifference...patronizing
(B) partiality...morose
(C) cruelty...sensitive
(D) impartiality...vulnerable
Ⓐ Ⓑ Ⓒ Ⓓ

31. _______ Margie saved the signed program as a _______ of her first prom.
(A) Sensible...momentum
(B) Thoughtless...souvenir
(C) Sentimental...memento
(D) Methodical...reminder
Ⓐ Ⓑ Ⓒ Ⓓ

32. _______ of the lifeguard's warnings, _______ Adam swam out beyond his depth.
(A) Heedless...rash
(B) Headful...incautious
(C) Disdainful...prudent
(D) Because...sensible
Ⓐ Ⓑ Ⓒ Ⓓ

33. Because of the increased activity of the outlaw gangs, a _______ of soldiers was stationed at Fort Laramie to protect the _______ settlers.
(A) group...invulnerable
(B) platoon...absent
(C) garrison...vulnerable
(D) regiment...departed
Ⓐ Ⓑ Ⓒ Ⓓ

34. The newcomer's _______ manner made the girls in the class ask _______, "Who does she think she is?"
(A) genial...impatiently
(B) cordial...bitterly
(C) haughty...indignantly
(D) offhand...sympathetically

Ⓐ Ⓑ Ⓒ Ⓓ

35. Because of her physical handicap, Louise has to _______ many more _______ problems than I do.
(A) alternate...convenient
(B) face...vexing
(C) create...insurmountable
(D) sensitize...trivial

Ⓐ Ⓑ Ⓒ Ⓓ

36. The _______ remarks of the onlookers did not please the owner, who insisted on repairing the _______ car while dressed in her Sunday best.
(A) sympathetic...unimpaired
(B) inept...wrecked
(C) frivolous...stalled
(D) sententious...insensitive

Ⓐ Ⓑ Ⓒ Ⓓ

37. I hope that the smog and the air _______ will not make human beings as _______ as the dinosaurs.
(A) particles...invulnerable
(B) pollutants...extinct
(C) waves...gigantic
(D) pollution...ferocious

Ⓐ Ⓑ Ⓒ Ⓓ

38. My _______ cousin _______ allows one word to do the work of a dozen.
(A) reticent...seldom
(B) unrelated...intentionally
(C) inquisitive...always
(D) loquacious...never

Ⓐ Ⓑ Ⓒ Ⓓ

39. We were _______ to believe everything she told us until cold facts proved how much she was _______ the truth.
(A) taught...uttering
(B) prone...distorting
(C) inclined...substantiating
(D) unwilling...coloring

Ⓐ Ⓑ Ⓒ Ⓓ

40. The longer you _______ without making your mind up definitely one way or the other, the more difficult it will be to reach a(n) _______ decision.
(A) argue...inequitable
(B) concur...mature
(C) vacillate...valid
(D) cajole...inconceivable

Ⓐ Ⓑ Ⓒ Ⓓ

41. I wish I knew how to _______ this annoying error without making it _______ to the rest of the staff!
(A) correct...mystifying
(B) allay...fatal
(C) rectify...obvious
(D) reactivate...acceptable

Ⓐ Ⓑ Ⓒ Ⓓ

42. She offered to help without _______ ; just for the _______ of being part of our organization.
(A) remuneration...joy
(B) stint...pangs
(C) complaint...dissatisfaction
(D) payment...humility

Ⓐ Ⓑ Ⓒ Ⓓ

43. The _______ bulldozer soon pushed away from the building site the _______ that remained of the bombed-out factory.
(A) indestructible...fragments
(B) flimsy...impediments
(C) invincible...seepage
(D) indefatigable...rubble

Ⓐ Ⓑ Ⓒ Ⓓ

44. How could you be so _______ as to think that this _______ would cheat everyone but you!
(A) gullible...swindler
(B) unconscious...magician
(C) naive...magnate
(D) perceptive...evildoer

Ⓐ Ⓑ Ⓒ Ⓓ

45. The _______ dangers that beset the usual traveler through the jungle depths never _______ Tarzan.
(A) effusive...beset
(B) myriad...deferred
(C) continual...daunted
(D) untold...depleted

Ⓐ Ⓑ Ⓒ Ⓓ

46. When the _______ turned into a downpour, the baseball game had to be _______.
(A) shower...resumed
(B) sprinkles....postponed
(C) flash flood...rescheduled
(D) drizzle...inaugurated

Ⓐ Ⓑ Ⓒ Ⓓ

47. Only after a(n) _______ search did the district attorney unearth evidence _______ to the case.
(A) revelatory...irrelevant
(B) picayune...inappropriate
(C) haphazard...applicable
(D) exhaustive...pertinent

Ⓐ Ⓑ Ⓒ Ⓓ

48. Edna's tastes are so _______ that she _______ nothing better than pizza with meat sauce.
(A) epicurean...enjoys
(B) sophisticated...loves
(C) plebeian...relishes
(D) cultured...esteems

Ⓐ Ⓑ Ⓒ Ⓓ

49. After the visitors left, we had to drive to the supermarket to _______ our _______ supply of food.
(A) recover...intact
(B) decrease...inadequate
(C) replenish...diminished
(D) succor...increased

Ⓐ Ⓑ Ⓒ Ⓓ

50. The _______ impostor's _______ failed; the guards would not let him in even though he claimed to be a reporter.
(A) invincible...stratagem
(B) indecisive...scheme
(C) crafty...ruse
(D) ingenuous...resolution

Ⓐ Ⓑ Ⓒ Ⓓ

Answers—Diagnostic Test Sentence Completion

1. **C**	14. **C**	27. **C**	39. **B**
2. **D**	15. **D**	28. **A**	30. **C**
3. **D**	16. **B**	29. **C**	41. **C**
4. **A**	17. **D**	30. **B**	42. **A**
5. **B**	18. **C**	31. **C**	43. **D**
6. **C**	19. **D**	32. **A**	44. **A**
7. **B**	20. **D**	33. **C**	45. **C**
8. **C**	21. **A**	34. **C**	46. **B**
9. **D**	22. **C**	35. **B**	47. **D**
10. **D**	23. **D**	36. **C**	48. **C**
11. **A**	24. **C**	37. **B**	49. **C**
12. **D**	25. **C**	38. **D**	50. **C**
13. **C**	26. **B**		

Rating Your Results

If you are in grade 5, 6, or 7 (Middle Level):

Superior	40–50 correct
Average	29–39 correct
Below Average	28 or fewer correct

If you are in grade 8, 9, 10, or 11 (Upper Level):

Superior	43–50 correct
Average	36–42 correct
Below Average	35 or fewer correct

STUDY PLAN

The key to improving your score on the Verbal Section is the amount of time you can spend on the exercises and practice tests in Chapter 4, Vocabulary, beginning on page 89.

Long-Term Program

1. Look through a dictionary, and try to learn several new words every day. Check the words you are unfamiliar with, and review them four or five at a time. You will be pleasantly surprised at how quickly you will master them! A 10-minute session each day is the secret to success.

2. Do not skip the varied mastery exercises and practice tests. They will reinforce your control of your growing vocabulary and increase your speed in handling the actual examination items.

3. Use the Practice ISEEs beginning on page 560 as your final step in preparation.

Crash Program

1. Concentrate your study time on doing many of the drills, exercises, and tests in Chapter 4, Vocabulary, beginning on page 89. Several short sessions are much more effective than one long one. The varied exercises will help you gain speed and accuracy in handling vocabulary questions.
2. Use the Practice ISEEs beginning on page 560 as your final step.

Mathematics

The two Mathematics Sections have a total of 90 questions: 40 quantitative ability and 50 mathematics achievement. You are allowed 35 minutes for the former type and 40 minutes for the latter.

In general, the quantitative ability subtest measures aptitude for mathematical learning; the mathematics achievement subtest seeks to determine strengths and weaknesses in specific areas. The best preparation for the test involves coverage of the wide range of basic arithmetic, algebra, and geometry.

WHAT YOU NEED TO KNOW

The outline below lists the areas to be covered. All of these are developed in this book with a considerable amount of practice material. Answers are given for all exercises and practice tests, and explanations are also provided for the Diagnostic Test in this chapter and the model ISEE exams at the back of the book.

1. Basic mathematical operations with whole numbers, fractions, decimals, and percents.
2. Common units of measure and operations with these measures.
3. The metric system.
4. Ratio and proportion.
5. Mathematical applications and problem solving:
   - A. Using basic operations.
   - B. Percentage problems.
   - C. Profit and loss.
   - D. Taxation.
   - E. Commission.
   - F. Discount.
   - G. Interest.
   - H. Averages.
6. Basic algebra:
   - A. Algebraic representation.
   - B. Exponents and evaluation of algebraic expressions.
   - C. Evaluation of formulas.
   - D. Solving equations.
   - E. Solving problems by using equations.
   - F. Solving inequalities.
7. Numbers and number systems:
   - A. Sets.
   - B. Numeration.
   - C. Exponents and expanded form.
8. The set of natural numbers and the set of whole numbers:
   - A. Factors and primes.
   - B. Divisibility.
   - C. Symbols of inequality.
   - D. Order in the set of integers.
9. The set of rational numbers.
10. The set of real numbers.
11. Laws of operation for real numbers.
12. Interpreting tables, maps, and graphs.
13. Geometry:
    - A. The basics.
    - B. Perimeter, area, and volume.
    - C. Indirect measurement:
      - Pythagorean Theorem and square root.
      - Congruence and similarity.
      - Coordinate geometry.
14. Mathematical reasoning.
15. Venn diagrams.
16. Quantitative comparisons.

Sample Mathematics Questions

The topics listed above are used in solving such typical problems as the following.

EXAMPLE 1: If $\frac{4}{7}$ of a number = 24, then $\frac{5}{3}$ of the number =

(A) 42 (B) 7 (C) 70 (D) 21

SOLUTION: If $\frac{4}{7}$ of a number is 24, then $\frac{1}{7}$ of the number is 6.
Therefore, the number is $7 \times 6 = 42$.

$$\frac{5}{3} \times 42 = \frac{210}{3} = 70$$

(C) is the correct choice.

EXAMPLE 2: In the product (3□4)6 = 2,304, what digit does □ represent?

(A) 9 (B) 4 (C) 6 (D) 8

SOLUTION: If we divide both sides of the given equation by 6, we have 3□ = 384
Thus, □ = 8
(D) is the correct choice.

EXAMPLE 3: A plane travels at a steady speed of 480 miles per hour. How many miles does the plane cover between 11:00 A.M. and 2:15 P.M.?

(A) 1,440 (B) 1,560 (C) 1,600 (D) 1,460

SOLUTION: The plane travels 1 hour until noon and $2\frac{1}{4}$ hours after noon. Thus, the plane travels a total of $3\frac{1}{4}$ hours. To find the distance covered, we multiply 480 by $3\frac{1}{4}$.

$480 \times 3\frac{1}{4} = 480 \times \frac{13}{4} = 1{,}560$ miles

(B) is the correct choice.

EXAMPLE 4: Triangle *ABC* is an isosceles triangle with $AB = AC$. If the measure of $\angle B$ is 54°, what is the measure of = $\angle A$?

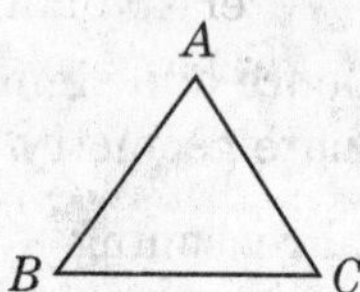

(A) 54° (B) 62° (C) 72° (D) 70°

SOLUTION: If $AB = AC$, then the measure of $\angle B$ = the measure of $\angle C$. Therefore, the measure of $\angle C = 54°$. Since the sum of the measures of the angles of a triangle is 180°, we have

$54° + 54° +$ measure of $\angle A = 180°$
$108° +$ measure of $\angle A = 180°$
measure of $\angle A = 180° - 108°$
$= 72°$

(C) is the correct choice.

The quantitative ability subsection includes a type of question called quantitative comparison, which requires you to determine which of two quantities is greater. Thus, in Examples 5, 6, and 7, you should note the given information, if any, and then compare the quantity in Column A to the quantity in Column B. Next to the number of each question you are asked to write

A if the quantity in Column A is greater,
B if the quantity in Column B is greater,
C if the two quantities are equal,
D is the relationship cannot be determined from the information given

EXAMPLE 5:

Column A		Column B
	$2x + 3 = 11$ $3y + 2 = 14$	
x		y

SOLUTION:

$$2x + 3 = 11$$
$$2x + 3 - 3 = 11 - 3$$
$$2x = 8$$
$$x = 4$$
$$3y + 2 = 14$$
$$3y + 2 - 2 = 14 - 2$$
$$3y = 12$$
$$y = 4$$

Thus, $x = y$.
(C) is the correct choice.

EXAMPLE 6:

Column A | Column B

ABCD and *RSTV* are rectangles.

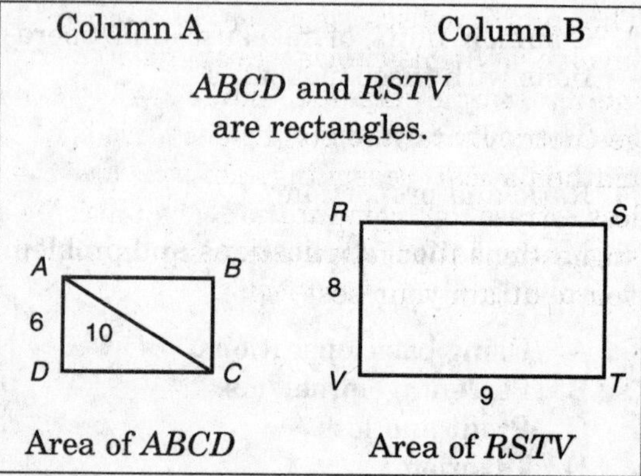

Area of *ABCD* | Area of *RSTV*

SOLUTION: $\triangle ABD$ is a right triangle. Therefore,

$(AB)^2 = (BD)^2 - (AD)^2$
$(AB)^2 = 10^2 - 6^2$
$(AB)^2 = 100 - 36 = 64$
$AB = 8$
Area of rectangle $ABCD = 8 \times 6$
$= 48$ square units.
Area of rectangle $RSTV = 8 \times 9$
$= 72$ square units.

In this case, the quantity in Column B (72) is greater than the quantity in Column A (48).

(B) is the correct choice.

EXAMPLE 7:

Column A		Column B
	x is an integer	
$1 - x$		$x - 1$

SOLUTION: Let $x = 5$

Then $1 - x = 1 - 5$ and $x - 1 = 5 - 1$

$x = -4$ $\quad$ $x = 4$

In this case, the quantity in Column B is greater than the quantity in Column A.

Let $x = -4$

Then $1 - x = 1 - (-4)$ and $x - 1 = -4 - 1$

$x = 5$ $\quad$ $x = -5$

In this case, the quantity in Column A is greater than the quantity in Column B.

Thus, we cannot tell whether $1 - x$ or $x - 1$ is the greater. The answer depends upon the value chosen for x.

(D) is the correct choice.

STRATEGIES FOR SUCCESS

The mathematics sections of the ISEE involve multiple-choice questions in arithmetic, simple algebra, and basic plane geometry. By far the greatest emphasis is on mathematical reasoning ability; there is less stress on computational ability. The suggestions that follow are designed to help you to attain your best score.

➤ ***Tactic 1:*** Read each question carefully. Every word in a mathematical statement is precise and important.

➤ ***Tactic 2:*** Determine what information is given and exactly what must be found. This analysis will give you the gist of the problem.

➤ ***Tactic 3:*** Develop a plan for a solution. Such a plan will involve a link between the given information and what you must find.

➤ ***Tactic 4:*** Use your plan as a guide to complete the solution to the problem.

➤ ***Tactic 5:*** Check your answer.

➤ ***Tactic 6:*** Be sure that your answer is given in the units specified in the question.

➤ ***Tactic 7:*** Do not get upset if you cannot answer a question. You do not have to answer every question to get a good score. If you do not see an immediate approach to the solution of a problem, leave it and return to it later if time permits.

➤ ***Tactic 8:*** Do not spend too much time on any one question. Since you have 35 minutes to answer 40 quantitative ability questions, and 40 minutes to answer 60 mathematics achievement questions, you cannot afford to dwell on a troublesome problem.

➤ ***Tactic 9:*** On this test, there is no penalty for an incorrect answer. Therefore, you should answer every question.

Diagnostic Test Mathematics

The purpose of the Diagnostic Test that follows is not to provide an exact equivalent of the real test but rather to pinpoint areas where you need additional learning. No time limit is given, and the 40 questions may be slightly easier than those on sample tests in later chapters or on the actual test. After taking the test, be sure to use the "Material to Review" section on page 67 as a guide for further study.

Four possible answers follow each question below. You may work out each problem in your head or use the margins of the test pages for scratch work. Decide which of the possible answers is best, and block out the corresponding letter on the answer grid.

> DIRECTIONS: For questions 1–32 read each problem carefully and decide on the correct answer choice. Then fill in the corresponding circle in the answer grid.
>
> **SAMPLE PROBLEM:**
>
> $5.09 \times 3.7 =$
>
> (A) 18.773 (B) 18.833 (C) 18.793 (D) 18.073

1. If $\frac{1}{3}$ of a number is less than 12, then the number must be

   (A) less than 12 (B) more than 12 (C) less than 4 (D) less than 36

   Ⓐ Ⓑ Ⓒ Ⓓ

2. Mr. Licuri bought 80 shares of XYZ stock at \$37 $\frac{5}{8}$ per share. A year later he sold the stock at \$43 $\frac{1}{4}$ per share. What was his profit before deductions for commission and tax?

   (A) \$400 (B) \$450 (C) \$420 (D) \$480

   Ⓐ Ⓑ Ⓒ Ⓓ

3. Mr. Crane earns x dollars per hour. How many dollars does he earn in 8 hours?

   (A) $x + 8$ (B) $x - 8$ (C) $8x$ (D) $8 \div x$

   Ⓐ Ⓑ Ⓒ Ⓓ

4. In the right triangle below, what is the value of x?

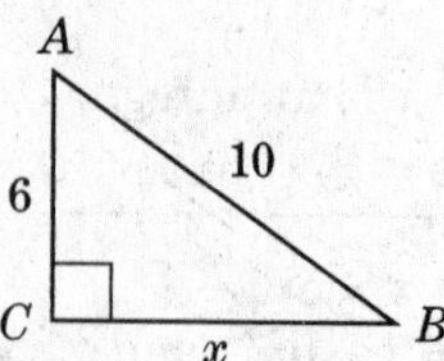

   (A) 6 (B) 10 (C) 8 (D) 95

   Ⓐ Ⓑ Ⓒ Ⓓ

5. Which of the following is closest to 0.49×99?

   (A) $\frac{1}{2} \times 100$ (B) 2×100 (C) 50×100 (D) 5×100

   Ⓐ Ⓑ Ⓒ Ⓓ

6. If $87 + \square = 401 - 189$, then $\square =$

   (A) 125 (B) 105 (C) 115 (D) 135

   Ⓐ Ⓑ Ⓒ Ⓓ

7. If $3x + 2 = 20$, then $x =$

   (A) 4 (B) 7 (C) 10 (D) 6

   Ⓐ Ⓑ Ⓒ Ⓓ

8. In the diagram below, $AC = 12$ inches, $BD = 15$ inches, and $BC = 4$ inches. What is the length of $\overline{AD}$?

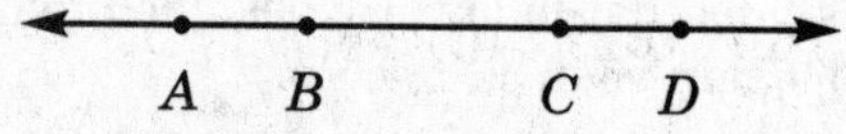

   (A) 23 inches (B) 25 inches (C) 27 inches (D) 31 inches

   Ⓐ Ⓑ Ⓒ Ⓓ

9. Bill has x dollars, and Juan has \$8 more than Bill. If Juan gives Bill \$5, how many dollars will Juan have left?

   (A) $x + 13$ (B) $x + 5$ (C) $x + 3$ (D) $x + 11$

   Ⓐ Ⓑ Ⓒ Ⓓ

10. A club collected $500 by assessing each member the same whole number of dollars. Which of the following could be the amount each member was assessed?

(A) $8 (B) $12 (C) $15 (D) $4

Ⓐ Ⓑ Ⓒ Ⓓ

11. If $8 \times 9 \times y = 0$, then the value of y is

(A) 0 (B) $\frac{1}{72}$ (C) $\frac{1}{17}$ (D) 72

Ⓐ Ⓑ Ⓒ Ⓓ

12. If $x + 3 = y + 5$, then

(A) $y > x$ (B) $y = x + 2$ (C) $x > y$ (D) $x = y$

Ⓐ Ⓑ Ⓒ Ⓓ

13. Last year the XYZ corporation's volume of business was $6.4 billion. The preceding year the XYZ corporation's volume of business was $5.8 billion. The percent of increase in volume of business was approximately

(A) 10% (B) 12% (C) 15% (D) 18%

Ⓐ Ⓑ Ⓒ Ⓓ

14. If $15 > N > 8$ and N is a multiple of 6, then $N =$

(A) 14 (B) 10 (C) 12 (D) 4

Ⓐ Ⓑ Ⓒ Ⓓ

15. All of the following are less than $\frac{5}{6}$ EXCEPT

(A) 0.7 (B) $\frac{3}{4}$ (C) 80% (D) 0.9

Ⓐ Ⓑ Ⓒ Ⓓ

16. When N is divided by 9, the quotient is 8 and the remainder is 5. $N =$

(A) 70 (B) 77 (C) 75 (D) 87

Ⓐ Ⓑ Ⓒ Ⓓ

17. If $\frac{6}{17} = \frac{y}{68}$, then $y =$

(A) 36 (B) 48 (C) 10 (D) 24

Ⓐ Ⓑ Ⓒ Ⓓ

18. What is the area of the figure below?

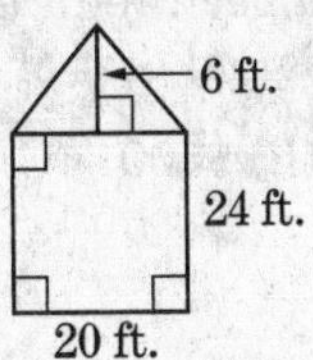

(A) 420 sq. ft. (B) 480 sq. ft. (C) 510 sq. ft. (D) 600 q. ft.

Ⓐ Ⓑ Ⓒ Ⓓ

19. If $2x - 3 < 1$, which of the following satisfies the inequality?

(A) 2 (B) 3 (C) –1 (D) 5

Ⓐ Ⓑ Ⓒ Ⓓ

20. Which of the following is not equal to the others?

(A) $3\frac{1}{2}$% (B) 0.035 (C) 3.5 (D) 3.5%

Ⓐ Ⓑ Ⓒ Ⓓ

21. At a concert an auditorium is $\frac{2}{3}$ full. To fill the auditorium completely, 400 more seats would have to be occupied. How many seats does the auditorium have?

(A) 1,100 (B) 1,200 (C) 1,500 (D) 1,250

Ⓐ Ⓑ Ⓒ Ⓓ

22. A piece of beef weighs 4 pounds 6 ounces. At $3.20 per pound, what is the cost of the piece of beef?

(A) $14.00 (B) $1.40 (C) $12.40 (D) $14.50

Ⓐ Ⓑ Ⓒ Ⓓ

23. A tank holds 50 gallons of a mixture of acid and water that is 40% acid. If 10 gallons of water are added, the percent of acid in the tank is

(A) 40% (B) 50% (C) 30% (D) $33\frac{1}{3}$%

Ⓐ Ⓑ Ⓒ Ⓓ

24. If $2x + 1 = 7$, then $2x^2 + 5x =$

(A) 51 (B) 33 (C) 44 (D) 50

Ⓐ Ⓑ Ⓒ Ⓓ

25. Mr. Steinfeld bought a VCR for $375 after it had been reduced by 25%. What was the original cost of the VCR?

(A) $450 (B) $500 (C) $475 (D) $600

Ⓐ Ⓑ Ⓒ Ⓓ

26. A scout troop hiked 5 miles due north. Then the troop hiked 12 miles due east. At that point, how many miles was the troop from its starting point?

(A) 17 (B) 12 (C) 13 (D) 15

Ⓐ Ⓑ Ⓒ Ⓓ

27. A family spends $\frac{4}{9}$ of its income for rent and food. In a circle graph showing the way the family budgets its income, the sector of the circle representing rent and food should have a central angle measuring

(A) 90° (B) 150° (C) 160° (D) 175°

Ⓐ Ⓑ Ⓒ Ⓓ

28. If $3x + y = 40$ and $x = 3y$, then $y =$

(A) 4 (B) 6 (C) 10 (D) 12

Ⓐ Ⓑ Ⓒ Ⓓ

29. If ballpoint pens sell at 3 for $0.49, how much do 51 pens cost?

(A) $8.23 (B) $7.33 (C) $8.03 (D) $8.33

Ⓐ Ⓑ Ⓒ Ⓓ

30. Brian and Kevin together earn $122. If Brian earns $24 more than Kevin, how much does Kevin earn?

(A) $49 (B) $59 (C) $73 (D) $60

Ⓐ Ⓑ Ⓒ Ⓓ

31. For the current year the town of Springville has a budget of 2.75 million dollars. If this is $320,000 greater than last year's budget, how much was last year's budget?

(A) $2,430,000 (B) $2,030,000 (C) $2,130,000 (D) $2,225,000

Ⓐ Ⓑ Ⓒ Ⓓ

32. Which number is a prime factor of both 56 and 91?

(A) 8 (B) 7 (C) 13 (D) 9

Ⓐ Ⓑ Ⓒ Ⓓ

DIRECTIONS: For questions 33–40 note the given information, if any, and then compare the quantity in Column A to the quantity in Column B. On the answer grid, fill in

A if the quantity in Column A is greater,
B if the quantity in Column B is greater,
C if the two quantities are equal,
D is the relationship cannot be determined from the information given.

	Column A	Column B
33.	$8\frac{1}{3} \div 4\frac{1}{6}$	$9\frac{1}{6} \div 4\frac{1}{2}$

Ⓐ Ⓑ Ⓒ Ⓓ

34.

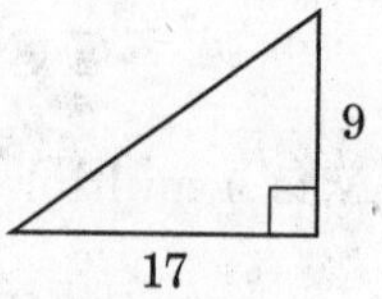

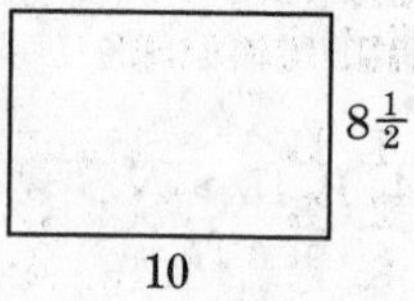

Column A	Column B
Area of this triangle	Area of this rectangle

Ⓐ Ⓑ Ⓒ Ⓓ

35.

$3x - 1 = 14$
$2y + 5 = 14$

Column A	Column B
Value of x	Value of y

Ⓐ Ⓑ Ⓒ Ⓓ

36. A carpenter and his helper earn $192 for an 8-hour work day. The carpenter earns twice as much as his helper.

Column A	Column B
Helper's hourly pay	$8

Ⓐ Ⓑ Ⓒ Ⓓ

	Column A	Column B
37.	A baseball batter has been at bat 150 times and has hit safely 30% of the time. On his next 50 times at bat he hits safely 25 times.	
	New percent of safe hits	35%
		Ⓐ Ⓑ Ⓒ Ⓓ
38.	$5 > x > -3$	
	$\frac{x}{2}$	$\frac{2}{x}$
		Ⓐ Ⓑ Ⓒ Ⓓ
39.	$x - y = 7$ $x + y = 5$	
	x	y
		Ⓐ Ⓑ Ⓒ Ⓓ
40.	$3^2 + 4^2$	$(3 + 4)^2$
		Ⓐ Ⓑ Ⓒ Ⓓ

Answers—Diagnostic Test Mathematics

1. **D**	11. **A**	21. **B**	31. **A**
2. **B**	12. **C**	22. **A**	32. **B**
3. **C**	13. **A**	23. **D**	33. **B**
4. **C**	14. **C**	24. **B**	34. **B**
5. **A**	15. **D**	25. **B**	35. **A**
6. **A**	16. **B**	26. **C**	36. **C**
7. **D**	17. **D**	27. **C**	37. **C**
8. **A**	18. **C**	28. **A**	38. **D**
9. **C**	19. **C**	29. **D**	39. **A**
10. **D**	20. **C**	30. **A**	40. **B**

Rating Your Results

If you are in grade 5, 6, or 7 (Middle Level):

Superior	23–25 correct
Average	18–22 correct
Below Average	21 or fewer correct

If you are in grade 8, 9, 10, or 11 (Upper Level):

Superior	35–40 correct
Average	28–34 correct
Below Average	27 or fewer correct

Material to Review: Chapters 8–14

Explanations

1. **D** Let x = the number.
Then $\frac{x}{3} < 12$.
If we multiply both sides of this inequality by 3, we have
$\frac{x}{3} \times 3 < 12 \times 3$
$x < 12 \times 2$, or $x < 36$

2. **B** $43\frac{1}{4} - 37\frac{5}{8} = \$5\frac{5}{8}$, profit per share
$5\frac{5}{8} = \frac{45}{8} \times 80 = \$450$

3. **C** To find Mr. Crane's earnings for 8 hours we must multiply his earnings per hour (x dollars) by 8. The result is $8x$ dollars.

4. **C** In right triangle ABC we use the Pythagorean Theorem to obtain the equation
$$x^2 + 6^2 = 10^2$$
$$x^2 + 36 = 100$$
$$x^2 = 100 - 36 = 64$$
$$x = 8$$

5. **A** 0.49 is close to 0.5, or $\frac{1}{2}$.
99 is close to 100.
Therefore, 0.49×99 is close to $\frac{1}{2} \times 100$.

6. **A** $87 + \square = 401 - 189$
$\square = 401 - 189 - 87$
$\square = 125$

7. **D** $3x + 2 = 20$
$3x = 20 - 2 = 18$
$x = 6$

8. **A**

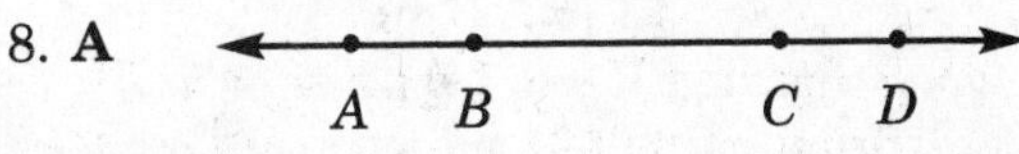

$AC = 12$
$BC = 4$
$AB = 12 - 4 = 8$
$BD = 15$
$BC = 4$
$CD = 15 - 4 = 11$
$AD = AB + BC + CD$
$AD = 8 + 4 + 11 = 23$

9. **C** Bill has x dollars.
Juan has 8 dollars more, or $(x + 8)$ dollars. If Juan gives Bill \$5, then Juan will have left $x + 8 - 5$ dollars, or $x + 3$ dollars.

10. **D** The amount assessed each member must be a factor of 500. Of the choices given, only 4 can be divided into 500 without leaving a remainder.

11. **A** Only if $y = 0$ can this product equal 0.

12. **C** $x + 3 = y + 5$
If we subract 3 from each side of this equation, we have
$x + 3 - 3 = y + 5 - 3$, or $x = y + 2$
This tells us that x is 2 more than y, or $x > y$.

13. **A** The increase in volume of business was 6.4 billion minus 5.8 billion.
$6.4 - 5.8 = 0.6$ billion
$\frac{0.6}{5.8} = \frac{6}{58}$
$\frac{6}{58}$ is approximately 10%

14. **C** $15 > N > 8$ tells us that N is greater than 8 but less than 15, thereby eliminating choice (D). Of the remaining choices, only 12 is a multiple of 6.

15. **D** $\frac{5}{6}$ is approximately equal to 0.83. Of the choices given, only 0.9 is greater than 0.83.

16. **B** $\frac{N}{9} = 8 + \frac{5}{9}$
If we multiply both sides of this equation by 9, we have
$N = 9 \times 8 + 5$
$N = 72 + 5 = 77$

17. **D** $\frac{6}{17} = \frac{y}{68}$
In this proportion we set the product of the means equal to the product of the extremes to obtain
$17 \times y = 6 \times 68$
$17y = 408$
$y = 24$

18. **C** Area of rectangle $= 20 \times 24$
$= 480$ sq. ft.
Area of triangle $= \frac{1}{2}(6)(10) = 30$ sq. ft.
Total area $= 480 + 30 = 510$ sq. ft.

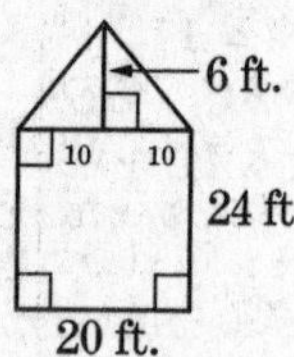

19. **C** $2x - 3 < 1$
If we add 3 to each side of the inequality, we have
$2x - 3 + 3 < 1 + 3$
$2x < 4$
$x < 2$
Of the choices given, only -1 is less than 2.

20. **C** (A) $3\frac{1}{2}\%$ may be written as 0.035.
(B) is 0.035
(C) 3.5 is greater than the other choices
(D) $3\frac{1}{2}\%$ may be written as 0.035.

21. **B** If the auditorium is $\frac{2}{3}$ full, it is $\frac{1}{3}$ empty. Thus, $\frac{1}{3}$ of the auditorium is equivalent to 400 seats. The full auditorium has $\frac{3}{3}$ or $3 \times 400 = 1{,}200$ seats.

22. **A** 6 ounces $= \frac{6}{16} = \frac{3}{8}$ of a pound
$4\frac{3}{8} = \frac{35}{8}$ pounds
$\frac{35}{8} \times 3.20 = \$14.00$

23. **D** The tank contains 50 gallons of a mixture of water and acid that is 40% acid.
40% of $50 = 0.4 \times 50 = 20$ gallons of acid.
After 10 gallons of water are added, the tank holds 60 gallons, of which 20 gallons are acid.
$\frac{20}{60} = \frac{1}{3}$, or $33\frac{1}{3}\%$.

24. **B** $2x + 1 = 7$
If we add -1 to each side of the equation, we have
$2x + 1 - 1 = 7 - 1$
$2x = 6$
$x = 3$
$2x^2 + 5x = 2(3)(3) + 5(3)$
$= 18 + 15 = 33$

25. **B** Let x = original cost of the VCR
Then $0.75x$ = amount paid for VCR
$0.75x = 375$
$x = 375 \div 0.75 = \$500$

26. **C** In the right triangle ABC we use the Pythagorean Theorem:
$x^2 = 5^2 + 12^2$
$x^2 = 25 + 144 = 169$
$x = 13$

12
C B
5 x
A

27. **C** In drawing a circle graph, we note that the sum of the measures of the angles about a point in a plane is 360°. In this case we wish to draw a sector

that represents $\frac{4}{9}$ of the circle. Therefore, the measure of the angle at the center must be $\frac{4}{9} \times 360 = 160°$.

28. **A** $3x + y = 40$
$x = 3y$
$3x = 9y$
$9y + y = 40$
$10y = 40$
$y = 4$

29. **D** Let x = cost of 51 pens.
We set up the proportion
$\frac{3}{0.49} = \frac{51}{x}$
$3x = 5 \times 0.49$
$x = 51 \times \frac{49}{3} = \frac{24.99}{3} = \$8.33$
The cost of 51 pens is $8.33.

30. **A** Let x = Kevin's earnings
And $x + 24$ = Brian's earnings
$x + x + 24 = 122$
$2x + 24 = 122$
$2x + 24 - 24 = 122 - 24$
$2x = 98$
$x = 49$
Kevin earns $49.

31. **A** To find last year's budget we subtract $320,000 from $2.75 million.
$2,750,000
320,000
$2,750,000
Last year's budget was $2,430,000.

32. **B** $56 = 7 \times 8$, $91 = 7 \times 13$
7 is a prime number, and a factor of both 56 and 91.

33. **B** $8\frac{1}{3} = \frac{25}{3}$ $9\frac{1}{6} = \frac{55}{6}$
$4\frac{1}{6} = \frac{25}{6}$ $4\frac{1}{2} = \frac{9}{2}$
$\frac{25}{3} \div \frac{25}{6}$ $\frac{55}{6} \div \frac{9}{2}$
$\frac{25}{3} \times \frac{6}{25} = 2$ $\frac{55}{6} \times \frac{2}{9} = \frac{55}{27} = 2\frac{1}{27}$
The quantity in Column B ($2\frac{1}{27}$) is greater than the quantity in Column A (2).

34. **B** Area of triangle $= \frac{9 \times 17}{2}$ Area of rectangle $= 10 \times 8\frac{1}{2}$
Area of triangle $= 76\frac{1}{2}$ Area of rectangle $= 85$
The quantity in Column B (85) is greater than the quantity in Column A ($76\frac{1}{2}$).

35. **A** $3x - 1 = 14$ $2y + 5 = 14$
$3x - 1 + 1 = 14 + 1$ $2y + 5 - 5 = 14 - 5$
$3x = 15$ $2y = 9$
$x = 5$ $y = 4\frac{1}{2}$
The quantity in Column A (5) is greater than the quantity in Column A ($4\frac{1}{2}$).

36. C Let x = helper's hourly pay
And $2x$ = carpenter's hourly pay
$8x + 8(2x) = 192$
$8x + 16x = 192$
$24x = 192$
$x = 8$
Helper's pay is $8 per hour.
The quantities in Column A and Column B are equal.

37. **C** 30% of $150 = 0.3 \times 150 = 45$
The batter has hit safely 45 times.
$45 + 25 = 70$
He has hit safely a total of 70 times.
He has batted $150 + 50$ = a total of 200 times
New percent of safe hits $= \frac{70}{200} = \frac{35}{100} = 35\%$.
The quantities in Column A and Column B are equal.

38. **D** $5 > x > -3$
x is a number less than 5 and greater than -3.
Let $x = 4$
Then $\frac{x}{2} = \frac{4}{2} = 2$ and $\frac{2}{x} = \frac{2}{4} = \frac{1}{2}$
In this case, the quantity in Column A (2) is greater than the quantity in Column B ($\frac{1}{2}$).
Now, let $x = 1$
Then $\frac{x}{2} = \frac{1}{2}$ and $\frac{2}{x} = \frac{2}{1} = 2$

In this case, the quantity in Column B (2) is greater than the quantity in Column A ($\frac{1}{2}$).
Thus, we cannot tell whether the quantity in Column A or the quantity in Column B is greater or whether the two quantities are equal. The answer depends upon the value of x.

39. **A** $x - y = 7$
$x + y = 5$
If we add these two equations we have
$2x = 12$
$x = 6$
If $x = 6$, we have
$6 - y = 7$
$y = -1$
The quantity in Column A (6) is greater than the quantity in Column B (–1).

40. **B** $3^2 + 4^2 = 9 + 16 = 25$
$(3 + 4)^2 = 7^2 = 49$
The quantity in Column B (49) is greater than the quantity in Column A (25).

STUDY PLAN

The amount of time necessary for a thorough study program to prepare for the Mathematics sections of the ISEE will vary greatly from individual to individual. It is not necessary to work through all the detailed exercise material given in the book. On any given topic it is suggested that you take one of the practice tests. If you can answer correctly at least 80% of the questions on the test, there is no need for you to linger; you may proceed to the next topic. Such a plan of procedure will enable you to concentrate on the areas in which you are weak. In general, there are three major areas to cover.

1. ***Basic arithmetic.*** This topic, which involves fundamental operations with whole numbers, fractions, decimals, and percents, is covered completely in Chapter 8.

   It is recommended that you cover Chapter 9, "Applications of Basic Mathematical Skills," in some detail. The emphasis in this chapter on verbal problems and special topics will be very helpful in developing problem-solving skills.

2. ***Algebra.*** The algebra content on the ISEE is limited and is thoroughly covered in Chapters 10 and 11. In preparing for the test, you are advised to study these chapters carefully. The exercise material is good preparation for the test.

   Chapter 12 on tables, maps, and graphs also anticipates likely test questions.

3. ***Geometry.*** The geometry content required on the ISEE is also limited and is concisely covered in Chapter 13, which should be studied in detail.

   Chapter 14, titled "Reasoning Skills," will help you develop resourcefulness in tackling a typical mathematical situation. It will also prepare you for the quantitative comparison questions on the ISEE.

Reading Comprehension

A basic key to academic success is information from the written word. Even though many students now spend more time watching television than reading printed matter, our schools are geared to using books as the primary communication medium. The ISEE, therefore, tests your ability to handle the study-type reading materials you will meet in high school.

The passages in the Reading Comprehension section of the ISEE are selected from the following content areas:

Social Studies:	history, economics, sociology
Science:	medicine, astronomy, physics, anthropology, psychology

The test section consists of nine reading passages selected from varied reading matter—books, magazines, and newspapers. Each passage is followed by a series of questions, 40 in all. The questions are of five basic types:

1. ***Factual:*** These questions test your direct understanding of what is stated or not stated in the paragraph:

EXAMPLE:
The main source of energy for the experimental engine is (A) ... (B) ... etc.

2. ***Vocabulary:*** These questions test your understanding of key words as used in he selection. Usually these terms are defined through examples, synonyms, or explanations.

EXAMPLE:
As used in this passage "perspicacious" most nearly means (A) ... (B) ... etc.

3. ***Implication or inference:*** These questions test your ability to read between the lines. Since the author says such and such, then ________ will also be true.

EXAMPLES:
The passage implies that (A) ... (B) ... etc.

The passage suggests that (A) ... (B) ... etc.

Which of the following can be inferred from the passage? (A) ... (B) ... etc.

4. ***Author's attitude:*** These questions test your ability to recognize the author's attitude (skeptical, factual, judgmental, humorous, biased) toward the subject matter.

EXAMPLE:
Which of the following best describes the author's attitude toward the subject? (A) ... (B) ... etc.

5. ***Best title:*** These questions test your ability to recognize the difference between the main idea and supporting ideas.

EXAMPLE:
Which of the following is the most appropriate title for the selection? (A) ... (B) ... etc.

Sample Questions

The directions and sample questions below are typical of those encountered on the Reading Comprehension section of the ISEE.

DIRECTIONS: The passage below is followed by questions based on its content. On the basis of what is stated or implied in that passage, circle the letter of the word or words that best answer the question.

Late in the seventeenth century, William Penn came into control of the area that later became Pennsylvania and Delaware. It already had a number of English, Dutch, and Swedish settlers. He set out to establish a model commonwealth based on the principles of the Quakers. He satisfied the Indian claims to the land by friendly treaties of purchase. He assured all settlers that they could obtain land on liberal terms and pledged that they would live in justice and equality with their neighbors. In 1682, William Penn came to these shores, bringing about a hundred colonists to join the thousands of other European immigrants enjoying the peace and prosperity that reigned in Pennsylvania.

1. In line 6, which of the following definitions of "commonwealth" is most appropriate?

   (A) a group of nations
   (B) a state of the United States
   (C) a political unit
   (D) a British union of states

2. The passage implies that Penn paid the Indians for the land because

   (A) it was the custom to do so
   (B) the British king had no right to take the land away from the natives
   (C) the British king suggested such a payment
   (D) Penn honored the Indians' claim to the land

3. When did European immigrants begin to move into Pennsylvania?

   (A) after the signing of the treaties with the Indians
   (B) after Penn and his colonists had settled there
   (C) before the land had been granted to Penn
   (D) after the Revolutionary War

4. Which of the following could not be inferred from the passage to be a governing principle of Quaker conduct?

   (A) Quakers and non-Quakers were entitled to equal justice.
   (B) All persons had a right to settle in the territory.
   (C) The laws applied to all classes of society.
   (D) European white people were superior beings.

5. Why did Penn develop his colony?

   (A) He wanted to gain more wealth.
   (B) He wanted to put his Quaker principles into practice.
   (C) He wanted to gain more power.
   (D) He wanted adventure.

Answers and Analysis

1. **C** The region eventually became two states of the United States. In the seventeenth century it was a political unit controlled by William Penn.

2. **D** Even though the king of England had made the land legally his by claiming sovereignty over it, Penn believed that the original inhabitants also had a claim to it.

3. **C** "It [the area in question] already had a number of English, Dutch, and Swedish settlers."

4. **D** This statement cannot be inferred because the Quakers stress "justice and equality with their neighbors."

5. **B** "He set out to establish a model commonwealth based on the principles of the Quakers." In other words, he wanted to put his Quaker principles into practice.

STRATEGIES FOR SUCCESS

- Zero in on the paragraph to be read. Clear your mind of everything else.
- Since this is a test of your ability to read, do not rely on your own knowledge as the basis of your answer. Each passage contains all the information you will need to answer the questions.
- Read the passage quickly to decide what it is about.
- Before you turn to the questions, read the passage a second time, sentence by sentence.
- Take the questions in order. Read all the choices before you select the best answer.
- Do not hesitate to turn back to the paragraph to verify your choices.
- Passages about familiar subjects or areas of your interest take less time than others. However, if you find a passage that seems too difficult, go on to the next; come back to it later if you have time. When you return to the passage, it may seem much easier to grasp.
- Often picking out the key sentence will organize your thinking about the selection.

- Some people find that looking at the questions first can point out the meaning of a difficult paragraph. Others find this approach very time-consuming; they prefer to get the main ideas in the selection before looking at the questions. While taking the practice tests, try both methods to see which one works better for you.
- Some people find underlining key phrases helpful. This process can slow your reading down too much. It may be better to concentrate on the sentence-by-sentence reading approach to find principal ideas, facts, and author's point of view.
- There is no substitute for practice. The more varied your reading, the better your score. Set aside some time each day for recreational reading and reading for information. The editorial page of the daily newspaper is an ideal source. And so are your textbooks!

Diagnostic Test Reading Comprehension

This test is planned for both the Middle and Upper forms of the test. When you take this Diagnostic Test, simulate examination conditions as closely as you can. Choose a quiet time of the day and a quiet room. Try to avoid interruptions. Concentrate on the test and give it your undivided attention.

DIRECTIONS: Each passage below is followed by questions based on its content. On the basis of what is *stated* or *implied* in that passage, select the word or words that best answer the question and fill in the circle that has the same letter as your answer choice.

A rain forest receives over 100 inches of rain, distributed throughout the year. Its temperature is warm enough to permit year-round growing, and many kinds of plants grow together here in jungle density. Yet there is no violent competition for light. The main inhabitants, the trees, fall into groups with certain height and illumination limits. Once the trees have grown beyond the sapling stage, there is a beautifully balanced organization. The members of the different tiers do not try to overtop each other. The real struggle is for root room. The runoffs caused by the heavy rain keep the feeding soil thin, and the roots cannot settle for different levels. Because the ground around is packed with other roots, they cannot run out widely. The dense growth of low shrubs around the tree base and the vines that twine from tree to tree help to keep the towering older trees from toppling.

1. As used in line 13, the word "tiers" means
(A) species
(B) levels
(C) temperature zones
(D) bases

Ⓐ Ⓑ Ⓒ Ⓓ

2. The severest competition in a rain forest is for
(A) anchorage
(B) altitude
(C) protection
(D) water

Ⓐ Ⓑ Ⓒ Ⓓ

3. Why is there little rich soil in a rain forest?
(A) There are too many plants to feed.
(B) The rains are so torrential.
(C) The sunlight rarely reaches the soil.
(D) The natives remove the soil.

Ⓐ Ⓑ Ⓒ Ⓓ

4. When people cut their way through the vines and low bushes,
(A) they endanger the trees.
(B) they give the trees a chance to breathe.
(C) they run the risk of meeting wild animals.
(D) they bring more sunlight into the dark jungle.

Ⓐ Ⓑ Ⓒ Ⓓ

5. Trees in a rain forest are in greatest danger when
(A) there is a forest fire.
(B) there is too much rain.
(C) they are young and growing up.
(D) they are mature.

Ⓐ Ⓑ Ⓒ Ⓓ

Alexander III of Macedon, better known as Alexander the Great, lived from 356 to 323 B.C. When he was 20, he succeeded his father as king. He was the greatest field commander the world has ever seen. His amazing conquests began with his gaining control of all of Greece. When he died of a fever at the age of 33 in 323 B.C., he had overthrown the mighty Perisan Empire and had conquered most of the known world. His empire included vast portions of Europe, Africa, and Asia. He was stopped, not by enemy troops, but by his men, who refused to go any further into Asia. Historians have been fascinated by the power and breadth of this world conqueror. The question that many have asked but have not found the final answer to is a simple one: Why did he push for control of his world? Through the centuries many theories have been explored. Did he want to make Greeks of all living people? Did he want to become so powerful that war would no longer exist? Was he motivated by religious zeal—or by mental illness?

6. What was Alexander the Great's most important asset as a general?

(A) his dreams
(B) his weaponry
(C) the size of his army
(D) his battle strategy

Ⓐ Ⓑ Ⓒ Ⓓ

7. As used in line 27, the word "zeal" means

(A) interest
(B) belief
(C) fervor
(D) cynicism

Ⓐ Ⓑ Ⓒ Ⓓ

8. The passage questions the reason for Alexander the Great's

(A) ambition
(B) manpower
(C) wealth
(D) successes

Ⓐ Ⓑ Ⓒ Ⓓ

9. Which of the following best describes the author's attitude toward Alexander the Great?

(A) admiration
(B) fear
(C) dislike
(D) envy

Ⓐ Ⓑ Ⓒ Ⓓ

10. Which of the following can be inferred from this selection?

(A) Alexander caused untold deaths and vast destruction.
(B) Alexander's forces never questioned his orders.
(C) The ancient Greeks were not proud of Alexander's accomplishments.
(D) Before he died, Alexander regretted his vast scheme for world conquest.

Ⓐ Ⓑ Ⓒ Ⓓ

It wasn't until the 1950s that scientists became interested in developing a language that would enable them to communicate with the great apes. Two American researchers suspected that the reason why the apes did not talk verbally was not lack of intelligence. Beatrice and Allan Gardner felt that difference between the vocal chords of human beings and apes made it difficult for the apes to pronounce words. The Gardners set out to experiment with chimpanzees because they are reputed to be easily trained. In 1966, they started to teach the standard American sign language, Ameslan, to an infant chimpanzee named Washoe. The Gardners installed Washoe in a trailer in their backyard. They spoke no English in the trailer, communicating solely by signing. In time, Washoe, through imitation and direct teaching of gestures, had developed a basic vocabulary that continued to enlarge. Scientists have accepted the challenge in this beginning and are continuing to develop language bonds with the great apes.

11. Why did the Gardners isolate Washoe in the trailer?

(A) They wanted to keep her healthy.
(B) They could then control the learning process.
(C) They did not want Washoe to escape.
(D) They did not want others to see what they were doing.

Ⓐ Ⓑ Ⓒ Ⓓ

12. In line 20, which of the following definitions of "signing" is most appropriate?
(A) initialing
(B) using hand signals
(C) holding up lettered placards
(D) showing approval
Ⓐ Ⓑ Ⓒ Ⓓ

13. At which point in the experiment does the selection end?
(A) When the Gardners selected Washoe
(B) When the experiment was abandoned
(C) When the experiment proved a success
(D) Before the results were known
Ⓐ Ⓑ Ⓒ Ⓓ

14. Which of the following is an inference that the Gardners did not make?
(A) Washoe was willing to learn.
(B) Washoe would object to confinement in the trailer.
(C) Washoe was intelligent enough to learn Ameslan.
(D) Washoe could thrive in the selected environment.
Ⓐ Ⓑ Ⓒ Ⓓ

A hundred years ago, our economy was expanding. New industries were being developed throughout our country. The basis for this growth was our cities. Untold numbers of immigrants flooded into the job market to feed the needs of growing production lines. Today, the story is much different. Other countries have caught up with the United States in the race to manufacture goods. Our cities have deteriorated into pools of ever-increasing poverty and crime. Industries have deserted the cities for the hinterlands, where costs are lower. Computerization and mechanization of production lines have lessened the need for trained workers. The more affluent have moved out of the city into the suburbs, leaving too few with too little to pay the burden of the tax load.

15. The author places some of the blame for the decay in our cities on
(A) overproduction of manufactured goods
(B) drugs and poverty
(C) industries' change of location
(D) lack of untrained workers
Ⓐ Ⓑ Ⓒ Ⓓ

16. As used in line 17, the work "affluent" means
(A) well-to-do
(B) skilled
(C) ambitious
(D) fortunate
Ⓐ Ⓑ Ⓒ Ⓓ

17. Which group had flocked to the cities a hundred years ago?
(A) the educated
(B) the ambitious
(C) the unskilled
(D) the religious
Ⓐ Ⓑ Ⓒ Ⓓ

18. In this selection the author is
(A) optimistic
(B) factual
(C) condemnatory
(D) argumentative
Ⓐ Ⓑ Ⓒ Ⓓ

The exhibit that attracts most visitors today in aquariums throughout the world is not the killer whales or even the snorting, playful seals. It is one of the world's oldest surviving inhabitants, the horseshoe crab. Its ancestors were flourishing on earth over 300 million years ago, when mists and endless rains covered all the land! Because of its outer shell and five pairs of walking legs, which it uses in swimming and burrowing, this animal received the common name of horseshoe crab or king crab. However, it is not a member of the crab family. Scientifically, it is classified as a distant sea-relative of the common spider.

Why has this species outlived so many others? The fact that it has two distinct pairs of eyes may be a partial answer. One set is compound, many lensed, and the other is small and simple. The compound eye is similar to that in the eyes of the bee. With it, the horseshoe crab can see polarized light rays, even ultraviolet and infrared, rays invisible to human beings. With such visual command, it can scurry away in time from situations that could become dangerous.

19. In line 5, the word "oldest" refers to
(A) specimens found in museums
(B) the species, not the individual
(C) horseshoe crabs found on beaches
(D) horseshoe crabs swimming in the ocean

Ⓐ Ⓑ Ⓒ Ⓓ

20. The horseshoe crab received its common name because of
(A) its marine habitat
(B) its two sets of eyes
(C) its colors and its five sets of legs
(D) its case and means of locomotion

Ⓐ Ⓑ Ⓒ Ⓓ

21. Which of the following inferences is most likely to be true?
(A) The horseshoe crab can see objects more clearly than human beings can.
(B) Fossils found in rocks help date the horseshoe crab.
(C) The earth is a more favorable habitat for this animal today than it was in the distant past.
(D) The horseshoe crab has survived because of its high level of intelligence.

Ⓐ Ⓑ Ⓒ Ⓓ

22. Which of the following is the most appropriate title for this selection?
(A) A Denizen of the Deep
(B) Facts and Fiction about the Horseshoe Crab
(C) The Oldest Animal on Earth
(D) Favorite Aquarium Exhibits

Ⓐ Ⓑ Ⓒ Ⓓ

Antoine Lavoisier was typical of the many intellectuals who joined the rebellious forces that overthrew the monarchy in the French Revolution at the end of the eighteenth century.

Lavoisier was a brilliant scientist. Modern chemistry came into being with the publication of his *Elements of Chemistry* in 1789. He did more than explain the role of oxygen in combustion and in respiration. He stressed the principle of the conservation of matter, which states that nothing is lost or gained during a chemical change: the weight of the products equals the weight of the starting materials. Also, he established the definition of chemical elements as substances that cannot be broken down by chemical means into anything simpler.

It is futile to try to guess how much more he could have added to our scientific knowledge had not the French Revolution intervened. Deeply concerned with improving social and economic conditions in France, he postponed his scientific research and held various posts in the revolutionary government. His career came to an abrupt end when he was guillotined during the Reign of Terror.

23. According to Lavoisier, carbon dioxide cannot be a chemical element because
(A) it contains both carbon and oxygen
(B) it is a gas
(C) it is colorless
(D) it is abundant in nature

Ⓐ Ⓑ Ⓒ Ⓓ

24. Which of the following is the most appropriate title for this selection?
(A) Casualties of War
(B) A Fallen Hero
(C) Excesses of the French Revolution
(D) The Father of Modern Chemistry

Ⓐ Ⓑ Ⓒ Ⓓ

25. Lavoisier discovered that the weight of a log that has been burned to ash in the fireplace
    (A) equals that of the remaining ash
    (B) is less than that of the remaining ash
    (C) equals the weights of the ash and of the gases that have escaped
    (D) is greater than the weights of the ash and of the gases that have escaped

    Ⓐ Ⓑ Ⓒ Ⓓ

26. From the facts stated in the selection, the reader is able to infer that Lavoisier was a(n)
    (A) idealist
    (B) school teacher
    (C) self-centered dreamer
    (D) incompetent researcher

    Ⓐ Ⓑ Ⓒ Ⓓ

George Washington was most fortunate in his choice of Alexander Hamilton as his Secretary of the Treasury. Hamilton's policies created a vast army of wealthy merchants who enthusiastically supported the national government and were ready to resist any effort to weaken it.

Many politicians were willing to repudiate the national debt of 56 million dollars, although such an act would have destroyed any confidence the bankers had in the new government. Hamilton overrode the opposition and put into effect a plan to repay the money in full. In addition, he had the federal government take over the unpaid debts incurred by the states while aiding the Revolution—a sum of 18 million more. This 74 million turned out to be a very small price to pay for the confidence and support it created.

Hamilton further strengthened the country's financial structure by setting up a national mint that made the federal government the sole source of currency, and by creating a Bank of America, modeled on the Bank of England, to serve as a center for federal borrowing.

27. Which of the following is the most appropriate title for this selection?
    (A) Strengthening the Power of U.S. Merchants
    (B) George Washington and Finances
    (C) Creating the Federal Financial Structure of a New Nation
    (D) Weakening State Controls on Banking and Finance

    Ⓐ Ⓑ Ⓒ Ⓓ

28. As used in this passage, the word "repudiate" in line 10 means to
    (A) refuse to lower
    (B) settle by negotiation
    (C) recalculate the amount of
    (D) refuse to pay

    Ⓐ Ⓑ Ⓒ Ⓓ

29. The reader can infer from Hamilton's program that our first Secretary of the Treasury
    (A) was planning to become a candidate for the presidency
    (B) disliked the English intensely
    (C) wanted to establish a strong federal government
    (D) disregarded the wishes of the politicians

    Ⓐ Ⓑ Ⓒ Ⓓ

30. The assumption of the debts incurred during the creation of the United States proved to the world of business that
    (A) the new country was rich and prosperous
    (B) no one was going to profit from war
    (C) the country was going to become a true democracy
    (D) honorable leaders were running the country

    Ⓐ Ⓑ Ⓒ Ⓓ

For several hundred years, European traders in the products of China and India were compelled to send their ships along the southern routes around Africa or South America. The ocean voyages were long in both distance and time; and the hazards were great: fearful storms, sudden calms, pirate raiders. A northern route was dreamed of, but none had been discovered.

The shippers had to wait until the nineteenth century for the first breakthrough. In 1878, a Swedish explorer, Nils Nordenskjold, led the first ship through a passage along the northern coast of Europe eastward to Asia. The Northeast Passage was ready for business! Today, Russian ice-breakers keep this passage open from June to October.

Twenty-five more years had to pass before a Northwest Passage was developed. As early as the sixteenth century, the English had begun to explore along the coast of North America for a route connecting the Atlantic and Pacific oceans. Not until 1903, however, did a Norwegian, Roald Amundsen, actually traverse and map out the first Northwest Passage. In recent years, the development of oil fields in Alaska and northern Canada has given this route additional commercial importance. Today short east and west itineraries to India and China are a reality, thanks to the courage and perseverance of international explorers.

31. Which of the following definitions is most appropriate for the word "hazards" in line 7?
   (A) games of chance played with two dice
   (B) sources of danger
   (C) scenic routes
   (D) monetary rewards

Ⓐ Ⓑ Ⓒ Ⓓ

32. Which of the following statements is true of both the Northwest and Northeast passages?
   (A) Canals had to be built for their completion.
   (B) They are icebound part of the year.
   (C) Only ships of English and American registry can use them.
   (D) They led to the discovery of oil in Alaska.

Ⓐ Ⓑ Ⓒ Ⓓ

33. The word "traverse" in line 28 most nearly means
   (A) reveal
   (B) plan
   (C) extol
   (D) navigate

34. The main purpose of the Northwest and Northeast passages is to
   (A) colonize the Northern Hemisphere
   (B) conserve natural resources
   (C) explore the Arctic region
   (D) provide a shorter waterway between oceans

Ⓐ Ⓑ Ⓒ Ⓓ

35. Which of the following best describes the tone of this selection?
   (A) condemnatory
   (B) evaluative
   (C) biased
   (D) objective

Ⓐ Ⓑ Ⓒ Ⓓ

A rock is solid matter composed of one or more of the minerals forming the earth's outer surface. There are three major classes of rock, depending on their origin. Granite, obsidian, and pumice are examples of igneous rocks, which result from the cooling and solidification of molten matter from the earth's interior. Limestone, clay, coal, and sandstone are sedimentary rocks originating from the consolidation of sediment deposited chiefly through the action of erosion on older rocks of all kinds. The third type—metamorphic rocks—originated from the alteration of the texture and mineral content of existing rocks of any kind under extreme heat and pressure within the earth. Marble, slate, and schist belong in this category.

36. Rocks are classified according to their
   (A) mineral content
   (B) mass and weight
   (C) outer surface
   (D) process of formation

Ⓐ Ⓑ Ⓒ Ⓓ

37. Which of the following is the most appropriate definition for the word "molten" in line 8?
   (A) molded by pressure
   (B) having warmth and brilliance
   (C) liquefied by heat
   (D) lacking an outer cover

Ⓐ Ⓑ Ⓒ Ⓓ

38. Which of the following is basic to the formation of marble?
    (A) high temperature and compression
    (B) the presence of air
    (C) a specific mineral
    (D) the wearing away of older rocks
    Ⓐ Ⓑ Ⓒ Ⓓ

39. Obsidian is found most often
    (A) in sand
    (B) around volcanoes
    (C) on farmland
    (D) in riverbeds
    Ⓐ Ⓑ Ⓒ Ⓓ

40. The tone of this selection can best be described as
    (A) authoritative
    (B) argumentative
    (C) casual
    (D) emotional
    Ⓐ Ⓑ Ⓒ Ⓓ

Answers—Diagnostic Test Reading Comprehension

1. **B**	11. **B**	21. **B**	31. **B**
2. **A**	12. **B**	22. **B**	32. **B**
3. **B**	13. **D**	23. **A**	33. **D**
4. **A**	14. **B**	24. **D**	34. **D**
5. **C**	15. **C**	25. **C**	35. **D**
6. **D**	16. **A**	26. **A**	36. **D**
7. **C**	17. **C**	27. **C**	37. **C**
8. **A**	18. **B**	28. **D**	38. **A**
9. **A**	19. **B**	29. **C**	39. **B**
10. **A**	20. **D**	30. **D**	40. **A**

Rating Your Results

If you are in grade 5, 6, or 7
(Middle Level):

Superior	31–40 correct
Average	24–30 correct
Below Average	23 or fewer correct

If you are in grade 8, 9, 10, or 11
(Upper Level):

Superior	34–40 correct
Average	28–33 correct
Below Average	27 or fewer correct

Material to Review: Chapter 5

Explanations

1. **B** Dictionary definition
2. **A** "The real struggle is for root room" (line 14).
3. **B** "The runoffs caused by the heavy rain keep the feeding soil thin...." (lines 15 and 16).
4. **A** Cutting away the vines and bushes removes the supports for the trees (last sentence), which may then topple.
5. **C** "Once the trees have grown beyond the sapling stage, there is a beautifully balanced organization" (line 10).
6. **D** "He was the greatest field commander..." (line 4).
7. **C** "Was he motivated by religious zeal...or mental illness?" (last sentence) "Zeal" implies deep devotion and drive.
8. **A** "Why did he push for control of his world?" (line 20).
9. **A** The author uses such phrases as "the greatest field commander," "His amazing conquests," and "the power and breadth of this world conqueror" to describe Alexander and his exploits.
10. **A** His armies and the vast territories they conquered ("most of the known world") lead to the inference of death and destruction.
11. **B** The Gardners wanted to communicate with the chimpanzee only through sign language; they did not want her to hear spoken English.
12. **B** The dictionary definition of sign language as a system of hand gestures is appropriate.
13. **D** Nowhere is the selection are the scientific conclusions revealed.
14. **B** The Gardners do not appear to have considered that the chimpanzee might rebel at the learning conditions.
15. **C** "Other countries have caught up with the United States in the race to manufacture goods" (line 8). In other words, some industrial production has moved.

16. **A** Dictionary definition. Also, the fact that those left "have too little to pay" implies that it was the well-to-do who fled the city.

17. **C** "...immigrants flooded into the job market to feed the needs of the growing production line." Those who worked the production lines were mainly unskilled.

18. **B** The article is a factual presentation.

19. **B** The age of the species, not of an individual crab, is told.

20. **D** "Because of its outer shell and five pairs of walking legs, this animal received the common name..." (lines 9–13).

21. **B** The only records we have of animal life millions of years ago are in rocks.

22. **B** The article describes facts and misconceptions about the horseshoe crab.

23. **A** "...chemical elements...substances that cannot be broken down" (lines 14 and 18). Carbon dioxide is made up of (and can be broken down into) carbon and oxygen, which are elements.

24. **D** The passage deals with Lavoisier, creator of modern chemistry (line 1).

25. **C** "...nothing is lost or gained during a chemical change" (lines 13 and 14).

26. **A** "Deeply concerned with improving social and economic conditions in France...," Lavoisier held various government posts.

27. **C** The article describes steps taken by Hamilton to create the federal financial structure of the United States.

28. **D** "Many politicians were willing to repudiate the national debt..." and "Hamilton...plan to repay the money in full."

29. **C** Every step described in the selection stresses Hamilton's desire to have a strong federal government.

30. **D** In that the leaders took no advantage of any group, they were playing fair with all.

31. **B** The list of hazards reveals the meaning of the word.

32. **B** Russian icebreakers keep this passage open from June to October, "...Alaska and Northern Canada...."

33. **D** Dictionary definition.

34. **D** The passages are in contrast to the older southern routes, which were "long in both distance and time" (lines 5 and 6).

35. **D** The passage states the facts objectively.

36. **D** "There are three major classes of rocks, depending on their origin" (lines 3 and 4).

37. **C** The passage refers to "extreme heat...within the earth" (lines 17 and 18) and to "cooling...of molten matter from the earth's interior" (lines 7 and 8).

38. **A** "...alteration...under extreme heat and pressure...." "Marble...belong[s] in this category" (lines 15–20).

39. **B** "Granite, obsidian,...igneous rocks which result from the cooling and solidification of molten matter from the earth's interior" (lines 5–9).

40. **A** The author lists definite categories of rocks, definitions, examples, and specific methods of formation in an authoritative manner.

STUDY PLAN

The key to raising your score in this area is the amount of time you can spend on the exercises and practice tests in Chapter 5, Reading, beginning on page 140.

Long-Term Program

1. The pages on Work-Study Skills consist of exercises and techniques to improve your speed and comprehension. Typical examination questions are analyzed in the sections that follow. The Mastery Exams will assure increased ability and speed.

2. The lists of things to do and facts to master in this section are long—and rewarding! All you have to do is to budget your time properly. Browse through the Reading chapter and decide where to begin. Spend no more than 25 minutes on each practice session. Do not skip the varied exercises and practice tests. They lead to confidence and speed in handling the actual ISEE.
3. Use the Practice ISEEs beginning on page 560 as your final step in preparation.

Crash Program

1. Turn to Chapter 5, Reading, beginning on page 140. Do as many of the exercises and practice tests as you can to gain speed and accuracy. Several short sessions are always more productive than one long haul.
2. Use the Practice ISEEs beginning on page 560 as your final step.

Writing the Essay

Success in high school depends heavily upon the ability to express oneself in Written Standard American English. Therefore, in this last section of the ISEE you are asked to write a 30-minute essay that will enable the middle or high schools of your choice to compare your writing ability with that of the other candidates.

Along with your results on the multiple-choice questions, copies of your essay will be forwarded to the schools of your choice. While the short-answer sections of the test will be given numerical ratings, your essay will be sent on unmarked. Evaluation of the essay is left to readers at the receiving schools.

STRATEGIES FOR SUCCESS

➤ Take the Essay Writing Diagnostic Test under time and place conditions that approximate as closely as possible those of the actual test.

➤ Pick a time and a quiet place where you will not be interrupted for 30 minutes. Plan to complete the test at one sitting.

➤ Sit at a desk or table bare of everything but a timer, a pen, pencils, erasers, and this book. No dictionaries or notes should be available.

➤ When you are ready, note the time you start and begin immediately to read the instructions. Pace yourself.

➤ If you have not finished by the end of the 30 minutes allotted, note in your essay where you should have stopped. Then continue to the end.

➤ Rate your essay for the 30-minute performance. If you had to extend your time, rate the essay with the extended time as well.

➤ Turn to page 86 to Monday-quarterback your results.

Diagnostic Test Essay Writing

The purpose of the Diagnostic Test that follows is to help you decide how much time you should devote to improving your ability to handle this part of the test. Therefore, contrary to the directives for the other tests, for this one you will set a time limit since you must divide the 30 minutes into four distinct parts:

1. Reading the prompt.
2. Planning the essay.
3. Writing the essay.
4. Proofreading the essay.

> Time Began: _____
> Time Ended: _____
>
> DIRECTIONS: Using your own 2 sheets of theme paper, write an essay in which you express your point of view on the topic developed in the following prompt:
>
> *Prompt:* The end of the twentieth century has brought serious changes in family life. Because of the dramatic increase in the divorce rate, there are many more singles living independent lives. Many of these individuals in their thirties and forties have been seeking to become adoptive parents of children ranging from infants to adolescents. Write an essay in which you agree or disagree that singles should be allowed to adopt children.
>
> Your response will be evaluated for organization and development of ideas, appropriateness of examples and supporting details, and technique (spelling, punctuation, usage).

RATING THE ESSAY

Ideally at this point, your essay would be evaluated by an experienced reader. Instead, there follows a series of essays to which yours can be compared by you and/or by your parents to obtain a rough estimate of its standing in relation to those written by other students. The ratings are based solely on organization and content. You will need to have an experienced reader proofread your essay for technical errors.

Here is the best way to proceed:

1. In the space provided, briefly analyze and then rate each of the following essays. Use the rating scale below.
2. Compare your ratings with those on pages 85–86.
3. Compare your own essay with the ones you rated.
4. Rate your own essay. Try to be objective.

Rating Scale	Writing Characterized By
Superior	originality of thought freshness of expression aptness of illustrations
Above Average	clarity of organization soundness of thought
Average	no attempt at a thesis fulfillment of the assigned topic
Below Average	weak organization irrelevant arguments rambling style

Evaluating Student Essays

Essay 1

I am so delighted that this topic appeared on the test. I've been thinking about the problem for a long time. I know many other students just as enthusiastic as I am in wanting to express our opinions on so important a subject. In these troubled times it can come up again and again. The sooner it is faced, the sooner many people will be truly happy.

In conclusion I should once again express my approval of your selection. There must be many very intelligent people on your staff.

ANALYSIS ______________________________

____

____

RATING ______________________________

Essay 2

Present-day social workers all agree that children brought up in institutions develop psychological scars that complicate their entire lives. That is why adoption agencies are so numerous in our country. They offer a practical solution to the problem of how society can best help children without parents or relatives to bring them up.

However, will giving these children into the care of single parents be of lasting benefit to both the child and the substitute mother or father? Again we turn to the social workers who investigate the applicants for both financial and psychological fitness. Here, too, the evidence that they present is overwhelmingly in favor of creating such bonds. In the vast majority of cases, both human beings involved in the newly created family thrive.

How do I know so much about this unusual form of adoption? You've guessed it! I know all about it from first-hand experience. I was adopted by a single parent!

ANALYSIS ______________________________

____

____

RATING ______________________________

Essay 3

If you ever watched Public Television and saw a program dealing with children who have been abandoned or children whose parents have died, you realize the seriousness of the problem society has in trying to give them a normal upbringing. Should singles living alone be given that responsibility?

Singles who work for a living have a sufficient number of problems of their own. They have to do everything for themselves. If they become sick, they have no one to turn to for help. They have to go to hospitals for care. There is sufficient psychological stress in their lives without their taking on the very heavy burden of caring for others. Because they do not have children of their own around, they lack the experience needed to care for an adopted child.

As you can see I feel sympathetic toward both these children and the singles who would want to take them on. However, I would leave well enough alone and have society look elsewhere for tender, loving care for these children.

ANALYSIS ______________________________

____

____

RATING ______________________________

Essay 4

Wars and recessions have certainly raised havoc with the end of this century. A sign of the times is found in the vast number of homes broken up by divorce. Many, too many of the resulting single men and women in their midyears are leading lonely lives in homes of their own.

Some of these people are seeking to break the awful loneliness for themselves while doing a good deed for others. They want to fulfill their lives and their responsibilities by adopting one of the unfortunate children lacking parents to support and guide them.

After thinking the problem over a long time, I can conclude that I am in favor. I enthusiastically agree that encouraging such adoptions would be for the benefit of both the children and the adoptive parents.

ANALYSIS ______________________________

____

____

RATING ______________________________

Essay 5

One of the most important problems facing our society today is whether single unmarrieds should adopt children. How do you feel about it?

There are many children living in institutions. If the singles had their way, a large group of these children would be living with people who loved them. Instead of feeling like outsiders, unloved and unwanted, these children could feel important and willing to make something of themselves.

Why not give the kids a chance to be somebody? It couldn't hurt them worse than they are hurt now. And in case the single parent substitute is unable to give the child a good home, the child could be taken back by the institution.

So, come on and do some good. Let the qualified singles empty the institutions. It will please the children, and the government will save a bundle of money.

ANALYSIS ______________________________

____

____

RATING ______________________________

Essay 6

There has been a significant increase today in the number of people living alone as singles and in the number of children who are without parents to care for them. Should a living-alone adopt one of these children?

Loneliness is one of the worst diseases of our times. Both the single adult and the adoptee could greatly benefit if they established themselves as a family. With television and TV dinners and day nurseries available, I can see them getting along very smoothly, of course, after the social worker has approved of the arrangement. Between them, they could so easily lick loneliness!

ANALYSIS ______________________________

____

____

RATING ______________________________

Ratings of Student Essays

Essay 1

The essay is organized into two units of thought. The second paragraph acts as a summary. However, the candidate ignored the directives given in the prompt. The essay never identifies the topic. The sentences are separate statements with no connections to bind them together.

Rating: Below Average

Essay 2

The essay is divided into three paragraphs. The first paragraph presents one of the problems central to the topic. The second paragraph argues in favor of adoption by single applicants. The third paragraph summarizes with a clincher.

The one weakness in this essay is that, except for the personal evidence in the last paragraph, the argument is based on unproved generalizations. However, we do not expect perfection or even the reasoning that we ourselves would offer.

Rating: Superior

Essay 3

The first paragraph gives the scope of the problem. The question that it ends with very skillfully leads into the second paragraph. In the second paragraph logical reasons are presented for not favoring such adoptions. In the third paragraph the writer summarizes her reasons and rejects the proposal.

One weakness in the essay is that no solution is offered other than that society should continue trying. The other weakness is that the arguments are merely listed. The writer failed to show, for example, how serious illness of the adopting parent would affect the child.

Rating: Above average

Essay 4

The presentation is divided appropriately into three units as signified by the paragraphing. The candidate displays an excellent command of words. The problem is clearly presented and a conclusion is given, but no reasons are offered to support the conclusion reached. The approach does not get down to cases or facts. It is all on the surface. It is superficial. Much of the essay is a rewording of the prompt.

Rating: Average

Essay 5

The essay is well organized. The writer develops a sound, logical argument in favor of a thesis. However, the opening is unfortunate since the problem involved is not one of society's most important. Also, the tone of the essay is flawed by too many informal expressions.

Rating: Above Average

Essay 6

The essay has a clearly focused introduction, ending with a question pointing to a logically developed thesis. Lacking, however, is a conclusion containing the answer to the question in the first paragraph.

Rating: Average

Rating Your Own Essay

ANALYSIS ______________________________

____

It is closest to Essay __________ because

____

RATING ______________________________

PREPARATION PLAN FOR WRITING THE ESSAY

1. If you found your confidence disappearing as you wrote your essay, of if the experience revealed that you could have done better if you had known better, turn to Chapter 7, Essay Writing, beginning on page 289. You will find techniques and study aids there.
2. Write as many of the practice essays as you have time for. Continued practice pays excellent dividends!
3. Have your teacher or a parent evaluate your practice essays for organization, spelling, and usage.

   If too many spelling errors are found, turn to the drills and exercises on pages 212–229.

   If too many questionable usages are found, turn to the drills and exercises on pages 248–277.

   The Study Aids in the chapters on communication skills can make the difference between weakness and strength in essay writing!

DIGEST OF COMMUNICATION SKILLS

Vocabulary

The high school entrance examinations usually contain four types of questions to evaluate your range of vocabulary control. This section will review the question types and the best strategies for handling each. The practice tests and Mastery Exams will help you evaluate you knowledge and ability. Use the Answer Keys at the end of this chapter, pages 138–139.

Synonym Questions

A *synonym* is a word that has the same meaning, or almost the same meaning, as another word. Each synonym question asks you to identify the word that comes closest in meaning to the capitalized, or key, word.

EXAMPLE

BRAGGART: (A) support (B) brigand (C) ignorant (D) boaster (E) veteran

Ⓐ Ⓑ Ⓒ ● Ⓔ

ANALYSIS: Study the key word for clues to its meaning. Notice that it contains the word *brag*. Because *brag* means *boast*, choice D is a possible answer. Choice A, *support*, may have been listed because one of its synonyms, *bracket*, sounds a bit like *braggart*. Although choice B, *brigand* (an outlaw), contains many of the same letters as the key word, don't let similar spelling fool you into picking it. Notice that C is an adjective. Because the key word is a noun, and four of the five choices are also nouns, C is not a likely answer. The remaining choice is E, but *veteran* is not related to the key word. Because a *braggart* tends to boast quite a lot, D is the correct answer.

HOW TO HANDLE SYNONYM QUESTIONS

Before you look at the answers, read the key word carefully. If you know the word, find the answer among the choices. If the word is vaguely familiar, perhaps you have a general sense of its meaning. Think of a synonym, if possible. While you may not think of an exact synonym, you may come up with something close. If you have no idea of the word's definition, try the following:

- Look for word parts—prefixes, suffixes, roots. These may help you detect the meaning.
- Say the word silently to yourself. "Hearing" the word may open its meaning to you.
- As you read the choices, try to eliminate any that are definitely wrong. Be wary of words that sound the same or are spelled like the key word. They may have been put there to mislead you.

- ➤ If you know the word but cannot find a synonym among the choices, remember that many words have more than one meaning. Go back to the key word and think of other definitions for it. (The verb *sow*, for example, means to plant; the noun *sow* refers to a female pig.)
- ➤ Be sure your answer is the same part of speech as the key word. If the key word is a verb, for example, the answer will also be a verb, never a noun, adjective, or other part of speech.

It is better to guess than leave the item blank. You might get lucky and choose the right answer.

PRACTICE TEST 1

DIRECTIONS: For each of the following, choose the word or phrase that most nearly means the SAME as the capitalized word. Circle the letter of the correct answer.

EXAMPLE:

ENRAGED: (A) involved (B) furious (C) troubling (D) betrothed (E) defeated

1. ACCOMPLISH: (A) redo (B) struggle (C) conspire (D) achieve (E) continue
2. APPAREL: (A) reality (B) garb (C) umbrella (D) style (E) appearance
3. BRAND: (A) trait (B) premium (C) trademark (D) relative (E) novelty
4. COLOSSAL: (A) immense (B) queer (C) frantic (D) superior (E) tasty
5. CLEAVE: (A) erupt (B) control (C) depart (D) grind (E) split
6. GHASTLY: (A) massively destructive (B) frighteningly terrible (C) primitive (D) royal (E) deeply offensive
7. MORTGAGE: (A) heavy fog (B) debt on a property (C) prospect (D) mortality (E) estate
8. TREACHEROUS: (A) traitor (B) betrayal (C) danger (D) disloyal (E) terrorist
9. GRUDGING: (A) hateful (B) clumsy (C) anticipation (D) doubting (E) reluctant
10. COUNSEL: (A) cash register (B) advice (C) city governing body (D) pluck (E) comfort
11. VAIN: (A) beautiful (B) fun-loving (C) valiant (D) desperate (E) conceited
12. ORATORY: (A) dignity (B) eloquence (C) purity (D) musical solo (E) trickery
13. REALIZE: (A) bring (B) analyze (C) accomplish (D) conquer (E) consume
14. RELISH: (A) mutilate (B) refrain (C) enjoy (D) replenish (E) recite
15. EGRESS: (A) bird (B) exit (C) leak (D) departure (E) excuse
16. SHUN: (A) avoid (B) attend (C) pursue (D) shudder (E) wander
17. INFRACTION: (A) violation (B) portion (C) command (D) design (E) denial
18. TERMINATE: (A) inflate (B) persecute (C) imitate (D) end (E) rule
19. SYNONYMOUS: (A) murmuring (B) meaning the same (C) persistent (D) inciting to sin (E) common
20. ULTIMATE: (A) next to last (B) petty (C) final (D) mimicking (E) essential
21. SUBMISSIVE: (A) obedient (B) marauding (C) mythical (D) pertaining to marine life (E) wintry
22. UNEMPLOYED: (A) insecure (B) unsure (C) without employees (D) jobless (E) wandering
23. VEHICLE: (A) spectacle (B) conveyance (C) flight (D) dexterity (E) cabin

24. VULGAR: (A) angry (B) coarse (C) vigorous (D) fervid (E) offhand

25. MALADY: (A) tune (B) flattery (C) sickness (D) reputation (E) mood

26. UNDISPUTED: (A) arguing (B) plain (C) unchallenged (D) wretched (E) victorious

27. MERE: (A) not more than (B) total (C) motherly (D) frantic (E) pertaining to horses

28. ACKNOWLEDGE: (A) write (B) admit (C) wisdom (D) advice (E) represent

29. UNCOMPROMISING: (A) pleading (B) meeting half-way (C) unyielding (D) tiresome (E) untruthful

30. LEGAL: (A) manufactured (B) pertaining to a limb (C) papal (D) lawful (E) expensive

31. TIMID: (A) faint-hearted (B) punctual (C) prompt (D) tasteless (E) controlled

32. OBLIGATORY: (A) pleasing (B) required (C) excessively polite (D) untiring (E) defective

33. GROUCH: (A) bungler (B) bag (C) optimist (D) grumbler (E) bully

34. ENVIOUS: (A) previous (B) jealous (C) joyful (D) inquisitive (E) unforgiving

35. ADMONISH: (A) befit (B) abandon (C) promote (D) rebuke (E) imprision unlawfully

36. BLEAK: (A) sleek (B) playful (C) desolate (D) wistful (E) noisy

37. CONSPIRACY: (A) circulation (B) secret plot (C) shaded terrace (D) fight to the death (E) treason

38. BOUNDLESS: (A) preceding (B) explicit (C) without limit (D) immense (E) energetic

39. BLUFF: (A) triumphant (B) trying (C) secretive (D) frank (E) timorous

40. ENRICH: (A) befall (B) arouse (C) adore (D) resolve (E) improve

41. ABRIDGE: (A) cross over (B) cover (C) elevate (D) straddle (E) shorten

42. ANALYZE: (A) disturb (B) paralyze (C) examine closely (D) praise insincerely (E) develop

43. ENDURE: (A) detour (B) last (C) occupy (D) exceed (E) harden

44. BRACKET: (A) nature (B) supporting piece (C) loud noise (D) tennis equipment (E) inclusion

45. EMBRACE: (A) love (B) resist (C) hug (D) recover (E) certify

46. SUPERB: (A) questionable (B) splendid (C) fairly good (D) scant (E) relevant

47. CRITICAL: (A) harmful (B) fault-finding (C) thoughtful (D) highly emotional (E) essential

48. REVITALIZE: (A) capture (B) trust (C) return (D) furnish (E) strengthen

49. SULLEN: (A) excessive (B) natural (C) rational (D) ill-tempered (E) soiled

50. INTERMINABLE: (A) powerful (B) endless (C) taut (D) tiresome (E) boastful

Words-in-Context Questions

Here your vocabulary is being tested in actual use. Therefore, these questions ask you to identify the word that comes closest in meaning to a word that appears in a phrase, a sentence, or a short paragraph.

EXAMPLE:

Choose the word that means the same as the word in boldface type in the following sentence:

The waters were **ruffled** by the wind.

(A) frozen (B) smoothed (C) disturbed
(D) driven (E) cooled

Ⓐ Ⓑ ● Ⓓ Ⓔ

ANALYSIS: Since *ruffled* means upset or disturbed, the correct answer is *disturbed.*

PATTERNS TO WORDS-IN-CONTEXT QUESTIONS

1. The entire sentence or paragraph may be a definition of the word.

EXAMPLE:

Anatomy is the science that deals with the study of the physical structure of an organism.

Anatomy

(A) is a recent discovery
(B) is based on physics
(C) describes how to dissect animals
(D) deals with the makeup of a body

ANALYSIS: The selection does not tell us how old anatomy is; therefore (A) is wrong. The selection does not describe where anatomy comes from; therefore (B) is not correct. Anatomy may involve dissections, but that aspect is not stressed in the sentence; therefore (C) is eliminated. (D) paraphrases "the study of the physical structure of an organism" and is the correct choice.

2. The key word may be followed by a synonym.

EXAMPLE:

Manumission, the liberation of slaves, was practiced by many people when the slave had served adequately for a definite period of time.

Manumission means most nearly

(A) purchase (B) freeing (C) capturing
(D) elevation

Ⓐ ● Ⓒ Ⓓ

ANALYSIS: Liberation, manumission, and freeing are synonyms; therefore (B) is the correct choice.

3. The selection may contain an example or illustration that explains the key word.

EXAMPLE:

The reasoning that leads to the *traitorous* deeds of a Benedict Arnold is beyond my comprehension.

Traitorous means

(A) kindly (B) deadly (C) disloyal
(D) patriotic

Ⓐ Ⓑ ● Ⓓ

ANALYSIS: The key to the answer—Benedict Arnold, who went over to the enemy—is in the given sentence. Therefore, *patriotic* is wrong. Arnold is not known for being *kindly* or *deadly*. The only possible answer is *disloyal*, as proved by Arnold's actions.

4. The action in the rest of the sentence serves as a clue to the meaning of the test word.

EXAMPLE:

Marjorie's skill in handling words made her speech most *stimulating.*

Stimulating means

(A) dull (B) wordy (C) intelligent
(D) exciting

Ⓐ Ⓑ Ⓒ ●

ANALYSIS: The sentence is in praise; therefore *dull* and *wordy* can be eliminated. Intelligence is not under discussion; therefore, *intelligent* can be eliminated. *Exciting* is correct by the process of elimination, and because *exciting* fits in with *skill* and *speech.*

HOW TO HANDLE WORDS-IN-CONTEXT QUESTIONS

- ➤ Don't even think about answering the question without first reading the whole passage, sentence, or paragraph.
- ➤ Look for clues to the correct answer. Clues often lie hidden in definitions, in carefully placed synonyms, and in examples. Sometimes a description will contain a clue to the right answer.
- ➤ Once you've found a promising clue, read all four choices (A–D) before determining your answer.
- ➤ Use the process of elimination to prove the other choices wrong.
- ➤ Once you have chosen an answer, check it by substituting it in the phrase, sentence, or paragraph. If it doesn't make sense, pick another answer.
- ➤ If you are stumped, don't dawdle. Go on to the next question, but make a note to come back later and try again. If you still can't answer the question, give it a guess. You may get lucky. You have a 25 percent chance of guessing the correct answer.

PRACTICE TEST 2

DIRECTIONS: Each of the following sentences is followed by an incomplete statement. Circle the letter of the choice that best completes the statement.

1. Alison walked her bicycle across the *heath* because there were no trails to ride on.

   A *heath* is most like a

   (A) flat meadow (B) stream (C) road (D) small park

2. In recent years motorists have grown *accustomed* to additives which are said to increase the power of gasoline.

   Accustomed means most nearly

   (A) wise (B) hardened (C) used (D) similar

3. The storm *baffled* the weather forecaster, who couldn't figure out what caused the snow to fall nonstop for three days and nights.

   Baffled most nearly means

   (A) threatened (B) advised (C) puzzled (D) delighted

4. Habits are learned behavior which has become automatic because of repetition.

   Actions become habits when

   (A) they are taught
   (B) they are mastered
   (C) they are avoided
   (D) they are done often enough

5. The first method for producing an electric current involved batteries, but batteries are not practical as sources of current on a large and continuous scale.

   Batteries will not

   (A) store electricity
   (B) produce electricity
   (C) store an indefinite amount of electricity
   (D) store a sufficient amount of electricity

DIRECTIONS: Select the correct SYNONYM for the italicized word in each sentence.

6. The defenders tried in vain to *expel* the invaders

   (A) conquer (B) meet (C) force out (D) envelop

7. The successful sales person is always *punctual* for appointments.

   (A) on time (B) prepared (C) anxious (D) anticipating

8. The criminal and his *accomplice* were captured by the alert detectives.

   (A) lawyer (B) helper (C) driver (D) victim

9. The angry father *chastised* his disobedient son.

   (A) scolded (B) praised (C) discovered (D) beat

10. Because the students were *boisterous* during the assembly, the principal kept them after school.
(A) unruly (B) unafraid
(C) uninterested (D) lethargic

11. The coach *lauded* his assistant for planning the winning play.
(A) rewarded (B) praised
(C) publicized (D) ignored

12. Only a *dolt* would believe such a ridiculous story.
(A) coward (B) friend (C) fool
(D) small child

13. Do not be so *rash* that you feel compelled to climb the mountain with them.
(A) reckless (B) insensitive
(C) sensitive (D) foolish

14. A *titanic* wave battered the small boat and drove it toward the rocks.
(A) tremendous
(B) produced by a storm (C) sudden
(D) unexpected

15. The president *rescinded* the order when he realized it would cause too much friction.
(A) enforced (B) broke (C) repealed
(D) issued

DIRECTIONS: Select the correct SYNONYM for the italicized word in each phrase.

16. appear *unconcerned* when told the news
(A) interested (B) fearful
(C) uninterested (D) disturbed

17. arrange a *truce* between the two warring groups
(A) treaty (B) temporary peace
(C) lasting agreement (D) contest

18. *replenish* their arms supply
(A) create (B) refill
(C) purchase illegally (D) uncover

19. a *minute* defect
(A) very small (B) serious
(C) trivial (D) costly

20. *quell* their fears
(A) analyze (B) quiet (C) show (D) hide

Antonym Questions

An *antonym* is a word that means the *opposite* of another word. An antonym question requires that you identify a word opposite in meaning to a given word.

EXAMPLE:

PRESERVE: (A) observe (B) destroy (C) enjoy (D) present (E) disregard
Ⓐ●ⒸⒹⒺ

ANALYSIS: To *preserve* liberty means to protect it. Therefore, *destroy* is the closest to the opposite of *preserve*. Let's look at the other choices: *enjoy* and *disregard* are unrelated to *preserve*. *Observe* contains many of the same letters. So does *present*. But neither word is related to the key word, *preserve*.

HOW TO HANDLE ANTONYM QUESTIONS

➤ Read the instructions carefully. Are you required to find a word that is the same (synonym) or the opposite (antonym) in meaning?

➤ Eliminate the obviously wrong answers. Narrow down your choices. Then select the answer most nearly or most usually correct.

PRACTICE TEST 3

DIRECTIONS: This a test of your ability to find words that mean the OPPOSITE of other words. For each of the fifty words below, there are five choices. Circle the letter of the best choice.

EXAMPLE:

FLIGHTY: (A) soaring (B) whirling (C) level-headed (D) lucky (E) imaginative

1. GENUINE: (A) banished (B) average (C) insincere (D) economical (E) greedy

2. OUTSTANDING: (A) condensed (B) interior (C) commonplace (D) reckless (E) innocent

3. MOCK: (A) fling (B) startle (C) fail (D) mutilate (E) praise

4. TARDY: (A) smooth (B) bristly (C) strong (D) punctual (E) concealed

5. EXCLUDE: (A) admit (B) excuse (C) console (D) excel (E) separate

6. IMPAIR: (A) import (B) improve (C) console (D) deceive (E) separate

7. GRAVITY: (A) cemetery (B) thankfulness (C) attraction (D) indebtedness (E) unimportance

8. DRAB: (A) humid (B) exorbitant (C) vivid (D) rigid (E) restful

9. RESENT: (A) intrude (B) prefer (C) send again (D) misaddress (E) welcome

10. PRUDENT: (A) novel (B) considerate (C) careless (D) sane (E) insurable

11. FORMAL: (A) neat (B) casual (C) obscure (D) apprehensive (E) presentable

12. BOISTEROUS: (A) deplorable (B) fretful (C) bright (D) placid (E) childish

13. TENSE: (A) miserable (B) calm (C) adopted (D) partial (E) unnoticed

14. JOVIAL: (A) melancholy (B) curious (C) inert (D) subsequent (E) failing

15. RESPONSE: (A) notation (B) rest (C) stimulus (D) rally (E) stature

16. FRIGID: (A) in bondage (B) imprisoned (C) adapted (D) torrid (E) dreamy

17. ORIGIN: (A) conflict (B) universe (C) outcome (D) ordinance (E) resource

18. DON: (A) lead (B) yield (C) doff (D) yearn (E) molest

19. OBVIOUS: (A) dubious (B) certified (C) suspicious (D) apart (E) ardent

20. LAUNCH: (A) sail (B) conclude (C) explain (D) stumble (E) finance

21. MOURNFUL: (A) majestic (B) visual (C) cheerful (D) supreme (E) minor

22. RADIATE: (A) absorb (B) elate (C) denounce (D) restrict (E) examine

23. JUSTICE: (A) cheerfulness (B) blame (C) hysteria (D) partiality (E) recklessness

24. WANE: (A) please (B) wax (C) gauge (D) strive (E) conceal

25. PARTICIPATE: (A) hesitate (B) counsel (C) abstain (D) coach (E) employ

26. VACANT: (A) occupied (B) sanctified (C) decorated (D) desolate (E) surrounded

27. CLASSIFY: (A) commence (B) disarrange (C) discover (D) ratify (E) enumerate

28. GENERAL: (A) superlative (B) indifferent (C) chronic (D) specific (E) elegant

29. HAMPER: (A) hurdle (B) impress (C) encase (D) assist (E) enforce

30. PATIENT: (A) docile (B) restless (C) uncooperative (D) pliable (E) polite

31. OBEDIENCE: (A) observance (B) commencement (C) rebellion (D) extravagance (E) management

32. ENORMOUS: (A) minute (B) momentary (C) drab (D) pompous (E) selective

33. IDEAL: (A) improbable (B) craven (C) imperfect (D) critical (E) momentous

34. SLUGGISH: (A) insignificant (B) powerless (C) brisk (D) willing (E) particular

35. TERRIFY: (A) reassure (B) control (C) strengthen (D) restore (E) empower

36. UNIFORM: (A) varied (B) conventional (C) total (D) dyed (E) universal

37. CHECK: (A) release (B) retrain (C) hover (D) repay (E) diminish

38. QUELL: (A) extol (B) correspond (C) incite (D) whisper (E) defer

39. AFFILIATE: (A) confer (B) separate (C) deter (D) consign (E) arrest

40. LIBERATE: (A) lend (B) falsify (C) enslave (D) settle (E) continue

41. PURCHASER: (A) contender (B) seller (C) monopolizer (D) consumer (E) agent

42. HAGGARD: (A) young at heart (B) companionable (C) well-nourished (D) dependable (E) edible

43. REJECT: (A) resist (B) abound (C) accept (D) flit (E) finance

44. LADEN: (A) wound up (B) delighted (C) gladdened (D) unburdened (E) stooped

45. BARREN: (A) pleasant (B) brooding (C) productive (D) calm (E) sultry

46. SHREWD: (A) serene (B) hypocritical (C) considerate (D) stupid (E) insulting

47. INDENT: (A) bend (B) project (C) ignite (D) punch (E) purify

48. SPECIFIC: (A) calm (B) slavish (C) vague (D) concentrate (E) innocent

49. UNIMPRESSIVE: (A) invaluable (B) placid (C) outstanding (D) subversive (E) free

50. ACQUIRE: (A) lose (B) placate (C) gratify (D) inspire (E) refine

Word Analogy Questions

A *word analogy* is a relationship between two words. The word analogy question requires that you determine the relationship between a pair of words, then, given another word, you are to complete a second pair of words by finding a word that relates to the given word *in the same way* that the words in the first pair relate.

EXAMPLE 1:

NOSE:SMELL::eye:
(A) people (B) animals (C) heart (D) sight (E) distance

ⒶⒷⒸ●Ⓔ

ANALYSIS: The symbol : means *is to* and the symbol :: means *as.* The words can be read as follows: NOSE *is to* SMELL *as* eye *is to* ....

The main function of the nose is to smell. Another way to put it is, a nose is a tool used for smelling. Similarly, the eye is used for sight. Therefore, *sight* is the correct answer.

EXAMPLE 2:

ROOSTER:HEN::ram:
(A) cow (B) lamb (C) heifer (D) ewe (E) boar

Analysis: Read the analogy this way: "Rooster is to hen as ram is to ______. *Rooster* is male, *hen* is female. Because *ram* is also male, the answer must be female. Choice A is female. So is choice D. Since both *ram* and *ewe* belong to the sheep family, however, *ewe* is a better choice than *cow*. D is the correct answer.

EXAMINATION FAVORITES

As you might imagine, there are more possibilities for word relationships than you can count. But there are favorites that show up over and over on examinations. Among them are:

1. SYNONYMS:
   hate/despise brave/couragous gale/storm
2. ANTONYMS:
   hot/cold humble/proud real/artificial
3. TOOL AND WORKER:
   wrench/plumber brush/artist glove/shortstop
4. TOOL AND OBJECT WORKED ON:
   hammer/nail mop/floor pen/paper
5. WORKER AND FUNCTION:
   teacher/instruct coach/train violinist/play
6. ACTION AND MEANING:
   wave/greeting yawn/tired fever/illness
7. SYMBOL AND MEANING
   wings/angel ring/marriage wreath/Christmas
8. DEGREE OF SIZE OR INTENSITY:
   chilly/freezing old/ancient damaged/destroyed
9. CLASS AND MEMBER:
   amphibian/frog clergy/priest furniture/bed
10. DEFINING QUALITY:
    mouse/quiet fire/hot razor/sharp
11. PART AND WHOLE:
    keyboard/computer finger/hand street/city

HOW TO HANDLE ANALOGY QUESTIONS

- Before looking at the answer choices, try to find the relationship between the words in the first pair. Put that relationship into words. Then find among the choices a pair that has the most similar or parallel relationship.
- Treat the choices as *pairs,* that is, consider *both* words. Do not try to find a relationship between the first word of a given pair and the first word of any of the choices.
- If the relationship between the words in a given pair seems difficult to find, proceed as follows:
  - Remember that a word can have several meanings. Often checking whether a key word has a second meaning can reveal the relationship.
- Stay alert to parts of speech. If both the given words are nouns, for example, then the answer must also be nouns. If the pair of given words is made up of an adjective and a noun, your answer must also be adjective and noun—and in the *same order* as the given pair.
- Sometimes two words spelled the same change meaning when pronounced differently. A *contract*, for example, is a type of legal document when the accent is on the first syllable. When the accent switches to the second syllable, the word becomes a verb that means to grow smaller.
- Watch for words that have more than one meaning. *Seal*, for example, can be that playful animal found in coastal waters or what you do after you lick an envelope. If you set your mind only on the first definition when the second is intended, you may not answer correctly
- If you have difficulty in selecting one of two choices, the criterion to use is clear: Select as the correct answer the choice that has most nearly the same relationship as the given pair.

EXAMPLE:

Tree is to Seed as
(A) gasoline is to automobile
(B) bear is to cave
(C) farmer is to livestock
(D) starling is to egg
(E) inventor is to device

Ⓐ Ⓑ Ⓒ ● Ⓔ

ANALYSIS: The relationship seems to be between *tree,* a natural object, and *seed,* its origin or its offspring: a tree develops from a seed *(origin),* and its *offspring* (seed) develops from the tree.

Eliminating:

(A) *Gasoline* is not involved in the creation of an *automobile.*
(B) A *bear* may raise its cubs in a *cave,* but the cave is neither an offspring nor a parent.
(C) A *farmer* cares for his *livestock* but does not create it.

Making the choice: The choice is between (E), an inventor who originates a device, and (D) a starling that creates or originates an egg. However, the tree-seed process is biological and so is the starling-egg; the inventor-device is not. Also, as in the tree-seed case, there may be a twofold relationship between the starling and the egg: the starling develops from an egg, and a female starling produces eggs. Therefore, the correct answer is (D).

PRACTICE TEST 4

DIRECTIONS: In each item the first two words can be combined as a pair. Find the alternative that combines with the remaining word to form a similar pair, and circle the letter that corresponds to your choice.

EXAMPLE:

MAN:TORSO::tree:
(A) roots (B) trunk (C) leaves (D) leaf (E) branch

1. COMB:TOOTH::fork:
(A) knife (B) food (C) point (D) prong (E) tone

2. CIRCUMFERENCE:BALL::perimeter:
(A) circle (B) arc (C) track (D) train (E) walker

3. ADOLESCENT:YOUTHFUL::adult:
(A) teenager (B) childish (C) citizen (D) infantile (E) mature

4. ASTRONOMER:PLANET::botanist:
(A) earth (B) tree (C) disease (D) plant (E) science

5. COW:BARN::bear:
(A) cub (B) cube (C) prairie (D) cave (E) mountaintop

6. AXE:CHOP::scissors:
(A) sew (B) tear (C) cut (D) repair (E) patch

7. LETTER:ENVELOPE::dollar:
(A) store (B) wallet (C) pennies (D) coins (E) bank teller

8. COAL:MINE::marble:
(A) farm (B) cave (C) plant (D) quarry (E) factory

9. SAME:OPPOSITE::timid:
(A) shy (B) backward (C) bold (D) quick (E) reluctant

10. AUTOMOBILE:WHEEL::boat:
(A) rudder (B) sail (C) portable (D) stern (E) steerage

11. DUCK:FLOCK::sheep:
(A) ewe (B) lamb (C) crowd (D) bevy (E) flock

12. QUIET:NOISY::safe:
(A) distant (B) dangerous (C) home (D) protected (E) lovely

13. NEAR:CLOSE::large:
(A) small (B) minute (C) distant (D) oral (E) gigantic

14. SWITZERLAND:SWISS::Denmark:
(A) Danish (B) Flemish (C) French (D) Dutch (E) Swedish

15. CLOTH:GARMENT::leather:
(A) soul (B) shoe (C) hide (D) tan (E) animal

16. RULER:DISTANCE::gauge:
(A) pressure (B) fire (C) press
(D) number (E) direction

17. ACTOR:PLAY::musician:
(A) music (B) score (C) baton
(D) orchestra (E) pit

18. FUEL:HEAT::food:
(A) delight (B) hunger (C) energy
(D) money (E) digestion

19. FALLS:WATER::avalanche:
(A) aviator (B) snow (C) height
(D) winter (E) danger

20. CRANE:LIFT::bulldozer:
(A) destroy (B) convert (C) move
(D) build (E) recover

Verbal Classification

This particular kind of question may not appear on the test you'll be taking. However, as you prepare for your test, you will find the exercises that follow helpful in increasing you word power and your understanding of examination-level vocabulary.

In the Practice Test that follows, you are given a list of four words. Three of them are related. You are asked to identify the fourth (unrelated) word.

EXAMPLE:

Which word does not belong with the others?
(A) comma (B) letter (C) semicolon
(D) dash

ANALYSIS: Three of the words refer to marks of punctuation: *comma, semicolon, dash. Letter* is different, since it is not a mark of punctuation. Therefore, **B** is the correct answer.

EXAMINATION FAVORITES

Word relationships come in countless varieties. Some exam favorites include

1. Synonyms: *spot, speck, blot*
2. Parts of a whole: *spokes, rim, hub*
3. Function: *timer, barometer, thermometer*
4. Unfavorable qualities: *cowardly, unfaithful, boorish*
5. Favorable qualities: *honest, courageous, charitable*
6. Related types: *opera, symphony, cantata*
7. Homophones: *weigh, whey, way*
8. Texture: *coarse, smooth, nubby*
9. Parts of speech: *of, between, for*
10. Composition: *cotton, wool, silk*
11. Occupation: *salesperson, computer programmer, writer*

On your own you could probably think of many other word relationships within a few minutes.

HOW TO HANDLE VERBAL CLASSIFICATION QUESTIONS

➤ Concentrate on the group of four words. Look for the related three. Don't turn to the Answer Key until you have tested the fourth word to make certain that it does not bear a similar relationship to any one of the other three.

➤ Look for obvious relationships first: synonyms, parts of a whole, functions. Don't begin by looking for complicated connections.

➤ Spotlight one word at a time, and compare it with the other three. This approach can often point to the clue that will reveal the related groups of three. The unrelated word may be an antonym of the other three.

➤ Very often, if the meaning of the one word is not clear, you can find the answer by working with the other three only. If two of the words bond together and the third is clearly unrelated or is an antonym of the pair, then the logical guess is to assume that the unknown word is unrelated to the two that bond. The same logic works if three words clearly bond together and the fourth is the unknown word.

- If the relationship does not become evident quickly, look for a word that has several meanings. You may be hung up on just one of the possible meanings: *drone* as a sound, *drone* as a type of bee.
- If you have difficulty with one item, do not dawdle over it. Go on to the next, which may be easier. You can always go back if there is time.
- Do not place speed over accuracy in handling relationship questions. Work for accuracy first; speed will follow with practice.

PRACTICE TEST 5

DIRECTIONS: Circle the letter of the unrelated word in each of the following groups of four.

1. (A) chew (B) nibble (C) gulp (D) munch
2. (A) waterwheel (B) utensil (C) generator (D) windmill
3. (A) totality (B) entirety (C) wholeness (D) segment
4. (A) sheriff (B) desperado (C) brigand (D) swindler
5. (A) handcuffs (B) uniform (C) manacles (D) fetters
6. (A) old (B) aged (C) juvenile (D) venerable
7. (A) worsen (B) mend (C) recuperate (D) heal
8. (A) slovenly (B) neat (C) messy (D) grubby
9. (A) spinach (B) asparagus (C) cauliflower (D) apple
10. (A) sentence (B) theme (C) chapter (D) paragraph
11. (A) golf (B) football (C) baseball (D) basketball
12. (A) praise (B) extol (C) laud (D) criticize
13. (A) oculist (B) pharmacist (C) gardener (D) chiropractor
14. (A) cautiously (B) boldly (C) recklessly (D) imprudently
15. (A) announce (B) herald (C) proclaim (D) suppress
16. (A) shutter (B) microscope (C) lens (D) film
17. (A) nylon (B) orlon (C) cotton (D) polyester
18. (A) condominium (B) house (C) palace (D) pastures
19. (A) check (B) goad (C) prod (D) spur
20. (A) lily (B) spruce (C) aster (D) rose

Building Your Vocabulary

A big vocabulary will help you read better, speak better, and of course, do better on the exam. Vocabulary is like money. You can never have too much of it.

While no single technique for building vocabulary works for everyone, a tried-and-true method that helps just about everyone is studying word parts, namely *prefixes, suffixes, roots,* and *stems*. For example, the prefix of a word can often give you at least a general sense of the word. The very word *prefix* contains the common prefix *pre*, meaning before, as in *prewar* (before the war) and *predict*—to foretell something before it happens.

A prefix is the name of a group of letters at the beginning of some words that help convey the meaning of the word. You can't speak English without using words that contain prefixes, such as

re, meaning *again*, as in *re*peat, *re*read, and *re*visit
co meaning *together*, as in *co*operate and *co*captain
mis meaning *bad* or *improper*, as in *mis*take and *mis*demeanor

Suffixes, like prefixes, also convey meaning, but suffixes are found at the ends of words such as:

oid, meaning *resembling*, as in ov*oid* (like an egg) and human*oid* (like a human)
er or *eer* or *or*, meaning *a person who*, as in mountain*eer* (a person who climbs mountains) and sail*or* (a person who sails)

A great many words contain roots or stems. Roots are word parts that originated in other languages, mostly Latin and Greek, that have been absorbed by English. Stems are a variety of roots that have evolved into new forms. Both stems and roots convey meaning, just as though they were prefixes or suffixes. For example:

tempor, meaning *time*, as in temporary (for a short time) and contemporary (at the same time)
terr, meaning *land*, as in terrestrial (of the earth) and subterranean (underground)

There are literally hundreds of prefixes, suffixes, roots, and stems. Knowing many of them can help you figure out the meaning of unfamiliar words. Not all of them can be listed in this book, but here is a basic list that could help you to improve your score on the exam.

PREFIX	DEFINITION	EXAMPLE
a, an	without, not	*amoral*, without morals *anarchy*, without government *anemia*, lack of blood
ab, abs	away, from	*absent*, not here *abduct*, take away
ambi	both	*ambiguous*, two meanings *ambidextrous*, both hands
ante	before	*anteroom*, entryway or foyer *antebellum*, before the war
anti	against	*antiwar*, opposed to war *antiseptic*, against germs or infection
arch	first, head	*archbishop*, head bishop *arch-rival*, main competitor
bi	two	*bicycle*, two-wheeler *bimonthly*, twice a month
circum	around	*circumnavigate*, sail around (the world) *circumspect*, careful, cautious
co, con, col	together, with	*confer*, talk with *combine*, join with *collaborate*, plan with
de	down, away	*depart*, go away *defer*, put off
di	two	*divide*, split in two *diverge*, spreading in two directions
dia	across	*diagonal*, from one side to another (at a slant) *diameter*, across a circle
dis	not, apart	*disappear*, to not appear, vanish *distant*, away from
e, ex	out of	*expel*, to throw out *emit*, to send out

PREFIX	DEFINITION	EXAMPLE
extra, extro	outside	*extraterrestrial*, out of the world *extraordinary*, beyond the ordinary
in, im	not	*invalid*, not valid *imperfect*, not perfect
inter	between	*interfere*, to come between *interscholastic*, between schools
intra, intro	within	*intramural*, within the walls *introspective*, looking within
micro	small	*microscopic*, tiny *microbe*, tiny organism
mis	not, bad	*misaligned*, not lined up properly *misjudge*, to judge badly
mono	one	*monarch*, single ruler *monopoly*, one owner or controller
multi	many	*multitude*, big crowd *multinational*, many nations
neo	new	*neophyte*, beginner *neonatal*, newborn
non	not	*nonsense*, no sense *nonhuman*, not human
ob, opp	against	*obstruct*, to stop or interfere with *oppose*, to be against
para	beyond	*paranormal*, beyond normal *paragon*, outstanding example
peri	around	*periphery*, outside edge *perimeter*, outside boundary
poly	many	*polygon*, many-sided figure *polyglot*, speaking many languages
post	after	*postwar*, after the war *posterior*, rear end
pre	before	*preface*, forword to a book, etc. *prejudice*, prejudgment
prim	first	*primary*, first or most important *prime*, first or best
pro	forward, in favor of	*propose*, to put forward an idea *promote*, to advance or support
re	backward, again	*repeat*, to do again *return*, to go back, bring back
se	away, aside	*secret*, hidden, concealed *seclude*, shut away
sub	under	*subway*, underground passage *subzero*, below zero
super	above	*supermarket*, store bigger than others *superior*, above or better than others

PREFIX	DEFINITION	EXAMPLE
trans	across	*transfer*, to go from one to the other *transport*, to take across
ultra	beyond, extreme	*ultramodern*, extremely modern *ultrasound*, beyond sound, unheard
un	not	*unknown*, not known *unaware*, not aware
uni	one	*uniform*, always the same *united*, together as one

SUFFIX	DEFINITION	EXAMPLE
able, ible	capable of being done	*washable*, able to be washed *drinkable*, able to be drunk
acious, icious	full of	*malicious*, full of malice (hatred) *delicious*, full of good taste
ate	to make	*penetrate*, to make a hole through *dilate*, to make larger
ation, ition	that which is	*conflagration*, that which is on fire *position*, that which is in a certain place
cy	state of being	*lunacy*, state of being crazy *accuracy*, state of being correct
fy	to make	*terrify*, to make scared *sanctify*, to make holy
ism	belief	*extremism*, belief in extremes *monotheism*, belief in one god
ist	one who does or believes	*artist*, one who does art *communist*, one who believes in communism
ity	state of being	*amiability*, state of being friendly *ability*, state of being able
ize, ise	make	*familiarize*, make familiar *realize*, make a reality
ous	full of	*ridiculous*, full of foolishness *porous*, full of holes

ROOTS/STEMS	DEFINITION	EXAMPLE
alt	high	*altitude*, height *exalted*, having high honor
alter	other	*alternating*, every other *altruistic*, considerate of others
am	love	*amity*, friendliness *amorous*, loving
ann, enn	year	*annual*, every year *perennial*, yearly
anthrop	man	*anthropology*, study of man *anthropomorphic*, in man's form
apt, ept	fit	*aptitude*, able *inept*, unfit

ROOTS/STEMS	DEFINITION	EXAMPLE
aqua	water	*aquatic*, of the water *aqueduct*, passage for water
aster	star	*astronomy*, study of stars *asteroid*, starlike object
aud	hear	*auditorium*, place to hear others *auditory*, related to hearing
auto	one	*autocrat*, one ruler *automatic*, unassisted or without help
belli	was	*antebellum*, before the war *belligerent*, inclined to fight
ben, bon	good	*benefit*, something good *bonus*, reward or extra pay
biblio	book	*bibliography*, list of books *bibliophile*, lover of books
bio	life	*biology*, study of life *biography*, story of a person's life
carn	meat	*carnal*, of the flesh *carnivorous*, meat-eating
ced, cess	give up, to go	*accede*, to agree, to give in *antecedent*, that which goes before
cent	one hundred	*cent* (1/100th) of a dollar *century*, one hundred years
chron	time	*chronicle*, history of events *anachronistic*, out of time's sequence
cide, cis	cut, kill	*suicide*, to kill oneself *excise*, to cut out
corp, corpor	body	*corpse*, dead body *corporation*, unified body of many parts
cred	believe	*incredible*, hard to believe *credible*, believable
curr, curs	run	*current*, ongoing at the present *cursive*, flowing (handwriting)
dem	people	*democracy*, government by the people *epidemic*, spread through the people
derm	skin	*dermatologist*, skin doctor *epidermis*, skin
dict	say	*diction*, speech *verdict*, statement by judge/jury
duc, duct	lead	*duct*, passage *conductor*, one who leads
eu	good, pleasant	*eulogy*, praise *euphemism*, pleasant way of saying something unpleasant
fid	truth, belief	*confidence*, belief in *fidelity*, truth

ROOTS/STEMS	DEFINITION	EXAMPLE
fin	end	*finish*, end *infinite*, having no end
flect	bend	*flexible*, able to bend *inflection*, change in speech
frag, fract	break	*fragile*, breakable *infraction*, violation
gen	classification	*gender*, classification by sex *general*, with no specific class
gress	go	*digress*, to depart from *regress*, to go backward
graph, gram	writing	*pictograph*, writing with pictures *autograph*, written signature
jec, ject	throw	*projectile*, missile *eject*, to throw out
loqu, locut	talk	*locquacious*, talkative *elocution*, speech
luc	light	*lucid*, clear *translucent*, letting light in
magn	large, great	*magnify*, to enlarge *magnificent*, great
mal	bad	*malodorous*, smelling bad *malicious*, nasty
mar	sea	*marine*, having to do with the sea *submarine*, under the sea
mater, matr	mother	*maternity*, related to mother *matricide*, to kill one's mother
mit, miss	send	*remit*, to send in *missionary*, one sent out
mor	die	*immortal*, never dying *morgue*, place for the dead
morph	shape	*amorphous*, shapeless *metamorphosis*, change of shape
nat	born	*nativity*, birth *neonatal*, newborn
nov	new	*novice*, beginner *novelty*, something new
omni	all, many	*omnivorous*, eating everything *omnicient*, all-knowing
pater, patr	father	*patriot*, one who loves his or her country *patricide*, killing one's father
path	feeling	*sympathy*, feeling for others *pathetic*, feeling of pity or sadness
ped, pod	foot	*pedestal*, base for a statue *podiatrist*, foot doctor

ROOTS/STEMS	DEFINITION	EXAMPLE
ped	child	*pediatrician*, children's doctor *pedagogue*, teacher of children
pel, puls	drive	*repel*, to withstand *repulse*, to drive back
phil	love	*bibliophile*, lover of books *philanthropist*, lover of humanity
port	carry	*transport*, to carry across *portable*, able to be carried
psych	mind	*psychologist*, one who studies minds and behavior *psyche*, workings of the mind
quer, quir	ask	*inquire*, to ask *inquisition*, investigation
reg, rect	rule	*regal*, pertaining to rulers *correct*, according to the rules
rupt	break	*interrupt*, to break into *corruption*, breaking of rules or law
sci	know	*conscious*, aware *science*, knowledge
scrib	write	*transcribe*, to write down *scribble*, to write aimlessly
sect	cut	*section*, piece cut from a whole *bisect*, to cut in two
sequi, secut	follow	*sequel*, something that follows *consequence*, result
soph	wisdom	*sophomoric*, without wisdom *sophisticated*, knowing or worldly
spec, spect	see, look	*spectator*, onlooker *spectacle*, something to see
tang, tact	touch	*tangent*, touching *tactile*, touchable
tempor	time	*temporary*, short time *contemporaneous*, same time
tort, tors	twist, turn	*distort*, to twist the truth *tortuous*, winding
tract	pull, drag	*tractor*, machine that drags a plow *distract*, to pull (attention) from
urb	city	*urban*, citylike *suburban*, outside the city
vac	empty	*vacuum*, empty of air *vacate*, to leave empty
vent	come	*advent*, arrival *convene*, to come together
ver	true	*veracity*, truthfulness *verify*, to check the truth of
viv, vit	alive	*revive*, to bring back to life *vitality*, liveliness

Words Commonly Confused

The following groups of pairs and triplets cause confusion of meaning and spelling. Do not run through the list in one sitting. Do study a column at a time. Check the items that cause you difficulty. Each time you turn to a new column, review the ones you checked previously. Use the Practice Test that follows to see how effectively your study time was spent.

accept *v.* to receive
except *prep.* leaving out
except *v.* to leave out

access *n.* approach
excess *n.* more than enough

addition *n.* increase, a term in arithmetic
edition *n.* printing, a term in publishing

advice *n.* counsel
advise *v.* to notify

affect *v.* to influence
effect *n.* a result
effect *v.* to bring about a result

aisle *n.* a passage between rows of seats
isle *n.* a small island
I'll *pron* and *v.* contraction of "I shall"

allowed *v.* gave permission
aloud *adv.* loud enough to be heard

all ready *pro.* plus *adj.* everybody prepared
already *adv.* by now

allusion *n.* reference
illusion *n.* something that deceives the eye or mind

altar *n.* an elevated structure for worship
alter *v.* to change

arc *n.* any part of a circle
ark *n.* a ship

ascent *n.* an upward slope
assent *v.* to agree

assistance *n.* aid, a helping hand
assistants *n.* plural of "assistant"; people who help

band *n.* a group of people; a narrow strip for holding things together
banned *v.* forbidden

bare *adj.* naked
bear *v.* to carry, endure
bear *n.* an animal

base *n.* foundation; a sack or plate in baseball
bass *n.* deepest voice in singing

beach *n.* a sandy shore
beech *n.* a tree with smooth gray bark

beau *n.* an escort, a sweetheart, a steady boyfriend
bow *n.* a knot; a weapon to propel an arrow; a wooden rod used in playing a musical instrument; a simple curve

berry *n.* a small juicy fruit
bury *v.* to cover up

berth *n.* a bed
birth *n.* beginning of life

blew *v.* past tense of "to blow"
blue *adj.* or *n.* a color

boar *n.* a male pig or hog
bore *v.* to pierce
bore *v.* to be uninteresting to (people)

born *v.* brought to life
borne *v.* carried

bough *n.* a branch
bow *v.* to bend

brake *n.* part of an automobile
break *v.* to smash or injure

bread *n.* food made of wheat
bred *v.* raised, brought up

bridal *adj.* relating to a bride or wedding
bridle *n.* head harness for horse

canvas *n.* cloth
canvass *v.* to solicit

capital *n.* the chief city
capitol *n.* a building in which a state or national legislature meets

carat *n.* a unit of weight
caret *n.* a mark showing where something was omitted
carrot *n.* a vegetable

cede *v.* to give up
seed *n.* a part of a plant

cell *n.* a small room
sell *v.* to get money for (an object)

cellar *n.* a room under a building
seller *n.* one who sells

cent *n.* a coin
scent *n.* an odor
sent *v.* did send

cite *v.* to quote or refer to
sight *n.* a view
site *n.* a place

climb *v.* to ascend; mount
clime *n.* a climate

coarse *adj.* rough
course *n.* a route

colonel *n.* an army officer
kernel *n.* a grain of corn or wheat

core *n.* the central part
corps *n.* a body of troops

council *n.* a meeting
counsel *v.* to advise

councilor *n.* a member of a council
counselor *n.* an advisor; lawyer

creak *v.* to squeak
creek *n.* a small stream

dear *adj.* beloved; expensive
deer *n.* an animal

descent *n.* a downhill slope
dissent *n.* disagreement

desert *v.* to abandon
dessert *n.* last course, usually sweet, of a meal

dew *n.* moisture from air
due *adj.* owed

die *v.* to lose one's life
dye *v.* to change color

doe *n.* a female deer
dough *n.* a mixture of flour for baking bread or cake

dual *adj.* double
duel *n.* a fight between two combatants

earn *v.* to receive pay for work
urn *n.* a vase with a pedestal

faint *v.* to lose consciousness
feint *v.* to move in such a way as to trick the opponent

fair *adj.* just; honest
fare *n.* money paid for transportation

fate *n.* destiny
fete *n.* festival

find *v.* to come upon
fined *v.* penalized (past tense of "to fine")

fir *n.* an evergreen
fur *n.* soft hair covering skin of certain animals

flea *n.* a small insect
flee *v.* to run away

flew *v.* past tense of "to fly"
flue *n.* a chimney; an air-shaft

flour *n.* wheat that has been ground into powder
flower *n.* a blossom

for preposition
four *n.* or *adj.* 2 times 2 or 3 plus 1

formally *adv.* properly; ceremoniously
formerly *adv.* in the past

forth *adv.* forward
fourth *adj.* following the third and before the fifth

foul *adj.* nasty; outside the playing field
fowl *n.* a chicken

gait *n.* manner of walking or running
gate *n.* the moveable part of a fence

gamble *v.* to bet
gambol *v.* to dance

gilt *n.* gold paint
guilt *n.* the opposite of innocence

grate *n.* framework of iron to hold a fire
great *adj.* big; large

groan *n.* a short moan
grown *adj.* increased in size

guessed *v.* past tense of "to guess"
guest *n.* a visitor in the house

hail *v.* to greet
hale *adj.* strong and well

hair *n.* the threadlike outgrowths from the head
hare *n.* a rabbit

hall *n.* a passageway
haul *v.* to move by pulling

hart *n.* a male deer
heart *n.* the blood-pumping organ of the body

heal *v.* to become well
heel *n.* the back of the foot

hear *v.* to listen
here *adv.* in this place

heard *v.* past tense of "to hear"
herd *n.* a group of animals

higher *adj.* further up (comparative of "high")
hire *v.* to pay for the use of something; to use

him *pron.* objective case of "he"
hymn *n.* a religious song of praise

hoarse *adj.* harsh in sound
horse *n.* animal

hole *n.* a hollow place
whole *adj.* entire

holy *adj.* sacred
wholly *adv.* entirely

hour *n.* sixty minutes
our *pron.* belonging to us

idle *adj.* doing nothing
idol *n.* an image for worship

in *prep.* within; not outside
inn *n.* a tavern or hotel

instance *n.* an example
instants *n.* moments

its *pron.* belonging to it; possessive of "it"
it's *pron.* and *v.* contraction of "it is"

knight *n.* a man with the title of Sir; a man on horseback
night *n.* the time between evening and morning

know *v.* to be sure of; to have information
no *adv.* opposite of yes

lain *v.* rested (past participle of "to lie")
lane *n.* a narrow path

lead *n.* metal
led *v.* past tense of "to lead"

lessen *v.* to diminish; make smaller
lesson *n.* something to be learned or studied

lie *v.* to recline
lye *n.* a strong alkaline

load *v.* to pile on a truck
lode *n.* a vein of metallic ore

loan *n.* something lent
lone *adj.* by oneself; solitary

mail *n.* and *v.* letters; to post
male *adj.* and *n.* masculine; a man or boy

main *adj.* most important
mane *n.* long hair on the neck of animals

meat *n.* flesh
meet *v.* to come together

metal *n.* a substance such as iron or gold
mettle *n.* high spirit; courage

miner *n.* one who digs coal
minor *n.* one who is under 21 years of age

morn *n.* morning
mourn *v.* to grieve

one *adj.* less than two
won *v.* gained; past tence of "to win"

pail *n.* a container for liquids
pale *adj.* without much color

pain *n.* feeling of being hurt
pane *n.* a sheet of glass

pair *n.* a set of two
pare *v.* to trim off
pear *n.* fruit

pour *v.* to cause to flow
paw *n.* the foot of an animal

peal *n.* a loud sound
peel *n.* the skin of fruit

peace *n.* quietness; absence of strife
piece *n.* a part

plain *adj.* easy to understand
plane *n.* flat or level surface; machine that flies

pray *v.* to speak to God in worship
prey *n.* victim

principal *adj.* and *n.* chief
principle *n* a truth; a rule of conduct

profit *n.* gain
prophet *n.* one who predicts the future

rain *n.* shower
reign *v.* to rule

rap *v.* to knock
wrap *v.* to fold a covering around

read *v.* to understand written words
reed *n.* a hollow stalk

read *v.* past tence of "to read"
red *adj.* or *n.* a color

real *adj.* actual; true
reel *n.* spool

right *adj.* correct
rite *n.* ceremony
write *v.* to put words on paper

ring *n.* a circle
wring *v.* to twist

road *n.* a highway
rode *v.* past tense of "to ride"
rowed *v.* past tense of "to row"

role *n.* actor's part in play
roll *v.* to revolve

root *n.* source; the part of a plant in the ground
route *n.* course

rote *n.* fixed routine
wrote *n.* past tense of "to write"

sail *v.* to travel on a ship
sale *n.* exchange of goods for money

scene *n.* a part of a play
seen *v.* past participle of "to see"

sea *n.* a large body of salt water
see *v.* to use the eyes

seam *n.* line where edges join
seem *v.* to appear

sew *v.* to stitch
so *adv.* in this way
sow *v.* to scatter seed in the ground

slay *v.* to kill
sleigh *n.* a sled

soar *v.* to fly upward
sore *adj.* painful

sold *v.* past tense of "to sell"
soled *adj.* having a sole, like a shoe

sole *adj.* one and only
soul *n.* spirit

some *adj.* few; not many
sum *n.* total; amount

son *n.* a male offspring
sun *n.* the star that gives us daylight

stake *n.* a post driven into ground
steak *n.* a slice of choice meat

stare *v.* to gaze at
stair *n.* a step

stationary *adj.* standing still
stationery *n.* writing materials

steal *v.* to take
steel *n.* to metal made from iron

straight *adj.* without a bend or curve
strait *n.* narrow passage of water between two seas

suite *n.* a set of rooms; a musical composition
sweet *adj.* sugary

tail *n.* part of an animal's body
tale *n.* a story

team *n.* a group of players
teem *v.* to swarm

their *pron.* belonging to them
there *adv.* 1. not here; in that place 2. an expletive (introductory word)
they're *pron.* and *v.* contraction of "they are"

threw *v.* past tense of "to throw"
through *prep.* all the way in or past

throne *n.* a chair for a king or queen
thrown *v.* past participle of "to throw"

tide *n.* alternate rise and fall of the ocean
tied *v.* past tense of "to tie"

toe *n.* a digit of the foot
tow *v.* to pull by a rope or chain

told *v.* said; past tense of "to tell"
tolled *v.* rang; past tense of "to ring"

vain *adj.* conceited
vane *n.* blade of a windmill
vein *n.* blood vessel

vale *n.* a valley
veil *n.* a covering for the face

vial *n.* small glass bottle
vile *adj.* very bad

wade *v.* to walk through shallow water
weighed *v.* past tense of "to weigh"

wail *n.* lament or cry
whale *n.* a large sea animal

waist *n.* the middle part of the body
waste *v.* to make poor use of

wait *v.* to remain
weight *n.* heaviness

ware *n.* anything for sale
wear *v.* to use as clothing
where *adv.* at what place

weak *adj.* not strong
week *n.* seven days

weather *n.* the daily changes in climate
whether *conj.* if

which *pron.* this or that?
witch *n.* a supernatural woman with evil powers

whine *v.* to complain in a sniveling way
wine *n.* fermented grape juice

wood *n.* timber
would *v.* should

your *adj.* belonging to you
you're *pron.* and *v.* contraction of "you are"

PRACTICE TEST 6

DIRECTIONS: In the sentences below fill in the blank space with the appropriate word.

1. **accept, except**

   We shall ____________ applications on Monday.

   This homework is correct ____________ for two mistakes.

2. **access, excess**

   We have ____________ to the Senator's record.

   The last person in the row will bring up any ____________ papers.

3. **addition, edition**
This is the fourth __________ of this book.
John is a welcome __________ to this honor class.

4. **affect, effect - n., effect - v.**
The different shades of blue create a beautiful __________.
The failing mark will __________ your average.
With the mayor's help, the union and the employer will __________ a settlement of the dispute.

5. **aisle, isle, I'll**
The bride walked down the __________ in the church.
I should like to spend my vacation on a beautiful __________.
__________ see you at the theater.

6. **allowed, aloud**
Read that passage __________.
I am __________ to stay up every evening until 10 P.M.

7. **all ready, already**
We are __________ to join in the game.
Has the game __________ started?

8. **allusion, illusion**
We found an __________ to myths on page 230.
The green lights in the dark room created an eerie __________.

9. **altar, alter**
The __________ was decorated with flowers for the wedding.
We will __________ the dress to fit you.

10. **arc, ark**
A pop fly to the first baseman describes a short high __________.
Noah's __________ floated on the water for forty days.

11. **ascent, assent**
The __________ up the mountain side was very steep.
Mother has given her __________; I may have my ears pierced.

12. **assistance, assistants**
The surgeon will have two __________ in the operating room.
Will you need my __________ in order to finish the job?

13. **band, banned**
The __________ of rebels captured the city.
Smoking is __________ in public libraries.

14. **bare, bear, bear**
The big brown __________ was in the cage.
The __________ walls made the room look gloomy.
__________ these rules in mind when you take the test.

15. **base, bass**
The __________ of the lamp is made of brass.
Our quartet has one tenor, two baritones, and a __________.

16. **beach, beech**
We sat under the shade of the __________ tree.
In the summer we go to the __________ to keep cool.

17. **beat, beet**
The __________ of the drum was steady.
The __________ is a red root vegetable.

18. **beau, bow**
At sixteen I had a very handsome young __________.
Please tie a __________ in my shoelace.

19. **berry, bury**

    The dog will __________ his bone and eat it later.

    A ______ is good to eat only when ripe.

20. **berth, birth**

    The __________ of the child brought joy to the family.

    I reserved a ______________ on the overnight train for Chicago.

21. **blew, blue**

    Tom __________ the candles out.

    The sky is __________.

22. **boar, bore, bore**

    The uninteresting story will ______ you.

    The carpenter will __________ a hole in the wood.

    In the hog family, the ________ is the father, the sow is the mother, the pigs are children.

23. **born, borne**

    George Washington was __________ on Feb. 22, 1732.

    A kite is _______ upward by the wind.

24. **bough, bow**

    A bird was standing on a __________ of the tree.

    The boys will __________ to the girls.

25. **brake, break**

    To stop the car, he applied his ______.

    Be careful not to ____________ the dishes.

26. **bread, bred**

    Tom is a very well ______ young man.

    I like whole wheat __________.

27. **bridal, bridle**

    On her wedding day Linda looked beautiful in her __________ gown.

    The jockey put the ________ on the horse.

28. **canvas, canvass**

    We slept in a __________ tent.

    Salesmen ___________ our neighborhood for new business.

29. **capital, capitol**

    Albany is the __________ of New York State.

    Each Congressman is given office space in the __________.

30. **carat, caret, carrot**

    May's ring had a two ____________ diamond.

    The rabbit's favorite treat was a ______.

    He placed a __________ between the two words to note a missing word.

31. **cede, seed**

    At the end of World War I, Germany agreed to __________ Alsace-Lorraine to France.

    In the spring I will plant the ______.

32. **cellar, seller**

    The buyer and _________ drew up an agreement.

    The furnace is in the ________ of the house.

33. **cent, scent, sent**

    Gum costs one __________ a slice.

    The book was ___________ to you by air mail.

    Perfume has a pleasant __________.

34. **cell, sell**

    The prisoner was asleep in his ______.

    We are going to _________ our house.

35. **cite, sight, site**

    The ____________ for the new school has been selected.

    The view from the hill was a beautiful __________.

    The officer will _________ John for bravery.

36. **climb, clime**
Ralph will ___________ the mountain.
In the winter the sunny ___________ of Florida attracts many visitors.

37. **coarse, course**
The scout master mapped out the ___________ for our hike.
___________ salt is used on slippery roads to melt ice.

38. **colonel, kernel**
Mr. Hamilton is a _________ in the army.
The ___________ of the corn is a seed.

39. **council, counsel**
My teacher offered me some wise _____.
The city ___________ voted against the sales tax.

40. **core, corps**
Michael is an officer in the air _______.
We eat most of the apple and throw the ___________ away.

41. **councilor, counselor**
Only one _____________ voted against the bill to install traffic lights on Main Street.
After graduation, he opened an office as ___________ at law.

42. **creak, creek**
The door will ____________ when you open it.
There weren't many fish in the ______.

43. **descent, dissent**
___________ by one juror can hold up a verdict.
There is a steep ___________ down the mountain side.

44. **dear, deer**
The _______ is a very graceful animal.
Memories of my grandparents are very ___________ to me.

45. **desert, dessert**
Chocolate pudding is a popular ______.
Mary did not ______ her friend in need.

46. **dew, due**
Pay the salesman what is _________ him.
The ___________ on the ground in the morning makes the grass wet.

47. **die, dye**
The plants will _______ without water.
I am going to _________ my dress red.

48. **doe, dough**
The ___________ is ready to be baked into bread.
The ___________ is a female deer.

59. **dual, duel**
He holds the ____________ job of secretary-treasurer.
Zorro never loses a ___________.

50. **earn, urn**
He will ___________ his day's pay.
This beautiful _____________ was used for water.

51. **faint, feint**
Linda thought she would ___________ when she heard the bad news.
The boxer will ___________ a punch in order to fool his opponent.

52. **fair, fare**
The referee made a _______________ decision.
We paid our __________________ on the bus.

53. **fate, fete**
Mary's _________________ was already decided.
The Mardi Gras is a gay ___________ in New Orleans.

54. **find, fined**

Jack was __________ ten dollars for speeding.

It is hard to __________ your way in the dark.

55. **fir, fur**

There were tall __________ trees in the forest.

A __________ coat is very warm.

56. **flea, flee**

We had to __________ from the burning house.

There was a __________ on the dog.

57. **flew, flue**

The parakeet __________ out of the cage.

The smoke escapes through a __________.

58. **flour, flower**

Bread is made of __________ .

A rose is a beautiful __________.

59. **for, four**

I will buy it __________ you.

I have __________ minutes to leave the house.

60. **formally, formerly**

Mary was __________ introduced to her future-in-laws.

The house was __________ a one family house.

61. **forth, fourth**

Bring __________ the gifts.

I was __________ on line; you are fifth.

62. **foul, fowl**

The __________ ball rolled outside the third-base line.

Chickens and turkeys are __________.

63. **gait, gate**

Close the __________ when you enter the yard.

The pony trotted with a steady __________.

64. **gamble, gambol**

It is unwise to __________.

The lambs __________ in the pasture.

65. **gilt, guilt**

The painter put __________ around the edge of the chair.

The concrete evidence proved the man's __________.

66. **grate, great**

We built an outdoor __________ to barbecue our steaks.

There was a __________ celebration when we won.

67. **groan, grown**

The sick man let out a __________.

The boy has __________ two inches this year.

68. **guessed, guest**

From this clue you might have __________ the answer.

Frances is a __________ in our house.

69. **hail, hale**

The doorman will __________ a cab for your.

The old man appeared __________ and hearty.

70. **hair, hare**

The __________ hopped away through the field.

She wears her __________ in a bun.

71. **hall, haul**

I walked through the __________ of the school.

The sailor will __________ in the rope.

72. **hart, heart**
The __________ is a male deer.
The __________ pumps blood.

73. **heal, heel**
This new medicine will __________ the wound.
The shoe has a very high __________.

74. **hear, here**
I can __________ his voice above the others'.
Bring the man in __________.

75. **heard, herd**
I __________ the telephone ring.
The __________ of sheep was grazing in the hills.

76. **higher, hire**
Place the picture __________ on the wall.
The store will __________ more help for Christmas.

77. **him, hymn**
Give __________ the book.
Mahalia Jackson sang a beautiful __________.

78. **hoarse, horse**
I love to go __________ back riding.
She talked so much her voice was __________.

79. **hole, whole**
The men dug a big __________.
I want to hear the __________ story.

80. **holy, wholly**
Sandra visited the __________ shrines in Europe.
He does his work __________ and thoroughly.

81. **hour, our**
__________ car is being repaired.
We can park here for only one __________.

82. **idle, idol**
__________ hands get into mischief.
Before modern religion, __________ worship was common.

83. **in, inn**
We stopped at an __________ for dinner.
The keys are __________ my purse.

84. **instance, instants**
Several __________ passed before anyone spoke.
The __________ you cited in your report is important.

85. **its, it's**
__________ raining.
The wolf bared __________ fangs.

86. **knight, night**
Stories of long ago tell tales of many a brave __________.
It was late at __________.

87. **know, no**
I __________ you will do a good job.
There is __________ time to waste.

88. **lain, lane**
The beautiful __________ was lined with trees.
The newspaper has __________ on the doorstep all day.

89. **lead, led**
The pipe was made of __________.
The firemen __________ the family to safety.

90. **lessen, lesson**
Today we shall have a __________ on safety.
If you give me one package, it will __________ your burden.

91. **lie, lye**

The ________ burned a hole in the floor.

Let the book ________ on the desk.

92. **load, lode**

It is too heavy a ______ for one man.

A rich ________ of silver was discovered in the mine.

93. **loan, lone**

Mary will repay the ________ in six weeks.

He was the ________ survivor of the crash.

94. **mail, male**

Please ________ the letter.

We need a deep ________ voice to sing in the choir.

95. **main, mane**

The horse has a shiny, black ______.

The ________ role goes to the leading lady.

96. **meat, meet**

The children ate ______ and potatoes.

I will ________ you at two o'clock.

97. **metal, mettle**

The knives are made of ________.

A good team shows its ________ when it is losing.

98. **miner, minor**

A ________ works hard digging coal.

Florence is a ________ and therefore cannot sign legal papers.

99. **morn, mourn**

How pleasant to hear the chirping of birds on a summer ________.

We shall ________ the loss of our great leader.

100. **one, won**

I will carry ________ carton at a time.

Our bowling team ________ the game.

101. **pail, pale**

Lou carried a ________ of water to the horse.

Because Fred was ill, he looked rather ________.

102. **pain, pane**

The ball shattered the window ______.

The sprain caused a sharp ________ in his ankle.

103. **pair, pare, pear**

I bought a ________ of bookends.

I enjoy eating a juicy ________.

Sheila will ________ the apples for the applesauce.

104. **pour, paw**

Mrs. Johnson will ________ the tea.

The bear has a large ________.

105. **peal, peel**

He slipped on a banana ________.

The bells ________ loud and long.

106. **peace, piece**

When you do the right thing you have ________ of mind.

Please cut a ________ of cake for me.

107. **plain, plane**

It takes only four hours by ________ to reach Florida.

His reasons are quite ________.

108. **pray, prey**

We all ________ for peace on earth.

The eagle has as its ________ small birds and mammals.

109. **principal, principle**

We must adhere to the __________ of our constitution.

Mr. Smith is __________ of the new elementary school.

110. **profit, prophet**

Elijah was a great __________.

We __________ from our experiences.

111. **rain, reign**

The __________ of Queen Victoria was very long.

The __________ wet the clothes on the line.

112. **rap, wrap**

The __________ on the door disturbed the silence.

I will __________ a blanket around the shivering girl.

113. **read, reed**

I need a new ________ for my clarinet.

I want to __________ *Little Women.*

114. **read, red**

Hunters usually wear ________ hats.

I __________ two books last week.

115. **real, reel**

Tell of a __________ experience.

The fisherman let out his __________.

116. **right, rite, write**

Graduation is an important ________ of passage.

I cannot think of the ________ word.

__________ me a letter.

117. **ring, wring**

__________ out the wash before hanging it on the line.

__________ the bell.

118. **road, rode, rowed**

Joe and I __________ the boat.

The __________ was very bumpy.

We __________ for an hour in the car.

119. **role, roll**

The __________ of the lawyer was the biggest part in the play.

I __________ the ball to the child.

120. **root, route**

We chose the fastest __________ to Pittsburgh.

The __________ of the tree was buried deep in the earth.

121. **rote, wrote**

I __________ a letter to my friend.

We memorized the formulas by _____.

122. **sail, sale**

The dresses on __________ were very cheap.

I like to __________ a boat on the lake.

123. **scene, seen**

The first __________ of *Hamlet* occurs at midnight.

I have __________ Jimmy frequently.

124. **sea, see**

The __________ was very rough.

It is nice to __________ old friends.

125. **seam, seem**

It doesn't ________ to be a wise plan.

The tear in the __________ was easily sewed.

126. **sew, so, sow**

It was ________ easy I was surprised.

Please ________ a button on my shirt.

In March the farmer will __________ his seeds.

127. **slay, sleigh**

The ________ came down the snowy hill.

A merciful knight does not ________ his opponent.

128. **soar, sore**

The pilot loves to ________ above the clouds.

Our pitcher had a ________ arm.

129. **sold, soled**

The shoemaker ________ my shoes.

They ________ the cars at a profit.

130. **sole, soul**

He had the ________ of a saint.

The ________ reason for his coming was his concern for her welfare.

131. **some, sum**

I will buy ________ of your candy.

The ________ of two and four is six.

132. **son, sun**

Bob is Mrs. Jones's ________.

The ________ sets in the west.

133. **stake, steak**

The horse was tied to a ________.

I like a nice, juicy ________ for supper.

134. **stare, stair**

Do not jump down the ________ case.

I love to ________ at the beautiful countryside.

135. **stationary, stationery**

I am going to use my new ________ to write the letter.

The sink is ________ and cannot be moved.

136. **steal, steel**

Coal and iron ore are required to make ________.

Thou shalt not ________.

137. **straight, strait**

A narrow ________ separated the two islands.

He went ________ home from school.

138. **suite, sweet**

The king and queen occupied a ________ of rooms in the hotel.

Peaches taste ________.

139. **tail, tale**

A monkey has a ________.

This is a ________ of intrigue.

140. **team, teem**

Our football ________ lost every game.

Polluted waters ________ with germs.

141. **their, there, they're**

________ are two new boys standing ________.

________ house was newly decorated.

________ the first tenants to live in the new house.

142. **threw, through**

He ________ the ball ________ the window.

143. **throne, thrown**

The halfback was ________ for a loss.

Prince Rainier sits on a ________.

144. **tide, tied**

The ocean is at low ________.

The boy scout ________ the knot.

145. **toe, tow**
The bat fell on his __________.
We had to __________ the car to a garage.

146. **told, tolled**
The bell __________ for fifteen minutes.
The storyteller __________ an amusing tale.

147. **vain, vane, vein**
It was a __________ attempt to save the man's life.
A __________ carries blood to the heart.
We have a weather __________ on our roof.

148. **vale, veil**
We trudged down the hill and through the __________.
The mother wore a dark __________.

149. **vial, vile**
The small __________ held expensive medicine.
Rotten food has a __________ odor.

150. **wade, weighed**
I took off my shoes to __________ in the brook.
The grocer __________ the cheese.

151. **wail, whale**
The __________ of sick children kept us up at night.
The __________ is a huge mammal.

152. **waist, waste**
It is sinful to __________ food.
The belt was too tight around her __________.

153. **wait, weight**
I will __________ for you on the corner.
Pat is gaining __________.

154. **ware, wear, where**
I will __________ a new dress tonight.
We polished the silver __________.
Show us __________ the new books are kept.

155. **weak, week**
John made a __________ effort to get up.
It will take a __________ for the watch to be repaired.

156. **weather, whether**
The game will be postponed if the __________ is bad.
Tell us __________ you will help us or not.

157. **which, witch**
__________ dress will you wear?
On Halloween, Maggie dressed up as a __________.

158. **whine, wine**
The lonely dog's __________ was heard all night.
The men drank a glass of __________ at dinner.

159. **wood, would**
They brought __________ for the fireplace.
__________ you be interested in learning the guitar?

160. **your, you're**
__________ not leaving, are you?
__________ taxi is waiting.

Mastery Exams

FOR THE LOWER GRADES—EXAMS 1–15

EXAM 1

DIRECTIONS: For each word in capitals, select the word or phrase that means most nearly the SAME, then circle the letter of the correct answer.

EXAMPLE:

ABSENT: (A) present (B) soak in (C) not here (D) jumping (E) late

ANALYSIS: The correct meaning is "not here." Therefore the answer is (C).

1. BEVERAGE: (A) supper (B) lunch (C) food (D) animal (E) drink
2. ENERGY: (A) ability to do work (B) slowness (C) speed (D) unwillingness (E) ohm
3. ADMIRABLE: (A) naval officer (B) excellent (C) sunset (D) masterpiece (E) terrible
4. EMPLOYEE: (A) fiancee (B) worker (C) hire (D) slave (E) peasant
5. CARGO: (A) auto (B) ship (C) shipment (D) small bundle (E) envelope
6. ADULT: (A) dilute (B) voter (C) very old (D) grown-up (E) invalid
7. ENLARGE: (A) diminish (B) reduce (C) picture (D) expand (E) package
8. COLLIDE: (A) slide (B) hurting (C) glide (D) hunt (E) crash
9. DEPEND: (A) rely (B) protect (C) survival (D) help (E) request
10. CEMENT: (A) burial ground (B) rock (C) earth (D) sea (E) paving material
11. BLIZZARD: (A) bird of death (B) humming sound (C) drought (D) snowstorm (E) desert
12. CABARET: (A) nightclub (B) playboy (C) taxi (D) two-wheeled carriage (E) plow
13. DEBATE: (A) defeat (B) thwart (C) discussion (D) needle (E) obstruct
14. ADOLESCENT: (A) child (B) grown-up (C) perfume (D) adult (E) teenager
15. CANDIDATE: (A) elector (B) canned fruit (C) dandy (D) appointment (E) office-seeker
16. BALLET: (A) leap (B) spiral (C) vote (D) opera (E) dramatic dance
17. ENORMOUS: (A) fatness (B) very large (C) abnormal (D) glorious (E) preferring
18. CHICK: (A) duck (B) yearling (C) baby rooster (D) throw (E) watch out
19. DAZZLE: (A) fizzle (B) bewilder (C) flurry (D) bubble (E) ray
20. ADVISER: (A) voice (B) influence (C) speak (D) provider (E) counselor

EXAM 2

DIRECTIONS: For each word in capitals, select the word or phrase that means most nearly the SAME, then circle the letter of the correct answer.

1. BESEECH: (A) search (B) forgive (C) prove (D) beg (E) desert
2. BESIEGE: (A) beg (B) hinder (C) prove (D) surround (E) betray

3. BIAS: (A) cut in two (B) opinion (C) ribbon (D) persecute (E) sew

4. BLEAK: (A) desolate (B) beak (C) dispute (D) line (E) whiten

5. BLISS: (A) darkness (B) disposition (C) joy (D) humming (E) courage

6. BLUFF: (A) storm (B) outspoken (C) mountain (D) suave (E) cloud

7. BOISTEROUS: (A) noisy (B) frank (C) begging (D) rough (E) courageous

8. SOLEMN: (A) grave (B) holy (C) sunny (D) soft (E) peaceful

9. ABSURD: (A) leave out (B) eject (C) happy (D) foolish (E) critic

10. ABUSE: (A) injure (B) use (C) independence (D) poor (E) cubicle

11. CHAMPION: (A) runner-up (B) winner (C) brigadier (D) sparkling wine (E) breeding

12. EMERGENCY: (A) brilliant (B) crisis (C) brink (D) dilemma (E) escape

13. BANQUET: (A) formal dinner (B) speeches (C) tuxedo (D) deprive (E) forerunner

14. CHEF: (A) chief (B) chop (C) insert (D) choir (E) cook

15. BATCH: (A) spoil (B) rapture (C) bring out of shell (D) quantity (E) quality

16. ADMIRAL: (A) general (B) captain (C) commander (D) frightful (E) naval officer

17. EMBRACE: (A) ashes (B) strengthen (C) hug (D) love (E) hate

18. FLIMSY: (A) airborne (B) fragile (C) floating (D) aged (E) peaceful

19. COLT: (A) bravery (B) baby horse (C) protector (D) raccoon (E) mare

20. BARGAIN: (A) advantage (B) rally (C) low-priced purchase (D) gain (E) small, flat ship

EXAM 3

DIRECTIONS: For each word in capitals, select the word or phrase that means most nearly the OPPOSITE, then circle the letter of the correct answer.

EXAMPLE:

HIGH: (A) tall (B) low (C) way up (D) lofty

ANALYSIS: The opposite of "high" is "low"; therefore the answer is (B).

1. CAPTIVE: (A) inmate (B) persecuted (C) imprisoned (D) free

2. BID: (A) random (B) order (C) obey (D) refrain

3. DELAY: (A) accelerate (B) slow-down (C) cause (D) soften

4. ACCOMPLISH: (A) fail (B) solve (C) achieve (D) suicide

5. EAGER: (A) African bird (B) unwilling (C) slow (D) desirous

6. DEFINITE: (A) vague (B) exact (C) solemn (D) finished

7. BOLDNESS: (A) insolence (B) cowardliness (C) merciless (D) rashness

8. DECENT: (A) inexpensive (B) improper (C) ugly (D) rashness

9. ACCELERATE: (A) pedal (B) deceive (C) speed up (D) retard

10. EFFECT: (A) touch (B) result (C) physical law (D) cause

11. ELIMINATE: (A) dehydrate (B) include (C) elementary (D) get rid of

12. DECAY: (A) spoil (B) grow (C) boil (D) oxidized

13. DEMONSTRATE: (A) examine (B) reveal (C) rally (D) conceal

14. CHAFE: (A) bake (B) irritate (C) collect (D) soothe

15. DESERT: (A) course of a meal (B) moisture (C) stay with (D) leave

16. ACQUIRE: (A) lose (B) obtain (C) gain (D) prevent

17. DEFENDANT: (A) attorney (B) judge (C) witness (D) plaintiff

18. BENEFIT: (A) infection (B) reward (C) injury (D) help

19. ELIGIBLE (A) not serious enough (B) unqualified (C) old enough (D) able to serve

20. ABSORB: (A) take in (B) discharge (C) retain (D) sponge

EXAM 4

DIRECTIONS: Circle the letter of the word or phrase that means most nearly the SAME as the phrase above.

EXAMPLE:

To keep from harm or change.
(A) repress (B) preserve (C) forbid (D) unchanging (E) harmless

1. A story intended to teach a moral truth
(A) narrative poem (B) sonnet (C) satire (D) fable (E) tall story

2. A solemn promise that God is called on to witness
(A) blood pledge (B) oath (C) reform (D) testimony (E) evidence

3. One who pretends to have a skill that he does not possess
(A) expert (B) demon (C) authority (D) legerdemain (E) quack

4. Something made by combining two different elements
(A) hybrid (B) fragment (C) conspiracy (D) paradigm (E) method

5. Careful and economical
(A) miser (B) frugal (C) rigid (D) inexpensive (E) shoddy

6. To hold up to great admiration
(A) magnify (B) martyrize (C) glorify (D) clarify (C) certify

7. The wormlike form in which insects hatch from the egg
(A) larva (C) chick (E) earthworm (D) butterfly (E) eel

8. One who joins metals by melting and pressing
(A) hod-carrier (B) welder (C) mason (D) alchemist (E) physicist

9. State of being adult or fully grown
(A) futurity (B) adolescence (C) old age (D) maturity (E) minority

10. A record of proceedings
(A) newspaper report (B) magazine article (C) journal (D) ledger (E) notebook

11. One who goes on foot
(A) motorist (B) veterinarian (C) vegetarian (D) footsore (E) pedestrian

12. A firm belief serving as a rule of conduct
(A) principle (B) whim (C) impulse (D) austerity (E) emotion

13. To give up in order to gain some other object
(A) save (B) sacrifice (C) exhaust (D) dispair (E) revolt

14. Well-known in a bad sense
(A) famous (B) notorious (C) celebrated (D) criminal (E) foolhardy

15. One who builds with brick
(A) carpenter (B) contractor (C) mason (D) machinist (E) artisan

16. An outbreak of wild emotionalism
(A) disorder (B) disobedience (C) frantic (D) hysteria (E) revolution

17. Proud and overbearing
(A) haughty (B) prejudicial (C) selfish
(D) pliable (E) docile

18. To approach with a request or plea
(A) sell (B) purchase (C) bargain
(D) suggest (E) solicit

19. Involving strong effort or exertion
(A) invigorating (B) lackadaisical
(C) painful (D) strenuous
(E) disturbing

20. A graceful, privately owned pleasure ship
(A) frigate (B) galleon (C) cruiser
(D) yacht (E) motorboat

EXAM 5

DIRECTIONS: For each question determine which of the choices most nearly means the SAME as the word in **boldface** type. Circle the letter of your answer.

EXAMPLE:

The Williams sisters became **proficient** in tennis at an early age.
(A) aggressive (B) wary (C) unimpressive
(D) mediocre (E) skillful

1. Once again France has a **flourishing** tourist trade.
(A) prospering (B) fluid (C) blazing
(D) slumping (E) rigid

2. Weekend football games have become a **fixture** in American life.
(A) frivolity (B) weakness (C) firm part
(D) ideal (E) idleness

3. Humankind possesses only a **fragmentary** history of ancient times.
(A) authoritative (B) indispensable
(C) incomprehensible (D) incomplete
(E) invaluable

4. Sending a human being into space is a **formidable** enterprise.
(A) contemptible (B) frightening
(C) simple (D) loathsome (E) alien

5. In his second year, the rookie went on to **fulfill** our highest expectations.
(A) disappoint (B) splinter (C) stir up
(D) revive (E) satisfy

6. In the last inning, our team made a **futile** attempt to win the game.
(A) giddy (B) vain (C) successful
(D) breathtaking (E) genuine

7. Many people were **gratified** when this style passed out of fashion.
(A) pleased (B) in style
(C) unconcerned (D) saddened
(E) alarmed

8. Smoking is **habitual** with some teenagers.
(A) taboo (B) unhealthy (C) necessary
(D) customary (E) popular

9. Patrick Henry uttered the **immortal** words: "Give me liberty or give me death."
(A) human (B) native (C) rebellious
(D) never dying (E) famous

10. Alex Rodriquez wore a **jaunty** air as he came to bat.
(A) taunting (B) irritable (C) placid
(D) serious (E) cheerful

EXAM 6

DIRECTIONS: For each question determine which of the choices most nearly means the OPPOSITE of the word in **boldface** type. Circle the letter of your answer.

EXAMPLE:

UNTRUSTWORTHY: (A) sly
(B) dependable (C) rash
(D) confidence (E) savings bank

1. FLEECY: (A) silky (B) sulky
(C) flighty (D) fiery (E) dense

2. GIDDY: (A) poised (B) flashing
(C) vivacious (D) spherical
(E) grateful

3. CORPULENT: (A) gaunt (B) hale
(C) desecrated (D) hampered (E) shy

4. ILLUMINATE: (A) shave (B) darken
(C) remove (D) imply (E) illegal

5. JEER: (A) sneer (B) taunt (C) mock
(D) cheer (E) mimic

6. KINDRED: (A) kind (B) relative (C) neighborly (D) alien (E) laden

7. LEGITIMATE: (A) improper (B) impoverish (C) inflated (D) theatrical (E) fervent

8. LOATHE: (A) dote on (B) lofty (C) detest (D) protest (E) liberate

9. JOVIAL: (A) Jupiter (B) isolated (C) frugal (D) evil (E) stern

10. INTIMATE: (A) tolerate (B) hint (C) proclaim (D) close (E) variable

EXAM 7

DIRECTIONS: In each of the items below, decide which word or phrase has the SAME or nearly the same meaning as the underlined word. Circle the letter of your choice.

EXAMPLE:

a cheerful face (A) sad (B) bashful (C) rough (D) happy

ANALYSIS: Letter D has been circled because a cheerful face is a happy face, rather than a sad, bashful, or rough face. The letter before "happy" is "D"; therefore, letter D is circled.

1. a massive structure (A) trifling (B) tremendous (C) isolated (D) lovely

2. drawing nigh (A) away (B) near (C) up (D) water

3. a startling observation (A) remark (B) view (C) service (D) claim

4. punctual arrival (A) late (B) early (C) on time (D) pointed

5. quelled the uprising (A) located (B) incited (C) approved (D) put down

6. radiated light (A) sent forth (B) obscured (C) rained (D) heated

7. replenish the supply (A) use up (B) drain off (C) lose (D) replace

8. of the finest quality (A) number (B) price (C) grade (D) worthlessness

9. pierce the skin (A) penetrate (B) hand from (C) burn (D) stretch

10. a deep resentment (A) kindness (B) animosity (C) obligation (D) corruption

11. a notable success (A) outstanding (B) notice (C) taking notes (D) musical

12. for medicinal purposes (A) final (B) digestive (C) solving (D) curative

13. a minute detail (A) hourly (B) very small (C) timed (D) quick

14. necessary requirements (A) essential (B) plausible (C) partial (D) fulfilling

15. an obedient pupil (A) rebellious (B) happy (C) dutiful (D) bright

16. a rugged pioneer (A) colonist (B) conservative (C) radical (D) flower

17. a quaint restaurant (A) dirty (B) unpleasant (C) a la carte (D) old-fashioned

18. the rehabilitated convict (A) remorseful (B) reformed (C) self-destructive (D) incorrigible

19. a respected doctor (A) highy regarded (B) experienced (C) famous (D) engaged in research

20. quickened our interest (A) explained (B) modified (C) deadened (D) aroused

EXAM 8

DIRECTIONS: Below are twenty pairs of words. The two words in a pair may be the same or nearly the same in meaning, or may be opposite or nearly opposite in meaning, or may be unrelated to each other. Circle S to the right of the question if the words in the pair have the same meaning; circle O if the words are opposite in meaning; and circle U if the two words are unrelated to each other.

EXAMPLES:

subside—sink (S) O U
yonder—writhe S O (U)
sentimental—unemotional S (O) U

1. maim—wound S O U
2. massive—light S O U
3. mental—physical S O U
4. melancholy—exhilarated S O U
5. minute—huge S O U
6. monotonous—ruinous S O U
7. mutual—joint S O U
8. observation—inspection S O U
9. optimism—suspense S O U
10. overseer—supervisor S O U
11. pamphlet—booklet S O U
12. panicky—cool S O U
13. parliament—congress S O U
14. patronage—support S O U
15. perpetual—temporary S O U
16. pious—indolent S O U
17. preamble—preface S O U
18. reward—penalty S O U
19. prevalent—uncommon S O U
20. prominent—obscure S O U

EXAM 9

DIRECTIONS: Below are twenty pairs of words. The two words in a pair may be the same or nearly the same in meaning, or may be opposite or nearly opposite in meaning, or may be unrelated to each other. Circle S to the right of the question if the words in the pair have the same meaning; circle O if the words are opposite in meaning; and circle U if the two words are unrelated to each other.

1. prow—stern S O U
2. qualify—fit S O U
3. quicken—die S O U
4. quaint—renovated S O U
5. endless—limited S O U
6. rapture—apathy S O U
7. rare—raw S O U
8. ration—allowance S O U
9. recruit—veteran S O U
10. recuperation—decline S O U
11. rejoice—grieve S O U
12. relative—absolute S O U
13. replace—supplant S O U
14. reply—answer S O U
15. resident—inhabitant S O U
16. resolution—firmness S O U
17. respectful—courteous S O U
18. route—defeat S O U
19. rumor—evil S O U
20. rural—cunning S O U

EXAM 10

DIRECTIONS: In the exercises below, complete each sentence by selecting the one right answer from the five choices that follow. Circle the letter of the right answer, as in the example below.

EXAMPLE:

A *narrative* is a
(A) composition (B) musicale ((C)) story
(D) mystery (E) vehicle

1. A *manual* control would be operated
   (A) automatically (B) rapidly
   (C) quietly (D) by hand
   (E) electrically

2. An *objective* report by a committee would be
   (A) prejudiced (B) subjective
   (C) personal (D) offensive (E) fair

3. A colorful *pageant* is
   (A) a public entertainment (B) a party
   (C) a disorderly gathering
   (D) a client (E) a platter

4. To *account* for one's actions means to ________ them.
   (A) explain (B) prevent (C) plan
   (D) reject (E) add up

5. A man of *prowess* is
   (A) proud (B) excessively humble
   (C) extraordinarily able (D) cowardly
   (E) none of these

6. His *pugilistic* skill means ________ skill.
   (A) athletic (B) musical
   (C) lack of (D) boxing
   (E) none of these

7. An *imposter* is a(an)
   (A) fraud (B) expert (C) model
   (D) specialist (E) none of these

8. A corrupt *regime* is
   (A) unheard of (B) for reform
   (C) a fine government
   (D) a democracy
   (E) none of these

9. To *resist* tyranny is to ________ tyranny.
   (A) fight against (B) submit to
   (C) suffer (D) worship
   (E) none of these

10. A *robust* woodsman is
    (A) anemic (B) sturdy (C) pallid
    (D) frail (E) none of these

EXAM 11

DIRECTIONS: For each item, determine whether the underlined word is used correctly. If it is, circle T, if not, circle F.

EXAMPLE:

An uninhabited country is one that has a huge population. T (F)

1. A rapier is a type of short, broad sword. T F
2. Rebellion is a peaceful change of government. T F
3. I can recollect events that happened when I was five years old. T F
4. As security guard, you need a person of reliability. T F
5. A repentant drunkard feels no remorse for his wasted life. T F
6. Snakes and lizards are reptiles. T F
7. *X* represents an unknown quantity in algebra. T F
8. A scoundrel resorts to trickery. T F
9. Restraint is required when criticizing our benefactors. T F
10. Plaid is a colorless strip of material used as trimming. T F
11. By using a ruse, he was able to gain his ends openly and fairly. T F
12. The light snow scorched her face gently. T F
13. Sculpture is one of the fine arts, the art of building beautiful structures. T F
14. The knife was placed in a sheath to keep it away from the children. T F

15. After a day in the desert, our food was sodden. T F

16. A spendthrift saves money regularly. T F

17. Spontaneous applause came all night from the paid applauders. T F

18. The cattle remained calm during the stampede. T F

19. There is no more steadfast friend than a fickle girl. T F

20. His boorish manners were uncouth. T F

EXAM 12

DIRECTIONS: For the underlined word in each phrase, select the lettered word or phrase that means most nearly the SAME. Circle the letter of the correct answer.

EXAMPLE:

an overcast sky
(A) brilliant (B) cloudy (C) windy (D) clear (E) starry

1. a noble sacrifice
(A) impulse (B) act of truth (C) gaiety (D) response (E) act of unselfishness

2. with great tact
(A) ability to say and do the right thing (B) inconvenience (C) exertion (D) facility at touching (E) piece of information

3. as a consequence
(A) cause (B) arch (C) hook (D) agent (E) result

4. the bright sash
(A) bloody wound (B) ribbon (C) dance step (D) battle (E) money

5. the talented singer
(A) beautiful (B) boastful (C) gifted (D) scout (E) poor

6. conventional wisdom
(A) common (B) unorthodox (C) unsuitable (D) disgusting (E) tardy

7. the vague answer
(A) complete (B) stylish (C) stupid (D) unclear (E) scarlet

8. the vacant lot
(A) parking (B) stupid (C) empty (D) whole (E) cultivated

9. the unabridged dictionary
(A) incomplete (B) specialized (C) Webster's (D) unadulterated (E) unshortened

10. a typical teenager
(A) rock 'n' roll (B) mature (C) happy (D) delinquent (E) average

11. the significant event
(A) unhappy (B) wedding (C) following (D) important (E) last

12. a noble sentiment
(A) feeling (B) sadness (C) cry (D) lament (E) silliness

13. the turmoil in the hills
(A) quiet (B) confusion (C) girl (D) elephant (E) crowd

14. unsound reasoning
(A) ringing (B) untested (C) intelligent (D) precocious (E) faulty

15. a hidden hazard
(A) trail (B) peril (C) explosive (D) ice storm (E) disease

16. a vision of success
(A) story (B) break (C) dream (D) fulfillment (E) example

17. with uncommon fervor
(A) ordinary (B) dreamy (C) noisy (D) unrealistic (E) more than usual

18. the important transaction
(A) business man (B) result (C) method of communication (D) piece of business (E) proceeding

19. the third <u>stanza</u>
(A) song (B) repetition (C) lyric
(D) portion of a poem (E) scale

20. the <u>subsequent</u> events
(A) in place of (B) following
(C) preceding (D) important
(E) significant

EXAM 13

DIRECTIONS: For the underlined word in each phrase, select the lettered word or phrase that means most nearly the SAME. Circle the letter of the correct answer.

EXAMPLE:

an <u>ambitious</u> man
(A) lazy (B) energetic (C) purposeful
(D) cruel (E) fine

1. the <u>customary</u> costume
(A) young (B) ideal (C) tattered
(D) traditional (E) colorful

2. <u>utilize</u> your talents
(A) make use of (B) utilities (C) sing
(D) modernize (E) undo

3. his <u>vigorous</u> objection
(A) unhappy (B) strong (C) sunny
(D) false (E) vivacious

4. the <u>vulgar</u> remark
(A) coarse (B) poorly timed (C) vintage
(D) wrong (E) tasteful

5. her <u>sullen</u> mood
(A) happy (B) silly (C) brooding
(D) sunny (E) distasteful

6. the <u>vast</u> garden
(A) empty (B) outdoor (C) expansive
(D) lovely (E) springy

7. <u>terminate</u> the business
(A) start (B) remodel (C) refinance
(D) exterminate (E) put an end to

8. a <u>cumbersome</u> package
(A) erect (B) inverted (C) immovable
(D) wrong (E) bulky

9. <u>veto</u> the bill
(A) sign (B) withdraw (C) debate on
(D) pass (E) refuse to sign

10. <u>variety</u> of acts
(A) show (B) hall (C) sequence
(D) assortment (E) poor quality

EXAM 14

DIRECTIONS: For each item choose the word or phrase that is closest in meaning to the capitalized word. Then circle the letter of the word or phrase you have selected.

EXAMPLE:

OBLIQUE: (A) blinking (B) scarce
(C) level (D) criss-cross (E) diagonal

1. STUMP: (A) glide (B) walk noisily
(C) imprint (D) strut (E) blast loose

2. PONDER: (A) sink (B) come after
(C) drive a horse carriage
(D) think (E) commute

3. SURGE: (A) swell (B) take a view of
(C) influence (D) remove (E) excel

4. TAUNT: (A) placate (B) mimic
(C) tangle (D) tease (E) tighten

5. TEMPO: (A) storm (B) largo
(C) rhythm (D) tendency
(E) symphony

6. THRIVE: (A) dishevel (B) push
(C) bounce (D) confess (E) flourish

7. PLEAT: (A) beg (B) offer (C) crease
(D) discuss (E) cry out

8. TUMULT: (A) wretchedness
(B) noise and confusion
(C) exciting anticipation
(D) multiplication
(E) deep and violent anger

9. TYRANT: (A) despot (B) ruler
(C) sovereign (D) viceroy
(E) premier

10. UNIQUE: (A) 100% (B) not basic
(C) alone of its kind (D) changeable
(E) extraordinarily large

EXAM 15

DIRECTIONS: Each of the following groups contains five pairs of words labeled (A), (B), (C), (D), and (E). For each group, select the pair of words that are OPPOSITE in meaning to each other. Circle the letter that corresponds to the pair of words you have chosen.

EXAMPLE:

(A) nag—annoy
(B) precaution—care
(C) scent—odor
((D)) social—self-centered
(E) subside—sink

1. (A) sadden—depress
(B) sanitary—dirty
(C) scarce—rare
(D) sentinel—picket
(E) serene—unclouded

2. (A) sequence—succession
(B) sever—separate
(C) shrill—dull
(D) sift—separate
(E) significant—meaningful

3. (A) solicit—entreat
(B) solitary—joint
(C) soothe—please
(D) souvenir—keepsake
(E) stature—standing

4. (A) stress—strain
(B) sturdy—robust
(C) submit—offer
(D) supreme—utmost
(E) tedious—stimulating

5. (A) tempest—storm
(B) terminal—end
(C) thrift—economy
(D) tolerant—prejudiced
(E) tributary—branch

6. (A) tropical—arctic
(B) truancy—absence
(C) trivial—unimportant
(D) turmoil—confusion
(E) unabridged—complete

7. (A) unaware—unconscious
(B) undoubted—certain
(C) unceasing—continuous
(D) unruffled—disturbed
(E) upright—honest

8. (A) urban—city
(B) utility—usefulness
(C) vagrant—tramp
(D) van—front
(E) violence—gentleness

9. (A) vision—dream
(B) vital—living
(C) vivacious—spiritless
(D) wary—cautious
(E) waver—hesitate

10. (A) wharf—dock
(B) woeful—joyous
(C) wrath—anger
(D) yarn—wool
(E) yield—produce

FOR THE UPPER GRADES—TESTS 16–22

EXAM 16

DIRECTIONS: Circle the letter of the best definition.

1. COARSE: (A) subject (B) track (C) rough (D) spotted (E) massive

2. ANTITHESIS: (A) grave (B) unfriendliness (C) part of flower (D) opposite (E) oration

3. ETHICAL: (A) causing sleep (B) racial (C) linguistic (D) moral (E) sensible

4. PREROGATIVE: (A) command (B) right (C) contradiction (D) early animal (E) haggard

5. INDEMNITY: (A) exemption (B) conviction (C) accusation (D) compensation (E) quell

6. CONCILIATORY: (A) winning over (B) undoing (C) advisory (D) defeating (E) subsequent

7. SALABLE: (A) marketable (B) healthful (C) easily soiled (D) old (E) preliminary

8. BOUNTEOUS: (A) beautiful (B) elastic (C) liberal (D) heavenly (E) mutinous

9. VANITY: (A) envy (B) saintliness (C) humility (D) excessive pride (E) urge

10. IMPERIAL: (A) royal (B) like an empire (C) empirical (D) principality (E) descendant

11. PORTLY: (A) from side to side (B) oblong (C) fat (D) perpendicular (E) vertical

12. JAUNTY: (A) subdued (B) retarded (C) phlegmatic (D) unconcerned (E) apathetic

13. VOID: (A) forested (B) unfilled (C) colonial (D) chaotic (E) substitute

14. ANTIDOTE: (A) against war (B) against vivisection (C) against poison (D) against liquor (E) against communism

15. PEEVISH: (A) frightened (B) amiable (C) screaming (D) complaining (E) juvenile

16. PLUMMET: (A) plunge (B) submerge (C) walk through water (D) tread water (E) hobble

17. WARRANT: (A) authorize (B) arrest (C) guarantee (D) digest (E) dawdle

18. TAINT: (A) heir (B) spoil (C) tyranny (D) poor taste (E) keen perception

19. VITAL: (A) propaganda (B) acceleration (C) sudden pain (D) essential (E) conscience

EXAM 17

DIRECTIONS: Circle the letter of the best definition.

1. DETER: (A) halt (B) steer (C) sting (D) turn (E) hinder

2. DELVE: (A) halve (B) hide (C) dig (D) divide (E) serve

3. NOMAD: (A) savage (B) fool (C) cloak (D) wanderer (E) insect

4. EBB: (A) weave (B) flow (C) fill (D) stretch (E) decrease

5. CARNAGE: (A) battle (B) war (C) slaughter (D) theft (E) charge

6. CULPABLE: (A) innocent (B) able (C) helpless (D) at fault (E) young

7. DISPENSE: (A) distribute (B) fling (C) disgust (D) desert (E) scatter

8. FIASCO: (A) failure (B) plot (C) carriage (D) comedy (E) loss

9. ERODE: (A) travel (B) wear down (C) soothe (D) erupt (E) evoke

10. ALLUDE: (A) aid (B) plan (C) deceive (D) escape (E) refer

11. GYRATE: (A) cheat (B) whirl (C) sting (D) threaten (E) fly

12. MELEE: (A) mess (B) mix (C) mar (D) mellow (E) fight

13. SEETHE: (A) storm (B) boil (C) stir (D) placate (E) save

14. ENNUI: (A) entry (B) youth (C) illness (D) boredom (E) energy

15. CELERITY: (A) speed (B) fame (C) courtesy (D) health (E) purity

16. YIELD: (A) want (B) need (C) subdue (D) give up (E) token

17. STATURE: (A) image (B) height (C) sculpture (D) law (E) radio interference

18. RELINQUISH:
(A) abandon (B) vacant (C) profound
(D) vast (E) triangular

19. SENTINEL: (A) middle (B) sentence
(C) guard (D) tangle (E) legend

20. GENESIS: (A) tendency (B) ration
(C) freight (D) insurance (E) beginning

EXAM 18

DIRECTIONS: For each word given, find the CORRECT meaning among the words or phrases labeled (A), (B), (C), and (D).

EXAMPLE:

HEAVY: (A) sorry (B) interested
(C) weighty (D) well

1. PAGAN: (A) sprightly (B) playful
(C) worried (D) heathen

2. AFFECTATION: (A) illness
(B) wordiness (C) oath (D) air

3. IMPLY: (A) suggest (B) furnish
(C) deceive (D) oil

4. SUBMISSIVE: (A) obedient
(B) angry (C) forlorn (D) total

5. DEFER: (A) second (B) postpone
(C) give (D) propose

6. ADORN: (A) agree to (B) assist
(C) decorate (D) communicate

7. TREAD: (A) help (B) swim
(C) turn back (D) step

8. TESTIFY: (A) oath (B) legal trick
(C) exam (D) report

9. IMMENSE: (A) object (B) huge
(C) torn (D) decrepit

10. CONVERSE: (A) change (B) talk
(C) fill (D) break into

11. SPLICE: (A) join (B) sell
(C) give up (D) turn down

12. HAMPER: (A) notify (B) curse
(C) find (D) obstruct

13. CONFUSE: (A) electrify (B) bewilder
(C) make up (D) anger

14. DELUXE: (A) of note (B) temporary
(C) selected (D) luxurious

15. REGAL: (A) royal (B) late
(C) difficult (D) gold

16. PLEA: (A) command (B) note
(C) barrier (D) request

17. SIFT: (A) alter (B) sort (C) thread
(D) maneuver

18. GAUNT: (A) empty (B) vivid (C) thin
(D) spiral

19. SUBSEQUENT: (A) in and out
(B) in order (C) afterward
(D) in reversed order

20. EXERT: (A) clamp (B) open (C) apply
(D) create tone

21. INCARCERATE: (A) imprison
(B) jailer (C) apply (D) captive

22. METROPOLITAN: (A) of note
(B) with people (C) pertaining to order
(D) pertaining to a large city

23. OBLIQUE: (A) compressed
(B) scattered (C) overt (D) slanted

24. PATRON: (A) fool (B) store-keeper
(C) braggart (D) supporter

25. METHODICAL: (A) frantic
(B) careless (C) orderly (D) askew

26. ECSTATIC: (A) light-bearing
(B) upright (C) being part of
(D) supremely joyous

27. VISUAL: (A) round (B) partial
(C) concerning time
(D) dealing with sight

28. STATUTE: (A) order (B) candle
(C) folder (D) law

29. REGIME: (A) bow shape (B) feathery coat (C) agreement (D) government

30. STAMPEDE: (A) make mild (B) force (C) run away (D) penetrate

31. CONFLICT: (A) will (B) battle (C) memory (D) convenant

32. DEFICIENCY: (A) excess (B) lack (C) quantity (D) falseness

33. PRECLUDE: (A) prevent (B) turn over (C) justify (D) convey

34. CHAPERON: (A) alien (B) student (C) learner (D) supervisor

35. TIMOROUS: (A) fearful (B) silly (C) generous (D) tenfold

36. TRANSFORM: (A) threaten (B) predict (C) convert (D) propose

37. PURLOIN: (A) withdraw (B) fulfill (C) pinpoint (D) steal

38. SCOWL: (A) frown (B) insist (C) dispel (D) picture

39. CONGENIAL: (A) baffling (B) loving (C) friendly (D) thoughtful

40. RAPTURE: (A) ecstasy (B) truth (C) worth (D) hostility

EXAM 19

DIRECTIONS: For each word given, find the CORRECT meaning among the words or phrases labeled (A), (B), (C), and (D). Circle the correct letter from choices given.

1. HEIR: (A) hither (B) successor (C) dam (D) predecessor

2. DETRIMENTAL: (A) perpetual (B) confident (C) harmful (D) idealistic

3. TAUNT: (A) be frivolous (B) tease cruelly (C) query (D) ply

4. RUGGED: (A) smooth (B) fertile (C) wavy (D) uneven

5. ABUNDANCE: (A) large amount (B) profundity (C) scarcity (D) country dance

6. INCLINATION: (A) mountain (B) prairie (C) preference (D) plane

7. GOBBLE: (A) talk a lot (B) eat greedily (C) rinse (D) mix up

8. REPOSE: (A) model (B) decline (C) hide (D) rest

9. PROHIBIT: (A) forestall (B) command (C) forbid (D) stain

10. TAINT: (A) pursue (B) infect (C) taunt (D) keep in step

11. BISECT: (A) go away (B) go in (C) divide in two (D) prescribe

12. COUNCIL: (A) lawyer (B) advice (C) governing body (D) will

13. BOLSTER: (A) rasher (B) support (C) rugged (D) persistent

14. TREPIDATION: (A) olden (B) fear (C) comical (D) trivial

15. STATURE: (A) standing (B) state (C) involvement (D) proclamation

16. PROMOTE: (A) backslide (B) support (C) reorganize (D) react

17. EMINENCE: (A) personality (B) decline (C) high position (D) sensation

18. PORTRAY: (A) settle (B) depict (C) take action (D) light up

19. ALLURING: (A) painted (B) attractive (C) sturdy (D) female

20. BAR: (A) fill (B) cohere (C) recede (D) prevent

21. CELESTIAL: (A) earthy (B) watery (C) heavenly (D) tempting

22. AGGRAVATE: (A) make worse (B) irritate (C) destroy (D) imitate

23. PLUCK: (A) adhere (B) entice (C) pull out (D) have good fortune

24. ADVOCATE: (A) lender of money (B) borrower of money (C) supporter (D) mortgage

25. PRELUDE: (A) preamble (B) loneliness (C) gaiety (D) aptitude

26. RETORT: (A) answer (B) garble (C) interfere (D) simulate

27. FACSIMILE: (A) imitate (B) copy (C) fabricate (D) send

28. BARD: (A) translator (B) religious leader (C) poet (D) gain

29. APPROXIMATE: (A) inexact (B) abridged (C) horizontal (D) suitable

30. CONSOLE: (A) adopt (B) comfort (C) disturb (D) grieve

31. CLANDESTINE: (A) outstanding (B) piddling (C) surreptitious (D) secret

32. TWINGE: (A) torture (B) sudden pain (C) extravagance (D) drive

33. SQUANDER: (A) support (B) bracket (C) purchase (D) waste

34. INTERCHANGEABLE: (A) luxurious (B) unreturnable (C) equal (D) familiar

35. GLOBAL: (A) conical (B) heavy (C) square (D) round

36. CRISIS: (A) trial (B) emergency (C) hurricane (D) sad effort

37. BRAWL: (A) fight (B) basement (C) bargain (D) saloon

38. APPARATUS: (A) personnel (B) reasoning (C) equipment (D) fantasy

39. BARBAROUS: (A) winsome (B) feminine (C) shrewd (D) savage

40. ALLEGE: (A) blackmail (B) claim (C) vow (D) deny

EXAM 20

DIRECTIONS: In each question below, one of the four words or phrases given as choices means almost the SAME as the italicized word in the preceding sentence. Circle the correct answer.

EXAMPLE:

Next to our house there is an *empty* lot.
(A) cluttered (B) full of flowers
(C) vacant (D) dirty

1. A *diligent* student is well rewarded.
(A) rich (B) skilled (C) punctual (D) conscientious

2. The mayor read his *proclamation* from the steps of city hall.
(A) amnesty (B) freedom of slaves (C) denial (D) government announcement

3. The cheerleaders *strutted* at the head of the parade.
(A) swindled (B) swaggered (C) waved batons (D) leaped high

4. My parents want me to *sever* ties with my friend Steve.
(A) strengthen (B) trade (C) cut (D) imprive

5. Her *untimely* death robbed us of a great philosopher.
(A) accidental (B) cruel (C) premature (D) merciful

6. *Vanity* keeps us from seeing our own faults.
(A) success (B) excessive pride (C) friends (D) relatives

7. The May Day *pageant* was held on the lawn.
(A) arena (B) exhibition (C) contest (D) race

8. Lucy finally succeeded in *unraveling* the wool thread.
(A) untangling (B) knitting (C) selling (D) buying

9. We must learn to *stress* goodness above beauty.
(A) emphasize (B) see (C) practice (D) foretell

10. Lila ate a *paltry* breakfast
(A) enormous (B) nutritious (C) meager (D) hurried

11. It is time to *replenish* our supply of coal.
(A) sell (B) buy (C) use up (D) make full again

12. You will not accomplish much with a *defiant* attitude.
(A) friendly (B) discreet (C) placid (D) antagonistic

13. He wasted his time on *trivial* matters.
(A) significant (B) metropolitan (C) unimportant (D) unsuccessful

14. Jerusalem is an *venerable* city.
(A) holy (B) deserted (C) distinguished (D) old

15. Pioneers *thrust* westward across the mountains.
(A) climbed (B) pushed (C) struggled (D) flew

16. We admired the graceful beauty of the *edifice*.
(A) apartment house (B) large building (C) ranch (D) church

17. He was arrested as a *vagrant*.
(A) homeless, unemployed person (B) traveler (C) immigrant (D) criminal

18. An *insolent* child is an unhappy one.
(A) cooperative (B) hard-working (C) fresh (D) sickly

19. Once burned, twice *wary*.
(A) nonchalant (B) careful (C) sunburned (D) warlike

20. His posture was erect and his *tread* firm.
(A) confidence (B) rubber tire (C) stance (D) step

21. Civilians were trained as *combatants* in six months.
(A) warriors (B) air-raid wardens (C) public officials (D) security guards

22. We are sending our *surplus* butter abroad.
(A) rancid (B) excess (C) useless (D) spoiled

23. The newspaper received an *laudatory* letter.
(A) complaining (B) full of praise (C) unsigned (D) critical

24. You cannot *withstand* progress.
(A) gainsay (B) praise enough (C) fight off (D) compel

25. Proceed with *vigilance*.
(A) business as usual (B) alterations (C) bidding contest (D) caution

26. *Pious* thoughts and generous actions characterize the good person.
(A) pure (B) violent (C) faithless (D) patient

27. Hilary made a *brash* remark in class.
(A) cheeky (B) boastful (C) irrelevant (D) funny

28. He used a *ruse* to gain admission.
(A) ticket (B) free pass (C) trick (D) gun

29. *Valiant* efforts were exerted to elect our candidate.
(A) vain (B) futile (C) courageous (D) foolish

30. This evidence will *vindicate* the defendant.
(A) condemn (B) exonerate (C) implicate (D) reform

Answers to All Practice Tests and Mastery Exams

PRACTICE TESTS

TEST 1, p. 90

1. D	11. E	21. A	31. A	41. E
2. B	12. B	22. D	32. B	42. C
3. C	13. C	23. B	33. D	43. B
4. A	14. C	24. B	34. B	44. B
5. E	15. B	25. C	35. D	45. C
6. B	16. A	26. C	36. C	46. B
7. B	17. A	27. A	37. B	47. B
8. D	18. D	28. B	38. C	48. E
9. E	19. B	29. C	39. D	49. D
10. B	20. C	30. D	40. E	50. B

TEST 2, p. 93

1. A	5. C	9. D	13. A	17. B
2. C	6. C	10. A	14. A	18. B
3. C	7. A	11. B	15. C	19. A
4. D	8. B	12. C	16. C	20. B

TEST 3, p. 95

1. C	11. B	21. C	31. C	41. B
2. C	12. D	22. A	32. A	42. C
3. E	13. B	23. D	33. C	43. C
4. D	14. A	24. B	34. C	44. D
5. A	15. C	25. C	35. A	45. C
6. B	16. D	26. A	36. A	46. D
7. E	17. C	27. B	37. A	47. B
8. C	18. C	28. D	38. C	48. C
9. E	19. A	29. D	39. B	49. C
10. C	20. B	30. B	40. C	50. A

TEST 4, p. 98

1. D	5. D	9. C	13. E	17. D
2. A	6. C	10. A	14. A	18. C
3. E	7. B	11. E	15. B	19. B
4. D	8. D	12. B	16. A	20. C

TEST 5, p. 100

1. C	5. B	9. D	13. C	17. C
2. B	6. C	10. B	14. A	18. D
3. D	7. A	11. A	15. D	19. A
4. A	8. B	12. D	16. B	20. B

TEST 6, p. 111

1. accept, except
2. access, excess
3. edition, addition
4. effect, affect, effect
5. aisle, isle, I'll
6. aloud, allowed
7. all ready, already
8. allusion, illusion
9. altar, alter
10. arc, ark
11. ascent, assent
12. assistants, assistance
13. band, banned
14. bear, bare, Bear
15. base, bass
16. beech, beach
17. beat, beet
18. beau, bow
19. bury, berry
20. birth, berth
21. blew, blue
22. bore, bore, boar
23. born, borne
24. bough, bow
25. brake, break
26. bred, bread
27. bridal, bridle
28. canvas, canvass
29. capital, capitol
30. carat, carrot, caret
31. cede, seed
32. seller, cellar
33. cent, sent, scent
34. cell, sell
35. site, sight, cite
36. climb, clime
37. course, coarse
38. colonel, kernel
39. counsel, council
40. corps, core
41. councilor, counselor
42. creak, creek
43. dissent, descent
44. deer, dear
45. dessert, desert
46. due, dew
47. die, dye
48. dough, doe
49. dual, duel
50. earn, urn
51. faint, feint
52. fair, fare
53. fate, fete
54. fined, find
55. fir, fur
56. flee, flea
57. flew, flue
58. flour, flower
59. for, four
60. formally, formerly
61. forth, fourth

62. foul
fowl
63. gate
gait
64. gamble
gambol
65. gilt
guilt
66. grate
great
67. groan
grown
68. guessed
guest
69. hail
hale
70. hare
hair
71. hall
haul
72. hart
heart
73. heal
heel
74. hear
here
75. heard
herd
76. higher
hire
77. him
hymn
78. horse
hoarse
79. hole
whole
80. holy
wholly
81. our
hour
82. idle
idol
83. inn
in
84. instants
instance
85. it's
its
86. knight
night
87. know
no
88. lane
lain
89. lead
led
90. lesson
lessen
91. lye
lie
92. load
lode
93. loan
lone
94. mail
male
95. mane
main
96. meat
meet
97. metal
mettle
98. miner
minor
99. morn
mourn
100. one
won
101. pail
pale
102. pane
pain
103. pair
pear
pare
104. pour
paw
105. peel
peal
106. peace
piece
107. plane
plain
108. pray
prey
109. principle
principal
110. prophet
profit
111. reign
rain
112. rap
wrap
113. reed
read
114. red
read
115. real
reel
116. rite
right
write
117. wring
ring
118. rowed
road
rode
119. role
roll
120. route
root
121. wrote
rote
122. sale
sail
123. scene
seen
124. sea
see
125. seem
seam
126. so
sew
sow
127. sleigh
slay
128. soar
sore
129. soled
sold
130. soul
sole
131. some
sum
132. son
sun
133. stake
steak
134. stair
stare
135. stationery
stationary
136. steel
steal
137. strait
straight
138. suite
sweet
139. tail
tale
140. team
teem
141. there
there
their
they're
142. threw
through
143. thrown
throne
144. tide
tied
145. toe
tow
146. tolled
told
147. vain
vein
vane
148. vale
veil
149. vial
vile
150. wade
weighed
151. wail
whale
152. waste
waist
153. wait
weight
154. wear
ware
where
155. weak
week
156. weather
whether
157. which
witch
158. whine
wine
159. wood
would
160. you're
your

MASTERY EXAMS

Rating Your Results

On exams with 10 questions:

Superior	9–10 correct
Average	7–8 correct
Below Average	6 or fewer correct

On exams with 20 questions:

Superior	18–20 correct
Average	14–17 correct
Below Average	13 or fewer correct

On exams with 30 questions:

Superior	27–30 correct
Average	21–26 correct
Below Average	20 or fewer correct

On exams with 40 questions:

Superior	36–40 correct
Average	28–35 correct
Below Average	27 or fewer correct

EXAM 1, p. 121

1. **E** 5. **C** 9. **A** 13. **C** 17. **B**
2. **A** 6. **D** 10. **E** 14. **E** 18. **C**
3. **B** 7. **D** 11. **D** 15. **E** 19. **B**
4. **B** 8. **E** 12. **A** 16. **E** 20. **E**

EXAM 2, p. 121

1. **D** 5. **C** 9. **D** 13. **A** 17. **C**
2. **D** 6. **B** 10. **A** 14. **E** 18. **B**
3. **B** 7. **A** 11. **B** 15. **D** 19. **B**
4. **A** 8. **A** 12. **B** 16. **E** 20. **C**

EXAM 3, p. 122

1. **D** 5. **B** 9. **D** 13. **D** 17. **D**
2. **C** 6. **A** 10. **D** 14. **D** 18. **C**
3. **A** 7. **B** 11. **B** 15. **C** 19. **B**
4. **A** 8. **B** 12. **B** 16. **A** 20. **B**

EXAM 4, p. 123

1. **D** 5. **B** 9. **D** 13. **B** 17. **A**
2. **B** 6. **C** 10. **C** 14. **B** 18. **E**
3. **E** 7. **A** 11. **E** 15. **C** 19. **D**
4. **A** 8. **B** 12. **A** 16. **D** 20. **D**

EXAM 5, p. 124

1. **A** 3. **D** 5. **E** 7. **A** 9. **D**
2. **C** 4. **B** 6. **B** 8. **D** 10. **E**

EXAM 6, p. 124

1. **E** 3. **A** 5. **D** 7. **A** 9. **E**
2. **A** 4. **B** 6. **D** 8. **A** 10. **C**

EXAM 7, p. 125

1. **B** 5. **D** 9. **A** 13. **B** 17. **D**
2. **B** 6. **A** 10. **B** 14. **A** 18. **B**
3. **A** 7. **D** 11. **A** 15. **C** 19. **A**
4. **C** 8. **C** 12. **D** 16. **A** 20. **D**

EXAM 8, p. 126

1. **S** 5. **O** 9. **U** 13. **S** 17. **S**
2. **O** 6. **U** 10. **S** 14. **S** 18. **O**
3. **O** 7. **S** 11. **S** 15. **O** 19. **O**
4. **O** 8. **S** 12. **O** 16. **U** 20. **O**

EXAM 9, p. 126

1. **O** 5. **O** 9. **O** 13. **S** 17. **S**
2. **S** 6. **O** 10. **O** 14. **S** 18. **U**
3. **O** 7. **S** 11. **O** 15. **S** 19. **U**
4. **O** 8. **S** 12. **O** 16. **S** 20. **U**

EXAM 10, p. 126

1. **D** 3. **A** 5. **C** 7. **A** 9. **A**
2. **E** 4. **A** 6. **D** 8. **E** 10. **B**

EXAM 11, p. 127

1. **F** 5. **F** 9. **T** 13. **F** 17. **F**
2. **F** 6. **T** 10. **F** 14. **T** 18. **F**
3. **T** 7. **T** 11. **F** 15. **F** 19. **F**
4. **T** 8. **T** 12. **F** 16. **F** 20. **T**

EXAM 12, p. 128

1. **E** 5. **C** 9. **E** 13. **B** 17. **E**
2. **A** 6. **A** 10. **E** 14. **E** 18. **D**
3. **E** 7. **D** 11. **D** 15. **B** 19. **D**
4. **B** 8. **C** 12. **A** 16. **C** 20. **B**

EXAM 13, p. 129

1. **D** 3. **B** 5. **C** 7. **E** 9. **E**
2. **A** 4. **A** 6. **C** 8. **E** 10. **D**

EXAM 14, p. 129

1. **B** 3. **A** 5. **C** 7. **C** 9. **A**
2. **D** 4. **D** 6. **E** 8. **B** 10. **C**

EXAM 15, p. 130

1. **B** 3. **B** 5. **D** 7. **D** 9. **C**
2. **C** 4. **E** 6. **A** 8. **E** 10. **B**

EXAM 16, p. 130

1. **C** 5. **D** 9. **D** 13. **B** 17. **A**
2. **D** 6. **A** 10. **B** 14. **C** 18. **B**
3. **D** 7. **A** 11. **C** 15. **D** 19. **D**
4. **B** 8. **C** 12. **D** 16. **A**

EXAM 17, p. 131

1. **E** 5. **C** 9. **B** 13. **B** 17. **B**
2. **C** 6. **D** 10. **E** 14. **D** 18. **A**
3. **D** 7. **A** 11. **B** 15. **A** 19. **C**
4. **E** 8. **A** 12. **E** 16. **D** 20. **E**

EXAM 18, p. 132

1. **D**	9. **B**	17. **B**	25. **C**	33. **A**
2. **D**	10. **B**	18. **C**	26. **D**	34. **D**
3. **A**	11. **A**	19. **C**	27. **D**	35. **A**
4. **A**	12. **D**	20. **C**	28. **D**	36. **C**
5. **B**	13. **B**	21. **A**	29. **D**	37. **D**
6. **C**	14. **D**	22. **D**	30. **C**	38. **A**
7. **D**	15. **A**	23. **D**	31. **B**	39. **C**
8. **D**	16. **D**	24. **D**	32. **B**	40. **A**

EXAM 19, p. 133

1. **B**	9. **C**	17. **C**	25. **A**	33. **D**
2. **C**	10. **B**	18. **B**	26. **A**	34. **C**
3. **B**	11. **C**	19. **B**	27. **B**	35. **D**
4. **D**	12. **C**	20. **D**	28. **C**	36. **B**
5. **A**	13. **B**	21. **C**	29. **A**	37. **A**
6. **C**	14. **B**	22. **A**	30. **B**	38. **C**
7. **B**	15. **A**	23. **C**	31. **C**	39. **D**
8. **D**	16. **B**	24. **C**	32. **B**	40. **B**

EXAM 20, p. 134

1. **D**	7. **B**	13. **C**	19. **B**	25. **D**
2. **D**	8. **A**	14. **D**	20. **D**	26. **A**
3. **B**	9. **A**	15. **B**	21. **A**	27. **A**
4. **D**	10. **C**	16. **B**	22. **B**	28. **C**
5. **C**	11. **D**	17. **A**	23. **B**	29. **C**
6. **B**	12. **D**	18. **C**	24. **C**	30. **B**

Reading

Improving Your Work-Study Skills

Here is a sound self-help plan for reading improvement.

1. Have a daily, varied reading program:
   browse through the encyclopedias,
   read sections of the daily newspaper (news stories, editorials, special columns),
   become interested in the lives of memorable people and read their biographies,
   read books dealing with hobbies,
   read and reread supplementary textbooks.
2. Be word-conscious. Add daily to your store of worthwhile words.
3. Concentrate when you read. *Nothing* should be able to distract you!
4. Read as fast as you can comfortably—and no faster. Speed comes from practice; don't let your anxieties rush you into skimming or scanning.

Below are key work-study skills designed to bring you up to the level of competency required to do well on the reading comprehension sections of standard examinations. Following each work-study skill is an exercise that will help you master it. After you have completed this section of this chapter, you will be ready to tackle the reading comprehension section that follows. Go through the latter section step by step. Use the diagnostic test in the beginning of the book to pinpoint your particular weakness in reading comprehension, and focus on that weakness. Do not, however, skip any part of the reading comprehension section if you wish to achieve the best results on a standard examination. Use the answer key at the end of the chapter to check your performance on exercises, practice tests, and Mastery Exams.

COMPOUND WORDS

Compound words are words made by combining two or more words:

haircut watchman nevertheless

While most compound words have a meaning derived from their parts, this is not true of all of them. Nevertheless, the skilled reader very often gains the meaning of an unfamiliar term by recognizing one or more of its elements.

EXERCISE 1

In the space provided write yes *if the meaning of the given compound word is derived from the words combined, write* no *if the word has an independent meaning*

_____ 1. sandtrap

_____ 2. handsome

_____ 3. kneecap

_____ 4. airline

_____ 5. carload

_____ 6. railroad

_____ 7. mastermind

_____ 8. commonplace

_____ 9. tenderfoot

_____ 10. (to) pinpoint

_____ 11. nowadays

_____ 12. icecap

_____ 13. hoodwink

_____ 14. sweetheart

_____ 15. babysitter

_____ 16. (to) softsoap

_____ 17. textbook

_____ 18. nevertheless

_____ 19. meantime

_____ 20. bulldozer

_____ 21. outraged

_____ 22. kneeguard

_____ 23. showdown

_____ 24. eyeglasses

_____ 25. tombstone

_____ 26. elsewhere

_____ 27. typewriter

_____ 28. searchlight

_____ 29. eyesore

_____ 30. notwithstanding

_____ 31. hairpiece

_____ 32. shoestring

_____ 33. within

_____ 34. daytime

_____ 35. runaway

_____ 36. headlights

_____ 37. warship

_____ 38. piecemeal

_____ 39. newspaper

_____ 40. manmade

WORD SUBSTITUTION

All too often hasty readers see on the printed page the words that they think should be there rather than what the author has actually put there. The exercise that follows will sharpen your ability to read accurately.

EXERCISE 2

Underline the misused word in each of the following sentences. Then, in the space provided, write the intended word.

1. Who was the artichoke who designed our State Capitol? _____

2. Since we are having too many rejects, we must find a butter way to make this product. _____

3. One of the causes of climate is the emotion of the Earth. _____

4. In order to learn more about television sets, Alice bought herself a duet yourself kit. _____

5. Since the cow chews its cub, it is classified as a ruminant. _____

6. To err is humor, to forgive divine. _____

7. The florist rangers searched the woods for the missing children. _____

8. The Earth makes a resolution every twenty-four hours. _____

9. The discussion leader said that we were invading the issue when we changed the topic under discussion. _____

10. When you are in need of cash, do not become involved with a lone shark. _____

11. She was so desperate that she decided to beg, burro, or steal a copy of the book. _____

12. Is the zebra a horse of a different choler? ______

13. Give me whatever you decide. I know that beggars cannot be cruisers. ______

14. When the enemy approached, the farmers lighted the deacons as signal fires to warn the countryside. ______

15. The engineer's flame spread throughout the county. ______

16. All of the political leaders have office space in our local City Haul. ______

17. It was not the heat but the humility of the moisture-filled air that made us so uncomfortable. ______

18. When you are in doubt, your superiors should always be insulted. ______

19. My cousin Alvin is a lizard at fixing TV sets. ______

20. The chickens have certainly come home to roast. ______

21. Although I had long considered him a friend, that traitor has turned out to be nothing more than a sneak in the grass! ______

22. The larvae that develop from flies' eggs are called magnets. ______

23. How many miles can the new car go on a galleon? ______

24. She proudly proclaimed, "All people are created eagle!" ______

25. The contestant really did say that a consonant is a large body of land surrounded by water. ______

Reading Comprehension Questions

TACTICS FOR ANSWERING READING QUESTIONS

Test-taking style varies from person to person. Not every tactic presented in this chapter will work equally well for every student. What works for you may not work for your best friend, and vice versa. That's why you should practice with this book. By experimenting with different methods, you'll find the one that produces the best results for you.

➤ *Option A. Read the passage carefully from start to finish before answering the questions.* Don't try to remember every detail, but ask yourself: What is this passage really about? When you are finished reading, try to state the author's main point in your own words. Then start answering the questions, referring back to the passage as often as necessary.

➤ *Option B. Skim the passage rapidly for its general idea.* Read faster than you normally would, just intently enough to get an impression of its contents. Don't expect to remember every detail. Then start to answer the questions, referring back to the passage as often as necessary.

➤ *Option C. Skim the passage to get its general meaning, then go back and read it more thoroughly*. Two readings, one fast and one slow, will help you grasp the passage better than if you read it only once. Then proceed to the questions. Because you've read the passage twice, you may not find it necessary to refer to it as often as someone using Option A or B.

Try each of the options as you prepare for the exam. Gradually you will discover the one that helps you answer the most questions correctly.

Regardless of which option works best for you:

1. *Get psyched for success*. Be confident that you can answer the questions. You can go far by thinking positively. The test questions are straightforward. They are not meant to trick or confuse you. Don't look for hidden meanings where there are none to be found.

2. *Read each passage from start to finish*. It may be tempting to start answering questions as quickly as you can, but since the meaning of the passage can change as it goes on, be sure to read the whole thing in the order it was written before answering the questions.

3. *Pay close attention to what you are reading*. Even if the topic of the passage doesn't appeal to you, force yourself to concentrate. Don't let your mind wander. Think of the passage as something important that you must know about, almost as though your life depended on it.

4. *Concentrate on the opening and closing sentences of each paragraph*. That's where you are most likely to find the topic sentence, the sentence that contains the key to the overall purpose of the paragraph. Most of the time the topic sentence is located near the beginning. Sometimes, the final sentence states or suggests the main point of the passage. But remember, too, that some paragraphs do not have topic sentences, especially when the author's intent is clear without one.

5. *Use paragraph organization as a clue to comprehension*. Writers generally take pains to organize their material. They decide what goes first, second, third, and so forth. Usually the arrangement follows a logical order, usually from the most general statement to the most specific. The paragraph you are now reading follows that pattern. The first sentence is the most general. The sentences that follow become increasingly specific.

6. *Underline key ideas and phrases*. Since you have a pencil in your hand during the test, use it to highlight important points in the passage. When you come to an idea that sounds important, quickly draw a line under it or put a check mark next to it in the margin. Underlining should be selective. There's no point in underlining the whole paragraph.

   To illustrate how to underline key points in a passage, here is a sample passage about stuttering. The first sentence is the topic sentence. The remainder of the paragraph lists several theories of the cause of stuttering. Each theory is underlined.

> While the symptoms of stuttering are easy to recognize, the <u>underlying cause remains a mystery</u>. Hippocrates thought that stuttering was due to <u>dryness of the tongue</u>, and he prescribed blistering substances to drain away the black bile responsible. A Roman physician recommended gargling and massages to strengthen a <u>weak tongue</u>. Seventeenth-century scientist Francis Bacon suggested hot wine to thaw a <u>"refrigerated" tongue</u>. <u>Too large a tongue</u> was the fault, according to a nineteenthth-century Prussian physician, so he snipped pieces of stutterers' tongues. Alexander Melville Bell, the father of the telephone inventor, insisted stuttering was simply <u>a bad habit</u> that could be cured by reeducation. Some theorists today attribute stuttering to problems in the control of the <u>muscles of speech</u>. Others think that stuttering arises from <u>deep-rooted personality problems</u> that may be lessened with drugs and therapy.

7. *Read all the questions at one time.* Some students find that reading all the questions before reading the passage gives them something to focus on as they read the passage. Sometimes they find answers to some questions right off the bat. Other students do better by reading all the questions right after finishing the passage. With the passage fresh in their minds, they might be able to answer a question or two immediately. In either case, reading the questions as a group instead of one by one may improve your score on the test. Try it.

8. *Forget what you already know about the topic in the passage.* The questions are derived from the passages. Answers are based on what the passage says, not on what you may know or think about the topic.

9. *Don't get bogged down on questions you find hard to answer.* This applies to all the questions on the test, but it's particularly easy to get stuck on reading questions. If you find yourself returning to the passage again and again in order to answer a question, you may be better off skipping it and making a note to try again later. Returning to the question with fresh eyes may help you answer it immediately.

THE MAIN IDEA QUESTION

You can recognize the main idea question because it is typically worded in one of the following ways:

1. The paragraph deals mainly with ...
2. The main idea of this selection may be best expressed as ...
3. The title that best expresses the ideas of this paragraph is ....
4. The writer's main purpose is apparently ...
5. The best name for this story is ...
6. The best title for this paragraph is ...

How successful are you in handling this type of question? Read the following paragraph and select, from the choices given, a suitable title for it. An analysis of the choices follows.

EXAMPLE:

One of the main traits desired in workers is dependability. The less supervision the employee needs, the more he or she is worth to the firm. Employees should be willing to do a full day's work even though they are not being watched. Supervisors will supply the necessary leadship and direction. Dependable employees will do their job well without complaining or trying to find unfair shortcuts.

The most suitable title for the paragraph is

(A) Supervisors on the Job
(B) A Job Well Done
(C) The Dependable Worker
(D) Success on the Job

ANALYSIS: Let's analyze the choices to see how to arrive at the correct answer:

Choice A empasizes the supervisor, not the worker who is discussed in the paragraph.

Choice B refers to one task properly completed. The paragraph is devoted to general behavior in the workplace, not to a specific job.

Choices C and D are possibilities. However, there are many different ways to succeed on the job. Choice D is much more general than Choice C. Therefore, *The dependable worker* is the best title. Each sentence in the paragraph in some way or other explains the advantages of being dependable.

HOW TO HANDLE A MAIN IDEA QUESTION

➤ Locate the topic sentence, the sentence that summarizes the passage. It is usually at the beginning of the passage, but sometimes you'll find it at the end, or even in the middle. If you can't find it, it may be implied. In that case, ask yourself:

What is the main topic of the passage? What point is the author making about the topic?

➤ Watch out for choices that are more general than the material in the passage.

➤ Similarly, be alert for choices that are too narrow, choices that refer to specific examples or to material used only to support or develop the main idea of the passage.

SPEED AND ACCURACY

It is true that speed will be a factor in determining your score. However, the way to gain speed is through practice and not through rushing. The more of the exercises in this book you do, the faster you will complete them. Speed will come—after accuracy! Do not dawdle. Do not rush. Concentrate every minute of the time, and speed will come.

EXERCISE 3

Read each of the following paragraphs carefully. Then, from the choices given, circle the letter of the title that is most appropriate for each. Also, complete each sentence under "Analysis" by inserting the correct letter.

1. A new plastic bandage has been developed to help those suffering from burns. Antibiotic ointments are manufactured into the bandage. When the burns are covered with this material, the antibacterial action of the ointment develops slowly. The antibiotic action of the salve can be continued for two or more weeks. Used on extensive burns, this bandage eliminates frequent and painful changes of dressings. The dressing may also be used for skin infections such as poison ivy where one application would provide the full course of treatment.

   A suitable title for this paragraph is
   (A) Antibiotics
   (B) Treating Burns
   (C) Sure Cures
   (D) A New Germ-Killing Dressing

ANALYSIS:

The suggested title that is wrong because it refers to only one of the uses of the new bandage is ____________.

The suggested title that is wrong because it refers to claims not made in the article is ____________.

The title that is wrong because it refers to a large field of germ killers when only one of these is mentioned briefly is ____________.

The title that is correct is ____________ ____________ because ____________.

2. No one can claim to be a "pure American." Even the Indians whom Columbus found here have been traced to the tribes that invaded the lands now occupied by the Chinese. Our people have come from all nations and all races. They came here to establish a home that they could be proud of, a home for their children. Unfortunately the word *minority* creeps too often into the speech of some communities that claim to have a majority group. The majority group looks upon their minority neighbors with doubt or suspicion. We must ever remember that if we want our nation to be strong we cannot afford the luxury of having second-class citizens. A man or woman must be judged as an individual, as one of the many who make up our nation. There is no room in the heart of America for prejudice.

   A suitable title for this paragraph is
   (A) Pure Americans
   (B) Melting Pots
   (C) American Minorities
   (D) A Source of Prejudice

ANALYSIS:

The title that is wrong because the article proves such persons do not exist is ____________.

The title that is wrong because no such expression is ever used is ____________.

The title that is wrong because it is too general for the article is _________.

The title that is correct is ______________________________________

because __________.

3. The development of the aluminum pram has given the American sportsman more mobility than he has ever had. This lightweight, sturdy boat usually weighs in the neighborhood of fifty pounds. It can easily be set securely on top of a car by one man. It can then be transported to any lake or stream within the reach of a road. Its draft is so shallow that it can be rowed through marshland and shallow inlets close to the waters inhabited by the largest of game fish. It is strong enough to be the basis for a blind built by the duckhunter who lies in wait for the unsuspecting wild mallards. With the coming of the new light weight outboard motors, it can even be propelled at slow speeds for the fisherman who prefers trolling. This boat is indeed the answer to the wishes of many sportsmen.

A suitable title for this paragraph is
(A) Drafting a Boat
(B) Traveling by Boat
(C) Hunting and Fishing
(D) An Ideal Boat for Sportsmen

ANALYSIS:

The title that is wrong because it includes many more types than mentioned in this selection is _________.

The title that is wrong because it is based on a misinterpretation of a word in the text is _________.

The title that is wrong because it stresses sports in general rather than an activity in sports is _________.

The title that is correct is ______________________________________

because __________.

4. Total color-blindness is most uncommon among the people who are classified as color-blind. Actually, this disability covers three different types. Some color-blind people see all colors as we normally do—except for an inability to see green or red. These are the people who must memorize that the top light in a traffic signal is always the red one. Then there are others who are unable to distinguish yellows and blues. The person who is unable to see any colors at all sees the world in shades of light and dark grays. The world to him is much like a black and white movie.

A suitable title for this selection is
(A) Total Blindness
(B) Total Color-Blindness
(C) Distinguishing Colors
(D) Types of Color-Blindness

ANALYSIS:

The title that is wrong because it deals with a completely different type of eye difficulty is _________.

The title that is wrong because it deals with only one of the three classifications is _________.

The title that is wrong because it is much too general is _________.

The title that is correct is ______________________________________

because __________.

5. In 1957 the United States Congress passed a highway construction program. At the time it seemed a wise and far-sighted measure. States did not have the funds to build enough good roads and traffic jams were an ever present headache. A national program of superhighway construction seemed a necessity and the only solution. What seemed wise in 1957 was called unwise and preposterous by many environmentalists in the early 1970s. Their argument was that the 1957 program was an unbalanced transport program. Superhighways

encourage the use of automobiles, and cars are one major source of pollution. Their use, especially by single operators, should not be encouraged. The environmentalists believe that the United States Congress in 1957 should have passed a comprehensive transportation program. Such a program, they maintain, should have included, in addition to highway construction, the development of mass transport facilities such as new interstate trains and commuter lines from suburbs to cities. They believe such a program would have reduced the use of the private car and that this would have substantially reduced air pollution. We will never know what might have happened if Congress had passed in 1957 the measure the environmentalists suggest.

A suitable title for this paragraph is
(A) Environmentalists
(B) Cars as Polluters
(C) Highway Act of 1957
(D) A Balanced Transportation Program

ANALYSIS:

A title that is wrong because it is too general is ________.

The title that is wrong because it deals with only one idea presented in the paragraph is ________.

The title that is wrong because it refers to only one type of transportation is ________.

The title that is correct is ________ ________ because ________.

PRACTICE TEST 1

DIRECTIONS: Beneath each of the following paragraphs you will find five descriptive expressions. After reading each paragraph, select the expression that contains the main idea of the passage. Circle the corresponding letter.

1. Do you really believe that the ostrich buries its head in the sand so that it cannot see the trouble that it is in? Nobody knows just when this strange belief was started, but there are very few people who have not heard it. If the ostrich were silly enough to follow this procedure, it would suffocate, once its head was buried in the sand. The ostrich really has no need for such a defense. It can kick with the full power of a mule, and it can run faster than a horse. It would be foolish indeed for the bird to stand without protecting itself when in danger.
(A) Stranger than fiction
(B) False belief
(C) Heading into sand
(D) Ostrich power
(E) Mules and ostriches

2. When speaking to the governor of a state, a visitor addresses him as "Your Excellency." The proper address to use when before a judge is "Your Honor." However, the President of the United States is simply "Mr. President." One of the earliest debates in Congress was on the issue. A Senate Committee voted that the President be addressed as "His Highness, the President of the United States of America, and Protector of their Liberties." James Madison objected. He claimed that the Constitution limited the title to just "President of the United States." James Madison and his supporters won, and that is why when a letter is sent to our chief executive in Washington it is addressed to "The President, The White House."
(A) Titles of honor
(B) The President's title
(C) Paying respect
(D) Madison's revenge
(E) A quaint idea

3. As one of the safety measures taken in the house, a package of baking soda should be kept near the kitchen range. There is always the danger of grease catching fire during the cooking process. Water must not be used on the burning grease. The water will only scatter the fiery grease and spread the fire. Baking soda scattered on the flaming grease has a different effect, however. The soda absorbs the grease and releases carbon dioxide that smothers the fire. If the fire is confined to a

greasy pan, putting a tight lid on it will also smother the flames quickly.
(A) Fire fighting
(B) Baking soda to the rescue
(C) The cooking process
(D) Handling grease
(E) Handling grease fires on the stove

4. The variety of behaviors insects show toward their eggs after laying them is almost without number. Some insects just lay their eggs anywhere and forget all about them. Many others set their eggs near food material and then go off. Butterflies, for example, lay their eggs on a plant which the young, when hatched, will feed on. The ants and the bees, on the other hand, give their young the greatest protection. The young have nursemaids to feed them and soldiers to protect them while they are carefully tended in their individual cells in the beehive or antnest.
(A) Ants and bees
(B) Insect variety
(C) Protection of baby insects
(D) Egg laying
(E) Careful butterflies

5. When considered in the light of the needs of pupils both in their present lives and as adults, oral expression merits greater time and attention than written expression. But, for the sake of economy of instruction time, the initial process and the drill that leads to the eradication of errors can tend toward written exercises rather than oral drill. Written work guarantees more individual student participation when the average class size is large.
(A) Meeting pupil needs
(B) Oral and written class-work
(C) Economy of effort
(D) Eradication of errors
(E) Oral instruction

PRACTICE TEST 2

DIRECTIONS: Read each of the following paragraphs carefully. Then select from the choices given, the title that is most appropriate for each, and circle the corresponding letter.

1. Meat is an ideal food for humans—and for mold and bacteria as well. When it is fresh, it is one of the best culture mediums. It consists of 20 percent protein, fats, mineral matter, and organic compounds. The rest of it is water. This combination of moisture and solids makes it one of the most perishable of foods. The bacteria produces discoloration and bad odors. The mold fills the meat with black spots and other discolorations.

The most appropriate title is
(A) Spoilage of Meat
(B) Meat and Molds
(C) Ideal Food for Humans
(D) Fresh Meat

2. Georges Claude of France invented a process for extracting neon and other gases from the air at reasonable prices. In 1920 he began to make neon tubes for commercial purposes. Although the tubes are called neon, they may contain many different gases. Neon itself gives a brilliant red light while argon and mercury give a bright blue light. Krypton and mercury give a green light when in a yellow tube. Helium in a yellow tube gives a yellow light. The neon tubes can be made in enormous lengths.

The most appropriate title is
(A) Georges Claude
(B) Rare Gases at Work
(C) Neon Light
(D) Reasonable Tubes

3. There are many essentials of life that we are willing to take for granted. Our families and continuing good health are not questioned. Even food and shelter are rarely causes of troubling thoughts. However, if most teenagers were asked to list the one or two things most important to their happiness, high on the list would be friends or friendships. Life, so they seem to feel, would lose its sparkle and vitality if friends were not present. This intense need for being part of a group or being accepted by one's equals in age lessens with maturity.

   The most appropriate title is
   (A) Essential Life
   (B) Troubling Thoughts
   (C) Friendly Youths
   (D) Need for Friends in Adolescence

4. Early in the sixteenth century the Spanish explorers reached a part of Mexico that they called Yucatan. There they found more than sixty cities that were no longer inhabited. The cities were all in ruin. They had been built by the Maya people. There were temples, palaces and great underground reservoirs. The Mayas had developed a civilization of which the people of Europe had known nothing. Mayan culture had grown and then decayed without ever having spread far afield. Will future explorers who travel into space have similar experiences? Will they too come upon cities in ruins on distant shores—of other planets?

   The most appropriate title is
   (A) Civilizations of the Future
   (B) Spanish Explorers
   (C) Unknown Civilizations
   (D) Exploring the Future

5. The Renaissance was a movement away from medieval ideals. There were many ways in which this movement away from the medieval period manifested itself. It can be seen in the copying of antique Roman and Greek ideas in literature and philosophy, in the developing of new approaches in science, in the discovering of new trade routes and the New World, in the using of more luxuries and new inventions. Most important, however, it can be seen in the way humanity was regarded by the people of the Renaissance period. To them man was important as an individual. We see his individuality in the realism of art, in the new centralized government, in philosophy, in attitudes toward religion, and in the emphasis on personal talent.

   The most appropriate title is
   (A) Medieval Ideals
   (B) Renaissance Philosophy
   (C) Individualism in the Renaissance
   (D) Rebirth of Greek and Roman Ideas

WORDS IN CONTEXT

Can you figure out the meaning of unfamiliar words when they are used in sentences? This is called obtaining the meaning of words it context. Read the following paragraph carefully, then complete the sentence below it.

EXAMPLE:

The trilobites, ancient relatives of the present-day lobster, ruled the seas millions of years ago. These sea-animals were usually just about three inches long. However, some of them grew to two feet long, weighing as much as fifteen pounds. They usually lived in shallow water near the shore. They walked over the floor of the sea on their jointed legs. Their multiple eyes and long feelers helped them to find their prey. The trilobites were in evidence in the seas for some three hundred million years. These sea-dwellers died out about two hundred million years ago. The fossils that we find in rocks tell their story.

The fossils are
(A) alive (B) remains (C) dangerous
(D) photographs

ANALYSIS: Let's analyze this first one together. See if you agree with our reasons for selecting the answer we think is correct.

The key sentence is "The fossils that we find in rocks tell their story." Add to this the sentence "These sea-dwellers died out about two hundred million years ago."

(A) *alive* must be wrong because the trilobites died out years ago.

(B) *remains* is the only answer left and rocks could contain the remains of the skeletons of these animals.

(C) *dangerous* must be wrong since the trilobites are no longer living.

(D) *photographs* must be wrong because these fossils are found in rocks, which do not contain photographs.

HOW TO HANDLE A WORD-IN-CONTEXT QUESTION

- Read the entire paragraph before answering the question. The context in which the word appears may alter its usual meaning.
- Find the word. Sometimes the word is underlined or printed in boldface type.
- Look for clues to the meaning of the word by rereading the sentence in which the word appears. Look particularly for a synonym, a definition, or an example.
- If no clue is given, reread the sentences that come before and after that sentence, looking for synonyms, a definition, or an example.

SPEED AND ACCURACY

Once again, you cannot sacrifice accuracy for speed. It is useless to be able to boast that you were the first one to finish—and fail. Fight against carelessness. Train yourself to be accurate. Don't dawdle, and speed will come eventually.

EXERCISE 4

The following paragraphs will help you to increase your speed and accuracy. Read the directions. After you have answered the question, analyze your answer.

Read each of the following paragraphs carefully. Then complete each of the incomplete statements under "Analysis." Most of the statements can be completed by selecting the correct lettered choices.

1. Over fifty million years ago the ancestor of the modern horse, the eohippus, lived in the swampy woodlands of western North America and of Europe. The eohippus, no bigger than the modern fox, was well fitted for living in swamplands. Its feet with definite toes helped it walk across the soggy terrain. Its teeth were well adapted to eating the leaves on the bushes and on the lower branches of the trees. Its swiftness saved it from the enemy that lurked among the trees.

   Soggy terrain is typical of
   (A) life fifty million years ago
   (B) the present day horse
   (C) swamplands
   (D) the eohippus

ANALYSIS:

When used to complete the sentence, three answers do not make sense. They are ______, ______, and ______.

The correct answer is __________ because the eohippus lived __________ and walked ________.

2. The employment of mercenaries was not unusual at the time of the American Revolution. Several small German states and Swiss cantons would let out all or part of their armed forces for hire. When George III of England was unable to recruit many Englishmen to fight the rebellious colonials, he made an agreement with Frederick II of Hesse-Kassel. The ruler of Hesse-Kassel received about 1,500,000 pounds for his 22,000 men. Of these an estimated 10,000 never returned to Germany. About 1,000 were killed in action. Almost 5,000 died from disease and accidents in the service. Approximately 4,000 settled in the United States when the hostilities were over. Since most of the mercenaries came from Hesse-Kassel, those that fought in America were called Hessians.

The hostilities were over when
(A) George III paid for the use of the soldiers
(B) the fighting ceased
(C) the mercenaries came to America
(D) the mercenaries were called Hessians

ANALYSIS:

The sentence that is the key to the answer is ________.

The three suggestions that are wrong because they are not connected with the key sentence are ________, ________, and ________.

The correct answer is ________ because the Hessians could never have ________ unless the end of hostilities meant that ________.

3. Naturalists may dispute about which trees are the largest in the world. One giant eucalyptus in Australia, measured after it had been felled, was more than 500 feet long. A giant sequoia of California, called the Father of the Forest, measured a mere 400 feet when it fell. However, scientists agree that the tallest plants are not among these trees. The seaweed of the ocean can tower over any of the trees so far measured. Seaweed over 600 feet tall has been found in the ocean at the Straits of Magellan, near the southern tip of South America. These plants are more than twice as tall as the Statue of Liberty!

People who dispute
(A) argue
(B) agree
(C) tell tales about trees
(D) measure carefully

ANALYSIS:

The sentence that is the key to the answer is ________.

The suggested answer that is an antonym of *dispute* is ________.

A suggested answer that is wrong because it is unrelated to the word *dispute* is ________.

The correct answer is ________ because the paragraph offers as a contrast to the fact that "Naturalists may dispute" the fact that ________.

4. We are never alone. We cannot claim that any of our actions involve only ourselves and no other people. At all times the frame of reference for our conduct must be the group most closely involved with the activity. Sometimes the team that we are part of is our family. At other times it is the group of friends that we have or even our school or community. When, in time of emergency, we fight as a member of the armed forces, we are part of a national unit. How right was the poet who said that no man is an island isolated from his fellow humans. Therefore, in all of our decisions, we must take into consideration the degree to which others are involved in our actions.

According to the author, a selfish person would be
(A) a frame of reference
(B) a national unit
(C) time of emergency
(D) an isolated island

ANALYSIS:

The suggested answer that is wrong because it confuses a person and war is ________.

The suggested answer that is wrong because it confuses a person with a philosophical term is ________.

The suggested answer that is wrong because it confuses a person with a group of many people is ________.

Since the author describes a person who is the opposite of ________, what this person is not would be correct; therefore, ________ is, correct.

5. Polyethylene was a war-time product first developed in England during World War II. It was first used to encase radar cables to protect them from being shattered by shells explod-

ing nearby. After the war, many additional uses for this synthetic were developed. At first it was used to insulate electric wires and cables. Then it was manufactured as bags for use in the deepfreeze. Because it is waterproof, millions of miles of tubes and pipes have been made from this product that has to be manufactured under thousands of pounds of pressure.

Polyethylene is a synthetic product because
(A) it is waterproof
(B) it is manufactured
(C) thousands of pounds of pressure are required
(D) it has so many uses

ANALYSIS:

The sentence that is the key to the answer is ____________.

The suggested answer that is wrong because it gives only one of polyethylene's qualities is ____________.

The suggested answer that is wrong because it involves an interesting but unimportant detail is ____________.

The suggested answer that is wrong because it is not mentioned in the paragraph is ____________.

The portion of the key sentence that explains *synthetic* is ____________.

The correct answer is ____________.

PRACTICE TEST 3

DIRECTIONS: Below each of the following paragraphs you will find an incomplete sentence and five descriptive expressions. After reading each paragraph, select the expression that best completes the sentence, and circle the corresponding letter.

1. In the 1600s the region between the lower Hudson and Connecticut rivers was inhabited by the Wappinger Confederacy, a small group of Algonquin tribes. The Manhattans, one of these nine tribes, had its main village in the vicinity of present day Yonkers. The Manhattans used Manhattan Island as a fishing and hunting preserve, and they built temporary huts there. The name Manhattan itself may have been derived from Algonquin words that mean "island of the hills."

   Preserve *as used in paragraph refers to*
   (A) conservation
   (B) icing foods
   (C) canning foods
   (D) canned fruits
   (E) none of the above

2. Marco Polo in his famous *Travels* makes no mention of the important invention of paper, a product first introduced by the Chinese. The Moors are credited with having brought paper into Europe by way of Samarkand, a remote land in central Asia. The Moors were taught by two Chinese paper makers captured during one of their raids. By the twelfth century Spain and then France knew the art of paper-making thanks to their Moorish invaders. However, at that time, most of the European printing continued to be done on parchment, since the paper was considered too fragile.

   Early European printers avoided paper because
   (A) it tore easily
   (B) the Moors were invaders
   (C) it had not as yet been invented
   (D) it was too costly
   (E) the Moors had made it

3. Early human beings had to concentrate all of their energies to secure food, shelter, and freedom from dangerous attackers. Human development from this state has been a slow and painful process. Today, man has advanced so far that he can control natural forces so immense that his power for good or evil is lightening. Today humans need have little fear of annihilation by the forces against which early man had to fight. Man no

longer fears greatly the violence of the elements or of creatures many times his own size or strength. The only cause of fear for the humans of today is man himself.

The annihilation of human beings would result in
(A) the disappearance of humans
(B) the victory of humans
(C) violence of the elements
(D) immense power for good or evil
(E) a painless process

4. One of the most astonishing tricks of the amateur magician involves a mixture of tincture of iodine and cornstarch dissolved in water. Before the very eyes of his onlookers, he writes boldy on a piece of paper a long message. Then a look of annoyance fills his countenance. He exclaims that he wished that he had not written the missive. He slowly looks for a cloth, in order to allow the ink to dry. When he is certain that it has dried, he finds his handkerchief and wipes the entire message clean off the paper. He does not, of course, tell his audience that the cornstarch has prevented the ink from penetrating the paper.

The missive is the
(A) magician
(B) ink
(C) paper
(D) letter
(E) book

5. The English language has achieved its richness and forcefulness as a result of its being a mixture of many tongues rather than the purified result of the endeavors of one people. The base of present-day English is a core of words used by the Angles, Jutes and Frisians, the basis of what is called Old English. To this were added direct borrowings from French and Latin. Once this amalgam had grown into a useful language, the English borrowed from all of the known word-patterns used throughout the world. Since English is made up of words from all languages, many scholars have urged that English be the universal language of the United Nations of the world.

An amalgam is a
(A) language
(B) mixture
(C) borrowing
(D) core
(E) people

PRACTICE TEST 4

DIRECTIONS: Read each of the following paragraphs carefully. Choose the most appropriate completion for the incomplete sentence that follows each, and circle the corresponding letter.

1. Near the edge of the water, snails crawled along the ground. Near the edges of the nearby swamplands were animals of a more important kind—amphibians. Most amphibians live a part of their lives in water and a part on land.

Amphibians are
(A) swamp snails
(B) types of land and water animals
(C) land and water dwellers
(D) types of snakes that crawl

2. Mediation is a means of maintaining peace between employers and employees. The agreement or settlement reached is made only by and between the members of each of these groups. The community or law enforcement agencies are not party to settlement other than as interested parties.

Mediation results when
(A) a strike is declared
(B) a strike is won
(C) both sides talk over their problems
(D) a strike is settled

3. The Russian intelligentsia had the advantage of wealth and education. They are often considered together as a group but there were many different attitudes held by the members. Some supported the Bolshevik revolutionar-

ies while others strongly supported conservative Tsarist policies. None were considered, however, merely members of the business or working class.

When a person is a member of the intelligentsia, he
(A) supports revolutionaries
(B) is a business man
(C) belongs to a wealthy and educated group
(D) likes conservatives

4. The Olympic Oath is repeated by all the contestants during the commencement exercises. "We swear that we will take part in the Olympic games in loyal competition, respecting the regulations which govern them and desirous of participating in them in the true spirit of sportsmanship for the honor of our country and for the glory of sport."

This oath is taken when
(A) the contests begin
(B) the contests are over
(C) the players prove their sportsmanship
(D) there is glory in the sport

5. Since 1871 smoking has been prohibited on the floor of the House of Representatives. Previously only a few legislators had smoked while listening to the debate among their fellow members. However it was generally felt that smoking during a legislative session was incompatible with the dignity of Congress.

Smoking has been prohibited among Representatives when the House is in session because the practice was thought to be
(A) undignified
(B) filled with dignity
(C) unsanitary
(D) unhealthful

THE FACT QUESTION

Students usually find the fact question the easiest to handle, since it is the most definite one in the group. The author makes a definite statement somewhere in the paragraph. The reader is asked to find the statement.

There are pitfalls, however. Students who try to gain speed by reading the questions first are too often trapped when the questioner skillfully repeats some phrases that can be found in the paragraph, but that do not lead to the correct answers.

To add difficulty to the level of the question, the examiner will often substitute synonyms for the words in the paragraph. The question then almost becomes a word-in-context question (see preceding section). The student must be alert and be ready to find such changes in the wording.

Because fact questions are often found in clusters, two or three of them to a paragraph, students are prone, through haste or carelessness, to skip some of them. A question not answered or omitted is the same as an incorrect answer. In your haste to make speed, do not overlook what you have to do!

HOW TO HANDLE A FACT QUESTION

- ➤ Read the entire paragraph before answering the question. By familiarizing yourself with the paragraph, you will know approximately where to seek your answer.
- ➤ Determine from the wording of the question that it is a fact question rather than another type.
- ➤ Search the paragraph to find the exact phrase or sentence or idea that contains the answer.
- ➤ After making your choice, review the other answers just in case you missed the point of the question.

EXERCISE 5

Read each of the following paragraphs carefully. Then complete the incomplete sentences below the paragraph.

There are many reasons that people can give for wanting to go to college. Some of those reasons are based on snobbishness. "Cousin John or Aunt Harriet went, and my parents would be embarrassed endlessly if I didn't go." "Everyone who is anybody goes to college, you know." Some people want to go to college out of fear, fear that when depressions come, they will lose out to college graduates. Some others go to college to choose a future mate or to avoid going to work. All these reasons are sincere and honest ones, but college is a miracle worker. Regardless of the reasons that moved people to attend college, the training given there teaches them to think better, to plan better, and to live better. A higher education is a must, then, for everyone who has the ability to gain from it.

1. The snob wants to go to college to
   (A) live better
   (B) earn more money
   (C) imitate his relatives
   (D) get married
   (E) plan better

   The sentence that answers this question is ____________.

   Therefore, the correct answer is ____________.

2. College teaches all who attend how to
   (A) be snobbish
   (B) be better human beings
   (C) choose a mate
   (D) earn money
   (E) think

   The sentence that answers this question is ____________.

   Therefore, the correct answer is ____________.

Each group in society develops a vocabulary, a group of words to describe the tools and operations involved in its trade or profession. These words are part of the daily lives of the group. Just listen to the waitress in the diner speak to the short-order cook or the shoe salesman talk to the manager. The words all sound familiar, but they just do not make sense to anyone who is not in the trade. This jargon, as it is called, is different from slang which is used by many groups in society. Jargon is usually limited to only one group of workers.

3. When two workers describe to each other an operation in their work, they use
   (A) slang
   (B) vocabulary
   (C) jargon
   (D) short-order
   (E) familiar sense

   The sentence that contains the answer is ____________.

   The correct answer is ____________.

4. Slang is different from jargon because
   (A) only workers use it
   (B) it is used by many groups
   (C) it is filled with trade terms
   (D) salesmen use it
   (E) it is unacceptable in polite society

   The sentence that contains the answer is ____________.

   The correct answer is ____________.

Amber began as resin that oozed from pine trees. Water, pressure, and time changed the gum into a clear, glasslike yellow substance. Human beings have long used amber to make varnish or ornamental jewelry. This lightest of all precious gems differs from the other jewels in that it has a plant origin rather than a mineral base. In ancient times amber was supposed to have worth as a medicine for treating diseases. The people of the Near East thought that amber prevented infections from spreading from person to person. That is the reason for its popularity as the material used in making cigarette holders.

5. Amber came originally from
   (A) water
   (B) trees
   (C) pressure
   (D) the Near East
   (E) precious gems

   The sentence that contains the answer is ____________.

   The correct answer is ____________.

6. Amber was used in the making of cigarette holders because
   (A) it kept the user from getting sick
   (B) it was light
   (C) it was pretty
   (D) it was worth much money
   (E) it was used in the making of varnish

   The sentence that contains the answer is ____________.

   The correct answer, therefore, is ____________.

The cold is the most common human ailment, yet it has stumped medical authorities. Many more dread diseases have come under control as the result of knowledge gained in research laboratories. Investigators have assumed that the cold is usually caused by a virus. However, no method of studying this virus has been devised. The chimpanzee is the only amimal to which the disease can be given experimentally. The use of this animal is limited by its cost and by the fact that so many of the animals die of pneumonia during the experiments. This leaves for all practical purposes only human volunteers to be used in research projects. Many inmates of prisons have aided in this work, but because of these limitations research into the cause and cure of colds has progressed very slowly.

7. Research into the cause and cure of colds has
   (A) gone ahead very slowly
   (B) gone ahead very rapidly
   (C) been filled with dread
   (D) been very common
   (E) been impossible

   The sentence that contains the answer is ____________.

   The correct answer, therefore, is ______.

When out-of-state Americans think of Kentucky, they always imagine fleet, young thoroughbreds frisking in the blue grass fields under the watchful eyes of men well-trained in the art of winning on the racetracks of the world. They also imagine that they can see tobacco toasting in the sun. The farms are large, and the work is carried on under most pleasant circumstances. The workers go from task to task humming or singing aloud gentle sentimental tunes. Every once in a while, the entire staff will come together and harmonize—while the work waits. Kentucky has come to mean a happy way of country life filled with horses, sunshine, and tobacco leaf. These beliefs did not come about accidentally. The romantic writers of stories and of popular music deserve full credit for what Kentucky is supposed to be. Stephen Foster was only one of the many who idealized this eastern state.

8. The picture of life in Kentucky is
   (A) true
   (B) false
   (C) filled with hard work
   (D) the work of writers
   (E) a lazy one

   The sentence that contains the answer is ____________.

   The correct answer, therefore, is ______.

9. This picture of life in Kentucky is in the minds of
   (A) all workers
   (B) many Americans
   (C) young thoroughbreds
   (D) Kentuckians
   (E) singers

   The sentence that contains the answer is ____________.

   The correct answer is ____________.

PRACTICE TEST 5

DIRECTIONS: After each of the following paragraphs, you will find three incomplete statements about the paragraph. Each statement is followed by five words or phrases lettered (A) to (E). After reading the paragraph, read the statements. Then select the word or phrase that most satisfactorily completes each statement, and circle the corresponding letter.

In 1910 Congress appropriated enough money to have the *Maine* raised. The sinking of the *Maine* in the harbor of Havana was one of the immediate causes of the Spanish-American War. No one ever determined what had caused the fatal explosion. The American newspapers blamed the Spanish commander in Cuba. The Spanish claimed that they had not put any mines into the harbor and denied any responsibility for the explosion. When the *Maine* was raised and examined by naval experts, they were unable to determine the cause of the explosion that had cost the lives of 229 Navy men. Since the wreck was a danger to ships sailing in and out of the harbor of Havana, what was left of the *Maine* was towed into the Gulf of Mexico, where it was sunk in 600 fathoms of water, while its flag fluttered in the breeze and American Navy vessels fired farewell salutes.

1. The *Maine* was a
   (A) state
   (B) Spanish Commando
   (C) Spanish boat
   (D) American Navy vessel
   (E) harbor

2. The ship was raised
   (A) to save the men
   (B) to make money
   (C) to punish the Spanish
   (D) to please the Spanish
   (E) to help determine causes

3. The Americans sank the ship
   (A) in deep water
   (B) in the Havana harbor
   (C) in Mexico
   (D) in Maine
   (E) after an explosion

The status quo antebellum was the basis of the peace settlement developed at the Congress of Vienna. The victorious nations had fought France and the new ideas of the French Revolution for twenty-five years. They were glad to be rid of their enemy leader of the last sixteen years, Napoleon, and they wanted peace based on the conditions of the old days. They really believed they could wipe out the new ideas and restore Europe to the conditions of 1789. Metternich, the Austrian leader and most important person at the Congress, presented plans for the peace settlement. The plans have been summed up in the terms legitimacy, restoration of former rulers to their legitimate throne, and compensation, donation of added territory to those nations bordering on France which suffered heavily during the war.

4. The restoration of former rulers to their thrones was referred to at the Congress of Vienna as
   (A) legitimacy
   (B) Metternich
   (C) compensation
   (D) status quo antebellum
   (E) the old days

5. The leader of the Congress of Vienna was
   (A) Napoleon
   (B) the victorious nations
   (C) France
   (D) Metternich
   (E) Austria

6. The nations that met at the Congress of Vienna had been
   (A) writing a peace treaty
   (B) supporting the French Revolution
   (C) fighting France for twenty-five years
   (D) fighting Napoleon
   (E) restoring Europe to the conditions of 1789

In his *Autobiography,* John Stuart Mill revealed the unusual method of education that his father had planned for him. By the time he was three, he was being taught Greek, arithmetic, and English grammar. He began the study of Latin when he was eight. Before he was twelve, he had read much Greek and Roman literature in the original. He was well-acquainted with the philosophers and writers of history. His recreation consisted chiefly of taking walks with his father and in reading works of history, fiction, and poetry, all selected for him. Since his health remained good during most of his life, this manner of living probably agreed with him. Could the child of today accept such a rigid training? Or are the temptations that radio, television, and theater place in our paths too great?

7. Mill learned his first foreign language when he
   (A) wrote his *Autobiography*
   (B) was three
   (C) was taking walks with his father
   (D) was eight
   (E) was twelve

8. For relaxation, he would
   (A) do more reading
   (B) take long walks by himself
   (C) play ball
   (D) listen to the radio
   (E) watch old movies

9. When Mill was growing up there were no
   (A) schools
   (B) teachers
   (C) writers
   (D) manners
   (E) radio sets

Modern philosophers differ greatly from those of earlier ages. The modern philosophers are usually scientific in their attitudes. The ancient ones were concerned with the pursuit of beauty while the thinkers of the Middle Ages were primarily interested in theology. Truth, beauty, and goodness were the centers of thought for the ancients. The man of the Middle Ages placed the doctrines of religion above concern about pure philosophy. Philosophy existed to clarify religious doctrines. Today, philosophy has freed itself from the search for truth in terms of beauty or goodness or theology. The main path of the modern philosopher pursues the need for interpreting the rapidly advancing sciences.

10. According to the author of this paragraph, modern philosophers study
   (A) beauty
   (B) religion
   (C) science
   (D) theology
   (E) goodness

11. The philosophers of Greece two thousand years ago were concerned with the study of
   (A) religion
   (B) the Middle Ages
   (C) science
   (D) beauty
   (E) doctrines

12. Philosophy existed in the Middle Ages to
   (A) strengthen religious beliefs
   (B) explore science
   (C) study the meaning of pure philosophy
   (D) reveal goodness wherever it may be
   (E) explain the terms of beauty

PRACTICE TEST 6

DIRECTIONS: Read each of the following paragraphs carefully. Then choose the letter of the word or phrase that best completes each of the incomplete sentences, and circle it.

The early English swimmers soon developed two strokes. The preferred stroke was the breast stroke which was alternated with the side stroke. These two for long remained the English style. They were used in all of the races among the competitors from the six swimming pools that developed in London in the early nineteenth century. This English style of swimming was far different from that of Native Americans, who thrashed the water violently with their arms and beat rapidly downward with their feet.

1. Most English swimmers used
   (A) the Native American stroke
   (B) freestyle
   (C) the breaststroke
   (D) the sidestroke
   (E) thrashing the water

2. The style of swimming of the Native American
   (A) resembled that of the English
   (B) resembled that of London in the early nineteenth century
   (C) was smooth and silent
   (D) was noisy and splashing
   (E) was unnecessary

The wagon cook had to carry two months' provisions for a crew of men through the heat of the western summer, without refrigeration. Therefore fresh vegetables and eggs were never present in the chuck wagon. The basic foods that the cook stored were dried varieties. The cowboys had to learn to survive on such starchy foods as beans, bread, corn, potatoes, rice. The cowboy rarely grew stout on such fare, however. The long hours of hard work in the saddle burned up all the energy the food gave him. Yet, something can be said in favor of the simplicity of the cowman's menu. The man in the saddle was not afflicted with stomach ailments and ulcers.

3. One of the main difficulties facing the wagon cook was
   (A) storage
   (B) quality of the food
   (C) dried varieties
   (D) menus
   (E) ulcers

4. The diet of the cowboy was
   (A) dried
   (B) unvaried
   (C) lacking in starch
   (D) refrigerated
   (E) fresh eggs and vegetables

Red tape is a term used today to refer to unusual amounts of complications filled with paper work, and procedures that seem to hinder rather than help when work must be done. The expression had its origin in England where official papers and packages of documents were tied in red tape. This cord was constantly being tied and untied. Thomas Carlyle and Charles Dickens used the phrase red tape so often in their writings that it is part of the common vocabulary of everyday people.

5. *Red tape* was really used in
   (A) Russia
   (B) America
   (C) England
   (D) Thomas Carlyle
   (E) complications

6. *Red tape* refers to
   (A) writers
   (B) Communists
   (C) Americans
   (D) helpful procedures
   (E) hindering complications

Bats are found throughout the world from the Arctic Circle almost into Antarctica. They are mammals with relatively large brains. They branched off the main stem of the mammalian family tree millions of years ago. They are the second largest order of mammals. Millions have been found sleeping in one cave. Almost all bats rest and sleep in the same position. They hang upside down, suspended by either one or both hind feet. Despite the reputation of the vampire bats that live exclusively on the blood of other animals, most bats feed on insects which they catch and eat while they are flying.

7. Bats are found
   (A) only in Africa
   (B) almost everywhere
   (C) in the Arctic Circle
   (D) in cold climates
   (E) in northern regions only

8. Most bats
   (A) are vampires
   (B) live on insects
   (C) live on flies
   (D) eat little
   (E) are large

For hundreds of years the madder plant was our sole source of yellow dye. The dye was extracted from the roots of the plant and sold all over the world. The great plantations in southern France were devoted to the cultivation of the madder plant until 1869. In that year German scientists discovered that the dye could be produced artificially. A chemical that was extracted from coal tar was their answer. Alizarine, as it is called, was cheaper to produce, easier to use and more permanent in coloring. The dyers of cloth turned to this new product, and the madder growers of France had to seek new crops to cultivate.

9. Our only source in former times for yellow dye was
   (A) chemicals
   (B) German plantations
   (C) dyers of cloth
   (D) coal tar
   (E) plant

10. The chemists discovered
   (A) a better dye
   (B) coal tar
   (C) the madder plant
   (D) French plantations
   (E) yellow dye

THE INFERENCE QUESTION

Inferring involves passing from one proposition, statement, or judgment to another whose truth follows from that of the former. In the inference question, you are asked to draw a conclusion based on what you have read in a passage.

The basic purpose of this type of question is to rate your ability to:

- detect a hidden meaning in a paragraph
- use the information conveyed in a reading selection
- extend the author's statements to other cases

HOW TO HANDLE AN INFERENCE QUESTION

➤ Read the entire paragraph before answering the question. Keep asking yourself, "What is the author's intent?" This is important to understand because inference questions ask you to "read between the lines."

➤ Once you've read the question, reread the section of the paragraph likely to contain the clues on which to base your judgment.

➤ Locate the words from which to draw your inference.

➤ Ask yourself whether your understanding of the author's intent is consistent with the answer you chose; that is, would the author be likely to agree with you?

➤ Avoid falling for an answer that simply restates material in the passage. Although the idea comes from the passage, it may not be the answer to the specific inference question.

➤ Eliminate the wrong answers. Have a logical reason for eliminating each one.

➤ Check the answer that is left. Test it against the facts in the paragraph.

SPEED AND ACCURACY

Do not fall into the trap of rushing through a judgment question. It is useless to be able to boast that you were the first to finish—and fail! Fight against the desire to pounce on the first likely answer. Concentrate on accuracy. Speed will come with practice.

EXERCISE 6

The following paragraphs will help you increase your speed and accuracy. Read the directions. After you have answered the question, analyze your answer.

Read each of the following paragraphs carefully. Circle the letter of the correct choice. Then complete each of the incomplete statements below.

Mars and Venus are the two planets that are the next door neighbors of Earth. Venus circles the Sun at an average distance of about 67 million miles. The average distance between the Earth and the Sun is 93 million miles. Mars, on the other hand, circles around the Sun in an ellipse that averages 141 million miles away from the Sun. At times the planets are on opposite sides of the Sun. Earth and Venus at such a time are 167 million miles apart. When they are closest, they are about 30 million miles away from each other. The nearest that Mars comes to Earth as they swing in their orbits that center around the Sun is about 35 million miles.

1. The closest neighbor to Earth among the planets is
(A) the Moon
(B) the Sun
(C) Mars
(D) Jupiter
(E) Venus

ANALYSIS:

The two choices that are wrong because they are not planets are ________ and ________.

The choice that is wrong because it is a planet not mentioned in the article is ________.

The closest neighbor is ________ because it is ________ million miles closer than ________.

2. Closest to the Sun is
(A) the Moon
(B) the stars
(C) Mars
(D) Earth
(E) Venus

ANALYSIS:

Since they are not mentioned in the article, I can eliminate ________ and ________.

The average distance away from the Sun for the Earth is ________ million miles, for the planet Mars is ________ million miles, and for Venus is ________ million miles. Therefore, the closest to the Sun is ________.

One of the tests that are basic to chemical analysis involves litmus paper. The name means *colored moss,* since it is obtained from certain primitive plants called lichens. If litmus paper comes into contact with an acid liquid, it turns reddish. The degree of reddishness depends on the concentration of the acid in the liquid. If litmus paper is dipped into an alkaline liquid, it turns various shades of blue. Many students remember the phrase "in a base, blue litmus" to associate the colors with the correct reactions.

3. Lichens are a type of
(A) paper
(B) litmus
(C) moss
(D) acid

ANALYSIS:

Since lichens are ________ which belong to the ________ family, the answer is ________.

4. If the litmus paper turns blue, it has been previously
(A) wet
(B) red
(C) white
(D) alkaline

ANALYSIS:

Since litmus paper is either ________ or ________ in color, ________ must be wrong.

Since both acid and base must be ________ for the litmus paper to react, ________ is wrong.

Since the color for acid is ________ and the color for base is ________ and another name for base is ________, therefore ________ is wrong.

Since the litmus paper turns from ________ to ________ in color, the answer must be ________.

An eternal weariness seemed to settle over his entire being. The strong, quick movements were replaced by the slow-motion of a tired old, old man. The glow was gone from his skin, and a pasty, sickly, whiteness colored its moistness. It was incredible that just a few minutes ago he had been so confident of the outcome of his encounter with his adversary. He had been positive that his youth and energy would be more than the age and experience of the other could overcome. How wrong he had been! Yet, all that he had done was to make one error, a slight one, but one that his crafty opponent had taken full advantage of. His guard had slipped for a brief second, the power-packed right had snaked through, and the end had come.

5. The main character in this incident had just
   (A) been knocked out
   (B) been injured badly in an accident
   (C) hurt another
   (D) found old age

ANALYSIS:

If he is facing a "crafty opponent," then _________ must be wrong.

Since he had "youth and energy" in facing an opponent, ___________ must be wrong.

Since he is the one who is a sickly white, _________ must be wrong.

The description in the _________ sentences shows that he is a boxer who is about to lose ___________; therefore _________ is right.

6. The cause of his condition was
   (A) his slow movements
   (B) lack of experience
   (C) inability to drive
   (D) trickery

ANALYSIS:

Since he had allowed___________, the correct answer must be ________.

Missouri was first explored by the French under Joliet and Marquette in 1673. It was part of the Louisiana Purchase Territory of 1803 and was included in the section then known as Upper Louisiana. Louisiana separated itself from the rest of the territory on April 8, 1812, when it became one of the states of the Union. For nearly two months, the territory, excluding Louisiana, continued to be called the Louisiana Territory. On June 4, 1812, its name was changed to Missouri. Part of this Missouri territory became the state of Missouri on August 10, 1821.

7. By 1732, Louisiana was known as
   (A) Upper Louisiana
   (B) French territory
   (C) Missouri
   (D) a state of the Union

ANALYSIS:

Since Louisiana became a state in _________, _________ is wrong.

The article does not give enough information to allow verification or denial of _________ and _________.

Since the Louisiana Purchase took place in __________ and it was purchased from the _________, the correct answer must be _________.

8. The territory of Missouri
   (A) became the state of Louisiana
   (B) became the state of Missouri
   (C) was too large to become one state
   (D) was too small to become a state

ANALYSIS:

The sentence that is the key to this answer is _________.

Since only _________ of the Missouri Territory became the _________, the correct answer must be _________.

The tourist suddenly brought his car to a stop, and just in time, too. He had heard the beginning hiss of the escaping air, and his foot had pressed hard on the brake. When the car stopped, he walked out of the car and stared at the tire that was going flat. Suddenly he realized that he had stopped close to a Utah rattlesnake den. A thirteen-footer was fast approaching the tire. The man retreated as he saw the rattler strike the flattened end. The poison in the venom of the snake was so strong that the solid rubber swelled back to normal size and the tourist was able to drive more than 200 miles to Salt Lake City and a repair station.

9. Stories of this type prove
   (A) the toughness of rubber
   (B) the deadliness of rattlesnakes
   (C) the imaginative powers of Americans
   (D) the stupidity of some people

ANALYSIS:

The reader must realize that this is a _________ story.

If the reader sees the _________ in the story, then _________ must be the correct answer.

PRACTICE TEST 7

DIRECTIONS: Below each of the following paragraphs, you will find two incomplete statements. Each statement is followed by five words or phrases lettered (A) to (E). After reading each paragraph, read the statements beneath it. Then select the word or phrase that most satisfactorily completes each statement, and circle the corresponding letter.

Corn in its original state had grown wild. Primitive human beings must have found a simple way to cultivate it while it was a wild grass. Although it still resembles two of the wild grasses found today, the origin of our corn plant is lost somewhere in the long-distant past. If the corn stalks are not harvested, the cobs will, in time, fall to the ground, and the kernels on the cob will start to grow. The closely packed young plants will soon smother and choke each other. For this reason corn is thought to have been cultivated longer than other farm products.

1. Corn must be hand-planted because
   (A) it will not grow wild
   (B) the seeds must be separated
   (C) the seeds must be put into the ground
   (D) the kernels are delicate
   (E) the kernels are young

2. Primitive corn did not have
   (A) a cob
   (B) kernels
   (C) so many kernels
   (D) a stalk
   (E) few kernels

Francois René de Chateaubriand was born in 1768, and died in 1848. He devoted his life to the writing of novels. He marked the change from the old classical to the modern romantic French literature. He helped to continue the naturalism of Rousseau in two of his significant novels, *Atala* and *Rene*. Like so many others in the history of literature, he is little read today. He is important historically because he influenced so many later French writers, but his stories have lost their appeal to the reading public. They are to be found only on the shelves of the universities and not in the bookstores.

3. Chateaubriand
   (A) lived before Rousseau
   (B) was influenced by Rousseau
   (C) influenced Rousseau
   (D) disliked Rousseau
   (E) was disregarded by Rousseau

4. Chateaubriand's stories are
   (A) old-fashioned
   (B) not true to life
   (C) illogical
   (D) without merit
   (E) unreadable

Shall is derived from the Anglo-Saxon word *sceal,* which means *I am compelled* or *obliged. Will,* on the other hand, comes from *willan,* another Anglo-Saxon word, which means *I intend* or *plan.* Over the years, tradition has established certain rules for the use of *shall* and *will. Will* used with *I* or *we* shows internal resolve, as does *shall* used with the second or third person. When the two words are reversed, however, they express simple futurity. In other words, simple futurity is intended when *shall* is used with *I* or *we* or when *will* is used with other persons. However, in present-day usage, these fine distinctions between *shall* and *will,* which are still found in some grammar books, are no longer observed. Thus, this is an area in which the careful student of language must learn to find new means of expressing fine shades of difference.

5. Many writers of today
   (A) follow the rules for *shall* and *will* as found in grammar books
   (B) do not follow any of the rules in grammar books
   (C) do not follow the rules for *shall* and *will*
   (D) make up their own rules for *shall* and *will*
   (E) are slow to change

6. *Will*
   (A) had only one meaning
   (B) has so many meanings that it has lost all meaning
   (C) can be used as a helping verb
   (D) cannot be used as a helping verb
   (E) can be used only with *shall*

The man who boasted that he grew pumpkins so large that his wife hollowed one out and used half as a cradle, met his master. When he told his story, the other man told of two full-grown policemen in his city being found asleep on one beat. The latter added that in one of the backyards, the cornstalks were cut after harvest and sold as telephone poles.

7. From this you can conclude that
   (A) both men are married
   (B) only one is married
   (C) neither one is married
   (D) both men may be married
   (E) none of these

8. The master was a
   (A) policeman
   (B) farmer
   (C) citizen-farmer
   (D) townsman
   (E) truthseeker

An allegory is a story in which the characters are symbols of ideas. The actions and the settings may also be symbolical. A fable, on the other hand, is a short tale meant to convey a useful lesson. The characters are usually birds or animals that speak and act like human beings. The most famous fables are those of the Greek slave, Aesop. A parable, finally, is a short narrative designed to convey a useful lesson, a moral or spiritual truth. The characters and the actions are like those in our everyday surroundings. An example of a famous parable is that of the prodigal son in the *New Testament.*

9. The story of the Three Little Pigs, in this classification, would be
   (A) tale
   (B) allegory
   (C) fable
   (D) parable
   (E) narrative

10. A parable could be
    (A) an allegory but not a fable
    (B) a fable but not an allegory
    (C) a fable but not a story
    (D) an allegory and a fable
    (E) neither an allegory nor a fable

PRACTICE TEST 8

DIRECTIONS: Read each of the following paragraphs carefully. Then choose the phrase that best completes each of the statements below, and circle the corresponding letter.

The connection between the amount of cholesterol in the body and heart disease has not as yet been definitely proved. Much research is being conducted to determine whether this fat-hormone-like substance that floats around in the blood stream actually is a factor causing some forms of heart trouble and arterial disease. All that can be said now about this substance is that cholesterol can be made from food products already stored in the body.

1. Cholesterol is being investigated because
   (A) it causes heart disease
   (B) it is found in the blood stream
   (C) it is a fat-hormome-like substance
   (D) it can be stored in the body.

2. As a result of reading this paragraph doctors should tell their patients
   (A) to avoid foods containing cholesterol
   (B) to forget all about cholesterol
   (C) to eat less fatty food
   (D) nothing about cholesterol

The tourist was obviously one who was greatly amused by the countrified atmosphere of the lake district. He turned to one of the natives who was passing by. "I am most anxious," he said slowly, "to find accommodations for the night. Could you tell me which way the village lies?"

The man whom he had stopped looked at him unsmilingly. "It's likely to lie in almost any direction," he replied. "However, since this is the summer, it's usually about the size of the fish that we catch."

3. The villager replied to the visitor in this fashion
   (A) to be polite
   (B) to show off
   (C) to teach him a lesson
   (D) to sell him vegetables

4. As a result of the villager's reply, the tourist
   (A) had to ask more questions
   (B) became angry and left
   (C) went to the tourist home
   (D) was willing to buy the vegetables

The unbroken silence filled the vast plant that had been filled with the thunderous noises of modern machinery only a few hours ago. Time was when the giant wheels never ceased their grinding and shaping of cold metal under thousands of tons of pressure. The footsteps of trained mechanics had been muffled for years by the pounding conveyor-belt pulleys. But the mastermind of humanity had never left the plant during those busy productive years. However, now that the economy of the entire nation had slowed down, daily periods of silence filled the vast auditorium with uneasy emptiness. Occasional gusts of fresh night air eddied down the long corridors.

5. The time of this paragraph is
   (A) late morning
   (B) summertime
   (C) late evening
   (D) wintertime

6. The cause of the silence is
   (A) strikes
   (B) war
   (C) death
   (D) economic depression

Fear filled the eyes of the silent farmhand as he took a second glance skyward. He had not been mistaken. There it was growing larger and larger in all of its black ugliness. Like a giant funnel made of billowing cloth that could not hold its shape, it loomed larger and larger. The man no longer could control his panic as he rushed toward the house. If he could only have enough time to warn the others of the awful danger bearing down on them. His plan of action was clear. He would first awaken the others, and then he would rush to the barn and lead the animals to the comparative safety of the storm cellar. His breath was coming in sobs now as he bent down and grabbed a large stone that he hurled at the upper story window. He shouted, "Hurry! Get up!" as he stumbled against the door and pushed it open. "Hurry, if you want to live, hurry! A twister!"

7. The other people were most likely in
   (A) the kitchen
   (B) the barn
   (C) the bedroom
   (D) the cellar

8. The man was
   (A) a coward because he cried
   (B) a coward because he ran
   (C) brave because he ran to the cellar
   (D) brave because he tried to save others

As he left the room, he knew that he had been wrong. If he could only control his temper! He had let his anger flare up too quickly. His father did not let the remark go by. His mother as usual had sent the warning glance too late. She had kept her customary silence while the loud tones flew across the table. Then came the usual command. As he walked to his room, that familiar sense of unhappiness took the place of his spent anger. All this was so unnecessary. If only he could learn control! If only he could go beck into the room and tell them that it was all a mistake. He had let his tongue run away from him. He really did love his parents. They really were trying to do their best to help him grow up with self-respect.

9. The boy is most likely
   (A) four years old
   (B) eight years old
   (C) fourteen years old
   (D) twenty years old

10. The boy went to his room
   (A) to avoid continuing the fight
   (B) to get over his feeling of misery
   (C) because he had been told to
   (D) to receive his punishment

Improving Your Reading Skills

Here is a sound self-help plan for reading improvement.

1. Have a daily, varied reading program:
   browse through the encyclopedias,
   read sections of the daily newspaper (news stories, editorials, special columns),
   become interested in the lives of memorable people and read their biographies,
   read books dealing with hobbies,
   read and reread supplementary textbooks.
2. Be word-conscious. Add daily to your store of worthwhile words.
3. Concentrate when you read. *Nothing* should be able to distract you!
4. Read as fast as you can comfortably—and no faster. Speed comes from practice; don't let your anxieties rush you into skimming or scanning.

Below are key work-study skills designed to bring you up to the level of competency required to do well on the reading comprehension sections of standard examinations. Following each work-study skill is an exercise that will help you master it. After you have completed this section of this chapter, you will be ready to tackle the reading comprehension section that follows. Go through the latter section step by step. Use the diagnostic test in the beginning of the book to pinpoint your particular weakness in reading comprehension, and focus on that weakness. Do not, however, skip any part of the reading comprehension section if you wish to achieve the best results on a standard examination. Use the answer key at the end of the chapter to check your performance on exercises, practice tests, and Mastery Exams.

COMPOUND WORDS

Compound words are words made by combining two or more words:

haircut *watchman* *nevertheless*

While most compound words have a meaning derived from their parts, this is not true of all of them. Nevertheless, the skilled reader very often gains the meaning of an unfamiliar term by recognizing one or more of its elements.

LITERAL AND FIGURATIVE MEANINGS

Literal means true to the word-by-word meaning. The coach or the doctor may tell you to "go soak your head," meaning that you are to douse yourself with water.

Figurative denotes an implied meaning. When a friend angrily refuses your request and tells you to "go soak your head," he is telling you what he thinks of your request.

If the writer intends a figurative interpretation, readers will be out in left field if they take the statement literally. Let the next two sets of exercises help you to evaluate your ability in this area.

EXERCISE 7

If the italicized phrase in each of the following sentences is to be taken literally, then write literal *in the space provided; if it is meant to be understood figuratively, then write* figurative.

1. Within a few minutes, the skillful lecturer had his youthful audience *eating out of his hand.* ________
2. When I say *"Hands off!"* I mean just that! ________
3. I have to *hand it to you;* you certainly knew just what had to be said. ________
4. *All hands* on deck! ________
5. Give the new singer *a big hand!* ________
6. Keep your *big hands* out of the cookie jar! ________
7. The store on the corner *changed hands* four times in the past two years. ________
8. The fretful baby is *more than a handful* even for an experienced baby-sitter. ________
9. Please *hand me* a copy of the textbook. ________
10. Keep *the change!* ________
11. We arrived just when the train was *pulling out* of the station. ________
12. The pressure was so great on the fishing line that I felt that my arm was *being pulled out of its socket.* ________
13. You'll have to get up much earlier if you want to *pull the wool over her eyes!* ________
14. The storekeeper said that he *has enough pull* to have the police overlook the violation. ________
15. The car skidded and *turned turtle* before it smashed into the retaining wall. ________
16. *Turn into* Gelton Street and stop near the corner. ________
17. She has had a *splitting headache* all day. ________
18. How much did they pay you for *splitting the logs?* ________
19. If she ever *gets wind* of this, we will truly be in a *mess!* ________
20. How long does it take to *wind up* the clock? ________
21. I need two more hours *to wind up* my business with them. ________
22. I am not ready to *play second fiddle* to anyone! ________
23. Stop *playing with* your food! ________
24. To treat your friends that way is not my idea of *playing fair.* ________
25. He *has more heart* than any other player I know. ________

EXERCISE 8

Literal statements are usually easier to understand than ones requiring a figurative interpretation. The exercise that follows will help you sharpen your control of sentences that gain in meaning when taken figuratively.

Circle the letter of the word or phrase that most appropriately completes each of the following sentences.

1. Well done is better than well ________.
   (A) made (B) said (C) furnished
   (D) finished

2. They do not always ________ who put their boots on.
   (A) pay (B) sigh (C) shine (D) ride

3. They who feel the benefit should feel the ________.
   (A) time (B) cloth (C) burden (D) anger

4. The bell calls others but never minds the ________.
   (A) sermon (B) cost (C) danger
   (D) weather

5. The fuel removed, the fire will ________.
   (A) rise (B) begin (C) spread (D) die

6. The goodness of a thing is known when it is ________.
   (A) stored (B) lacking (C) described
   (D) totaled

7. Learning has no enemy but ________.
   (A) ignorance (B) time (C) waste
   (D) use

8. Promises and pie crusts are made to be ________.
   (A) seen (B) eaten (C) broken
   (D) well-baked

9. Drive the nail that will ________.
   (A) bend (B) loosen (C) rust (D) go

10. Suspicions are ________ the guilty.
    (A) natural to (B) unusual to
    (C) evidence to (D) wrong for

11. They that stay in the ________ will never get over the hill.
    (A) struggle (B) saddle (C) wagon
    (D) valley

12. It is impossible to ________ what never was good.
    (A) improve (B) spoil (C) destroy
    (D) discover

13. In crossing the ocean, we change the climate, not the ________.
    (A) cost (B) danger (C) person (D) joy

14. A grain of ________ is worth a pound of medicine.
    (A) sand (B) caution (C) food (D) gold

15. Do not ________ two rabbits with one dog.
    (A) hunt (B) house (C) compare
    (D) train

16. The coat does not make the ________.
    (A) cost (B) paint (C) brush (D) person

17. They must ________ who cannot sit upright.
    (A) argue (B) weep (C) stoop
    (D) explain

18. Wine has ________ more people than the sea ever did.
    (A) fancied (B) drowned (C) saved
    (D) enriched

19. The spider extracts ________ where the bee gathers honey.
    (A) poison (B) air (C) fear
    (D) goodness

20. Doing things by halves is ________; it may be the other half that counts.
    (A) sensible (B) valuable (C) poetic
    (D) worthless

21. If you have nothing to ________, you can try anything.
    (A) offer (B) say (C) lose (D) reveal

22. Don't ________ ideas; put them to work.
    (A) execute (B) entertain (C) interpret
    (D) request

23. The great ________ of life is not knowledge but action.
    (A) end (B) cause (C) person (D) loss

24. Real ________ is when you don't try to make the best of a bad bargain.
    (A) success (B) failure (C) worry (D) joy

25. ________ makes time fly swiftly.
    (A) Lectures (B) Happiness (C) Homework (D) Illness

SPECIFIC AND GENERAL MEANINGS

A *specific statement* is based on a given instance.

At three o'clock, I went shopping.

A *general statement* (generalization) deals with a group or class of actions as a principle, a rule.

I always go shopping at three o'clock.
All the students go shopping at three o'clock.

Specific statements are usually easier to comprehend; they require less of the reader. The general statement demands an additional step; the alert reader must examine it for a possible range of exceptions that may weaken its validity. Use the exercises that follow to check your control of specific statements and generalizations.

EXERCISE 9

In the space provided, label each of the following statements as either specific (S) *or* general (G).

__ 1. Just when the TV play reached its most exciting moment, our set went out of order.

__ 2. I always have to do the dishes when my sister forgets.

__ 3. Every student should support our school teams.

__ 4. The coach praised the captain of the team for his wise decision.

__ 5. Our football coach never forgets to give credit where credit is due.

__ 6. I would no more keep an animal in a cage in a zoo than I would so imprison myself as a spectacle behind bars!

__ 7. The officers did not have time yesterday to react to our list of complaints.

__ 8. The sound of the TV program is so loud, I can't hear myself think!

__ 9. Why must you always play your radio so loud!

__ 10. The first of the disarmament conferences was the Washington Conference for the Limitation of Armaments in 1921.

__ 11. The great advances in medical science have produced one of our major problems—the population explosion.

__ 12. Every generation has felt that it was progressing too fast for its own benefit.

__ 13. The doctor checked my glasses when I told him I was having trouble reading.

__ 14. Teenagers tend to imitate their friends rather than their elders.

__ 15. My sister generously offered to help me when I told her that I couldn't do my math homework.

__ 16. You always become irritable when someone tries to help you!

__ 17. I can't do the problem!

__ 18. That type of problem always gives me trouble.

__ 19. The truth will out!

__ 20. The more you have the more you lose!

EXERCISE 10

General statements are usually more difficult to handle than specific statements. Try your hand at the following.

Following each of the given generalizations is a group of words or phrases. Circle the letter of the word or phrase that most satisfactorily completes each sentence.

1. Think like a person of action, act like a person of ________.
(A) activity (B) wealth (C) thought (D) fear

2. When you see a snake, never ________ where it came from.
(A) tell (B) mind (C) depict (D) gaze at

3. A hero is no braver than others; he is only ________ five minutes longer.
(A) present (B) fearful (C) concerned (D) brave

4. I am always ready to learn, although I do not always like being ________.
(A) taught (B) right (C) seen (D) lenient

5. There is no ________ in any job. The future lies in the person who holds the job.
(A) greatness (B) future (C) promotion (D) wealth

6. The way to win a nuclear war is to make certain it never ________.
(A) starts (B) ends (C) is encouraged (D) is negotiated

7. We have to live today by what truth we can get today, and be ready tomorrow to call it ________.
(A) honestly (B) falsehood (C) everlasting (D) narrow

8. Most people like hard work, especially when they are ________ for it.
(A) paid (B) paying (C) dressed (D) punished

9. Every age is ________ to those living in it.
(A) stern (B) useless (C) humorous (D) modern

10. The chief cause of human errors is to be found in the ________ picked up in childhood.
(A) prejudices (B) toys (C) friends (D) joys

11. People have one thing in common: they are ________.
(A) generous (B) different (C) thoughtful (D) concerned

12. A proverb is a short sentence based on long ________.
(A) words (B) days (C) ideals (D) experience

13. Words are the signs of our ________ only and are not things themselves.
(A) times (B) ideas (C) property (D) concerns

14. Even if you are on the right track, you will get ________ if you just sit there.
(A) run over (B) ahead (C) in trouble (D) tired

15. If you want the present to be different from the past, ________ the past.
(A) reject (B) flee (C) study (D) live in

16. You get the chicken by ________ the egg, not smashing it.
(A) eating (B) boiling (C) finding (D) hatching

17. Pride makes some people appear ________ but prevents others from becoming so.
(A) clever (B) ridiculous (C) wealthy (D) sensible

18. A city on a hill cannot be ________.
(A) hidden (B) bombed (C) developed (D) excavated

19. Books that are kept on a shelf and never read will help ________.
(A) nobody (B) solve problems (C) prevent war (D) the poor student

20. The process of learning is neither _________ nor always pleasant.
    (A) inspired (B) easy (C) productive (D) constructive

21. _________ makes no distinction between good and evil.
    (A) Justice (B) Government (C) Nature (D) Punishment

22. It is possible to __________ too much. A person with one watch knows the time; a person with two watches is never quite sure.
    (A) know (B) own (C) develop (D) tell

23. Today the real test of power is not the capacity to make war but the capacity to _________ it.
    (A) analyze (B) foresee (C) encircle (D) prevent

24. _________ boats must keep near shore.
    (A) Sturdy (B) Big (C) Cargo (D) Little

25. The hen is the egg's way of producing another _________.
    (A) roast (B) error (C) egg (D) meal

EXERCISE 11

Examination items on figurative language often require the candidate to explain a generalization.

Following each of the proverbs presented below is a series of sentences. Circle the letter of the sentence that is the most appropriate application of the proverb.

1. Little boats should keep near shore.
   (A) Children should be seen and not heard.
   (B) The smaller you are, the more fearful you must be.
   (C) Never take chances.
   (D) Know your own limits and act accordingly.

2. We boil at different degrees.
   (A) Not everyone can be a good cook.
   (B) Some people are much more tolerant than others.
   (C) The sun affects different people differently.
   (D) We are all brothers under the skin.

3. When all else is lost, the future yet remains.
   (A) Tomorrow is always another day.
   (B) We learn too slowly where our fortunes lie.
   (C) Always hope for the best.
   (D) Always do your best.

4. When the blind carry the banner, woe to those that follow.
   (A) It is always better to be modest and not boastful.
   (B) The wise learn from the mistakes of others.
   (C) Success of a group effort depends on the skill of the leaders.
   (D) Prejudice can make the efforts of any group a failure.

5. They know the water best who have waded through it.
   (A) Perseverance is the secret of success.
   (B) Water should be tested before it is used for drinking purposes.
   (C) Even the best swimmers must be cautious.
   (D) Practice is the best teacher.

6. The dog that trots about finds the bone.
   (A) Hours of dreaming are hours of accomplishing.
   (B) Dogs make the best pets.
   (C) Nothing comes without toil.
   (D) Talking things over can lead to successful planning.

7. Old foxes want no tutors.
   (A) Animals learn through imitation how to do things.
   (B) It is not hard to teach an old dog new tricks.
   (C) Elderly people are set in their ways.
   (D) Senior citizens deserve special considerations.

8. The smallest worm will turn, being trodden on.
   (A) Even the most timid can be made to fight back.
   (B) Every worm has its turn.
   (C) One good turn deserves another.
   (D) Good things come in small packages.

9. The shell must break before the bird can fly.
   (A) We must do first things first.
   (B) The early bird catches the worm.
   (C) We must keep our houses in order.
   (D) Birds of a feather flock together.

10. It never troubles the wolf how many sheep there are.
   (A) The one who works alone does best.
   (B) Evil doers are not concerned about their victims.
   (C) There is comfort in numbers.
   (D) You can't tell a wolf by its clothing.

11. All sunshine makes the desert.
   (A) Water is essential to life.
   (B) Rome was not built in a day.
   (C) Too much of a good thing can be harmful.
   (D) Study thoroughly; work hard; enjoy much.

12. Small to great matters must give way.
   (A) In an emergency, you must set priorities.
   (B) Little children, little worries; big children, big worries.
   (C) It is the purpose, not the deed, that decides worth.
   (D) Success waits for no person.

13. They who seek truth should be of no country.
   (A) Patriotism must not be questioned.
   (B) There is no American chemistry, no Russian biology, no English physics.
   (C) Research contradicts the brotherhood of man.
   (D) Prejudice can injure us.

14. Vanity is the fruit of ignorance.
   (A) Those who are in love with themselves are on the way to lose themselves.
   (B) The more we know, the more we realize how insignificant we are.
   (C) The greater the task, the greater the person who must do it.
   (D) Pride leads to humility.

15. Wealth consists not in having great possessions but in having few wants.
   (A) The miser is always poor.
   (B) Count your good deeds as your true wealth.
   (C) Need not, want not.
   (D) He is rich who is in control of his desire.

SIGNAL WORDS

Signal words are words or phrases that do not contain the main ideas but show relationships.

Time: when, before, soon, during
Order: least, of most importance, next
Joining: and, in addition, also
Separating: but, on the other hand, yet
Summarizing: therefore, all-in-all, now

The list of signal words is endless, but the alert reader looks for these words and phrases because they group ideas and aid in anticipating the author's intent.

EXERCISE 12

Circle the letter of the word or phrase that best fits each of the following descriptions.

1. A word that introduces secondary rather than main ideas
   (A) the (B) a (C) while (D) however

2. A phrase that begins a qualifying or contradictory statement
   (A) on the other hand
   (B) in the meantime
   (C) whichever comes first
   (D) rising to the occasion

3. A word or phrase that does *not* usually introduce equal elements
(A) and (B) either (C) or (D) since

4. A word that does *not* usually signal cause
(A) since (B) consequently
(C) altogether (D) because

5. A word that is *not* used to signal time
(A) when (B) since (C) while (D) what

6. A word that is *not* used to point out
(A) that (B) this (C) those (D) any

7. The word among the following that shows least frequency
(A) seldom (B) customarily
(C) usually (D) rarely

8. A word that shows both place and action at the same time
(A) in (B) into (C) on (D) by

9. A word that can be used to signal either time or place
(A) and (B) in (C) but (D) nor

10. A word used to refer mainly to people rather than to places or things
(A) which (B) that (C) who (D) what

11. A word or phrase that signals a change in thought direction
(A) however (B) of course
(C) continuing (D) in addition

12. A word or phrase that does *not* show that the end is approaching
(A) hence (B) lastly (C) in conclusion
(D) in order that

13. A word that does *not* point toward a specific time of the day
(A) sun-up (B) sunset (C) daily
(D) twilight

14. A word *not* used to point out location
(A) from (B) over (C) if (D) by

15. A word used to point out an exception
(A) and (B) if (C) but (D) consequently

16. A word rarely used to point out cause or result
(A) because (B) even (C) for (D) since

17. Two words or phrases *not* usually used as a pair
(A) both...and (B) not only...but also
(C) neither...together (D) either...or

18. A word that rarely introduces a question
(A) who (B) which (C) what (D) there

FACTS AND OPINIONS

Facts are beliefs that are widely accepted as having been proved or capable of being proved for a given group. At one time, that the world was flat was an accepted fact!

Opinions are beliefs that are accepted by a limited portion of a group. Evidence must be presented to convince others. "*I think it is wrong (right) because . . .*" is always involved with opinions. Alert readers must always be ready to classify authors' statements as facts or opinions. Having our critical reasoning thus involved in what we read always increases our concentration and makes the material easier to understand.

EXERCISE 13

In the space provided, label each of the following statements as either fact (F) *or* opinion (O).

__ 1. Four ounces of cottage cheese contains fewer calories than four ounces of cheddar cheese.

__ 2. Cottage cheese is tastier than cheddar cheese.

__ 3. Beginning in July 1940, German aircraft bombarded England day and night.

__ 4. The British held out throughout 1940–41 despite all the destruction caused by the German round-the-clock bombing.

__ 5. The unconquered British showed more courage than did their Allies whom the Germans had conquered.

__ 6. The class that people belong to in South America is generally based on the amount of money they make.

__ 7. Few of the South American countries in 1979 had much industry or mechanization.

__ 8. People may someday conquer the Amazon the way they have gained control over the other major rivers of the world.

__ 9. Elementary school students wear uniforms in many South American countries.

__ 10. The University of San Marcos in Lima, Peru, began in 1551.

__ 11. Haiti won its independence in 1863, years before any of the other Latin American colonies.

__ 12. There should be no charge for parking in small-town business sections.

__ 13. People today spend too much of their spare time watching television programs.

__ 14. There are more suburbanites today than there are central city residents.

__ 15. People years ago were convinced that the sun revolved around the earth.

__ 16. We should think twice before contacting creatures living in outer space because they might come and conquer us as we have conquered the other creatures on earth.

__ 17. Anything that significantly changes the composition of the air around us can be a threat to our survival.

__ 18. All who are willing to work hard and do what they are told will get ahead and make it to the top.

__ 19. People cannot be hypnotized against their will.

__ 20. If others have survived experimenting with dangerous drugs, so will I!

PICKING THE SUBJECT

The *subject* is what the sentence or paragraph deals with. Usually the subject is a single noun or a noun phrase.

The *price* is much too high.

Scientific ingenuity has both simplified and complicated our lives.

The author does not always signal the subject by putting it at the beginning of the sentence or even in the first sentence.

On the floor next to the large carton was the missing *notebook*.

After long hours of bitter anxiety, it suddenly dawned on me! There was no longer any doubt where the *key* was hidden.

Often the grammatical subject of the sentence can be different from the logical subject of the sentence or sentences.

The creation of new weaponry has resulted in dynamic changes of army strategy.

In the above sentence, *creation* is the grammatical subject, but *new weaponry* is the logical subject of the thought content.

Your first task, as a reader, is to find the logical subject of a selection. Once you have located the key word or phrase, following the author's thoughts becomes much simpler. How skillful are you at unraveling sentences?

EXERCISE 14

Circle the word or phrase that is the logical (not necessarily the grammatical) subject of each of the following sentences.

1. Even at very early stages of development, human beings lived together in social groups.
2. When underground water comes in contact with lava, it will often emerge as a hot spring when it flows to the earth's surface.
3. Within the enlarged base of the flower are tiny white structures known as ovules.
4. In July 1945, on a remote desert spot in New Mexico, there occurred an event that will affect countless generations to come—the explosion of the first atomic bomb.
5. Not too many years ago, airplane travel was avoided by many people who considered it dangerous and uncertain.
6. In many local elections, the school budget becomes one of the major issues.
7. More than any other court in the United States, the Supreme Court creates precedents through its decisions and interpretations.
8. Finally in July 1953, shortly after the death of Stalin, a cease-fire agreement was reached in Korea.
9. One of the pressing problems of our times has been the alarming increase in crimes of violence.
10. A second industrial revolution is being brought about by automation, the use of machines to control other machines and to take the place of human effort, observation, and even judgment.
11. In most instances, inventions consist mainly of combining a number of already known ideas into something new.
12. Specifically, urban renewal consists of much more that just the construction of public housing for low-income families.
13. In the other countries of the world, too, there has been a startling and rapid development of mass communication.
14. In the foundation years of the United States, there was practically no free public education as we know it today.
15. That success in life does not necessarily bring happiness or a sense of security has long been shown by psychological and sociological investigations.
16. One of the remarkable political developments of our history is the way in which the powers of the president have increased.
17. In general, however, inorganic compounds have relatively simple chemical structures.
18. Although some types of bacteria cause human diseases, others assist us by causing the decay of dead plants and animals, thus returning organic matter and minerals to the soil.
19. Because Hinduism does not insist that all its adherents agree on what they believe or in how they worship, the chief ideas of Hinduism are difficult to describe.
20. Even though more than 15 major languages are recognized in India, the government has declared English and Hindi as the two official languages.

SENTENCE SENSE

The sentence is a unit of thought. It is the building block in the development of a paragraph. If the reader of a selection understands the thought content sentence by sentence, he or she soon grasps the meaning of the paragraph.

The following exercises will help you judge your control of sentence meanings.

EXERCISE 15

Circle the letter of the pair of words or phrases that most appropriately completes each of the following sentences.

1. In the early days of the factory system, people thought that the government had no right to _______ with business, and so no one forced the factory owners to treat their workers_________.
(A) combine...poorly
(B) interfere...fairly
(C) deal...consistently
(D) discuss...as partners

2. President Franklin D. Roosevelt _____ the Good Neighbor policy, which called for action by all the American governments, rather than by the United States alone, when _________ arose in any of the American nations.
(A) condemned...dictators
(B) praised...peace
(C) ended...prosperity
(D) established...difficulties

3. _______ of refuse and garbage at open dumps long remained a major _______ of air pollution in many of our cities.
(A) Purchasing...result
(B) Burning...cause
(C) Consideration...concern
(D) Collection...benefit

4. More than 2,000 years ago, the Chinese emperors _________ a postal system so that they could send official ________ throughout the empire.
(A) imagined...programs
(B) instituted...decrees
(C) improved...judges
(D) destroyed...agents

5. Thomas Jefferson _________ the role of the President as the party leader who _________ the legislative branch of the government.
(A) rejected...joined
(B) ridiculed...rejected
(C) relied on...established
(D) established...dominated

6. Children have to be _________ slowly and patiently the skills which are needed to deal with the _________ of living.
(A) taught...problems
(B) allowed...art
(C) denied...cost
(D) clarified...possibilities

7. The emphasis on violence and crime in so many TV programs has led young people to ________ violence as a means of _________ problems.
(A) reject...causing
(B) accept...solving
(C) use...making
(D) realize...dissolving

8. When India gained its __________, the organization and principles of the new nation _____________ basic features of American, British, French, and other democratic governments.
(A) reputation...formed
(B) independence...reflected
(C) wealth...rejected
(D) power...desired

9. When a bar magnet is _________ at the center so that it may ________ freely, it always comes to rest pointing north and south.
(A) fastened...not move
(B) split...spin
(C) painted...settle
(D) suspended...swing

10. Because of political and military _____ the United States has always been eager to _______ stable, friendly, peace-loving governments throughout the Western Hemisphere.
(A) considerations...see
(B) dictators...vote for
(C) dangers...reject
(D) power...combine

11. The small force under Cortez was _____ to conquer the Aztec empire because Indian war clubs were so ________ to cannon and muskets.
(A) foolish...incomparable
(B) unwilling...superior
(C) seen...comparable
(D) able...inferior

12. When a stream of water flows in a ________ path, it tends to wear away the softer and looser material to ______ a ditch or gully.
(A) slow...elevate
(B) downward...form
(C) swift...erect
(D) steady...destroy

13. Customs tend to remain ________ once they become firmly ________ a group.
(A) weak...developed
(B) effective...rejected by
(C) colorful...discussed by
(D) unchanged...established in

14. As modern life becomes more complex, government ________ its functions and becomes more ________.
(A) enforces...unacceptable
(B) slows down...effective
(C) multiplies...powerful
(D) considers...considerate

15. The modern period of African history ________ in the fifteenth century with the ________ of Portuguese sailors, explorers, and settlers.
(A) ended...loss
(B) flourished...atrocities
(C) lasted...destruction
(D) began...coming

EXERCISE 16

From the list of words below each of the following sentences, select the two that most appropriately complete the sentence. Write them in the spaces provided.

1. What is needed in Alaska today is not the complete ___(A)___ of productive activities but a ___(B)___ of such activities to make sure that they do not destroy our last fontier.
ownership government control
source banning
(A) ________
(B) ________

2. In Lamarck's theory, millions of years ago the giraffes were ___(A)___ animals that ate leaves from lower branches, and as they stretched their necks to reach the higher branches, their necks tended to grow longer; the ___(B)___ done by the parents gave their children longer necks before they were born.
intelligent thinking stretching
mischief short-necked
(A) ________
(B) ________

3. When DDT was first used, there were very few flies which were immune to this poison. The only ones that survived were those few that spread rapidly without the ___(A)___ of the others. Soon DDT-resistant types ___(B)___ a large part of the total fly population.
destroyed competition destruction
made up aid
(A) ________
(B) ________

4. In the past, most of the peoples of Africa grew their own food and made their own clothing. They had little use for ___(A)___. Whatever ___(B)___ was done was on the barter system. Products and crops were traded for foreign goods and bright clothing.
travel trading agriculture
money wealth
(A) ________
(B) ________

5. A vaccine obtained from the blood of calves that have had cowpox is injected into people's arms. If the people are susceptible to the disease they develop a mild case of smallpox. Their bodies produce antitoxin to ___(A)___ the virus, and they soon recover. The antitoxin remains in their bloodstream for several years, thus protecting them from further ___(B)___ of smallpox.
destroy reproduce injections
protect attacks
(A) ________
(B) ________

6. The Supreme Court by a unanimous vote in 1954 declared that racially segregated education can never be truly ___(A)___ education. The Court further ordered local school boards to set up programs of ___(B)___ with all deliberate speed.

significance integration valuable equal irrigation

(A) ____________

(B) ____________

7. Most of the year, the ports of the former Soviet Union that border on the Arctic Ocean are icebound and much of the coast is closed to ___(A)___. Because it is adjacent to the North Atlantic Drift, a warm current which ___(B)___ from the Gulf Stream, Murmansk is Russia's only northern-most harbor that is free from ice throughout the year.

empties into flows from attack industry navigation

(A) ____________

(B) ____________

8. Experimental study of animal behavior has shown that the behavior of animals can be ___(A)___ when changes in the environment so dictate. Animals have shown amounts of intelligence beyond our expectations. The differences between human beings and other animals is a matter of degree, not in the kind of ___(B)___.

brutality modified causation behavior sensed

(A) ____________

(B) ____________

9. Plastics are an increasingly ___(A)___ element in solid wastes. Many of them cannot be reduced to simpler forms that then can be put back into the life cycle. In incinerators most plastics foul the grate because they melt rather than ___(B)___.

disappear beneficial dissolve troublesome burn

(A) ____________

(B) ____________

10. The kerosene lamp works on the same principle as the candle. However, the fuel in the lamp starts as a liquid rather than a ___(A)___. The kerosene is drawn up through the wick and is vaporized by the heat of the ___(B)___.

solid flame candle gas draft

(A) ____________

(B) ____________

SENTENCE RELATIONSHIPS

Each sentence in the paragraph is related in thought content to the others. The reader must be trained to look for this relationship, which reveals the meaning of the entire selection. The exercises that follow will help you to review three of the more usual sentence connections.

EXERCISE 17

Main Ideas and Related Details

In the space provided, label each sentence in each of the following sets as main idea (M) *or* detail (D).

1. __ (A) More than 70% of the people of Japan live in big cities.
   __ (B) The islands of Japan contain more than 100 million people.

2. __ (A) Superiority based on arms is at best relative and temporary.
   __ (B) The advantage gained by a nation when it acquires a new weapon disappears when its rival acquires a similar weapon.

3. __ (A) Almost a century of campaigning was necessary before the women's liberation movement brought about significant changes.
   __ (B) Often a great deal of opposition must be overcome before changes are made in our society.

4. __ (A) To keep an idea alive, propagandists present it over and over, again and again.
   __ (B) One of the basic principles of propaganda is repetition.

5. __ (A) Dogs seem to suffer from the same types of air pollutants as human beings do.
   __ (B) Many of the air pollutants have proved to be highly poisonous to animals.

6. __ (A) The beneficial as well as the pest varieties of insects are killed.
   __ (B) When DDT is spread through an area, it kills all insects.

7. __ (A) Iron ore, coal, and oil are said to be found in great amounts.
   __ (B) Russia claims that it has mineral wealth beyond measure.

8. __ (A) A number of organisms are used in the study of heredity and genetics.
   __ (B) The fruit fly *Drosophila* has long been a major experimental animal.

9. __ (A) Radiation time-clock methods have been used to study the age of the older layers of rocks in the earth.
   __ (B) The uranium-lead ratio and the potassium-argon ratio have been most accurate.

10. __ (A) Under Genghis Khan, the Mongols were organized into one of the most dreaded war machines in human history.
    __ (B) The Mongols conquered or destroyed all that stood in their path.

11. __ (A) Peter the Great wanted to make Russia into a rich commercial country.
    __ (B) Peter the Great established many new industries.

12. __ (A) The greatest of all eroding forces is running water.
    __ (B) Waterfalls, rivers, and ocean waves have done more to alter the surface of the earth than any other factor.

13. __ (A) Corn, for example, is the most important cereal grown in the United States.
    __ (B) Cereals are grasses that yield a grain that is used for food.

14. __ (A) The dhoti is worn by men and the sari by women in the villages of India.
    __ (B) In the villages of India, custom has decreed a traditional dress.

15. __ (A) With one Representative and two Senators, Alaska has three electors in the Electoral College.
    __ (B) Each state is allowed the same number of electors in the Electoral College as it has members in Congress.

EXERCISE 18

Cause and Effect

In the space provided, label each sentence in each of the following pairs as cause (C) *or* effect (E) *(result).*

1. __ (A) The nomads in the Sahara in Africa spend their lives in search of waterholes and green grazing grass.
   __ (B) There is never enough plant life in the Sahara to feed the goats and cattle on which their lives depend.

2. __ (A) Parents could do almost anything to their children.
   __ (B) Children were regarded as property of their parents.

3. __ (A) Women had been taught that their major role was to do what their fathers and husbands told them to do.
   __ (B) For generations women destroyed their ability to think and act for themselves.

4. __ (A) At present levels of TV advertising, the typical 17-year-old will have been exposed to more than 350,000 commercials.
   __ (B) Young people watch more than 24 hours of TV a week.

5. __ (A) Until 1947, princes ruled about 40% of India.
   __ (B) The maharajahs had the power of life and death over their subjects.

6. __ (A) Nitrogen neither burns nor supports combustion.
   __ (B) Nitrogen is a rather inactive element.

7. __ (A) We may someday live in a world without the necessity of work.
   __ (B) As more and more industries become automated, machines are taking over the means of production.

8. __ (A) A true pacifist feeling appeared in wide evidence among the Japanese people.
   __ (B) It is unlikely that any large scale revival of military aggression against its neighbors would be considered.

9. __ (A) The general flow of air on the earth's surface is toward the equator away from both poles.
   __ (B) There are great differences in temperature between the polar regions and the equatorial zone.

10. __ (A) People who have experienced severe poverty in childhood may be haunted for the rest of their lives by a fear of being poor.
    __ (B) The fear of poverty may show up later on as a drive to be better than all the other workers in the factory.

11. __ (A) During his lifetime Buddha did not put his teachings in written form.
    __ (B) After Buddha's death, his faithful followers collected his beliefs in books called *Sutras.*

12. __ (A) French governors often removed African rulers and chiefs.
    __ (B) French policy showed little respect for the traditional way of life in their colonies.

13. __ (A) The tsar's greatest ambition was to make Russia like the nations of Western Europe.
    __ (B) Peter the Great developed many new industries.

14. __ (A) Islam regulates all aspects of life.
    __ (B) Islam is an all-embracing religion.

15. __ (A) Whenever the vice presidency becomes vacant, the President nominates a new Vice President.
    __ (B) The person nominated by the President takes office after being confirmed by a majority vote of both houses of Congress.

EXERCISE 19

Reaching Conclusions

From the lettered statements below each of the following sentences, choose the one that is the most logical conclusion that can be drawn from the sentence. Circle the letter of that conclusion.

1. The nation's industries use very large quantities of fresh water for cooling during many manufacturing processes.
   (A) Only purified water can be used in cooling processes.
   (B) The manufacturers can use the same water over and over.
   (C) Industry must develop systems for disposing of considerable amounts of hot water.
   (D) The water used by industry is polluted and cannot be used again.

2. Planet Earth is a closed system with limited space and limited resources.
   (A) Earth is continually shrinking.
   (B) There is no limit to the number of human beings Earth can support.
   (C) Life on Earth is doomed.
   (D) A point could be reached at which Earth could no longer support life.

3. In traditional Japanese ink drawings, the artist tries to paint a state of mind rather than an exact copy of some object.
   (A) Japanese ink drawings resemble camera snapshots.
   (B) Japanese ink drawings have vivid colors.
   (C) Most Japanese ink drawings are of people.
   (D) Japanese ink drawings give the feeling rather than the appearance of some living quality.

4. Very little of the Aztec goldwork remains because the Spaniards melted it down into bars.
   (A) The Aztec jewelry was all of gold.
   (B) The Spaniards felt that the Aztec gold designs were not beautiful.
   (C) The Aztec jewelry was in thin, leaflike designs.
   (D) Gold bars are easier to transport than gold jewelry.

5. Only about one in ten of the known microbes is harmful to human beings.
   (A) There are more beneficial than harmless microbes.
   (B) There are more harmful than harmless microbes.
   (C) There are more harmful than beneficial microbes.
   (D) None of the above statements can be inferred from the given sentence.

6. About one fourth of the workers in the United States belong to some kind of labor union.
   (A) Most older workers belong to unions.
   (B) Most workers do not belong to unions.
   (C) Unions have bettered the living conditions of workers.
   (D) Unions encourage young people to learn trades.

7. In Russia, parents are often blamed by the authorities if children misbehave.
   (A) Russian children are the wards of the state.
   (B) Russian children are given more freedom than are American children.
   (C) Russian parents can be fined if children cross against a traffic light.
   (D) Russian parents are better than are American parents.

8. The greater number of men than women working in such areas as business and government is due to social rather than biological factors.
   (A) Women are physically weaker than men.
   (B) Women are better workers than men.
   (C) Custom has kept women out of politics.
   (D) There is proof that women could not do as well as men do as mayors, governors, or President.

9. The machinery of the Industrial Revolution made the production of goods easier and quicker.
   (A) Machinery improved the appearance of the goods being sold.
   (B) Machinery speeded up the manufacturing process.
   (C) Machinery added to the cost of production.
   (D) Machinery lessened the cost of production.

10. There are many more divorces today than in the first half of the twentieth century.
   (A) People now are less happy than they were then.
   (B) Divorce as a solution is more acceptable today.
   (C) There are more people living today.
   (D) People are marrying at an earlier age today.

EXERCISE 20

Review of Sentence Relationships

In the spaces provided write the words that are missing in each of the following groups of sentences.

1. At the close of World War II, the Soviet Union created a belt of satellite states in Eastern Europe. The key purpose was to create a ____(A)____ zone to absorb any possible ____(B)____ attack from the West.

   (A) ______________

   (B) ______________

2. Agriculture had long been the major occupation of Canada. Because of its vast expanses of ___(A)___ soil, it is one of the world's ___(B)___ exporters of wheat.
   (A) ____________
   (B) ____________

3. The very existence of nuclear weapons confonts humanity with the most fateful choice in its history on earth. Steps must be taken to ___(A)___ their use by irresponsible governments to bring about the inevitable ___(B)___ of life on earth.
   (A) ____________
   (B) ____________

4. Labor's efforts to bring more people into unions have not had marked success in recent years. The high wage scales for blue-collar workers ___(A)___ workers' interest in joining unions; clerical workers usually are by and large ___(B)___ to unionization.
   (A) ____________
   (B) ____________

5. In the fourth century, the people of Ghana created a vast empire because they were able to exploit their advantage over their neighbors. They alone knew the secret of making iron ___(A)___ and ___(B)___.
   (A) ____________
   (B) ____________

6. While the League of Nations controlled the ambitions of smaller nations, it was not powerful enough to enforce obedience among the larger countries. It could not ___(A)___ Japan from ___(B)___ Manchuria from China or ___(A)___ Italy from seizing Ethiopia.
   (A) ____________
   (B) ____________

7. The deep snow and ice of Russian winter stopped the tanks and motorized units of the Germans, but the Soviet soldiers, who were ___(A)___ to these conditions, were able to ___(B)___ and retake many important places.
   (A) ____________
   (B) ____________

8. We seek peace—enduring peace. More than an ___(A)___ to war, we want an end to this brutal, inhuman method of ___(B)___ the differences between governments.
   (A) ____________
   (B) ____________

9. The pictures that the ancient Egyptian artists drew in their temples and tombs are still considered beautiful and are greatly ___(A)___ today. The colors they used were so good that in most cases they have not ___(B)___ through all the centuries that have passed.
   (A) ____________
   (B) ____________

10. The family is the most important unit of society in Latin America. The father is the recognized ___(A)___ of the family with the mother next in ___(B)___.
    (A) ____________
    (B) ____________

11. In Japan there was a heavy demand after World War II for wood products because the bombings had destroyed many structures. To save their forests from being wiped out, the Japanese ___(A)___ the steel and concrete industries to aid in new ___(B)___.
    (A) ____________
    (B) ____________

12. All streams normally carry amounts of soil and rock particles. Only when the siltation becomes ___(A)___ does a pollution ___(B)___ exist.
    (A) ____________
    (B) ____________

13. The use of the energy of flowing or falling water to create electrical power is ideal from the ecological point of view. Power derived from water creates no ___(A)___ and uses up no ___(B)___ fuel resources.
    (A) ____________
    (B) ____________

14. The public expects the police and the law courts to enforce the law and punish lawbreakers. These agencies cannot do an ___(A)___ job unless they have the full support of the ___(B)___.
(A) ______________
(B) ______________

15. An audience is different from a crowd. Audience refers to ___(A)___ come together for the purpose of listening to or observing some proceedings in accordance with a ___(B)___ set in advance.
(A) ______________
(B) ______________

PARAGRAPH UNITS

Effective readers rarely go through a paragraph word by word. Rather, they see the paragraph as a series of connected word groups. The smaller groups, phrases, flow together into a thought unit, a sentence. When readers come to the end of each sentence, they pause, if necessary, to make certain that they have followed the trend of thought. They thus continue from sentence to sentence through the paragraph.

Use the following exercise to evaluate your ability to recognize thought units in a paragraph.

EXERCISE 21

Place the missing periods and capital letters in each of the following paragraphs and then fill in the blanks in the sentences below.

Psychologists taught Washoe to communicate in a sign language used by deaf people it took five years for her to learn 160 words five years is a long period of time Washoe, however, was the first chimpanzee to use sign language.

1. The paragraph contains ___________ sentences.
2. The second sentence begins with _____.
3. The last sentence begins with _______.

The Gypsies probably originated in India there are more than three million Gypsies throughout the world the word *Gypsy* derives from the false idea that the group came from Egypt Gypsies call themselves *Rom,* their word for man.

4. The paragraph contains ___________ sentences.
5. The last word in the first sentence is ___________.
6. The third sentence ends with the word ___________.

There are 35 to 40 known varieties of electric fish capable of discharging electricity that they produce themselves all except two, the electric eel and the torpedo ray, are harmless the torpedo ray and the electric eel when full grown are capable of injuring large mammals the electric eel is probably the only one capable of killing a full-grown person in good health.

7. The number of sentences in the paragraph is __________.
8. The second sentence begins with _____.
9. ___________ is a word below that does not begin a sentence.
there the all that
10. The last word of the third sentence is ___________.

Uri Geller became known throughout the world for his claims as a person having psychic power he says that he bends spoons, pins, and other things through the power of his mind some scientists claim that he has shown his abilities under laboratory conditions others call him a clever trickster out for fame and fortune.

11. The number of sentences in this paragraph is __________.
12. __________ is a letter below that does not begin a sentence.
S H O A

13. The last word of the third sentence is ________.

14. The first word of the second sentence is ________.

Benito Juarez led the Mexicans to victory over the French who tried to establish Maximilian of Austria as Emperor of Mexico Juarez has often been compared to Abraham Lincoln Lincoln and Juarez had many of the same liberal ideals Juarez tried to make land ownership possible for wealthy farmers he tried to spread the tax burden more evenly he wanted the same justice for both rich and poor.

15. The number of sentences is ________.

16. No sentence begins with________.
    Benito who Juarez Lincoln

17. The first sentence ends with ________.

18. The third sentence ends with ________.

19. The last sentence begins with ________.

20. The word below that seems to have been used in error is ________.
    Juarez wealthy Lincoln ideals

EXERCISE 22

Decide, from the lettered choices, the best order in which to arrange the sentences in each of the following groups to form a well-organized paragraph. Circle the letter of your choice.

1. A. To the astonishment of the nearby farmers, the mountain began to move down the valley.
   B. In 1972, a strange event occurred in the Soviet Caucasus.
   C. The mountain slid over a mile in eight days.
   D. Heavy rains had swelled the underground river.
   E. As it often happens, there was a river flowing below a large mountain.
   (A) ECDBA
   (B) EBCAD
   (C) BEDAC
   (D) BDAEC
   (E) ABDCE

2. A. That's how *tip* came into the language.
   B. Printed on the box was *To Insure Promptness.*
   C. It was to remind customers to leave something for the waiter—if the service was good.
   D. In no time at all the phrase was abbreviated as *T.I.P.*
   E. Old-English inns kept a box near the entrance door.
   (A) EADBC
   (B) BCAED
   (C) ABDCE
   (D) DACBE
   (E) ECBDA

3. A. At the river mouth, the soil spreads out into a triangular shape.
   B. When a river flows through the countryside, it picks up soil.
   C. The river loses speed as it approaches the sea, and it drops the soil.
   D. The triangular shape resembles the fourth letter of the Greek alphabet, *delta.*
   E. How did the land at the mouth of a river get the name of delta?
   (A) AECBD
   (B) DBECA
   (C) BCADE
   (D) EBCAD
   (E) CABDE

4. A. One of the latter is the most famous chair handed down to us from the past.
   B. It is the one called *Chair of St. Peter.*
   C. It is exhibited once every 100 years.
   D. Some are kept on exhibition while others are stored in carefully guarded vaults.
   E. The Vatican possesses many unusual and rare treasures.
   (A) BECAD
   (B) EDABC
   (C) CEDAB
   (D) ACBDE
   (E) ECBAD

5. A. Knowing us, Susanna did not break down!
   B. She refused to show us what it was.
   C. We were all very curious and promised not to tell Adam her secret.
   D. To honor Adam's return, we all planned to give him presents.
   E. Susanna told us that she had made a gift for him.
   (A) EDBAC
   (B) BECDA
   (C) EABDC
   (D) DECBA
   (E) BCEAD

6. A. Our house was the only one for miles around.
   B. Our woodlands gradually were replaced by houses and paved streets.
   C. Then a big factory was built in the nearby town.
   D. Many of the workers wanted to live in the country
   E. When we moved into the neighborhood, woods surrounded our property.
   (A) EACDB
   (B) ACEDB
   (C) BDACE
   (D) CEDBA
   (E) AECBD

7. A. Others like Matt Dillon and Doc never really existed.
   B. According to the script writers, each of them polished off scores of bad men.
   C. Bat Masterson and Wyatt Earp were real lawmen.
   D. Some of the sheriffs made famous in western movies really existed.
   E. But according to fact, each of them was in only one fatal fight.
   (A) EDBAC
   (B) DCEAB
   (C) CBADE
   (D) DACBE
   (E) EDCAB

8. A. We knew that our lives, however, could never be the same.
   B. The sun rose as usual the next day.
   C. Only time will tell but we fervently hope so.
   D. Our neighbors continued to follow the routines of their daily lives.
   E. Relatives and friends told us that the ache would grow more bearable in the weeks ahead
   (A) BECAD
   (B) ABDCE
   (C) DCEBA
   (D) BDAEC
   (E) BACED

9. A. It is now west of the date line and thousands of miles west of San Francisco.
   B. The tip of the island of Hawaii, South Point, has the honor.
   C. For many years it was Key West, Florida.
   D. The title changed when our 49th state joined the Union.
   E. What is the southern most spot in the United States?
   (A) EBDCA
   (B) CABDE
   (C) ACEBD
   (D) DBECA
   (E) DCEBA

10. A. History proves that Rome did suffer from a devastating fire.
    B. The violin was invented a thousand years after Nero's death.
    C. It is also true that Nero had been Emperor of Rome.
    D. Legends and facts often differ considerably.
    E. However, he never could have fiddled on a violin during the fire.
    (A) BCADE
    (B) DACEB
    (C) ACDBE
    (D) DBAEC
    (E) ABECD

IRRELEVANT SENTENCES

Irrelevant sentences are sentences that are not related to the other sentences in a paragraph. This exercise will help you to evaluate your ability to see the logical building blocks in the construction of paragraphs and to recognize unrelated material.

EXERCISE 23

Each of the following groups of sentences contains one sentence that is not related to the others. Circle the letter of the unrelated sentence.

1. (A) Democracy came to Great Britain in gradual stages.
   (B) It came by means of laws.
   (C) The democratizing laws were called reform acts.
   (D) Parliament passed laws to reduce the working hours of children
   (E) The laws were passed in response to the demands of the people.

2. (A) The Incas were far advanced as farmers.
   (B) Agriculture has long been the backbone of the economy of South America.
   (C) They used nitrates for fertilizers.
   (D) They had planned irrigation to insure a proper amount of water for crops.
   (E) Despite their technology, the Incas' crops were not large enough to support their population.

3. (A) The village council in India is the local governing organization.
   (B) Called the panchayat, it is elected by the entire adult population of the village.
   (C) A villager who breaks a law can be fined or even expelled from the village.
   (D) It is responsible for the smooth functioning of the village.
   (E) It is in charge of the roads, water system, medical care, and child welfare.

4. (A) There are many Shinto shrines throughout Japan.
   (B) They are usually located in a lovely natural setting.
   (C) Shinto is based on people's response to the world around them.
   (D) The shrine is usually simple in design and without elaborate decorations.
   (E) Some of the shrines reflect Chinese rather than Japanese architecture.

5. (A) Growth goes on despite reverses or disappointments.
   (B) It is sometimes necessary to get angry and let others know it.
   (C) It always means giving up what is familiar and comfortable.
   (D) It is ever accompanied by difficulties and pains as well as by rewards.
   (E) Whether it will be distorted or proceed in a natural way depends on the strength of the individual.

6. (A) The craft guilds resembled the National Manufacturers Association rather than modern unions.
   (B) The guild membership consisted of the employers and not the workers.
   (C) The workers were called journeymen and apprentices.
   (D) The guilds controlled all phases of the industry.
   (E) Inspectors checked up on the members, who could be fined if they lowered the price or the quality of the goods produced.

7. (A) The total cost of air pollution in the United States amounts to many billions a year.
   (B) However, it cannot be calculated precisely.
   (C) Damage to buildings and agricultural crops is estimated at more than $900 million a year.
   (D) The time lost from work as the result of illness caused by air pollution is incalculable.
   (E) The cost of safety devices in motor vehicles cannot be calculated in dollars and cents.

8. (A) The physical features of Africa have kept the peoples of Africa apart.
   (B) The desert, rain forests, and mountains prevented the coastal groups from exploring the interior.
   (C) Africa's rivers have many spectacular falls, rapids, sandbars, and swamps, making them difficult to navigate.
   (D) The vast deserts contain no roads and a people who are not interested in building any.
   (E) The soil and irregular rainfall pose great obstacles to large-scale agricultural productivity.

9. (A) In ancient times China was ruled by a series of dynasties.
   (B) The dynasties consisted of a succession of rulers who were members of the same family.
   (C) The Hsia Dynasty, for example, ruled for over 500 years almost 3,500 years ago.
   (D) During this time there was a written language and most of the people were farmers.
   (E) The Hsia Dynasty consisted of a group of related princes, each of whom controlled specific areas.

10. (A) In Southeast Asia, titles and names of respect are given to individuals of great merit.
    (B) The title *U* is one of respect and is given only to those of outstanding accomplishment.
    (C) The Secretary General of the UN was named U Thant because of his role in keeping world peace.
    (D) In Moslem areas the title *Haji* is added to the names of those who have made the religious pilgrimage to Mecca.
    (E) Throughout Southeast Asia, people are still addressed formally by their first names.

TOPIC SENTENCES

The topic sentence is the sentence that contains the main idea in a paragraph. It is the sentence that the other sentences explain, prove, expand, develop, illustrate. Most frequently, the topic sentence is placed first in a selection. However, this is not always the case. It can be set anywhere in the selection. It can even be inferred—and not be stated in the paragraph. Use the exercise that follows to test your ability to locate the topic sentence.

EXERCISE 24

Each of the following groups of sentences belongs in a single paragraph, but the individual sentences are not presented in their logical order. Circle the letter of the topic sentence.

1. (A) The most common form is that of walking over a shallow trench filled with glowing coal.
   (B) In some areas the performer walks over a bed of hot stones.
   (C) Fire walking takes various forms.
   (D) Some fire walkers go through a log fire.

2. (A) The tsar relied on aristocratic advisers who were interested in mainly receiving bribes.
   (B) The soldiers went into battle without essential equipment.
   (C) When the people demanded food, they were ignored.
   (D) The government of Russia in 1914 was cruel, inefficient, and corrupt.

3. (A) Power from the atom will keep our wheels of industry going.
   (B) In the years ahead, nuclear energy may change our lives more profoundly than did the Industrial Revolution.
   (C) The atom is becoming even now increasingly important in diagnosis and treatment of diseases.
   (D) Controlled nuclear explosions can make possible stupendous engineering feats.

4. (A) Native Americans have witnessed the almost total obliteration of their cultures.
   (B) The victims of cruel injustice, most Native Americans have been torn away from their physical heritage.
   (C) Blundering federal policies led to the violation of solemn treaties.
   (D) The original American has been a tragic figure in American history.

5. (A) The League was formed to bring in to reality one of humanity's strongest hopes, peace among nations.
   (B) The League was doomed almost from the start when the United States failed to join.
   (C) The League was an idea whose time had almost arrived.
   (D) The League proved to be only a first attempt at the prevention of war.

6. (A) The land mass of the islands covers more than 700,000 square miles.
   (B) There are over 3,000 islands in the chain.
   (C) There are so many islands in the Republic of Indonesia that no textbook can do justice to all of them.
   (D) The Republic of Indonesia is one of the largest island chains in the world.

7. (A) It was a war on every front.
   (B) The Chinese declared war on "rats, flies, mosquitoes, and grain-eating sparrows."
   (C) The death rate of newborn infants and their mothers was drastically reduced.
   (D) Thousands of tons of precious grain were saved for human consumption.

8. (A) Knowledge, however, in Zen comes from within the individual.
   (B) Introduced by way of China, Zen had a profound effect on the Japanese.
   (C) The followers of Zen must lead a simple life close to nature.
   (D) Zen is a branch of Buddhism.

9. (A) City dwellers looked to his leadership because of his background of experience.
   (B) Gandhi won the support of large segments of the Indian population.
   (C) The Indian villagers gave him unquestioning loyalty because he crusaded to improve their lives.
   (D) Political leaders were impressed by his depth of understanding.

10. (A) The Aztecs believed that they had to offer human blood to their god Quetzalcoatl as repayment for his protection.
    (B) The supply of victims for their sacrifices came from the enemy captured.
    (C) When more victims were needed, the Aztecs went to war to get them.
    (D) The debt to Quetzalcoatl was great, and so the sacrifices had to be many.

11. (A) The patient is made to feel guilty and ashamed of his condition, thus retarding his path to recovery.
    (B) Families will often hide the fact that one of their members is suffering from such an ailment.
    (C) The attitude of the average family toward mental illness must be changed.
    (D) The chance of treating the patient at an early and easier stage is lost.

12. (A) Many of the pesticides that break down rapidly kill all insects where applied, whether the insects are beneficial or harmful.
    (B) These nonpersistent pesticides lead to the development of insect varieties that are not harmed by them.
    (C) Many of these poisons are extremely deadly.
    (D) Even the pesticides that last for just a few days have serious disadvantages.

Mastery Exams

Now that you have studied each type of question likely to appear in the Reading Comprehension Section of any standard examination, it is time to put everything together. The following are Mastery Examinations. Take each exam under conditions similar to those you will meet when you take the one that counts—no TV, no radio, no food, no cooperation! Let the score represent the best you can do now.

EXAM 1

DIRECTIONS: Carefully read each passage below, and then answer the questions that follow. Select the choice that, on the basis of the passage, best answers the question. Then circle the letter that corresponds to the correct answer.

Hatting was one of the first domestic industries to develop in the colonies. As early as 1640, American hats were one of the homemade articles used for barter and exchange. By the beginning of the eighteenth century, hatting had become one of New England's important industries; in the 1730s hats were being exported from the colonies in sufficient numbers to arouse uneasiness among hatters in the mother country and to cause them to exert successful pressure on Parliament for a law prohibiting the export of hats from one colony to another, and from any colony to Great Britain or any other country.

Wool was the principal raw material, but a considerable proportion of the hats were made of fur felt, using beaver fur as the base. The average price of wool hats during the eighteenth century ranged from 40 to 80 cents, and beaver hats ranged fom \$2.50 to \$3.50.

1. The phrase that best expresses the main idea or subject of this selection is:
   (A) Raw materials for hats
   (B) Colonial exports
   (C) How hats were made
   (D) Kinds of hats in America
   (E) An early American industry

2. A law regarding the hat trade was enacted by Parliament in response to a complaint by
   (A) colonists
   (B) Indians
   (C) English noblemen
   (D) citizens of foreign countries
   (E) English hatmakers

3. This law made it illegal for
   (A) Great Britain to export hats
   (B) the colonies to import hats
   (C) the hatters to use beaver fur
   (D) the colonies to export hats
   (E) the colonies to change the price of hats

4. American hats
   (A) were made principally of wool
   (B) did not suit the customers in Great Britain
   (C) were an unimportant part of New England industry
   (D) were sent only to Great Britain
   (E) were not made until 1730

5. Beaver hats
   (A) were unpopular
   (B) were much cheaper than those of wool
   (C) were made mainly for barter with the Native Americans
   (D) cost more than wool hats
   (E) were not exported

The Republic of India is one of the largest nations in the world. It has a large population made up of many ethnic groups. Each of the major racial divisions, Negroid, Australoid, Mongoloid, and Caucasoid, can be found on the Indian subcontinent

The land mass of India is a peninsula that juts into the Indian Ocean from the Asian heartland. It is separated from the heartland by the Himalayas, the world's greatest mountain mass. These mountains plus the ocean provide the subcontinent with good natural borders. Unfortunately, the subcontinent contains another nation besides the Republic of India. The nation of Pakistan rules two sections in the northern part of the peninsula, making it the only nation in the world with two separated areas, East and West Pakistan, to be ruled as one nation.

The division of the subcontinent took place in 1947. The British granted independence to the subcontinent, but the inhabitants could not agree on one nation to rule them. The widely diversified ethnic groups were committed to only two religions—Hindu and Muslim. The adherents of each faith demanded their own nation. The natural borders and great ethnic variety were ignored and the borders of divided Pakistan were drawn to include most Muslims. The Republic of India is a predominantly Hindu nation.

The division satisfied neither the Muslims nor the Hindus. Warfare broke out and many lives were lost. Tensions still exist between the two nations which might have shared the natural borders and ethnic diversity of the region. Instead, time, effort, and money has been devoted to military actions. This has prevented the Republic of India from being as significant a world power as its size suggests it could be.

6. The title that best expresses the main idea or subject of this selection is:
(A) India
(B) Muslims and Hindus
(C) Races of India
(D) Division of the Subcontinent
(E) Pakistan

7. The Himalayas are
(A) mountains
(B) hills
(C) a plateau
(D) India's border
(E) Pakistan's border

8. A fact stated by the writer about Pakistan is that
(A) it has no mountains
(B) the nation is divided into two parts
(C) it is one of the largest nations in the world
(D) it juts into the sea
(E) the people are Hindus

9. The Indian subcontinent
(A) is hilly
(B) is overcrowded
(C) juts into the Indian Ocean
(D) is attached to Africa
(E) contains one nation

10. The Republic of India has
(A) all Australoids
(B) mainly Hindus
(C) more Muslims than Hindus
(D) mainly Muslims
(E) equal numbers of Hindus and Muslims

11. Pakistan and India were
(A) separated according to natural borders
(B) ancient nations
(C) separated by the British to keep them weak
(D) divided on ethnic grounds
(E) divided by themselves on religious lines

Freedom of the press is often taken for granted in our nation. It is hard for Americans to realize that in many countries, publishers and writers are not always allowed to criticize and comment upon the way the country is run. We are so used to reading different opinions and to hearing praise or criticism of our government quoted from newspapers we do not recall that it was not always this way.

In colonial days there were few newspapers. People read them with care as they were almost the only source of news. Colonial governors realized how important the newspapers were in forming opinions. They often wished to suppress or prevent stories from appearing. The governors did not like to be criticized but such criticism is essential to democracy.

One governor who tried to control the press was Governor Cosby in New York. John Peter Zenger published in his paper, the *Weekly Journal,* criticism of the Governor. Zenger was arrested. The Governor stated Zenger was printing lies. Zenger's lawyer, Alexander Hamilton, at the trial in 1735 proved to the jury's satisfaction that Zenger was speaking and writing the truth. The spectators at the trial cheered this decision which is the basic decision establishing freedom of the press in our country.

12. The title that best expresses the main idea or subject of this selection is:
    (A) Colonial Newspapers
    (B) Governor Cosby's Attack
    (C) Freedom of the Press
    (D) John Peter Zenger
    (E) The Trial

13. John Peter Zenger was arrested for
    (A) telling lies
    (B) writing stories about New York
    (C) criticizing Governor Cosby
    (D) printing the *Weekly Journal*
    (E) writing Alexander Hamilton

14. The author of the selection believes that
    (A) Zenger was wrong
    (B) many Americans take freedom of the press for granted
    (C) colonial newspapers were poor
    (D) Governor Cosby was right
    (E) many countries have freedom of the press

15. The trial of Zenger established the
    (A) basis of the freedom of the press in America
    (B) reputation of the *Weekly Journal*
    (C) reputation of Alexander Hamilton
    (D) importance of Governor Cosby
    (E) role of juries in trials

The regular unit of European life in the Middle Ages was not the city or the open farmstead. It was the feudal castle—a fortification situated if possible upon a lofty hill, and often with a little village of the crude huts of the lord's peasants clustered close beside it. During the earlier feudal period the castle in most cases would be simply a single huge tower, round or square, with merely a crude palisade and a ditch for outworks. The height would baffle any scaling-ladder. There would be no opening in its blank masonry until a considerable distance from the ground. Then the narrow door would be entered only by a flimsy wooden bridge, easy to demolish, or by a frail ladder, drawn up every night. Inside the tower there would be a series of dark, cavernous rooms, one above another, communicating by means of ladders. The sole purpose of such a comfortless castle was defense, and that defense by mere height and mass, not by any special skill in arranging the various parts.

Little by little this simple donjon became more complicated. The original tower was kept, but enclosed by other lines of defense. To force the outer barriers meant simply that you had a far stronger inner bulwark before you. The best kind of medieval castle needed only a very small number of soldiers. From behind its walls even an inferior baron could protect himself from a kingly army.

16. European life in medieval times centered around the
    (A) king's army
    (B) farm
    (C) city
    (D) castle
    (E) peasant village

17. The most important part of the fortifications was the
    (A) palisade
    (B) ditch
    (C) tower
    (D) drawbridge
    (E) hill

18. The chief value of the castle was
    (A) strategy in attack
    (B) a good view
    (C) simple defense
    (D) warmth
    (E) comfortable living

19. To defend a well-built castle the lord needed a
    (A) small group of soldiers
    (B) kingly arms
    (C) peasant family
    (D) great deal of skill
    (E) more complicated system

20. A true statement about the medieval castle is that
    (A) a hill was its ideal situation
    (B) the peasants lived in the tower
    (C) its innermost fortifications were its weakest parts
    (D) it was entered through a wide door
    (E) it was made completely of wood

EXAM 2

DIRECTIONS: Carefully read each passage below, and then answer the questions that follow. Select the choice that, on the basis of the passage, best answers the question. Then circle the letter that corresponds to the correct answer.

Money has now become so important that we often lose sight of what lies behind it. The usual way to regain our focus is to ask a question like this: "If you were without food on a desert island with no chance of rescue for a long time and had to choose between a million dollars in gold or a fifty-pound Wisconsin cheese, which would you take?" I think it is extremely necessary to see clearly and simply what lies behind the dollars. I doubt if we can solve our financial problems unless we see the people, the land, the machines, the houses, the freight cars, the loaves of bread which alone give dollars any meaning. In the long run it is human labor, capital investment, raw materials, mechanical energy and scientific knowledge which form the chief parts of the economic machine.

1. The phrase that best expresses the main idea or subject of this selection is:
   (A) Solving our financial problems
   (B) The real meaning of dollars
   (C) Wisconsin cheese
   (D) Money and the machine
   (E) Living on a desert island

2. The author suggests that if one were away from civilization
   (A) money would be the most important possession
   (B) one would miss the economic machine
   (C) food would be of greater value than money
   (D) it would be necessary to solve financial problems
   (E) human labor would be unnecessary

You may think that totem poles were some sort of strange idol used in religious services. That is not true. Among the Pacific Coast Native Americans totem poles were like the coats-of-arms used by medieval knights in Europe. Each figure carved on the wooden pole had some meaning. It stood for a title held by the owner or for some family connection of the chief. The Native Americans raised their totem poles in front of their houses. To them they were very natural and did not seem strange at all. The totem pole was part of their life and everyone in the village understood what it meant.

3. Totem poles are similar to
   (A) coats-of-arms
   (B) religious symbols
   (C) idols
   (D) medieval knights
   (E) a title

4. The figures on the totem pole were
   (A) scratched
   (B) grotesque
   (C) carved
   (D) colored blue
   (E) Indians

5. The story assumes that things that are not familiar to us often appear
   (A) unappealing
   (B) strange
   (C) European
   (D) medieval
   (E) forbidding

Liberia, the tiny republic on the west coast of Africa, has long been of interest to the United States. This is partly because it was founded as a sovereign state by little bands of freed slaves from the United States and the West Indies who settled there over a century ago, and partly because of its fast-developing rubber plantations.

Only slightly larger than Ohio, Liberia is unique in that it is the only part of the African continent remaining in black hands and under black control. Its name refers to the new-found liberation of the former slaves who colonized its shores, and whose descendants today rule the little nation. Besides some 2,000,000 primitive natives who live in the tropical inland areas, there are about 70,000 civilized inhabitants with a standard of living patterned after that of the United States or Europe. Only blacks may be citizens of Liberia.

Although tiny, Liberia is of some military importance. It has no good ports, but its capital, Monrovia (named for President Monroe), is practically next door to the great British naval base at Freetown. Liberia exports some $3,000,000 worth of crude rubber annually.

6. The phrase that best expresses the main idea or subject of this selection is:
   (A) Rubber from Liberia
   (B) The west coast of Africa
   (C) Descendants of the slaves
   (D) A black republic
   (E) A colony of the United States

7. Liberia was settled
   (A) before the United States
   (B) twenty-five years ago
   (C) more than one hundred years ago
   (D) about eighty years ago
   (E) two hundred years ago

8. The name "Liberia" was chosen because
   (A) it described the small size of the country
   (B) the founders had recently been freed from slavery
   (C) the United States was interested in it
   (D) rubber was an important crop
   (E) President Monroe suggested it

9. The citizens of Liberia are
   (A) of many races
   (B) American slaves
   (C) all blacks
   (D) British subjects
   (E) mostly civilized inhabitants

10. From the selection we may conclude that
   (A) Liberia has no military importance
   (B) the Liberian landscape is similar to that of Ohio
   (C) the seaports of Liberia are exceptionally good
   (D) the United States has had no influence on Liberia
   (E) Liberia is important for its export of rubber

It was none too soon that a national forest should bear the name of Gifford Pinchot, and it was appropriate that the forest selected for this honor was the Columbia National Forest on the slopes of the Cascade Range in Washington. This national forest was originally established and named when Clifford Pinchot was Chief of the United States Forest Service, and its administration was begun under his direction. In June of 1949, President Truman signed a proclamation officially changing the name to Gifford Pinchot National Forest, and in October the million and one-quarter acres were officially dedicated when the Society of American Foresters held its annual meeting in Seattle. Mr. Pinchot was born in the greatest era of waste of national resources in our country's history. And he chose a profession then almost unknown in America—forestry. As the country's first "consulting forester" he discovered, however, that there were many who felt some concern for the future of our forest resources. In 1898 Mr. Pinchot became Chief of the Division of Forestry in the Department of Agriculture; in 1900 he helped organize the Society of American Foresters; in 1905 he became Chief of the new United States Forest Service and took over the administration of the forest reserves of the public domain. The rest of his life was devoted to public service, with conservation ever foremost in his mind. No memorial to his contribution could be more appropriate than a great forest of green and growing trees.

11. The phrase that best expresses the main idea or subject of this selection is:
    (A) The boyhood of Gifford Pinchot
    (B) A memorial to a great conservationist
    (C) The United States Forest Service
    (D) The importance of our national forests
    (E) The waste of natural resources

12. It was appropriate to name this forest after Mr. Pinchot because
    (A) it is more beautiful than any other forest in the country
    (B) it is the only national forest
    (C) it is the one Mr. Pinchot wanted
    (D) it is one of those forests he supervised when they first became national forests
    (E) it is in the state of Washington

13. Mr. Pinchot devoted his life to
    (A) satisfying his own selfish desires
    (B) serving the public in the field of forestry
    (C) withdrawing from public contact
    (D) choosing a suitable memorial
    (E) encouraging lumbermen

14. The author of the selection shows clearly that he
    (A) admires the work that Mr. Pinchot did
    (B) does not approve of changing the names of forests
    (C) thinks the need for conservation is overrated
    (D) is himself a "consulting forester"
    (E) was a close friend of Gifford Pinchot

EXAM 3

DIRECTIONS: Carefully read each passage below and then answer the questions that follow. Select the choice that, on the basis of the passage, best answers the question. Then circle the letter that corresponds to the correct answer.

The Gulf Stream, which runs like a friendly blue river across the cold, green Atlantic Ocean, is one of the mightiest powers in the world. By comparison, the Mississippi and the mighty Amazon are but small rivers. Two million tons of coal burned every minute would not equal the heat that the Stream gives forth in its Atlantic crossing. Without the Stream's warmth England's pleasant green countryside would be as cold as Labrador, which is no farther north than England. If this "river of blue" were cooled as much as 15 degrees, England, Scandinavia, northern France and Germany would probably become a region for the Eskimos.

The general course of the blue river has never been known to change. From Florida north the Stream follows the curve of the coast but stays well away from the shore. When the warm waters meet the icy Labrador currents, the Stream loses some speed and heat, but even with icebergs at its margin it stays warm enough for tropical sea life.

As the Stream nears Europe it divides north and south. The northern drift mixes with the Arctic Ocean. The southern drift comes again into the path of Africa's hot trade winds, and the waters hurry back to the Gulf of Mexico, gathering again their store of heat. The complete course of the Stream, therefore, is like a tremendous 12,000-mile whirlpool.

Scientists think that it takes three years for the Stream to make a complete trip. Their belief is based on the courses of bottles that have been thrown into the Stream to drift. These bottles contain papers, printed in many languages, requesting the finders to note the places and dates of finding and mail them back. Government experts on ocean currents have records of thousands of these "bottle papers."

Other oceans have such currents. In the North Pacific, for example, the Japanese Current makes the climate of coastal Alaska and our west coast moderate. Science is still not satisfied with what it knows about these currents. But for most of us it is enough to know that the Gulf Stream and similar currents give warmth to countries that would otherwise be very cold indeed.

1. The phrase that best expresses the main idea or subject of this selection is:
   (A) Interesting facts about the Gulf Stream
   (B) Currents similar to the Gulf Stream
   (C) What Florida owes to the Gulf Stream
   (D) Scientific experiments on the Gulf Stream
   (E) Tropical sea life in the Gulf Stream

2. The water in the Gulf Stream is
   (A) cold and green
   (B) coal-colored
   (C) icy and blue
   (D) warm and blue
   (E) pleasantly green

3. The effect of the Gulf Stream on England is to
   (A) cool the air pleasantly
   (B) make possible the green countryside
   (C) make necessary the burning of two million tons of coal
   (D) cool England's rivers 15 degrees
   (E) make England a region for Eskimos

4. The number of miles covered by the waters of the Gulf Stream is
   (A) considerably different each year
   (B) about 100 billion
   (C) about 12 thousand
   (D) undetermined
   (E) about 2 million

5. Scientists have used papers in bottles to determine the number of
   (A) languages spoken along the course of the Gulf Stream
   (B) people who are alert to such things
   (C) government experts on ocean currents
   (D) beliefs about the course of the bottles
   (E) years needed for the Gulf Stream to make a complete round trip

6. The author says that a person who finds one of the bottles is asked to tell
   (A) his name and birth date
   (B) where and when the bottle was found
   (C) how many languages he speaks
   (D) how many other bottles he has found
   (E) how far he was from home at the time

7. Many countries should be thankful to the Gulf Stream and similar currents for
   (A) cool summers
   (B) moderate climates
   (C) thousands of specific records
   (D) scientific progress
   (E) trade winds

8. Scientists believe that
   (A) their knowledge of these currents is complete
   (B) these currents are of little use
   (C) they need to know more about these currents
   (D) only one ocean has such a current as the Gulf Stream
   (E) their "bottle papers" have not been useful

Tom Sawyer said to himself that it was not such a hollow world after all. He had discovered a great law of human action without knowing it—namely, that in order to make a man or boy desire a thing it is only necessary to make the thing difficult to attain. If he had been a great and wise philosopher, he would now have understood that work consists of whatever a body is obliged to do, and that play consists of whatever a body is not obliged to do. And this would help him to understand why constructing artificial flowers or performing on a treadmill is work, while rolling tenpins or climbing Mont Blanc is only amusement. There are wealthy men in England who drive four-horse passenger coaches 20 or 30 miles on a daily line in the summer, because the privilege costs them considerable money; but if they were offered wages for the service, that would turn it into work, and then they would resign.

9. The "law of human action" discovered by Tom could be stated as follows: A man wants most that which
   (A) he already has
   (B) he is obliged to do
   (C) he cannot easily attain
   (D) no one else likes
   (E) he can get for nothing

10. According to the author, play consists of
   (A) the things a person does of his own free will
   (B) the things a person has to do
   (C) jobs such as working a treadmill
   (D) the things that make this a hollow world
   (E) tasks done for wages

11. A man who does such a thing as drive a coach for amusement would resign if offered wages for the activity because
(A) he doesn't want to earn money
(B) it is a dangerous activity
(C) he would lose money
(D) he doesn't have time
(E) the activity would then become work

Many people know that Ben Franklin's kite experiment helped to prove that lightning is electricity. Kites have been used for scientific purposes since the middle 1700s—for testing weather conditions, taking aerial photographs, and so on. They have also been employed in many interesting ways during wartime. Centuries ago, a Korean general sent a kite, with a line attached, to the opposite bank of a river. A cable followed the line, forming the nucleus from which a bridge was built. The Japanese developed a man-carrying kite, invaluable in scouting the enemy's position. Many armies used to employ kites for signaling purposes. Now some airplane lifeboats are equipped with kites carrying radio antennas which automatically signal S.O.S.

12. The phrase below that best expresses the main idea or subject of this selection is:
(A) Kite making as a hobby
(B) Methods of signaling
(C) Uses of kites through the years
(D) Our debt to Ben Franklin
(E) Wartime use of kites

13. The author tells us that the Japanese used kites for
(A) photography
(B) scouting
(C) radio signaling
(D) scientific studies
(E) weather predicting

14. The most recent use of kites mentioned is carrying
(A) bridge cables
(B) soldiers
(C) photographers
(D) electricity
(E) radio antennas

On the whole the Inuit are a coastal people. Their total number is not more than 35,000. Of these about 14,500 live along the coast of Greenland. Inuit settlements are scattered along the northern coast of North America from Labrador to Alaska's Panhandle. On Baffin Island and on other large islands there are Inuit villages. The Inuit spend most of their time near the sea and get much of their living from the sea. However, one tribe, the Caribou Inuit, live inland west of Hudson Bay. Some of them have never seen the sea.

Although life in one village is, in many ways, very much like life in another, there are some differences. The reason is that the Inuit must use what they find in the particular district where they live. The Copper Inuit who live beside Coronation Gulf build thick-walled winter houses of snow blocks. Alaskan Inuit do not use such houses and most of them have never even seen one. Their winter homes are made of turf and mud. The Inuit of southern Greenland are expert in handling a kayak, or Inuit canoe. They fish in the open water of the sea. The Inuit of northern Greenland have little chance to use kayaks because the water along the coast is frozen almost all the year. All tribes, however, have one thing in common. They are primarily fishermen and hunters.

15. The phrase below that best expresses the main idea or subject of this selection is:
(A) The Caribou Inuit
(B) The Inuit
(C) Inuit fishing
(D) Inuit homes
(E) The Copper Inuit

16. Most Inuit live
(A) near the water
(B) on the plains
(C) in the forests
(D) inland
(E) on islands

17. The Caribou Inuit are
    (A) from the coast of Greenland
    (B) not hunters and fishermen
    (C) scattered along the coast of North America
    (D) not coastal people
    (E) skilled at gaining their living from the sea

18. A comparison of different Inuit villages shows that the way of life in each
    (A) is quite similar to that in the others
    (B) is very unlike that in the others
    (C) has nothing to do with the location
    (D) is very civilized
    (E) is much like our own way of life

19. Alaskan Inuit make their winter homes of
    (A) snow blocks
    (B) skins and furs
    (C) wood
    (D) turf and mud
    (E) stones

20. A kayak is a kind of
    (A) sled
    (B) house
    (C) boat
    (D) animal
    (E) spear

21. All Inuit tribes
    (A) are skilled in the use of the kayak
    (B) hunt and fish for a living
    (C) make homes of snow blocks
    (D) live in Greenland
    (E) depend on the ocean for a living

EXAM 4

DIRECTIONS: Carefully read each passage below, and then answer the questions that follow. Select the choice that, on the basis of the passages, best answers the question. Then circle the letter that corresponds to the correct answer.

Education was free. That subject my father had written about repeatedly, as comprising his chief hope for us children, the essence of American opportunity, the treasure that no thief could touch, not even misfortune or poverty. It was the one thing he was able to promise us when he sent for us, more sure, safer than bread or shelter. On our second day I was thrilled with the realization of what this freedom of education meant. A little girl from across the alley came and offered to conduct us to school. My father was out, but we five among us had a few words of English by this time. We knew the word *school.* We understood. This child, who had never seen us till yesterday, who could not pronounce our names, who was not much better dressed that we, was able to offer us the freedom of the schools of Boston! The doors stood open for every one of us. The smallest child could show us the way. This incident impressed me more than anything I had heard in advance about the freedom of education in America. It was a concrete proof—almost the thing itself. One had to experience it to understand it.

1. The phrase below that best expresses the main idea or subject of this selection is:
   (A) My first day in America
   (B) The schools of Boston
   (C) My father's education
   (D) Our greatest opportunity in America
   (E) The little girl next door

2. When the father sent for his children, the only thing he could surely promise them was
   (A) bread
   (B) friends
   (C) shelter
   (D) schooling
   (E) wealth

3. The father believed that
   (A) he should have stayed in Europe
   (B) education was not worth while
   (C) the children could not learn English
   (D) he would always live in poverty
   (E) education was one possession that could not be stolen

4. The word *school*
   (A) was unknown to the children
   (B) frightened the children
   (C) was one of the first English words the children had learned
   (D) reminded the children of unhappy days in Europe
   (E) was difficult for the children to understand

5. The children fully realized the meaning of their father's words when they discovered that
   (A) the little girl across the way had better clothes than they did
   (B) they could not understand the little girl
   (C) the Boston schools didn't want them
   (D) in America even a little girl could take them to school
   (E) the little girl could not pronounce their names

High in the Swiss Alps long years ago, there lived a lonely shepherd boy who longed for a friend to share his vigils. One night, he beheld three wrinkled old men, each holding a glass. The first said: "Drink this liquid and you shall be victorious in battle."

The second said: "Drink this liquid and you shall have countless riches."

The last man said: "I offer you the happiness of music—the alphorn."

The boy chose the third glass. Next day, he came upon a great horn, ten feet in length. When he put his lips to it, a beautiful melody floated across the valley. He had found a friend.

So goes the legend of the alphorn's origin. Known in the ninth century, the alphorn was used by herdsmen to call cattle, for the deep tones echoed across the mountainsides. And even today, on, a quiet summer evening, its music can be heard floating among the peaks.

6. The story tells us that of the three old men, the one whose glass the boy chose was the
   (A) smallest in size
   (B) most wrinkled
   (C) first to speak
   (D) oldest
   (E) last to speak

7. One liquid offered to the boy would have brought him
   (A) defeat in battle
   (B) great wealth
   (C) lonely vigils
   (D) another boy to help him
   (E) three wishes

8. To the boy, the alphorn
   (A) seemed too heavy to play
   (B) seemed like a real friend
   (C) brought unhappiness
   (D) sounded unpleasant
   (E) brought great riches

9. The practical use of the alphorn is to
   (A) summon the three old men
   (B) make friends
   (C) call cattle
   (D) give summer concerts
   (E) tell the legends of the Alps

The region that lies between the Tigris and Euphrates Rivers was once a rich and flourishing land. The people built great cities such as Ur and Babylon. They established government and the world's first empires grew up in the region. They developed fine arts and some of the gold cups and jewelry from the area are as beautiful as any ever made. Agriculture was highly developed with extensive and complex irrigation systems. The reign of Hammurabi (often dated at around 1750 B.C. but historians differ on the exact date of his reign) was one of the high points of ancient civilization.

But all of this changed. The decline was gradual, and the reasons offered are many. Among them are climatic changes brought about by such geological events as the change in size of the ice cap at the North Pole. Another suggested reason is the way the people treated their environment. They cut down the forests outside the cities thus exposing the land to eroding rains at certain seasons, and to the rapid runoff of water which lowers the underground water level. They may also have overgrazed the grasslands. A third suggestion is the action or raids of enemy groups which wrecked or blocked the irrigation canals. These canals were the basis of survival for the society.

The food needed by the many city dwellers could only be supplied if the canals were working. If the farmers had to spend their time repairing the canals, they could not grow food and the city population starved or left the cities. Thus the level of civilization declined. The land was left without trees and open to erosion. With little demand for food from cities, farmers took little care of the land.

10. Agriculture in the age of Hammurabi was highly developed with
    (A) extensive irrigation
    (B) use of horses
    (C) steel plows
    (D) priests running the farms
    (E) control by the King

11. Historians differ about the exact date of Hammurabi's reign but the author suggests as a date
    (A) around 2000 B.C.
    (B) the second millennium
    (C) 1750
    (D) around 1750 B.C.
    (E) around 1750 A.D.

12. The region described lies between the Tigris and the
    (A) Nile
    (B) Euphrates
    (C) Danube
    (D) Congo
    (E) Euhate

13. When forests were cut down, the land in this region was exposed to
    (A) eroding rains
    (B) sunshine
    (C) irrigation
    (D) enemy raids
    (E) the plow

14. With the decline of the city population the author suggests the farmers took
    (A) advantage of the people
    (B) little care of the land
    (C) the chance to buy city homes
    (D) over the canals
    (E) the grazing areas

15. One possible geological explanation of the change in fertility of the region described is due to the
    (A) rainfall
    (B) level of the rivers
    (C) river flooding
    (D) ice cap size
    (E) erosion

The word *atom* has captured the human imagination. In addition to atomic bombs and atomic energy, we see signs advertising products with names such as "atomic-energized gasoline." Who invented the word *atom,* and what does it mean?

The inventor was a Greek philosopher named Democritus, who lived about 400 B.C. Even then, Greek physicists were wondering about the structure of matter. Democritus suggested that matter is not what it seems—a continuous mass of material. He thought that matter could be broken up into finer and finer parts until finally it could be broken no further. These basic particles he called atoms, something which could not be cut or divided.

We can see for ourselves that Democritus did have a good idea. When a teaspoonful of sugar is put into a cup of coffee, the sugar dissolves and disappears. If coffee—or water—were solid and continuous, there would be no room for the sugar. But since the sugar does disappear, we must conclude that the water and sugar are both made up of tiny particles with spaces between them. The sugar particles slip into the spaces between the water particles.

In one way, however, we have come to disagree with Democritus. Following his lead, for hundreds of years men thought of atoms as solid little bits of matter. Newton spoke of them as being "so very hard as never to wear or break into pieces." John Dalton, an English chemist, in 1807 called atoms "indivisible, eternal and indestructible."

Today we know that atoms are not solid and not indestructible. We now think of an atom as a miniature solar system, with a central nucleus or "sun" around which tiny particles revolve.

16. The word *atom* was first used by
    (A) an English chemist
    (B) a Greek philosopher
    (C) an American scientist
    (D) an advertising writer
    (E) a Greek physician

17. The author indicates that Democritus' theory of the atom was
    (A) partly right
    (B) completely wrong
    (C) never accepted by others
    (D) too imaginative
    (E) contradicted by Dalton's theory

18. Sugar is believed to dissolve in water because
    (A) the water is solid and continuous
    (B) the sugar is solid and continuous
    (C) they are both solid and continuous
    (D) only a teaspoonful is used
    (E) there is room for sugar particles between the water particles

19. For centuries men believed that atoms
    (A) were destructive
    (B) had revolving parts
    (C) were really unimportant
    (D) could not be divided
    (E) were like sugar particles

20. An atom can be compared to a solar system because an atom
    (A) is round
    (B) is unbreakable
    (C) has particles revolving around a center
    (D) is "indivisible, eternal and indestructible"
    (E) is a continuous mass of material

EXAM 5

DIRECTIONS: Carefully read each passage below, and then answer the questions that follow. Select the choice that, on the basis of the passage, best answers the question. Then circle the letter that corresponds to the correct answer.

One of the most fascinating questions of technology is how the great pyramids of Egypt were built. These great tombs of the Old Kingdom Pharaohs still stand as monuments to a civilization that many people think of as primitive. They were built without electricity, internal combustion engines, cranes, bulldozers, or any of the many machines used by men today. The builders did not attend engineering schools and not one of them knew calculus or modern mathematics. How could such huge monuments—for the pyramid of Pharaoh Cheops (also spelled in English, Khufu or Kheops) is twice as high as the capitol in Washington and covers thirteen acres—have been built?

For many years scholars believed that the pyramids were built by slaves working in the hot sun under harsh slave drivers. Plans were drawn showing how ramps of sand built around the pyramid would allow the slaves, using log rollers, to pull the two and a half ton stone blocks up to their location. Archaeologists have found the remains of dwellings around the pyramids where scholars suggested the slaves lived.

Recently, the slave theory has been questioned. The numbers that would be required, the amount of earth that would have to be moved to build ramps, and the difficulty of getting the top stone in place present problems. Also, the source of so many slaves is debated since there is little evidence of international warfare at the time.

A new theory suggests that the builders worked in the flood season when they could not farm. They worked voluntarily for the Pharaoh in return for food and shelter in the dwellings around the pyramids. Instead of ramps on which to pull the stones, it is now suggested the Egyptians used simple machines employing levers and weights. Such devices are still used in Egypt to raise water for irrigation from one level to the next. It is possible that with such simple technology and a small number of workers, the great pyramids of Egypt were built.

1. The pyramids were built as
    (A) training exercises in technology
    (B) tombs
    (C) capitols
    (D) slave quarters
    (E) monuments

2. Some scholars believed that the pyramids were built by slaves using
   (A) ramps of sand
   (B) bulldozers
   (C) floods
   (D) calculus
   (E) slave drivers

3. A new theory suggests the pyramids were built using
   (A) slaves
   (B) simple machines employing levers and weights
   (C) food and shelter
   (D) simple machines
   (E) the flood season

4. Compared with the capitol at Washington the pyramid of Pharaoh Cheops is
   (A) similar to the capitol
   (B) has more tourists
   (C) was built later
   (D) twice as high
   (E) built of larger stones

The famous Pony Express started at St. Joseph, Missouri, and followed the Oregon and California trail for the most part, with many short cuts because mountain-bred horses, sure-footed as goats, could travel where no stagecoach could go. It ended at Sacramento, California where a river steamer carried the mail on to San Francisco. Post stations were built along the trail at intervals of about 70 miles in open country, or 35 miles in the mountains. Each station was provided with food, shelter, a corral of horses, and two keepers. Between post stations, at intervals of about ten miles (which is as far as they wished their horses to run at high speed) were several relay stations, each with a keeper and a few extra horses, one of which was always saddled and ready to run.

Coming with a rush into the relay station, the post rider would swing down from his lathered mount, swing up on a fresh horse with his precious *mochila* (saddle bag), and be off without a moment's delay. He was expected to reach the next post station on time, and he did it or died trying. More than one rider came at dawn or dusk to find the post station burned, its keepers killed, its horses run off by Indians; and in that case he had to keep on to the next station without food or rest. The longest continuous run, 384 miles, was made by "Buffalo Bill," then a boy of 18; the fastest by Jim Moore, another youngster, who rode 280 miles in 22 hours.

Ninety riders were running the long trail at all hours of the day or night, often taking their lives in their hands to get the mail through within the time limit set for the run. Ten days was the time set, but the job was regularly done in eight. The average speed was eleven miles an hour, which was fast in a region where at one hour a horse might run his best and the next hour be swimming a river or cat-footing along a trail where a misstep meant death for horse and rider.

This daring Pony Express ran for less than two years; it ended in 1861, when a telegraph line offered a swifter means of communication.

5. The Pony Express ran between
   (A) St. Joseph and San Francisco
   (B) Oregon and California
   (C) St. Joseph and Sacramento
   (D) Sacramento and San Francisco
   (E) St. Joseph and Oregon

6. The greatest distance between post stations along the Pony Express run was about
   (A) 10 miles
   (B) 35 miles
   (C) 50 miles
   (D) 70 miles
   (E) 105 miles

7. The principal duty of a keeper of a relay station was to
   (A) guard the mail pouches
   (B) prepare meals
   (C) hunt Indians
   (D) plan short cuts for riders
   (E) have a horse ready for an incoming rider

8. The Pony Express riders waited at relay stations only long enough to
   (A) allow a stagecoach to pass
   (B) get a fresh mount
   (C) catch a few hours' sleep
   (D) escape thieving Indians
   (E) sort the mail

9. From this passage it would seem that most of the riders were
   (A) surefooted
   (B) faithful to duty
   (C) middle-aged
   (D) mountain-bred
   (E) carefree

10. A Californian sending mail by Pony Express could expect his mail to reach the eastern end of the run
    (A) within 22 hours
    (B) between dawn and dusk
    (C) within 10 days
    (D) in about a month
    (E) in about 90 days

11. The Pony Express ended in 1861 because
    (A) messages could be sent more quickly by wire
    (B) fast horses had become scarce
    (C) riders would not work under such conditions
    (D) river boats had come into wider use
    (E) so many stations had been attacked by Indians

One of America's famous and interesting shrines is the National Baseball Hall of Fame and Museum located in the village of Cooperstown, New York, also celebrated as the home of James Fenimore Cooper, the novelist. Dedicated in 1939, the building attracts thousands of visitors who come from far and wide each year to see the birthplace and mementos of "America's national pastime." Cooperstown was chosen as the site of this museum because baseball is said to have been originated there by General Abner Doubleday in 1839 when he was a student at a military academy.

The museum houses a collection of baseball relics that are the delight of all sports lovers. Here also can be found the names and pictures—as well as some of the equipment they used—of the "Immortals" who have been elected to the Baseball Hall of Fame by the nation's sportswriters. One of the interesting displays, the locker of former Yankee great, Lou Gehrig, holds his old uniform and some of the playing equipment used when he gained his fame as baseball's "iron man." Another popular attraction is an exhibit of duplicates of the diamond rings awarded annually to World Series participants.

The accomplishments of such classic heroes as Babe Ruth, Cy Young, Ty Cobb, Christy Matthewson, and Lou Gehrig will live on forever in this popular shrine, which is a sanctuary for thousands of budding young athletes.

12. Cooperstown was chosen as the site of a baseball museum because
    (A) sportswriters had selected it
    (B) baseball is said to have originated there
    (C) World Series trophies are on display there
    (D) James Fenimore Cooper had lived there
    (E) several baseball "Immortals" had been born there

13. The baseball museum was first opened to the public about
    (A) three years ago
    (B) twenty-five years ago
    (C) a half century ago
    (D) sixty years ago
    (E) over a hundred years ago

14. Baseball is said to have been originated by a
    (A) sportswriter
    (B) novelist
    (C) former Yankee player
    (D) military student
    (E) group of sportswriters

15. Baseball's "iron man" was
    (A) Babe Ruth
    (E) Ty Cobb
    (C) Abner Doubleday
    (D) Cy Young
    (E) Lou Gehrig

Milk is a suspension of nourishing materials in water, which constitutes about 86 percent of the total weight. The total 14 percent of nutrient solids consist of the following: milk sugar, 5 percent; fat, about 4 percent; protein just a fraction less than that; and finally minerals and vitamins. It can readily be seen that milk is a kind of natural combination containing most of the body's requirements for growth and health. What is unique about milk is its richness in minerals and vitamins. Fat, sugar, and protein can come from other sources, but the vitamin A and the minerals of milk cannot be easily obtained elsewhere. It is also rich in the vitamin B group so urgently needed for health. Calcium and phosphorus are two minerals contained in milk that are of primary importance. These minerals are essential for normal development and maintenance of bones and teeth. Not only is milk rich in bone-forming calcium and phosphorus but also it carries them in a form that is much more readily assimilated than the same minerals found in vegetables. Yet it is fortunate for us that we do not have to subsist on milk alone. Milk does not supply the body with the iron needed to prevent anemia. Milk also lacks vitamin D, although sunshine easily compensates for that shortage. Under our conditions of preparing milk, it also lacks vitamin C, which is the antiscurvy vitamin of many fruits and vegetables. Cream and butter contain the fat of the milk, while cheese contains its solidified protein plus some fat, its vitamin A, and some minerals. We also have, of course, the concentrated forms of milk, such as evaporated, condensed, and powdered. These are whole-milk equivalents minus some or all of the water.

16. The phrase that best expresses the main idea or subject of this selection is:
    (A) A history of milk
    (B) The sources of milk
    (C) Milk, a perfect food
    (D) Food values in milk
    (E) Popular milk products

17. The largest part of milk is composed of
    (A) fat
    (B) sugar
    (C) water
    (D) minerals
    (E) vitamins

18. Milk is an especially important food because
    (A) it is cheap
    (B) it is easily available
    (C) it contains so much protein
    (D) its fat content is so large
    (E) its minerals cannot be readily obtained otherwise

19. Milk is deficient in
    (A) phosphorus
    (B) iron
    (C) fat
    (D) protein
    (E) vitamin A

20. In order to have good teeth, a person should have plenty of
    (A) calcium
    (B) iron
    (C) protein
    (D) sugar
    (E) cheese

21. Sunshine is a good source of
    (A) vitamin A
    (B) vitamin C
    (C) vitamin D
    (D) phosphorus
    (E) calcium

EXAM 6

DIRECTIONS: Carefully read each passage below, and then answer the questions that follow. Select the choice that, on the basis of the passage, best answers the question. Then circle the letter that corresponds to the correct answer.

The Homestead Act was a great boon to western settlement. Two acts passed by Congress in the early 1860s were the keys to the rapid settlement of the West. The first was the Pacific Railway Act, which authorized the building of a transcontinental railroad. The route, completed in 1869, provided rapid and easy transportation westward for many settlers.

The second act, the Homestead Act, had to do with public lands; that is, land that belonged to the federal government. Before this act land was sold to settlers for as little as $1.25 per acre but each settler had to buy many acres. Thus many poor families could not afford to settle in the West. The new act stated that any head of a family could become the owner of a farm or homestead of 160 acres if he lived on it and worked the land for five years. The act made it possible for many Civil War veterans to move west and settle on their own land. Together with the Pacific Railway Act the act made it certain the West would be settled rapidly.

1. The phrase that best expresses the main idea or subject of this selection is:
   (A) Pacific Railway Act
   (B) Two acts
   (C) Homestead Act
   (D) The opening of the West
   (E) Land ownership

2. Before the Homestead Act, a settler could
   (A) not buy public land
   (B) take any homestead
   (C) not travel by railroad to the West
   (D) buy land at $1.25 an acre
   (E) own land by working it

3. The Pacific Railway Act provided for
   (A) rapid transportation
   (B) a transcontinental railroad
   (C) quick western settlement
   (D) public lands
   (E) unemployed Civil War veterans

4. Public lands are
   (A) lands owned by each state
   (B) lands used by the government
   (C) lands open to sale by the government
   (D) lands owned by the federal government
   (E) lands owned by a government

For the colonists of Portugal and Spanish America, self-government began during the period of the Napoleonic Wars. Brazil, the colony of Portugal, became a separate nation without any war of independence. The Portuguese king fled from Napoleon to Brazil. When he returned to Europe after the wars, the basis of Brazil's independent existence as a free nation was established.

The Spanish colonies had to fight for their independence in the same way the United States had done. Napoleon conquered Spain in 1808 and deposed the King, Ferdinand VII. Napoleon made his own brother King of Spain. When this happened, Spanish colonists in different areas of South America formed governing groups called juntas and declared they would rule in the name of King Ferdinand VII until he could get his throne back. In 1814 Ferdinand regained his throne in Spain but the juntas refused to give up the power they had originally seized in the name of the King. The colonists had found that their independence gave them advantages they did not wish to give up. They were able to trade freely with England and the United States. They were no longer under the rule of Spanish nobles sent out by the King as governors. These nobles often ruled badly and took advantage of the colonists. Finally, the non-Spanish inhabitants believed they would have more rights if they were not ruled by nobles from Spain.

King Ferdinand sent troops to help his appointed governors reestablish their authority. The result was a war for independence that lasted ten years. By 1824 the brilliant military leadership of Simón Bolívar and José de San Martín had freed all of the Spanish territory in South America from the rule of the Spanish King. Only three small areas in northeastern South America were not self-governing. These three areas, ruled by the English, French, and Dutch, finally gained their independence after World War II.

5. The phrase that best expresses the main idea or subject of this selection is:
   (A) Origin of self-government in South America
   (B) Bolívar and San Martín
   (C) King Ferdinand VII
   (D) Reasons for South American Wars of Independence
   (E) Spanish self-government

6. Napoleon deposed
   (A) San Martín
   (B) his brother
   (C) King Frederick VI
   (D) Frederick the Great
   (E) the King of Spain

7. The Spanish colonists in South America began their war of independence in
   (A) 1814
   (B) 1824
   (C) 1808
   (D) 1945
   (E) 1834

8. Simón Bolívar and José de San Martín were
   (A) Spanish nobles
   (B) advisers to the King
   (C) outlaws
   (D) military leaders
   (E) Brazilians

9. A junta is
   (A) a committee
   (B) a group formed to govern
   (C) a Spanish word
   (D) a military group
   (E) a Spanish nobleman

10. By 1824 all of South America was self-governing except for three small areas ruled by the
    (A) French, English, Spanish
    (B) Spanish, Brazilians, French
    (C) English, French, Dutch
    (D) Germans, French, Spanish
    (E) English, French, Portuguese

Harriet Tubman was, perhaps, the most remarkable of many remarkable people who worked on the Underground Railroad. She was called the "Moses of her people" because she led so many slaves out of bondage just as Moses had done for his people. She had been born a slave and at 25 managed to escape. She then organized escape routes over which she led out her sisters and brothers and her parents. She led more than three hundred of her fellow slaves to freedom. Each trip was tightly organized and her word was law. The route was more important than any individual, since runaway slaves, if caught, would be tortured and they might reveal the escape patterns.

Slaveholders hated and feared Harriet Tubman. They offered $40,000 in reward money for her capture dead or alive but she was never caught. During the Civil War she served as a nurse. After the war she continually worked for rights for her people.

11. The phrase that best expresses the main idea or subject of this selection is:
    (A) Harriet Tubman's escape
    (B) The way to freedom
    (C) Harriet Tubman and the Underground Railway
    (D) The Underground Railway
    (E) Moses of her people

12. Slave owners showed their feelings toward Harriet Tubman by
    (A) freeing three hundred slaves
    (B) offering a reward for her capture
    (C) offering her a reward
    (D) calling her "Moses of her people"
    (E) torturing runaway slaves

13. The purpose of the Underground Railway was to
    (A) give Harriet Tubman a job
    (B) anger slave holders
    (C) organize slaves
    (D) free runaway slaves
    (E) provide an escape route for slaves

From earliest times, eggs have been an important human food. The Eskimos gather the eggs of ducks that visit the Arctic in the spring. African Bushmen and Hottentots eat ostrich eggs. The eggs of sea birds are the chief and favorite native food of the Easter Islanders. Turtle eggs are eaten in South America. Eggs of fishes are considered a great delicacy. The eggs or roe of the sturgeon of the Caspian sea are salted and appear on our tables as caviar.

Since eggs must give rise to full-fledged organisms, it is not surprising that their yolks are extremely rich in minerals, such as phosphorus and particularly iron. Milk, perhaps the most valuable of protective foods, has a weak spot in its shortage of iron. Eggs have a far richer supply of iron, but they have less calcium proportionately than milk. Young chicks get their calcium from the eggshells. Eggs also have a good supply of phosphorus, which is as badly needed in the formation of bones and teeth as is calcium. So far as vitamins are concerned, eggs are about as rich and varied a source as can be found. They contain all the vitamins but C. There is an abundance of vitamin A in them and they also form an excellent source of the several components of the vitamin B group. Besides, eggs also contain the precious sunshine vitamin known as vitamin D. Their principal nutrient is protein. All of these nutrients—minerals, vitamins and proteins—make eggs an excellent protective food.

14. The phrase that best expresses the main idea or subject of this selection is:
(A) A comparison of milk with eggs
(B) The formation of an egg
(C) Various kinds of eggs
(D) Eggs as a food
(E) Vitamins in eggs

15. Ostrich eggs form an article of diet among the
(A) South Americans
(B) Eskimos
(C) Easter Islanders
(D) Europeans
(E) Hottentots

16. Milk as a food is deficient in
(A) water
(B) fat
(C) iron
(D) calcium
(E) vitamins

17. The part of the egg that provides the young chicken with the needed calcium is the
(A) white
(B) yolk
(C) shell
(D) watery content
(E) membrane lining the shell

18. Most of the food substance of the egg is composed of
(A) proteins
(B) fats
(C) carbohydrates
(D) calcium
(E) phosphorus

19. Eggs lack vitamin
(A) A
(B) B_1
(C) B_2
(D) C
(E) D

Were all mosquitoes males, the human race would doubtless pay them small attention, for the male mosquito's food is vegetable juice. It is only the female mosquito that has an appetite for animal blood and an apparatus for procuring it. The female mosquito's proboscis (feeding organ) is a flexible tube with a groove on the upper side. Within this groove are sheathed six needle-keen stylets with points like lancets. It is these with which the tapping of the blood streams is done. When the mosquito has discovered a good feeding-site, she presses her proboscis against it until the external sheath is bent back and the stylets are allowed to plunge into the flesh. Upon the uppermost of these piercing organs there is a tiny trough or channel through which the blood of the victim is drawn up. So tiny and quick is the mosquito's puncture that in itself it would cause no distress to human being or other animal. The distress is caused by a different operation. As she draws in the blood, she pours out also the secretion of her salivary glands—a fiercely irritant spittle which she injects deep into the wound. The purpose of this is to delay the coagulation of the blood until her feeding is completed.

20. The phrase that best expresses the central idea of this paragraph is:
(A) The mosquito appetite
(B) Male vs. female mosquitoes
(C) The structure of a male mosquito
(D) Why mosquitoes bite human beings
(E) How a mosquito bites

21. The male mosquito lives on
 (A) dew
 (B) vegetable juice
 (C) blood
 (D) grass leaves
 (E) spittle

22. The female mosquito pierces the skin of her victim by means of her
 (A) lancets
 (B) stylets
 (C) groove
 (D) glands
 (E) sheath

23. The irritation resulting from a mosquito bite is due to
 (A) pressure of the proboscis
 (B) coagulation of the blood
 (C) puncture of the skin
 (D) sucking of the blood
 (E) injection of a liquid

Answers to All Exercises, Practice Tests, and Mastery Exams

EXERCISES

EXERCISE 1, p. 140

1. yes	11. yes	21. no	31. yes
2. no	12. yes	22. yes	32. no
3. yes	13. no	23. no	33. no
4. no	14. no	24. yes	34. yes
5. yes	15. yes	25. yes	35. yes
6. yes	16. no	26. yes	36. yes
7. yes	17. yes	27. yes	37. yes
8. no	18. no	28. yes	38. no
9. no	19. no	29. no	39. yes
10. no	20. no	30. no	40. yes

EXERCISE 2, p. 141

1. artichoke—architect
2. butter—better
3. emotion—motion
4. duet—do-it
5. cub—cud
6. humor—human
7. florist—forest
8. resolution—revolution
9. invading—evading
10. lone—loan
11. burro—borrow
12. choler—color
13. cruisers—choosers
14. deacons—beacons
15. flame—fame
16. Haul—Hall
17. humility—humidity
18. insulted—consulted
19. lizard—wizard
20. roast—roost
21. sneak—snake
22. magnets—maggots
23. galleon—gallon
24. eagle—equal
25. consonant—continent

EXERCISE 3, p. 145

1. **B**; **C**; **A**; **D** ... each sentence helps to explain the germ-killing quality of the bandage.
2. **A**; **B**; **C**; **D** ... the article explains the meaning of minority and how prejudice gathers around it.
3. **B**; **A**; **C**; **D** ... the article shows the advantages of the boat to the sportsman.
4. **A**; **B**; **C**; **D** ... the article explains the three types of color blindness.
5. **A**; **B**; **D**; **C** ... the paragraph shows how the 1957 Act has affected U.S. transportation.

EXERCISE 4, p. 150

1. **A**, **B**, and **D**; **C** ...lived "in the swampy woodlands," ... walked "across the soggy terrain."
2. "Approximately 4,000 settled in the United States when the hostilities were over." **A**, **C**, and **D**; **B** ... have "settled in the United States" ... meant that fighting had ceased.
3. "Naturalists may dispute about which trees are the largest in the world." **B**; **C** or **D**; **A** ... "However, scientists agree ..."
4. **C**; **A**; **B**; selfish ... **D**.
5. "Polyethylene was a war-time product first developed in England during World War II." **A**; **C**; **D**; war-time product; **B**.

EXERCISE 5, p. 154

1. "Cousin John ... go." **C**.
2. Regardless of the reasons ... better." **B**.
3. "Jargon ... workers." **C**.
4. "This jargon ... society." **B**.
5. "Amber ... trees." **B**.
6. "The people ... person." **A**.
7. "Many inmates ... slowly." **A**.
8. "The romantic ... be." **D**.
9. "When out-of-state ... world." **B**.

EXERCISE 6, p. 160

1. **A** and **B**; **D**; **E** Venus... 5 ... Mars.
2. **A** and **B**; 93 (Earth), 141 (Mars), 67 (Venus). Closest is **E**.
3. plants ... moss ... **C**.
4. blue ... red ... **C**; wet ... **A**; red ... blue ... alkaline ... **D**; red to blue ... **B**.
5. **B**; **D**; **C**; first three sentences ... consciousness ... **A**.
6. his guard to slip for a brief second ... **B**.
7. 1812 ... **D**; (**A**) ... (**C**) 1803 ... French ... **B**.
8. Part of ... 1821; part ... state of Missouri ... (**C**).
9. tall (humorous)
10. Humor ... **C**.

PRACTICE TESTS

TEST 1, p. 147

1. **B** 2. **B** 3. **E** 4. **C** 5. **B**

TEST 2, p. 148

1. **A** 2. **B** 3. **D** 4. **C** 5. **C**

TEST 3, p. 152

1. **E** 2. **A** 3. **A** 4. **D** 5. **B**

TEST 4, p. 153

1. **C** 2. **C** 3. **C** 4. **A** 5. **A**

TEST 5, p. 156

1. **D**	2. **E**	3. **A**
4. **A**	5. **D**	6. **C**
7. **B**	8. **A**	9. **E**
10. **C**	11. **D**	12. **A**

TEST 6, p. 158

1. **C**	2. **D**
3. **A**	4. **B**
5. **C**	6. **E**
7. **B**	8. **B**
9. **E**	10. **A**

TEST 7, p. 163

1. **B**	2. **C**
3. **B**	4. **A**
5. **C**	6. **C**
7. **B**	8. **D**
9. **C**	10. **A**

TEST 8, p. 164

1. **B**	2. **D**
3. **C**	4. **A**
5. **C**	6. **D**
7. **C**	8. **D**
9. **C**	10. **C**

EXERCISE 7, p. 167

1. figurative	14. figurative
2. literal	15. figurative
3. figurative	16. literal
4. figurative	17. figurative
5. figurative	18. literal
6. literal	19. figurative
7. figurative	20. literal
8. figurative	21. figurative
9. literal	22. figurative
10. literal	23. literal
11. literal	24. figurative
12. literal	25. figurative
13. figurative	

EXERCISE 8, p. 168

1. **B**	6. **B**	11. **D**	16. **D**	21. **C**
2. **D**	7. **A**	12. **B**	17. **C**	22. **B**
3. **C**	8. **C**	13. **C**	18. **B**	23. **A**
4. **A**	9. **D**	14. **B**	19. **A**	24. **B**
5. **D**	10. **A**	15. **A**	20. **D**	25. **B**

EXERCISE 9, p. 169

1. S	11. G
2. G	12. G
3. G	13. S
4. S	14. G
5. G	15. S
6. G	16. G
7. S	17. S
8. S	18. G
9. G	19. G
10. S	20. G

EXERCISE 10, p. 170

1. **C**	6. **A**	11. **B**	16. **D**	21. **C**
2. **B**	7. **D**	12. **D**	17. **B**	22. **B**
3. **D**	8. **B**	13. **B**	18. **A**	23. **D**
4. **A**	9. **D**	14. **A**	19. **A**	24. **D**
5. **B**	10. **A**	15. **C**	20. **B**	25. **C**

EXERCISE 11, p. 171

1. **D**	4. **C**	7. **C**	10. **B**	13. **B**
2. **B**	5. **D**	8. **A**	11. **C**	14. **B**
3. **A**	6. **C**	9. **A**	12. **A**	15. **D**

EXERCISE 12, p. 172

1. **C** 2. **A** 3. **D** 4. **C** 5. **D** 6. **D** 7. **D** 8. **B** 9. **B** 10. **C** 11. **A** 12. **D** 13. **C** 14. **C** 15. **C** 16. **B** 17. **C** 18. **D**

EXERCISE 13, p. 173

1. F
2. O
3. F
4. F
5. O
6. F
7. F
8. O
9. F
10. F
11. F
12. O
13. O
14. F
15. F
16. O
17. O
18. O
19. F
20. O

EXERCISE 14, p. 175

1. human beings
2. underground water
3. ovules
4. first atomic bomb
5. airplane travel
6. school budget
7. Supreme Court
8. cease-fire agreement
9. crimes of violence
10. automation
11. inventions
12. urban renewal
13. mass communication
14. public education
15. success in life
16. powers of the President
17. inorganic compounds
18. bacteria
19. chief ideas of Hinduism
20. official languages

EXERCISE 15, p. 176

1. **B** 2. **D** 3. **B** 4. **B** 5. **D** 6. **A** 7. **B** 8. **B** 9. **D** 10. **A** 11. **D** 12. **B** 13. **D** 14. **C** 15. **D**

EXERCISE 16, p. 177

1. (A) banning (B) control
2. (A) short-necked (B) stretching
3. (A) competition (B) made up
4. (A) money (B) trading
5. (A) destroy (B) attacks
6. (A) equal (B) integration
7. (A) navigation (B) flows from
8. (A) modified (B) behavior
9. (A) troublesome (B) burn
10. (A) solid (B) flame

EXERCISE 17, p. 178

1. (A) D (B) M
2. (A) M (B) D
3. (A) D (B) M
4. (A) D (B) M
5. (A) D (B) M
6. (A) D (B) M
7. (A) D (B) M
8. (A) M (B) D
9. (A) M (B) D
10. (A) M (B) D
11. (A) M (B) D
12. (A) M (B) D
13. (A) D (B) M
14. (A) D (B) M
15. (A) D (B) M

EXERCISE 18, p. 179

1. (A) E (B) C
2. (A) E (B) C
3. (A) C (B) E
4. (A) E (B) C
5. (A) C (B) E
6. (A) E (B) C
7. (A) E (B) C
8. (A) C (B) E
9. (A) C (B) E
10. (A) C (B) E
11. (A) C (B) E
12. (A) E (B) C
13. (A) C (B) E
14. (A) C (B) E
15. (A) C (B) E

EXERCISE 19, p. 180

1. **C** 2. **D** 3. **D** 4. **D** 5. **D** 6. **B** 7. **C** 8. **C** 9. **B** 10. **B**

EXERCISE 20, p. 181

(In this exercise appropriate synonyms for the indicated answers can be acceptable for credit.)

1. (A) safety (B) future
2. (A) fertile (B) greatest
3. (A) prevent (B) destruction
9. (A) admired (B) faded
10. (A) head (B) authority
11. (A) developed (B) construction

4. (A) lessened
   (B) cool
5. (A) tools*
   (B) weapons*
6. (A) stop
   (B) seizing
7. (A) accustomed
   (B) advance
8. (A) end
   (B) settling
12. (A) excessive
   (B) problem
13. (A) pollution
   (B) irreplaceable
14. (A) effective
   (B) people
15. (A) people
   (B) program

(*reversible answers)

EXERCISE 21, p. 183

1.	four	11.	four
2.	It	12.	A
3.	Washoe	13.	conditions
4.	four	14.	He
5.	India	15.	six
6.	Egypt	16.	who
7.	four	17.	Mexico
8.	All	18.	ideals
9.	That	19.	He
10.	mammals	20.	wealthy

EXERCISE 22, p. 184

1. **C**	3. **D**	5. **D**	7. **D**	9. **A**
2. **E**	4. **B**	6. **A**	8. **D**	10. **B**

EXERCISE 23, p. 186

1. **D**	3. **C**	5. **B**	7. **E**	9. **D**
2. **B**	4. **C**	6. **C**	8. **E**	10. **E**

EXERCISE 24, p. 187

1. **C**	4. **D**	7. **B**	9. **B**	11. **C**
2. **D**	6. **C**	8. **D**	10. **A**	12. **D**
3. **B**	6. **D**			

MASTERY EXAMS

Rating Your Results

On exams with 17 questions:

Superior	15–17 correct
Average	12–14 correct
Below Average	11 or fewer correct

On exams with 19–20 questions:

Superior	17–20 correct
Average	14–16 correct
Below Average	13 or fewer correct

On exams with 21–22 questions:

Superior	19–22 correct
Average	15–18 correct
Below Average	14 or fewer correct

EXAM 1, p. 189

1. **E**	5. **D**	9. **C**	13. **C**	17. **C**
2. **E**	6. **D**	10. **B**	14. **B**	18. **C**
3. **D**	7. **A**	11. **E**	15. **A**	19. **A**
4. **A**	8. **B**	12. **C**	16. **D**	20. **A**

EXAM 2, p. 192

1. **B**	4. **C**	7. **C**	10. **E**	13. **B**
2. **C**	5. **B**	8. **B**	11. **B**	14. **A**
3. **A**	C. **D**	9. **C**	12. **D**	

EXAM 3, p. 194

1. **A**	6. **B**	10. **A**	14. **E**	18. **A**
2. **D**	7. **B**	11. **E**	15. **B**	19. **D**
3. **B**	8. **C**	12. **C**	16. **A**	20. **C**
4. **C**	9. **C**	13. **B**	17. **D**	21. **B**
5. **E**				

EXAM 4, p. 197

1. **D**	5. **D**	9. **C**	13. **A**	17. **A**
2. **D**	6. **E**	10. **A**	14. **B**	18. **E**
3. **E**	7. **B**	11. **D**	15. **D**	19. **D**
4. **C**	8. **B**	12. **B**	16. **B**	20. **C**

EXAM 5, p. 200

1. **B**	6. **D**	10. **C**	14. **D**	18. **E**
2. **A**	7. **E**	11. **A**	15. **E**	19. **B**
3. **B**	8. **B**	12. **B**	16. **D**	20. **A**
4. **D**	9. **B**	13. **D**	17. **C**	21. **C**
5. **C**				

EXAM 6, p. 203

1. **D**	6. **E**	11. **C**	16. **C**	20. **E**
2. **D**	7. **A**	12. **B**	17. **C**	21. **B**
3. **B**	8. **D**	13. **E**	18. **A**	22. **B**
4. **D**	9. **B**	14. **D**	19. **D**	23. **E**
5. **A**	10. **C**	15. **E**		

Language Arts

This chapter contains digests of what you should know about:

- Spelling
- Punctuation and Capitalization
- Standard English Usage

Each section includes exercises and practice tests that will not only familiarize you with typical examination questions but also give you maximum control of the subject matter.

However, the areas covered in this chapter are those that receive the most varied treatments on examinations. Before you spend time reviewing any particular area, therefore, you should make certain that it is included in the examination you plan to take.

Answer Keys for all exercises and tests, except for spelling, are given at the end of the chapter. In the spelling section, the answers follow immediately after each test.

Spelling Aids and Rules

This section contains a review of basic rules and aids to correct spelling. Probably there is much here that you already know. The various tests will help you to identify the areas that require continued attention.

HOW TO MASTER SPELLING

Write. Every time you write a word, you are taking a spelling test. The more you write (notes, letters, homework, compositions), the more you are practicing spelling.

Check. As you write, you will be in doubt about the spelling of some words. Check these immediately in your dictionary.

Carry. Carry a pocket dictionary with you whenever possible, so that you can look up the spelling of a word immediately.

List. On a special page in your notebook list every word you misspell.

***Rewrite.** (the asterisk is for emphasis). Rewrite every misspelled word five times CAREFULLY and CORRECTLY. Cover the word each time; don't copy.

Memorize. Memorize the correct spellings of the words you have misspelled so that you never make the same mistake twice.

Study. Study lists of spelling demons, words that have given everybody trouble for a long time.

Analyze. Analyze each spelling demon and try to figure out a way to remember the difficult part. Invent a mnemonic (memory) device for each word. (See page 214.)

Learn. Learn the rules and their exceptions. One rule and ten exceptions may help you learn fifty to one hundred words.

Test. Test yourself frequently on those words that bother you most. Mother, Dad, Brother, Sister, or a friend will dictate to you. Since spelling is a writing technique, write the words from dictation. Do not spell aloud.

Spelling Diagnostic Test: The 100 Demons

DIRECTIONS: In each of the following groups of words, one word is misspelled. Find the word, and spell it correctly in the blank space.

1. finaly, original, criticism, expense, further ______
2. written, excelent, purchased, returning, decision ______
3. comittee, merely, secretary, interested, busy ______
4. awfuly, particularly, character, addressed, stating ______
5. usual, recommendation, possibly, due, alright ______
6. correspondence, customers, allowed, realy, representative ______
7. expect, accordingly, existance, suggest, experience ______
8. extremely, character, reciept, organization, material ______
9. cancel, considerably, useing, assume, bearing ______
10. definate, commission, decided, literature, entitled ______
11. imagine, balance, doubt, acquainted, refered ______
12. executive, preferrence, surprised, library, concerning ______
13. experiment, sincerly, disappoint, satisfactorily, course ______
14. sufficient, returning, different, truely, accepted ______
15. forward, guarantee, recomend, attaching, planning ______
16. similiarly, catalog, memorandum, approximately, association ______
17. accordingly, bulletin, mortgage, therefore, conection ______
18. delivery, begining, waste, inquiry, superintendent ______
19. business, remittance, extension, occured, actually ______
20. terrible, haveing, disposition, obliged, apparently ______

Answers—Diagnostic Test

1. finally
2. excellent
3. committee
4. awfully
5. all right
6. really
7. existence
8. receipt
9. using
10. definite
11. referred
12. preference
13. sincerely
14. truly
15. recommend
16. similarly
17. connection
18. beginning
19. occurred
20. having

Score
(number CORRECT multiplied by 5)____

Plan for 100%! Begin your own list of words to study now.

Misspellings I overlooked: __________

Correct spellings I was mistaken about: __________

Correct spellings I was not sure of: __________

Practice the REWRITE rule now! On a separate sheet of paper:

1. Carefully and correctly write each word from your list five times.
2. Cover the word each time you write it.
3. Don't copy.

MNEMONIC DEVICES, OR TRICKY WAYS TO REMEMBER TRICKY WORDS

Here are just a few examples of some clever, original ways to remember the kind of spellings we call demons because they have a way of tripping you up, and they keep on doing it. You can make up your own mnemonic device for any word that gives you particular trouble.

piece	Everyone likes a piece of pie. Look for PIE in PIEce.
theirs	The heirs will get theirs. Look for HEIRS in tHEIRS.
believe	Would you believe a lie? How strange to find a LIE in beLIEve.
principal	(head of a school) The principal of the school is everybody's pal. Look for PAL in princiPAL.
principle	(a law of conduct or *rule)* Look for the *le* in ruLE and principLE.
there	(over there; not here; in that place) Look for HERE in tHERE.
there	(introductory word) There is no spelling difference between "there" (introductory word) and "there" meaning "in that place."

Memorize these trick sentences:

*There*④ is no room over *there*③ for *their*① coats, so *they're*② going to wear them.

1. their belonging to them
2. they're they are
3. there in that place
4. there introductory

It's *too*③ bad that when you *two*② boys came *to*① the party you didn't bring your *two*② friends *too*④.

1. to in the direction of
2. two more than one
3. too very
4. too also

*It's*① too bad the cat caught *its*② tail in the door.

1. it's it is
2. its belonging to it

stationery	PapER for a lettER is called stationERy.
stationary	Something that stAys in the sAme plAce is stationAry.
cemetery	There are three E's buried in cEmEtEry.

Now make up your own mnemonic devices for your own spelling demons, devils, and friends.

SPELLING RULES AND TESTS

RULE 1:

*Place **i** before **e** (except after **c**) when sounded like **e** as in **he, she,** and **me.***

EXAMPLES: -ie-

field	believe	collie
brief	prairie	pier
shriek	movie	grief
fiend	fierce	frontier

-cei-

receive	deceive	ceiling
conceit	receipt	deceit

EXCEPTIONS: -ei-

either	weird	sheik
neither	seizure	protein
seize	leisure	

-cie-

financier		species

Memorize the rule plus these ten exceptions and you will be able to spell over fifty difficult words. See test on Rule 1 for other e-sounding words, below.

RULE 2:

*Place **e** before **i** when sounded like **a** as in **neighbor** and **weigh.***

EXAMPLES:

beige	heinous	skein
deign	inveigle	sleigh
eight	lei	veil
feign	neigh	vein
feint	neighbor	weigh
freight	reign	weight
geisha	rein	weighty

Note: There are no exceptions to this rule.

Test on Rules 1 and 2

DIRECTIONS: In the space beneath each of the following groups, rewrite the misspelled word correctly. There is one misspelled word in each group.

EXAMPLE: believe deceive preist

ANSWER: priest

1. peice relieve either ______
2. thief receipt breif ______
3. shriek financeir neither ______
4. seizure achieve protien ______
5. movie caddie greif ______
6. deciet relief fierce ______
7. pier fronteir wield ______
8. receive beleif besiege ______
9. bier perceive wierd ______
10. sieze siege field ______
11. hygiene cieling masterpiece ______
12. peirce fiend leisure ______
13. brigadier liege concieve ______
14. conceit prairie repreive ______
15. neice yield inveigle ______
16. wieghty heinous sleigh ______
17. rien vein feint ______
18. skein frieght neighbor ______

19. geisha	collie	niegh
		______________
20. eight	reign	decieve
		______________

Answers—Rules 1 and 2

1. piece	8. belief	15. niece
2. brief	9. weird	16. weighty
3. financier	10. seize	17. rein
4. protein	11. ceiling	18. freight
5. grief	12. pierce	19. neigh
6. deceit	13. conceive	20. deceive
7. frontier	14. reprieve	

Words I missed:

____

RULE 3:

Adding a suffix to a word ending in a vowel and consonant

When a one-syllable word ends in a vowel and consonant, double the consonant when adding a suffix beginning with a vowel.

EXAMPLES: "beg" + "-ed" equals "beGGed."

bag	baggy	baggage
clan	clannish	
bid	bidding	
squat	squatted	
sad	sadder	saddest
drug	druggist	
war	warrior	

Note: There are no exceptions to this rule.

When a two-syllable word ends in a vowel and consonant, double the consonant if the suffix begins with a vowel and the accent remains on the second syllable.

refer	referring	rebut	rebuttal
occur	occurrence	rebel	rebellion
compel	compelled	concur	concurrent

Complicated as it sounds, the rule is simple to apply once it is understood.

Note: There are very few exceptions to this rule. Here they are:

inferable	(accent on second syllable, yet no doubling)
transferable	(accent on second syllable, yet no doubling)
cancellation	(accent on third syllable, yet the "l" is doubled)
excellent	(accent on first syllable, yet the "l" is doubled)

Other Advantages of Rule 3: If you learn Rule 3, it will help you in spelling dozens of other words. For example, take words like *cool, weep, chirp, happen, offer, repeat, extend, annex, allow,* and *display.* Do they ever double the final letter? NEVER, because they do not come under the rule for doubling.

cool	weep	repeat
cooling	weeping	repeater

No doubling, *because there are two vowels before the consonant.*

cost	chirp	extend
costing	chirping	extending

No doubling, *because these words end in two consonants.*

happen	offer
happened	offered

No doubling, *because the accent is always on the first syllable.*

annex	allow	display
annexed	allowed	displaying

No doubling of "**w**," "**x**," or "**y**" ever takes place ("**x**" is really two consonants, "**ks**"; "**w**" and "**y**" act like vowels at the end of words).

patrol	equip	defer
patrolman	equipment	deferment

No doubling, *because the suffix begins with a consonant.*

infer	inference

No doubling, *because the accent shifts from second to first syllable.*

refer	referee

No doubling, *because the accent shifts from second to third syllable.*

Test on Rule 3

DIRECTIONS: *Supply the missing letters where needed*

EXAMPLES: bag_age equip_ ment

ANSWER: baggage (Supply "g" in the blank space.)
equipment (Supply nothing in the blank space.)

1. ship_ment
2. stun_ing
3. want_ing
4. bat_er
5. wrap_ing
6. drag_ed
7. wit_y
8. drug_ist
9. tan_ing
10. begin_ing
11. bid_er
12. commit_ee
13. blur_ed
14. happen_ed
15. war_ior
16. stand_ing
17. suffer_er
18. depend_ence
19. offer_ed
20. cool_ing
21. prefer_ence
22. occur_ing
23. omit_ing
24. infer_ing
25. occur_ence
26. prefer_ed
27. remit_ance
28. refer_ee
29. control_able
30. compel_ed
31. allot_ing
32. allot_ment
33. regret_ed
34. admit_ing
35. admit_ance
36. plan_ed (intended)
37. stop_ed
38. infer_ence
39. recur_ent
40. rebel_ion
41. get_ing
42. got_en
43. credit_or
44. edit_or
45. profit_ing
46. profit_eer
47. prefer_ential
48. mention_ed
49. succeed_ing
50. avail_able
51. appear_ance
52. await_ing
53. benefit_ed
54. exist_ence
55. allow_ance
56. annex_ed
57. dispel_ed
58. defer_ed
59. defer_ence
60. defer_ment

DIRECTIONS: *Fill in the blanks where necessary.*

61. commit_ee
62. equip_ing
63. defer_ence
64. concur_ent
65. refer_endum
66. begin_er
67. regret_ed
68. admis_ion
69. big_er
70. chop_ing
71. patrol_man
72. profit_ed
73. suffer_ance
74. chat_y
75. differ_ence
76. hot_est
77. repeat_er
78. extend_ing
79. acquit_al
80. impel_ed
81. rebel_ious
82. emis_ion
83. permis_ion
84. begot_en
85. rebut_al
86. beg_ar
87. transfer_ed
88. refer_ence
89. quit_er
90. deter_ent

Answers—Rule 3

2. stunning
4. batter
5. wrapping
6. dragged
7. witty
8. druggist
9. tanning
10. beginning
11. bidder
12. committee
13. blurred
15. warrior
22. occurring
23. omitting
24. inferring
25. occurrence
26. preferred
27. remittance
29. controllable
30. compelled
31. allotting
33. regretted
34. admitting
35. admittance
36. planned
37. stopped
39. recurrent
40. rebellion
41. getting
42. gotten
57. dispelled
58. deferred
59. deference
60. deferment

61. committee
62. equipping
64. concurrent
66. beginner
67. regretted
69. bigger
70. chopping
74. chatty
76. hottest
79. acquittal
80. impelled
81. rebellious
82. emission
83. permission
84. begotten
85. rebuttal
86. beggar
87. transferred
89. quitter
90. deterrent

Words I missed: ____________________

Rule 4:

*Adding a suffix to a word ending in a silent **e**.*

Add the suffix to the whole word if the suffix begins with a consonant.

Examples:

immediate	resource	whole
immediately	resourceful	wholesome
manage	cruel	noise
management	cruelly	noiseless

Exceptions:

abridge	awe	due
abridgment	awful	duly
acknowledge	argue	true
acknowledgment	argument	truly
judge	wise	whole
judgment	wisdom	wholly

*Drop the **e** and add the suffix if the suffix begins with a vowel.*

Examples:

dine	force	shine
dining	forcible	shiny
love	struggle	blue
lovable	struggling	bluish
continue	style	
continuous	stylish	

Exceptions:

agree	dye	singe
agreeable	dyeing	singeing

(to avoid confusion with dying and singing)
(Tests on Rules 4 to 10 follow Rule 10.)

Rule 5:

*When a word ends in **-le,** change silent **e** to **y** to form the adverb.*

Examples:

possible	audible	wile
possibly	audibly	wily
considerable	scale	
considerably	scaly	

Exceptions: whole wholly

Rule 6:

*When a word ends in **-ll,** add **y** to the original word to form the adverb.*

Examples:

dull	full	smell	chill
dully	fully	smelly	chilly

Note: There are no exceptions.

Rule 7:

*When a word ends in **-l,*** form the adverb as follows:

*For adjectives ending in **-l** add **-ly** to the original word.*

Examples:

cruel	natural	foul
cruelly	naturally	foully
actual	cool	beautiful
actually	coolly	beautifully

*For nouns ending in **-l,** add **y.***

curl	oil	steel
curly	oily	steely
meal	pearl	wool
mealy	pearly	wooly or woolly

RULE 8:

Adding a suffix to a word ending in **-ce** *or* **-ge.**

Drop the **e** *before* **e, i,** *or* **y.**

EXAMPLES:

arrange	arranged	arranging
change	changing	
charge	charger	charging
encourage	encouraging	
manage	managing	
notice	noticing	
range	rangy	
service	servicing	
trace	tracing	

Keep the **e** *before (1)* **a** *or* **o** *and (2) before a* consonant.

(1) Before **a** or **o**	(2) Before a consonant
advantageous	
arrangeable	arrangement
changeable	changeling
chargeable	
courageous	
	encouragement
manageable	management
noticeable	
outrageous	
peaceable	
serviceable	
traceable	

PRONUNCIATION RULES THAT AFFECT SPELLING

To understand Rule 8 more fully, it is advisable to consider several pronunciation rules.

1. **C** is pronounced like *s* before *e, i,* and *y.*
   *ce*iling *Ci*nderella Nan*cy*
2. **C** is pronounced like *k* before *a, o,* and *u* and before consonants.
   *ca*t *co*mic *cu*t le*c*ture *c*rease
3. **G** is pronounced like *j* before *e, i,* and *y.*
   *Ge*orge reli*gi*on *gy*roscope
4. **G** is pronounced like the *g* in *go* before *a, o, u,* and any consonant.
   *ga*ve *go*t *gu*n e*gg* se*gm*ent reco*gn*ize
5. The letters **dg**, when sounded as one, are always pronounced like *j.*
   ju*dg*e ri*dg*e acknowle*dg*ment

Examine these pronunciation rules now for their effect on spelling. The word *manage* under Rule 8 ends in a *soft g* or *j* sound. It drops the final *e* before *-ing* because the *g* in both *manageing* and *managing* would retain the *j* sound of the original word. Therefore, the correct spelling (Rule 8) is *managing,* without the *e.* On the other hand, *manageable* must keep the *e* (Rule 8, 1) to have the soft *g* (*j*) sound of *manage.* If the word were spelled managable, it would have the hard *g* of gun. The same rule of pronunciation guides us in the spelling of management. *G* before *m* (a consonant) would be hard. We need a soft *j* sound and therefore the *e* must be kept in management (Rule 8, 2).

Test any other word under Rule 8 by these pronunciation rules.

RULE 9:

When a word ends in **-dge,** *drop the silent* **e** *before any suffix.*

abridgment acknowledgment judgment

In the past, these words were spelled with the silent *e* since the suffix started with a consonant *(m).* However, in view of Pronunciation Rule 5 above, the combination *dg* is pronounced like *j* anyway. Since the *e* is not needed, modern spelling experts have recommended that it be dropped before any suffix. Nevertheless, students will still see the old spellings (judgement, knowledgeable, lodgement) because the writers went to school before the changes were adopted. British writers usually retain the *e.*

RULE 10:

Adding a suffix to a word ending in **-c.**

Add **k** *before* **e, i** *or* **y.**

frolic	panic	picnic
frolicking	panicky	picnicked

Frolic + ing (without a *k)* would have had *c* before *i.* According to Pronunciation Rule 1, *c* before *i* is pronounced like an *s.* To keep the *k* sound of the *c* in frolic, a *k* must be added to the *c.* The same is true for *panic + y* and *picnic + ed.*

*Add nothing before **a, o,** or **u.***

critic — critical — critically
fantastic — fantastically
comic — comical — comically
basic — basically
organic — organically

Here again, pronunciation decides spelling: *c* keeps its *k* sound before *a o, u*—hence, needs no "support."

Test on Rules 4 to 10

DIRECTIONS: Circle the letter of one misspelled word in each of the following groups of five.

EXAMPLE:

(A) circling (B) refuseing (C) dully (D) pearly (E) purely

ANSWER:

Letter (B) has been circled because *refuseing* is a misspelling of *refusing*.

1. (A) resourcful (B) wisdom (C) argument (D) cruelly (E) changeable
2. (A) curly (B) singeing (C) singing (D) politly (E) politically
3. (A) artistically (B) basically (C) professionally (D) pokeing (E) racing
4. (A) receding (B) arrangment (C) realizing (D) receiving (E) mealy
5. (A) grieving (B) rhetorically (C) retirement (D) rhythmically (E) rideing
6. (A) immediatly (B) shiny (C) shrilly (D) normally (E) dining
7. (A) pitifully (B) plentifully (C) judgment (D) useable (E) factually
8. (A) serviceable (B) believable (C) wholly (D) dodgeing (E) timing
9. (A) mercifully (B) duely (C) grateful (D) noticeably (E) masterfully
10. (A) agreeable (B) fuly (C) wholesome (D) rhyming (E) sensibly
11. (A) unruly (B) ably (C) possibly (D) decideing (E) forcible
12. (A) fancifully (B) peaceable (C) amusement (D) noiseless (E) achievment
13. (A) abridgment (B) actualy (C) dutifully (D) bereavement (E) struggling
14. (A) frilly (B) truly (C) naturally (D) hilly (E) considerablely
15. (A) fantastically (B) capitally (C) cruelly (D) regionally (E) outragous
16. (A) advantageous (B) really (C) stylish (D) vaguly (E) lovable
17. (A) physically (B) managment (C) smelly (D) parallel (E) rebel
18. (A) dyeing (B) dying (C) audibly (D) continual (E) chargable
19. (A) aweful (B) careful (C) wonderfully (D) beautiful (E) trifle
20. (A) curlly (B) acknowledgment (C) radiating (D) wooly (E) enforceable

DIRECTIONS: Supply the missing letters where necessary.

EXAMPLE: picnic_ed

ANSWER: picnic<u>k</u>ed

21. rac_ing
22. saf_ty
23. fat_ful
24. arriv_al
25. mov_ment
26. peac_ful
27. abridg_ing
28. ach_ing
29. blu_ish
30. su_ing
31. cano_ing
32. amus_ment
33. argu_ment
34. excit_ing
35. tru_ly
36. mov_able
37. griev_ance
38. forc_ible

39. lov_able
40. argu_ing
41. tast_ful
42. creat_or
43. admir_able
44. manag_able
45. ting_ing
46. ho_ing
47. charg_able
48. du_ly
49. wis_dom
50. valu_able
51. notic_able
52. outrag_ous
53. arrang_able
54. picnic_ing
55. fantastic_ly
56. judg_ment
57. wool_y
58. chang_ing
59. critic_ly
60. mimic_ry
61. encourag_ing
62. abridg_ment
63. traffic_ed
64. peac_able
65. possibl_y
66. servic_able
67. unrul_y
68. aw_ful
69. grat_ful
70. cruel_y
71. full_y
72. considerabl_y
73. colic_y
74. basic_ly
75. continu_ous
76. shin_y
77. styl_ish
78. dull_y
79. undu_ly
80. chronic_ly

DIRECTIONS: Next to each word, write *c* if it is correctly spelled. Rewrite the word correctly if it is misspelled.

EXAMPLES:

mimicked	c
panicy	panicky

81. arrangable ________
82. fantasticly ________
83. encouraging ________
84. picnicking ________
85. peaceably ________
86. noticeable ________
87. colicky ________
88. shellaced ________
89. advantageous ________
90. charged ________
91. panicked ________
92. changing ________
93. chronically ________
94. frolicking ________
95. frantically ________
96. arranging ________
97. artisticly ________
98. noticing ________
99. courageous ________
100. trafficing ________
101. changeably ________
102. tracable ________
103. basically ________
104. judging ________
105. acknowledgeing ________
106. encouragment ________
107. abridgment ________
108. outragous ________
109. acknowledgment ________
110. judgement ________

Answers—Rules 4 to 10

1. **A**	5. **E**	9. **B**	13. **B**	17. **B**
2. **D**	6. **A**	10. **B**	14. **E**	18. **E**
3. **D**	7. **D**	11. **D**	15. **E**	19. **A**
4. **B**	8. **D**	12. **E**	16. **D**	20. **A**

22. safety
23. fateful
25. movement
26. peaceful
31. canoeing
32. amusement
41. tasteful
44. manageable
45. tinging or tingeing
46. hoeing
47. chargeable
51. noticeable
52. outrageous
53. arrangeable
54. picnicking
55. fantastically
57. wooly or woolly
59. critically
63. trafficked
64. peaceable
65. possibly
66. serviceable
69. grateful
70. cruelly
73. colicky
74. basically
80. chronically

(The other words on the test needed no letters added.)

81. arrangeable
82. fantastically
83. c
84. c
85. c
86. c
87. c
88. shellacked
89. c
90. c
91. c
92. c
93. c
94. c
95. c
96. c
97. artistically
98. c
99. c
100. trafficking
101. c
102. traceable
103. c
104. c
105. acknowledging
106. encouragement
107. c
108. outrageous
109. c
100. judgment

Words I missed:

1.–20. ____________________

21.–80. ____________________

____

____

81.–110. ____________________

RULE 11:

*Adding suffixes to words ending in **-y**, and forming plurals and some verb forms.*

*If the **y** follows a consonant, as in*

dut*y*	victor*y*	magnif*y*	appl*y*
carr*y*	bus*y*	laz*y*	ic*y*

*change the **y** to **i** when you add a suffix, as in*

dut*i*ful	victor*i*ous	magn*i*ficent
appl*i*cant	carr*i*age	bus*i*ness
laz*i*ness	ic*i*ness	

*Also, change **y** to **i** and add **es** for the plural of nouns, and for some verb forms, as in*

lady	carry	reply	sky	supply
ladies	carries	replies	skies	supplies

EXCEPT: 1. *When the suffix begins with an **i**, the **y** is kept:*

hurry	bury	defy	copy
hurrying	burying	defying	copyist

EXCEPT: 2. *When the **y** keeps the **i** sound before a consonant, the **y** is kept.*

dry	shy	sly	spry
dryness	shyness	slyness	spryness

*Do not change **y** to **i** when adding a suffix to a word ending in a vowel + **y**.*

bu*y*	buyer	buying
jo*y*	joys	joyful
da*y*	days	
monke*y*	monkeys	
pay	payable	
emplo*y*	employed	employable

EXCEPTIONS:

day	lay	pay	say	slay
daily	laid	paid	said	slain

Note: When the word ending in **-y** combines with another word, the **y** is kept.

anyone	drypoint	copywrite

(Test on Rule 11 follows Rule 12.)

RULE 12:

*When a word ends in **-ie**, change **ie** to **y** when adding **-ing**.*

lie	tie	belie	vie
lying	tying	belying	vying

Test on Rules 11 and 12

DIRECTIONS: Supply the missing letters.

EXAMPLE:

juicy juic_ness

ANSWER:

juiciness

any 1. an_thing

2. an_where

birthday 3. birthda_s

beauty 4. beaut_s

5. beaut_ful

carry	6. carr_ing
	7. carr_ed
	8. carr_age
city	9. cit__s
	10. cit__zen
die	11. d__ing
	12. d__d
donkey	13. donk__s
dye	14. d__ing
	15. d__d
easy	16. eas__ly
	17. eas__er
	18. eas__est
employ	19. emplo__ees
	20. emplo__er
	21. emplo__ment
emergency	22. emergenc__s
Friday	23. Frida__s
funny	24. funn__er
	25. funn__est
gloomy	26. gloom__ness
	27. gloom__er
greedy	28. greed__ness
hobby	29. hobb__s
history	30. histor__an
	31. histor__cal
icy	32. ic__ness
	33. ic__cle
injury	34. injur__s
	35. injur__ous
key	36. k__s
kindly	37. kindl__ness
lay	38. la__d
lie	39. l__d
	40. l__ing

library	41. librar__s
	42. librar__ian
marry	43. marr__d
	44. marr__age
memory	45. memor__s
	46. memor__al
necessary	47. necessar__ly
necessity	48. necessit__s
obey	49. ob__ing
	50. ob__ed
ordinary	51. ordinar__ly
pay	52. pa__d
plenty	53. plent__ful
pony	54. pon__s
ready	55. read__ness
reply	56. repl__d
	57. repl__ing
responsibility	58. responsibilit__s
say	59. sa__d
	60. sa__s
Saturday	61. Saturda__s
stay	62. sta__d
	63. sta__ing
strawberry	64. strawberr__s
they	65. the__r
try	66. tr__ing
	67. tr__d
	68. tr__al
university	69. universit__s
unnecessary	70. unnecessar__ly
vary	71. var__d
	72. var__ous
	73. var__ing
vie	74. v__ing
volley	75. voll__s
	76. voll__ing

worry	77. worr_d
	78. worr_ing
	79. worr_s
worthy	80. worth_ness

DIRECTIONS: In each group of five words, one is misspelled. Pick out the incorrect word and write it correctly in the space below.

81. defied layed days copying lying

____

82. iciness spys beautiful carrying joyful

____

83. luckyly curliness colonies readily days

____

84. playful giddiness business birthdaies applies

____

85. loveliness modifies courtesies countries spriness

____

86. swaying supplies buying lieing buried

____

87. moneys accompanies dryness armys slain

____

88. slyly playing colonies difficulties payed

____

89. delaid wryness earliness applying easiest

____

90. employed buyers defied steadiness familys

____

Answers—Rules 11 and 12

1. anything
2. anywhere
3. birthdays
4. beauties
5. beautiful
6. carrying
7. carried
8. carriage
9. cities
10. citizen
11. dying
12. died
13. donkeys
14. dyeing
15. dyed
16. easily
17. easier
18. easiest
19. employees
20. employer
21. employment
22. emergencies
23. Fridays
24. funnier
25. funniest
26. gloominess
27. gloomier
28. greediness
29. hobbies
30. historian
31. historical
32. iciness
33. icicle
34. injuries
35. injurious
36. keys
37. kindliness
38. laid
39. lied
40. lying
41. libraries
42. librarian
43. married
44. marriage
45. memories
46. memorial
47. necessarily
48. necessities
49. obeying
50. obeyed
51. ordinarily
52. paid
53. plentiful
54. ponies
55. readiness
56. replied
57. replying
58. responsibilities
59. said
60. says
61. Saturdays
62. stayed
63. staying
64. strawberries
65. their
66. trying
67. tried
68. trial
69. universities
70. unnecessarily
71. varied
72. various
73. varying
74. vying
75. volleys
76. volleying
77. worried
78. worrying
79. worries
80. worthiness

81. laid
82. spies
83. luckily
84. birthdays
85. spryness
86. lying
87. armies
88. paid
89. delayed
90. families

Words I missed:

1.–80. ____________________

____

____

81.–90. ____________________

RULE 13:

*Distinguishing between **fore-** and **for**.*

*Spell the prefix **fore-** in words meaning **before.***

To *foretell* the future means to *tell* about a future happening *before* it happens.

forebode	foreknowledge	foresight
forecast	foreman	forestall
foreclose	foremost	foretaste
forefather	forenoon	forethought
forefinger	forerunner	forewarn
forefront	foresee	forewoman
foreground	foreshadow	foreword
forehand	foreshorten	aforesaid
forehead		

*Spell the prefix **for-** in words meaning **off, away,** or **without.***

To *forbid* means to *bid* some action *away,* that is, to bid some action not be done.

forbear	forget	forsake
forfeit	forlorn	forswear
forgive		

EXCEPTION: forward
This word has the meaning *before,* but it contains no *e.*

Be aware that two words are commonly spelled either way.

forgather	forgo
foregather	forego

Forgo means *to go without; forego* means *to go before.*

STUDY HINT:
Memorize the nine *for-* words. Then you will know that any other word is spelled *fore-*. Memorizing nine words will give you control of thirty-eight words.

Test on Rule 13

DIRECTIONS: Supply the missing *e* in the words that require it.

1. afor_said
2. for_sake
3. for_bode
4. for_swear
5. for_get
6. for_cast
7. for_word
8. for_close
9. for_man
10. for_bear
11. for_hand
12. for_noon
13. for_head
14. for_feit
15. for_lorn
16. for_stall
17. for_see
18. for_sight
19. for_ground
20. for_most

Answers—Rule 13

1. aforesaid
3. forebode
6. forecast
7. foreword
8. foreclose
9. foreman
11. forehand
12. forenoon
13. forehead
16. forestall
17. foresee
18. foresight
19. foreground
20. foremost

(All the other words are spelled without the *e*.)

Words I missed:

____

____

RULE 14:

*When adding the word **full** as a suffix to another word, drop the final **l**.*

cup + full = cupful
spoon + full = spoonful

awful	handful	masterful	plentiful
beautiful	fanciful	merciful	sorrowful
dutiful	grateful	pitiful	wonderful

(There are many other *full* compounds; they are all spelled -ful.)

STUDY HINTS:

1. The only word in the language ending in f-u-l-l is the word *full* itself.
2. Note the demons *awful* (without an *e*) and *grateful* (with an *e*).
3. Notice that *beauty, duty, fancy, mercy, pity,* and *plenty* drop *y* and add *i* before *-ful.* See Rule 11.

Test on Rule 14

DIRECTIONS: Add the word *full* as a suffix to each of the words below.

1. skill __________
2. wonder __________
3. hand __________
4. ear __________
5. beauty __________
6. purpose __________
7. forget __________
8. barrel __________
9. soul __________
10. duty __________
11. fancy __________
12. grace __________
13. shovel __________
14. pity __________
15. tear __________
16. wake __________
17. mourn __________
18. care __________
19. venge(ance) __________
20. rest __________

Answers—Rule 14

1. skillful	11. fanciful
2. wonderful	12. graceful
3 handful	13. shovelful
4. earful	14. pitiful
5. beautiful	15. tearful
6. purposeful	16. wakeful
7. forgetful	17. mournful
8. barrelful	18. careful
9. soulful	19. vengeful
10. dutiful	20. restful

Words I missed: ________________

Spelling Mastery Test 1

DIRECTIONS: On the line provided, rewrite correctly the misspelled word in each group.

EXAMPLE:
breakfast thier children's neighbor
ANSWER: their

1. faucet, picnic, series, sieze __________
2. pastime, tomatoes, supprised, imaginary __________
3. devine, mischief, ridiculous, haven't __________
4. definate, machinery, descendant, contemptible __________

5. cathedral, discription, stationery, simile

____

6. eight, marriage, reciept, choir

____

7. consistent, genuine, muscle, Febuary

____

8. glimpse, dairy, dissipline, creature

____

9. transfered, successful, village, woman

____

10. becoming, earnest, embarass, suite

____

11. ninteenth, supersede, persuade, circular

____

12. bureau, forehead, momentous, mischeivous

____

13. missionary, suspicious, thoroughly, perserverance

____

14. colleague, heros, minimizing, itemized

____

15. humane, pitifully, garranty, eliminate

____

16. harrass, monotonous, lightning, hymn

____

17. compelled, mobilize, submitted, volenteer

____

18. bycicle, monetary, reference, prestige

____

19. courteous, neccesity, inadequate, unconsciously

____

20. colonel, angle, antique, liesure

____

Answers—Mastery Test 1

1. seize
2. surprised
3. divine
4. definite
5 description
6. receipt
7. February
8. discipline
9. transferred
10. embarrass
11. nineteenth
12. mischievous
13. perseverance
14. heroes
15. guarantee
16. harass
17. volunteer
18. bicycle
19. necessity
20. leisure

Words I missed: ____________

Spelling Mastery Test 2

DIRECTIONS: In each of the following groups, 1 to 20, one word is misspelled. In each case spell correctly, on the line provided, the misspelled word.

1. attach, voucher, twins, assistence, cordial

____

2. faculties, people's, indetedness, ignorant, resource

____

3. wholly, apitite, twelfth, unauthorized, embroider

____

4. certified, attorneys, foggy, potato, extravagent

____

5. hysterics, simelar, intelligent, label, salaries

____

6. apponants, we're, finely, herald, continuous

____

7. cancellation, athletic, perminant, preference, utilize

____

8. urns, zephir, tuition, incidentally, acquisition

____

9. kinsman, bazaar, foliage, wretched, asassination

____

10. insignia, bimonthly, typewriting, notariety, psychology

____

11. lieutenant, abandoned, successor, phisycal, inquiries

____

12. nuisance, coranation, voluntary, faculties, herald

____

13. indipendance, notwithstanding, tariff, opportunity, accompanying

____

14. statutes, rhubarb, corset, unauthorized, subsedy

____

15. partisan, initiate, colonel, ilness, errand

____

16. acquired, wrapped, propriater, screech, duly

____

17. sufraige, countenance, fraternally, undo, fireman

____

18. ladies', chef (cook), spirituel, Sabbath, itemized

____

19. ere, interests, cheesecloth, paridoxical, assessment

____

20. bulletin, everlasting, porttiere, discretion, inconvenienced

____

Answers—Mastery Test 2

1. assistance	11. physical
2. indebtedness	12. coronation
3. appetite	13. independence
4 extravagant	14. subsidy
5. similar	15. illness
6. opponents	16. proprietor
7. permanent	17. suffrage
8. zephyr	18. spiritual
9. assassination	19. paradoxical
10. notoriety	20. portiere

Words I missed: ____________

Spelling Mastery Test 3

DIRECTIONS: In each of the following groups, 1 to 20, one word is misspelled. In each case, rewrite the misspelled word correctly on the line provided.

1. advising, recognize, seize (grasp), supply, tradegy

____

2. intensive, stationary (fixed), benifit, equipped, preferring

____

3. predjudice, pervade, excel, capitol (building), chimneys

____

4. all right, ninty, cronies, nervous, separate

____

5. atheletic, queue (waiting line), furl, schedule, abusing ____________
6. skein, wholesome, witches, coherent, defenite ____________
7. aggravate, counsel (advice), deplorable, proficiancy, interested ____________
8. suppressed, lugubrious, pecuniary, boulevard, fourty-fourth ____________
9. militarism, pilot, crimnal, monotonous, tendency ____________
10. prevalent, berth (for sleeping), auxiliary, priveleges, women's ____________
11. acquired, mercury, stetistics, thought, vassal ____________
12. tempature, calendar, series, gout, alcohol ____________
13. important, foreigner, Australia, leggend, rhythm ____________
14. height, achevment, monarchial, axle, fertile ____________
15. falsity, prestige, conquer, arketecture, Jerusalem ____________
16. magniffecent, bacteria, holly, diseases, cellar ____________
17. medicine, grievous, beaker, benefits, attendents ____________
18. military, vacancy, weird, feudalism, hybird ____________
19. adopted, agrigate, Renaissance, tournament, colonies ____________
20. vivisection, penitentiary, candadacy, ere, Sabbath ____________

Answers—Mastery Test 3

1. tragedy
2. benefit
3. prejudice
4. ninety
5. athletic
6. definite
7. proficiency
8. forty-fourth
9. criminal
10. privileges
11. statistics
12. temperature
13. legend
14. achievement
15. architecture
16. magnificent
17. attendants
18. hybrid
19. aggregate
20. candidacy

Words I missed: ____________

Punctuation and Capitalization

If you are using this book to prepare for a specific test, make certain that the material in this section is included in the test items before you begin to allot time to study sessions.

This section contains a review of basic rules of punctuation and capitalization. There is much here that you already know. Use the exercises and practice tests to find the areas that require your continued attention.

Turn to pages 285–288 for Answer Keys to all exercises and practice tests in this section.

PUNCTUATION MARKS: REVIEW AND RULES

The Apostrophe (')

The apostrophe shows where sounds or letters have been left out.

can't (cannot)
B'klyn (Brooklyn)

The plurals of letters and numbers need an apostrophe.

How many *6's* are there in your phone number?
My name is spelled with two *l's*.

The possessive case of nouns and pronouns (except personal pronouns) needs the apostrophe.

Harry's hat	the Joneses' house
the cat's paw	the owls' nests
someone's cry	

Use no apostrophe with personal pronouns!

his	yours	theirs
hers	ours	its

To understand the use of the apostrophe with the possessive case more clearly, it is necessary to know a few rules. The following will explain what you must know:

Singular Possessive

If a singular word ends in a letter other than **s**, *add an apostrophe and* **s**.

man	man's
coat	coat's

When a name ends in the letter **s**, *add either just an apostrophe or an apostrophe and* **s**.

CORRECT: *Dickens'* books or *Dickens's* books.

If a word ends in *s*, sometimes you add only the apostrophe. It is usually the sound that determines the choice.

goodness' *cross's*

Compound or hyphenated nouns have the apostrophe and **s** added to the last word in the group.

John, Mary, and *Sal's* project
My sister-in-*law's* cake

Plural Possessive

If the plural form of the word or name ends in the letter **s**, *just add an apostrophe after the* **s**.

horses	*horses'*
schools	*schools'*
Murphys	*Murphys'*

If the plural form does not end in the letter **s**, *add an apostrophe and* **s**.

men's
mice's

EXERCISE 1

Read the following paragraph carefully. Look at the word preceding each number. Next to the same number below, write the letter C *if an apostrophe has been correctly used, or if an apostrophe has been omitted where none belongs. If an apostrophe has been incorrectly omitted or used, write out the full word, placing the apostrophe where it belongs.*

In many ways the ancient Greeks' (1) coins were different from our's (2). Their coins werent (3) made for utility only, but were also works (4) of art. Artists commissioned to fashion these coins drew their material from nature and mythology. An interesting coin from Agrigentum pictured eagles paired in 2s (5), while another had four dolphins surrounded by dots. Often a great mans (6) portrait was used, or that of a relative. One famous Syracusan coin bears the kings (7) mother-in-laws (8) likeness. The coins (9) edges were more uneven than they are on today's (10) coins, because money then was handmade.

1. ________ 6. ________
2. ________ 7. ________
3. ________ 8. ________
4. ________ 9. ________
5. ________ 10. ________

EXERCISE 2

On the line provided, rewrite correctly any word that requires an apostrophe or that contains an apostrophe incorrectly used. Write the letter C *if no correction is needed.*

1. Is that really the latest in mens' hats? ________
2. It was really theirs and not ours. ________
3. The policemens' lot can really be a happy one. ________
4. The lady's hats are over there. ________
5. Place it near that officers documents. ________
6. His work is as good as anyones. ________
7. My French teachers notes were left on the shelf. ________
8. The razors edge has been dulled by exposure to the dampness. ________
9. Phyllis answers are as good as yours. ________
10. Please learn to dot your is. ________
11. Did you see Paul and Harriets latest project? ________
12. Its an old story by this time. ________
13. Its fine finish is the result of James hard work. ________
14. Hes the best swimmer in camp. ________
15. Wont you please listen to my side of the story! ________
16. Youd have done the same yourself. ________
17. It was just the worms turn to turn. ________
18. The trees leaves are turning pale with the cold. ________
19. The hurt animals cry filled my dreams for many nights after that incident. ________
20. The boys father and mother told his friends the entire story. ________

The Semicolon (;)

The semicolon is used where a conjunction has been left out of a sentence.

Alexander Pope was a classical poet; he used the heroic couplet.

The semicolon is used before certain words, such as

moreover	consequently
however	nevertheless
hence	thus
subsequently	as a result

when they introduce an additional thought to an otherwise complete statement. Notice that a comma usually follows such an introductory word.

> He told me it would be advisable to join; however, I used my own judgment and refused.

EXERCISE 3

One sentence in each group of four is incorrectly punctuated. Circle the answer choice of that sentence.

1. (A) Rocket ships will eventually explore new worlds. They will penetrate far into outer space.
   (B) A person who wishes to be an astronaut must be in perfect physical condition; however, more than physical stamina will be needed to qualify.
   (C) Imagine the feelings of the command pilot; when she guides her ship into sky roads never before traveled by human beings.
   (D) Space travelers will probably be fearful at first; then, when they gain experience, they will gain courage.

2. (A) The distance between Earth and Mars varies; consequently, any space flight to our sister planet will start when she is closest to us.
   (B) Scientists feel that some form of life may well exist on Mars; since they have detected what seem to be signs of water and vegetation.
   (C) Many people wonder if there are any strange, purple-hued beings on Mars; they forget that bug-eyed monsters are the creation of fiction and songwriters.
   (D) The hazards of a trip to Mars will be great; nevertheless, many will be eager to go.

3. (A) Scientists believe that there are millions of planets capable of supporting life; they feel that it is far from unlikely that animal life of some kind exists on many planets.
   (B) There are also many planets whose chemistry is vastly different from ours; it's possible that weird and fantastic forms of plant life exist on these.
   (C) Human beings know so little of the vast sea of space that surrounds them; however, one day they will certainly know much more!
   (D) Many people now are so thrilled by the possibility of exploring outer space that they cannot wait; until they soar off into the limitless sea of stars beyond us.

EXERCISE 4

HW

For each of the following, write A *if the semicolon is used correctly. Write* B *if the semicolon is used incorrectly.*

___ 1. Don't come any closer; the shell can explode at any moment.

___ 2. I told him the facts; and he believed everything I said.

___ 3. Listen to him; then, follow his plan.

___ 4. The man almost lost his life; and his car as well.

___ 5. Mike knows the answer to our problem; and we should ask him to help us.

___ 6. Only one sentence is incorrect; the other contains no error.

___ 7. We will have to see her soon; because she left her notebook in our locker.

__ 8. Tell him to see me; or the custodian.

__ 9. Over on the shelf; you will find the missing cover.

__ 10. Play fair; let the others break the rules.

__ 11. I could have left early; since I had finished my work hours ago.

__ 12. The recorder supplied all of our music; but it was just a bit too low for my comfort.

__ 13. The price is reasonable; however, I shall have to think your proposition over for a day or so.

__ 14. The melody is a haunting one; I just cannot forget it.

__ 15. Watch me; and I'll show you how to operate the tape deck.

The Comma (,)

The comma is used to separate words, phrases, or clauses in a series of three or more.

Words: He decided to take French, elementary algebra, English, and science.

Phrases: The horse galloped furiously over the hill, across the valley, through the meadow, and into the lake.

Clauses: The brothers worked steadily. John sawed the wood, Harry planed it, and Fred stacked it.

A comma is used to separate adjectives modifying the same noun, or adverbs modifying the same verb.

The rambling, old, colonial house was charming.
He advanced slowly, stealthily.

A comma is used after an introductory word, phrase, or clause.

Word: Nevertheless, the view was beautiful.

Phrase: After long hours of waiting, we found the solution.

Clause: When I saw him enter the room, I realized that our troubles were over.

Clause: Although nothing was changed, the room somehow looked different.

A comma is used to set off words or phrases in apposition.

Mr. Edmonds, my teacher, speaks very effectively.
The Golden Leopard, largest and most luxurious liner of its class, makes a transatlantic crossing in record time.

A comma is used to set off a clause that could be dropped out of the sentence without damaging its meaning

Edwards, who has a great deal of wisdom, was elected president.

The clause "who has a great deal of wisdom" merely tells us a little more about Edwards; it is not absolutely necessary to the main statement, "Edwards was elected president." Compare this with the following:

The person whom we elect to the presidency must have widsom.

The clause "whom we elect to the presidency" is indispensable. To say "The person must have wisdom" would be incomplete and even meaningless; the reader would instantly say "What person?" Therefore, no commas should be used.

A comma is used after an interjection.

Ah, so you have decided to come!

A comma is used after the name of a person who is addressed directly.

John, will you please turn off your radio?

Commas are used to set off adjectives that are placed after words they modify.

The umbrella, torn and flimsy, was no protection against the sweeping rain.

HW

EXERCISE 5

In each sentence you will find a word in italics. If you think that there should be a comma after the word in italics, write the letter C *next to the number. If you feel there should be no comma write the letter* N.

___ 1. It was a *very* difficult journey.

___ 2. The *cloud* dark and threatening, hovered over the town.

___ 3. "John," said the *teacher* "you are late."

___ 4. He preferred *fruit* and cheese for dessert.

___ 5. The *game* which I like best is basketball.

___ 6. *Eagerly* he volunteered to go.

___ 7. *Oh* you are much too kind to me.

___ 8. The Concorde, the latest advance in aeronatical *science* is twice as fast as a regular jet plane.

___ 9. *Tony* who is the youngest member of the class, is also the best baseball player.

___ 10. The team worked as a perfect unit. The fielding was *excellent* the batting was powerful, and the pitching was superb.

___ 11. Oh, puppy, *puppy* come here.

___ 12. The *college* that I choose to attend must have a first-rate science department.

___ 13. The *very* old book is a valuable antique.

___ 14. He was most interested in stamp collecting *and* photography.

___ 15. While the skipper watched the horizon for signs of storm *clouds* the passengers laughed, unaware of danger.

EXERCISE 6

For each of the following pairs, circle A *if the first sentence needs a comma. Circle* B *if the second sentence needs a comma.*

1. (A) I saw Helen and called to her.
   (B) I saw Helen and she spoke to me.

2. (A) Alexander the Great is one of my heroes.
   (B) Lincoln was a great president a man who truly loved his country.

3. (A) Yes I will definitely be there on time.
   (B) No is a word I use frequently.

4. (A) I love my cream cheese and olive sandwich.
   (B) I lived for two weeks on jelly cream cheese, and milk.

5. (A) Helen will please do as she was told.
   (B) Helen please do as you are told.

6. (A) Incidentally I could have told you that myself.
   (B) Next in line was the winner of the contest.

7. (A) Because he would not listen to me he found himself in difficulty.
   (B) He soon found himself in difficulty because he would not listen to me.

8. (A) Coming to my last reason I found that the facts are not in his favor.
   (B) Coming to my last reason was the most difficult thing for me to do.

9. (A) We told the story to my brother who had been in the next room.
   (B) We told the story to the officer who was in charge of the investigation.

10. (A) I can still see her standing there teary-eyed and smiling.
    (B) She was teary-eyed and smiling all during the interview.

The Colon (:)

A colon is used after the salutation in a formal letter.

Dear Mr. Evans:

A colon is used to separate chapter and verse when referring to Biblical quotations.

Matthew 2:3

A colon is used to separate hours and minutes when expressing the time of day in numbers.

It is now 3:25.

A colon is used after an introductory clause that precedes a listing or enumeration of items.

I believe in these truths: a person has freedom of will; a person is obligated to act in accord with one's own conscience; a person must respect others in order to respect oneself.

The curriculum included the following subjects: accounting, bookkeeping, commercial law, computer usage, and record analysis.

EXERCISE 7

Each sentence in the paragraph below is numbered, and the number is repeated, with a line beside it, below the paragraph. Read each sentence. If you think that the sentence should have a colon, write in the proper numbered space the word or expression from the sentence that should be followed by a colon. If you think that the sentence needs no colon, write the letter N *in the numbered space.*

(1) It is now 11 43 of a moonless, cold night on the desert. (2) Having spent months and months of incessant and often useless toil exploring this region, I am reminded of Job's words, "So am I made to possess months of vanity, and wearisome nights appointed to me." Job 7 3. (3) In my painstaking researches, I have discovered much evidence that this desert was once a vast ocean bottom. (4) A list of the evidence would include the following shellfish deposits, many salt lakes, beds of rock salt, and large areas filled with saline clay. (5) It seems indisputable to me that this region was once wave covered. (6) I planned to write you a letter. (7) It would have begun with these words. (8) Dear Dr. Evans I am adrift in the Sea of the Sahara, seeking the ghosts of departed fish. (9) Yet, today, water is indeed the scarcest commodity for hundreds and hundreds of miles. (10) I have, however, seen the following a violet tinted fog, a furious, destructive hot wind, and endless clouds of hot dust.

1. ____________ 6. ____________

2. ____________ 7. ____________

3. ____________ 8. ____________

4. ____________ 9. ____________

5. ____________ 10. ____________

End Punctuation—The Period (.)

The period puts a stop to a complete statement, or sentence.

He is the oldest boy in the group. (A statement)

Leave the room as quickly as possible. (A quiet order)

They wished to know what his name was. (An indirect question)

Kindly enclose a sample of the product. (A request)

End Punctuation—The Question Mark (?)

The question mark follows a direct question.

When will you go?

End Punctuation—The Exclamation Mark (!)

The exclamation mark ends a statement that is either a strong command or an expression of strong feeling

Keep still and mind your own business! (A command)

How dare you!
(Notice that this is not really a question, though it is phrased like one, but an expression of anger.)

Look, there's a man falling from the roof!
(An outcry)

EXERCISE 8

Some of the following sentences have the correct end punctuation, others have not. Next to the number, write the letter C *if the end punctuation is correct; if it is not correct, write the correct punctuation mark on the line provided.*

__ 1. Will you please leave the room quietly and immediately?

__ 2. They wanted to know how old he was.

__ 3. Leave this room at once.

__ 4. He is the smartest boy in the class!

__ 5. Where do you plan to go for your vacation?

__ 6. Are you, a private, telling your sergeant how this should be done!

__ 7. I want to know the simple facts.

__ 8. Please do as you are told!

__ 9. What are you planning to do at the end of this term?

__ 10. The general wanted to know how the enemy troops were disposed of.

EXERCISE 9

In each of the following sentences, on the line provided: Write A *if a period should precede* Margie. *Write* B *if a question mark should precede* Margie. *Write* C *if an exclamation mark should precede* Margie. *Write* D *if no punctuation mark should precede* Margie.

__ 1. You will have to tell that story to us again Margie was not listening.

__ 2. Leave now Margie will never wait for you!

__ 3. They plan to visit Margie when they arrive in San Francisco.

__ 4. How can I ever thank you Margie will be ever grateful to you for your kindness.

__ 5. Will you help me carry the package Margie plans to use as one of the items on the stage during the rehearsal.

__ 6. He will have to be the one who will help Margie to rewrite the entire second act.

__ 7. When is the report due Margie said that she would help me do the typing.

__ 8. They asked that we remind you to complete the assignment Margie was also absent today.

__ 9. Will you kindly come this way Margie is in charge of the next demonstration.

__ 10. What can I do now Margie left with the keys to the car!

__ 11. Listen to that racket Margie is practicing again.

__ 12. He will be able to help Margie if he is told just what work must be done.

__ 13. The music is hauntingly beautiful Margie must get us that record the next time she goes to the city.

__ 14. Which one is mine Margie had said that I would be given one.

__ 15. Copy the homework assignment quickly Margie will explain how to do the fourth problem.

Quotation Marks (" ")

A pair of quotation marks is used to set off a direct quotation.

John said, "I don't really have the qualifications for the job, but I'll try."

"I don't really have the qualifications," said John, "but I'll try." (broken quotation)

Single quotation marks are used for a quotation within a quotation.

John said, "Mother's exact words were, 'Dust the furniture carefully,' and I'll do just as she said."

The titles of books, magazines, newspapers, plays, movies, television series, and long (epic) poems should be italicized. Titles of chapters, articles, television shows, and works of art and music require quotation marks.

Did you read "On Language" in last Sunday's *New York Times*?

"Walnuts" was one of the funnier episodes on the old *Dick Van Dyke Show*.

"Mona Lisa" is a lovely work of art, as Nat King Cole sang in the 1950's song, "Mona Lisa."

Quotation marks are used to set off words used sarcastically or words of a technical nature, or to show the attitude of the author, usually ironical.

We call him "Skinny." He weighs 284 pounds.

Since he began studying chemistry, all he talks of is "isotopes" and "valences."

Quotation Patterns for Dialogues

1. He said, "We ____________."
2. "We ____________," he said.
3. He asked, "Are we ____________?"
4. "Are we ____________?" he asked.
5. "We ____________," he said. "We ____________. We ____________. They ____________." (four sentences)
6. He said, "We ____________. They ____________. Then ____________." (three sentences)
7. "We ____________." (one speaker)
   "Are ____________?" (a second speaker)
   "Yes, we ____________." (first speaker)

CHECK YOUR ABILITY TO USE QUOTATION MARKS CORRECTLY.

EXERCISE 10

In the following paragraph there are numbered, italicized word groups. If you think that quotation marks belong around the italicized group, then place the letter Q *after the corresponding number at the end of the paragraph. If you think that there should be no quotation marks, write the letter* N.

Did you ever read (1) *This Earth of Ours* by (2) *Jean Henri Fabre?* It is a fascinatng account of the earth's geography and (3) *physiography.* Reading it, you may wonder why Fabre calls the (4) *Sahara Desert* (5) *the Sahara Ocean.* You may be surprised to find that he said (6) *that volcanoes are really helpful to humanity.* In Fabre's words, (7) *they furnish a vent for confined gases.* He also informs us that (8) *many mountains began as masses of lava.* He wrote, (9) *these masses erupted from early volcanoes.*

1. ______ 4. ______ 7. ______
2. ______ 5. ______ 8. ______
3. ______ 6. ______ 9. ______

EXERCISE 11

For each of the following sentences, on the line provided: Write A *if quotation marks are needed. Write* B *if a comma is needed. Write* C *if a period is needed. Write* D *if the sentence is punctuated correctly.*

___ 1. He said that Paul would not be allowed to visit us.

___ 2. How could you ever do a thing like that! I said.

___ 3. I just finished reading *Tom Sawyer.*

__ 4. Ever since I read the book, Tom Sawyer has been one of my best friends.

__ 5. I shouted "Don't walk in that direction!"

__ 6. The book was written by Mark Twain.

__ 7. We subscribe to The New York Times.

__ 8. "Why did you do that!" he demanded angrily.

__ 9. He demanded to know why I had done it.

__ 10. Rowena is one of the main characters in *Ivanhoe*.

__ 11. Did you ever do the Funky Monkey? she demanded.

__ 12. He told me that I could do all of the experiments by myself.

__ 13. Do all of the work yourself, he told me quietly.

__ 14. I said I could never leave them.

__ 15. He is called the intellectual monster of the century.

__ 16. He asked why I had left so early.

__ 17. "When do we leave for the party?" asked Helen.

__ 18. "To tell the truth," Paul said "I never thought he could do it."

__ 19. "Why should I listen" demanded Helen, "since you never do what I tell you anyway."

__ 20. "Come early," he suggested, "Alan will be here."

The Hyphen

WITH NUMBERS

The hyphen is used with compound numbers from twenty-one to ninety-nine, when such numbers are spelled out.

twenty-seven sixty-six
eighty-five thirty-two

The hyphen is used to separate the numerator from the denominator in fractions that are spelled out.

One-seventh eight-fourteenths

The hyphen is used between the words in certain compound nouns.

brother-in-law mayor-elect
author-teacher

WITH PREFIXES

Usually no hyphen is used when such prefixes as anti-, ex-, extra-, mid-, non-, pre-, post-, trans-, ultra-, *and* un- *are added to complete words.*

antislavery midnight
preseason extraordinary
nonviolent transcontinental

There are, however, four exceptions to this general rule:

1. The word to which the prefix is added is a proper (capitalized) noun or adjective.
   all-American pro-Canadian
   ex-President Clinton
2. The word that is formed when the prefix is added must be distinguished from a homonym.
   re-cover (recover) un-ionized (unionized).
3. The prefix is added to more than one word.
   non-steel-producing nations
   (Note that the original term is "steel-producing nations.")
4. The prefix causes confusion because the same vowels are placed next to each other.
   pre-engineered anti-inflammatory

But: cooperation coauthors reentry

(These words are familiar because of long-established usage; the hyphen will probably be dropped from many other similar words in the future, for the same reason.)

Note: The prefix *self-* is always followed by a hyphen.

self-control self-centered

WITH COMPOUND MODIFIERS

A hyphen is used to join two or more words used as a single adjective preceding a noun.

dual-purpose cleanser
tried-and-true leader
well-qualified applicant

But:

If the first of the compound modifiers ends in *ly,* then no hyphen is used.

thoroughly researched paper
quietly conceived solution

If the compound modifier does not precede the noun, no hyphen is used.

A cleanser that is all purpose
An applicant who is well qualified
A leader called tried and true

FOR SYLLABICATION

The hyphen is used to indicate the division of a word at the end of a line—not at the beginning of the next line. It is usually placed at the end of a syllable, but it is best to consult the dictionary to discover the preferred breakpoints.

EXERCISE 12

In each sentence you will find a word in italics. If you think there should be a hyphen joining it to the word that precedes it, write H *in the space provided. If you think that there should be no hyphen, write the letter* N. *Then write the word as it should appear.*

__ 1. Two post *graduate* students are assisting in the dean's office.

____

__ 2. It is a never *ending* struggle to make ends meet.

____

__ 3. The total is two *hundred.*

____

__ 4. One out of every *ten* will fail this test.

____

__ 5. He is a self *appointed* leader of the group.

____

__ 6. Is it *all* right for us to leave now?

____

__ 7. This is a definitely *incorrect* entry.

____

__ 8. He is the sixty *third* candidate on the list.

____

__ 9. He claims that he is a self *made* man.

____

__ 10. He is working on an anti *pollution* device.

____

__ 11. He attended the post *season* dinner.

____

__ 12. The spectators were a pro *Austrian* crowd.

____

__ 13. He bemoaned his never *realized* dreams.

____

__ 14. These plans of his were never *realized.*

____

__ 15. Three *fifths* of the produce never went to market.

____

EXERCISE 13

Write A *if the hyphen is used correctly in each of the following. Write* B *if the hyphen is incorrectly used in each of the following. Then write the word correctly.*

__ 1. He sold me an all-purpose cream.

____

__ 2. The team consists of all-seniors.

____

__ 3. You will have to apply for re-exemption.

____

__ 4. He fired all twenty-two of the assistants.

____

__ 5. This is a pre-trial hearing.

____

__ 6. This book is by ex-President Bush.

____

__ 7. It was a cleverly-plotted scheme to cheat the villagers.

____

__ 8. I ate a piece of the so-called pie.

____

__ 9. The task is all-completed.

____

__ 10. He turned out to be a never-to-be trusted salesman.

____

The Dash

WITH ADDITIONS

The dash is used to set off parenthetical phrases, explanatory insertions, and lists of examples.

> The visitors—ambassadors, generals, leaders of business—all had to wait their turn before being introduced to the new government leaders.
> The visitors—all of our friends—were treated with the greatest courtesy.

The dash is used to show a sudden break, change, or pause in thought.

> Do you—can you—allow unqualified personnel to inspect the final products?
> The best of all possible worlds—what a cynical phrase—does not describe what our country is going through today!

CAUTION: *The dash is a mark of emphasis; it must be used sparingly. When it is used within a sentence, it is used in pairs. It is not used after a comma, colon, or semicolon. When used at the end of a sentence, the period replaces the second dash.*

> We will take full advantage of this opportunity—if it ever comes.

WITH SUMMARIES

The dash is used before a word or phrase that summarizes what has gone before.

> Ability to survive by living off the land, knowledge of the ways of the weather, skill in swimming, boating, fishing—all of these and more are needed assets of the professional guide who leads groups through our mountains.

WITH OMISSIONS

A shorter dash is used to mark the omission of the word to *between two words or numbers.*

> April–September 1865
> pages 3–132 inclusive
> 1901–1933
> $5.00–$35.00

Note: If the word from *is used, the word* to *should not be omitted.*

> *From* April *to* September 1865

EXERCISE 14

On the line provided, write the word or words that should be preceded by dashes in each of the following—if dashes are required. If no dash is required, then write No.

__ 1. How could we even consider standing by and allowing millions of others to live in misery and degradation this is my primary concern!

__ 2. My classmates those who were still in the city came to offer me their assistance.

__ 3. My closest friends, Henry, Milton, Arthur, and Stanley, agreed to share in the expense.

__ 4. There were from 3 to 303 others who could have done just as well as I did.

__ 5. Read carefully all of the figures on pages 37 and 39.

__ 6. If the company fails and I truly hope it will not he will lose all of his inheritance.

__ 7. I shall now tell you exactly what happened but that would be the wrong thing to do at this moment!

__ 8. These explorations of the moon, outerspace, planets, and the inner core of the earth must be carried on with greatest efficiency if man is to survive for long.

__ 9. The clock ticked loudly oh ever so loudly as the fatal moment approached.

__ 10. Camping, touring, fishing, hunting these are the major outdoor sports of the rural population.

__ 11. Alan actually so he wants us to believe spoke to the President about the plight of the beaver in our valley.

__ 12. Ben Wunder shall we call him friend or foe introduced the bill at our last meeting.

__ 13. Rob Lowe, a the skilled actor, is a most accomplished painter as well.

__ 14. Just when we least expected it, the end came.

__ 15. He left without saying his farewells to any of us, and he left without taking any of the money we had accumulated it had to be that way!

Parentheses

ENCLOSING FIGURES

Parentheses may be used to enclose figures after a spelled-out number.

Fifteen dollars ($15.00)

Parentheses are used around figures or letters to mark divisions of enumerations, especially those run into the text.

The reasons for this request are (1) the lateness of the delivery, (2) the cost of replacement parts, (3) the need for training our staff, and (4) the apathy of the public.

INSERTED ELEMENTS

Parentheses are used to set off inserted elements that do not affect the structure of this sentence, matter that has not been added for emphasis.

He gave a halting (and somewhat obscure) explanation of the process.

EXERCISE 15

On the line provided, write the word that should be preceded by parentheses in each of the following—if parentheses are required. If no parentheses are needed, then write N.

____ 1. We wished them as you would have all the happiness and good fortune possible.

____ 2. Two students probably Martin and Louis will be named the winners of the contest.

____ 3. The owner of the parts-factory, Joe Schwab, will interview the successful candidates.

____ 4. My sister Helen you met her in the school library last week has requested this exchange of supplies.

____ 5. It is believed in some areas at least that the mayor is responsible for this mix-up.

____ 6. This sweater is expensive it is hand knitted but so very practical.

____ 7. We ordered kayaks one-man canoes for the expedition down the Colorado.

____ 8. May we—do we have the right to—question so high an official?

____ 9. Edna refused to assist I don't blame her and let them stew all afternoon.

____10. The coat cost six pounds about fifteen dollars and was worth every penny.

PRACTICE TEST 1

> DIRECTIONS: In the following paragraphs, you will find numbers in parentheses. If numbers appear where punctuation marks have been used or omitted correctly, write the letter C next to the same number in the answer column at the right. Where punctuation marks have been used or omitted incorrectly, write the correct punctuation mark next to the same number in the answer column.

It(1) s a strange(2) yet true fact that the first discoverers(3) of gold in California'(4)s rich soil weren(5)'t looking for it. There was Francisco Lopez(6) who discoved a nugget clinging to the roots of a wild onion he'd plucked(7) there was Baptista Ruelle, who found gold near Los Angeles in 1841(8) and General Vallejo, (whose name is always spelled with two l(9)s) who claimed that as early as 1824 gold had been found in the hills(10) of the Sierras(11)! (12)Many people knew these facts,(13) however, no mad stampede was begun.

(14)The tenacious resistance of the Indians in the Sierras,(15) said General Vallejo, (16)prevented people from searching for gold."(17) Many people feel(18) that California would have been discovered there.

In any event, the Gold Rush had it(19)s beginning when a man named Marshall(20) who was building a sawmill for John Augustus Sutter, picked up a piece of gold. Then the rush started. What a rush it was!(21) All types of people came,(22) Puritians from England, noblemen from France, convicts, and reckless adventurers from all over the world. Do you think you would like to have been there?(23) I wonder if that question can be answered?(24) The inhabitants'(25) days in the temporary towns were filled with danger and violence. "In the days of the Gold Rush(26) wrote Philip Henna,(27) in(28) California. Through Four Centuries,(29) (30)no coward ever started for California and no weakling ever got there." Steadfastly, grimly(31) those men dug for gold that was part of a 300 mile belt(32) which had been deeply buried for thousands and thousands of years. When geological disturbances deep underground pushed the Sierra Mountains up, this buried treasure was also upheaved. Rough(33) unshaven men dug for it(34) they blasted for it, and at times,(35) they even scratched for it with bare fingers. Creeks(36) beds were scraped clean and fortunes(37) were washed into the panners(38) waiting hands.

1. ___
2. ___
3. ___
4. ___
5. ___
6. ___
7. ___
8. ___
9. ___
10. ___
11. ___
12. ___
13. ___
14. ___
15. ___
16. ___
17. ___
18. ___
19. ___
20. ___
21. ___
22. ___
23. ___
24. ___
25. ___
26. ___
27. ___
28. ___
29. ___
30. ___
31. ___
32. ___
33. ___
34. ___
35. ___
36. ___
37. ___
38. ___

Tough[39] rough towns grew up in the wilderness wastes[40] as miners moved in. Often, the names of the towns[41] were vivid and picturesque. Some of those names were[42] Hangtown, Flea Town, Mosquito Alley[43] Drunkards[44] Bar, and Poker Flat.

Incredible amounts of money were made in amazingly brief times. Four hundred thousand dollars was taken out of Bear Gulch in four days[45] by a few miners. American Bar surrendered $3,000,000 in gold in a matter of weeks. A single pan yielded $1500. The owner of the hotel spent a couple of hours daily[46] just digging under his building[47] and made at least $100 a day. I would like to know if anyone ever heard of making money that easily!

Even today[48] old prospectors[49] weary and grizzled, search for gold and it can still be found. In the midst of the depression[50] unemployed workers prospected in the sawdust of an old '49 saloon and found enough gold dust, probably fallen from the clothes of old time celebrating miners, to make it worth their while.

39. ___
40. ___
41. ___
42. ___
43. ___
44. ___
45. ___
46. ___
47. ___
48. ___
49. ___
50. ___

PRACTICE TEST 2

DIRECTIONS: Read each of the following carefully and then if the sentence contains an error in punctuation, write A. If the sentence contains no error in punctuation, write B.

___ 1. We saw the game and enjoyed it very much.

___ 2. We saw the game but we did not enjoy the score at the end.

___ 3. I ordered fish and chips.

___ 4. Will you send me some refills some erasers and a blotter?

___ 5. I enjoy bread and butter and pickles and sweet cream.

___ 6. It is his wont to take a walk every morning before breakfast.

___ 7. Before breakfast every morning when the weather is fine, he takes a long walk.

___ 8. It is all part of a days work.

___ 9. Its paw was hurt in the accident.

___ 10. You could do it yourself; however I would not advise you to try.

___ 11. Push both levers at the same time, then it will work.

___ 12. I told him "That the problem was solved."

___ 13. I told him, "The problem is solved!"

___ 14. Because he has not followed directions, the problem became overcomplicated.

___ 15. How could you dare think I would not help.

___ 16. Did you see the firemen's new uniforms?

___ 17. It was called Lady's Day.

__ 18. I ordered neither a new book nor another copy of that old one.

__ 19. Now, is the time for you to see how much you can help him.

__ 20. He spells his name with two i's.

__ 21. He borrowed the children's coats for the play.

__ 22. Did I ever show you my brother-in-law's new car?

__ 23. I ate the piece of cake; moreover, I was the one who paid for it!

__ 24. You shall regret this, henceforth, I shall never come to your assistance.

__ 25. Black and white, left and right and tall and short are three examples of extremes.

__ 26. Into the room as quickly as we could; we rushed to save the rest of our supplies.

__ 27. The picture is an unforgettable one; I shall always see that smile on his face.

__ 28. The teams competed against each other in volleyball, and relays.

__ 29. We kept score and the winner received a prize.

__ 30. I had lost the race; I just couldn't run any faster.

__ 31. Ill never forget the look on her face.

__ 32. Willing to learn the rules Phil listened to our advice.

__ 33. Skating over thin ice is a very dangerous pastime.

__ 34. Smoothly silently we glided over the ice.

__ 35. On the morning of the third day the rescue team finally reached us.

__ 36. Harry Smith, my father's best friend, teaches in one of the nearby towns.

__ 37. No, I just can't see how you could ask me to do that.

__ 38. The scouts, tired and hungry, came into the camp at the end of the long hike.

__ 39. Lake Luzerne a town in the foothills of the Adirondacks, is just south of Lake George.

__ 40. My brother, who is a senior in high school, plans to become an electrical engineer.

__ 41. Wishing to please his parents has been the principal cause of his efforts.

__ 42. Franklin D. Roosevelt a victim of polio could have escaped that disease if he had lived twenty years later.

__ 43. Yes is a word that is rarely used by him.

__ 44. I saw Helen but she failed to see me.

__ 45. His request included the following four handkerchiefs, two pairs of woolen gloves and a copy of the Manual.

__ 46. The basic requirements are: goodwill, willingness to help others, and time to devote to our work.

__ 47. I read the New York "Times" regularly.

__ 48. "Must I follow his advice?" I asked. "I am fully capable of doing it on my own!"

__ 49. How many 9's are there in the answer.

__ 50. Cant I help you now?

PRACTICE TEST 3

DIRECTIONS: Read each of the following carefully and then, if the sentence contains an error
In the use of an apostrophe, write A.
In the use of a period, write B.
In the use of a comma, write C.
In the use of quotation marks, write D.
If the sentence contains no error write E.

__ 1. What he doesnt know should be his chief concern.

__ 2. He has a part-time job selling mens' ties.

__ 3. He is not well-trained; nevertheless he plans to do the work all by himself this time.

__ 4. That he had missed the last bus was no reason for his refusing to attend the meeting.

__ 5. Because he had missed the last bus he did not come to the meeting.

__ 6. Peanut butter and jelly or cream cheese and olives can make the most tempting sandwiches.

__ 7. Samuel Clemens, better known as Mark Twain is my favorite humorist.

__ 8. Listen to the music; let its quiet soothing strains melt away your cares.

__ 9. When he finally arrived it was too late.

__ 10. It was much too late when he finally arrived.

__ 11. Seeing that all of the work had been done I decided to take the afternoon off.

__ 12. Seeing that all of the work was completed was my principal concern.

__ 13. The package, bulky and heavy blocked the entrance to the room.

__ 14. Mr. Edwards, my homeroom teacher is very understanding.

__ 15. Paul, who is my favorite cousin, is a member of the varsity baseball team.

__ 16. Our present needs include a first-baseman's mitt.

__ 17. I wondered whether I could ever be as generous as Milton.

__ 18. "If he solves the problem, I said, he will win the prize!"

__ 19. "Give me one chance!" I pleaded, "I know I can do it."

__ 20. "When," I asked, "will you learn to be more patient!"

__ 21. Who said that this was a man's world!

__ 22. Its really time for his plans to be successful.

__ 23. "Here's to your good health!" he shouted.

__ 24. I know that I shall try but never succeed.

__ 25. I know that I shall try but he will be the successful one.

CAPITALIZATION

Rules

We capitalize words as follows:

Proper names of people and animals.

*M*arty and *R*ose *C*orbett went for a walk with their dog *S*potty.

(Notice that *dog* is not capitalized but that *Spotty* is.)

Days of the week and months of the year.

During the summer, Steve spends *S*aturdays and *S*undays in the country.

(Note that the names of seasons—summer, etc.—are not capitalized.)

Every *J*uly and *A*ugust, we close our dress shop and do not reopen until the fall.

Nouns and adjectives referring to religious or political holidays.

*C*hristmas, *H*anukkah, *D*ay of *A*tonement, *T*hanksgiving, *E*lection *D*ay

Nouns and adjectives denoting nationality, race, or language.

*F*rance, *F*ilipino, *I*ndian, *H*ispanic, *S*cottish, *African*-*A*merican, *O*riental

Names of countries states, and cities.

*G*ermany
*W*ashington, *D. C.*
*I*ndiana
*D*es *M*oines, *I*owa
*T*okyo, *J*apan

Names of regions, but not directions.

In the Civil War, the *S*outh fought the *N*orth for four long years.

But:

We turned off the main road and headed south.
The prairie starts west of the Mississippi River.

Titles of persons and family titles.

*P*rofessor Allesandro was assisted by *D*octor Griffith and *C*olonel Gold.
Aunt *J*essie came with *G*randfather.

But:

Francis Allesandro is a professor.
Ian Griffith is a doctor.
Michael Gold is a colonel.

(Note that the title is not capitalized unless it precedes a person's name.)

First letter of every sentence, title of literature, and line of poetry.

Recently, I read *Of Mice and Men* by John Steinbeck.

"*W*ho has seen the wind?"
*N*either I nor you:
*B*ut when the leaves hang trembling,
*T*he wind is passing through.

The pronoun I, the exclamation O.

Words that refer to the Bible or the Deity.

God revealed *H*is wishes through the *S*criptures.
The *B*ible is the most widely read book in the world.

Important words in titles (nouns, pronouns, verbs, adverbs, and adjectives).

The *O*ld *M*an and the *S*ea
The *T*ruth about *F*lying *M*issiles
*M*y *V*acation in the *M*ountains
*H*ow *G*reen *W*as *M*y *V*alley

A few parts of the letter form.

3016 *E*ast *S*ixth *S*treet
*O*akland, *CA* 94618
*J*une 17, 2001
*D*ear *S*ir:
*G*entlemen:
*T*o *W*hom *I*t *M*ay *C*oncern:
*V*ery truly yours, (only the first word)
*C*ordially yours, (only the first word)

The first word of a sentence in a direct quotation.

"*H*ow are you?" asked Joe.
Joe asked, "*H*ow are you?"

All parts of a hyphenated proper noun except articles or short prepositions or conjunctions.

*F*orty-*S*econd *S*treet

The names of organizations, institutions, and schools.

The *M*emphis *C*hamber of *C*ommerce
The *S*mithsonian *I*nstitution
*G*rover *C*leveland *H*igh *S*chool
*H*arvard *U*niversity

The names of political parties, governmental groups, clubs and societies, corporations, religious groups.

*R*epublican *P*arty
the *S*enate
*A*udubon *S*ociety
*S*ears, *R*oebuck and *C*ompany
*L*atter-*D*ay *S*aints

The names of courses but not of subjects.

*C*hemistry I comes before *C*hemistry II in the study of chemistry.

But:

Of all the sciences, I enjoyed physics and biology the most.
In many schools, *M*athematics 5 is intermediate algebra while *M*athematics 6 is trigonometry.

PRACTICE TEST 4

DIRECTIONS: On the lines provided, rewrite the words that require capitalization.

1. next year, i will study english, math, french, and history.

 ____

2. the boy asked, "would you please let me look at your bible?"

 ____

3. tomorrow will be new year's day, the first of january.

 ____

4. there was a cold spell in the northwest last spring.

 ____

5. the jacksons are traveling south for the winter.

 ____

6. the best book i ever read is *the call of the wild* by jack london.

 ____

7. last Wednesday we visited aunt ann.

 ____

8. "don't trust doug," leo warned me. "he's a chronic liar.

 ____

9. mildred asked martha to join the young women's christian association.

 ____

10. tom laughton and harold o'connor belong to the united automobile workers of america.

 ____

11. we celebrated the fourth of july in philadelphia, pennsylvania.

 ____

12. the near east is rich in oil deposits.

 ____

13. protestants, catholics, and jews work together in the national conference of Christians and jews.

 ____

14. there are very few arabs living in south america.

 ____

15. rosaline told us that she would be leaving in the morning.

 ____

16. rosaline said, "i'll be leaving in the morning."

 ____

17. the united states of america needed a new flag when alaska and hawaii were admitted to the union as new states.

 ____

18. if professor lewis debates senator garlan, dr. fawcett will serve as moderator.

____

19. among my friends, larry wants to be a doctor and roy wants to be a baseball player.

____

Standard English Usage

GLOSSARY OF THE BASIC TERMS OF GRAMMAR

This alphabetical list of grammatical terms has been included for your convenience when reviewing the sections on Standard English Usage that follow. Grammatical explanations there have been kept to a minimum. However, if any are not clear to you, checking the definitions of the terms involved can clear up many difficulties.

active verb An active verb is one that shows the subject performing some action. (Contrast this with PASSIVE VERB.)

The boy *chopped* wood.

adjective An adjective is a word that modifies a noun or pronoun; the adjective changes the meaning of the word it modifies by making it more definite.

An old brick Colonial house.

Each adjective contributes to making the picture of "house" more and more definite.

adverb An adverb is a word that modifies a verb. An adverb usually tells *where, when, how,* or to *what extent* a verb performs its action.

The girl walked *there. (where)*
The girl walked *yesterday. (when)*
The girl walked *slowly. (how)*
The girl walked *much. (to what extent).*

An adverb can also modify an adjective:

I am *very* tired,

or another adverb:

I exercised *too* strenuously.

agreement Agreement refers to use of the singular form of the verb with a singular subject and the plural form of the verb with a plural subject.

He goes. (Singular subject—singular verb form)
They go. (Plural subject—plural verb form)
Everyone goes. (A collective pronoun, *everyone* is considered singular and takes the singular form of the verb.)
The class goes. (The word *class* is a collective noun and takes the singular form of the verb when the individuals are thought of as a group.)

Agreement between pronoun and antecedent refers to the use of the same number, person, and gender for a pronoun as for its antecedent.

Elaine is president of *her* class.

antecedent An antecedent is a word whose place a pronoun takes. Since it would be awkward to say, "John hurried because John was late," we say,

John hurried because *he* was late.

The pronoun *he* is used instead of *John.* Therefore we say that *John* is the antecedent of *he.*

apposition A word or phrase is said to be in apposition with another word when it is another way of naming that word.

The Constitution, *a body of laws,* outlines our system of government.

article The article is a kind of adjective used before most nouns.

The house.
A car.
An automobile.

The three examples are the only articles in English.

auxiliary verb Sometimes called a HELPING VERB, the auxiliary is used with a participial form of another verb. Together, they are called the COMPLETE VERB, and the participial form, which always follows the auxiliary, is called the MAIN VERB. The auxiliary form is usually some form of the verb *to be* or *to have.*

I *have* gone
auxiliary main

In this connection, it is important to remember that the participial form of a verb (present or past participle) may never be used as the main verb in a clause unless it is preceded by a helping verb.

case Every noun or pronoun in a sentence is related to some other word in that sentence (as subject, object, or indicator of possession). The CASE of a noun or pronoun is a name for that relationship. In English there are only three cases. For further information, see NOMINATIVE, OBJECTIVE, POSSESSIVE CASE.

clause A clause is a group of words, related in meaning, containing a subject and verb. When a clause makes a completed statement (or has a complete thought), it is a sentence. A clause may be a sentence in itself or, joined by a connecting word to another clause, may be part of a compound or complex sentence.

I went home. (A clause that makes a completed statement—a sentence)

When I went home. (Not a completed statement—therefore not a sentence. This is usually called a DEPENDENT or SUBORDINATE clause.)

I went home, and Mary stayed in school. (Part of a compound sentence)

I went home while Mary stayed in school. (Part of a complex sentence)

There are three types of DEPENDENT or SUBORDINATE clauses: ADJECTIVE, ADVERBIAL, and NOUN.

adjective clause An adjective clause modifies a noun or pronoun, and is connected to the main clause by a relative pronoun.

He is a man *whom I like.* (The clause modifies the noun *man.)*

adverbial clause An adverbial clause modifies a verb (or an adverb) and is connected to the main clause by a subordinate conjunction (sometimes called a RELATIVE CONJUNCTION or CONJUNCTIVE ADVERB).

He went *when the sun rose.* (The clause modifies the verb *went* by telling *when* he went.)

noun clause A noun clause is a clause that serves any function served by a noun.

Whoever discovered America was a fearless navigator.

The subject of the verb *was* is the whole clause.

I know *who committed the crime.*

The object of the verb is the whole clause.

collective noun (pronoun) A collective noun is a word for a group of individuals (people, animals, or objects). It may describe the group under circumstances where it acts as a single unit.

The *flock* of sheep *is* large.

At other times, the individuals may not be acting as a unit.

The *flock* of sheep *were* wandering in many directions.

compound object Two or more nouns, joined by a coordinating conjunction, both objects of the same verb, form a compound object.

He liked *baseball* and *tennis.*

compound sentence Two or more clauses, joined by a coordinate conjunction, make a compound sentence.

The satellite will revolve around earth for an indefinite period of time, *and* then it will descend like a flaming meteor.

compound subject Two or more subjects of the same verb form a compound subject.

John and *Jane* went together.

compound verb Two or more verbs, joined by a coordinating conjunction, each relating to the same subject, form a compound verb.

The pitcher *wound up* and *threw!*

complex sentence A complex sentence consists of two or more clauses joined by one or more subordinating conjunctions or relative pronouns.

Don't shoot *'til* you see the whites of their eyes.

Grammar is one subject *that* I may never completely understand.

Grammar is one subject I may never completely understand.

(The relative pronoun may be omitted when the meaning is clear without it.)

comparison of adjectives In addition to modifying nouns, adjectives also show comparison. There are three degrees of comparison: the adjective itself, which is called the POSITIVE degree, the adjective with the suffix *-er* or the word *more* in front of it called the COMPARATIVE degree, and the adjective with the suffix *-est* or the word *most* in front of it called the SUPERLATIVE degree.

POSITIVE:	*tall*	*intelligent*	*good*
COMPARATIVE:	*taller*	*more intelligent*	*better*
SUPERLATIVE:	*tallest*	*most intelligent*	*best*

comparison of adverbs The adverb, usually spelled the same as the adjective with the suffix *-ly* added to it, has the same three degrees. However, in all cases, it is compared by prefixing it with the words *more* or *most.*

POSITIVE:	*quickly*	*happily*
COMPARATIVE:	*more quickly*	*more happily*
SUPERLATIVE:	*most quickly*	*most happily*

Note: In some contexts, *slow* may be used as adverb: Go *slow* (or *slowly*).

conjugate Conjugation is the process of giving the form of a verb in any tense, indicating the changes that follow the use of each person and number.

SIMPLE PRESENT: *I go. You go. He, she,* or *it goes. We go. You go. They go.*

SIMPLE PAST: *I went. You went. He, she* or *it went. We went. You went. They went.*

conjunction A conjunction is a word that joins. It may join two single words, two phrases, or two clauses.

Juan *and* Maria went. (words)

They traveled through the woods *but* not across the river. (phrases)

Juan didn't find the treasure, *nor* did Maria. (clauses)

coordinating conjunction A coordinating conjunction is one type of conjunction. It is used to join independent clauses or words and phrases. See the examples above, which all illustrate the use of coordinating conjunctions. The six coordinating conjunctions are *and, but, or, nor, so* and *yet.*

copulative verb A copulative verb depicts a state of being, and not an action. The most commonly used copulative verb is *to be* and all its forms. Other verbs such as *seems, feels, appears,* and *smells* are copulative when they are used to express a state of being rather than an action.

He *seems* happy.

Everything *appears* in order.

dangling participle When a participle is used as an adjective, it must always modify a noun.When a participle is used in a sentence without a noun to modify, it is said to be dangling. Walking through the streets, the traffic lights are very confusing. The participle *walking* has no noun to modify. We correct it by inserting a noun or pronoun as in the following sentence:

Walking through the streets, *I* found the traffic lights very, confusing.

demonstrative pronoun A demonstrative pronoun points out a specific noun, and is used somewhat like an adjective. In fact, the two demonstrative pronouns are sometimes called DEMONSTRATIVE ADJECTIVES.

SINGULAR:

this pencil

that pencil

PLURAL:

these pencils

those pencils

direct object A direct object receives the action of the verb:

Kevin *threw* the ball.

gender Some nouns and pronouns refer to males or females. Those referring to males are in the MASCULINE GENDER, while those that refer to females are in the FEMININE GENDER. Those that refer to neither are NEUTER. Those that refer to both are COMMON.

MASCULINE:	*Brian*	*rooster*	*he*
FEMININE:	*Sarah*	*hen*	*she*
NEUTER:	*automobile*		
COMMON:	*cousin*	*poultry*	*they*

gerund Sometimes called a noun participle, the gerund is a participle used as a noun.

Swimming is fun.

idiom An idiom is an expression that is peculiar to or characteristic of a language.

We *catch a cold, toss our heads, throw an idea out.*

imperative See MOOD.

indicative See MOOD.

indirect object An indirect object receives the benefit of the action described by the verb. It is placed between the verb and the direct object, and is never preceded by a preposition.

He gave *me* the pencil.

Throw *John* a ball.

Bake *her* a cake.

infinitive The infinitive is the form of the verb that is preceded by the word *to,* as in *to dance, to sing, to work.* Although never used as a verb, it may be modified by an adverb: *To think quickly is* an asset. It may also take a subject:

I want *Jerry to go,*

or an object:

I want *to see Jerry.*

The infinitive is usually used as a noun.

To dance well was her ambition. (*To dance* is subject of the verb *was).*

He wanted *to dance. (To dance* is object of the verb *wanted.)*

Note: The word *to* is sometimes omitted:

He did nothing but *(to) cry.*

interrogative adverb In an interrogative sentence, an adverb that asks the question is an interrogative adverb.

When are you going?

Where are you going?

Why are you going?

interrogative pronoun In some interrogative sentences the word that asks the question is a pronoun. Such a pronoun is an interrogative pronoun.

Who are you?

Whom did I choose?

interrogative sentence An interrogative sentence is one that asks a question. For examples, see INTERROGATIVE ADVERB and INTERROGATIVE PRONOUN above.

interjection An interjection is an exclamation, a word usually expressive of feeling that has no grammatical relationship with the rest of the sentence.

Oww! That hurts!

Alas! Poor Yorick, I knew him well.

intransitive verb An intransitive verb takes no object. Some verbs are naturally intransitive and never take an object.

He *sleeps.*

Others may be transitive or intransitive depending on their use in the sentence.

misplaced modifier A modifier should be as close to the word it modifies as possible. Confusion and sometimes ridiculous sentences result when this rule is broken.

I *only* want the money.

What does this sentence mean? It could signify that only *you* and no other person wants the money. It could signify that you only *want* the money, but don't deserve it. It certainly does not mean that you want the money and nothing else.

I like the jockey on the horse *who smokes a cigar.*

Obviously the modifying clause *who smokes a cigar* should be closer to *jockey,* which it modifies.

modify (modifier) Literally, to modify means to change. A word that modifies changes the meaning of the word that it modifies by changing it from the general to the specific. Usually the more modifiers that are used, the more narrow becomes the meaning of the modified word.

Huge, ramshackle, lonely wooden house.

The modifiers have changed the original idea of house to a specific picture of a definite house.

Modifiers are divided into two classes: ADJECTIVES, which modify nouns or pronouns, and ADVERBS, which modify verbs and adjectives.

mood Mood is the form of a verb that changes according to the manner in which the writer or speaker regards the action. There are three recognized moods in English: INDICATIVE MOOD, SUBJUNCTIVE MOOD, and IMPERATIVE MOOD. The following shows the verb *to be* in its three moods:

INDICATIVE MOOD:

I *am* busy.

Is there a doctor in the house?

The speaker regards his statement or question as a fact.

SUBJUNCTIVE MOOD:

If I were President of *the* United States, I'd declare Benjamin Franklin's birthday a holiday. (But *I'm* not President.)

If you were young again, would you

do things differently? (But you are not young again.)

The speaker regards his statement or question as definitely not true.

IMPERATIVE MOOD:

Be still.

The speaker is issuing a command.

nominative case The nominative is one of the three cases in which nouns or pronouns may be used. A noun or pronoun may be in the nominative case for any of the following reasons: SUBJECT OF THE VERB, APPOSITION WITH THIS SUBJECT, or PREDICATE NOMINATIVE.

noun A noun is a word that names a person, place, or thing. A proper noun names a particular person, place, or thing.

	PERSON	PLACE	THING
COMMON:	*boy*	*park*	*statue*
PROPER:	*Joe*	*Prospect Park*	*Statue of Liberty*

number Nouns or pronouns may be singular or plural. Therefore, nouns or pronouns have number, which indicates whether an object referred to is only one, or is more, of its kind. Although verbs change their form and spelling to agree with singular or plural subjects, they do not actually have "number."

object The object of a verb is the noun or pronoun that receives the verb's action.

John slammed the *ball.* (The noun *ball* receives the action of slamming.)

The object of a preposition is the noun or pronoun that first appears after that preposition.

He went to the *store.* (Object of the preposition is *store.)*

objective case Any noun or pronoun that is an object, either of a preposition or verb, is said to be in the objective case. An indirect object is also in the objective case.

objective complement An objective complement completes the meaning of an object.

They elected him *president.*

They made him *chief assistant.*

parallel construction When two words, phrases, or clauses perform the same grammatical function, they should be in the same form.

He likes *dancing* and *to sing.*

Both *dancing* and *to sing* have the same grammatical function; they are objects of the verb *likes.* Therefore, they should have the same form. They should both be participles:

He likes *dancing* and *singing.*

Or they should both be infinitives:

He likes *to sing* and *dance.*

participle The participle is a form of a verb made by dropping the *to* and adding *-ing* to the infinitive.

INFINITIVE:	*to go*	*to pause*
PARTICIPLE (PRESENT):	*going*	*pausing*

The participle is never used as a verb in a sentence unless it is preceded by a helping verb. The PAST PARTICIPLE is a form of the verb usually made by adding the letters *-ed* to the first person singular of the verb, but sometimes the past participle is irregular in form. The past participle of the regular verb *walk* is *walked.* The past participle of the irregular verb *go* is *gone.* A past participle may never be used as a verb unless it is preceded by a helping verb.

When the past participle is not preceded by a helping verb, it is used as an adjective.

The *broken* vase was mended.

parts of speech The eight parts of speech—NOUN, PRONOUN, ADJECTIVE, VERB, ADVERB, CONJUNCTION, PREPOSITION, INTERJECTION—cover the eight basic functions that words may have in a sentence.

passive verb A passive verb is always preceded by some form of the verb *to be (was, is, will be, etc.)* and shows action performed upon, rather that by, the subject.

Andrew *was hurt.* (The subject, Andrew, receives the action.)

person There are three "persons" in English *grammar.* The *word* PERSON as used in grammar is a convenient way of identifying a noun or pronoun. The one who speaks is FIRST PERSON, the one spoken to is SECOND PERSON, and the one spoken about is THIRD PERSON.

SINGULAR:

I go. (*I* is the speaker; and is in the first person.)

You go. (*You* is the one spoken *to,* and is in the second person.)

He goes. (He is the one spoken about, and is in the third person.)

PLURAL:

We go. (first person)

You go. (second person)

They go. (third person)

personal pronoun The personal pronoun is the word *I,* in all its form. Since the forms vary as the person, number, and case vary, the best way to see it in all its forms is through a chart.

	SINGULAR		
	Nominative	Objective	Possessive
First Person	*I*	*me*	*mine*
Second Person	*you*	*you*	*yours*
Third Person	*he, she, it*	*him, her, it*	*his, hers, its*

	PLURAL		
	Nominative	Objective	Possessive
First Person	*we*	*us*	*ours*
Second Person	*you*	*you*	*yours*
Third Person	*they*	*then*	*theirs*

phrase A phrase is a group of connected words without a subject or verb.

He went *to the damp, marshy country* to hunt snakes *for his collection.*

To the damp, marshy country is one prepositional phrase, and *for his collection* is another.

possessive case The possessive is one of the three cases in English grammar. It is used to show ownership and is usually indicated by adding an apostrophe and an *s* to the nominative form.

NOMINATIVE: *ship*

POSSESSIVE: *ship's*

He watched the ship's departure.

predicate The predicate is the main verb of the sentence in its complete form, with all its helping verbs.

He *had been playing. (Had been playing* is the predicate.)

predicate adjective A predicate adjective is an adjective that is found in the predicate and that modifies the subject. It occurs only in sentences with copulative verbs.

He was *late.*

predicate noun A predicate noun, sometimes called a PREDICATE NOMINATIVE, is a noun that follows immediately after a copulative verb. It is usually another way of naming the subject.

George Washington was our first *president.*

preposition A preposition is a word that shows a relationship between two nouns or a noun and a verb. Usually this relationship signifies *direction, distance, nearness, ownership,* or *purpose.*

The chalk *is near* the blackboard.

The bridge *is over* the river.

The *proprietor of* the store called the police.

principal parts The principal parts of a verb are the forms of the verb from which the different tenses are derived.

INFINITIVE:	*to watch*	*to think*	*to see*
PRESENT:	*watch*	*think*	*see*
PRESENT PARTICIPLE:	*watching*	*thinking*	*seeing*
PAST:	*watched*	*thought*	*saw*
PAST PARTICIPLE:	*watched*	*thought*	*seen*

pronoun A pronoun is a word used instead of a noun. We could say:

Susan went to school. Susan was late.

Instead we simplify it by saying:

Susan went to school. *She* was late.

relative pronoun A relative pronoun has a double function. It connects two clauses and also replaces a noun in the subordinate clause.

I know a man *who* is an excellent artist.

Who joins the two clauses and also replaces the noun *man.*

run-on sentence A run-on sentence is a form of sentence error in which two or more clauses are improperly connected, or not connected at all.

The ocean pounded at the shore it hurled mighty waves high on the beach.

This is incorrect because there are two clauses and no connecting word.

sentence A sentence is a group of words that are related in meaning, contain a subject and a verb, and make a completed statement or a completed question.

John went.

All three requirements for a sentence are present: a subject, a verb, and a completed statement.

sentence fragment A sentence fragment (incomplete sentence) is incomplete because it lacks one or more of the three ingredients necessary to a sentence.

John, eager to be certain, carefully approaching the stranger and asking his name.

This is a sentence fragment because it lacks a verb.

simple sentence A simple sentence is a sentence with only one clause.

Patiently waiting in the shadows, the tiger listened for its prey.

Standard English Expressions, word forms, and sentence structures in general use and acceptance are labeled as STANDARD ENGLISH. FORMAL ENGLISH includes those forms used on state occasions and solemn occasions. COLLOQUIAL ENGLISH is the level of everyday speech and writing. NONSTANDARD is the label applied to items in usage not in widespread acceptance. Slang terms and ungrammatical forms are considered nonstandard. The examinations for which you are preparing test your mastery of Standard English.

subordinating conjunction A subordinating conjunction is used to connect a modifying or subordinate clause to a main clause.

He went *when* it rained.

He went *since* I did.

superlative degree See COMPARISON OF ADJECTIVES and COMPARISON OF ADVERBS.

syntax Syntax refers to the grammatical relationships among words in sentences. To give the syntax you must explain how a word is used in a particular sentence. Syntax deals with phrase and clause patterns while MORPHOLOGY, the other major component of grammatical study, concentrates on words.

tense TENSE is a grammatical term used only with verbs. It means time, and refers to the time of action of a verb.

PRESENT: *I go*

PRESENT PROGRESSIVE: *I am going*

PAST: *I went*

FUTURE: *I shall go*

PRESENT PERFECT: *I have gone*

PAST PERFECT: *I had gone*

FUTURE PERFECT: *I shall have gone*

transitive verb See INTRANSITIVE VERB. A transitive verb is one that does or can take an object.

I hit the *ball.*

The action of hitting is transferred directly to the object, *ball.*

Mary opened the *window.*

The action of opening is transferred directly to the object, *window.*

usage Usage describes how words and groups of words are employed to convey meaning. It stresses idioms, language conventions, and the level of acceptability of those conventions.

verb Basically, a verb is a word of action or state of being. It tells what the subject does or is.

The *runner,* carefully holding his strength in reserve and waiting for his rivals to tire, suddenly *sprinted* into the lead.

It is easy to see that *runner* is the subject. What word placed after it will make sense and convey the basic action of the sentence? Obviously, it is *sprinted.*

Standard English is the currently accepted usage in which our laws and regulations are written. It is the level of language used in textbooks, newspaper stories, news broadcasts, and television interviews. Because it prevails in our schools and colleges, students must know how to speak and write it if they are to obtain a formal education.

Your knowledge of Standard English Usage is tested in two different ways on entrance examinations: One type of question evaluates your ability to identify standard and nonstandard forms, while the other type tests your ability to change nonstandard forms into standard ones.

This section contains a review of the problem in Standard English Usage. A form that may be acceptable or correct in another dialect is labeled as nonstandard or incorrect if it is not acceptable in Standard English Usage. The terms *error, correct* and *incorrect* as used in this chapter apply only to Standard English.

After working the Exercises, Practice Tests, and Mastery Exams, be sure to check your results with the Answer Key at the end of the chapter.

SENTENCE SENSE ERRORS

Run-ons

I looked everywhere I just couldn't fnd the missing pin.

Analysis: This is a sentence error since it contains two complete ideas (1. I looked everywhere. 2. I just couldn't find the missing pin.) that are not separated by a period or joined together by a conjunction *(in, and, or, but, nor)*. This is an example of a *run-on sentence.*

Methods of Correction:

Separate into two sentences.

I looked everywhere. I just couldn't find the missing pin.

Use a conjunction to join properly.

I looked everywhere, and (or but) I just couldn't find the missing pin.

Subordinate one of the ideas.

Although I looked everywhere, I just couldn't find the missing pin.

Comma Splice

I looked everywhere, I just couldn't find the missing pin.

Analysis: This is still a sentence error since a comma cannot serve to separate two complete ideas. This is a variation of the run-on sentence, which is sometimes called a comma-splice or comma sentence, since a comma is incorrectly used to separate two complete ideas.

Methods of Correction: Same as for run-on sentences.

Sentence Fragments (Incomplete Sentences)

In the corner.
Coming to the end of the examination.
Since he would not listen to me.
Who is my very best friend.

Analysis: None of these examples is a complete sentence. The first is a prepositional phrase, the second is a participial phrase, the third is an adverbial clause, and the fourth is a relative clause. As they stand now, they are not sentences because they lack one or more of the following: verb, subject, independent clause, question mark.

These are examples of sentence fragments or incomplete sentences.

Methods of Correction: Since these groups of words lack complete meaning, there are two possible methods of correction.

Join the group of words to the preceding or following sentence.

Place the package in the corner near the end of table.

Add a sufficient number of words to complete the meaning of the group.

I was pleased when I saw that we were coming to the end of the examination.

Since he would not listen to me, he continued to make the same fundamental errors.

May I tell you about Henry, who is my very best friend?

EXERCISE 16

In the space provided write A *if the sentence is correct. Write* B *if the sentence is a run-on sentence. Write* C *if the sentence is a comma splice. Write* D *if the sentence is a sentence fragment.*

___ 1. I could never have succeeded without the kind assistance I had received from you.

__ 2. Who would have been able to foresee such an ending he is certainly a genius.

__ 3. I have just read the life story of John Paul Jones, the great American naval hero.

__ 4. Seeing that the ending was just a matter of seconds.

__ 5. Don't tell me the answer, I really want to see whether I can work the problem out myself.

__ 6. You stay where you are I will send for you soon.

__ 7. Couldn't the ending have been a happier one why did he have to disappoint me so!

__ 8. From one end of the campus to the other, there was only one name being mentioned.

__ 9. Whenever he tried to tell that story to one of his friends.

__ 10. Because of the difficulty, he could not reach home until very late.

__ 11. You tell him I just can't be that cruel.

__ 12. I planned to use the fishing rod with which he had so much luck.

__ 13. If I could just see him for one moment before he begins to take the test.

__ 14. A book of fun with puzzles.

__ 15. Whichever one you really want me to choose.

__ 16. Send the book to him today he has just finished reading the one I had lent him.

__ 17. Margie plans to go to college, she wants to follow in her sister's footsteps.

__ 18. Frances is my favorite aunt, we get along well for hours at a time.

__ 19. I really wish I knew what I wanted to be my parents would be very much relieved.

__ 20. Because I had not left the room all evening.

__ 21. If you so wish, I will write the note for you.

__ 22. Could we go over the last measure I don't think that it had the right tempo.

__ 23. Arriving on time, we were there to greet the incoming freshmen.

__ 24. Into the lives of all of us at some time or another.

__ 25. Between you and me.

Two of the sentences in each of the following groups contain no errors. Circle the letters of the correct sentences.

26. (A) After the entire incident had died down. We tried to discover what had been the cause.
    (B) After the entire incident had died down, we tried to discover. What had been the cause.
    (C) After the entire incident had died down, we tried to discover what had been the cause.
    (D) Joe Louis. A veteran boxer of many years' standing with a reputation for honesty and integrity.
    (E) Joe Louis was a veteran boxer of many years' standing with a reputation for honesty and integrity.

27. (A) We had to do all of the calculations without the aid of the machine since we were uncertain of how to operate it.
    (B) We had to do all of the calculations. Without the aid of the machine since we were uncertain of how to operate it.
    (C) Since we were uncertain of how to operate it, we had to do all of the calculations without the aid of the machine.
    (D) Since we were uncertain of how to operate it. We had to do all of the calculations without the aid of the machine.
    (E) Uncertain of how to operate it. We had to do all of the calculations without the aid of the machine.

28. (A) I should like to meet David Warshauer. A famous American psychologist.
    (B) Coming to the end of the story is always a painful experience for me.
    (C) I should like to tell you the entire story. Because I really respect your opinion.
    (D) How could you do such a thing! I am really annoyed with you!
    (E) If you follow the directions. You will become as confused as I!

29. (A) I had just completed reading one of the best books I have ever read, *Hit and Run* by Duane Decker.
    (B I had just completed reading one of the best books I have ever read. *Hit and Run* by Duane Decker.
    (C) It is a story of a ball player. Who must learn to control his temper.
    (D) He had perfect control of his playing ability, but he just couldn't control his tongue.
    (E) He finally learned a lesson it cost him too much to learn it the hard way.

30. (A) Ken taught me how to swim, he insisted on my learning not to be afraid of the water from the very start.
    (B) I like him very much he is one of the most patient men I have ever met.
    (C) We belonged to a class-group, but he seemed to have time to treat us as individuals at all times.
    (D) When I finally passed the beginner's test, it was one of the proudest moments of my life.
    (E) Everyone should know how to swim, don't you agree with me?

31. (A) Dave has always been afraid to be second best in whatever he does.
    (B) When we were learning how to water-ski. He insisted on receiving as much attention as he felt he needed from the instructor.
    (C) Sometimes Jerry had planned to give him that amount of time, sometimes he hadn't.
    (D) We all sensed that his need did not arise from selfishness it seemed to stem from his intense desire to be first.
    (E) I felt that he would have been one of the best, anyway, without his making such an obvious nuisance of himself.

32. (A) George Pulver. Who had owned a store in our neighborhood. Was a very good friend of our family.
    (B) Because he was so understanding, we often went to him with our problems.
    (D) Regardless of how busy he was in his store. He always seemed to find time to listen to our troubles.
    (D) He was so different from others, he rarely offered definite advice.
    (E) He would ask simple questions that would soon make us realize what the correct solution would be—for us.

33. (A) Margie has always found time to practice playing her guitar. Even during examination season.
(B) At first she had studied it as a musical instrument. Trying to imitate the great Segovia.
(C) When she realized that she would never be able to spend all of the time required for real study, she took stock of the situation.
(D) She enjoyed playing the instrument she enjoyed singing the tunes that she played.
(E) She soon reached her present compromise, to continue playing the instrument, not for its own sake, but as an accompanying musical instrument for social singing.

34. (A) Joel soon learned an important lesson. One that affected his attitude toward many things.
(B) He noticed the intensity with which Harold had approached everything he did.
(C) Harold did not push others out of his way, he only insisted that he himself try his best whenever he did anything.
(D) Joel soon saw that if Harold became involved in an activity, he would devote all of his attention to it.
(E) Joel now agrees with Harold, whatever is worth doing at all is worth doing well.

THE DOUBLE NEGATIVE

Typical Nonstandard Form

I don't want no one else to know the combination of the lock

Analysis: Standard English does not allow two negatives to control one negative idea. Only one negative verb, adjective, adverb, pronoun, or conjunction can be used in one sentence to convey a negative idea. The example has a negative adverb *(don't)* and a negative adjective *(no)*. One of them must go!

Method of Correction: Eliminate one of the negatives.

I want no one to know ... or I don't want anyone to know ...

Typical Nonstandard Form

I have hardly no money left in that account.

Analysis: Words like *hardly, scarcely, but a,* and *barely* (when it means hardly) are negative in meaning. Therefore, they cannot be used along with another negative to convey a *negative* idea.

Method of Correction: Eliminate one of the negatives.

I have hardly any money left in that account.

EXERCISE 17

Write A *if the sentence is standard. Write* B *if the sentence is nonstandard.*

__ 1. He won't listen to nobody in this matter.

__ 2. I can't hardly see the speck on the horizon anymore.

__ 3. It wasn't the double negative that bothered me.

__ 4. That can't be done no more by any member of our team.

__ 5. I would scarcely call that "No time at all!"

__ 6. We hadn't barely enough money to pay for the train fare.

__ 7. We would never ask nobody to do that type of assisting.

__ 8. Can't you never do the right thing the first time you try!

__ 9. I never want to see you again!

__ 10. Don't you want to see the doctor now?

__ 11. I haven't but a single word to say to you—"Courage!"

__ 12. They don't want nothing to do with him.

__ 13. They don't want nothing for nothing.

__ 14. Nobody in his right mind would accept no money for so valuable an object.

__ 15. I don't want either your compliments nor your favors.

Two of the sentences in each of the following groups contain nonstandard forms. Circle the letters of the standard sentences in each group.

16. (A) Harold doesn't want no one to help him.
    (B) Harold wants no one to help him.
    (C) Harold doesn't want anyone to help him.
    (D) Harold doesn't want help from no one.
    (E) Harold doesn't want help any more from anybody.

17. (A) I could scarcely see the end of the pier.
    (B) I couldn't scarcely see the end of the pier.
    (C) I had barely enough time to make the train.
    (D) I hadn't barely enough time to make the train.
    (E) We wouldn't want to do it either.

18. (A) Either you come with me, or I just won't go.
    (B) We hadn't but a moment to spare.
    (C) We could hardly follow his directions.
    (D) We couldn't hardly follow his directions.
    (E) We had but a moment to spare.

19. (A) I have just learned my lesson, and I won't bother him no longer.
    (B) I have learned my lesson, and I won't bother him ever again.
    (C) Don't forget that this letter doesn't belong to you.
    (D) I won't want to see him neither.
    (E) There is scarcely an ounce of flour left in the bin.

20. (A) We couldn't hardly wait for the reply from the advertiser.
    (B) Who said that we could never find the answer?
    (C) We could hardly wait for the reply from the advertiser.
    (D) I am not going there no more.
    (E) No isn't the politest of replies.

PAST TENSE OR PAST PARTICIPLE

Typical Nonstandard Form

I done whatever was expected of me.

ANALYSIS: In Standard English, the past participle *done* cannot be used by itself as a verb. It needs a helping *(auxiliary)* verb.

METHODS OF CORRECTION:

Add a helping verb.

I have *done whatever was expected of me.*

Use the past tense instead.

I did *whatever was expected of me.*

Typical Nonstandard Form

He had never *broke his promise before.*

ANALYSIS: The past tense of the verb cannot be used with a helping verb.

METHODS OF CORRECTION:

Remove the helping verb.

He never broke *his promise before.*

Use the past participle instead of the past tense.

He had *never* broken *his promise before.*

EXERCISE 18

Write A *if the sentence is standard. Write* B *if the sentence contains a nonstandard verb form.*

__ 1. I was so thirsty that I could have drank two quarts of milk then and there.

__ 2. The dog had hurt its paw.

__ 3. I would never chosen that copy of the text to give to the principal.

__ 4. When my term come, I was too nervous to begin.

__ 5. What is done is done and nothing further need be said.

__ 6. The pipe had bursted into three parts.

__ 7. An argument had arose very early in the evening.

__ 8. He had been stricken ill during the third act.

__ 9. You should never have wore so flimsy a jacket on such a cold evening.

__ 10. The case has been thrown out of court.

__ 11. I am glad that you had brung that matter up for discussion.

__ 12. My jacket shrank three inches after the soaking it received in the rain last night.

__ 13. He could never have teached me how to do that without your help.

__ 14. The net had been torn into shreds by the struggling, frantic bird.

__ 15. A cold breeze sprang up during the night to hamper the rescue workers.

__ 16. I wish you had seen his face when I rung the bell at three in the morning.

__ 17. I wish I knew now what I had knew then at the time of the test.

__ 18. He did not feel too well after he had ate fourteen pieces of pizza pie.

__ 19. The river had frozen overnight so we could go skating without any danger of falling in.

__ 20. The fun begun when he tried to disregard our suggestions.

__ 21. The river had slowly rose above its banks.

__ 22. He said that I had brang all of the spare parts with me on the first trip.

__ 23. I could have burst with pride when my experiment was described.

__ 24. I awoke with a terrific headache because I had forgot to open the window the night before.

Some of the sentences in each of the following groups contain standard forms. Circle the letters of the standard sentences only.

25. (A) How could I have knew what he had on his mind?
    (B) How could I have known what he had on his mind?
    (C) You should never have chose that topic to write on.
    (D) The toast was burnt to a crisp.
    (E) You should never have chosen that topic to write on.

26. (A) The news of my success bursted the shell that kept me in isolation.
    (B) He had spoke to me about you.
    (C) I could have sworn that you had told me the formula.
    (D) We had drove all night to reach Lake Luzerne by morning.
    (E) I sprung to my feet in protest.

27. (A) This river can be swam during the spring floods.
    (B) This river can be swum during the spring floods.
    (C) He has stoled all of the jokes that I had planned to tell.
    (D) An unpleasant situation has arose.
    (E) I had done all of the work without complaining to anyone.

28. (A) All that I know is that I run as fast as I could to get the message to the officer in charge.
    (B) The bell has already rung.
    (C) The bell has already rang.
    (D) He had never eaten so much in so little time before.
    (E) He said that I had mistook a suggestion for a command.

29. (A) You could never have wrote so unpleasant a note.
    (B) After he had wrang the mop almost dry, he hung it up in the closet.
    (C) The ship was sank when it hit the iceberg.
    (D) I hope you seen what I had been describing to you.
    (E) The record is really broken.

30. (A) He had took the dishes from this closet.
    (B) He sprang to his feet and shouted with joy when he saw us coming toward his cabin.
    (C) I have swum in colder water than this, but I just can't recall when.
    (D) I never would have beat him if he hadn't been so annoyed with himself.
    (E) The picture was stolen as a foolish prank.

31. (A) He has went to see whether we can join the group this afternoon.
    (B) Overnight he become a world famous pianist.
    (C) Overnight he has became a world famous pianist.
    (D) Overnight he has become a world famous pianist.
    (E) Overnight he could have become a world famous pianist.

32. (A) He drunk deeply from the cup of bitter experience and gained sober wisdom.
    (B) I could have swore that you had been with us during the visit.
    (C) I am glad that you were the one who had brought that matter up.
    (D) I am glad that you were the one who had brung that matter up.
    (E) I am glad you were the one who brought that matter up.

33. (A) Yesterday the sun had shone only for a few minutes.
    (B) I wish I could have wrung his neck before he uttered those words.
    (C) I really seen it with my own eyes.
    (D) I had really saw it with my own eyes.
    (E) I could have told you that I had seen it with my own eyes.

34. (A) I am glad that you have spoke to him about this matter.
    (B) The mill has run this way for over one hundred years.
    (C) The mill run this way for over one hundred years.
    (D) The mill has ran this way for over one hundred years.
    (E) The mill ran this way for over one hundred years.

ERRORS IN AGREEMENT

This area is one in which students make a great many of their errors. Test yourself to see whether you are a master or a novice.

Typical Error

Only one of the onlookers (WAS, WERE) *willing to help us.*

ANALYSIS: A verb agrees with its subject in number. Here the subject is *one,* not *onlookers. Onlookers* is the object of the preposition *of. One,* the subject, is singular and should be followed by the singular form of the verb, *was,* not the plural form, *were.*

CORRECT ANSWER: Only one of the onlookers *was* willing to help us.

Typical Error

Somebody in the class (IS, ARE) *going with me.*

ANALYSIS: *Someone, everyone, no one, somebody, everybody, nobody,* and *each* are singular and should be followed by the singular form of the verb. *Are* is plural; *is* is singular.

CORRECT ANSWER: Somebody in the class *is* going with me.

Typical Error

Alice with her three friends (WRITE, WRITES) *a weekly column for the school newspaper.*

ANALYSIS: Additional phrases introduced by *with, in addition to, including, as well as,* and *together with* are not part of the subject. The subject is still *Alice,* a singular noun. *Write* is plural; *writes* is singular.

CORRECT ANSWER: Alice with her three friends *writes* a weekly column for the school newspaper.

Typical Error

Neither the pen nor the books (WAS, WERE) *on the desk.*

ANALYSIS: With *neither ... nor, either ...or,* the verb form is determined by the noun (or pronoun) that is closest to the verb. *Books* is plural; *were* is the plural verb form.

CORRECT ANSWER: Neither the pen nor the books *were* on the desk.

Typical Error

He is one of the students who (HAVE, HAS) *been elected to the student body executive committee.*

ANALYSIS: In a relative clause, the noun before the *who, whom, which,* or *that* determines the verb form. In the example, *students* precedes *who. Students* is plural; therefore we must use *have,* which is plural.

CORRECT ANSWER: He is one of the students who *have* been elected to the student body executive committee.

Typical Error

Everyone should use (HIS OR HER, THEIR) *own notebook.*

ANALYSIS: *His or her* is singular; *their is* plural. *His* or *her* should be used to refer to a singular antecedent. *Their* should be used to refer to a plural antecedent. Since *everyone* is singular, *his or her* must be used.

CORRECT ANSWER: Everyone should use *his or her* own notebook.

EXERCISE 19

Write A *if the sentence is standard. Write* B *if the sentence contains a nonstandard verb form.*

__ 1. One of the students have my homework.

__ 2. Are any of you going to see the game today?

__ 3. One-fourth of the crew was injured in that game.

__ 4. One-fourth of the members are ready to vote now.

__ 5. Any one of the four is as good as these.

__ 6. A box of oranges were received at the depot early this morning.

__ 7. Neither you nor he is responsible for my errors.

__ 8. Either of the men know the combination to the safe.

__ 9. She is one of the girls who is to speak at the rally.

__ 10. Every one of the solutions were rejected by the judges.

__ 11. Either this group or several of those was the object of his search.

__ 12. Pauline together with her four friends wish to see you immediately.

__ 13. The carton of old magazines were placed in the basement.

__ 14. Everyone except the members of the laboratory squad see this as a major problem.

__ 15. Milton and Jerome without the aid of anyone of their friends has solved the problem within the time limits set by the rules.

__ 16. There is only one set of rules that I ever follow.

__ 17. Here are the set of records that he bought for me.

__ 18. Each of the boys who sell newspapers has to have an identification badge.

__ 19. Why don't someone fix the switch for the electric trains?

__ 20. Why don't he mind his own business!

__ 21. Edna accompanied by Margie and her friend has left for the station.

__ 22. No longer do his incessant cries for assistance bother his calloused guards.

__ 23. Neither the time nor the energy is his at this moment.

__ 24. Each of the contestants have three minutes to work out the puzzle.

__ 25. Are there anyone of the players ready to join me in a practice session?

Some of the sentences in each of the following groups contain no errors. Circle the letters of the correct sentences only.

26. (A) Some of the students see an advantage in not going to the game.
(B) Someone among the students know how to handle this engine.
(C) Someone among the students knows how to handle this engine.
(D) Some of the students sees an advantage in not going to the game.
(E) Is anyone of the students present now?

27. (A) A group of boys was seen walking toward the gymnasium.
(B) Some of the boys was seen walking toward the gymnasium.
(C) A group of boys were seen walking toward the gymansium.
(D) Some of the boys were seen walking toward the gymnasium.
(E) Someone among the boys were seen walking toward the gymnasium.

28. (A) Each of you are going to use your own notes.
(B) Each of them are going to use your notes.
(C) Each of them is going to use your notes.
(D Each of you is going to use your own notes.
(E) Everyone wished to use their own notes.

29. (A) None of my friends do the work in just that way.
(B) None of my friends carried their skates with them.
(C) Have there been any lessening of effort on his part?
(D) None of my friends does the work in just that way.
(E) Has there been any lessening of effort on his part?

30. (A) One of the spectators who was watching the game knows the answer to our question.
    (B) One of the spectators who were watching the game knows the answer to our question.
    (C) One of the spectators were watching the game know the answer to our question.
    (D) One of the spectators who was watching the game know the answer to our question.
    (E) One of the spectators who was watching.

31. (A) Neither your help nor my assistance are needed by him.
    (B) Was there any of them available for our use at that time?
    (C) Were there any of them available for our use at that time?
    (D) Here lie the remnants of my fondest hopes.
    (E) Here lies the remnants of my fondest hopes.

32. (A) Joel along with his parents enter through those doors every day.
    (B) Joel along with his parents enters through those doors every day.
    (C) He is one of those people who always sees the bright side in everything.
    (D) He is one of those people who always see the bright side in everything.
    (E) Is there anyone among you who can explain this problem to me?

33. (A) Everybody, including the three strangers, knows the path through the woods.
    (B) Everybody, including the three strangers, know the path through the woods.
    (C) Are any of you interested in taking a walk with me?
    (D) Did everyone use their own pen?
    (E) Did everyone use his own pen?

34. (A) A group of trees were destroyed by the storm.
    (B) Jack as well as Lucy were invited to join the group.
    (C) Jack as well as Lucy was invited to join the group.
    (D) Neither your sense of humor nor your cruelty affect me much.
    (E) One of the soldiers left his supplies near our cabin.

35. (A) Everyone of the candidates who applies now is going to be approved.
    (B) A set of carving knives, no matter how sharp they may be, are better than the ability of the user.
    (C) Dave with Phyllis and Lewis is coming toward our house.
    (D) Dave with Phyllis and Lewis are coming toward our house.
    (E) Everyone of the candidates who apply now are going to be approved.

ERRORS IN CASE

Typical Error

Paul and (I, ME) *will attend the conference.*

ANALYSIS: The subject is always in the nominative case, whether it is simple or compound. *Paul* will attend; I will attend.

CORRECT: Paul and *I* will attend the conference.

Typical Error

The cake was baked for Allan and (WE, US).

ANALYSIS: The object of a verb or of a preposition is always in the objective case, whether it is simple or compound. The sentence means: The cake was baked for *Allan;* the cake was baked for us.

CORRECT: The cake was baked for Allan and *us.*

Typical Error

She is a better scholar than (HE, HIM).

ANALYSIS: After *than* or *as,* part of the sentence is often omitted. If we complete the sentence, the correct answer becomes obvious.

CORRECT: She is a better scholar than he *(is).*

Typical Error

It is (HE, HIM).

ANALYSIS: A pronoun that comes after any form of the verb *to be* (except the infinitive) is a predicate nominative and such a form uses the nominative case. (Usage has allowed *It is me* to be accepted as a correct colloquial form parallel to the more formal *It is I.* However, this is the only exception.) *Him* is the object form; *he* is the predicate nominative form; therefore, *he* is correct.

CORRECT: It is *he.*

Typical Error

(WE, US) *seniors will have an award assembly this week.*

ANALYSIS: The pronoun is in apposition to the noun *seniors.* The appositive must be in the same case as the noun it is in apposition with. *Seniors* is in the nominative case; therefore, we must choose *we,* which is the nominative form.

CORRECT: *We* seniors will have an award assembly this week.

Typical Error

She asked Henry and (I, ME) *to attend the meeting.*

ANALYSIS: Both the subject and the object of an infinitive are in the objective case. *Me* is the objective form; therefore it is the correct form. The difficulty arises from the fact that the (I, ME) is part of a compound group. Treat it separately. (She asked Henry to attend the meeting. She asked *me* to attend the meeting.) Treated separately, the correct form becomes obvious.

CORRECT: She asked Henry and *me* to attend the meeting.

Special Note: Errors are frequently made with the objective form of the pronouns that should follow the prepositions *between, like, except,* and *but* (when it means except). *Memorize as correct:* Between you and me!

EXERCISE 20

Write A *if the sentence is correct. Write* B *if the italicized pronoun should be in the nominative case. Write* C *if the italicized pronoun should be in the objective case.*

__ 1. He left the work for you and *I.*

__ 2. You will have to decide between Paula and *us.*

__ 3. Everyone except *they* had heard the shocking news.

__ 4. Hank and *me* decided to handle these matters in our own way.

__ 5. *Who* did you want to see?

__ 6. You are a better peacemaker than *me.*

__ 7. No one but Morris and *us* had any right to handle the matter on hand.

__ 8. For *whom* did you intend that insult?

__ 9. Her brother really looks like *her.*

__ 10. They requested Addie and *we* to visit the dean's office.

__ 11. It is all over between them and *me.*

__ 12. Is it she *whom* you wanted to see?

__ 13. It was *them* all right.

__ 14. She can write as effectively as *him.*

__ 15. He told the truth to *we* members of the club.

__ 16. *Us* sophomores must not lose our identity.

__ 17. After Edna and *me* had played golf, we went to the conference.

__ 18. It was difficult for Lenny and *we* to find the correct solution.

__ 19. Was it they *who* you wished to see?

__ 20. Between you and *I,* I think there is a much better road than this.

__ 21. Did you want to see Alice or *me?*

__ 22. *Who* in your opinion should be chosen to lead the group?

__ 23. *Us* members of the team must be loyal to the coach.

__ 24. She asked him and *I* to speak to you.

__ 25. Everyone except John and *I* had brought skates to the rink.

Some of the sentences in each of the following groups contain errors. Circle the letters of the incorrect sentences only.

26. (A) Neither Henry nor me could see our way clear to joining them.
    (B) He is by far a more skillful driver than me.
    (C) Mother spoke to Phyllis and I about the coming party.
    (D) We men must learn to handle the ax more skillfully.
    (E) Between you and they, I shall never be able to do my own work

27. (A) Tell me whom I must see.
    (B) Tell me who I must see.
    (C) Everybody but me had been invited.
    (D) Everybody but I had been invited.
    (E) Does this ruling apply to Frank and I?

28. (A) He will never be able to swim as well as I.
    (B) He will never be able to swim as well as me.
    (C) He will never be able to swim as well as us.
    (D) He will never be able to swim as well as we.
    (E) He spoke to her as well as to me.

29. (A) He said that it was she.
    (B) He said that it was her.
    (C) He said that it was I.
    (D) He said that is was me.
    (E) He said that it could have been them.

30. (A) He spoke slowly to us beginners.
    (B) He spoke slowly to we beginners.
    (C) We girls must practice if we ever expect to win the game.
    (D) Us girls must practice if we ever expect to win the game.
    (E) Give us leaders some credit for experience and intelligence.

CORRECT USE OF ADJECTIVES AND ADVERBS

Good *is normally the adjective form, and* **well** *the adverb form, but when applied to health,* **well** is an adjective.

ADJECTIVE: She looks *good* in that dress!
ADJECTIVE: She looks *well* now that she has recovered.
ADVERB: The machine runs *well.*

A verb that indicates state of being, not action, is followed by a predicate adjective describing the subject rather than by an adverb, which would describe the action in the verb. Whether the verb indicates action or state of being in a particular sentence depends upon the meaning of the sentence since most of these verbs can be used in both senses. Some of these verbs are

sound	grow	look
seem	smell	become
taste	feel	be

ADVERB: This plant grew quickly. (Quickly tells how the plant grew.)
PREDICATE ADJECTIVE: The room grew quiet. (Quiet describes the room.)

The form **an** *is used instead of* **a** *before a word beginning with a vowel sound.*

an actress *an* uncle *an* honor
But: *a* union man *a* hotel

Just as **ain't** *has been declared unacceptable, certain adjective forms are wrong because they are classified as errors of illiteracy.*

WRONG:	CORRECT:
kind of a	kind of
this here	this
these here	these
that there	that
those there	those
these kind	this kind *(or* these kinds)
those kind	that kind *(or* those kinds)
these sort	this sort
those sort	that sort
them (as an adjective)	that, those

When two persons or things are being compared, use the **comparative**.

WRONG: He is the *brightest* of the two brothers.
CORRECT: He is the *brighter* of the two brothers.

When three persons or things are being compared, use the **superlative**.

WRONG: Of the three, he is the *slower.*
CORRECT: Of the three, he is the *slowest.*

Never combine both methods of forming either the comparative or the superlative in a given instance.

WRONG: She is the *most quietest* girl in the class.
CORRECT: She is the *quietest* (or the *most quiet)* girl in the class.

Use the word **other** *or* **else** *when a person, place, or thing is compared with the entire group to which it belongs.*

WRONG: He is more capable than *any* boy in his group.
(He cannot be more capable than himself; yet he is part of the group!)
CORRECT: He is more capable than *any other* boy in his group.

Some adverbs have the same form as their corresponding adjectives. Some of these are

ill slow fast deep sweet

CORRECT:
Go *slow.*
Drive *slow.*
Take a *slow* train.

Note: Usage has made the following also acceptable.
Go *slowly.*
Drive *slowly.*

EXERCISE 21

Write A *if the sentence is correct. Write* B *if the sentence contains an error in the use of an adjective or an adverb.*

__ 1. That suit sure fits him well!

__ 2. You will have to do more better than that if you expect to remain on the first team.

__ 3. Do not put them there!

__ 4. This is the kind of a sentence that I enjoy reading.

__ 5. Go slow as you approach the curves, and you will do good.

__ 6. This here is as far as I can go now.

__ 7. He doesn't look so good tonight.

__ 8. Go quick, and get Mr. Hammond here as soon as you can.

__ 9. I always enjoy reading those kind of books.

__ 10. May I have one of those over there?

__ 11. He is the best player on his team, without any doubt.

__ 12. These kinds of records must be handled with additional care.

__ 13. She is more capable than any girl in her clique.

__ 14. She took an onion so that she could have a good cry.

__ 15. It was the most noisiest party that I have ever attended, but I enjoyed it.

__ 16. We found that there boat at the end of the lake.

__ 17. Is this the sort of remark that you should make?

__ 18. The machine now runs very quiet.

__ 19. The flowers smelled so sweet that I could not leave the garden.

__ 20. You did good when you really tried.

__ 21. He showed me a real good copy of the picture.

__ 22. She is most funniest when her audience applauds at the right moments.

__ 23 Give him one of those there reports when he comes in.

__ 24. She is brighter than any of her friends.

__ 25. How could you have put that bottle over there!

Some of the sentences in each of the following groups contain no errors. Circle the letters of the correct sentences only.

26. (A) The VCR operates good now that he has fixed it.
    (B) He sure looks well now that he has recovered from his illness.
    (C) Look sharp and breathe deep if you want to survive the crisis.
    (D) Be quiet when you enter that corridor.
    (E) Walk quiet when you go through that corridor.

27. (A) The torch of freedom burns bright throughout the world.
    (B) He drives so careful that I have full confidence in his ability.
    (C) The torch of freedom burns brightly throughout the world.
    (D) He drives so recklessly that I fear for his life.
    (E) They played well during the rehearsal.

28. (A) Please be prompt for tonight's rehearsal.
    (B) Arrive prompt, and you will leave on time.
    (C) Go direct to my office when you arrive.
    (D) Go directly to my office when you arrive.
    (E) That new suit looks good on him.

29. (A) Them words express my feelings exactly.
    (B) Them words express my exact feelings.
    (C) That there was a foul ball.
    (D) That was a foul ball.
    (E) That there sure was a foul ball.

30. (A) Helen is more capable than anyone in her family.
    (B) Helen is the most capable one in her family.
    (C) Jonathans are the most tastiest of all apples.
    (D) Jonathans are more tasty than any apples.
    (E) It was a argument that I just could not answer.

VERBS OFTEN CONFUSED

accept a verb that means to *take* or *receive*. Please *accept* my apology.

except as a preposition means *other than*. Everyone *except* Dan had done the work. Except as a verb means to *omit* or *exempt*. Paul was *excepted* from the ruling.

borrow you borrow *from*. I *borrowed* a book from the library.

lend you lend *to*. Mary needed money so I had to *lend* a dollar to her.

isn't–ain't *ain't* may be in the dictionary, but society has ruled it an outcast. Eliminate *ain't* from your vocabulary!

don't–doesn't *does* and *doesn't* are the third person singular *(he, she, it, body, one,* etc.) Use *does* in the affirmative and *doesn't (does not)* in the negative. *Do* and *don't* are used with the first and second persons (*I* or *you do)* and the third person plural *(they don't)*. When in doubt, substitute *do not* for *don't* and *does not* for *doesn't.*

bring–take *bring* means to carry to the person who is speaking. *Bring* the book to me. *Take* means to carry away from the speaker. *Take* it upstairs to my room.

learn–teach you learn *from* someone and teach *to* someone.

stay–stand *stay* means to remain. *Stand* refers to a physical position, being erect. Memorize this incorrect sentence and you will not make the mistake again:
WRONG: When he broke his ankle, he *stood* in bed for three weeks. (How cruel!)
CORRECT: When he broke his ankle, he *stayed* in bed for three weeks.

beat–beat meaning to *defeat,* does not change its form whether it is in the present or the past.
PRESENT: Today I *beat* him in a game of chess. PAST: Yesterday I beat him in a game of chess. (Bet always means to wager. It never means to defeat.)
WRONG: They *bet* us by a score of 8-1.
CORRECT: They *beat* us by a score of 8-1.

let–leave *let* means to allow. *Leave* is not a substitute for *let.*

WRONG:	CORRECT:
Leave him go.	Let him go.
Leave it be.	Let it be.
Leave him do it.	Let him do it.

sit–set the only thing that sets itself is either the sun or a hen. Someone sits himself down; someone sets something else down.
WRONG: *Set* down on that chair.
CORRECT: *Sit* down on that chair.

lie–lay these are by far the most difficult verbs on the list for people who refuse to memorize some simple facts. Here are the facts:
Lie means to *rest* or *recline.*
Lay means to *place* or *put.*
PRESENT: Today I *lie* down. Today I *lay* the package down.
PAST: Yesterday I *lay* down. Yesterday I *laid* the package down.
PAST PARTICIPLE: I have (had) *lain* down. I have (had) *laid* the package down.
Note: The past *of lie* and the present of *lay* are the same. Otherwise, the forms are completely different.
WRONG:
Lay down for a while
I laid down when I had a headache.
I laid in bed all morning.
It has *laid* on the table for three hours.
CORRECT:
Lie down for a while.
I *lay* down when I had a headache.
I *lay* in bed all morning.
It has *lain* on the table for three hours.

shall–will in formal usage, shall is used to show future action with I and we.
In informal usage, will is used with all pronouns to show simple future. I (He, She, They, We, You) *will* leave soon.
To express determination, promise, threat, or emphasis, shall is used with all pronouns. I (He, She, They, We, You) *shall* do it!
For examinations, follow formal usage.

should–would *should* follows the rules for *shall,* and *would* follows the rules for *will.*
SIMPLE CONDITION: *I should* like to be able to solve the problem. They *would* prefer to sit with us.
EMOTION EMPHASIZED: We *would* never talk to him in that language. They *should* have listened to her!
To express obligation or duty, *should* is used with all persons. He *should* go there much more often.
To express repeated or customary actions, *would* is used with all persons. I *would* go there every morning.

can–may this is another distinction that belongs in formal usage.
Can implies the ability to do something. He *can* swim across the lake.
May implies permission to do something. *May* I leave as soon as I complete the examination?
In formal usage, *can* and *may* are used interchangeably with *can* being preferred.

EXERCISE 22

Write A *if the sentence is correct. Write* B *if the sentence contains an error in choice of correct verb.*

__ 1. It don't seem right to me.

__ 2. May I lend your assignment pad for a moment?

__ 3. Bring that to me as soon as you have finished painting it.

__ 4. Everyone except Paula had voted for the resolution.

__ 5. I have stood for as much of your nonsense as I can take!

__ 6. He bet us decisively when I challenged him to a race.

__ 7. Let the pillow lay where it has fallen.

__ 8. She set down on the edge of the sofa as she talked to her son.

__ 9. Don't they want to see the end of misery for others?

__ 10. May we borrow a copy of the book from you?

__ 11. The word ain't is not an acceptable one in formal English.

__ 12. Did he learn you to work the outboard motor?

__ 13. I except your challenge, and we shall play this afternoon to see who is the champion of Lakeside Avenue.

__ 14. The theme has laid on her desk for three hours.

__ 15. Bring the valise to his room as soon as you can.

__ 16. Don't he seem overworked to you?

__ 17. Leave me go!

__ 18. Don't bet him that he doesn't know the answer to that riddle.

__ 19. How can you leave him do all of that heavy work without assistance!

__ 20. Do you think that he knows enough to be able to learn me how to drive with safety?

__ 21. The pen was laying on the table all the while we looked for it.

__ 22. Borrow little and gossip less.

__ 23. When he hurt his arm, he stood in the hospital overnight.

__ 24. Just leave it to me.

__ 25. Why don't she try to understand my position in this matter!

Some of the sentences in each of the following contain no errors. Circle the letters of the correct sentences only.

26. (A) May I have a lend of your pen for a moment?
(B) May I lend your pen for a moment?
(C) Can I lend your pen for a moment?
(D) May I borrow your pen for a moment?
(E) Can I borrow your pen for a moment?

27. (A) The present company excepted, the members of the freshman class must be taught how to respect the rights of others.
(B) How could you have accepted his offer of assistance!
(C) How could you refuse to except his offer of assistance!
(D) Everyone except you had watched the televised program.
(E) I except the gift in the name of the senior class.

28. (A) It ain't right to let it lie there.
(B) It isn't right to let it lay there.
(C) It isn't right to let it lie there.
(D) It ain't right to let it lay there.
(E) Let it lay where it has fallen.

29. (A) Set the package on the table.
    (B) I set before the television screen, entranced by the play.
    (C) He bet us in three games of tennis.
    (D) May I learn him how to fix the switch?
    (E) He stood at home for three days, hoping to cure his cold.

30. (A) You can't bring your notes with you into the examination room.
    (B) Shall I bring my camera with me?
    (C) He should have listened to me.
    (D) It doesn't mean that much to me, now.
    (E) In two hours I will have completed my homework.

31. (A) They shall be there on time.
    (B) We would receive a note from her every day.
    (C) You should not have left so early!
    (D) She shall not fail this time!
    (E) How would you have done it?

CONJUNCTIONS AND PREPOSITIONS OFTEN CONFUSED

between–among In formal usage, *between* is used when two (persons, things, ideas, groups) are involved. Divide the profits *between* the two owners. In formal usage, *among* is used when three or more items or people or groups are involved. Divide the profits *among* the four owners.

like–as–as if In formal usage, *like* is a preposition. It is followed by an object. It looks *like* an old battleship. *Like* cannot be used as a conjunction in place of *as* or *as if*.
WRONG: It looks like it is going to rain.
He looks *like* the captain of a battleship should.
CORRECT: It looks *as if* it is going to rain.
He looks *as* the captain of a battleship should.

being–being that–because–since Neither *being* nor *being that* can be used as a substitute for *because. Since* is sometimes used and is not wrong, but *because* is preferred.
WRONG: *Being* I didn't feel well, I left early.
Being that he is my friend, I asked him for some advice.
CORRECT: *Because (since)* I didn't feel well, I left early.
Because (since) he is my friend, I asked him for some advice.

write up–write down Since the process of writing goes in one direction, onto the paper, *up* and *down* should not follow the word *write* to show direction.
WRONG: Write *down* the directions.
CORRECT: Write the directions.

Memorize the Following Correct Usages

WRONG:	CORRECT:
leap off of, fall off of	leap off, leap from, fall from, fall off
lose out, win out	lose, win
inside of the, outside of the	inside the, outside the
different than	different from
try and, be sure and	try to, be sure to
to graduate school	to be graduated from or graduate from school
is where, is when	occurs where, occurs when
reason is because…	reason is that …
blame on somebody	blame somebody
place something in something else	place something into something else
come over to my house	come to my house
finish up, divide up, polish up, rest up, dress up	finish, divide, polish, rest, dress
refer back, descend down, ascend up, rise up	refer, descend, ascend, rise
cannot help but	cannot help

EXERCISE 23

Some of the sentences in each of the following groups contain no errors. Circle the letters of the correct sentences only.

1. (A) I plan to write up the entire story of the accident.
   (B) I will have to write up to the very last minute.
   (C) Please come over to my house before dinner time.
   (D) It smells like a cigar should.
   (E) The results are so different from what I had expected.

2. (A) Put the dog in the observation cage.
   (B) May I borrow his pen off him for one moment?
   (C) Being a citizen, he refused to be terrorized by threats of imprisonment without trial or revealed charges.
   (D) I hope to graduate elementary school this June.
   (E) I cannot help but regret that I did not listen to his advice.

3. (A) I plan to finish up all of the work today.
   (B) If you lose your head, you will never be able to win out.
   (C) Please refer to the instructions on the back of the carton.
   (D) I found the missing envelope just outside of the house.
   (E) Being that I had not had lunch, my tension increased.

4. (A) I am so tired I will just have to rest up until the very last moment before the contest.
   (B) Divide the profits up among all the members of the club.
   (C) He spoke up like I thought he would.
   (D) The reason he acts that way is because he hadn't been told the reason for our decision.
   (E) Please try and then you will know whether you can do the work.

5. (A) Don't blame your carelessness on someone else.
   (B) Why don't you try and be cooperative?
   (C) Being that I could do the work rapidly, I was put in charge of the crew.
   (D) It seemed like time would never pass.
   (E) Distribute the booklets among the members of the audience.

6. (A) The book fell off of the chair.
   (B) The most exciting scene was when I forgot how to stop the motor.
   (C) The most exciting scene was where I forgot how to stop the motor.
   (D) We polished up the handle on the front door until it shone.
   (E) The cat leaped off of the chair and onto me when she saw me.

WORDS OFTEN CONFUSED IN MEANING

affect to influence. *Affect* by a decision.

effect a result; to produce a result. See the *effect* of watering a plant. The new law will *effect* a change.

angel a spiritual being. An *angel* of mercy.

angle a figure formed by two lines coming together in a point. A sharp *angle.*

besides in addition to. I don't want to see that movie and *besides,* I am too tired to go out.

beside alongside. Lucy sat *beside* Mel during the performance.

capital chief city; money; of first quality. Washington is the *capital* of the United States. Business requires *capital.* She paid a high price for *capital* seats.

capitol chief governmental building. The *Capitol* in Washington has a dome.

costume dress, apparel. The *costume* of a clown is funny.

custom usage. The *customs* of teenagers are often strange to adults.

desert to abandon; a barren region. The bear *deserted* her cubs. The great Sahara *Desert.*

dessert the last course of a meal. We like pie for *dessert.*

everywheres unacceptable substitute for everywhere. Look *everywhere* for the lost ring.

fewer refers specifically to number. *Fewer* books were sold today than yesterday.

less refers to quantity. She bought a hat for *less* money at a sale.

formerly at an earlier time; heretofore. She was *formerly* a resident here but she moved away.

formally in a stately manner. She introduced the man *formally* to her parents.

later comparative degree of late. Mary arrived *later* than John.

latter second of two. I prefer the *latter* to the former.

loan something lent. Repay a *loan.*

lone single, alone. A *lone* diner in a lunchroom.

miner one who digs ore from the ground. Work as a coal *miner.*

minor one under age; of little importance. A five-year-old is a *minor.* A *minor* injury.

moral ethical meaning. A story with a *moral* teaches good behavior.

morale state of mind in respect to confidence. High *morale* is necessary for the team.

number refers to individual units. A large *number* of questions.

amount refers to quantity. A large *amount* of gold is in Fort Knox.

principal head of a school; money at interest; most important. Mr. Jones is the *principal* of school No. 2. Banks pay interest on your *principal* which is on deposit. My *principal* reason is that I have not enough money.

principle rule, truth. We try to live by high *principles.*

reign to rule. Let wisdom *reign* over us.

rein strap of a bridle. Hold the horse's *rein.*

rain shower. Caught in a summer *rain* storm, the boy got wet.

slay to kill. *Slay* a dragon.

sleigh sled. Go for a *sleigh* ride during the winter.

stationary not moving. A *stationary* car is used for display.

stationery writing material. Personal *stationery* is monogrammed.

weather atmospheric conditions. Stormy *weather.*

whether a choice between two alternatives. She did not know *whether* to play or to study.

who, whose, whom refer to people. A man *whom* I know.

which refers to animals or things. A house *which I* saw.

EXERCISE 24

Some of the sentences in each of the following groups contain no errors. Circle the letters of the correct sentences only.

1. (A) Let me sit besides you.
   (B) You must show your birth certificate to prove that you are not a minor.
   (C) I am glad that the goldfish-eating costume has become a thing of the past.
   (D) What was his principle argument?
   (E) He has less friends now than ever.

2. (A) You just sleigh me!
   (B) I know you from somewheres else!
   (C) The morale of the wounded soldier was excellent.
   (D) The moral of the wounded soldier was excellent.
   (E) He was formerly in the employ of the government.

3. (A) My favorite desert is the Kalihari.
   (B) He always carries a large amount of singles with him.
   (C) He always carries a large number of singles with him.
   (D) I didn't know weather to believe him after the previous incident.
   (E) How many degrees are there in that acute angel?

4. (A) The effect of the storm was considerable.
   (B) He is the man which I came to see.
   (C) What is the capitol of New York?
   (D) Hold the reins lightly.
   (E) If I were offered yogurt and ice cream, I would choose the latter.

5. (A) The loan star state is a land of bigness.
   (B) When dieting, I skip my second dessert.
   (C) She owes me less money than she thinks.
   (D) He has a small amount of unused three-cent stamps.
   (E) He decided to sit down beside me.

CAUSES OF LACK OF CLARITY

Dangling Participle When the *ing* form of the verb is used as an adjective, there must be a word in the sentence for it to modify logically. If there isn't, then the participle dangles.

DANGLING PARTICIPLE: *Rushing* into the room, the unconscious man lay on the floor. (The word *rushing* as used here refers to the *unconscious man.)*

CORRECT: *Rushing* into the room, we saw the unconscious man lying on the floor. (The word *rushing* as used here refers to *we.)*

Dangling Gerund When the *ing* form of the verb is preceded immediately by *when, after, before,* or *since,* the entire phrase must logically modify some noun in that sentence. If it doesn't, then the entire phrase dangles and the name given to that construction is *dangling gerund phrase.*

DANGLING GERUND: When *swimming* long distances, your breathing must be under constant control.

CORRECT: *When you swim* long distances, you must keep your breathing under constant control.

Dangling Infinitive When an infinitive (the *to* verb form) is used as an adjective, there should be a word in the sentence which indicates the performer of the action. If such a word is too distant or absent, then the infinitive is said to dangle.

DANGLING INFINITIVE: *To do* well on the test, your training must be thorough.

CORRECT: *To do* well on the test, you must be thoroughly trained.

Pronoun with Indefinite Antecedent When a pronoun can refer to two or more possible nouns, the sentence must be rephrased.

INDEFINITE ANTECEDENT: Margie told Edna that she had passed the test.

CORRECT: Margie told Edna that Edna had passed the test.

or

Margie said to Edna, "I passed that test."

Impersonal Pronoun In the phrase *In this book, they say, they* is a pronoun without any antecedent and is wrongly used. It is not clear who *they* means.

WITHOUT ANTECEDENT: In the newspaper they say that teenagers are maturing faster these days.

CORRECT: The writer of the newspaper article asserts that teenagers mature faster these days.

Dangling Prepositional Phrase Prepositional phrases must logically modify a word or phrase in the rest of the sentence. Otherwise they are said to dangle.

DANGLING PREPOSITIONAL PHRASE: At the age of seven, his family moved to Brooklyn.

CORRECT: When he was seven, his family moved to Brooklyn.

Possessive Case with the Gerund The *ing* form of a verb used as a noun is called a *gerund.* The gerund, being a noun form, requires the possessive case of a noun or pronoun modifying it.

WRONG: I approve of *him* being chosen moderator.

CORRECT: I approve of *his* being chosen moderator.

Singular Compound Subject When a compound subject is thought of as a unit, then it takes a singular verb.

WRONG: Fish and chips are a favorite New England dish.

CORRECT: Fish and chips is a favorite New England dish.

EXERCISE 25

Some of the sentences in each of the following groups contain no errors. Circle the letters of the correct sentences only.

1. (A) When fishing, care must be taken not to entangle your line.
   (B) Coming to my next point, your attitude is completely wrong.
   (C) Coming to my next point is a tedious process.
   (D) Coming to my next point, he attacked it calmly and with logic.
   (E) To be able to drive a car has been my ambition for years.

2. (A) Paul told us that he would not go with us.
   (B) Phyllis told Edna that she could not go with us.
   (C) Phyllis told Dave that she could not go with us.
   (D) Harold told Jerry that he could not go with us.
   (E) We told them that they could not go with us.

3. (A) To solve the problem correctly, algebra should be used.
   (B) To solve the problem correctly is not an easy task.
   (C) To solve the problem correctly, our knowledge had to be pooled.
   (D) To solve the problem correctly, we used trial and error.
   (E) To solve the problem correctly, the instructor gave us two hints.

4. (A) Peanut butter and jelly are the favorite sandwich ingredients for many.
   (B) Peanut butter and jelly is my favorite sandwich mix.
   (C) On this page, it says that all accidents are preventable.
   (D) I just can't stand his trying to appear better than he really is.
   (E) I just can't stand him trying to appear better than we are.

5. (A) When coming into city traffic, your speed should be reduced.
   (B) After seeing the fire break out, I rushed to send in the alarm.
   (C) At the age of nineteen, he was a virtuoso at the piano.
   (D) At the age of ten, his family moved to Newcomb.
   (E) Before washing the dishes, the sink must be cleaned thoroughly.

OTHER ERRORS IN USAGE

Incorrect Sequence

Misplaced Adverbs Words like *not, only, merely, almost* should be placed almost always before the expressions they modify.

MISPLACED: I lost my *breath almost* when he came toward me.

CLEAR: *I almost lost* my breath when he came toward me.

Misplaced Phrases and Clauses Misplaced phrases and clauses are often the basis of unintentional humor. A phrase or clause should be placed as closely as possible to the word that it modifies in the sentence.

WRONG: Lauren stated that she would definitely arrive on Monday in her first paragraph.

CORRECTED: In her first paragraph Lauren stated that she would definitely arrive on Monday.

WRONG: I spent hours looking for the picture of the collie that had been hanging in the attic. (What was hanging, the picture or the collie?)

CORRECTED: I spent hours looking for the picture that had been hanging in the attic. It was the picture of a collie.

Misplaced Correlatives Pairs of correlatives should be placed directly before the words that they bring into comparison. The most frequently used correlative conjunctions are *either ... or, neither ... nor, both ... and, not only ... but also.*

WRONG: *Either* Mary wants the book *or* the pencil.
CORRECT: Mary wants *either* the book *or* the pencil.

Confusion of Tenses

Present and Past Tenses Confused *Do* not shift from the present to the past tense without having a definite reason for doing so.

WRONG: They *come* into the house and *told* me the news.
CORRECT: They *came* into the house and *told* me the news.

Present Perfect and Past Confused The past tense denotes action completed in the past. The present perfect denotes an action perfected (completed) in the present without specification of exactly when it occurred. The present perfect tense denotes action begun in the past and continued up to or into the present.

PAST: I *took* the examination yesterday.
PRESENT PERFECT: I *have taken* the driving test three times in the past six months.

Past and Perfect Confused Two actions are usually involved in this error. When both actions occurred about the same time in the past, the past tense is used for *both verbs.*

We *saw* him the moment he *arrived.*

The past perfect tense is used to indicate an action that was completed *before* the time of other past action.

We *had* already seen him by the time you *arrived.*

Confusion of Pronouns

Pronoun Mixup When using pronouns like *you, we,* and *one* to refer to people in general, do not shift from one to another.

CONFUSING: If *we* wish to remain at peace, one must not use threatening words.
CORRECT: If *we* wish to remain at peace, we must not use threatening words.

or

If *one* wishes to remain at peace, one must not use threatening words.

Miscellaneous Errors

WRONG:	CORRECT:
not as … as…	not so … as …
If I would have…	If I had …
kind of (meaning somewhat)	somewhat, rather
providing (meaning if)	provided
due to (as a preposition)	because of, since, as
My friends, they do …	My friends do …
without (meaning unless)	unless
most (meaning nearly)	almost
hadn't ought	ought not

EXERCISE 26

Some of the sentences in each of the following groups contain no errors. Circle the letters of the correct sentences only.

1. (A) We lived in that house for the past five years.
   (B) I smiled when he nodded his head merely.
   (C) If you had gone with us, we could have solved the entire problem then and there.
   (D) It was the money on the shelf that I needed to pay for the lesson.
   (E) Either you eat the fish or you leave the table now.

2. (A) Providing you help us, we cannot lose.
   (B) Provided you help us, we cannot lose.
   (C) He was most out of breath by the time he arrived in school.
   (D) You are not so smart as you claim to be.
   (E) You are not as smart as you claim to be.

3. (A) Due to circumstances beyond our control, this performance must be discontinued.
   (B) If you had done your work properly, this would not have happened.
   (C) If you would have done your work properly, this could not have happened.
   (D) I was kind of surprised when they decided to elect me chairman.
   (E) He changed his attitude after I told him our side of the story.

4. (A) He told me I was to leave in the morning in the afternoon.
   (B) If one does his work on time, one will receive a just reward in a clear conscience.
   (C) If you do what your training bids, one can make mistakes.
   (D) After he had seen me, I was able to leave the building.
   (E) After he saw me, I was able to leave the building.

5. (A) Helen not only took my pen but also my copy of the textbook.
   (B) Neither a borrower nor a lender be.
   (C) You can either go to see the museum exhibition or attend the lecture.
   (D) Either you listen to me or to him.
   (E) You cannot both talk about a person and have him as a friend.

6. (A) Paul yelled that he needed us to help him badly.
   (B) The children stared into the store windows with wide eyes.
   (C) We found the door to the attic in the bedroom.
   (D) You did not do so badly as you thought you had.
   (E) I want a copy of the picture of the man that is hanging on the wall.

Mastery Exams

EXAM 1

DIRECTIONS: Following each group of given sentences is a series of statements, designated as A, B, C, D, E. Some of these statements are true. Some are false. Circle the letters of the true statements only.

1. Wanting to see the end of the contest.
   He came early, he sat down in the jury box.
   I had hardly any time to see the end results.
   We scarcely never go there any more.
   We hadn't but one moment to spare.
   (A) Two of the sentences contain sentence errors.
   (B) Three of the sentences contain double negatives.
   (C) Only two of the sentences contain no errors.
   (D) One of the sentences is a sentence fragment.
   (E) Two of the examples contain run-on sentences.

2. His answer is different from ours.
   Everyone of the soldiers want to volunteer for this duty.
   Someone in this group left their books in the last room.
   You must either see Paul or Henry immediately.
   Please try to view this matter calmly.
   (A) Two of the sentences contain sentence errors.
   (B) One of the sentences contains an error in the placement of correlatives.
   (C) Two of the sentences are correct.
   (D) Two of the sentences contain errors in agreement.
   (E) One of the sentences contains an error in case.

3. Wishing to end the quarrel, a note of pleading entered my voice.
   Ham and eggs are the ingredients of my favorite breakfast dish.
   Only I had seen the picture once.
   They bet us by a score of 2-1 in a close game yesterday.
   We lived in Brooklyn for the past six years.

(A) One of the sentences contains a dangling gerund.
(B) Two of the sentences are correct.
(C) One of the sentences contains a misused verb.
(D) Two of the sentences contain errors in tense.
(E) One of the sentences contains a misplaced adverb.

4. Bring the book to my room now, before I reach there.
My father said when I left for school I should take the package with me.
He has less friends now than ever before.
Go slow, please, when rounding the corners of the corridors.
Don't he know how to spell *separate* correctly?
(A) Three of the sentences contain no errors.
(B) One sentence contains a misplaced modifier.
(C) One of the sentences contains an adjective form used instead of the adverb form.
(D) One of the sentences contains a sentence error.
(E) Two of the sentences contain errors in verb forms.

5. I object to him being elected chairman.
Being elected chairman is one of my fondest ambitions.
It tastes like chocolate cake should.
I sure appreciate your cooperation.
I lay in bed all day yesterday with a frightful headache.
(A) One of the sentences contains an error in agreement.
(B) Three of the sentences are correct.
(C) One of the sentences contains an error in case.
(D) Two of the sentences contain wrong verb forms.
(E) One of the sentences contains a misused adjective.

EXAM 2

DIRECTIONS: One, two, or three of the sentences in each of the following groups may be correct. Circle the letters of the correct ones only.

1. (A) May I borrow your pen off you for a moment?
(B) Due to unforeseen circumstances, I shall be unable to be with you tonight.
(C) He was graduated from college last year.

2. (A) We lived in this house ever since my father had bought it three years ago.
(B) How shall we write up the accident report?
(C) He is the kind of person whom I enjoy being with.

3. (A) He gave me final instructions after I saw you.
(B) Everybody in our class knows his part in the pageant thoroughly.
(C) He hasn't looked good ever since he had that cold three weeks ago.

4. (A) You hadn't ought to have listened to him.
(B) If you had left earlier, this could not have been the result.
(C) The ship sunk into the mud.

5. (A) Put your money back into your pocket.
(B) You may either choose this one or the other.
(C) I came to the end of the road nearly before they saw me.

6. (A) He has scarcely any money left.
(B) If one wants to succeed, you have to try and try again and again.
(C) Polish the stairs up to the first landing only.

7. (A) The purse has laid on the sidewalk for hours.
   (B) This *here* is out of place.
   (C) They could have done without our aid.

8. (A) There was three boats at the dock when I had arrived.
   (B) Pauline together with her three friends was waiting for us.
   (C) He is one of the men who is responsible for the new bridge.

9. (A) Between you and I, he is definitely the stronger candidate.
   (B) It was me whom they had asked for.
   (C) Us fishermen must plan the entire trip.

10. (A) He works faster than her.
    (B) She is brighter than anyone in her entire family.
    (C) The machine certainly runs smoothly now.

11. (A) Give me one of them books to read.
    (B) You will have to decide between Jack and him.
    (C) Drive slowly around the corners.

12. (A) These here answers are the only acceptable ones.
    (B) He is the most quiet boy in the group.
    (C) She is the more intelligent of the two.

13. (A) Can I leave the room now?
    (B) May I leave the room now?
    (C) Just leave me be, please!

14. (A) Wait a moment, I want to go with you.
    (B) In this pamphlet it says that a new system of geometry has just been devised.
    (C) Wishing to solve the problem alone, he went over the evidence again with even greater care than ever before.

15. (A) I did say that the reason is because you had left too early.
    (B) He sometimes acts like a real infant.
    (C) I want to win real bad.

EXAM 3

DIRECTIONS: Circle the letter of the choice that best completes each of the following.

1. I don't know _________ there.
   (A) anybody (B) nobody

2. May I have three of this, _________ notebook.
   (A) kind of a (B) kind of

3. The program had _________ by the time we arrived.
   (A) began (B) begun

4. The record was _________ by the Australian team.
   (A) broke (B) broken

5. The thief had _________ in through the half-opened door.
   (A) sneaked (B) snook

6. The river has _________ over early this year.
   (A) froze (B) frozen

7. I could have _________ it by myself.
   (A) did (B) done

8. We could _________ gone to the store without him.
   (A) 've (B) of

9. _________ my carelessness, we lost the game.
   (A) Due to (B) Because of

10. Between you and _________, I have met this phrase before.
    (A) me (B) I

11. I put the coins _________ my pocket.
    (A) in (B) into

12. The bottle fell _________ the shelf.
    (A) off of (B) from

13. It looks _________ it is going to clear up.
    (A) as if (B) like

14. Distribute the extra copies _________ the students in the other school.
    (A) among (B) between

15. ________ I don't feel well, I should like to be excused early.
(A) Being that (B) Since

16. This is much different ________ mine.
(A) from (B) than

17. Why don't you try ________ understand my position?
(A) and (B) to

18. Neither Philip nor his sisters ________ planning to attend the affair.
(A) was (B) were

19. Neither Paul nor Enid ________ ready to debate the issue now.
(A) are (B) is

20. Why not come ________ my house after the performance?
(A) over to (B) to

EXAM 4

DIRECTIONS: Circle the letter of the choice that best completes each of the following.

1. I can't ________ remembering how pleasant the entire evening was.
(A) help but (B) help

2. The best scene in the story ________ when the bridge collapses.
(A) is (B) occurs

3. Be sure ________ go into the exhibition room when you reach the museum.
(A) to (B) and

4. I don't see why you have to ________ me.
(A) blame it on (B) blame

5. Just place the lumber ________ my window.
(A) outside of (B) outside

6. The cat leaped ________ the chair and onto my lap.
(A) off of (B) off

7. There was a ________ star in the sky when I looked up at twilight.
(A) lone (B) loan

8. What will be the ________ of the court decision?
(A) affect (B) effect

9. Everyone except Larry and ________ could swim that distance.
(A) I (B) me

10. Go ________ to your seats.
(A) quick (B) quickly

11. She is definitely the ________ one of the two.
(A) politest (B) politer

12. These ________ of apples make me think of lemons.
(A) kinds (B) kind

13. These flowers smell ________.
(A) sweet (B) sweetly

14. Will you please ________ it to me?
(A) make a loan of (B) lend

15. Did you ________ their invitation?
(A) accept (B) except

16. He ________ in the country for a month during the summer.
(A) stood (B) stayed

17. What shall we have for ________ to end the meal?
(A) desert (B) dessert

18. He gave me ________ cards than he kept for himself.
(A) fewer (B) less

19. I could find it ________ in the house.
(A) nowheres (B) nowhere

20. It was ________ known as Fourth Lake, before its name was changed.
(A) formerly (B) formally

EXAM 5

DIRECTIONS: Circle the letter of the word that best completes each of the following.

1. Bread and butter ____________ my favorite filler.
(A) is (B) are

2. Will you please sit ____________ me.
(A) besides (B) beside

3. Did you visit the __________ in Albany?
(A) capital (B) capitol

4. Will the horse remain ____________ while I try to mount the saddle?
(A) stationery (B) stationary

5. Long may genial humor ____________ in our comic strips.
(A) reign (B) rain

6. Let us _________ the dragon of tyranny.
(A) sleigh (B) slay

7. Neither Paul nor Edgar __________ going to leave with us.
(A) is (B) are

8. You will have to do it without assistance from Will or ____________.
(A) we (B) us

9. He has tried to learn many of the popular American ____________.
(A) costumes (B) customs

10. It was, fortunately, just a ___________ accident.
(A) minor (B) miner

11. What is his ____________ reason for refusing our offer?
(A) principal (B) principle

12. If you __________ followed instructions, this could not have been.
(A) would have (B) had

13. He is not ________ patient as he thinks he is.
(A) so (B) as

14. ____________ you do the work properly, the results will be worthwhile.
(A) Provided (B) Providing

15. He is ___________ shy some of the time.
(A) kind of (B) somewhat

16. You _________ to listen to such rumors.
(A) ought not (B) hadn't ought

17. I am ___________ exhausted from trying to argue with her.
(A) almost (B) most

18. The motor runs so ___________ that you can scarcely hear its hum.
(A) quiet (B) quietly

19. They had ___________ across the river early this morning.
(A) swam (B) swum

20. She is one of the girls who ___________ being considered for membership.
(A) is (B) are

EXAM 6

DIRECTIONS: In each of the following groups, one of the four sentences contains an error in usage. Circle the letter of the incorrect sentence.

EXAMPLE:

(A) It don't do no good. [circled]
(B) Everyone brought his book.
(C) They thought we boys had done it.
(D) Did you expect the winner to be him?

1. (A) The work was more difficult than I had expected.
(B) My assignment was different from what I had expected.
(C) Everybody except she agreed to the plan.
(D) It was too bad the two other boys couldn't come too.

2. (A) He hadn't ought to have done it.
(B) She feels all right now.
(C) None of us is ready.
(D) She wanted to go last week.

3. (A) Why do you like Francine better than me?
   (B) She is taller than I.
   (C) A bushel of potatoes have been picked by the children.
   (D) Is there any chance of this coming in time?

4. (A) There should be no quarreling between her and you.
   (B) The part I liked best was when Lassie opened the stable door.
   (C) If I were president, I'd raise taxes.
   (D) If he was there, why didn't we see him?

5. (A) He took my book, which makes me angry.
   (B) None of them did his homework.
   (C) The reason Allen left was that he was hungry.
   (D) Of the two, Joan is neater.

6. (A) Running around during lunchtime is where you can get hurt.
   (B) He would've helped us, if we had asked.
   (C) If it weren't for Al, where would we be now?
   (D) Why doesn't Anne care for rock music?

7. (A) Frank and Tom were nearly pushed off the train.
   (B) He borrowed the money off me yesterday.
   (C) If it was permissible last week, why isn't it permissible this week?
   (D) Ruth, please take this message to the principal's office.

8. (A) They're going to eat their lunch as soon as they get there.
   (B) Whose is this?
   (C) I'm sure you would of done the same thing in my place.
   (D) Such weather! It's raining again.

9. (A) Why weren't you there when we needed you?
   (B) On your way back, bring home some ice cream.
   (C) More time has passed than I care to remember.
   (D) If it was you, wouldn't you feel bad?

10. (A) If the truth be known, I had forgotten all about the appointment.
    (B) Hugh chose David for his team.
    (C) The boat sank before we could reach it.
    (D) We have bought a large amount of toys for the children.

11. (A) It couldn't have been we who did it.
    (B) The bell has already rung.
    (C) Divide the candy evenly between the five girls.
    (D) Every student is expected to show his loyalty to Madison High School.

12. (A) He was all shaken up in the accident.
    (B) I've eaten more than I should have.
    (C) You should not let him play with fire.
    (D) I'll be glad to bring your shoes to the shoemaker. I'm going past the shoestore.

13. (A) Joan felt bad when her boy friend did not phone her.
    (B) Each one of the golfers had his golf clubs carried by his own caddie.
    (C) A neighborhood with no slums has less cases of juvenile delinquency.
    (D) Because Mr. Lyons is kind but firm, he has fewer problems with his students than any of the other teachers.

14. (A) Why don't you try to improve your batting and fielding?
    (B) Five of we boys have formed a basketball team.
    (C) The person in the snapshot is not he.
    (D) The winners of the contest are she and you.

15. (A) Not having anything to do, the movies seemed the best place for us to spend the evening.
    (B) Louise acts as though she were the teacher.
    (C) Set your things down on the desk, and sit in the first seat.
    (D) Try to finish what you start.

16. (A) Please let me go.
    (B) These papers have lain in the closet for months.
    (C) May I leave the room?
    (D) I could of done it for you more cheaply.

17. (A) As for his attendance, he has been absent fewer times than might have been expected.
    (B) Yesterday when Dad came into the house, I saw that he was angry.
    (C) Paul saw nothing wrong in asking for help.
    (D) We ordered a large number of trucks.

18. (A) I'm mad at you for kicking my dog.
    (B) Did you receive the correct number of articles?
    (C) Senator Douglas was the principal speaker at the conference.
    (D) Only a man of principle should hold the high office of mayor.

19. (A) Mr. Jeffers becomes very angry when anyone contradicts him.
    (B) When I seen *The Gladiator,* I liked the chariot race best.
    (C) He suffered a great setback, due to his inexperience.
    (D) Because of illness, he was unable to attend.

20. (A) You must do as I tell you.
    (B) I saw nothing.
    (C) If Geraldine would have come to the party, Jock would have danced with her.
    (D) Frances is taller than I.

EXAM 7

DIRECTIONS: In each of the following groups, one of the four sentences contains an error in usage. Circle the letter of the incorrect sentence.

EXAMPLE:

(A) It don't do no good.
(B) Everyone brought his book.
(C) They thought we boys had done it.
(D) Did you expect him to be the winner?

1. (A) On New Year's Eve we stood up late to greet the New Year.
   (B) I had rather spend a little more and get better quality.
   (C) When he laid his money on the counter, the agent gave him a ticket.
   (D) When the patient lay on his side, he didn't feel the pain so much.

2. (A) We borrowed it from him.
   (B) Tabby, our cat, lays on the rug near the radiator.
   (C) May I borrow your tennis racket please?
   (D) Since it's late, we'll have to leave now.

3. (A) Nothing could've changed the result.
   (B) You hadn't ought to have done that.
   (C) We had better turn back now.
   (D) Is it all right if we sit on this couch?

4. (A) You better not come late to school.
   (B) She would've arrived earlier, if she had known.
   (C) Are you all ready?
   (D) We've laid fifty miles of pipe through the desert.

5. (A) I knew it to be him as soon as I heard his voice.
   (B) Please teach us how to multiply by eleven.
   (C) If you were I, would you do it?
   (D) To build a fire, only dry wood should be selected.

6. (A) What's the idea of his coming here?
   (B) He is the kind of a person who causes trouble wherever he goes.
   (C) You can expect his friends to raise a storm when they hear his rabble-rousing speeches.
   (D) To make money, you must work hard and faithfully.

7. (A) Eric fell off the ladder.
   (B) Bring the dirty dog out of this house immediately!
   (C) I can scarcely believe your story.
   (D) Uncle George is one of the cleverest bridge players at the club.

8. (A) Africa has risen up to throw off its oppressors.
   (B) The doctor has torn the adhesive tape off.
   (C) He is one of the fastest, if not the fastest, baserunner in baseball.
   (D) Have you written home lately?

9. (A) If only Phil were more careful, we could trust him with the car.
   (B) May I borrow your glove?
   (C) With one person excepted, all those attending had a good time.
   (D) While watching the dull basketball game, my attention wandered.

10. (A) After cleaning the sink, please take the garbage out.
   (B) What kind of person do you think I am?
   (C) It's a matter of his solving his own problems.
   (D) The work having been completed, the laborers picked up their tools and left.

11. (A) Beat it.
   (B) We thought it to be her.
   (C) We have not done anything wrong.
   (D) Ain't I right in believing peace is better than war?

12. (A) There were Arthur and Murray, standing in the rain.
   (B) I should greatly appreciate the loan of your lawn mower.
   (C) They should have been here by now.
   (D) Betty doesn't care for these kind of stockings.

13. (A) I hardly know how to begin.
   (B) All term long there has been many examples of mischief in this class.
   (C) This sort of thing must stop.
   (D) I don't know how to begin.

14. (A) If he had been more prudent, he would not have gotten into this difficulty.
   (B) Neither Mr. Cowan nor his business partners is interested in buying any more property.
   (C) Please bring me back a souvenir from the fair.
   (D) He has not stirred in the past half hour.

15. (A) Either Ben or Jerry are going to be elected.
   (B) Phoebe, as well as all the other girls, is welcome to join our club.
   (C) We should've been home half an hour ago.
   (D) It's quality, not quantity, that counts.

16. (A) Except for him, nobody likes me.
   (B) There is altogether too much confusion here.
   (C) Those kind of people don't think for themselves.
   (D) Please leave. Take your things with you.

17. (A) The irritation on his heel was aggravated by his wearing of sneakers.
   (B) This secret is just for you and me.
   (C) What will be the effects of disarmament?
   (D) That there house is the oldest in the neighborhood.

18. (A) How will disarmament affect the world?
   (B) Spring is here already.
   (C) Some people say Fred Astaire was more graceful than any dancer.
   (D) If they are all ready, we ought to leave.

19. (A) Almost all the books have been borrowed.
   (B) Being that it's Saturday, you may go out tonight.
   (C) They accepted our gift.
   (D) Pat ate most of the grapes.

20. (A) Will you raise their salaries?
   (B) In science, we Americans are spending less time and training fewer students than the Japanese.
   (C) Let us give you a token of our affection.
   (D) Those Globetrotters sure know how to dribble.

Answers to All Exercises, Practice Tests, and Mastery Exams

EXERCISES

EXERCISE 1, p. 230

1. C
2. ours
3. weren't
4. C
5. 2's
6. man's
7. king's
8. mother-in-law's
9. coins'
10. C

EXERCISE 2, p. 231

1. men's
2. C
3. policemen's
4. C
5. officer's
6. anyone's
7. teacher's
8. razor's
9 Phyllis'
10. i's
11. Harriet's
12. It's
13. James' or James's
14. He's
15. Won't
16. You'd
17. worm's
18. trees' or tree's
19. animal's
20. boy's

EXERCISE 3, p. 232

1. **C** 2. **B** 3. **D**

EXERCISE 4, p. 232

1. **A**	4. **B**	7. **B**	10. **A**	13. **A**
2. **B**	5. **B**	8. **B**	11. **B**	14. **A**
3. **A**	6. **A**	9. **B**	12. **B**	15. **B**

EXERCISE 5, p. 234

1. N	4. N	7. C	10. C	13. N
2. C	5. N	8. C	11. C	14. N
3. C	6. C	9. C	12. N	15. C

EXERCISE 6, p. 234

1. **B**	3. **A**	5. **B**	7. **A**	9. **A**
2. **B**	4. **B**	6. **A**	8. **A**	10. **A**

EXERCISE 7, p. 235

1. 11
2. 7
3. N
4. following
5. N
6. N
7. words
8. Evans
9. N
10. following

EXERCISE 8, p. 236

1. period
2. C
3. !
4. C
5. C
6. C
7. C
8. C
9. C
10. C

EXERCISE 9, p. 236

1. **A** or **C**	6. **D**	11. **A** or **C**
2. **C** or **A**	7. **B**	12. **D**
3. **D**	8. **A**	13. **A**
4. **C** or **A**	9. **A**	14. **B**
5. **A** or **B**	10. **B** or **C**	15. **A**

EXERCISE 10, p. 237

1. Q	4. N	7. Q
2. N	5. Q	8. N
3. N	6. N	9. Q

EXERCISE 11, p. 237

1. **D**	5. **B**	9. **D**	13. **A**	17. **D**
2. **A**	6. **D**	10. **D**	14. **D**	18. **B**
3. **D**	7. **A**	11. **A**	15. **A**	19. **B**
4. **D**	8. **D**	12. **D**	16. **D**	20. **C**

EXERCISE 12, p. 239

1. (N) postgraduate
2. (H) never-ending
3. (N) two hundred
4. (N) every ten
5. (H) self-appointed
6. (N) all right
7. (N) definitely incorrect
8. (H) sixty-third
9. (H) self-made
10. (N) antipollution
11. (N) postseason
12. (H) pro-Austrian
13. (H) never-realized dreams
14. (N) never realized
15. (H) three-fifths

EXERCISE 13, p. 239

1. (A) all-purpose
2. (B) all seniors
3. (B) reexemption
4. (A) twenty-two
5. (B) pretrial
6. (A) ex-President
7. (B) cleverly plotted
8. (A) so-called
9. (B) all completed
10. (A) never-to-be trusted

EXERCISE 14, p. 240

1. — this
2. — those — came
3. No
4. No
5. No
6. — and — he
7. — but
8. — of — must
9. — oh — as
10. — these
11. — so — spoke
12. — shall
    — introduced
13. No
14. No
15. — it

EXERCISE 15, p. 241

1. as all
2. probably will
3. N
4. you has
5. in that
6. it but
7. one for
8. N
9. I and
10. about and

EXERCISE 16, p. 255

1. **A**	6. **B**	11. **B**	16. **B**	21. **A**
2. **B**	7. **B**	12. **A**	17. **C**	22. **B**
3. **A**	8. **A**	13. **D**	18. **C**	23. **A**
4. **D**	9. **D**	14. **D**	19. **B**	24. **D**
5. **C**	10. **A**	15. **D**	20. **D**	25. **D**

26. **C, E**	29. **A, D**	32. **B, E**
27. **A, C**	30. **C, D**	33. **C, E**
28. **B, D**	31. **A, E**	34. **B, D**

EXERCISE 17, p. 258

1. **B**	6. **B**	11. **B**	16. **B, C, E**
2. **B**	7. **B**	12. **B**	17. **A, C, E**
3. **A**	8. **B**	13. **B**	18. **A, C, E**
4. **B**	9. **A**	14. **B**	19. **B, C, E**
5. **A**	10. **A**	15. **B**	20. **B, C, E**

EXERCISE 18, p. 260

1. **B**	6. **B**	11. **B**	16. **B**	21. **B**
2 **A**	7. **B**	12. **A**	17. **B**	22. **B**
3. **B**	8. **A**	13. **B**	18. **B**	23. **A**
4. **B**	9. **B**	14. **A**	19. **A**	24. **B**
5. **A**	10. **A**	15. **A**	20. **B**	

25. **B, D, E**	29. **E**	32. **C, E**
26. **C**	30. **B, C, E**	33. **A, B, E**
27. **B, E**	31. **D, E**	34. **B, E**
28. **B, D**		

EXERCISE 19, p. 262

1. **B**	6. **B**	11. **B**	16. **A**	21. **A**
2. **A**	7. **A**	12. **B**	17. **B**	22. **A**
3. **A**	8. **B**	13. **B**	18. **A**	23. **A**
4. **A**	9. **B**	14. **B**	19. **B**	24. **B**
5. **A**	10. **B**	15. **B**	20. **B**	25. **B**

26. **A, C, E**	31. **C, D**
27. **A, D**	32. **B, D, E**
28. **C, D**	33. **A, C, E**
29. **D, E**	34. **C, E**
30. **B**	35. **C**

EXERCISE 20, p. 265

1. **C**	6. **B**	11. **A**	16. **B**	21. **A**
2. **A**	7. **A**	12. **A**	17. **B**	22. **A**
3. **C**	8. **A**	13. **B**	18. **C**	23. **B**
4. **B**	9. **A**	14. **B**	19. **C**	24. **C**
5. **C**	10. **C**	15. **C**	20. **C**	25. **C**

26. **A, B, C, E**	29. **B, E**
27. **B, D, E**	30. **B, D**
28. **B, C**	

EXERCISE 21, p. 267

1. **B**	6. **B**	11. **A**	16. **B**	21. **B**
2. **B**	7. **B**	12. **A**	17. **A**	22. **B**
3 **A**	8. **B**	13. **B**	18. **B**	23. **B**
4 **B**	9. **B**	14. **A**	19. **A**	24. **A**
5. **B**	10. **A**	15. **B**	20. **B**	25. **A**

26. **C, D**	29. **D**
27. **C, D, E**	30. **B**
28. **A, D, E**	

EXERCISE 22, p. 270

1\. **B** 6. **B** 11. **A** 16. **B** 21. **B**
2\. **B** 7. **B** 12. **B** 17. **B** 22. **A**
3\. **A** 8. **B** 13. **B** 18. **A** 23. **B**
4\. **A** 9. **A** 14. **B** 19. **B** 24. **A**
5\. **A** 10. **A** 15. **B** 20. **B** 25. **B**

26\. **D** 29. **A**
27\. **A, B, D** 30. **C, D, E**
28\. **C** 31. **A, B, C, D, E**

EXERCISE 23, p. 272

1\. **B, E** 4. **E**
2\. **C** 5. **E**
3\. **C** 6. none

EXERCISE 24, p. 273

1\. **B** 4. **A, D, E**
2\. **C, E** 5. **B, C**
3\. **A, C**

EXERCISE 25, p. 275

1\. **C, D, E** 4. **A, B, D**
2\. **A, C, E** 5. **B, C**
3\. **B, D**

EXERCISE 26, p. 276

1\. **C** 4. **D**
2\. **B, D** 5. **B, C, E**
3\. **B** 6. **D**

PRACTICE TESTS

TEST 1, p. 242

1\. ’ 11. C 21. C 31. , 41. C
2\. C 12. C 22. C 32. C 42. :
3\. C 13. ; 23. C 33. , 43. ,
4\. C 14. “ 24. . 34. , 44. ’s
5\. ’ 15. ” 25. C 35. C 45. C
6\. , 16. “ 26. ,” 36. s’ 46. ,
7\. .T 17. C 27. C 37. C 47. ,
8\. , 18. C 28. “ 38. s’ 48. ,
9\. ’ 19. C 29. ” 39. , 49. ,
10\. C 20. , 30. “ 40. C 50. ,

TEST 2, p. 243

1\. **B** 11. **A** 21. **B** 31. **A** 41. **B**
2\. **A** 12. **A** 22. **B** 32. **A** 42. **A**
3\. **B** 13. **B** 23. **B** 33. **B** 43. **B**
4\. **A** 14. **B** 24. **A** 34. **A** 44. **B**
5\. **B** 15. **A** 25. **A** 35. **A** 45. **A**
6\. **B** 16. **B** 26. **A** 36. **B** 46. **B**
7\. **A** 17. **A** 27. **B** 37. **B** 47. **A**
8\. **A** 18. **B** 28. **A** 38. **B** 48. **B**
9\. **B** 19. **A** 29. **A** 39. **A** 49. **A**
10\. **A** 20. **B** 30. **B** 40. **B** 50. **A**

TEST 3, p. 245

1\. **A** 6. **E** 11. **C** 16. **E** 21. **E**
2\. **A** 7. **C** 12. **E** 17. **E** 22. **A**
3\. **C** 8. **C** 13. **C** 18. **D** 23. **E**
4\. **E** 9. **C** 14. **C** 19. **B** 24. **E**
5\. **C** 10. **E** 15. **E** 20. **E** 25. **C**

TEST 4, p. 247

1. Next, I, English, French.
2. The, Would, Bible.
3. Tomorrow, New Year’s Day, First of January.
4. There, Northwest.
5. The Jacksons.
6. The, I, *The Call of the Wild*, Jack London.
7. Last, Wednesday, Aunt Ann.
8. Don’t, Doug, Leo, He’s.
9. Mildred, Martha, Young Women’s Christian Association.
10. Tom Laughton, Harold O’Connor, United Automobile Workers of America.
11. We, Fourth of July, Philadelphia, Pennsylvania.
12. The Near East.
13. Protestants, Catholics, Jews, National Conference of Christians and Jews.
14. There, Arabs, South America.
15. Rosaline.
16. Rosaline, I’ll.
17. The United States of America, Alaska, Hawaii, Union.
18. If, Professor Lewis, Senator Garlan, Dr. Fawcett.
19. Among, Larry, Roy.

MASTERY EXAMS

Rating Your Results

On exams with 5 questions:

Superior	5 correct
Average	4 correct
Below Average	3 or fewer correct

On exams with 15 questions:

Superior	14–15 correct
Average	11–13 correct
Below Average	10 or fewer correct

On exams with 20 questions:

Superior	18–20 correct
Average	14–17 correct
Below Average	13 or fewer correct

EXAM 1, p. 277

1. **A**
2. **B, C, D**
3. **C, E**
4. **B, E**
5. **C, E**

EXAM 2, p. 278

1. **C**	5. **A**	9. **B**	13. **A, B**
2. **C**	6. **A, C**	10. **C**	14. **C**
3. **B**	7. **B, C**	11. **B, C**	15. **B**
4. **B**	8. **B**	12. **B, C**	

EXAM 3, p. 279

1. **A**	5. **A**	9. **B**	13. **A**	17. **B**
2. **B**	6. **B**	10. **A**	14. **A**	18. **B**
3. **B**	7. **B**	11. **B**	15. **B**	19. **B**
4. **B**	8. **A**	12. **B**	16. **A**	20. **B**

EXAM 4, p. 280

1. **B**	5. **B**	9. **B**	13. **A**	17. **B**
2. **B**	6. **B**	10. **B**	14. **B**	18. **A**
3. **A**	7. **A**	11. **B**	15. **A**	19. **B**
4. **B**	8. **B**	12. **A**	16. **B**	20. **A**

EXAM 5, p. 281

1. **A**	5. **A**	9. **B**	13. **A**	17. **A**
2. **B**	6. **B**	10. **A**	14. **A**	18. **B**
3. **B**	7. **A**	11. **A**	15. **B**	19. **B**
4. **B**	8. **B**	12. **B**	16. **A**	20. **B**

EXAM 6, p. 281

1. **C**	5. **A**	9. **D**	13. **C**	17. **B**
2. **A**	6. **A**	10. **D**	14. **B**	18. **A**
3. **C**	7. **B**	11. **C**	15. **A**	19. **B**
4. **B**	8. **C**	12. **D**	16. **D**	20. **C**

EXAM 7, p. 283

1. **A**	5. **D**	9. **D**	13. **B**	17. **D**
2. **B**	6. **B**	10. **D**	14. **B**	18. **C**
3. **B**	7. **B**	11. **D**	15. **A**	19. **B**
4. **A**	8. **C**	12. **D**	16. **C**	20. **D**

Essay Writing

Although all students may benefit from the material that follows, do not spend your study time on this chapter unless you are preparing to take the ISEE, the Hunter High School Entrance Examination, or another test that requires you to write an essay.

The essay question is a practical test of your mastery of the basic aspects of writing. It measures your ability to

- use Standard American English.
- express your ideas clearly and effectively.
- organize your ideas.
- marshall evidence and present proof to support opinions.

How the Entrance-Test Essay and Classroom Compositions Differ

The entrance-test theme and the usual classroom composition differ in several important aspects.

Most classroom compositions are of the narrative variety. You are required to recall an incident or retell a highlight in your experience. The classroom composition, in short, tends to deal with concrete incidents or facts. It can be organized around the original timetable of the events you describe.

The entrance-test essay, on the other hand, requires an ability to discuss ideas, generalizations, abstractions. Incidents and highlights from your own experiences are relevant only briefly, as proof or support of a point of view. This essay requires an explanation of why you think the way you do about a definite concept or question. Orderly development of your thesis, or main viewpoint, rather than presentation of events in chronological sequence, becomes the basis of organization.

The typical classroom composition is written under teacher direction. It most often follows a lively class discussion and exchange of ideas. The test essay is not planned to allow you to read widely, to listen to the ideas of other students, to ask questions, or to weigh and consider for a substantial length of time. All you have is 30 minutes to plan and to write!

How Essays Are Rated

Although the testmakers will score your answers on the multiple-choice questions in the test, they will not read or rate your essay. Instead, an unmarked copy of your essay is sent along with your test scores to each of the schools you designate.

The admissions committee at each school then uses your essay to judge how well you compare in two important aspects with the other students who took the test: (1) how well you organized your thoughts and (2) how well you express yourself in writing. They will not look for right or wrong statements, broad knowledge of facts, or sophisticated arguments. The essays will not be given a numerical rating.

The admissions committee readers take into account the grade level of the candidate. The comparative rating given each essay is a composite result of the negative and positive factors listed below, as well as the frequency and seriousness of errors.

Positive Factors

Content:

- adequate development of ideas
- logical presentation
- appropriate examples and supporting details

Technique:

- logical organization
- proper choice of words
- correct sentence structure
- correct punctuation, capitalization, and spelling

Negative Factors

Content:

- vagueness
- inconsistency
- undeveloped ideas
- inadequate development of basic argument

Technique:

- inexactness
- ineffective expression
- failure to use Standard American English
- lack of variety in sentence structure
- inept choice of words

Technical Errors

1. Sentence errors—run-ons, comma splices, sentence fragments
2. Misspelling of common demons such as *to-too, their-there, than-then, separate, receive, doesn't*
3. Misuse of apostrophe—omission or addition
4. Word confusion: *altogether-all together, council-counsel, than-then*
5. Errors in case and agreement
6. Dangling elements
7. Vague reference
8. Misspelling of technical terms and words in general use
9. Additional errors in punctuation
10. Incorrect paragraphing: over- or underparagraphing
11. Incorrect capitalization
12. Trite expressions
13. Mixed metaphors
14. Lack of sentence variety: too many simple or compound sentences

See Digest of Communication Skills, beginning on page 87, for a discussion of the preceding items.

Errors in Content

These are errors in what the student says. The major stress in high school composition training is on developing the discipline that improves the content of themes.

1. Irrelevancies—additions to content that are not related to the subject, lack of unity
2. Needless repetition of ideas
3. Superficiality—saying only the obvious
4. Incorrect statements of fact
5. Illogical deductions
6. Facile generalizations, overgeneralizing

Errors in Style and Organization

1. Lack of discernible three-part organization that includes an introduction, a development, and a conclusion
2. Incorrect level of diction or usage: for example, inappropriate inclusion of slang or nonstandard usage
3. Lack of coherence—lack of transitional words or phrases
4. Oversimplification or overelaborateness of sentence structure—overuse of short, staccato sentences or pompous, complex sentences

Some Questions and Answers About Essay Writing

How can I do my best on the essay question?

You cannot change yourself or your outlook for the moments of examination taking. Plan to express your own thoughts with honesty and sincerity. Do not try to guess what the markers want you to say; you do not know what their opinions are. They are looking primarily for the methods that you use to express your ideas, and for the basis of these ideas.

The ideal preparation takes time. The more time you can spend on each section of this book, the more effectively you will be able to express yourself. Do not waste time, however, in drilling yourself on items you already know. Check for those that you do not have under control, and then review these until you know them thoroughly.

How much time should I spend in planning? in writing? in proofreading?

You are allowed 30 minutes for the essay. How much of this time should you spend on each step? Of course there is no pat answer to this question.

However, you should know generally how much time you need to plan, to write, and then to proofread a one- or two-page theme. The only way that you can find out is by timing yourself under practice examination conditions. The exercises and practice tests that follow will allow you to do just that, so that you can discover how much of your time should be spent in becoming familiar with the directions, how much time you need to plan the paragraph-by-paragraph development of your ideas, how much time you need for the actual writing, and, equally important, how much time you will need to check spelling, choice of words, punctuation and capitalization, sentence structure, and usage, and how much time you will need to double-check for errors of omission and carelessness.

Shall I plan a rough draft and then a finished copy?

In the 30 minutes allotted to you, you will not be able to write and then rewrite. Not only will you not have time, but also you will not be given the paper to do such writing. If, however, you plan in advance the content of each paragraph or section, you will not need to write a rough draft.

Where can I do my scratch work in planning the essay?

The proctor will indicate where space has been provided in the examination book for your initial planning. Remember, however, that the essay itself must be written on the paper provided.

Shall I write a formal outline?

Your outline will not be rated. You will be given two pages on which to write. Since your notes will have to be made in the examination booklet, the outline or rough draft that you think through must be just that. If you are more comfortable in working with a formal outline, then of course do so. If you have no preference, train yourself to plan just what you want to say in each paragraph and then begin to write the essay.

Should I plan a title?

Usually, a title is not called for. Do not waste your time, therefore, in trying to think of one unless the question requires it.

Is it better to agree or disagree with the topic?

It is not your point of view that will be rated. The essay is planned to show how well you can express your thoughts. The subject of the essay is usually one that you can explore on the basis of your personal experience, observation, or reading. The specific examples or details that you use to support your opinion are much more important than whether you agree or disagree with a stated viewpoint.

May I both agree and disagree with the topic?

Again, you are not being rated on your point of view. The clarity of your expression and the forcefulness of your statements are what count. Therefore, if you find that there are some aspects to agree with and some aspects to disagree with, fine!

How many points should I make?

Remember: you are not being asked to write a book! You do not have time to explore all aspects of the topic. Choose a limited thesis; stick with what you think is most important—and then explain that clearly.

Shall I favor polysyllabic words over shorter, simpler ones?

Be yourself. However, remember that this is a test of formal written English. A familiar tone and slang expressions should be avoided. On the other hand, don't try to impress the reader with the extent of your vocabulary. A short word used properly is much more effective than a longer word that does not express your meaning. The key test is whether the word fits appropriately into the tone and message of the essay.

If a quotation is included, shall I copy it?

Do not waste valuable time in copying verbatim. Try to reach your discussion as quickly as possible. If you need to quote from the question, do so as concisely as possible.

What shall I do if I make an error?

Make changes by lining out and substituting. One line through the material to be omitted and then a neat interlinear change placed above will lead to no misunderstandings.

Do handwriting and neatness count?

Usually, these elements are not taken into consideration; however, the reader will be inclined more favorably toward a paper that is easier to read than toward one that requires much time and effort to decipher.

You cannot expect to change your handwriting overnight; yet, if you are careful, you can produce a legible script. The following are some precautionary measures to be taken if your handwriting tends to be less than clear.

Letter formation

1. Your *i*'s should be dotted, and your *e*'s kept open.

   Confusing: wuird

   Improved: weird

2. An *a, d, b, q, o,* or *s* should be closed.

   Confusing: odobe

   Improved: adobe

3. A *k* should be closed so that it is not confused with *h*.

   Confusing: kill

   Improved: kill

4. An *r* should not resemble *i*, nor should *m* look like *n*.

   Confusing: run

   Improved: rum

5. The letters like *l, b, f, h,* and *y* should be looped, while *t* should be closed.

   Confusing: blot

   Improved: blot

6. The letters *g, q, f, y* should contain bottom loops.

   Confusing: foggy

   Improved: foggy

7. Letters like *m, n, u,* and *w* should be rounded, not pointed.

   Confusing: numb

   Improved: numb

Additional fundamentals

1. Keep your letters on the line; do not write uphill or downhill.
2. Avoid flourishes at the beginning or end of words.
3. Keep the space between letters and the spaces between words uniform.

Shall I skip lines between paragraphs?

Since the amount of space offered you is limited, do not skip lines. Begin to write on the first line and keep your margins very narrow.

Must I fill the two pages?

Some people can say much in few words; others can never find enough words to express themselves. It is more important that you state clearly and forcefully what you have to say than that you completely fill the two pages. Make sure that your essay encompasses the beginning, development, and conclusion of an idea.

Would a one-page essay be sufficient?

The instructions will not tell you how long or short the essay should be. Concentrate on expressing your thoughts in an orderly fashion with clarity and correctness. The 30-minute limitation will take care of the length. One page could be sufficient if what you have written says all that you should have said. Again, what counts is what you say and how you say it, not how many words or how much paper you use.

Can my essay run to more than two pages?

The proctor will make provision for additional paper; however, your major limitation is not space for writing, but time in which to write, and proofread. Do not write so much that you are forced to omit that essential last step, catching unintentional errors.

Four Ways to Improve Your Essay Score

Most students are unaccustomed to writing an essay that must be completed in 30 minutes. The following four steps should help you to master the essay form unique to the entrance test.

1. Treat the exercises that follow as you would the drills in a workbook. Do them!
2. Keep in mind that several shorter sessions are more productive than one cram session.
3. At intervals, in order to assess your progress, take the practice tests that follow.
4. Reread the explanations and redo the exercises and tests where necessary. Overlearning will give you the speed and confidence required to do your best.

Improving Prose Style and Organization

When writing the essay, you will probably be most aware of avoiding errors in usage, diction, and sentence structure. However, you should also attempt to display a sensitivity to the use of language and an effectiveness in organizing thoughts. Effective organization of thoughts comes through systematic consideration of the topic, compilation of evidence to support or attack a point of view, and planned presentation of this evidence.

SENTENCE VARIETY

An experienced writer conveys a message most effectively by varying the types of sentences he or she uses. By varying your sentence types, you will achieve a certain rhythm and flow to your writing. Consider the following sentence patterns:

Simple sentence: *Maria walked to the store.*

Simple sentence with compound subject: *Maria and Sylvia walked to the store.*

Simple sentence with compound verb: *Maria walked to the store and bought two onions.*

Simple sentence with compound object: *Maria walked to the store and bought two onions and three potatoes.*

Compound sentence: *Maria walked to the store, and Sylvia followed her.*

Complex sentence: *As soon as Maria left for the store, Sylvia began to follow her.*

Compound-complex sentence: *If Maria walks to the store, Sylvia will follow her; but Maria wants to be alone.*

Practice changing simple sentences to complex; change compound sentences to complex. Remember that an essay with only simple sentences will sound immature, so vary your sentences!

EXERCISE 1

DIRECTIONS: Using all of the types of sentences illustrated above, rewrite each of the following selections to gain maximum emphasis and variety.

1. Jonas Salk is a true hero in my opinion. He worked unselfishly. He worked for humanity. The grateful public gave him many honors. He was not interested in being a popular person. He gave the money prizes to charity. He praised those who helped him in the laboratory. Salk's main request was a simple one. He repeated it often. He only wanted to continue his research. He wanted to work in quiet. He did not want to be interrupted. Jonas Salk set a good example. Many young people have followed in his footsteps. He is a hero in the best sense.

2. Cowardice has many meanings today. The word was easier to define years ago. The test was clear. It was easy to apply. Then it meant not being able to face a situation. The coward ran away. The brave person stayed to face the consequences.

   We now realize more subtle values. The picture changes. One person may run and be brave. Another may stay and be a coward. The person may run, and he can plan to face the enemy at a better time. The person may stay, and he may cover his cowardice by blustering and shouting. The person may stay, and he can sacrifice the lives of others and protect himself. This sacrifice could even be unnecessary, and all it would do would be to protect the coward.

   We know more today. We know that just staying is not always a sign of bravery. It is the motive and not the deed that should decide what is to be labeled cowardice.

3. The nineteenth century had its physical frontiers, and we today have political, social, and scientific frontiers. The pioneers settled our country, and they faced the dangers of the frontiers of our land. The pioneers of today face similar dangers, and these dangers require similar courage.

   Some people see social injustice around us, and they devote their lives to fighting for equality for others. Some people see political tyranny, and they see others deprived by trickery of their right to vote. They plan long campaigns, and they try to educate the public. Freedom cannot belong to a few. Freedom must belong to all.

Some people explore these political and social frontiers, and others explore the frontiers of space, and still others explore the frontiers found in the laboratory. These are not our least important explorers. They are conquering disease, and they are making our lives longer and fuller. There are many frontiers today, and no one can say that frontiers no longer exist.

4. High school has a fundamental purpose. The purpose is to help the next generation meet the challenges of the years ahead. It prepares us for living together. It prepares us for making a living. It has many offerings. How can the entering students take best advantage of what high school has to offer?

   There are two simple rules. These rules have helped generations of students. They could be the key to your success. The first one consists of six words. It is "Don't be afraid to ask questions." Ask questions. Get all the possibilities before making an important decision. Ask questions when you are having difficulty with school work. You must be careful in selecting the person you turn to. Pick someone who knows. Speak to people who are knowledgeable. Choose a moment when they can really listen to you. Don't let a bad response discourage you. Instead, try again. Turn to someone else.

   The second rule is even simpler. It is "Do each day's work each day." Don't let assignments pile up. The accumulation can become so massive that you will be swamped.

   There are many more rules. Rules can help a beginner. They can help a beginner to a successful start in high school. These are the ones that made high school a success story for me.

5. War is a costly luxury, and people must realize this. The winner loses, and so does the loser. There is no victor in war, and we should realize this. Inflation is an unavoidable part of war. Inflation eats away the life savings in the land of the winner, and it does the same in the land of the conquered.

   Some of the men and women who were in the armed forces during the war feel that they have missed part of their lives. They become civilians, and they look for the good times they missed. Morality reaches a low level, and the winners talk about a lost generation, and the losers complain about a generation that has low moral standards. Fads sweep the country, and social advances are neglected.

   Money is spent on more and more armaments, and needed civic improvements are neglected. War does not end with the firing of the last gun. It continues to destroy for years afterward. We should realize this, and we should be determined to fight the concept of war at all costs, and we should fight it at all turns.

   We should fight poverty, hunger, and ignorance, and we should not fight other human beings. The fight against other human beings is wasteful and all who are in it suffer.

Note: Answers in this exercise will vary too greatly to allow for an Answer Key.

PROPER PARAGRAPHING

In writing the essay, you face a practical test of your ability to express ideas and to arrange and relate them in paragraphs with appropriate connectives. The material that follows will give you practice in developing the correct habits for mature thought sequences. It will familiarize you with the level of development expected of you in your paragraph work on the high school level.

Elements of Correct Paragraphing

UNITY A theme has unity when each sentence and each paragraph in it is related to the topic under discussion. Unrelated sentences or paragraphs are irrelevant. Unity is obtained in a paragraph by excluding extraneous material.

COHERENCE Each part of a theme should lead logically to the next. Each thought should lead to the one that follows. Each sentence in a paragraph should follow this logical type of pattern. Coherence is gained by the logical arrangement of material and by the judicious use of transitional words and phrases to indicate the relationships between ideas.

Coherence is gained through the use of linking expressions such as the following:

therefore, moreover, consequently, in addition to, furthermore, for example, for instance, as a result, nevertheless, obviously, first, on the whole, at any rate, naturally, of course, however, yet, at length, in conclusion, finally, next, first

LENGTH There is no prescribed length for a paragraph. The average length, however, is about 100 words. An essay should normally consist of more than one paragraph. A paragraph should normally consist of more than one sentence.

The rule of thumb used by most students is that a paragraph of more than a page in longhand is probably too long; a paragraph of one or two sentences is probably too brief.

TOPIC SENTENCE The usual paragraph contains one sentence that summarizes the ideas of the paragraph. That sentence is called the topic sentence. If all of the ideas of the paragraph relate to that sentence, then the paragraph has unity. If the ideas of the paragraph lead to or from that sentence, then the paragraph has coherence. Although the topic sentence is usually found at the beginning of the paragraph, it may be placed at the end or at any other point in the paragraph.

DEVELOPING THE PARAGRAPH A typical paragraph usually deals with only one of the ideas to be developed in the essay. Each paragraph may explain, develop, defend, attack, or illustrate a single idea. The paragraph may be developed by:

1. giving examples of the idea stated in the topic sentence
2. defining one or more of the terms in the topic sentence
3. giving details to support the topic sentence
4. giving cause and effect
5. giving the steps in a process
6. using comparison and contrast
7. presenting details or facts and also conclusions to be drawn from those details or facts

INTRODUCTORY PARAGRAPH The introductory paragraph serves two main functions. The first is to delimit the topic, to explain just what the writer hopes to accomplish by writing the theme. The second is to interest the reader. Too often students are overconcerned with the need to interest the reader. If the introductory paragraph states the purpose of the theme succinctly, that should be sufficient to create reader interest.

CONCLUDING PARAGRAPH The final paragraph should not contain new ideas. It should serve to summarize the theme. It should also contain a concluding sentence that restates the writer's main point.

RHETORICAL QUESTION A rhetorical question is one that a writer uses in an essay for dramatic purposes but does not expect the reader to answer. A rhetorical question at the end of the introductory paragraph acts as an excellent connective. It joins the body of the composition to the introduction when the body actually is an answer to that question.

TRANSITIONS *Transitions* are words and expressions that make the direction and organization of the theme absolutely clear to the reader. A good example of a transitional phrase is the use of *in conclusion* or *therefore* as part of the topic sentence in the conclusion. Other transitional expressions are given above under "Coherence."

EMPHASIS Emphasis can be gained within a paragraph by employing the unexpected. Some ways of gaining emphasis are as follows:

Rhetorical question: Who is responsible for the resurgence of the United Nations?

Repetition: His coach refused him. His teachers refused him. His parents had refused him. Now his best friend had just refused him!

Words placed out of the usual order: *Tired and frightened,* the prisoner was thrust into a cell.

In September, I expect to leave for Europe.

Swiftly came the night.

EXERCISE 2

A

DIRECTIONS: Underline the irrelevant sentence in each of the following paragraphs.

1. I look forward to the time that I can retire. I shall seek a cabin somewhere and let others worry about budgets. He who has been gifted with the love of retirement possesses as it were another sense. I then shall do all the reading that I have missed for the past three years.
2. The wise disregard nothing that concerns the welfare of mankind. Proverbs are but rules, and rules do not create character. They prescribe conduct, but do not furnish a full and proper motive. They are usually but half-truths and seldom contain the principle of the action they teach.
3. The morality of an action depends upon the motive from which we act. Let us with caution indulge the supposition that morality can be maintained without religion. Let us suppose that I fling a few dollars to a beggar with the intention of breaking his head. He escapes my intention and picks the money up. If he buys food with the money, the physical effect of my deed is good. However, with respect to me, the action was morally wrong.
4. Of course there is no one facet of a person's activities that can reveal him completely to others. However, what a person praises is perhaps a surer standard, even, than what he condemns. His praise can so often reveal his character, information, and abilities. No ashes are lighter than those of incense, and a few burn out sooner. No wonder, then, that most people are so shy of praising anything.
5. Do not wait for a day of reckoning. Sum up at night what you have done by day. In the morning, plan reflectively what you are to do during that day. It is easier to enrich ourselves with a thousand virtues than to correct ourselves of a single fault. Dress and undress your inner being; mark well its decay and growth. You never know when your conscience will catch up with your deeds. Judged you will be, but by yourself, and on that day, beware of finding yourself wanting. There can be no sterner judge of your true accounts than you.

B

DIRECTIONS: Underline the topic sentence in each of the following.

1. Hail can destroy one farmer's prospects of a harvest in a matter of seconds. It can leave his neighbor's unimpaired. It can slay a flock of sheep in one field, while the sun continues to shine in the next. To the harassed meteorologist its behavior is even more Machiavellian than that of the ice storm. He cannot predict the onset of a hailstorm, nor can he tell its course or duration once it has started. He is not even too sure any more about the way in which hail forms. Hail is at once the cruelest weapon in Nature's armory, and the most incalculable.
2. The preservation of even small bits of marshlands or woods representing the last stands of irreplaceable biotic communities is interwoven with the red tape of law, conflicting local interests, the overlapping jurisdiction of governmental and private conservation bodies, and an intricate tangle of economic and social considerations. The problems we face in conserving the natural resources are laborious and complex. During the time spent in resolving these factors, it often happens that the area to be preserved is swallowed up. Even more formidable is the broad-scale conservation problem raised by the spread of urban belts. The pressures of human growth are so acute in such instances that they raise issues which would tax the wisdom of Solomon.

3. Farmers raising crops from the same type of seed will often band together into an association. The purpose of the association is to spread the cost of advertising their product. The growers of navel oranges in California have helped to make Sunkist known in every home in the land. Similarly, the American growers of one of the pima cottons have banded together in the SuPima Association of America, and garments made of this superior cotton often carry the SuPima label.

4. I have a rich neighbor who is always so busy that he has no leisure to laugh. The entire business of his life is to get money. The more money he amasses, the more he seems to want. He fails to consider that it is not in the power of riches to make a man happy. How wise were they that said, "There are as many miseries beyond riches as on this side of them." The search for happiness or contentment must not center upon worldly wealth.

5. I am so tired of having to argue with others on unequal terms. The moment my adversary centers his thoughts upon self-interest, how can I continue to discuss with him! I am lost from the start. He will never accept my premises, as I cannot accept his. My facts are not facts to him. My conclusions are just as absurd when he weighs them in terms of only himself. Yet, how can humanity strive to reach a goal in which all will have an equal chance to live fully unless we keep our thoughts centered upon all, not one? We can march forward together only when we think of *we* and not *me*.

C

DIRECTIONS: Rearrange the following sentences into logical order. In the space to the left, write the number that would represent that sentence's place in the paragraph.

___ 1. (a) Great Britain declared war against the Netherlands a few months later.

___ (b) He was a former vice president of South Carolina and president of the Continental Congress.

___ (c) Laurens was put into the Tower of London when the British discovered the projected treaty.

___ (d) In 1778 Henry Laurens was chosen to go to Holland to negotiate a $10,000,000 loan and a treaty of amity.

___ (e) He was captured off Newfoundland by the British frigate Vestal.

___ 2. (a) For many years it was described as a hereditary disease, the result of some unknown defect in the germ plasm.

___ (b) Down's syndrome is a congenital malformation that blights approximately one in 650 births.

___ (c) Proof is now at hand that the disease is neither typically hereditary nor environmental.

___ (d) Other investigators have often argued an opposite explanation, that the disease was environmental, caused by accidents during gestation.

___ (e) It arises from a defect in the mechanism by which the hereditary material is passed on from parent to offspring.

___ 3. (a) One of the topics discussed was the development of methods that would elevate world fishing from a hunting industry to an agricultural technology.

___ (b) The group, known as the Conference of Science and World Affairs, convened for its seventh conference.

___ (c) Another topic discussed was the internationalization of the moon under the basic principles of the International Antarctic Treaty.

___ (d) The first conference had been held at Pugwash in Nova Scotia in 1957.

___ (e) In September 1961, 41 scientists from 12 countries met under skies darkened by distrust among nations.

___ (f) The purpose of these conferences is to foster the constructive use of science and help in preventing its destructive use.

___ 4. (a) Its width varies from 1,200 miles to 2,500 miles.
___ (b) The waters of the Pacific off North and South America conceal a low bulge in the crust of the earth.
___ (c) The Rise runs roughly north and south for 8,000 miles.
___ (d) But it is not its size that is at present considered so significant; its crest is a region of high earthquake activity.
___ (e) This bulge is as extensive as both of the continents.
___ (f) The East Pacific Rise is the name given to this vast feature.

___ 5. (a) They were supposed to live in the land of the Alps in houses built on stilts out over the water of the lakes.
___ (b) Recent findings tend to disprove Keller.
___ (c) These dwellings seemed to resemble those of South Sea Islanders.
___ (d) For over a century anthropologists have believed that there were prehistoric Swiss lake dwellers.
___ (e) This comparison resulted from the findings of Ferdinand Keller in 1854 along the shore of the Lake of Zurich.
___ (f) Research seems to point to these houses having been built on the shores of lakes that have since grown larger.

PRACTICE TESTS IN ORGANIZATION

Test 1

Suggested Time: 18 minutes

DIRECTIONS: The sentences in each of the following units A–D, belong in a well-organized paragraph. However they are presented here out of their correct order. You are to rearrange them in the best possible order. In the space provided before each sentence, write the number of its place in the paragraph, that is, whether it should be sentence 1, 2, 3, 4, or 5.

A

___ (a) Early men and women could do little more than hunt for berries, fruits, and edible animals.
___ (b) Later, agriculture emerged as the dominant activity of human beings, and they learned to control and direct the living matter around them.
___ (c) Primitive people lived in bondage to nature.
___ (d) The complex and broad interaction between human beings and nature is still going on today.
___ (e) They did nothing to interfere with the course of natural processes.

B

___ (a) The average number of moves is usually somewhere around forty-five, although the shortest game can consist of only two moves.
___ (b) A common saying among those who know the game best is that the winner is the one who makes the next-to-the-last blunder.
___ (c) It is rare, therefore, that a game lasts for considerably more than 100 moves.
___ (d) The end of the game is forecast by the opponent's skillful taking advantage of a mistake made at any point in the game.
___ (e) Even among grand masters, the secret of success is not superior planning but the persistent omission of errors in tactics.

C

___ (a) Our present research has enabled us to identify the sun as a large body of gas with a surface temperature of about 11,000 degrees Fahrenheit.
___ (b) Artificial satellites tell us that the corona envelops the earth and extends far out into the solar system.
___ (c) Above this visible sun is a thinner layer called the chromosphere, where, our rocket-directed cameras reveal, the temperature rises to about 30,000 degrees Fahrenheit.
___ (d) Probing into space with rockets and satellites has helped to add much to our knowledge about the star nearest us, the sun.

___ (e) Beyond is the corona, an extremely hot region with a kinetic temperature of millions of degrees.

D

___ (a) The great majority of bills die in committee.
___ (b) When a proposed law—bill—is introduced in either house, it is identified by a number and then referred to a committee.
___ (c) It may, on the other hand, decide to ignore the measure altogether—in other words, let it die.
___ (d) The committee may amend or even rewrite a bill before reporting it for final debate and vote.
___ (e) Congress is the legislative, or law making, branch of our government.

Test 2

Suggested Time: 20 minutes

DIRECTIONS: The sentences in each of the following units, A–D, belong in a well-organized paragraph. However, they are presented here out of their correct order. You are to rearrange them in the best possible order. In the space provided before each sentence, write the number of its place in the paragraph, that is, whether it should be sentence 1, 2, 3, 4, or 5.

A

___ (a) He thus had to find his way from the artificial conventions of the theater to a more simplified film style.
___ (b) He gave visible form to the inner conflicts of human beings in a realistic film language.
___ (c) He rejected the theatrical traditions that for too long had dominated filmmaking.
___ (d) At its best, the result was a realism in both plot and characters not achieved by any other contemporary film director.
___ (e) Films as a separate art form achieved a high peak under the direction of Sweden's Ingmar Bergman.

B

___ (a) Much later, with Lincoln and Theodore Roosevelt the choice was largely luck.
___ (b) It cannot be said that Franklin Roosevelt was an unknown quality when he was first elected president.
___ (c) American democracy has always managed to find a great leader in time of crisis.
___ (d) Yet few who voted for him realized that as an advocate of democracy he ranked with Lincoln and as a leader toward a better world he was an equal of Wilson.
___ (e) In the case of our first president, Washington, the choice was based on a proven record of solid achievements.

C

___ (a) The impurity may lower the effectiveness of the finished product.
___ (b) In ancient Greece and Rome, there were laws against such abuses and merchants were punished for coloring and flavoring wine.
___ (c) In most instances addition of an adulterant to foods and drinks has only one aim—to increase the profit of the seller.
___ (d) In our country today, the federal government has accepted the responsibility of safeguarding the public from such practices in both food and drinks.
___ (e) More dangerously, it may pose a threat to the health of the consumer.

D

___ (a) According to some scholars, this decline, which began in 1914, was the result of the failure of the alliance system which the political leaders had toiled to create.
___ (b) Gradually, before our very eyes Europe has disappeared as the overlord of the world.
___ (c) These scholars claim that the nineteenth century was not a period of calm stability, as is commonly assumed, but one of deep and bitter disagreements.
___ (d) Others seem to feel that the basic cause lies in the undermining of tradi-

tional beliefs by the intellectual giants of the preceding century—Darwin, Marx, Nietzsche.

___ (e) Its cultural, political, and economic achievements had been accepted universally as the measure of human progress.

Test 3

Suggested Time: 20 minutes

DIRECTIONS: The sentences in each of the following units, A–D, belong in a well-organized paragraph. However, they are presented here out of their correct order. You are to rearrange them in the best possible order. In the space provided before each sentence, write the number of its place in the paragraph, that is, whether it should be sentence 1, 2, 3, 4, or 5.

A

___ (a) The Confederates almost succeeded in their plans, for on its first day in action the *Merrimac* quickly destroyed two wooden warships, and would have wiped out more of them if it had not met the *Monitor* on the second day.

___ (b) For four hours the ironclads pounded each other with shot and shell, with little apparent damage.

___ (c) As an act of desperation in an attempt to end the Federal blockade that was strangling its commerce, the Confederacy placed all of its hopes in the *Merrimac*.

___ (d) However, when the action ceased the *Merrimac* was leaking badly, unable to attack any more warships, and thus failing to accomplish its primary mission.

___ (e) This was a 3,500-ton steam-propelled vessel that had been abandoned and then sunk by the Federals before it was refitted by the Confederates with a coating of four inches of railroad iron.

B

___ (a) When a proposal is introduced in either the House of Representatives or the Senate, it is called a bill.

___ (b) Once it has been passed by that House, it is reprinted as an act.

___ (c) An act becomes a law when it has passed both houses and been signed by the President.

___ (d) It remains a bill while it is under consideration by that House of Congress.

___ (e) An act, therefore, is a measure that has been enacted by one branch of the legislature.

C

___ (a) A portrait furnished a faithful image of the deceased to aid his survival in the afterworld.

___ (b) Etruscan sculptors preferred to work in clay or bronze rather than in stone.

___ (c) The art of portraiture played an important role in their funeral rites.

___ (d) Their best work took the form of portraits.

___ (e) They were particularly fond of the bas-relief, in which they filled the scene with delightfully animated figures.

D

___ (a) This snake, an inhabitant of the southwestern United States, is usually found on soft soil or sand, bad surfaces for a thick-bodied snake to travel across by the usual snake methods of movement.

___ (b) The snake overcomes the difficulty by throwing forward, sidewise loops of its body.

___ (c) However, it is the only way in which the snake can move satisfactorily over the yielding surfaces.

___ (d) One member of the rattlesnake family is called the sidewinder because of its method of traveling across the terrain in which it lives.

___ (e) The effect of this "sidewinding" makes it appear as if the snake were trying to walk.

Test 4

Suggested Time: 20 minutes

DIRECTIONS: In each of the following units, the sentences form the sentence outline for an essay. However, the sentences are out of their proper order. By filling in the appropriate letter in the answer column, mark

A if the sentence contains the central idea of the theme,
B if the sentence contains a main supporting idea that points directly to the central idea,
C if the sentence contains an example or illustrative fact that acts as proof,
D if the sentence contains a statement that is unrelated to the central idea.

A

1. The peasantry were overburdened by taxes from many sources.

Ⓐ Ⓑ Ⓒ Ⓓ

2. Monarchs such as Peter the Great of Russia and Frederick II of Prussia supported the arts and sciences.

Ⓐ Ⓑ Ⓒ Ⓓ

3. All men were subject to military duty in the destructive wars carried on by these rulers.

Ⓐ Ⓑ Ⓒ Ⓓ

4. They spent millions of dollars in building magnificent palaces as monuments to remind people of their greatness.

Ⓐ Ⓑ Ⓒ Ⓓ

5. While the eighteenth century saw many advances in literature, science, and art, the common people were oppressed by continuing burdens.

Ⓐ Ⓑ Ⓒ Ⓓ

6. Voltaire was one of the intellectual leaders who revolted against the oppressive forces of the current rulers.

Ⓐ Ⓑ Ⓒ Ⓓ

7. These enlightened despots sponsored writers and artists who praised their reigns.

Ⓐ Ⓑ Ⓒ Ⓓ

8. They refused to change old, obsolete forms of government.

Ⓐ Ⓑ Ⓒ Ⓓ

B

9. The earth could be blanketed in the space of an hour with a deadly cloud of radioactive fall-out poisons.

Ⓐ Ⓑ Ⓒ Ⓓ

10. Nearly half the population of America live or work in environments polluted to some degree by man-made fumes.

Ⓐ Ⓑ Ⓒ Ⓓ

11. Unfriendly nations have at their disposal even more dangerous pollutive forces.

Ⓐ Ⓑ Ⓒ Ⓓ

12. Bombs filled with bacterial agents can be exploded over the vast areas, spreading disease and death for months and years.

Ⓐ Ⓑ Ⓒ Ⓓ

13. Modern industrialized society has forced equally large segments of peoples of other countries to breathe in chemical fumes, from factories, automobile exhausts and processing plants.

Ⓐ Ⓑ Ⓒ Ⓓ

14. Air pollution has become a social evil of widespread consequences.

Ⓐ Ⓑ Ⓒ Ⓓ

15. The average person breathes daily about twenty pounds of air.

Ⓐ Ⓑ Ⓒ Ⓓ

16. Airborne contaminants blanket large portions of the world.

Ⓐ Ⓑ Ⓒ Ⓓ

C

17. The reasons for public indifference reach deep into the private lives of the citizens.

Ⓐ Ⓑ Ⓒ Ⓓ

18. In midterm Congressional elections even fewer people take the trouble to cast their ballots.

Ⓐ Ⓑ Ⓒ Ⓓ

19. The average person is so deeply absorbed in his personal affairs that he sees little connection between what he is doing and governmental operations.

Ⓐ Ⓑ Ⓒ Ⓓ

20. Too often elections reveal an apathy on the part of the voters.

Ⓐ Ⓑ Ⓒ Ⓓ

21. The strength of a democracy lies in the intelligence of its citizens.

Ⓐ Ⓑ Ⓒ Ⓓ

22. America suffers from a widespread indifference to political affairs.

Ⓐ Ⓑ Ⓒ Ⓓ

23. Fewer than 65% of those eligible to vote take the trouble to do so in important presidential election years.

Ⓐ Ⓑ Ⓒ Ⓓ

24. Governmental agencies do not reach the people with the facts and figures needed to dispel ignorance of their principles and practices, so that the importance of their actions is unknown to the average voters.

Ⓐ Ⓑ Ⓒ Ⓓ

D

25. Silver and gold coins are milled around the edges because they contain valuable metal.

Ⓐ Ⓑ Ⓒ Ⓓ

26. No one can pare a quarter or half-dollar without it being seen at once by anyone handling the coin.

Ⓐ Ⓑ Ⓒ Ⓓ

27. Unless they were so treated, people could pare the edges of these coins and sell the precious metal.

Ⓐ Ⓑ Ⓒ Ⓓ

28. Pennies and nickels have smooth edges, however.

Ⓐ Ⓑ Ⓒ Ⓓ

29. Have you ever wondered why some coins have grooved edges while others do not?

Ⓐ Ⓑ Ⓒ Ⓓ

30. Pennies and nickels are not milled because it would not be economically worthwhile to the thieves to pare the edges of these coins.

Ⓐ Ⓑ Ⓒ Ⓓ

31. The cost of coinage is kept to a minimum because it is done exclusively by the government with no middleman to make a profit.

Ⓐ Ⓑ Ⓒ Ⓓ

Test 5

Suggested Time: 20 minutes

DIRECTIONS: In each of the following units, the sentences form the sentence outline for an essay. However, the sentences are out of their proper order. By filling in the appropriate letter in the answer column, mark

A if the sentence contains the central idea of the theme,
B if the sentence contains a main supporting idea that points directly to the central idea,
C if the sentence contains an example or illustrative fact that acts as proof,
D if the sentence contains a statement that is unrelated to the central idea.

A

1. The nuclear physicist holds a high priority in the group who center their interests in discovering more and more of the universe's until-now unknown principles.

Ⓐ Ⓑ Ⓒ Ⓓ

2. The teacher of science and mathematics in schools and colleges prepares the next generation for the tasks ahead.

Ⓐ Ⓑ Ⓒ Ⓓ

3. The scientist plays just as important a role in the practical world of everyday.

Ⓐ Ⓑ Ⓒ Ⓓ

4. The theoretical mathematician and the biochemist searching for the cure of people's physical ills meet here to exchange their ideas for the betterment of humanity.

Ⓐ Ⓑ Ⓒ Ⓓ

5. The student interested in science and mathematics has many areas open to him, depending upon his interests and aptitudes.

Ⓐ Ⓑ Ⓒ Ⓓ

6. The technician, the pharmacist, the laboratory assistant, and the nurse have their roles to play in safeguarding people from physical ills.

Ⓐ Ⓑ Ⓒ Ⓓ

7. Those who decide to go into research may work in private or public laboratories.

Ⓐ Ⓑ Ⓒ Ⓓ

8. The paths that lead to science and mathematics begin in the earliest school grades.

Ⓐ Ⓑ Ⓒ Ⓓ

9. The physician makes her daily rounds, applying her knowledge to the immediate health problems that cannot wait for a future solution.

Ⓐ Ⓑ Ⓒ Ⓓ

B

10. The bells also signified the passing of every half hour during each watch.

Ⓐ Ⓑ Ⓒ Ⓓ

11. The time between four in the afternoon and eight in the early evening was often divided into two two-hour periods called dogwatches.

Ⓐ Ⓑ Ⓒ Ⓓ

12. Each watch consisted of four hours, and there were six watches in each day.

Ⓐ Ⓑ Ⓒ Ⓓ

13. One bell meant the passing of the first half hour in each watch.

Ⓐ Ⓑ Ⓒ Ⓓ

14. Time on board ship was once based solely on the bell system.

Ⓐ Ⓑ Ⓒ Ⓓ

15. Eight bells marked the end of each watch and the beginning of the next, when the man who was on duty departed and the next man came to relieve him.

Ⓐ Ⓑ Ⓒ Ⓓ

16. Three bells meant, for example, that an hour and a half had passed during the watch.

Ⓐ Ⓑ Ⓒ Ⓓ

17. The bells were used to signal the end of the watches.

Ⓐ Ⓑ Ⓒ Ⓓ

18. Eight bells then meant that eight half hours had passed.

Ⓐ Ⓑ Ⓒ Ⓓ

C

19. The impermanence of federal employment discouraged the more qualified and pressured them to seek employment elsewhere, where their salaries and position would depend more upon their ability as workers.

Ⓐ Ⓑ Ⓒ Ⓓ

20. Before 1883 the spoils system prevailed, and nearly all positions in the federal service were filled on the basis of political patronage.

Ⓐ Ⓑ Ⓒ Ⓓ

21. By 1933, nearly 80% of the positions in the executive branches of government were under the merit system.

Ⓐ Ⓑ Ⓒ Ⓓ

22. To maintain his job, the officeholder had to contribute money and time to the political party in power.

Ⓐ Ⓑ Ⓒ Ⓓ

23. It has only been within recent years that government service has attracted career workers and highly qualified personnel.

Ⓐ Ⓑ Ⓒ Ⓓ

24. With the passage of the Pendleton Act and the establishment of the Civil Service Commission, the end of the spoils system began.

Ⓐ Ⓑ Ⓒ Ⓓ

25. Even then, when the party that had given him his job was defeated at the polls, he would most likely lose his job, regardless of how competent he might be.

Ⓐ Ⓑ Ⓒ Ⓓ

26. In recent years there has been considerable criticism directed against the administration of the federal civil service system.

Ⓐ Ⓑ Ⓒ Ⓓ

27. However, there are still thousands of positions that are filled by the politicians who are interested in votes, not in ability to produce on the job.

Ⓐ Ⓑ Ⓒ Ⓓ

D

28. Ability to receive sounds varies not only from person to person but from age group to age group.

Ⓐ Ⓑ Ⓒ Ⓓ

29. Sound is the result of air-molecule motion and cannot spread faster than the air's molecules move collectively.

Ⓐ Ⓑ Ⓒ Ⓓ

30. Sound waves are waves of energy that are received differently by different organisms.

Ⓐ Ⓑ Ⓒ Ⓓ

31. Sounds are audible to the average adult as continuous tones when they contain between twenty and thirty vibrations per second.

Ⓐ Ⓑ Ⓒ Ⓓ

32. Cats, small dogs, and guinea pigs detect better than thirty thousand vibrations per second.

Ⓐ Ⓑ Ⓒ Ⓓ

33. For ordinary sounds the energy involved is incredibly small.

Ⓐ Ⓑ Ⓒ Ⓓ

34. Brown bats have given evidence of hearing vilbrations that are as high as a hundred thousand vibrations per second.

Ⓐ Ⓑ Ⓒ Ⓓ

35. Young children catch the more shrill sounds, sounds with the highest number of vibrations, much better than adults do.

Ⓐ Ⓑ Ⓒ Ⓓ

36. Five thousand people speaking over the telephone for one year would develop only enough energy to bring a gallon of water to boil.

Ⓐ Ⓑ Ⓒ Ⓓ

37. Animals, particularly the small mammals, hear sounds even higher than those heard by children.

Ⓐ Ⓑ Ⓒ Ⓓ

Test 6

Suggested Time: 12 minutes

DIRECTIONS: In each of the following units, the sentences form the sentence outline for an essay. However, the sentences are out of their proper order. By filling in the appropriate letter in the answer column, mark

A if the sentence contains the central idea of the theme,
B if the sentence contains a main supporting idea that points directly to the central idea,
C if the sentence contains an example or illustrative fact that acts as proof,
D if the sentence contains a statement that is unrelated to the central idea.

A

1. The lawyers, dentists, and doctors continue to receive their initial college training in the liberal arts.

Ⓐ Ⓑ Ⓒ Ⓓ

2. Other four-year institutions have been springing up.

Ⓐ Ⓑ Ⓒ Ⓓ

3. Parents have led their children to realize that within a rather short period of time the average white-collar worker will be college-trained.

Ⓐ Ⓑ Ⓒ Ⓓ

4. The liberal arts college is still a stepping-stone to traditional professional training.

Ⓐ Ⓑ Ⓒ Ⓓ

5. The many fields of business education can now be pursued following training in a college of business.

Ⓐ Ⓑ Ⓒ Ⓓ

6. Not only are there colleges of engineering, but some institutions now offer a four-year course in technology, the handmaiden to engineering.

Ⓐ Ⓑ Ⓒ Ⓓ

7. Formal education beyond high school has been undergoing a rapid change within recent years.

Ⓐ Ⓑ Ⓒ Ⓓ

B

8. A jet pilot trying to leave a disabled plane has little chance of climbing out against the pressure of the hurricane of air rushing by.

Ⓐ Ⓑ Ⓒ Ⓓ

9. Ejecting him with a charge of gunpowder only partially solves the difficulties.

Ⓐ Ⓑ Ⓒ Ⓓ

10. Human survival after a supersonic bailout has been a serious problem when a failure occurs in jet planes.

Ⓐ Ⓑ Ⓒ Ⓓ

11. An unprotected man cannot depend on surviving the effects of being hit by the wind of present plane speeds.

Ⓐ Ⓑ Ⓒ Ⓓ

12. The speed generated by the plane is a basic cause of the difficulty.

Ⓐ Ⓑ Ⓒ Ⓓ

13. In February 1955, a test pilot was the first person to survive a forced bailout while his plane was traveling at supersonic speeds.

Ⓐ Ⓑ Ⓒ Ⓓ

14. Even if he did succeed in getting out of the cabin, the tail assembly would most probably cut him in two.

Ⓐ Ⓑ Ⓒ Ⓓ

C

15. Hitler and his corps of followers destroyed the machinery that allowed nations to live at peace with each other.

Ⓐ Ⓑ Ⓒ Ⓓ

16. Six million Jews were not their only victims.

Ⓐ Ⓑ Ⓒ Ⓓ

17. Deceit and bullying, treachery and war replaced humanitarianism and Christian ethics as the principles the Nazis brought to the conference table when countries met to iron out their differences.

Ⓐ Ⓑ Ⓒ Ⓓ

18. Each succeeding generation must be taught to recoil at the horror that was unleased on the world by the forces of Nazism.

Ⓐ Ⓑ Ⓒ Ⓓ

19. Many millions more from Russia, Poland, France, and England were slaughtered like cattle and burned in ovens built to convert their bodies into fertilizer.

Ⓐ Ⓑ Ⓒ Ⓓ

20. Innocent people throughout Europe were ground into slavery and dust because they stood in the path of these ruthless would-be conquerors of the world.

Ⓐ Ⓑ Ⓒ Ⓓ

21. By January 1933, the Nazis had formed the largest single political party in Germany.

Ⓐ Ⓑ Ⓒ Ⓓ

Test 7

Suggested Time: 20 minutes

DIRECTIONS: In each of the following units, the sentences form the sentence outline for an essay. However, the sentences are out of their proper order. By filling in the appropriate letter in the answer column, mark

- **A** if the sentence contains the central idea of the theme,
- **B** if the sentence contains a main supporting idea that points directly to the central idea,
- **C** if the sentence contains an example or illustrative fact that acts as proof,
- **D** if the sentence contains a statement that is unrelated to the central idea.

A

1. He hurried his family out of the house and into the cyclone cellar.

Ⓐ Ⓑ Ⓒ Ⓓ

2. Before he realized what had happened, the great funnel was hanging directly over him.

Ⓐ Ⓑ Ⓒ Ⓓ

3. Not many men have been as fortunate as the Kansas farmer, Will Keller, who escaped unharmed even though a tornado passed directly over him.

Ⓐ Ⓑ Ⓒ Ⓓ

4. All wind had ceased, and he caught a very distinctive pungent odor.

Ⓐ Ⓑ Ⓒ Ⓓ

5. He took one last look through the barn and hurried to the cellar himself.

Ⓐ Ⓑ Ⓒ Ⓓ

6. When he saw a greenish black cloud in the southwest, Keller suspected a tornado.

Ⓐ Ⓑ Ⓒ Ⓓ

7. A line of thunderheads, at first low on the horizon, soon appeared in the west.

Ⓐ Ⓑ Ⓒ Ⓓ

8. He looked directly into the circular opening of the tornado and saw small twisters form and writhe their way around inside the rim of the funnel.

Ⓐ Ⓑ Ⓒ Ⓓ

9. He stopped at the cellar door before going down to safety.

Ⓐ Ⓑ Ⓒ Ⓓ

B

10. The late eighteenth and early nineteenth centuries were characterized by a relatively simple agricultural economy that did not require economic controls.

Ⓐ Ⓑ Ⓒ Ⓓ

11. To outlaw practices which endangered the public health, Congress enacted the Meat Inspection Act.

Ⓐ Ⓑ Ⓒ Ⓓ

12. The role of the government in assuring social justice for all has undergone marked changes during the last 100 years.

Ⓐ Ⓑ Ⓒ Ⓓ

13. The important issues of that day seemed to be mainly political rather than in the area of the national economy.

Ⓐ Ⓑ Ⓒ Ⓓ

14. The leaders felt that the government should try to encourage agriculture and commerce without restricting the individual farmer.

Ⓐ Ⓑ Ⓒ Ⓓ

15. The earlier approach was based on the Jeffersonian idea that the best form of government is the one which disturbs the individual the least.

Ⓐ Ⓑ Ⓒ Ⓓ

16. The government must exert controls in our social and economic organization to protect the individual.

Ⓐ Ⓑ Ⓒ Ⓓ

17. The government must concern itself with everyday factors of living and earning a living.

Ⓐ Ⓑ Ⓒ Ⓓ

18. The basic issues which confront the nation today are mainly economic, the outgrowth of a highly complex industrial civilization.

Ⓐ Ⓑ Ⓒ Ⓓ

C

19. The freshwater angler who enjoys walking along rocks or streambeds wanders with a box of flies into isolated areas in search of trout.

Ⓐ Ⓑ Ⓒ Ⓓ

20. He casts his heavily weighted line out beyond the breakers and trolls it in, catching unwary fish that have come close to the beach in search of food.

Ⓐ Ⓑ Ⓒ Ⓓ

21. The fisherman of today has a variety of tackle and types of fishing activities to choose from.

Ⓐ Ⓑ Ⓒ Ⓓ

22. The surfcaster, equipped with heavy boots and the longest rod of them all, stands in the white water on the beach's edge.

Ⓐ Ⓑ Ⓒ Ⓓ

23. The sportsman with the big-game hunter instinct is usually attracted to the swivel chair and the deepsea launches.

Ⓐ Ⓑ Ⓒ Ⓓ

24. The fly-fisherman can use either the traditional long bamboo pole or the modern spinning equipment with a spun-glass rod.

Ⓐ Ⓑ Ⓒ Ⓓ

25. The laker finds fun and enjoyment in a sport that has some of the characteristics usually found mainly among the other three types of fishing.

Ⓐ Ⓑ Ⓒ Ⓓ

26. The fishing widow is the wife who has resigned herself to being left stranded by her husband while he searches for the big one and for release of his tensions.

Ⓐ Ⓑ Ⓒ Ⓓ

D

27. Many seeds are water travelers, for those that are lighter than water are able to float.

Ⓐ Ⓑ Ⓒ Ⓓ

28. Birds, tempted by pleasantly flavored fruit, feast and then drop and scatter the seeds.

Ⓐ Ⓑ Ⓒ Ⓓ

29. Many seeds have wings that cause them to be carried by the wind.

Ⓐ Ⓑ Ⓒ Ⓓ

30. In the tumbleweeds, the whole plant breaks off from the roots when it stops growing.

Ⓐ Ⓑ Ⓒ Ⓓ

31. Nature's means of seed dispersal are many and varied.

Ⓐ Ⓑ Ⓒ Ⓓ

32. Dandelion seeds sail long distances, wafted by the breeze on delicate parachutes composed of a crown of silky hairs.

Ⓐ Ⓑ Ⓒ Ⓓ

33. Although the dustlike seeds of the orchids have no special flying equipment, because of their small size, they are carried great distances by even gentle breezes.

Ⓐ Ⓑ Ⓒ Ⓓ

34. Coconuts can float many miles before the seed is landed on a distant shore.

Ⓐ Ⓑ Ⓒ Ⓓ

35. Fruits of the arrowhead have air chambers that help them on their voyage and enable the seeds to settle far from the parent plant.

Ⓐ Ⓑ Ⓒ Ⓓ

36. For many seeds, birds serve as the means of transportation.

Ⓐ Ⓑ Ⓒ Ⓓ

Test 8

Suggested Time: 20 minutes

DIRECTIONS: In each of the following units, the sentences form the sentence outline for an essay. However, the sentences are out of their proper order. By filling in the appropriate letter in the answer column, mark

A if the sentence contains the central idea of the theme,
B if the sentence contains a main supporting idea that points directly to the central idea,
C if the sentence contains an example or illustrative fact that acts as proof,
D if the sentence contains a statement that is unrelated to the central idea.

A

1. Over 8,000,000 men died in battle or of wounds sustained in battle.

Ⓐ Ⓑ Ⓒ Ⓓ

2. Many cities and villages were destroyed completely.

Ⓐ Ⓑ Ⓒ Ⓓ

3. The loss in human life far exceeded that caused in all previous wars combined.

Ⓐ Ⓑ Ⓒ Ⓓ

4. The immediate effects of World War I were almost unbelievable in their magnitude.

Ⓐ Ⓑ Ⓒ Ⓓ

5. Material losses can be estimated only in billions of dollars.

Ⓐ Ⓑ Ⓒ Ⓓ

6. Over 22,000,000 soldiers were wounded.

Ⓐ Ⓑ Ⓒ Ⓓ

7. Economic nationalism cut down world trade in a futile effort to rebuild destroyed manufacturing centers.

Ⓐ Ⓑ Ⓒ Ⓓ

8. Almost 20,000,000 civilians died because of the famine, disease, and the direct destructive forces of war.

Ⓐ Ⓑ Ⓒ Ⓓ

9. Trade and manufacturing as well as farming ceased in large areas.

Ⓐ Ⓑ Ⓒ Ⓓ

B

10. At one time sponges were considered as worm houses built by worms much as bees build honeycombs.

Ⓐ Ⓑ Ⓒ Ⓓ

11. The skeleton, when the animal is alive, contains many tiny cells.

Ⓐ Ⓑ Ⓒ Ⓓ

12. The sponge is an intricate structure that once was regarded as one of nature's puzzles.

Ⓐ Ⓑ Ⓒ Ⓓ

13. There are many mistaken beliefs about the sponge.

Ⓐ Ⓑ Ⓒ Ⓓ

14. The dry material that we buy is really a skeleton.

Ⓐ Ⓑ Ⓒ Ⓓ

15. One ancient writer asserted that sponges were from the foam of the sea.

Ⓐ Ⓑ Ⓒ Ⓓ

16. A stream of water carries food and oxygen around the cells.

Ⓐ Ⓑ Ⓒ Ⓓ

17. Actually the sponge is an animal.

Ⓐ Ⓑ Ⓒ Ⓓ

18. Some even consider the sponge a type of seaweed.

Ⓐ Ⓑ Ⓒ Ⓓ

19. The sponges are of many different colors.

Ⓐ Ⓑ Ⓒ Ⓓ

C

20. Foreign governments could not deal with a government lacking this function.

Ⓐ Ⓑ Ⓒ Ⓓ

21. Any predatory group could attempt to seize power and run the government.

Ⓐ Ⓑ Ⓒ Ⓓ

22. The individual would be without protection for his personal liberties.

Ⓐ Ⓑ Ⓒ Ⓓ

23. The property of foreigners could not be protected, nor would their businessmen be able to deal with ours lest just debts be ignored by gangster groups.

Ⓐ Ⓑ Ⓒ Ⓓ

24. Criminal elements could seize from the weaker citizens their wealth and property.

Ⓐ Ⓑ Ⓒ Ⓓ

25. Policing is one of the chief functions of government.

Ⓐ Ⓑ Ⓒ Ⓓ

26. Anarchy is the type of social structure in which there are no governmental structures or restrictions.

Ⓐ Ⓑ Ⓒ Ⓓ

27. Organized group activities would be at a standstill if governments did not have policing.

Ⓐ Ⓑ Ⓒ Ⓓ

D

28. The glands connected to the fang in the harmless snake look like those of the deadly snakes; yet they produce nothing to hurt anyone.

Ⓐ Ⓑ Ⓒ Ⓓ

29. The amount of poison is slight, but the venom of many of our poisonous snakes is among the most deadly of all poisons.

Ⓐ Ⓑ Ⓒ Ⓓ

30. The fang in the harmless snakes lacks the hollow slit.

Ⓐ Ⓑ Ⓒ Ⓓ

31. The snake's fang is an eye or canine tooth, corresponding to the sharp- pointed tooth that humans have between the front teeth and the back teeth.

Ⓐ Ⓑ Ⓒ Ⓓ

32. Those who fear snakes should learn to recognize the harmless ones that are beneficial to man.

Ⓐ Ⓑ Ⓒ Ⓓ

33. In poisonous snakes the fang has a hollow channel running through it.

Ⓐ Ⓑ Ⓒ Ⓓ

34. The fang in a poisonous snake has one significant difference from that found in the non-poisonous snakes.

Ⓐ Ⓑ Ⓒ Ⓓ

35. Where the snake bites, drops of poison are forced through the channel and into the victim's body.

Ⓐ Ⓑ Ⓒ Ⓓ

Answers to all exercises and practice tests begin on page 328.

Analysis of a Typical Essay Question

The essay is assigned to give you an opportunity to show how well you can write. You should, therefore, take care to express your thoughts on the topic clearly and effectively. How well you write is much more important than how much you write, but to cover the topic adequately you will want to write at least three paragraphs. Be specific.

Your essay must be written on the two lined sheets provided. You will receive no other paper on which to write. You will find that you have enough space if you write on every line, avoid wide margins, and keep your handwriting to a reasonable size. Remember that what you write will be read by someone who is not familiar with your handwriting, and to write or print so that what you have to say is legible.

DO NOT WRITE IN YOUR TEST BOOK. You will receive credit only for what you write on the sheets provided.

TYPICAL QUESTION

The essay question usually consists of three parts: directions, a quotation or statement, and the prompt, which acts as an assignment.

DIRECTIONS: You have 30 minutes to plan and write an essay on the topic assigned below. DO NOT WRITE ON ANOTHER TOPIC. AN ESSAY ON ANOTHER TOPIC IS NOT ACCEPTABLE.

Consider carefully the following quotation and the prompt (that is, the part of the question that narrows the topic and directs your thinking).

Experience is the best teacher.

Prompt: Do you agree or disagree with this statement? Write an essay in which you support your opinion with specific examples from history, contemporary affairs, literature, or personal observation.

Spotlight on Directions

The directions are the least productive part of the question. Usually they consist of one or more generalized statements of procedure. However, you must not skip or skim over them. The directions on the form of the test that you take may differ significantly from those in the samples in the official information bulletin.

Read the directions carefully with pen in hand to underline statements that signal a change from the usual or that contain information you need to keep in mind.

Spotlight on Statement or Quotation

The statement or quotation provides the topic that you are to write about and is planned to stimulate you to agree or disagree wholly or in part. You are expected to discuss it from your experience, observations, or reading. It should lead you to explanations and generalizations supported by specific examples as you explore its implications according to your own knowledge or experience.

Before allowing your mind to explore, you must be able to answer these questions.

What do the key words mean?
What is the literal meaning of the statement or quotation?
What are some figurative meanings?
How do you react to its implications?
To what extent is the statement true?

With the given proverb, "Experience is the best teacher," for example, you could

1. disagree completely, and show that experience may lead to a disaster that can be avoided if the warnings or examples of others are heeded. A child need not learn from experience that fire can cause severe burns. This approach uses an extreme though not unusual example to challenge the validity of the proverb.
2. agree completely, and show that the best way to learn how to replace a carburetor in a car is not through listening to a lecture or reading a manual, but through doing it yourself—under the supervision of an experienced mechanic. You could give endless effective examples as long as you deal with areas in which the experience is constructive and is limited in its demands.
3. agree in part and disagree in part, again citing examples. You could conclude that all generalizations, including this one about experience, tell only part of the truth.

However, once you have begun to explore the statement or quotation and have come up with some ideas, you are not ready to write your essay! First you must carefully consider the prompt.

Spotlight on the Prompt

Given the bewildering flow of ideas that may overwhelm you when you begin to examine the given statement or quotation, the prompt becomes the key to your organization. It indicates which areas you are to explore and what type of conclusion you should reach.

Let us now return to our example.

Prompt: Do you agree or disagree with this statement? Write an essay in which you support your opinion with specific examples from history, contemporary affairs, literature, or personal observation.

As the prompt, or assignment, is worded, you are asked to decide to what extent and in which ways you agree or disagree with the given proverb. Now you are ready to return to your preliminary thinking on and reactions to "Experience is the best teacher." Of all the arguments you mustered while reading the quotation, which seem most compelling? They do not have to be the ones you have always believed in or will believe in in the future. They should be ones that you presently accept. Since the essay is necessarily a brief one, do not attempt an exhaustive listing. Limit yourself to the one or two arguments that you find most compelling at the time of the examination.

If you find yourself unable to be selective and too many ideas continue to churn around, imagine what the reaction to the proverb would be for some favorite person—a teacher, friend, parent. Then write the response from that person's point of view.

When you have decided on the major thoughts you are planning to present, you are ready to formulate your *thesis,* that is, the main point you want to bring out in your essay. Usually the thesis answers the question *why* and is formulated in a *because* sentence. For the given prompt, the thesis could begin like these examples:

The proverb is a justifiable generalization because...

The proverb is not justifiable because...

I both agree and disagree with the proverb because...

Remember that you are not going to be rated on the quality of the reasons or proof. You do not have time to search for highly original examples or arguments. At best, the essay is a rough instrument for separating the applicants into groups, not a method for showing unique excellence.

When you have selected your thesis, you are ready to organize and write your essay. The time for selection of your point of view and the major reasons for doing so has passed!

Organizing Your Essay

You are not ready for this step until you

1. understand the quotation,
2. have used the assignment to formulate your thesis, and
3. have selected your explanation and illustrations.

Probably, you will not have time to plan a formal outline. Your thinking, however, must be developed around the three parts of your essay: introduction, development, conclusion. You should have a minimum, therefore, of three paragraphs.

THE INTRODUCTION

Avoid elaborate flourishes. The introduction should indicate to the reader the direction of your theme. It may contain a definition, an example, a statement of the problem, a statement of the present situation, a quotation, and/or a dramatization of the problem.

The transition from the introduction to the body can very well be a rhetorical question based on the topic being discussed. If you are discussing heroes of today, then the transitional sentence may be, "Is it true then, that there is no hero in our world of today?" The section of the essay that follows will be your answer to the question.

DO'S AND DON'T'S FOR INTRODUCTIONS

1. Avoid the trite, the forced, the unrelated.
2. Be simple and direct.
3. Strive to be accurate, clear, emphatic.
4. Be modest and unassuming, but confident.
5. Do not strive to be funny.
6. Be positive. Cynicism is to be avoided.
7. Try to achieve appropriate mood and manner.

PRACTICE IN WRITING AND ANALYZING INTRODUCTIONS

To obtain maximum benefit, write, under strict examination conditions, an introduction for the practice essay question given below. Then, following the directions provided, compare what you have written with the six student introductions given. An evaluation of these introductions follows the samples.

DIRECTIONS: Following the given essay question are the introductions of essays typical of those submitted by high school applicants. In the space provided, write your analysis of the strengths and weaknesses in each. Confine your criticism to organization and content.

The Person I Admire Most

Prompt: Hero worship is not confined to teenagers. At all ages, from infancy through maturity, we choose individuals as models to admire and to imitate. Who is the person that you admire most at present? Explain and defend your choice, using illustrations from your observation or your reading.

STUDENT INTRODUCTIONS

1. I am delighted that this topic is the one chosen for us to write on. It is a topic of special concern to teenagers. We are in the stage of finding out who we are and what paths we will take in the future. Which person do I admire most?

ANALYSIS ______________________

____

____

2. As a teenager about to enter high school, I have to begin to prepare myself for my future. I have to decide on who I want to be and what career I shall choose. The person whom I admire most has helped me greatly in my choices. That person is our family doctor. Let me explain why I chose her as the person I admire most.

ANALYSIS ______________________

____

____

3. In these troubled times, there are many issues that can leave us torn by fears and doubts. We look in all directions for help. These issues must be solved and solved quickly if we are to survive. As a teenager I must turn to my personal problems, the problems involving my future. One person has spent many hours helping me make decisions. This person is my dad. Why do I admire him most?

ANALYSIS ______________________

____

____

4. Teenagers have an endless number of people to choose from when picking the person they admire most. Many of them choose among athletes, from the most valuable professional player to the star of the high school team. Others confine their choices to the entertainment world. They choose the most popular singer, actor, or even composer as their idol. I'm different! Let me tell you about the person I admire most and why I chose her.

ANALYSIS ______________________

____

____

5. The person I admire most is the manager of our local supermarket. He has the respect of all of the workers. He never raises his voice or utters a harsh word. He is always available to listen to customers when they complain. He always sees things from the other person's point of view. I enjoy working for him after school. When I grow up, I hope to be like him.

ANALYSIS ______________________

____

____

6. There is nothing unusual about his appearance. I don't think he would stand out in a crowd of people. In fact, because he is only 5 feet 10, he is just about average. He has never been mentioned in the news or had his picture taken for a newspaper story. Yet, he is the person I admire most. Let me explain why!

ANALYSIS ______________________

____

____

EVALUATION OF STUDENT INTRODUCTIONS

1. The writer shows an awareness of the purpose of an introductory paragraph. Although the opening statement may arouse reader interest, it is too self-conscious, directing attention unnecessarily to the writer rather than to the topic. The last sentence does point toward what is going to be discussed in the next paragraph; however, it is not thought-connected to the preceding sentence.
2. The paragraph is well organized and clearly defines the topic. The last sentence indicates the direction of what is to follow. The major weakness of the paragraph is that the thought content is close to being a mere restatement of the question.
3. The writer shows a firm grasp of the question. You can readily see the plan or organization. What will follow must be the reasons why Dad was chosen. However, there is no justification for beginning with the old chestnut "In these troubled times..." A less global approach would be more effective.
4. The paragraph is well organized and begins with a sentence intended to arouse the interest of the reader. The sense flows smoothly from one sentence to the next. This introduction may be a bit wordy, but it touches all bases.
5. The writer does explain why the person chosen is worthy of admiration. However, this is an answer to a test question; it is not the introduction to an essay.
6. The paragraph is well organized. From the attention-getting first sentence to the forward-directing last sentence, the writer adheres closely to the prompt.

EVALUATION OF YOUR OWN INTRODUCTION

Weakness ____________________

Strength ____________________

It is closest to number __________ of the student introductions because __________

____

I could have improved it if I had __________

____

THE DEVELOPMENT

Don't attempt to turn the development into a listing of reasons, facts, and examples; it is *not* a test of your memory. It is a test of your ability to explain and defend a point of view or a serious topic. The key to an adequate development lies in stressing the word *because*. The major portion of this section of your essay should consist of reasoning and *selected* examples or illustrations. You should support your statements by referring to your own experience or to the world of literature.

PRACTICE IN WRITING AND ANALYZING DEVELOPMENTS

To obtain maximum learning, write, under strict examination conditions, a development that could evolve from the introduction given in the following question. Then, following the directions provided, compare what you have written with the five student developments given. An evaluation of these developments follows the samples.

DIRECTIONS: Below is a practice essay question. It is followed by a completed introduction and by five developments written by different students. In the space provided, write your analysis of each of these developments. Confine your criticism to organization and content.

Consider carefully the following quotation: "Good sportsmanship, doing unto others what you would have done unto yourself, is an idea basic to the American way. Yet many business people do not hesitate to disregard this ideal when money is involved. Even our athletes often believe that winning is all that counts. Youth is rightfully confused about which moral standards to follow."

Prompt: Are these statements justified? What do they tell about our way of life? Explain and defend your answer, using illustrations from your observations, reading, or personal experience.

Completed introduction:

No one will deny that in many activities our society does not practice what it preaches. To make a profit, corporations put

harmful additives into baby food. They charge not what will result in a fair profit, but whatever people are willing to pay. To win, athletes take drugs, injure opponents, and break rules when authorities are not looking. Yet at the same time, we talk about the need for high moral standards in our conduct toward others. What does this reveal about our way of life?
(For best results, now write your own development based on this introduction.)

Student Developments

1. Greed is the cause of all difficulties in our society. If people were not so selfish, they would not disregard the welfare of others. We live in a world of dog eat dog and let the devil take the hindmost. If people were not so greedy for wealth and power, this would be a much better world to live in. How can manufacturers live with themselves when they make and sell life-endangering products? Is it worth it when a young athlete's entire future is ruined by an injury intentionally inflicted on the football field?

   ANALYSIS ______________________________

   ____

   ____

2. If these examples of greed and selfishness were true of all our businesses and all of our athletes, our country is really in a bad way. However, even our worst critics cannot claim that such practices are engaged in by all of our business leaders and athletes. All of us can name corporations that spend millions on research to make their products more beneficial to the consumer. All of us can name companies that share their profits with the public by giving huge sums to charities and worthwhile nonprofit organizations. For every athlete that injures an opponent intentionally, we can name thousands that play the game fairly.

   ANALYSIS ______________________________

   ____

   ____

3. Youth is confused about good sportsmanship. On one hand, we are told that we have to treat others as we ourselves want to be treated. On the other hand, business leaders do not care about who gets hurt so long as their companies can show huge profits. Athletes try any tactic that they can get away with so long as they win. They even go so far as to injure their opponents if they have to in order to win. This is the world we live in!

   ANALYSIS ______________________________

   ____

   ____

4. The fact that some people do not follow the Golden Rule does not prove much about our way of life. Unfortunately, not all of us have the moral strength to avoid the temptation to profit illegally at the expense of others. The fact that we have the machinery to punish those who attempt to do so shows strength rather than weakness in our way of life. Our government is on the alert and passes regulations to correct practices that endanger the welfare of the people.

   ANALYSIS ______________________________

   ____

   ____

5. Do the above facts prove that democracy is a failure and should be replaced by some form of dictatorship that could better control those who violate the Golden Rule? The practices would have to be more widespread for such a drastic conclusion. To me what these practices reveal is the true strength of democracy. We have agencies that curb erring corporations when the public health is threatened. The rules and regulations for games are modified when the well-being of the players is endangered. We have the ability in our country to make changes when we discover that some practices endanger the public.

   ANALYSIS ______________________________

   ____

   ____

EVALUATION OF STUDENT DEVELOPMENTS

1. The paragraph does answer the question: "What does this reveal about our way of life?" However, it employs the examples given in the introduction to present an overgeneralized condemnation of all people. This is a barely adequate development.

2. The paragraph is developed to answer the question in the prompt: "Are these statements justified?" It cites examples to support the writer's conclusion that it is wrong to condemn the many for the actions of the few. There is much more that could have been said, but in a brief essay the writer must limit his or her treatment. This is a better than average development.

3. The paragraph does tell us something about our way of life. However, it is a series of unconnected sentences that repeat the thought content of the introduction. This is an inadequate development.

4. The paragraph has answers to the two questions in the prompt: "Are these statements justified?" and "What do they tell us about our way of life?" It then reverses the argument and uses the evidence to prove strength rather than weakness. A deficiency is that no examples are given to support the conclusion. This is a better than adequate development.

5. The paragraph expands the questions in the prompt into one that begins the paragraph and then is answered in the sentences that follow. A clear explanation is given of how, in our democracy, the public is protected from endangerment. This is a superior development.

EVALUATION OF YOUR OWN DEVELOPMENT

Weakness ______________________

Strength ______________________

It is closest to number ____________ of the student developments because ______________________

____

I would rate it as ______________________

I could have improved it if I had ______________________

____

THE CONCLUSION

The conclusion should not introduce any new ideas. It should serve as a summary of what you have said before. It should end on a strong emotional note—if such a note is appropriate.

PRACTICE IN WRITING AND ANALYZING CONCLUSIONS

To obtain maximum benefit, write, under simulated examination conditions, a conclusion that could evolve from the introduction and development given below for the practice question. Then, following the directions provided, compare what you have written with the five student conclusions given. An evaluation of the conclusions follows the samples.

DIRECTIONS: Following the given essay question are an introduction and development and then five conclusions. In the space provided, write your analysis of the strengths and weaknesses in each conclusion. Confine your criticism to organization and content.

Television viewing has become the opiate of the masses. It has turned us into a people with flabby bodies overstuffed with junk food, and with flabby minds overstuffed with repetitive stories of violence and endless athletic contests that require only passive watching.

Prompt: Comment on the opening statement, using your personal experience or reading as the basis for your opinion. To what extent do you think the statement is correct or incorrect? Support your opinion by using specific illustrations.

Introduction and development:

Untold sets of statistics have been evolved to show how completely we as a nation have incorporated television viewing into our way of life. The direst of all analyses are those that, like the opening statement given for this essay, view us as being converted into a nation of zombies. Is this a fair representation of the effect of television?

It is true that many people view the endless detective series and become glued to the weekend football games, the evening baseball series, and basketball tournaments. Almost as bad are those addicted to the often repeated reruns of old movies. But the picture is not so bad as the quotation suggests.

Television has helped to popularize fitness. The news programs and special series stress health topics, especially the recognition and prevention of disease. Such programming offsets somewhat the deleterious effects of too much sitting before the one-eyed monster's usual fare.

Then too, public television has grown. Great literature, serious music, and expert discussion of timely topics form the major bill of fare offered. These channels show how television, used effectively, can raise the cultural level and social consciousness of the viewers. The commercial and cable networks also have their share of opera, special musical spectaculars, weekly forums, and special coverage of outstanding events, such as the Senate confirmation hearings for Supreme Court justices and other high officials.

STUDENT CONCLUSIONS

1. The biggest problem with television viewing is how to handle the conflicts of interest that arise in a family. In some homes, each member has a personal television set in addition to the one in the living room or playroom. Sometimes, usually not too often, all the individuals in the family get together and watch the same program. Most of the time, each goes a separate way. Sometimes, kindred souls who like the same program join the lone watcher. The alternatives to such compromise are violence, dictatorship, or even divorce!

ANALYSIS ______________________

____

____

2. I am always pleased when the mandated topic for an essay is on a timely issue that thinking people must be made aware of. The topic for this essay is just that kind. We were made aware of a problem that must be handled if we are to survive as a world leader. I offer you my sincerest congratulations for giving us this timely topic to write on. Thank you for giving me an opportunity to discuss how television has affected our lives.

ANALYSIS ______________________

____

____

3. It is true that too many of us spend too much of our time watching television programs that add nothing to our lives. Yet, television is constantly changing. It has so many possibilities for being an effective force for improving our lives. Public television in its entirety and network and cable systems with their cultural and special events programs point up the fact that not all of television is bad. And public television will continue to offer new and challenging issues and exciting programming concepts. I have faith that television is a force for the good!

ANALYSIS ______________________

____

____

4. Therefore just saying that TV viewing has become an opiate of the masses tells only part of the story. The other part is much more encouraging. Selective TV viewing is possible. Junk TV can be limited or even eliminated. The educational system, therefore, along with parents and civic leaders, has an obvious obligation. The youth of today must be taught to shun programs that are sensational and overcommer-

cialized. I am certain that our adult guides will show us the way!

ANALYSIS ______________________

____

____

5. As you can see, I believe that this condemnation of current TV fare has a large piece of the truth in it. However, not all is negative. Much of current programming, especially in public television, is wholesome, constructive, educational. As consumers, we must hope that the percentage of these better programs increases.

ANALYSIS ______________________

____

____

EVALUATION OF STUDENT CONCLUSIONS

1. Another aspect of the effect of television is introduced in this paragraph. It effectively presents a serious problem that television has caused. However, this is not a summary of what has already been said. It is not a conclusion. A summarizing paragraph is still needed. This is an inadequate conclusion.
2. This generalized statement does include in the concluding sentence a reference to television. However, this is not a summary; it does not reinforce the thesis developed in the previous sections. Such a conclusion is given the lowest possible rating.
3. The paragraph begins with a summary of the aspects that the writer has discussed. It ends with a thesis-statement and a hope for the future. This is a superior conclusion.
4. The first two sentences begin as an effective summary even though the writer feels obligated to repeat the wording of the quotation. However, a new undeveloped aspect is introduced with the discussion of the role of educators, parents, and civil leaders, weakening the impact of the conclusion. This conclusion is barely adequate.
5. In the first three sentences, the paragraph summarizes the main ideas of the essay. The final sentence is an attempt to give an application of previous data. This conclusion is very good.

EVAULATION OF YOUR OWN CONCLUSION

Weakness ______________________

Strength ______________________

It is closest to number __________ of the student conclusions because __________

____

I would rate it as ______________

I could have improved it if I had __________

____

Strategies for Success in Essay Writing

1. Clear your head of the preceding (multiple choice) portion of the test.
2. Read the directions and the prompt carefully. Underline the key words.
3. Remember that you have never written on this topic before in just the way that the prompt directs you. Do *not* answer with a memorized essay that you wrote previously!
4. Keep in mind that what you write must be in accord with the prompt and the directions. If you write on any other topic, or treat the topic in any other way, you will be severely penalized when the essay is rated by the admissions committees.
5. Don't begin to write the essay immediately. Instead, jot down in the question booklet key words and ideas that come to your mind.
6. Now decide what one or two points you want to make.
7. Next, block out your essay into three or four paragraphs: introduction, main ideas, conclusion.
8. Now begin to write. All of the process up to this point should have taken no more than 8 minutes.
9. When you have finished, proofread what you have written. Catch the pen-slips, misspellings, and omissions. Check that every idea is clearly expressed. Indicate a revision by drawing a single line through the wrong word or phrase and writing the correction neatly above it.

Practice in Writing the Essay

To obtain maximum benefit from the following exercise:

1. Write, under strict examination conditions, a 30-minute essay based on the question.
2. Analyze the student responses that follow.
3. Compare your analysis of each essay with the evaluation given.
4. Evaluate your own essay.

Time begun ____ Time ended ____

Time used ____

Did you complete the essay on time? ____

DIRECTIONS: You have 30 minutes to plan and write an essay on the topic assigned below. DO NOT WRITE ON ANOTHER TOPIC. AN ESSAY ON ANOTHER TOPIC IS NOT ACCEPTABLE.

The wise argue causes; fools decide them.

Prompt: Do you agree or disagree with this statement? Write an essay in which you support your opinion with specific examples from history, contemporary affairs, literature, or personal observation.

STUDENT ESSAYS FOR ANALYSIS

The following essays are typical of those submitted by applicants. In the space below each, write your analysis of the strengths and weaknesses of the essay. Confine your criticism to elements of content and organization. Rate each essay on this scale of 1 to 6:

5–6 *Generally excellent:* Originality of thought and freshness of expression.

4–5 *Competent:* Soundness of thought and clear organization.

3 *Interesting but flawed:* Imagination and ability to think clearly combined with irrelevancies and weakness in organization.

1–2 *Inadequate:* Borderline in thought, content, and organization; triteness of thought coupled with lack of organization.

1. I find the topic most interesting. It forces you to think about how people behave in the world around us. If more people would allow sayings like this one to govern their lives, there would be fewer fights in families and among nations.

   Wise sayings come from the experiences of millions of people through the ages. If they are used as guides, they benefit individuals and the world of people around them.

   We must learn to use sayings like this one, "The wise argue causes; fools decide them." In that way we will best be able to find answers to the problems around us.

   ANALYSIS ______________________________

   ____

   ____

2. The given proverb contains two different meanings for *causes.* In the first half, *causes* means *those things that bring about a result.* In the second half, *causes* means *issues.* To me, the saying thus means that the best approach to an issue is to find that which brought it about. The worst way to handle a problem is to take sides before knowing what caused the problem.

   The world around us is filled with many horrifying threats. We seem to be rushing toward disaster. With the weapons of war that we now have, we can wipe out all life from the surface of our planet. We can even destroy the planet itself. When will we learn that we are not the masters of the Earth and that we are only a small part of a larger pattern that we cannot control?

   ANALYSIS ______________________________

   ____

   ____

3. "The wise argue causes; fools decide them." During an examination, I find difficulty in describing my thought as clearly as I should like to. Yet, in this world filled with responsibilities we cannot stand still and let things just happen to us. We must rise to the occasion and do our best. Our best under such circumstances may prove unsatisfactory, but that is all that society can expect from us.

   Like all generalizations, the proverb given for this essay has a piece of the truth. When facing an issue we are wise if we look for the underlying cause before taking sides. Taking sides means that there must be a winner and a loser; but in many social issues there cannot always be winners and losers. You cannot just be against slums, disease, poverty. You have to do more than just argue; you have to attack causes and try to overcome them through positive action.

   Looking for causes is good as far as it goes. However, if we stop there, nothing can be accomplished We must take a firm stand and fight if necessary once we have a clear idea of causes. That is the piece of the truth that the quotation misses.

   ANALYSIS ______________________________

   ____

   ____

4. Proverbs have been guides to human action for thousands of years. They have been tested and proved by millions of people. Yet, we do not look to them for the complete truth. As with any generalization, we cannot expect them to be true under all circumstances. Rather we look to proverbs and folk sayings for insights that can help us to understand other people and ourselves. The saying "The wise argue causes; fools decide them" is an excellent illustration to prove my point.

   The proverb can be punched full of holes. It is not always wise to *argue causes.* When a child is drowning in a bathtub, you do not stand there arguing about what or who caused the accident. It is not *always* foolish to take a stand on an unresolved issue. If the blacks at Birmingham had not decided to act, instead of analyzing causes, our march toward social and economic democracy would not have taken giant steps forward.

   However, the proverb does contain a valuable insight. If we want to solve a problem that has a solution, it is better to approach its causes and handle them. For example, when parents and children quarrel over curfew, chores, or allowances, the problems are more easily controlled when the family discusses the reasons for the rulings and for the objections to them. Nothing is truly resolved when each side takes a stand stating that one side is right and the other wrong. The reason for the position, rather than the rightness or wrongness, is key to a satisfactory solution.

   ANALYSIS ______________________________

   ____

   ____

5. Every human being has to face problems, personal, social, and economic. Proverbs can guide us through such difficulties.

   Right now, my big problem involves my choice of career. I think I would like to become a medical doctor. My parents have approved my choice. However, the cost of a medical education is so high that my family will not be able to see me through. I really do not want to put such a burden on them. I have three brothers and sisters all younger than me. They too should have the right to go to college when the time comes for them. My parents have said that if I do well enough in high school and undergraduate college courses, scholarships and loans could see me through.

   By reading the proverb "The wise argue causes; fools decide them," I have been helped to see what my problem is and how to resolve it. Proverbs can truly guide us through our difficulties.

   ANALYSIS ______________________________

   ____

   ____

EVALUATION OF STUDENT ESSAYS

1. At no point did the student discuss the given topic. The generalizations, while applicable, could be a form response to all similar topics. The answer contains no supportive illustrations. While the essay is divided into three paragraphs, the second is primarily a repetition of the first.

   RATING: Inadequate—1

2. The essay is divided into two unconnected paragraphs. The first paragraph shows an excellent approach to the topic; a workable explanation of the proverb is presented. The second paragraph is completely unrelated to the first and apparently unrelated to the topic. The writer may have had a strong thread of connection planned, but it was never realized in the presentation.

   RATING: Inadequate—2

3. There are two unrelated sections to the essay. The first paragraph begins with the proverb, but it is not related to the following sentence. What follows in the first paragraph is unrelated to the topic and to the next two paragraphs; it contains a self-conscious attempt at an introduction.

The second and third paragraphs are very well organized, and they deal cogently with the ideas the writer related to the statement. More could have been done to illustrate the candidate's thesis that the proverb has only a piece of the truth.

RATING: Competent—4

4. This is a more ambitious essay that only a student who can think and write quickly can consider writing. The writer develops the concept that proverbs are valuable for the insights they give us and not for the truth, or lack of it, in a particular generalization. The second paragraph shows the weakness in the proverb's message. In the third paragraph the writer presents evidence of the insight obtained from the proverb.

RATING: Generally excellent—5-6

5. The essay has a three-part organization. The main idea in the first paragraph is repeated in the conclusion. But at no one point did the writer carry out the given assignment. There is no clarification of the quotation, presentation of a thesis, or proof to support a thesis.

RATING: Inadequate—2

EVALUATION OF YOUR OWN ESSAY

Weaknesses ______________________

Strengths ______________________

It is closest to number _____ of the student essays because ______________________

____

I would rate it as ______________________

I could have improved it if I had ______________________

____

ADDITIONAL ESSAY ASSIGNMENTS

The following set of assignments is for those who have the time or need for additional practice in planning and organizing a 30-minute essay.

The assumption here, as throughout this chapter, is that you can write without making costly technical errors. If, however, you do need additional practice in that area, work on the material in *Digest of Communication Skills*, beginning on page 87. Unless you have command of sentence structure, everyday spelling, word meanings, and Standard American Usage, you are not ready to do the level of essay writing required for an "excellent" rating in essay writing.

Step 1. Plan three-part essays.

What will you put in the introduction? In the development? In the conclusion?

What will be your main point or thesis?

What will be your major examples and supporting points?

Step 2. Now, if time permits, write fully one or more of the three parts of several essays, choosing from the topics that follow. Write some introductions, some developments, and some conclusions; don't concentrate on any one part.

If you complete an essay, limit yourself to two sides of the usual $8^1/2$ by 11 theme paper.

Essay Topics

GROUP ONE: PAIRS IN CONTRAST

Prompt: As we grow older, we develop more and more respect for the nuggets of wisdom passed on from generation to generation in proverbs and wise sayings. Unfortunately, some of these sage maxims come in seemingly contradictory pairs.

To what extent does each of the following pairs express part of the truth? Are the sayings really contradictory? Support your opinion with specific examples from history, contemporary affairs, literature, or personal observation.

1. Eat, drink and be merry; who knows what the future will bring?
   Never fail to save for the rainy day.
2. Hitch your wagon to a star.
   They will endure who ask nothing out of life.
3. Self-preservation is the first law of life.
   One for all; all for one.

4. I am the captain of my soul; I am the master of my fate.
   We are all pawns in the hands of Fate.
5. If you are not truthful with your friends, when can you be trusted?
   A little flattery cements friendships.
6. Look before you leap.
   He who hesitates is lost.
7. Nothing ventured; nothing gained.
   If you want to survive, don't stick your neck out.

GROUP TWO: QUESTIONS TO ANSWER

Prompt: The topics in this group explore responsibilities to yourself and to the society of which you are a part. Support your opinions with specific examples from history, contemporary affairs, literature, or personal observation.

1. What should be the role of TV in our lives?
2. How can we help the homeless?
3. How can school be made more attractive to potential dropouts?
4. Now that legal lotteries have had their chance, should they be abolished?
5. Does violence on TV cause violence in real life?
6. Should teenagers be barred from viewing the afternoon soap operas?
7. Should members of high school varsity team be given a contract and a salary?

GROUP THREE: SETTING VALUES

Prompt: A most important part of growing up is identifying your own values, finding out how you feel about some of the basic issues of the day. In writing an essay on any of the following topics, do not try to cover every aspect you can think of. Pick the one or two points that you feel are most important. Then support your opinions with specific examples from history, contemporary affairs, literature, or personal observation.

1. A formula for success (failure)
2. How to be a successful gift-giver at Christmas time
3. People I could easily do without
4. A cure for laziness (lateness, dawdling, procrastination)
5. Advice to new entrants into high school
6. Adjusting to a new school
7. My "never, never again" list
8. What adolescents need most
9. What I expect of a friend
10. What I value most

GROUP FOUR: "HOW-TO" TOPICS

Prompt: We can list many reasons why others should behave in a particular way, and almost as many explaining how we ourselves should act. However, in writing a 30-minute essay on a "how-to" topic, you must limit yourself. The best approach is to select the one or two aspects that you consider most important and then concentrate on why you believe that way. Support your opinions with specific examples from history, contemporary affairs, literature, or personal observation.

1. How to become a successful babysitter
2. How to live with siblings
3. How to keep friends
4. How to please both your parents and yourself
5. How to give advice
6. How to influence parents
7. How to pick a career
8. How to keep an afterschool job
9. How to budget your time
10. How to make even your best friend mad

GROUP FIVE: MORE TOPICS FOR ESSAYS

Prompt: Growing-up is a serious business. During this coming-out time, when the adolescent's world widens to include so many others outside the immediate family, teenagers are called on to make judgments that will affect their adult way of life. In a

30-minute essay on one of the following topics, support your opinions with specific examples from history, contemporary affairs, literature, or personal observation.

1. Surviving in a world menaced by drugs
2. Teenagers are conformists
3. Pity the poor consumer
4. Settling family quarrels
5. What teenagers value most
6. The meaning of "well dressed"
7. Handling first impressions
8. Acting your age
9. Handling hurt pride
10. Handling prejudice in others
11. Recognizing a prejudice of your own
12. My changing heroes
13. Handling moods
14. In defense of rainy days
15. Television and family life
16. Advice to a new teacher
17. Handling anger
18. Breaking a bad habit

Answers to All Exercises and Practice Tests

EXERCISES

EXERCISE 1, p. 294

(No Answer Key can be given for this exercise)

EXERCISE 2, p. 297

A

1. He who has been gifted with the love of retirement possesses as it were another sense.
2. The wise disregard nothing that concerns the welfare of mankind.
3. Let us with caution indulge the supposition that morality can be maintained without religion.
4. No ashes are lighter than those of incense, and few burn out sooner.
5. It is easier to enrich ourselves with a thousand virtues than to correct ourselves of a single fault.

B

1. Hail is at once the cruelest weapon in Nature's armory, and the most incalculable.
2. The problems we face in conserving natural resources are laborious and complex.
3. Farmers raising crops from the same type of seed will often band together into an association.
4. The search for happiness or contentment must not center upon worldly wealth.
5. We can march forward together only when we think of *we* and not *me*.

C

(1) 5, 2, 4, 1, 3
(2) 3, 1, 5, 4, 2
(3) 5, 2, 6, 3, 1, 4
(4) 5, 1, 4, 6, 2, 3
(5) 2, 5, 3, 1, 4, 6

PRACTICE TESTS

TEST 1, p. 299

A	B	C	D
1. (c)	1. (b)	1. (d)	1. (e)
2. (a)	2. (e)	2. (a)	2. (b)
3. (e)	3. (d)	3. (c)	3. (d)
4. (b)	4. (c)	4. (e)	4. (c)
5. (d)	5. (a)	5. (b)	5. (a)

TEST 2, p. 300

A	B	C	D
1. (e)	1. (c)	1. (c)	1. (b)
2. (c)	2. (e)	2. (a)	2. (a)
3. (a)	3. (a)	3. (e)	3. (c)
4. (b)	4. (b)	4. (b)	4. (e)
5. (d)	5. (d)	5. (d)	5. (d)

TEST 3, p. 301

A	B	C	D
1. (c)	1. (a)	1. (b)	1. (d)
2. (e)	2. (d)	2. (d)	2. (a)
3. (a)	3. (b)	3. (e)	3. (b)
4. (b)	4. (e)	4. (c)	4. (e)
5. (d)	5. (c)	5. (a)	5. (c)

TEST 4, p. 302

A	B	C	D
1. **C**	9. **C**	17. **B**	25. **B**
2. **B**	10. **C**	18. **C**	26. **C**
3. **C**	11. **B**	19. **C**	27. **C**
4. **C**	12. **C**	20. **B**	28. **B**
5. **A**	13. **C**	21. **D**	29. **A**
6. **D**	14. **A**	22. **A**	30. **C**
7. **C**	15. **D**	23. **C**	31. **D**
8. **B**	16. **B**	24. **C**	

TEST 5, p. 303

A	B	C	D
1. **C**	10. **B**	19. **C**	28. **B**
2. **C**	11. **D**	20. **B**	29. **D**
3. **B**	12. **C**	21. **C**	30. **A**
4. **C**	13. **C**	22. **C**	31. **C**
5. **A**	14. **A**	23. **A**	32. **C**
6. **C**	15. **C**	24. **B**	33. **B**
7. **B**	16. **C**	25. **C**	34. **C**
8. **D**	17. **B**	26. **D**	35. **C**
9. **C**	18. **C**	27. **C**	36. **C**
			37. **C**

TEST 7, p. 307

A	B	C	D
1. **C**	10. **C**	19. **B**	27. **B**
2. **B**	11. **D**	20. **C**	28. **C**
3. **A**	12. **A**	21. **A**	29. **B**
4. **C**	13. **C**	22. **B**	30. **D**
5. **C**	14. **C**	23. **B**	31. **A**
6. **B**	15. **B**	24. **C**	32. **C**
7. **D**	16. **C**	25. **B**	33. **B**
8. **C**	17. **C**	26. **D**	34. **C**
9. **C**	18. **B**		35. **C**
			36. **B**

TEST 6, p. 306

A	B	C
1. **C**	8. **C**	15. **B**
2. **B**	9. **B**	16. **C**
3. **D**	10. **A**	17. **C**
4. **B**	11. **C**	18. **A**
5. **C**	12. **B**	19. **C**
6. **C**	13. **D**	20. **B**
7. **A**	14. **C**	21. **D**

TEST 8, p. 309

A	B	C	D
1. **C**	10. **C**	20. **B**	28. **C**
2. **C**	11. **B**	21. **C**	29. **C**
3. **B**	12. **A**	22. **B**	30. **B**
4. **A**	13. **B**	23. **B**	31. **A**
5. **B**	14. **B**	24. **C**	32. **D**
6. **C**	15. **C**	25. **A**	33. **C**
7. **D**	16. **C**	26. **D**	34. **B**
8. **C**	17. **B**	27. **B**	35. **C**
9. **C**	18. **C**		
	19. **D**		

DIGEST OF MATHEMATICAL SKILLS

Mathematical Skills

In this chapter, many topics of mathematics are reviewed. Most of the topics are followed by three exercise sets. If you do sufficiently well on the first set of practice exercises, you do not need further practice on that topic. If you do not do well on the first set, use the second set, which is usually longer, to build your skill on that topic. Use the third set of exercises to determine that you have mastered the skill. This approach allows you to review the necessary topics in a reasonable amount of time while building skills where they are needed. Answers to All Exercises and Practice Tests begin on page 391.

Whole Numbers

Practice—Addition

EXERCISE 1

In addition, the *addends* are the numbers that are added. The *sum* is the answer.

Add the following.

1.	2.	3.	4.
235	109	890	523
482	537	112	909
706	628	509	347
859	140	438	400
121	216	785	571
360	935	363	686
718	147	184	195
+ 525	+ 423	+ 717	+ 230

5.	6.	7.	8.
641	958	1,369	73
825	139	275	159
796	264	2,501	8
104	382	138	807
378	195	976	42
909	617	23	87
264	820	3,085	291
+ 540	+ 463	+ 1,603	+ 352

If you got seven or eight of these problems correct, go on to the next section on Subtraction. If you got more than one wrong, use Exercise 2 to build your skill.

EXERCISE 2

Add the following.

1.	2.	3.	4.	5.
325	455	904	628	773
472	137	357	119	508
814	904	816	247	379
352	768	749	583	425
719	319	998	402	667
115	250	843	380	321
247	763	122	955	790
+ 598	+ 275	+ 640	+ 371	+ 112

6.	7.	8.	9.	10.
403	775	829	3,174	418
725	804	173	429	211
170	576	729	738	1,074
819	132	485	1,902	92
624	849	540	2,400	724
137	921	277	93	2,225
950	687	348	329	258
+ 528	+ 459	+ 104	+ 1,207	+ 29

Now be sure of your skill. Try Exercise 3.

EXERCISE 3

Add the following.

1.	2.	3.	4.
349	158	414	587
123	324	752	104
405	605	395	793
768	789	470	658
841	457	867	720
527	593	903	119
664	640	288	246
+ 970	+ 898	+ 176	+ 335

5.	6.	7.	8.
782	124	756	2,073
596	387	2,897	152
350	359	592	1,270
829	931	84	732
111	855	739	409
478	129	78	381
502	770	840	72
+ 227	+ 258	+ 2,016	+ 1,208

Practice—Subtraction

The *subtrahend* is the number to be subtracted. The *minuend* is the number from which the subtrahend is to be subtracted.

EXERCISE 4

Subtract the following.

1. 85765 − 43512
2. 56324 − 28473
3. 90521 − 38149
4. 65093 − 30247
5. 71585 − 38618
6. 90150 − 30072
7. 85214 − 7847
8. 50638 − 27040
9. 94003 − 37512
10. 82513 − 4162
11. 74391 − 53618
12. 80203 − 7016
13. 45214 − 34806
14. 15792 − 13849
15. 70506 − 30507

If you got 13 or more correct, go on to the next section on Multiplication. If you got more than 2 wrong, use Exercise 5 to build your skill.

EXERCISE 5

Subtract the following.

1. 62451 − 31236
2. 85137 − 23489
3. 60529 − 37158
4. 28507 − 13759
5. 77293 − 30572
6. 85917 − 7645
7. 40321 − 37512
8. 59001 − 32694
9. 94052 − 7916
10. 48302 − 25769
11. 80405 − 32906
12. 70091 − 52304
13. 76051 − 32592
14. 30000 − 25619
15. 48256 − 3957
16. 80304 − 1205
17. 92003 − 21798
18. 46387 − 9059
19. 53040 − 17629
20. 65702 − 3982
21. 80059 − 30078
22. 92011 − 38562
23. 35712 − 28903
24. 89053 − 6778
25. 56893 − 30276
26. 40932 − 2569
27. 68439 − 19572
28. 50370 − 2056
29. 10059 − 2006
30. 60507 − 53079

Now be sure of your skill. Try Exercise 6.

EXERCISE 6

Subtract the following.

1. 43795 − 12482
2. 35672 − 12895
3. 82950 − 34729
4. 79053 − 46704
5. 30070 − 21563
6. 92053 − 56427
7. 32470 − 8956
8. 47304 − 39567
9. 46300 − 32495
10. 10563 − 7429
11. 58923 − 38759
12. 80530 − 79286
13. 92004 − 89007
14. 36029 − 9583
15. 70012 − 6904

Practice—Multiplication

When two or more numbers are multiplied the result is called a *product.* The numbers that are multiplied to form a product are *factors.* For example, 6 × 7 = 42. In this case, 42 is the product and 6 and 7 are factors. Since the product (42) may also be written as 3 × 2 × 7, the numbers 3 and 2 are also factors of 42. The numbers 3, 2, and 7 are called *prime numbers* because they have no factors except themselves and 1. The numbers 3, 2, and 7 are said to be the *prime factors* of 42.

EXERCISE 7

Multiply the following.

1. 5843 × 7
2. 6028 × 8
3. 5704 × 9
4. 3012 × 6
5. 6824 × 37
6. 4850 × 49
7. 6057 × 82
8. 7850 × 56
9. 3852 × 134
10. 4037 × 208
11. 7590 × 356
12. 2859 × 470

If you got 11 or 12 of these problems correct, go on to the next section on Division. If you got more than one wrong, use Exercise 8 to build your skill.

EXERCISE 8

Multiply the following.

1. 6843 × 5
2. 5803 × 9
3. 7246 × 8
4. 5098 × 7
5. 6008 × 4
6. 1207 × 6
7. 3850 × 3
8. 5205 × 2
9. 5831 × 19
10. 7046 × 94
11. 5103 × 57
12. 6009 × 38
13. 2904 × 63
14. 9017 × 82
15. 3578 × 59
16. 7124 × 98
17. 2853 × 124
18. 3715 × 286
19. 4029 × 617
20. 7108 × 509
21. 9007 × 680
22. 3592 × 847
23. 2570 × 319
24. 6853 × 708

Now be sure of your skill. Try Exercise 9.

EXERCISE 9

Multiply.

1. 6234 × 9
2. 5037 × 6
3. 2509 × 8
4. 2053 × 7
5. 7839 × 29
6. 6350 × 47
7. 4059 × 58
8. 6830 × 72
9. 8512 × 128
10. 5069 × 302
11. 6380 × 274
12. 3157 × 940

Practice—Division

When we divide 35 by 5 the result is 7. In this case 35 is called the *dividend,* 5 is called the *divisor,* and 7 is called the *quotient.*

Sometimes, when we divide one number by another there will be a quotient and a *remainder.*

EXAMPLE: Divide 429 by 17.

```
                 25 →quotient
divisor → 17)429 →dividend
             34
             89
             85
              4→ remainder
```

In this case, the divisor is 17, the dividend is 429, the quotient is 25, and the remainder is 4. The answer may be written $25\frac{4}{17}$.

EXERCISE 10

Divide the following (express remainders, if any, as the numerators of fractions).

EXAMPLE: 7)4853 = $693\frac{2}{7}$

1. 4)5828
2. 7)6146
3. 8)2464
4. 6)4623
5. 24)8232
6. 37)7411
7. 89)8633
8. 29)9109
9. 46)14352
10. 92)37265
11. 63)42218
12. 87)51595
13. 352)164384
14. 740)176123
15. 589)414690
16. 416)164320

If you got 14 or more correct, go on to the Practice Tests that follow. If you got more than two wrong, use Exercise 11 to build your skill.

EXERCISE 11

Divide the following (express remainders, if any, as the numerators of fractions).

1. 6)3474	2. 5)7320
3. 9)8200	4. 7)1764
5. 8)4635	6. 6)3402
7. 4)3841	8. 3)1168
9. 7)8042	10. 9)4639
11. 5)8424	12. 6)5395
13. 4)6845	14. 8)1047
15. 9)4938	16. 7)2103
17. 36)1728	18. 49)1813
19. 23)2001	20. 97)8051
21. 45)2617	22. 19)5792
23. 51)3550	24. 64)4997
25. 37)6420	26. 63)13049
27. 89)65504	28. 71)57439
29. 378)231336	30. 465)368280
31. 729)609470	32. 956)666373
33. 508)354179	34. 297)180899
35. 816)613632	36. 470)283410

Now be sure of your skill. Try Exercise 12.

EXERCISE 12

Divide the following (express remainders, if any, as the numerators of fractions).

1. 6)3564	2. 9)6039
3. 7)3247	4. 8)9403
5. 36)8892	6. 49)8580
7. 27)2646	8. 73)6397
9. 68)24276	10. 97)39891
11. 54)39937	12. 19)17998
13. 464)148016	14. 630)338397
15. 379)228200	16. 532)247380

Before you attempt these Practice Tests, be sure to review Test-Taking Tips on page vii.

PRACTICE TEST 1

DIRECTIONS: Circle the letter that corresponds to the correct answer.

1. 2,919 + 3,151 =

   (A) 607 (B) 670 (C) 6,070 (D) 6,060 (E) 6,065

2. The sum of 387, 58, and 101 =

   (A) 1,061 (B) 546 (C) 536 (D) 446 (E) 542

3. The difference between 1,001 and 997 is:

   (A) 104 (B) 14 (C) 41 (D) 40 (E) 4

4. 716 is greater than 409 by:

   (A) 207 (B) 406 (C) 703 (D) 227 (E) none of these

5. The product of 6 and 268 is:

   (A) 1,608 (B) 1,628 (C) 1,604 (D) 1,508 E) 274

6. The result of multiplying 17 by 98 is:

   (A) 1,766 (B) 1,666 (C) 1,667 (D) 1,278 (E) 1,756

7. When 405 is multiplied by 24 the result is:

   (A) 972 (B) 2,430 (C) 9,720 (D) 9,070 (E) 9,620

8. When 1,748 is divided by 7 the dividend is:

   (A) 1,874 (B) 1,478 (C) 1,778 (D) 1,758 (E) 1,748

9. When 9,747 is divided by 48 the remainder is:

   (A) 1 (B) 20 (C) 5 (D) 52 (E) none of these

10. If 62,220 is divided by 204 the result is:

    (A) 325 (B) 305 (C) 345 (D) 35 (E) none of these

PRACTICE TEST 2

DIRECTIONS: Circle the letter that corresponds to the correct answer.

1. 687 + 313 =

   (A) 1,100 (B) 1,010 (C) 990 (D) 1,000 (E) none of these

2. The sum of 706, 33, and 111 =

   (A) 850 (B) 1,147 (C) 1,120 (D) 950 (E) none of these

3. 605 – 97 =

   (A) 58 (B) 518 (C) 608 (D) 508 (E) none of these

4. If 3,079 is subtracted from 5,903 the result is:

   (A) 2,834 (B) 1,824 (C) 1,823 (D) 2,924 (E) 2,824

5. The product of 8 and 325 =

   (A) 2,610 (B) 2,605 (C) 1,600 (D) 2,400 (E) 2,600

6. When 315 is multiplied by 50 the result is:

   (A) 1,575 (B) 15,750 (C) 10,575 (D) 57,510 (E) 3,069

7. The product of 89 and 47 is:

   (A) 4,283 (B) 3,183 (C) 2,183 (D) 4,083 (E) none of these

8. If 1,116 is divided by 9 the result is:

   (A) 104 (B) 124 (C) 140 (D) 114 (E) 122

9. When 3,480 is divided by 57 the remainder is:

   (A) 6 (B) 60 (C) 3 (D) 7 (E) 5

10. If 91,020 is divided by 370 the result is:

    (A) 2,460 (B) 246 (C) 264 (D) 240 (E) none of these

PRACTICE TEST 3

DIRECTIONS: Circle the letter that corresponds to the correct answer.

1. 1,783 + 517 =

   (A) 2,310 (B) 1,390 (C) 2,300 (D) 2,290 (E) 2,320

2. The sum of 682, 98, and 350 =

   (A) 1,230 (B) 1,130 (C) 1,030 (D) 930 (E) 1,040

3. 512 – 309 =

   (A) 213 (B) 113 (C) 103 (D) 203 (E) none of these

4. When 1,758 is subtracted from 2,063 the result is:

   (A) 1,305 (B) 315 (C) 1,215 (D) 1,315 (E) 305

5. The product of 6 and 150 =

   (A) 90 (B) 650 (C) 903 (D) 300 (E) none of these

6. When 246 is multiplied by 65 the product is:

   (A) 15,090 (B) 1,599 (C) 15,990 (D) 16,090 (E) 15,980

7. The product of 99 and 81 is:

   (A) 8,019 (B) 7,119 (C) 7,019 (D) 7,919 (E) none of these

8. If 6,040 is divided by 8 the result is:

   (A) 750 (B) 705 (C) 755 (D) 745 (E) 850

9. When 28,849 is divided by 69 the remainder is:

   (A) 9 (B) 19 (C) 5 (D) 17 (E) none of these

10. When 156,510 is divided by 235 the result is:

    (A) 650 (B) 616 (C) 665 (D) 666 (E) 606

Fractions

MEANING OF FRACTIONS

The box below is divided into 5 equal parts.

Using a fraction, we say that $\frac{2}{5}$ of the box is shaded. In the fraction $\frac{2}{5}$, 2 is the *numerator* and 5 is the *denominator*. The denominator, 5, indicates that the box has been divided into 5 equal parts. The numerator, 2, indicates that 2 of these parts have been shaded.

A **proper fraction** is a fraction in which the numerator is less than the denominator. Examples of proper fractions are $\frac{7}{8}$ and $\frac{4}{9}$.

An **improper fraction** is a fraction in which the numerator is equal to, or greater than, the denominator. Examples of improper fractions are $\frac{5}{5}$ and $\frac{7}{3}$.

A **mixed number** is a number such as $4\frac{2}{3}$ or $2\frac{5}{6}$ representing.the sum of a whole number and a fraction. The number $4\frac{2}{3}$ means $4 + \frac{2}{3}$.

EXERCISE 13

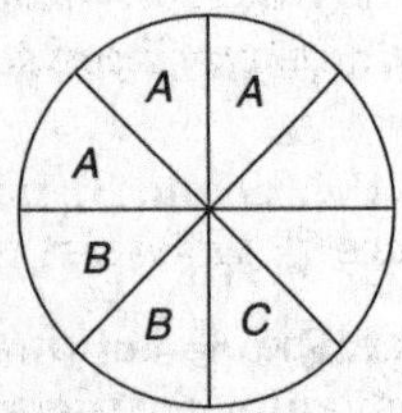

1. (a) Into how many parts is the circle divided?
   (b) What fractional part of the circle is marked with *A*?
   (c) What fractional part of the circle is marked with *B*? Write this fraction in two ways.
   (d) What fractional part of the circle is marked with *C*?

		X	X
X	X		B

2. (a) Into how many parts is the box divided?
   (b) What fractional part of the box is marked with *B*?
   (c) What fractional part of the box is shaded? Write this fraction in two ways.
   (d) What fractional part of the box is marked with *X*? Write this fraction in two ways.

3. (a) Mark with *C* the parts that would add up to $\frac{1}{2}$ of the box.
   (b) Mark with *D* the parts that would make up $\frac{1}{6}$ of the box.
   (c) Write, as a fraction, the part of the box that is left unmarked.

4. A major league team has a squad of 24 men consisting of 10 pitchers, 6 infielders, 5 outfielders, and 3 catchers. Express, as fractions, the part of the squad represented by: (a) pitchers (b) infielders (c) outfielders (d) catchers

5. The Stamp Club at the Benton Junior High School has 36 members. In electing a president of the club, all 36 members cast votes. The final total showed the following:

   John Andrews—20 votes
   Philip Verone—12 votes
   Louis Sellers —4 votes

   Express as fractions the part of the total vote obtained by each boy.

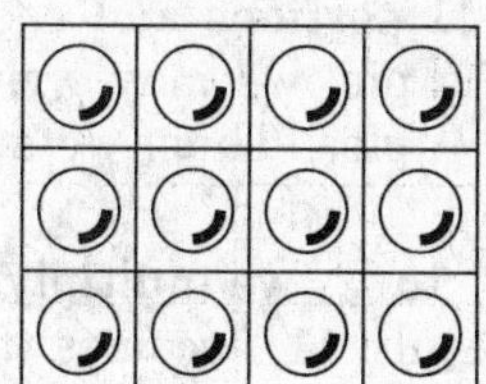
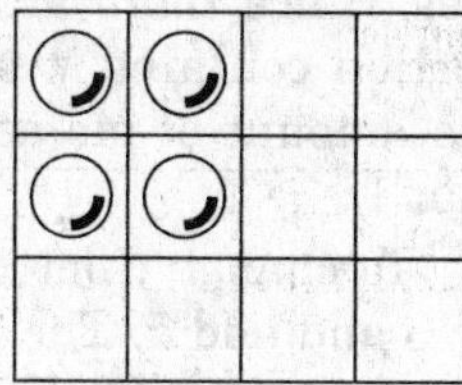

6. Use a mixed number to indicate the number of dozens of golf balls in these boxes.

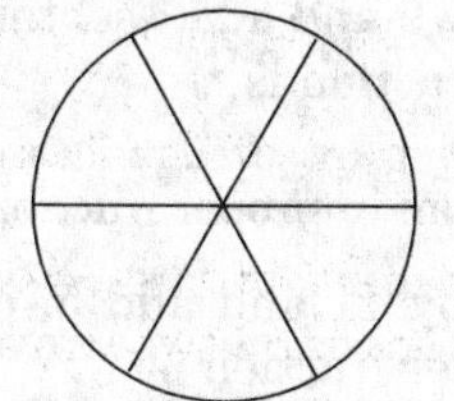
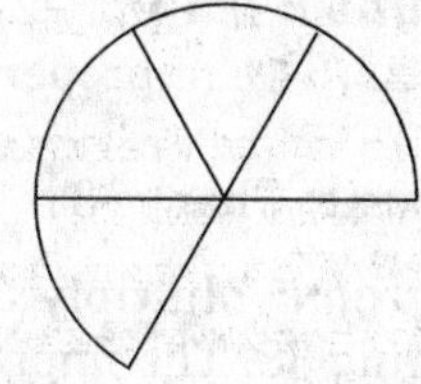

7. Use a mixed number to indicate the number of pies shown above.

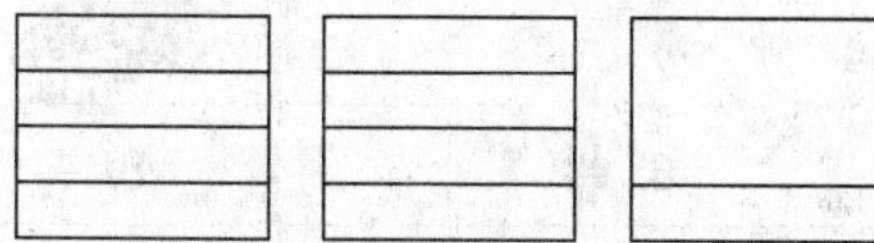

8. Use a mixed number to indicate the number of cups of milk.

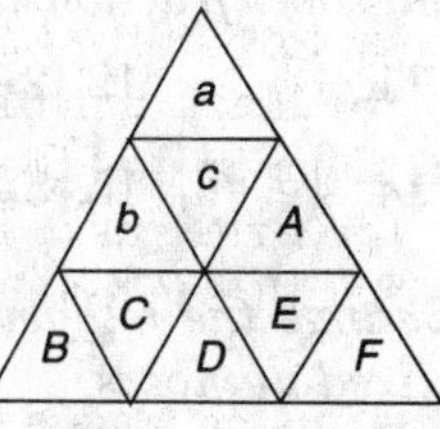

9. (a) Into how many parts is the triangle divided?
(b) Express, in two ways, the fractional part of the triangle marked by lower case letters of the alphabet.
(c) Express, in two ways, the fractional part of the triangle marked by upper case letters of the alphabet.
(d) Express, as a fraction, the part of the triangle marked by the letters *B C D E F*.

CHANGING THE FORM OF A FRACTION

Reducing Fractions to Lowest Terms

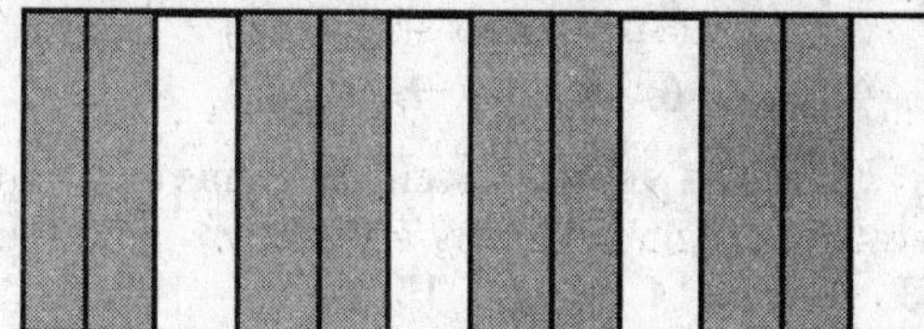

The fact that 8 of the 12 boxes in this diagram are shaded can be represented by the fraction $\frac{8}{12}$.

Also, you can see that two out of every 3 boxes, or $\frac{2}{3}$ of the boxes are shaded. In other words, $\frac{8}{12} = \frac{2}{3}$. This process of writing a fraction with a smaller denominator equivalent to another fraction is called reducing a fraction to lower terms. When the new fraction has the smallest possible denominator, we say that the fraction is *reduced to its lowest terms.* Note that the change from $\frac{8}{12}$ to $\frac{2}{3}$ is performed by dividing both the numerator and denominator of the fraction $\frac{8}{12}$ by 4. This change is based upon the following principle:

THE FUNDAMENTAL PRINCIPLE OF FRACTIONS

The numerator and denominator of a fraction may be multiplied or divided by the same number without changing the value of the fraction.

If n and b are not zero, $\frac{a}{b} = \frac{a \times n}{b \times n}$

If n and b are not zero, $\frac{a}{b} = \frac{a \div n}{b \div n}$

Fractions generated by using this principle are called *equivalent fractions*. That is $\frac{12}{20}$ and $\frac{3}{5}$ are equivalent because $\frac{12}{20} = \frac{12 \div 4}{20 \div 4} = \frac{3}{5}$. If the numerator and denominator cannot be divided by any number other than 1, the fraction is said to be *reduced to lowest terms* or *simplified*.

EXAMPLE: Reduce $\frac{15}{25}$ to lowest terms.

SOLUTION: To reduce $\frac{15}{25}$ to lowest terms, we divide both numerator and denominator by 5.

$$\frac{15}{25} = \frac{15 \div 5}{25 \div 5} = \frac{3}{5}$$

EXAMPLE: Reduce $\frac{36}{48}$ to lowest terms.

SOLUTION: We note that 36 and 48 may both be divided by 2, 3, 4, 6, and 12. Since we wish to reduce $\frac{36}{48}$ to lowest terms, we must divide both the numerator and denominator by the largest number that is contained in them evenly. In this case, the largest number is 12.

$$\frac{36}{48} = \frac{36 \div 12}{48 \div 12} = \frac{3}{4}$$

This reduction can also be done in stages:

$$\frac{48}{72} = \frac{6}{9} = \frac{2}{3}$$

Changing from Improper Fractions to Mixed Numbers

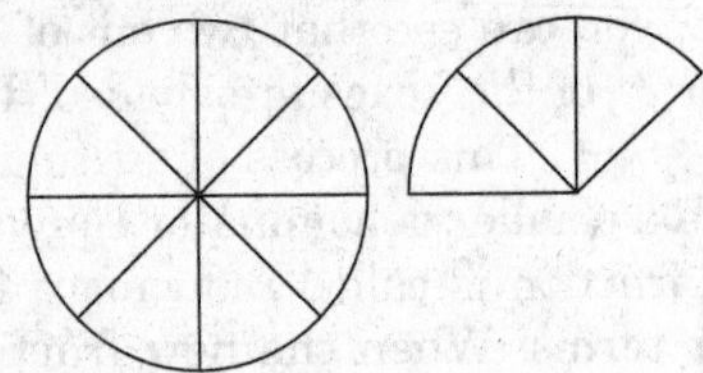

In the diagram, the whole pie is divided into 8 equal portions. The other piece of pie contains 3 additional portions. There is a total of 11 portions or $\frac{11}{8}$ pies. This may also be written as 1 whole pie and $\frac{3}{8}$ of another pie. The amount of pie may thus be written as $\frac{11}{8}$ or $1\frac{3}{8}$, or the improper fraction $\frac{11}{8}$ equals the mixed number $1\frac{3}{8}$. In general, an improper fraction may be changed to a whole or mixed number by dividing the numerator of the improper fraction by its denominator. The quotient is the whole number part of the mixed number and the remainder is the numerator of the fraction part.

Example: Change $\frac{19}{7}$ to a mixed number.

Solution: To change $\frac{19}{7}$ to a mixed number we divide 19 by 7, obtaining the result $2\frac{5}{7}$.

Example: Change $\frac{40}{12}$ to a mixed number.

Solution: To change $\frac{40}{12}$ to a mixed number, we divide 40 by 12, obtaining the result $3\frac{4}{12}$. If we reduce $\frac{4}{12}$ to $\frac{1}{3}$, the result, $3\frac{4}{12}$, may be written in simplest terms as $3\frac{1}{3}$.

The improper fraction $\frac{40}{12}$ may be simplified first by dividing the numerator and denominator by 4, obtaining $\frac{10}{3}$. Now, if we divide 10 by 3 we obtain the result $3\frac{1}{3}$.

Changing from Mixed Numbers to Improper Fractions

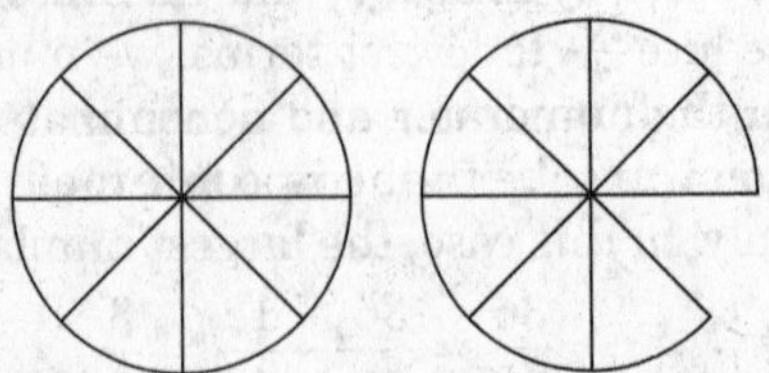

In the diagram, we have 1 whole pie and $\frac{5}{6}$ of another pie. This may be written as $1\frac{5}{6}$ pies. Since there are 11 portions and each portion contains $\frac{1}{6}$ of a pie, we may write the amount of pie as $\frac{11}{6}$ pies. Thus, we see that $1\frac{5}{6} = \frac{11}{6}$.

To change from $1\frac{5}{6}$ to $\frac{11}{6}$, we multiply 1 by 6 and add 5. The result, 11, becomes the numerator of the improper fraction $\frac{11}{6}$.

Example: Change $2\frac{4}{9}$ to an improper fraction.

Solution: Multiply 2 by 9 and add 4, obtaining 22. The improper fraction is $\frac{22}{9}$.

Example: Change $3\frac{5}{11}$ to an improper fraction.

Solution: Multiply 3 by 11 and add 5, obtaining 38. The improper fraction is $\frac{38}{11}$.

EXERCISE 14

Reduce the following fractions to lowest terms.

1. $\frac{3}{9}$ 2. $\frac{4}{10}$ 3. $\frac{6}{16}$ 4. $\frac{9}{12}$
5. $\frac{12}{20}$ 6. $\frac{16}{18}$ 7. $\frac{24}{32}$ 8. $\frac{8}{14}$
9. $\frac{21}{28}$ 10. $\frac{35}{45}$

Change the following mixed numbers to improper fractions.

11. $1\frac{1}{3}$ 12. $2\frac{3}{8}$ 13. $3\frac{6}{7}$
14. $4\frac{3}{5}$ 15. $5\frac{4}{9}$ 16. $7\frac{3}{4}$

Change the following improper fractions to mixed numbers.

17. $\frac{5}{4}$ 18. $\frac{7}{3}$ 19. $\frac{17}{6}$
20. $\frac{28}{12}$ 21. $\frac{31}{9}$ 22. $\frac{42}{16}$

If you got 20 or more correct, go on to the next section on Addition of Fractions and Mixed Numbers. If you got more than three wrong, use Exercise 15 to build your skill.

EXERCISE 15

Reduce the following fractions to lowest terms.

1. $\frac{2}{4}$ 2. $\frac{8}{10}$ 3. $\frac{6}{9}$ 4. $\frac{8}{12}$
5. $\frac{3}{6}$ 6. $\frac{10}{14}$ 7. $\frac{15}{20}$ 8. $\frac{20}{24}$
9. $\frac{18}{30}$ 10. $\frac{14}{16}$ 11. $\frac{22}{32}$ 12. $\frac{16}{40}$
13. $\frac{32}{36}$ 14. $\frac{16}{28}$ 15. $\frac{12}{18}$ 16. $\frac{14}{22}$
17. $\frac{12}{27}$ 18. $\frac{18}{20}$ 19. $\frac{15}{21}$ 20. $\frac{25}{35}$

Change the following mixed numbers to improper fractions.

1. $1\frac{3}{4}$ 2. $2\frac{5}{6}$ 3. $3\frac{2}{7}$ 4. $2\frac{4}{5}$

5. $4\frac{2}{9}$ 6. $1\frac{1}{7}$ 7. $2\frac{5}{8}$ 8. $6\frac{1}{3}$

9. $7\frac{5}{6}$ 10. $3\frac{7}{8}$ 11. $4\frac{3}{11}$ 12. $5\frac{7}{12}$

13. $2\frac{7}{9}$ 14. $1\frac{1}{2}$ 15. $6\frac{3}{7}$

Now be sure of your skill. Try Exercise 16.

EXERCISE 16

Reduce the following fractions to lowest terms.

1. $\frac{4}{8}$ 2. $\frac{2}{6}$ 3. $\frac{10}{12}$ 4. $\frac{14}{16}$

5. $\frac{16}{20}$ 6. $\frac{10}{18}$ 7. $\frac{6}{14}$ 8. $\frac{15}{24}$

9. $\frac{28}{32}$ 10. $\frac{25}{35}$

Change the following mixed numbers to improper fractions.

11. $1\frac{1}{4}$ 12. $2\frac{5}{6}$ 13. $3\frac{7}{8}$

14. $2\frac{5}{9}$ 15. $1\frac{5}{6}$ 16. $2\frac{5}{7}$

Change the following improper fractions to mixed numbers.

17. $\frac{19}{6}$ 18. $\frac{9}{4}$ 19. $\frac{11}{9}$

20. $\frac{32}{12}$ 21. $\frac{22}{3}$ 22. $\frac{50}{24}$

ADDITION OF FRACTIONS AND MIXED NUMBERS

In learning to add fractions we make use of the general principle that only like quantities may be combined. For example,

3 eggs + 4 eggs = 7 eggs
5 books + 6 books = 11 books
one-fifth + three-fifths = four-fifths

or

$$\frac{1}{5} + \frac{3}{5} = \frac{4}{5}$$

Thus, we can see that fractions that have the same denominator may be added directly by simply adding the numerators and placing this sum of the numerators over the common denominator.

EXAMPLES: $\frac{4}{9} + \frac{3}{9} = \frac{7}{9}$

$$\frac{2}{7} + \frac{1}{7} = \frac{3}{7}$$

We may not add two fractions with unlike denominators by the same method since we would then be adding two unlike quantities. For example, we may not add the fractions $\frac{1}{2}$ and $\frac{1}{4}$ directly. Before this addition is performed, we must change each of these fractions to an equivalent fraction with the same denominator, as follows:

$$\frac{1}{2} = \frac{2}{4}$$
$$\frac{1}{4} = \frac{1}{4}$$
$$\text{Sum} = \frac{3}{4}$$

The smallest denominator that can be used as a common denominator for combining two or more fractions is called the *least common denominator* (LCD, for short). It is the smallest number that is exactly divisible by the denominators of the given fractions.

To add fractions with unlike denominators, use the Fundamental Principle of Fractions to find their LCD and to change each of the fractions to an equivalent fraction having the LCD as denominator. Then, add the fractions by adding the numerators and writing the sum over the common denominator.

A simple method for finding the LCD is explained in the following examples. You will often be able to find the LCD by inspection.

EXAMPLE: Find the LCD for adding the fractions $\frac{5}{6}$ and $\frac{3}{8}$.

SOLUTION: First, we write the set of multiples of the denominator of the first fraction.

{6, 12, 18, 24, 30, 36, . . .}

Then we write the set of multiples of the denominator of the second fraction.

{8, 16, 24, . . .}

The first multiple that appears in both sets of multiples is the LCD. In this case, the LCD is 24.

EXAMPLE: Find the LCD for adding the fractions $\frac{5}{9}$, $\frac{7}{12}$, and $\frac{3}{4}$.

SOLUTION:
The set of multiples of 9 is:

{9, 18, 27, 36, 45, 54, . . .}

The set of multiples of 12 is:

{12, 24, 36, 48, 60, . . .}

The set of multiples of 4 is:

{4, 8, 12, 16, 20, 24, 28, 32, 36, . . .}

The first multiple that appears in all three sets of multiples is the LCD. In this case, the LCD is 36.

EXAMPLE: $\frac{3}{5} = \frac{6}{10}$.

SOLUTION: We multiply the numerator and denominator of the fraction $\frac{3}{5}$ by 2, obtaining the result $\frac{6}{10}$.

EXAMPLE: $\frac{5}{8} = \frac{?}{16}$.

SOLUTION: In this example, we must write $\frac{5}{8}$ as an equivalent fraction with denominator 16. We must therefore multiply the numerator and denominator of $\frac{5}{8}$ by 2, obtaining

$$\frac{5 \times 2}{8 \times 2} = \frac{10}{16}$$

EXERCISE 17

Change the following fractions to equivalent fractions having the indicated denominators.

1. $\frac{1}{2} = \frac{?}{6}$ 2. $\frac{1}{3} = \frac{?}{12}$ 3. $\frac{3}{4} = \frac{?}{8}$
4. $\frac{2}{5} = \frac{?}{15}$ 5. $\frac{7}{8} = \frac{?}{24}$ 6. $\frac{1}{4} = \frac{?}{16}$
7. $\frac{5}{12} = \frac{?}{36}$ 8. $\frac{3}{5} = \frac{?}{20}$ 9. $\frac{2}{7} = \frac{?}{28}$
10. $\frac{5}{6} = \frac{?}{12}$ 11. $\frac{2}{3} = \frac{?}{24}$ 12. $\frac{5}{9} = \frac{?}{18}$
13. $\frac{7}{9} = \frac{?}{27}$ 14. $\frac{1}{5} = \frac{?}{40}$ 15. $\frac{1}{3} = \frac{?}{15}$
16. $\frac{5}{7} = \frac{?}{21}$ 17. $\frac{7}{12} = \frac{?}{48}$ 18. $\frac{2}{3} = \frac{?}{9}$
19. $\frac{3}{7} = \frac{?}{42}$ 20. $\frac{4}{5} = \frac{?}{30}$

EXAMPLE: Add the fractions $\frac{1}{4}$ and $\frac{3}{8}$.

SOLUTION: The LCD is 8. Therefore, we must write each fraction with denominator 8.

$$\frac{1}{4} = \frac{2}{8}$$
$$\frac{3}{8} = \frac{3}{8}$$
$$\text{Sum} = \frac{5}{8}$$

EXAMPLE: Add $\frac{1}{6}$ and $\frac{4}{9}$.

SOLUTION: The LCD is 18. Therefore, we must write each fraction with denominator 18.

$$\frac{1}{6} = \frac{3}{18}$$
$$\frac{4}{9} = \frac{8}{18}$$
$$\text{Sum} = \frac{11}{18}$$

EXAMPLE: Add $\frac{7}{8}$ and $\frac{11}{12}$.

SOLUTION: The LCD is 24. Therefore, we must write each fraction with denominator 24.

$$\frac{7}{8} = \frac{21}{24}$$
$$\frac{11}{12} = \frac{22}{24}$$
$$\text{Sum} = \frac{43}{24} = 1\frac{19}{24}$$

EXAMPLE: Add $2\frac{5}{12}$ and $3\frac{8}{9}$.

SOLUTION: The LCD is 36. Therefore, we must write each fraction with denominator 36.

$$2\frac{5}{12} = 2\frac{15}{36}$$
$$3\frac{8}{9} = 3\frac{32}{36}$$
$$\text{Sum} = 5\frac{47}{36} = 5 + 1 + \frac{11}{36} = 6\frac{11}{36}$$

EXAMPLE: Add $3\frac{2}{3}$, $2\frac{2}{5}$,and $4\frac{5}{6}$.

SOLUTION: The LCD is 30. Therefore, we must write each fraction with denominator 30.

$$3\frac{2}{3} = 3\frac{20}{30}$$
$$2\frac{2}{5} = 2\frac{12}{30}$$
$$4\frac{5}{6} = 4\frac{25}{30}$$
$$\text{Sum} = 9\frac{57}{30} = 10\frac{27}{30} = 10\frac{9}{10}$$

EXERCISE 18

Add the following fractions and mixed numbers.

1. $\frac{1}{2} + \frac{1}{4}$ 2. $\frac{1}{3} + \frac{1}{2}$ 3. $\frac{1}{3} + \frac{1}{4}$ 4. $\frac{2}{3} + \frac{1}{6}$
5. $\frac{2}{5} + \frac{1}{10}$ 6. $\frac{1}{6} + \frac{3}{4}$ 7. $\frac{3}{5} + \frac{2}{3}$ 8. $\frac{3}{4} + \frac{5}{6}$
9. $\frac{3}{8} + \frac{5}{12}$ 10. $1\frac{1}{3} + \frac{1}{6}$ 11. $2\frac{4}{5} + 3\frac{8}{15}$ 12. $4\frac{7}{10} + 5\frac{5}{6}$

13. $2\frac{3}{4} + 3\frac{2}{7}$ 14. $\frac{1}{2} + \frac{1}{3} + \frac{1}{4}$ 15. $\frac{2}{5} + \frac{5}{6} + 3\frac{1}{3}$ 16. $1\frac{1}{2} + 2\frac{5}{8} + 3\frac{5}{16}$

17. $2\frac{3}{8} + 3\frac{2}{3} + 6\frac{5}{12}$ 18. $6\frac{7}{10} + \frac{3}{4} + 5\frac{3}{20}$

If you got 16 or more correct, go on to the next section on Subtraction of Fractions and Mixed Numbers. If you got more than three wriong, use Exercise 19 to build your skill.

EXERCISE 19

Add the following fractions and mixed numbers.

1. $\frac{1}{2} + \frac{1}{6}$ 2. $\frac{1}{4} + \frac{1}{3}$ 3. $\frac{3}{4} + \frac{1}{6}$ 4. $\frac{3}{8} + \frac{1}{4}$

5. $\frac{5}{6} + \frac{1}{8}$ 6. $\frac{4}{9} + \frac{1}{3}$ 7. $\frac{3}{8} + \frac{1}{6}$ 8. $\frac{1}{12} + \frac{2}{3}$

9. $\frac{5}{12} + \frac{2}{9}$ 10. $\frac{1}{6} + \frac{2}{15}$ 11. $\frac{7}{8} + \frac{1}{12}$ 12. $\frac{5}{9} + \frac{1}{6}$

13. $\frac{2}{3} + \frac{7}{12}$ 14. $\frac{2}{9} + \frac{3}{4}$ 15. $\frac{3}{7} + \frac{1}{2}$ 16. $\frac{1}{4} + \frac{1}{10}$

17. $\frac{7}{8} + \frac{5}{6}$ 18. $\frac{3}{10} + \frac{5}{6}$ 19. $\frac{8}{15} + \frac{7}{10}$ 20. $\frac{3}{8} + \frac{11}{12}$

21. $2\frac{1}{3} + \frac{8}{9}$ 22. $3\frac{1}{5} + 6\frac{1}{2}$ 23. $4\frac{1}{2} + 3\frac{1}{6}$ 24. $5\frac{1}{3} + 2\frac{1}{2}$

25. $2\frac{5}{12} + 1\frac{1}{9}$ 26. $4\frac{2}{3} + 3\frac{1}{6}$ 27. $7\frac{3}{8} + 2\frac{5}{6}$ 28. $4\frac{3}{5} + 3\frac{3}{4}$

29. $6\frac{3}{10} + \frac{1}{2}$ 30. $5\frac{3}{7} + 2\frac{1}{2}$ 31. $3\frac{4}{5} + 4\frac{1}{3}$ 32. $4\frac{7}{9} + \frac{5}{12}$

33. $\frac{1}{2} + \frac{1}{4} + \frac{1}{8}$ 34. $\frac{1}{3} + \frac{1}{6} + \frac{4}{9}$ 35. $\frac{5}{6} + \frac{7}{12} + \frac{1}{2}$ 36. $\frac{3}{8} + \frac{11}{12} + \frac{1}{4}$

37. $\frac{2}{3} + \frac{7}{9} + \frac{1}{12}$ 38. $1\frac{1}{2} + 2\frac{1}{4} + 2\frac{1}{3}$ 39. $3\frac{1}{5} + 6\frac{3}{10} + 4\frac{7}{15}$ 40. $2\frac{1}{6} + 3\frac{2}{3} + 6\frac{5}{9}$

41. $3\frac{7}{10} + 2\frac{5}{6} + 9\frac{1}{4}$ 42. $3\frac{5}{8} + 2\frac{11}{12} + 8\frac{5}{16}$

Now be sure of your skill. Try Exercise 20.

EXERCISE 20

Add the following fractions and mixed numbers.

1. $\frac{1}{2} + \frac{1}{3}$ 2. $\frac{1}{2} + \frac{1}{8}$ 3. $\frac{2}{3} + \frac{1}{4}$ 4. $\frac{5}{8} + \frac{1}{4}$

5. $\frac{3}{5} + \frac{3}{10}$ 6. $\frac{1}{9} + \frac{5}{6}$ 7. $\frac{3}{4} + \frac{2}{3}$ 8. $\frac{5}{6} + \frac{1}{2}$

9. $\frac{7}{9} + \frac{5}{12}$ 10. $1\frac{1}{5} + \frac{7}{10}$ 11. $2\frac{2}{3} + 2\frac{11}{12}$ 12. $3\frac{1}{4} + 4\frac{6}{7}$

13. $2\frac{3}{10} + 7\frac{5}{6}$ 14. $\frac{1}{4} + \frac{1}{6} + \frac{1}{3}$ 15. $\frac{2}{3} + \frac{5}{8} + \frac{7}{12}$ 16. $3\frac{1}{3} + 2\frac{3}{4} + 1\frac{5}{6}$

17. $2\frac{7}{9} + 3\frac{1}{6} + 4\frac{2}{3}$ 18. $3\frac{1}{5} + 2\frac{3}{4} + 5\frac{9}{10}$

SUBTRACTION OF FRACTIONS AND MIXED NUMBERS

In subtracting fractions we again make use of the general principle that only like quantities may be combined. For example, when we subtract $\frac{1}{9}$ from $\frac{8}{9}$ we obtain the result $\frac{7}{9}$. If we have unlike quantities, we proceed as in the following example.

EXAMPLE: Subtract $\frac{1}{6}$ from $\frac{5}{9}$.

SOLUTION: We note that the LCD of these two fractions is 18.

$$\frac{5}{9} = \frac{10}{18}$$
$$\frac{1}{6} = \frac{3}{18}$$
$$\text{Difference} = \frac{7}{18}$$

In subtracting one fraction or mixed number from another mixed number it is sometimes necessary to borrow, as is shown in the following examples.

EXAMPLE: From $5\frac{1}{8}$ subtract $\frac{3}{8}$.

SOLUTION: We cannot subtract $\frac{3}{8}$ from $\frac{1}{8}$. Therefore, it is necessary to borrow 1 from 5. Since $1 = \frac{8}{8}$ we may write $5\frac{1}{8}$ as $4 + \frac{8}{8} + \frac{1}{8}$ or $4\frac{9}{8}$. Now, we may subtract $\frac{3}{8}$ from $4\frac{9}{8}$, obtaining the result $4\frac{6}{8}$, or $4\frac{3}{4}$. The work may be arranged as follows.

$$\begin{array}{rl} 5\frac{1}{8} = 4 + 1 + \frac{1}{8} = & 4\frac{9}{8} \\ \frac{3}{8} \qquad\qquad \frac{3}{8} & \frac{3}{8} \\ \hline \text{Difference} = 4\frac{6}{8} = & 4\frac{3}{4} \end{array}$$

EXAMPLE: Subtract $2\frac{7}{9}$ from $6\frac{5}{12}$.

SOLUTION: The LCD of the two fractions is 36.

$$\begin{array}{rl} 6\frac{5}{12} = 6\frac{15}{36} = 5 + 1 + \frac{15}{36} = & 5\frac{51}{36} \\ 2\frac{7}{9} = 2\frac{28}{36} = \qquad 2\frac{28}{36} = & 2\frac{28}{36} \\ \hline \text{Difference} = & 3\frac{23}{36} \end{array}$$

EXERCISE 21

Subtract the following fractions and mixed numbers.

1. $\frac{4}{5} - \frac{1}{5}$ 2. $\frac{5}{8} - \frac{1}{8}$ 3. $\frac{3}{4} - \frac{1}{3}$ 4. $\frac{5}{6} - \frac{2}{9}$

5. $\frac{7}{8} - \frac{5}{6}$ 6. $\frac{5}{8} - \frac{5}{12}$ 7. $4 - \frac{1}{6}$ 8. $3\frac{1}{2} - 1\frac{1}{4}$

9. $5\frac{5}{6} - 2\frac{3}{8}$ 10. $7\frac{9}{10} - 3\frac{1}{4}$ 11. $6\frac{1}{4} - \frac{1}{2}$ 12. $8 - 2\frac{3}{5}$

13. $7\frac{1}{3} - 6\frac{3}{4}$ 14. $8\frac{1}{2} - 3\frac{2}{3}$ 15. $5\frac{2}{9} - 4\frac{7}{12}$ 16. $9\frac{5}{16} - 3\frac{3}{4}$

If you got 15 or 16 of these problems correct, go on to the next section on Comparison of Fractions. If you got more than two wrong, use Exercise 22 to build your skill.

EXERCISE 22

Subtract the following fractions and mixed numbers.

1. $\frac{2}{3} - \frac{1}{3}$ 2. $\frac{7}{9} - \frac{2}{9}$ 3. $\frac{5}{6} - \frac{1}{6}$ 4. $\frac{1}{2} - \frac{1}{4}$

5. $\frac{2}{3} - \frac{1}{6}$ 6. $\frac{3}{4} - \frac{1}{8}$ 7. $\frac{5}{12} - \frac{1}{3}$ 8. $\frac{7}{10} - \frac{2}{5}$

9. $\frac{1}{2} - \frac{1}{3}$ 10. $\frac{3}{4} - \frac{1}{6}$ 11. $\frac{2}{3} - \frac{2}{9}$ 12. $\frac{4}{5} - \frac{2}{3}$

13. $\frac{6}{7} - \frac{1}{2}$ 14. $\frac{8}{9} - \frac{5}{12}$ 15. $7 - \frac{1}{3}$ 16. $4\frac{3}{5} - 2\frac{1}{5}$

17. $9\frac{7}{8} - 3\frac{1}{8}$ 18. $6\frac{7}{9} - 2\frac{1}{9}$ 19. $8\frac{3}{4} - 2\frac{9}{10}$ 20. $6\frac{1}{3} - 4\frac{3}{4}$

21. $8 - \frac{4}{7}$ 22. $5\frac{1}{8} - 4\frac{1}{2}$ 23. $7\frac{1}{3} - 6\frac{1}{2}$ 24. $5\frac{1}{10} - 4\frac{3}{4}$

25. $6\frac{5}{9} - 2\frac{5}{6}$ 26. $6\frac{5}{8} - 5\frac{1}{6}$ 27. $4\frac{1}{9} - 3\frac{5}{12}$ 28. $3\frac{1}{3} - 2\frac{4}{7}$

29. $8\frac{1}{4} - 6\frac{2}{3}$ 30. $5\frac{4}{9} - 3\frac{1}{2}$ 31. $3\frac{5}{16} - 2\frac{3}{4}$ 32. $7\frac{2}{3} - 5\frac{11}{15}$

33. $6\frac{3}{8} - 2\frac{2}{3}$ 34. $1\frac{1}{6} - \frac{7}{8}$ 35. $7\frac{1}{7} - 2\frac{1}{2}$

Now be sure of your skill. Try Exercise 23.

EXERCISE 23

Subtract the following fractions and mixed numbers.

1. $\frac{5}{7} - \frac{1}{7}$ 2. $\frac{9}{10} - \frac{3}{10}$ 3. $\frac{1}{2} - \frac{1}{3}$ 4. $\frac{7}{8} - \frac{1}{4}$

5. $\frac{5}{6} - \frac{1}{3}$ 6. $\frac{1}{3} - \frac{1}{4}$ 7. $\frac{7}{8} - \frac{5}{12}$ 8. $5 - \frac{1}{8}$

9. $\begin{array}{r} 4\frac{1}{2} \\ -2\frac{1}{8} \\ \hline \end{array}$ 10. $\begin{array}{r} 6\frac{2}{3} \\ -2\frac{1}{6} \\ \hline \end{array}$ 11. $\begin{array}{r} 7\frac{4}{5} \\ -2\frac{1}{4} \\ \hline \end{array}$ 12. $\begin{array}{r} 7\frac{1}{8} \\ -6\frac{1}{4} \\ \hline \end{array}$

13. $\begin{array}{r} 9 \\ -3\frac{2}{3} \\ \hline \end{array}$ 14. $\begin{array}{r} 3\frac{1}{2} \\ -1\frac{4}{7} \\ \hline \end{array}$ 15. $\begin{array}{r} 7\frac{1}{12} \\ -6\frac{7}{9} \\ \hline \end{array}$ 16. $\begin{array}{r} 8\frac{1}{6} \\ -3\frac{3}{4} \\ \hline \end{array}$

COMPARISON OF FRACTIONS

Equivalent Fractions

Consider these fractions.

$$\frac{8}{14} \text{ and } \frac{36}{63}$$

Suppose we wish to determine whether these fractions name the same rational number. We could, of course, reduce each fraction to lowest terms and then compare. However, there is a simpler method.

PRINCIPLE OF EQUIVALENCE OF FRACTIONS

If we have two fractions $\frac{a}{b}$ and $\frac{c}{d}$, then $\frac{a}{b} = \frac{c}{d}$ if, and only if, a × d = b × c.

EXAMPLE: $\frac{2}{3} = \frac{12}{18}$ because 2 × 18 = 3 × 12.

But $\frac{7}{8} \neq \frac{5}{6}$ because 7 × 6 ≠ 8 × 5.

EXERCISE 24

By using the Principle of Equivalence of Fractions, determine which of the following pairs of fractions name the same rational number and which do not name the same rational number.

1. $\frac{3}{5}$ and $\frac{21}{35}$
2. $\frac{6}{8}$ and $\frac{51}{68}$
3. $\frac{7}{9}$ and $\frac{21}{35}$
4. $\frac{29}{37}$ and $\frac{10}{12}$
5. $\frac{22}{26}$ and $\frac{44}{52}$
6. $\frac{21}{49}$ and $\frac{24}{55}$
7. $\frac{25}{45}$ and $\frac{45}{81}$
8. $\frac{24}{39}$ and $\frac{56}{89}$
9. $\frac{63}{98}$ and $\frac{81}{126}$
10. $\frac{68}{84}$ and $\frac{153}{189}$
11. $\frac{27}{66}$ and $\frac{63}{154}$
12. $\frac{35}{84}$ and $\frac{45}{110}$
13. $\frac{63}{81}$ and $\frac{91}{127}$
14. $\frac{49}{105}$ and $\frac{77}{165}$
15. $\frac{43}{79}$ and $\frac{54}{132}$

Ordering the Fractions

Here is a rule to determine which of two fractions is greater. (The symbol ">" means "is greater than.")

PRINCIPLE OF COMPARISON OF FRACTIONS

If we have two fractions $\frac{a}{b}$ and $\frac{c}{d}$, then $\frac{a}{b} > \frac{c}{d}$ if, and only if, $a \times d > b \times c$.

EXAMPLES:

1. $\frac{3}{4} > \frac{5}{8}$ because 3 × 8 > 4 × 5
2. $\frac{7}{9} > \frac{1}{3}$ because 7 × 3 > 9 × 1
3. $\frac{4}{5} > \frac{2}{9}$ because 4 × 9 > 5 × 2

EXERCISE 25

Use the Principle of Comparison of Fractions to determine which fraction is greater.

1. $\frac{1}{3}$ and $\frac{5}{17}$
2. $\frac{2}{5}$ and $\frac{4}{9}$
3. $\frac{3}{7}$ and $\frac{6}{11}$
4. $\frac{8}{15}$ and $\frac{9}{16}$
5. $\frac{9}{11}$ and $\frac{5}{6}$
6. $\frac{5}{13}$ and $\frac{3}{11}$
7. $\frac{9}{14}$ and $\frac{12}{19}$
8. $\frac{6}{7}$ and $\frac{8}{9}$
9. $\frac{12}{23}$ and $\frac{8}{17}$
10. $\frac{16}{25}$ and $\frac{21}{46}$
11. $\frac{7}{18}$ and $\frac{8}{21}$
12. $\frac{9}{31}$ and $\frac{6}{23}$
13. $\frac{16}{27}$ and $\frac{9}{14}$
14. $\frac{15}{37}$ and $\frac{13}{29}$
15. $\frac{14}{19}$ and $\frac{27}{37}$

In each case, use the Principle of Comparison of Fractions to arrange each of the following sets of fractions in order from least to greatest. For example, $\frac{1}{3} < \frac{1}{2} < \frac{3}{4}$ (the symbol "<" means "is less than").

16. $\frac{2}{5}, \frac{3}{8}, \frac{3}{4}$
17. $\frac{5}{8}, \frac{3}{5}, \frac{11}{20}$
18. $\frac{7}{12}, \frac{5}{9}, \frac{5}{6}$
19. $\frac{17}{24}, \frac{2}{3}, \frac{5}{8}$
20. $\frac{3}{8}, \frac{2}{9}, \frac{4}{11}$
21. $\frac{6}{7}, \frac{7}{9}, \frac{5}{8}$
22. $\frac{8}{11}, \frac{12}{17}, \frac{13}{16}$
23. $\frac{11}{21}, \frac{10}{19}, \frac{20}{41}$
24. $\frac{8}{18}, \frac{6}{17}, \frac{11}{31}$
25. $\frac{7}{23}, \frac{8}{27}, \frac{9}{32}$

Reciprocal Fractions

Before discussing the methods for multiplying and dividing fractions, we will define *reciprocal* fractions. Two numbers are reciprocals of each other if their product is 1. For example, $\frac{2}{5}$ and $\frac{5}{2}$, 7 and $\frac{1}{7}$, and $\frac{8}{3}$ and $\frac{3}{8}$ are pairs of reciprocals. It is clear that every number except 0 has a reciprocal.

If b and d are not zero, $\frac{a}{b} \times \frac{c}{d} = \frac{a \times c}{b \times d}$.

MULTIPLICATION OF FRACTIONS AND MIXED NUMBERS

In multiplying two or more fractions, we multiply the numerators of the fractions to obtain the new numerator, and multiply the denominators of the fractions to obtain the new denominator.

EXAMPLE: Multiply $\frac{2}{5}$ by $\frac{4}{9}$.

SOLUTION: $\frac{2}{5} \times \frac{4}{9} = \frac{2 \times 4}{5 \times 9} = \frac{8}{45}$

Many times the answer must be reduced to lowest terms. This can be done by *cancellation*. Before the multiplication is actually done, divide any numerator and denominator by a common factor. Then multiply what remains. The following examples illustrate cancellation.

EXAMPLE: Multiply $\frac{3}{8}$ by $\frac{4}{9}$.

SOLUTION: Before multiplying the numerators and denominators we may divide the numerator 3 and the denominator 9 by 3. We may also divide the numerator 4 and the denominator 8 by 4. This work may be shown as follows.

$$\frac{\overset{1}{\cancel{3}}}{\underset{2}{\cancel{8}}} \times \frac{\overset{1}{\cancel{4}}}{\underset{3}{\cancel{9}}} = \frac{1 \times 1}{2 \times 3} = \frac{1}{6}$$

EXAMPLE: Multiply $\frac{8}{27}$ by $\frac{15}{16}$.

SOLUTION: $\frac{\overset{1}{\cancel{8}}}{\underset{9}{\cancel{27}}} \times \frac{\overset{5}{\cancel{15}}}{\underset{2}{\cancel{16}}} = \frac{5}{18}$

In multiplying a whole number by a fraction we may regard the whole number as a fraction whose denominator is 1. Then we proceed as we did in multiplying two fractions.

EXAMPLE: Multiply 48 by $\frac{7}{8}$.

SOLUTION: $\frac{\overset{6}{\cancel{48}}}{1} \times \frac{7}{\underset{1}{\cancel{8}}} \times \frac{42}{1} = 42$

EXAMPLE: Multiply 72 by $\frac{5}{28}$.

SOLUTION: $\frac{\overset{18}{\cancel{72}}}{1} \times \frac{5}{\underset{7}{\cancel{28}}} = \frac{5 \times 18}{7} = \frac{90}{7}$ *or* $12\frac{6}{7}$

To multiply (or divide) fractions, all whole numbers or mixed numbers must first be changed to improper fractions.

EXAMPLE: Multiply $3\frac{1}{8}$ by $\frac{4}{5}$.

SOLUTION: $3\frac{1}{8} \times \frac{4}{5}$

Changing $3\frac{1}{8}$ to $\frac{25}{8}$ we have:

$$\frac{\overset{5}{\cancel{25}}}{\underset{2}{\cancel{8}}} \times \frac{\overset{1}{\cancel{4}}}{\underset{1}{\cancel{5}}} = \frac{5}{2} \text{ or } 2\frac{1}{2}$$

EXAMPLE: Multiply $2\frac{2}{3}$ by $2\frac{5}{8}$.

SOLUTION: $2\frac{2}{3} \times 2\frac{5}{8}$

Changing the mixed numbers to improper fractions, we have:

$$\frac{\overset{1}{\cancel{8}}}{\underset{1}{\cancel{3}}} \times \frac{\overset{7}{\cancel{21}}}{\underset{1}{\cancel{8}}} = 7$$

EXAMPLE: Multiply $5\frac{1}{3}$ by $2\frac{7}{10}$.

SOLUTION: $5\frac{1}{3} \times 2\frac{7}{10}$

$$\frac{\overset{8}{\cancel{16}}}{\underset{1}{\cancel{3}}} \times \frac{\overset{9}{\cancel{27}}}{\underset{5}{\cancel{10}}} = \frac{72}{5} \text{ or } 14\frac{2}{5}$$

EXAMPLE: Multiply $\frac{3}{10} \times \frac{8}{9} \times \frac{5}{16}$.

SOLUTION: $\frac{\overset{1}{\cancel{3}}}{\underset{2}{\cancel{10}}} \times \frac{\overset{1}{\cancel{8}}}{\underset{3}{\cancel{9}}} \times \frac{\overset{1}{\cancel{5}}}{\underset{2}{\cancel{16}}} = \frac{1}{12}$

EXAMPLE: Multiply $\frac{6}{7} \times 2\frac{4}{5} \times 1\frac{1}{3}$.

SOLUTION: $\frac{6}{7} \times 2\frac{4}{5} \times 1\frac{1}{3}$

$$\frac{\overset{2}{\cancel{6}}}{\underset{1}{\cancel{7}}} \times \frac{\overset{2}{\cancel{14}}}{5} \times \frac{4}{\underset{1}{\cancel{3}}} = \frac{16}{5} = 3\frac{1}{5}$$

EXERCISE 26

Multiply.

1. $\frac{1}{4} \times \frac{3}{5}$
2. $\frac{1}{2} \times \frac{5}{9}$
3. $\frac{3}{8} \times \frac{2}{7}$
4. $\frac{2}{3} \times \frac{9}{16}$
5. $\frac{3}{4} \times \frac{8}{15}$
6. $\frac{9}{10} \times \frac{2}{3}$
7. $\frac{4}{21} \times \frac{7}{8}$
8. $\frac{5}{8} \times \frac{16}{45}$
9. $10 \times \frac{1}{5}$
10. $16 \times \frac{3}{4}$
11. $12 \times \frac{7}{9}$
12. $60 \times \frac{11}{15}$
13. $\frac{3}{8} \times 2$
14. $\frac{5}{12} \times 16$
15. $18 \times \frac{4}{9}$
16. $5 \times \frac{2}{3}$
17. $24 \times 2\frac{5}{8}$
18. $6 \times 7\frac{1}{2}$
19. $3\frac{1}{7} \times \frac{7}{8}$
20. $6\frac{2}{3} \times \frac{5}{8}$
21. $6\frac{1}{4} \times 1\frac{3}{5}$
22. $3\frac{3}{4} \times 3\frac{1}{3}$
23. $1\frac{5}{7} \times 2\frac{5}{8}$
24. $2\frac{2}{3} \times 1\frac{5}{16}$
25. $\frac{2}{3} \times \frac{5}{8} \times \frac{6}{7}$
26. $\frac{5}{6} \times \frac{3}{4} \times \frac{8}{9}$
27. $4\frac{1}{2} \times 3\frac{1}{9} \times 1\frac{1}{3}$

If you got 24 or more correct, go on to the next section on Division of Fractions and Mixed Numbers. If you got more than 3 wrong, use Exercise 27 to build your skill.

EXERCISE 27

Multiply.

1. $\frac{2}{3} \times \frac{1}{7}$
2. $\frac{1}{2} \times \frac{3}{5}$
3. $\frac{3}{4} \times \frac{7}{10}$
4. $\frac{1}{5} \times \frac{3}{4}$
5. $\frac{3}{4} \times \frac{5}{6}$
6. $\frac{4}{5} \times \frac{1}{2}$
7. $\frac{3}{8} \times \frac{4}{7}$
8. $\frac{5}{6} \times \frac{9}{10}$
9. $\frac{3}{4} \times \frac{8}{15}$
10. $\frac{7}{9} \times \frac{3}{14}$
11. $\frac{5}{12} \times \frac{3}{10}$
12. $\frac{3}{8} \times \frac{5}{6}$
13. $\frac{3}{7} \times \frac{14}{15}$
14. $\frac{1}{8} \times \frac{4}{9}$
15. $\frac{9}{20} \times \frac{10}{27}$
16. $\frac{3}{4} \times \frac{6}{7}$
17. $20 \times \frac{2}{5}$
18. $18 \times \frac{4}{9}$
19. $\frac{1}{3} \times 24$
20. $\frac{3}{4} \times 16$
21. $18 \times \frac{1}{4}$
22. $24 \times \frac{3}{8}$
23. $28 \times \frac{5}{6}$
24. $\frac{7}{10} \times 45$
25. $\frac{7}{24} \times 60$
26. $\frac{5}{12} \times 40$
27. $\frac{6}{7} \times 4$
28. $5 \times \frac{5}{6}$
29. $4\frac{1}{2} \times \frac{6}{7}$
30. $\frac{5}{6} \times 3\frac{3}{5}$
31. $\frac{1}{2} \times 3\frac{1}{3}$
32. $\frac{5}{12} \times 2\frac{1}{10}$
33. $25 \times 1\frac{1}{5}$
34. $2\frac{1}{4} \times 18$
35. $5\frac{1}{3} \times 6$
36. $24 \times 2\frac{5}{8}$
37. $3 \times 7\frac{1}{2}$
38. $12 \times 5\frac{1}{4}$
39. $3\frac{1}{7} \times 4$
40. $9 \times 2\frac{5}{6}$
41. $2\frac{1}{4} \times 1\frac{1}{3}$
42. $3\frac{1}{5} \times 2\frac{5}{8}$
43. $5\frac{5}{6} \times 7\frac{1}{5}$
44. $2\frac{3}{16} \times 1\frac{3}{5}$
45. $4\frac{5}{7} \times 1\frac{3}{11}$
46. $\frac{2}{9} \times \frac{3}{5} \times \frac{1}{4}$
47. $8\frac{4}{5} \times 11\frac{1}{4}$
48. $6\frac{3}{7} \times 4\frac{2}{3}$
49. $3\frac{1}{5} \times 5\frac{1}{6}$
50. $\frac{5}{6} \times \frac{3}{7} \times \frac{2}{9}$
51. $2\frac{4}{5} \times 3\frac{1}{7} \times \frac{3}{11}$
52. $6\frac{2}{3} \times 1\frac{3}{5} \times 4\frac{1}{2}$
53. $1\frac{4}{5} \times 2\frac{1}{2} \times 3\frac{1}{3}$
54. $2\frac{2}{3} \times 1\frac{1}{4} \times 3\frac{1}{5}$

Now be sure of your skill. Try Exercise 28.

EXERCISE 28

Multiply.

1. $\frac{1}{5} \times \frac{2}{3}$
2. $\frac{5}{7} \times \frac{1}{3}$
3. $\frac{3}{4} \times \frac{2}{5}$
4. $\frac{5}{8} \times \frac{4}{15}$
5. $\frac{5}{9} \times \frac{3}{10}$
6. $\frac{7}{16} \times \frac{4}{9}$
7. $\frac{1}{2} \times \frac{6}{11}$
8. $\frac{3}{10} \times \frac{5}{9}$
9. $15 \times \frac{1}{3}$
10. $18 \times \frac{5}{6}$
11. $20 \times \frac{3}{8}$
12. $30 \times \frac{5}{12}$
13. $\frac{5}{6} \times 12$
14. $\frac{7}{8} \times 24$
15. $28 \times \frac{5}{7}$
16. $8 \times \frac{2}{3}$
17. $36 \times 1\frac{3}{4}$
18. $8 \times 3\frac{1}{2}$
19. $\frac{3}{8} \times 2\frac{1}{3}$
20. $4\frac{2}{5} \times \frac{10}{11}$
21. $3\frac{1}{8} \times 1\frac{1}{3}$
22. $1\frac{1}{7} \times 5\frac{1}{4}$
23. $4\frac{1}{6} \times 3\frac{5}{8}$
24. $3\frac{1}{9} \times 2\frac{1}{16}$
25. $\frac{2}{3} \times \frac{4}{5} \times \frac{9}{10}$
26. $\frac{4}{9} \times \frac{3}{7} \times \frac{5}{8}$
27. $2\frac{2}{5} \times 3\frac{1}{3} \times \frac{3}{4}$
28. $4\frac{1}{5} \times 1\frac{1}{3} \times 3\frac{4}{7}$

DIVISION OF FRACTIONS AND MIXED NUMBERS

In dividing one fraction by another we invert the divisor and multiply.

EXAMPLE: Divide $\frac{5}{8}$ by $\frac{1}{3}$.

SOLUTION: $\frac{5}{8} \div \frac{1}{3}$

$$\frac{5}{8} \times \frac{3}{1} = \frac{15}{8} \text{ or } 1\frac{7}{8}$$

EXAMPLE: Divide $\frac{8}{9}$ by $\frac{2}{3}$.

SOLUTION: $\frac{8}{9} \div \frac{2}{3}$

$$\frac{\overset{4}{\cancel{8}}}{\underset{3}{\cancel{9}}} \times \frac{\overset{1}{\cancel{3}}}{\underset{1}{\cancel{2}}} = \frac{4}{3} \text{ or } 1\frac{1}{3}$$

In dividing a fraction, mixed number, or whole number by a mixed number we change mixed numbers and whole numbers into improper fractions and divide.

EXAMPLE: Divide $1\frac{1}{8}$ by $\frac{3}{16}$.

SOLUTION: $1\frac{1}{8} \div \frac{3}{16}$

$$\frac{9}{8} \div \frac{3}{16}$$

$$\frac{\overset{3}{\cancel{9}}}{\underset{1}{\cancel{8}}} \times \frac{\overset{2}{\cancel{16}}}{\underset{1}{\cancel{3}}} = 6$$

EXAMPLE: Divide 8 by $3\frac{1}{3}$.

SOLUTION: $8 \div 3\frac{1}{3}$

$$8 \div \frac{10}{3}$$

$$8 \times \frac{3}{10}$$

$$\frac{\overset{4}{\cancel{8}}}{1} \times \frac{3}{\underset{5}{\cancel{10}}} = \frac{12}{5} \text{ or } 2\frac{2}{5}$$

EXAMPLE: Divide $2\frac{2}{5}$ by $8\frac{7}{10}$.

SOLUTION: $2\frac{2}{5} \div 8\frac{7}{10}$

$$\frac{12}{5} \div \frac{87}{10}$$

$$\frac{\overset{4}{\cancel{12}}}{\underset{1}{\cancel{5}}} \times \frac{\overset{2}{\cancel{10}}}{\underset{29}{\cancel{87}}} = \frac{8}{29}$$

EXAMPLE: Divide $3\frac{8}{9}$ by $2\frac{1}{12}$.

SOLUTION: $3\frac{8}{9} \div 2\frac{1}{12}$

$$\frac{35}{9} \div \frac{25}{12}$$

$$\frac{\overset{7}{\cancel{35}}}{\underset{3}{\cancel{9}}} \times \frac{\overset{4}{\cancel{12}}}{\underset{5}{\cancel{25}}} = \frac{28}{15} \text{ or } 1\frac{13}{15}$$

EXERCISE 29

Divide

1. $\frac{1}{5} \div \frac{1}{3}$
2. $\frac{3}{4} \div \frac{7}{8}$
3. $\frac{1}{4} \div \frac{2}{3}$
4. $\frac{11}{12} \div \frac{5}{6}$
5. $\frac{9}{10} \div \frac{3}{5}$
6. $\frac{2}{7} \div 3$
7. $6 \div \frac{1}{2}$
8. $8 \div \frac{4}{9}$
9. $12 \div \frac{2}{5}$
10. $\frac{3}{8} \div 9$
11. $\frac{1}{2} \div 2\frac{1}{4}$
12. $\frac{3}{10} \div 2\frac{2}{5}$
13. $4\frac{1}{6} \div \frac{2}{3}$
14. $1\frac{2}{3} \div \frac{5}{6}$
15. $12 \div 6\frac{2}{3}$
16. $25 \div 3\frac{3}{4}$
17. $3\frac{1}{2} \div 2\frac{1}{3}$
18. $9\frac{1}{3} \div 1\frac{1}{6}$
19. $5\frac{3}{5} \div 2\frac{1}{10}$
20. $6\frac{3}{4} \div 2\frac{1}{2}$

If you got 19 or 20 correct, go on to the next section on Complex Fractions. If you got more than two wrong, use Exercise 30 to build your skill.

EXERCISE 30

Divide

1. $\frac{1}{2} \div \frac{1}{3}$
2. $\frac{2}{5} \div \frac{1}{2}$
3. $\frac{5}{8} \div \frac{3}{4}$
4. $\frac{2}{3} \div \frac{3}{8}$
5. $\frac{3}{7} \div \frac{9}{14}$
6. $\frac{5}{12} \div \frac{3}{10}$
7. $\frac{4}{9} \div \frac{1}{3}$
8. $\frac{2}{5} \div \frac{7}{15}$
9. $\frac{9}{10} \div \frac{3}{4}$
10. $\frac{7}{12} \div \frac{14}{15}$
11. $\frac{1}{2} \div 2\frac{1}{4}$
12. $\frac{3}{10} \div 2\frac{2}{5}$
13. $\frac{3}{4} \div 2$
14. $\frac{6}{7} \div 3$
15. $8 \div \frac{1}{3}$
16. $12 \div \frac{2}{5}$
17. $20 \div \frac{4}{7}$
18. $48 \div \frac{8}{9}$
19. $36 \div \frac{9}{11}$
20. $18 \div \frac{8}{9}$
21. $21 \div \frac{7}{8}$
22. $\frac{5}{12} \div 10$
23. $\frac{7}{9} \div 14$
24. $\frac{4}{15} \div 10$
25. $\frac{1}{3} \div 1\frac{1}{6}$
26. $\frac{7}{8} \div 2\frac{1}{3}$
27. $\frac{9}{10} \div 4\frac{1}{2}$
28. $\frac{7}{9} \div 5\frac{1}{4}$
29. $3\frac{1}{5} \div \frac{4}{5}$
30. $3\frac{1}{3} \div \frac{2}{9}$
31. $6\frac{2}{3} \div \frac{5}{6}$
32. $8\frac{2}{5} \div \frac{3}{10}$
33. $5\frac{1}{4} \div 2\frac{1}{2}$
34. $3\frac{3}{8} \div 4\frac{1}{2}$
35. $4\frac{1}{8} \div 3\frac{1}{7}$
36. $8\frac{1}{3} \div 1\frac{1}{9}$
37. $9\frac{3}{4} \div 1\frac{1}{2}$
38. $2\frac{11}{12} \div 4\frac{1}{6}$
39. $6\frac{1}{4} \div 5\frac{5}{8}$
40. $7\frac{1}{2} \div 4\frac{1}{6}$

Now be sure of your skill. Try Exercise 31.

EXERCISE 31

Divide

1. $\frac{1}{4} \div \frac{1}{3}$
2. $\frac{5}{6} \div \frac{2}{3}$
3. $\frac{3}{10} \div \frac{5}{9}$
4. $\frac{9}{16} \div \frac{3}{4}$
5. $\frac{3}{7} \div \frac{9}{14}$
6. $\frac{5}{7} \div 2$
7. $9 \div \frac{1}{3}$
8. $15 \div \frac{5}{9}$
9. $10 \div \frac{4}{7}$
10. $\frac{7}{8} \div 14$
11. $\frac{1}{3} \div 4\frac{1}{6}$
12. $\frac{7}{9} \div 4\frac{2}{3}$
13. $4\frac{1}{5} \div \frac{9}{10}$
14. $7\frac{1}{2} \div \frac{3}{4}$
15. $18 \div 4\frac{1}{2}$
16. $30 \div 5\frac{1}{4}$
17. $2\frac{1}{2} \div 1\frac{2}{3}$
18. $8\frac{1}{3} \div 2\frac{1}{2}$
19. $2\frac{5}{8} \div 1\frac{3}{4}$
20. $11\frac{1}{4} \div 3\frac{3}{5}$

COMPLEX FRACTIONS

Sometimes we are required to simplify fractions.

EXAMPLE: Simplify $\dfrac{\frac{1}{2} + \frac{1}{3}}{\frac{3}{4}}$

SOLUTION: First, we find the LCD of all the fractions within the numerator and the denominator. In this case, the LCD is 12.

Second, we multiply both the numerator and the denominator of the complex fraction by 12. This does not change the value of the fraction.

$$\frac{12\left(\frac{1}{2} + \frac{1}{3}\right)}{12\left(\frac{3}{4}\right)} = \frac{6 + 4}{9} = \frac{10}{9} \text{ or } 1\frac{1}{9}$$

EXERCISE 32

Simplify the following complex fractions.

1. $\dfrac{\frac{5}{6} + \frac{2}{3}}{\frac{1}{4}}$
2. $\dfrac{\frac{5}{9} - \frac{1}{12}}{\frac{5}{6}}$
3. $\dfrac{\frac{4}{5} - \frac{3}{10}}{\frac{7}{15}}$
4. $\dfrac{\frac{5}{6} - \frac{3}{8}}{\frac{7}{12}}$

Review Test-Taking Tips on page vii.

PRACTICE TEST 4

1. The fraction $\frac{36}{54}$ reduced to lowest terms is equal to:

   (A) $\frac{3}{7}$ (B) $\frac{6}{9}$ (C) $\frac{5}{8}$ (D) $\frac{2}{3}$ (E) $\frac{16}{27}$

2. The fraction $\frac{20}{30}$ reduced to lowest terms is equal to:

   (A) $\frac{3}{7}$ (B) $\frac{4}{5}$ (C) $\frac{4}{7}$ (D) $\frac{2}{3}$ (E) $\frac{7}{4}$

3. $\frac{1}{3} + \frac{1}{4} =$

   (A) $\frac{1}{6}$ (B) $\frac{7}{12}$ (C) $\frac{2}{7}$ (D) $\frac{7}{4}$ (E) $\frac{7}{6}$

4. $\frac{5}{6} + \frac{5}{9} =$

   (A) $\frac{2}{3}$ (B) $\frac{5}{54}$ (C) $\frac{25}{54}$ (D) $1\frac{2}{9}$
   (E) none of these

5. $2\frac{6}{7} + \frac{2}{3} =$

   (A) $3\frac{1}{11}$ (B) $2\frac{8}{21}$ (C) $3\frac{11}{21}$ (D) $2\frac{3}{4}$ (E) $2\frac{4}{7}$

6. $\frac{5}{8} + \frac{3}{4} + \frac{5}{6} =$

   (A) $\frac{13}{18}$ (B) $\frac{25}{64}$ (C) $2\frac{5}{12}$ (D) $2\frac{5}{24}$ (E) $\frac{17}{18}$

7. $1\frac{1}{4} + 3\frac{4}{5} + 2\frac{7}{10} =$

   (A) $7\frac{1}{10}$ (B) $7\frac{3}{4}$ (C) $6\frac{3}{5}$ (D) $8\frac{1}{5}$ (E) $6\frac{1}{2}$

8. $\frac{7}{8} - \frac{5}{6} =$

   (A) $\frac{1}{7}$ (B) 1 (C) $\frac{1}{12}$ (D) $\frac{3}{8}$ (E) $\frac{1}{24}$

9. $2\frac{1}{6} - \frac{2}{3} =$

   (A) $\frac{1}{3}$ (B) $1\frac{1}{2}$ (C) $2\frac{1}{9}$ (D) $2\frac{5}{18}$
   (E) none of these

10. $3\frac{3}{8} - 1\frac{7}{12} =$

    (A) $2\frac{1}{12}$ (B) $1\frac{9}{24}$ (C) $1\frac{1}{3}$ (D) $1\frac{19}{24}$ (E) $1\frac{1}{4}$

11. $\frac{9}{10} \times \frac{8}{15} =$

    (A) $\frac{17}{15}$ (B) $\frac{12}{25}$ (C) $1\frac{7}{10}$ (D) $1\frac{2}{15}$ (E) $1\frac{11}{16}$

12. $1\frac{5}{16} \times 4\frac{2}{3} =$

    (A) $4\frac{5}{24}$ (B) $4\frac{1}{8}$ (C) $6\frac{3}{4}$ (D) $6\frac{5}{16}$ (E) $6\frac{1}{8}$

13. $4\frac{1}{2} \times \frac{7}{9} \times \frac{3}{14} =$

    (A) $1\frac{1}{2}$ (B) $\frac{3}{4}$ (C) $4\frac{1}{6}$ (D) $5\frac{1}{7}$
    (E) none of these

14. $2\frac{1}{2} \times 3\frac{3}{4} \times 5\frac{1}{3} =$

    (A) $30\frac{1}{2}$ (B) 25 (C) $30\frac{1}{8}$ (D) 50
    (E) none of these

15. $\frac{2}{3} \div \frac{5}{12} =$

    (A) $\frac{5}{8}$ (B) $\frac{5}{18}$ (C) $1\frac{3}{5}$ (D) $\frac{5}{9}$ (E) $\frac{7}{36}$

16. $6\frac{1}{4} \div 5\frac{5}{12} =$

(A) $1\frac{5}{12}$ (B) $1\frac{1}{5}$ (C) $1\frac{1}{14}$ (D) $\frac{4}{5}$

(E) none of these

PRACTICE TEST 5

1. The fraction $\frac{28}{32}$ reduced to lowest terms is equal to:

(A) $\frac{4}{7}$ (B) $\frac{14}{16}$ (C) $\frac{3}{4}$ (D) $\frac{7}{8}$ (E) $\frac{5}{8}$

2. The fraction $\frac{30}{45}$ reduced to lowest terms is equal to:

(A) $\frac{3}{5}$ (B) $\frac{2}{3}$ (C) $\frac{5}{7}$ (D) $\frac{4}{5}$ (E) $\frac{3}{4}$

3. $\frac{1}{3} + \frac{1}{5} =$

(A) $\frac{8}{15}$ (B) $\frac{1}{4}$ (C) $\frac{2}{8}$ (D) $\frac{4}{5}$ (E) $\frac{2}{3}$

4. $\frac{7}{8} + \frac{5}{6} =$

(A) $\frac{6}{7}$ (B) $1\frac{12}{24}$ (C) $1\frac{19}{24}$ (D) $1\frac{17}{24}$ (E) $1\frac{1}{4}$

5. $2\frac{5}{7} + \frac{1}{2} =$

(A) $2\frac{3}{14}$ (B) $2\frac{2}{3}$ (C) $3\frac{5}{14}$ (D) $2\frac{5}{9}$

(E) none of these

6. $\frac{1}{4} + \frac{4}{5} + \frac{7}{10} =$

(A) $\frac{3}{5}$ (B) $1\frac{1}{2}$ (C) $\frac{11}{20}$ (D) $1\frac{3}{4}$ (E) $1\frac{3}{10}$

7. $1\frac{2}{3} + 2\frac{3}{4} + 1\frac{5}{6} =$

(A) $4\frac{5}{6}$ (B) $6\frac{1}{4}$ (C) $4\frac{1}{2}$ (D) $6\frac{1}{3}$

(E) none of these

8. $\frac{11}{12} - \frac{5}{8} =$

(A) $\frac{7}{24}$ (B) $\frac{6}{4}$ (C) $\frac{1}{2}$ (D) $\frac{5}{16}$ (E) $\frac{6}{10}$

9. $2\frac{5}{7} - \frac{2}{3} =$

(A) $1\frac{5}{21}$ (B) $2\frac{3}{4}$ (C) $2\frac{1}{21}$ (D) $2\frac{4}{21}$ (E) $2\frac{1}{7}$

10. $3\frac{1}{9} - 1\frac{5}{6} =$

(A) $1\frac{1}{3}$ (B) $1\frac{7}{18}$ (C) $2\frac{5}{18}$ (D) $2\frac{2}{3}$ (E) $1\frac{5}{18}$

11. $\frac{4}{15} \times \frac{9}{16} =$

(A) $\frac{3}{10}$ (B) $\frac{6}{10}$ (C) $\frac{3}{20}$ (D) $\frac{13}{60}$ (E) $\frac{7}{30}$

12. $3\frac{3}{4} \times 5\frac{1}{3} =$

(A) $15\frac{1}{4}$ (B) 16 (C) $15\frac{3}{4}$ (D) 15 (E) 20

13. $2\frac{2}{3} \times \frac{5}{9} \times 3\frac{3}{5} =$

(A) $6\frac{2}{3}$ (B) $5\frac{1}{3}$ (C) $6\frac{8}{15}$ (D) $4\frac{7}{9}$

(E) none of these

14. $2\frac{1}{4} \times 3\frac{1}{3} \times 1\frac{1}{5} =$

(A) 9 (B) $6\frac{1}{2}$ (C) $6\frac{7}{15}$ (D) $7\frac{2}{3}$ (E) $8\frac{1}{2}$

15. $\frac{3}{8} \div \frac{5}{16} =$

(A) $\frac{5}{6}$ (B) $1\frac{1}{3}$ (C) $\frac{3}{5}$ (D) $1\frac{1}{5}$ (E) $1\frac{3}{8}$

16. $10\frac{2}{3} \div 3\frac{1}{5} =$

(A) $3\frac{1}{15}$ (B) $3\frac{1}{3}$ (C) $2\frac{2}{15}$ (D) $2\frac{2}{3}$

(E) none of these

PRACTICE TEST 6

1. The fraction $\frac{24}{42}$ reduced to lowest terms is equal to:

(A) $\frac{6}{7}$ (B) $\frac{1}{2}$ (C) $\frac{4}{7}$ (D) $\frac{3}{7}$ (E) $1\frac{3}{7}$

2. The fraction $\frac{32}{48}$ reduced to lowest terms is equal to:

(A) $\frac{2}{3}$ (B) $\frac{3}{4}$ (C) $\frac{4}{6}$ (D) $\frac{6}{16}$ (E) $\frac{5}{6}$

3. $\frac{1}{2} + \frac{1}{3} =$

(A) $\frac{2}{5}$ (B) $\frac{2}{6}$ (C) $\frac{1}{6}$ (D) $\frac{4}{6}$

(E) none of these

4. $\frac{4}{5} + \frac{3}{4} =$

(A) $\frac{7}{20}$ (B) $\frac{7}{9}$ (C) $1\frac{11}{20}$ (D) $1\frac{7}{9}$ (E) $1\frac{17}{20}$

5. $1\frac{5}{6} + \frac{7}{8} =$

(A) $2\frac{5}{12}$ (B) $2\frac{17}{24}$ (C) $1\frac{23}{24}$ (D) $2\frac{3}{8}$

(E) none of these

6. $\frac{1}{2} + \frac{1}{6} + \frac{4}{9} =$

(A) $1\frac{5}{18}$ (B) $2\frac{1}{18}$ (C) $1\frac{4}{9}$ (D) $2\frac{1}{9}$ (E) $1\frac{1}{9}$

7. $2\frac{2}{3} + 3\frac{4}{5} + 1\frac{7}{10} =$

(A) $6\frac{1}{6}$ (B) $7\frac{17}{30}$ (C) $8\frac{1}{6}$ (D) $6\frac{5}{6}$

(E) none of these

8. $\frac{8}{9} - \frac{5}{6} =$
(A) $\frac{1}{18}$ (B) $\frac{2}{3}$ (C) $\frac{1}{9}$ (D) $\frac{1}{3}$ (E) $\frac{1}{12}$

9. $2\frac{3}{8} - \frac{1}{2} =$
(A) 2 (B) $1\frac{1}{2}$ (C) $1\frac{3}{4}$ (D) $\frac{1}{3}$
(E) none of these

10. $5\frac{4}{9} - 3\frac{11}{12} =$
(A) $2\frac{38}{72}$ (B) $1\frac{19}{36}$ (C) $2\frac{1}{3}$ (D) $1\frac{1}{3}$ (E) $1\frac{1}{2}$

11. $\frac{3}{8} \times \frac{2}{9} =$
(A) $\frac{1}{2}$ (B) $\frac{2}{3}$ (C) $\frac{3}{4}$ (D) $\frac{1}{6}$
(E) none of these

12. $2\frac{5}{8} \times 3\frac{1}{7} =$
(A) $8\frac{1}{4}$ (B) $6\frac{5}{56}$ (C) $7\frac{1}{2}$ (D) $4\frac{1}{8}$ (E) $6\frac{1}{7}$

13. $7\frac{1}{2} \times \frac{4}{5} \times \frac{2}{3} =$
(A) 8 (B) $2\frac{2}{3}$ (C) 4 (D) $8\frac{4}{15}$ (E) 6

14. $1\frac{5}{6} \times 3\frac{3}{4} \times 1\frac{7}{11} =$
(A) $4\frac{1}{4}$ (B) $10\frac{1}{4}$ (C) $5\frac{3}{8}$ (D) $22\frac{1}{2}$ (E) $11\frac{1}{4}$

15. $\frac{5}{9} \div \frac{2}{3} =$
(A) $\frac{10}{27}$ (B) $1\frac{1}{5}$ (C) $\frac{5}{18}$ (D) $\frac{5}{6}$
(E) none of these

16. $4\frac{1}{6} \div 1\frac{2}{3} =$
(A) $2\frac{1}{2}$ (B) $\frac{2}{5}$ (C) $12\frac{5}{18}$ (D) $2\frac{1}{5}$
(E) none of these

Decimal Fractions

DECIMALS

The place values to the right of the decimal point are:

0.__ __ __ __ __ __ __ __

TENTHS, HUNDREDTHS, THOUSANDTHS, TEN-THOUSANDTHS, HUNDRED-THOUSANDTHS, MILLIONTHS, TEN-MILLIONTHS, HUNDRED-MILLIONTHS

After the millionths period are billionths, trillonths, quadrillionths, and so on corresponding to the names of the periods of whole numbers. To read such a number, read the digits to the right of the decimal point as if they were a whole number and then name the place value of the right-most digit.

EXAMPLES:

Read 5.0258.
Read: "Five *and* two hundred fifty-eight *ten-thousandths*." The only place where *and* should be read in any number is where the decimal point is located.

Read: 27.120453. (The 3 sits in the millionths' position.)
Read: "Twenty-seven and one hundred twenty thousand four hundred fifty-three millionths."

When the whole number part of the decimal number is zero, the zero is used only for emphasis; it may be deleted. For example, 0.23 may be written merely as .23. Zeros to the right of the right-most nonzero digit may be deleted. Such decimal numbers are equivalent.

$$2.5700 = 2.57$$

COMPARING DECIMAL FRACTIONS

In comparing the sizes of decimal fractions we compare tenths first. If necessary we compare hundredths, thousandths, etc., until the larger value is determined.

EXAMPLE: Which is larger, 0.63 or 0.59?

SOLUTION: Since the first decimal contains 6 tenths and the second decimal contains 5 tenths, the first decimal is larger than the second decimal.

EXAMPLE: Which is larger, 0.137 or 0.45?

SOLUTION: Since the first decimal contains 1 tenth and the second decimal contains 4 tenths, the second decimal is larger than the first decimal.

EXAMPLE: Which is larger, 0.853 or 0.8512?

SOLUTION: The two decimals have the same number of tenths (8) and the same number of hundredths (5). However, the first decimal contains 3 thousandths and the second decimal contains 1 thousandth. Therefore, the first decimal is larger than the second decimal.

ROUNDING OFF DECIMAL FRACTIONS

In writing a decimal fraction to a given number of decimal places, examine the digit in the decimal place that is one place to the right of the decimal required. If this digit is 5 or more, increase the digit to the left by 1. If this digit is less than 5, the digit to the left is not changed. Drop all digits to the right of the required place.

The decimal fraction 0.26, rounded off correctly to the nearest tenth, is 0.3, because 0.26 is closer to 0.3 than it is to 0.2. The decimal fraction 0.762, rounded off correct to the nearest hundredth, is 0.76, because 0.762 is closer to 0.76 than it is to 0.77.

EXAMPLE: Round off 0.83 to the nearest tenth.

SOLUTION: Since 3 is less than 5, 8 is left unchanged and the 3 is dropped. The answer is 0.8.

EXAMPLE: Round off 0.42781 to the nearest hundredth.

SOLUTION: The digit to the right of the hundredths place is 7. Since 7 is more than 5, we increase the 2 to 3 and drop all other digits. The answer is 0.43.

EXERCISE 33

Round off the following decimals as indicated.

1. 0.46 (nearest tenth)
2. 0.307 (nearest hundredth)
3. 0.982 (nearest hundredth)
4. 0.3568 (nearest thousandth)

Arrange each of the following sets of decimal fractions in order of their size, with the largest decimal fraction first.

5. 0.653, 0.67, 0.619
6. 0.712, 0.721, 0.716
7. 0.237, 0.2, 0.218
8. 0.467, 0.4009, 0.4102

If you got 7 or 8 correct, go on to the next section on Addition of Decimals. If you got more than one wrong, use Exercise 34 to build your skill.

EXERCISE 34

Round off the following decimals as indicated.

1. To the nearest tenth
   (a) 0.32 (b) 0.691 (c) 0.052 (d) 0.93 (e) 0.487 (f) 0.709 (g) 0.85 (h) 0.4172 (i) 0.9128 (j) 0.63
2. To the nearest hundredth
   (a) 0.163 (b) 0.038 (c) 0.685 (d) 0.701 (e) 0.854
3. To the nearest thousandth
   (a) 0.6579 (b) 0.4032 (c) 0.8175 (d) 0.0952 (e) 0.5437

Arrange each of the following sets of decimal fractions in order of their size, with the largest decimal fraction first.

4. 0.309, 0.295, 0.416
5. 0.857, 0.875, 0.902
6. 0.7, 0.605, 0.713
7. 0.489, 0.492, 0.516
8. 0.3, 0.128, 0.41
9. 0.57, 0.712, 0.7
10. 0.914, 0.832, 0.823
11. 0.096, 0.088, 0.123

Now be sure of your skill. Try Exercise 35.

EXERCISE 35

Round off the following decimals as indicated.

1. 0.53 (nearest tenth)
2. 0.209 (nearest hundredth)
3. 0.768 (nearest hundredth)
4. 0.8513 (nearest thousandth)

Arrange each of the following sets of decimal fractions in order of their size, with the largest decimal fraction first.

5. 0.461, 0.47, 0.418
6. 0.385, 0.319, 0.391
7. 0.6, 0.602, 0.59
8. 0.7031, 0.7103, 0.7301

ADDITION OF DECIMALS

The addition of decimal fractions is a much simpler operation than the addition of ordinary fractions since the denominators are 10, 100, 1,000, etc. Arrange the decimals in a column so that the decimal points are aligned. Then add the decimals in the same manner as whole numbers. The decimal point in the answer is in line with the decimal points of the numbers that were added.

EXAMPLES: Add the following.

0.3	4.7	5.73
0.6	3.2	6.04
0.5	0.9	2.59
+ 0.4	+ 1.5	+ 3.60
1.8	10.3	17.96

0.918	28.47
2.403	3.62
0.759	809.03
+ 6.572	+ 37.94
10.652	879.06

EXAMPLE: Add the following:

16.237 + 48.051 + 9.003 + 67.215 + 3.790

SOLUTION: Arrange these numbers, keeping the decimal points in a line.

```
   16.237
   48.051
    9.003
   67.215
+   3.790
  144.296
```

SUBTRACTION OF DECIMALS

In subtracting decimals, we arrange them in a column, aligning the decimal points. Then we subtract as with whole numbers. The decimal point in the answer appears in the same column as in the numbers that were subtracted.

EXAMPLES: Subtract

0.9	0.63	3.5
− 0.5	− 0.49	− 0.7
0.4	0.14	2.8

48.07	720.72
− 7.68	− 69.58
40.39	651.14

EXAMPLE: Subtract 0.53 from 0.81.

SOLUTION:

```
  0.81
− 0.53
  0.28
```

EXAMPLE: From 4.821 subtract 1.367.

SOLUTION:

```
  4.821
− 1.367
  3.454
```

EXERCISE 36

Add the following.

1.	2.	3.	4.
0.42	6.01	28.3	128.304
0.39	5.29	7.8	7.927
+ 0.75	0.67	65.4	63.518
	+ 3.40	+ 0.2	+ 0.479

5. Add 38.42 + 1.65 + 3.29 + 80.07.
6. Add 5.01 + 7.92 + 63.78 + 40.80.

Subtract

7.	8.	9.	10.
0.83	5.07	34.561	290.103
− 0.49	− 3.48	− 7.483	− 83.561

11. From 2.67 subtract 1.08.
12. Subtract 56.314 from 89.057.

If you got 11 or 12 correct, go on to the next section on Multiplication of Decimals. If you got more than one wrong, use Exercise 37 to build your skill.

EXERCISE 37

Find each sum.

1.	2.	3.
0.53	0.85	6.38
0.29	0.30	5.02
0.48	0.17	0.49
0.65	0.69	3.15
+ 0.34	+ 0.92	+ 4.30

4. 9.12
6.73
5.28
0.09
+ 1.25

5. 39.2
41.3
6.8
59.6
+ 7.1

6. 50.32
67.19
8.57
32.08
+ 9.10

7. 32.95
68.17
91.24
2.39
+ 0.46

8. 159.01
36.57
216.28
8.09
+ 78.65

9. 459.83
60.19
203.05
75.16
+ 2.58

10. 2.069
47.135
68.926
4.007
+ 15.298

11. 25.712
6.059
31.207
9.895
+ 67.156

12. 3.050
2.716
85.018
16.009
+ 07.502

13. 786.14
95.07
139.18
26.49
+ 18.80

14. 230.04
17.98
169.07
598.82
+ 68.75

15. Add 8.1 + 3.7 + 6.5 + 7.9 + 2.4
16. Add 5.3 + 2.5 + 6.9 + 3.8 + 2.7
17. Add 9.52 + 8.76 + 4.37 + 5.09 + 1.06
18. Add 8.75 + 4.69 + 3.06 + 7.27 + 2.58
19. Add 67.34 + 75.08 + 59.17 + 63.92 + 71.47
20. Add 58.51 + 63.47 + 5.94 + 7.83 + 95.82

Subtract.

21. 0.48 − 0.15　22. 0.72 − 0.38　23. 0.51 − 0.29　24. 0.68 − 0.49

25. 4.52 − 1.37　26. 8.14 − 3.59　27. 7.08 − 3.16　28. 5.03 − 2.19

29. 79.91 − 43.67　30. 82.15 − 45.29　31. 63.168 − 15.712

32. 75.065 − 38.173　33. 50.012 − 18.564　34. 841.07 − 68.59

Now be sure of your skill. Try Exercise 38.

EXERCISE 38

Add.

1. 0.38
0.57
+ 0.62

2. 8.03
7.59
0.72
+ 4.56

3. 57.2
9.7
38.8
+ 00.6

4. 387.207
8.158
59.623
+ 0.385

5. Add 63.79 + 3.48 + 1.67 + 60.06.
6. Add 7.02 + 8.95 + 71.64 + 85.07.

Subtract.

7. 0.62 − 0.38　8. 6.03 − 1.59　9. 68.382 − 9.597　10. 560.208 − 79.472

11. From 3.84 subtract 2.07.
12. Subtract 37.516 from 95.028.

MULTIPLICATION OF DECIMALS

In multiplying decimals, follow the procedure used in multiplying whole numbers. It is not necessary to arrange the numbers so that the decimal points are in a line. The number of decimal places (the places to the right of the decimal point) in the answer is equal to the total of the decimal places in the two numbers that were multiplied.

EXAMPLE: Multiply 75 by 0.8.

SOLUTION:
75
× 0.8 ← 1 decimal place
60.0 ← 1 decimal place

EXAMPLE: Multiply 84 by 0.03.

SOLUTION:
84
× 0.03 ← 2 decimal places
2.52 ← 2 decimal places

EXAMPLE: Multiply 0.27 by 9.

SOLUTION:
0.27
× 9
2.43

EXAMPLE: Multiply 65 by 0.87.

SOLUTION:
65
× .87
455
520
56.55

EXAMPLE: Multiply 3.82 by 5.7.

SOLUTION:
3.82 ← 2 decimal places
× 05.7 ← 1 decimal place
2674
1910
21.774 ← 3 decimal places

EXAMPLE: Multiply 68.2 by 0.79.

SOLUTION:
68.2
× 0.79
6138
4774
53.878

EXERCISE 39

Multiply.

1. 8×0.6 2. 0.9×7 3. 37×0.4

4. 2.9×0.8 5. 67×0.03 6. 85×0.47

7. 49×2.6 8. 6.8×79 9. 1.6×4.7

10. 0.38×59 11. 518×0.63 12. 5.07×0.682

13. 5.37×0.914 14. 6.409×0.076 15. 0.0496×3.7

If you got 14 or 15 correct, go on to the next section on Division of Decimals. If you got more than one wrong, use Exercise 40 to build your skill.

EXERCISE 40

Multiply.

1. 8×0.6 2. 7×0.9 3. 0.5×7

4. 0.8×4 5. 9×0.3 6. 0.3×7

7. 24×0.04 8. 39×0.46 9. 67×0.34

10. 78×0.59 11. 81×0.67 12. 59×4.5

13. 73×6.8 14. 82×3.6 15. 43×9.7

16. 3.5×48 17. 6.7×69 18. 2.9×53

19. 5.1×3.2 20. 6.8×8.4 21. 0.19×63

22. 0.53×0.29 23. 0.77×0.48 24. 386×0.28

25. 503×0.92 26. 890×0.25 27. 463×0.78

28. 257×0.416 29. 409×0.324 30. 667×0.469

31. 8.07×0.624 32. 7.46×0.389 33. 8.167×0.534

34. 6.809×0.247 35. 7.020×0.309 36. 0.035×7.8

37. 2.035×3.9 38. 0.0659×4.7

Now be sure of your skill. Try Exercise 41.

EXERCISE 41

Multiply:

1. 8×0.7 2. 0.6×9 3. 58×0.6

4. 3.9×0.7 5. 797×0.04 6. 76×0.38

7. 43×7.9 8. 8.1×93 9. 5.6×3.7

10. 0.47×69 11. 384×0.76 12. 608×0.483

13. 7.29×0.827 14. 9.308×0.063 15. 0.0384×2.7

DIVISION OF DECIMALS

In dividing a decimal by a whole number, divide as in division of whole numbers, placing the decimal point of the result in line with the decimal point in the dividend.

EXAMPLE: Divide $9\overline{)74.835}$

SOLUTION: Perform the division, placing the decimal point in the result in line with the decimal point in the dividend between 4 and 8.

$$\begin{array}{r} 8.315 \\ 9\overline{)74.835} \end{array}$$

The result is 8.315.

To divide any number by a decimal, first move the decimal point in the divisor to the right as many places as is necessary to make it a whole number. Then move the decimal point in the dividend the same number of places to the right. Divide as in whole number division and place the decimal point in the quotient immediately above the decimal point in the dividend.

Example: Divide $0.028\overline{)3.1407}$, correct to the nearest tenth.

Solution: Make the divisor a whole number by moving the decimal point three places to the right. Also move the decimal point in the dividend three places to the right. The decimal point in the dividend is now between 0 and 7. Proceed with the division as with whole numbers, annexing a zero on the right in the dividend so that we may find the digit in the hundredths place. This will enable us to state the quotient correct to the nearest tenth.

```
          112.16
0.028)3.140.70
       28
        34
        28
         60
         56
          47
          28
          190
          168
```

The result is 112.2, correct to the nearest tenth.

Example: Divide $4.17\overline{)162.3180}$ finding the quotient correct to the nearest tenth.

Solution: We move the decimal point in both the divisor and the dividend two places to the right. Then we annex a zero on the right to find the digit in the hundredths place. This will enable us to state the quotient correct to the nearest tenth.

```
          38.92
4.17)162.31.80
     1251
      3721
      3336
       3858
       3753
        1050
         834
```

The result is 38.9, correct to the nearest tenth.

EXERCISE 42

Divide. When necessary, round as indicated.

1. $8\overline{)38.4}$
2. $7\overline{)45.63}$ (to nearest tenth)
3. $39\overline{)685.7}$ (to nearest tenth)
4. $56\overline{)2.057}$ (to nearest hundredth)
5. $0.7\overline{)58.36}$ (to nearest tenth)
6. $0.6\overline{)0.2349}$ (to nearest tenth)
7. $0.03\overline{)5.697}$
8. $0.009\overline{)3.17862}$
9. $8.7\overline{)3.0795}$ (to nearest hundredth)
10. $0.36\overline{)92.052}$
11. $0.59\overline{)7.0269}$
12. $0.048\overline{)0.76504}$ (to nearest hundredth)
13. $5.12\overline{)80.532}$ (to nearest hundredth)
14. $60.7\overline{)431.052}$ (to nearest tenth)
15. $0.168\overline{)0.05479}$ (to nearest hundredth)

If you got 14 or 15 correct, go on to the next sections on Multiplication and Division by 10, 100, 1000, etc. If you got more than one wrong, use Exercise 43 to build your skill.

EXERCISE 43

Divide. When necessary, round as indicated.

1. $9\overline{)32.67}$
2. $6\overline{)47.16}$
3. $8\overline{)68.48}$
4. $5\overline{)30.05}$
5. $7\overline{)53.78}$ (to nearest tenth)
6. $4\overline{)28.07}$ (to nearest tenth)
7. $9\overline{)47.06}$ (to nearest tenth)
8. $67\overline{)980.7}$ (to nearest tenth)
9. $74\overline{)80.56}$ (to nearest tenth)
10. $83\overline{)5.927}$ (to nearest hundredth)

11. $57\overline{)7.604}$ (to nearest hundredth)
12. $19\overline{)5.782}$ (to nearest tenth)
13. $0.9\overline{)47.32}$ (to nearest tenth)
14. $0.7\overline{)85.19}$
15. $0.4\overline{)0.1758}$ (to nearest tenth)
16. $0.8\overline{)0.1609}$ (to nearest tenth)
17. $0.06\overline{)7.236}$
18. $0.07\overline{)8.015}$
19. $0.03\overline{)5.106}$
20. $0.008\overline{)4.10648}$
21. $0.004\overline{)5.6704}$
22. $5.3\overline{)4.1682}$ (to nearest hundredth)
23. $3.9\overline{)5.7106}$ (to nearest hundredth)
24. $0.48\overline{)15.648}$
25. $0.67\overline{)27.336}$
26. $0.91\overline{)64.792}$
27. $0.73\overline{)18.834}$
28. $0.039\overline{)0.65712}$ (to nearest hundredth)
29. $0.017\overline{)0.38706}$ (to nearest hundredth)
30. $3.14\overline{)67.085}$ (to nearest hundredth)
31. $7.08\overline{)91.307}$ (to nearest tenth)
32. $37.6\overline{)582.705}$ (to nearest tenth)
33. $49.3\overline{)609.487}$ (to nearest tenth)
34. $0.234\overline{)0.06789}$ (to nearest hundredth)
35. $0.857\overline{)0.70138}$ (to nearest hundredth)

Now be sure of your skill. Try Exercise 44.

EXERCISE 44

Divide. When necessary, round the quotient to the place indicated.

1. $9\overline{)50.4}$
2. $6\overline{)37.47}$ (to nearest tenth)
3. $47\overline{)593.8}$ (to nearest tenth)
4. $79\overline{)3.068}$ (to nearest hundredth)
5. $0.8\overline{)73.15}$ (to nearest tenth)
6. $0.7\overline{)0.3482}$ (to nearest tenth)
7. $0.04\overline{)6.792}$
8. $0.009\overline{)4.07934}$
9. $7.9\overline{)5.6023}$ (to nearest hundredth)
10. $0.42\overline{)33.012}$
11. $0.67\overline{)3.4103}$
12. $0.052\overline{)18.173}$ (to nearest hundredth)
13. $3.79\overline{)92.036}$ (to nearest hundredth)
14. $58.3\overline{)389.619}$ (to nearest tenth)
15. $236\overline{)68.42}$ (to nearest hundredth)

MULTIPLYING BY 10, 100, 1,000, ETC.

To multiply a number by 10, move the decimal point in the number one place to the right. In some cases, it may be necessary to annex a zero to complete the operation. Similarly, to multiply a number by 100, move the decimal point in the number two places to the right. In some cases, it may be necessary to annex one or two zeros to complete the operation. Similar procedures are followed when multiplying a number by 1,000, 10,000, etc.

EXAMPLES:

Multiply.

	ANSWERS
(a) 10 × 3.5—Move the decimal point 1 place to the right.	35
(b) 10 × 69—Annex a zero to 69.	690
(c) 100 × 0.47—Move the decimal point 2 places to the right.	47
(d) 100 × 8.72—Move the decimal point 2 places to the right	872
(e) 10 × 0.018—Move the decimal point 1 place to the right.	0.18
(f) 100 × 0.9—Move the decimal point 2 places to the right.	90
(g) 100 × 65.3—Move the decimal point 2 places to the right.	6,530
(h) 1,000 × 4.7—Move the decimal point 3 places to the right.	4,700
(i) 1,000 × 0.0019—Move the decimal point 3 places to the right.	1.9

(j) 1,000 × 0.056—Move the decimal point 3 places to the right. 56

(k) 1,000 × 2.78—Move the decimal point 3 places to the right. 2,780

(l) 1,000 × 8.5—Move the decimal point 3 places to the right. 8,500

DIVIDING BY 10, 100, 1,000, ETC.

To divide a number by 10, move the decimal point in the number one place to the left. In some cases, it may be necessary to insert a zero between the decimal point and the first digit on the left, to complete the operation. Similarly, to divide a number by 100, move the decimal point in the number two places to the left. In some cases, it may be necessary to insert one or two zeros between the decimal point and the first digit on the left, to complete the operation. Similar procedures are followed when dividing a number by 1,000, 10,000, etc.

EXAMPLES:

Divide. **ANSWERS**

(a) 68 ÷ 10—Move the decimal point 1 place to the left. 6.8

(b) 759 ÷ 10—Move the decimal point 1 place to the left. 75.9

(c) 37.5 ÷ 10—Move the decimal point 1 place to the left. 3.75

(d) 0.47 ÷ 10—Move the decimal point 1 place to the left and insert a zero. 0.047

(e) 0.003 ÷ 10—Move the decimal point 1 place to the left and insert a zero. 0.0003

(f) 5,670 ÷ 100—Move the decimal point 2 places to the left. 56.7

(g) 38.5 ÷ 100—Move the decimal point 2 places to the left. 0.385

(h) 0.24 ÷ 100—Move the decimal point 2 places to the left and insert 2 zeros. 0.0024

(i) 4.97 ÷ 100—Move the decimal point 2 places to the left and insert a zero. 0.0497

(j) 7,000 ÷ 1,000—Move the decimal point 3 places to the left. 7

(k) 806 ÷ 1,000—Move the decimal point 3 places to the left. 0.806

(l) 5.31 ÷ 1,000—Move the decimal point 3 places to the left and insert 2 zeros. 0.00531

EXERCISE 45

Perform the following multiplications.

1. 10 × 6.7	2. 10 × 58
3. 10 × 0.05	4. 10 × 736
5. 10 × 0.482	6. 100 × 3.2
7. 100 × 0.725	8. 100 × 356
9. 100 × 0.051	10. 100 × 65.9
11. 1,000 × 0.015	12. 1,000 × 34
13. 1,000 × 2.69	14. 1,000 × 85
15. 1,000 × 3.14	

Perform the following divisions.

16. 85 ÷ 10	17. 0.69 ÷ 10
18. 0.043 ÷ 10	19. 68.72 ÷ 10
20. 0.4951 ÷ 10	21. 3,720 ÷ 100
22. 78.4 ÷ 100	23. 3.72 ÷ 100
24. 0.016 ÷ 100	25. 643.7 ÷ 100
26. 9,000 ÷ 1,000	27. 675 ÷ 1,000
28. 4.07 ÷ 1,000	29. 58.62 ÷ 1,000
30. 0.015 ÷ 1,000	

If you got 27 or more correct, go on to the next section on Operations With United States Money. If you got more than three wrong, use Exercise 46 to build your skill.

EXERCISE 46

Multiply the following numbers by 10.

1. 3.2	2. 58	3. 7
4. 0.68	5. 57	6. 0.035
7. 2.14	8. 60.5	9. 4.273
10. 285	11. 0.452	12. 2.83
13. 350	14. 6.805	15. 0.0058

Multiply the following numbers by 100.

1. 6.2	2. 351	3. 0.012
4. 750	5. 0.1572	6. 8.531
7. 0.00039	8. 51.32	9. 4
10. 3.79	11. 1,275	12. 0.02
13. 65	14. 3.002	15. 27.1

Multiply the following numbers by 1,000.

1. 25	2. 6.48	3. 583.2
4. 0.0016	5. 9.075	6. 21.7
7. 0.123	8. 0.01534	9. 3.1416
10. 62.5	11. 0.72	12. 0.00035
13. 2.91	14. 0.05	15. 9.126

Divide the following numbers by 10.

1. 58	2. 400	3. 375
4. 0.625	5. 87.5	6. 125
7. 0.46	8. 250	9. 0.02
10. 75	11. 0.0035	12. 8,532
13. 63.7	14. 1.05	15. 5,780

Divide the following numbers by 100.

1. 750	2. 64.5	3. 0.032
4. 8.73	5. 0.0058	6. 297
7. 3,500	8. 0.167	9. 4,850
10. 9.87	11. 0.5036	12. 90.4
13. 8,610	14. 0.53	15. 65.03

Divide the following numbers by 1,000.

1. 5,300	2. 2,070	3. 6.25
4. 0.015	5. 952	6. 3.14
7. 0.67	8. 2.975	9. 75
10. 125	11. 0.025	12. 65.72
13. 8.75	14. 0.0065	15. 0.833

Now be sure of your skill. Try Exercise 47.

EXERCISE 47

Perform the following multiplications.

1. 10×3.5	2. 10×0.69
3. 10×56	4. 10×0.389
5. 10×506	6. 100×0.463
7. 100×5.2	8. 100×0.063
9. 100×875	10. 100×73.4
11. $1{,}000 \times 58$	12. $1{,}000 \times 0.018$
13. $1{,}000 \times 6.2$	14. $1{,}000 \times 3.87$
15. $1{,}000 \times 57$	

Perform the following divisions.

16. $97 \div 10$	17. $0.035 \div 10$
18. $0.48 \div 10$	19. $0.6532 \div 10$
20. $52.8 \div 10$	21. $4{,}680 \div 100$
22. $58.3 \div 100$	23. $6.97 \div 100$
24. $0.018 \div 100$	25. $548.3 \div 100$
26. $315 \div 1{,}000$	27. $4{,}000 \div 1{,}000$
28. $8.73 \div 1{,}000$	29. $43.78 \div 1{,}000$
30. $0.026 \div 1{,}000$	

OPERATIONS WITH UNITED STATES MONEY

United States money, always preceded by a dollar sign ($), is written as a whole number and a two-place decimal, as a two-place decimal either preceded by a zero or not, or as a whole number. Amounts such as $12.96, $5.00, $1.27, $0.48, $.32, and $26 are examples. The operations of addition, subtraction, multiplication, and division with U.S. money follow the methods used with decimals. Note that $.32 = 32¢.

EXERCISE 48

Add.

1.	2.
$3.68	$0.79
0.49	5.03
15.06	127.45
8.52	69.76
+ 0.58	+ 5.21

3.	4.
$580.18	$43.62
91.37	120.04
0.84	98.73
602.06	6.96
+ 3.75	+ 9.09

Subtract.

5.	6.	7.
$685.47	$209.57	$500.08
− 26.19	− 143.73	− 379.46

8. $1,467.12
− 708.59

Multiply.

9.	10.	11.
$275.08	$65.47	$8.79
× 9	× 38	× 107

12. $657.08
× 17

Divide.

13. $843.22 ÷ 7	14. $1,290.09 ÷ 23
15. $701.04 ÷ $0.69	16. $2,671.80 ÷ $8.76

If you got 15 or 16 correct, go on to the following Practice Tests. If you got more than one wrong, use Exercise 49 to build your skill.

EXERCISE 49

Add.

1.	2.	3.
$4.73	$23.89	$897.45
18.29	47.21	673.79
143.06	650.04	44.83
0.29	9.15	2.07
+ 6.52	+ 78.46	+ 385.26

4. $2.03
4.79
367.85
412.06
+ 69.98

5. $59.91
248.05
374.77
25.69
+ 87.03

6. $901.11
8.99
653.48
0.98
+ 5.04

7. $240.01
59.89
3.45
82.16
+ 302.47

8. $ 85.50
69.07
125.48
304.96
+ 2.57

Subtract.

1. $2.07 − 0.39
2. $6.50 − 1.68
3. $79.12 − 42.39
4. $90.01 − 69.59
5. $432.72 − 58.87
6. $890.07 − 367.78
7. $1,240.70 − 589.86
8. $3,282.03 − 1,569.18

Multiply.

1. $650.03 × 7
2. $507.19 × 8
3. $84.37 × 29
4. $70.09 × 36
5. $5.80 × 205
6. $9.06 × 125
7. $428.45 × 78
8. $902.06 × 23

Divide the following, finding results to the nearest cent.

1. $930.78 ÷ 9
2. $1,569.50 ÷ 7
3. $3,897.10 ÷ 18
4. $910.78 ÷ 26
5. $95.45 ÷ $0.83
6. $74.48 ÷ $0.76
7. $267.52 ÷ $3.52
8. $1,333.71 ÷ $6.57

Now be sure of your skill. Try Exercise 50.

EXERCISE 50

Add.

1. $4.37
0.69
28.43
7.14
+ 8.48

2. $0.68
4.07
249.79
78.53
+ 0.49

3. $54.69
837.28
403.07
0.65
+ 8.42

4. $180.07
65.58
7.92
94.65
+ 8.01

Subtract.

5. $379.46 − 39.18
6. $407.62 − 239.57
7. $700.02 − 523.39
8. $2,650.14 − 905.76

Multiply.

9. $587.04 × 6
10. $79.48 × 47
11. $9.48 × 209
12. $306.17 × 29

Divide. Round to the nearest cent.

13. $694.18 ÷ 9
14. $3,462.05 ÷ 29
15. $119.13 ÷ $0.57
16. $1,412.43 ÷ $5.29

PRACTICE TEST 7

1. The sum of $0.97, $0.68, and $0.04 =

(A) $2.35 (B) $1.52 (C) $1.62
(D) $1.69 (E) $1.72

2. The sum of $38.09, $0.57, and $7.44 =

(A) $56.10 (B) $46.00 (C) $51.23
(D) $36.10 (E) $46.10

3. When $12.67 is subtracted from $40.05 the result is:

(A) $28.18 (B) $38.28 (C) $27.28
(D) $37.18 (E) none of these

4. The difference between $18.79 and $6.98 =

(A) $12.81 (B) $11.81 (C) $1.81
(D) $25.77 (E) $12.77

5. When $0.48 is multiplied by 15 the result is:

(A) $0.72 (B) $6.20 (C) $0.032
(D) $7.20 (E) $5.40

6. When $19.89 is multiplied by 24 the result is:

(A) $47.74 (B) $467.36 (C) $477.36
(D) $377.36 (E) $367.36

7. When $163.45 is divided by 7 the result is:

(A) $2.35 (B) $2.34 (C) $23.35
(D) $21.92 (E) $23.15

8. When $88.37 is divided by 29 the result, correct to the nearest cent, is:

   (A) $3.05 (B) $3.04 (C) $3.47 (D) $3.46 (E) $3.36

9. When $30.71 is divided by $0.83 the result is:

   (A) 3.70 (B) 31 (C) 37 (D) 37.10 (E) none of these

10. When $206.50 is divided by $8.26 the result is:

    (A) 2.50 (B) 250 (C) .25 (D) 25 (E) 50

PRACTICE TEST 8

1. The sum of $0.69, $0.47, and $0.05 =

   (A) $1.01 (B) $1.10 (C) $1.21 (D) $1.11 (E) $1.20

2. The sum of $46.07, $0.98, and $5.03 =

   (A) $51.08 (B) $52.08 (C) $51.98 (D) $52.28 (E) $51.18

3. When $18.08 is subtracted from $30.14 the result is:

   (A) $11.06 (B) $12.16 (C) $48.22 (D) $11.16 (E) none of these

4. The difference between $31.25 and $7.98 is:

   (A) $23.33 (B) $24.23 (C) $24.27 (D) $23.27 (E) $24.57

5. When $0.36 is multiplied by 35 the result is:

   (A) $10.60 (B) $12.60 (C) $2.80 (D) $11.61 (E) $.71

6. When $17.69 is multiplied by 32 the result is:

   (A) $566.08 (B) $566.18 (C) $567.08 (D) $565.18 (E) none of these

7. When $153.09 is divided by 9 the result is:

   (A) $16.01 (B) $17.21 (C) $10.71 (D) $17.01 (E) $14.01

8. When $101.48 is divided by 37 the result, correct to the nearest cent, is:

   (A) $3.72 (B) $2.75 (C) $2.65 (D) $2.74 (E) $2.94

9. When $60.03 is divided by $0.69 the result is:

   (A) 0.87 (B) 88 (C) 87 (D) 81 (E) 85

10. When $209.96 is divided by $7.24 the result is:

    (A) 0.38 (B) 29. (C) 2.9 (D) 290 (E) 0.31

PRACTICE TEST 9

1. The sum of $0.24, $0.89, and $0.07 is:

   (A) $1.10 (B) $13.00 (C) $1.20 (D) $1.11 (E) $1.31

2. The sum of $0.73, $34.05, and $6.89 is:

   (A) $40.67 (B) $41.57 (C) $40.57 (D) $40.51 (E) none of these

3. When $10.78 is subtracted from $26.15 the result is:

   (A) $15.37 (B) $15.47 (C) $16.37 (D) $16.47 (E) $37.93

4. The difference between $20.62 and $6.57 is:

   (A) $13.05 (B) $13.15 (C) $14.05 (D) $13.95 (E) $13.80

5. When $0.48 is multiplied by 75 the result is:

   (A) $3.60 (B) $36.00 (C) $36.60 (D) $35.00 (E) $35.60

6. When $19.32 is multiplied by 42 the result is:

   (A) $801.44 (B) $810.44 (C) $811.54 (D) $811.44 (E) none of these

7. When $684.32 is divided by 8 the result is:

   (A) $86.64 (B) $80.54 (C) $85.54 (D) $86.54 (E) $86.64

8. When $305.37 is divided by 49 the result, correct to the nearest cent, is:

   (A) $6.23 (B) $6.24 (C) $6.14 (D) $6.03 (E) none of these

9. When $41.28 is divided by 96 the result is:

   (A) 42 (B) $43 (C) $0.43 (D) $42 (E) $47

10. When $111.01 is divided by $6.53 the result is:

    (A) 27 (B) 19 (C) 38 (D) 17 (E) none of these

Operations with Fractions, Mixed Numbers, and Decimals

CHANGING FRACTIONS AND MIXED NUMBERS TO DECIMALS

A fraction may be considered as a division of one whole number by another. For example, the fraction $\frac{4}{9}$ indicates that 4 is to be divided by 9. The following examples will indicate the details of this operation.

EXAMPLE: Change $\frac{3}{4}$ to a decimal.

SOLUTION: Divide 3 by 4.

$$4\overline{)3.00}\quad 0.75$$

Thus, $\frac{3}{4} = 0.75$

EXAMPLE: Change $\frac{5}{8}$ to a decimal.

SOLUTION: Divide 5 by 8.

$$8\overline{)5.000}\quad 0.625$$

Thus, $\frac{5}{8} = 0.625$

EXAMPLE: Change $\frac{4}{7}$ to a decimal.

SOLUTION: Divide 4 by 7.

$$7\overline{)4.00}\quad 0.57\tfrac{1}{7}$$

The quotient in this division will be an endlessly repeating decimal. The answer rounded to the nearest hundreth is 0.57.

EXAMPLE: Change $2\frac{5}{6}$ to a decimal, correct to two decimal places.
SOLUTION: Divide 5 by 6.

$$6\overline{)5.00}\quad 0.83\tfrac{2}{6}$$

Thus, $2\frac{5}{6}$

Rounded to the nearest hundredth, $2\frac{5}{6}$ is 2.83.

CHANGING DECIMALS TO FRACTIONS

In changing decimals to fractions it is helpful to remember that a decimal is a fraction whose denominator is 10, 100, 1,000, etc. Thus, to change a decimal to a fraction we write a fraction whose numerator is the given decimal without the decimal point, and whose denominator is 10, 100, 1,000, etc., as indicated by the placement of the decimal point. The fraction thus obtained is then reduced to its lowest terms.

EXAMPLE: Change 0.6 to a fraction.

SOLUTION: $0.6 = \frac{6}{10}$

$\frac{6}{10}$ may be reduced to $\frac{3}{5}$.

EXAMPLE: Change 0.48 to a fraction.

SOLUTION: $0.48 = \frac{48}{100}$

$\frac{48}{100} = \frac{12}{25}$

EXAMPLE: Change 0.015 to a fraction.

SOLUTION: $0.48 = \frac{15}{1{,}000}$

$\frac{15}{1{,}000} = \frac{3}{200}$

EXAMPLE: Change $0.663\frac{2}{3}$ to a fraction.

SOLUTION: $0.66\frac{2}{3} = \dfrac{66\frac{2}{3}}{100}$

Consider this as a division of fractions problem.

$$66\tfrac{2}{3} \div 100 = \frac{200}{3} \div \frac{100}{1} = \frac{200}{3} \times \frac{1}{100} = \frac{2}{3}$$

EXAMPLE: Change 3.625 to a mixed number.

SOLUTION: $3.625 = 3\frac{625}{1000} = 3\frac{5}{8}$

The following fractions and their decimal equivalents occur frequently. You are advised to memorize these equivalents.

Fraction	$\frac{1}{2}$	$\frac{1}{3}$	$\frac{2}{3}$	$\frac{1}{4}$	$\frac{3}{4}$	$\frac{1}{5}$
Decimal	0.5	$0.33\frac{1}{3}$	$0.66\frac{2}{3}$	0.25	0.75	0.2

Fraction	$\frac{2}{5}$	$\frac{3}{5}$	$\frac{4}{5}$	$\frac{1}{6}$	$\frac{5}{6}$	$\frac{1}{8}$
Decimal	0.4	0.6	0.8	$0.16\frac{2}{3}$	$0.83\frac{1}{3}$	0.125

Fraction	$\frac{3}{8}$	$\frac{5}{8}$	$\frac{7}{8}$	$\frac{1}{10}$	$\frac{3}{10}$	$\frac{7}{10}$	$\frac{9}{10}$
Decimal	0.375	0.625	0.875	0.1	0.3	0.7	0.9

EXERCISE 51

Express the following fractions or mixed numbers as decimals. Where a remainder occurs, give the decimal correct to two decimal places.

1. $\frac{1}{4}$ 2. $\frac{3}{5}$ 3. $\frac{5}{6}$ 4. $\frac{3}{8}$
5. $\frac{2}{7}$ 6. $\frac{7}{9}$ 7. $2\frac{5}{12}$ 8. $\frac{18}{25}$
9. $\frac{9}{14}$ 10. $\frac{7}{15}$ 11. $\frac{4}{11}$ 12. $3\frac{6}{17}$

Express the following decimals as fractions or mixed numbers.

13. 0.7 14. 0.04 15. 0.45
16. 2.4 17. 0.625 18. 0.245
19. $1.33\frac{1}{3}$ 20. $0.12\frac{1}{2}$ 21. $0.08\frac{1}{3}$
22. 0.008 23. $5.37\frac{1}{2}$ 24. $2.83\frac{1}{3}$

If you got 22 or more correct, go on to the next section on Operations With Fractions and Decimals. If you got more than two wrong, use Exercise 52 to build your skill.

EXERCISE 52

Express the following fractions or mixed numbers as decimals. Where a remainder occurs, give the decimal correct to two decimal places.

1. $\frac{1}{2}$ 2. $\frac{1}{5}$ 3. $\frac{5}{8}$ 4. $\frac{1}{3}$
5. $\frac{1}{6}$ 6. $\frac{3}{7}$ 7. $\frac{2}{9}$ 8. $\frac{7}{10}$
9. $\frac{3}{11}$ 10. $3\frac{1}{8}$ 11. $\frac{9}{20}$ 12. $\frac{4}{15}$
13. $\frac{5}{6}$ 14. $2\frac{1}{12}$ 15. $\frac{3}{4}$ 16. $\frac{3}{14}$
17. $\frac{8}{17}$ 18. $\frac{6}{7}$ 19. $\frac{7}{25}$ 20. $\frac{3}{19}$

Express the following decimals as fractions or mixed numbers.

1. 0.3 2. 0.09 3. 0.11 4. 0.65
5. 3.8 6. 0.275 7. $0.83\frac{1}{3}$ 8. 0.036
9. $2.12\frac{1}{2}$ 10. 0.48 11. $1.33\frac{1}{3}$ 12. 0.375
13. 2.25 14. $2.16\frac{2}{3}$ 15. 3.72 16. 0.625
17. 4.8 18. 2.32 19. $2.66\frac{2}{3}$ 20. 5.85

Now be sure of your skill. Try Exercise 53.

EXERCISE 53

Express the following fractions or mixed numbers as decimals. Where a remainder occurs, give the decimal correct to two decimal places.

1. $\frac{2}{5}$ 2. $\frac{3}{4}$ 3. $\frac{7}{8}$ 4. $\frac{1}{6}$
5. $\frac{5}{9}$ 6. $3\frac{7}{12}$ 7. $\frac{8}{9}$ 8. $\frac{11}{20}$
9. $1\frac{8}{15}$ 10. $\frac{3}{14}$ 11. $2\frac{4}{17}$ 12. $\frac{8}{11}$

Express the following decimals as fractions or mixed numbers.

13. 0.9 14. 0.06 15. 0.85 16. 3.8
17. 0.375 18. 3.485 19. $2.66\frac{2}{3}$ 20. $0.41\frac{2}{3}$
21. 0.018 22. $3.62\frac{1}{2}$ 23. $1.16\frac{2}{3}$ 24. 6.64

OPERATIONS WITH FRACTIONS AND DECIMALS

It is sometimes required to perform operations involving both fractions and decimals. In such cases, we change all quantities either to fractions or to decimals as directed.

EXAMPLE: Add $\frac{1}{4}$ and 0.59. Express the result as a decimal.

SOLUTION:

$$\frac{1}{4} = .25$$
$$0.59 = 0.59$$
$$\frac{1}{4} + 0.59 = 0.84$$

EXAMPLE: From 4.09 subtract $\frac{5}{8}$.

SOLUTION:

$$4.09 = 4.090$$
$$-\frac{5}{8} = 0.625$$
$$4.09 - \frac{5}{8} = 3.465$$

EXAMPLE: Multiply $\frac{4}{9}$ by 0.36. Express the result as a fraction.

SOLUTION: $\frac{4}{9} = \frac{4}{9}$, $0.36 = \frac{36}{100}$

$$\frac{\overset{1}{\cancel{4}}}{\underset{1}{\cancel{9}}} \times \frac{\overset{4}{\cancel{36}}}{\underset{25}{\cancel{100}}} = \frac{4}{25}$$

EXAMPLE: Find $0.83\frac{1}{3}$ of 27.

SOLUTION: Before performing this multiplication it is advisable to change $0.83\frac{1}{3}$ to the fraction $\frac{5}{6}$.

$$\frac{5}{\underset{2}{\cancel{6}}} \times \overset{9}{\cancel{27}} = \frac{45}{2} = 22\frac{1}{2}$$

EXAMPLE: Divide $9.37\frac{1}{2}$ by $\frac{5}{16}$.

SOLUTION: $9.37\frac{1}{2} = 9\frac{3}{8} = \frac{75}{8}$

$$\frac{75}{8} \div \frac{5}{16} = \frac{\overset{15}{\cancel{75}}}{8} \times \frac{\overset{2}{\cancel{16}}}{5} = 30$$

EXAMPLE: Divide $15\frac{3}{4}$ by $4.08\frac{1}{3}$.

SOLUTION: $15\frac{3}{4} = \frac{63}{4}$

$$4.08\frac{1}{3} = 4\frac{1}{12} = \frac{49}{12}$$

$$\frac{63}{4} \div \frac{49}{12} = \frac{\overset{9}{\cancel{63}}}{\underset{1}{\cancel{4}}} \times \frac{\overset{3}{\cancel{12}}}{\underset{7}{\cancel{49}}} = \frac{27}{7} = 3\frac{6}{7}$$

EXERCISE 54

Perform the following operations. Express the results as decimals.

1. Add $\frac{3}{5}$ and 0.46.
2. Add $\frac{7}{8}$ and 0.09.
3. From 3.27 subtract $\frac{3}{4}$.
4. From $8\frac{7}{100}$ subtract 2.59.
5. Multiply $\frac{7}{20}$ by 6.2.
6. Divide $8\frac{1}{5}$ by 2.05.
7. Find $0.16\frac{2}{3}$ of 45.
8. Divide 90 by $2.08\frac{1}{3}$.

Perform the following operations. Express the results as decimals.

9. Add $\frac{5}{12}$ and 0.15.
10. Add $0.83\frac{1}{3}$ and $\frac{4}{9}$.
11. From 6.4 subtract $\frac{1}{2}$.
12. From $5\frac{1}{3}$ subtract $2.16\frac{2}{3}$.
13. Multiply $\frac{8}{15}$ by 0.15.
14. Find $0.37\frac{1}{2}$ of 76.
15. Divide 8 by 0.24.
16. Divide $37\frac{1}{2}$ by $1.12\frac{1}{2}$.

If you got 15 or 16 correct, go on to the following Practice Tests. If you got more than two wrong, use Exercise 55 to build your skill.

EXERCISE 55

Perform the following operations. Express the results as decimals.

1. Add $\frac{1}{2}$ and 0.79.
2. Add $\frac{3}{8}$ and 2.16.
3. Add 5.03 and $\frac{1}{4}$.
4. Add 2.57 and $\frac{3}{5}$.
5. From 6.81 subtract $\frac{1}{8}$.
6. From 3.2 subtract $\frac{9}{20}$.
7. From $7\frac{3}{5}$ subtract 1.09.
8. From $6\frac{3}{8}$ subtract 2.14.
9. Multiply 48 by $0.08\frac{1}{3}$.
10. Multiply 72 by $0.66\frac{2}{3}$.
11. Find $0.33\frac{1}{3}$ of 42.3.
12. Find $0.62\frac{1}{2}$ of 44.
13. Divide 76 by 3.04.
14. Divide 156 by 2.08.
15. Divide 47.5 by $3.16\frac{2}{3}$.
16. Divide 57 by $2.37\frac{1}{2}$.

Perform the following operations. Express the results as fractions.

1. Add $\frac{5}{9}$ and $0.83\frac{1}{3}$.
2. Add $0.62\frac{1}{2}$ and $\frac{7}{12}$.
3. Add $0.33\frac{1}{3}$ and $\frac{2}{5}$.
4. Add $0.58\frac{1}{3}$ and $\frac{11}{15}$.
5. From 9.5 subtract $\frac{3}{4}$.
6. From 4.7 subtract $\frac{2}{5}$.

7. From $9\frac{1}{8}$ subtract $3.37\frac{1}{2}$.
8. From $7\frac{1}{6}$ subtract $4.66\frac{2}{3}$.
9. Multiply $\frac{4}{5}$ by 0.35.
10. Multiply $\frac{6}{7}$ by $0.33\frac{1}{3}$.
11. Multiply $0.16\frac{2}{3}$ by 64.
12. Find 0.45 of 75.
13. Divide 16 by 0.48.
14. Divide 18 by 0.36.
15. Divide 80 by $4.16\frac{2}{3}$.
16. Divide 30 by 1.2.

Now be sure of your skill. Try Exercise 56.

EXERCISE 56

Perform the following operations. Express the results as decimals.

1. Add $\frac{1}{4}$ and 0.38.
2. Add $\frac{3}{8}$ and 0.07.
3. From 6.58 subtract $\frac{3}{5}$.
4. From $7\frac{3}{10}$ subtract 3.46.
5. Multiply $\frac{8}{15}$ by 3.6.
6. Divide $26\frac{4}{5}$ by 3.35.
7. Find $0.83\frac{1}{3}$ of 57.
8. Divide 105 by $0.87\frac{1}{2}$.

Perform the following operations. Express the results as decimals.

9. Add $\frac{3}{4}$ and 0.56.
10. Add $0.37\frac{1}{2}$ and $\frac{7}{12}$.
11. From 7.5 subtract $\frac{1}{6}$.
12. From 7.8 subtract $3.62\frac{1}{2}$.
13. Multiply $\frac{9}{14}$ by 0.35.
14. Find $0.83\frac{1}{3}$ of 40.
15. Divide 36 by 0.15.
16. Divide $24\frac{1}{2}$ by $4.08\frac{1}{3}$.

PRACTICE TEST 10

1. 3.876, correct to the nearest tenth =

   (A) 3.8 (B) 3.88 (C) 3.9 (D) 3.90 (E) 3.95

2. 2.053, correct to the nearest hundredth =

   (A) 2.15 (B) 2.06 (C) 2.13 (D) 2.03 (E) none of these

3. Of the following sets of decimals, the set that is ordered, with the largest decimal first, is:

   (A) 0.583, 0.538, 0.835
   (B) 0.538, 0.853, 0.583
   (C) 0.835, 0.583, 0.538
   (D) 0.835, 0.538, 0.583
   (E) 0.538, 0.583, 0.835

4. The sum of 0.32, 0.09, and 0.76 =

   (A) 1.07 (B) 1.27 (C) 1.98 (D) 1.17 (E) none of these

5. The sum of 8.032, 7.165, and 3.897 =

   (A) 18.994 (B) 19.094 (C) 19.084 (D) 19.184 (E) 18.184

6. The difference between 8.03 and 5.19 =

   (A) 2.94 (B) 3.84 (C) 3.16 (D) 2.84 (E) 3.22

7. When 14.803 is subtracted from 207.312 the result is:

   (A) 192.509 (B) 192.519 (C) 193.509 (D) 182.519 (E) 193.519

8. The product of 0.03 and 8 is:

   (A) 0.024 (B) 24 (C) 2.4 (D) 0.24 (E) none of these

9. When 60 is multiplied by 0.65 the result is:

   (A) 3.9 (B) 36 (C) 30.9 (D) 30.09 (E) 39

10. The product of 72 and 0.035 is:

    (A) 5.76 (B) 57.6 (C) 2.52 (D) 25.2 (E) 2.54

11. When 40.16 is divided by 8 the quotient is:

    (A) 5.2 (B) 5.02 (C) 40.02 (D) 50.2 (E) 5.22

12. When 0.901 is divided by 0.017 the result is:

    (A) 0.53 (B) .053 (C) 530 (D) 53 (E) 52.8

13. When 6.852 is divided by 2.7 the quotient, correct to the nearest tenth, is:

(A) 25.4 (B) 2.5 (C) 2.6 (D) 26.3 (E) 2.63

14. When 3.75 is multiplied by 1,000 the result is:

(A) 375,000 (B) 375 (C) 37,500 (D) 3,750 (E) 37.5

15. When 6.85 is divided by 100 the result is:

(A) 685 (B) 68.5 (C) 0.0685 (D) 0.685 (E) 6.85

PRACTICE TEST 11

1. 54.832, correct to the nearest tenth =

(A) 54.9 (B) 54.83 (C) 54.82 (D) 54.8 (E) 54.85

2. 6.185, correct to the nearest hundredth =

(A) 6.18 (B) 6.2 (C) 6.19 (D) 6.16 (E) 6.25

3. Of the following sets of decimals, the one in correct order of their size, with the largest first, is:

(A) 0.728, 0.827, 0.782
(B) 0.827, 0.782, 0.728
(C) 0.827, 0.728, 0.782
(D) 0.782, 0.827, 0.728
(E) 0.728, 0.782, 0.827

4. The sum of 0.48, 0.07, and 0.64 =

(A) 1.09 (B) 2.09 (C) 1.19 (D) 1.21 (E) none of these

5. The sum of 6.138, 2.009, and 3.715 =

(A) 11.962 (B) 11.952 (C) 12.862 (D) 12.962 (E) 11.862

6. The difference between 7.12 and 4.09 =

(A) 2.03 (B) 3.03 (C) 3.13 (D) 3.3 (E) 2.3

7. When 17.069 is subtracted from 109.347 the result is:

(A) 102.278 (B) 92.288 (C) 82.278 (D) 92.278 (E) 91.278

8. The product of 0.07 and 9 is:

(A) 6.3 (B) 0.063 (C) 0.16 (D) 63 (E) none of these

9. When 85 is multiplied by 0.24 the result is:

(A) 204 (B) 240 (C) 20.4 (D) 2400 (E) 230

10. The product of 120 and 0.065 is:

(A) 78 (B) 7.8 (C) 7.08 (D) 780 (E) 78.08

11. When 35.91 is divided by 7 the result is:

(A) 5.03 (B) 5.11 (C) 5.31 (D) 5.13 (E) none of these

12. When 0.32048 is divided by 0.0016 the quotient is:

(A) 20.3 (B) 2.30 (C) 200.3 (D) 230 (E) 2,300

13. When 10.237 is divided by 3.9 the quotient, correct to the nearest tenth, is:

(A) 2.4 (B) 2.6 (C) 2.7 (D) 0.27 (E) 260

14. When 4.869 is multiplied by 100 the result is:

(A) 4,869 (B) 48.69 (C) 48,690 (D) 0.4869 (E) 486.9

15. When 73.2 is divided by 1,000 the result is:

(A) 0.732 (B) 0.0732 (C) 73.2 (D) 7.32 (E) 730.2

PRACTICE TEST 12

1. 68.708, correct to the nearest tenth =

(A) 68.8 (B) 68.71 (C) 68.7 (D) 68.88 (E) 68.08

2. 3.537, correct to the nearest hundredth =

(A) 3.54 (B) 3.57 (C) 3.58 (D) 3.53 (E) 3.56

3. Of the following sets of decimals, the set that is ordered, with the largest decimal first, is:

(A) 0.697, 0.967, 0.769
(B) 0.967, 0.697, 0.769
(C) 0.967, 0.769, 0.697
(D) 0.769, 0.967, 0.697
(E) 0.697, 0.769, 0.967

4. The sum of 0.87, 0.39, and 0.06 is:

   (A) 1.12 (B) 1.32 (C) 1.02 (D) 2.12 (E) 0.92

5. The sum of 6.043, 3.918, and 5.307 is:

   (A) 15.258 (B) 14.268 (C) 15.368 (D) 14.368 (E) none of these

6. The difference between 7.15 and 3.06 is:

   (A) 4.19 (B) 3.09 (C) 3.19 (D) 4.09 (E) 10.21

7. When 89.17 is subtracted from 340.02 the result is:

   (A) 250.85 (B) 260.85 (C) 250.95 (D) 260.95 (E) 260.75

8. The product of 0.004 and 9 is:

   (A) 0.36 (B) 3.6 (C) 0.036 (D) 36 (E) 0.013

9. When 0.92 is multiplied by 85 the result is:

   (A) 77.2 (B) 78.02 (C) 78.12 (D) 78.2 (E) none of these

10. The product of 650 and 0.042 is:

    (A) 273 (B) 2,730 (C) 27.3 (D) 2.73 (E) 27,300

11. When 63.09 is divided by 9 the quotient is:

    (A) 7.1 (B) 7.01 (C) 70.01 (D) 70.1 (E) 7.001

12. When 1.022 is divided by 0.014 the quotient is:

    (A) 0.73 (B) 703 (C) 7.3 (D) 730 (E) none of these

13. When 69.42 is divided by 4.7 the quotient, correct to the nearest tenth, is:

    (A) 13.8 (B) 14.7 (C) 14.8 (D) 14.0 (E) 15

14. When 2.64 is multiplied by 1,000 the result is:

    (A) 26.4 (B) 2,640 (C) 264 (D) 26,400 (E) 2.64

15. When 3.75 is divided by 100 the result is:

    (A) 375 (B) 3,750 (C) 0.375 (D) 0.0375 (E) 37.5

Percentage

MEANING OF PERCENT

The word *percent* means "hundreths." To change a percent to a decimal, move the decimal point two places to the left and omit the percent sign.

EXAMPLES:

17% = 0.17 28.3% = 0.283
6% = 0.06 250% = 2.5

To change a decimal to a percent, just reverse the procedure.

EXAMPLES:

0.69 = 69%
0.8333 = 83.33%
1.53 = 153%

CHANGING DECIMALS TO PERCENTS AND PERCENTS TO DECIMALS

EXAMPLES:

Express the following as percents.	**ANSWERS**
1. 18 hundredths	18%
2. 7 hundredths	7%
3. 134 hundredths	134%
4. $\frac{1}{2}$ hundredth	$\frac{1}{2}$%
5. 6$\frac{1}{4}$ hundredths	6$\frac{1}{4}$%
6. 0.09	9%
7. 0.63	63%
8. 0.12$\frac{1}{2}$	12$\frac{1}{2}$%

9. $3.16\frac{2}{3}$	$316\frac{2}{3}\%$
10. 0.625	$62\frac{1}{2}\%$ or 62.5%

EXAMPLES:

Express the following as decimals.	**ANSWERS**
1. 19%	0.19
2. $6\frac{1}{2}\%$	$0.06\frac{1}{2}$ or 0.065
3. 375%	3.75
4. $\frac{1}{2}\%$	$0.00\frac{1}{2}$ or 0.005
5. 150%	1.5

EXERCISE 57

Express the following percents as decimals.

1. 73%	2. 4%	3. 80%
4. 127%	5. $7\frac{1}{2}\%$	6. $3\frac{1}{4}\%$
7. $2\frac{3}{4}\%$	8. $112\frac{1}{2}\%$	9. 4.3%
10. 0.25%	11. $\frac{1}{2}\%$	12. 5.07%

Express the following decimals as percents.

13. 0.48	14. 0.08	15. 0.3
16. 2.07	17. $0.13\frac{1}{2}$	18. $3.83\frac{1}{3}$
19. 0.025	20. 0.009	21. 6.5
22. $4.08\frac{1}{3}$	23. 1.875	24. 0.004

If you got 22 or more correct, go on to the next section on Changing Percents to Fractions. If you got more than three wrong, use Exercise 58 to build your skill.

EXERCISE 58

Express the following percents as decimals.

1. 68%	2. 47%	3. 30%
4. 90%	5. 132%	6. 165%
7. $8\frac{1}{2}\%$	8. $4\frac{1}{2}\%$	9. $1\frac{1}{4}\%$
10. $5\frac{1}{4}\%$	11. $8\frac{3}{4}\%$	12. $6\frac{3}{4}\%$
13. 6.2%	14. $124\frac{1}{2}\%$	15. 7.8%
16. $144\frac{1}{2}\%$	17. 0.75%	18. $\frac{1}{5}\%$
19. 0.35%	20. 6.4%	21. 7.08%
22. $\frac{1}{4}\%$	23. 3.18%	24. 0.3%

Express the following decimals as percents.

25. 0.62	26. 0.38	27. 0.02
28. 0.7	29. 5.09	30. 0.27
31. 3.05	32. $0.08\frac{1}{2}$	33. 6.09
34. $0.24\frac{1}{2}$	35. $2.37\frac{1}{2}$	36. 0.067
37. $7.83\frac{1}{3}$	38. 0.089	39. 0.002
40. 7.4	41. $3.04\frac{1}{2}$	42. 0.007
43. 3.9	44. 1.125	45. 0.005
46. $8.06\frac{2}{3}$	47. 7.8	48. 3.175

Now be sure of your skill. Try Exercise 59.

EXERCISE 59

Express the following percents as decimals.

1. 57%	2. 8%	3. 60%
4. 149%	5. $2\frac{1}{2}\%$	6. $1\frac{1}{4}\%$
7. $5\frac{3}{4}\%$	8. $128\frac{1}{2}\%$	9. 6.2%
10. 0.5%	11. $\frac{1}{8}\%$	12. 3.08%

Express the following decimals as percents.

13. 0.62	14. 0.03	15. 0.8
16. 5.02	17. $0.18\frac{1}{2}$	18. $2.17\frac{1}{3}$
19. 0.067	20. 0.002	21. 8.2
22. $3.02\frac{1}{3}$	23. 2.625	24. 0.009

CHANGING PERCENTS TO FRACTIONS

In changing a percent to a fraction we recall that a percent can be written as a fraction whose denominator is 100. For example, 73% is equal to the fraction $\frac{73}{100}$, and 24% is equal to the fraction $\frac{24}{100}$. The fraction $\frac{24}{100}$ may be reduced to the fraction $\frac{6}{25}$.

Since certain percents appear very frequently, it is best to memorize their fractional equivalents. The following chart contains the most frequently used percents and their equivalents.

$\frac{1}{2} = 50\%$	$\frac{1}{6} = 16\frac{2}{3}\%$	$\frac{1}{10} = 10\%$
$\frac{1}{3} = 33\frac{1}{3}\%$	$\frac{5}{6} = 83\frac{1}{3}\%$	$\frac{3}{10} = 30\%$
$\frac{2}{3} = 66\frac{2}{3}\%$	$\frac{1}{7} = 14\frac{2}{7}\%$	$\frac{7}{10} = 70\%$
$\frac{1}{4} = 25\%$	$\frac{1}{8} = 12\frac{1}{2}\%$	$\frac{9}{10} = 90\%$
$\frac{3}{4} = 75\%$	$\frac{3}{8} = 37\frac{1}{2}\%$	$\frac{1}{12} = 8\frac{1}{3}\%$
$\frac{1}{5} = 20\%$	$\frac{5}{8} = 62\frac{1}{2}\%$	$\frac{1}{16} = 6\frac{1}{4}\%$
$\frac{2}{5} = 40\%$	$\frac{7}{8} = 87\frac{1}{2}\%$	$\frac{1}{20} = 5\%$
$\frac{3}{5} = 60\%$		$\frac{1}{25} = 4\%$
$\frac{4}{5} = 80\%$		$\frac{1}{50} = 2\%$
		$\frac{1}{100} = 1\%$

EXAMPLE: Express 84% as a fraction.

SOLUTION: $84\% = \frac{84}{100}$

$\frac{84}{100}$ may be reduced to $\frac{21}{25}$.

Thus, $84\% = \frac{21}{25}$

EXAMPLE: Express $37\frac{1}{2}\%$ as a fraction.

SOLUTION: We may recall that $37\frac{1}{2}\% = \frac{3}{8}$; or

$$37\tfrac{1}{2}\% = \frac{37\frac{1}{2}}{100}$$

Do this operation as a division of fractions problem.

$$\frac{37\frac{1}{2}}{100} = 37\tfrac{1}{2} \div 100 = \frac{75}{2} \div \frac{100}{1} = \frac{75}{2} \times \frac{1}{100} = \frac{\overset{3}{\cancel{75}}}{2} \times \frac{1}{\underset{4}{\cancel{100}}} = \frac{3}{8}$$

EXAMPLE: Express 125% as a mixed number.

SOLUTION: $125\% = \frac{125}{100}$

$\frac{125}{100}$ may be reduced to $\frac{5}{4}$.

Written as a mixed number,

$$\frac{5}{4} = 1\tfrac{1}{4}$$

CHANGING FRACTIONS TO PERCENTS

To change a fraction to a percent, divide the numerator of the fraction by its denominator, finding the quotient correct to two decimal places. Then write the resulting decimal as a percent.

EXAMPLE: Express $\frac{9}{25}$ as a percent.

SOLUTION: Divide 9 by 25.

```
   0.36
25)9.00
   7 5
   1 50
   1 50
```

$$\frac{9}{25} = 0.36 = 36\%$$

EXAMPLE: Write $\frac{7}{8}$ as a percent.

SOLUTION: Recall that $\frac{7}{8}$ is equal to $0.87\frac{1}{2}\%$.

$$0.87\tfrac{1}{2}\% = 87\tfrac{1}{2}\%$$

Or we may change $\frac{7}{8}$ to $.87\frac{1}{2}$ by dividing 8 into 7.

EXAMPLE: Change $\frac{5}{9}$ to a percent.

SOLUTION:

```
  0.55 5/9
9 )5.00
```

$$0.55\tfrac{5}{9} = 55\tfrac{5}{9}\%$$

EXAMPLE: Change $2\frac{7}{16}$ to a percent.

SOLUTION: Write the mixed number $2\frac{7}{16}$ as the improper fraction $\frac{39}{16}$.

Now divide 39 by 16:

```
    2.43
16)39.00
   32
    70
    64
     60
     48
     12
```

$$2\tfrac{7}{16} = 2.43\tfrac{12}{16} = 2.43\tfrac{3}{4} = 243\tfrac{3}{4}\%$$

or 244% to the nearest whole-number percent.

EXAMPLE: Change 3 to a percent.

SOLUTION: 3 = 3.00
3.00 = 300%

EXERCISE 60

Change the following percents to fractions.

1. 72%	2. $62\frac{1}{2}\%$	3. 40%
4. 55%	5. 120%	6. 8%
7. $137\frac{1}{2}\%$	8. $208\frac{1}{3}\%$	

Change the following fractions and mixed numbers to percents.

9. $\frac{3}{4}$	10. $\frac{5}{7}$	11. $\frac{11}{20}$
12. $\frac{5}{8}$	13. $1\frac{2}{3}$	14. $\frac{4}{9}$
15. $2\frac{4}{5}$	16. $3\frac{1}{6}$	

If you got 15 or 16 correct, go on to the next section on Finding a Percent of a Number. If you got more than one wrong, use Exercise 61 to build your skill.

EXERCISE 61

Change the following percents to fractions or mixed numbers.

1. 56% 2. $83\frac{1}{3}$% 3. 35%
4. $33\frac{1}{3}$% 5. 70% 6. 48%
7. 140% 8. 6% 9. $287\frac{1}{2}$%
10. $41\frac{2}{3}$% 11. $2\frac{1}{2}$% 12. 67%
13. 12% 14. 125% 15. $16\frac{2}{3}$%
16. 220%

Change the following fractions and mixed numbers to percents.

17. $\frac{8}{25}$ 18. $\frac{1}{4}$ 19. $\frac{17}{20}$
20. $\frac{3}{8}$ 21. $\frac{5}{6}$ 22. $\frac{2}{7}$
23. $1\frac{1}{3}$ 24. $\frac{4}{15}$ 25. $1\frac{2}{5}$
26. $\frac{7}{9}$ 27. $3\frac{7}{12}$ 28. $2\frac{4}{11}$
29. $1\frac{3}{5}$ 30. $\frac{2}{3}$ 31. $1\frac{1}{8}$
32. $2\frac{7}{10}$

Now be sure of your skill. Try Exercise 62.

EXERCISE 62

Change the following percents to fractions or mixed numbers.

1. 48% 2. $83\frac{1}{3}$% 3. 60%
4. 85% 5. 140% 6. 6%
7. $187\frac{1}{2}$% 8. $216\frac{2}{3}$%

Change the following fractions and mixed numbers to percents.

9. $\frac{4}{5}$ 10. $\frac{8}{9}$ 11. $\frac{3}{8}$
12. $\frac{7}{20}$ 13. $\frac{2}{7}$ 14. $1\frac{1}{3}$
15. $3\frac{3}{5}$ 16. $2\frac{1}{12}$

FINDING A PERCENT OF A NUMBER

To find a percent of a number, change the percent to a fraction or decimal, whichever is more convenient. Then multiply the given number by the fraction or decimal.

EXAMPLE: Find 37% of 84.

SOLUTION: 37%, written as a decimal, is 0.37.

$$\begin{array}{r} 84 \\ \underline{0.37} \\ 5\,88 \\ \underline{25\,2} \\ 31.08 \end{array}$$

EXAMPLE: Find $62\frac{1}{2}$% of 28.

SOLUTION: $62\frac{1}{2}$%, written as a fraction, is $\frac{5}{8}$.

$$\frac{5}{\underset{2}{\cancel{8}}} \times \frac{\overset{7}{\cancel{28}}}{1} = \frac{35}{2} = 17\frac{1}{2}$$

EXAMPLE: Find $4\frac{1}{2}$% of 68.

SOLUTION: $4\frac{1}{2}$%, written as a decimal, is 0.045.

$$\begin{array}{r} 68 \\ \underline{0.045} \\ 340 \\ \underline{272} \\ 3.060 = 3.06 \end{array}$$

EXAMPLE: Find 3.4% of \$48.12 to the nearest cent.

SOLUTION: 3.4%, written as a decimal, is 0.034.

$$\begin{array}{r} \$48.12 \\ \underline{0.034} \\ 19248 \\ \underline{14436} \\ 1.63608 = \$1.64 \end{array}$$

EXAMPLE: Find $116\frac{2}{3}$% of 4.5.

SOLUTION: $116\frac{2}{3}$%, written as a mixed number, is $1\frac{1}{6}$.

$$1\frac{1}{6} = \frac{7}{6}$$

$$\frac{7}{\underset{2}{\cancel{6}}} \times \frac{\overset{1.5}{\cancel{4.5}}}{1} = \frac{10.5}{2} = 5.25$$

EXERCISE 63

Find the following.

1. 23% of 56 2. 8% of 72
3. 63% of 12.5 4. $3\frac{1}{2}$% of 24
5. 118% of 48 6. $37\frac{1}{2}$% of 90
7. 2.8% of 140 8. $133\frac{1}{3}$% of 153
9. $\frac{3}{4}$% of 96 10. 79% of 18.4
11. 200% of 82 12. $4\frac{1}{2}$% of \$65.38 to the nearest cent

If you got 11 or 12 correct, go on to the next section on Finding What Percent One Number is of Another. If you got more than one wrong, use Exercise 64 to build your skill.

EXERCISE 64

Find the following.

1. 68% of 72
2. 43% of 115
3. 19% of 38.5
4. 27% of 46.8
5. 9% of 137
6. 76% of 114.2
7. 7% of 16.2
8. $5\frac{1}{2}$% of 78
9. $2\frac{1}{2}$% of 48.6
10. 127% of 66
11. 152% of 72
12. $33\frac{1}{3}$% of 112.2
13. $8\frac{1}{3}$% of 64
14. $\frac{3}{4}$% of 170
15. 12.8% of 95
16. $183\frac{1}{3}$% of 108
17. 175% of 84
18. $\frac{1}{2}$% of 628
19. 300% of 29
20. $\frac{1}{5}$% of 58
21. 76% of 14.2
22. $187\frac{1}{2}$% of 240
23. $4\frac{1}{4}$% of 80
24. 35% of 1.28
25. 5% of $37.23 to the nearest cent
26. 9% of $65.48 to the nearest cent
27. $3\frac{1}{2}$% of $87.64 to the nearest cent
28. $2\frac{1}{4}$% of $35.60 to the nearest cent

Now be sure of your skill. Try Exercise 65.

EXERCISE 65

Find the following.

1. 29% of 72
2. 6% of 48
3. 59% of 14.5
4. $4\frac{1}{2}$% of 38
5. 123% of 64
6. $62\frac{1}{2}$% of 76
7. $\frac{3}{4}$% of 160
8. $166\frac{2}{3}$% of 171
9. $\frac{1}{4}$% of 52
10. 83% of 26.4
11. 500% of 43
12. $3\frac{1}{2}$% of $32.74 to the nearest cent

FINDING WHAT PERCENT ONE NUMBER IS OF ANOTHER

To find what percent one number is of another, follow these steps:

1. Make a fraction with the first number as the numerator and the second number as the denominator.
2. Change this fraction to a decimal by dividing the numerator of the fraction by its denominator.
3. Write this decimal as a percent.

EXAMPLE: 48 is what percent of 60?

SOLUTION: $\frac{48}{60} = \frac{4}{5}$

$\frac{4}{5} = 80\%$

EXAMPLE: 17 is what percent of 39?

SOLUTION: $\frac{17}{39}$

$$\begin{array}{r} 0.43 \\ 39\overline{)17.00} \\ \underline{15\ 6} \\ 1\ 40 \\ \underline{1\ 17} \\ 23 \end{array}$$

$0.43\frac{23}{39} = 43\frac{23}{39}\%$

EXAMPLE: What percent of 74 is 90?

SOLUTION: $\frac{90}{74} = \frac{45}{37}$

$$\begin{array}{r} 1.21 \\ 37\overline{)45.00} \\ \underline{37} \\ 80 \\ \underline{74} \\ 60 \\ \underline{37} \\ 23 \end{array}$$

$1.21\frac{23}{37} = 121\frac{23}{37}\%$

FINDING A NUMBER WHEN A PERCENT OF IT IS GIVEN

In this case, we are given part of a number and are required to find the number. The part given may be expressed as a fraction, a decimal, or a percent.

EXAMPLE: One month a man found that he had saved 20% of his income. If he saved $414, what was his monthly income?

SOLUTION: 20% of income = $414

Since 20% = $\frac{1}{5}$, $\frac{1}{5}$ of income = $414

Therefore, total income or

$\frac{5}{5} = 5 \times 414 = \$2,070$

EXAMPLE: At a high school dance, $66\frac{2}{3}\%$ of the students attended. If 156 students attended, how many students were enrolled in the school?

SOLUTION: $66\frac{2}{3}\%$ of the students = 156

Since $66\frac{2}{3}\% = \frac{2}{3}$, $\frac{2}{3}$ of the students = 156

Therefore, $\frac{1}{3}$ of the students = 78

Total number or $\frac{3}{3} = 3 \times 78 = 234$ students.

Note that the same result could have been obtained by dividing 156 by $\frac{2}{3}$.

$$156 \div \frac{2}{3} = 156 \times \frac{3}{2} = 234 \text{ students}$$

EXAMPLE: Mr. Hunter bought a suit in a sale for \$63. This was $87\frac{1}{2}\%$ of the original price. What was the original price?

SOLUTION: $87\frac{1}{2}\%$ of the original price = \$63

Since $87\frac{1}{2}\% = \frac{7}{8}$, $\frac{7}{8}$ of the original price = \$63

Therefore, $\frac{1}{8}$ of the original price = \$9

Total number or $\frac{8}{8} = 8 \times \$9 = \$72$

Note that the same result could have been obtained by dividing \$63 by $\frac{7}{8}$.

$$\$63 \div \frac{7}{8} = \$63 \times \frac{8}{7} = \$72$$

In general, we may find a number when a percent of it is given by (*a*) changing the percent to a fraction or (*b*) dividing the given number by the fraction.

EXAMPLE: 24% of what number is 30?

SOLUTION: $24\% = \frac{24}{100} = \frac{6}{25}$

$$30 \div \frac{6}{25} = \frac{\overset{5}{\cancel{30}}}{1} \times \frac{25}{\cancel{6}} = 125$$

EXAMPLE: 21 is $83\frac{1}{3}\%$ of what number?

SOLUTION: $83\frac{1}{3}\% = \frac{5}{6}$

$$21 \div \frac{5}{6} = \frac{21}{1} \times \frac{6}{5} = \frac{126}{5} = 25\frac{1}{5}$$

EXERCISE 66

1. 18 is what percent of 24?
2. 28 is what percent of 40?
3. What percent of 32 is 22?
4. What percent of 44 is 36?
5. 54 is what percent of 40?
6. What percent of 53 is 79?
7. 18% of what number is 63?
8. 22.4 is 35% of what number?
9. $62\frac{1}{2}\%$ of what number is 35?
10. $133\frac{1}{3}\%$ of what number is 74?

If you got 18 or more correct, go on the following Practice Tests. If you got more than two wrong, use Exercise 67 to build your skill.

EXERCISE 67

1. 15 is what percent of 75?
2. 17 is what percent of 68?
3. What percent of 98 is 56?
4. What percent of 135 is 81?
5. 19 is what percent of 67?
6. 32 is what percent of 92?
7. 96 is what percent of 78?
8. 65 is what percent of 80?
9. What percent of 96 is 60?
10. 49 is what percent of 40?
11. 69 is what percent of 75?
12. What percent of 42 is 77?
13. 16% of what number is 17?
14. 45% of what number is 17.1?
15. $16\frac{2}{3}\%$ of what number is 17?
16. 98.7 is 47% of what number?
17. 95 is 125% of what number?
18. 64 is $66\frac{2}{3}\%$ of what number?
19. 51 is 68% of what number?
20. 45 is $112\frac{1}{2}\%$ of what number?

Now be sure of your skill. Try Exercise 68.

EXERCISE 68

1. 16 is what percent of 20?
2. 48 is what percent of 80?
3. What percent of 34 is 17?
4. What percent of 56 is 38?
5. 78 is what percent of 60?
6. What percent of 47 is 61?
7. 24% of what number is 84?
8. 37.8 is 45% of what number?
9. $37\frac{1}{2}\%$ of what number is 45?
10. $183\frac{1}{3}\%$ of what number is 132?

PRACTICE TEST 13

1. Find 35% of 250.
2. Write $\frac{3}{8}$ as a percent.
3. 16 is 40% of what number?
4. Write $12\frac{1}{2}\%$ as a fraction reduced to lowest terms.
5. What percent of 24 is 18?

6. Write 5% as a fraction reduced to lowest terms.
7. Find 83 $\frac{1}{3}$% of 384.
8. Write 0.2 as a percent.
9. 63 is 37 $\frac{1}{2}$% of what number?
10. Write 48% as a decimal fraction.
11. Write $\frac{7}{20}$ as a percent.
12. Write 3.4 as a percent.
13. What percent of 72 is 27?
14. What is $\frac{1}{2}$% of 40?
15. 60 is what percent of 48?
16. Write 16% as a fraction reduced to lowest terms.
17. Find 120% of 8.
18. Write $\frac{5}{12}$ as a percent.
19. What percent of 48 is 32?
20. Write 87 $\frac{1}{2}$% as a decimal fraction.
21. What percent of 72 is 12?
22. Write 0.245 as a percent.
23. Write 62 $\frac{1}{2}$% as a fraction reduced to lowest terms.
24. 18% of what number is 54?
25. Write 125% as a decimal fraction.
26. Find 6% of 350.
27. What is 4.2% of 85?
28. 2 $\frac{1}{2}$% of what number is 75?
29. Write $\frac{7}{9}$ as a percent.
30. 22.5 is what percent of 15?
31. 16 $\frac{2}{3}$% of what number is 3.2?
32. Find $\frac{3}{5}$% of 2,000.
33. 24 is what percent of 30?
34. Find 134 $\frac{1}{2}$% of 80.
35. Write 0.402 as a percent.
36. 28% of what number is 1.4?
37. Write $\frac{7}{200}$ as a percent.
38. Write 15 $\frac{1}{2}$% as a fraction reduced to lowest terms.
39. 42% of what number is 21?
40. Write 1.052 as a percent.
41. Find 112 $\frac{1}{2}$% of 48.
42. Write $\frac{8}{5}$ as a percent.
43. 16 is what percent of 2.5?
44. Write $\frac{17}{32}$ as a percent.
45. Find 42 $\frac{1}{2}$% of 200.
46. 96 is what percent of 72?
47. Write 137 $\frac{1}{2}$% as a fraction reduced to lowest terms.
48. Find 0.3% of 450.
49. 4 $\frac{1}{2}$% of what number is 2.7?
50. Write 0.0035 as a percent.

PRACTICE TEST 14

1. 68%, expressed as a decimal =

   (A) 68 (B) 0.068 (C) 6.8 (D) 0.68 (E) 680

2. 7 $\frac{1}{2}$%, expressed as a decimal =

   (A) 750 (B) 0.075 (C) 0.75 (D) 7 $\frac{1}{2}$ (E) 7.5

3. 125%, expressed as a decimal =

   (A) 1.25 (B) 125 (C) 0.125 (D) 12.5 (E) none of these

4. 0.92, expressed as a percent =

   (A) 0.92% (B) 0.092% (C) 92% (D) 9.2% (E) 920%

5. 0.06 $\frac{2}{3}$, expressed as a percent =

   (A) 66 $\frac{2}{3}$% (B) 67% (C) 6 $\frac{2}{3}$% (D) 0.06 $\frac{2}{3}$% (E) .6 $\frac{2}{3}$%

6. 0.35%, expressed as a fraction =

   (A) 3 $\frac{1}{2}$ (B) $\frac{7}{2000}$ (C) $\frac{5}{14}$ (D) $\frac{2}{7}$ (E) none of these

7. 83 $\frac{1}{3}$%, expressed as a fraction =

   (A) $\frac{7}{8}$ (B) $\frac{4}{5}$ (C) $\frac{8}{9}$ (D) $\frac{5}{6}$ (E) $\frac{5}{8}$

8. $\frac{3}{5}$, expressed as a percent =

   (A) 30% (B) 75% (C) 6% (D) $\frac{3}{5}$% (E) none of these

9. 1 $\frac{5}{8}$, expressed as a percent =

   (A) 162 $\frac{1}{2}$% (B) 1 $\frac{5}{8}$% (C) 183 $\frac{1}{3}$% (D) 175% (E) 137 $\frac{1}{2}$%

10. 12% of 95 =

    (A) 114 (B) 10.4 (C) 11.04 (D) 10.14 (E) 11.4

11. $3\frac{1}{2}$% of 218 =

    (A) 763 (B) 7.63 (C) 7.53 (D) 8.63 (E) 7.625

12. $116\frac{2}{3}$% of 84 =

    (A) 91 (B) 112 (C) 72 (D) 98 (E) 102

13. 48 is what percent of 60?

    (A) 125% (B) 48% (C) 60% (D) 75% (E) none of these

14. What percent of 36 is 48?

    (A) 75% (B) 125% (C) $133\frac{1}{3}$% (D) 80% (E) 130%

15. $87\frac{1}{2}$% of what number is 56?

    (A) 49 (B) 64 (C) 35 (D) 63 (E) none of these

16. $133\frac{1}{3}$% of what number is 96?

    (A) 72 (B) 128 (C) 144 (D) 120 (E) 160

PRACTICE TEST 15

1. 47%, expressed as a decimal =

   (A) 4.7 (B) 0.047 (C) 0.47 (D) 470 (E) 47

2. $3\frac{1}{2}$%, expressed as a decimal =

   (A) 3.5 (B) 350 (C) $3\frac{1}{2}$ (D) $1\frac{2}{5}$ (E) none of these

3. 140%, expressed as a decimal =

   (A) 140 (B) 1.40 (C) 14.0 (D) $1\frac{2}{5}$ (E) 1.04

4. 0.47, expressed as a percent =

   (A) 0.047% (B) 0.47% (C) 4.7% (D) 47% (E) 470%

5. $0.08\frac{1}{3}$, expressed as a percent =

   (A) $83\frac{1}{3}$% (B) 83% (C) $8\frac{1}{3}$% (D) 803% (E) 0.083%

6. 24%, expressed as a fraction =

   (A) $\frac{1}{4}$ (B) $\frac{6}{20}$ (C) $\frac{4}{12}$ (D) $\frac{1}{3}$ (E) none of these

7. $37\frac{1}{2}$%, expressed as a fraction =

   (A) $\frac{1}{6}$ (B) $\frac{3}{8}$ (C) $\frac{5}{12}$ (D) $\frac{5}{8}$ (E) $\frac{2}{5}$

8. $\frac{3}{4}$, expressed as a percent =

   (A) 80% (B) 85% (C) 70% (D) 75% (E) 90%

9. $1\frac{5}{6}$%, expressed as a percent =

   (A) $183\frac{1}{3}$% (B) 180% (C) $187\frac{1}{2}$% (D) 185% (E) 18.3%

10. 16% of 75 =

    (A) 120 (B) 11 (C) 102 (D) 12 (E) 110

11. $4\frac{1}{2}$% of 148 =

    (A) 66 (B) 6.66 (C) 660 (D) 5.66 (E) 5.76

12. $162\frac{1}{2}$% of 96 =

    (A) 15.6 (B) 146 (C) 14.6 (D) 156 (E) none of these

13. 32 is what percent of 40?

    (A) 75% (B) 70% (C) 80% (D) 125% (E) 150%

14. What percent of 44 is 55?

    (A) 120% (B) 80% (C) $36\frac{4}{11}$% (D) 130% (E) 125%

15. $66\frac{2}{3}$% of what number is 72?

    (A) 48 (B) 108 (C) 90 (D) 96 (E) 102

16. $112\frac{1}{2}$% of what number is 216?

    (A) 182.8 (B) 243 (C) 270 (D) 192 (E) 252

PRACTICE TEST 16

1. 81%, expressed as a decimal =

(A) 0.081 (B) 0.0081 (C) 0.81 (D) 81 (E) 8.1

2. $6\frac{1}{2}$%, expressed as a decimal =

(A) 6.5 (B) 0.065 (C) 65 (D) 0.65 (E) 6.05

3. 105%, expressed as a decimal =

(A) 1.5 (B) 105 (C) 10.5 (D) 1.50 (E) 1.05

4. 0.19, expressed as a percent =

(A) 1.9% (B) 109% (C) 19% (D) 190% (E) 0.19 %

5. $0.42\frac{1}{3}$, expressed as a percent =

(A) $0.42\frac{1}{3}$% (B) $42\frac{1}{3}$% (C) $423\frac{1}{3}$% (D) $4.2\frac{1}{3}$% (E) none of these

6. 48%, expressed as a fraction =

(A) $\frac{48}{50}$ (B) $\frac{12}{20}$ (C) $\frac{3}{8}$ (D) $\frac{12}{25}$ (E) $\frac{12}{18}$

7. $87\frac{1}{2}$%, expressed as a fraction =

(A) $\frac{8}{9}$ (B) $\frac{5}{6}$ (C) $\frac{7}{8}$ (D) $\frac{3}{4}$ (E) $\frac{5}{8}$

8. $\frac{2}{5}$, expressed as a percent =

(A) 40% (B) 20% (C) 25% (D) 250% (E) none of these

9. $1\frac{2}{3}$, expressed as a percent =

(A) $133\frac{1}{3}$% (B) 120% (C) 175% (D) $166\frac{2}{3}$% (E) $162\frac{1}{2}$%

10. 35% of 78 =

(A) 26.30 (B) 27.30 (C) 62.40 (D) 27.34 (E) 27.4

11. $6\frac{1}{2}$% of 132 =

(A) 85.8 (B) 7.58 (C) 0.858 (D) 14.52 (E) none of these

12. $183\frac{1}{3}$% of 54 =

(A) 18 (B) 99 (C) 102 (D) 90 (E) 104.8

13. 36 is what percent of 96?

(A) $33\frac{1}{3}$% (B) 35% (C) 40% (D) $37\frac{1}{2}$% (E) 42%

14. What percent of 32 is 56?

(A) 175% (B) $57\frac{1}{7}$% (C) 150% (D) 140% (E) none of these

15. $62\frac{1}{2}$% of what number is 40?

(A) 25 (B) 65 (C) 64 (D) 30 (E) 20

16. 120% of what number is 90?

(A) 108 (B) 75 (C) 72 (D) 180 (E) none of these

PRACTICE TEST 17

1. The sum of 3,070, 256, and 4,938 is:

(A) 8,164 (B) 7,264 (C) 7,164 (D) 8,264 (E) 8,254

2. When 697 is subtracted from 2,050 the result is:

(A) 1,453 (B) 1,363 (C) 1,353 (D) 1,463 (E) 1,443

3. The product of 385 and 79 is:

(A) 29,415 (B) 29,315 (C) 30,315 (D) 30,115 (E) 30,415

4. When 3,540 is divided by 6 the result is:

(A) 59 (B) 590 (C) 509 (D) 599 (E) none of these

5. When 13,357 is divided by 19 the result is:

(A) 703 (B) 73 (C) 730 (D) 7,003 (E) 733

6. The sum of 5.03, 2.79, 6.85 is:

(A) 13.67 (B) 14.57 (C) 13.57 (D) 15.67 (E) none of these

7. The difference between 80.13 and 29.87 is:

(A) 51.26 (B) 50.26 (C) 50.36 (D) 51.36 (E) 51.26

8. The sum of $\frac{3}{4}$ and $\frac{2}{3}$ is:

   (A) $\frac{5}{7}$ (B) $\frac{5}{12}$ (C) $\frac{1}{2}$ (D) $1\frac{5}{12}$
   (E) none of these

9. The difference between $3\frac{1}{4}$ and $1\frac{2}{5}$ is:

   (A) $2\frac{1}{9}$ (B) $1\frac{17}{20}$ (C) $2\frac{17}{20}$ (D) $1\frac{3}{5}$
   (E) $4\frac{1}{3}$

10. The product of $4\frac{2}{3}$ and $2\frac{1}{7}$ is:

    (A) $6\frac{3}{10}$ (B) $6\frac{17}{21}$ (C) $8\frac{2}{21}$ (D) $9\frac{2}{21}$
    (E) 10

11. When $\frac{2}{3}$ is divided by $\frac{5}{6}$ the result is:

    (A) $\frac{4}{5}$ (B) $\frac{5}{9}$ (C) $\frac{5}{4}$ (D) $\frac{3}{4}$ (E) $\frac{7}{9}$

12. $\frac{1}{3} \times 24 \times 6.03$ is equal to:

    (A) 120.06 (B) 434.16 (C) 49
    (D) 48.24 (E) none of these

13. The product of 36 and $15\frac{1}{2}$ is:

    (A) 540 (B) $540\frac{1}{2}$ (C) 558 (D) 548
    (E) $555\frac{1}{2}$

14. When $42.37 is divided by 17 the result correct to the nearest cent, is:

    (A) $24.90 (B) $2.49 (C) $2.50 (D) $249
    (E) $24.91

15. The product of 3.24 and 2.5 is:

    (A) 8.1 (B) 71 (C) 7.01 (D) 70.1
    (E) none of these

16. When 273.6 is divided by 7.2 the result is:

    (A) 0.38 (B) 3.8 (C) 380 (D) 38
    (E) 37

17. The product of 0.058 and 100 is:

    (A) 58 (B) 0.58 (C) 580 (D) 0.00058
    (E) 5.8

18. 40% written as a fraction reduced to lowest terms is:

    (A) $\frac{1}{2}$ (B) $\frac{40}{100}$ (C) $\frac{2}{5}$ (D) $2\frac{1}{2}$
    (E) none of these

19. $\frac{8}{25}$ written as a percent is:

    (A) 8% (B) 32% (C) 25% (D) 40%
    (E) 48%

20. 76.5 divided by 100 is equal to:

    (A) 7.65 (B) 7,650 (C) 0.0765
    (D) 0.765 (E) 765

21. 0.859 written as a percent is:

    (A) 0.859% (B) 8.59% (C) 85.9%
    (D) 859% (E) none of these

22. $\frac{1}{7}$ divided by 5 is equal to:

    (A) $\frac{5}{7}$ (B) $\frac{7}{5}$ (C) $\frac{6}{7}$ (D) $\frac{1}{35}$ (E) $1\frac{5}{7}$

23. 18% of 45 is equal to:

    (A) 81 (B) 810 (C) 0.63 (D) 8.01
    (E) none of these

24. 12 is what percent of 16?

    (A) 125% (B) 75% (C) 12% (D) 28%
    (E) 200%

25. 48 is 32% of what number?

    (A) 300 (B) 15.34 (C) $\frac{3}{200}$ (D) 150
    (E) 120

26. $3\frac{5}{9}$ divided by $2\frac{2}{3}$ is equal to:

    (A) 12 (B) $1\frac{1}{3}$ (C) $\frac{3}{4}$ (D) $10\frac{2}{3}$
    (E) none of these

PRACTICE TEST 18

1. The sum of 2,857, 406, and 5,793 is:

   (A) 7,956 (B) 8,056 (C) 8,146
   (D) 9,056 (E) 8,046

2. When 859 is subtracted from 3,020 the result is:

   (A) 2,741 (B) 3,241 (C) 2,141
   (D) 2,241 (E) 2,161

3. The product of 496 and 75 is:

   (A) 37,210 (B) 36,200 (C) 36,210
   (D) 5,952 (E) 37,200

4. When 4008 is divided by 8 the result is:

   (A) 51 (B) 501 (C) 510 (D) 500 (E) 520

5. The sum of 3.89, 2.05, and 7.14 is:

   (A) 12.98 (B) 13.98 (C) 12.08 (D) 13.08 (E) none of these

6. The difference between 65.03 and 49.18 is:

   (A) 15.95 (B) 16.85 (C) 16.95 (D) 25.85 (E) none of these

7. When 9,407 is divided by 23 the result is:

   (A) 490 (B) 409 (C) 49 (D) 419 (E) 4,090

8. The sum of $\frac{5}{8}$ and $\frac{5}{6}$ is:

   (A) $\frac{10}{14}$ (B) $\frac{5}{7}$ (C) $\frac{25}{48}$ (D) $\frac{10}{48}$ (E) $1\frac{11}{24}$

9. The difference between $5\frac{1}{4}$ and $2\frac{2}{3}$ is:

   (A) $3\frac{3}{7}$ (B) $3\frac{1}{12}$ (C) $2\frac{7}{12}$ (D) $3\frac{7}{12}$ (E) none of these

10. The product of $3\frac{2}{5}$ and $1\frac{1}{4}$ is:

    (A) $3\frac{2}{9}$ (B) $4\frac{1}{4}$ (C) $6\frac{2}{3}$ (D) $3\frac{1}{10}$ (E) $4\frac{1}{10}$

11. When $\frac{3}{8}$ is divided by $\frac{5}{6}$ the result is:

    (A) $\frac{3}{20}$ (B) $\frac{5}{16}$ (C) $\frac{4}{7}$ (D) $\frac{9}{20}$ (E) none of these

12. $\frac{3}{4} \times 36 \times 8.12$ is equal to:

    (A) 218.24 (B) 73.08 (C) 219.24 (D) 119.24 (E) 210.24

13. The product of 57 and $16\frac{1}{3}$ is:

    (A) $912\frac{1}{3}$ (B) $917\frac{1}{3}$ (C) 1,102 (D) 912 (E) none of these

14. When $58.03 is divided by 19 the result, correct to the nearest cent, is:

    (A) 35 (B) $3.05 (C) $3.06 (D) $3.15 (E) $3.47

15. The product of 4.85 and 3.6 is:

    (A) 16.46 (B) 17.406 (C) 1.746 (D) 17.46 (E) 0.1746

16. When 460.2 is divided by 11.8 the result is:

    (A) 309 (B) 390 (C) 39 (D) 3090 (E) none of these

17. The product of 7.8 and 100 is:

    (A) 78 (B) 780 (C) 7080 (D) 7,800 (E) 0.078

18. 35% written as a fraction reduced to lowest terms is:

    (A) $\frac{1}{3}$ (B) $\frac{7}{25}$ (C) $\frac{35}{100}$ (D) $\frac{7}{20}$ (E) $\frac{7}{30}$

19. $\frac{3}{7}$ written as a percent is:

    (A) 40% (B) $42\frac{6}{7}$% (C) 30% (D) 21% (E) 37%

20. 3.69 divided by 100 is equal to:

    (A) 0.369 (B) 369 (C) 36.9 (D) 0.0369 (E) none of these

21. 1.57 written as a percent is:

    (A) 1.57% (B) 0.0157% (C) 15.7% (D) 1,570% (E) 157%

22. $\frac{2}{3}$ divided by 9 is equal to:

    (A) $\frac{3}{2}$ (B) $\frac{2}{27}$ (C) 6 (D) $13\frac{1}{2}$ (E) $\frac{2}{3}$

23. 27% of 52 is equal to:

    (A) 14.04 (B) 4.78 (C) 15.41 (D) 15.04 (E) 14.14

24. 24 is what percent of 40?

    (A) 24% (B) 40% (C) 60% (D) 64% (E) 10.37

25. 144 is 72% of what number?

    (A) 2 (B) 103.68 (C) 20 (D) 200 (E) 10.37

26. $7\frac{2}{9}$ divided by $3\frac{1}{3}$ is equal to:

    (A) $2\frac{1}{6}$ (B) $2\frac{2}{3}$ (C) $21\frac{2}{7}$ (D) $4\frac{1}{9}$ (E) none of these

Common Units of Measure

The following tables of common units of measure should be memorized.

Measures of Length

12 inches = 1 foot
3 feet = 1 yard
36 inches = 1 yard
5,280 feet = 1 mile
1,760 yards = 1 mile

Measures of Weight

16 ounces = 1 pound
2,000 pounds = 1 ton

Liquid Measures

4 gills = 1 pint
16 ounces = 1 pint
2 pints = 1 quart
4 quarts = 1 gallon
8 pints = 1 gallon

Dry Measures

2 pints = 1 quart
8 quarts = 1 peck
4 pecks = 1 bushel
32 quarts = 1 bushel

Measures of Time

60 seconds = 1 minute
60 minutes = 1 hour
24 hours = 1 day
7 days = 1 week
30 days = 1 month (approx.)
12 months = 1 year

CONVERSION OF UNITS

Each of the relationships above can be expressed as unit fractions to help in conversion from one measurement to another

EXAMPLE: Convert 7 feet to inches.

SOLUTION: Since 12 inches = 1 foot, we can write either unit fraction $\frac{12\ in}{1\ ft}$ or $\frac{1\ ft}{12\ in}$.

Then to convert a measurement such as 7 feet to inches, just multiply by whichever unit fraction cancels the appropriate units. Then multiply by any number that appears on top and divide by any number that appears on the bottom.

$$7\ ft = \frac{7\ ft}{1} \times \frac{12\ in}{1\ ft} = (7 \times 12)in = 84\ in$$

EXAMPLE: Convert 112 ounces to quarts.

SOLUTION: The relationship, 16 ounces = 1 pint can be written $\frac{1\ pt}{16\ oz}$, and the relationship 2 pints = 1 quart can be written $\frac{1\ qt}{2\ pt}$. Therefore,

$$112\ oz = \frac{112\ oz}{1} \times \frac{1\ pt}{16\ oz} \times \frac{1\ qt}{2\ pt} = 3.5\ qt$$

EXAMPLE: Change 5 pounds to ounces.

SOLUTION: 16 ounces = 1 pound

$$\frac{5\ lb}{1} \times \frac{16\ oz}{1\ lb} = 80\ oz$$

EXAMPLE: Change 4 feet to inches.

SOLUTION: 12 inches = 1 foot

$$\frac{4\ ft}{1} \times \frac{12\ in}{1\ ft} = 48\ in$$

EXAMPLE: Find the number of ounces in 9 pints.

SOLUTION: 16 ounces = 1 pint

$$\frac{9\ pt}{1} \times \frac{16\ oz}{1\ pt} = 144\ oz$$

EXAMPLE: Change $3\frac{1}{2}$ hours to minutes.

SOLUTION: 60 minutes = 1 hour

$$\frac{3\frac{1}{2}\ hr}{1} \times \frac{60\ min}{1\ hr} = 210\ min$$

EXAMPLE: Change 66 inches to feet.

SOLUTION: 12 inches = 1 foot

$$\frac{66\ in}{1} \times \frac{1\ ft}{12\ in} = 5\frac{1}{2}\ ft$$

EXAMPLE: Change 124 ounces to pounds.

SOLUTION: 16 ounces = 1 pound

$$\frac{124\ oz}{1} \times \frac{1\ lb}{16\ oz} = 7\tfrac{3}{4}\ lb$$

EXAMPLE: Change 180 liquid ounces to quarts.

SOLUTION: 32 liquid ounces = 1 quart

$$\frac{180\ oz}{1} \times \frac{1\ pt}{16\ oz} \times \frac{1\ qt}{2\ pt} = 5\tfrac{5}{8}\ qt$$

EXAMPLE: Change 1,470 seconds to minutes.

SOLUTION: 60 seconds = 1 minute

$$\frac{1470\ sec}{1} \times \frac{1\ min}{60\ sec} = 24.5\ min$$

EXERCISE 69

Make the following changes.

1. 48 ounces to pounds
2. 3 feet to inches
3. 2 hours to minutes
4. 6 quarts to gallons
5. 33 inches to feet
6. 90 seconds to minutes
7. 4 pints to ounces
8. $1\frac{1}{2}$ miles to feet
9. 144 liquid ounces to quarts
10. $2\frac{1}{4}$ pounds to ounces

If you got 9 or 10 correct, go on to the next section on Operations with Units of Measure. If you got more than one wrong, use Exercise 70 to build your skill.

EXERCISE 70

Make the following changes.

1. 64 ounces to pounds
2. 40 ounces to pounds
3. 4 feet to inches
4. $2\frac{1}{2}$ feet to inches
5. 5 hours to minutes
6. $3\frac{1}{4}$ hours to minutes
7. 10 quarts to gallons
8. 14 quarts to gallons
9. 28 inches to feet
10. 21 inches to feet
11. 150 seconds to minutes
12. 100 seconds to minutes
13. 2 pints to ounces
14. 6 pints to ounces
15. $1\frac{1}{8}$ miles to feet
16. $2\frac{1}{4}$ miles to feet
17. 64 liquid ounces to quarts
18. 40 liquid ounces to quarts
19. $3\frac{1}{2}$ pounds to ounces
20. $5\frac{1}{4}$ pounds to ounces

Now be sure of your skill. Try Exercise 71.

EXERCISE 71

Make the following changes.

1. 32 ounces to pounds
2. 5 feet to inches
3. 3 hours to minutes
4. 9 quarts to gallons
5. 39 inches to feet
6. 150 seconds to minutes
7. 3 pints to ounces
8. $1\frac{3}{4}$ miles to feet
9. 112 liquid ounces to quarts
10. $3\frac{3}{4}$ pounds to ounces

OPERATIONS WITH UNITS OF MEASURE

It is sometimes necessary to perform the fundamental operations with common units of measures.

Addition

To add common units of measure, arrange the units in columns, add each column, and simplify the results.

EXAMPLE: Add 3 ft. 5 in., 4 ft. 6 in., and 2 ft. 7 in.

SOLUTION:

3 ft. 5 in.
4 ft. 6 in.
2 ft. 7 in.
9 ft. 18 in.

Since 12 in. = 1 ft., 9 ft. 18 in. = 9 ft. 12 in. + 6 in. = 10 ft. 6 in.

EXAMPLE: Add 5 hr. 12 min., 3 hr. 47 min., 2 hr. 35 min., and 4 hr. 38 min.

SOLUTION:

5 hr. 12 min.
3 hr. 47 min.
2 hr. 35 min.
4 hr. 38 min.
14 hr. 132 min. = 16 hr. 12 min.

Since 60 min. = 1 hr., 14 hr. 132 min. = 14 hr. 120 min. + 12 min. = 16 hr. 12 min.

EXAMPLE: Add 3 lb. 11 oz., 2 lb. 8 oz., and 1 lb. 7 oz.

SOLUTION:

```
3 lb. 11 oz.
2 lb.  8 oz.
1 lb.  7 oz.
------------
6 lb. 26 oz. = 7 lb. 10 oz.
```

Since 16 oz. = 1 lb., 6 lb. 26 oz. = 6 lb. 16 oz. + 10 oz. = 7 lb. 10 oz.

Subtraction

To subtract common units of measure, arrange the units in columns, and subtract each column, starting with the smallest unit. It is necessary to borrow if the number in the subtrahend is larger than the number in the minuend.

EXAMPLE: From 30 min. 12 sec. subtract 19 min. 47 sec.

SOLUTION:

```
30 min. 12 sec. = 29 min. 72 sec.
19 min. 47 sec. = 19 min. 47 sec.
---------------------------------
                  10 min. 25 sec.
```

EXAMPLE: Subtract 2 gal. 3 qt. from 6 gal. 1 qt.

SOLUTION:

```
6 gal. 1 qt. = 5 gal. 5 qt.
2 gal. 3 qt. = 2 gal. 3 qt.
---------------------------
               3 gal. 2 qt.
```

EXAMPLE: Subtract 3 yd. 2 ft. 11 in. from 9 yd. 1 ft. 3 in.

SOLUTION:

```
9 yd. 1 ft.  3 in. = 8 yd. 4 ft.  3 in. = 8 yd. 3 ft. 15 in.
3 yd. 2 ft. 11 in. = 3 yd. 2 ft. 11 in. = 3 yd. 2 ft. 11 in.
------------------------------------------------------------
                                          5 yd. 1 ft.  4 in.
```

Multiplication

To multiply common units of measure by a number, multiply each unit by the multiplier and simplify the result.

EXAMPLE: Multiply 3 lb. 9 oz. by 6.

SOLUTION:

```
 3 lb.  9 oz.
           6
-------------
18 lb. 54 oz. = 21 lb. 6 oz.
```

Since 16 oz. = 1 lb., 18 lb. 54 oz. = 21 lb. 6 oz.

EXAMPLE: Multiply 8 min. 29 sec. by 9.

SOLUTION:

```
 8 min.  29 sec.
              9
----------------
72 min. 261 sec.
  = 1 hr. 16 min. 21 sec.
```

Since 60 min. = 1 hr., and 60 sec. = 1 min., 72 min. 261 sec. = 1 hr. 12 min. + 4 min. 21 sec. = 1 hr. 16 min. 21 sec.

Division

To divide common units of measure by a number divide each unit by the divisor, starting with the largest unit. If a remainder is obtained in dividing, convert the remainder to the next smaller unit and add the result to the given number of smaller units. Continue the division.

EXAMPLE: Divide 8 ft. 6 in. by 3.

SOLUTION:

```
   2 ft. 10 in.
3)8 ft.  6 in.
  6 ft.
  ------------
  2 ft. 6 in. = 30 in.
                30 in.
```

The result is 2 ft. 10 in.

EXAMPLE: Divide 7 lb. 8 oz. by 4.

SOLUTION:

```
   1 lb. 14 oz.
4)7 lb.  8 oz.
  4 lb.
  ------------
  3 lb. 8 oz. = 56 oz.
                56 oz.
```

The result is 1 lb. 14 oz.

EXERCISE 72

1. Add 4 ft. 2 in., 3 ft. 7 in., and 8 ft. 5 in.
2. Add 6 hr. 28 min., 4 hr. 15 min., and 2 hr. 49 min.
3. Add 1 lb. 12 oz., 3 lb. 7 oz., and 5 lb. 5 oz.
4. Add 4 gal. 2 qt., and 2 gal. 3 qt.
5. Multiply 4 lb. 5 oz. by 7.
6. Multiply 5 min. 17 sec. by 8.
7. Multiply 4 yd. 2 ft. by 9.
8. From 6 lb. 15 oz. subtract 2 lb. 8 oz.
9. From 3 hr. 14 min. subtract 1 hr. 45 min.
10. From 2 gal. 1 qt. subtract 3 qt.

11. Divide 3 hr. 36 min. by 4.
12. Divide 15 lb. 8 oz. by 8.

If you got 9 or 10 correct, go on to the following Practice Tests. If you got more than one wrong, use Exercise 73 to build your skill.

EXERCISE 73

1. Add 3 hr. 8 min., 2 hr. 37 min., and 1 hr. 43 min.
2. Add 1 lb. 3 oz., 2 lb. 9 oz., and 5 lb. 11 oz.
3. Add 4 gal. 1 qt., 2 gal. 3 qt., and 3 gal. 2 qt.
4. Add 4 min. 8 sec., 3 min. 49 sec., and 5 min. 31 sec.
5. Add 2 ft. 5 in., 3 ft. 9 in., and 2 ft. 7 in.
6. Add 2 lb. 7 oz., 8 lb. 4 oz., and 3 lb. 11 oz.
7. Multiply 3 min. 43 sec. by 7.
8. Multiply 2 lb. 7 oz. by 5.
9. Multiply 2 hr. 34 sec. by 4.
10. Multiply 1 gal. 3 qt. by 9.
11. From 5 lb. 11 oz. subtract 2 lb. 3 oz.
12. From 3 hr. 14 min. subtract 1 hr. 37 min.
13. From 3 gal. 1 qt. subtract 1 gal. 2 qt.
14. From 17 min. 12 sec. subtract 5 min. 48 sec.
15. From 8 lb. 1 oz. subtract 3 lb. 8 oz.
16. Divide 8 hr. 56 min. by 4.
17. Divide 6 lb. 2 oz. by 7.
18. Divide 7 gal. 2 qt. by 3.
19. Divide 16 ft. 3 in. by 5.
20. Divide 10 yd. 2 ft. by 4.

Now be sure of your skill. Try Exercise 74.

EXERCISE 74

1. Add 3 ft. 4 in., 5 ft. 11 in., and 2 ft. 7 in.
2. Add 5 hr. 38 min., 7 hr. 25 min., and 1 hr. 57 min.
3. Add 2 lb. 4 oz., 3 lb. 5 oz., and 4 lb. 6 oz.
4. Add 1 gal. 3 qt. and 4 gal. 2 qt.
5. Multiply 6 lb. 8 oz. by 9.
6. Multiply 8 min. 37 sec. by 7.
7. Multiply 3 yd. 1 ft. by 8.
8. From 4 lb. 14 oz. subtract 1 lb. 10 oz.
9. From 4 hr. 12 min. subtract 1 hr. 53 min.
10. From 5 gal. 2 qt. subtract 1 gal. 3 qt.
11. Divide 2 hr. 39 min. by 3.
12. Divide 7 lb. 14 oz. by 9.

Time

Some examinations require you to find the time required to complete a job or the number of days between two calendar dates.

EXAMPLE: A carpenter started a job a 9:15 A.M. and completed it at 4:45 P.M. If she took 45 minutes for lunch, how many hours did it take the carpenter to complete the job?

SOLUTION: From 9:15 A.M. to 12:00 (noon) is 2 hours and 45 minutes, or $2\frac{3}{4}$ hours. From noon to 4:45 P.M. is 4 hours and 45 minutes, or $4\frac{3}{4}$ hours.

$$2\frac{3}{4} + 4\frac{3}{4} = 6\frac{6}{4} \text{ hours, or } 7\frac{1}{2} \text{ hours}$$

If we subtract the lunch time of $\frac{3}{4}$ hour, we have

$$7\frac{1}{2} - \frac{3}{4} = 6\frac{3}{4} \text{ hours}$$

It took the carpenter $6\frac{3}{4}$ hours to complete the job.

EXAMPLE: A man went on a business trip. He left on the morning of April 29 and returned home on the afternoon of May 16. How many nights was he away from home?

SOLUTION: He was away on the nights of April 29 and 30 as well as 15 nights in May. Thus, he spent 17 nights away from home.

EXERCISE 75

1. A boy borrowed a library book on September 26. The book had to be returned within two weeks. By what date did the book have to be returned?
2. A train running between Cedarville and Mountainville left Cedarville at 8:47 A.M. and reached Mountainville at 10:12 A.M. How many minutes did the trip take?
3. A plane leaves Miami at 4:35 P.M. and arrives at Boston at 7:05 P.M. How many hours did the trip take?
4. A cargo vessel left home port on August 25 and returned on December 7 of the same year. How many weeks was the boat away?
5. A movie showing starts at 8:50 P.M. and lasts 2 hours and 45 minutes. At what time is the showing over?

PRACTICE TEST 19

1. The number of feet in 18 in. is:

   (A) $\frac{2}{3}$ (B) 2 (C) 3 (D) $1\frac{1}{2}$ (E) $1\frac{1}{3}$

2. The number of pounds in 24 oz. is:

   (A) 2 (B) 3 (C) $\frac{2}{3}$ (D) $\frac{3}{4}$
   (E) none of these

3. The number of pints in a gallon is:

   (A) 4 (B) 8 (C) 2 (D) 16 (E) 10

4. The number of hours in 45 min. is:

   (A) $\frac{2}{3}$ (B) $1\frac{1}{2}$ (C) $\frac{5}{9}$ (D) $\frac{3}{4}$ (E) $\frac{5}{8}$

5. The number of ounces in $2\frac{1}{2}$ lb. is:

   (A) 50 (B) 40 (C) 24 (D) 32 (E) 38

6. The sum of 3 ft. 9 in. and 6 ft. 8 in. is:

   (A) 9 ft. 7 in. (B) 10 ft. 7 in.
   (C) 10 ft. 5 in. (D) 9 ft. 5 in.
   (E) none of these

7. The number of ounces in a 2 gal. jug is:

   (A) 256 (B) 128 (C) 32 (D) 64 (E) 250

8. When 2 hr. 57 min. is multiplied by 5 the result is:

   (A) 13 hr. 15 min. (B) 10 hr. 35 min.
   (C) 14 hr. 45 min. (D) 11 hr. 15 min.
   (E) none of these

9. The number of feet in 4 yd. 2 ft. is:

   (A) 6 (B) 14 (C) 8 (D) $4\frac{1}{2}$ (E) 12

10. When 3 lb. 8 oz. is subtracted from 5 lb. 1 oz. the result is:

    (A) 2 lb. 9 oz. (B) 1 lb. 11 oz.
    (C) 7 lb. 9 oz. (D) 2 lb. 7 oz.
    (E) none of these

11. The number of pounds in 76 oz. is:

    (A) $4\frac{1}{2}$ (B) $4\frac{2}{3}$ (C) $4\frac{3}{4}$ (D) $4\frac{1}{4}$
    (E) none of these

12. When 8 yd. 4 ft. is divided by 4 the result is:

    (A) 21 yd. (B) 21 ft. (C) 2 yd.
    (D) 2 yd. 1 ft. (E) 3 yd.

13. The sum of 1 hr. 14 min., 3 hr. 59 min., and 2 hr. 37 min. is:

    (A) 6 hr. 10 min. (B) 7 hr. 50 min.
    (C) 7 hr. 10 min. (D) 6 hr. 50 min.
    (E) none of these

14. The number of yards in 7 ft. 6 in. is:

    (A) 2 (B) $2\frac{1}{4}$ (C) $2\frac{2}{3}$ (D) $2\frac{1}{2}$
    (E) none of these

15. When 5 lb. 7 oz. is multiplied by 7 the result is:

    (A) 39 lb. (B) 35 lb. 7 oz.
    (C) 38 lb. 1 oz. (D) 37 lb. 1 oz.
    (E) 40 lb.

16. When 3 hr. 48 min. is subtracted from 6 hr. 20 min. the result is:

    (A) 3 hr. 28 min. (B) 2 hr. 32 min.
    (C) 10 hr. 2 min. (D) 3 hr. 32 min.
    (E) none of these

17. The number of minutes in $1\frac{1}{4}$ hr. is:

    (A) 45 (B) 75 (C) 62 (D) 125 (E) 80

18. The sum of 2 lb. 5 oz., 3 lb. 7 oz., and 6 lb. 11 oz. is:

    (A) 12 lb. 7 oz. (B) 12 lb. 11 oz.
    (C) 12 lb. 2 oz. (D) 13 lb. 2 oz.
    (E) none of these

19. The number of yards in $1\frac{1}{4}$ miles is:

    (A) 6,600 (B) 1,200 (C) 1,500
    (D) 2,200 (E) 2,000

20. When 6 hr. 30 min. is divided by 5 the result is:

    (A) 1 hr. 6 min. (B) 1 hr. 26 min.
    (C) 1 hr. 18 min. (D) 1 hr. 16 min.
    (E) none of these

PRACTICE TEST 20

1. The number of hours in 100 minutes is:

   (A) 1 (B) $1\frac{3}{4}$ (C) $1\frac{1}{2}$ (D) $1\frac{2}{3}$
   (E) none of these

2. The number of gallons in 50 pints is:

   (A) $12\frac{1}{2}$ (B) $6\frac{1}{4}$ (C) $12\frac{1}{4}$ (D) $6\frac{1}{2}$
   (E) none of these

3. The number of ounces in $3\frac{1}{4}$ pounds is:

 (A) 50 (B) 48 (C) 34 (D) 36
 (E) none of these

4. The number of feet in 30 inches is:

 (A) $2\frac{1}{4}$ (B) $1\frac{7}{8}$ (C) $2\frac{1}{2}$ (D) 3
 (E) none of these

5. The number of minutes in 140 seconds is:

 (A) $2\frac{1}{2}$ (B) $2\frac{1}{3}$ (C) $2\frac{1}{4}$ (D) $2\frac{2}{3}$
 (E) none of these

6. The number of pounds in 72 ounces is:

 (A) $7\frac{1}{5}$ (B) $4\frac{1}{4}$ (C) $4\frac{1}{3}$ (D) $4\frac{1}{2}$
 (E) none of these

7. The sum of 5 ft. 9 in. and 2 ft. 6 in. is:

 (A) 8 ft. 5 in. (B) 8 ft. 3 in.
 (C) 9 ft. 3 in. (D) 9 ft. 1 in.
 (E) none of these

8. When 2 lb. 11 oz. is multiplied by 8 the result is:

 (A) $20\frac{1}{2}$ lb. (B) $20\frac{1}{4}$ lb. (C) $21\frac{1}{2}$ lb.
 (D) $24\frac{1}{2}$ lb. (E) none of these

9. The number of inches in $3\frac{1}{4}$ feet is:

 (A) 40 (B) 39 (C) $38\frac{1}{2}$ (D) $36\frac{1}{3}$
 (E) none of these

10. When 2 hr. 52 min. is subtracted from 5 hr. 10 min. the result is:

 (A) 3 hr. 58 min. (B) 2 hr. 58 min.
 (C) 3 hr. 18 min. (D) 2 hr. 18 min.
 (E) none of these

11. The number of quarts in 2 gal. 1 pt. is:

 (A) 9 (B) 5 (C) $2\frac{1}{2}$ (D) $4\frac{1}{2}$
 (E) none of these

12. When 6 lb. 12 oz. is divided by 3 the result is:

 (A) $2\frac{1}{2}$ lb. (B) $2\frac{1}{3}$ lb. (C) $2\frac{1}{4}$ lb.
 (D) $2\frac{2}{3}$ lb. (E) none of these

13. The sum of 2 hr. 18 min., 3 hr. 43 min., and 1 hr. 19 min. is:

 (A) 6 hr. 20 min. (B) 6 hr. 48 min.
 (C) 7 hr. 40 min. (D) 7 hr. 20 min.
 (E) none of these

14. The number of feet in 3 yd. 8 in. is:

 (A) $9\frac{2}{3}$ (B) 11 (C) $6\frac{1}{2}$ (D) $9\frac{3}{4}$
 (E) none of these

15. When 3 lb. 9 oz. is multiplied by 6 the result is:

 (A) $21\frac{1}{2}$ (B) $23\frac{1}{3}$ (C) $19\frac{1}{3}$ (D) $21\frac{3}{8}$
 (E) none of these

16. When 5 ft. 8 in. is subtracted from 9 ft. 3 in. the result is:

 (A) 4 ft. 3 in. (B) 3 ft. 7 in.
 (C) 3 ft. 5 in. (D) 4 ft. 5 in.
 (E) none of these

17. The number of seconds in $3\frac{1}{4}$ minutes is:

 (A) 325 (B) 225 (C) 315 (D) 195
 (E) none of these

18. The sum of 3 lb. 9 oz., 2 lb. 6 oz., and 4 lb. 11 oz. is:

 (A) 10 lb. 8 oz. (B) 9 lb. 10 oz.
 (C) 10 lb. 6 oz. (D) 10 lb. 9 oz.
 (E) none of these

19. The number of yards in $2\frac{1}{5}$ miles is:

 (A) 2,250 (B) 3,960 (C) 3,872
 (D) 2,500 (E) none of these

20. When 7 hr. 30 min. is divided by 6 the result is:

 (A) 1 hr. 22 min. (B) 1 hr. 15 min.
 (C) 1 hr. 5 min. (D) 1 hr. 20 min.
 (E) none of these

The Metric System

The metric system is the system of measurement that is used in most European countries, and is also used extensively in scientific laboratories and in industry. The great advantage in using the metric system is that its units are related by powers of 10 and thus it resembles the decimal system.

The basic unit of **length** in the metric system is the *meter*. The meter is a bit larger than the yard.

1 meter = 39.37 inches approximately.

The *millimeter,* which is equal to $\frac{1}{1,000}$ of a meter, is often used in science to measure very small distances. 1 millimeter is approximately 0.04 inch. The *centimeter* is $\frac{1}{100}$ of a meter and is approximately 0.4 inch. The centimeter is useful in measuring short distances. The *kilometer* is used to measure long distances. The kilometer is approximately equal to $\frac{5}{8}$ of a mile. To sum up:

1 meter ≈ 39.37 inches
1 centimeter ≈ 0.4 inch
1 kilometer ≈ $\frac{5}{8}$ mile

The basic unit of **mass** in the metric system is the *gram*. The *milligram* is equal to $\frac{1}{1,000}$ of a gram and is often used in prescribing medicines. Since the gram is very small, the unit used most often in practical situations is the *kilogram*.

1 kilogram = 1,000 grams exerts a force due to gravity approximately 2.2 pounds

The basic unit of **liquid measure** in the metric system is the *liter*.

1 liter ≈ 1.1 quarts

EXAMPLE: The cost of a kilogram of butter is \$3.20. What is the cost of 700 grams of butter?

SOLUTION: 1 kilogram = 1,000 grams

$$700 \text{ grams} = \frac{700}{1000} \text{ kilograms} = \frac{7}{10} \text{ kilogram}$$

$$\frac{7}{10} \times \$3.20 = \$2.24$$

EXAMPLE: A city posts a speed limit of 48 kilometers per hour. What is the approximate speed in miles per hour?

SOLUTION: Since 1 kilometer ≈ $\frac{5}{8}$ of a mile, 48 kilometers per hour is

$$\frac{5}{8} \times 48 \approx 30 \text{ miles per hour.}$$

PRACTICE TEST 21

DIRECTIONS: Solve each of the following problems and then circle the letter that corresponds to the right answer.

1. Five kilograms exerts approximately how many pounds due to gravity?

   (A) 3 (B) 10 (C) 11 (D) 15 (E) 12

2. The distance between two cities in Europe is 96 kilometers. The approximate distance in miles is:

   (A) 50 (B) 48 (C) 156 (D) 90 (E) 60

3. A gallon of milk is approximately how many liters?

   (A) .5 (B) 4.4 (C) 2.5 (D) 3.6 (E) 4

4. One hundred centimeters is approximately equal to:

   (A) a quarter of a mile
   (B) a little more than a yard
   (C) a foot (D) 4 inches
   (E) 400 inches

5. If a man is 2 meters tall, his height in feet is approximately:

   (A) 6 (B) 5 (C) $6\frac{1}{2}$ (D) 7 (E) $5\frac{1}{2}$

6. Approximately how many grams exerts 1 pound of force due to gravity?

   (A) 450 (B) 150 (C) 1,000 (D) 500
   (E) 200

7. A motorist in Europe fills his tank with 50 liters of gasoline. About how many gallons is this?

   (A) 12 (B) $13\frac{3}{4}$ (C) 15 (D) 10 (E) 8

8. A plane in Italy flies at the rate of 600 kilometers per hour. About how fast is this, in miles per hour?

   (A) 300 (B) 500 (C) 250 (D) 450 (E) 375

9. A woman's mass is 52 kilograms. In pounds, this corresponds to:

   (A) 110 (B) 108 (C) 114 (D) 120 (E) 125

10. The distance along the right field foul line in a baseball field is marked 108 meters in length. In feet, this is about:

    (A) 354 (B) 300 (C) 420 (D) 320 (E) 375

11. One millimeter is equal to:

    (A) 10 centimeters (B) $\frac{1}{100}$ of a meter (C) $\frac{1}{10}$ of a centimeter (D) $\frac{1}{100}$ of a kilometer (E) $\frac{1}{1,000}$ of a kilometer

12. One milligram is equal to:

    (A) $\frac{1}{10}$ of a kilogram (B) 10 grams (C) $\frac{1}{10}$ of a gram (D) $\frac{1}{1,000}$ of a gram (E) $\frac{1}{100}$ of a kilogram

Ratio and Proportion

RATIO

When two quantities are compared by dividing one quantity by the other the comparison is called a *ratio*. A ratio may be expressed as a fraction or by the use of the symbol ":" (colon).

EXAMPLES:

Express the following as ratios:

1. \$5.00 to \$6.00	1. $\frac{5}{6}$ or 5:6
2. 3 hours to 7 hours	2. $\frac{3}{7}$ or 3:7
3. 4 ft. to 12 ft.	3. $\frac{4}{12} = \frac{1}{3}$ or 1:3
4. 9 lb. to 15 lb.	4. $\frac{9}{15} = \frac{3}{5}$ or 3:5

EXAMPLE: Express as a ratio 10 in. to 2 ft.

SOLUTION: Since the quantities must be expressed *in the same units of measure* we change 2 ft. to 24 in. The ratio is 10:24. Since a ratio is a fraction we may divide both 10 and 24 by the common factor 2 to obtain the result 5:12.

EXAMPLE: Express as a ratio 3 lb. to 9 oz.

SOLUTION: Before writing the ratio, we change 3 lb. to 48 oz. The ratio is 48:9. This may be reduced to 16:3.

EXAMPLE: Express as a ratio 3 days to 8 hours.

SOLUTION: Before writing the ratio, we change 3 days to 72 hours. The ratio is 72:8. This may be reduced to 9:1.

EXAMPLE: Express as a ratio $\frac{3}{8}$ to $\frac{15}{16}$.

SOLUTION:

$$\frac{3}{8} : \frac{15}{16} = \frac{3}{8} \div \frac{15}{16} = \frac{\overset{1}{\cancel{3}}}{\underset{1}{\cancel{8}}} \times \frac{\overset{2}{\cancel{16}}}{\underset{5}{\cancel{15}}}$$

This result may be written as 2:5.

EXAMPLE: Wilson High School defeated Lincoln High School at football by a score of 27 points to 18 points. What is the ratio of the number of points scored by Wilson High to the number of points scored by Lincoln High School?

SOLUTION:

$$\frac{\text{number of points scored by Wilson H.S.}}{\text{number of points scored by Lincoln H.S.}} = \frac{27}{18}$$

This result may be reduced to $\frac{3}{2}$ by dividing the numerator and denominator of the fraction $\frac{27}{18}$ by 9.

The result may be written as 3:2 or $\frac{3}{2}$.

PRACTICE TEST 22

1. The ratio of 7 to 9 is:

   (A) 9:7 (B) $\frac{9}{7}$ (C) 7:9 (D) $\frac{2}{9}$
   (E) none of these

2. The ratio of 12 to 16 is:

   (A) 2:3 (B) 3:4 (C) 4:3 (D) 3:2
   (E) 1 and $\frac{1}{3}$

3. The ratio 1:3 is equal to:

   (A) 3:12 (B) 9:3 (C) 6:12 (D) 3:1
   (E) 5:15

4. The ratio of 3.2 to 2.4 is:

   (A) 3:2 (B) 2:3 (C) 3:4 (D) 4:3
   (E) 2:1

5. The ratio of $\frac{5}{6}$ to $\frac{5}{12}$ is:

   (A) 25:72 (B) 72:25 (C) 1:2 (D) 2:1
   (E) none of these

6. The ratio of 4 yards to 2 feet is:

   (A) 4:2 (B) 2:1 (C) 1:6 (D) 1:4
   (E) none of these

7. The ratio of 20 minutes to $2\frac{1}{2}$ hours is:

   (A) 8:1 (B) 2:15 (C) 4:1 (D) 1:4
   (E) 1:7

8. A man had 12 dress shirts and 3 sport shirts. The ratio of sport shirts to dress shirts is:

   (A) 1:4 (B) 1:5 (C) 4:1 (D) 4:5
   (E) 5:4

9. A football team scored 12 points in the first half and 28 points in the second half. The ratio of the number of points scored in the first half to the total number of points is:

   (A) 3:7 (B) 7:3 (C) 7:10 (D) 3:10
   (E) 10:7

10. On a test, a pupil did 24 problems correctly and 6 problems incorrectly. The ratio of incorrect problems to correct problems is:

    (A) 4:1 (B) 1:5 (C) 1:4 (D) 5:1
    (E) none of these

PRACTICE TEST 23

1. The ratio of 15 to 2 is:

   (A) 15:17 (B) 15:2 (C) 2:15 (D) 13:2
   (E) none of these

2. The ratio 16:36 is equal to:

   (A) 4:9 (B) 4:5 (C) 9:4 (D) 5:4
   (E) 4:13

3. The ratio 1:7 is equal to:

   (A) 1:8 (B) 6:1 (C) 1:6 (D) 3:21
   (E) 28:1

4. The ratio of 4.8 to 4 is:

   (A) 12:1 (B) 3:10 (C) 1:12 (D) 2:1
   (E) 6:5

5. The ratio of $\frac{3}{8}$ to $\frac{5}{4}$ is:

   (A) 15:32 (B) 3:10 (C) 10:3 (D) 32:15
   (E) none of these

6. The ratio of 1 lb. to 6 oz. is:

   (A) 1:6 (B) 6:1 (C) 3:8 (D) 4:1
   (E) 8:3

7. The ratio of 10 in. to $1\frac{1}{2}$ ft. is:

   (A) 20:3 (B) 3:20 (C) 5:9 (D) 1:2
   (E) 10:1

8. Bill caught 9 fish and Henry caught 15 fish. The ratio of the number of fish caught by Bill to the number of fish caught by Henry is:

   (A) 3:8 (B) 3:5 (C) 8:3 (D) 2:3
   (E) none of these

9. A class has 18 boys and 12 girls. The ratio of the number of the girls to the number of boys is:

   (A) 3:2 (B) 2:5 (C) 5:2 (D) 3:4
   (E) none of these

10. A man bought a shirt for \$22.50 and a tie for \$12.50. The ratio of the cost of the tie to the total amount spent is:

    (A) 5:9 (B) 9:14 (C) 5:14 (D) 14:9
    (E) 1:3

PROPORTION

Let us consider the ratios 3:5 and 12:20. If we write these ratios in fraction form, we have $\frac{3}{5}$ and $\frac{12}{20}$. Now if we apply the Principle of Equivalency of Fractions, we have $3 \times 20 = 5 \times 12$. Thus, the fractions $\frac{3}{5}$ and $\frac{12}{20}$ are equivalent. We can also say that the ratios 3:5 and 12:20 are equivalent.

Thus, we may write 3:5 = 12:20. This statement is called a proportion.

DEFINITION

A *proportion* is a statement that two ratios are equivalent.

EXAMPLES: (*a*) 1:2 = 4:8
(*b*) 5:6 = 15:18
(*c*) $\frac{3}{8} = \frac{9}{24}$

Extremes and Means

In a proportion, the first and fourth numbers are called the *extremes* and the second and third numbers are called the *means*. In example (*a*) above, 1 and 8 are the extremes and 2 and 4 are the means. In example (*b*) above, 5 and 18 are the extremes and 6 and 15 are the means. In example (*c*) above, 3 and 24 are the extremes and 8 and 9 are the means. Thus, if we have a proportion $a:b = c:d$, then

extremes

$a:b = c:d$

means

Let us consider the following true proportions.

Proportion	Product of Means	Product of Extremes
2:3 = 4:6	3 × 4 = 12	2 × 6 = 12
3:7 = 9:21	7 × 9 = 63	3 × 21 = 63
4:3 = 12:9	3 × 12 = 36	4 × 9 = 36
10:16 = 5:8	16 × 5 = 80	10 × 8 = 80

Do you notice that, in a true proportion, the product of the means is equal to the product of the extremes? This principle will not hold in a proportion that is not true. This leads us to the following principle:

PRINCIPLE OF PROPORTIONS

In a proportion, the product of the means is equal to the product of the extremes.

EXERCISE 76

Use the Principle of Proportions to determine which of the following are true proportions.

1. 5:7 = 15:21
2. 9:4 = 17:10
3. 6:11 = 12:24
4. 18:12 = 51:34
5. 1.4:3.5 = 4.6:11.5
6. 56:32 = 49:28
7. 63:81 = 77:99
8. 14.5:29 = 8.7:17.4
9. 64:28 = 96:40
10. 58:74 = 174:222

It is often necessary to find the fourth member of a proportion when three members are known. Consider the proportion $3:4 = 6:y$. In this proportion, we know that the first three terms are 3, 4, and 6. We do not know the fourth term, which we have called y. If we use the Principle of Proportions we know that $3 \times y = 4 \times 6$, or $3y = 24$. You can see that if 3 times y is equal to 24, then y must be equal to 8. Now, let us replace y in the original proportion to obtain 3:4 = 6:8, a true proportion.

EXAMPLE: What number should replace n to make the following a true proportion?

$$5:6 = n:12$$

According to the Principle of Proportions

$$6 \times n = 5 \times 12$$
$$6n = 60$$
$$n = \frac{60}{6}$$
$$n = 10$$

EXAMPLE: What number should replace n to make the following a true proportion?

$$7:n = 9:20$$

According to the Principle of Proportions

$$9 \times n = 7 \times 20$$
$$9n = 140$$
$$n = \frac{140}{9}$$
$$n = 15\tfrac{5}{9}$$

EXERCISE 77

In each of the following, what number should replace n *to make each a true proportion?*

1. $n:5 = 6:10$
2. $n:4 = 12:8$
3. $3:n = 9:36$
4. $5:8 = 35:n$
5. $6:14 = n:7$
6. $17:n = 6:8$
7. $9:15 = 12:n$
8. $7:n = 11:18$
9. $12:28 = n:14$
10. $15:35 = 4:n$

Proportions are often useful in solving certain types of problems.

EXAMPLE: If 12 sport shirts cost $54, how much will 15 sport shirts cost at the same rate?

The ratio $\frac{54}{12}$ or 54:12 tells us how much each sport shirt costs. If we let n represent the cost of 15 sport shirts, then the ratio $n/15$ or $n:15$ also tells us how much each sport shirt costs. Since these ratios are equal we have

$$54:12 = n:15$$

According to the Principle of Proportions, we have

$$\begin{aligned} 12 \times n &= 54 \times 15 \\ 12n &= 810 \\ n &= \frac{810}{12} \\ n &= 67\tfrac{1}{2} \end{aligned}$$

Thus, the 15 sport shirts cost $67.50.

EXERCISE 78

1. If a dealer buys 24 pairs of shoes for $300, how much does he pay for a shipment of 36 pairs of shoes at the same rate?
2. If a carpenter's helper earns $704 for 8 days of work how much does he earn for 11 days of work at the same rate of pay?
3. If ballpoint pens sell for 3 for 65 cents how many pens may be bought for $9.75?
4. A motorist paid $11.88 for 8 gallons of gasoline. How much would she pay for 14 gallons of gasoline at the same rate?
5. A school pays $116.80 for a set of 32 textbooks. How much did the school pay for a set of 47 textbooks at the same rate?
6. A major league baseball player gets 81 hits in 96 games. How many hits will this baseball player get in 160 games if he continues to hit at the same rate?
7. A motorist uses 34 gallons of gasoline in traveling 629 miles. On another trip, he uses 42 gallons of gasoline at the same rate of use. How many miles did the second trip cover?
8. At a special sale, 392 TV sets were sold during the first $3\frac{1}{2}$ hours. How many sets were sold during the first $5\frac{1}{2}$ hours at the same rate?

Scales and Scale Drawing

Before a building is constructed, a plan is drawn on paper. On this plan each measurement in the building is reduced in size. For example, the length of a 30-foot hallway might be represented by a line 2 inches long. On the other hand, it is sometimes necessary to enlarge the drawing of an object. For example, in a dictionary the drawing of an ant might be 5 times the size of an ant. This process is called drawing to scale. The reduced or enlarged drawing is called a *scale drawing*.

A scale used on a drawing may be indicated in several ways.

EXAMPLES:

(*a*) 1″ = 5′
means that every inch on the drawing represents 5 feet in actual size.

(*b*) $\frac{1}{20}$ means that every measurement on the drawing is equal to $\frac{1}{20}$ of the actual size.

(*c*) 1:15 means that every measurement on the drawing is equal to $\frac{1}{15}$ of the actual size.

EXAMPLE: Using a scale of $\frac{1}{4}$ in. = 1 ft., how long is a line representing a distance of 16 ft.?

SOLUTION: Establish a proportion:

$$\frac{\frac{1}{4}\ in}{1\ ft} = \frac{n\ in}{16\ ft}$$

Cross multiply:

$$1 \times n = \frac{1}{4} \times 16 = 4$$

So a line 4 inches long represents a length of 16 feet.

EXAMPLE: On a scale drawing $\frac{1}{8}''$ = 60 miles. What is the distance represented by a line $2\frac{1}{4}''$ long?

SOLUTION: Establish a proportion:

$$\frac{\frac{1}{8}\ in}{60\ mi} = \frac{2\frac{1}{4}\ in}{n\ mi}$$

Cross multiply:

$$\frac{1}{8} \times n = 2\frac{1}{4} \times 60$$

$$\frac{1}{8} \times n = 135$$

$$n = 1080$$

So a line $2\frac{1}{4}$ inches long represents a length of 1080 miles.

PRACTICE TEST 24

1. The scale of miles on a certain map is 1 inch = 40 miles. The distance between two cities that are $3\frac{1}{4}$ inches apart on the map is:

   (A) 120 miles (B) $12\frac{4}{13}$ miles (C) 130 miles (D) 170 miles (E) none of these

2. A map is drawn to a scale of 12 miles = 1 inch. The distance represented by $5\frac{3}{4}$ inches is:

   (A) 60 miles (B) 68 miles (C) $2\frac{2}{23}$ miles (D) 69 miles (E) none of these

3. On a certain house plan a line 5 inches long represents 20 feet. The number of inches representing 30 feet is:

   (A) 4 (B) $7\frac{1}{2}$ (C) 6 (D) $3\frac{1}{3}$ (E) none of these

4. The picture of a moth in a dictionary is drawn to the scale 1:6. If the length of the moth in the picture is $\frac{3}{8}''$ the actual length of the moth in inches is:

   (A) 2″ (B) $2\frac{1}{8}''$ (C) $1\frac{7}{8}''$ (D) $2\frac{1}{2}''$ (E) none of these

5. The dimensions of a living room are 14′ by 22′. In drawing this room to scale the scale $\frac{1}{16}$ is used. The length of the room on the scale drawing is:

   (A) $1\frac{3}{8}''$ (B) $1\frac{1}{4}''$ (C) $\frac{5}{8}''$ (D) $1\frac{7}{8}''$ (E) none of these

6. The scale used on a map is 1 inch = 9 feet. This scale expressed as a ratio is:

   (A) 1:9 (B) 1:27 (C) 1:108 (D) 12:1 (E) none of these

7. The ratio used in making the scale drawing of a machine part is 1:24. The length of the part is 6 feet. The number of inches required to show this length is:

   (A) 4 (B) 6 (C) $2\frac{1}{2}$ (D) 3 (E) none of these

8. In printing the picture of a gnat the scale $\frac{32}{5}$ is used. If the picture is $\frac{1}{4}''$ long the actual length of the gnat is:

   (A) $1\frac{3}{5}''$ (B) $\frac{5}{128}''$ (C) $6\frac{2}{5}''$ (D) $\frac{1}{24}''$ (E) none of these

9. The scale used on a drawing is 1:15. This scale may be expressed as:

   (A) 1″ = 15 feet (B) 1 ft. = 54 miles (C) $\frac{1}{2}''$ = 25 miles (D) $\frac{1}{4}''$ = 6 miles (E) none of these

10. Two cities are 216 miles apart. The distance between them on the map is $4\frac{1}{2}$ inches. The scale used on this map is:

    (A) 1″ = 48 miles (B) 1″ = 54 miles (C) $\frac{1}{2}''$ = 25 miles (D) $\frac{1}{4}''$ = 6 miles (E) none of these

PRACTICE TEST 25

1. The scale of miles on a certain map is 1 inch = 36 miles. The distance between two cities that are $2\frac{3}{4}$ inches apart on the map is:

   (A) 100 miles (B) 96 miles (C) 99 miles (D) 98 miles (E) none of these

2. A map is drawn to a scale of 32 miles = 1 inch. The distance represented by $6\frac{5}{8}$ inches is:

   (A) 202 miles (B) 180 miles (C) 192 miles (D) 212 miles (E) none of these

3. On a blueprint a line 4 inches long represents 32 feet. The number of inches representing 80 feet is:

   (A) $6\frac{1}{2}$ (B) 8 (C) 12 (D) 16
   (E) none of these

4. The picture of a bookcase in a catalogue is drawn to the scale 1:18. If the length of the bookcase in the picture is $1\frac{1}{2}''$, the actual length of the bookcase is:

   (A) 2 ft. (B) $2\frac{1}{4}$ ft. (C) 20 in.
   (D) 30 in. (E) none of these

5. The dimensions of a garage are 20′ × 30′. In drawing this garage to scale the scale $\frac{1}{24}$ is used. The length of the garage on the scale drawing is:

   (A) $1\frac{1}{6}'$ (B) $1\frac{1}{8}'$ (C) $1\frac{1}{2}'$ (D) $1\frac{1}{4}'$
   (E) none of these

6. The scale used on a map is 1 inch = 8 feet. This scale expressed as a ratio is:

   (A) 1:96 (B) 1:8 (C) 1:32 (D) 1:12
   (E) none of these

7. The ratio used in making the scale drawing of a steel beam is 1:36. The length of the beam is 15 feet. The number of inches required to show this length is:

   (A) 36 (B) 10 (C) 5 (D) 8
   (E) none of these

8. In enlarging a picture the scale used is $\frac{8}{3}$. If the original picture is 9″ long, the length of the enlargement is:

   (A) $1\frac{1}{2}'$ (B) 2′ (C) 3′ (D) 8′
   (E) none of these

9. The scale used on a blueprint is 1:48. This scale may be expressed as:

   (A) 1″ = 48 ft. (B) 1 ft. = 4 ft.
   (C) 1″ = 16″ (D) 1″ = 4 ft.
   (E) none of these

10. Two cities are 420 miles apart. The distance between them on a map is $1\frac{3}{4}$ inches. The scale used on this map is:

    (A) 1″ = 735 miles (B) 1″ = 250 miles
    (C) 1″ = 240 miles (D) 1″ = 300 miles
    (E) none of these

Answers to All Exercises and Practice Tests

EXERCISES

EXERCISE 1

1. 4,006 3. 3,998 5. 4,457 7. 9,970
2. 3,135 4. 3,861 6. 3,838 8. 1,819

EXERCISE 2

1. 3,642 5. 3,975 8. 3,485
2. 3,871 6. 4,356 9. 10,272
3. 5,429 7. 5,203 10. 5,031
4. 3,685

EXERCISE 3

1. 4,647 3. 4,265 5. 3,875 7. 7,702
2. 4,464 4. 3,562 6. 3,813 8. 6,297

EXERCISE 4

1. 42,253 6. 60,078 11. 20,773
2. 27,851 7. 77,367 12. 73,187
3. 52,372 8. 23,598 13. 10,408
4. 34,846 9. 56,491 14. 1,943
5. 32,967 10. 78,351 15. 39,999

EXERCISE 5

1. 31,215 11. 47,499 21. 49,981
2. 61,648 12. 17,787 22. 53,449
3. 23,371 13. 43,459 23. 6,809
4. 14,748 14. 4,381 24. 82,275
5. 46,721 15. 44,299 25. 26,617
6. 78,272 16. 79,099 26. 38,363
7. 2,809 17. 70,205 27. 48,867
8. 26,307 18. 37,328 28. 48,314
9. 86,136 19. 35,411 29. 8,053
10. 22,533 20. 61,720 30. 7,428

EXERCISE 6

1. 31,313 6. 35,626 11. 20,164
2. 22,777 7. 23,514 12. 1,244
3. 48,221 8. 7,737 13. 2,997
4. 32,349 9. 13,805 14. 26,446
5. 8,507 10. 3,134 15. 63,108

EXERCISE 7

1. 40,901 5. 252,488 9. 516,168
2. 48,224 6. 237,650 10. 839,696
3. 51,336 7. 496,674 11. 2,702,040
4. 18,072 8. 439,600 12. 1,343,730

EXERCISE 8

1. 34,215 9. 110,789 17. 353,772
2. 52,227 10. 662,324 18. 1,062,490
3. 57,968 11. 290,871 19. 2,485,893
4. 35,686 12. 228,342 20. 3,617,972
5. 24,032 13. 182,952 21. 6,124,760
6. 7,242 14. 739,394 22. 3,042,424
7. 11,550 15. 211,102 23. 819,830
8. 10,410 16. 698,152 24. 4,851,924

EXERCISE 9

1. 56,106 5. 227,331 9. 1,089,536
2. 30,222 6. 298,450 10. 1,530,838
3. 20,072 7. 235,422 11. 1,748,120
4. 14,371 8. 491,760 12. 2,967,580

EXERCISE 10

1. 1,457 5. 343 9. 312 13. 467
2. 878 6. 200R11 10. 405R5 14. 238R3
3. 308 7. 97 11. 670R8 15. 704R34
4. 770R3 8. 314 $\frac{3}{29}$ 12. 593 $\frac{4}{87}$ 16. 395

EXERCISE 11

1. 579 13. 1,711R1 25. 173R19
2. 1,464 14. 130R7 26. 207R8
3. 911R1 15. 548R6 27. 736
4. 252 16. 300R3 28. 809
5. 579R3 17. 48 29. 612
6. 567 18. 37 30. 792
7. 960R1 19. 87 31. 836R26
8. 389R1 20. 83 32. 697R41
9. 1,148R6 21. 58R7 33. 697R103
10. 515R4 22. 304R16 34. 609R26
11. 1,684R4 23. 69R31 35. 752
12. 899R1 24. 78R5 36. 603

EXERCISE 12

1. 594
2. 671
3. 463R6
4. 1,175R3
5. 247
6. 175R5
7. 98
8. 87R46
9. 357
10. 411R24
11. 739R31
12. 947R5
13. 319
14. 537R87
15. 602R42
16. 465

EXERCISE 13

1. a. 8 b. $\frac{3}{8}$ c. $\frac{2}{8}, \frac{1}{4}$ d. $\frac{1}{8}$
2. a. 12 b. $\frac{1}{12}$ c. $\frac{3}{12}, \frac{1}{4}$ d. $\frac{4}{12}, \frac{1}{3}$
3. c. $\frac{1}{3}$
4. a. $\frac{5}{12}$ b. $\frac{1}{4}$ c. $\frac{5}{24}$ d. $\frac{1}{8}$
5. John Andrews— $\frac{5}{9}$
   Philip Verone— $\frac{1}{3}$
   Louis Sellers— $\frac{1}{9}$
6. $1\frac{1}{3}$
7. $1\frac{2}{3}$
8. $2\frac{1}{4}$
9. a. 9 b. $\frac{3}{9}, \frac{1}{3}$ c. $\frac{6}{9}, \frac{2}{3}$ d. $\frac{5}{9}$

EXERCISE 14

1. $\frac{1}{3}$
2. $\frac{2}{5}$
3. $\frac{3}{8}$
4. $\frac{3}{4}$
5. $\frac{3}{5}$
6. $\frac{8}{9}$
7. $\frac{3}{4}$
8. $\frac{4}{7}$
9. $\frac{3}{4}$
10. $\frac{7}{9}$
11. $\frac{4}{3}$
12. $\frac{19}{8}$
13. $\frac{27}{7}$
14. $\frac{23}{5}$
15. $\frac{49}{9}$
16. $\frac{31}{4}$
17. $1\frac{1}{4}$
18. $2\frac{1}{3}$
19. $2\frac{5}{6}$
20. $2\frac{1}{3}$
21. $3\frac{4}{9}$
22. $2\frac{5}{8}$

EXERCISE 15

1. $\frac{1}{2}$
2. $\frac{4}{5}$
3. $\frac{2}{3}$
4. $\frac{2}{3}$
5. $\frac{1}{2}$
6. $\frac{5}{7}$
7. $\frac{3}{4}$
8. $\frac{5}{6}$
9. $\frac{3}{5}$
10. $\frac{7}{8}$
11. $\frac{11}{16}$
12. $\frac{2}{5}$
13. $\frac{8}{9}$
14. $\frac{4}{7}$
15. $\frac{2}{3}$
16. $\frac{7}{11}$
17. $\frac{4}{9}$
18. $\frac{9}{10}$
19. $\frac{5}{7}$
20. $\frac{5}{7}$

1. $\frac{7}{4}$
2. $\frac{17}{6}$
3. $\frac{23}{7}$
4. $\frac{14}{5}$
5. $\frac{38}{9}$
6. $\frac{8}{7}$
7. $\frac{21}{8}$
8. $\frac{19}{3}$
9. $\frac{47}{6}$
10. $\frac{31}{8}$
11. $\frac{47}{11}$
12. $\frac{67}{12}$
13. $\frac{25}{9}$
14. $\frac{3}{2}$
15. $\frac{45}{7}$

EXERCISE 16

1. $\frac{1}{2}$
2. $\frac{1}{3}$
3. $\frac{5}{6}$
4. $\frac{7}{8}$
5. $\frac{4}{5}$
6. $\frac{5}{9}$
7. $\frac{3}{7}$
8. $\frac{5}{8}$
9. $\frac{7}{8}$
10. $\frac{5}{7}$
11. $\frac{5}{4}$
12. $\frac{17}{6}$
13. $\frac{31}{8}$
14. $\frac{23}{9}$
15. $\frac{11}{6}$
16. $\frac{19}{7}$
17. $3\frac{1}{6}$
18. $2\frac{1}{4}$
19. $1\frac{2}{9}$
20. $2\frac{2}{3}$
21. $7\frac{1}{3}$
22. $2\frac{1}{12}$

EXERCISE 17

1. $\frac{3}{6}$
2. $\frac{4}{12}$
3. $\frac{6}{8}$
4. $\frac{6}{15}$
5. $\frac{21}{24}$
6. $\frac{4}{16}$
7. $\frac{15}{36}$
8. $\frac{12}{20}$
9. $\frac{8}{28}$
10. $\frac{10}{12}$
11. $\frac{16}{24}$
12. $\frac{10}{18}$
13. $\frac{21}{27}$
14. $\frac{8}{40}$
15. $\frac{5}{15}$
16. $\frac{15}{21}$
17. $\frac{28}{48}$
18. $\frac{6}{9}$
19. $\frac{18}{42}$
20. $\frac{24}{30}$

EXERCISE 18

1. $\frac{3}{4}$
2. $\frac{5}{6}$
3. $\frac{7}{12}$
4. $\frac{5}{6}$
5. $\frac{1}{2}$
6. $\frac{11}{12}$
7. $1\frac{4}{15}$
8. $1\frac{7}{12}$
9. $\frac{19}{24}$
10. $1\frac{1}{2}$
11. $6\frac{1}{3}$
12. $10\frac{8}{15}$
13. $6\frac{1}{28}$
14. $1\frac{1}{12}$
15. $4\frac{17}{30}$
16. $7\frac{7}{16}$
17. $12\frac{11}{24}$
18. $12\frac{3}{5}$

EXERCISE 19

1. $\frac{2}{3}$
2. $\frac{7}{12}$
3. $\frac{11}{12}$
4. $\frac{5}{8}$
5. $\frac{23}{24}$
6. $\frac{7}{9}$
7. $\frac{13}{24}$
8. $\frac{3}{4}$
9. $\frac{23}{36}$
10. $\frac{3}{10}$
11. $\frac{23}{24}$
12. $\frac{13}{18}$
13. $1\frac{1}{4}$
14. $\frac{35}{36}$
15. $\frac{13}{14}$
16. $\frac{7}{20}$
17. $1\frac{17}{24}$
18. $1\frac{2}{15}$
19. $1\frac{7}{30}$
20. $1\frac{7}{24}$
21. $3\frac{2}{9}$
22. $9\frac{7}{10}$
23. $7\frac{2}{3}$
24. $7\frac{5}{6}$
25. $3\frac{19}{36}$
26. $10\frac{1}{9}$
27. $10\frac{5}{24}$
28. $8\frac{7}{20}$
29. $6\frac{4}{5}$
30. $7\frac{13}{14}$
31. $8\frac{2}{15}$
32. $8\frac{7}{36}$
33. $\frac{7}{8}$
34. $\frac{17}{18}$
35. $1\frac{11}{12}$
36. $1\frac{13}{24}$
37. $1\frac{19}{36}$
38. $6\frac{1}{12}$
39. $13\frac{29}{30}$
40. $12\frac{7}{18}$
41. $15\frac{47}{60}$
42. $14\frac{41}{48}$

EXERCISE 20

1. $\frac{5}{6}$
2. $\frac{5}{8}$
3. $\frac{11}{12}$
4. $\frac{7}{8}$
5. $\frac{9}{10}$
6. $\frac{17}{18}$
7. $1\frac{5}{12}$
8. $1\frac{1}{3}$
9. $1\frac{7}{36}$
10. $1\frac{9}{10}$
11. $5\frac{7}{12}$
12. $8\frac{3}{28}$
13. $10\frac{2}{15}$
14. $\frac{3}{4}$
15. $1\frac{7}{8}$
16. $7\frac{11}{12}$
17. $10\frac{11}{18}$
18. $11\frac{17}{20}$

EXERCISE 21

1. $\frac{3}{5}$
2. $\frac{1}{2}$
3. $\frac{5}{12}$
4. $\frac{11}{18}$
5. $\frac{1}{24}$
6. $\frac{5}{24}$
7. $3\frac{5}{6}$
8. $2\frac{1}{4}$
9. $3\frac{11}{24}$
10. $4\frac{13}{20}$
11. $5\frac{3}{4}$
12. $5\frac{2}{5}$
13. $\frac{7}{12}$
14. $4\frac{5}{6}$
15. $\frac{23}{36}$
16. $5\frac{9}{16}$

EXERCISE 22

1. $\frac{1}{3}$
2. $\frac{5}{9}$
3. $\frac{2}{3}$
4. $\frac{1}{4}$
5. $\frac{1}{2}$
6. $\frac{5}{8}$
7. $\frac{1}{12}$
8. $\frac{3}{10}$
9. $\frac{1}{6}$
10. $\frac{7}{12}$
11. $\frac{4}{9}$
12. $\frac{2}{15}$
13. $\frac{5}{14}$
14. $\frac{17}{36}$
15. $6\frac{2}{3}$
16. $2\frac{2}{5}$
17. $6\frac{3}{4}$
18. $4\frac{2}{3}$
19. $5\frac{17}{20}$
20. $1\frac{7}{12}$
21. $7\frac{3}{7}$
22. $\frac{5}{8}$
23. $\frac{5}{6}$
24. $\frac{7}{20}$
25. $3\frac{13}{18}$
26. $1\frac{11}{24}$
27. $\frac{25}{36}$
28. $\frac{16}{21}$
29. $1\frac{7}{12}$
30. $1\frac{17}{18}$
31. $\frac{9}{16}$
32. $1\frac{14}{15}$
33. $3\frac{17}{24}$
34. $\frac{7}{24}$
35. $4\frac{9}{14}$

EXERCISE 23

1. $\frac{4}{7}$
2. $\frac{3}{5}$
3. $\frac{1}{6}$
4. $\frac{5}{8}$
5. $\frac{1}{2}$
6. $\frac{1}{12}$
7. $\frac{11}{24}$
8. $4\frac{7}{8}$
9. $2\frac{3}{8}$
10. $4\frac{1}{2}$
11. $5\frac{11}{20}$
12. $\frac{7}{8}$
13. $5\frac{1}{3}$
14. $1\frac{13}{14}$
15. $\frac{11}{36}$
16. $4\frac{5}{12}$

EXERCISE 24

1. Equal
2. Equal
3. Unequal
4. Unequal
5. Equal
6. Unequal
7. Equal
8. Unequal
9. Equal
10. Equal
11. Equal
12. Unequal
13. Unequal
14. Equal
15. Unequal

EXERCISE 25

1. $\frac{1}{3}$ larger
2. $\frac{4}{9}$ larger
3. $\frac{6}{11}$ larger
4. $\frac{9}{16}$ larger
5. $\frac{5}{6}$ larger
6. $\frac{5}{13}$ larger
7. $\frac{9}{14}$ larger
8. $\frac{8}{9}$ larger
9. $\frac{12}{23}$ larger
10. $\frac{16}{25}$ larger
11. $\frac{7}{18}$ larger
12. $\frac{9}{31}$ larger
13. $\frac{9}{14}$ larger
14. $\frac{13}{29}$ larger
15. $\frac{14}{19}$ larger
16. $\frac{3}{8} < \frac{2}{5} < \frac{3}{4}$
17. $\frac{11}{20} < \frac{3}{5} < \frac{5}{8}$
18. $\frac{5}{9} < \frac{7}{12} < \frac{5}{6}$
19. $\frac{5}{8} < \frac{2}{3} < \frac{17}{24}$
20. $\frac{2}{9} < \frac{4}{11} < \frac{3}{8}$
21. $\frac{5}{8} < \frac{7}{9} < \frac{6}{7}$
22. $\frac{12}{17} < \frac{8}{11} < \frac{13}{16}$
23. $\frac{20}{41} < \frac{11}{21} < \frac{10}{19}$
24. $\frac{6}{17} < \frac{11}{31} < \frac{8}{19}$
25. $\frac{9}{32} < \frac{8}{27} < \frac{7}{23}$

EXERCISE 26

1. $\frac{3}{20}$
2. $\frac{5}{18}$
3. $\frac{3}{28}$
4. $\frac{3}{8}$
5. $\frac{2}{5}$
6. $\frac{3}{5}$
7. $\frac{1}{6}$
8. $\frac{2}{9}$
9. 2
10. 12
11. $9\frac{1}{3}$
12. 44
13. $\frac{3}{4}$
14. $6\frac{2}{3}$
15. 8
16. $3\frac{1}{3}$
17. 63
18. 45
19. $2\frac{3}{4}$
20. $4\frac{1}{6}$
21. 10
22. $12\frac{1}{2}$
23. $4\frac{1}{2}$
24. $3\frac{1}{2}$
25. $\frac{5}{14}$
26. $\frac{5}{9}$
27. $18\frac{2}{3}$

EXERCISE 27

1. $\frac{2}{21}$
2. $\frac{3}{10}$
3. $\frac{21}{40}$
4. $\frac{3}{20}$
5. $\frac{5}{8}$
6. $\frac{2}{5}$
7. $\frac{3}{14}$
8. $\frac{3}{4}$
9. $\frac{2}{5}$
10. $\frac{1}{6}$
11. $\frac{1}{8}$
12. $\frac{5}{16}$
13. $\frac{2}{5}$
14. $\frac{1}{18}$
15. $\frac{1}{6}$
16. $\frac{9}{14}$
17. 8
18. 8
19. 8
20. 12
21. $4\frac{1}{2}$
22. 9
23. $23\frac{1}{3}$
24. $31\frac{1}{2}$
25. $17\frac{1}{2}$
26. $16\frac{2}{3}$
27. $3\frac{3}{7}$
28. $4\frac{1}{6}$
29. $3\frac{6}{7}$
30. 3
31. $1\frac{2}{3}$
32. $\frac{7}{8}$
33. 30
34. $40\frac{1}{2}$
35. 32
36. 63
37. $22\frac{1}{2}$
38. 63
39. $12\frac{4}{7}$
40. $25\frac{1}{2}$
41. 3
42. $8\frac{2}{5}$
43. 42
44. $3\frac{1}{2}$
45. 6
46. $\frac{1}{30}$
47. 99
48. 30
49. $16\frac{8}{15}$
50. $\frac{5}{63}$
51. $2\frac{2}{8}$
52. 48
53. 15
54. $10\frac{2}{3}$

EXERCISE 28

1. $\frac{2}{15}$	8. $\frac{1}{6}$	15. 20	22. 6
2. $\frac{5}{21}$	9. 5	16. $5\frac{1}{3}$	23. $15\frac{5}{48}$
3. $\frac{3}{10}$	10. 15	17. 63	24. $6\frac{5}{12}$
4. $\frac{1}{6}$	11. $7\frac{1}{2}$	18. 28	25. $\frac{12}{25}$
5. $\frac{1}{6}$	12. $12\frac{1}{2}$	19. $\frac{7}{8}$	26. $\frac{5}{42}$
6. $\frac{7}{36}$	13. 10	20. 4	27. 6
7. $\frac{3}{11}$	14. 21	21. $4\frac{1}{6}$	28. 20

EXERCISE 29

1. $\frac{3}{5}$	6. $\frac{2}{21}$	11. $\frac{2}{9}$	16. $6\frac{2}{3}$
2. $\frac{6}{7}$	7. 12	12. $\frac{1}{8}$	17. $1\frac{1}{2}$
3. $\frac{3}{8}$	8. 18	13. $6\frac{1}{4}$	18. 8
4. $1\frac{1}{10}$	9. 30	14. 2	19. $2\frac{2}{3}$
5. $1\frac{1}{2}$	10. $\frac{1}{24}$	15. $1\frac{4}{5}$	20. $2\frac{7}{10}$

EXERCISE 30

1. $1\frac{1}{2}$	11. $1\frac{2}{9}$	21. 24	31. 8
2. $\frac{4}{5}$	12. $\frac{1}{8}$	22. $\frac{1}{24}$	32. 28
3. $\frac{5}{6}$	13. $\frac{3}{8}$	23. $\frac{1}{18}$	33. $2\frac{1}{10}$
4. $1\frac{7}{9}$	14. $\frac{2}{7}$	24. $\frac{2}{75}$	34. $\frac{3}{4}$
5. $\frac{2}{3}$	15. 24	25. $\frac{2}{7}$	35. $1\frac{5}{16}$
6. $1\frac{7}{18}$	16. 30	26. $\frac{3}{8}$	36. $7\frac{1}{2}$
7. $1\frac{1}{3}$	17. 35	27. $\frac{1}{5}$	37. $6\frac{1}{2}$
8. $\frac{6}{7}$	18. 54	28. $\frac{4}{27}$	38. $\frac{7}{10}$
9. $1\frac{1}{5}$	19. 44	29. 4	39. $1\frac{1}{9}$
10. $\frac{5}{8}$	20. $20\frac{1}{4}$	30. 15	40. $1\frac{4}{5}$

EXERCISE 31

1. $\frac{3}{4}$	6. $\frac{5}{14}$	11. $\frac{2}{25}$	16. $5\frac{5}{7}$
2. $1\frac{1}{4}$	7. 27	12. $\frac{1}{6}$	17. $1\frac{1}{2}$
3. $\frac{27}{50}$	8. 27	13. $4\frac{2}{3}$	18. $3\frac{1}{3}$
4. $\frac{3}{4}$	9. $17\frac{1}{2}$	14. 10	19. $1\frac{1}{2}$
5. $\frac{2}{3}$	10. $\frac{1}{16}$	15. 4	20. $3\frac{1}{8}$

EXERCISE 32

1. 6	2. $\frac{17}{30}$	3. $1\frac{1}{14}$	4. $\frac{11}{14}$

EXERCISE 33

1. 0.5	5. 0.67, 0.653, 0.619
2. 0.31	6. 0.721, 0.716, 0.712
3. 0.98	7. 0.237, 0.218, 0.2
4. 0.357	8. 0.467, 0.4102, 0.4009

EXERCISE 34

1. (a) 0.3 (b) 0.7 (c) 0.1 (d) 0.9 (e) 0.5 (f) 0.7 (g) 0.9 (h) 0.4 (i) 0.9 (j) 0.6
2. (a) 0.16 (b) 0.04 (c) 0.69 (d) 0.70 (e) 0.85
3. (a) 0.658 (b) 0.403 (c) 0.818 (d) 0.095 (e) 0.544
4. 0.416, 0.309, 0.295
5. 0.902, 0.875, 0.857
6. 0.713, 0.7, 0.605
7. 0.516, 0.492, 0.489
8. 0.41, 0.3, 0.128
9. 0.712, 0.7, 0.57
10. 0.914, 0.832, 0.823
11. 0.123, 0.096, 0.088

EXERCISE 35

1. 0.5	5. 0.47, 0.461, 0.418
2. 0.21	6. 0.391, 0.385, 0.319
3. 0.77	7. 0.602, 0.6, 0.59
4. 0.851	8. 0.7301, 0.7103, 0.7031

EXERCISE 36

1. 1.56	5. 123.43	9. 27.078
2. 15.37	6. 117.51	10. 206.542
3. 101.7	7. 0.34	11. 1.59
4. 200.228	8. 1.59	12. 32.743

EXERCISE 37

1. 2.29	13. 1,065.68	24. 0.19
2. 2.93	14. 1,084.66	25. 3.15
3. 19.34	15. 28.6	26. 4.55
4. 22.47	16. 21.2	27. 3.92
5. 154	17. 28.8	28. 2.84
6. 167.26	18. 26.35	29. 36.24
7. 195.21	19. 336.98	30. 36.86
8. 498.6	20. 231.57	31. 47.456
9. 800.81	21. 0.33	32. 36.892
10. 137.435	22. 0.34	33. 31.448
11. 140.029	23. 0.22	34. 772.48
12. 114.295		

EXERCISE 38

1. 1.57
2. 20.9
3. 106.3
4. 455.373
5. 129
6. 172.68
7. 0.24
8. 4.44
9. 58.785
10. 480.736
11. 1.77
12. 57.512

EXERCISE 39

1. 4.8
2. 6.3
3. 14.8
4. 2.32
5. 2.01
6. 39.95
7. 127.4
8. 537.2
9. 7.52
10. 22.42
11. 326.34
12. 3.45774
13. 4.90818
14. 0.487084
15. 0.18352

EXERCISE 40

1. 4.8
2. 6.3
3. 3.5
4. 3.2
5. 2.7
6. 2.1
7. 0.96
8. 17.94
9. 22.78
10. 46.02
11. 54.27
12. 265.5
13. 496.4
14. 295.2
15. 417.1
16. 168
17. 462.3
18. 153.7
19. 16.32
20. 57.12
21. 11.97
22. 0.1537
23. 0.3696
24. 108.08
25. 462.76
26. 222.5
27. 361.14
28. 106.912
29. 132.516
30. 312.823
31. 5.03568
32. 2.90194
33. 4.361178
34. 1.681823
35. 2.16918
36. 0.273
37. 7.9365
38. 0.30973

EXERCISE 41

1. 5.6
2. 5.4
3. 34.8
4. 2.73
5. 31.88
6. 28.88
7. 339.7
8. 753.3
9. 20.72
10. 32.43
11. 291.84
12. 293.664
13. 6.02883
14. 0.586404
15. 0.10368

EXERCISE 42

1. 4.8
2. 6.5
3. 17.6
4. 0.04
5. 83.4
6. 0.4
7. 189.9
8. 353.18
9. 0.35
10. 255.7
11. 11.91
12. 15.94
13. 15.73
14. 7.1
15. 0.33

EXERCISE 43

1. 3.63
2. 7.86
3. 8.56
4. 6.01
5. 7.7
6. 7
7. 5.2
8. 14.6
9. 1.1
10. 0.07
11. 0.13
12. 0.30
13. 52.6
14. 121.7
15. 0.4
16. 0.2
17. 120.6
18. 114.5
19. 170.2
20. 513.31
21. 1417.6
22. 0.79
23. 1.46
24. 32.6
25. 40.8
26. 71.2
27. 25.8
28. 16.85
29. 22.77
30. 21.36
31. 12.9
32. 15.5
33. 12.4
34. 0.29
35. 0.82

EXERCISE 44

1. 5.6
2. 6.2
3. 12.6
4. 0.04
5. 91.4
6. 0.5
7. 169.8
8. 453.26
9. 0.71
10. 78.6
11. 5.09
12. 349.48
13. 24.28
14. 6.7
15. 0.29

EXERCISE 45

1. 67
2. 580
3. 0.5
4. 7,360
5. 4.82
6. 320
7. 72.5
8. 35,600
9. 5.1
10. 6,590
11. 15
12. 34,000
13. 2,690
14. 85,000
15. 3,140
16. 8.5
17. 0.069
18. 0.0043
19. 6.872
20. 0.04951
21. 37.2
22. 0.784
23. 0.0372
24. 0.00016
25. 6.437
26. 9
27. 0.675
28. 0.00407
29. 0.05862
30. 0.000015

EXERCISE 46

1. 32
2. 580
3. 70
4. 6.8
5. 570
6. 0.35
7. 21.4
8. 605
9. 42.73
10. 2,850
11. 4.52
12. 28.3
13. 3,500
14. 68.05
15. 0.058

1. 620
2. 35,100
3. 1.2
4. 75,000
5. 15.72
6. 853.1
7. 0.039
8. 5.132
9. 400
10. 379
11. 127,500
12. 2
13. 6,500
14. 300.2
15. 2,710

1. 25,000 6. 21,700 11. 720
2. 6,480 7. 123 12. 0.35
3. 583,200 8. 15.34 13. 2,910
4. 1.6 9. 3,141.6 14. 50
5. 9.075 10. 62,500 15. 9,126

1. 5.8 6. 12.5 11. 0.00035
2. 40 7. 0.046 12. 853.2
3. 37.5 8. 25 13. 6.37
4. 0.0625 9. 0.002 14. 0.105
5. 8.75 10. 7.5 15. 578

1. 7.5 6. 2.97 11. 0.005036
2. 0.645 7. 35 12. 0.904
3. 0.00032 8. 0.00167 13. 86.1
4. 0.0873 9. 48.5 14. 0.0053
5. 0.000058 10. 0.0987 15. 0.6503

1. 5.3 6. 0.00314 11. 0.000025
2. 2.07 7. 0.00067 12. 0.06572
3. 0.00625 8. 0.002975 13. 0.00875
4. 0.000015 9. 0.075 14. 0.0000065
5. 0.952 10. 0.125 15. 0.000833

EXERCISE 47

1. 35 11. 58,000 21. 46.8
2. 6.9 12. 18 22. 0.583
3. 560 13. 6,200 23. 0.0697
4. 3.89 14. 3,870 24. 0.00018
5. 5,060 15. 57,000 25. 5.483
6. 46.3 16. 9.7 26. 0.315
7. 520 17. 0.0035 27. 4
8. 6.3 18. 0.048 28. 0.00873
9. 87,500 19. 0.06532 29. 0.04378
10. 7,340 20. 5.28 30. 0.000026

EXERCISE 48

1. $28.33 9. $2,475.72
2. $208.24 10. $2,487.86
3. $1,278.20 11. $940.53
4. $278.44 12. $11,170.36
5. $659.28 13. $120.46
6. $65.84 14. $56.09
7. $120.62 15. $1,016
8. $758.53 16. $305

EXERCISE 49

1. $172.89 5. $795.45
2. $808.75 6. $1,569.60
3. $2,003.40 7. $687.98
4. $856.71 8. $587.58

1. $1.68 5. $373.85
2. $4.82 6. $522.29
3. $36.73 7. $650.84
4. $20.42 8. $1,712.85

1. $4,550.21 5. $1,189
2. $4,057.52 6. $1,132.50
3. $2,446.73 7. $33,419.10
4. $2,523.24 8. $20,747.38

1. $103.42 5. $115
2. $224.21 6. $98
3. $216.51 7. $76
4. $35.03 8. $203

EXERCISE 50

1. $49.11 9. $3,522.24
2. $333.56 10. $3,735.56
3. $1,304.11 11. $1,981.32
4. $356.23 12. $8,878.93
5. $340.28 13. $77.13
6. $168.05 14. $119.38
7. $176.63 15. $209
8. $1,744.38 16. $267

EXERCISE 51

1. 0.25 7. 2.42 13. $\frac{7}{10}$ 19. $1\frac{1}{3}$
2. 0.6 8. 0.72 14. $\frac{1}{25}$ 20. $\frac{1}{8}$
3. 0.83 9. 0.64 15. $\frac{9}{20}$ 21. $\frac{1}{12}$
4. 0.38 10. 0.47 16. $2\frac{2}{5}$ 22. $\frac{1}{125}$
5. 0.29 11. 0.36 17. $\frac{5}{8}$ 23. $5\frac{3}{8}$
6. 0.78 12. 3.35 18. $\frac{49}{200}$ 24. $2\frac{5}{6}$

EXERCISE 52

1. 0.5 8. 0.7 15. 0.75
2. 0.2 9. 0.27 16. 0.21
3. 0.63 10. 3.13 17. 0.47
4. 0.33 11. 0.45 18. 0.86
5. 0.17 12. 0.27 19. 0.28
6. 0.43 13. 0.83 20. 0.16
7. 0.22 14. 2.08

1. $\frac{3}{10}$ 2. $\frac{9}{100}$ 3. $\frac{11}{100}$ 4. $\frac{13}{20}$ 5. $3\frac{4}{5}$
6. $\frac{11}{40}$ 7. $\frac{5}{6}$ 8. $\frac{9}{250}$ 9. $2\frac{1}{8}$ 10. $\frac{12}{25}$
11. $1\frac{1}{3}$ 12. $\frac{3}{8}$ 13. $2\frac{1}{4}$ 14. $2\frac{1}{6}$ 15. $3\frac{18}{25}$
16. $\frac{5}{8}$ 17. $4\frac{4}{5}$ 18. $2\frac{8}{25}$ 19. $2\frac{2}{3}$ 20. $5\frac{17}{20}$

EXERCISE 53

1. 0.4 2. 0.75 3. 0.88 4. 0.17 5. 0.56 6. 3.58
7. 0.89 8. 0.55 9. 1.53 10. 0.21 11. 2.24 12. 0.73
13. $\frac{9}{10}$ 14. $\frac{3}{50}$ 15. $\frac{17}{20}$ 16. $3\frac{4}{5}$ 17. $\frac{3}{8}$ 18. $3\frac{97}{200}$
19. $2\frac{2}{3}$ 20. $\frac{5}{12}$ 21. $\frac{9}{500}$ 22. $3\frac{5}{8}$ 23. $1\frac{1}{6}$ 24. $6\frac{16}{25}$

EXERCISE 54

1. 1.06 2. 0.965 3. 2.52 4. 5.48 5. 2.17 6. 4
7. 7.5 8. 43.2 9. $\frac{17}{30}$ 10. $1\frac{5}{18}$ 11. $5\frac{9}{10}$
12. $3\frac{1}{6}$ 13. $\frac{2}{25}$ 14. $28\frac{1}{2}$ 15. $33\frac{1}{3}$ 16. $33\frac{1}{3}$

EXERCISE 55

1. 1.29 2. 2.54 3. 5.28 4. 3.17 5. 6.69 6. 2.75
7. 6.51 8. 4.24 9. 4 10. 48 11. 14.1
12. $27\frac{1}{2}$ 13. 25 14. 75 15. 15 16. 24

1. $1\frac{7}{16}$ 2. $1\frac{5}{24}$ 3. $\frac{11}{15}$ 4. $1\frac{19}{60}$ 5. $8\frac{3}{4}$ 6. $4\frac{3}{10}$
7. $5\frac{3}{4}$ 8. $2\frac{1}{2}$ 9. $\frac{7}{25}$ 10. $\frac{2}{7}$ 11. $10\frac{2}{3}$
12. $33\frac{3}{4}$ 13. $33\frac{1}{3}$ 14. 50 15. $19\frac{1}{5}$ 16. 25

EXERCISE 56

1. 0.63 2. 0.45 3. 5.98 4. 3.84 5. $1\frac{23}{25}$ 6. 8
7. $47\frac{1}{2}$ 8. 120 9. 1.31 10. $\frac{23}{24}$ 11. $7\frac{1}{3}$
12. $4\frac{7}{40}$ 13. $\frac{9}{40}$ 14. $33\frac{1}{3}$ 15. 240 16. 6

EXERCISE 57

1. 0.73 2. 0.04 3. 0.8 4. 1.27 5. 0.075 6. 0.0325 7. 0.0275 8. 1.125
9. 0.043 10. 0.0025 11. 0.005 12. 0.0507 13. 48% 14. 8% 15. 30% 16. 207%
17. $13\frac{1}{2}$% 18. $383\frac{1}{3}$% 19. 2.5% 20. 0.9% 21. 650% 22. $408\frac{1}{3}$% 23. $187\frac{1}{2}$% 24. 0.4%

EXERCISE 58

1. 0.68 2. 0.47 3. 0.3 4. 0.9 5. 1.32 6. 1.65 7. 0.085 8. 0.045 9. 0.0125 10. 0.0525 11. 0.0875 12. 0.0675 13. 0.062 14. 1.245 15. 0.078 16. 1.445
17. 0.0075 18. 0.005 19. 0.0035 20. 0.064 21. 0.0708 22. 0.0025 23. 0.0318 24. 0.003 25. 62% 26. 38% 27. 2% 28. 70% 29. 509% 30. 27% 31. 305% 32. $8\frac{1}{2}$%
33. 609% 34. $24\frac{1}{2}$% 35. $237\frac{1}{2}$% 36. 6.7% 37. $783\frac{1}{3}$% 38. 8.9% 39. 0.2% 40. 740% 41. $304\frac{1}{2}$% 42. 0.7% 43. 390% 44. $112\frac{1}{2}$% 45. 0.5% 46. $806\frac{2}{3}$% 47. 780% 48. $317\frac{1}{2}$%

EXERCISE 59

1. 0.57
2. 0.08
3. 0.6
4. 1.49
5. 0.025
6. 0.0125
7. 0.0575
8. 1.285
9. 0.062
10. 0.005
11. 0.0125
12. 0.0308
13. 62%
14. 3%
15. 80%
16. 502%
17. $18\frac{1}{2}\%$
18. $217\frac{1}{3}\%$
19. 6.7%
20. 0.2%
21. 820%
22. $302\frac{1}{3}\%$
23. 262.5%
24. 0.9%

EXERCISE 60

1. $\frac{18}{25}$
2. $\frac{5}{8}$
3. $\frac{2}{5}$
4. $\frac{11}{20}$
5. $1\frac{1}{5}$
6. $\frac{2}{25}$
7. $1\frac{3}{8}$
8. $2\frac{1}{12}$
9. 75%
10. $71\frac{3}{7}\%$
11. 55%
12. $62\frac{1}{2}\%$
13. $166\frac{2}{3}\%$
14. $44\frac{4}{9}\%$
15. 280%
16. $316\frac{2}{3}\%$

EXERCISE 61

1. $\frac{14}{25}$
2. $\frac{5}{6}$
3. $\frac{7}{20}$
4. $\frac{1}{3}$
5. $\frac{7}{20}$
6. $\frac{12}{25}$
7. $1\frac{2}{5}$
8. $\frac{3}{50}$
9. $2\frac{7}{8}$
10. $\frac{5}{12}$
11. $\frac{1}{40}$
12. $\frac{67}{100}$
13. $\frac{3}{25}$
14. $1\frac{1}{4}$
15. $\frac{1}{6}$
16. $2\frac{1}{5}$
17. 32%
18. 25%
19. 85%
20. $37\frac{1}{2}\%$
21. $83\frac{1}{3}\%$
22. $28\frac{4}{7}\%$
23. $133\frac{1}{3}\%$
24. $26\frac{2}{3}\%$
25. 140%
26. $77\frac{7}{9}\%$
27. $358\frac{1}{3}\%$
28. $236\frac{4}{11}\%$
29. 160%
30. $66\frac{2}{3}\%$
31. $112\frac{1}{2}\%$
32. 270%

EXERCISE 62

1. $\frac{12}{25}$
2. $\frac{5}{6}$
3. $\frac{3}{5}$
4. $\frac{17}{20}$
5. $\frac{7}{5}$
6. $\frac{3}{50}$
7. $1\frac{7}{8}$
8. $2\frac{1}{6}$
9. 80%
10. $88\frac{8}{9}\%$
11. $37\frac{1}{2}\%$
12. 35%
13. $28\frac{4}{7}\%$
14. $133\frac{1}{3}\%$
15. 360%
16. $208\frac{1}{3}\%$

EXERCISE 63

1. 12.88
2. 5.76
3. 7.875
4. 0.84
5. 56.64
6. 33.75
7. 3.92
8. 204
9. 0.72
10. 14.536
11. 164
12. $2.94

EXERCISE 64

1. 48.96
2. 49.45
3. 7.315
4. 12.636
5. 12.33
6. 86.792
7. 1.134
8. 4.29
9. 1.215
10. 83.82
11. 109.44
12. 37.4
13. 5.33
14. 1.275
15. 12.16
16. 198
17. 147
18. 3.14
19. 87
20. 0.116
21. 10.792
22. 450
23. 3.4
24. 0.448
25. $1.86
26. $5.89
27. $3.07
28. $0.80

EXERCISE 65

1. 20.88
2. 2.88
3. 8.555
4. 1.71
5. 78.72
6. 47.5
7. 1.2
8. 285
9. 0.13
10. 21.912
11. 215
12. $1.15

EXERCISE 66

1. 75%
2. 70%
3. $68\frac{3}{4}\%$
4. $81\frac{9}{11}\%$
5. 135%
6. $149\frac{3}{53}\%$
7. 350
8. 64
9. 56
10. 55.5

EXERCISE 67

1. 20%
2. 25%
3. $57\frac{1}{7}\%$
4. 60%
5. $28\frac{24}{67}\%$
6. $34\frac{18}{23}\%$
7. $123\frac{1}{13}\%$
8. $81\frac{1}{4}\%$
9. $62\frac{1}{2}\%$
10. $122\frac{1}{2}\%$
11. 92%
12. $183\frac{1}{3}\%$
13. 106.25
14. 38
15. 102
16. 210
17. 76
18. 96
19. 75
20. 40

EXERCISE 68

1. 80%
2. 60%
3. 50%
4. $67\frac{6}{7}\%$
5. 130%
6. $129\frac{37}{47}\%$
7. 350
8. 84
9. 120
10. 72

EXERCISE 69

1. 3 lb.
2. 36 in.
3. 120 min.
4. $1\frac{1}{2}$ gal.
5. $2\frac{3}{4}$ ft.
6. $1\frac{1}{2}$ min.
7. 64 oz.
8. 7,920 ft.
9. $4\frac{1}{2}$ qt.
10. 36 oz.

EXERCISE 70

1. 4 lb.
2. $2\frac{1}{2}$ lb.
3. 48 in.
4. 30 in.
5. 300 min.
6. 195 min.
7. $2\frac{1}{2}$ gal.
8. $3\frac{1}{2}$ gal.
9. $2\frac{1}{3}$ ft.
10. $1\frac{3}{4}$ ft.
11. $2\frac{1}{2}$ min.
12. $1\frac{2}{3}$ min.
13. 32 oz.
14. 96 oz.
15. 5, 940 ft.
16. 11, 880 ft.
17. 2 qt.
18. $1\frac{1}{4}$ qt.
19. 56 oz.
20. 84 oz.

EXERCISE 71

1. 2 lb.
2. 60 in.
3. 18 min.
4. $2\frac{1}{4}$ gal.
5. $3\frac{1}{4}$ ft.
6. $2\frac{1}{2}$ min.
7. 48 oz.
8. 9,240 ft.
9. $3\frac{1}{2}$ qt.
10. 60 oz.

EXERCISE 72

1. 16 feet 2 inches
2. 13 hours 32 minutes
3. 10 pounds 8 ounces
4. 7 gallons 1 quart
5. 30 pounds 3 ounces
6. 42 minutes 16 seconds
7. 42 yards
8. 4 pounds 7 ounces
9. 1 hour 29 minutes
10. 1 gallon 2 quarts
11. 54 minutes
12. 1 pound 15 ounces

EXERCISE 73

1. 7 hours 28 minutes
2. 9 pounds 7 ounces
3. 10 gallons 2 quarts
4. 13 minutes 28 seconds
5. 8 feet 9 inches
6. 14 pounds 6 ounces
7. 26 minutes 1 second
8. 12 pounds 3 ounces
9. 10 hours 16 minutes
10. 15 gallons 3 quarts
11. 3 pounds 8 ounces
12. 1 hour 37 minutes
13. 1 gallon 3 quarts
14. 11 minutes 24 seconds
15. 4 pounds 9 ounces
16. 2 hours 14 minutes
17. 14 ounces
18. 2 gallons 2 quarts
19. 3 feet 3 inches
20. 2 yards 2 feet

EXERCISE 74

1. 11 feet 10 inches
2. 15 hours
3. 9 pounds 15 ounces
4. 6 gallons 1 quart
5. 58 pounds 8 ounces
6. 1 hour 19 seconds
7. 26 yards 2 feet
8. 3 pounds 4 ounces
9. 2 hours 19 minutes
10. 3 gallons 3 quarts
11. 53 minutes
12. 14 ounces

EXERCISE 75

1. October 10
2. 1 hr. 25 min.
3. 2 hr. 30 min.
4. 15 weeks
5. 11:35 P.M.

EXERCISE 76

1. True
2. False
3. False
4. True
5. True
6. True
7. True
8. True
9. False
10. True

EXERCISE 77

1. 3
2. 6
3. 12
4. 56
5. 3
6. $22\frac{2}{3}$
7. 20
8. $11\frac{5}{11}$
9. 6
10. $9\frac{1}{3}$

EXERCISE 78

1. $450
2. $968
3. 45
4. $20.79
5. $171.55
6. 135
7. 777 miles
8. 616 sets

PRACTICE TESTS

TEST 1

1. C	3. E	5. A	7. C	9. E
2. B	4. E	6. B	8. E	10. B

TEST 2

1. D	3. D	5. E	7. E	9. C
2. A	4. E	6. B	8. B	10. B

TEST 3

1. C	3. D	5. E	7. A	9. E
2. B	4. E	6. C	8. C	10. D

TEST 4

1. D	5. C	9. B	13. B
2. D	6. D	10. D	14. D
3. B	7. B	11. B	15. C
4. E	8. E	12. E	16. E

TEST 5

1. D	5. E	9. C	13. B
2. B	6. D	10. E	14. A
3. A	7. B	11. C	15. D
4. D	8. A	12. E	16. B

TEST 6

1. C	5. B	9. E	13. C
2. A	6. E	10. B	14. E
3. E	7. C	11. E	15. D
4. C	8. A	12. A	16. A

TEST 7

1. D	3. E	5. D	7. C	9. C
2. E	4. B	6. C	8. A	10. D

TEST 8

1. C	3. E	5. B	7. D	9. C
2. B	4. D	6. A	8. D	10. B

TEST 9

1. C	3. A	5. B	7. C	9. C
2. E	4. C	6. D	8. A	10. D

TEST 10

1. C	4. D	7. A	10. C	13. B
2. E	5. B	8. D	11. B	14. D
3. C	6. D	9. E	12. D	15. C

TEST 11

1. D	6. B	11. D
2. C	7. D	12. C
3. B	8. E	13. B
4. C	9. C	14. E
5. E	10. B	15. B

TEST 12

1. C	6. D	11. B
2. A	7. A	12. E
3. C	8. C	13. C
4. B	9. D	14. B
5. E	10. C	15. D

TEST 13

1. 87.5	18. $41\frac{2}{3}\%$	35. 40.2%
2. $37\frac{1}{2}\%$	19 $66\frac{2}{3}\%$	36. 5
3. 40	20. 0.875	37. $3\frac{1}{2}\%$
4. $\frac{1}{8}$	21. $16\frac{2}{3}\%$	38. $\frac{31}{200}$
5. 75%	22. $24\frac{1}{2}\%$	39. 50
6. $\frac{1}{20}$	23. $\frac{5}{8}$	40. 105.2%
7. 320	24. 300	41. 54
8. 20%	25. 1.25	42. 160%
9. 168	26. 21	43. 640%
10. 0.48	27. 3.57	44. $53\frac{1}{8}\%$
11. 35%	28. 3,000	45. 85
12. 340%	29. $77\frac{7}{9}\%$	46. $133\frac{1}{3}\%$
13. $37\frac{1}{2}\%$	30. 150%	47. $1\frac{3}{8}$
14. 0.2	31. 19.2	48. 1.35
15. 125%	32. 12	49. 60
16. $\frac{4}{25}$	33. 80%	50. 0.35%
17. 9.6	34. 107.6	

TEST 14

1. D	5. C	9. A	13. E
2. B	6. B	10. E	14. C
3. A	7. D	11. B	15. B
4. C	8. E	12. D	16. A

TEST 15

1. C	5. C	9. A	13. C
2. E	6. E	10. D	14. E
3. B	7. B	11. B	15. B
4. D	8. D	12. D	16. D

TEST 16

1. C	5. B	9. D	13. D
2. B	6. D	10. B	14. A
3. E	7. C	11. E	15. C
4. C	8. A	12. B	16. B

TEST 17

1. D	7. B	12. D	17. E	22. D
2. C	8. D	13. C	18. C	23. E
3. E	9. B	14. B	19. B	24. B
4. B	10. E	15. A	20. D	25. D
5. A	11. A	16. D	21. C	26. B
6. E				

TEST 18

1. D	7. B	12. C	17. B	22. B
2. E	8. E	13. E	18. D	23. A
3. E	9. C	14. B	19. B	24. C
4. B	10. B	15. D	20. D	25. D
5. D	11. D	16. C	21. E	26. A
6. E				

TEST 19

1. D	6. C	11. C	16. B
2. E	7. A	12. D	17. B
3. B	8. C	13. B	18. A
4. D	9. B	14. D	19. D
5. B	10. E	15. C	20. C

TEST 20

1. D	6. D	11. E	16. B
2. B	7. B	12. C	17. D
3. E	8. C	13. D	18. E
4. C	9. B	14. A	19. C
5. B	10. D	15. D	20. B

TEST 21

1. C	4. B	7. B	10. A
2. E	5. C	8. E	11. C
3. D	6. A	9. C	12. D

TEST 22

1. C	3. E	5. D	7. B	9. D
2. B	4. D	6. E	8. A	10. C

TEST 23

1. B	3. D	5. B	7. C	9. E
2. A	4. E	6. E	8. B	10. C

TEST 24

1. C	3. B	5. A	7. D	9. E
2. D	4. E	6. C	8. B	10. A

TEST 25

1. C	3. E	5. D	7. C	9. D
2. D	4. B	6. A	8. B	10. C

Application of Basic Mathematical Skills

Verbal Problems

THE BASICS

In solving verbal problems the student must:

1. Read the problem carefully.
2. Determine which facts are given.
3. Determine what must be found.
4. Decide upon a plan that will yield a solution.
5. Solve the problem.
6. Answer the question.

Using Addition

EXAMPLE: A fully loaded coal truck dumped 1,500 pounds of coal at house A and 2,530 pounds at house B. It then had 2,470 pounds left. If the truck when empty weighed 7,200 pounds, what was the weight of the truck when fully loaded?

SOLUTION: The weight of the fully loaded truck consisted of the weight when empty plus the weight of all the coal that was in the truck. We therefore add all the given weights.

$$\begin{array}{r} 1{,}500 \\ 2{,}530 \\ 2{,}470 \\ \underline{7{,}200} \\ 13{,}700 \end{array}$$

The weight of the truck fully loaded was 13,700 pounds.

PRACTICE TEST 1

1. A pole is made by glueing together pieces of wood measuring $6\frac{3}{4}$ inches, $19\frac{5}{6}$ inches, and $28\frac{2}{3}$ inches respectively. Find the length of the pole.
2. A man's bank balance reads \$128.72 after a \$23.38 withdrawal. Find the amount he had in the beginning.
3. The weight of chemical A is 6.29 grams more than that of chemical B. If chemical B weighs 17.3 grams, chemical A weighs how many grams?
4. The tax receipts of a certain city for 5 years were as follows: In 1987, \$7,426,725.23; in 1988, \$17,384,725.68; in 1989, \$11,889,979; in 1990, \$23,299,864.92; and in 1991, \$17,642,746.71. What was the total tax collection over the 5 years?
5. A tank holds $17\frac{3}{5}$ gallons after losing $36\frac{2}{3}$ gallons, $4\frac{5}{6}$ gallons, and $27\frac{7}{12}$ gallons in 3 consecutive days. If at the beginning the tank was $20\frac{3}{4}$ gallons short of capacity, what is the capacity of the tank?
6. The usual price of an electric stapler is \$49.75. One store sells the stapler for \$4.35 above the usual price, while a second store sells it at a discount of \$7.95. What is the difference in the prices set by the two stores?

Using Subtraction

EXAMPLE: Osna's bank deposits exceed Peggy's by \$3,679. If Osna has \$10,000 in the bank, how much does Peggy have?

SOLUTION: Peggy has less in the bank than Osna. We must therefore subtract from Osna's sum to find Peggy's.

$$\begin{array}{r} \$10{,}000 \\ \underline{-\quad 3{,}679} \\ \$\ 6{,}321 \end{array}$$

Peggy has \$6,321 on deposit.

PRACTICE TEST 2

1. Peg goes to the store and buys $1.84 worth of apples. How much change will she get from a five-dollar bill?

2. At the start of the trip Mr. Prest's speedometer read 23,214.3 miles. If the reading was exactly 25,000 miles at his destination, how many miles did he travel?

3. How much less does Bob earn than Bill, if Bill's salary is $62 and Bob's is $55.80?

4. How many more feet longer is a pipe that is $13\frac{5}{8}$ feet in length than one that is 6 feet 11 inches?

5. A truck that weighs 6,248 pounds when empty now weighs 13,440 pounds. What is the weight of its contents?

6. Last year Nancy weighed $37\frac{5}{8}$ pounds. This year she weighs 42.7 pounds. How much did she gain?

7. A radio lists for $37 but is sold for $29.98. What is the discount?

8. The population of New York City in a certain year was 7,892,463 and that of Los Angeles was 1,974,564. How much larger was New York's population?

9. The weight of chemical *A* is 6.29 grams more than that of chemical *B*. If chemical *A* weighs 17.3 grams, chemical *B* weighs how many grams?

Using Multiplication

EXAMPLE: A manuscript averages 36 words to a line and 24 lines to a page. There are 100 pages to the manuscript. If only $\frac{7}{8}$ of the words can be incorporated into a book, how many words will there be in the book?

SOLUTION: One line has 36 words. To find the words in 24 of these lines (one page), we multiply 24 by 36. Now that we have the words for one page, we multiply by 100 to find the words on all the printed pages. Since only $\frac{7}{8}$ of the words are to be included in the book, we multiply the result by $\frac{7}{8}$.

$$\frac{36}{1}\times\frac{\overset{3}{\cancel{24}}}{1}\times\frac{100}{1}\times\frac{7}{\cancel{8}}=75,600$$

The book will contain 75,600 words.

PRACTICE TEST 3

1. Stan earns $8.80 per hour for an 8-hour day's work. How much does he earn in a 5-day week?

2. Each battalion has 250 soldiers. A regiment consists of 12 battalions. A division has 10 regiments. How many soldiers are there in a division?

3. Each of Mrs. Bernstein's 4 boys averages $15.60 a week by delivering papers. How much do the 4 boys earn each week?

4. A boy cuts up a stick so that he has 16 pieces each $2\frac{3}{4}$ inches long. What was the original length of the stick if there was no waste in cutting?

5. May's rainfall was 0.52 inch. In June the rainfall was 0.13 as much. How much rain, in inches, fell in June?

6. Last year the city's revenue from taxes was $4,723,213. This year the revenue is 0.78 as much. What is the revenue this year?

7. What is the weight of 320 jars if each weighs 3 pounds 2 ounces?

8. How many feet of cloth are needed to manufacture 48 shirts if each shirt requires $2\frac{1}{3}$ yards of the cloth?

9. How far does Judy travel in $2\frac{3}{4}$ hours if she travels at the rate of $5\frac{1}{2}$ miles per hour?

10. A cricket chirps 15 times a minute. How many chirps will it give forth in 2 hours?

11. A car averages 16.8 miles per gallon and uses 265 gallons traveling cross-country. What was the distance the car traveled?

12. A map scale reads 1 inch = 200 miles. How many miles are represented by a line 44 inches long?

Using Division

EXAMPLE: A school has 3,698 children. If there are 86 classrooms in the school, what is the average number of students in each classroom?

SOLUTION: To find the number of students in one classroom, we divide the number of children in the school by the number of classrooms.

$$\begin{array}{r} 43 \\ 86\overline{)3,698} \\ \underline{344} \\ 258 \\ \underline{258} \end{array}$$

There is an average of 43 students per classroom.

EXAMPLE: A vat holds 695 gallons. If the contents are used to fill flasks each of which has the capacity of $2\frac{1}{2}$ gallons, how many flasks can be filled?

SOLUTION: Each flask holds $2\frac{1}{2}$ gallons. To find how many "$2\frac{1}{2}$ gallons" are contained in 695 gallons, we divide 695 by $2\frac{1}{2}$.

$$695 \div 2\frac{1}{2} = 695 \div \frac{5}{2} = \frac{\overset{139}{\cancel{695}}}{1} \times \frac{2}{\underset{1}{\cancel{5}}} = 278$$

The number of flasks that can be filled is 278.

PRACTICE TEST 4

1. Phyllis's mother has 6 pounds of candy to divide evenly among her 8 children. This is an average of how many pounds per child?

2. Mr. O'Neill's fence is 425 feet long. How many yards long is it?

3. How many school rooms are needed for 595 children, if each room can hold 35 children?

4. How many $\frac{3}{8}$-inch strips of cloth can a tailor cut out of a piece of cloth 48 inches long?

5. If notebooks cost $15.00 a dozen, what is the price for one?

6. Each bolt weighs 0.14 gram. How many bolts are there in a batch that weighs 50.4 grams?

7. In $2\frac{3}{4}$ hours Steve traveled $1\frac{1}{2}$ miles. What was his rate in miles per hour?

8. Mrs. Colson bought a TV set for $\frac{4}{5}$ of its original value. If she paid $80 for the set, what did it cost originally?

9. Evelyn buys 24 pounds of chocolate and packs it into $\frac{3}{4}$-pound packages. How many packages can she make?

10. Light travels 186,000 miles a second. How long, to the nearest hundredth of a second, will it take a ray of light to travel from the earth to the moon if the approximate distance between them is 242,000 miles?

Using Mixed Operations

EXAMPLE: A plane started a flight at 7:30 A.M. and arrived at its destination at 11:45 A.M. The distance covered was 612 miles. What was the average rate of speed of the plane?

SOLUTION: In order to find the average rate of speed we must divide the distance covered by the time spent. The distance covered is 612 miles. The time spent may be found by subtracting 7:30 from 11:45.

$$\begin{array}{rr} & 11{:}45 \\ & \underline{7{:}30} \\ \text{Time spent} = & 4{:}15 \text{ or } 4\frac{1}{4} \text{ hours} \end{array}$$

$$612 \div 4\frac{1}{4} = 612 \div \frac{17}{4} = \overset{36}{\cancel{612}} \times \frac{4}{\cancel{17}} = 144$$

The average rate of speed was 144 miles per hour.

EXAMPLE: A gas station operator's gasoline sales for one week were as follows: Monday, 255 gallons; Tuesday, 280 gallons; Wednesday, 235 gallons; Thursday, 375 gallons; Friday, 370 gallons; Saturday, 465 gallons; Sunday, 690 gallons. He paid $117 for 100 gallons of the gasoline and sold it at 6 gallons for $9.15. What was his profit for the week?

SOLUTION: The number of gallons sold may be found by adding: 255 + 280 + 235 + 375 + 370 + 465 + 690 = 2,670 gallons. The cost of $117 per 100 gallons may be regarded as $1.17 per gallon.

If we multiply 2,670 by $1.17, we obtain $3,123.90, the total cost.

To find the selling price we can calculate the number of 6-gallon units in 2,670 gallons by dividing 2,670 by 6. The result is 445.

Since each 6-gallon unit was sold for $9.15, the total selling price is $9.15 × 445 = $4,071.75.

Profit = Selling price – Cost
= $4,071.75 – $3,123.90
= $947.85

EXAMPLE: A man worked as follows during a week: Monday, 8 hr. 45 min.; Tuesday, 9 hr.; Wednesday, 8 hr. 50 min.; Thursday, 9 hr. 35 min.; Friday, 9 hr. 40 min.; Saturday, 5 hr. 40 min. He earned $8.80 an hour for each of the first 40 hours and $13.20 for each additional hour over 40 hours that he worked. What were his total earnings for the week?

SOLUTION: Total time the man worked may be obtained as follows:

8 hr. 45 min.
9 hr.
8 hr. 50 min.
9 hr. 35 min.
9 hr. 40 min.
5 hr. 40 min.
48 hr. 210 min.

= 48 hr. + 180 min. + 30 min.
= 51 hr. 30 min. = $51\frac{1}{2}$ hr.

At $8.80 for 40 hr., earnings = $352.00
At $13.20 for $11\frac{1}{2}$ hr., earnings = $151.80
Total earnings = $503.80

EXAMPLE: A farmer had some chickens to sell. On August 15 they weighed 240 pounds and could have been sold at $0.42 a pound. He kept them until October 1 and fed them at a cost of $18. He then sold them, a total weight of 265 pounds, at $0.48 a pound. How much did he gain or lose by keeping them?

SOLUTION: On August 15, he could have sold 240 pounds of chicken at $0.42 a pound for a total of $100.80.

On October 1, he sold 265 pounds of chicken at $0.48 a pound for a total of $127.20. From this must be deducted expenses of $18, leaving $109.20.

By keeping the chickens until October 1 he gained $109.20 – $100.80 = $8.40.

EXAMPLE: A boy's club with a membership of 22 decides to go camping for one week. The estimated expenses are as follows: transportation $115, rent for the camp $132, food $295, incidentals $74. The boys have $88 in the treasury and vote to raise the balance necessary by taxing each member an equal amount.

(a) What will their total expenses be?
(b) How much must be raised by taxing the members?
(c) How much must each member be taxed?

SOLUTION:

(a) The expenses may be found by adding:
$115 + $132 + $295 + $74 = $616.
(b) The amount needed by taxing the members is $616 – $88 = $528.
(c) To find the tax per member we must divide the total tax of $528 by 22. The result is $24.

EXAMPLE: During December and January, Bill, Tom, and Dick shoveled snow from the sidewalks in front of several stores. They agreed to divide their pay according to the number of hours each worked. Bill worked 6 hours. Tom worked 15 hours, and Dick worked 9 hours. They received $135 for their work. How much did each boy receive?

SOLUTION: Since Bill contributed 6 parts, Tom 15 parts, and Dick 9 parts the total number of parts into which the money was to be divided was 30.

Bill's share $= \frac{6}{30} = \frac{1}{5}$
Tom's share $= \frac{15}{30} = \frac{1}{2}$
Dick's share $= \frac{9}{30} = \frac{3}{10}$
Bill received $\frac{1}{5} \times \$135 = \$27$
Tom received $\frac{1}{2} \times \$135 = \$67.50$
Dick received $\frac{3}{10} \times \$135 = \$40.50$

EXAMPLE: The list price of a radio is \$90, with a discount of $\frac{1}{10}$ for cash. The same radio can also be purchased on the installment plan for a down payment of \$10 and payments of \$7.50 a month for one year. How much more does the radio cost when purchased on the installment plan than when cash is paid?

SOLUTION: We must compare price for cash with price on the installment plan.

Price for cash = \$90 less discount
Discount = $\frac{1}{10}$ of \$90 = \$9
Price for cash = \$90 − \$9 = \$81
Price on the installment plan = \$10 + 12 × \$7.50
= \$10 + \$90
= \$100

The difference in price is \$100 − \$81, or \$19 more on the installment plan.

PRACTICE TEST 5

1. Twenty gallons of a liquid weigh 400 lb. What is the weight of 1 quart?

2. A. man spends \$88 for gas and oil in making a trip. He used 10 quarts of oil at \$1.50 per quart. If gasoline was \$1.46 a gallon and he averaged 18 miles to the gallon, how many miles did he travel?

3. John bought 240 pens at \$3 a dozen, spent \$16 on advertising, and sold the pens at 75 cents each. What was his profit?

4. Linda has 26 feet of ribbon. She uses $2\frac{1}{3}$ feet for each of 4 dresses and decides to make 10 hair ornaments, using an equal amount of ribbon for each. How many inches of ribbon are used for each ornament?

5. Barry buys a used car for \$2,500. He pays $\frac{1}{5}$ down and the remainder is to be paid monthly for 3 years. What is the monthly payment?

6. Bill is paid \$8.00 an hour for a 40-hour week. For every hour over 40 hours, he is paid at a rate that is $1\frac{1}{2}$ times his usual rate. One week he worked 48 hours and the next week 36 hours. What did he earn in the 2 weeks?

7. Jack bought 4 oz. of butter at \$1.92 a pound, 12 cans of juice at \$0.25 per can, and 8 oranges at \$1.26 a dozen. How much did he spend?

8. Lenore gets a monthly check of \$1,250 and Millie a weekly check of \$980. What is the difference in their yearly earnings?

9. From an 18-pound cut of meat, Mr. Rand cuts off steaks weighing 1 pound 15 ounces, $3\frac{1}{8}$ pounds, and $4\frac{1}{2}$ pounds. He divides up the rest into 9-ounce patties, and sells them at 3 for \$3.12. How much does he receive for the patties?

10. Joan worked from 7:20 A.M. to 4:05 P.M. What is her salary if she is paid \$5.60 an hour?

11. A carton contains 5 pounds of cookies. If each cookie weighs $\frac{5}{8}$ of an ounce, how many cookies are in the box?

12. A mountain climber ascends 264 feet in 45 minutes. What is her rate in miles per hour?

13. A truckowner pays \$120 for the first 100 gallons of gasoline, \$1.12 a gallon for the next 300 gallons, and \$1.08 a gallon for any additional purchase of gasoline. What is his bill for 700 gallons of gasoline?

14. A man buys 3,400 boxes at \$12.50 a hundred and sells them at a profit of 6 cents each. What does he receive for the boxes?

15. Paul Allen lost $\frac{2}{3}$ of his money and has \$12 left. How much did he have?

16. Sue's dad opened a bank account for her, depositing \$25.00 a month for the first year. He promised to increase the deposit by $\frac{1}{5}$ each year. After three increases, what was the monthly deposit?

17. A man buys 48 quarts of cider at \$1.20 a quart and sells it in $\frac{1}{2}$-pint jars at 40 cents a jar. What was his profit?

18. Ronnie sold his bicycle for \$35. He had spent \$10 on repairs and \$4 for a new horn. If he suffered a \$6 loss on the sale, what was the original cost of the bicycle?

19. Miriam bought 64 pounds of popcorn. She kept $\frac{1}{4}$ for her family, gave $\frac{1}{8}$ of the remainder to her club, and distributed the rest equally among 8 friends. How many ounces did each friend get?

20. Henry hired a painter and agreed to pay him \$26.00 an hour. He supplied him with $1\frac{1}{2}$ gallons of paint that cost \$5.70 a quart and 2 quarts of paint thinner that sold for \$2.20 a quart. The painter started at 8 A.M. and finished at 4:30 P.M. What was the cost of painting the room?

Percentage Problems

Finding a percent of a number—Type I

EXAMPLE: From a group of 1,200 students $12\frac{1}{2}\%$ took a scholarship examination. Of those who took the test 20% qualified for the semifinals. How many qualified for the semifinals?

SOLUTION: The 1,200 students constitute the whole. To find $12\frac{1}{2}\%$ or $\frac{1}{8}$ of the whole we must take $\frac{1}{8}$ of 1,200; $\frac{1}{8} \times 1{,}200$ is 150 students. The 150 students represent the whole group who took the test. Of these 150 students, 20% or $\frac{1}{5}$ qualified for the semifinals. Therefore $\frac{1}{5}$ of 150, or 30 students, qualified.

PRACTICE TEST 6

1. Forty percent of the people in a certain class of 35 students are girls. How many girls are in the class?

2. Nina saves $37\frac{1}{2}\%$ of her weekly salary of \$520. How much does she spend?

3. Reggie bought 32 pairs of slacks at \$25 each and sold them at an increase of 25%. What did he receive for the slacks?

4. The population of a town increased $16\frac{2}{3}\%$ in 1990 and 10% in 1991. If the population at the beginning of 1990 was 30,000, what was its population at the end of 1991?

5. A vat contains 360 gallons of water. Of this, 10% is removed from the vat. Alcohol is then added equal to 10% of the amount of water left in the vat. How many gallons of solution are now in the vat?

6. Mr. Gardner has \$30,000 on deposit and receives $9\frac{3}{4}\%$ interest annually. What annual interest does he receive the first year?

7. An iceberg weighs 450,000 pounds. If it loses 0.2% of its weight in a day, what is its new weight at the end of the day?

8. Travelers' checks have a service charge of $\frac{3}{4}\%$. If Leon buys \$3,000 worth of checks, what is the service charge?

Finding what percent one number is of another—Type II

EXAMPLE: Karen's weight went up from 60 to 70 pounds in a year. What was the percent of increase?

SOLUTION: In finding the percent of increase, we compare the amount of increase to the original whole and change the resulting fraction to a percent. In this case the amount of increase was 70 – 60, or 10 pounds.

$$\text{Percent of increase} = \frac{\text{Amount of increase}}{\text{Original whole}}$$

$$= \frac{10}{60} = \frac{1}{6} = 16\frac{2}{3}\%$$

The percent of increase was $16\frac{2}{3}\%$.

EXAMPLE: A football team won 26 games in 1996, 34 games in 1997, and 36 games in 1998. What percent of the games did it win in 1998?

SOLUTION: We are asked to compare the number of games won in 1990 to all the games.

Percent of games won in 1990

$$= \frac{\text{Number of games won in 1990}}{\text{Total number of games}}$$

$$= \frac{36}{96} = \frac{3}{8} = 37\tfrac{1}{2}\%$$

The team won $37\frac{1}{2}\%$ of its games in 1990.

PRACTICE TEST 7

1. Bertha bought 2 apples, 6 pears, and 10 bananas. What percent of the fruit were the pears?
2. The population of a town increased from 560 to 630 people. What was the percent of increase?
3. Mr. Richardson won 36 out of the 108 games he played. What percent of the games did he lose?
4. Ross catches 4 fish and his son catches 12 fish. The son's catch was what percent of his father's?
5. In a test Louise has 64 examples correct and 8 wrong. What percent did she have wrong?
6. A bank paid Mr. Sporn $132 interest on deposits that amounted to $2,400. At what rate of interest was Mr. Sporn being paid?
7. Adele buys a scarf that usually sells for $10.50 at a sale price of $7. What percent was the price reduced?
8. In 1996 Sid weighed 120 pounds. In 1997 his gain in weight was $16\frac{2}{3}\%$. In 1998 he weighed 150 pounds. The increase in his weight from 1997 to 1998 is what percent of his 1996 weight?
9. Paula's salary was raised from $600 to $1,800 in the course of 5 years. What was the percent of increase in salary?
10. Of the 480 children in a school, 180 were absent in a flu epidemic. What percent of the children attended?

Finding the whole if the percent of it is given—Type III

EXAMPLE: Cynthia buys an encyclopedia at an 18% discount and saves $54. What did she pay for the encyclopedia?

SOLUTION: The saving of $54 is the part and represents 18% of the whole or original price. To find the whole we divide the part by the rate.

$$\$54 \div 18\% = 54 \div \frac{18}{100} = \frac{\overset{3}{\cancel{54}}}{1} \times \frac{100}{\underset{1}{\cancel{18}}} = \$300$$

The original price was $300. Since Cynthia saved $54, she paid $300 – 54, or $216.

EXAMPLE: Central Tire Corporation raised the price of heavy-duty truck tires by $16\frac{2}{3}\%$. If the present price is $168, what was the original price?

SOLUTION: The original price (the whole) was increased by $16\frac{2}{3}\%$, or $\frac{1}{6}$ of itself. The price of $168, which is the new price, therefore represents $\frac{6}{6} + \frac{1}{6}$, or $\frac{7}{6}$, of the original price. To find the original whole we divide the $168 by the fraction of the whole that the $168 represents.

$$168 \div \frac{7}{6} = \frac{168}{1} \times \frac{6}{7} = 144$$

The original price of the tire was $144.

PRACTICE TEST 8

1. Twenty-three percent of a town's population owns cars. If the number of cars owned is 5,290, what is the population of the town?
2. Mr. Hall saved $15 by buying a tool at a 10% discount. What did the tool list for?

3. A salesman earned $750 in making sales that paid him a $7\frac{1}{2}\%$ commission. What was the value of his sales?

4. The population of a city dipped $\frac{1}{2}\%$ last year. If the decrease amounted to 2,453 people, what was the population of the town after the decrease?

5. The Continental Office Supply found that a markup of $37\frac{1}{2}\%$ on a desk resulted in making a $48 profit. What was the original cost of the desk?

6. Martin had 14 examples wrong on a test. His score was 72% correct. How many examples were there on the test?

7. A bank pays Sally $6\frac{1}{4}\%$ interest yearly. If the yearly interest payment she receives amounts to $50, how much does she have on deposit?

8. Roy found that after receiving a 25% discount he had to pay $72 for a tape recorder. How much was the discount?

9. Vicki traveled 90 miles and found she had completed $83\frac{1}{3}\%$ of her trip. How many miles did she still have to go?

10. Gladys paid $25.48 for a tablecloth. If the price included a 4% sales tax, what was the price of the cloth itself?

Special Topics in Percent

PROFIT AND LOSS

A merchant's *profit* or loss represents the difference between the *total (gross)* cost and the *selling price* of the goods sold. The gross cost includes the first cost of the merchandise plus the overhead. The *overhead* is the expenses of doing business, such as rent, light, salaries, taxes, insurance. If the selling price is less than the total cost, then of course the merchant suffers a loss. The difference between the original cost of the goods and the selling price is known as the *markup.* It equals the overhead expenses plus the profit. The relationship in the case of profit can be shown as follows:

First cost + Overhead + Profit = Selling price

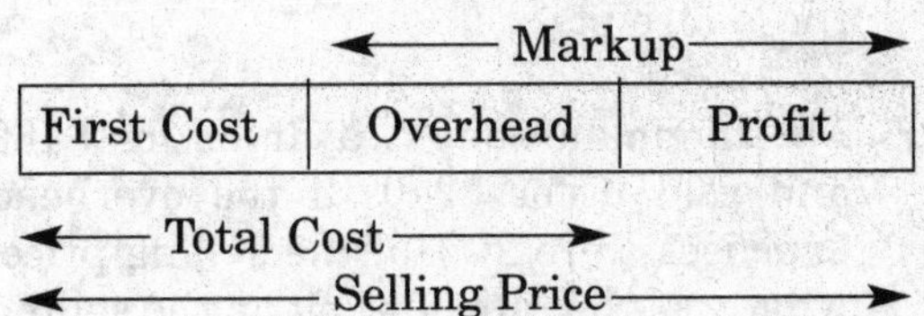

EXAMPLE: Eve buys a bicycle for $11. She spends $6 for repairs and $2 to ship it. If she sells the bicycle for $26, what profit does she make?

SOLUTION: The total cost of the article was $11 + $6 + $2 = $19. The profit Eve made was $26 – $19 or $7.

EXAMPLE: A table costs Mr. Lustig $90. The operating expense is 20% of the cost of the table. He wishes to make a profit of $33\frac{1}{3}\%$ of the first cost. At what price should the table sell?

SOLUTION: Mr. Lustig's overhead expenses are 20% of $90 or $18. His profit is to be $33\frac{1}{3}\%$ or $\frac{1}{3}$ of $90 or $30. The selling price must be $90 + $18 + $30, or $138.

EXAMPLE: Carol buys a tape recorder for $120. After spending $30 for repairs she sells it at a price that is $16\frac{2}{3}\%$ more than what she paid for it. What was the profit or loss on the transaction?

SOLUTION: Carol's total cost was $120 + $30 or $150. The price increase equals $16\frac{2}{3}\%$ of $120, which equals $\frac{1}{6} \times$ $120, or $20. The selling price was, therefore, $120 + $20 or $140. Since the selling price was less than the total cost, Carol suffered a loss of $150 – $140, or $10.

EXAMPLE: If an article costs $12 and sells for $18, what is the percent of profit?

SOLUTION: If just the cost is given we assume that either there are no operating expenses or they are included in the cost. This is a type II percentage problem. Unless otherwise stated, any increase or decrease is based on the original whole. Thus,

$$\text{Percent profit} = \frac{\text{Amount of profit}}{\text{Cost}}$$

$$= \frac{18-12}{12} = \frac{6}{12} = \frac{1}{2} = 50\%$$

EXAMPLE: Barry Metal Products pays \$12,000 for raw materials. Its manufacturing expenses are 200% of the cost of these materials. If the amount received for the sale of the finished products is \$50,000, what percent of the total cost is the profit?

SOLUTION:

Manufacturing expenses
= 200% × \$12,000
= 2(\$12,000) = \$24,000
The total cost is \$12,000 + \$24,000
= \$36,000
The profit is \$50,000 – \$36,000
= \$14,000

The percentage of profit

$$= \frac{14{,}000}{36{,}000} = \frac{7}{18}$$

$$\frac{7}{18} = \frac{7}{18} \times 100\% = 38\frac{8}{9}\%$$

EXAMPLE: The Recco Gift Shop wishes to make a 30% profit on the cost of its merchandise. If the profit amounts to \$600, what does the merchandise cost?

SOLUTION: This is a type III problem in which the part and the percent that the part represents are known.

$$\text{Cost} = \text{Profit} \div \text{Rate of profit}$$

$$= \$600 \div 30\% = \$600 \div \frac{3}{10}$$

$$= \$600 \times \frac{10}{3} = \$2{,}000$$

The cost of the merchandise is \$2,000.

EXAMPLE: Jesse's toy store sells a doll for \$8.00 which represents a profit of 15% of the cost. If the average overhead is 5% of the cost, what profit does Jesse make on the doll?

SOLUTION: The markup is 15% + 5% or 20% of the cost. Since the cost is the base and represents 100%, the selling price is 100% + 20% or 120% of the cost. This is a type III problem. When we wish to find the original whole, in this case the cost, we divide the part by the rate.

$$\text{Cost} = \$8 \div 120\% = \$8 \div \frac{120}{100}$$

$$= \$8 \times \frac{5}{6} = \frac{20}{3} = \$6.66\frac{2}{3}$$

The cost to the nearest cent is \$6.67.
The profit is \$8.00 – \$6.67 = \$1.33.

PRACTICE TEST 9

1. What is the selling price of a radio that costs \$30 and has a markup of $8\frac{1}{3}\%$?

2. During a blizzard a tire dealer sold a pair of skid chains that cost him \$7.50 at a price that netted him a 350% profit. What did the pair of chains sell for?

3. A variety store listed the cost of the goods sold as \$50,000, its operating overhead as 20% of the cost, and the value of its sales as \$75,000. What percent of the total cost was the profit?

4. A hotel suffered a loss of \$45,000 during a season. If the rate of loss was $37\frac{1}{2}\%$ of the gross receipts, what was the value of these receipts?

5. Mr. Lippman bought a dryer for \$160 and sold it for \$240. If the overhead expenses were 20% of the selling price, what was the rate of profit on the selling price?

6. A music shop sold twenty-five \$50 radios at a profit of 8% and six \$30 radios at a loss of 15%. How much was the profit or loss on the combined transaction?

7. Mrs. Gold buys a stock of $300 worth of vegetables, which she sells at a 30% markup. If $75 worth of the vegetables spoils and cannot be sold, does Mrs. Gold make a profit or a loss? How much?

8. Alice bought 20 baseball cards at a cost of $1.00 each. She is now willing to sell the whole lot for a total of $12. What will be Alice's percent of loss?

9. The Joneses bought a house 3 years ago for which they paid $65,000. They spent $5,000 repairing it, $1,000 on insurance premiums, and $8,000 in taxes, heat, and light. In order to make a final profit of 5% of his outlay, for how much must Mr. Jones sell his house?

10. After selling twelve books for $180, Bill finds that he has made a profit on them amounting to 25% of the cost and incurred expenses amounting to 10% of the cost. How much did Bill pay for the books?

TAXATION

In order to pay for the government services we must pay taxes. In most communities the greatest source of government income is real estate taxes. Each building and plot of ground is given an assessed valuation. The total assessed valuation is used to fix the tax rate for a community. Let us suppose that a town has a budget of $75,000 for a certain year and the assessed valuation of the taxable property in the town is $1,875,000. The tax rate is computed as follows:

$$\text{Tax rate} = \frac{\text{Amount of money needed}}{\text{Assessed valuation}}$$

In the above case

$$\text{Tax rate} = \frac{\$75,000}{\$1,875,000} = 0.04$$

Thus the tax rate for this community is 4%.

The rate is stated in several ways, such as the following:

4% of the assessed value
$4 on each $100 of assessed value
$40 on each $1,000 of assessed value
$0.04 on each $1 of each assessed value
40 mills on each $1 of assessed value (A mill is equal to $\frac{1}{10}$ of 1 cent.)

EXAMPLE: It is necessary to raise $55,648 by tax in a village with an assessed valuation of $3,478,000. What will be the tax rate per $1,000?

SOLUTION:

$$\text{Tax rate} = \frac{\text{Amount of money needed}}{\text{Assessed valuation}}$$

$$= \frac{\$55,648}{\$3,478,000}$$

```
                 0.016
3,478,000)55,648.000
          34 780 00
          20 868 000
          20 868 000
```

The tax rate is 1.6%, or $0.016 per $1, or $16 per $1,000.

EXAMPLE: In the same village a man owns a home with an assessed valuation of $42,500. How much village tax will he pay?

SOLUTION: For each $1,000 of assessed valuation the tax is $16. The assessed valuation of this home is $42.5 thousand. Therefore, the tax is

```
  $42.50
×     16
  255 00
  425 0
 $680.00
```

Some communities have other taxes, such as sales taxes, to bring in additional revenue. A sales tax is computed as a percent of the selling price of an article.

COMMISSION

Some salespeople receive salary in the form of a *commission* based on the value of the goods sold. The commission is usually computed by taking an agreed upon percent of sales. Sometimes, the salesperson deducts the commission from the money received and turns the balance over to the employer. The money turned over to the employer is called the *net proceeds.*

EXAMPLE: A farmer shipped 2,650 bushels of apples to market. His agent sold the apples at \$8.40 per bushel and deducted $4\frac{1}{2}\%$ commission. What were the net proceeds?

SOLUTION: The total sales were

$$\$8.40 \times 2{,}660 = \$22{,}260.00$$

The commission was $4\frac{1}{2}$ of \$22,260 = 1,001.70

The net proceeds were \$21,258.30

EXAMPLE: A book salesman receives a commission of 7% on sales. If his commission amounted to \$168 on an order, what was the amount of the order?

SOLUTION: 7% of the order was \$168.

To find the size of the order we divide the part (\$168) by the rate.

$$\frac{\$168}{7\%} = \frac{168}{0.07}$$

$$0.07.\overline{)168.00.} = 2400.$$

The amount of the order was \$2,400.

EXAMPLE: In buying a jacket, a man pays a sales tax of 3%. If his tax amounted to \$1.95, what was the cost of the jacket?

SOLUTION: \$1.95 represents 3% of the cost of the jacket. To find the total cost we divide the part by the rate.

$$\$1.95 \div 3\% = \frac{1.95}{0.03} = \frac{195}{3} = \$65$$

The jacket cost \$65.

EXAMPLE: A real estate agent sold a house for \$85,000 and received a commission of \$3,825. What was her rate of commission?

SOLUTION: To find the rate of commission we divide the commission received by the selling price of the house.

$$\frac{\$3{,}825}{\$85{,}000}$$

$$\begin{array}{r} 0.045 \\ 85{,}000\overline{)3{,}825.000} \\ \underline{3\ 400\ 00} \\ 425\ 000 \\ \underline{425\ 000} \end{array}$$

The rate of commission was $4\frac{1}{2}\%$.

DISCOUNT

During sales, articles are usually marked down in price. Sometimes, a buyer will save money by buying for cash. Whenever an article is sold for less than its regular price it is sold at a *discount.* The original price is called the *marked price* or *list price.* The percent of the marked price that is deducted is called the *rate of discount.* Thus,

$$\text{Discount} = \text{List price} \times \text{Rate of discount}$$
$$\text{Sale price} = \text{List price} - \text{Discount}$$

EXAMPLE: At a clearance sale, the Fashion Shop sold a \$69.50 raincoat at a discount of 15%. What was the sale price of the raincoat?

SOLUTION: In order to obtain the discount we find 15% of \$69.50.

$$\begin{array}{r} \$69.50 \\ \times\ \ 0.15 \\ \hline 34750 \\ 6950\ \ \\ \hline \end{array}$$

\$10.4250 = \$10.43 to the nearest cent

The sale price is obtained by subtracting the discount from the list price.

$$\begin{array}{r} \$69.50 \\ -\ 10.43 \\ \hline \$59.07 \end{array} = \text{Sale price of the coat}$$

EXAMPLE: A chair was priced at \$47.50. During a sale the chair sold for \$38.00. What was the rate of discount on the chair?

SOLUTION: The discount on the chair was \$47.50 – \$38.00 = \$9.50.

$$\text{The rate of discount} = \frac{\text{Discount}}{\text{List Price}} = \frac{\$9.50}{\$47.50}.$$

```
          0.2
47.50.)9.50.0
       9.50 0
```

The rate of discount was 0.2, or 20%.

EXAMPLE: On a furniture order, a merchant received a discount of \$115 for cash. This represented $2\frac{1}{2}\%$ of the purchase price. What was the purchase price?

SOLUTION: \$115 represents $2\frac{1}{2}\%$.

To find the purchase price we divide the part (\$115) by the rate ($2\frac{1}{2}\%$).

$$\frac{\$115}{2\frac{1}{2}\%} = \frac{115}{0.025}$$

```
            4600.
0.025.)115.000.
       100
        15 0
        15 0
```

The purchase price was \$4,600.

EXAMPLE: A school wishes to buy baseball equipment that is listed at \$600. A.M. Smith Co. quotes discounts of 15% and 10%. C.A. Jones Co. quotes a single discount of 25%. Which offer is better and by how much?

SOLUTION:

A.M. Smith Co. offer

```
  $600   (list price)
× 0.15
 $90.00  (first discount)

  $510   (price after discount)
× 0.10
   $51   (second discount)

  $510
 –  51   (second discount)
  $459   (net price)
```

C.A. Jones Co. offer:

```
  $600     (list price)
   0.25
  3000
 1200
$150.00   (discount)

$600.00   (list price)
–150.00
$450      (net price)
```

The C.A. Jones offer is better by \$9.

INTEREST

Business people sometimes need money to buy new equipment or stock. The business person usually borrows this money from a bank. The bank charges the business person interest for the use of the money borrowed. Thus, at the end of the period for which the loan was made, the borrower repays the original amount borrowed, or principal, plus the interest charged. For example, Mr. Barry borrows \$6,000 from the National Bank for a period of 3 years. He agrees to pay interest at the rate of 14% annually. In this case,

\$6,000 = Principal
14% = Rate of interest
3 years = Time

The rule for finding the interest is

Interest = Principal × Rate × Time

The interest on Mr. Barry's loan is computed as follows:

$$\begin{aligned}\text{Interest} &= \text{Principal} \times \text{Rate} \times \text{Time}\\ \text{Interest} &= \$6{,}000 \times 14\% \times 3\\ &= \$6{,}000 \times \tfrac{14}{100} \times 3\\ &= \$2{,}520\end{aligned}$$

At the end of 3 years Mr. Barry will repay the bank the principal (\$6,000) plus the interest (\$2,520). The sum of the principal and the interest is called the *amount.*

EXAMPLE: Find the interest on \$2,500 for 2 years at 12%.

SOLUTION:

$$\begin{aligned}\text{Interest} &= \text{Principal} \times \text{Rate} \times \text{Time}\\ &= \$2{,}500 \times \tfrac{12}{100} \times 2 = \$600\end{aligned}$$

EXAMPLE: Find the interest on $3,125 for 4 years at $12\frac{1}{2}\%$.

SOLUTION:

$$\text{Interest} = \text{Principal} \times \text{Rate} \times \text{Time}$$
$$= \$3{,}125 \times \tfrac{1}{8} \times 4 = \$1{,}562.50$$

$$\text{NOTE: } 12\frac{1}{2}\% = \frac{12\frac{1}{2}}{100} = \frac{25}{200} = \frac{1}{8}$$

EXAMPLE: Find the interest on $82.50 for 1 year and 3 months at 6%.

SOLUTION:

$$\text{Interest} = \text{Principal} \times \text{Rate} \times \text{Time}$$
$$= \$82.50 \times \tfrac{6}{100} \times \tfrac{5}{4}$$
$$= \$6.19 \text{ to the nearest cent}$$

NOTE: 1 year and 3 months =
$1 + \frac{3}{12} = 1\frac{1}{4} = \frac{5}{4}$ years

EXAMPLE: Mr. Crane borrowed $875 to buy a car. The money was borrowed for a period of 2 years and 4 months at 15% interest. What amount did Mr. Crane pay back?

SOLUTION:

$$\text{Interest} = \text{Principal} \times \text{Rate} \times \text{Time}$$
$$= \$875 \times \tfrac{15}{100} \times \tfrac{7}{3} = \$306.25$$
$$\text{Amount} = \text{Principal} + \text{Interest}$$
$$= \$875 + \$306.25 = \$1{,}181.25$$

Mr. Crane paid back $1,181.25.

EXAMPLE: Mrs. James placed $120 in a bank. At the end of the year Mrs. James received $7.80 in interest. What rate of interest did the bank pay Mrs. James?

SOLUTION: To find the rate of interest we divide the interest ($7.80) by the principal ($120).

$$\frac{\$7.80}{\$120} \qquad 120\overline{)7.800}^{\,0.065}$$

```
     0.065
120)7.800
    7.200
      600
      600
```

The rate of interest paid by the bank was $6\frac{1}{2}\%$.

EXAMPLE: Mr. Sloan paid $2,520 in interest on a mortgage loan. If the interest rate was $10\frac{1}{2}\%$, what was the amount of the mortgage loan?

SOLUTION: $2,520 is equal to $10\frac{1}{2}\%$ of the amount of the loan. To find the amount of the loan we divide the part ($2,520) by the rate.

$$\frac{\$2{,}520}{10\frac{1}{2}\%} = \frac{2{,}520}{0.105}$$

```
         24 000.
0.105.)2520.000.
       210
        420
        420
```

The amount of the loan was $24,000.

PRACTICE TEST 10

1. The budget for a certain town requires a tax collection of $58,940. The assessed valuation of taxable property in the town is $1,684,000. What is the tax rate?

2. A real estate agent receives a commission of $2\frac{1}{2}\%$ on the sales price of a lot. Find the agent's commission on a lot that sold for $16,250.

3. An agent sold a shipment of 72 radio sets at $23.48 per set. His commission was $92.98. What was his rate of commission?

4. Mrs. Ames bought a chair at a discount of 18%. If the amount of the discount was $75.60, what was the cost of the chair?

5. Mr. Albert bought some merchandise for his business for $8,125. To do this he paid $2,500 in cash and borrowed the balance from his bank for one year at 16% annual interest. What was the actual cost of the merchandise?

6. An agent sold a shipment of 38 dozen golf balls at $14.70 per dozen. What was the agent's commission at $5\frac{1}{2}\%$?

7. The cost of a used car was $2,884.00. This included a sales tax of 3%. Find the cost of the car without the tax.

8. A lot is assessed for \$11,500. The real estate tax on the lot is \$287.50. What is the tax rate?

9. Money is borrowed for one year at $12\frac{1}{2}\%$ interest. If the interest payment was \$850, what was the size of the loan?

10. A salesman sold 42 dozen shorts at \$22.50 per dozen. What was the salesman's commission at the rate of $4\frac{1}{2}\%$?

11. By receiving a discount of 15% a buyer saved \$28.44 on a table. What was the price of the table before the discount was taken off?

12. A farmer shipped 196 dozen eggs to market. His agent sold the eggs at \$0.82 per dozen and charged the farmer 6% of the selling price for his services. How much did the farmer receive?

13. A hat was priced at \$10.80. During a sale, the hat sold for \$9.18. What was the rate of discount on the hat?

14. A man's tax on his home is \$1,952. The tax rate is \$3.20 per \$100 of assessed value. What is the assessed value of the home?

15. Mr. Fisher deposited \$3,210 in his bank for a period of 8 months at $5\frac{1}{2}\%$ annual interest. What amount did Mr. Fisher withdraw at the end of the 8 months?

16. The sales tax on a table was \$2.70. If the tax rate was 2% what was the cost of the table?

17. Mr. Leonard bought a shipment of goods for \$7,250. He paid \$3,000 in cash and agreed to pay the balance in 9 months with interest at $12\frac{1}{2}\%$. What was the total cost of the shipment?

18. A coat was priced at \$68.50. At a sale, the coat sold for \$54.80. What was the rate of discount on the coat?

19. A real estate agent collected \$4,250 in rents. She gave the owner \$3,910 and retained the balance as commission. What was her rate of commission?

20. A refrigerator was marked down in price from \$249.50 to \$199.60 during a sale. What was the rate of discount?

PRACTICE TEST 11

1. Of 480 students in a high school, 180 were in the ninth year. What percent of the students in the school were in the ninth year?

2. A car dealer made 35% of his annual car sales during the months of April and May. If he sold 133 cars during these months, how many cars did he sell during the year?

3. A boy had to save \$12.40 to buy a new shirt. What percent of the needed amount had he saved when he had \$7.75?

4. A clothing store made sales of \$8,560 during a certain month. If $3\frac{1}{2}\%$ of the sales amount was profit, how much profit did the store earn during this month?

5. During the year 1988 a certain type of TV set sold for \$368. This was $133\frac{1}{3}\%$ of the price of the same type of TV set in 1998. What was the price of this set in 1998?

6. The Rivera family planned to save 14% of its income. If the total annual income is \$55,500, how much do they plan to save each month?

7. In a certain election district 684 voters cast their ballots. This was 60% of the total number of voters in the district. How many voters were in the district?

8. Mr. Denning bought a jacket for \$67.50 and a tie for \$12.50. If a sales tax of 3% was added to the price of his purchase, what was his total bill?

9. The Blue Sox baseball team won 40 games of 48 games played. The Green Sox won 27 games of 45 games played. Which team won the greater percentage of games? By what percent?

10. A car is insured for $12,000 or 80% of its actual value. What is its actual value?

11. On a snowy day, 85% of the pupils of Wilson High School were present. If 527 pupils were present, how many pupils were enrolled at the school?

12. An oil tank contains 580 gallons. When 87 gallons of oil have been used, what percent of the 580 gallons are left in the tank?

13. Of 580 students in a high school graduating class 45% are planning to go to college. How many of the graduates are planning to go to college?

14. Mr. Albert sold his car for $6,240. This was 65% of the original cost. What was the original cost of Mr. Albert's car?

15. A theater has 1,450 seats. If 42% of these seats are balcony seats, how many balcony seats does the theater have?

16. A motorist planned a trip covering 920 miles. After he had traveled 598 miles, what percent of the mileage planned had he covered?

17. A department store placed 980 overcoats on sale for one week. On Monday 298 overcoats were sold, on Tuesday 312 overcoats were sold, and on Wednesday 223 overcoats were sold. What percent of the 980 overcoats were left unsold?

18. The value of a new car decreases 35% in the first year. If a car costs $9,800, how much would it be worth at the end of the first year?

19. When Mrs. Rogers had paid $374 for her sofa she had paid 68% of the total cost. What was the total cost of the sofa?

20. A homeowner figured that 62% of his expenses were taxes. If his tax bill was $775, what was the total expense of running his house?

21. A machine part manufacturer found that $2\frac{1}{2}$% of the parts made in his factory were defective. If 12 parts were defective, how many parts were made in the factory?

22. A class library contained 325 books. Of these, 36% were history books. How many history books did the class library contain?

23. A TV dealer received a shipment of TV sets that cost him $192 per set. At what price did he sell each of these sets if he made a profit of $12\frac{1}{2}$%?

24. The total admissions in a movie house were 1,550 during one week. If 527 attended the movie house on Saturday, what percent of the total admissions for the week occurred on Saturday?

25. A sporting goods store sells its goods so that the profit is 12% of its sales. What must be the amount of sales if the profit is to be $42,000?

26. A man keeps $2,800 in a savings bank for 1 year at 5% interest compounded semiannually. How much does the man get when he withdraws his money?

27. A manufacturer wishes to make a profit of $1.80 on an article. If this profit is to be 15% of the wholesale price of the article, what is the wholesale price of the article?

28. A woman bought a dress at a discount of $16\frac{2}{3}$%. If the woman paid $32.50, what was the original price of the dress?

29. The price of heating oil was raised from $1.40 to $1.47 per gallon. What was the percent of increase?

30. Cement used for concrete contains 64% lime. How many pounds of lime are there in 650 pounds of cement?

31. A lot is assessed at $15,800 and the tax is $711. What is the tax rate?

32. When 100 new students enrolled in a certain high school its enrollment was increased by 8%. What was the original enrollment of the high school?

33. Ms. Polanski has a $5,000 bond on which she receives annual interest of $450. What rate of interest does the bond pay?

34. A man bought a car for $12,800. He paid 40% down and arranged to pay the balance in 24 equal monthly installments. How much was each installment?

35. On an electricity bill of $40.80, Mrs. Miller pays only $38.76 because she pays before a certain date. What percent discount is Mrs. Miller allowed?

36. On a family income of $29,600 the Burton family saved $8\frac{1}{2}$% one year. How much did the Burton family spend that year?

37. By hiring 45 new employees a department store increased its help by 18% during the Christmas season. How many employees did the store have before the increase?

38. In a high school enrollment of 1,580 students, 1,501 joined the student organization. What percent of the students joined the student organization?

39. A camera usually sells for $68. Because it was slightly damaged it sold for $59.50. What was the rate of discount?

40. Last year, a man earned $19,200. This year, his salary was increased to $20,736. What was the percent of increase?

41. One year, a star baseball player got 220 hits. If 45% of these hits were for extra bases, how many extra base hits did the player get?

42. In a certain high school, $62\frac{1}{2}$% of the students are taking science courses. If 650 students are in science classes in this school, what is the total enrollment of the school?

43. A salesman of machinery sold 148 machines at $79.50 each. If he received a commission of $7\frac{1}{2}$%, how much was his commission?

44. A manufacturer decided to spend 18% of her expense budget for advertising. If she spent $2,700 for advertising, what was her total expense budget?

45. A dealer sold 112 cars during the month of May and 96 cars during the month of June. What was the percent of decrease?

46. At an evening performance 85% of the seats in a movie house were occupied. If 731 people attended this performance what was the seating capacity of the movie house?

47. A bookstore sold 762 books at $3.95 each. If the dealer makes a profit of 40% on each sale, what is his total profit on the sale of the books?

48. In a high school graduating class of 125 students, 35 students received athletic awards. What percent of the graduating class received athletic awards?

49. Mr. Rodriguez bought a jacket at $69.50, a tie at $15.50, and a raincoat at $72.35. If he received a discount of $12\frac{1}{2}$% on each of these items, what was his bill?

50. A merchant sold articles of clothing at 140% of what he paid for them. What did he pay for an article that he sold for $84?

Averages

To find the average of several numbers, we find the sum of the numbers and divide this sum by the number of addends.

Example: A boys marks on 6 tests where 90, 85, 82, 68, 84, and 77. What was the average of the boy's marks?

Solution:

$$\begin{array}{r} 90 \\ 85 \\ 82 \\ 68 \\ 84 \\ \underline{77} \\ 486 \end{array} \qquad 6\overline{)486}^{\;81}$$

The boy's average was 81.

Example: A traveling salesman clocked his daily mileages for 7 days as follows:

327, 462, 184, 217, 92, 149, 198.

Find the average daily mileage to the nearest mile.

Solution:

$$\begin{array}{r} 327 \\ 462 \\ 184 \\ 217 \\ 92 \\ 149 \\ \underline{198} \\ 1629 \end{array} \qquad 1629 \div 7 = 232\tfrac{5}{7}$$

$232\frac{5}{7}$ = 233 miles to the nearest mile.

The average daily mileage was 233.

Example: In a small company, 9 workers each received \$72 per day and 6 workers each received \$82 per day. What was the average daily wage per worker?

Solution: The total amount of wages was

$$\begin{array}{rr} 9 \times \$72 = & \$\,648 \\ 6 \times \$82 = & \underline{492} \\ & \$1140 \end{array}$$

Since there were 15 workers we divide \$1140 by 15.

$$\begin{array}{r} 76 \\ 15\overline{)1140} \\ \underline{105} \\ 90 \\ \underline{90} \end{array}$$

The average daily wage was \$76 per worker.

Example: The Roosevelt High School football team played a schedule of 7 games. The total attendance for the 7 games was 9,443. Find the average attendance per game.

Solution:

$$\begin{array}{r} 1,349 \\ 7\overline{)9,443} \end{array}$$

The average attendance was 1,349.

PRACTICE TEST 12

1. Find the average of 49, 15, 9, 75.

2. A student received the following grades in a series of tests: 78, 85, 92, 65, 71, and 83. What was her average on these tests?

3. A student's budget showed that he spent the following amounts over a period of several weeks: \$3.01, \$2.89, \$4.17, \$1.67, \$3.96, and \$2.06. What was his average expenditure per week over this period of time, to the nearest cent?

4. The Star Theater had an attendance of 5,803 for 7 performances. What was the average attendance per performance?

5. A boy had an average of 84% on 4 tests. He received a mark of 94% on a fifth test. What was his average for the five tests?

6. A garage attendant made the following sales of gasoline: \$23.70, \$30.80, \$39.20, \$28.90, \$34.70, and \$29.50. What was his average sale, to the nearest cent?

7. After 6 games a man's average bowling score was 186. After 3 other games his average score was 201. What was his average score for all 9 games?

8. On a basketball team, the heights of the players are 6′6″, 5′7″, 6′2″, 5′11″, and 6′3″. What is the average of these heights?

9. A TV set dealer made the following number of sales daily during the holiday season: 87, 67, 38, 47, 79, 82, 99, and 101. What was the average daily number of sales?

10. The average of 5 numbers is 37. What must a sixth number be if the average of the six numbers is to be 46?

ONE HUNDRED VERBAL PROBLEMS

1. Mrs. Abbate wishes to make a dozen towels. If each towel is to be $\frac{3}{4}$ yard long, how many yards of material should Mrs. Abbate buy?

2. On a trip, Mr. Moore drove at an average speed of 42 miles per hour. If the trip took $3\frac{1}{2}$ hours, how far did Mr. Moore drive?

3. Mr. Evans paid $10.60 each for 72 shirts. He sold the shirts for $14.20 each. What was his total profit on the shipment?

4. A plumber had a piece of pipe 5 feet long. He used 2 pieces, each $1\frac{3}{4}$ feet long. How big a piece of pipe was left?

5. Jose spent 6 hours in school. Each school period is $\frac{3}{4}$ hour long. How many periods did Jose spend in school?

6. Mr. Abrams earns $480 per week. He saves 5% of his earnings. How much does Mr. Abrams spend in a year?

7. Anne earns $2.50 per hour for babysitting. At the end of a month she had earned $95.00. How many hours did Anne work?

8. The telephone bills for a family for five months were $25.83, $26.02, $27.34, $26.56, and $25.54. What was the average telephone bill per month?

9. On a map $\frac{1}{8}$ of an inch stands for 24 miles. On this map two cities are $2\frac{1}{4}$ inches apart. What is the actual distance between the cities?

10. A 5-gallon can of motor oil costs $28.00. What is the cost of 1 quart of the oil?

11. A department store placed 144 suits on sale. By the end of the day 108 suits had been sold. What percent of the suits were sold on the day?

12. Mr. Foote placed a cement walk along the side of his house. The walk is 18 inches wide and 32 feet long. What was the cost of the walk at $2.10 a square foot?

13. A car will travel 17.4 miles on a gallon of gas. How many gallons of gas will be needed for a trip of 435 miles?

14. Mrs. Santos buys $3\frac{1}{2}$ pounds of beef at $2.68 per pound and $8\frac{1}{4}$ pounds of turkey at $0.96 per pound. How much did Mrs. Santos spend?

15. The rainfall for three months in a certain city was 4.87 inches, 6.08 inches, and 5.49 inches. What was the average rainfall for the three months?

16. A home was valued at $73,500. It was insured for 80% of its value at a premium of $0.40 per $100. Find the yearly premium.

17. A woman buys 2 pounds of butter at $1.85 per pound and 3 pounds of cheese at $2.15 per pound. She gives the clerk as $20 bill. How much does she receive in change?

18. A traveling salesman drives his car 30,000 miles a year. His car travels 16 miles to the gallon of gas. How many gallons of gas does he use in a year?

19. What will it cost to send a 15-word telegram, if the first 10 words cost 85 cents and each additional word costs 7 cents?

20. A basketball team won 10 of its first 20 games. It then won its next 5 games. What fractional part of its total number of games did it win?

21. At 20 miles per hour, how long does it take to travel 1 mile?

22. In the shop, a boy was given a board 16 feet long and was asked to cut it into pieces, each $1\frac{1}{2}$ feet long. How many full pieces did he get?

23. If 4 oranges cost 66 cents, what will one dozen cost, at the same rate?

24. On a test taken by 96 pupils, $\frac{1}{8}$ of the pupils failed. How many pupils passed?

25. If a space of 18 inches is allowed for each person, how many persons can be seated in a row of bleacher seats 90 feet long?

26. If John can save $0.25 per day, how many days will it take him to save $9.50?

27. If a discount of 16% is allowed on a work shirt that ordinarily sells for $8.50, what is the sales price?

28. Meghan makes a profit of $4\frac{1}{2}$ cents on each paper that she sells. How much profit will she make on 60 papers?

29. A bunch of bananas weighs 3 pounds and 8 ounces. What is the cost of the bananas at $0.60 per pound?

30. A worker receives $7.20 per hour. What is his pay for $42\frac{1}{2}$ hours of work?

31. By paying $10 cash and the balance at $3 per week, how long would it take to pay for a used bicycle costing $64?

32. During the past season, a basketball team won 18 games and lost 7 games. What percent of the games did the team win?

33. A concrete floor 3 inches thick is to be laid in a cellar 30 feet by 24 feet. How many cubic feet of concrete are needed?

34. A babysitter worked from 8:30 P.M. to 11:00 P.M. At the rate of $2.10 per hour, how much did she earn?

35. If there are 7 frankfurters to the pound, how many pounds of frankfurters are needed for a picnic to supply 19 pupils with 2 frankfurters each?

36. An army is organized as follows:

    250 soldiers in a company
    4 companies in a battalion
    3 battalions in a regiment

    How many soldiers are there in a regiment?

37. A homeowner uses 5,015 gallons of oil during the heating season. How much does she spend for oil, if she pays $1.46 per gallon?

38. What must be the length of a box that is 4 feet wide and 3 feet deep, if it has a volume of 96 cubic feet?

39. A saleswoman received $40 per day, plus a commission of 2% on all sales over $300 per week. What was her salary for a 5-day week during which her sales amounted to $1,260?

40. A high school has 480 pupils of whom 80% attend a school concert. If each pupil paid $1.05 for a ticket, find the total receipts.

41. A notebook listed at $2 is sold to the school at a discount of 25%. What is the selling price?

42. A data-entry clerk spends $86 per week for food. This is 20% of his weekly income. What is the weekly income?

43. Mr. Smith owns a lot valued at $12,000. It is assessed at 80% of its value. How much tax does he pay if the tax rate is $1\frac{1}{2}$% of the assessed value?

44. Mr. Adamski's daily pay was $84. He received an increase of $6.30. What is the percent of increase?

45. If 5 ounces of cheese cost $0.85, what is the cost of 24 ounces at the same rate?

46. What will be the cost of 50 feet of hose at 0.55\frac{1}{2}$ per foot?

47. If $\frac{1}{4}$ inch represents 5 yards, how many inches long must a scale drawing be to show a football field 100 yards long?

48. If, on the average, 1 potato out of every 50 in a bin spoils, what percent of the potatoes spoil?

49. A certain grade in a school contains 96 pupils. If there are 40 boys, what is the ratio of boys to girls in this grade?

50. A man borrowed $65 from the bank for one year. He paid $7.80 in interest. What rate of interest was charged by the bank?

51. A merchant paid $40 for 5 dozen notebooks and sold them for $1.25 each. What was her profit?

52. How many stakes $5\frac{1}{2}$ feet long can be cut from 10 lengths of lumber each 12 feet long?

53. If a boy walks 6 miles in 2 hours, how far will he walk in 5 hours, at the same rate?

54. How many square yards of carpeting are needed to cover a floor 18 feet long by 12 feet wide?

55. If a mixture of water and alcohol contains 20% alcohol, what percent of the mixture is water?

56. At the rate of 360 miles per hour, how far would an airplane travel in 1 hour and 20 minutes?

57. A page in an average newspaper has 8 columns of print. Each column consists of 160 lines and each line averages 6 words. Find the average number of words on a full page.

58. A boy spends 45% of his allowance for lunches and 10% for carfare. What percent of his allowance does he have left?

59. At the rate of $0.80 per $100, how much does it cost to insure a car against fire and theft for $1,650?

60. A dealer purchased tee shirts at $2.40 each and sold them for $4.25 each. His overhead was $0.60 per shirt. How much money did he make on each shirt?

61. How much money would you have if you had 2 quarters, 3 dimes, 7 nickels, and 14 pennies?

62. An agent sold 250 boxes of apples at $6.50 each. He charged a commission of 5%. What was his commission?

63. A concrete sidewalk 3 feet wide, 18 feet long, and 4 inches thick contains how many cubic feet of concrete?

64. A boy scores an average of 6 out of every 10 shots. At the same rate, how many scoring shots should he make out of 100 attempts?

65. A baseball team lost 4 games, which were 20% of the total number of games played. How many games did the team play?

66. Maria's class purchased 10 boxes of candy for $43.20. If each box contained 24 candies, what was the cost of each candy?

67. How much profit does a grocer make if he buys a case of beans containing 24 cans for $7.50 and sells it for $0.42 per can?

68. Ms. Delilio borrowed $1,200 from a bank for 90 days at 12% annual interest. How much interest did she pay?

69. If a dress factory uses $3\frac{1}{8}$ yards of cloth to make a dress, how many yards will it take to make 12 dresses?

70. The sales tax in a certain city is 2%. A man buys a camera and pays a sales tax of $3.20. What was the cost of the camera, exclusive of the sales tax?

71. John's father bought 2 turkeys. One weighed $12\frac{1}{2}$ pounds and the other $13\frac{3}{4}$ pounds. How much did they weigh together?

72. A man pays a water bill of $6.75 every three months. How much does he pay in a year?

73. If a car travels 357 miles and uses 21 gallons of gas, how many miles does it average per gallon of gas?

74. Mary receives $2.00 weekly as an allowance. If she saves $0.70 of it, what percent does she save?

75. In six tests Joshua had scores of 80, 90, 100, 70, 90, and 80. What was his average score?

76. If a boy makes 16 free throws out of 20 tries, what percent of his throws are made?

77. A plane traveled 510 miles in $1\frac{1}{2}$ hours. What was the average rate of speed of the plane?

78. Mrs. Jones buys a refrigerator. She pays $230 down and $16.50 a month for 18 months. What was the cost of the refrigerator?

79. A boy spent one third of his money for a tennis racket and one fifth of his money for balls. What fractional part of his money did he spend?

80. By Thursday a family had spent $148, which was 80% of its weekly budget. How much was the budget?

81. Mr. White's farm is mortgaged for $52,000. At a rate of 8% what is the first year's annual interest charge for the mortgage?

82. If 30 inches of leather will make one belt, how many feet of leather would be needed to make 12 belts?

83. Of 75 dozen eggs sold by a dealer, 60 dozen were white eggs. What percent of the eggs sold were white eggs?

84. At a sale, all clothing was marked down 15%. Beth Steinfeld bought a blouse for $10.95 and a scarf for $8.85. What was the discount on her purchase?

85. A certain airplane uses 28.6 gallons of fuel per hour of flight. How many hours can the plane fly if its tank contains 214.5 gallons of fuel?

86. A plumber has a 12-foot length of pipe. From this length he cuts two pieces, each measuring $3\frac{1}{4}$ feet in length. How many feet of pipe remain?

87. A fuel oil bill for 350 gallons amounted to $518. What was the price per gallon of oil?

88. Mr. Frank spent $\frac{3}{8}$ of his savings for a new refrigerator. If the refrigerator cost $540, what were Mr. Frank's savings?

89. A school librarian can buy books at a 20% discount from the list price. One month she spent $72 for books. What was the list price value of the books?

90. At a sale, a furniture dealer sold a sofa for $144. The sofa cost the dealer $150. What was his percent of loss?

91. How many sheets of copper each 0.024 inches thick will make a pile 7.2 inches high?

92. Mr. Downs bought a camera for $56. This was 80% of the list price. What was the list price?

93. Ms. Rojas's yearly income is $23,400 a year. If she decides to save 10% of her yearly income, how much must she save each month?

94. A gallon of paint will cover 420 square feet. How many gallons of paint are needed to paint a porch 45 feet long and 14 feet wide?

95. At a special sale counter, notebooks were sold for $0.98 each. If the cash register at this counter showed sales of $109.76, how many notebooks were sold?

96. The mileage meter on Mr. Sanford's car read 5,684.9 at the start of the month, and 6,512.3 at the end of the month. How many miles did Mr. Sanford drive during the month?

97. Mrs. Frost bought a roast weighing $4\frac{1}{2}$ pounds. If she serves the roast to 6 people, what fraction of a pound of meat per person will the roast provide?

98. On a trip, Mrs. Ahmed drove 188 miles in 4 hours. On the return trip, she took a different route and traveled 197 miles in $4\frac{1}{4}$ hours. What was the average rate of speed for the trip?

99. At an election for class president, the winning candidate received 91 votes. This was 65% of the total vote cast. How many votes were cast?

100. Of 76 pupils in a certain grade, 57 passed a test. What percent of the pupils passed the test?

Mastery Exams

EXAM 1

1. A cab driver uses 18 gallons of gas in driving 264.6 miles. The average number of miles per gallon of gas used is:
(A) 15.2 (B) 16.7 (C) 14.7 (D) 12.9 (E) 14.9

2. Mr. Allan gave the clerk a $5 bill to pay for two dozen pencils at $0.59 per dozen. The amount of change he received was:
(A) $4.41 (B) $4.51 (C) $3.92 (D) $3.82 (E) $3.85

3. A new paperback sells for $2.48. The cost of a class set of 30 at a discount of 25% is:
(A) $62.00 (B) $56.55 (C) $55.80 (D) $74.40 (E) $52.00

4. Ms. Shapiro borrowed $500 for 3 months at 15% annual interest. The amount she paid back at the end of 3 months was:
(A) $518.75 (B) $520.50 (C) $512.25 (D) $518.25 (E) $95.25

5. A grocer bought one dozen key rings for $3.48. He sold the key rings for $0.37 each. His profit was:
(A) $1.08 (B) $4.44 (C) $3.11 (D) $0.60 (E) none of these

6. A school district with an assessed valuation of $2,480,500 has a tax rate of $12 per $1,000. The amount raised by taxes was:
(A) $2,976.60 (B) $2,976.06 (C) $29,760 (D) $29,766 (E) none of these

7. A boy earned $5.50 per hour for time worked up to 40 hours and $1\frac{1}{2}$ as much for all time worked over 40 hours. The amount of money he earned during one week when he worked 52 hours was:
(A) $253 (B) $249.60 (C) $319
(D) $324 (E) $195.40

8. A plane started on a flight at 9:30 A.M. and arrived at its destination at 1:45 P.M. The plane used 51 gallons of gas. The number of gallons used per hour was:
(A) 216.25 (B) 12 (C) 12.75 (D) 204
(E) none of these

9. A boy traveled 17 miles on his bicycle in 2 hours. At the same rate the time it will take him to travel 42.5 miles is:
(A) $2\frac{1}{2}$ hours (B) 3 hours (C) $4\frac{1}{2}$ hours
(D) 5 hours (E) none of these

10. A man bought a house for $75,000. He had it painted and paid the painter $162 per day for 5 days. He also paid a carpenter $174 a day for 3 days of work. Additional expenses amounted to $1,392. He then sold the house for $87,500. His profit was:
(A) $10,995 (B) $9,796 (C) $9,662
(D) $10,128 (E) none of these

11. A tank is 22 inches long, 14 inches wide, and 12 inches high. If 1 gallon contains 231 cubic inches the number of gallons the tank will hold is:
(A) 8 (B) 10 (C) 12 (D) 15
(E) none of these

12. A man borrowed $650 from the bank for one year. He paid $94.25 in interest. The rate of interest charged by the bank was:
(A) 14% (B) $14\frac{1}{2}$% (C) $15\frac{1}{2}$% (D) 12%
(E) none of these

13. A man bought a set of furniture listed at $2,350. He received a discount of 5% and then paid a 3% sales tax on the selling price. The sales tax was:
(A) $2,232.60 (B) $70.50 (C) $66.98
(D) $68.39 (E) $72.40

14. A farmer shipped 2,000 bushels of potatoes to a commission merchant. The farmer paid $480 for freight and $140 for trucking. The potatoes were sold for $8.90 a bushel by the merchant, who charged 4% commission. The farmer's net return was:
(A) $16,468 (B) $17,088 (C) $17,708
(D) 19,132 (E) none of these

15. A farmer insured her stock of goods for $27,000 at a rate of $1.85 per $100. The cost of the insurance was:
(A) $4,996 (B) $9.95 (C) $499.50
(D) $409.50 (E) $501

16. Henry won first place in the shot-put with a heave of 37 feet 1 inch. John won second place with a heave of 35 feet 9 inches. Henry defeated John by:
(A) 2 feet 2 inches (B) 1 foot 2 inches
(C) 1 foot 4 inches (D) 2 feet 4 inches
(E) none of these

17. If $\frac{1}{4}$ inch represents 5 yards, the number of inches needed to show a football field 100 yards long is:
(A) 4 inches (B) 5 inches (C) 20 inches
(D) 5 inches (E) 6 inches

18. The dimensions of a living room are 18 ft. by 15 ft. by 8 ft. If air weighs 0.08 lb. per cu. ft., the weight of the air in this room is:
(A) 2,160 lb. (B) 216 lb. (C) 172.8 lb.
(D) 17.28 lb. (E) 175 lb.

19. A radiator contains 8 gallons of water and 3 gallons of alcohol. The percent of alcohol in the radiator is:
(A) $27\frac{3}{11}$% (B) $37\frac{1}{2}$% (C) $72\frac{8}{11}$%
(D) 30% (E) 29%

20. A grocer paid $31 for 200 lb. of cabbage and sold it at the rate of 2 lb. for $0.39. His profit was:
(A) $47.00 (B) $16.00 (C) $39.00
(D) $8.00 (E) none of these

EXAM 2

1. The price of eggs decreased from $0.65 per dozen to $0.59 per dozen. The decrease per egg was:
(A) $0.06 (B) $0.02 (C) $0.01
(D) $0.005 (E) $0.03

2. A train was scheduled to arrive at 2:35 P.M. but was 40 minutes late. The train arrived at:
(A) 1:50 P.M. (B) 3:15 P.M.
(C) 3:05 P.M. (D) 1:45 P.M.
(E) 4:00 P.M.

3. If rock salt sells for $7.20 per hundred pounds, the cost of 750 pounds is:
(A) $49.00 (B) $49.50 (C) $52.00
(D) $54.00 (E) $56.00

4. At the rate of 360 miles per hour, the number of miles a plane will travel in 20 minutes is:
(A) 72 miles (B) 240 miles (C) 180 miles
(D) 144 miles (E) none of these

5. A man receives a salary of $3,150 per month. During the year he spends $4,800 for rent, $8,200 for food, $3,750 for clothing, and $7,500 for other expenses. The amount he saves in one year is:
(A) $24,250 (B) $12,550 (C) $13,550
(D) $14,500 (E) $14,000

6. A motorist left New York City at 9:40 A.M. and arrived at his destination at 1:00 P.M. If he traveled at an average speed of 42 miles per hour the total distance he covered was:
(A) 150 miles (B) 140 miles
(C) 126 miles (D) 168 miles
(E) none of these

7. Ms. Talento bought some household furnishings. She paid 40% down and agreed to pay the balance in 12 equal installments of $10 each. The total cost of the furnishings was:
(A) $240 (B) $250 (C) $160 (D) $300
(E) none of these

8. At the rate of 2 bushels of seed per acre, the number of bushels of seed required to plant 28 acres is:
(A) 75 (B) 10 (C) 56 (D) 73 (E) 70

9. In a recent basketball game one team made 21 successful shots and missed 66. The percent of successful shots was approximately:
(A) 33% (B) 24% (C) 25% (D) 32%
(E) 30%

10. The cost of 8 pounds of cabbage at 3 pounds for $0.65 is:
(A) $1.30 (B) $5.20 (C) $1.08 (D) $1.73
(E) $1.75

11. A homeowner bought 1,500 gallons of heating oil at $1.47 a gallon. The total cost was:
(A) $220.50 (B) $2,205.00 (C) $2,105.00
(D) $1,205.00 (E) $2,200.00

12. A salesman worked on a weekly salary of $180.00. To this was added a commission of 5% on all sales over $500. If his sales for one week were $750, his total salary for the week was:
(A) $217.50 (B) $205.00 (C) $212.50
(D) $192.50 (E) $210.00

13. A dealer has 12 pounds of peanuts. The number of 4-ounce bags she can fill is:
(A) 48 (B) 30 (C) 36 (D) 60
(E) none of these

14. The number of cubic feet of concrete contained in a sidewalk 3 ft. wide, 18 ft. long, and 4 in. thick is:
(A) 54 (B) 162 (C) 216 (D) 27
(E) none of these

15. At the start of a 1,565 mile trip there were 17 gallons of gasoline in the tank. During the trip 89 gallons of gasoline were bought. At the end of the trip 5 gallons of gasoline were left in the tank. The number of miles, to the nearest tenth, that the car averaged per gallon of gasoline, was:
(A) 16.4 (B) 15.5 (C) 17.1 (D) 16.5
(E) 16.1

16. At the rate of $0.72 for the first 10 minutes and $0.09 for each additional minute the cost of a 15-minute phone call is:
(A) $1.35 (B) $1.27 (C) $1.07 (D) $1.17
(E) none of these

17. A young man earns $1,350 a month. He pays $\frac{1}{5}$ of this amount for rent, $\frac{1}{3}$ of this amount for food, and $\frac{1}{6}$ for other household expenses. The amount of money he has left is:
(A) $40.50 (B) $94.50 (C) $945
(D) $480 (E) none of these

18. A man bought a lot for $1,200 and sold it for $1,500. His percent of gain based on the selling price was:
(A) 25% (B) 80% (C) 75% (D) 20%
(E) 22%

19. A room in a public building is to have a floor area of 770 square feet. If its length is 35 feet, then its width is:
(A) 350 ft. (B) 44 ft. (C) 22 ft. (D) 20 ft.
(E) none of these

20. Jerry's class purchased 10 boxes of candy for $43.20. If each box contained 24 candy bars the cost of each was:
(A) $0.08 (B) $0.15 (C) $0.06 (D) $0.18
(E) $0.12

EXAM 3

1. A salesman receives a salary of $20,900 per year and 2% commission on his sales. During the past year his sales amounted to $125,000. His average weekly salary was:
(A) $420 (B) $450 (C) $400 (D) $459.50
(E) $475

2. Mr. Thomas borrowed $1,200 from a bank for 90 days at $12\frac{1}{2}$% annual interest. The interest he paid was:
(A) $37 (B) $60 (C) $42 (D) $37.50
(E) $37.40

3. The cost of 36 pencils at the rate of 2 pencils for $0.37 is:
(A) $13.32 (B) $6.96 (C) $6.66
(D) $8.64 (E) none of these

4. A dealer sold 13 quart containers and 11 pint containers of ice cream in one day. The number of gallons of ice cream he sold was:
(A) 6 (B) $4\frac{5}{8}$ (C) $5\frac{1}{8}$ (D) 5 (E) 6

5. In a school cafeteria hamburgers were sold at 65 cents each. During the week, 60 pounds of meat were sold that averaged 12 hamburgers to the pound. The value of the hamburgers sold was:
(A) $486 (B) $720 (C) $780 (D) $568
(E) none of these

6. A plane left Atlanta at 11:30 A.M. and flew to an airport near Boston. The plane was due at Boston 3:15 P.M. The plane arrived 25 minutes late. The time of the trip was:
(A) 3 hr. 42 min. (B) 4 hr. 20 min.
(C) 4 hr. 10 min. (D) 3 hr. 50 min.
(E) none of these

7. The number of hours and minutes it will take a boy to ride his bicycle a distance of 10 miles at the rate of 6 miles per hour is:
(A) 1 hr. 45 min. (B) 1 hr. 40 min.
(C) 1 hr. 4 min. (D) 1 hr. 24 min.
(E) none of these

8. Ms. Sanchez drove 198 miles in 5 hours and 30 minutes. Her average rate of speed per hour was:
(A) 38 (B) 40 (C) 35 (D) 42
(E) none of these

9. If a man pays a water bill of $6.75 every three months, the amount he pays in a year is:
(A) $27 (B) $24.70 (C) $25.25
(D) $26.50 (E) $25.00

10. A watermelon weighs 4 pounds 6 ounces. The cost of the watermelon at $0.40 per pound is:
(A) $1.80 (B) $1.84 (C) $1.75 (D) $1.92
(E) none of these

11. The ratio of 1 pint to 4 gallons is:
(A) 1:4 (B) 1:32 (C) 1:16 (D) 1:8
(E) 1:40

12. At $15 per square yard, the cost of a rug that is 18 feet long and 10 feet wide is:
(A) $900 (B) $1,200 (C) $600 (D) $300
(E) $400

13. On a plane trip, baggage over 40 pounds is charged at the rate per pound of 1% of the one-way fare. The charge for a bag weighing 52 pounds on a trip where the one-way fare is $98 is:
(A) $11.76 (B) $4.90 (C) $25.48
(D) $5.88 (E) $8.72

14. When Mr. Green bought a used car he made a down payment of $825. This was 30% of the total cost. The total cost was:
(A) $2,475 (B) $2,750 (C) $3,200
(D) $2,650 (E) none of these

15. Mr. Kelly allows 6% of his sales dollar for profit and 69% of his sales dollar for cost. The percent of his sales dollar he allows for other expenses is:
(A) 31% (B) 94% (C) 75% (D) 63%
(E) none of these

16. One year a businesswoman made a profit of $15,000. The next year the profit was increased by 11% and the following year was decreased by 5%. The profit during the last year was:
(A) $15,750 (B) $15,850 (C) $17,250
(D) $15,675 (E) none of these

17. Mrs. Dana can buy a coat for $187.50 cash or for $25 down and $15 per month for 12 months. The charge for buying on the installment plan is:
(A) $12.50 (B) $17.50 (C) $22.50
(D) $27.50 (E) $18.50

18. After saving his allowance each week for nine weeks, Billy bought a jacket for $48.50. He found that he had $5.50 left. The amount of Billy's allowance each week was:
(A) $4.83 (B) $5.50 (C) $5.75 (D) $6.00
(E) none of these

19. A swimming pool 75 ft. long and 30 ft. wide is filled to an average depth of 6 ft. If $7\frac{1}{2}$ gal. of water occupy 1 cu ft., the number of gallons of water the pool contains is:
(A) 101,250 (B) 300 (C) $18\frac{3}{4}$ (D) 150
(E) none of these

20. Mr. Wang bought $800 worth of travelers' checks. The service charge was $\frac{3}{4}$ of 1% of the value of the checks. The service charge was:
(A) $5.00 (B) $4.00 (C) $3.00 (D) $8.00
(E) none of these

EXAM 4

1. Mr. Hall bought a car for $12,000. He made a down payment for $4,440 and agreed to pay the balance at the rate of $70 per month. The car was completely paid for in:
(A) 8 yr. (B) 10 yr. (C) 7 yr. 6 mo.
(D) 9 yr. (E) none of these

2. Mr. Stanley received a check for $240. This was the interest for 1 year at 6% on money he had lent to Mr. Stein. The amount he had lent to Mr. Stein was:
(A) $5,000 (B) $1,440 (C) $2,400
(D) $400 (E) none of these

3. At a school play 248 student tickets were sold at $0.75 each. If the total receipts were $250 the number of adult tickets sold at $1 each was:
(A) 2 (B) 68 (C) 64 (D) 76 (E) 80

4. Mr. Roll can insure his household silver for $10,500 at $0.32 for $100 for 1 year. A 3-year policy costs $2\frac{1}{2}$ times as much. By buying a 3-year policy instead of three 1-year policies, Mr. Roll saves:
(A) $33.60 (B) $16.80 (C) $25.00
(D) $1.60 E) none of these

5. A train covers 24 miles in 36 minutes. Its rate of speed in miles per hour is:
(A) 60 (B) 45 (C) 48 (D) 40 (E) 38

6. In one state, the income tax law provides for a tax of 1% on the first $1,000 of taxable income and 2% on the second $1,000 of taxable income. Mr. Cable has a taxable income of $1,850. His income tax is:
(A) $37 (B) $27 (C) $17 (D) $27.75
(E) $28.50

7. The cost of a ticket to a school concert is $0.90. This includes a tax of 20% on the actual price of the ticket. The tax is:
(A) $0.20 (B) $0.10 (C) $0.12 (D) $0.15
(E) $0.18

8. Ballpoint pens sell for 2 for $0.33. A box of pens containing 72 pens sells for:
(A) $11.88 (B) $23.76 (C) $11.52
(D) $12.48 (E) none of these

9. The cost of cementing a walk 8 feet wide and 24 feet long at $14.40 a square yard is:
(A) $31.20 (B) $2,764.80 (C) $307.20
(D) $921.60 (E) none of these

10. Taxi fare is $1.20 for the first $\frac{1}{4}$ mile and $0.10 for each additional $\frac{1}{8}$ mile. A man pays a fare of $3.00. The number of miles he has traveled is:
(A) 2 miles (B) $2\frac{1}{4}$ miles (C) $1\frac{3}{4}$ miles
(D) $2\frac{1}{2}$ miles (E) 3 miles

11. If a TV set is bought on the installment plan there is a down payment of $25 and 12 monthly payments of $15 each. The same set may be bought for cash at 12% less than the installment price. The amount saved by making a cash payment is:
(A) $20 (B) $21.60 (C) $24.00
(D) $24.60 (E) $22

12. One state has a tax of $0.04 on each gallon of gasoline sold. One month the tax amounted to $50,013.68. The number of gallons of gasoline sold during the month was:
(A) 125,342 (B) 1,250,342 (C) 1,205,042
(D) 1,253,042 (E) 1,023,796

13. A rectangular box is to have a volume of 66 cubic feet. If its length is 8′3″ and its width is 4′ then its height must be:
(A) 1 ft. (B) 2 ft. 6 in. (C) 2 ft.
(D) 2 ft. 3 in. (E) 3 ft.

14. The scale on a map is $\frac{3}{4}$ inch equals 24 miles. The actual distance between 2 cities that are $5\frac{1}{4}$ inches apart on this map is:
(A) 126 mi. (B) $31\frac{1}{2}$ mi. (C) 63 mi.
(D) 168 mi. (E) 170 mi.

15. A major league baseball team has won 24 games and lost 20 games. Out of the next 16 games the team wins 12 games. The percentage of games it has won is:
(A) 60% (B) 36% (C) 50% (D) 75%
(E) 55%

16. One year an automobile sales agency sells 3,200 cars. The following year sales are increased by 5%. The year after that sales decreased 15%. The number of cars sold that third year was:
(A) 3,360 (B) 2,880 (C) 2,740 (D) 2,856
(E) 2,800

17. A man buys furniture that has a list price of $255. He is allowed a discount of 12% but must pay a sales tax of 3% on the cost. The amount he actually pays is:
(A) $217.67 (B) $231.13 (C) $224.40
(D) $232.50 (E) none of these

18. A school has 510 students. They are to be divided into 18 classes so that, as far as possible, each class has the same number of students. After the students have been divided:
(A) all classes have exactly the same number of students
(B) 12 of the classes are smaller than the other 6
(C) each class has over 30 students
(D) one class is larger than all the others
(E) none of these

19. A man traveled to his country home, a distance of 150 miles, and then back. His average rate of speed going was 50 miles an hour and his average return speed was 30 miles an hour. His average rate of speed for the entire trip was:
(A) 40 miles per hour
(B) 42 miles per hour
(C) $37\frac{1}{2}$ miles per hour
(D) 35 miles per hour
(E) 30 miles per hour

20. A garden is 18 feet 3 inches long and 10 feet 8 inches wide. The amount of fencing needed to enclose the garden is:
(A) 36 feet 11 inches
(B) 47 feet 2 inches
(C) 39 feet 7 inches
(D) 57 feet 10 inches
(E) none of these

EXAM 5

1. A strip of molding is 20 inches long. Five pieces each $3\frac{1}{2}$ inches long are cut from the strip. The amount of molding remaining is:
(A) 3 inches (B) $3\frac{1}{2}$ inches
(C) $2\frac{1}{2}$ inches (D) 2 inches
(E) none of these

2. A man's income is $14,904 a year. He pays $138 a month for rent. The part of this income spent for rent per year is:
(A) $\frac{1}{54}$ (B) $\frac{1}{9}$ (C) $\frac{1}{12}$ (D) $\frac{2}{9}$ (E) $\frac{1}{11}$

3. A pantry contains 6 shelves each 42 inches long. The shelves are to be relined with fresh paper. The paper is sold in 1 yard rolls. The number of 1 yard rolls needed is:
(A) 6 (B) 7 (C) 3 (D) 5 (E) 9

4. A machine is bought for $4,125. It loses 20% of its value each year. The value of the machine at the end of 2 years is:
(A) $2640 (B) $2475 (C) $3300
(D) $825 (E) $2500

5. Bill gets up at 7:15 A.M. every morning. The time he must get to sleep if he is to get $9\frac{1}{2}$ hours of sleep is:
(A) 10:15 P.M. (B) 10:45 P.M.
(C) 9:45 P.M. (D) 11:00 P.M.
(E) none of these

6. Round-trip fare between two cities is $68.40 plus 15% tax. At the same rate, one-way fare is:
(A) $34.20 (B) $78.66 (C) $73.53
(D) $53.40 (E) none of these

7. Ms. Sun bought a 145-acre farm at $76 an acre. Her down payment was 25% of the cost. The down payment was:
(A) $11,020 (B) $10,120 (C) $2,755
(D) $2,900 (E) none of these

8. Betty admired a blouse that was marked at $12.80. She figured that she could make the blouse herself for 35% less than the marked price. The cost of making the blouse was:
(A) $4.48 (B) $8.32 (C) $21.12
(D) $10.58 (E) $8.40

9. Mr. Adams harvested 936 bushels of wheat from 52 acres. If the pattern continues, the number of bushels of wheat harvested from 79 acres is:
(A) 1,015 (B) 1,264 (C) 1,186 (D) 1,422
(E) 1,500

10. Mr. Stavropoulos owns a cottage worth $68,500. He insured it for 80% of its value at $0.42 per $100. His premium was:
(A) $2,301 (B) $287.70 (C) $230.16
(D) $240 (E) none of these

11. Mr. Bates bought a television set for $148. He paid $30 down and the balance in 15 equal payments of $8.50 each. The amount of the carrying charge was:
(A) $20.50 (B) $9.50 (C) $2.00
(D) $7.50 (E) $9.00

12. The distance between Seattle and Denver is 1,020 miles. Mr. Riley travels between the two cities by car at an average rate of 45 miles per hour. Mr. Moto made the same trip by plane at the average rate of 306 miles per hour. The number of hours Mr. Moto saved by using the plane was:
(A) $19\frac{1}{3}$ (B) $28\frac{1}{3}$ (C) 24 (D) 20 (E) 30

13. Mr. Corbin is a salesman. He gets a 5% commission on all sales between $100 and $500 and a 10% commission on all sales above $500. His commission on sales of $783 was:
(A) $53.30 (B) $98.30 (C) $48.30 (D) $102.45 (E) $49.00

14. Of the students who tried out for the baseball team, $\frac{1}{8}$ tried out as catchers, $\frac{1}{3}$ as infielders, and $\frac{1}{4}$ as outfielders. The fraction of the students who tried out as pitchers was:
(A) $\frac{2}{3}$ (B) $\frac{5}{8}$ (C) $\frac{7}{8}$ (D) $\frac{7}{24}$ (E) $\frac{7}{25}$

15. John wishes to make a picture frame 2′3″ long and 1′8″ wide. The amount of molding John will need is:
(A) 3′11″ (B) 7′10″ (C) 8′2″ (D) 8′6″ (E) 8′

16. In a foul shooting contest Mario sank 11 out of 16 tries, Plato sank 10 out of 15 tries, Fred sank 15 out of 20 tries, Sam sank 9 out of 17 tries, and Karen sank 15 out of 21 tries. The winner was:
(A) John (B) Bill (C) Fred (D) Sam (E) Karen

17. A dozen golf balls were priced at $7.20. The tax was 15% of the selling price. The cost of each golf ball was:
(A) $0.65 (B) $0.69 (C) $0.72 (D) $0.80 (E) $0.75

18. At the rate of 50 miles per hour a car can travel 14.6 miles for each gallon of gas used. On a trip Mr. Hanson used 12.5 gallons of gas traveling at a speed of 50 miles per hour. The number of miles covered during the trip was:
(A) 62.5 (B) 100 (C) 1,250 (D) 365 (E) none of these

19. For a local talent show, orchestra seats sell for $8.50 and balcony seats sell for $4.50. The box office took in $2,616. If 128 balcony seats were sold, then the number of orchestra seats sold was:
(A) 256 (B) 240 (C) 320 (D) 280 (E) 350

20. On a camping vacation trip of 12 days the Otis family spent $579.84. If $63.48 was spent for automobile expenses then the daily expenses for other items were:
(A) $516.36 (B) $42.93 (C) $48.32 (D) $43.03 (E) none of these

EXAM 6

1. A gallon of a certain kind of paint will cover 224 square feet of surface. In painting two walls, one 36′ by 8′ and the other 24′ by 9′, the number of gallons of paint used is:
(A) 3 (B) $2\frac{1}{2}$ (C) $4\frac{1}{4}$ (D) $2\frac{1}{4}$ (E) $2\frac{1}{2}$

2. At a television station 46% of the workers are employed in the technical department, 23% in the program department, and the rest in other departments. The percent of the workers employed in other departments is:
(A) 21% (B) 41% (C) 31% (D) 69% (E) 32%

3. Mrs. Roberts needs material for four curtains. Each curtain requires 3 yards 1 foot of material. At $3 per yard the cost for material is:
(A) $37 (B) $40 (C) $45 (D) $80 (E) $42

4. Morad finds he can walk a mile in 12 minutes 15 seconds. The time it would take him to walk 8 miles is:
   (A) 1 hr. 38 min. (B) 2 hr. 4 min. (C) 1 hr. 36 min. (D) 1 hr. 30 min. (E) none of these

5. A kitchen floor is 9 feet long and 6 feet wide. The number of yards of molding needed to hold the linoleum around the outside edge is:
   (A) 30 (B) 15 (C) 21 (D) 5 (E) none of these

6. The weights of the members of the backfield of the Adams High School are 184 lb., 178 lb., 191 lb., and 167 lb. Bill Walters weighs 183 lb. Bill's weight is:
   (A) 5 lb. above the average of the backfield
   (B) 2 lb. below the average of the backfield
   (C) 3 lb. above the average of the backfield
   (D) equal to the average weight of the backfield
   (E) none of these

7. The basketball team of Martin Luther King High School won 12 of its first 15 games. It then won its next 3 games. Its winning percentage was then:
   (A) 80% (B) 75% (C) 60% (D) $83\frac{1}{3}$% (E) 78%

8. Bob got 34 questions right on a test and received a mark of 85%. The number of questions on the test was:
   (A) 38 (B) 40 (C) 29 (D) 50 (E) 45

9. Mr. Baker earns $448 a week. He spends 86% of this amount for expenses. The amount he saves in a year of 52 weeks is:
   (A) $3,361.18 (B) $1,792.48 (C) $3,136 (D) $3,261.44 (E) none of these

10. In a high school there are 768 pupils. Of these, $\frac{3}{8}$ are girls. If $\frac{5}{6}$ of the girls are below the senior class, the number of senior girls is:
    (A) 44 (B) 56 (C) 59 (D) 39 (E) none of these

11. A car is driven at the rate of 30 miles per hour. The distance the car covers in 1 minute is:
    (A) $\frac{1}{4}$ mile (B) 2 miles (C) $\frac{1}{2}$ mile (D) 4 miles (E) 5 miles

12. Mrs. Smiros went on a trip of 780 miles. The first day she covered 297 miles and the second day 379 miles. The part of the trip left was:
    (A) $\frac{1}{3}$ (B) $\frac{2}{15}$ (C) $\frac{1}{7}$ (D) $\frac{1}{9}$ (E) $\frac{1}{10}$

13. A package of books weighs 48 pounds. The packing case weighs 3 pounds. If each book weighs $1\frac{1}{4}$ pounds the number of books is:
    (A) 40 (B) 44 (C) 32 (D) 36 (E) 40

14. Mr. Sherman earns $7.20 per hour. On Monday he works $8\frac{1}{2}$ hours, Tuesday $7\frac{3}{4}$ hours, Wednesday $7\frac{1}{2}$ hours, Thursday 7 hours, and Friday $7\frac{3}{4}$ hours. His earnings for the week are:
    (A) $273.60 (B) $277.20 (C) $280.80 (D) $278.00 (E) none of these

15. Mrs. Simon has a piece of cloth 15 yards long. From this cloth she cuts towels 27 inches long. The number of towels she obtains is:
    (A) 12 (B) 16 (C) 18 (D) 20 (E) 25

16. Mr. Barry works on an 8% commission basis. One week his pay was $336. His sales amounted to:
    (A) $420 (B) $4,200 (C) $2,688 (D) $2,736 (E) none of these

17. The distance from Los Angeles to Denver is 810 miles. If the scale on the map is 1″ = 180 miles, the distance between these cities on the map is:
    (A) $3\frac{1}{2}$″ (B) $5\frac{1}{4}$″ (C) $4\frac{1}{2}$″ (D) $3\frac{1}{4}$″ (E) 4″

18. A store received a shipment of 3 dozen shirts that cost $162. If the shirts are to be sold at a profit of 40%, each shirt must be marked at:
    (A) $4.90 (B) $5.20 C) $6.30 (D) $6.00 (E) $6.50

19. A town has a population of 153,000. There are 50,490 telephones in the town. The number of telephones per 100 of population is:
(A) 50.49 (B) 33 (C) 5.04 (D) 0.504
(E) 35

20. Mr. Seto borrowed some money from a bank at 15% interest. At the end of the year he made a payment of $517.50 to cover the entire capital plus interest. The amount he had borrowed from the bank was:
(A) $480 (B) $500 (C) $456.80 (D) $450
(E) none of these

EXAM 7

1. A bus traveled 156 miles in 3 hours and 15 minutes. The distance the bus traveled in 5 hours and 40 minutes at the same rate of speed was:
(A) 250 miles (B) 264 miles
(C) 280 miles (D) 260 miles
(E) none of these

2. A dealer bought a used car for $270. She spent $50 in repairs and then sold the car for $400. The percent of profit she made on her investment was:
(A) 29% (B) $33\frac{1}{2}$% (C) 25% (D) 30%
(E) none of these

3. A man bought a house for $76,000. He made a down payment of $26,000 and agreed to pay $2,500 each year with interest of 14% on the unpaid balance. His payment at the end of the second year was:
(A) $6,650 (B) $8,150 (C) $7,500
(D) $9,150 (E) none of these

4. Mr. Fry was paid partly on a commission basis. His commission earnings for 4 weeks were $120, $132, $108, and $116. In order to have an average commission salary of $125 for the 5 weeks his commission earnings for the fifth week must be:
(A) $137 (B) $149 (C) $151 (D) $119
(E) $150

5. A ball team won 15 games and lost 22 games. It plays 13 more games and wins 12 of them. The percent of games won is now:
(A) 27% (B) 80% (C) 92% (D) 66%
(E) none of these

6. A homeowner buys 450 gallons of oil at $1.49 per gallon and 350 gallons of oil at $1.51 per gallon. His total cost is:
(A) $670.50 (B) $528.50 (C) $1,199.00
(D) $764.00 (E) none of these

7. A woman bought a steak weighing 5 pounds 6 ounces at $3.20 per pound and oranges weighing 3 pounds 4 ounces at $0.68 per pound. The amount she received in change from a $20 bill was:
(A) $1.58 (B) $19.41 (C) $2.43
(D) $0.59 (E) $0.49

8. Mr. Stone and Mr. Alvin grow potatoes on their farms. Mr. Stone has 168 acres and averages 127.4 bushels to the acre. Mr. Alvin has 149 acres and averages 130.7 bushels to the acre. Together the number of bushels of potatoes grown is:
(A) 39,877 (B) 40,877.5 (C) 41,877.5
(D) 1,928.9 (E) none of these

9. Mr. Saul bought a used car for $9,600. Over a 5-year period he paid $289.60 per year for insurance, $948 for repairs, $5,048 for gas, and $690 for other expenses. If he drove 60,000 miles and then sold the car for $3,200 his driving cost per mile was:
(A) less than $0.20 (B) about $0.24
(C) between $0.26 and $0.27
(D) about $0.30 (E) none of these

10. Ms. Russo spent $\frac{2}{3}$ of her income for rent and food and saved $\frac{1}{2}$ of the remainder. The part of her income saved was:
(A) $\frac{1}{3}$ (B) $\frac{1}{5}$ (C) $\frac{1}{6}$ (D) $\frac{1}{4}$ (E) $\frac{1}{8}$

11. In driving between 2 cities Mr. Bayne drove a distance of 180 miles. The trip took 5 hours including a one-half hour stop for food. The average driving speed on the trip was:
(A) 36 mph (B) 40 mph (C) 45 mph
(D) 38 mph (E) 42 mph

12. A city has a 3% sales tax. A motorist buys 8 gallons of gas at $1.289 cents per gallon plus tax. His total cost is:
(A) $10.62 (B) $10.60 (C) $10.31
(D) $10.00 (E) $10.75

13. A state's budget for a certain year is $78,500,000. Of this amount 28.7% is spent for education. The amount spent for education is:
(A) $2,252,950 (B) $225,295
(C) $22,529,500 (D) $32,419,500
(E) none of these

14. There are 630 pupils in a high school. If 20% of the pupils are seniors the number who are not seniors is:
(A) 126 (B) 630 (C) 315 (D) 404
(E) none of these

15. The weight of a certain type of copper wire is 12.8 lb. per 1,000 ft. The weight of 375 ft. of this wire is:
(A) 4,800 lb. (B) 480 lb. (C) 4.8 lb.
(D) 48 lb. (E) 5.2 lb.

16. Joe is 5′4″ tall and his father is 6′ tall. The ratio of Joe's height to his father's height is:
(A) 9:8 (B) 9:10 (C) 10:9 (D) 8:9 (E) 8:7

17. The thickness of one sheet of a certain type of sheet aluminum is 0.03 inch. The number of sheets in a pile 6 inches high is:
(A) 20 (B) 200 (C) 180 (D) 2,000
(E) 250

18. A movie house shows 5 continuous performances over a period of 12 hours. The length of each showing is:
(A) 2 hr. and 20 min.
(B) 2 hr. and 40 min.
(C) 2 hr. and 30 min.
(D) 2 hr. and 24 min.
(E) none of these

19. A plane has a fuel tank that holds 5,250 gallons of gas. With a full tank, the plane can cover 4,200 miles. The number of miles the plane can cover for each gallon of gas is:
(A) 1.25 (B) 0.8 (C) 12 (D) 8 (E) 1.2

20. One gallon of water is equal to 231 cubic inches. The number of gallons needed to fill a tank 22″ by 9″ by 7″ is:
(A) 5 (B) 7 (C) 9 (D) 6 (E) 8

EXAM 8

1. A student's college education costs $8,500 per year. He saves $1,200 while working during the summer. His father agrees to pay $\frac{1}{2}$ of his expenses. The amount the student still needs is:
(A) $4,250 (B) $3,650 (C) $3,050
(D) $2,450 (E) none of these

2. Mr. Gage buys furniture valued at $975. He makes a down payment of $260 and agrees to pay the balance in installments of $25 each. The number of installments he pays is:
(A) 29 (B) 39 (C) 17 (D) 32 (E) 35

3. A certain type of plane uses 4.75 gallons of gas per hour while cruising. If a pilot has 22.8 gallons of gas he can cruise for:
(A) 4 hours and 8 minutes
(B) 4 hours and 24 minutes
(C) 4 hours and 48 minutes
(D) 4 hours and 40 minutes
(E) none of these

4. In a high school, $\frac{1}{3}$ of the students are freshmen and $\frac{1}{6}$ of the students are seniors. There are equal numbers of sophomores and juniors. The fraction representing the part of the students who are juniors is:
(A) $\frac{1}{5}$ (B) $\frac{1}{3}$ (C) $\frac{1}{2}$ (D) $\frac{3}{8}$
(E) none of these

5. In a certain state, a taxpayer is permitted a deduction of $2,500. On the balance of his income he pays 2% on his first $1,000, 3% on the next $2,000, and 5% on the rest of his income. His tax on an income of $16,700 is:
(A) $740 (B) $680 (C) $640 (D) $720
(E) $800

6. Mr. Van Dyke sells two cars costing $12,000 and $7,600. On the first sale he makes a profit of 8% and on the second he suffers a loss of 10%. The result is:
(A) a loss of $200 (B) a loss of 2%
(C) a gain of 2% (D) a gain of $200
(E) none of these

7. A city has a budget of $6,480,000. It marks 8.45% for public welfare. The amount available for public welfare is:
(A) $534,320 (B) $547,560 (C) $54,432
(D) $533,320 (E) none of these

8. Mr. Paul insures his house for $90,000 at $0.38 per $100. The amount he can save by taking a policy for 5 years for a total premium of $1,580 is:
(A) $30 (B) $230 (C) $150 (D) $130
(E) $200

9. A dealer buys a shipment of 60 radios for a total of $2,280. If he wishes to make a profit of 30% on the shipment, the sale price of each radio should be:
(A) $38 (B) $31.80 (C) $49.40
(D) $34.20 (E) $35.00

10. The Martin Fruit Co. charges 7% commission for selling fruit. The commission for selling 516 crates of oranges at $16.30 per crate is:
(A) $5,887.56 (B) $58.88 (E) $608.36
(D) $588.76 (E) $600.00

11. A dealer sold an overcoat for $96. This was at a profit of $33\frac{1}{3}$% of the cost. The cost of the overcoat was:
(A) $64 (B) $72 (C) $128 (D) $68
(E) $84

12. A steel bar which is 17 feet long weighs 52.53 pounds. A similar bar 19 feet long weighs:
(A) 55.91 pounds (B) 56.81 pounds
(C) 58.71 pounds (D) 60.61 pounds
(E) none of these

13. Ms. Choung had $1,200. She bought a desk for $158.98, and spent half of what she had left for a sofa. The amount she had left was:
(A) $1,041.02 (B) $520.01 (C) $520.51
(D) $679.29 (E) $600

14. A mechanic started working on a car at 10:45 A.M. and finished the job at 12:15 P.M. If the charge for labor is $17.50 per hour, the labor charge for this job was:
(A) $35.00 (B) $26.25 (C) $25.00
(D) $33.75 (E) $28.00

15. A boy answered 12 questions on a test correctly and received a rating of 80%. The number of questions on the test was:
(A) 20 (B) 16 (C) 18 (D) 25
(E) none of these

16. Bob weighed 96 pounds last year and now weighs 112 pounds. His gain in weight is:
(A) $16\frac{2}{3}$% (B) 16% (C) 12% (D) $10\frac{1}{2}$%
(E) none of these

17. A woman bought curtain material 25 yards long. Each curtain takes $5\frac{1}{2}$ yards. After she has made as many curtains as she has material for, the amount of material left is:
(A) $2\frac{1}{4}$ yards (B) 3 yards (C) 4 yards
(D) $2\frac{1}{2}$ yards (E) 5 yards

18. A school has 8 classes of 32 pupils and 7 classes of 33 pupils. The school has room for 520 pupils. The number of additional pupils the school can admit is:
(A) 13 (B) 15 (C) 33 (D) 47 (E) 35

19. Mr. Moran drove his car 2,254 miles one month. His insurance on the car was $61.27 per month. The cost of insurance per mile was approximately:
(A) $0.29 (B) 0.35\frac{1}{3}$ (C) $0.36
(D) 0.32\frac{1}{2}$ (E) none of these

20. Mr. Lopez priced ties selling for $4.50 per tie. During a sale the ties were reduced in price by 20%. The number of ties Mr. Lopez bought for $18.00 during the sale was:
(A) 4 (B) 6 (C) 5 (D) 8 (E) 9

Answers to All Practice Tests, Verbal Problems, and Mastery Exams

PRACTICE TESTS

TEST 1

1. $55\frac{1}{4}$ in.
2. $152.10
3. 23.59 g.
4. $77,644,041.54
5. $107\frac{13}{30}$ gal.
6. $12.30

TEST 2

1. $3.16
2. 1,782.7 mi.
3. $6.20
4. $6\frac{17}{24}$ ft.
5. 7,192 lb.
6. 5.075 or $5\frac{3}{40}$ lb.
7. $7.02
8. 5,917,899
9. 11.01 g.

TEST 3

1. $352
2. 30,000
3. $62.40
4. 44 in.
5. 0.0676 in.
6. $3,684,106
7. 1,000 lb.
8. 336 ft.
9. $15\frac{1}{8}$ mi.
10. 1800
11. 4452 mi.
12. 950 mi.

TEST 4

1. $\frac{3}{4}$ lb.
2. $141\frac{2}{3}$ yd.
3. 17
4. 128
5. $1.25
6. 360
7. $\frac{6}{11}$ m.p.h.
8. $100
9. 32
10. 1.30 sec.

TEST 5

1. 5 lb.
2. 900 mi.
3. $104
4. 20 in.
5. $55.56
6. $704
7. $4.32
8. $3240
9. $15.60
10. $49
11. 128
12. $\frac{1}{15}$ or 0.067 m.p.h.
13. $780
14. $629
15. $36
16. $43.20
17. $19.20
18. $27
19. 84 oz.
20. $233.95

TEST 6

1. 14
2. $325
3. $1,000
4. 38,500
5. 356.4 gal.
6. $2,925
7. 449,100 lb.
8. $22.50

TEST 7

1. $33\frac{1}{3}$%
2. $12\frac{1}{2}$%
3. $66\frac{2}{3}$%
4. 300%
5. $11\frac{1}{9}$%
6. $5\frac{1}{2}$%
7. $33\frac{1}{3}$%
8. $83\frac{1}{3}$%
9. 200%
10. $62\frac{1}{2}$%

TEST 8

1. 23,000
2. $150
3. $10,000
4. 490,600
5. $128
6. 50
7. $800
8. $24
9. 18 mi.
10. $24.50

TEST 9

1. $32.50
2. $33.75
3. 25%
4. $120,000
5. $13\frac{1}{3}$%
6. $73 profit
7. $7.50 loss
8. 8.40%
9. $82,950
10. $144

TEST 10

1. $3\frac{1}{2}$%
2. $406.25
3. $5\frac{1}{2}$%
4. $420
5. $9,025
6. $30.72
7. $2,800
8. $2\frac{1}{2}$%
9. $6,800
10. $42.53
11. $189.60
12. $151.08
13. 15%
14. $61,000
15. $3,327.70
16. $135
17. $7,648.44
18. 20%
19. 8%
20. 20%

TEST 11

1. $37\frac{1}{2}$%
2. 380
3. $62\frac{1}{2}$%
4. $299.60
5. $276
6. $647.50
7. 1,140
8. $82.40
9. The Blue Sox by $23\frac{1}{3}$%
10. $15,000
11. 620
12. 85%
13. 261
14. $9,600
15. 609
16. 65%
17. 15%
18. $6,370
19. $560
20. $1,250
21. 480
22. 117
23. $216
24. 34%
25. $350,000
26. $2,941.75
27. 12
28. $39
29. 5%
30. 416
31. $4\frac{1}{2}$%
32. 1,250
33. 9%
34. $320
35. 5%
36. $27,084
37. 250
38. 95%
39. $12\frac{1}{2}$%
40. 8%
41. 99
42. 1,040
43. $882.45
44. $15,000
45. $14\frac{2}{7}$%
46. 860
47. $1,203.96
48. 28%
49. $138.21
50. $60

TEST 12

1. 37
2. 79
3. $2.96
4. 829
5. 86%
6. $31.13
7. 191
8. 6′ 1″
9. 75
10. 91

ONE HUNDRED VERBAL PROBLEMS

Rating Your Results

Superior	90–100 correct
Average	70–89 correct
Below Average	69 or fewer correct

1. 9 yards
2. 147 miles
3. $259.20
4. $1\frac{1}{2}$ feet
5. 8
6. $23,712
7. 38 hours
8. $26.26
9. 432 miles
10. $1.40
11. 75%
12. $100.80
13. 25 gallons
14. $17.30
15. 5.48 inches
16. $235.20
17. $9.85
18. 1,875 gallons
19. $1.20
20. $\frac{3}{5}$
21. 3 minutes
22. 10
23. $1.98
24. 84
25. 60
26. 38
27. $7.14
28. $2.70
29. $2.10
30. $306
31. 18 weeks
32. 72%
33. 180 cubic feet
34. $5.25
35. $5\frac{3}{7}$ pounds
36. 3,000
37. $7,321.90
38. 8 feet
39. $219.20
40. $403.20
41. $1.50
42. $430
43. $144
44. $7\frac{1}{2}$%
45. $4.08
46. $27.75
47. 5 inches
48. 2%
49. 5:7
50. 12%
51. $35
52. 20
53. 15 miles
54. 24 square yards
55. 80%
56. 480 miles
57. 7,680
58. 45%
59. $13.20
60. $1.25
61. $1.29
62. $81.25
63. 18 cubic feet
64. 60
65. 20
66. $0.18
67. $2.58
68. $36
69. $37\frac{1}{2}$ yards
70. $160
71. $26\frac{1}{4}$ pounds
72. $27
73. 17 miles
74. 35%
75. 85
76. 80%
77. 340 miles per hour
78. $527
79. $\frac{8}{15}$
80. $185
81. $4,160
82. 30 feet
83. 80%
84. $2.97
85. $7\frac{1}{2}$ hours
86. $5\frac{1}{2}$ feet
87. $1.48
88. $1,440
89. $90
90. 4%
91. 300
92. $70
93. $195
94. $1\frac{1}{2}$ gallons
95. 112
96. 827.4 miles
97. $\frac{3}{4}$ pound
98. 44 miles per hour
99. 140
100. 75%

MASTERY EXAMS

Rating Your Results

Superior	18–20 correct
Average	14–17 correct
Below Average	13 or fewer correct

EXAM 1

1. **C**
2. **D**
3. **C**
4. **A**
5. **E**
6. **D**
7. **C**
8. **B**
9. **D**
10. **E**
11. **E**
12. **B**
13. **C**
14. **A**
15. **C**
16. **C**
17. **B**
18. **C**
19. **A**
20. **D**

EXAM 2

1. **D**
2. **B**
3. **D**
4. **E**
5. **C**
6. **B**
7. **A**
8. **C**
9. **B**
10. **D**
11. **B**
12. **D**
13. **A**
14. **E**
15. **B**
16. **D**
17. **E**
18. **D**
19. **C**
20. **D**

EXAM 3

1. **B**	5. **E**	9. **A**	13. **A**	17. **B**
2. **D**	6. **C**	10. **C**	14. **B**	18. **D**
3. **C**	7. **B**	11. **B**	15. **E**	19. **A**
4. **B**	8. **E**	12. **A**	16. **E**	20. **E**

EXAM 4

1. **D**	5. **D**	9. **D**	13. **C**	17. **B**
2. **E**	6. **B**	10. **D**	14. **D**	18. **B**
3. **C**	7. **D**	11. **D**	15. **A**	19. **C**
4. **B**	8. **A**	12. **B**	16. **D**	20. **D**

EXAM 5

1. **C**	5. **C**	9. **D**	13. **C**	17. **B**
2. **B**	6. **E**	10. **E**	14. **D**	18. **E**
3. **B**	7. **C**	11. **B**	15. **B**	19. **B**
4. **A**	8. **B**	12. **A**	16. **C**	20. **D**

EXAM 6

1. **D**	5. **E**	9. **D**	13. **D**	17. **C**
2. **C**	6. **C**	10. **E**	14. **B**	18. **C**
3. **B**	7. **D**	11. **C**	15. **D**	19. **B**
4. **A**	8. **B**	12. **B**	16. **B**	20. **D**

EXAM 7

1. **E**	5. **E**	9. **B**	13. **C**	17. **B**
2. **C**	6. **C**	10. **C**	14. **E**	18. **D**
3. **D**	7. **D**	11. **B**	15. **C**	19. **A**
4. **B**	8. **B**	12. **A**	16. **D**	20. **D**

EXAM 8

1. **C**	5. **C**	9. **C**	13. **C**	17. **B**
2. **A**	6. **D**	10. **D**	14. **B**	18. **C**
3. **C**	7. **B**	11. **B**	15. **E**	19. **D**
4. **E**	8. **D**	12. **C**	16. **A**	20. **C**

Algebra

Representing Numbers by Letters

We know that we can find the average of three numbers by finding the sum of the numbers and dividing this sum by 3. This idea may be expressed by the following formula:

$$N = \frac{x+y+z}{3}$$

In this formula

N represents the average
x represents the first number
y represents the second number
z represents the third number

Letters used to represent numbers in this manner are called *variables*.

The advantage in writing this formula is that it tells us how to find the average of any three numbers.

The product of two numbers may be expressed by using the × symbol or the raised dot. For example, the product of 4 and 7 may be written as 4×7, or as $4 \cdot 7$. If n represents a number in algebra we may express the product of 5 and n as $5 \times n$, or as $5 \cdot n$, or simply as $5n$. Similarly, $9y$ means "9 times y" and ab means "a times b."

The operations of addition, subtraction, and division are expressed by using the same symbols as used in arithmetic. For example,

$x + y$ means "the sum of x and y"

$a - b$ means "the difference between a and b"

$c \div d$, or $\frac{c}{d}$, means "c divided by d"

In order to learn how to use algebra in solving problems, we must learn how to translate ordinary language into algebraic language.

EXAMPLE: A man has x dollars in the bank. He deposits 100 dollars more. How many dollars does he have in the bank after the deposit?

SOLUTION: x + \$100

EXAMPLE: A dealer has b television sets in stock. During a sale the dealer sells y of these sets. How many sets does she have left?

SOLUTION: $b - y$

EXAMPLE: A movie theater has z rows with 28 seats in each row. How many seats does the movie theater have?

SOLUTION: The theater has z times 28 seats, or 28 times z seats. This may be expressed as $28 \times z$, or $28 \cdot z$, or $28z$. The expression "$28z$" is preferred.

EXAMPLE: If 7 apples cost y cents, what is the cost of a apples?

SOLUTION: The cost of one apple is $\frac{y}{7}$ cents. The cost of a apples is $a \times \frac{y}{7}$, or $\frac{ay}{7}$ cents.

EXAMPLE: Express the product of the number $c + 5$ and the number k.

SOLUTION: In order to express this product, we must regard $c + 5$ as one number. To do this, we use parentheses. The result is $k(c + 5)$.

PRACTICE TEST 1

DIRECTIONS: Solve each of the following problems, and then circle the letter that corresponds to the right answer.

1. A man bought a shirt for x dollars and a tie for \$6. The total cost for the two items is:
(A) $6x$ (B) $x - 6$ (C) $x \div 6$ (D) $x + 6$
(E) $6 - x$

2. A motorist drives between two cities that are 120 miles apart. After he has covered y miles the remaining distance is:
(A) $120 + y$ (B) $120 - y$ (C) $y - 120$
(D) $120y$ (E) $120 \div y$

3. A woman buys b pounds of apples at 59 cents per pound. The cost of the apples is:
(A) b + 59¢ (B) 59¢ − b (C) b − 59¢
(D) 59¢ ÷ b (E) 59¢b

4. A girl has \$5.00. She buys 4 notebooks at c cents each. The amount she receives in change is:
(A) \$5.00 − $4c$ (B) \$5.00 + $4c$
(C) $4c$ − \$5.00 (D) $4c$ · \$5.00
(E) \$5.00 ÷ $4c$

5. A Boy Scout troop hikes z miles in 4 hours. The number of miles per hour covered by the troop is:
(A) $4z$ (B) $z + 4$ (C) $z \div 4$ (D) $4 \div z$
(E) $z - 4$

6. Luigi is x years old. His father is 30 years older. The age of Luigi's father is:
(A) $30 - x$ (B) $30 \div x$ (C) $30x$ (D) $x + 30$
(E) $x - 30$

7. If 10 pencils cost y cents, what is the cost of x pencils?
(A) $10xy$ (B) $xy \div 10$ (C) $x + y + 10$
(D) $10x \div y$ (E) $10y \div x$

8. Mr. Burns deposited n dollars in a bank and received 7% interest per year. His interest for one year was:
(A) $7n$ (B) $0.7n$ (C) $7 + n$ (D) $n - 7$
(E) $0.07n$

9. If y dozen eggs cost x cents, how many dozen eggs can be bought for k cents?
(A) $\frac{xk}{y}$ (B) $\frac{ky}{x}$ (C) $\frac{xy}{k}$ (D) $\frac{y}{kx}$ (E) $\frac{x}{ky}$

10. A train travels b miles in 8 hours. What is the average rate of speed of the train?
(A) $8b$ (B) $b + 8$ (C) $b \div 8$ (D) $8 \div b$
(E) $b - 8$

Exponents and Evaluating Algebraic Expressions

When we multiply the number 9 by itself we may express the multiplication by the expression 9×9, or by the expression 9^2. In this case, the 2 is called an *exponent* and 9 is called the *base*. In the same way, $5 \times 5 \times 5 \times 5$ may be expressed as 5^4. The expression b^3 means $b \times b \times b$.

EXAMPLES: a^5 means $a \times a \times a \times a \times a$
$2c^3$ means $2 \times c \times c \times c$

It is necessary to be able to find the numerical value of an algebraic expression when we know the numerical value of each letter of the expression. When an expression has several operations, it is necessary to follow the proper order of operations.

ORDER OF OPERATIONS RULES

1. Do all operations inside grouping symbols first. Grouping symbols include parentheses ( ), brackets [ ], braces { }, and a bar as in $\sqrt{9 + 16}$ or $\frac{3 + 5}{8}$.
2. Do all roots and exponents in order from left to right.
3. Do all multiplications and divisions in order from left to right. This rule does *not* say do all multiplications and then do all divisions—do them as they appear in order from left to right.
4. Do all additions and subtractions in order from left to right. This also does not say do

additions before subtractions—do them as they appear in order from left to right.

EXAMPLE: Find the value of $3a + b - 2c$ when $a = 5$, $b = 3$, and $c = 1$.

$$\begin{aligned} 3a + b - 2c &= 3 \cdot 5 + 3 - 2 \cdot 1 \\ &= 15 + 3 - 2 \\ &= 16 \end{aligned}$$

EXAMPLE: Find the value of $5x^2 - 2y^3 + z$ when $x = 4$, $y = 3$, and $z = 7$.

$$\begin{aligned} 5x^2 - 2y^3 + z &= 5 \cdot 4 \cdot 4 - 2 \cdot 3 \cdot 3 \cdot 3 + 7 \\ &= 80 - 54 + 7 \\ &= 33 \end{aligned}$$

EXAMPLE: Find the value of $6(4y^3 - 3x^2)$ when $x = 5$ and $y = 3$.

$$\begin{aligned} 6(4y^3 - 3x^2) &= 6(4 \cdot 3^3 - 3 \cdot 5^2) \\ &= 6(108 - 75) \\ &= 6(\pm 33) \\ &= \pm 198 \end{aligned}$$

PRACTICE TEST 2

DIRECTIONS: Solve each of the following problems, then circle the letter that corresponds to the right answer.

In the following examples $x = 6$, $y = 5$, $z = 4$, $a = 3$, and $b = 1$.

1. The value of $2x^2 + 2y - 7a$ is:
(A) 133 (B) 175 (C) 39 (D) 61 (E) 51

2. The value of $x^3 - 2z^2 + b$ is:
(A) 183 (B) 185 (C) 249 (D) –13 (E) 153

3. The value of $2xa^2b^3$ is:
(A) 111 (B) 180 (C) 1,296 (D) 105 (E) 108

4. The value of $a(b + x^2)$ is:
(A) 111 (B) 108 (C) 39 (D) 101 (E) 105

5. The value of $12y^2 \div b^2x$ is:
(A) 12 (B) 50 (C) 2 (D) 25 (E) $5\frac{5}{6}$

6. The value of $abx^2 - 2y$ is:
(A) 29 (B) 30 (C) 98 (D) 101 (E) 118

7. The value of $xy^2 + 2yz^2 - 4ab$ is:
(A) 1,048 (B) 250 (C) 322 (D) 300 (E) 298

8. The value of $z(a + b)^2$ is:
(A) 12 (B) 32 (C) 144 (D) 64 (E) 20

9. The value of $2b(x - a)^2$ is:
(A) 18 (B) 12 (C) 162 (D) 27 (E) 36

10. The value of $x^2y^2 - az^3$ is:
(A) 608 (B) 708 (C) 852 (D) 7 (E) 800

Formulas

In our work in geometry we use formulas such as

$$P = 2l + 2w$$

to find the perimeter of a rectangle and

$$A = \tfrac{1}{2}bh$$

to find the area of a triangle. Formulas are used frequently in science, in engineering, and in business. In this section, we will work with several different types of formulas.

EXAMPLE: The formula $E = IR$ (Ohm's law) is used in electricity. Find the value of E when $I = 5$ and $R = 28$.

SOLUTION:

$$\begin{aligned} E &= IR \\ E &= 5 \times 28 = 140 \end{aligned}$$

EXAMPLE: The formula $C = \frac{5}{9}(F - 32)$ is used to convert Fahrenheit temperature readings to Celsius temperature readings. Find the Celsius reading when the Fahrenheit reading is 68°.

SOLUTION:

$$\begin{aligned} C &= \tfrac{5}{9}(F - 32) \\ C &= \tfrac{5}{9}(68 - 32) \\ C &= \tfrac{5}{9}(36) = 20 \end{aligned}$$

PRACTICE TEST 3

DIRECTIONS: Solve each of the following problems, then circle the letter that corresponds to the right answer.

1. The formula $A = \frac{a+b+c+d}{4}$ is used to find the average of four numbers *a, b, c,* and *d.* The average of 68, 73, 47, and 84 is:
(A) $65\frac{1}{2}$ (B) 68 (C) 47 (D) 71 (E) 69

2. The formula $D = 16t^2$ is used to find the distance, in feet, of a freely falling body where *t* represents the number of seconds during which the body falls. The number of feet covered by a freely falling body in 9 seconds is:
(A) 144 (B) 288 (C) 2,304 (D) 400 (E) 1,296

3. The formula $C = 35 + 5(n - 3)$ is used to find the cost of borrowing a book from a circulating library where *n* represents the number of days during which the book is borrowed. The cost, in cents, of borrowing a book for 12 days is:
(A) 70 (B) 80 (C) 90 (D) 95 (E) 85

4. The formula $S = 5{,}000 + 20(n - 100)$ is used to find the yearly salary of a machine salesman where *n* represents the number of machines sold. If the salesman sold 678 machines during a certain year, his salary for that year was:
(A) \$5,678 (B) \$17,500 (C) \$16,560 (D) \$17,000 (E) \$17,800

5. The formula for finding the area of an open rectangular box with a square base is $A = b^2 + 4bh$. If $b = 8$ ft. and $h = 6$ ft., the area of the box, in square feet, is:
(A) 256 (B) 246 (C) 204 (D) 208 (E) 212

6. The recommended weight of an adult man is given by the formula $W = \frac{11}{2}(h - 60) + 100$ where W = weight in pounds and h = height in inches. If a man is 72 inches tall, his weight, in pounds, should be:
(A) 232 (B) 178 (C) 192 (D) 166 (E) 160

Solving Equations

The ability to solve equations enables us to solve many different types of problems.

An *equation* is a statement that two quantities are equal.

Consider the equation

$$2x + 5 = 11$$

This equation tells us that $2x + 5$ and 11 name the same number. Since this is the case, the value of x must be 3, since $2 \cdot 3 + 5 = 11$. And 3 is the only number that balances the equation. The number 3, which represents x and balances or satisfies the equation, is called the solution of the equation.

PRACTICE TEST 4

DIRECTIONS: Solve each of the following problems, then circle the letter that corresponds to the right answer.

Select the letter that represents a solution of the given equation.

1. $x + 3 = 7$
(A) 10 (B) 5 (C) 4 (D) 7 (E) –10

2. $x - 2 = 8$
(A) 6 (B) 4 (C) –6 (D) –10 (E) 10

3. $2x + 1 = 11$
(A) 6 (B) 5 (C) 4 (D) –5 (E) 3

4. $3x - 2 = 4$
(A) $1\frac{1}{2}$ (B) $1\frac{1}{3}$ (C) 2 (D) 3 (E) –1

5. $\frac{x}{2} + 1 = 5$
(A) 8 (B) 2 (C) 3 (D) 5 (E) 7

6. $\frac{x}{3} - 2 = 2$
(A) 0 (B) 1 (C) 4 (D) 12 (E) 6

7. $3x + 1 = 19$
(A) 5 (B) 6 (C) $6\frac{2}{3}$ (D) 3 (E) 2

8. $5x - 4 = 11$
(A) 5 (B) 15 (C) 2 (D) $1\frac{2}{5}$ (E) 3

9. $x^2 + 2x = 3$
(A) 2 (B) −2 (C) 1 (D) 3 (E) 4

10. $y^2 - y - 6 = 0$
(A) 3 (B) −3 (C) 4 (D) 2 (E) 1

11. $x^2 = 5x$
(A) 3 (B) 5 (C) 1 (D) 4 (E) 2

12. $y^2 + 3y - 10 = 0$
(A) 5 (B) 4 (C) 0 (D) 2 (E) 1

We will now consider systematic methods of solving equations.

Consider the equation $x + 1 = 6$. This tells us that when a certain number is added to 1, the result is 6. It is clear that the unknown number is 5, since $5 + 1 = 6$. Thus, $x = 5$. To go from $x + 1$ to x we subtract 1 from $x + 1$, or $x + 1 - 1 = x$. Since $x + 1$ and 6 name the same number, we must subtract the same number from $x + 1$ and from 6 to obtain equal results. We write this process as follows:

$$\begin{aligned} x + 1 &= 6 \\ x + 1 - 1 &= 6 - 1 \\ x &= 5 \end{aligned}$$

Consider the equation $x - 3 = 1$. In order to obtain x on the left side of the equation, we add 3 to $x - 3$. Since $x - 3$ and 1 name the same number, we must add 3 to both $x - 3$ and 1 to obtain equal results.

$$\begin{aligned} x - 3 &= 1 \\ x - 3 + 3 &= 1 + 3 \\ x &= 4 \end{aligned}$$

Consider the equation $3x = 12$. In order to obtain x on the left side of the equation, we must divide $3x$ by 3. Since $3x$ and 12 name the same number, we divide both $3x$ and 12 by 3 and we obtain equal results.

$$\begin{aligned} 3x &= 12 \\ \tfrac{1}{3}(3x) &= \tfrac{1}{3}(12) \\ x &= 4 \end{aligned}$$

Consider the equation $\frac{y}{4} = 5$. In order to obtain y on the left side of the equation, we must multiply $\frac{y}{4}$ or $\frac{1}{4}y$ by 4. Since $\frac{y}{4}$ and 5 represent the same number, we multiply both $\frac{y}{4}$ and 5 by 4 and we obtain equal results.

$$\begin{aligned} \frac{y}{4} &= 5 \\ \frac{4 \times y}{4} &= 4 \times 5 \\ y &= 20 \end{aligned}$$

The results of this discussion may be summarized as follows:

To Find the Solution to an Equation

1. Subtract where there is a sum. For example:

$$\begin{aligned} x + 1 &= 6 \\ x + 1 - 1 &= 6 - 1 \\ x &= 5 \end{aligned}$$

2. Add when there is a difference. For example:

$$\begin{aligned} x - 3 &= 1 \\ x - 3 + 3 &= 1 + 3 \\ x &= 4 \end{aligned}$$

3. Divide when there is a product. For example:

$$\begin{aligned} 3x &= 12 \\ \frac{3x}{3} &= \frac{12}{3} \\ x &= 4 \end{aligned}$$

4. Multiply when there is a quotient. For example:

$$\begin{aligned} \frac{x}{4} &= 5 \\ 4\left(\frac{x}{4}\right) &= 4(5) \\ x &= 20 \end{aligned}$$

PRACTICE TEST 5

DIRECTIONS: Solve the following equations.

1. $x + 2 = 5$ $x =$ ________

2. $x - 2 = 3$ $x =$ ________

3. $3x = 15$ $x =$ ________

4. $\frac{x}{2} = 7$ $x =$ ________

5. $x - 6 = 3$ $x =$ ________

6. $x + 4 = 7$ $x =$ ________

7. $2x = 8$ $x =$ ______
8. $\frac{x}{3} = 5$ $x =$ ______
9. $4x = 20$ $x =$ ______
10. $x - 2 = 7$ $x =$ ______
11. $x + 7 = 9$ $x =$ ______
12. $2x = 16$ $x =$ ______
13. $x - 7 = 1$ $x =$ ______
14. $\frac{x}{4} = 5$ $x =$ ______
15. $5x = 10$ $x =$ ______
16. $x - 2 = 2$ $x =$ ______
17. $x + 7 = 10$ $x =$ ______
18. $7x = 35$ $x =$ ______
19. $x - 8 = 2$ $x =$ ______
20. $x + 9 = 9$ $x =$ ______

To solve some equations it is sometimes necessary to combine similar terms. Terms that have the exact same variable factors are called similar (or like) terms, and they can be combined by adding or subtracting the numerical factors of the similar terms.

EXAMPLES:

$$3x + 5x = (3 + 5)x = 8x$$
$$4y - y = (4 - 1)y = 3y$$

In solving some problems it is useful to be able to find the solutions of more difficult equations.

EXAMPLE: Solve the equation $3x + 4x = 35$. Since $3x + 4x = 7x$, we have

$$7x = 35$$
$$x = \frac{35}{7}$$
$$x = 5$$

EXAMPLE: Solve the equation $\frac{3}{4}x = 12$. In order to obtain x on the left side of the equation, we must multiply $\frac{3}{4}x$ by $\frac{4}{3}$. Since $\frac{3}{4}x$ and 12 name the same number, we multiply both $\frac{3}{4}x$ and 12 by $\frac{4}{3}$ to obtain equal results.

$$\frac{4}{3} \cdot \frac{3}{4}x = \frac{4}{3} \cdot 12$$
$$x = 16$$

EXAMPLE: Solve the equation $3x + 2 = 20$.

$$3x + 2 = 20$$
$$3x + 2 - 2 = 20 - 2$$
$$3x = 18$$
$$\frac{3x}{3} = \frac{18}{3}$$
$$x = 6$$

EXAMPLE: Solve the equation $\frac{2}{3}x - 4 = 6$.

$$\frac{2}{3}x - 4 = 6$$
$$\frac{2}{3}x - 4 + 4 = 6 + 4$$
$$\frac{2}{3}x = 10$$
$$\frac{3}{2} \cdot \frac{2}{3}x = \frac{3}{2} \cdot 10$$
$$x = 15$$

PRACTICE TEST 6

DIRECTIONS: Solve the following equations.

1. $3x + 4x = 14$ $x =$ ______
2. $x + 5x = 30$ $x =$ ______
3. $4x + 1 = 25$ $x =$ ______
4. $3x - 4 = 14$ $x =$ ______
5. $\frac{x}{3} + 2 = 7$ $x =$ ______
6. $7x - 3x = 32$ $x =$ ______
7. $2x + 5 = 7$ $x =$ ______
8. $\frac{3}{5}x + 2 = 8$ $x =$ ______
9. $3x + 4x + 2 = 16$ $x =$ ______
10. $2x - 5 = 1$ $x =$ ______
11. $5x + 1 = 31$ $x =$ ______
12. $\frac{2}{3}x - 4 = 8$ $x =$ ______
13. $3x - 7 = 2$ $x =$ ______
14. $6x - x = 25$ $x =$ ______
15. $2x + x + 3 = 15$ $x =$ ______
16. $\frac{4}{3}x - 2 = 6$ $x =$ ______
17. $7x - 5 = 9$ $x =$ ______
18. $x + 3x - 1 = 11$ $x =$ ______
19. $5x + 7 = 22$ $x =$ ______
20. $4x - 5 = 11$ $x =$ ______

Solving Problems by the Use of Equations

Since we now know how to solve equations, we may solve a great variety of problems. Consider the following:

EXAMPLE: During a football game 45 points were scored. If the winning team scored 9 points more than the losing team, how many points did each team score?

SOLUTION: Let x = the number of points scored by the losing team.

And $x + 9$ = the number of points scored by the winning team.

Since the total number of points scored was 45, we have

$$x + (x + 9) = 45$$
$$2x + 9 = 45$$
$$2x + 9 - 9 = 45 - 9$$
$$2x = 36$$
$$x = \frac{36}{2} = 18$$
$$x + 9 = 18 + 9 = 27$$

Thus, the losing team scored 18 points and the winning team scored 27 points.

EXAMPLE: Two cars leave Washington, DC traveling in opposite directions. The faster car travels at an average speed of 40 miles per hour and the slower car travels at the rate of 30 miles per hour. In how many hours will the cars be 630 miles apart?

SOLUTION: Let x = the number of hours it takes the cars to be 630 miles apart.

Then $40x$ = the number of miles covered by the faster car.

And $30x$ = the number of miles covered by the slower car. At this point, it is helpful to collect our information in a box.

Rate	×	Time	=	Distance
40	×	x	=	$40x$
30	×	x	=	$30x$

According to the conditions of this problem, the distance covered by the faster car plus the distance covered by the slower car = 630 miles. Thus, we have the equation

$$40x + 30x = 630$$
$$70x = 630$$
$$x = 630 \div 70 = 9$$

It will take 9 hours of driving before the cars are 630 miles apart.

EXAMPLE: Green, Adams, and Burns were the three top scorers in a basketball game. Green scored twice as many points as Adams, and Burns scored 7 points more than Adams. Together the three men scored 75 points. How many points did each man score?

SOLUTION: Let x = the number of points scored by Adams.

And $2x$ = the number of points scored by Green.

And $x + 7$ = the number of points scored by Burns.

Since the total scored by the three men was 75 points, we have

$$x + 2x + x + 7 = 75$$
$$4x + 7 = 75$$
$$4x + 7 - 7 = 75 - 7$$
$$4x = 68$$
$$x = \frac{68}{4} = 17$$
$$2x = 2 \times 17 = 34$$
$$x + 7 = 17 + 7 = 24$$

Thus, Adams scored 17 points, Green scored 34 points, and Burns scored 24 points.

EXAMPLE: The ratio of two numbers is 5:3. If 7 is added to the larger number and 1 is added to the smaller number, the numbers are in the ratio of 2:1. Find the two original numbers.

SOLUTION: Let $5x$ = the larger number.

And $3x$ = the smaller number.

After 7 is added to the larger number and 1 is added to the smaller number, the resulting numbers are $(5x + 7)$ and $(3x + 1)$.

According to the conditions of the problem, the resulting numbers are in the ratio 2:1. This gives us the equation

$$(5x + 7) : (3x + 1) = 2:1$$

In this proportion, if we set the product of the means equal to the product of the extremes we have

$$2(3x + 1) = (5x + 7)$$
$$6x + 2 = 5x + 7$$
$$6x - 5x + 2 = 5x - 5x + 7$$
$$x + 3 = 7$$
$$x + 2 - 2 = 7 - 2$$
$$x = 5$$

The larger number $= 5x = 5 \cdot 5 = 25$.
The smaller number $= 3x = 3 \cdot 5 = 15$.

Thus, the original numbers are 25 and 15.

EXAMPLE: Mr. Barnes has \$25,000 to invest. He plans to invest part of his money at 6% yearly interest and the rest at 7% yearly interest. If his total yearly income from both investments is \$1,600, how much did he invest at each rate?

SOLUTION: Let x = the amount invested at 6%.

Then \$25,000 – x = the amount invested at 7%.

The sum of the two incomes is \$1,600 yearly.

Thus, we have the equation

$$.06x + .07\,(25{,}000 - x) = \$1{,}600$$

If we multiply both sides of this equation by 100, we have

$$6x + 7\,(250{,}000 - x) = 160{,}000$$
$$6x + 1{,}750{,}000 - 7x = 160{,}000$$
$$-x = -1{,}590{,}000$$
$$x = 1{,}590{,}000$$
$$25{,}000 - x = 10{,}000$$

Thus, Mr. Barnes invested \$15,000 at 6% and \$10,000 at 7%.

EXAMPLE: The difference between $\frac{1}{3}$ of a number and $\frac{1}{8}$ of the same number is 15. Find the number.

SOLUTION: Let x = the number.

Then $\frac{1}{3}x$, or $\frac{x}{3}$, = $\frac{1}{3}$ of the number.

And $\frac{1}{8}x$, or $\frac{x}{8}$, = $\frac{1}{8}$ of the number.

According to the conditions of the problem, the difference between $\frac{1}{3}$ of the number and $\frac{1}{8}$ of the number is 15. This gives the equation

$$\frac{x}{3} - \frac{x}{8} = 15$$

If we multiply all members of the equation by 24 we will obtain the following equation, which does not contain fractions:

$$8x - 3x = 360$$
$$5x = 360$$
$$x = \frac{360}{5} = 72$$

Thus, the number is 72.

PRACTICE TEST 7

DIRECTIONS: Solve the following problems.

1. The measure of one angle of a triangle is 6 degrees greater than the measure of a second angle of the triangle. And the measure of the third angle of the triangle is equal to the sum of the measures of the first two angles. Find the measures of the three angles of the triangle.
2. Find four consecutive odd numbers such that the difference between three times the fourth and the first exceeds the third by 31.
3. A man invests \$20,000 to yield \$1,280 interest annually. If part of his investment pays 6% annually and the rest of his investment pays 7% annually, how much does he invest at each rate?
4. Five less than seven times a certain number is 58. Find the number.
5. A plumber wishes to cut a piece of pipe 32 inches long into two parts so that the smaller part is 4 inches less than three times the larger part. What are the lengths of the two parts of the pipe?
6. A mechanic earns \$5 more per hour than his helper. On a six-hour job the two men earn a total of \$114. How much does each earn per hour?
7. The sum of two numbers is 26. If the larger number is 2 less than three times the smaller number, what is the smaller number?
8. The perimeter of a triangle is 44 inches. If one side is 5 inches longer than the smallest side and the largest side is 1 inch less than twice the smallest side, how many inches are there in the smallest side?

9. The sum of $\frac{1}{2}$ a certain number and $\frac{1}{3}$ of the same number is 30. Find the number.

10. The ratio of John's money to Fred's money is 8:3. If John gives Fred \$6, John will have twice as much money as Fred. How much money does John have before he gives Fred money?

11. Two motorists start at the same time to drive toward each other from cities that are 360 miles apart. If the first motorist averages 48 miles per hour and the second motorist averages 42 miles per hour, in how many hours will they meet?

12. If 19 is subtracted from 4 times a number, the result is 73. Find the number.

13. Two planes start from the same airport at the same time and travel in opposite directions. If the first plane travels at an average speed of 240 miles per hour and the second plane travels at an average speed of 320 miles per hour, in how many hours will the planes be 1,400 miles apart?

14. The difference between $\frac{1}{2}$ of a number and $\frac{1}{5}$ of the same number is 24. Find the number.

15. The ratio of two numbers is 7:4. If 8 is added to the larger number and 4 is subtracted from the smaller number, the ratio of the numbers is 5:2. Find the two original numbers.

16. A man died and left his estate of \$125,000 to his wife, his daughter, and his son. If the wife received twice as much as his son, and his daughter received \$5,000 more than his son, how much did the man leave to his son?

17. The length of a room, rectangular in shape, is 8 feet greater than its width. If the perimeter of the room is 64 feet, what are the dimensions of the room?

18. A professional baseball player makes 168 hits over a season. Of these, the number of singles is 5 less than three times the number of extra base hits. How many extra base hits did the player make?

19. Two motorists start toward each other from cities 400 miles apart at 1 P.M. If one motorist travels at an average rate of 42 miles per hour and the other motorist travels at an average rate of 38 miles per hour, at what time will the cars meet?

20. If 5 more than a certain number is tripled, the result is 72. What is the number?

21. Two numbers are in the ratio of 5:7. If 12 is added to each number the ratio is 4:5. What are the original two numbers?

Solving Inequalities

An *inequality* is a statement that two quantities are unequal. For example, $7 > 3$ and $2 < 6$. (Recall that the symbol $>$ means "is greater than," and $<$ means "is less than.")

Consider the inequality

$$3x + 5 > 17$$

This inequality tells us that $3x + 5$ represents a number that is greater than 17. To solve this inequality we must find the value or values of x such that the expression "$3x + 5$" has a value greater than 17. Before we develop systematic methods of solving inequalities, we will use trial methods.

If $x = 1$, then $3x + 5 = 3 \cdot 1 + 5 = 8$
If $x = 2$, then $3x + 5 = 3 \cdot 2 + 5 = 11$
If $x = 3$, then $3x + 5 = 3 \cdot 3 + 5 = 14$
If $x = 4$, then $3x + 5 = 3 \cdot 4 + 5 = 17$
If $x = 5$, then $3x + 5 = 3 \cdot 5 + 5 = 20$

Thus, 5 is a solution of the inequality $3x + 5 > 17$. Also, we can see that when $x > 4$ the inequality is satisfied. For example, $x = 4.1$, $x = 6$, and $x = 7.03$. The inequality has an infinite number of solutions and all these solutions are numbers greater than 4. We may express this result by saying that the solution of the inequality is $x > 4$.

PRACTICE TEST 8

DIRECTIONS: In each case, select the letter that is a solution of the given inequality.

1. $x + 1 > 3$
   (A) 0 (B) 1 (C) 2 (D) 5 (E) –2

2. $x + 2 < 5$
   (A) 3 (B) 2 (C) 4 (D) 5 (E) 7

3. $2x + 1 > 6$
   (A) 2 (B) $2\frac{1}{2}$ (C) 3 (D) –2 (E) 1

4. $3x - 1 < 7$
   (A) 3 (B) 4 (C) $3\frac{1}{2}$ (D) 5 (E) 2

5. $5x + 3 > 18$
   (A) 3 (B) 2 (C) $3\frac{1}{2}$ (D) 0 (E) 1

6. $2x - 1 < 3$
   (A) 0 (B) 2 (C) 3 (D) 5 (E) 6

We are now ready to consider systematic methods of solving inequalities.

The rules for generating equivalent inequalities are similar to those for solving equations.

The following rules are stated using < (less than) but they could be stated using any of the symbols > (greater than), ≤ (less than or equal), or ≥ (greater than or equal).

1. If $A < B$, then $A + C < B + C$. Adding (or subtracting) the same number to both sides of an inequality generates an equivalent inequality.

EXAMPLE: Solve $x - 4 < 5$.

$$x - 4 < 5$$
$$x - 4 + 4 < 5 + 4$$
$$x < 9$$

2. If $A < B$, then:
   a. $AC < BC$, if C is a positive number.
   b. $AC > BC$, if C is a negative number.

   This rule that you can multiply (or divide) both sides of an inequality by the same positive number maintaining the same direction of the inequality. But if you multiply (or divide) both sides of an inequality by a negative number, you must reverse the direction of the inequality.

EXAMPLES: Solve $3x > 15$.

$$3x > 15$$
$$\frac{3x}{3} > \frac{15}{3}$$
$$x > 5$$

Solve $1 - 2x \leq 7$.

$$1 - 2x \leq 7$$
$$1 - 2x - 1 \leq 7 - 1$$
$$-2x \leq 6$$
$$\frac{-2x}{-2} \geq \frac{6}{-2}$$
$$x \geq -3$$

Consider the inequality

$$x - 3 < 5$$

In order to solve this inequality, we must add 3 to both numbers. In general, if we add the same quantity to both members of an inequality, we do not change the direction of the inequality. Thus, we have

$$x - 3 + 3 < 5 + 3$$

or

$$x < 8$$

Consider the inequality

$$3x < 12$$

In order to obtain x on the left side of the inequality, we must divide $3x$ by 3. We must also divide the right side of the inequality by 3 in order to maintain the balance of the inequality. In general, we may divide both members of an inequality by the same *positive* number without changing the direction of the inequality. Thus, we have

$$\frac{3x}{3} < \frac{12}{3}$$

or

$$x < 4$$

EXAMPLE: Solve the inequality $x + 5 > 7$.

$$x + 5 > 7$$
$$x + 5 - 5 > 7 - 5$$
$$x > 2$$

EXAMPLE: Solve the inequality $x - 1 < 5$.

$$x - 1 < 5$$
$$x - 1 + 1 < 5 + 1$$
$$x < 6$$

EXAMPLE: Solve the inequality $5x > 15$.

$$5x > 15$$
$$\frac{5x}{5} > \frac{15}{5}$$
$$x > 3$$

EXAMPLE: Solve $2 - 5x > 12$.

$$2 - 5x > 12$$
$$2 - 5x - 2 > 12 - 2$$
$$-5x > 10$$
$$\frac{-5x}{-5} < \frac{10}{-5}$$
$$x < -2$$

PRACTICE TEST 9

DIRECTIONS: Solve the following inequalities.

1. $x + 4 > 7$ $x >$ ________
2. $x - 2 > 4$ $x >$ ________
3. $x + 1 < 10$ $x <$ ________
4. $x - 3 < 6$ $x <$ ________
5. $2x < 8$ $x <$ ________
6. $3x > 18$ $x >$ ________
7. $x - 5 > 1$ $x >$ ________
8. $x + 4 < 7$ $x <$ ________
9. $3x + 5 > 23$ $x >$ ________
10. $\frac{x}{3} + 1 \leq 4$ $x \leq$ ________

In solving inequalities involving two operations, it is generally desirable to add or subtract before dividing. The following examples show how this is done.

EXAMPLE: Solve the inequality

$$2y + 1 > 9$$
$$2y + 1 - 1 > 9 - 1$$
$$2y > 8$$
$$\frac{2y}{2} > \frac{8}{2}$$
$$y > 4$$

EXAMPLE:

$$3y - 2 < 4$$
$$3y - 2 + 2 < 4 + 2$$
$$3y < 6$$
$$\frac{3y}{3} < \frac{6}{3}$$
$$y < 2$$

PRACTICE TEST 10

DIRECTIONS: Solve the following inequalities.

1. $2x + 3 > 11$ $x >$ ________
2. $3y - 1 > 14$ $y >$ ________
3. $4y + 1 > 29$ $y >$ ________
4. $2x - 5 < 9$ $x >$ ________
5. $3x + 7 < 13$ $x <$ ________
6. $5y - 2 > 28$ $y >$ ________
7. $6x + 1 > 25$ $x >$ ________
8. $4y - 5 < 23$ $y <$ ________
9. $4 - 2y < 10$ $y <$ ________
10. $\frac{1}{2}x - 3 > 2$ $x >$ ________

Answers to All Practice Tests

TEST 1

1. **D** 3. **E** 5. **C** 7. **B** 9. **B**
2. **B** 4. **A** 6. **D** 8. **E** 10. **C**

TEST 2

1. **D** 3. **E** 5. **B** 7. **E** 9. **A**
2. **B** 4. **A** 6. **C** 8. **D** 10. **B**

TEST 3

1. **B** 3. **B** 4. **C** 5. **A** 6. **D**
2. **E**

TEST 4

1. **C** 4. **C** 7. **B** 9. **C** 11. **B**
2. **E** 5. **A** 8. **E** 10. **A** 12. **D**
3. **B** 6. **D**

TEST 5

1. 3	6. 3	11. 2	16. 4
2. 5	7. 4	12. 8	17. 3
3. 5	8. 15	13. 8	18. 5
4. 14	9. 5	14. 20	19. 10
5. 9	10. 9	15. 2	20. 0

TEST 6

1. 2	6. 8	11. 6	16. 6
2. 5	7. 1	12. 18	17. 2
3. 6	8. 10	13. 3	18. 3
4. 6	9. 2	14. 5	19. 3
5. 15	10. 3	15. 4	20. 4

TEST 7

1. 42, 48, and 90
2. 17, 19, 21, 23
3. \$12,000 at 6% and \$8,000 at 7%
4. 9
5. 9 inches, 23 inches
6. \$12 per hour for mechanic
   \$7 per hour for helper
7. 7
8. 10 inches
9. 36
10. \$72
11. 4
12. 23
13. $2\frac{1}{2}$ hours
14. 80
15. 42, 24
16. \$30,000
17. 12 feet by 20 feet
18. 43
19. 6 P.M.
20. 19
21. 20, 28

TEST 8

1. **D** 3. **C** 5. **C**
2. **B** 4. **E** 6. **A**

TEST 9

1. $x > 3$	5. $x < 4$	9. $x > 6$
2. $x > 6$	6. $x > 6$	10. $x \leq 9$
3. $x < 9$	7. $x > 6$	
4. $x < 9$	8. $x < 3$	

TEST 10

1. $x > 4$	5. $x < 2$	9. $y > -3$
2. $y > 5$	6. $y > 6$	10. $x > 10$
3. $y > 7$	7. $x > 4$	
4. $x < 7$	8. $y < 7$	

Numbers and Number Systems

If you are using this book to prepare for a specific examination, make certain that the material in this chapter is included in the test items *before* you begin studying this section.

Sets

The idea of a set is basic in modern mathematics. In much of our ordinary speaking and writing we talk about collections of objects. For example, we talk about a *set* of checkers, a *deck* of cards, a *circle* of friends, and a *team* of basketball players.

A set is a collection of objects. Each item of a set is called an *element* or a *member* of the set. In defining a set, we must make clear which objects are members of the set and which objects are not members of the set. For convenience, we use braces { } to enclose the members of a set. Thus, we may describe a set in words or by the use of braces. A set may have one or more members, or a set may have no members. A set that has no members is called an *empty* set. Either of two symbols may be used to designate an empty set: Ø or { }.

EXAMPLE: A = {Monday, Tuesday, Wednesday, Thursday, Friday, Saturday, Sunday}

A is the set consisting of the names of the days of the week.

EXAMPLE: B = {July 4}

B is the set consisting of the names of the legal United States holidays in the month of July.

EXAMPLE: C = { }

C is the set of the names of women presidents of the United States (an empty set).

EXERCISE 1

1. *Write the following sets by listing their members enclosed in braces.*
   (a) The set of names of months of the year beginning with the letter J.
   (b) The set of the names of the members of your family.
   (c) The set consisting of the names of the first three letters of the English alphabet.
   (d) The set of the names of professional football players who are women.
   (e) The set consisting of the names of the days of the week when you do not attend school.
   (f) The set consisting of the name of the first president of the United States.

2. *Describe each of the following sets in words:*
   (a) {x, y, z}
   (b) {1¢, 5¢, 10¢, 25¢, 50¢}
   (c) {New York, Chicago, Los Angeles}
   (d) {2, 4, 6, 8, 10}
   (e) {right forward, left forward, center, right guard, left guard}

The *union* of two sets, *A* and *B*, is the set consisting of all members of *A* together with all members of *B*. The symbol used to designate union is ∪.

EXAMPLE: $A = \{1, 3, 5, 7\}$
$B = \{2, 4, 5, 6, 7\}$
$A \cup B = \{1, 2, 3, 4, 5, 6, 7\}$

The *intersection* of two sets, *A* and *B*, is a set containing the members that are in both set *A* and set *B*. The symbol used to designate the intersection is ∩.

EXAMPLE: $A = \{a, b, c, e, f, o\}$
$B = \{a, e, i, o, u\}$
$A \cap B = \{a, e, o\}$
$A \cup B = \{a, b, c, e, f, i, i, o, u\}$

EXERCISE 2

1. *Write the union of the following pairs of sets:*
   (a) $C = \{5, 10, 15, 20\}$,
   $D = \{10, 20, 30, 35\}$
   (b) $F = \{$John, Bill, Mary$\}$,
   $G = \{$John, Fred, Nancy$\}$
   (c) $K = \{$June, July, August, September$\}$,
   $L = \{$June, October, December$\}$
   (d) $P = \{$the set of names of days of the week beginning with T$\}$
   $Q = \{$the set of names of days of the week beginning with S$\}$

2. *Write the intersection of the following pairs of sets:*
   (a) $B = \{2, 4, 6, 8, 10\}$,
   $E = \{4, 8, 12, 16\}$
   (b) $F = \{$Frank, Edna, Sally, Don$\}$,
   $G = \{$Ben, Sally, Don, Stella$\}$
   (c) $H = \{$Monday, Wednesday, Friday$)$,
   $R = \{$Tuesday, Wednesday, Sunday$\}$
   (d) $K = \{$the set of even numbers$\}$,
   $L = \{$the set of odd numbers$\}$

3. *If $A = \{1, 2, 3, 4\}$ and $B = \{2, 4, 6, 8\}$, write the set that is obtained by performing the following operations:*
   (a) $A \cup B$
   (b) $A \cap B$

4. *If $X = \{a, b, c\}$ and $Y = \{d, e\}$, write the set that is obtained by performing the following operations:*
   (a) $X \cup Y$
   (b) $X \cap Y$

Numeration

It is clear that the number 7 may be written in many different ways.

EXAMPLE: $8 - 1$, VII, $\frac{14}{2}$, $4 + 3$, $\sqrt{49}$
The number 7 is an idea that we have in our minds. The symbols that we put on paper to designate 7 are called numerals. Thus,

$8 - 1$, VII, $4 + 3$, and $\sqrt{49}$

are numerals. Numerals are names for numbers. And numbers may have many different names just as people may have more than one name. For example, John Smith may be known to some of his friends as Johnnie, to other friends as Smittie, to his baseball coach as Lefty, and to his father as Sonny.

READING AND WRITING NUMBERS

MILLIONS	HUNDRED THOUSANDS	TEN THOUSANDS	THOUSANDS	HUNDREDS	TENS	UNITS	TENTHS	HUNDREDTHS	THOUSANDTHS
1,	3	5	8,	7	0	2.	4	6	9

The number at the bottom is read as one million three hundred fifty-eight thousand seven hundred two *and* four hundred sixty-nine thousandths. Note that the decimal point is indicated by the use of the word *and.*

Note that the positions of the various digits determine the values the digits possess. This may be seen if we write the number 1,358,702.469 as follows:

$$\begin{array}{r} 1{,}000{,}000.000 \\ +\ 300{,}000.000 \\ +\ 50{,}000.000 \\ +\ 8{,}000.000 \\ +\ 700.000 \\ +\ 00.000 \\ +\ 2.000 \\ +\ .400 \\ +\ .060 \\ +\ .009 \end{array}$$

For example, we see that 3 represents 300,000 and that 7 represents 700. This is due to the positions of the 3 and the 7 in writing the number. The zero between the 7 and the 2 is merely a place holder and indicates that the number is written with no tens.

EXAMPLE: Which of the following numbers has 5 in the hundreds place and 9 in the tenths place?

(A) 3,516.29 (B) 5,317.94 (C) 6,501.92 (D) 3,519.32

SOLUTION: The answer is (C).

EXAMPLE: Precisely how many tens does the number 5,469 have?

SOLUTION: We may find the precise number of tens by dividing the number 5,469 by 10. The result is 546.9.

EXERCISE 3

Use numerals to write the following numbers:

1. Five thousand sixty and four hundredths
2. Six million four hundred fifty thousand nine hundred and six tenths
3. Two hundred seventy thousand five hundred ninety three
4. Forty million seven hundred sixteen thousand two hundred eighty-four and nineteen thousandths

EXPONENTS AND EXPANDED FORM

Consider the number 537. In this case, the 5 represents 500, the 3 represents 30, and the 7 represents 7. Thus, the number 537 may be written by using the following numerals:

$$537 = (5 \times 100) + (3 \times 10) + 7$$
$$\text{or}\quad 537 = (5 \times 10 \times 10) + (3 \times 10) + 7$$

When numbers are written in this form they are said to be written in *expanded form.*

EXAMPLE: Write 6,942 in expanded form.

$$6{,}942 = (6 \times 1000) + (9 \times 100) + (4 \times 10) + 2$$
$$\text{or } (6 \times 10 \times 10 \times 10) + (9 \times 10 \times 10) + (4 \times 10) + 2$$

EXAMPLE: Write 3,050 in expanded form.

$$3{,}050 = (3 \times 1000) + (0 \times 100) + (5 \times 10) + 0$$
$$\text{or } (3 \times 10 \times 10 \times 10) + (0 \times 10 \times 10) + (5 \times 10) + 0$$

Notice that there is a zero in the hundreds place. However, we do not leave this place blank as it would be just as confusing as writing 3,050 as 3 5.

EXERCISE 4

Write each of the following in expanded form, as shown in the preceding examples:

1. 28	6. 193	11. 35,729
2. 17	7. 2,486	12. 12,063
3. 40	8. 7,031	13. 70,519
4. 359	9. 1,908	14. 93,702
5. 406	10. 6,007	15. 10,046

In the examples given you have noticed that it was necessary to write numerals such as 10 × 10 × 10, or 10 × 10 × 10 × 10. There is a shorter way of writing such numerals. 10 × 10 × 10 may be written as 10^3. The small, raised "3" written to the right of 10 is called an *exponent* and indicates the number of times 10 is to be used as a factor.

An *exponent* is defined as follows:

For whole numbers n,

$$a^n = \underbrace{a \cdot a \cdot a \cdots\cdots a}_{n \text{ factors of } a}.$$

In the expression a^n, a is called the base and n is an exponent. When n is greater than 1, the exponent indicates the number of factors of the base that are multiplied.

$a^1 = a$
$a^0 = 1$

EXAMPLES: $2^4 = 2 \cdot 2 \cdot 2 \cdot 2 = 16$
$3^0 = 1$

Factor is defined as follows:

If *a, b,* and c are whole numbers, then *b* is a factor of *c* if $a \times b = c$, and *a is* also a factor of c.

EXAMPLE: Write 9^5 in expanded form.

$9^5 = 9 \times 9 \times 9 \times 9 \times 9$

EXAMPLE: Write $7 \times 7 \times 7 \times 7 \times 7$ by using exponents.

$7 \times 7 \times 7 \times 7 \times 7 = 7^5$

EXAMPLE: Write 4,689 in expanded form using exponents.

$$\begin{aligned} 4{,}689 &= (4 \times 10 \times 10 \times 10) + (6 \times 10 \times 10) \\ &\quad + (8 \times 10) + 9 \\ &= (4 \times 10^3) + (6 \times 10^2) + (8 \times 10) + 9 \end{aligned}$$

Notice that when 10 is taken once as a factor, we do not use the exponent 1. Thus, $80 = 8 \times 10$, not 8×10^1. It is not incorrect to write 80 as 8×10^1, but the number is not customarily written that way.

EXERCISE 5

1. *Write in expanded form:*
   (a) 3^4 (b) 5^3 (c) 2^5 (d) 10^4

2. *Use exponents to write each of the following:*
   (a) $9 \times 9 \times 9 \times 9$
   (b) $4 \times 4 \times 4$
   (c) $6 \times 6 \times 6 \times 6 \times 6$
   (d) 7×7
   (e) $10 \times 10 \times 10 \times 10 \times 10$
   (f) $3 \times 3 \times 3 \times 3 \times 3 \times 3$

3. *Use exponents to write each of the following in expanded form:*

(a) 359	(e) 5,307	(i) 90,350
(b) 7,648	(f) 75,123	(j) 15,026
(c) 3,052	(g) 890	(k) 43,100
(d) 704	(h) 6,080	(l) 70,051

The Set of Natural Numbers and the Set of Whole Numbers

The set of numbers {1, 2, 3, 4, 5, ...} is composed of the numbers that are used in counting. This set is called the set of natural numbers or, more simply, the set of *counting numbers.* The set {0, 1, 2, 3, 4, 5, ...} is called the set of *whole numbers.*

It is often helpful to associate sets of numbers with points on a line called the *number line.* This is done as follows: We draw a line, take a point on this line, and label some point 0. Then we take another point to the right of this point and label it 1. We use the distance between 0 and 1 as a unit and mark off other counting numbers on it as follows:

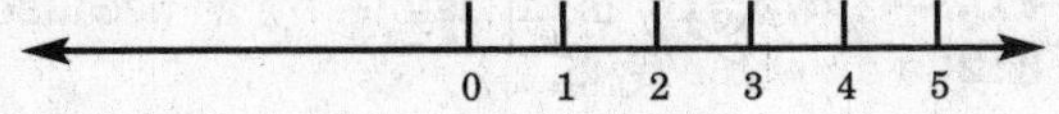

FACTORS AND PRIMES

As we saw in the preceding section, when two numbers are multiplied to form a product each of the numbers is called a *factor* of that product. Thus, 3 and 5 are factors of 15. We say that 8 is a factor of 32, or that 32 is *divisible* by 8.

A *prime number* is any counting number other than 1 that is divisible only by itself and 1. For example, the numbers 2, 3, 5, 7, and 11 are the five smallest prime numbers. A *composite number* is a counting number that can be expressed as the product of two smaller counting numbers other than 1. For example, 6 is a composite number because $6 = 3 \times 2$. A *multiple* of a counting number is the product of that number and a counting number.

EXAMPLE: 4, 8, 12, 16, 20, 24, 28, and 32 are multiples of 4.

Every composite number can be written as a product of prime numbers. The process of determining the prime factors of a given composite number is called *factoring*. The result is the prime factorization of the composite number.

EXAMPLES:

$$12 = 2 \cdot 2 \cdot 3$$
$$80 = 2 \cdot 2 \cdot 2 \cdot 2 \cdot 5$$
$$98 = 2 \cdot 7 \cdot 7$$

One convenient way of determining the prime factorization of a number is to use a factor tree. Name any two factors of the number and write them at the ends of branches below the number. Keep factoring each composite number at the ends of the branches until the numbers at the ends of the branches are all prime. The numbers at the ends of the branches constitute the prime factorization.

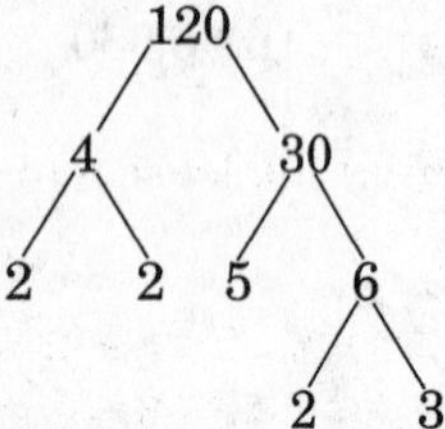

The prime factorization of 120 is $2 \cdot 2 \cdot 2 \cdot 3 \cdot 5$.

EXAMPLE: Write the prime factorization of 150.

$$150 = 2 \times 3 \times 5 \times 5$$

EXERCISE 6

1. *Write all the prime numbers greater than 10 and less than 20.*
2. *Which of the following numbers are prime and which are composite?*
   (a) 23 (b) 25 (c) 37 (d) 31 (e) 36
   (f) 51 (g) 53 (h) 61
3. *Name the four smallest multiples of the following counting numbers:*
   (a) 3 (b) 5 (c) 7 (d) 9
4. *Tell whether each of the following is true or false:*
   (a) 21 is a multiple of 7.
   (b) 2 is the only even prime number.
   (c) 3 is a factor of 10.
   (d) 20 is divisible by 5.
   (e) 3 and 4 are both factors of 12.
   (f) 6 is a prime factor of 42.
5. *Write the prime factorizations of the following numbers:*
   (a) 30 (b) 63 (c) 132 (d) 280 (e) 350

DIVISIBILITY

A number is *divisible by 2* if it is an even number. In other words, a number is divisible by 2 if the digit in the one's place is 0, 2, 4, 6, or 8.

EXAMPLE: The numbers 48, 76, 580, and 394 are divisible by 2.

A number is *divisible by 3* if the sum of its digits is divisible by 3.

EXAMPLE: 71,259 is divisible by 3 because 7 + 1 + 2 + 5 + 9 = 24, and 24 is divisible by 3.

A number is *divisible by 4* if the number formed by the last two digits on the right is divisible by 4.

EXAMPLE: 30,428 is divisible by 4 because 28 is divisible by 4.

A number is *divisible by 5* if the last digit on the right is either 5 or 0.

EXAMPLE: 795 is divisible by 5 because the last digit on the right in 795 is 5.

A number is *divisible by 6* if it is an even number and if the sum of its digits is divisible by 3.

EXAMPLE: 25,794 is divisible by 6 because 25,794 is an even number, and it is divisible by 3 because 2 + 5 + 7 + 9 + 4 = 27, which is divisible by 3.

A number is *divisible by 8* if the number formed by the last three digits on the right is divisible by 8.

EXAMPLE: 75,312 is divisible by 8 because 312 is divisible by 8.

A number is *divisible by 9* if the sum of its digits is divisible by 9.

EXAMPLE: 205,731 is divisible by 9 because 2 + 0 + 5 + 7 + 3 + 1 = 18, which is divisible by 9.

A number is *divisible by 10* if the digit in the one's place is 0.

EXAMPLE: 569,280 is divisible by 10 because the number in the one's place is 0.

EXERCISE 7

1. *Find the smallest prime factor of each of the following:*
   (a) 79,048 (b) 16,251 (c) 32,485
   (d) 1,337 (e) 649 (f) 1,343
   (g) 1,659 (h) 2,231

2. *Let X = {2, 3, 4, 5, 6, 8, 9, 10}. By which members of set X is each of the following numbers divisible?*
   (a) 6,480 (b) 1,756 (c) 5,432
   (d) 2,415 (e) 10,344 (f) 6,513
   (g) 7,002 (h) 4,618

3. *In each of the following, replace □ by a digit that will make the resulting number divisible by the number in the parentheses.*
   (a) 41 □ (2) (g) □ (9)
   (b) 32 □ (3) (h) 6, □ 12 (3)
   (c) 6, 7 □ 2 (4) (i) 7, □ 12 (4)
   (d) 4, 05 □ (5) (j) 6, 5 □ 0 (8)
   (e) 8, □ 12 (6) (k) 1, 23 □ (9)
   (f) 4, 3 □ 6 (8) (l) 9, 21 □ (6)

GREATEST COMMON FACTOR

The *greatest common factor* of two counting numbers is the greatest counting number that is a factor of each of them.

EXAMPLE: 8 is the greatest common factor of 24 and 32.

In order to find the greatest common factor of two counting numbers, we write each number as the product of its prime factors. Then we select the smallest power of each prime factor that appears in each set of prime factors. The product of these prime factors is the greatest common factor of the two numbers.

EXAMPLE: Find the greatest common factor of 60 and 90.

$$60 = 2 \cdot 2 \cdot 5 \cdot 3 = 2^2 \cdot 5 \cdot 3$$

$$90 = 2 \cdot 3 \cdot 3 \cdot 5 = 2 \cdot 3^2 \cdot 5$$

The greatest common factor of 60 and 90 is $2 \cdot 3 \cdot 5 = 30$.

LEAST COMMON MULTIPLE

The *least common multiple* of two counting numbers is the smallest counting number that is a multiple of each of them.

EXAMPLE: 24 is the least common multiple of 6 and 8.

In order to find the least common multiple of two counting numbers, we write each number as the product of its prime factors. Then we find the product of all of the prime factors, with each prime factor raised to the highest power that appears in any of the factors.

EXAMPLE: Find the least common multiple of 12 and 18.

$$12 = 2 \cdot 2 \cdot 3 = 2^2 \cdot 3$$

$$18 = 2 \cdot 3 \cdot 3 = 2 \cdot 3^2$$

The least common multiple of 12 and 18 is $2^2 \cdot 3^2 = 4 \cdot 9 = 36$.

EXERCISE 8

1. *Find the greatest common factor of each of the following pairs of numbers:*
   (a) 8, 12 (e) 49, 70 (i) 12, 30
   (b) 16, 24 (f) 72, 120 (j) 68, 170
   (c) 15, 20 (g) 36, 84 (k) 35, 49
   (d) 32, 48 (h) 96, 132 (l) 81, 108

2. *Find the least common multiple of each of the following pairs of numbers:*
   (a) 6, 8 (e) 4, 5 (i) 12, 16
   (b) 9, 12 (f) 14, 21 (j) 20, 25
   (c) 15, 20 (g) 8, 10 (k) 18, 32
   (d) 7, 14 (h) 10, 15 (l) 30, 40

THE SET OF INTEGERS

In locating the set of whole numbers on the number line, we did not consider points to the left of 0. Such points are located and shown on the number line below.

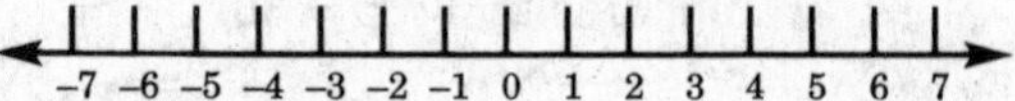

The numbers located on the number line to the left of zero are called *negative integers*. Negative integers are used to indicate temperatures below zero, to indicate a loss in business as opposed to a profit, etc. The set {..., –4, –3, –2, –1, 0, 1, 2, 3, 4, ...} is called the *set of integers*.

Addition of Integers

We may learn how to add integers by using the number line.

EXAMPLE: Find the sum of 2 + 3.

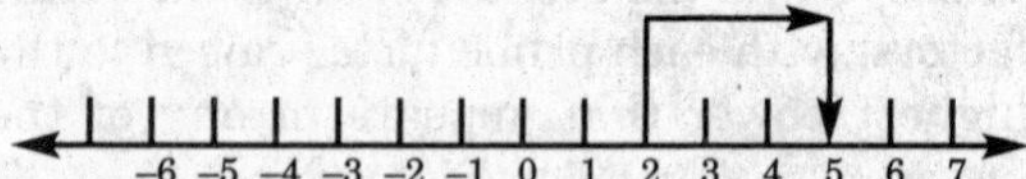

Locate 2 on the number line and then move 3 units to the right. We will interpret a move to the right as positive and a move to the left as negative. The result is 2 + 3 = 5.

EXAMPLE: Find the sum of 3 + (–5)

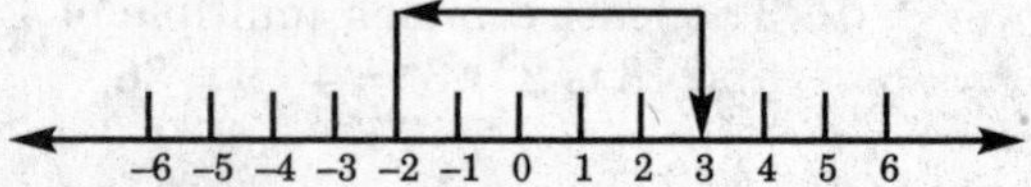

Locate 3 on the number line and then move 5 units to the left. The result is 3 + (–5) = –2.

EXAMPLE: Find the sum of –1 + (–3)

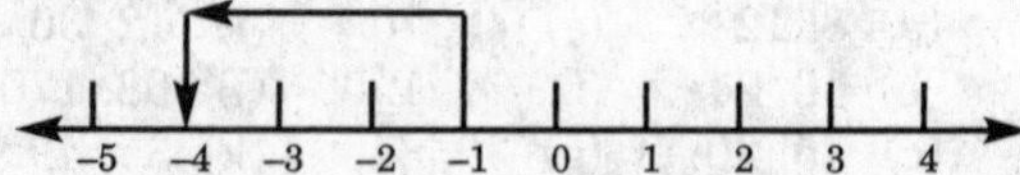

Locate –1 on the number line and then move 3 units to the left. The result is –1 + (–3) = –4.

EXAMPLE: Find the sum of –2 + 6.

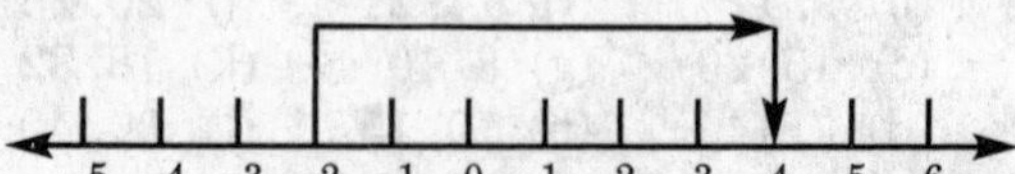

Locate –2 on the number line and then move 6 units to the right. The result is –2 + 6 = 4.

Signed Numbers

The opposite (or additive inverse) of any number is the number located the same distance from 0 on the number line in the opposite direction.

EXAMPLE: Write in symbols, "the opposite of negative seven." –(–7)

The opposite of negative seven is positive seven. –(–7) = +7 = 7

The absolute value of any number is the distance that the number is from 0 on the number line. Remember that distance is positive. The absolute value of –3 is written |–3|.

EXAMPLES: |3| = 3
|–5| = 5
|0| = 0

Addition

1. If two numbers have the same sign, add their absolute values and attach the common sign to the result.

EXAMPLES: 5 + 7 = 12
–3 + (–8) = –11

2. If two numbers have opposite signs, subtract their absolute values, the smaller from the larger, and attach the sign of the number with the larger absolute value to the result.

EXAMPLES: –9 + 3 = –6
–8 + 13 = 5
15 + (–25) = –10

EXERCISE 9

1. *Find the following sums. You may use the number line to help you.*

(a) 1 + 4
(b) 1 + (–4)
(c) 2 + (–3)
(d) 3 + (–5)
(e) –3 + 5
(f) –2 + (–5)
(g) 6 + (–4)
(h) –1 + 4
(i) –2 + (–3)
(j) 5 + (–3)

2. *Represent the following quantities by using positive or negative integers.*
   (a) A loss of 3 pounds in weight.
   (b) A gain of 3 yards in football.
   (c) A bank deposit of $20.
   (d) A bank withdrawal of $20.
   (e) Ten degrees below zero.

Subtraction of Integers

Every positive integer may be paired with a negative integer and every negative integer may be paired with a positive integer as shown below. We say that

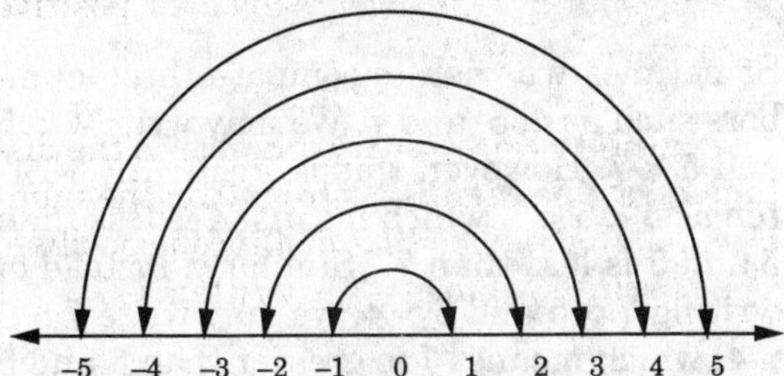

1 and –1 are opposites, 2 and –2 are opposites, 3 and –3 are opposites, etc.

In order to subtract integer b from integer a, we add a to the opposite of b.

$$a - b = a + (-b)$$

EXAMPLE: Subtract –5 from 7.
$7 - (-5) = 7 + 5 = 12$

EXAMPLE: Subtract –2 from –6.
$-6 - (-2) = -6 + 2 = -4$

EXAMPLE: Subtract 3 from –4.
$-4 - 3 = -4 + (-3) = -7$

EXERCISE 10

Perform the following subtractions:

1. $3 - 5$
2. $9 - 3$
3. $-1 - 4$
4. $6 - (-2)$
5. $-8 - 2$
6. $10 - 2$
7. $-3 - 7$
8. $6 - 9$
9. $7 - (-4)$
10. $-8 - (-3)$

Multiplication of Integers

To multiply two numbers, multiply their absolute values and attach a sign to the result according to the following rule:

1. If the two numbers have the same sign, the result is positive.
2. If the two numbers have opposite signs, the result is negative.

EXAMPLE: $5 \times 9 = 45$
$-5 \times (-9) = 45$
$5 \times (-9) = -45$
$-5 \times 9 = -45$

EXERCISE 11

Find the following products:

1. $6 \cdot (-3)$
2. $2 \cdot 7$
3. $-4 \cdot 5$
4. $-2 \cdot (-8)$
5. $1 \cdot (-5)$
6. $-4 \cdot 3$
7 $(-7) \cdot (-5)$
8. $0 \cdot (-6)$
9. $4 \cdot (-8)$
10. $(-3) \cdot (-7)$

Division of Integers

To divide two numbers, divide their absolute values and attach a sign to the result according to the rule for multiplication.

EXAMPLE: $15 \div 5 = 3$
$-15 \div (-5) = 3$
$15 \div (-5) = -3$
$-15 \div 5 = -3$

EXERCISE 12

Perform the indicated operations:

1. $6 + (-4)$
2. $(-3) + (-5)$
3. $8 + (-2)$
4. $-5 - 9$
5. $8 - (-2)$
6. $6 \times (-2)$
7. $-4 \times (-7)$
8. $-8 \div -2$
9. $-12 \div 4$
10. $18 \div -6$

Symbols of Inequality

In working with numbers, we often wish to indicate that one number is greater than another or that one number is less than another. For this purpose, as you have learned, we use the following symbols:

$>$ means "is greater than"
$<$ means "is less than"

Example: $5 > 3$ means "5 is greater than 3."
$2 < 7$ means "2 is less than 7."

EXERCISE 13

Use one of the symbols >, =, < in the place of the □ to make each of the following statements true.

1. $5 + 7 \square 5 + 4$
2. $9 - 6 \square 2 + 8$
3. $3 \times (6 + 5) \square (3 \times 6) + (3 \times 5)$
4. $7 \times (5 + 1) \square (7 \times 5) \times 1$
5. $5 + (8 + 3) \square (8 + 3) - 5$
6. $8 \times 9 \square 8 \times (6 + 3)$
7. $17 - 1 \square 6 + (9 + 3)$
8. $6 \times (8 \times 3) \square 17 + 2 \times (5 + 9)$
9. $25 - 3 \times (6 + 1) \square 2 + 7$
10. $15 + (3 + 9) \square (4 \times 6) + 3$

Example: If set $A = \{1, 2, 3, 4, 5\}$, *write the set of natural numbers contained in set A* that can be used to replace n to make the statement true.

1. $n + 2 > 5$

We note that when n is replaced by 4 or 5 of set A, then the statement becomes true. Thus, the correct result is $\{4, 5\}$.

2. $7 + n < 11$

We note that when n is replaced by 1, 2, or 3 of set A then the statement becomes true. Thus, the correct result is $\{1, 2, 3\}$.

EXERCISE 14

In each case, select the set of numbers from set A = {1, 2, 3, 4, 5, 6} that will make the statement true.

1. $n + 1 > 4$
2. $n - 1 > 3$
3. $n + 5 = 7$
4. $2 + n < 5$
5. $6 - n > 3$
6. $2 \times n < 8$
7. $3 + n < 4 + 5$
8. $7 < 2 \times n$
9. $5 + (3 + 7) = (5 + n) + 7$
10. $(6 \times 4) \times 3 < (6 \times 4) \times n$

Sometimes we wish to compare three numbers such as 4, 5, and 7. We may write $4 < 5$ and $5 < 7$. However, this is frequently written as $4 < 5 < 7$, which means "4 is less than 5 and 5 is less than 7." Similarly, instead of writing $7 > 5$ and $5 > 4$, we may write $7 > 5 > 4$, which means "7 is greater than 5 and 5 is greater than 4." In each case we note that 5 is between 4 and 7.

EXERCISE 15

1. *Use symbols to write each of the following:*
   (a) 6 is greater than 3 and 3 is greater than 2.
   (b) 4 is less than 5 and 5 is less than 9.
   (c) 1 is less than 8 and 8 is less than 11.
   (d) 9 is greater than 7 and 7 is greater than 3.
   (e) 5 is between 4 and 8.
   (f) 6 is between 3 and 12.

2. *State each of the following in words:*
   (a) $7 > 6 > 1$
   (b) $4 < 12 < 15$
   (c) $14 > 10 > 3$
   (d) $5 < 16 < 20$

3. *In each case, select the set of numbers from set B = {5, 6, 7, 8, 9, 10} that will make the statement true.*
   (a) $4 < n < 7$
   (b) $9 > n > 6$
   (c) $6 < n < 9$
   (d) $8 > n > 5$

ORDER IN THE SET OF INTEGERS

We have seen that the set of integers may be represented on the number line with the set of negative integers represented to the left of 0 and the set of positive integers represented to the right of 0. We observe that of two integers represented on the number line, the integer to the right is greater than the integer to the left. For example, 8 > 5, 0 < 3, 4 > –6, and –1 > –5.

EXERCISE 16

Copy the two integers and insert the correct symbol (> or <):

EXAMPLE: –7 < 3

1. 2 5	6. 0 –4
2. 8 4	7. 7 –9
3. 6 –2	8. –2 –5
4 –5 –9	9. –3 0
5. –1 3	10. –6 1

Consider the compound sentence:

$$5 > 0 > -4$$

This sentence states that 5 > 0 *and* 0 > –4.

EXAMPLE: In the following sentence, replace *n* by the set of integers that satisfy the sentence

$$-3 < n < 2$$

This sentence states that –3 is less than *n* and *n* is less than 2.

The integers that are less than 2 are 1, 0, –1, –2, –3, –4, ... The integers that satisfy the above compound sentence are greater than –3. Thus, the set of integers that satisfy the compound set is

{1, 0 –1, –2}

EXERCISE 17

Write the set of integers that satisfy the sentence:

1. 4 > *n* > 0
2. 3 > *n* > –3
3. –2 > *n* > –5
4. 2 < *n* < 7
5. –1 < *n* < 3
6. –5 < *n* < 1

The Set of Rational Numbers

A rational number is a number that can be expressed by a fraction which is the quotient of two integers, with the exception that division by zero is not permissible.

EXAMPLE: $\frac{2}{3}, -\frac{9}{5}, \frac{4}{1}$, and 3.2 are rational numbers.

Note that all integers are rational numbers since they can be expressed as fractions that are quotients of two integers.

EXAMPLE: 7 can be expressed as $\frac{7}{1}$, and –3 can be expressed as $-\frac{3}{1}$.

On the number line below, there are located some rational numbers that are not integers.

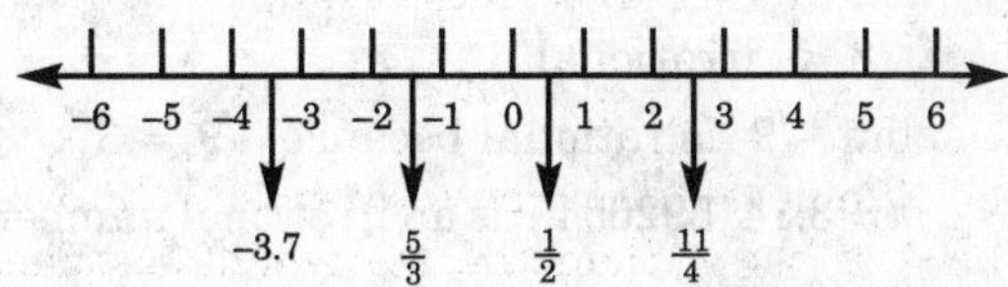

Operations with rational numbers are discussed in Chapter 8, "Mathematical Skills."

The Set of Real Numbers

Some rational numbers can be expressed as terminating decimals.

EXAMPLE: $\frac{1}{2} = 0.5$ $\frac{2}{5} = 0.4$
$\frac{3}{4} = 0.75$ $\frac{7}{8} = 0.875$

Some rational numbers can be expressed as repeating decimals. By repeating decimals we mean decimals that have a repeating block of digits.

EXAMPLE: $\frac{1}{3} = 0.333....$ This may be written as $0.\overline{3}$. The bar indicates that the "3" is repeated infinitely.

$\frac{5}{6} = 0.8\overline{3}$ $\frac{5}{9} = 0.\overline{5}$ $\frac{3}{11} = 0.\overline{27}$

All rational numbers may be expressed either as terminating decimals or as repeating decimals.

An *irrational number* is a number whose decimal representation is neither a terminating decimal nor a repeating decimal.

EXAMPLE: $\sqrt{2} = 1.4142135....$ This decimal representation is not terminating; it will never come to an end. Nor is this decimal representation repeating; there is no block of digits that is repeating.

$\sqrt{5} = 2.23606....$ Similarly, this decimal representation is neither a terminating decimal nor a repeating decimal.

All such *radicals* represent irrational numbers.

$\sqrt{7}$ is irrational
$\sqrt{8}$ is irrational
but $\sqrt{9}$ is rational because $\sqrt{9} = 3$.
$\pi = 3.141592654...$ is an irrational number.

The set of *real numbers* is composed of the set of rational numbers and the set of irrational numbers. Thus, the set of real numbers includes the set of counting numbers, the set of integers, the set of rational numbers and the set of irrational numbers.

EXERCISE 18

1. *Identify each of the following real numbers as rational or irrational:*
(a) 7 (d) $\sqrt{4}$ (g) $\sqrt{16}$
(b) $\sqrt{6}$ (e) $\sqrt{10}$ (h) –5
(c) $-2\frac{1}{2}$ (f) –3.7 (i) $\sqrt{8}$

2. *The numbers in the first column of the following chart are members of one or more of the sets of numbers given. Copy the chart in your notebook and complete it by placing a check in the box that applies. The first number is checked as a sample.*

NUMBER	COUNTING NUMBER	INTEGER	RATIONAL NUMBER	IRRATIONAL NUMBER	REAL NUMBER
–6		✔	✔		✔
$\sqrt{7}$					
$3\frac{1}{2}$					
0					
$-2\frac{1}{4}$					
0.37					
$\sqrt{3}$					
$-0.\overline{12}$					
–19					
$\sqrt{25}$					

LAWS OF OPERATION FOR REAL NUMBERS

You know from experience that 3 + 4 = 4 + 3 and 7 + 9 = 9 + 7. In fact, the order in which two real numbers are added makes no difference as far as the results are concerned. Mathematicians call this principle the *commutative law for addition of real numbers.* We state this law formally as follows:

Commutative Law for Addition of Real Numbers

If a and b represent real numbers, then

$$a + b = b + a.$$

Similarly, the order of multiplication may be changed without affecting the result.

Commutative Law for Multiplication of Real Numbers

If a and b represent real numbers, then

$$a \times b = b \times a.$$

It is also true that if three numbers are to be added, the result doesn't change by altering the grouping.

$$(4 + 7) + 5 = 11 + 5 = 16$$
$$4 + (7 + 5) = 4 + 12 = 16$$

This is known as:

Associative Law for Addition of Real Numbers

If a, b, and c represent real numbers, then

$$(a + b) + c = a + (b + c).$$

Regrouping does not affect the result of multiplication either. So we have:

Associative Law for Multiplication of Real Numbers

If a, b, and c represent real numbers, then

$$(a \times b) \times c = a \times (b \times c).$$

A man bought 3 solid ties at $12 each and 6 striped ties at $12 each. In computing the total bill, the clerk proceeded as follows:

3 solid ties at $12 each = 3 × 12 = $36
6 striped ties at $12 each = 6 × 12 = $72
Total =$108

Of course, he could have computed the bill more simply as follows:

(6 + 3) ties at $12 each
= $12 × (6 + 3) = $12 × 9 = $108

This example illustrates the fact that

$$12 \times (6 + 3) = 12 \times 6 + 12 \times 3$$

Mathematicians call the principle described above the *distributive law for multiplication with respect to addition.* We shall simply call it the *distributive law.* We state this law formally as follows:

Distributive Law

If a, b, and c are any real numbers, then

$$a \times (b + c) = a \times b + a \times c.$$

EXERCISE 19

In each case, identify the law illustrated.

1. $5 + 3 = 3 + 5$
2. $(6 \times 7) \times 4 = 6 \times (7 \times 4)$
3. $9 \times (3 + 5) = 9 \times 3 + 9 \times 5$
4. $8 \times 2 = 2 \times 8$
5. $(4 + 7) + 1 = 4 + (7 + 1)$
6. $5 \times (6 + 3) = 5 \times 6 + 5 \times 3$
7. $7 + 3 = 3 + 7$
8. $(5 + 3) + 6 = 5 + (3 + 6)$
9. $1 \times 12 = 12 \times 1$
10. $6 \times (5 + 9) = 6 \times 5 + 6 \times 9$
11. $(7 \times 4) \times 2 = 7 \times (4 \times 2)$
12. $(3 + 12) + 4 = 3 + (12 + 4)$
13. $9 + 5 = 5 + 9$
14. $3 \times (1 + 5) = 3 \times 1 + 3 \times 5$
15. $(6 \times 5) \times 4 = 6 \times (5 \times 4)$
16. $8 \times 7 = 7 \times 8$
17. $(12 + 3) + 2 = 12 + (3 + 2)$
18. $7 \times (5 + 4) = 7 \times 5 + 7 \times 4$
19. $(3 + 5) + 9 = 3 + (5 + 9)$
20. $2 + 15 = 15 + 2$
21. $6 \times (12 + 8) = 6 \times 12 + 6 \times 8$
22. $(2 \times 8) \times 5 = 2 \times (8 \times 5)$
23. $19 \times 3 = 3 \times 19$
24. $(1 + 2) + 7 = 1 + (2 + 7)$
25. $9 + 3 = 3 + 9$

Answers to All Exercises

EXERCISE 1

1. (a) {January, June, July}
   (b) {This will vary.}
   (c) {a,b,c}
   (d) Ø or { }
   (e) {Saturday, Sunday}
   (f) {Washington}

2. (a) The set consisting of the names of the last three letters of the English alphabet.
   (b) The set consisting of the names of the coins in the U.S. money system.
   (c) The set consisting of the names of three American cities.
   (d) The set consisting of the names of the first five even numbers.
   (e) The set consisting of the names of the positions on a basketball court.

EXERCISE 2

1. (a) {5, 10, 15, 20, 30, 35}
   (b) {John, Bill, Mary, Fred, Nancy}
   (c) {June, July, August, September, October, December}
   (d) {Tuesday, Thursday, Saturday, Sunday}

2. (a) {4, 8}
   (b) {Sally, Don}
   (c) {Wednesday}
   (d) The empty set, { }.

3. (a) {1, 2, 3, 4, 6, 8}
   (b) {2, 4}

4. (a) {a, b, c, d, e}
   (b) The empty set, { }

EXERCISE 3

1. 5,060.04
2. 6,450,900.6
3. 270,593
4. 40,716,284.019

EXERCISE 4

1. $(2 \times 10) + 8$
2. $(1 \times 10) + 7$
3. 4×10
4. $(3 \times 100) + (5 \times 10) + 9$
5. $(4 \times 100) + (0 \times 10) + 6$
6. $(1 \times 100) + (9 \times 10) + 3$
7. $(2 \times 1{,}000) + (4 \times 100) + (8 \times 10) + 6$
8. $(7 \times 1{,}000) + (0 \times 100) + (3 \times 10) + 1$
9. $(1 \times 1{,}000) + (9 \times 100) + (0 \times 10) + 8$
10. $(6 \times 1{,}000) + (0 \times 100) + (0 \times 10) + 7$
11. $(3 \times 10{,}000) + (5 \times 1000) + (7 \times 100) + (2 \times 10) + 9$
12. $(1 \times 10{,}000) + (2 \times 1{,}000) + (0 \times 100) + (6 \times 10) + 3$
13. $(7 \times 10{,}000) + (0 \times 1{,}000) + (5 \times 100) + (1 \times 10) + 9$
14. $(9 \times 10{,}000) + (3 \times 1{,}000) + (7 \times 100) + (0 \times 10) + 2$
15. $(1 \times 10{,}000) + (0 \times 1{,}000) + (0 \times 100) + (4 \times 10) + 6$

EXERCISE 5

1. (a) $3 \times 3 \times 3 \times 3$
   (b) $5 \times 5 \times 5$
   (c) $2 \times 2 \times 2 \times 2 \times 2$
   (d) $10 \times 10 \times 10 \times 10$

2. (a) 9^4 (b) 4^3 (c) 6^5
   (d) 7^2 (e) 10^5 (f) 3^6

3. (a) $(3 \times 10^2) + (5 \times 10) + 9$
   (b) $(7 \times 10^3) + (6 \times 10^2) + (4 \times 10) + 8$
   (c) $(3 \times 10^3) + (0 \times 10^2) + (5 \times 10) + 2$
   (d) $(7 \times 10^2) + (0 \times 10) + 4$
   (e) $(5 \times 10^3) + (3 \times 10^2) + (0 \times 10) + 7$
   (f) $(7 \times 10^4) + (5 \times 10^3) + (1 \times 10^2) + (2 \times 10) + 3$
   (g) $(8 \times 10^2) + (9 \times 10)$
   (h) $(6 \times 10^3) + (0 \times 10^2) + (8 \times 10)$
   (i) $(9 \times 10^4) + (0 \times 10^3) + (3 \times 10^2) + (5 \times 10)$
   (j) $(1 \times 10^4) + (5 \times 10^3) + (0 \times 10^2) + (2 \times 10) + 6$
   (k) $(4 \times 10^4) + (3 \times 10^3) + (1 \times 10^2) + (0 \times 10)$
   (l) $(7 \times 10^4) + (0 \times 10^3) + (0 \times 10^2) + (5 \times 10) + 1$

EXERCISE 6

1. 11, 13, 17, 19

2. (a) Prime (b) Composite (c) Prime (d) Prime (e) Composite (f) Composite (g) Prime (h) Prime

3. (a) 3, 6, 9, 12 (b) 5, 10, 15, 20 (c) 7, 14, 21, 28 (d) 9, 18, 27, 36

4. (a) True (b) True (c) False (d) True (e) True (f) False

5. (a) $2 \times 3 \times 5$
(b) $3 \times 3 \times 7$
(c) $2 \times 2 \times 3 \times 11$
(d) $2 \times 2 \times 2 \times 5 \times 7$
(e) $5 \times 5 \times 2 \times 7$

EXERCISE 7

1. (a) 2 (b) 3 (c) 5 (d) 7 (e) 11 (f) 17 (g) 3 (h) 23

2. (a) {2, 3, 4, 5, 6, 8, 9} (b) {2, 4} (c) {2, 4, 8} (d) {3, 5} (e) {2, 3, 4, 6, 8} (f) {3} (g) {2, 3, 6, 9} (h) {2}

3. (a) 0, 2, 4, 6, or 8 (b) 1, 4, or 7 (c) 1, 3, 5, 7, or 9 (d) 0, or 5 (e) 1, 4, or 7 (f) 3, or 7 (g) 3 (h) 0, 3, 6, or 9 (i) any digit (j) 2, or 6 (k) 3 (l) 0, or 6

EXERCISE 8

1. (a) 4 (b) 8 (c) 5 (d) 16 (e) 7 (f) 24 (g) 12 (h) 12 (i) 6 (j) 34 (k) 7 (l) 27

2. (a) 24 (b) 36 (c) 60 (d) 14 (e) 20 (f) 42 (g) 40 (h) 30 (i) 48 (j) 100 (k) 288 (l) 120

EXERCISE 9

1. (a) 5 (b) –3 (c) –1 (d) –2 (e) 2 (f) –7 (g) 2 (h) 3 (i) –5 (j) 2

2. (a) –3 (b) 3 (c) \$20 (d) –\$20 (e) –10

EXERCISE 10

1. –2
2. 6
3. –5
4. 8
5. –10
6. 8
7. –10
8. –3
9. 11
10. –5

EXERCISE 11

1 –18
2. 14
3. –20
4. 16
5. –5
6. –12
7. 35
8. 0
9. –32
10. 21

EXERCISE 12

1. 2
2. –8
3. 6
4. –14
5. 10
6. –12
7. 28
8. 4
9. –3
10. –3

EXERCISE 13

1. >
2. <
3. =
4. >
5. >
6. =
7. <
8. <
9. >
10. =

EXERCISE 14

1. {4, 5 ,6}
2. {5, 6}
3. {2}
4. {1, 2}
5. {1, 2}
6. {1, 2, 3}
7. {1, 2, 3, 4, 5}
8. {1, 2, 3}
9. {3}
10. {4, 5, 6}

EXERCISE 15

1. (a) $6 > 3 > 2$
   (b) $4 < 5 < 9$
   (c) $1 < 8 < 11$
   (d) $9 > 7 > 3$
   (e) $4 < 5 < 8$ or $8 > 5 > 4$
   (f) $3 < 6 < 12$ or $12 > 6 > 3$

2. (a) 7 is greater than 6 and 6 is greater than 1.
   (b) 4 is less than 12 and 12 is less than 15.
   (c) 14 is greater than 10 and 10 is greater than 3.
   (d) 5 is less than 16 and 16 is less than 20.

3. (a) {5, 6}　　(c) {7, 8}
   (b) {8, 7}　　(d) {7, 6}

EXERCISE 16

1. $2 < 5$
2. $8 > 4$
3. $6 > -2$
4. $-5 > -9$
5. $-1 < 3$
6. $0 > -4$
7. $7 > -9$
8. $-2 > -5$
9. $-3 < 0$
10. $-6 < 1$

EXERCISE 17

1. {3, 2, 1}
2. {2, 1, 0, –1, –2}
3. {–3, –4}
4. {3, 4, 5, 6}
5. {0, 1, 2}
6. {–4, –3, –2, –1, 0}

EXERCISE 18

1. (a) rational
   (b) irrational
   (c) rational
   (d) rational
   (e) irrational
   (f) rational
   (g) rational
   (h) rational
   (i) irrational

NUMBER	COUNTING NUMBER	INTEGER	RATIONAL NUMBER	IRRATIONAL NUMBER	REAL NUMBER
-6		✔	✔		✔
$\sqrt{7}$				✔	✔
$3\frac{1}{2}$			✔		✔
0		✔	✔		✔
$-2\frac{1}{4}$			✔		✔
0.37			✔		✔
$\sqrt{3}$				✔	✔
$-0.\overline{12}$			✔		✔
-19			✔		✔
$\sqrt{25}$	✔	✔	✔		✔

EXERCISE 19

1. The commutative law for addition
2. The associative law for multiplication
3. The distributive law
4. The commutative law for multiplication
5. The associative law for addition
6. The distributive law
7. The commutative law for addition
8. The associative law for addition
9. The commutative law for multiplication
10. The distributive law
11. The associative law for multiplication
12. The associative law for addition
13. The commutative law for addition
14. The distributive law
15. The associative law for multiplication
16. The commutative law for multiplication
17. The associative law for addition
18. The distributive law
19. The associative law for addition
20. The commutative law for addition
21. The distributive law
22. The associative law for multiplication
23. The commutative law for multiplication
24. The associative law for addition
25. The commutative law for addition

Reading Tables, Maps, and Graphs

Tables

Tables are used to present numerical facts and relationships. Often it is easier to pick out needed information by looking at a table than by reading through written material. Thus, the ability to read tables quickly and accurately is a very useful skill.

PRACTICE TEST 1

DIRECTIONS: Base your answers to the following questions on the table below.

NUMBER OF CARS SOLD

	JAN.	FEB.	MARCH	APRIL	MAY	JUNE
ADAMS	5	6	8	15	18	25
SANCHEZ	8	7	10	12	19	28
GOTTLIEB	3	9	12	14	12	20
JAWORSKI	4	5	11	9	15	19
LUM	7	4	6	10	11	17

The Star Auto Sales Company employs five salespersons. Their sales record for the first six months of the year is shown in the table above. The numbers represent the number of cars sold.

1. The most cars were sold by the five salespersons during the month of
(A) March (B) May (C) June
(D) January (E) April

2. The salesperson with the least number of sales for the six-month period was
(A) Jaworski (B) Gottlieb (C) Sanchez
(D) Adams (E) Lum

3. The total number of cars sold by salesperson Sanchez for the six-month period was
(A) 84 (B) 80 (C) 27 (D) 82 (E) 78

4. The difference between the number of cars sold in March and the number of cars sold in February was
(A) 14 (B) 15 (C) 12 (D) 16 (E) 10

5. If the average car sold for about $12,000 the approximate value of the cars sold in April was
(A) $600,000 (B) $720,000
(C) $6,000,000 (D) $7,200,000
(E) $72,000

PRACTICE TEST 2

DIRECTIONS: Base your answers to the following questions on the table below.

JULY

MON.	TUES.	WED.	THURS.	FRI.	SAT.	SUN.
	1 [32]	2 [29]	3 [31]	4 [40]	5 [46]	6 [38]
7 [27]	8 [34]	9 [30]	10 [24]	11 [39]	12 [45]	13 [41]
14 [23]	15 [31]	16 [28]	17 [26]	18 [38]	19 [49]	20 [39]
21 [26]	22 [35]	23 [27]	24 [25]	25 [43]	26 [47]	27 [42]
28 [29]	29 [27]	30 [34]	31 [29]			

Ms. Rossi owns the Roadside Motel, which has 50 units. She wishes to keep a handy record of the number of units occupied. To do this she uses a calendar and writes the number of units occupied in a small box in the upper right-hand corner of each date. The following questions are based on the occupancy rate for July.

1. On which day of the week did the Roadside Motel have the best rate of occupancy?
(A) Wednesday (B) Friday
(C) Saturday (D) Monday
(E) Sunday

2. The total number of units occupied during the week of July 14 through July 20 was
(A) 23 (B) 240 (C) 239 (D) 244 (E) 234

3. The average occupancy rate throughout the month for Thursday was
(A) 27 (B) 31 (C) 29 (D) 28 (E) 25

4. On how many days during the month were less than one half of the units occupied?
(A) 4 (B) 5 (C) 0 (D) 2 (E) 3

5. Ms. Rossi regards a 90% occupancy rate as excellent. On how many dates during the month did the Roadside Motel have a 90% or better rate of occupancy?
(A) 5 (B) 4 (C) 6 (D) 1 (E) 3

Maps

Maps are used to show direction, size, and location and to measure distances between various points. The *scale* on a map tells you how great a distance is represented by each unit on the map. Thus, if the scale on a map says "1 inch = 20 miles," this means that one inch on the map represents a distance of 20 miles.

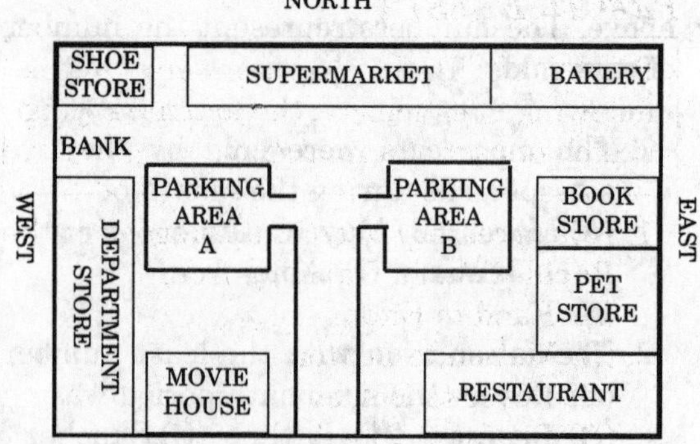

MIDWAY SHOPPING CENTER

PRACTICE TEST 3

DIRECTIONS: Base your answers to the following questions on the accompanying sketch of the Midway Shopping Center.

1. The store with the largest floor area in the Midway Shopping Center is the
   (A) Supermarket
   (B) Bakery
   (C) Movie House
   (D) Department Store
   (E) Shoe Store

2. In walking from the Movie House to the Restaurant the direction is
   (A) north (B) west (C) east (D) south
   (E) northeast

3. Of the following the one nearest Parking Area A is the
   (A) Restaurant (B) Bakery
   (C) Movie House (D) Supermarket
   (E) Book Store

4. The direction from the Shoe Store to the Pet Shop is
   (A) south (B) east (C) southwest
   (D) southeast (E) northeast

5. A shopper plans to park in Parking Area A, shop, and then return to his car. Of the following, which should he follow if he wishes to walk the least distance?
   (A) Book Store, Shoe Store, Bank, Bakery
   (B) Bakery, Bank, Book Store, Shoe Store
   (C) Shoe Store, Book Store, Bank, Bakery
   (D) Book Store, Bank, Bakery, Shoe Store
   (E) Bank, Shoe Store, Bakery, Book Store

PRACTICE TEST 4

DIRECTIONS: Base your answers to the following questions on the accompanying sketch of part of a road map.

1. It is necessary to cross a bridge over the Rapid River in traveling from
   (A) Rand to Elton
   (B) Vernon to Benton
   (C) Dover to Holden
   (D) Benton to Dover
   (E) Vernon to Rand

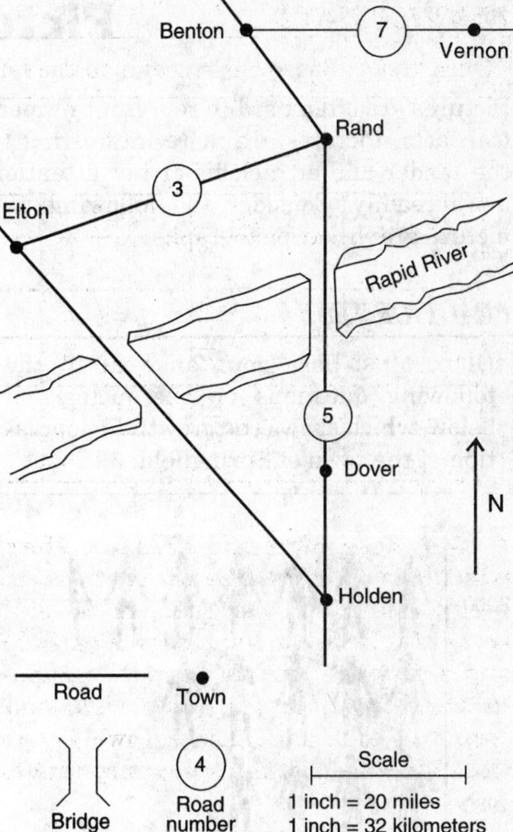

2. In traveling from Benton to Vernon the direction to take is
   (A) west (B) east (C) north
   (D) southeast (E) south

3. The distance from Rand to Dover, is approximately
   (A) 20 miles (B) 30 miles (C) 25 miles
   (D) 50 miles (E) 40 miles

4. Traveling from Vernon to Dover, a motorist takes
   (A) Route 7 and then Route 3
   (B) Route 5 and then Route 7
   (C) Route 7 and then Route 5
   (D) Route 2 and then Route 7
   (E) Route 3 and then Route 5

5. In driving from Holden to Elton a motorist travels
   (A) northwest (B) northeast (C) west
   (D) southeast (E) north

6. The distance from Benton to Vernon, in kilometers, is
   (A) 32 (B) 48 (C) 40 (D) 36 (E) 56

Pictographs

Pictures are often used to represent numerical facts. Pictures are more interesting to the reader and attract his or her attention more readily. Consider the following two picture graphs, or pictographs.

PRACTICE TEST 5

DIRECTIONS: Base your answers to the following questions on the pictograph below, which shows the growth in population of the town of Springfield.

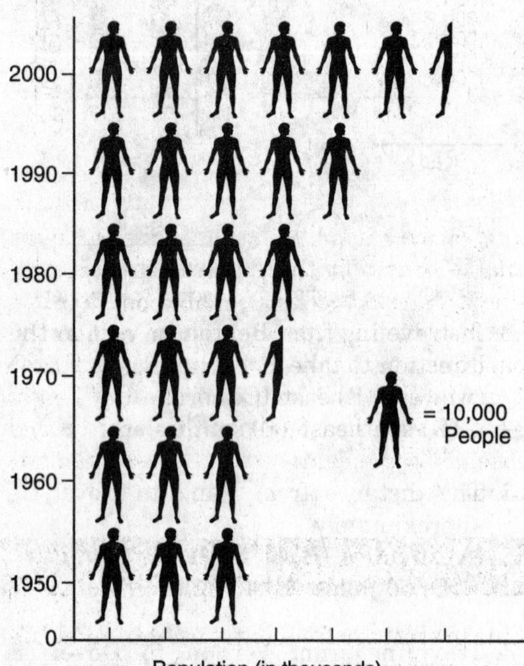

1. If the population of Springfield was 30,000 in 1960, how many people are represented by each symbol in the pictograph?
(A) 5,000 (B) 20,000 (C) 10,000
(D) 15,500 (E) 50,000

2. The population of Springfield in 2000 was about
(A) 30,000 (B) 49,000 (C) 52,000
(D) 60,000 (E) 39,000

3. The smallest population increase for a 10-year period occurred during
(A) 1960–1970 (B) 2000–2010
(C) 1990–2000 (D) 1970–1980
(E) 1980–1990

4. The increase in population in Springfield between 1960 and 2000 was about
(A) 38,000 (B) 45,000 (C) 48,000
(D) 50,000 (E) 35,000

5. The Springfield Town Planning Council predicted that the population will reach 80,000 by the year 2020. How many symbols would be needed on the pictograph to represent 80,000 population?
(A) 10 (B) 20 (C) 16 (D) 12 (E) 8

PRACTICE TEST 6

DIRECTIONS: Base your answers to the following questions on the pictograph below, which shows the number of feet required to stop a car, at various speeds, after applying the brakes.

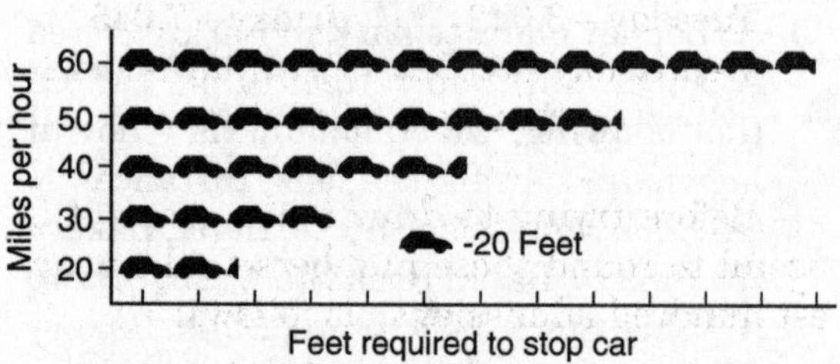

1. A motorist traveling at 30 miles per hour requires 80 feet to stop her car after applying the brakes. Therefore, each car in the pictograph represents how many feet?
(A) 10 (B) 15 (C) 20 (D) 40 (E) 25

2. If a motorist is traveling at 50 miles per hour, about how many feet are required to stop his car after applying the brakes?
(A) 180 (B) 160 (C) 200 (D) 195
(E) 185

3. How many more feet are needed to stop a car traveling at 50 miles per hour than a car going 40 miles per hour?
(A) 80 (B) 60 (C) 40 (D) 45 (E) 75

4. A motorist is traveling at the rate of 60 miles per hour. He sees a stop sign in the distance. About how many feet in advance must he apply the brake in order to stop at the stop sign?
(A) 100 (B) 150 (C) 200 (D) 250
(E) 300

Graphs

Graphs are also used to present numerical facts in visual form. Graphs enable a person to make comparisons and see relationships at a glance. In this section, we will consider three types of graphs: (a) bar graphs, (b) line graphs, (c) circle graphs.

BAR GRAPHS

Bar graphs are frequently used to make it easy to compare quantities.

EXAMPLE: Average attendance by days of the week at the Squire Movie Theater is given below:

Monday—2,407 Thursday—4,612
Tuesday—3,042 Friday—7,045
Wednesday—5,892 Saturday—9,812
Sunday—8,286

Before trying to draw a bar graph it is useful to round these numbers to the nearest hundred admissions, as follows:

Monday—2,400 Thursday—4,600
Tuesday—3,000 Friday—7,000
Wednesday—5,900 Saturday—9,800
Sunday—8,300

Next, we must decide upon a scale. In this case, it would be reasonable to let each box on the graph paper represent 1,000 admissions. Thus, Monday's admissions (2,400) would be represented by a height of 2.4 boxes, Tuesday's admissions (3,000) by 3 boxes, Wednesday's admissions (5,900) by almost six boxes, etc. The completed graph is shown in the next column.

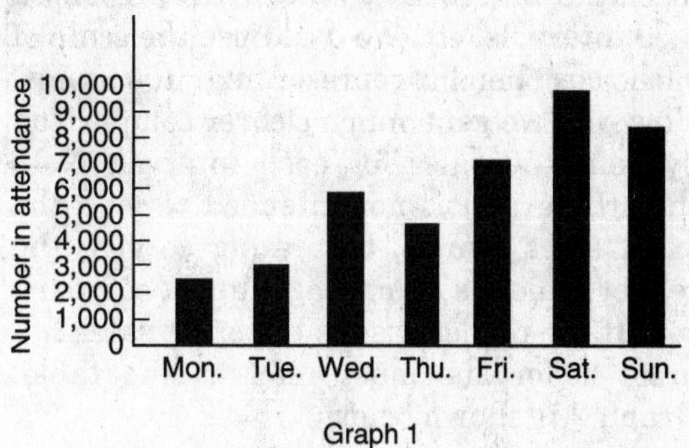

Graph 1

Notice that the scale selected must enable one to fit the graph on paper. Also, the scale selected must enable one to draw box heights so that it is easy to make comparisons at a glance. For example, on Graph 1 it would not be helpful if one box height were to represent 5,000 admissions. In that case, all box heights would be less than two units.

LINE GRAPHS

Line graphs are frequently used to show numerical changes over a period of time.

EXAMPLE: The Adams Motor Company sells automobiles. The number of cars sold during the first eight months of a certain year are shown in the table below:

January—203 May—679
February—316 June—548
March—461 July—412
April—537 August—362

Before drawing the graph it will be helpful to round these numbers to the nearest 50 cars, as shown on the next page:

January—200	May—700
February—300	June—550
March—450	July—400
April—550	August—350

Next, we must decide upon a scale. In this case, it is reasonable to let each interval on the y-axis (that is, the vertical axis on the left) represent 50 cars. Thus, January sales (200) are represented by 4 intervals, February sales (300) are represented by 6 intervals, March sales (450) are represented by 9 intervals, etc. We could use the scale of each box height representing 100 sales. However, we get a much clearer comparison by using 50 sales for each interval. Note that the graph is not intended to give the exact sales figures, but rather to give the reader a means of making a quick comparison. If the reader wishes the exact sales figures, he or she must refer to the table. Graph 2 is shown below.

MONTHLY SALES OF ADAMS MOTOR CO.

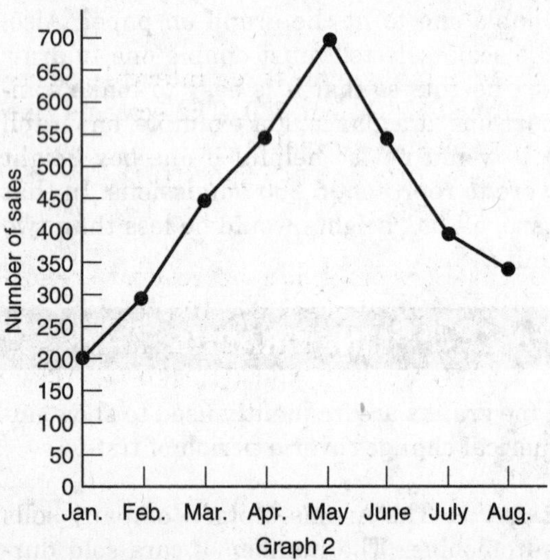

Graph 2

CIRCLE GRAPHS

Circle graphs are used when a whole quantity is divided into parts and we wish to make a comparison among the parts. In representing the parts we use the properties of a circle. Since the measure of a whole revolution is 360°, $\frac{1}{4}$ of a revolution is $\frac{1}{4}$ of 360° or 90°.

EXAMPLE: A city employs 6,000 workers distributed as follows:

Teachers—2,000	Sanitation—600
Police—1,000	Clerks—800
Firefighters—500	Miscellaneous—1,100

Draw a circle graph representing these figures.

GRAPH OF DISTRIBUTION OF CITY WORKERS

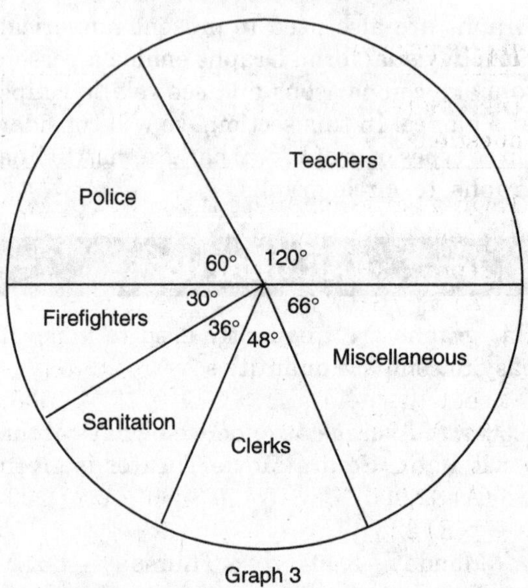

Graph 3

The sector of the circle representing the number of teachers is $\frac{2000}{6000} = \frac{1}{3}$. And $\frac{1}{3}$ of 360° = 120°. Thus the sector of the circle representing the number of teachers has an angle of 120° at the center.

The sector of the circle representing the number of police is $\frac{1000}{6000} = \frac{1}{6}$. And $\frac{1}{6}$ of 360° = 60°. Thus, the sector of the circle representing the number of police has an angle of 60° at the center.

The sector of the circle representing the number of firefighters is $\frac{500}{6000} = \frac{1}{12}$. And $\frac{1}{12}$ of 360° = 30°. Thus, the sector of the circle representing the number of firefighters has an angle of 30° at the center.

The sector of the circle representing the number of sanitation workers is $\frac{600}{6000} = \frac{1}{10}$. And $\frac{1}{10}$ of 360° = 36°. Thus, the sector of the circle representing the number of sanitation workers has an angle of 36° at the center.

The sector of the circle representing the number of clerks is $\frac{800}{6000} = \frac{2}{15}$. And $\frac{2}{15}$ of 360° = 48°. Thus, the sector of the circle representing the number of clerks has an angle of 48° at the center.

The sector of the circle representing the number of miscellaneous workers is $\frac{1100}{6000} = \frac{11}{60}$. And $\frac{11}{60}$ of 360° = 66°. Thus, the sector of the circle representing the number of miscellaneous workers has an angle of 66° at the center.

PRACTICE TEST 7

DIRECTIONS: Answer each of the following questions.

1. On a bar graph, the scale is 1 box = 600 people. The number of boxes needed to represent 2,000 people is
   (A) $2\frac{1}{2}$ (B) 3 (C) $3\frac{1}{2}$ (D) $3\frac{1}{3}$ (E) $3\frac{2}{3}$

2. On a bar graph it is necessary to represent the following: $850; $712; $1,548; $438; $903; $679. The best scale to use is 1 box =
   (A) $2,000 (B) $10 (C) $200 (D) $1,000 (E) $25

Answer questions 3–7 based on bar graph 4, which represents the number of traffic violations reported by the Traffic Division of the police department of a large city.

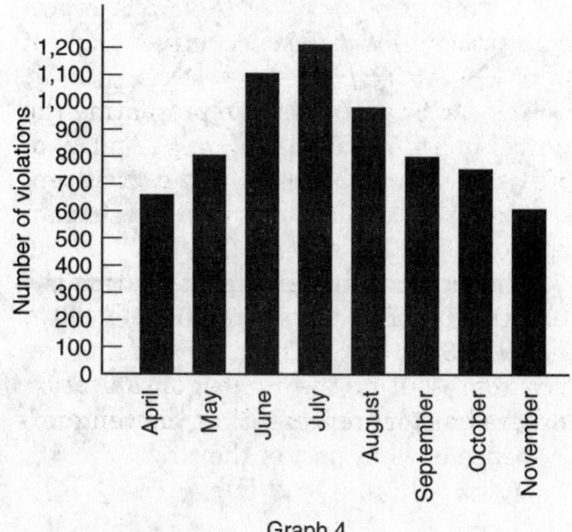

Graph 4

3. The scale on this graph is 1 box = __________ traffic violations.
   (A) 1,200 (B) 100 (C) 500 (D) 200 (E) 400

4. The number of traffic violations reported during the month of April was about
   (A) 600 (B) 700 (C) 650 (D) 550 (E) 575

5. The greatest number of violations occurred during the month of
   (A) May (B) November (C) June (D) August (E) July

6. The number of traffic violations reported during the month of August was about
   (A) 975 (B) 900 (C) 950 (D) 1,000 (E) 850

7. The month during which there were twice the number of traffic violations reported in November was
   (A) April (B) August (C) June (D) July (E) May

8. On a line graph, three intervals represent the number 750. The scale on this graph is 1 interval = ______________.
   (A) 200 (B) 300 (C) 350 (D) 100 (E) 250

9. On a line graph it is necessary to represent the numbers 87, 102, 53, 75, 68, 119. The best scale to use is 1 interval =
   (A) 10 (B) 40 (C) 50 (D) 120 (E) 100

Answer questions 10–14 based on line graph 5, which represents the number of tolls collected on the Cross Island Bridge during a certain week.

GRAPH OF NUMBER OF TOLLS COLLECTED ON CROSS ISLAND BRIDGE

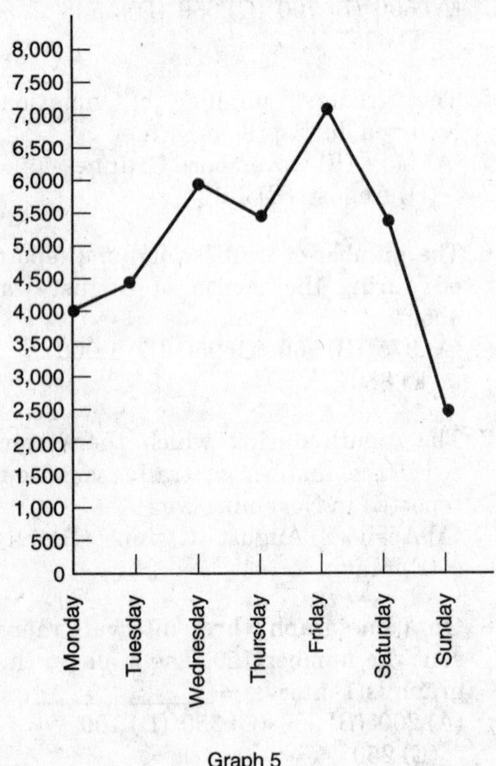

Graph 5

10. The scale on this graph is 1 interval = __________.
    (A) 1,000 (B) 2,000 (C) 1,500 (D) 500 (E) 700

11. The day on which the lowest number of tolls was collected was
    (A) Monday (B) Sunday (C) Friday (D) Tuesday (E) Saturday

12. The number of tolls collected on Friday was about
    (A) 7,500 (B) 7,000 (C) 6,500 (D) 6,000 (E) 8,000

13. The increase in the number of tolls collected between Tuesday and Wednesday was about
    (A) 1,000 (B) 2,500 (C) 2,000 (D) 1,500 (E) 500

14. The difference between the number of tolls collected on Saturday and the number of tolls collected on Sunday was about
    (A) 2,500 (B) 2,000 (C) 3,000 (D) 3,500 (E) 1,500

15. On a circle graph the angle at the center of a sector representing the fraction $\frac{10}{50}$ is
    (A) 72° (B) 20° (C) 50° (D) 10° (E) 100°

16. If an angle at the center of the sector of a circle graph measures 45° it represents the fraction
    (A) $\frac{1}{6}$ (B) $\frac{1}{9}$ (C) $\frac{9}{100}$ (D) $\frac{1}{4}$ (E) $\frac{1}{8}$

Answer questions 17–20 based on circle graph 6, which represents the number of dollars for various items in the monthly budget of the Green family. The Green family has a monthly income of $1,800.

GRAPH OF MONTHLY BUDGET OF THE GREEN FAMILY

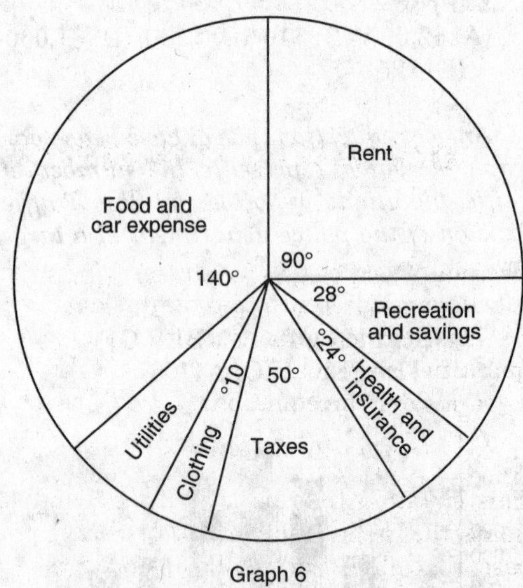

Graph 6

17. The monthly amount spent for rent is
    (A) $400 (B) $425 (C) $500 (D) $450 (E) $350

18. The sector representing clothing expense is what part of the circle?
    (A) $\frac{1}{10}$ (B) $\frac{1}{20}$ (C) $\frac{1}{36}$ (D) $\frac{1}{15}$ (E) $\frac{1}{25}$

19. One month the Green family spent $200 on the family car for repairs and gas. The amount left in the budget for food this month was
(A) $700 (B) $500 (C) $450
(D) $600 (E) $650

20. The monthly cost of taxes for the Green family was
(A) $200 (B) $50 (C) $150 (D) $300
(E) $250

Answers to All Practice Tests

TEST 1

1. **C** 2. **E** 3. **A** 4. **D** 5. **B**

TEST 2

1. **C** 2. **E** 3. **A** 4. **D** 5. **B**

TEST 3

1. **D** 2. **C** 3. **D** 4. **D** 5. **E**

TEST 4

1. **D** 3. **E** 4. **C** 5. **A** 6. **B**
2. **B**

TEST 5

1. **C** 2. **B** 3. **D** 4. **A** 5. **E**

TEST 6

1. **C** 2. **E** 3. **B** 4. **D**

TEST 7

1. **D**	5. **E**	9. **A**	13. **D**	17. **D**
2. **C**	6. **A**	10. **D**	14. **C**	18. **C**
3. **B**	7. **D**	11. **B**	15. **A**	19. **B**
4. **C**	8. **E**	12. **A**	16. **E**	20. **E**

Geometry

CHAPTER 13

The Basics

POINTS, LINES, RAYS

Geometry is the study of lines, angles, surfaces, and solids. A *point* in geometry is suggested by a dot on a piece of paper, first base on a baseball field, or a star in the sky. A *line* in geometry is a set of points. A line is suggested by an edge of this page, a sideline in football, or a telephone wire stretched between two poles. A line in geometry is always thought of as a straight line and extends infinitely in both directions. For this reason a line is often shown with two arrows, as below. A line is named by naming two points on it with a double arrow above the names of the points. For

example, $\overleftrightarrow{AB}$ is a line containing both points A and B.

Parallel lines are lines in the same plane (flat surface) that never meet regardless of how far they are extended. $\overleftrightarrow{CD}$ is parallel to $\overleftrightarrow{EF}$. This may be written as $\overleftrightarrow{CD} \parallel \overleftrightarrow{EF}$.

Perpendicular lines are lines that meet at right angles (from square corners). $\overleftrightarrow{TV}$ is perpendicular to $\overleftrightarrow{RS}$. This may be written as $\overleftrightarrow{TV} \perp \overleftrightarrow{RS}$.

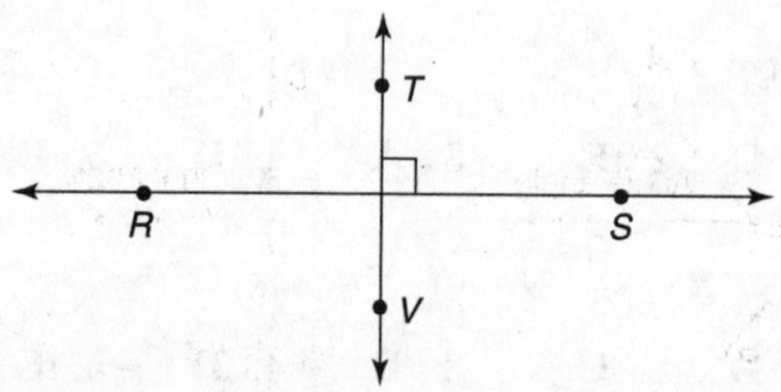

A *line segment* $\overline{AB}$ is a set of points of a line consisting of the points A and B and all the points between them.

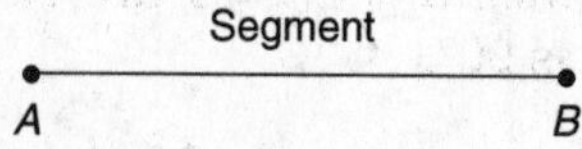

The points A and B are called the *endpoints* of the segment.

The length of $\overline{AB}$ is denoted by AB.

The figure below is a *ray*. A *ray* consists of

one endpoint and all the points on a line on one side of the endpoint.

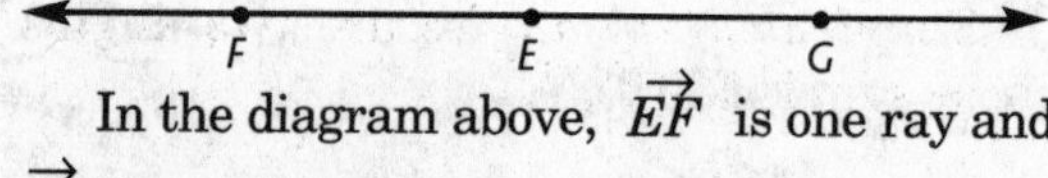

In the diagram above, $\overrightarrow{EF}$ is one ray and $\overrightarrow{EG}$ is another ray.

ANGLES

An *angle* is the union of two rays that have the same endpoint. The two rays are called the *sides* of the angle and their common endpoint is called the *vertex*. An angle is named by naming a point on one side, the vertex, and then a point on the other side. Where there is no ambiguity, an angle may be named by naming only its vertex.

EXAMPLE: In the diagram (right) the sides of the angle are $\overrightarrow{CA}$ and $\overrightarrow{CB}$, the vertex is C and the angle is named $\angle ACB$, or $\angle BCA$, or simply $\angle C$.

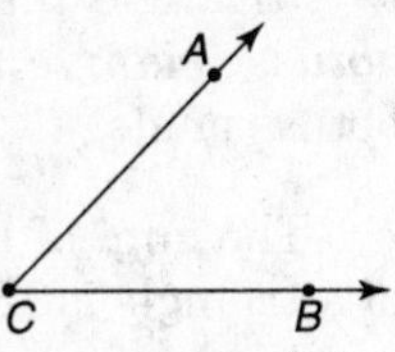

An angle is measured in degrees. An *acute* angle is an angle whose measure is less than 90°. A *right* angle is an angle whose measure is 90°. An *obtuse* angle is an angle whose measure is greater than 90° and less than 180°. A *straight* angle is an angle whose measure is 180°.

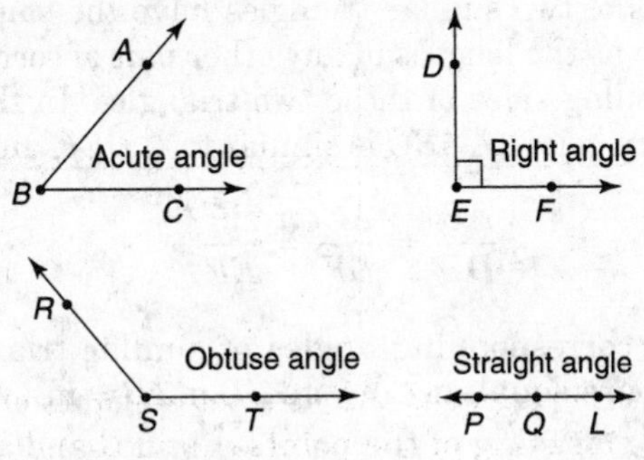

Complementary angles are two angles whose sum is 90°.

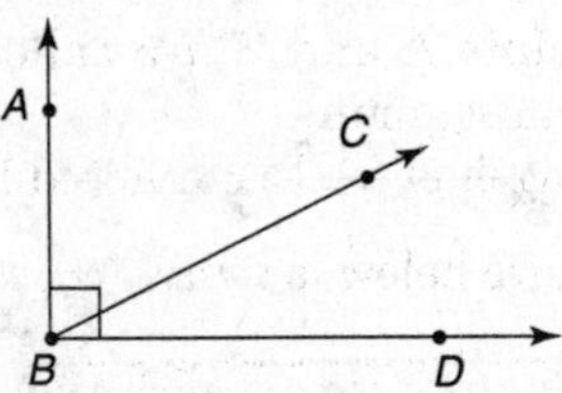

Thus in the diagram, $\angle ABC$ is complementary to $\angle CBD$.

Supplementary angles are two angles whose sum is 180°.

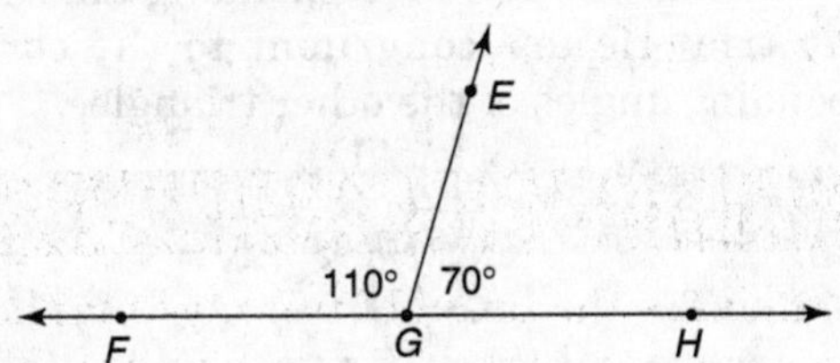

Thus, in the figure, $\angle EGF$ is supplementary to $\angle HGE$.

Two angles are said to be *congruent* if they have the same measure.

Thus, in the figure, $\angle CED$ is congruent to $\angle AFG$. This may be written as $\angle CED \cong \angle AFG$.

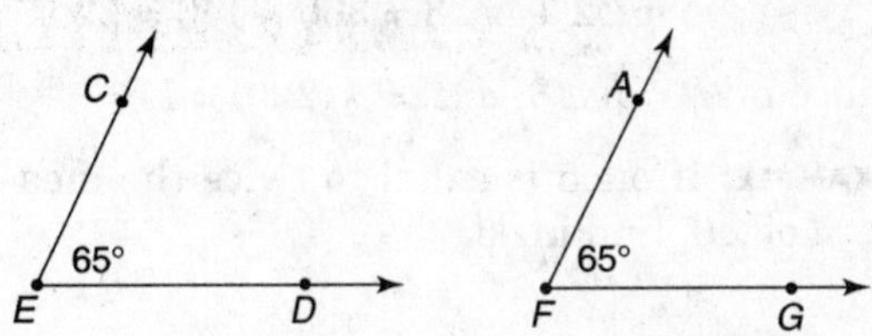

Vertical angles are pairs of opposite angles formed by two intersecting lines. Thus, in the figure, $\angle DAB$ and $\angle EAC$ are a pair of vertical angles. And $\angle BAC$ and $\angle EAD$ are another pair of vertical angles. Vertical angles are congruent.

Thus, in the figure, $\angle DAB \cong \angle EAC$, and $\angle BAC \cong \angle EAD$.

The sum of the measures (abbreviated as "m") of the angles around a point in a plane is 360°.

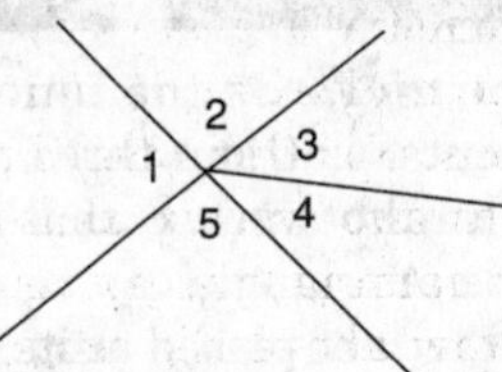

EXAMPLE: $m\angle 1 + m\angle 2 + m\angle 3 + m\angle 4 + m\angle 5 = 360°$.

The sum of the measures of the angles around a point in a plane on one side of a straight line is 180°.

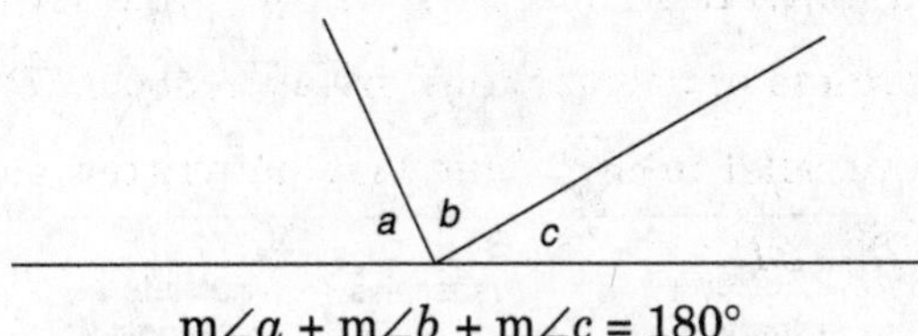

$m\angle a + m\angle b + m\angle c = 180°$

EXAMPLE: If $m\angle 1 = 140°$ and $m\angle 2 = m\angle 3$, find $m\angle 2$.

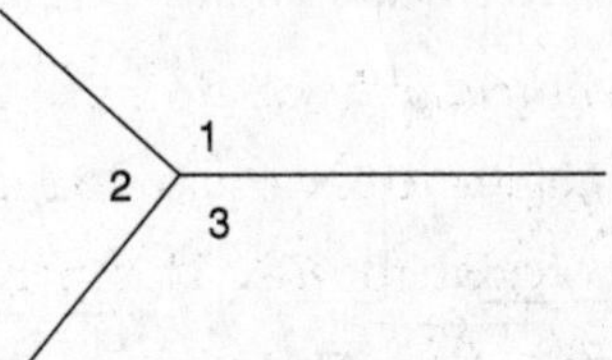

$$m\angle 1 + m\angle 2 + m\angle 3 = 360°$$
$$m\angle 1 = 140°$$
$$m\angle 2 + m\angle 3 = 360 - 140 = 220°$$

Since $m\angle 2 = m\angle 3$, $m\angle 2 = \frac{1}{2}(220) = 110°$

EXAMPLE: If $m\angle 5$ is equal to twice the measure of $\angle 6$, find $m\angle 5$.

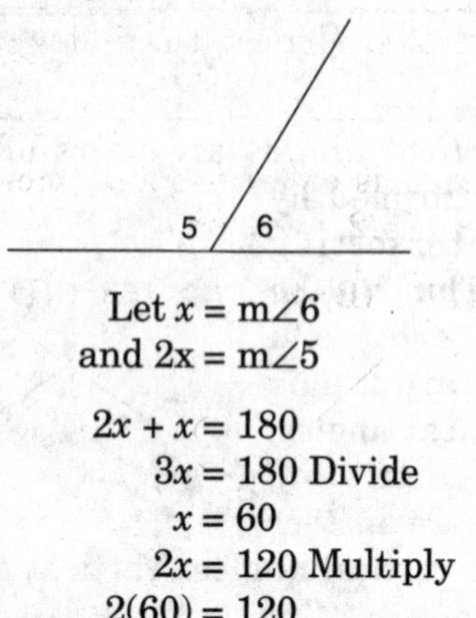

Let $x = m\angle 6$
and $2x = m\angle 5$

$2x + x = 180$
$3x = 180$ Divide
$x = 60$
$2x = 120$ Multiply
$2(60) = 120$

Thus, $m\angle 5 = 120°$.

TRIANGLES

A *triangle* is the union of three line segments that join three points called vertices (plural of vertex) that are not in a straight line. A triangle can be named by three capital letters placed at its vertices.

Triangles can be classified according to their *sides*. Thus, a *scalene triangle* is a triangle in which no two sides are congruent (equal). An *isosceles triangle* has two congruent sides. The base angles, opposite the congruent sides, are also congruent. An *equilateral triangle* has three congruent sides.

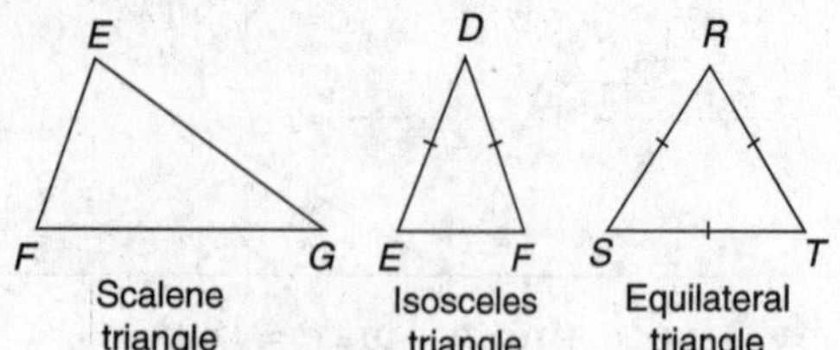

Triangles can also be classified according to their angles. An *acute triangle* is a triangle that has three acute angles. A *right triangle* is a triangle that has one right angle. An *obtuse triangle* is a triangle that has one obtuse angle.

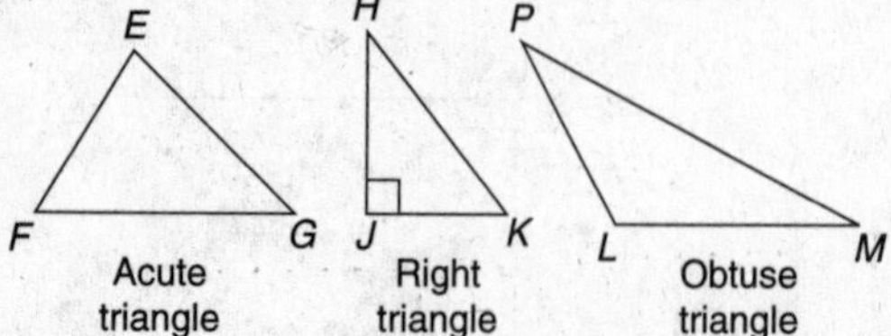

The sum of the measures of the angles of a triangle is 180°. Thus, if the measure of one angle of a triangle is 30°, and the measure of a second angle of the triangle is 80°, then the measure of the third angle is 180 – (30 + 80), or 180 – 110, or 70°.

Similar triangles are triangles that have the same shape but not necessarily the same size. The lengths of a pair of corresponding sides of two similar triangles have the same ratio as the lengths of any other pair of corresponding sides of those two triangles. In the figure below $\triangle ABC$ is similar to $\triangle DEF$, and

$$\frac{AB}{DE} = \frac{AC}{DF} = \frac{BC}{EF}.$$

The corresponding angles of similar triangles are equal: $m\angle A = m\angle D$, $m\angle B = m\angle E$, $m\angle C = m\angle F$.

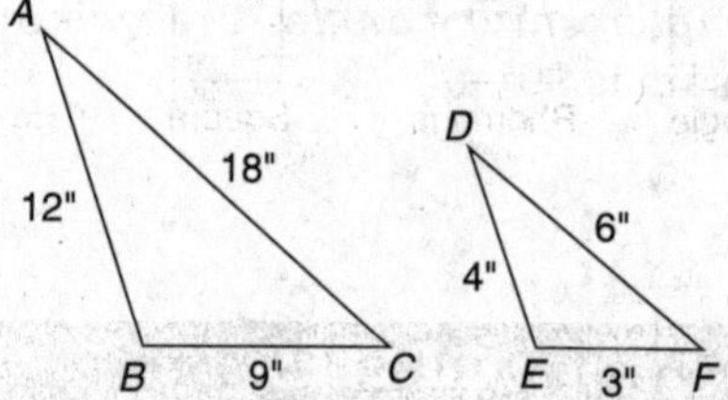

Congruent triangles have the same shape and the same size and can be made to coincide exactly. In the figure below, $\triangle ABC$ is congruent to $\triangle DEF$. Note that the corresponding sides of one triangle are congruent to the corresponding sides of the other triangle. The corresponding angles of one triangle are congruent to the corresponding angles of the other triangle.

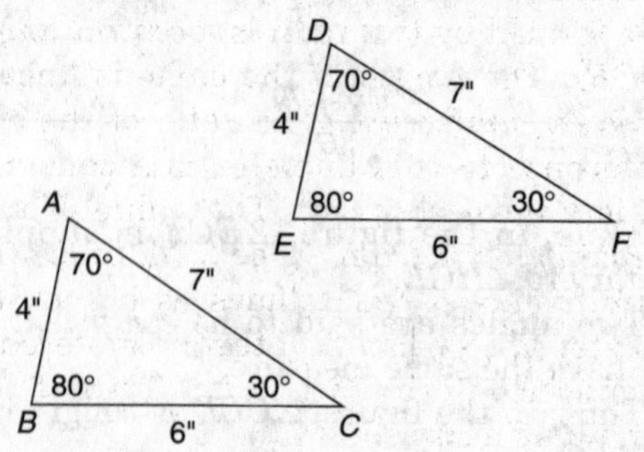

OTHER POLYGONS

A *polygon* is composed of a set of line segments in the same plane, each of which meets exactly two other line segments, one at each endpoint.

A *quadrilateral* is a polygon containing four segments as sides. A *trapezoid* is a quadrilateral with only one pair of sides parallel. Here the bases $\overline{AB}$ and $\overline{CD}$ are parallel. A *parallelogram* is a quadrilateral with two pairs of sides parallel. Here side $\overline{AB}$ is parallel to side $\overline{CD}$, and side $\overline{AD}$ is parallel to side $\overline{CB}$. A *rectangle* is a quadrilateral with four right angles. A *rhombus* is a quadrilateral with all sides congruent. A *square* is a quadrilateral with all sides congruent and all right angles. A *hexagon* is a polygon of six sides.

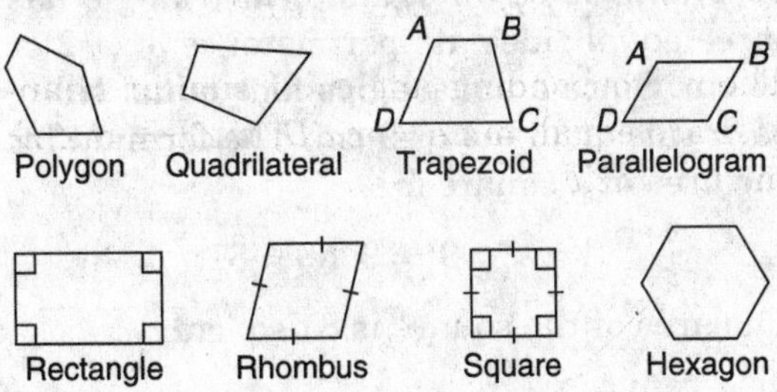

CIRCLES

A *circle* is the set of all points in a plane that are a given fixed distance from a fixed point called the *center*. Any segment from the center to a point on the circle is called a *radius*. Any segment connecting two points on the circle is called a *chord*. A chord that contains the center is called a *diameter*. The length of the diameter is twice that of the radius. An angle formed by two radii is a *central angle* $(\angle BOR)$. The length of the circle is known as the *circumference*. The ratio of the circumference to the diameter is a constant and is known as π (pi). The value of π is approximately $3\frac{1}{7}$ or $\frac{22}{7}$ or 3.14. Since the circumference (C) is π times as big as the diameter (d), we can find the circumference by using the formula $C = \pi d$. Thus if the diameter of a circle is 14,

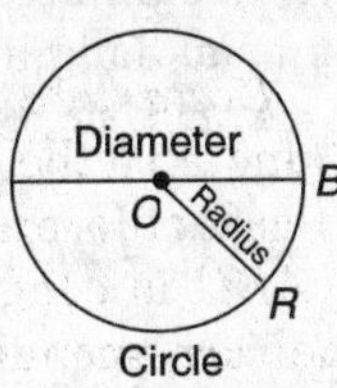

$$C = \pi d = \frac{22}{\underset{1}{\cancel{7}}} \times \frac{\overset{2}{\cancel{14}}}{1} = 44$$

PRACTICE TEST 1

DIRECTIONS: Answer the following questions.

1. If m∠1 is equal to four times the measure of ∠2, m∠1 is:

   (A) 36° (B) 48° (C) 154° (D) 144°

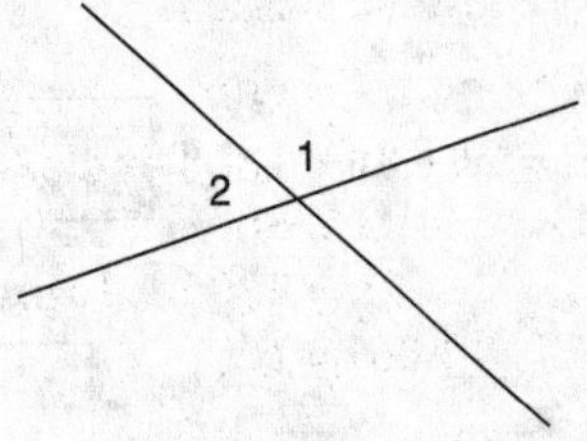

2. If m∠3 = 90° and m∠4 = m∠5, m∠4 is:

   (A) 90° (B) 45° (C) 50° (D) 135°

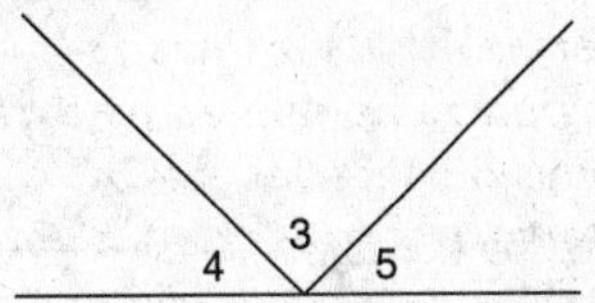

3. If m∠1 = m∠2 and m∠1 = 140°, m∠3 is:

   (A) 80° (B) 90° (C) 120° (D) 100°

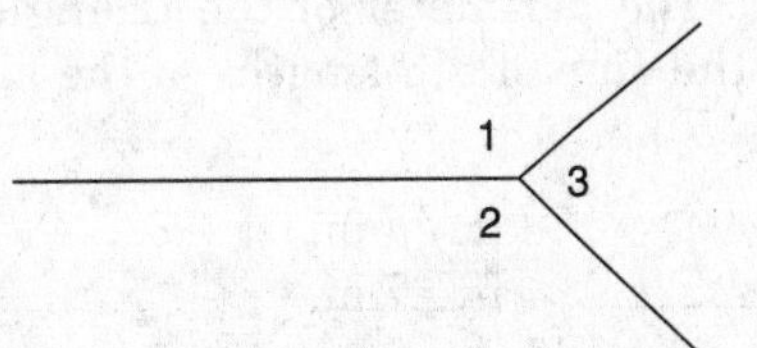

4. If m∠5 is equal to twice the measure of ∠4, m∠6 is:

   (A) 120° (B) 100° (C) 60° (D) 90°

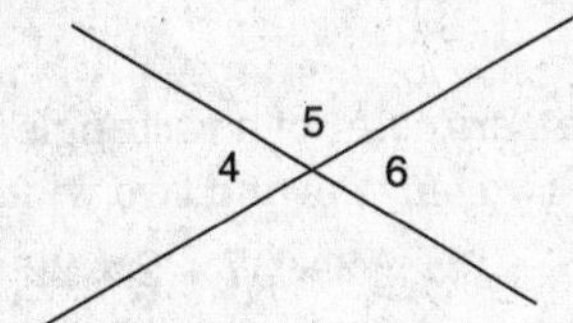

Perimeter, Area, and Volume

PERIMETER

The *perimeter* is the distance around a plane figure. The following formulas will prove helpful in determining perimeters.

Triangle: $P = a + b + c$

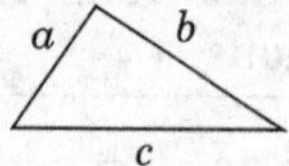

Equilateral triangle: $P = 3s$

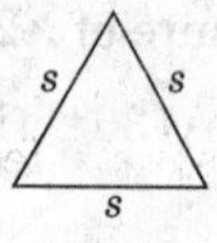

Rectangle: $P = 2l + 2w$

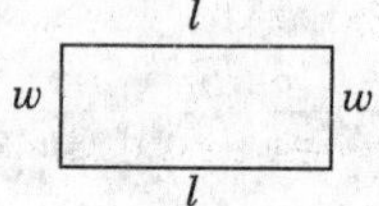

Square: $P = 4s$

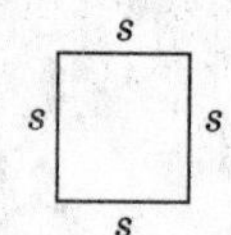

Regular or equilateral hexagon: $P = 6s$

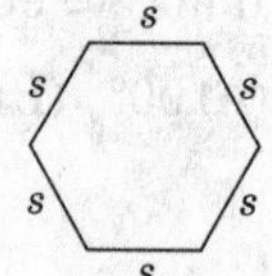

Circle: $C = \pi d$ or $C = 2\pi r$

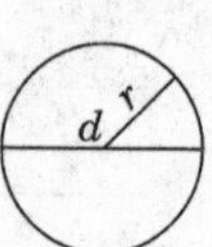

EXAMPLE: Find the perimeter of a triangle whose sides are 3 ft. 4 in., 4 ft. 7 in., and 5 ft. 6 in.

SOLUTION: The perimeter of the triangle is equal to the sum of the lengths of the sides or $P = a + b + c$.

3 ft. 4 in.
4 ft. 7 in.
5 ft. 6 in.
12 ft. 17 in.

The perimeter of the triangle is 13 ft. 5 in.

EXAMPLE: How many feet of fencing are required to enclose a rectangular yard that is 37 ft. by 22 ft. 6 in.?

SOLUTION: The perimeter of a rectangle is equal to the sum of two lengths and two widths.

$$P = 2l + 2w = 2 \times 37 + 2 \times 22\tfrac{1}{2}$$
$$= 74 + 45 = 119$$

The perimeter of the rectangle, and therefore the amount of fencing required, is 119 feet.

EXAMPLE: The perimeter of a rectangle is 82 ft. If the width of the rectangle is 17 ft., find the length.

SOLUTION: If we subtract two widths of the rectangle from the perimeter we will find the value of two lengths: $82 - 34 = 48$. Since the two equal lengths add up to 48 feet, the value of one length is 24 feet.

EXAMPLE: The side of an equilateral triangle is 12 cm. Find the area of a square whose perimeter is equal to that of the triangle.

SOLUTION: Since an equilateral triangle has three equal sides, its perimeter is 3×12 or 36 cm. Since a square has four equal sides, each side is $36 \div 4$ or 9 cm. The formula for the area of a square is

$$A = s^2 = 9^2 = 9 \times 9 = 81.$$

The area of the square is 81 sq. cm.

EXAMPLE: How much rope is needed to put along the edge of a circular pool that has a radius of 21 feet?

SOLUTION: The length of a circle is known as the circumference. The circumference is π times as long as the diameter, or $C = \pi d$ or $C = 2\pi r$. Use $\frac{22}{7}$ as the value of π.

$$C = 2\pi r = 2 \times \frac{22}{\cancel{7}_1} \times \cancel{21}^3 = 132$$

The length of the rope is 132 feet.

EXAMPLE: A circle has a circumference of 78.5 feet. Find the length of the diameter. (Let $\pi = 3.14$.)

SOLUTION: Since $C = \pi \times d$, then $d = C \div \pi$.

$$d = 78.5 \div 3.14$$

```
            25.
3.14.)78.50.
      62 8
      15 70
      15 70
```

The diameter is 25 feet in length.

AREA

The area of a plane figure is the number of square units that the figure contains. For example, the unit of measure used in measuring the area of the rectangle at the right is the square inch. A square inch is a square whose length is 1 inch and whose width is 1 inch. Since a square inch is contained in the rectangle 8 times, we say that the area of the rectangle is 8 square inches. It can be seen that the area of a rectangle is obtained by multiplying the number of units in its length by the number of units in its width. In converting units of area recall that 144 sq. in. = 1 sq. ft. and 9 sq. ft. = 1 sq. yd. The following formulas are useful in finding areas.

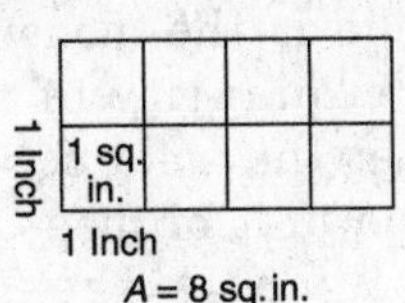

Rectangle: $A = lw$

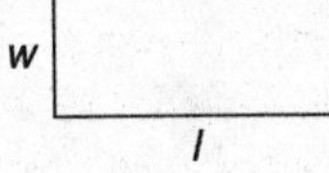

Parallelogram: $A = bh$

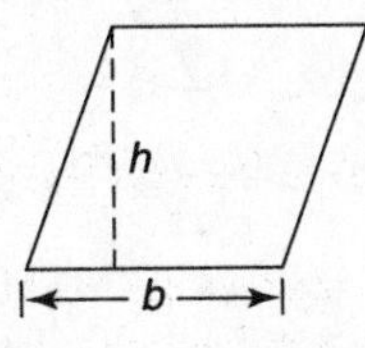

Square: $A = s^2$

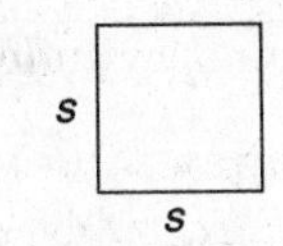

Triangle: $A = \frac{1}{2}bh$

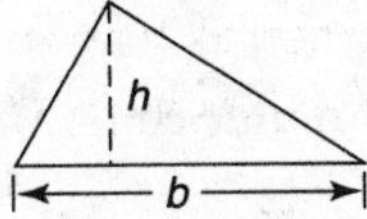

Trapezoid:
$A = \frac{1}{2}h(b_1 + b_2)$

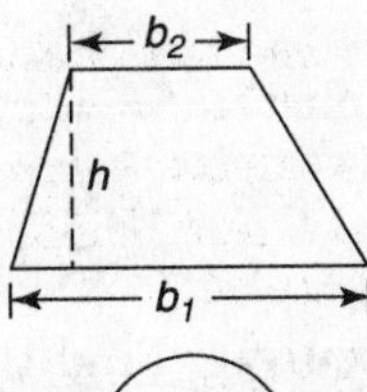

Circle: $A = \pi r^2$

EXAMPLE: A rectangular living room is 22 ft. long and 12 ft. 6 in. wide. How many square feet of carpet are needed to cover the floor of the living room?

SOLUTION: The area of the floor of the living room is found by obtaining the product of the number of units in the length and the number of units in the width.

$$22 \times 12\tfrac{1}{2}$$

$$\begin{array}{r} 22 \\ \times\ 12\frac{1}{2} \\ \hline 11 \\ 44 \\ 22 \\ \hline 275 \end{array}$$

275 square feet of carpet are needed.

EXAMPLE: The area of a rectangular room is 207 square feet. If the length of the room is 18 feet, find the width of the room.

SOLUTION: The width of the room is obtained by dividing the area of the room by its length.

$$\begin{array}{r} 11\frac{9}{18} \\ 18\overline{)207} \\ \underline{18} \\ 27 \\ \underline{18} \\ 9 \end{array}$$

The width of the room is $11\frac{9}{18}$ ft. = $11\frac{1}{2}$ ft. or 11 ft. 6 in.

EXAMPLE: A tile measures 6 inches by 6 inches. How many such tiles are needed to cover a floor 15 feet long and 12 feet wide?

SOLUTION: The floor area is obtained by multiplying the number of units in its length by the number of units in its width.

$$\text{Area} = 15 \times 12 = 180 \text{ sq. ft.}$$

Each tile has an area of 6 in. by 6 in. or 36 sq. in. Since 144 sq. in. is 1 sq. ft., then 3 sq. in. is $\frac{36}{144}$ or $\frac{1}{4}$ of a square foot. The number of tiles needed is $180 \div \frac{1}{4}$, or 180×4, or 720 tiles.

EXAMPLE: Find the area of a triangle whose base is 8 ft. 4 in. and whose altitude is 9 ft.

SOLUTION: The area of the triangle is equal to one-half the product of its base and altitude.

$$\begin{aligned} \text{Base} \times \text{Altitude} &= 8 \text{ ft. } 4 \text{ in.} \times 9 \text{ ft.} \\ &= 8\tfrac{1}{3} \times 9 = 75 \text{ sq. ft.} \end{aligned}$$

One-half of this product is $37\frac{1}{2}$ square feet.

EXAMPLE: A triangular-shaped cloth sail has a base of 10 meters and a height of 6 meters. If the cloth cost $4 a square meter, find the cost of the sail.

SOLUTION: The formula for the area of a triangle is $A = \frac{1}{2}bh$.

$$A = \tfrac{1}{2}bh = \tfrac{1}{2} \times 10 \times 6 = 30 \text{ square meters.}$$

Since each square meter costs $4, the cost of 30 square meters is 30 × 4, or $120.

EXAMPLE: Find the surface area of a box that measures 6 cm by 4 cm by 3 cm.

SOLUTION: The box has six rectangular surfaces. The bottom and top surfaces each have an area of 6 cm × 4 cm or 24 sq cm. The surfaces to the right and left each have an area of 3 cm × 4 cm or 12 sq. cm. The front and back rectangles each have an area of 6 cm. × 3 cm or 18 sq. cm.

$$\begin{aligned} 2 \times 24 + 2 \times 12 + 2 \times 18 &= 48 + 24 + 36 \\ &= 108 \text{ sq. cm} \end{aligned}$$

The total surface is therefore equal to 108 square centimeters.

EXAMPLE: Find the area of a circular garden whose diameter is 20 feet.

SOLUTION: The formula for the area of a circle is $A = \pi r^2$. Since the diameter is 20 feet, the radius is 10 feet. Since 7 does not divide evenly into 10, it is best to select 3.14 as the value of π.

$$A = \pi r^2 = 3.14 \times 10 \times 10 = 314$$

The area of the garden is 314 square feet.

EXAMPLE: The circumference of a circle is 88 inches. Find its area. (Let $\pi = \frac{22}{7}$.)

SOLUTION: The circumference of a circle is π times as long as its diameter. To find the diameter we divide the circumference by π.

$$d = C \div \pi = 88 \div \frac{22}{7} = \overset{4}{\cancel{88}} \times \frac{7}{\underset{1}{\cancel{22}}} = 28$$

Since the diameter is 28, the radius is 14 inches.

$$A = \pi r^2 = \frac{22}{\underset{1}{\cancel{7}}} \times \overset{2}{\cancel{14}} \times 14 = 616$$

The area of the circle is 616 square inches.

VOLUME

The dimensions of a solid are the length, the width, and the height. The volume of a solid is the measure of the quantity of space that the solid occupies. The unit of measure of volume is the *cubic unit*. The cubic inch is a cube whose length, width, and height each measure 1 inch. The following formulas for determining volumes of solids will prove helpful:

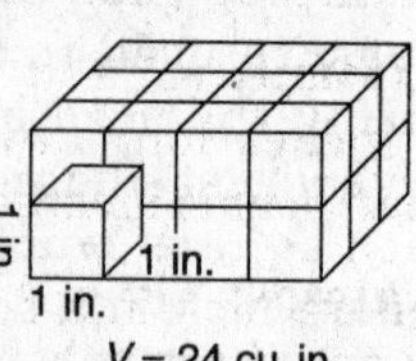

Rectangular solid (prism): $V = lwh$

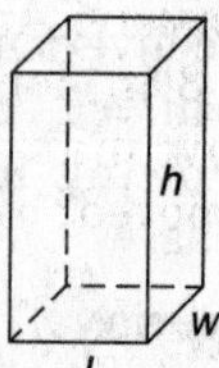

Cube: $V = e^3$

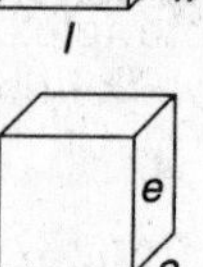

Circular cylinder: $V = \pi r^2 h$

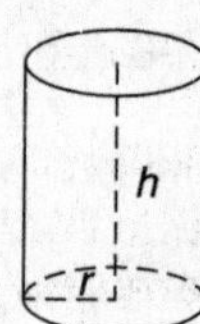

Circular cone: $V = \frac{1}{3}\pi r^2 h$

Sphere: $V = \frac{4}{3}\pi r^3$

EXAMPLE: Find the volume of a rectangular solid whose length is 2 ft. 3 in., whose width is 1 ft. 6 in., and whose height is 8 in.

SOLUTION: The volume of the rectangular solid is obtained by multiplying the number of units in its length by the number of units in its width by the number of units in its height.

Since 2 ft. 3 in. = $2\frac{1}{4}$ ft., 1 ft. 6 in. = $1\frac{1}{2}$ ft., and 8 in. = $\frac{2}{3}$ ft.,

$$\text{Volume} = 2\frac{1}{4} \times 1\frac{1}{2} \times \frac{2}{3} = \frac{9}{4} \times \frac{3}{2} \times \frac{2}{3} = \frac{9}{4}$$

The volume of the rectangular solid is $2\frac{1}{4}$ cubic feet.

EXAMPLE: A candy box is 2.5 inches high, 8 inches long, and 5.4 inches wide. How many cubic inches does the box contain?

SOLUTION: The volume is obtained by multiplying the number of units in the length by the number of units in the width by the number of units in the height.

$$\text{Volume} = 8 \times 5.4 \times 2.5 = 108$$

The candy box contains 108 cubic inches.

EXAMPLE: An excavation for a building is 48 ft. 3 in. long, 24 ft. wide, and 12 ft. deep. How many cubic feet of earth must be removed?

SOLUTION:

$$\text{Volume} = 48\frac{1}{4} \times 24 \times 12$$

$$\text{Volume} = \frac{193}{4} \times 24 \times 12 = 13{,}896$$

13,896 cubic feet must be removed.

EXAMPLE: A cubical tank in a ship's hold measures 30 feet on an edge. How many gallons of oil can be poured into it ($7\frac{1}{2}$ gal. = 1 cu. ft.)?

SOLUTION: The formula for the volume of a cube is $V = e^3$.

$$V = e^3 = 30^3 = 30 \times 30 \times 30 = 27{,}000 \text{ cu. ft.}$$

Since each cubic foot contains $7\frac{1}{2}$ gallons, the total number of gallons is $27{,}000 \times 7\frac{1}{2}$.

$$\frac{\overset{13{,}500}{\cancel{27{,}000}}}{1} \times \frac{15}{\underset{1}{\cancel{2}}} = 202{,}500$$

The tank will hold 202,500 gallons of oil.

EXAMPLE: Find the volume of a circular cylindrical tank that has a diameter of 20 feet and a height of 14 feet.

SOLUTION: The formula to find the volume of a circular cylinder is $V = \pi r^2 h$. Here the radius is 10 feet and the height is 14 feet. In this example it is best to use $\frac{22}{7}$ as the value of π since 7 divides evenly into 14.

$$V = \pi r^2 h = \frac{22}{\underset{1}{\cancel{7}}} \times \frac{10}{1} \times \frac{10}{1} \times \frac{\overset{2}{\cancel{14}}}{1} = 4{,}400$$

The volume of the cylinder is 4,400 cu. ft.

EXAMPLE: Find the volume of a circular cone-shaped pile of sand if its base has a diameter of 20 ft. and its height is 5 ft. 3 in.

SOLUTION: The formula for finding the volume of a circular cone is $V = \frac{1}{3}\pi r^2 h$. The radius is $\frac{1}{2}$ of 20 or 10 ft. The height is $5\frac{1}{4}$ ft.

$$V = \frac{1}{3}\pi r^2 h = \frac{1}{3} \times \frac{22}{7} \times 10 \times 10 \times \frac{21}{4} = 550$$

The volume of the sand pile is 550 cubic feet.

PRACTICE TEST 2

1. The sides of a triangle are 4′2″, 5′9″, and 3′8″. The perimeter of the triangle is:

   (A) 12′9″ (B) 13′9″ (C) 12′3″ (D) 13′7″ (E) 12′7″

2. The perimeter of a triangle is 20′. Two sides of the triangle are 6′8″ and 5′10″. The third side of the triangle is:

   (A) 9′6″ (B) 7′6″ (C) 12′6″ (D) 32′6″ (E) none of these

3. The length and width of a rectangle are 18′8″ and 7′6″. The perimeter of the rectangle is:

   (A) 52′4″ (B) 26′2″ (C) 50′8″ (D) 37′4″ (E) 15′

4. A room is 19′9″ long and 14′8″ wide. A strip of molding is fitted around the ceiling of the room. The length of molding used is:

   (A) 66′ (B) 54′2″ (C) 68′10″ (D) 69′4″ (E) 34′5″

5. The perimeter of a rectangle is 45′6″. The width of the rectangle is 8′6″. The length of the rectangle is:

   (A) 18′6″ (B) 108′ (C) 37′ (D) 74′ (E) 14′3″

PRACTICE TEST 3

1. The sides of a triangle are 6′3″ 3′8″ and 4′7″. The perimeter of the triangle is:

   (A) 13′8″ (B) 15′ (C) 14′8″ (D) 14′6″ (E) 72′

2. The perimeter of a triangle is 31′2″. Two sides of the triangle are 12′3″ and 10′6″. The other side of the triangle is:

   (A) 53′11″ (B) 9′3″ (C) 10′6″ (D) 8′5″ (E) 10′3″

3. A rectangle is 6′6″ long and 3′4″ wide. The area of the rectangle is:

   (A) $21\frac{2}{3}$ sq. ft. (B) 26 sq. ft. (C) 20 sq. ft. (D) $18\frac{2}{3}$ sq ft. (E) $18\frac{1}{3}$ sq. ft.

4. The base of a triangle is 15′9″. Its altitude is 5′4″ wide. The area of the triangle is:

   (A) 76 sq. ft. (B) 48 sq. ft. (C) 75 sq. ft. (D) 84 sq. ft. (E) 42 sq. ft.

5. The area of a rectangle is 110 square feet. The length of the rectangle is 15′. The width of the rectangle is:

   (A) 7′ (B) 7′3″ (C) 7′4″ (C) 22′ (E) 7′6″

6. A rectangular solid has a length of 9′6″, a width of 8′, and a height of 3′3″. The volume of the rectangular solid is:

   (A) 216 cu. ft. (B) 221 cu. ft. (C) $20\frac{3}{8}$ cu ft. (D) $226\frac{1}{4}$ cu. ft. (E) 247 cu. ft.

7. A drawer is 11.3 inches long, 4.4 inches wide, and 2.5 inches high. The volume of the drawer is:

   (A) 121 cubic inches
   (B) 124 cubic inches
   (C) 113 cubic inches
   (D) 124.3 cubic inches
   (E) 226 cubic inches

8. The volume of a rectangular solid is 156 cubic inches. The length of the solid is 6.5 inches and its width is 5 inches. The height of the solid is:

   (A) 4.8 inches (B) 5 inches (C) 5.2 inches (D) 10.2 inches (E) 2.8 inches

PRACTICE TEST 4

1. A right isosceles triangle has one angle of:

   (A) 60° (B) 30° (C) 45° (D) 75° (E) none of these

2. An obtuse triangle always has:

   (A) only one acute angle
   (B) three obtuse angles
   (C) two obtuse angles
   (D) two acute angles
   (E) equal sides

3. Two angles of a triangle are 20° and 40°. The third angle contains:

   (A) 120° (B) 60° (C) 30° (D) 40° (E) 100°

4. Two sides of a right triangle are always:

   (A) equal (B) perpendicular (C) oblique (D) vertical (E) horizontal

5. Triangles whose corresponding sides are equal in length are said to be:

   (A) congruent (B) equal (C) isosceles (D) almost alike (E) equilateral

6. A circle has a diameter of 42. Its circumference is (let $\pi = \frac{22}{7}$):

   (A) 264 (B) 1386 (C) 132 (D) 441 (E) none of these

7. The area of a circle whose diameter is 20 is (let $\pi = 3.14$):

   (A) 1256 (B) 314 (C) 400 (D) 62.8 (E) none of these

8. The volume of a circular cylinder whose diameter is 10 inches and whose height is 7 feet is (let $\pi = \frac{22}{7}$):

   (A) 2200 cu. in. (B) 550 cu. ft. (C) 6600 cu. ft. (D) 66,000 cu. in (E) none of these

9. A wire in the shape of a rectangle is twisted into the shape of a square. If the rectangle measures 10 inches by 6 inches, the area of the square is:

   (A) 32 sq. in. (B) 60 sq. in. (C) 225 sq. in. (D) 16 sq in. (E) 64 sq. in.

10. A cube 6 feet on an edge is filled with water. The water is poured into a container that is the shape of a rectangular solid. If the base measures 12 feet by 3 feet, to what height will the water rise?

    (A) 12 ft. (B) 1 ft. (C) 3 ft. (D) 6 ft. (E) 8 ft.

11. The diameter of the base of a circular cone is 3′6″ and the altitude is 5′. The volume of the cone, in cubic feet, is (let $\pi = \frac{22}{7}$):

    (A) 770 (B) 38.5 (C) 110 (D) $16\frac{1}{24}$ (E) none of these

12. A machine part is in the form of a semicircle with radius of $5\frac{1}{4}$″. The area of the machine part, in square inches, is (let $\pi = \frac{22}{7}$):

    (A) $16\frac{1}{8}$ (B) $32\frac{3}{4}$ (C) $43\frac{5}{16}$ (D) $86\frac{2}{7}$ (E) 33

PRACTICE TEST 5

1. The supplement of an acute angle is:

   (A) a right angle (B) an acute angle (C) an obtuse angle (D) a reflex angle (E) none of these

2. Two angles of a triangle are 68° and 75°. The value of the third angle is:

   (A) 57° (B) 37° (C) 47° (D) 143° (E) none of these

3. The length of a rectangle is 8 feet and its width is 7 feet. The length of a side of a square that has the same perimeter as the rectangle is:

   (A) $3\frac{3}{4}$ feet (B) 4 feet (C) 7 feet (D) $7\frac{1}{2}$ feet (E) 8 feet

4. The sum of an angle and its complement is:

   (A) an obtuse angle (B) a right angle (C) 135° (D) 180° (E) none of these

5. A vertex angle of an isosceles triangle is 52°. The value of each of the base angles is:

   (A) 52° (B) 62° (C) 60° (D) 64° (E) none of these

6. A circular cylindrical jar has a base diameter of 21 inches and a height of 14 inches. When it is half full of water, the volume of water contained in the jar is (let $\pi = \frac{22}{7}$):

   (A) 4,851 cu. in. (B) 462 cu. in. (C) 924 cu. in. (D) $2{,}425\frac{1}{2}$ cu. in. (E) none of these

7. If each side of a cube is doubled, the volume of the cube is multiplied by:

   (A) 8 (B) 4 (C) 2 (D) $1\frac{1}{2}$ (E) none of these

8. The perimeter of a rectangle is 28 inches. If its length is 8 inches then its width is:

   (A) 20 inches (B) 12 inches (C) 4 inches (D) 6 inches (E) none of these

9. The difference between the supplement of an angle and its complement is:

   (A) an acute angle (B) an obtuse angle (C) a right angle (D) a reflex angle (E) none of these

10. One of the equal angles of an isosceles triangle is 48°. The value of the vertex angle is

    (A) 84° (B) 48° (C) 104° (D) 4° (E) none of these

11. An oil tank in the form of a rectangular solid has a length of 15 feet and a width of 8 feet. If 300 cubic feet of oil are poured into the tank, what will be the height of the oil in the tank?

    (A) 2 feet (B) $2\frac{1}{2}$ feet (C) 3 feet (D) $13\frac{1}{23}$ feet (E) 20 feet

12. The acute angles of a right triangle are:
    (A) complementary
    (B) supplementary
    (C) 45° each
    (D) each greater than 45°
    (E) each less than 45°

Indirect Measurement

In measuring such distances as the height of an airplane or the distance across a lake it is not practical to use a ruler or a tape measure. Such measurements are made indirectly, as will be shown in this section.

In making measurements indirectly it is useful to know a property of right triangles called the *Pythagorean Theorem.*

PYTHAGOREAN THEOREM AND SQUARE ROOT

The Pythagorean Theorem states that in a right triangle the square of the length of the hypotenuse is equal to the sum of the squares of the lengths of the legs.

In the diagram, $c^2 = a^2 + b^2$.

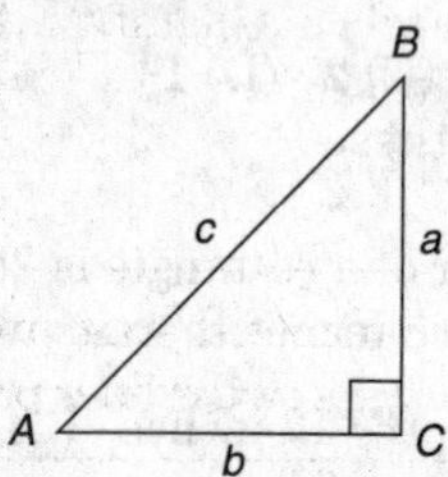

EXAMPLE: A boat travels 30 miles east and then 40 miles north. How many miles is the boat from its starting point?

SOLUTION:

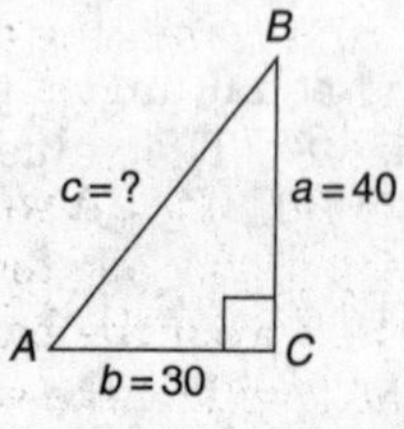

$$c^2 = a^2 + b^2$$

In this case, $a = 40$, $b = 30$, and the value of c must be determined. We have

$$c^2 = (40)^2 + (30)^2$$
$$c^2 = 1{,}600 + 900 = 2{,}500$$

The equation $c^2 = 2{,}500$ asks the question, What number multiplied by itself is equal to 2,500? The number that replaces c, to make the equation $c^2 = 2{,}500$ true, is 50.

The number 50 is called the *square root* of 2,500 since $50 \times 50 = 2{,}500$. We may write $\sqrt{2{,}500} = 50$.

Thus, the boat in this example is 50 miles from its starting point.

In this section, we will develop a systematic method for finding the square root of a number.

We may find the square root of a number by trial. For example, $\sqrt{9} = 3$, $\sqrt{36} = 6$, $\sqrt{81} = 9$. However, trial methods are not always satisfactory. Consider the following examples.

EXAMPLE: Find $\sqrt{289}$.

SOLUTION: We first estimate the answer. Suppose we estimate that the answer is 15. We next divide 15 into 289.

$$\begin{array}{r} 19 \\ 15\overline{)289} \\ \underline{15} \\ 139 \\ \underline{135} \end{array}$$

If 15 were the correct answer we would have obtained a quotient of 15. Since we did not, we get the average of the divisor (15) and the quotient (19).

$$\frac{15+19}{2} = \frac{34}{2} = 17$$

Now, we use 17 as a divisor.

$$\begin{array}{r} 17 \\ 17\overline{)289} \\ \underline{17} \\ 119 \\ \underline{119} \end{array}$$

Since the divisor and the quotient are identical, we have found the square root of the number.

Thus, $\sqrt{289} = 17$.

Consider $\sqrt{69}$. Since $8^2 = 64$ and $9^2 = 81$, $\sqrt{69}$ must have a value between 8 and 9. Actually, $\sqrt{69}$ cannot be written precisely in fractional or decimal form. A real number that cannot be written precisely in fractional or decimal form is called an *irrational number.* We may write the square root of an irrational number as a decimal to the nearest thousandth, etc.

EXAMPLE: Find $\sqrt{69}$ to the nearest tenth.

SOLUTION: Our first estimate is 8.2. Therefore we divide 69 by 8.2.

$$\begin{array}{r} 8.4 \\ 8.2\overline{)690.0} \\ \underline{656} \\ 340 \\ \underline{328} \end{array}$$

Next, we average the divisor (8.2) and the quotient (8.4).

$$\frac{8.2+8.4}{2} = \frac{16.6}{2} = 8.3$$

Next, we divide 69 by 8.3.

$$\begin{array}{r} 8.3 \\ 8.3\overline{)690.0} \\ \underline{664} \\ 260 \\ \underline{249} \end{array}$$

Since the divisor and the quotient are identical, we have $\sqrt{69} = 8.3$ to the nearest tenth.

PRACTICE TEST 6

1. Find the square roots of the following numbers.

   (A) $\sqrt{1,600}$ (B) $\sqrt{256}$ (C) $\sqrt{324}$ (D) $\sqrt{225}$
   (E) $\sqrt{729}$ (F) $\sqrt{1,024}$

2. Find the square root of each of the following correct to the nearest tenth.

   (A) $\sqrt{45}$ (B) $\sqrt{89}$ (C) $\sqrt{130}$ (D) $\sqrt{162}$
   (E) $\sqrt{116}$ (F) $\sqrt{243}$

EXAMPLE: A ladder is extended to a length of 17 feet and leaned against a wall. If the base of the ladder is 8 feet from the wall, how high up the wall does the ladder reach?

SOLUTION:

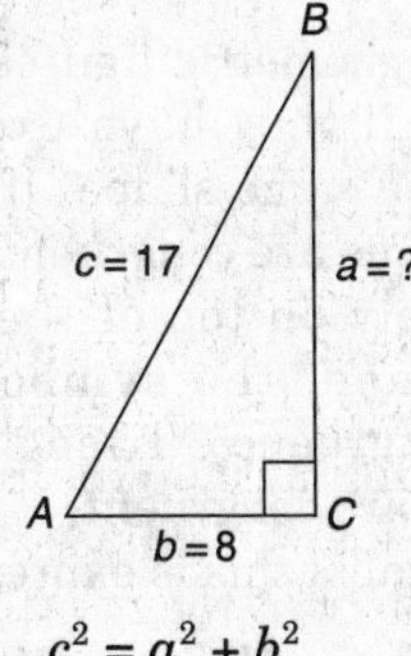

$$c^2 = a^2 + b^2$$

In this case, $b = 8$, $c = 17$, and the value of a must be found.

$$\begin{aligned} (17)^2 &= a^2 + (8)^2 \\ 289 &= a^2 + 64 \\ 289 - 64 &= a^2 + 64 - 64 \\ 225 &= a^2 \\ a &= \sqrt{225} \\ a &= 15 \end{aligned}$$

The ladder reaches a point on the wall 15 feet above the ground.

PRACTICE TEST 7

DIRECTIONS: Solve the following problems and write your answers on the lines provided.

1. A scout troop hikes 5 miles due west and then 12 miles due north. How many miles is the troop from its starting point? ______

2. A backyard is 20 feet long and 15 feet wide. What is the length of a diagonal path that cuts across the yard? ______

3. A pole is 24 feet high. A wire is stretched from the top of the pole to a point on the ground 7 feet from the base of the pole. What is the length of the wire? ______

4. A ladder 15 feet in length leans against the side of a building. If the base of the ladder is 9 feet from the building, how high up the building does the ladder reach?

____

5. A side of a packing box measures 24 inches in length and 18 inches in width. A piece of supporting tape is stretched diagonally across the side of the box. What is the length of this piece of tape?

____

Congruence and Similarity

Two plane geometric figures are said to be congruent if they have exactly the same size and the same shape. If two plane geometric figures are congruent, one can be fitted precisely on top of the other. As you have learned, the symbol ≅ is used to express congruence. Triangle *ABC* and triangle *RST* are congruent. If we use the congruence symbol this is expressed as

$$\triangle ABC \cong \triangle RST$$

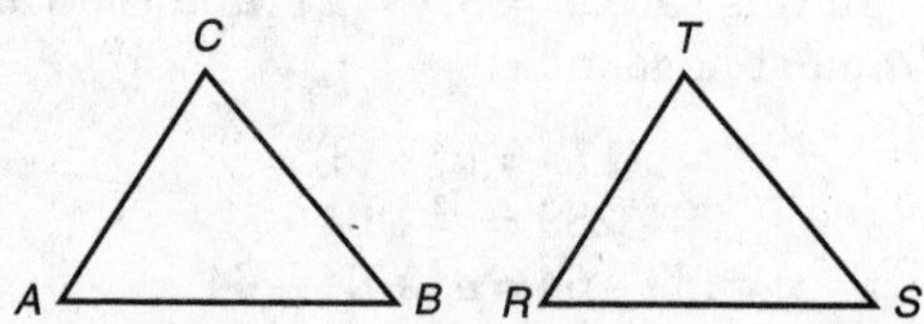

Since $\triangle ABC \cong \triangle RST$, the corresponding sides of these two triangles are equal in length; that is,

$$AB = RS,\ BC = ST,\ \text{and}\ AC = RT.$$

Congruent triangles can be used to measure distances indirectly.

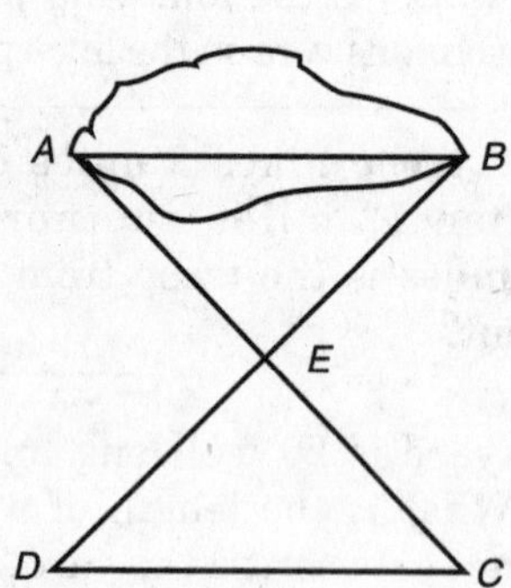

EXAMPLE: To find the distance *AB* across a pond we locate a convenient point, *E*. Then we draw a line, $\overleftrightarrow{AE}$ and extend this line to a point *C* so that $AE = EC$. Similarly, we draw a line, $\overleftrightarrow{BE}$, and extend this line to point *D* so that $BE = ED$. It can be proved that $\triangle ABE \cong \triangle CDE$. Since *DC* and *AB* are corresponding sides of congruent triangles, $DC = AB$. When we measure the length of *DC* on dry land, we are indirectly measuring the length of *AB*. If $DC = 150$ feet, $AB = 150$ feet.

Two geometric figures are said to be similar if they have the same shape. Since similar figures have the same shape, the measures of their corresponding angles are equal and the lengths of their corresponding sides are in proportion. The symbol for similarity is ~. In the diagram, $\triangle ABC$ and $\triangle PQR$ are similar, or $\triangle ABC \sim \triangle PQR$.

Since the lengths of corresponding sides of similar triangles are in proportion, we have

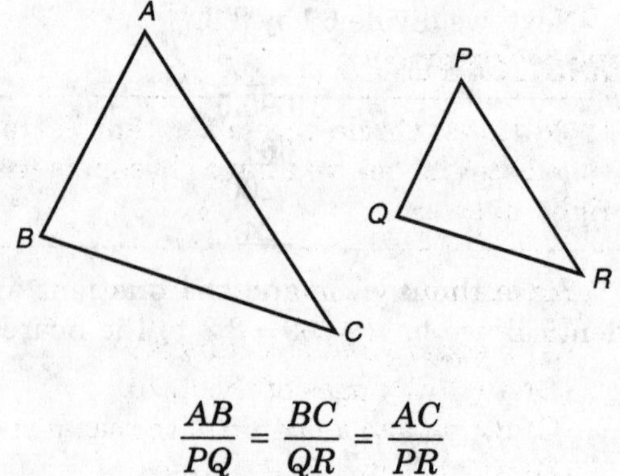

$$\frac{AB}{PQ} = \frac{BC}{QR} = \frac{AC}{PR}$$

We may use similar triangles to measure distances indirectly.

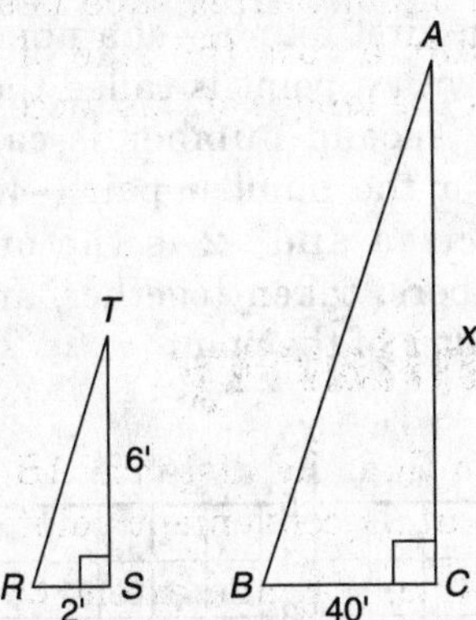

EXAMPLE: To find the height of the building (*AC*) we drive a stake (*TS*) into the ground. We then measure the height of the stake (*TS* = 6′), the length of its shadow (*RS* = 2′) and the length of the shadow of the building (*BC* = 40′). It can be proved that $\triangle ABC \sim \triangle TSR$. Therefore, the lengths of the corresponding sides of the two triangles are in proportion; that is,

$$\frac{AC}{TS} = \frac{BC}{RS}$$

or

$$\frac{x}{6} = \frac{40}{2}$$

$$2x = 6(40) = 240$$

$$x = 120$$

Thus, the height of the building is 120 feet.

PRACTICE TEST 8

DIRECTIONS: Circle the letter that corresponds to the one you have chosen as the right answer.

1. An example of congruent figures is

   (A) a square and a rectangle
   (B) any two pages of this book
   (C) a man and a picture of the same man
   (D) any two drinking glasses
   (E) any two music records

2. An example of similar figures is

   (A) any two triangles
   (B) any two rectangles
   (C) a wall and a picture on the wall
   (D) a TV picture on a 12-inch screen and the same TV picture on a 9-inch screen
   (E) a circle and a cylinder

3. If $\triangle EDC \cong \triangle PQR$, the value of x =

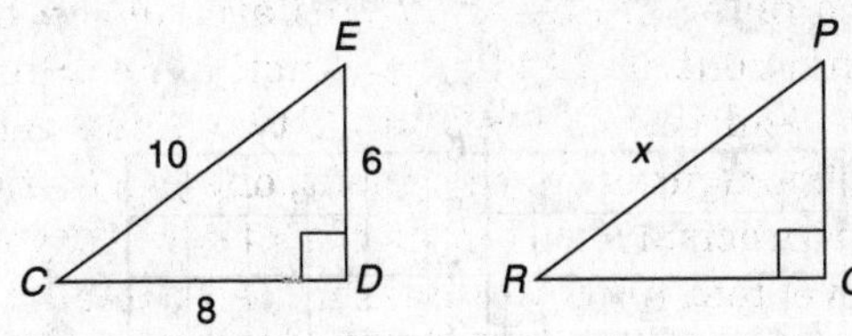

   (A) 6 (B) 8 (C) 10 (D) 7 (E) 9

4. If $\triangle STV \sim \triangle WZB$, then WB =

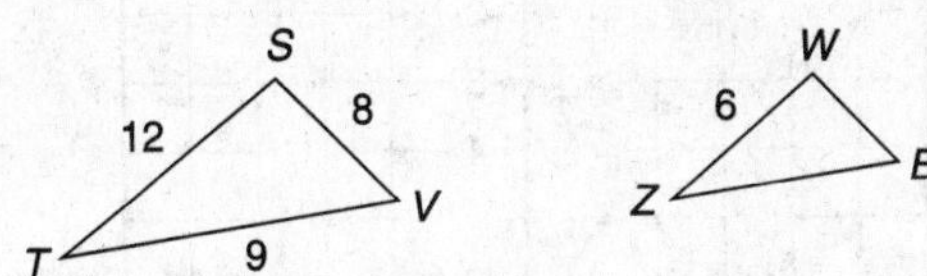

   (A) 6 (B) $4\frac{1}{2}$ (C) 5 (D) 7 (E) 4

5. At noon the shadow of a flagpole is 19 feet. At the same time the shadow of a wall 12 feet high is 4 feet. The height of the flagpole, in feet, is

   (A) 38 (B) $6\frac{1}{2}$ (C) 57 (D) 76 (E) 32

Coordinate Geometry

The diagram below represents a plan of the center of a town. To the right of North-South Street the streets are numbered 1, 2, 3, 4, etc. Similarly, the avenues above East-West Avenue are numbered 1, 2, 3, 4, etc. The avenues below East-West Avenue are numbered –1, –2, –3, –4, etc., and the streets to the left of North-South Street are numbered –1, –2, –3, –4, etc.

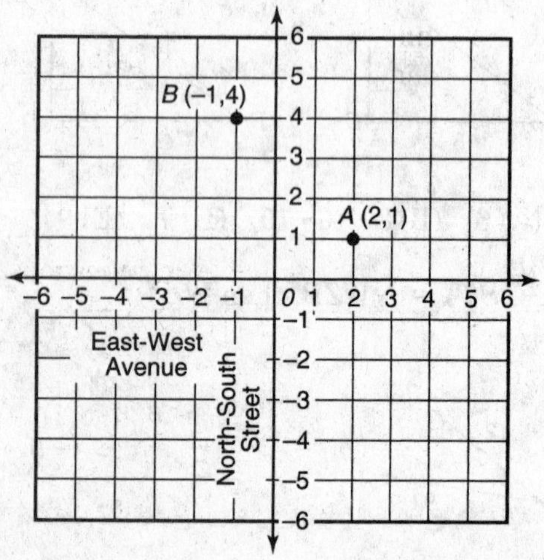

Point A, the point where 2nd Street and 1st Avenue meet, is named (2, 1) if we agree that, in the number pair (2, 1) the first number represents the street number and the second number represents the avenue number. Similarly, point B represents the point where –1 Street and 4th Avenue meet, or (–1, 4).

We have seen that we can associate points on the number line with real numbers. However, the number line is insufficient if we wish to locate points in the plane that are above or below the number line. To locate points in the plane that are not on the number line we draw two perpendicular number lines. These perpendicular number lines are called the x-axis and the y-axis, as shown in the diagram. The point where the x-axis and the y-axis meet is called the *origin,* and the number pair associated with the origin is (0, 0). Using this plan we associate the number pair (3, 2) with the point C and the number pair (–4, –2) with the point D. The first number of a number pair associated with a point is called the *abscissa* and the second number is called the *ordinate.* For the number pair (–4, –2), –4 is the abscissa and –2 is the ordinate. These numbers, taken together, are called the *coordinates* of the point.

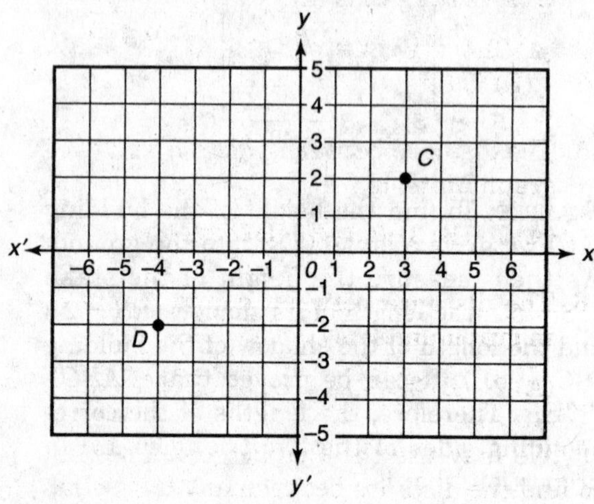

PRACTICE TEST 9

DIRECTIONS: Answer questions 1–6 based on the diagram below.

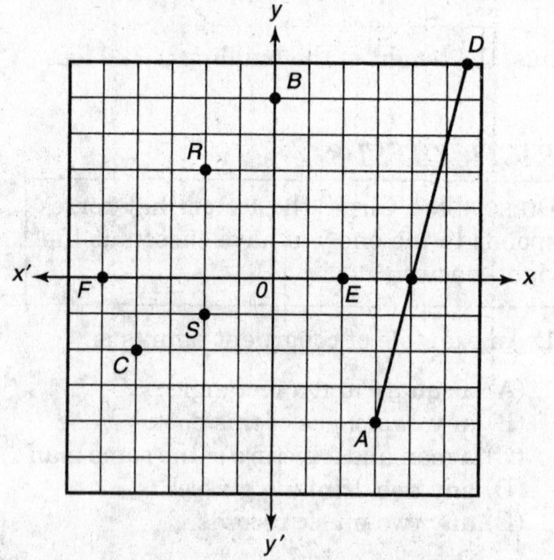

1. The coordinates of point A are

   (A) (–4, 3) (B) (4, 3) (C) (3, 4)
   (D) (3, –4) (E) (–4, –3)

2. The coordinates of point B are

(A) (5, 0) (B) (5, –5) (C) (0, 5)
(D) (5, 5) (E) (0, –5)

3. The coordinates of point C are

(A) (4, –2) (B) (–4, 2) (C) (4, 2)
(D) (–2, 4) (E) (–4, –2)

4. The coordinates of the point where $\overline{AD}$ crosses the x-axis are

(A) (0,4) (B) (4,0) (C) (3,–4) (D) (5,3)
(E) (0,0)

5. The distance between points E and F, in graph units, is

(A) 7 (B) 3 (C) –3 (D) 8 (E) –1

6. The distance between points R and S, in graph units, is

(A) 2 (B) 3 (C) 4 (D) 5 (E) 6

We may use the Pythagorean Theorem to find the distance between any two points whose coordinates are given.

EXAMPLE: Find the distance between point A (1, 2) and point B (7, 10).

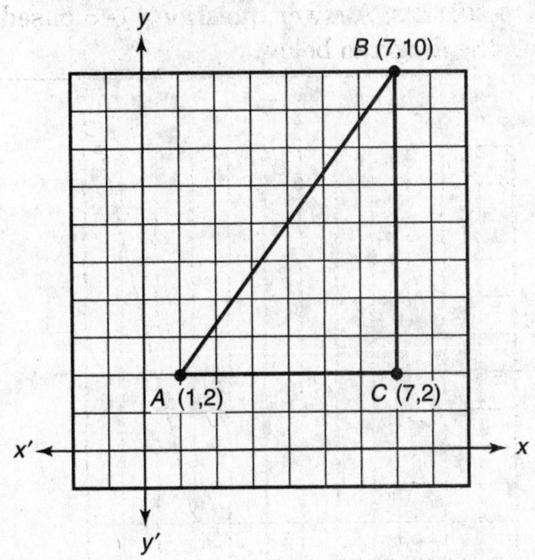

SOLUTION: If we draw $\overline{AC}$ parallel to the x-axis and $\overline{BC}$ parallel to the y-axis, we note that the coordinates of point C are (7,2). Since $\triangle ACB$ is a right triangle with hypotenuse AB, we have, by the Pythagorean Theorem,

$$(AB)^2 = (AC)^2 + (BC)^2$$

By counting we find that $AC = 6$ and $BC = 8$. Thus,

$$(AB)^2 = 6^2 + 8^2$$
$$(AB)^2 = 36 + 64 = 100$$
$$AB = \sqrt{100} = 10$$

Thus, the distance between point A and point B is 10.

PRACTICE TEST 10

DIRECTIONS: Answer the following questions.

1. The distance between A (1, 1) and B (4, 5) is

(A) 3 (B) 4 (C) 5 (D) 6 (E) 2

2. The distance between C (3, 2) and D (9, 10) is

(A) 5 (B) 10 (C) 8 (D) 6 (E) 9

3. The distance between E (0, 0) and F (–3, –4) is

(A) 5 (B) –5 (C) 10 (D) 7 (E) 6

4. The distance between R (–1, –2) and S (2, 2) is

(A) 3 (B) 4 (C) 10 (D) 6 (E) 5

5. The distance between T (–4, –3) and S (1, 9) is

(A) 12 (B) 13 (C) 10 (D) 8 (E) 6

Answers to All Practice Tests

TEST 1

1. **D** 2. **B** 3. **A** 4. **C**

TEST 2

1. **D** 2. **B** 3. **A** 4. **C** 5. **E**

TEST 3

1. **D** 2. **D** 3. **A** 4. **E**
5. **C** 6. **E** 7. **D** 8. **A**

TEST 4

1. **C** 2. **D** 3. **A** 4. **B**
5. **A** 6. **C** 7. **B** 8. **B**
9. **E** 10. **D** 11. **D** 12. **C**

TEST 5

1. **C** 2. **B** 3. **D** 4. **B**
5. **D** 6. **D** 7. **A** 8. **D**
9. **C** 10. **A** 11. **B** 12. **C**

TEST 6

1. (A) 40 (B) 16 (C) 18 (D) 15 (E) 27 (F) 32

2. (A) 6.7 (B) 9.4 (C) 11.4 (D) 12.7 (E) 10.8 (F) 15.6

TEST 7

1. 13 miles
2. 25 feet
3. 25 feet
4. 12 feet
5. 30 inches

TEST 8

1. **B** 2. **D** 3. **C** 4. **E** 5. **C**

TEST 9

1. **D** 2. **C** 3. **E** 4. **B** 5. **A** 6. **C**

TEST 10

1. **C** 2. **B** 3. **A** 4. **E** 5. **B**

Reasoning Skills

Seeing Number Relationships

Mathematical reasoning involves the ability to see relationships between quantities and to use these relationships in arriving at useful conclusions. The following examples will indicate how problems in mathematical reasoning may be analyzed and solved.

EXAMPLE: If $\frac{4}{9}$ of a number is 20, find the value of $\frac{3}{5}$ of the number.

SOLUTION: If $\frac{4}{9}$ of the number is 20, then $\frac{1}{9}$ of the number is equal to 20 divided by 4, or 5.

If $\frac{1}{9}$ of the number is 5, then $\frac{9}{9}$ or the whole number is equal to 5×9, or 45.

If the number is 45, then $\frac{3}{5}$ of the number is equal to $\frac{3}{5} \times 45 = 27$.

EXAMPLE: How many thirds are there in $\frac{5}{12}$?

SOLUTION: To find the number of thirds in $\frac{5}{12}$ we must divide $\frac{5}{12}$ by $\frac{1}{3}$.

$$\frac{5}{12} \div \frac{1}{3} = \frac{5}{12} \times \frac{3}{1} = \frac{5}{4}$$

There are $\frac{5}{4}$ or $1\frac{1}{4}$ thirds in $\frac{5}{12}$.

EXAMPLE: 18 is 24% of what number?

SOLUTION: 24%, or 24 of the number = 18 Then 0.01 of the number = $\frac{18}{24}$ and the number is equal to

$$\frac{18}{24} \times 100 = \frac{1800}{24}$$

The number is 75.

EXAMPLE: If 3 times a number is $4\frac{1}{8}$ what is the number?

SOLUTION: If 3 times a number is equal to $4\frac{1}{8}$ then the number may be found by dividing $4\frac{1}{8}$ by 3.

$$4\frac{1}{8} = \frac{33}{8}, \frac{33}{8} \div 3 = \frac{\overset{11}{\cancel{33}}}{9} \times \frac{1}{\underset{1}{\cancel{3}}} = \frac{11}{8}$$

The number is $\frac{11}{8}$ or $1\frac{3}{8}$.

PRACTICE TEST 1

DIRECTIONS: Answer the following questions.

1. A number that is closer to 73 than it is 49 is

   (A) 55 (B) 61 (C) 63 (D) 59 (E) 50

2. When 28 is subtracted from the sum of 17 and 36 the result is

   (A) 11 (B) 8 (C) 9 (D) 53 (E) none of these

3. The product of 8 and 49 is

   (A) less than 100 (B) greater than 400 (C) an odd number (D) less than 400 (E) greater than 500

4. Of the fractions $\frac{3}{7}$, $\frac{1}{2}$, $\frac{5}{8}$, $\frac{7}{12}$, and $\frac{4}{9}$ the largest one is

   (A) $\frac{7}{12}$ (B) $\frac{5}{8}$ (C) $\frac{4}{9}$ (D) $\frac{1}{2}$ (E) $\frac{3}{7}$

5. If $\frac{3}{4}$ of a number is 12, the number is

   (A) 9 (B) 8 (C) 16 (D) 15 (E) 14

6. The number in which 3 represents 300 is

 (A) 5,413 (B) 3,514 (C) 5,134 (D) 5,314 (E) 3,752

7. When 8,406 is divided by 7 the remainder is

 (A) 0 (B) 1 (C) 2 (D) 1,200 (E) none of these

8. If 3 times a number is $5\frac{1}{4}$ the number is

 (A) $1\frac{3}{4}$ (B) $2\frac{1}{4}$ (C) $8\frac{1}{4}$ (D) $16\frac{3}{4}$ (E) $\frac{4}{7}$

9. 5% means

 (A) 5 (B) $\frac{1}{5}$ (C) 500 (D) 0.05 (E) 0.5

10. When the sum of $\frac{1}{4}$ and $\frac{1}{6}$ is subtracted from 1 the result is

 (A) $\frac{5}{12}$ (B) $\frac{7}{12}$ (C) $\frac{4}{5}$ (D) $\frac{2}{10}$ (E) $\frac{1}{2}$

11. The number 59 means

 (A) 5 + 9 (B) 5 × 9 (C) 9 × 10 (D) 5 × 10 + 9 (E) none of these

12. The number that is equal to $\frac{1}{2}$ of $\frac{3}{5}$ is

 (A) $\frac{3}{7}$ (B) $\frac{2}{5}$ (C) $\frac{4}{7}$ (D) $\frac{3}{10}$ (E) $\frac{6}{5}$

13. When 5.17 is multiplied by 65 the result is closest to

 (A) 325 (B) 335 (C) 336 (D) 3,360 (E) 3,365

14. 16 is 25% of

 (A) 4 (B) 64 (C) 20 (D) 640 (E) none of these

15. The ratio of one hour to one minute is

 (A) 1:60 (B) 1:1 (C) 30:1 (D) 60:1 (E) 1:30

16. The fraction that is equal to $\frac{5}{6}$ is

 (A) $\frac{5}{11}$ (B) $\frac{10}{12}$ (C) $\frac{6}{5}$ (D) $\frac{2}{12}$ (E) none of these

17. The number of days from May 5 to June 15 is

 (A) 41 (B) 20 (C) 21 (D) 30 (E) 45

18. To discover how much bigger one number is than another we

 (A) add (B) divide (C) subtract (D) multiply (E) none of these

19. In the number 562.38 the digit 2 is in

 (A) the tens place (B) the tenths place (C) the hundreds place (D) the ones place (E) the hundredths place

20. When the sum of $\frac{1}{3}$, $\frac{1}{4}$, and $\frac{1}{6}$ is subtracted from 1 the result is

 (A) $\frac{10}{13}$ (B) $\frac{1}{2}$ (C) $\frac{3}{13}$ (D) $\frac{1}{4}$ (E) none of these

PRACTICE TEST 2

DIRECTIONS: Answer the following questions.

1. $\frac{5}{8}$ of 18 exceeds 11 by

 (A) 7 (B) 5 (C) 26 (D) .25 (E) 2

2. The percent that $\frac{1}{5}$ is of $\frac{1}{2}$ is

 (A) 250% (B) 10% (C) 40% (D) 20% (E) 30%

3. 4 hundredths written as a decimal is

 (A) 400 (B) 0.04 (C) 14 (D) 40.0 (E) none of these

4. The exact number of hundreds in 3,250 is

 (A) 300 (B) 325 (C) 3,250 (D) 3.25 (E) none of these

5. If $\frac{1}{3}$ of a number is 24, then twice the number is

 (A) 8 (B) 144 (C) 16 (D) 48 (E) 148

6. 0.7 written as a percent is

 (A) 7 (B) 7% (C) 0.07% (D) 70% (E) 700%

7. The number of tens in 1 thousand is

 (A) 3 (B) 100 (C) 10 (D) 1,000 (E) 990

8. In a short-cut method of multiplying 84 by 25, we annex 2 zeros and

   (A) divide by 25 (B) multiply by 4 (C) divide by 4 (D) add 25 (E) none of these

9. If 5 times a number is 135 then $\frac{1}{3}$ of the number is

   (A) 45 (B) 9 (C) 27 (D) 225 (E) 6

10. In the number 5,367, if the number in the thousands place is changed to 9, the number becomes

    (A) 5,967 (B) 5,369 (C) 5,397 (D) 9,367 (E) 5,900

11. 8 is 40% of

    (A) $3\frac{1}{5}$ (B) 12 (C) 16 (D) 18 (E) none of these

12. The sum of $\frac{1}{3}$ and $\frac{5}{12}$ is greater than $\frac{1}{6}$ by

    (A) $\frac{11}{12}$ (B) $\frac{1}{12}$ (C) $\frac{7}{12}$ (D) $\frac{7}{30}$ (E) none of these

13. In numerals, the number one thousand three is written as

    (A) 1,030 (B) 1,003 (C) 1,300 (D) 3,100 (E) 3,001

14. When the quotient of 16 ÷ 2 is added to 7 the result is

    (A) 25 (B) 39 (C) 30 (D) 15 (E) $7\frac{1}{8}$

15. The number that has 8 in the tenths place is

    (A) 485.2 (B) 348.03 (C) 162.85 (D) 91.08 (E) none of these

16. The next number in the series 4, 9, 14, 19, 24 is

    (A) 25 (B) 29 (C) 28 (D) 27 (E) 30

17. When a number is increased by 25% of itself the result is 30. The number is

    (A) 36 (B) 28 (C) 25 (D) 32 (E) none of these

18. To find what part one whole number is of another we

    (A) multiply (B) subtract (C) divide (D) add (E) none of these

19. The number that is equivalent to $\frac{32}{40}$ is

    (A) $\frac{9}{10}$ (B) $\frac{3}{4}$ (C) $\frac{4}{5}$ (D) $\frac{3}{5}$ (E) 0.7

20. To change $\frac{4}{7}$ to a decimal we

    (A) add 4 and 7 (B) divide 7 by 4 (C) multiply 4 by 7 (D) divide 4 by 7 (E) subtract 4 from 7

PRACTICE TEST 3

DIRECTIONS: Answer the following questions.

1. The next number in the series 1, 2, 4, 7, 11, 16 is

   (A) 18 (B) 19 (C) 22 (D) 25 (E) 15

2. $83\frac{1}{3}$% of a certain number is 30. The number is

   (A) 25 (B) $18\frac{3}{4}$ (C) 48 (D) 36 (E) 34

3. Pencils cost 2 for $0.15. The number of pencils that can be bought for $1.20 is

   (A) 30 (B) 16 (C) 1 dozen (D) 8 (E) 15

4. When 45 is divided by 1.23 the result will be closest to

   (A) 3.7 (B) 37 (C) 0.38 (D) 380 (E) 3.8

5. The sum of 8, 7, and 9 divided by their product is equal to

   (A) 21 (B) 24 (C) 504 (D) $\frac{5}{3}$ (E) none of these

6. The average of the numbers 12, 15, and 18 is equal to

   (A) their sum
   (B) their common difference
   (C) the middle number
   (D) their quotient
   (E) their sum divided by their common difference

7. The percent that $\frac{1}{12}$ is of $\frac{1}{3}$ is

   (A) 25% (B) 75% (C) 36% (D) 400% (E) 20%

8. 8% of a number is equal to

(A) $\frac{1}{8}$ of the number
(B) 0.8 of the number
(C) 4% of twice the number
(D) one-half of twice the number
(E) none of these

9. In order to find out how many inches there are in 5 feet 3 inches we

(A) first multiply then divide
(B) first multiply then add
(C) first divide than add
(D) first divide then subtract
(E) none of these

10. A boy's marks on three tests were 75%, 78%, and 82%. In order to raise his average to 80% his mark on a fourth test must be

(A) 81 (B) 76 (C) 80 (D) 82
(E) none of these

11. If 3 times a number is 48 then $\frac{1}{4}$ of the same number is

(A) 16 (B) 4 (C) 12 (D) 30 (E) 5

12. The smallest number into which the numbers 2, 3, 5, and 7 can be divided without leaving a remainder is

(A) 6 (B) 420 (C) 280 (D) 210
(E) 180

13. When half of a number is added to that number the result is 24. The number is

(A) 12 (B) 15 (C) 16 (D) 24
(E) 20

14. Of the following numbers, the one that has 0 in the tens place is

(A) 4,307 (B) 3,270 (C) 650 (D) 4,070
(E) 780

15. The ratio of 1 pound to 6 ounces is

(A) 1:6 (B) 6:1 (C) 3:8 (D) 8:3
(E) 5:3

16. 2% is equal to

(A) 200 (B) 2 (C) 0.2 (D) 2.0
(E) none of these

17. The smallest of the fractions $\frac{2}{7}$, $\frac{1}{3}$, $\frac{3}{10}$, $\frac{4}{9}$, and $\frac{2}{5}$ is

(A) $\frac{2}{5}$ (B) $\frac{3}{10}$ (C) $\frac{1}{3}$ (D) $\frac{4}{9}$ (E) $\frac{2}{7}$

18. If 8 books of the same thickness standing on a shelf occupy 1 foot then the thickness of each book is

(A) $\frac{2}{3}''$ (B) 1″ (C) $1\frac{1}{2}''$ (D) $1\frac{1}{3}''$
(E) none of these

19. The number of eighths in $87\frac{1}{2}$% is

(A) 1 (B) 3 (C) 8 (D) 7 (E) 6

20. It takes a man 15 days to do a job. The part of the job that he can do in 5 days is

(A) $\frac{1}{5}$ (B) $\frac{1}{3}$ (C) $\frac{1}{15}$ (D) 3.5 (E) $\frac{1}{4}$

PRACTICE TEST 4

DIRECTIONS: Answer the following questions.

1. The number of halves in $\frac{1}{5}$ is

(A) $\frac{1}{2}$ (B) $\frac{1}{10}$ (C) $\frac{1}{5}$ (D) $\frac{2}{5}$ (E) $\frac{3}{10}$

2. When a number is divided by 7 the quotient is 4 and the remainder is 3. The number is

(A) 14 (B) 31 (C) 28 (D) 25 (E) 19

3. It takes Mr. Blane 2 hours and 40 minutes to complete half a job. The time he will take to complete the whole job is

(A) 4 hours and 20 minutes
(B) 3 hours and 30 minutes
(C) 5 hours and 10 minutes
(D) 5 hours and 20 minutes
(E) none of these

4. When the fractions $\frac{2}{3}$, $\frac{3}{4}$, $\frac{5}{8}$, and $\frac{5}{7}$ are arranged in order of size, with the largest one first, the order is

(A) $\frac{5}{8}, \frac{5}{7}, \frac{3}{4}, \frac{2}{3}$ (B) $\frac{5}{7}, \frac{3}{4}, \frac{2}{3}, \frac{5}{8}$

(C) $\frac{3}{4}, \frac{5}{7}, \frac{2}{3}, \frac{5}{8}$ (D) $\frac{2}{3}, \frac{5}{7}, \frac{3}{4}, \frac{5}{8}$

(E) $\frac{3}{4}, \frac{5}{8}, \frac{5}{7}, \frac{2}{3}$

5. When 1 is divided by a fraction whose value is less than 1 the result is

   (A) 1 (B) less than 1 (C) less than $\frac{1}{2}$ (D) less than $\frac{2}{3}$ (E) greater than 1

6. The next number in the series 2, 5, 11, 23, 47 is

   (A) 95 (B) 71 (C) 59 (D) 53 (E) 101

7. 6% of 100 is what percent of 150?

   (A) 5% (B) 6% (C) 4% (D) 8% (E) 3%

8. When a certain fraction is added to $\frac{1}{4}$ the result is $\frac{5}{6}$. The fraction that is added is

   (A) $\frac{1}{6}$ (B) $\frac{1}{2}$ (C) $\frac{2}{3}$ (D) $\frac{7}{12}$ (E) $\frac{5}{12}$

9. The average of two fractions is $\frac{3}{10}$. One of the fractions is $\frac{1}{2}$. The other fraction is

   (A) $\frac{1}{2}$ (B) $\frac{1}{10}$ (C) $\frac{7}{10}$ (D) $\frac{4}{5}$ (E) $\frac{1}{20}$

10. The number in which the tens digit is greater than the ones digit is

    (A) 155 (B) 237 (C) 859 (D) 275 (E) 336

11. On a test 90% of the members of a class had passing grades. Of these, 10% had minimum passing grades. The percent of the class that had minimum passing grades was

    (A) 10% (B) 1% (C) 90% (D) 80% (E) none of these

12. The product of the numbers 15 and 3.4 exceeds their sum by

    (A) 27.4 (B) 32.6 (C) 69.4 (D) 65 (E) 30.6

13. The precise number of tens in the number 486 is

    (A) 400 (B) 480 (C) 86 (D) 48.6 (E) 4,860

14. Of the boys reporting for a high school baseball team, $\frac{1}{3}$ were trying out for the outfield and $\frac{4}{7}$ were trying out for the infield. Those not trying out for either infield or outfield were

    (A) more than half of those trying out
    (B) exactly half of those trying out
    (C) less than 10% of those trying out
    (D) more than $\frac{1}{3}$ of those trying out
    (E) none of these

15. 0.003 written as a percent is

    (A) 3% (B) 30% (C) 0.003% (D) 0.03% (E) none of these

16. The number which when divided by 7 leaves the largest remainder is

    (A) 615 (B) 305 (C) 714 (D) 1,001 (E) 701

17. If $\frac{1}{3}$ of a number is added to $\frac{5}{6}$ of a number the result is

    (A) greater than 1
    (B) less than 1
    (C) greater than the number
    (D) less than the number
    (E) none of these

18. We may multiply a number by $12\frac{1}{2}$ by annexing two zeros to the number and dividing the result by

    (A) 6 (B) 10 (C) 12 (D) 8 (E) 5

19. A football team gains 18 yards on one play, loses 3 yards on the next play, and loses 6 yards on a third play. The result is that the team has a

    (A) net loss of 11 yards
    (B) net gain of 9 yards
    (C) net gain of 29 yards
    (D) net gain of 23 yards
    (E) none of these

20. One-half the difference between 97 and 46 is

    (A) less than 25 (B) greater than 72 (C) 51 (D) greater than 25 (E) 100

PRACTICE TEST 5

DIRECTIONS: Answer the following questions.

1. 205 students are to be assigned to 7 classes so that, as far as possible the classes are of the same size. The result will be that

   (A) two of the classes will be larger than the others
   (B) all classes will be exactly the same size
   (C) one class will be smaller than all the others
   (D) no class will be larger than 28
   (E) none of these

2. A man invested $\frac{3}{5}$ of his money in bonds and $\frac{3}{10}$ of his money in stocks. He kept the balance of his money in a savings account. The part of his money in the savings account was

   (A) $\frac{9}{10}$ (B) $\frac{4}{5}$ (C) $\frac{3}{5}$ (D) $\frac{1}{10}$ (E) $\frac{1}{15}$

3. The next number in the series 2, 6, 18, 54 is

   (A) 57 (B) 108 (C) 162 (D) 72
   (E) 168

4. 3.12 written as a percent is

   (A) 312% (B) 3.12% (C) 31.2%
   (D) 0.0312% (E) none of these

5. In an election $\frac{5}{8}$ of the votes went to candidate A. Candidate B received $\frac{2}{3}$ of the remaining votes. The part of the votes received by candidate B was

   (A) $\frac{5}{12}$ (B) $\frac{1}{24}$ (C) $\frac{1}{12}$ (D) $\frac{4}{11}$
   (E) none of these

6. When a number is added to $\frac{1}{3}$ of itself the result is 60. The number is

   (A) 80 (B) 45 (C) 40 (D) $60\frac{1}{3}$
   (E) 50

7. Of its broadcast time, a radio station spends $\frac{1}{2}$ on music and $\frac{1}{5}$ on news and lectures. The percent of its time spent on other features is

   (A) 20% (B) 70% (C) 40% (D) 30%
   (E) 36%

8. The ratio between the sum of the numbers 18 and 12 and their difference is

   (A) 3:2 (B) $\frac{2}{3}$ (C) 6:1 (D) 1:6
   (E) none of these

9. The number in which the hundreds digit exceeds the ones digit by 4 is

   (A) 123 (B) 501 (C) 236 (D) 515
   (E) 620

10. A school has 7 classes with an average size of 31 students and 4 classes with an average size of 34 students. The average size of all classes is

    (A) less than 31 (B) greater than 33
    (C) greater than 34
    (D) greater than 32 (E) none of these

11. $66\frac{2}{3}$% of a number exceeds $16\frac{2}{3}$% of the same number by

    (A) $\frac{1}{3}$ of the number
    (B) $\frac{2}{3}$ of the number
    (C) $\frac{1}{2}$ of the number
    (D) $\frac{1}{4}$ of the number
    (E) $\frac{2}{5}$ of the number

12. Of the following statements the one that is correct is:

    (A) When an even number is divided by an odd number there is no remainder.
    (B) When an odd number is divided by an even number there is no remainder.
    (C) When an even number is multiplied by 3 the result is an odd number.
    (D) When an odd number is multiplied by 2 the result is an even number.
    (E) When an even number is subtracted from an even number the result is an odd number.

13. A lecture hall is $\frac{1}{2}$ full. After 20 people in the audience leave, the lecture hall is $\frac{1}{3}$ full. The seating capacity of the hall is

(A) 60 (B) 120 (C) 90 (D) 80 (E) 96

14. 8% of a number is 72. The number is

(A) 5.76 (B) 57.6 (C) 90 (D) 900 (E) 960

15. The number of halves in $\frac{4}{9}$ is

(A) $\frac{2}{9}$ (B) $\frac{1}{9}$ (C) $\frac{9}{8}$ (D) 9 (E) none of these

16. A mixture contains 12 gallons of water and 3 gallons of acid. If 6 more gallons of water is added, the part of the mixture that is acid is

(A) $\frac{1}{6}$ (B) $\frac{1}{7}$ (C) $\frac{2}{3}$ (D) $\frac{4}{7}$ (E) $\frac{1}{8}$

17. $\frac{1}{5}$ of a number is 2 less than 12. The number is

(A) 10 (B) 5 (C) 40 (D) 50 (E) 45

18. The precise number of tens in 305 is

(A) 0 (B) 3 (C) 30.5 (D) 305 (E) none of these

19. Among the numbers 2.11, $2\frac{1}{10}$, 2.057, $1\frac{9}{100}$, and 1.92 the number closest to 2 is

(A) 2.11 (B) $2\frac{1}{10}$ (C) 2.057 (D) $1\frac{9}{100}$ (E) 1.92

20. The sum of two numbers is 51. One number exceeds twice the other number by 9. The numbers are

(A) 42 and 9 (B) 24 and 33 (C) 33 and 18 (D) 37 and 14 (E) none of these

PRACTICE TEST 6

DIRECTIONS: Answer the following questions.

1. The next number in the series 9, 3, 1, $\frac{1}{3}$ is

(A) $\frac{1}{4}$ (B) $\frac{1}{6}$ (C) $\frac{1}{12}$ (D) $\frac{1}{5}$ (E) none of these

2. $\frac{2}{3}$ of one half of 48 is

(A) 32 (B) 16 (C) 8 (D) 24 (E) 30

3. The number that when multiplied by 2.8 yields 34.16 is

(A) 36.96 (B) 95.648 (C) 122 (D) 12.2 (E) 12.4

4. If the numerator of a fraction is doubled and its denominator is halved

(A) the value of the fraction is multiplied by 4
(B) the value of the fraction remains unchanged
(C) the value of the fraction is divided by 2
(D) the value of the fraction is decreased
(E) none of these

5. A building contractor uses 12 men to complete a job in 15 days. Had the contractor used 10 men the job would have been completed in

(A) 22 days (B) 10 days (C) 18 days (D) 12 days (E) 20 days

6. A cafeteria served milk in pint bottle portions. One day the cafeteria served 18 gallons and 2 quarts of milk. The number of portions served was

(A) 20 portions (B) 148 portions (C) 74 portions (D) 76 portions (E) none of these

7. 6.8% written as a decimal is

(A) 0.68 (B) 0.0068 (C) 0.680 (D) 0.068 (E) 0.6080

8. If $\frac{1}{3}$ of a number is 6 more than $\frac{1}{4}$ of the number, the number is

(A) $6\frac{1}{4}$ (B) 72 (C) 24 (D) 48 (E) $6\frac{7}{12}$

9. The average of 5 consecutive whole numbers is

(A) the sum of the first and last number
(B) twice the first number
(C) the difference between the last and the first number
(D) the second number
(E) the third number

10. A basketball team has won 18 games and lost 12 games. The number of games it must win in succession to have a winning percentage of 75% is

(A) 18 (B) 12 (C) 6 (D) 9 (E) 20

11. The fraction that when divided by $\frac{1}{2}$ yields $\frac{3}{7}$ is

(A) $\frac{1}{3}$ (B) $\frac{2}{21}$ (C) $\frac{7}{6}$ (D) $\frac{3}{14}$ (E) $\frac{1}{5}$

12. 3.05 written as a percent is

(A) 3.5% (B) 3.05% (C) 305% (D) 0.0305% (E) 3.005%

13. When a number is added to twice itself the result is 64 more than the number. The number is

(A) 96 (B) 64 (C) 48 (D) 32 (E) 36

14. A baseball pitcher has won 12 games and lost 5 games. The percent of the games he has won is

(A) $57\frac{1}{2}$% (B) $58\frac{1}{3}$% (C) 60% (D) 75% (E) none of these

15. A family spends $\frac{1}{3}$ of its income for food and $\frac{1}{5}$ of its income for rent. The part of its income left for other expenses is

(A) $\frac{3}{4}$ (B) $\frac{8}{15}$ (C) $\frac{7}{15}$ (D) $\frac{1}{4}$ (E) $\frac{5}{12}$

16. When a number is added to $\frac{1}{3}$ of itself the result is 72. The number is

(A) 60 (B) 54 (C) 65 (D) 90 (E) 64

17. The number in which the sum of the digits exceeds the tens digit by 15 is

(A) 932 (B) 846 (C) 689 (D) 767 (E) 585

Using Venn Diagrams to Solve Problems

It is often convenient to arrange given information in tables, charts, or diagrams. In mathematics we often arrange given information in circles, called Venn diagrams, in order to solve certain types of problems.

Let A = the set of members of the History Club. As you learned in Chapter 11, we may enclose the names of the members of the club in braces, as follows:

A = {Bill, Fred, Amy, Lois, Nicole, Juan, Rosita, Beth, Henry, Angelo}

and let B = the set of members of the Science Club. We may also enclose the names of the members of the club in braces, as follows.

B = {Mary, Paula, John, Lois, Yong, Andrew, Edna, Grace, Angelo, Ben, Charles, Juan}

Also, we may represent these sets in circles:

History	Science
Bill	Mary
Fred	Paula
Amy	John
Lois	Lois
Nicole	Yong
Juan	Andrew
Rosita	Edna
Beth	Grace
Henry	Angelo
Angelo	Ben
	Charles
	Juan

If we examine sets A and B we notice that Lois, Angelo, and Juan are members of both sets A and B. Therefore, it is logical to arrange our circles as follows:

History **Science**

Bill
Fred
Amy
Nicole
Rosita
Beth
Henry

Lois
Angelo
Juan

Mary
Paula
John
Yong
Andrew
Edna
Grace
Ben
Charles

The intersection of two sets *A* and *B* consists of the members common to both A and *B*. As you know, the symbol for intersection is $\cap$. Thus, in this case, $A \cap B$ = {Lois, Angelo, Juan}.

We may have three intersecting sets. Let *C* = the set of members of the debating team.

C = {Ed, Ella, Angelo, Tony, Lois}

We may now represent these three sets by circles, as follows:

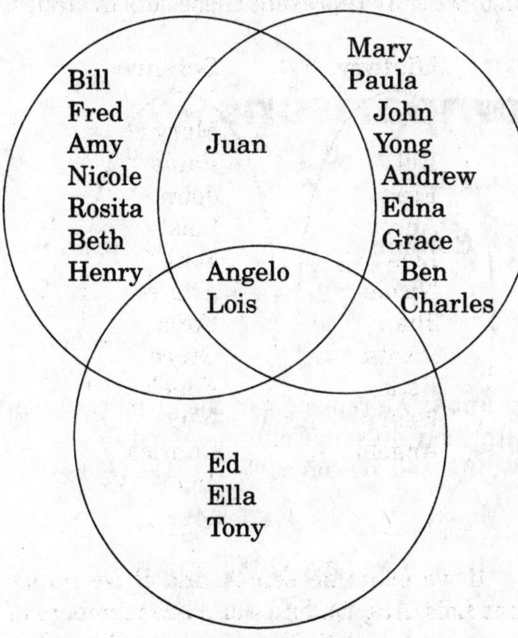

Debating Team

Venn diagrams may be used to solve problems.

Example: At Madison High School, enrollments in foreign language were as follows:

French: 148 French and Spanish: 18
Spanish: 96 French and German: 12
German: 67 Spanish and German: 8
French, Spanish, and German: 5

How many individual students were studying foreign languages?

Solution: In this problem, we have the intersection of three sets, those studying French, those studying Spanish, and those studying German.

First, we place 5 in the space that represents the intersection of the three sets. The intersection of the French and Spanish sets has 18 members. Therefore, we place 13 (18 – 5) in the space above the 5. The intersection of the French and German sets has 12 members. Therefore, we place 7 in the space to the left of 5. The intersection of the Spanish and German sets has 8 members. Therefore, we place 3 in the space to the right of 5.

There are 148 students in French classes. Since we have already placed 5 + 13 + 7 = 25 in the French circle, we place 148 – 25 = 123 in the rest of the circle.

There are 96 students in Spanish classes. Since we have already placed 5 + 13 + 3 in the Spanish circle, we place 96 – 21 = 75 in the rest of the circle.

There are 67 students in German classes. Since we have already placed 5 + 7 + 3 = 15 in the German circle, we place 67 – 15 = 52 in the rest of the circle.

French **Spanish**

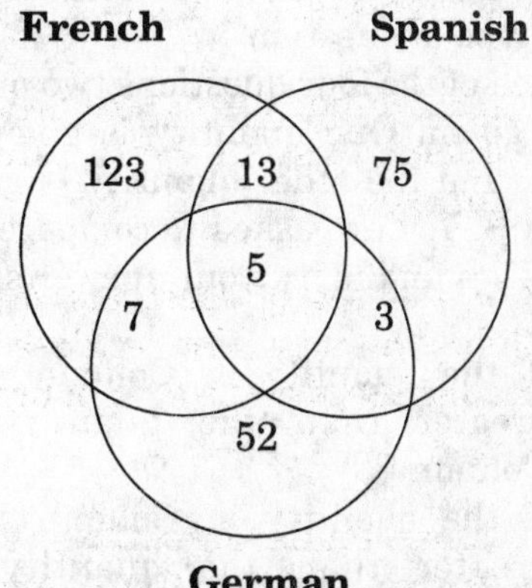

German

To obtain the total individual enrollment, we add *all* the numbers on the Venn diagram:

123 + 13 + 5 + 7 + 3 + 75 + 52 = 278

There are 278 individual students enrolled in foreign language classes.

PRACTICE TEST 7

DIRECTIONS: Use Venn diagrams to answer the following questions.

1. At the Fashion Shop there is a sale on sport coats. The colors of the sale items are as follows.

Gray:	48	Gray and blue:	20
Blue:	56	Gray and green:	12
Green:	32	Blue and green:	8

Gray, blue, and green: 5

How many coats are on sale?

2. At Springfield High School three popular sports are baseball, track, and football. The numbers of students on the squads are shown below:

Baseball:	32	Baseball and track:	10
Track:	26	Baseball and football:	18
Football:	45	Track and football:	11

Baseball, track, and football: 7

How many individual students are engaged in these sports?

3. The State Senate has three major committees, legal, budget, and education. The numbers of members of the Senate active on these committees are given below.

Legal:	38	Legal and Budget:	24
Budget:	46	Legal and Education:	16
Education:	22	Budget and Education:	12

Legal, Budget, and Education: 8

How many individual senators work on the committees?

4. At a certain college the enrollments in three major sciences are as follows:

Biology:	102	Biology and physics:	28
Physics:	48	Biology and chemistry:	35
Chemistry:	65	Physics and chemistry:	25

Biology, physics, and chemistry: 15

How many individual students are enrolled in these sciences?

Quantitative Comparisons

Quantitative comparison questions require you to compare two mathematical quantities. The four examples given below illustrate this type of question.

For each of the four questions two quantities are given. One quantity is given in Column A, and the other quantity is given in Column B. You are asked to compare the two quantities and mark your answer sheet as follows:

(A) if the quantity in Column A is greater than the quantity in Column B,

(B) if the quantity in Column B is greater than the quantity in Column A,

(C) if the quantities in Column A and Column B are equal,

(D) if the relationship cannot be determined from the information given.

EXAMPLE:

Column A		Column B
	$2x^2 - x + 1$	
$x = -1$		$x = 3$

SOLUTION: We replace x in the given equation with the values in Columns A and B.

If $x = -1$ we have $2(-1)(-1) - (-1) + 1$

$$2 + 1 + 1 = 4$$

If $x = 3$ we have $2(3)(3) - (3) + 1$:

$$18 - 3 + 1 = 16$$

The quantity in Column B (16) is greater than the quantity in Column A (4).

The correct answer is B.

EXAMPLE:

Column A	Column B
$x + y = 5$ $x - y = 1$	
x	y

SOLUTION: If we add the two given equations, we have

$$2x = 5 + 1 = 6$$
$$x = 3$$

Since $x = 3$ and $x + y = 5$, then $3 + y = 5$

$$y = 5 - 3$$
$$y = 2$$

Thus, $x = 3$ and $y = 2$

The correct answer is A.

EXAMPLE:

Column A	Column B

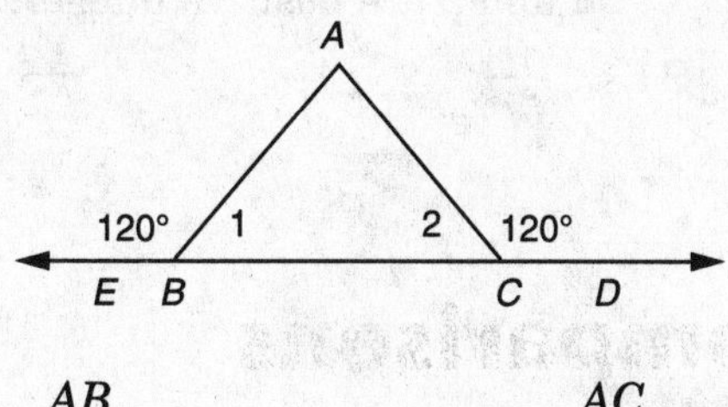

AB	AC

SOLUTION: Since the measure of $\angle ABE = 120°$, the measure of $\angle 1 = 60°$.

Similarly, since the measure of $\angle ACD = 120°$, the measure of $\angle 2 = 60°$.

Since the measures of $\angle 1$ and $\angle 2$ are each 60°, $AB = AC$.

The correct answer is C.

EXAMPLE:

Column A	Column B
x and y are positive integers.	
$\frac{x}{y}$	$\frac{y}{x}$

SOLUTION: Let $x = 3$ and $y = 5$.

$$\frac{x}{y} = \frac{3}{5} \text{ and } \frac{y}{x} = \frac{5}{3}.$$

In this case, the quantity in Column B is greater than the quantity in Column A.

Alternatively, since x and y are positive integers, we may let $x = 7$ and $y = 4$.

Then

$$\frac{x}{y} = \frac{7}{4} \text{ and } \frac{y}{x} = \frac{4}{7}.$$

In this case, the quantity in Column A is greater than the quantity in Column B.

In this example, therefore, we cannot tell whether the quantity in Column A or the quantity in Column B is greater.

The correct answer is D.

PRACTICE TEST 8

DIRECTIONS: Answer the following quantitative comparison questions by writing *A* if the quantity in Column A is greater than the quantity in Column B, *B* if the quantity in Column B is greater than the quantity in Column A, *C* if the two quantities are equal, *D* if the relationship cannot be determined.

	Column A	Column B
1.	3^4	4^3
2.	$6 + 18 \div 2 - 3 \times 5$	$7(5 - 2) + 6 \times 3$
3.	$2x + 1 = 7$	$2y - 1 = 9$
4.	The average of 75, 80, 90, 70	The average of 85, 80, 100, 70

	Column A	Column B
5.	36 minutes on the Internet with phone line charges of 8.2 cents per minute	$24\frac{1}{2}$ minutes on the Internet with phone line charges of 12 cents per minute

6.

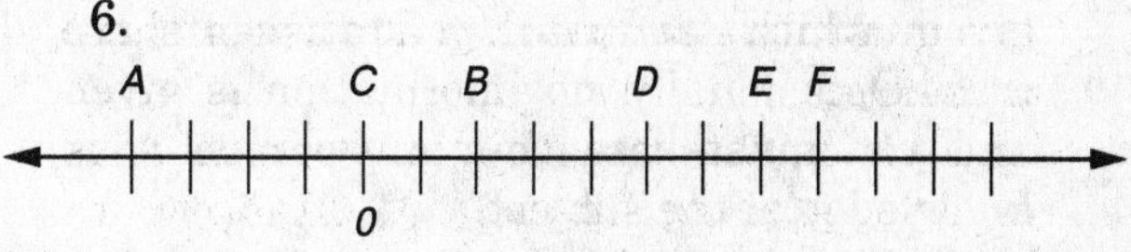

$AB + CD$	$CF + BE$

7.

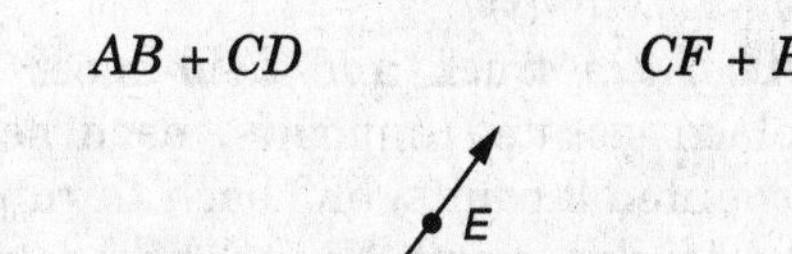

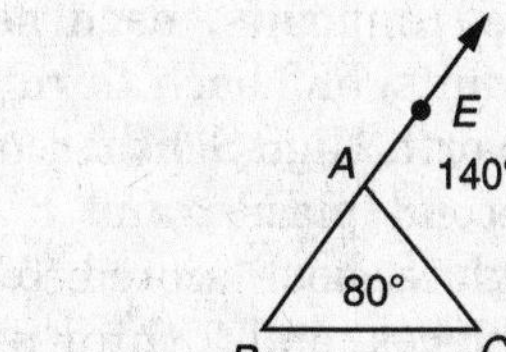

The measure of $\angle EAC = 140°$.
The measure of $\angle B = 80°$

AB	AC

	Column A	Column B
8.	$\frac{\frac{1}{2}+\frac{1}{6}}{\frac{2}{3}-\frac{1}{4}}$	2
9.	$x + 3 = y - 4$	
	y	x
10.	y is an integer	
	y	$1 - y$
11.	The remainder when 269 is divided by 17	The remainder when 318 is divided by 19
12.	$2 > x > -2$, x is an integer	
	$x^2 - x$	$x^2 + x$
13.	x is 85% of 70	y is 80% of 74
	x	y

	Column A	Column B
14.	Jack earns \$9 an hour with time and a half for overtime above 40 hours a week. One week he works 47 hours. John earns \$10.50 an hour with time and a half for overtime above 40 hours a week. One week he works 44 hours.	
	Jack's earnings for 47-hour week	John's earnings for 44-hour week
15.	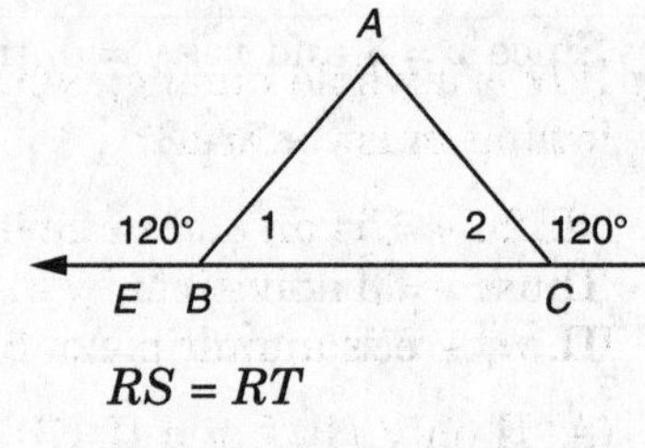	
	$RS = RT$	
	RT	RV
16.	a and b are positive integers.	
	$\frac{a+b}{a-b}$	$\frac{a-b}{a+b}$

I, II, III-Type Questions

Some tests, such as the SSAT, include questions with a special format. In a question of this type, usually information is presented and then is followed by three statements numbered I, II, and III. You are asked to decide, on the basis of the information given, which statement or statements are true. Occasionally, no information is given and you must base your answer on your knowledge of the subject.

EXAMPLE: At a track and field meet each first place counted 5 points, each second place counted 3 points, and each third place counted 1 point. North High School scored 6 first places, 4 second places, and 3 third places. West High School scored 5 first places, 7 second places, and 2 third places. Each High School scored 3 first places, 5 second places, and 4 third places.

Which of the following must be true?

I. North High School scored 11 more points than East High School.
II. West High School scored 48 points.
III. East High School scored 10 points less than West High School.

(A) I only (B) III only (C) I and III
(D) II and III (E) I and III

SOLUTION: North High School scored 45 points (30 + 12 + 3), West High School scored 48 points (25 + 21 + 2), and East High School scored 34 points (15 + 15 + 4). Thus, North High School scored 11 points more than East High School (statement I), West High School scored 48 points (statement II).

Since I is true and II is true, the correct choice is (C).

EXERCISE 1

DIRECTIONS: Answer the following questions.

1. If x is a positive integer and $A = x^2 - 3x + 2$, which of the following must be true?

   I. If $x = 5$, then $A = 12$
   II. If $x = -3$, then $A = 20$.
   III. If $x = 0$, then $A = 4$.

   (A) I only (B) II only (C) III only (D) I and II (E) I and III

2. If N is a whole number, which of the following must be true?

   I. $2n + 1$ is an odd number.
   II. $3n + 6$ is divisible by 3.
   III. $n^2 + 5$ is a multiple of 5.

   (A) II only (B) I and II (C) II and III (D) I and III (E) I, II, and III

3. Which of the following is (are) true?

   I. All quadrilaterals are squares.
   II. All squares are rectangles.
   III. All rectangles are quadrilaterals.

   (A) I only (B) II only (C) III only (D) I and II (E) I and III

4. If $y = x - 3$, then which of the following must be true?

   I. $x > y$.
   II. $x = y + 3$.
   III. $y - x = 3$.

   (A) III only (B) I and II (C) I and III (D) II and III (E) I, II, and III

5. A baseball team won 23 of the first 40 games it played. It then lost 3 games and won 7 games. Which of the following must be true?

   I. In all, the team won 30 games.
   II. The team won the last 10 games it played.
   III. The team won 70% of the games it played.

   (A) I and III only (B) II only (C) I and II (D) II and III (E) I, II, and III

Number Series

Another type of question requires you to select the next number in a series. To answer correctly, you must first determine the relationship between the given numbers.

EXAMPLE:

What is the next number in the series 1, 3, 7, 15, ________ ?

(A) 30 (B) 31 (C) 28 (D) 36 (E) 40

SOLUTION: 3 is *2* more than 1 (1 + 2), 7 is *4* more than 3 (3 + 4), 15 is *8* more than 7 (7 + 8), so the next number must be 31, which is *16* more than 15.

EXERCISE 2

DIRECTIONS: Supply the next number in each of the following series.

1. 2, 6, 18, 54, ________

   (A) 60 (B) 72 (C) 162 (D) 180 (E) 62

2. 32, 16, 8, 4, ________

   (A) –4 (B) 8 (C) 3 (D) 2 (E) 1

3. 5, 8, 11, 14, ________

   (A) 17 (B) 18 (C) 20 (D) 15 (E) 16

4. 1, 4, 9, 16, ________

   (A) 19 (B) 18 (C) 21 (D) 23 (E) 25

5. 2, 5, 10, 17, ________

   (A) 25 (B) 26 (C) 24 (D) 27 (E) 28

Answers to All Exercises and Practice Tests

PRACTICE TESTS

TEST 1

1. C	5. C	9. D	13. C	17. A
2. E	6. D	10. B	14. B	18. C
3. D	7. E	11. D	15. D	19. D
4. B	8. A	12. D	16. B	20. D

TEST 2

1. D	5. B	9. B	13. B	17. E
2. C	6. D	10. D	14. D	18. C
3. B	7. B	11. E	15. C	19. C
4. E	8. C	12. C	16. B	20. D

TEST 3

1. C	5. E	9. B	13. C	17. E
2. D	6. C	10. E	14. A	18. C
3. B	7. A	11. B	15. D	19. D
4. B	8. C	12. D	16. E	20. B

TEST 4

1. D	5. E	9. B	13. D	17. C
2. B	6. A	10. D	14. C	18. D
3. D	7. C	11. E	15. E	19. B
4. C	8. D	12. B	16. A	20. D

TEST 5

1. A	5. E	9. B	13. B	17. D
2. D	6. B	10. D	14. D	18. C
3. C	7. D	11. C	15. E	19. C
4. A	8. E	12. D	16. B	20. D

TEST 6

1. E	5. C	9. E	13. D	17. C
2. B	6. B	10. A	14. E	
3. D	7. D	11. D	15. C	
4. A	8. B	12. C	16. B	

TEST 7

1. 101 2. 71 3. 62 4. 142

TEST 8

1. A	5. A	9. A	13. A
2. B	6. B	10. D	14. B
3. B	7. B	11. C	15. A
4. B	8. B	12. D	16. A

EXERCISES

EXERCISE 1

1. D 2. C 3. B 4. B 5. A

EXERCISE 2

1. C 2. D 3. A 4. E 5. B

PRACTICE HIGH SCHOOL ENTRANCE EXAMINATIONS

Answer Sheet
Practice Secondary School Admission Test 1

SECTION 1

1. Ⓐ Ⓑ Ⓒ Ⓓ Ⓔ
2. Ⓕ Ⓖ Ⓗ Ⓙ Ⓚ
3. Ⓐ Ⓑ Ⓒ Ⓓ Ⓔ
4. Ⓕ Ⓖ Ⓗ Ⓙ Ⓚ
5. Ⓐ Ⓑ Ⓒ Ⓓ Ⓔ
6. Ⓕ Ⓖ Ⓗ Ⓙ Ⓚ
7. Ⓐ Ⓑ Ⓒ Ⓓ Ⓔ
8. Ⓕ Ⓖ Ⓗ Ⓙ Ⓚ
9. Ⓐ Ⓑ Ⓒ Ⓓ Ⓔ
10. Ⓕ Ⓖ Ⓗ Ⓙ Ⓚ
11. Ⓐ Ⓑ Ⓒ Ⓓ Ⓔ
12. Ⓕ Ⓖ Ⓗ Ⓙ Ⓚ
13. Ⓐ Ⓑ Ⓒ Ⓓ Ⓔ
14. Ⓕ Ⓖ Ⓗ Ⓙ Ⓚ
15. Ⓐ Ⓑ Ⓒ Ⓓ Ⓔ
16. Ⓕ Ⓖ Ⓗ Ⓙ Ⓚ
17. Ⓐ Ⓑ Ⓒ Ⓓ Ⓔ
18. Ⓕ Ⓖ Ⓗ Ⓙ Ⓚ
19. Ⓐ Ⓑ Ⓒ Ⓓ Ⓔ
20. Ⓕ Ⓖ Ⓗ Ⓙ Ⓚ
21. Ⓐ Ⓑ Ⓒ Ⓓ Ⓔ
22. Ⓕ Ⓖ Ⓗ Ⓙ Ⓚ
23. Ⓐ Ⓑ Ⓒ Ⓓ Ⓔ
24. Ⓕ Ⓖ Ⓗ Ⓙ Ⓚ
25. Ⓐ Ⓑ Ⓒ Ⓓ Ⓔ

SECTION 2

1. Ⓐ Ⓑ Ⓒ Ⓓ Ⓔ
2. Ⓕ Ⓖ Ⓗ Ⓙ Ⓚ
3. Ⓐ Ⓑ Ⓒ Ⓓ Ⓔ
4. Ⓕ Ⓖ Ⓗ Ⓙ Ⓚ
5. Ⓐ Ⓑ Ⓒ Ⓓ Ⓔ
6. Ⓕ Ⓖ Ⓗ Ⓙ Ⓚ
7. Ⓐ Ⓑ Ⓒ Ⓓ Ⓔ
8. Ⓕ Ⓖ Ⓗ Ⓙ Ⓚ
9. Ⓐ Ⓑ Ⓒ Ⓓ Ⓔ
10. Ⓕ Ⓖ Ⓗ Ⓙ Ⓚ
11. Ⓐ Ⓑ Ⓒ Ⓓ Ⓔ
12. Ⓕ Ⓖ Ⓗ Ⓙ Ⓚ
13. Ⓐ Ⓑ Ⓒ Ⓓ Ⓔ
14. Ⓕ Ⓖ Ⓗ Ⓙ Ⓚ
15. Ⓐ Ⓑ Ⓒ Ⓓ Ⓔ
16. Ⓕ Ⓖ Ⓗ Ⓙ Ⓚ
17. Ⓐ Ⓑ Ⓒ Ⓓ Ⓔ
18. Ⓕ Ⓖ Ⓗ Ⓙ Ⓚ
19. Ⓐ Ⓑ Ⓒ Ⓓ Ⓔ
20. Ⓕ Ⓖ Ⓗ Ⓙ Ⓚ
21. Ⓐ Ⓑ Ⓒ Ⓓ Ⓔ
22. Ⓕ Ⓖ Ⓗ Ⓙ Ⓚ
23. Ⓐ Ⓑ Ⓒ Ⓓ Ⓔ
24. Ⓕ Ⓖ Ⓗ Ⓙ Ⓚ
25. Ⓐ Ⓑ Ⓒ Ⓓ Ⓔ
26. Ⓕ Ⓖ Ⓗ Ⓙ Ⓚ
27. Ⓐ Ⓑ Ⓒ Ⓓ Ⓔ
28. Ⓕ Ⓖ Ⓗ Ⓙ Ⓚ
29. Ⓐ Ⓑ Ⓒ Ⓓ Ⓔ
30. Ⓕ Ⓖ Ⓗ Ⓙ Ⓚ
31. Ⓐ Ⓑ Ⓒ Ⓓ Ⓔ
32. Ⓕ Ⓖ Ⓗ Ⓙ Ⓚ
33. Ⓐ Ⓑ Ⓒ Ⓓ Ⓔ
34. Ⓕ Ⓖ Ⓗ Ⓙ Ⓚ
35. Ⓐ Ⓑ Ⓒ Ⓓ Ⓔ
36. Ⓕ Ⓖ Ⓗ Ⓙ Ⓚ
37. Ⓐ Ⓑ Ⓒ Ⓓ Ⓔ
38. Ⓕ Ⓖ Ⓗ Ⓙ Ⓚ
39. Ⓐ Ⓑ Ⓒ Ⓓ Ⓔ
40. Ⓕ Ⓖ Ⓗ Ⓙ Ⓚ
41. Ⓐ Ⓑ Ⓒ Ⓓ Ⓔ
42. Ⓕ Ⓖ Ⓗ Ⓙ Ⓚ
43. Ⓐ Ⓑ Ⓒ Ⓓ Ⓔ
44. Ⓕ Ⓖ Ⓗ Ⓙ Ⓚ
45. Ⓐ Ⓑ Ⓒ Ⓓ Ⓔ
46. Ⓕ Ⓖ Ⓗ Ⓙ Ⓚ
47. Ⓐ Ⓑ Ⓒ Ⓓ Ⓔ
48. Ⓕ Ⓖ Ⓗ Ⓙ Ⓚ
49. Ⓐ Ⓑ Ⓒ Ⓓ Ⓔ
50. Ⓕ Ⓖ Ⓗ Ⓙ Ⓚ
51. Ⓐ Ⓑ Ⓒ Ⓓ Ⓔ
52. Ⓕ Ⓖ Ⓗ Ⓙ Ⓚ
53. Ⓐ Ⓑ Ⓒ Ⓓ Ⓔ
54. Ⓕ Ⓖ Ⓗ Ⓙ Ⓚ
55. Ⓐ Ⓑ Ⓒ Ⓓ Ⓔ
56. Ⓕ Ⓖ Ⓗ Ⓙ Ⓚ
57. Ⓐ Ⓑ Ⓒ Ⓓ Ⓔ
58. Ⓕ Ⓖ Ⓗ Ⓙ Ⓚ
59. Ⓐ Ⓑ Ⓒ Ⓓ Ⓔ
60. Ⓕ Ⓖ Ⓗ Ⓙ Ⓚ

SECTION 3

1. Ⓐ Ⓑ Ⓒ Ⓓ Ⓔ
2. Ⓕ Ⓖ Ⓗ Ⓙ Ⓚ
3. Ⓐ Ⓑ Ⓒ Ⓓ Ⓔ
4. Ⓕ Ⓖ Ⓗ Ⓙ Ⓚ
5. Ⓐ Ⓑ Ⓒ Ⓓ Ⓔ
6. Ⓕ Ⓖ Ⓗ Ⓙ Ⓚ
7. Ⓐ Ⓑ Ⓒ Ⓓ Ⓔ
8. Ⓕ Ⓖ Ⓗ Ⓙ Ⓚ
9. Ⓐ Ⓑ Ⓒ Ⓓ Ⓔ
10. Ⓕ Ⓖ Ⓗ Ⓙ Ⓚ
11. Ⓐ Ⓑ Ⓒ Ⓓ Ⓔ
12. Ⓕ Ⓖ Ⓗ Ⓙ Ⓚ
13. Ⓐ Ⓑ Ⓒ Ⓓ Ⓔ
14. Ⓕ Ⓖ Ⓗ Ⓙ Ⓚ
15. Ⓐ Ⓑ Ⓒ Ⓓ Ⓔ
16. Ⓕ Ⓖ Ⓗ Ⓙ Ⓚ
17. Ⓐ Ⓑ Ⓒ Ⓓ Ⓔ
18. Ⓕ Ⓖ Ⓗ Ⓙ Ⓚ
19. Ⓐ Ⓑ Ⓒ Ⓓ Ⓔ
20. Ⓕ Ⓖ Ⓗ Ⓙ Ⓚ
21. Ⓐ Ⓑ Ⓒ Ⓓ Ⓔ
22. Ⓕ Ⓖ Ⓗ Ⓙ Ⓚ
23. Ⓐ Ⓑ Ⓒ Ⓓ Ⓔ
24. Ⓕ Ⓖ Ⓗ Ⓙ Ⓚ
25. Ⓐ Ⓑ Ⓒ Ⓓ Ⓔ

SECTION 4

1. Ⓐ Ⓑ Ⓒ Ⓓ Ⓔ
2. Ⓕ Ⓖ Ⓗ Ⓙ Ⓚ
3. Ⓐ Ⓑ Ⓒ Ⓓ Ⓔ
4. Ⓕ Ⓖ Ⓗ Ⓙ Ⓚ
5. Ⓐ Ⓑ Ⓒ Ⓓ Ⓔ
6. Ⓕ Ⓖ Ⓗ Ⓙ Ⓚ
7. Ⓐ Ⓑ Ⓒ Ⓓ Ⓔ
8. Ⓕ Ⓖ Ⓗ Ⓙ Ⓚ
9. Ⓐ Ⓑ Ⓒ Ⓓ Ⓔ
10. Ⓕ Ⓖ Ⓗ Ⓙ Ⓚ
11. Ⓐ Ⓑ Ⓒ Ⓓ Ⓔ
12. Ⓕ Ⓖ Ⓗ Ⓙ Ⓚ
13. Ⓐ Ⓑ Ⓒ Ⓓ Ⓔ
14. Ⓕ Ⓖ Ⓗ Ⓙ Ⓚ
15. Ⓐ Ⓑ Ⓒ Ⓓ Ⓔ
16. Ⓕ Ⓖ Ⓗ Ⓙ Ⓚ
17. Ⓐ Ⓑ Ⓒ Ⓓ Ⓔ
18. Ⓕ Ⓖ Ⓗ Ⓙ Ⓚ
19. Ⓐ Ⓑ Ⓒ Ⓓ Ⓔ
20. Ⓕ Ⓖ Ⓗ Ⓙ Ⓚ
21. Ⓐ Ⓑ Ⓒ Ⓓ Ⓔ
22. Ⓕ Ⓖ Ⓗ Ⓙ Ⓚ
23. Ⓐ Ⓑ Ⓒ Ⓓ Ⓔ
24. Ⓕ Ⓖ Ⓗ Ⓙ Ⓚ
25. Ⓐ Ⓑ Ⓒ Ⓓ Ⓔ
26. Ⓕ Ⓖ Ⓗ Ⓙ Ⓚ
27. Ⓐ Ⓑ Ⓒ Ⓓ Ⓔ
28. Ⓕ Ⓖ Ⓗ Ⓙ Ⓚ
29. Ⓐ Ⓑ Ⓒ Ⓓ Ⓔ
30. Ⓕ Ⓖ Ⓗ Ⓙ Ⓚ
31. Ⓐ Ⓑ Ⓒ Ⓓ Ⓔ
32. Ⓕ Ⓖ Ⓗ Ⓙ Ⓚ
33. Ⓐ Ⓑ Ⓒ Ⓓ Ⓔ
34. Ⓕ Ⓖ Ⓗ Ⓙ Ⓚ
35. Ⓐ Ⓑ Ⓒ Ⓓ Ⓔ
36. Ⓕ Ⓖ Ⓗ Ⓙ Ⓚ
37. Ⓐ Ⓑ Ⓒ Ⓓ Ⓔ
38. Ⓕ Ⓖ Ⓗ Ⓙ Ⓚ
39. Ⓐ Ⓑ Ⓒ Ⓓ Ⓔ
40. Ⓕ Ⓖ Ⓗ Ⓙ Ⓚ

Secondary School Admission Test (SSAT) Practice Tests

Overview

Total Time

Approximately $2\frac{1}{2}$ hours.

Type of Questions

The questions are multiple choice, with answers filled in on a machine-scored Answer Sheet.

Pacing

Students taking either the Upper Level or the Lower Level are not expected to complete all items. They are expected to work as fast as possible while maintaining accuracy. The general rule is this: Do not linger over questions you find too difficult.

Guessing

A blank answer receives no credit. However, because $\frac{1}{4}$ point is subtracted for each incorrect answer wild guessing is discouraged. Do not fill in a blank at random when you have no idea of the answer. Follow these guidelines:

1. If the answer would be a pure guess, leave it blank.
2. If you can eliminate one or more choices, then take the chance.
3. Since your first guess is usually the better one, stick with it unless you are positive that you have chosen incorrectly.

Rating Results

SSAT scores compare each student's test performance only with the performances of other students in the same grade level.

Exam Specifications

The forms of the exam are subject to change each year. Time limits given below and on the practice tests for the various portions are guidelines rather than strict specifications.

Test Content

At both the Lower and the Upper Levels, the test consists of the following parts; however, they may be given in a different order from the one shown here.

Section 1: Mathematics Computation
25 questions, 25 minutes

Section 2: Verbal Ability *25 minutes total*

Vocabulary—Synonyms *30 questions*

Vocabulary—Analogies *30 questions*

Section 3: Mathematics Concepts
25 questions, 25 minutes

Section 4: Reading Comprehension
40 questions, 25 minutes

Section 5: Experimental Section
This section may appear anywhere in the test. It may be similar in form or content to any one of the other sections, but answers to questions in this section are not counted in test scores. An experimental section is not included in the practice tests.

The two tests that follow are planned for both the Lower and the Upper Levels. The rating scores (pages 526 and 579) take into account the difference in preparation and training for the groups taking the tests.

Practice Secondary School Admission Test 1

SECTION 1

Time—25 minutes
25 questions

DIRECTIONS: Five possible answers follow each question below. You may work out each problem in your head or use the margins of the test pages for scratch work. Decide which of the five possible answers is best. On the Answer Sheet fill in the circle with the letter that corresponds to your answer choice.

SAMPLE PROBLEM:

7,524
−6,736

(A) 788 (B) 798 (C) 898 (D) 1,788 (E) 1,888

● Ⓑ Ⓒ Ⓓ Ⓔ

1. $8 \times 75 \times \square = 6$. The value of □ is

(A) 100 (B) 9.3 (C) 10 (D) 0.01 (E) 600

2. $0.4 + \frac{3}{100} + \frac{1}{2} =$

(F) 1.2 (G) 9.3 (H) 0.93 (J) 0.57 (K) 0.435

3. $\square + 89.1 = 1{,}005 - 906$. The value of □ is

(A) 9.9 (B) 99 (C) 0.99 (D) 99.1 (E) 9.91

4. 40% of 6 is equal to 75% of what number?

(F) 32 (G) 0.32 (H) 320 (J) 1.8 (K) 3.2

5. The coordinates of $\triangle ABC$ are $A(3, 1)$, $B(8, 1)$, and $C(5, 7)$. What is the area of $\triangle ABC$, in square units?

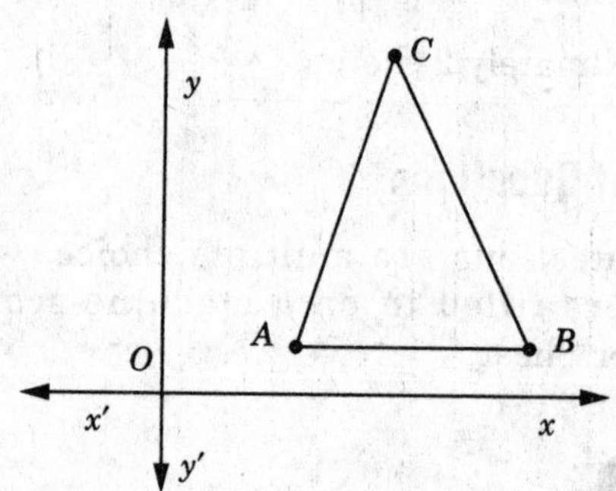

(A) 30 (B) 45 (C) 15 (D) 18 (E) 20

6. If $7 > N > 3$ and N is a multiple of 3, then $N =$

(F) 5 (G) 6 (H) −2 (J) 4 (K) 9

7. If the area of a rectangle is 240 square meters and the length of the rectangle is 20 meters then the perimeter of the rectangle, in meters, is

(A) 32 (B) 12 (C) 44 (D) 64 (E) 52

8. A lecture hall has 32 rows of seats with 15 seats in each row. How many seats are vacant when 75% of the seats are occupied?

(F) 150 (G) 360 (H) 180 (J) 240 (K) 120

9. Which one of the following does not have a value of 0.3?

(A) $\frac{3}{10}$ (B) 30% (C) 0.300 (D) $\frac{1}{3}$ (E) $\frac{6}{20}$

10. This graph represents attendance at the XYZ movie house on five days of the week. Each box represents 50 people. How many more people attended the XYZ movie house on Tuesday than on Thursday?

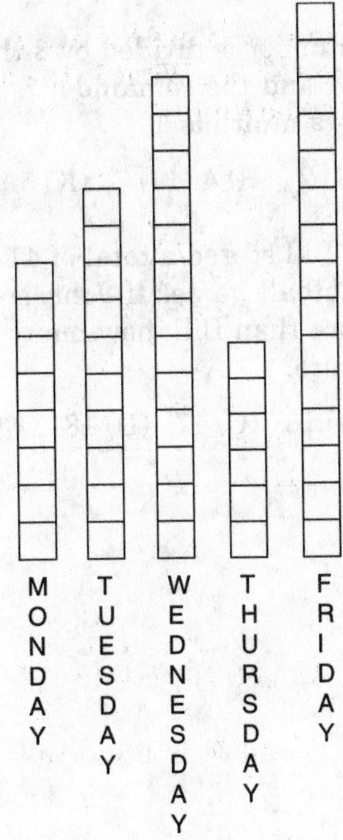

(F) 150 (G) 300 (H) 250 (J) 200 (K) 500

11. If □ – 4 = 3, then 6 times □ is

(A) 42 (B) 6 (C) 60 (D) 30 (E) 24

12. A baseball batter made 12 hits in 40 times at bat. In his next 10 times at bat he made 3 outs, 4 hits, and then 3 more outs. Which of the following must be true?

I. He had a total of 50 times at bat.
II. He had a total of 16 hits.
III. He made hits on 30% of his times at bat.

(F) I only
(G) I and II only
(H) I and III only
(J) I, II, and III
(K) II and III only

13. □ + 2 × △ = 16. If △ = 3, then the value of □ is

(A) 8 (B) 22 (C) 10 (D) 11 (E) 12

14. A number equal to $\frac{2}{5}$ is

(F) 0.04 (G) $\frac{2}{5}$% (H) $\frac{0.4}{10}$ (J) 5 ÷ 2 (K) 40%

15. If 2.7 × 0.96 = 27 × □, then the value of □ is

(A) 0.96 (B) 0.096 (C) 9.6 (D) 96 (E) 0.0096

16. All of the following are greater than $\frac{1}{3}$ but less than $\frac{1}{2}$ EXCEPT

(F) 0.48 (G) 40 percent (H) $\frac{3}{8}$ (J) $\frac{4}{7}$ (K) $\frac{4}{9}$

17. In driving 1 mile, how many seconds does a motorist save by driving at the rate of 50 miles per hour rather than at the rate of 40 miles per hour?

(A) 10 (B) 18 (C) 12 (D) 15 (E) 16

18. When a number is increased by one-half of itself, the result is greater than 45. The number is

(F) 67 $\frac{1}{2}$ (G) greater than 30 (H) 22 $\frac{1}{2}$
(J) greater than 67 $\frac{1}{2}$
(K) none of these

19. In an isosceles triangle the measure of the vertex angle is 68°. The measure of each of the equal base angles, in degrees, is

(A) 16 (B) 66 (C) 34 (D) 52 (E) 56

20. A man bought 6 pairs of slacks at n dollars per pair. The cost of the slacks, in dollars was

(F) $6 + n$ (G) $6n$ (H) $n \div 6$ (J) $6 \div n$ (K) $n - 6$

21. If each side of a square is doubled in length then

 (A) the area of the square is doubled
 (B) the perimeter of the square is multiplied by 4
 (C) the area of the square is multiplied by 8
 (D) the area of the square is multiplied by 4
 (E) none of the above is true

22. At midnight the temperature was 9 degrees below zero. By 8:00 A.M. the temperature had risen 6 degrees. What was the temperature at 8 A.M.?

 (F) 15 degrees above zero
 (G) 15 degrees below zero
 (H) 3 degrees below zero
 (J) 3 degrees above zero
 (K) 12 degrees above zero

23. Mr. James bought a jacket and paid a sales tax of $3.90. If the rate of the sales tax was 6%, what was the price of the jacket before the tax?

 (A) $234 (B) $66 (C) $65 (D) $90 (E) $55

24. When a number is divided by 8 the quotient is 24 and the remainder is 3. The number is a multiple of

 (F) 10 (G) 2 (H) 4 (J) 7 (K) 5

25. John and Bill scored a total of 41 points in a basketball game. If John scored 5 points more than Bill, how many points did Bill score?

 (A) 23 (B) 16 (C) 17 (D) 18 (E) 20

SECTION 2

Time—25 minutes
60 questions

DIRECTIONS: In this section there are two different types of questions. Directions and a sample question precede each type.

Select, from the lettered choices, the word or phrase closest in meaning to the word in capital letters. On the Answer Sheet, fill in the circle that has the same letter as your answer choice.

SAMPLE QUESTION:

NIMBLE:

(A) annoying (B) occasional
(C) lively (D) childish (E) somber

1. ENTREAT:

(A) entertain (B) employ (C) release
(D) reject (E) beg

2. CORRESPOND:

(F) request (G) relay (H) delight
(J) agree (K) cancel

3. SEVER:

(A) turn over (B) cut apart
(C) stop completely (D) drop off
(E) eat slowly

4. PREAMBLE:

(F) formal introduction
(G) instruction book
(H) lengthy notes (J) common law
(K) short message

5. YEARN:

(A) labor (B) regret (C) desire
(D) annul (E) consider

6. WITHSTAND:

(F) console (G) occur (H) weaken
(J) resist (K) construct

7. EMINENCE:

(A) good luck (B) total control
(C) high position (D) knowledge
(E) power

8. VERIFY:

(F) change form (G) make a claim
(H) foresee trouble (J) dream about
(K) prove true

9. CONCUR:

(A) happen (B) defeat (C) agree
(D) stop (E) invade

10. FULFILL:

(F) overflow (G) extent (H) control
(J) excel (K) accomplish

11. CLEFT:

(A) split (B) injury (C) ridge
(D) scar (E) birthmark

12. ELUCIDATE:

(F) show off (G) clear up (H) free from
(J) send away (K) escape from

13. DEFACE:

(A) detect (B) display (C) paint
(D) resist (E) spoil

14. DANK:

(F) dark and windy
(G) short and stocky
(H) moist and chilly
(J) noisy and dangerous
(K) hot and dusty

15. ENDURE:

(A) last (B) exceed (C) discover
(D) need (E) educate

16. DESPOT:

(F) vessel (G) general (H) tyrant
(J) ruler (K) subject

17. DATA:

(A) accident (B) facts (C) money (D) appointments (E) view

18. THRIVE:

(F) number (G) attempt (H) breathe (J) prosper (K) console

19. CONTEMPLATE:

(A) detest (B) time (C) agree (D) relate (E) consider

20. FLOURISH:

(F) flee (G) foil (H) prosper (J) feed (K) begin

21. TEDIOUS:

(A) sharp (B) wearisome (C) lonely (D) incorrect (E) hateful

22. FIERY:

(F) cautious (G) reliable (H) angry (J) stern (K) blazing

23. INKLING:

(A) letter (B) title (C) signature (D) hint (E) stain

24. DELUGE:

(F) flood (G) end (H) deposit (J) excite (K) release

25. OBLIGATORY:

(A) dangerous (B) watchful (C) required (D) timid (E) notable

26. REMINISCE:

(F) forget about (G) fight against (H) agree with (J) defend against (K) exchange memories

27. INCIDENT:

(A) tragedy (B) misfortune (C) event (D) wound (E) birth

28. DISTRUST:

(F) friendship (G) dishonesty (H) hatred (J) suspicion (K) envy

29. PANICKY:

(A) brief (B) alarmed (C) harmful (D) peevish (E) protective

30. FETE:

(F) cheese (G) sad occasion (H) lavish party (J) destruction (K) elaborate building

DIRECTIONS: Each of the following questions gives two words that relate in a certain way. You must determine this relationship, and then choose the answer that best completes the meaning of the sentence. On the Answer Sheet, fill in the circle that has the same letter as your answer choice.

SAMPLE QUESTION:

River is to stream as

(A) motor is to auto
(B) boulevard is to lane
(C) tire is to rim
(D) gravel is to concrete
(E) liquid is to solid

Ⓐ ● Ⓒ Ⓓ Ⓔ

Choice (B) is the best answer because, as a river is wider than a stream, so a boulevard is wider than a lane. Of all the choices, (B) expresses a relationship (based on size) most similar to the relationship between river and stream.

31. Coffee is to beverage as

(A) radio is to television
(B) straw is to mat
(C) profession is to doctor
(D) eclair is to pastry
(E) soda is to pop

32. Pale is to white as ashen is to

(F) disturbed (G) gray (H) sudden (J) moving (K) relaxed

33. Reservoir is to water as silo is to

(A) cattle (B) horses (C) fodder (D) cannery (E) barn

34. Publisher is to books as producer is to

(F) plays (G) toys (H) wealth
(J) plants (K) furniture

35. Acclaim is to praise as berate is to

(A) command (B) scold (C) evaluate
(D) confer (E) deny

36. Hangar is to airport as

(F) road is to truck
(G) outerspace is to rocket
(H) red is to green
(J) gulfstream is to ocean
(K) pier is to harbor

37. Level is to carpenter as

(A) estimate is to plumber
(B) director is to actor
(C) cattle is to butcher
(D) roller is to painter
(E) bridge is to engineer

38. Cabin is to passengers as

(F) lease is to superintendent
(G) airplane is to hovercraft
(H) hold is to cargo
(J) purse is to price
(K) saddle is to mount

39. Liter is to volume as

(A) pint is to quality
(B) inch is to weight
(C) foot is to distance
(D) kilometer is to speed
(E) yard is to pressure

40. Fare is to taxi driver as

(F) fee is to lawyer
(G) tip is to broker
(H) passbook is to teller
(J) profit is to storekeeper
(K) check is to counterfeiter

41. Script is to actor as score is to

(A) sculptor (B) painter (C) poet
(D) musician (E) novelist

42. Jar is to shake as prod is to

(F) sting (G) control (H) irritate
(J) push (K) help

43. Moon is to satellite as Mercury is to

(A) earth (B) planet (C) galaxy
(D) sun (E) comet

44. Battle is to weapons as

(F) bandage is to injuries
(G) glove is to fighters
(H) insult is to quarrels
(J) argument is to words
(K) choice is to champions

45. Decline is to elevate as

(A) more is to more (B) most is to least
(C) less is to more (D) less is to less
(E) more is to less

46. Pumpkin is to gourd as

(F) apple is to mackintosh
(G) lima bean is to legume
(H) cabbage is to head
(J) artichoke is to lettuce
(K) asparagus is to spear

47. Dalmatian is to dog as cobra is to

(A) house wren (B) venom (C) weasel
(D) asp (E) snake

48. Damper is to fireplace as

(F) oil is to furnace
(G) gauge is to engine
(H) needle is to thread
(J) valve is to pipe
(K) base is to statue

49. Small is to minute as little is to

(A) gigantic (B) tiny (C) sizable
D) light (E) masterly

50. Robin is to egg as

(F) horse is to pony (G) grass is to seed
(H) inventor is to manufacturer
(J) tiger is to den
(K) motor is to limousine

51. Somber is to cheerful as

(A) testy is to healthful
(B) loyal is to obedient
(C) mediocre is to ordinary
(D) counterfeit is to genuine
(E) shrill is to competent

52. Canon is to cathedral as

(F) soldier is to regiment
(G) architect is to stadium
(H) engineer is to blueprint
(J) artist is to painting
(K) supervisor is to factory

53. Police officer is to crime as

(A) doctor is to poverty
(B) miner is to coal
(C) Edison is to electricity
(D) philanthropist is to health
(E) teacher is to ignorance

54. Scale is to weight as thermometer is to

(F) height (G) health (H) strength
(J) temperature (K) pressure

55. Illiterate is to reading ability as

(A) ignorant is to knowledge
(B) infectious is to disease
(C) outrageous is to kindness
(D) positive is to certainty
(E) disobedient is to understanding

56. Evaluate is to critic as

(F) navigate is to stoker
(G) create is to novelist
(H) console is to organist
(J) prison is to officer
(K) profit is to accountant

57. Brain is to intelligence as

(A) scaffolding is to building
(B) conscience is to willpower
(C) skeleton is to bones
(D) teeth are to food
(E) muscle is to strength

58. Repel is to annoy as

(F) hatred is to dislike
(G) concern is to envy
(H) offend is to distrust
(J) please is to notice
(K) recede is to resent

59. Interval is to second as

(A) time is to distance
(B) definite is to indefinite
(C) distance is to time
(D) indefinite is to definite
(E) hour is to day

60. Ideals are to goals as

(F) nail is to board
(G) pen is to paper
(H) cloud is to sky
(J) track is to train
(K) sail is to wind

SECTION 3

Time—25 minutes
25 questions

DIRECTIONS: Five possible answers follow each question below. You may work out each problem in your head or use the margins of the test pages for scratch work. Decide which of the five possible answers is best. On the Answer Sheet fill in the circle with the letter that corresponds to your answer choice.

SAMPLE PROBLEM:

7,524
–6,736

(A) 788 (B) 798 (C) 898 (D) 1,788
(E) 1,888

● Ⓑ Ⓒ Ⓓ Ⓔ

1. If $\frac{2}{3}$ of a number is 24, then $\frac{5}{9}$ of this number is

   (A) 28 (B) 30 (C) 32 (D) 20 (E) 18

2. The base and the altitude of a triangle are each doubled. Which one of the following statements is true?

   (F) The area of the enlarged triangle is twice that of the original triangle.
   (G) The perimeter of the enlarged triangle is four times that of the original triangle.
   (H) The area of the enlarged triangle is four times as great as the area of the original triangle.
   (J) The enlarged triangle is an equilateral triangle.
   (K) The base of the enlarged triangle is equal to the altitude of the enlarged triangle.

3. The average of $\frac{3}{4}$ and $\frac{1}{6}$ is

   (A) $\frac{1}{5}$ (B) $\frac{11}{24}$ (C) $\frac{1}{8}$ (D) $\frac{2}{3}$ (E) $\frac{5}{12}$

4. At a sale of radio sets, $\frac{1}{3}$ of the sets were sold the first day, $\frac{1}{4}$ of the sets were sold the second day, and $\frac{1}{8}$ of the sets were sold the third day. What fractional part of the sets were left unsold after the third day?

   (F) $\frac{17}{24}$ (G) $\frac{5}{12}$ (H) $\frac{9}{16}$ (J) $\frac{7}{18}$ (K) $\frac{7}{24}$

5. 48 is 32% of what number?

   (A) 300 (B) 15.34 (C) $\frac{3}{200}$ (D) 150
   (E) 180

6. If we increase both the numerator and denominator of the proper fraction by the same positive number, then

   (F) the value of the fraction remains the same
   (G) the value of the fraction increases
   (H) the value of the fraction decreases
   (J) the value of the fraction becomes greater than 1
   (K) none of the above is true

7. If $y = 4x^3$ the value of y when $x = \frac{1}{2}$ is

   (A) $\frac{1}{2}$ (B) $\frac{1}{4}$ (C) $\frac{1}{8}$ (D) 1 (E) 2

8. Which of the following is closest in value to 6?

   (F) $2 \div 0.03$ (G) 3.6×1.8 (H) $(2.4)^2$
   (J) $8 \div 0.4$ (K) $3.8 + 4.2$

9. On a 600-mile trip between two cities, a plane averaged 400 miles per hour. On the return trip the plane averaged 300 miles per hour. The average rate of speed for the round trip, in miles per hour, was

   (A) 350 (B) 360 (C) 340 (D) 380
   (E) $342\frac{6}{7}$

10. If $6 < x < 10$ and $8 > x > 4$, then the value of x is

   (F) 5 (G) 7 (H) 8 (J) 9 (K) 12

11. If the sum of two numbers is y, and one of the numbers is 6 then twice the other number is

    (A) $2y - 6$ (B) $6 - 2y$ (C) $2(6 - y)$
    (D) $2(y - 6)$ (E) $2(2y - 6)$

12. The coordinates of a rectangle $ABCD$ are $A(-2, 3)$, $B(5, 3)$, $C(5, -1)$ $D(-2, -1)$. The perimeter of the rectangle is

    (F) 11 (G) 18 (H) 22 (J) 20 (K) 24

> DIRECTIONS: Questions 13–15 refer to the following definitions:
>
> For all real numbers x and y,
>
> $$\overline{x} \square \overline{y} = (x + y) + (x - y)$$
>
> **EXAMPLE**
>
> $$\overline{5} \square \overline{3} = (5 + 3) + (5 - 3) = 8 + 2 = 10$$

13. $\overline{6} \square \overline{2} =$

    (A) 8 (B) 12 (C) 32 (D) 4 (E) 6

14. If $\overline{N} \square \overline{6} = 10$, then $N =$

    (F) 8 (G) 4 (H) 1 (J) 5 (K) 3

15. If A and B are positive real numbers, which of the following must be true?

    I. $\overline{B} \square \overline{B} = \overline{B}$
    II. $\overline{A} \square \overline{B} = 2A$
    III. $\overline{A} \square \frac{1}{A} = 2A$

    (A) I only (B) I and II only (C) II only
    (D) II and III only (E) I, II, and III

16. A recipe calls for 8 ounces of butter and 3 ounces of sugar. If 6 ounces of butter are used, how many ounces of sugar should be used?

    (F) $\frac{4}{9}$ (G) 2 (H) $2\frac{1}{2}$ (J) $2\frac{3}{4}$ (K) $2\frac{1}{4}$

17. After driving 162 miles, a motorist had covered 36% of his planned mileage for the day. How many miles did this motorist plan to travel that day?

    (A) 58.32 (B) 450 (C) 486 (D) 495
    (E) 470

18. If $x + 5 = y + 3$ then

    (F) $x > y$ (G) $x = y$ (H) $y > x$
    (J) $x = y + 2$ (K) $y = x - 3$

19. An oil tank in the form of a rectangular solid has a length of 20 feet and a width of 12 feet. If 1,200 cubic feet of oil are poured into the tank, what will be the height, in feet, of the oil in the tank?

    (A) 6 (B) 5 (C) $4\frac{1}{2}$ (D) 9 (E) 12

20. How many sixths are there in $2\frac{3}{4}$?

    (F) $16\frac{1}{2}$ (G) $\frac{11}{24}$ (H) $12\frac{1}{2}$ (J) 15
    (K) 18

21. A room is 20 feet long, 12 feet wide, and 8 feet high. The walls of this room are painted. What is the area of the painted surface, in square feet?

    (A) 416 (B) 1,920 (C) 320 (D) 1,600
    (E) 512

22. $7 \times 9 \times 6 \times \square = 54 \times 56$. The value of $\square$ is

    (F) 6 (G) 8 (H) 4 (J) 5 (K) 3

23. At a price of $0.76 per pound, what is the cost of a bag of onions weighing 3 pounds 4 ounces?

    (A) $2.66 (B) $2.28 (C) $2.75
    (D) $2.47 (E) $2.68

24. A major league baseball player gets 87 hits in 96 games. How many hits will this baseball player get in 160 games if he continues to hit at the same rate?

    (F) 145 (G) 135 (H) 125 (J) 140
    (K) 150

25. A girl has $5.00. She buys 3 notebooks at x cents each. The amount she receives in change, in cents, is

    (A) $3x$ – $5.00 (B) $5.00 ÷ $3x$
    (C) $5.00 – $3x$ (D) $5.00 + $3x$
    (E) $3x$ ÷ $5.00

SECTION 4

Time—25 minutes
40 questions

DIRECTIONS: Carefully read each of the passages below and the questions that follow. Select the choice which, on the basis of the passage, best answers the question. On the Answer Sheet, fill in the circle that has the same letter as your answer choice.

In modern times there has been a revolutionary change in attitude toward death-dealing diseases. For many centuries people felt that some superior force—fate or destiny—decided whether a person would fall victim to any given disease. There was little or nothing that the intended victim could do to evade the course of the ailment.

Sometimes deeply concerned parents would keep the well in contact with the ill so that all the children would get the disease at the same time.

Slowly people began to realize that inevitability need not be involved in illness. The first preventive measure taken was isolation. The victim, if possible, would be separated from the others. Or the noninfected people would flee from the area in which the disease was prevalent.

Today, thanks to medical research, we have learned more about how diseases are contracted. We not only can prevent the attack but also have developed weapons that shorten the duration and lessen the severity. In many instances, preventive measures can delay the onset of the disease for a long period of time.

Medicines today are not the only weapons available. Attention to diet, exercise, and stress has also proved very effective. As a result, more and more people are living longer and enjoying living longer.

1. During the 1400s, most people felt that
   (A) supernatural forces controlled their state of health
   (B) germs caused disease
   (C) poor food caused illness
   (D) medicines were of no help in fighting a disease
   (E) rest and exercise helped to prevent disease

2. As used in the last line of paragraph 3, "prevalent" means
   (F) trivial (G) rare (H) unknown (J) widespread (K) noncontagious

3. As a rule, we separate the well from the ill today because we believe that
   (A) the ill then can get the necessary attention
   (B) many diseases are transmitted by germs
   (C) the well do not then bother the ill
   (D) the ill get better faster
   (E) it is easier on the parents when caring for their children

4. A life-prolonging practice *not* mentioned in this passage is
   (F) proper eating habits
   (G) planned, regular exercise
   (H) controlling tension and anxiety
   (J) regulating hours of sleep
   (K) prescribing drugs

5. The author's style is best described as
   (A) dramatic (B) argumentative (C) sarcastic (D) factual (E) doleful

The quickest way to success is not to come up with a very elaborate or complicated new idea. Most effective is the introduction of a simpler version of a process already proven to do what it is claimed to do. The world beats the path to the fortunate one who invents a better mousetrap!

One of the latest examples to prove these generalizations comes from an unusual area. A former big-city police officer moved out into the suburbs, where he decided to raise sheep on his limited number of acres. As his herd increased, he faced the need for more grazing land. The additional expense required would have eaten too deeply into the slim profits of his venture.

Then the idea came. He placed a small advertisement in the city newspaper. Knowing that there are many homeowners who hate the chore of mowing their lawns, he offered to rent a sheep to anyone who wanted an automatic lawnmower from April to September.

On the day the notice was printed, he received 95 telephone calls in one hour. Within a few days he rented over 75 sheep throughout his own state and the two adjoining ones. He charged $50 a season for each animal. Most of the renters picked up and returned the sheep themselves. One customer even hired a truck for much more than the $50 fee to get the sheep.

6. The better mousetrap described in this passage attracted

(F) people who live in big cities
(G) people with lawns
(H) condominium owners
(J) people with limited incomes
(K) owners of apartment houses

7. The major advantage to the sheep's owner was that

(A) he was paid to have his sheep fed
(B) he received many telephone calls
(C) his sheep were kept in good health
(D) he could buy more land
(E) he pleased many people

8. The owner offered only a limited number of months for renting because

(F) the sheep eat best during those months
(G) the weather is best then
(H) sheep should be outdoors during that time
(J) that is the period of greatest lawn growth
(K) transportation is easiest then

9. The rental system could not have worked so well

(A) if many more people had placed orders
(B) if the owner had fewer sheep
(C) if the owner had a partner
(D) if the owner wanted the scheme to make him wealthy
(E) if the owner possessed less land

10. According to the author, the rental system was successful because

(F) it was so unusual
(G) it was inexpensive
(H) people love sheep
(J) it was simple
(K) the owner used a publicity consultant

The American flag does not belong to any political group. Those of our citizens who want a change in government misuse the flag when they burn, rip, or drag it in the dust. They who insist that their point of view is represented by the "Stars and Stripes" also misuse it.

Our flag is a symbol of our patriotism. It stands for our unity as a country and a people. It brings together a varied countryside and millions from very different backgrounds.

Ours is a patriotism not of blood and soil but of liberal and humane values. We come from too many different racial backgrounds to claim that our ancestry is the unifying factor. We do not focus on tradition, like the British monarchy, to bind us into a strong nation. Nor do we have a group of martyrs—as do the Irish—to bring us into oneness.

Without the Constitution and the Bill of Rights, our very nationhood would vanish. We are bound together by the equality and liberty they define. Our love of country stems from our uniqueness as a nation. Citizenship means that you have to look after not only yourself but the other fellow as well because you know that the other fellow would look after you.

Our ability to accept social responsibility has made us a model for other nations. The American flag is the symbol of our hopes and achievements. It represents all of us. It is not the exclusive property of any division among us.

11. The most appropriate day for this passage to appear as a newspaper editorial would be

(A) Christmas Day
(B) Thanksgiving Day
(C) July 4
(D) Labor Day
(E) January 1

12. Which of the following is a suitable title for this selection?

(F) Respect for Our Flag
(G) Desecrating the Flag
(H) Our Beliefs and Achievements
(J) The American Flag, A Symbol
(K) Britain and the American Flag

13. In this passage, the author defines

(A) tradition
(B) patriotism
(C) liberty
(D) social responsibility
(E) political groups

14. One of the martyrs referred to in this passage is

(F) Nathan Hale
(G) a New York City police officer killed in the line of duty
(H) an Air Force pilot shot down in Vietnam
(J) a person who died in the struggle to unite his or her country
(K) a President shot by an assassin's bullet

15. The people of the United States are different from the citizens of the rest of the world because of

(A) our laws that protect the individual
(B) our military power
(C) our high standard of living
(D) our abundant natural resources
(E) our way of life

16. The American flag stands for

(F) our government leaders
(G) those who do not want to change our form of government
(H) ideas that bind, not divide
(J) our greatness as a nation
(K) our willingness to sacrifice in times of danger

Susanna was so upset that she tried to hide her turmoil from her family. A bit more silent than usual, she did her after-dinner chores as efficiently as ever. As soon as she could, she went to her room, supposedly to do her usual stint of work for school. Fortunately, no one had detected that she was in such anguish. Had her parents or her sister Ellen questioned her, she would not have been able to hold back the tears that had been threatening ever since the scene outside the science classroom.

In her room, she sat for a long time at her desk, staring with unseeing eyes. The paper before her was blank. The pen was clenched in her hand, but she made no move to begin to write.

As her thinking began to reach a direction for action, Susanna knew that she had made the right decision. She could not call Margie on the phone. She knew that she would be unable to control her voice or keep back the intense feelings she had. In writing, on the other hand, she could pour out her hurt at a pace she could control. Without interruption, she would be able to say what had to be said.

How could Margie have accused her of doing such a thing! Margie was her best friend. Susanna could never say or do anything to hurt her. Margie was the one she depended on, the one she always confided in. What hurt her most was not what Margie had said. Susanna knew that you must not build on what people say in anger. No, those bitter remarks could be swallowed; they were not at the basis of her unhappiness. What upset her most was that Margie could even think that her best friend would do such a thing!

Susanna was unaware that outside a threatening snowstorm had begun. The front lawn and pavement had already turned a uniform white. Finally, she lowered her pen and began

Dearest Margie,

17. Susanna's difficulty began

(A) at breakfast
(B) on the school bus
(C) in a school corridor
(D) after dinner
(E) in science class

18. This passage does *not* reveal
    (F) who Margie was
    (G) the mood Margie was in when she met Susanna
    (H) how Susanna reacted to Margie's statements during the meeting
    (J) what Susanna was supposed to have done
    (K) how Susanna felt toward Margie

19. The attitude of the author toward Susanna can best be described as
    (A) sympathetic
    (B) condemnatory
    (C) sentimental
    (D) critical
    (E) cynical

20. The snowstorm is described to emphasize
    (F) Susanna's outward calmness
    (G) the time of year of the story
    (H) Susanna's innocence
    (J) how absorbed Susanna was in her feelings
    (K) how concerned nature was with Susanna's problem

21. Humor can be found in
    (A) Margie's reactions
    (B) Susanna's being so upset
    (C) Susanna's sister's comments
    (D) the first line of Susanna's letter
    (E) Susanna's not telling her parents

Importation of birds, animals, and plants is often disastrous for a region because conditions can often permit expansion of foreign species. The natural limitations imposed by the ecological chain are broken, and an imported specimen without a natural enemy in its new environment soon multiplies out of control.

A member of the weaver bird family, misnamed the English sparrow, was introduced into the United States during the early 1800s. It soon became a great nuisance in our cities. Only when the introduction of the automobile eliminated the horses on our streets did the number of sparrows diminish.

The English starling was introduced into this country in 1890. Today it has replaced the sparrow as the nuisance bird. It gathers in large flocks, driving out other birds, and its constant noise is most disagreeable.

With just as unhappy results, the Australian pine was introduced into Florida from the Pacific islands. Along with the melaleuca and Brazilian pepper, both imports, this fast-growing tree threatens to wipe out native trees and shrubs.

22. The English starlings are considered pests because
    (F) they transmit dangerous diseases
    (G) they attack human beings
    (H) they discourage other birds
    (J) they are so large
    (K) they eat garden plants

23. Floridians want to control the Brazilian pepper shrubs because
    (A) their red berries attract too many birds
    (B) they replace the native palmetto
    (C) their leaves irritate the skin when touched
    (D) they are not attractive looking
    (E) they block out the sun

24. The importations that are discussed in this passage involve
    (F) buying and selling
    (G) use of pets
    (H) developing new species
    (J) scientific experimentation
    (K) unrestricted admission

25. The author explains
    (A) how the species were brought over
    (B) the measures taken to control the newcomers
    (C) why these species were brought in
    (D) why the newcomers multiplied
    (E) the average life of the newcomers

26. A conclusion that can be drawn from this article is that
    (F) all imported species do well in this country
    (G) we should not import new species
    (H) we cannot predict how an imported species will react
    (J) we should import very few foreign species
    (K) all imported species become pests

Throughout Israel patient archeologists are busy digging to find remnants of civilizations that flourished hundreds and thousands of years ago.

Dotting the landscape, especially along old caravan routes, are tels. A tel is a people-made hill built by successive settlements over centuries.

In ancient days, the protective outer walls and inner buildings of towns and cities were made of sun-dried bricks. In time these cities were destroyed by enemy troops or were abandoned and allowed to collapse through decay.

The site was usually elevated and close to a supply of water. Because of these advantages, a succeeding group would choose to build on the same location. Since the houses required neither elaborate foundations nor cellars, new dwellings were constructed on top of the ruins. Often coins, pots, and tools of the previous inhabitants were buried in the rubble underneath each structure.

Over the centuries, this process of raising, leveling, and again raising buildings was repeated many times. With each new town, the level of the mound, or tel, rose steadily above the surrounding plain. Each layer contained many remnants of the preceding group.

The lowest layer represents the earliest period while upper ones correspond to later times. The layers in Tel Anafa in Upper Galilee have been explored for many years. Researchers have uncovered traces that range from a 16th century Turkish settlement to a group that inhabited the area during the Early Bronze Age, about 3000 B.C.

The tels are protected by the Israeli government. Only officially approved groups are permitted to dig in specific areas for a limited amount of time.

Digging in four-by-four-meter squares, excavators carefully remove the soil layer by layer. They begin with small handpicks and trowels. When sifting, they use whisk brooms, dental picks, and medical tweezers. The depth of each level is measured. The remains of floor or walls are photographed. From the items measured and photographed, master plans are deduced by architects. The master plan helps the archeologists verify the period to which the findings belong.

The materials most frequently found are pieces of pottery and coins. Many of the broken pieces of pottery, called *shards,* can be glued back to form complete clay pots.

The bits and pieces belonging to past civilizations are carefully put together to give us a realistic glimpse into our past.

27. People built one city on top of another to
    (A) save money
    (B) raise the city higher
    (C) save time
    (D) take advantage of a good location
    (E) get the most benefit from slave labor

28. A disadvantage of the type of bricks used by ancient people was that
    (F) they could not be made nearby
    (G) they could not be put together by unskilled labor
    (H) they could crumble
    (J) they offered little protection from enemy attack
    (K) they did not keep out the cold

29. The Israeli government controls the digs around the tels
    (A) to prevent valuables from getting into enemy hands
    (B) to prevent the tels from being lowered
    (C) to learn as much as possible from each dig
    (D) to prevent the museums from becoming overcrowded
    (E) to increase the value of the findings

30. The earliest inhabitants of Tel Anafa were most likely identified by

 (F) the type of buildings they lived in
 (G) the clothing they wore
 (H) the type of food they grew
 (J) the date on the coins they left behind
 (K) the tools they used

31. The archeologists prove their patience by

 (A) working in four-by-four meter squares
 (B) the types of tools they use
 (C) gluing together complete clay pots
 (D) the photographs they take
 (E) working in the hot sun

As more and more people take to the outdoors, the remote wilderness becomes an attractive goal to thousands. They come back-packing, canoeing, walking, or even cycling and jogging along back country roads. The introduction of ultralight camping gear and dehydrated foods has made it possible for these adventurers to go farther and stay longer than ever before.

Too often, however, modern campers lack survival skills and are completely dependent on the food they carry in their packs. A simple accident that separates them from the contents of their pack could mean disaster ending in death.

Experienced guides urge all who walk through isolated woodlands to learn enough to avoid such fatal mistakes. The amount of time required is so little! Most books on camping contain the vital information. Even a very elementary knowledge of more common edible plants can enable the lost or strayed person not only to survive but also to thrive. In the woods a little knowledge can go a long way; it can get you out alive!

Dandelions in early spring and chickweed leaves throughout the growing season, when eaten raw, make a tasty combination. The cat-tail is also known as the cat-o-nine-tail, flag, and cossack asparagus. It is a year-round food source. In the spring, the young stems can be easily collected. When the leaves are pulled away, the crisp, white core can be eaten raw. Green immature flower spikes can be eaten as a cooked vegetable. With the outer husk removed, the spikes can be cooked in boiled water for a few minutes and then eaten like corn on the cob.

These are only three examples of the many familiar plants that can be the difference between survival and starvation. Once you become familiar with the food potential in the world of wild plants, you will discover that the best reason for learning about them is that any of them are delicious!

32. Which of the following statements is (are) true of the survival skills stressed in this passage?

 I. They are needed by all who hike in the woods.
 II. They can be learned through experience only.
 III. They involve avoiding the wildlife in the woods.

 (F) I only
 (G) II only
 (H) III only
 (J) I and II only
 (K) I, II, and III

33. This passage does *not* contain advice on

 (A) how to avoid hunger pangs while camping
 (B) where to find the necessary information on edible plants
 (C) how to prepare wild plants by cooking
 (D) how to get out of the woods
 (E) eating common weeds

34. Even those who will never go deep into the woods should know about edible wild plants

 (F) so that they can tell other people
 (G) because a little knowledge goes a long way
 (H) because many are very tasty
 (J) because the information is free
 (K) because the information is easy to locate

35. Many people gather dandelions to use as a food source

(A) all year round
(B) when the plant is fairly young
(C) mainly when the plant is mature
(D) after the plants have flowered
(E) because the plants are rich in vitamins

At once a voice arose among
The bleak twigs overhead
In a full-hearted evensong
Of joy illimited.
An aged thrush, frail, gaunt, and small,
In blast beruffled plume,
Had chosen thus to fling his soul
Upon the growing gloom,
So little cause for carolings
Of such ecstatic sound
Was written on terrestrial things
Afar or nigh around,
That I could think there trembled through
His happy goodnight air
Some blessed Hope, whereof he knew
And I was unaware.

36. The incident described in the selection occurred

(F) at daybreak
(G) during a storm
(H) on a wintry evening
(J) on a crowded city street
(K) high on a hill

37. To what was the thrush's song in sharp contrast?

I. The appearance of the bird
II. The mood of the speaker
III. The bleak surroundings

(A) I only
(B) II only
(C) III only
(D) I and II only
(E) I, II, and III

38. The "happy goodnight air" was

(F) the song the bird sang
(G) the appearance of the bird
(H) the surroundings
(J) Hope itself
(K) the attitude of the speaker

39. Which of the following does the speaker NOT tell us?

I. Why he was depressed
II. How long the bird sang
III. What the Hope could be

(A) I only
(B) II only
(C) III only
(D) I and II only
(E) I, II, and III

40. The "terrestrial things afar or nigh around" could *not* be

(F) fear of nuclear explosions
(G) aftermath of famine
(H) the speaker
(J) the bird itself
(K) the carolings

Answers to Practice SSAT 1

SECTION 1

1. D	6. G	11. A	16. J	21. D
2. H	7. D	12. G	17. B	22. H
3. A	8. K	13. C	18. G	23. C
4. K	9. D	14. K	19. E	24. K
5. C	10. J	15. B	20. G	25. D

Rating Your Results

Superior	23–25 correct
Average	18–22 correct
Below Average	17 or fewer correct

Material to Review: Chapters 8–14

SECTION 2

1. E	7. C	13. E	19. E	25. C
2. J	8. K	14. H	20. H	26. K
3. B	9. C	15. A	21. B	27. C
4. F	10. K	16. H	22. K	28. J
5. C	11. A	17. B	23. D	29. B
6. J	12. G	18. J	24. F	30. H

Rating Your Results

Lower Level

Superior	26–30 correct
Average	23–25 correct
Below Average	22 or fewer correct

Upper Level

Superior	27–30 correct
Average	24–26 correct
Below Average	23 or fewer correct

Material to Review: Chapter 4

31. D	37. D	43. B	49. B	55. A
32. G	38. H	44. J	50. G	56. G
33. C	39. C	45. C	51. D	57. E
34. F	40. F	46. G	52. K	58. F
35. B	41. D	47. E	53. E	59. D
36. K	42. J	48. J	54. J	60. J

Rating Your Results

Lower Level

Superior	25–30 correct
Average	20–24 correct
Below Average	19 or fewer correct

Upper Level

Superior	27–30 correct
Average	21–26 correct
Below Average	23 or fewer correct

Material to Review: Chapter 4

SECTION 3

1. D	6. G	11. D	16. K	21. E
2. H	7. A	12. H	17. B	22. G
3. B	8. H	13. B	18. H	23. D
4. F	9. E	14. J	19. B	24. F
5. D	10. G	15. D	20. F	25. C

Rating Your Results

Superior	23–25 correct
Average	18–22 correct
Below Average	17 or fewer correct

Material to Review: Chapters 8–14

SECTION 4

1. A	9. D	17. C	25. D	33. D
2. J	10. J	18. J	26. H	34. H
3. B	11. C	19. A	27. D	35. B
4. J	12. J	20. J	28. H	36. H
5. D	13. B	21. D	29. C	37. E
6. G	14. J	22. H	30. K	38. F
7. A	15. A	23. B	31. B	39. E
8. J	16. H	24. K	32. F	40. K

Rating Your Results

Lower Level

Superior	34–40 correct
Average	26–33 correct
Below Average	25 or fewer correct

Upper Level

Superior	36–40 correct
Average	28–35 correct
Below Average	27 or fewer correct

Material to Review: Chapter 5

Answers Explained

SECTION 1

1. **D** $8 \times 75 \times \square = 6$

$$8 \times 75 = 600$$
$$600 \times \square = 6$$
$$\square = \frac{6}{600} = \frac{1}{100} = 0.01$$

2. **H** $0.4 + \frac{3}{100} + \frac{1}{2} =$

$\frac{3}{100} = 0.03,\ \frac{1}{2} = 0.5$

$0.4 + 0.03 + 0.5 = 0.93$

3. **A** $\square + 89.1 = 1{,}005 - 906$

$1{,}005 - 906 = 99$

$\square + 89.1 = 99$

$\square = 99 - 89.1 = 9.9$

4. **K** $40\% = 0.4$ and $0.4 \times 6 = 2.4$

Let x = the number

$2.4 = \frac{3}{4}x$

$3x = 9.6$ and $x = 3.2$

5. **C**

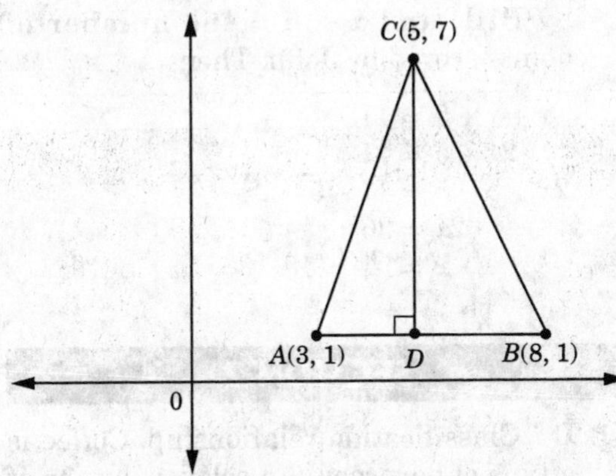

The area of $\triangle ABC = \frac{1}{2}$ base × altitude

Length of base (AB) = $8 - 3 = 5$

Length of altitude (CD) = $7 - 1 = 6$

Area = $\frac{1}{2} \times 5 \times 6 = 15$

6. **G** If $7 > N > 3$ then N is greater than 3 and less than 7. Thus, N could be 4, 5, or 6. Of these, only 6 is a multiple of 3.

7. **D** If the area of a rectangle is 240 square inches and the length of the rectangle is 20 inches, the width is $240 \div 20 = 12$ inches.

The perimeter is equal to twice the length plus twice the width.

Perimeter = $2(20) + 2(12) = 40 + 24 = 64$ inches

8. **K** The number of seats in the lecture hall is $32 \times 15 = 480$. If 75% of the seats are occupied, then 25% of the seats are vacant.

$25\% = \frac{1}{4}$ and $\frac{1}{4}$ of $480 = 120$

9. **D** Consider the choices in turn:

(A) $\frac{3}{10} = 0.3$

(B) $30\% = \frac{30}{100}$

(C) $0.300 = 0.3$

(D) $\frac{1}{3} = 0.33\frac{1}{3}$

(E) $\frac{6}{20} = \frac{3}{10} = 0.3$

10. **J** The number of people who attended on Tuesday is represented by 10 boxes, and the number who attended on Thursday by 6 boxes.

$10 - 6 = 4 \quad 4 \times 50 = 200$ people

11. **A** $\square - 4 = 3$

$\square = 3 + 4 = 7$

$6\square = 6 \times 7 = 42$

12. **G** The batter had a total of $40 + 10 = 50$ times at bat. He had a total of $12 + 4 = 16$ hits. Thus, I and II are true. To find his percent of hits, we set up the fraction $\frac{16}{50}$

$$\frac{16}{50} = \frac{32}{100} = 32\%$$

Thus, III is not true.

13. **C** $\square + 2 \times \triangle = 16$

If $\triangle = 3$, $\square + 6 = 16$

$\square = 16 - 6 = 10$

14. **K** $\frac{2}{5} = 0.40 = 40\%$

15. **B** $2.7 \times 0.96 = 27 \times \square$

$$\square = \frac{2.7 \times 0.96}{27}$$
$$27 = 2.7 \times 10$$

Thus, $\square = \frac{2.7 \times 0.96}{2.7 \times 10} = \frac{0.96}{10} = 0.096$

16. **J** $\frac{1}{3} = 0.33\frac{1}{3}$ and $\frac{1}{2} = 0.50$. Consider the choices in turn:

(F) 0.48 is greater than $\frac{1}{3}$ and less than $\frac{1}{2}$.

(G) 40% = 0.40. It is greater than $\frac{1}{3}$ and less than $\frac{1}{2}$.

(H) $\frac{3}{8} = 0.375$. It is greater than $\frac{1}{3}$ and less than $\frac{1}{2}$.

(J) $\frac{4}{7} = 0.57\frac{1}{7}$. It is greater than $\frac{1}{3}$ and *also* greater than $\frac{1}{2}$.

(K) $\frac{4}{9} = 0.44\frac{4}{9}$. It is greater than $\frac{1}{3}$ and less than $\frac{1}{2}$.

17. **B** Driving at the rate of 50 miles per hour, a motorist takes

$$\frac{1}{50}\text{ hour} = \frac{1}{50} \times 60 \times 60 = 72\text{ seconds}$$

to cover 1 mile. Driving 40 miles per hour, she takes

$$\frac{1}{40}\text{ hour} = \frac{1}{40} \times 60 \times 60 = 90\text{ seconds}$$

to cover 1 mile. The saving is 90 – 72 = 18 seconds.

18. **G** Let x = the number

Then $\frac{1}{2}x$ or $\frac{x}{2}$ = one-half the number

$$x + \frac{x}{2} > 45$$
$$2x + x > 90$$
$$3x > 90$$
$$x > 30$$

19. **E** The sum of the measures of the angles of a triangle is 180°.
180 – 68 = 112
The sum of the measures of the two equal base angles is 112°.
The measure of each base angle is 112 ÷ 2 = 56°.

20. **G** In order to find the cost of the slacks we must multiply 6 by the cost (n) of each pair: $6 \times n$ or $6 \cdot n = 6n$.

21. **D** Examine the diagram. When we double the length of each side of the square we obtain a square whose area is exactly four times the area of the original square.

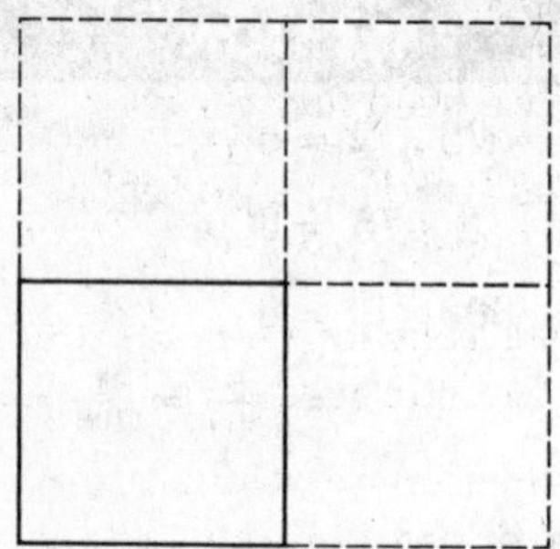

22. **H** In order to obtain the temperature at 8:00 A.M. we add: –9 + 6 = –3, or 3 degrees below zero.

23. **C** Let x = the price of the jacket

$$0.06x = \$3.90$$
$$x = \frac{3.90}{0.06} = \frac{390}{6} = \$65$$

24. **K** Let x = the number

$$\frac{x}{8} = 24 + \frac{3}{8}$$
$$x = 24 \times 8 + 3$$
$$x = 192 + 3 = 195$$

195 is a multiple of 5.

25. **D** Let x = the number of points scored by Bill, and $x + 5$ = the number of points scored by John. Then

$$x + x + 5 = 41$$
$$2x + 5 = 41$$
$$2x + 5 - 5 = 41 - 5$$
$$2x = 36$$
$$x = \frac{36}{2} = 18$$

SECTION 2

31. **D** Classification relationship. Coffee is a type of beverage. An eclair is a type of pastry.

32. **G** Synonym relationship. *Pale* means white and *ashen* means gray.

33. **C** Storage relationship. Water is stored in a reservoir; fodder is stored in a silo.

34. **F** Product relationship. What a publisher does for books, a producer does for plays.

35. **B** Synonym relationship. *Acclaim* and *praise* are synonyms; *berate* and *scold* are synonymous.

36. **K** Use relationship. Both hangars and piers are used for storage.

37. **D** Tool-user relationship. Both level and roller are tools.

38. **H** Use relationship. Both cabins and holds are storage places.

39. **C** Function relationship. A liter measures liquid volume; a foot measures linear distance.

40. **F** Payment relationship. Payment to a taxi driver is a fare while payment to a lawyer is a fee.

41. **D** Occupation relationship. The actor's lines are in the script; the musician's music is the score.

42. **J** Synonym relationship. When something is jarred, it is shaken. When something is prodded, it is pushed.

43. **B** Classification relationship. The moon is a satellite of the earth; Mercury is a planet of the sun.

44. **J** Instrument relationship. Battles are fought with weapons. Arguments are conducted mainly with words.

45. **C** Direction relationship. When something declines, it lessens. When something is elevated, it increases.

46. **G** Class relationship. In (F), mackintosh is a type of apple, not a class as are gourd and legume.

47. **E** Classification relationship. Dalmatian is a type of dog; cobra is a type of snake.

48. **J** Function relationship. The damper regulates air flow, and the valve regulates liquid or gas flow.

49. **B** Size relationship. As minute is less than small, so tiny is less than little.

50. **G** Origin relationship. The egg contains the embryo of the robin; the seed contains the embryo of grass.

51. **D** Antonym relationship. Somber is the antonym of *cheerful; counterfeit* and *authentic* are also opposites.

52. **K** Occupation relationship. A canon is the person in charge of a cathedral. A supervisor is the person in charge of a factory.

53. **E** Occupation relationship. A police officer targets crime; a teacher fights ignorance.

54. **J** Function relationship. A scale measures weight; a thermometer records temperature.

55. **A** Negative relationship. An illiterate person lacks ability to read. An ignorant person lacks knowledge.

56. **G** Function relationship. A critic's job is to determine the value of something. A novelist's job is to create with words.

57. **E** Source relationship. Intelligence is developed in the brain. Physical strength is developed in muscles.

58. **F** Intensity relationship. To repel is stronger than to annoy. Hatred is stronger than dislike.

59. **D** Definition relationship. An interval is an undetermined or indefinite period of time. A second is a measured or definite period of time.

60. **J** Guide relationship. As goals follow a pattern set by our ideals, so a train follows the tracks set for it.

SECTION 3

1. **D** If $\frac{2}{3}$ of a number = 24, then $\frac{1}{3}$ of the number = 12

   and $\frac{3}{3}$ of the number = $3 \times 12 = 36$

   $\frac{5}{9}$ of the number = $\frac{5}{9} \times 36 = 20$.

2. **H** Let the length of the base of the triangle be b and the length of the altitude be h. Then the area of the triangle is $\frac{1}{2}bh$. If we double the length of the base we have $2b$, and if we double the length of the altitude we have $2h$. The area of the enlarged triangle is $\frac{1}{2}(2b)(2h) = 2bh$.

Since $2bh$ is 4 times as great as $\frac{1}{2}bh$, the area of the enlarged triangle is 4 times as great as the area of the original triangle.

3. **B** To obtain the average of $\frac{3}{4}$ and $\frac{1}{6}$, we add these two fractions (the L.C.D. is 12) and divide the result by 2.

$\frac{3}{4} = \frac{9}{12}$, $\frac{1}{6} = \frac{2}{12}$

$\frac{9}{12} + \frac{2}{12} = \frac{11}{12}$

$\frac{1}{2} \times \frac{11}{12} = \frac{11}{24}$

4. **F** To find the fraction of the sets that were left unsold subtract. Let 1 represent the total number of sets.

$1 - \frac{1}{3} = \frac{2}{3} - \frac{1}{4} = \frac{5}{12} - \frac{1}{8} = \frac{7}{24}$

5. **D** Let x = the number

32% of $x = 48$

$0.32x = 48$

$x = \frac{48}{0.32} = 150$

6. **G** Consider the proper fraction $\frac{3}{8}$. If we add 2 to both numerator and denominator we have $\frac{5}{10}$, or $\frac{1}{2}$. Clearly, the value of the fraction has increased. Consider the proper fraction $\frac{a}{b}$ $(b > a)$. If we add n to both numerator and denominator we have $\frac{a+n}{b+n}$. Now, $\frac{a+n}{b+n}$ will be greater than $\frac{a}{b}$ if $b(a + n)$ is greater than $a(b + n)$. $ab + bn$ is greater than $ab + an$ because $bn > an$.

7. **A** $4x^3 = 4(x)(x)(x) = 4\left(\frac{1}{2}\right)\left(\frac{1}{2}\right)\left(\frac{1}{2}\right) = \frac{1}{2}$

8. **H** We evaluate each alternative:

(F) $2 \div 0.03 = \frac{200}{3} = 66\frac{2}{3}$

(G) $3.6 \times 1.8 = 6.48$

(H) $(2.4)^2 = 5.76$

(J) $8 \div 0.4 = \frac{80}{4} = 20$

(K) $3.8 + 4.2 = 8.0$

Clearly, $(2.4)^2$ is closest to 6.

9. **E** The average rate of speed is obtained by dividing the total mileage by the total time.

Time on trip out $= \frac{600}{400} = 1\frac{1}{2}$ hours

Time on return trip $= \frac{600}{300} = 2$ hours

Average speed $= \frac{1{,}200}{3\frac{1}{2}} = 1{,}200 \div \frac{7}{2}$

$= 1{,}200 \times \frac{2}{7} = \frac{2{,}400}{7} = 342\frac{6}{7}$

10. **G** $6 < x < 10$ tells us that x is greater than 6 but less than 10.

$8 > x > 4$ tells us that x is greater than 4 but less than 8.

The number 7 meets both conditions.

11. **D** If the sum of two numbers is y and one of the numbers is 6, then the other number is $y - 6$. Twice the number $y - 6$ is $2(y - 6)$.

12. **H** The perimeter of the rectangle $ABCD = AB + BC + CD + AD$.

$AB = 7, BC = 4, CD = 7, AD = 4$.

Perimeter = 22

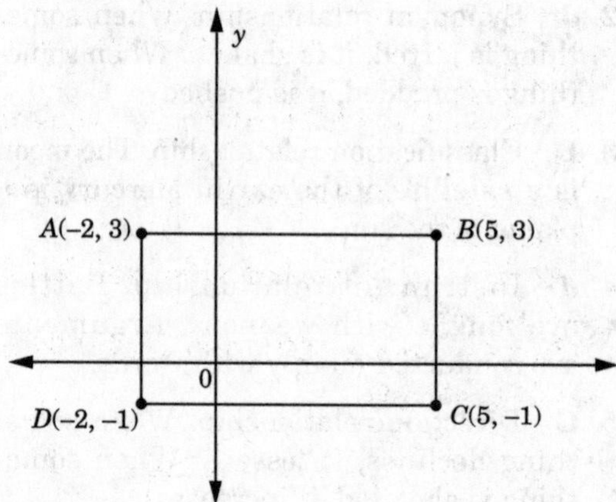

13. **B** $\overline{6} \square \overline{2} = (6 + 2) + (6 - 2) = 8 + 4 = 12$.

14. **J** $\overline{N} \square \overline{6} = (N + 6) + (N - 6) = N + 6 + N - 6 = 2N$

$2N = 10, N = 5$

15. **D** $\overline{B} \square \overline{B} = (B + B) + (B - B) = 2B$

$\overline{A} \square \overline{B} = (A + B) + (A - B) = 2A$

$\overline{A} \square \frac{1}{A} = \left(A + \frac{1}{A}\right) + \left(A - \frac{1}{A}\right) = 2A$

Only the second and third equations are true.

16. **K** If 6 ounces of butter are used instead of 8 ounces, we must use $\frac{6}{8}$, or $\frac{3}{4}$, of all other ingredients:

$\frac{3}{4} \times 3 = \frac{9}{4} = 2\frac{1}{4}$

17. **B** Let x = the mileage to be covered that day

$0.36x = 162$

$x = \frac{162}{0.36} = \frac{16{,}200}{36} = 450$

18. **H** If we subtract 3 from both members of this equation, we have

$x + 5 - 3 = y + 3 - 3$

$x + 2 = y$

If $x + 2 = y$, then $y > x$.

19. **B** Let x = the height of the oil in the tank, in feet.

Then $(20)(12)x = 1{,}200$

$240x = 1{,}200$

$x = \frac{1{,}200}{240} = 5$

20. **F** To find the number of sixths in $2\frac{3}{4}$ we must divide $2\frac{3}{4}$ by $\frac{1}{6}$.

$2\frac{3}{4} \div \frac{1}{6} = \frac{11}{4} \div \frac{1}{6} = \frac{11}{4} \times 6 = \frac{33}{2} = 16\frac{1}{2}$

21. **E** The area of the front wall = 8×20 = 160 square feet.
The area of the back wall = 160 square feet.
The area of a side wall = $8 \times 12 = 96$ square feet.
The area of the other side wall = 96 square feet.
The total area = $160 + 160 + 96 + 96$ = 512 square feet.

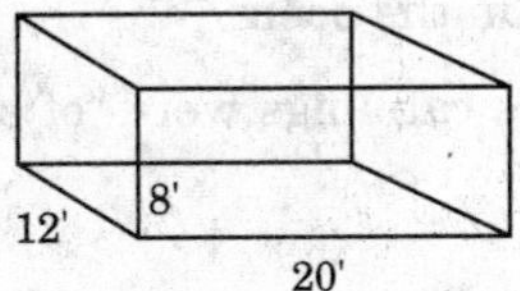

22. **G** $7 \times 9 \times 6 \times \square = 54 \times 56$

Since $9 \times 6 = 54$, we have

$7 \times 54 \times \square = 54 \times 56$

$7\square = 56$, $\square = 8$

23. **D** Since 4 ounces $= \frac{4}{16} = \frac{1}{4}$ pound, 3 pounds 4 ounces = $3\frac{1}{4}$ pounds.

$3\frac{1}{4} = 3.25$ and $3.25 \times \$0.76 = \$2.47$

24. **F** Let x = the number of hits the player will get in 160 games. We may now set up the following proportion:

$\frac{87}{96} = \frac{x}{160}$

$96x = 87 \times 160$

$x = \frac{87 \times 160}{96} = 145$

25. **C** The cost of the notebooks = $3x$ cents. Amount girl receives in change = $\$5.00 - 3x$.

SECTION 4

1. **A** "...some superior force—fate or destiny—decided whether a person would fall victim to any given disease."

2. **J** People fled the area because the disease was widespread. They would not have left if the disease had been trivial, rare, unknown, or noncontagious.

3. **B** Inferential answer based on third paragraph.

4. **J** Elimination of choices applied to last paragraph.

5. **D** The author gives facts calmly and objectively without being emotional.

6. **G** "Knowing that there are many home owners who hate the chore of mowing their lawns...."

7. **A** "He charged $50 a season for each animal."

8. **J** Process of elimination of choices based on third paragraph.

9. **D** "... he rented over 75 sheep...." "He charged $50 a season for each animal." These numbers don't imply wealth.

10. **J** "Most effective is the introduction of a simpler version ..."

11. **C** Elimination of choices based on third and fourth paragraphs.

12. **J** The entire selection deals with the qualities the flag symbolizes—equality, liberty, social responsibility.

13. **B** "Ours is a patriotism not of blood and soil but of liberal and humane values."

14. **J** "Nor do we have a group of martyrs —as do the Irish—to bring us into oneness."

15. **A** Fourth paragraph: "our uniqueness as a nation. Citizenship means...the other fellow as well...."

16. **H** "Our flag...stands for our unity as a country and a people." "It represents all of us."

17. **C** "...tears that had been threatening ever since the scene outside the science classroom."

18. **J** Elimination of choices based on entire selection.

19. **A** The author describes the entire incident from Susanna's point of view. Susanna's upset state is presented with understanding and sympathy.

20. **J** "Susanna was unaware that outside a threatening snowstorm had begun."

21. **D** In view of what has gone before, "*Dearest Margie*" is an unexpected salutation.

22. **H** Elimination of choices based on third paragraph.

23. **B** "...this fast-growing tree threatens to wipe out our native trees and shrubs."

24. **K** Elimination of choices based on first paragraph.

25. **D** "...an imported specimen without a natural enemy in its new environment soon multiplies out of control."

26. **H** "Importation of birds, animals, and plants is often disastrous..."

27. **D** "Because of these advantages, a succeeding group would choose to build on the same location."

28. **H** Third paragraph: "buildings were made of sun-dried bricks"; "... allowed to collapse through decay."

29. **C** Inferential answer based on last paragraph.

30. **K** Inferential answer based on: "... that range from...to a group that inhabited the area during the Early Bronze Age...."

31. **B** "When sifting, they use whisk brooms, dental picks, and medical tweezers."

32. **F** "Experienced guides urge all who walk through isolated woodlands to learn enough to avoid such fatal mistakes."

33. **D** Elimination of choices based on entire selection.

34. **H** ". . . you will discover that the best reason for learning about them is that many of them are delicious."

35. **B** "Dandelions in early spring and chickweed leaves ... make a tasty combination."

36. **H** "...The bleak twigs overhead ..."; "a fullhearted evensong."

37. **E** The song was a "happy goodnight air," the bird was "frail, gaunt" (I); the surroundings are characterized by "the growing gloom" (III); and the poet by "Hope [of which] I was unaware" (II).

38. **F** "Air" is a synonym for *tune*.

39. **E** None of the three choices is mentioned in the poem.

40. **K** The carolings were "of such ecstatic sound."

Answer Sheet Practice Secondary School Admission Test 2

SECTION 1

1. Ⓐ Ⓑ Ⓒ Ⓓ Ⓔ
2. Ⓕ Ⓖ Ⓗ Ⓙ Ⓚ
3. Ⓐ Ⓑ Ⓒ Ⓓ Ⓔ
4. Ⓕ Ⓖ Ⓗ Ⓙ Ⓚ
5. Ⓐ Ⓑ Ⓒ Ⓓ Ⓔ
6. Ⓕ Ⓖ Ⓗ Ⓙ Ⓚ
7. Ⓐ Ⓑ Ⓒ Ⓓ Ⓔ
8. Ⓕ Ⓖ Ⓗ Ⓙ Ⓚ
9. Ⓐ Ⓑ Ⓒ Ⓓ Ⓔ
10. Ⓕ Ⓖ Ⓗ Ⓙ Ⓚ
11. Ⓐ Ⓑ Ⓒ Ⓓ Ⓔ
12. Ⓕ Ⓖ Ⓗ Ⓙ Ⓚ
13. Ⓐ Ⓑ Ⓒ Ⓓ Ⓔ
14. Ⓕ Ⓖ Ⓗ Ⓙ Ⓚ
15. Ⓐ Ⓑ Ⓒ Ⓓ Ⓔ
16. Ⓕ Ⓖ Ⓗ Ⓙ Ⓚ
17. Ⓐ Ⓑ Ⓒ Ⓓ Ⓔ
18. Ⓕ Ⓖ Ⓗ Ⓙ Ⓚ
19. Ⓐ Ⓑ Ⓒ Ⓓ Ⓔ
20. Ⓕ Ⓖ Ⓗ Ⓙ Ⓚ
21. Ⓐ Ⓑ Ⓒ Ⓓ Ⓔ
22. Ⓕ Ⓖ Ⓗ Ⓙ Ⓚ
23. Ⓐ Ⓑ Ⓒ Ⓓ Ⓔ
24. Ⓕ Ⓖ Ⓗ Ⓙ Ⓚ
25. Ⓐ Ⓑ Ⓒ Ⓓ Ⓔ

SECTION 2

1. Ⓐ Ⓑ Ⓒ Ⓓ Ⓔ
2. Ⓕ Ⓖ Ⓗ Ⓙ Ⓚ
3. Ⓐ Ⓑ Ⓒ Ⓓ Ⓔ
4. Ⓕ Ⓖ Ⓗ Ⓙ Ⓚ
5. Ⓐ Ⓑ Ⓒ Ⓓ Ⓔ
6. Ⓕ Ⓖ Ⓗ Ⓙ Ⓚ
7. Ⓐ Ⓑ Ⓒ Ⓓ Ⓔ
8. Ⓕ Ⓖ Ⓗ Ⓙ Ⓚ
9. Ⓐ Ⓑ Ⓒ Ⓓ Ⓔ
10. Ⓕ Ⓖ Ⓗ Ⓙ Ⓚ
11. Ⓐ Ⓑ Ⓒ Ⓓ Ⓔ
12. Ⓕ Ⓖ Ⓗ Ⓙ Ⓚ
13. Ⓐ Ⓑ Ⓒ Ⓓ Ⓔ
14. Ⓕ Ⓖ Ⓗ Ⓙ Ⓚ
15. Ⓐ Ⓑ Ⓒ Ⓓ Ⓔ
16. Ⓕ Ⓖ Ⓗ Ⓙ Ⓚ
17. Ⓐ Ⓑ Ⓒ Ⓓ Ⓔ
18. Ⓕ Ⓖ Ⓗ Ⓙ Ⓚ
19. Ⓐ Ⓑ Ⓒ Ⓓ Ⓔ
20. Ⓕ Ⓖ Ⓗ Ⓙ Ⓚ
21. Ⓐ Ⓑ Ⓒ Ⓓ Ⓔ
22. Ⓕ Ⓖ Ⓗ Ⓙ Ⓚ
23. Ⓐ Ⓑ Ⓒ Ⓓ Ⓔ
24. Ⓕ Ⓖ Ⓗ Ⓙ Ⓚ
25. Ⓐ Ⓑ Ⓒ Ⓓ Ⓔ
26. Ⓕ Ⓖ Ⓗ Ⓙ Ⓚ
27. Ⓐ Ⓑ Ⓒ Ⓓ Ⓔ
28. Ⓕ Ⓖ Ⓗ Ⓙ Ⓚ
29. Ⓐ Ⓑ Ⓒ Ⓓ Ⓔ
30. Ⓕ Ⓖ Ⓗ Ⓙ Ⓚ
31. Ⓐ Ⓑ Ⓒ Ⓓ Ⓔ
32. Ⓕ Ⓖ Ⓗ Ⓙ Ⓚ
33. Ⓐ Ⓑ Ⓒ Ⓓ Ⓔ
34. Ⓕ Ⓖ Ⓗ Ⓙ Ⓚ
35. Ⓐ Ⓑ Ⓒ Ⓓ Ⓔ
36. Ⓕ Ⓖ Ⓗ Ⓙ Ⓚ
37. Ⓐ Ⓑ Ⓒ Ⓓ Ⓔ
38. Ⓕ Ⓖ Ⓗ Ⓙ Ⓚ
39. Ⓐ Ⓑ Ⓒ Ⓓ Ⓔ
40. Ⓕ Ⓖ Ⓗ Ⓙ Ⓚ
41. Ⓐ Ⓑ Ⓒ Ⓓ Ⓔ
42. Ⓕ Ⓖ Ⓗ Ⓙ Ⓚ
43. Ⓐ Ⓑ Ⓒ Ⓓ Ⓔ
44. Ⓕ Ⓖ Ⓗ Ⓙ Ⓚ
45. Ⓐ Ⓑ Ⓒ Ⓓ Ⓔ
46. Ⓕ Ⓖ Ⓗ Ⓙ Ⓚ
47. Ⓐ Ⓑ Ⓒ Ⓓ Ⓔ
48. Ⓕ Ⓖ Ⓗ Ⓙ Ⓚ
49. Ⓐ Ⓑ Ⓒ Ⓓ Ⓔ
50. Ⓕ Ⓖ Ⓗ Ⓙ Ⓚ
51. Ⓐ Ⓑ Ⓒ Ⓓ Ⓔ
52. Ⓕ Ⓖ Ⓗ Ⓙ Ⓚ
53. Ⓐ Ⓑ Ⓒ Ⓓ Ⓔ
54. Ⓕ Ⓖ Ⓗ Ⓙ Ⓚ
55. Ⓐ Ⓑ Ⓒ Ⓓ Ⓔ
56. Ⓕ Ⓖ Ⓗ Ⓙ Ⓚ
57. Ⓐ Ⓑ Ⓒ Ⓓ Ⓔ
58. Ⓕ Ⓖ Ⓗ Ⓙ Ⓚ
59. Ⓐ Ⓑ Ⓒ Ⓓ Ⓔ
60. Ⓕ Ⓖ Ⓗ Ⓙ Ⓚ

SECTION 3

1. Ⓕ Ⓖ Ⓗ Ⓙ Ⓚ
2. Ⓐ Ⓑ Ⓒ Ⓓ Ⓔ
3. Ⓕ Ⓖ Ⓗ Ⓙ Ⓚ
4. Ⓐ Ⓑ Ⓒ Ⓓ Ⓔ
5. Ⓕ Ⓖ Ⓗ Ⓙ Ⓚ
6. Ⓐ Ⓑ Ⓒ Ⓓ Ⓔ
7. Ⓕ Ⓖ Ⓗ Ⓙ Ⓚ
8. Ⓐ Ⓑ Ⓒ Ⓓ Ⓔ
9. Ⓕ Ⓖ Ⓗ Ⓙ Ⓚ
10. Ⓐ Ⓑ Ⓒ Ⓓ Ⓔ
11. Ⓕ Ⓖ Ⓗ Ⓙ Ⓚ
12. Ⓐ Ⓑ Ⓒ Ⓓ Ⓔ
13. Ⓕ Ⓖ Ⓗ Ⓙ Ⓚ
14. Ⓐ Ⓑ Ⓒ Ⓓ Ⓔ
15. Ⓕ Ⓖ Ⓗ Ⓙ Ⓚ
16. Ⓐ Ⓑ Ⓒ Ⓓ Ⓔ
17. Ⓕ Ⓖ Ⓗ Ⓙ Ⓚ
18. Ⓐ Ⓑ Ⓒ Ⓓ Ⓔ
19. Ⓕ Ⓖ Ⓗ Ⓙ Ⓚ
20. Ⓐ Ⓑ Ⓒ Ⓓ Ⓔ
21. Ⓕ Ⓖ Ⓗ Ⓙ Ⓚ
22. Ⓐ Ⓑ Ⓒ Ⓓ Ⓔ
23. Ⓕ Ⓖ Ⓗ Ⓙ Ⓚ
24. Ⓐ Ⓑ Ⓒ Ⓓ Ⓔ
25. Ⓕ Ⓖ Ⓗ Ⓙ Ⓚ

SECTION 4

1. Ⓐ Ⓑ Ⓒ Ⓓ Ⓔ
2. Ⓕ Ⓖ Ⓗ Ⓙ Ⓚ
3. Ⓐ Ⓑ Ⓒ Ⓓ Ⓔ
4. Ⓕ Ⓖ Ⓗ Ⓙ Ⓚ
5. Ⓐ Ⓑ Ⓒ Ⓓ Ⓔ
6. Ⓕ Ⓖ Ⓗ Ⓙ Ⓚ
7. Ⓐ Ⓑ Ⓒ Ⓓ Ⓔ
8. Ⓕ Ⓖ Ⓗ Ⓙ Ⓚ
9. Ⓐ Ⓑ Ⓒ Ⓓ Ⓔ
10. Ⓕ Ⓖ Ⓗ Ⓙ Ⓚ
11. Ⓐ Ⓑ Ⓒ Ⓓ Ⓔ
12. Ⓕ Ⓖ Ⓗ Ⓙ Ⓚ
13. Ⓐ Ⓑ Ⓒ Ⓓ Ⓔ
14. Ⓕ Ⓖ Ⓗ Ⓙ Ⓚ
15. Ⓐ Ⓑ Ⓒ Ⓓ Ⓔ
16. Ⓕ Ⓖ Ⓗ Ⓙ Ⓚ
17. Ⓐ Ⓑ Ⓒ Ⓓ Ⓔ
18. Ⓕ Ⓖ Ⓗ Ⓙ Ⓚ
19. Ⓐ Ⓑ Ⓒ Ⓓ Ⓔ
20. Ⓕ Ⓖ Ⓗ Ⓙ Ⓚ
21. Ⓐ Ⓑ Ⓒ Ⓓ Ⓔ
22. Ⓕ Ⓖ Ⓗ Ⓙ Ⓚ
23. Ⓐ Ⓑ Ⓒ Ⓓ Ⓔ
24. Ⓕ Ⓖ Ⓗ Ⓙ Ⓚ
25. Ⓐ Ⓑ Ⓒ Ⓓ Ⓔ
26. Ⓕ Ⓖ Ⓗ Ⓙ Ⓚ
27. Ⓐ Ⓑ Ⓒ Ⓓ Ⓔ
28. Ⓕ Ⓖ Ⓗ Ⓙ Ⓚ
29. Ⓐ Ⓑ Ⓒ Ⓓ Ⓔ
30. Ⓕ Ⓖ Ⓗ Ⓙ Ⓚ
31. Ⓐ Ⓑ Ⓒ Ⓓ Ⓔ
32. Ⓕ Ⓖ Ⓗ Ⓙ Ⓚ
33. Ⓐ Ⓑ Ⓒ Ⓓ Ⓔ
34. Ⓕ Ⓖ Ⓗ Ⓙ Ⓚ
35. Ⓐ Ⓑ Ⓒ Ⓓ Ⓔ
36. Ⓕ Ⓖ Ⓗ Ⓙ Ⓚ
37. Ⓐ Ⓑ Ⓒ Ⓓ Ⓔ
38. Ⓕ Ⓖ Ⓗ Ⓙ Ⓚ
39. Ⓐ Ⓑ Ⓒ Ⓓ Ⓔ
40. Ⓕ Ⓖ Ⓗ Ⓙ Ⓚ

Practice Secondary School Admission Test 2

SECTION 1

Time—25 minutes
25 questions

DIRECTIONS: Five possible answers follow each question below. You may work out each problem in your head or use the margins of the test pages for scratch work. Decide which of the five possible answers is best. On the Answer Sheet fill in the circle with the letter that corresponds to your answer choice.

SAMPLE PROBLEM:

$$\begin{array}{r} 7{,}524 \\ -6{,}736 \\ \hline \end{array}$$

(A) 788 (B) 798 (C) 898 (D) 1,788 (E) 1,888

● Ⓑ Ⓒ Ⓓ Ⓔ

1. 1,200 – 409 =

   (A) 801 (B) 891 (C) 791 (D) 881 (E) 781

2. One-third of a number is 2 less than 10. What is the number?

   (F) 11 (G) 4 (H) 36 (J) 20 (K) 24

3. At noon the temperature was 6 degrees above zero. By midnight the temperature had fallen 9 degrees. The temperature at midnight was

   (A) 15° below zero
   (B) 3° above zero
   (C) 3° below zero
   (D) 15° above zero
   (E) 6° below zero

4. The value of $2^8 \div 2^2$ is

   (F) 16 (G) 64 (H) 26 (J) 6 (K) 9

5. If $16 \times \frac{3}{8} \times \square = 15 \times 32$, then the value of $\square$ is

   (A) 80 (B) 8 (C) 40 (D) 60 (E) 64

6. $3{,}675 \div 0.07 =$

   (F) 525 (G) 5,250 (H) 5,050 (J) 52,500 (K) 525,000

7. $\dfrac{3\frac{1}{4} - \frac{5}{6}}{\frac{7}{12}} =$

   (A) $2\frac{5}{12}$ (B) $3\frac{4}{7}$ (C) $4\frac{1}{12}$ (D) $2\frac{7}{12}$ (E) $4\frac{1}{7}$

8. On a circle graph the angle at the center of a sector representing the fraction $\frac{1}{8}$ is

   (F) 90° (G) 60° (H) 80° (J) 75° (K) 45°

9. The circle graph shows how Fred spends a day. Approximately how many hours of sleep does he get?

   (A) 8 (B) 10 (C) 7 (D) 9 (E) 12

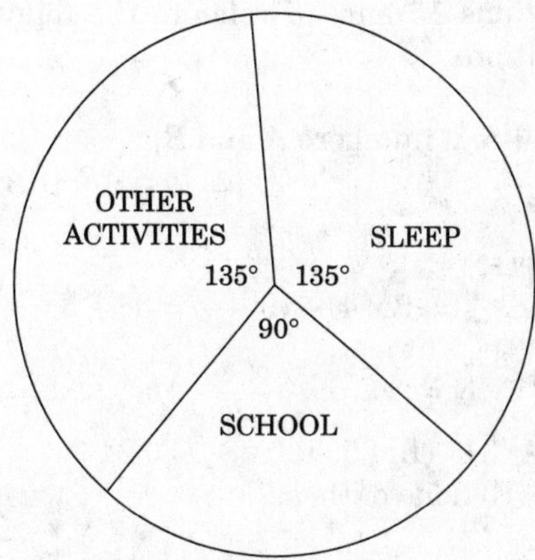

10. Of the numbers 3.01, 4.57, 6.02, and 7.75, the two that are closest in value to each other are

    (F) 3.01 and 6.02 (G) 4.57 and 7.75 (H) 3.01 and 4.57 (J) 4.67 and 6.02 (K) 6.02 and 7.75

11. A movie theater has $\frac{3}{4}$ of its seats occupied. After 100 people leave, $\frac{2}{3}$ of the seats are occupied. How many seats does the theater have?

    (A) 1,000 (B) 900 (C) 1,200 (D) 800 (E) 1,500

12. In the multiplication example below, the symbols △ and □ represent digits that give a correct product. What is the sum of these digits?

$$\begin{array}{r} 49 \\ \times\,\underline{\triangle 5} \\ 245 \\ \underline{\text{- - -}} \\ \square - 75 \end{array}$$

    (F) 7 (G) 8 (H) 9 (J) 10 (K) 12

13. If $\frac{a}{4} = \frac{2}{8}$ and $\frac{a + 4}{4} = \frac{b}{8}$, then $b =$

    (A) 4 (B) 6 (C) 5 (D) 2 (E) 10

14. An apple pie 10 cm in diameter costs $1.50. Then, an apple pie 20 cm in diameter should cost

    (F) $3.00 (G) $4.00 (H) $4.50 (J) $6.00 (K) $8.00

Questions 15 and 16 refer to the following definition:

For all real numbers A and B,

$$\underline{A|} \triangle \underline{B|} = AB + (A - B)$$

EXAMPLE:

$\underline{9|} \triangle \underline{4|} = (9 \times 4) + (9 - 4) = 36 + 5 = 41$

15. $\underline{7|} \triangle \underline{3|} =$

    (A) 31 (B) 25 (C) 38 (D) 24 (E) none of these

16. Which of the following equations is (are) true?

    I. $\underline{B|} \triangle \underline{B|} = B^2$
    II. $\underline{B|} \triangle \underline{0|} = 2B$
    III. $\underline{B|} \triangle \underline{1|} = B + 1$

    (F) I only (G) II only (H) I and II (J) I and III (K) I, II, and III

17. Mr. Brown sold a jacket for $120, thus making a profit of 20% on his cost. Later, he sold another jacket for $120, this time suffering a loss of 20% on his cost. The result of the two sales was

    (A) he broke even (B) he gained $10 (C) he lost $10 (D) he lost $4.00 (E) he gained $4.00

18. When a number is decreased by 25% of itself, the result is 15. If the same number is increased by 50% of itself, the result is

    (F) 25 (G) 30 (H) 40 (J) 70 (K) 50

19. We may multiply a number by 25 by annexing two zeros to the number and

    (A) multiplying the result by 4
    (B) dividing the result by 4
    (C) multiplying the result by 5
    (D) dividing the result by 5
    (E) multiplying the result by 2

20. The difference between one-third of a number and one-fourth of the same number is 6. What is the number?

    (F) 24 (G) 48 (H) 64 (J) 72 (K) 108

21. The length of a rectangle is 4 cm and the length of a diagonal of the rectangle is 5 cm. The perimeter of the rectangle, in centimeters, is

    (A) 18 (B) 3 (C) 7 (D) 16 (E) 14

22. If $\frac{1}{3}x = 30$, then $\frac{1}{6}x =$

    (F) 15 (G) 20 (H) 60 (J) 90 (K) 120

23. If $3x - 1 > 20$ then x^2 must be

    (A) equal to 49 (B) greater than 50 (C) less than 100 (D) greater than 49 (E) greater than $\frac{19}{3}$

24. If, in the expression $\frac{a}{bc}$, if a, b, and c are each doubled, then the expression is

(F) multiplied by 2 (G) multiplied by 4
(H) divided by 2 (J) divided by 4
(K) left unchanged

25. The measures of the two acute angles of a right triangle are in the ratio 1:4. The measure of the larger acute angle, in degrees, is

(A) 18 (B) 36 (C) 45 (D) 90 (E) 72

SECTION 2

Time—25 minutes
60 questions

DIRECTIONS: In this section there are two different types of questions. Directions and a sample question precede each type.

Select, from the lettered choices, the word or phrase closest in meaning to the word in capital letters. On the Answer Sheet, fill in the circle that has the same letter as your answer choice.

SAMPLE QUESTION:

STUPEFY:

(A) injure (B) astound (C) recall (D) study (E) replace

1. GALA:

(A) stormy (B) public C) rare (D) festive (E) costly

2. EXTOL:

(F) ring out (G) silence (H) praise highly (J) thunder (K) exile

3. DOCILE:

(A) talented (B) motionless (C) difficult (D) obedient (E) educated

4. CHERUB:

(F) patient (G) angel (H) student (J) client (K) starlet

5. SURMOUNT:

(A) saddle (B) torture (C) seize (D) free from (E) overcome

6. RECTIFY:

(F) build (G) sentence (H) fix (J) allow (K) explain

7. ERRONEOUS:

(A) futile (B) incorrect (C) answerable (D) impure (E) injured

8. CURTAIL:

(F) relate (G) deliver (H) conciliate (J) slander (K) shorten

9. COY:

(A) clever (B) fortunate (C) male (D) shy (E) frightful

10. GRATIS:

(F) without charge (G) infrequent (H) irritating (J) lunar (K) grateful

11. CORPULENT:

(A) wealthy (B) fat (C) hardworking (D) elderly (E) shrewd

12. ALOOF:

(F) tall (G) indistinct (H) apart (J) impolite (K) considerate

13. PINNACLE:

(A) branch (B) mast (C) feather (D) peak (E) wave

14. DISBURSE:

(F) plan for (G) scatter (H) pull apart (J) charge (K) pay out

15. MAXIM:

(A) report (B) resolution (C) gigantic (D) proverb (E) lecture

16. MORTIFY:

(F) humiliate (G) propitiate (H) kit (J) intend (K) smudge

17. MIRE:

(A) spectacle (B) glue (C) mud (D) exit (E) rate

18. APPREHENSIVE:

(F) total (G) incomplete (H) difficult
(J) timely (K) worried

19. MEANDER:

(A) foretell (B) inspire (C) seek
(D) wind (E) install

20. CORSAIR:

(F) pirate (G) vessel (H) pilot
(J) fort (K) captain

21. LOQUACIOUS:

(A) overlong (B) pedantic (C) brilliant
(D) content (E) talkative

22. AMALGAMATE:

(F) destroy (G) save from (H) realize
(J) unite with (K) explode

23. IMBIBE:

(A) tell (B) distrust (C) drink
(D) follow (E) feed

24. PREVARICATE:

(F) praise highly (G) be untruthful
(H) lose control (J) criticize severely
(K) quote freely

25. EMBEZZLE:

(A) steal (B) encumber (C) overcome
(D) educate (E) rain on

26. TEPID:

(F) tender (G) cloudy (H) lukewarm
(J) watery (K) weary

27. INTREPID:

(A) immortal (B) ingenious (C) timid
(D) fearless (E) tireless

28. ARDUOUS:

(F) impossible (G) partial (H) difficult
(J) adult (K) simple

29. MALIGNANT:

(A) evil (B) pert (C) fortunate
(D) puzzling (E) massive

30. SOMBER:

(F) well dressed (G) irate (H) sloppy
(J) foolhardy (K) gloomy

DIRECTIONS: Each of the following questions gives two words that relate in a certain way. You must determine this relationship, and then choose the answer that best completes the meaning of the sentence. On the Answer Sheet, fill in the circle that has the same letter as your answer choice.

SAMPLE QUESTION:

Potter is to clay as

(A) anchorperson is to news
(B) actor is to director
(C) poet is to novel
(D) politician is to democracy
(E) manager is to production

Choice (A) is the best answer because, as a potter molds clay, so an anchorperson takes a news story and molds it into something newsworthy. Of all the choices, (A) expresses the relationship most similar to the relationship between potter and the clay that she works.

31. Musician is to orchestra as

(A) cello is to baton
(B) soldier is to regiment
C) astronaut is to satellite
(D) mechanic is to blueprint
(E) worker is to union

32. Penguin is to flying as

(F) lion is to stalking
(G) antelope is to grazing
(H) dog is to tracking
(J) sheep is to cropping
(K) seal is to trotting

33. Pension is to retired person as

(A) bribe is to inspector
(B) bank is to depositor
(C) inheritance is to student
(D) gift is to lawyer
(E) salary is to civil service worker

34. Prod is to elephant as

(F) stirrup is to mule
(G) lariat is to pony
(H) chain is to bear
(J) whip is to colt
(K) fish is to seal

35. Future is to spaceship as past is to

(A) horseshoe (B) museum (C) tortoise (D) galleon (E) rocket

36. Rug is to sound as

(F) silk is to dress
(G) oil is to friction
(H) siren is to alarm
(J) sofa is to room
(K) gasoline is to chassis

37. Fine is to judge as

(A) summary is to orator
(B) paragraph is to writer
(C) reprimand is to parent
(D) lens is to optician
(E) typewriter is to secretary

38. Scarlet is to red as

(F) green is to topaz
(G) purple is to orange
(H) tinted is to blue
(J) tinge is to gray
(K) canary is to yellow

39. Automobile is to turnpike as

(A) cart is to rut
(B) spaceship is to log
(C) caravan is to route
(D) horse is to saddle
(E) jet is to trail

40. Apprentice is to learner as accomplice is to

(F) associate (G) crime (H) mastermind (J) attorney (K) victim

41. Father is to crony as daughter is to

(A) spouse (B) subordinate (C) confidante (D) acquaintance (E) sibling

42. Incessant is to occasional as

(F) impious is to irreligious
(G) perilous is to rewarding
(H) dormant is to active
(J) pensive is to actual
(K) permanent is to confident

43. Sullen is to smile as

(A) gleeful is to joy
(B) reluctant is to willingness
(C) respectful is to courtesy
(D) evasive is to fear
(E) composure is to conscience

44. Confusion is to frustrate as seasickness is to

(F) puzzle (G) nauseate (H) nourish (J) travel (K) overcome

45. Bond is to gilt-edged as clothing is to

(A) shoddy (B) exclusive (C) expensive (D) top quality (E) sturdy

46. Meadow is to prairie as

(F) river is to stream
(G) farm is to city
(H) pit is to grape
(J) mound is to plateau
(K) area is to neighborhood

47. Subside is to stoop as

(A) down is to up
(B) up is to down
(C) down is to down
(D) less is to more
(E) more is to less

48. Semicircle is to new moon as

(F) $\frac{1}{2}$ is to $\frac{1}{4}$ (G) $\frac{1}{2}$ is to $\frac{3}{4}$ (H) $\frac{1}{2}$ is to 0

(J) $\frac{1}{2}$ is to $\frac{1}{2}$ (K) $\frac{1}{4}$ is to 1

49. Congress is to statute as

(A) principal is to law
(B) supervisor is to monument
(C) governor is to restriction
(D) meeting is to resolution
(E) police is to citation

50. Supreme is to top as prior is to

(F) after (G) before (H) since
(J) subsequent (K) along with

51. Perpetual is to conclusion as awkward is to

(A) clumsiness (B) speed
(C) intelligence (D) grace
(E) meaning

52. Injure is to partial as annihilate is to

(F) severe (G) multiple (H) complete
(J) barbarous (K) relentless

53. Program is to pageant as agenda is to

(A) event (B) conference (C) secretary
(D) battleplan (E) strategy

54. Prudent is to miserly as

(F) engaged is to plighted
(G) energetic is to spiritless
(H) generous is to extravagant
(J) fatigued is to weary
(K) prominent is to well-known

55. Hence is to therefore as

(A) but is to unless
(B) consequently is to moreover
(C) nevertheless is to providing
(D) providing is to if
(E) since is to herein

56. Note is to letter as

(F) tie is to shirt
(G) smock is to gown
(H) dining is to eating
(J) soap is to detergent
(K) soldier is to marine

57. Impartial is to neutral as

(A) for is to for
(B) for is to against
(C) against is to for
(D) nonpartisan is to nonbiased
(E) unfair is to fair

58. Precaution is to disaster as

(F) surgery is to diagnosis
(G) exploration is to payment
(H) hospitalization is to cure
(J) consultation is to involvement
(K) antiseptic is to infection

59. Strange is to outlandish as

(A) many is to one
(B) noisy is to obvious
(C) elastic is to plastic
(D) unwilling is to obstinate
(E) former is to previous

60. Valiant is to courage as

(F) steadfast is to intelligence
(G) wavering is to faith
(H) rigid is to honesty
(J) robust is to good health
(K) reliable is to instinct

SECTION 3

Time—25 minutes
25 questions

DIRECTIONS: Five possible answers follow each question below. You may work out each problem in your head or use the margins of the test pages for scratch work. Decide which of the five possible answers is best. On the Answer Sheet fill in the circle with the letter that corresponds to your answer choice.

SAMPLE PROBLEM:

7,524
−6,736

(A) 788 (B) 798 (C) 898 (D) 1,788 (E) 1,888

● Ⓑ Ⓒ Ⓓ Ⓔ

1. A dealer buys chairs at 3 for $50. He intends to sell them at $24 each. How many chairs must he sell to make a profit of $1,100?

(F) 150 (G) 250 (H) 100 (J) 500 (K) 350

2. When the sum of $\frac{1}{4}$ and $\frac{1}{6}$ of a number is subtracted from the number, the result is

(A) $\frac{4}{5}$ of the number
(B) $\frac{5}{12}$ of the number
(C) 40 percent of the number
(D) 60 percent of the number
(E) $\frac{7}{12}$ of the number

3. If $2x - 1 > 5$, then a value of x that makes this inequality true is

(F) 3 (G) 2 (H) 10 (J) 0 (K) −3

4. In a school with 615 students, 18 classes are formed. If most of the classes are equal in size, how many classes are larger than the others?

(A) 1 (B) 0 (C) 2 (D) 4 (E) 3

5. If $x + y = 5$ and x and y are positive integers, what is the maximum possible value of $x - y$?

(F) 2 (G) 5 (H) 4 (J) 3 (K) 6

6. A city spends 40% of its budget for education. In drawing a circle graph of the city's budget, the measure of the angle at the center that represents education expense is, in degrees,

(A) 144 (B) 40 (C) 120 (D) 160 (E) 150

7. $0.0357 \times \square = 357 \times 2.\ \square =$

(F) 200 (G) 200,000 (H) 2,000 (J) 20,000 (K) 7,140

8. A girl's grades on four tests are 75, 80, 90, and 50. In order to have an average of 50 for the five tests, the grade she receives on the fifth test must be

(A) 95 (B) 90 (C) 100 (D) 80 (E) none of these

9. A man's salary is cut 10%. A year later his salary is increased 20%. The net effect is

(F) an increase of 10%
(G) an increase of 6%
(H) an increase of 8%
(J) an increase of 9%
(K) no increase or decrease

10. One bell rings every 20 minutes, a second bell rings every 30 minutes, and a third bell rings every 50 minutes. If all three bells ring at noon, at what time will all three bells ring again?

(A) 3:00 P.M. (B) 4:00 P.M. (C) 9:00 P.M. (D) 5:00 P.M. (E) 6:00 P.M.

11. The coordinates of $\triangle ABC$ are $A(2, 3)$, $B(7, 3)$ and $C(7, 9)$. The area of triangle ABC, in square units, is

(F) 30 (G) 15 (H) 12 (J) 18 (K) 24

12. A chemist has a 40-gallon solution of alcohol and water that is 5% alcohol. If 10 gallons of alcohol are added to the solution, the percentage of alcohol in the new solution is

(A) 25% (B) 20% (C) 30% (D) 24% (E) 35%

13. If a number is multiplied by 3, the product is 21. If the same number is increased by 5, result is

(F) 10 (G) 12 (H) 15 (J) 18 (K) 20

14. Numbers 1 through 9 are fitted into the boxes so that the sum of the numbers of each row, each column, and each diagonal are equal. The number that replaces x is

		4
	5	
x		

(A) 3 (B) 6 (C) 7 (D) 8 (E) 4

15. At a party there are 6 girls and 6 boys. The number of different couples that can pair off for dancing is

(F) 12 (G) 720 (H) 36 (J) 30 (K) 24

16. A man earns $8.50 per hour. If he works 6 hours and 40 minutes he earns

(A) $56.67 (B) $58.00 (C) $51.40 (D) $51.50 (E) $55.00

17. The formula expressing the relationship between x and y in the following table is:

x	1	2	3	4	5	6	7
y	3	5	7	9	11	13	15

(F) $y = 3x$ (G) $x = 2y + 1$ (H) $x = 2y - 1$ (J) $y = x + 2$ (K) $y = 2x + 1$

18. At a sale of TV sets, 80 sets were sold the first day and one-half of the remainder the next day. There were then 50 sets left. The number of TV sets originally put on sale was

(A) 130 (B) 230 (C) 180 (D) 30 (E) 210

19. If $a > b > c > d > 0$, which one of the following MUST be true if a, b, c, and d are positive numbers?

(F) $c + d > a + b$

(G) $\frac{a}{d} > \frac{b}{c}$

(H) $a + d > b + c$

(J) $\frac{a}{d} > \frac{c}{d}$

(K) $\frac{a}{d} > \frac{c}{b}$

20. When a certain number is divided by 9, the quotient is 30 and the remainder is 8. The number is

(A) 270 (B) 102 (C) $270\frac{8}{9}$ (D) 278 (E) 279

21. A restaurant has 9 pounds 12 ounces of chicken. How many portions of 6 ounces each will this amount of chicken yield?

(F) 24 (G) 25 (H) 26 (J) 27 (K) 28

22. Take any two-digit number whose tens digit is greater than its units digit. If the number with the digits reversed is subtracted from the original number, then the result is always divisible by

(A) 9 (B) 11 (C) 6 (D) 8 (E) 5

23. If $ABCD$ is a square and $AB = 14$ inches, find the area of the shaded portion in square inches (Let $\pi = \frac{22}{7}$)

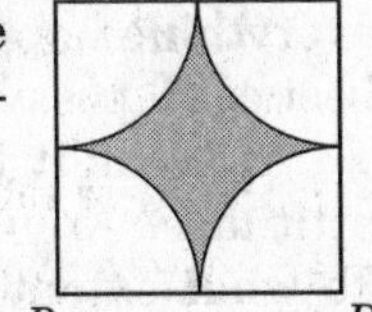

(F) 42 (G) 52 (H) 110 (J) 40 (K) 50

24. If $3N - 1 = 14$, then 8 more than twice N is

(A) 13 (B) 12 (C) 18 (D) 15 (E) 14

25. Two numbers are in the ratio 2:3. If 5 is added to each of these numbers, then the ratio of the numbers is 3:4. The smaller of the two numbers is

(F) 15 (G) 10 (H) 20 (J) 25 (K) 30

SECTION 4

Time—25 minutes
40 questions

DIRECTIONS: Carefully read each of the passages below and the questions that follow. Select the choice which, on the basis of the passage, best answers the question. On the Answer Sheet, fill in the circle that has the same letter as your answer choice.

Do you belong to the group that usually says, "The jar is half *empty*"? Or are you one who replies, "No, the jar is half *filled*"! The facts are the same for each; the difference is in the attitude the speakers.

The ones who see only that something is lacking usually belong to the sector called *pessimists.* They are the ones who believe that buttered bread always falls on its face. They urge you never to expect anything, and then you'll not be disappointed. They think that things are as bad as they can be; yet, they expect things to get worse.

On the other hand, those who look at the positive side, the *optimists,* say that when things are not as you like, like them as they are. They urge you to remember the teakettle: when it is up to its neck in hot water, it sings. They firmly believe that everything happens for the best; in this, the best of all possible worlds.

What is it that instills these opposing attitudes? Are we born with a set outlook? To what extent do our parents and friends influence the way we see things in general? Are we so constituted that we cannot or do not change our way of looking at things?

1. Those who say that a jar is half empty rather than half filled

   (A) are more correct than those who stress half filled
   (B) are less correct than those who stress half filled
   (C) hide their attitude
   (D) see the negative rather than the positive
   (E) respond without thinking

2. In this passage, the author

   (F) favors an optimistic outlook
   (G) favors a pessimistic outlook
   (H) favors neither pessimists nor optimists
   (J) is unable to make up his mind
   (K) dislikes both pessimists and optimists

3. The purpose of this passage is to

   (A) turn the reader into an optimist
   (B) turn the reader into a pessimist
   (C) show the reader how to solve problems
   (D) make the reader aware of the differences between pessimists and optimists
   (E) teach the reader how to handle people for the best advantage to all involved

4. When the teakettle in the example is compared to people, the hot water then means

   (F) boiling water
   (D) higher temperatures
   (H) trouble
   (J) examples
   (K) refreshments

5. The word "constituted" as used in the last sentence means

   (A) legalized (B) enacted
   (C) processed (D) made up
   (E) originated

Most Native American tribes created music in two ways—with the voice and the flute. Although some Native American music has been recorded in writing in both early and recent times, most of the sounds and rhythms have been handed down from generation to generation by voice.

Very few of the old flutes passed down through the tribes play at all today because of the cracks that soon develop in these fragile instruments. The Native American flutes were usually carved from pine, cedar, alderwood, or other softwood.

The flute had a variety of uses, depending on tribal traditions. In some tribes, it was used as a war signal. When it was played around the village it was clearly understood by the people as a call to arms. In other groups, it was used in religious ceremonies, in courting, or as an accompaniment in the daily work of grinding grain.

Most Native American flutes have a range of one octave, making the instrument limited in terms of Western music. However, those who have been privileged to hear it played say that there is no sound as entrancing and as soothing as that heard when the Native American flute is played with a throat or diaphragm vibrato.

6. The Native American flute was

   (F) usually made of metal
   (G) always hand made
   (H) always played to accompany a singer
   (J) developed to resemble the European musical instrument
   (K) invented in the eighteenth century

7. Very few museums contain examples of the Native American flute that still can be played because

   (A) so few were made
   (B) the wood dried out too quickly
   (C) they were so expensive
   (D) they were destroyed after they were used
   (E) the Indians hid them

8. The main tool used in making the Native American flute is a

   (F) hammer (G) saw
   (H) pair of scissors (J) knife
   (K) pair of pliers

9. The Native Americans did NOT use the flute

   (A) for background music while they worked
   (B) to call groups together
   (C) to amuse the children
   (D) during prayer meetings
   (E) as an accompaniment in the singing of love songs

10. Compared to instruments in a modern orchestra, the Native American flute

    (F) requires a longer training period in order to be played well
    (G) is sturdier
    (H) does not have a characteristic tone
    (J) is more limited in range
    (K) has only a shrill sound

Sight and sound records of the past have been available for a comparatively few years. Future generations will be able to use photographs and recordings to identify people, places, and events of our times. However, such proof cannot go back much before the middle of the nineteenth century. Written records of even earlier times are available only when they have been preserved and can be translated into current languages. But how can we reach across the centuries when no such data have been preserved?

Archeologists digging into the ruins of the past have patiently reconstructed flattened buildings and broken pottery to give us a glimpse of how the people of earlier civilizations lived.

Scientists studying cross-sections of tree trunks have been able to tell us about the climate changes and weather conditions that can go back more than a thousand years. The tree-ring calendar is based on the fact that trees grow only in summer when they get moisture. Growth stops each winter, and so a distinct yearly record is kept. One such record has been carried back to the 1300s through a study of California's long-lived sequoias. By studying beams of old Pueblo Indian homes, one dendrochronologist was able to develop a complete weather record back to the year A.D. 700.

Yet, as you can readily see, once we reach back before the miracle inventions of the camera and recording devices, we have meager pickings.

11. Posterity will never be able to see a photograph of

    (A) Abraham Lincoln
    (B) George Washington
    (C) Franklin Roosevelt
    (D) Mohammed Ali
    (E) Albert Einstein

12. A dendrochronologist is
    (F) an expert in photography
    (G) a Pueblo Indian
    (H) a recording artist
    (J) a specialist in handling old pottery
    (K) a researcher who decides the age of trees

13. Which of the following is a suitable title for this selection?
    (A) Scientists at Work
    (B) Pueblo Indian Homes
    (C) Sight and Sound
    (D) Glimpses of the More Remote Past
    (E) On Being an Archeologist

14. How people lived in the year 6000 B.C. can be determined today only through
    (F) written records
    (G) observation by trained specialists
    (H) deduction by researchers
    (J) fossils found in land sites
    (K) oral reports by researchers

15. The tree-ring calendar can reveal
    (A) why some people migrated from one land to another
    (B) when nations fought against each other
    (C) when a disease wiped out a nation
    (D) what grains the people planted
    (E) how long the average person lived

16. The author's style is best described as
    (F) critical (G) objective (H) dramatic (J) biased (K) argumentative

The bowfin is a fish that is found principally in the streams and rivers of the Mississippi Valley. The mature male reaches about 18 inches in length while the female averages about 24 inches. This freshwater fish has been studied by scientists because of two unusual characteristics.

In dry spells, the streams and rivers lose their vital supplies of water. The stream levels lower, and deep pools disappear. At such time, most water inhabitants suffocate, but not the bowfin. It has been nicknamed the mudfish for a very good reason.

When the surface water has all but disappeared, it buries itself in the mud. It gets its essential oxygen from the air bladder that acts as a lung. It survives for long periods of time in the mud until the water begins to flow again.

The bowfin also has the distinction of being one of the two varieties of fish in which the male takes over the entire task of caring for the offspring.

The male builds an elaborate nest in shallow water containing a heavy growth of plants. With his teeth, he cuts down the reeds in a circle of about two feet in diameter. The female then lays hundreds of eggs in the hollow that the male has dug in the cleared area. Having completed her share of the task, the female leaves. But the male remains, guarding the nest for the week or so that it takes for the young to hatch. When the young appear, the male becomes an ever-present guard. He swims constantly around the nest, herding the hundreds of tiny offspring back as they try to escape. He continues his vigil for the month or so that it takes the young to grow three or four inches long.

17. The bowfin reaches independence
    (A) in muddy pools
    (B) after a year of fighting for survival
    (C) after a week or so away from the nest
    (D) when the female leaves the nest
    (E) a month after birth

18. A bowfin lives through the dry season by
    (F) nibbling on grass
    (G) taking oxygen out of the air
    (H) living in shallow pools
    (J) hibernating
    (K) living among the roots of the reeds

19. Which of the following is a suitable title for this selection?
    (A) Fish of the Mississippi
    (B) Parenting by the Male Bowfin
    (C) In and Out of Danger
    (D) Mudfish Out of Water
    (E) Bowfin Survival Tactics

20. The word "vigil" in the last sentence means
    (F) indifference (G) search (H) imprisonment (J) watch (K) escape

Psychologists have found that hope plays a surprisingly potent role in giving people a measurable advantage in academic achievement. They found that the level of hope in students beginning their first semester is a more accurate predictor of their school grades than are their entrance examination scores or their previous school averages.

Students with high levels of hope share several attributes. Unlike people who are low in hope, they turn to their friends for advice on how to achieve their goals. They tell themselves that they can succeed at what they need to do. Even in tight spots they tell themselves that things will get better as time goes on. They are flexible enough to find different ways to reach their goals. If hope for one goal fades, they aim for another. Those low in hope, on the other hand, just keep the same goal and become increasingly frustrated. Those high in hope show an ability to break down a formidable task into specific achievable chunks. People low in hope, however, see only the large goal and not the small steps along the way.

21. Which of the following best states the main idea of the passage?

(A) Hope is the main factor in success.
(B) Hopefulness is an inherited trait.
(C) Parents should instill hope in their children.
(D) People low in hope cannot succeed.
(E) Hope is a significant factor in success.

22. The word "attributes" as used in the first sentence of the second paragraph means

(F) difficulties (G) characteristics (H) peculiarities (J) rewards (K) frustrations

23. According to the selection, students with hope

(A) don't change their goals in midstream
(B) welcome all obstacles as challenges
(C) set their goals early in life
(D) believe that there is more than one way to skin a cat
(E) enjoy giving advice

24. From this selection we can infer that the author believes that whenever difficulties arise, students should

(F) never call for assistance
(G) set an example for others
(H) cross one bridge at a time
(J) change their goals
(K) trust their instincts

25. Which of the following terms best expresses the tone of this selection?

(A) instructive (B) informal (C) ironic (D) emotional (E) humorous

At a few minutes past five, Dave noted that the blanket of darkness was lifting. He was able to distinguish the heavier masses that eventually appeared as the familiar trees that lined the automobile road at the base of the hill. The upper reaches of the sky showed lighter shades of gray.

Dave slipped quietly out of bed and dressed quickly. He mixed a spoonful of instant chocolate into a glass of cold water. He tried to sip slowly, but his impatience forced him to finish the drink in gulps.

As he walked down toward the lake, Dave paused to reach for the fishing rod and gear box on the bench where he had left them the night before.

By the time he reached the aluminum pram, a thick white mist had spread over the surface of the water. He stepped into the small boat, sat down, and used the oars to glide out of the weedbeds that lined the edge of the shore.

The outer fringe of the lake disappeared as the boat glided forward noiselessly. All he could see was the enveloping whiteness. He could not tell where the boat and the surrounding air met the surface of the lake.

Dave rowed steadily ahead, relying on a mental image of the surroundings. Then the mist began to rise, slowly. It soon rested inches above the still surface of the lake. The heavy silence was now being broken by the occasional bass breaking through the surface tension as they leaped out of the water for low-flying insects.

The magic time had arrived. Dave snapped his favorite lure onto the steel leader. He raised his rod and flipped the yellow flatfish close to the edge of the lily pads. The spell of dawn was broken. He was galvanized into expectancy.

26. The incident described in this passage opens
    (F) toward nightfall
    (G) during a rainstorm
    (H) on a foggy morning
    (J) just before dawn
    (K) just after dinnertime

27. As the day begins for Dave, he is
    (A) depressed by what he has to do
    (B) filled with fear of what is about to happen
    (C) overjoyed by what has happened
    (D) annoyed by what he was led to expect
    (E) filled with anticipation

28. Dave was planning to fish
    (F) off the dock at first
    (G) in a small pond
    (H) in the salt marshes
    (J) in a nearby lake
    (K) with two of his friends

29. The reader is NOT told
    (A) how old Dave is
    (B) the type of boat Dave used
    (C) where the boat was kept
    (D) how large a breakfast Dave ate
    (E) how well Dave knew the lake

30. Dave planned to be out on the lake
    (F) to take advantage of the mist
    (G) at feeding time
    (H) where he could be alone
    (J) to practice rowing
    (K) to see if he could find his way through the mist

When Alaska was purchased by the United States from Russia in 1867, it was a very poor area, a vast expanse of ice and tundra. It was inhabited mostly by native Americans—Aleuts, Inuits, and Indians. None of the natives were consulted in the purchase.

In 1896, gold was discovered in the streams and hills of Alaska. Thousands raced there, seeking quick wealth. But when the gold fever subsided, Alaska remained largely underdeveloped and underexplored. By 1959, there were only 200,000 people living there. It was a poor relation when it became the 49th state.

In the 1960s, Alaska had a swift turnaround. Oil was discovered on the state's north coast. The north slope at Prudhoe Bay was estimated to hold a third of our country's total reserve.

One of the crucial questions that must be addressed today is the fate of the land owned by the federal government. Over 225 million acres are at stake. The Alaskan government and various commercial interests would like to see hunting, mining, logging, and oil exploration permitted on much of this land. The environmentalists want the areas designated as wilderness and placed off limits.

The federal government has given million of acres to the Alaskan state government. The native inhabitants of Alaska were given 44 million acres and a billion dollars to settle their claims to the land. The environmentalists feel that the remaining acres under federal ownership should remain forever wild. Alaska is our last frontier. It is our last chance to preserve wild areas that, once altered, cannot be replaced.

31. Which of the following best states the main idea of the passage?
    (A) Alaska is a very wealthy state.
    (B) The wilderness areas of Alaska are endangered.
    (C) None of the natives were consulted when Russia sold their land to the United States.
    (D) Alaska is our last frontier.
    (E) The United States acted unwisely in buying Alaska.

32. The United States paid the Russians and not the inhabitants because
    (F) the inhabitants had sold the land to the Russians
    (G) it was part of Russia's European territories
    (H) the Russians claimed it was theirs by right of exploration
    (J) the Russians had conquered the inhabitants
    (K) the inhabitants had lost their case in court

33. Alaska's prosperity at the beginning of the twentieth century disappeared because

(A) there was a worldwide depression
(B) the factories closed down
(C) the streambeds ran out of gold
(D) it was too cold
(E) gold lost most of its value

34. Alaska has proved to be a valuable addition because

(F) it has rich natural resources
(G) the natives have scientific ability
(H) it brings the United States and Canada closer together
(J) it is a major year-round tourist attraction
(K) it has rich farmlands

35. Which of the following must occur if more sources of gold and oil are to be found in Alaska?

I. More land must be bought from the natives.
II. The physical appearance of public lands must change.
III. The government must do the exploring.

(A) I only
(B) II only
(C) III only
(D) I and II only
(E) I, II, and III

Tree at my window, window tree,
My sash is lowered when night comes on;
But let there never be curtain drawn
Between you and me.

Vague dream-head lifted out of the ground,
And thing next most diffuse to cloud,
Not all your light tongues talking aloud
Could be profound.

But, tree, I have seen you taken and tossed,
And if you have seen me when I slept,
You have seen me when I was taken and swept
And all but lost.

That day she put our heads together,
Fate had her imagination about her—
Your head so much concerned with outer,
Mine with inner, weather.

36. How can the "light tongues" be most easily identified?

I. As shafts of light
II. As leaves of the tree
III. As underground roots

(F) I only
(G) II only
(H) III only
(J) I and II only
(K) I, II, and III

37. The tree is pictured as being

(A) in a nearby meadow
(B) on the road in front of the house
(C) reaching high above the house
(D) newly planted
(E) none of the above

38. Under what circumstances was the speaker "taken and swept"?

I. He was emotionally distressed.
II. He had a nightmare.
III. He was almost shipwrecked.

(F) I only
(G) II only
(H) III only
(J) I and II only
(K) I, II, and III

39. The poet

(A) admires the tree for its fullness
(B) sees the tree as a fellow creature
(C) wants the tree to share his thoughts
(D) feels superior to the tree
(E) is awed by the tree's size

40. The tree looks like a "dream-head lifted out of the ground" because of

(F) the position of the speaker's room
(G) the lack of curtains on the window
(H) the open, unlocked window
(J) the coming of night
(K) the turning on of the lights

Answers to Practice SSAT 2

SECTION 1

1. **C**	6. **J**	11. **C**	16. **F**	21. **E**
2. **K**	7. **E**	12. **J**	17. **C**	22. **F**
3. **C**	8. **K**	13. **E**	18. **G**	23. **D**
4. **G**	9. **D**	14. **J**	19. **B**	24. **H**
5. **A**	10. **J**	15. **B**	20. **J**	25. **E**

Rating Your Results

Superior	23–25 correct
Average	18–22 correct
Below Average	17 or fewer correct

Material to Review: Chapters 8–14

SECTION 2

1. **D**	7. **B**	13. **D**	19. **D**	25. **A**
2. **H**	8. **K**	14. **K**	20. **F**	26. **H**
3. **D**	9. **D**	15. **D**	21. **E**	27. **D**
4. **G**	10. **F**	16. **F**	22. **J**	28. **H**
5. **E**	11. **B**	17. **C**	23. **C**	29. **A**
6. **H**	12. **H**	18. **K**	24. **G**	30. **K**

Rating Your Results

Lower Level

Superior	25–30 correct
Average	20–24 correct
Below Average	19 or fewer correct

Upper Level

Superior	26–30 correct
Average	23–25 correct
Below Average	22 or fewer correct

Material to Review: Chapter 4

31. **B**	37. **C**	43. **B**	49. **D**	55. **D**
32. **K**	38. **K**	44. **G**	50. **G**	56. **G**
33. **E**	39. **C**	45. **D**	51. **D**	57. **D**
34. **J**	40. **F**	46. **J**	52. **H**	58. **K**
35. **D**	41. **C**	47. **C**	53. **B**	59. **D**
36. **G**	42. **H**	48. **H**	54. **H**	60. **J**

Rating Your Results

Lower Level

Superior	25–30 correct
Average	21–24 correct
Below Average	20 or fewer correct

Upper Level

Superior	27–30 correct
Average	19–26 correct
Below Average	18 or fewer correct

Material to Review: Chapter 4

SECTION 3

1. **F**	6. **A**	11. **G**	16. **A**	21. **H**
2. **E**	7. **J**	12. **D**	17. **K**	22. **A**
3. **H**	8. **E**	13. **G**	18. **C**	23. **F**
4. **E**	9. **H**	14. **B**	19. **G**	24. **C**
5. **J**	10. **D**	15. **H**	20. **D**	25. **G**

Rating Your Results

Superior	23–25 correct
Average	18–22 correct
Below Average	17 or fewer correct

Material to Review: Chapters 8–14

SECTION 4

1. **D**	9. **C**	17. **E**	25. **A**	33. **C**
2. **H**	10. **J**	18. **G**	26. **J**	34. **F**
3. **D**	11. **B**	19. **E**	27. **E**	35. **B**
4. **H**	12. **K**	20. **J**	28. **J**	36. **G**
5. **D**	13. **D**	21. **E**	29. **A**	37. **E**
6. **G**	14. **H**	22. **G**	30. **G**	38. **J**
7. **B**	15. **A**	23. **D**	31. **B**	39. **B**
8. **J**	16. **G**	24. **H**	32. **H**	40. **F**

Rating Your Results

Lower Level

Superior	34–40 correct
Average	28–33 correct
Below Average	27 or fewer correct

Upper Level

Superior	36–40 correct
Average	31–35 correct
Below Average	30 or fewer correct

Material to Review: Chapter 5

Answers Explained

SECTION 1

1. **C** $\begin{array}{r} 1200 \\ -\ 409 \\ \hline 791 \end{array}$

2. **K** 2 less than 10 = 8
Let x = the number
$\frac{1}{3}x = 8$
$x = 24$

3. **C** When the temperature is 6 degrees above zero a drop of 6 degrees brings the temperature to 0. A drop of 3 more degrees brings the temperature to 3 degrees below zero.

4. **G** $2^8 \div 2^2 = 2^{8-2} = 2^6$
$2^6 = 2 \times 2 \times 2 \times 2 \times 2 \times 2$
$= 64$

5. **A** $16 \times \frac{3}{8} = 6$
$6\,\square = 15 \times 32$
$\square = \frac{15 \times 32}{6} = 80$

6. **J** $\frac{3{,}675}{0.07} \times \frac{367{,}500}{7} = 52{,}500$

7. **E** The L.C.D. of the fractions is 12. If we multiply the numerator and denominator of the fraction by 12, we have
$$\frac{12\left(\frac{13}{4} - \frac{5}{6}\right)}{12\left(\frac{7}{12}\right)} = \frac{39 - 10}{7} = \frac{29}{7} = 4\tfrac{1}{7}$$

8. **K** The sum of the measures of the angles around a point in a plane is 360°. To represent the fraction $\frac{1}{8}$, we must find an angle whose measure is $\frac{1}{8} \times 360 = 45°$.

9. **D** The angle at the center of the sector representing sleep is 135°. Thus, sleep is $\frac{135}{360}$ of the 24-hour day.
$$\frac{135}{\underset{30}{\cancel{360}}} \times \frac{\overset{2}{\cancel{24}}}{1} = \frac{260}{30} = 9$$

10. **J** If we examine the pairs of numbers we may eliminate F and G immediately since they are each 3+ units apart. If we examine the other pairs we see that the J pair differ by a little more than 1. The J pair are closer to each other than the H and K pairs.

11. **C** Let x = the number of seats in the theater.
$\frac{3}{4}x - 100 = \frac{2}{3}x$
We multiply both members of this equation by 12 to obtain
$$\begin{aligned} 9x - 1{,}200 &= 8x \\ 9x - 8x &= 1{,}200 \\ x &= 1{,}200 \end{aligned}$$

12. **J** In order to obtain 7 on the lowest line, the number directly above 7 must be 3.
In order to obtain 3 (above 7), △ must be 7 because △ × 9 will yield 3 only if △ is 7.
If △ is 7 then the product of 7 and 49 is 343.
Thus, □ must be 3.
Since △ = 7 and □ = 3,
then △ + □ = 10

$$\begin{array}{r} 49 \\ \times\,\triangle 5 \\ \hline 245 \\ -\,-\,- \\ \hline \square - 75 \end{array} \qquad \begin{array}{r} 49 \\ \triangle 5 \\ \hline 245 \\ 343 \\ \hline \boxed{3}675 \end{array}$$

13. **E** If $\frac{a}{4} = \frac{2}{8}$, then $8a = 8$, and $a = 1$.
$\frac{a + 4}{4} = \frac{b}{8}$
$\frac{1 + 4}{4} = \frac{b}{8}$
$\frac{5}{4} = \frac{b}{8}$, $4b = 40$, $b = 10$

14. **J** The area of a circle = πR^2.
For the 10-inch pie the radius is 5 inches.
The area of the 10-inch pie = 25π.
For the 20-inch pie the radius is 10 inches.
The area of the 20-inch pie = 100π.
Thus, the larger pie is 4 times the size of the smaller pie and its cost should be $4 \times 1.50 = \$6.00$.

15. **B** $\underline{7|} \triangle \underline{3|} = (7 \times 3) + (7 - 3) = 21 + 4 = 25$

16. **F** $\underline{B|} \triangle \underline{B|} = (B \times B) + (B - B) = B^2 + 0 = B^2$
$\underline{B|} \triangle \underline{0|} = (B \times 0) + (B - 0) = 0 + B = B$
$\underline{B|} \triangle \underline{1|} = (B \times 1) + (B - 1) = B + B - 1 = 2B - 1$
Thus only I is true.

17. **C** Since Mr. Brown made a profit of 20% on his first sale, he sold the first jacket at 120% of his cost.
Let x = cost of jacket

120% of $x = 120$
1% of $x = 1$
100% of $x = 100$
Thus, Mr. Brown made a profit of \$20 on the first jacket.
Since Mr. Brown had a loss of 20% of his second sale, he sold the second jacket at 80% of his cost.

80% of $x = 120$

1% of $x = \frac{120}{80}$

100% of $x = 100 \times \frac{120}{80} = 150$

Thus, Mr. Brown had a loss of 150 – 120 = \$30 on the second jacket. Mr. Brown lost 30 – 20 = \$10 on both sales.

18. **G** Let x = the number

$25\% = \frac{1}{4}$

$x - \frac{1}{4}x = 15$

$\frac{3}{4}x = 15$

$3x = 60, \quad x = 20$

50% of $20 = 10, \; 20 + 10 = 30$

19. **B** $25 = \frac{100}{4}$

Thus, multiplying a number by 25 is the same as multiplying by 100 and dividing by 4.

20. **J** Let x = the number

$\frac{1}{3}x - \frac{1}{4}x = 6$

We multiply both members of the equation by 12 to obtain

$12(\frac{1}{3})x - 12(\frac{1}{4})x = 12(6)$
$4x - 3x = 72$
$x = 72$

21. **E** Let x = the width of the rectangle
$x^2 + 4^2 = 5^2$
$x^2 + 16 = 25$
$x^2 = 25 - 16 = 9$
$x = 3$

The perimeter = 3 + 4 + 3 + 4 = 14 cm.

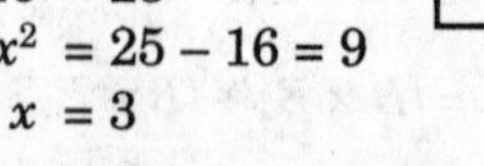

22. **F** $\frac{1}{3} = 2(\frac{1}{6})$, or $\frac{1}{6} = \frac{1}{2}$ of $\frac{1}{3}$

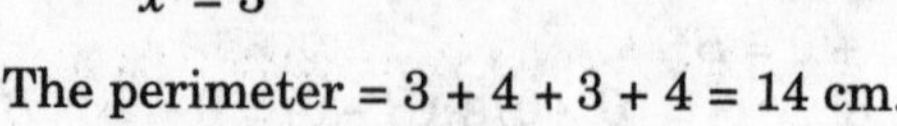

If $\frac{1}{3}x = 30$, then $\frac{1}{6}x = \frac{1}{2}(30) = 15$.

23. **D** $3x - 1 > 20$
$3x > 20 + 1$
$3x > 21$
$x > 7$
Therefore, x^2 is greater than 49.

24. **H** If a, b, and c are doubled, then we have

$$\frac{2a}{(2b) \times (2c)} = \frac{2a}{4bc} = \frac{a}{2bc}$$

The expression is divided by 2.

25. **E** The sum of the measures of the acute angles of a right triangle is 90°.

Let x = the measure of the smaller angle and $4x$ = the measure of the larger angle
$x + 4x = 90$
$5x = 90$
$x = 18$
$4x = 4(18) = 72$

SECTION 2

31. **B** Participant and group. A musician is a member of an orchestra. A soldier is a member of a regiment.

32. **K** Object to characteristic. A penguin cannot fly. Seals cannot trot.

33. **E** Object to receiver. A pension is money a retiree receives. A salary is money a civil service worker receives.

34. **J** Instrument and use. A prod directs an elephant. A whip directs a colt.

35. **D** Time and object. The spaceship is the means of transportation of the future. The sailing ship (galleon) is that of the past.

36. **G** Object and characteristic. A rug lessens sound. Oil lessens friction.

37. **C** Action (punishment) and doer. A judge can punish through fines. A parent can punish through a reprimand, a scolding.

38. **K** Item and class. Scarlet is a shade of red. Canary is a shade of yellow.

39. **C** Object and environment. An automobile travels along a turnpike. A caravan travels along a route.

40. **F** Synonyms. An apprentice learns. An accomplice is an associate.

41. **C** Synonyms. The friend of an older person may be called a crony. The friend of a young girl may be called her confidante.

42. **H** Antonyms. That which is *incessant* never stops; that which is *occasional* is never continual.

43. **B** Characteristic and action. When people are sullen, they do not smile. When people are reluctant, they do not show willingness.

44. **G** Action and result. Confusion frustrates. Seasickness nauseates.

45. **D** Object and characteristic. Both a gilt-edged bond and top-quality clothing are the best obtainable.

46. **J** Small is to large. Meadow is smaller than a prairie as a flat area. Mound is smaller than a plateau as an elevated area.

47. **C** Degree of action. When something subsides, it moves down. When people stoop, the movement is downward.

48. **H** Object and appearance (size). A semicircle is seen as one-half a circle. The new moon is invisible.

49. **D** Institution and function. Congress passes statutes (laws). A meeting passes resolution (motions).

50. **G** Synonyms. That which is supreme is at the top. That which is prior comes before.

51. **D** Adjective and characteristic. *Perpetual* means without conclusion. *Awkward* means without grace.

52. **H** Object and intensity. An injury may be partial damage, but annihilation is complete destruction.

53. **B** Name of activity. The plan of events for a pageant is its program. The plan of events for a conference is its agenda.

54. **H** Intensity of synonyms. As prudent is less than miserly, so generous is less than extravagant.

55. **D** Synonyms. *Hence* and *therefore* imply that a result follows. *Providing* and *if* imply that a condition follows.

56. **G** Synonyms. As a note is informal and a letter is formal, so a smock is informal and a gown is formal.

57. **D** Synonyms. Both *impartial* and *neutral* mean nonpartisan or nonbiased.

58. **K** Action and result. As a precaution can prevent disaster, so an antiseptic can prevent infection.

59. **D** Intensity of synonyms. As *outlandish* means more strange, so *obstinate* implies more unwilling.

60. **J** Adjective and quality. To be valiant is to have courage. To be robust is to have good health.

SECTION 3

1. **F** The dealer sells 3 chairs for \$72. Thus, on each sale of 3 chairs, the dealer makes a profit of 72 − 50 = \$22. To make a profit of \$1,100 the dealer must sell 1,100 ÷ 22, or 50 sets of 3 chairs. That is, he must sell 3 × 50, or 150 chairs.

2. **E** Let x = the number

$$\frac{1}{4} + \frac{1}{6} = \frac{3}{12} + \frac{2}{12} = \frac{5}{12}$$

$$x - \frac{5}{12}x = \frac{7}{12}x$$

3. **H** $2x - 1 > 5$

$$2x - 1 + 1 > 5 + 1$$
$$2x > 6$$
$$x > 3$$

4. **E** If we divide 615 by 18 we have a quotient of 34 and a remainder of 3. This means that 15 classes with 34 students in each, and 3 classes with 35 students in each, are formed.

5. **J** If x and y are positive integers and their sum is 5, with x greater than y, the only possibilities are

$x = 4,\ y = 1$

$x = 3,\ y = 2$

If $x = 4$ and $y = 1$, we have the maximum possible value of $x - y = 3$.

6. **A** The sum of the measures of the angles at the center of a circle is 360°. The sector representing 40% of the budget would require an angle whose measure is 0.4 of 360 = 144°.

7. **J** $0.0357 \times \square = 357 \times 2$

$$\square = \frac{357 \times 2}{0.0357}$$

If we multiply the numerator and the denominator of the fraction by 10,000 we have

$$\frac{357 \times 2 \times 10{,}000}{357} = 2 \times 10{,}000 = 20{,}000$$

8. **E** Let x = the grade needed on the fifth test.

$$\frac{75 + 80 + 90 + 50 + x}{5} = 80$$

$75 + 80 + 90 + 50 + x = 5(80) = 400$
$295 + x = 400$
$x = 400 - 295 = 105$

Since $x > 100$, it is impossible for the girl to obtain an average of 80 on the five tests.

9. **H** Let x = the man's original salary.
   After a cut of 10% his salary is $0.9x$.
   After a gain of 20% his salary is $(1.2) \times (0.9x) = 1.08x$.
   Thus, the net result is an increase of 8%.

10. **D** The first bell rings after 20, 40, 60, 80 100, 120, 140, 160, 180, 200, 220, 240, 260, 280, and 300 minutes.
    The second bell rings after 30, 60, 90, 120, 150, 180, 210, 240, 270, and 300 minutes.
    The third bell rings after 50, 100, 150, 200, 250, and 300 minutes.
    Thus, all three bells ring at 300 minutes after noon.
    Since 300 minutes is equal to 5 hours, all three bells will next ring at 5:00 P.M.

11. **G** In the right triangle *ABC,* the area is equal to one-half of the product of the legth of the base (*AB*) and the length of the altitude (*BC*).
    Area = $\frac{1}{2}(AB)(BC) = \frac{1}{2}(5)(6) = 15$

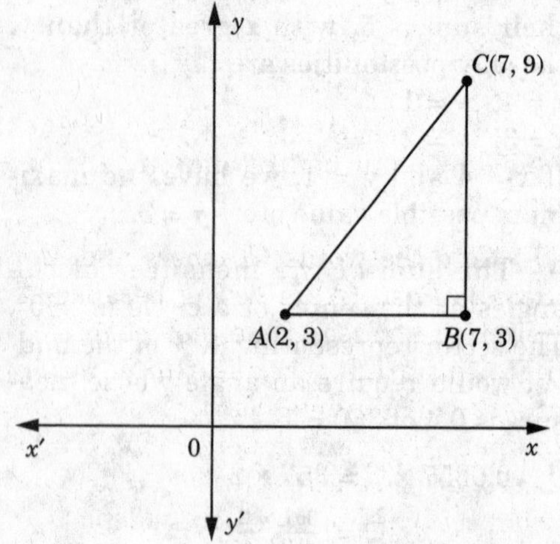

12. **D** 5% of 40 = $0.05 \times 40 = 2$
    The original solution contains 2 gallons of alcohol.
    If 10 gallons of alcohol are added, the new solution has 12 gallons of alcohol in a solution of 50 gallons.

$$\frac{12}{50} = \frac{24}{100} = 24\%$$

13. **G** Let n = the number.
    Then $3n = 21$
    $n = \frac{21}{3} = 7$
    $7 + 5 = 12$

14. **B** Numbers 1 through 9 are to be fitted into the boxes. The sum of these numbers is
    $1 + 2 + 3 + 4 + 5 + 6 + 7 + 8 + 9 = 45$
    Therefore the sum of each of the three columns must be 15 ($15 \times 3 = 45$).
    Since the sum of the numbers in a column is equal to the sum of the numbers in a diagonal, the sum of the numbers in the given diagonal is 15. Thus, x must be equal to 6.

		4
	5	
x		

15. **H** Each boy can dance with 6 different girls to form 6 different couples. Since there are 6 boys in the party, the number of different couples that can be set up is $6 \times 6 = 36$.

16. **A** 40 minutes = $\frac{40}{60} = \frac{2}{3}$ of an hour.
    The man works $6\frac{2}{3} = \frac{20}{3}$ hours.
    $\frac{20}{3} \times 8.50 = \frac{170.00}{3} = 56.67$

17. **K** If we examine the table carefully we see that each number in the y row is 1 more than twice the corresponding number in the x row. That is, $y = 2x + 1$.

18. **C** Since one-half of the remainder were sold on the second day and 50 were left, 50 is the other half of the remainder. Thus, the remainder on the second day was 100, and 100 plus the 80 sold the first day gives 180 as the original number.

19. **G** Since $a > b > c > d > 0$, a is the largest of the four positive numbers and d is the smallest.
    The ratio of the largest positive number (a) to the smallest positive number (d) is greater than the ratio of the two in-between numbers (b) and (c). That is, $\frac{a}{d} > \frac{b}{c}$.

20. **D** Let x = the required number.
    $\frac{x}{9} = 30 + \frac{8}{9}$
    If we multiply both members of this equation by 9, we have
    $x = 9(30) + 8 = 270 + 8 = 278$

21. **H** 1 pound = 16 ounces
 9 pounds 12 ounces = 9(16) + 12 ounces
 = 144 + 12
 = 156 ounces
 $156 \div 6 = 26$

22. **A** Let $10t + u$ represent the original number.
 Then, $10u + t$, or $t + 10u$, represents the number with the digits reversed.
 If we subtract the number with the digits reversed from the original number we have

$$\begin{array}{r} 10t + u \\ \underline{t + 10u} \\ 9t - 9u \end{array}$$

 $9t - 9u$ is divisible by 9.

23. **F** If AB = 14 inches, the area of the square is $14 \times 14 = 196$ square inches. Each curved area in the figure is a quarter-circle. The sum of the four curved areas is a complete circle.
 The radius of the circle is $\frac{1}{2}(14) = 7$ inches.
 The area of the circle = $\pi r^2 = \frac{22}{7} \times 7 \times 7$ = 154 square inches.
 The area of the shaded portion = area of square – area of circle.
 The area of the shaded portion = 196 – 154 = 42 square inches.

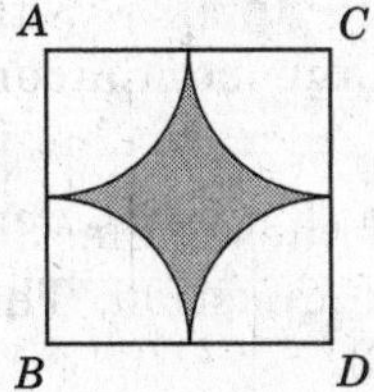

24. **C**

$$\begin{aligned} 3N - 1 &= 14 \\ 3N &= 14 + 1 = 15 \\ N &= 5 \end{aligned}$$

 Twice $N = 2(5) = 10$.
 8 more than twice $N = 8 + 10 = 18$.

25. **G** Let $2x$ = one number and $3x$ = the other number.

$$\frac{2x + 5}{3x + 5} = \frac{3}{4}$$

$$\begin{aligned} 3(3x + 5) &= 4(2x + 5) \\ 9x + 15 &= 8x + 20 \\ 9x - 8x &= 20 - 15 \\ x &= 5 \end{aligned}$$

 The smaller number is $2x = 2(5) = 10$.

SECTION 4

1. **D** Inference. *Half empty* stresses the negative; *half filled* accents the positive.
2. **H** Inference. The author gives equal explanations for both terms, *optimistic* and *pessimistic*.
3. **D** The selection does not go beyond explaining the two terms.
4. **H** Hot water is to teakettle as trouble is to people. Optimists believe people in trouble should also sing (rather than groan).
5. **D** The only definition of "constituted" that fits the sentence is "made up."
6. **G** "The Indian flutes were *carved* from pine...."
7. **B** "Very few of the old flutes...play... because of the cracks that soon develop in these fragile instruments."
8. **J** Inference. The only tool among the choices that could be used for carving is the knife.
9. **C** There is no mention in the selection of using the flute to amuse children.
10. **J** "Most Native American flutes have a range of one octave, making the instrument limited in terms of Western music."
11. **B** George Washington lived before the middle of the nineteenth century.
12. **K** Inference. 'By studying beams in old Pueblo Indian homes, one dendrochronologist..."
13. **D** Note the words *Glimpses* and *More Remote Past.* (A) is wrong because the selection stresses time, not people. (B) is eliminated because the selection deals with more than the Pueblo Indians. (C) is too general. (E) is wrong because the selection does not deal with what it means to be an archeologist.
14. **H** Researchers have to deduce, from whatever evidence is available, how people lived thousands of years ago.
15. **A** Inference. The tree rings reveal the water supply of each year. The people had to migrate when water was too scarce.

16. **G** The selection does not criticize (F); it is not dramatic (H), biased (J), nor argumentative (K). The author just gives facts and conclusions; therefore, (G) is correct.

17. **E** Inference. "He" [the male parent] continues his vigil for the month or so ..."

18. **G** "...it buries itself in the mud. It gets it essential oxygen from an air bladder that acts as a lung."

19. **E** The second, third, and fifth paragraph describe the characteristics that enable the bowfin to survive.

20. **J** "...the male becomes an ever-present guard. He swims constantly around the nest....He continues his vigil for the month..."

21. **E** The first sentence, as topic sentence, summarizes the paragraph: "... hope plays a...potent role...in academic achievement."

22. **G** The paragraph lists qualities (a synonym for "characteristics") that students with high levels of hope have in common. High levels of hope mean that these students share positive values, thus eliminating difficulties (F), peculiarities (H), and frustration (K). The paragraph does not describe several rewards (J).

23. **D** "They are flexible enough to find different ways to reach their goals."

24. **H** "Those high in hope show an ability to break a formidable task into specific achievable chunks"—figuratively speaking, to cross one bridge at a time.

25. **A** The purpose of the selection is to teach students how to use hope and an optimistic attitude as aids in achieving success.

26. **J** "At a few minutes past five, Dave noted that the blanket of darkness was lifting."

27. **E** Inferential answer based on "He tried to sip slowly, but his impatience forced him to finish the drink in gulps."

28. **J** "As he walked down toward the lake . . ."

29. **A** Choices (B), (C), (D), and (E) are described in the selection.

30. **G** "...the occasional bass...leaped out of water for low-flying insects....The magic time had arrived."

31. **B** The entire selection leads up to the last sentence: "It is our last chance to preserve wild areas that, once altered, cannot be replaced."

32. **H** Inference. No money had passed between the natives and Russians (F); Alaska is not part of Europe (G); the natives had not fought Russia (J); and no court had tried the case (K). As the French, English, and Spanish governments had claimed ownership to land through exploration, the Russians must have done the same.

33. **C** "...when the gold fever subsided, Alaska remained largely underdeveloped and underexplored."

34. **F** "Oil was discovered on the state's north coast"; see also next-to-last paragraph.

35. **B** When gold and oil are taken from the land, the land surfaces are altered.

36. **G** The image compares leaves to tongues.

37. **E** None of these selections (**A**)–(**D**) answers the question. Therefore, the answer is (**E**).

38. **J** Inference. There had to be some bad moment (emotional stress, nightmares) in his life ("I was...all but lost") while he remained in the room.

39. **B** Inference. The poet attributes many creature traits to the tree—it is able to talk, see, and be concerned.

40. **F** The position of the poet's room—far above the ground, so that the tree at his window lets him see the trunk and all of the branches and leaves rising from the ground.

Answer Sheet Practice Independent School Entrance Examination 1

TEST ONE

1. Ⓐ Ⓑ Ⓒ Ⓓ	11. Ⓐ Ⓑ Ⓒ Ⓓ	21. Ⓐ Ⓑ Ⓒ Ⓓ	31. Ⓐ Ⓑ Ⓒ Ⓓ
2. Ⓐ Ⓑ Ⓒ Ⓓ	12. Ⓐ Ⓑ Ⓒ Ⓓ	22. Ⓐ Ⓑ Ⓒ Ⓓ	32. Ⓐ Ⓑ Ⓒ Ⓓ
3. Ⓐ Ⓑ Ⓒ Ⓓ	13. Ⓐ Ⓑ Ⓒ Ⓓ	23. Ⓐ Ⓑ Ⓒ Ⓓ	33. Ⓐ Ⓑ Ⓒ Ⓓ
4. Ⓐ Ⓑ Ⓒ Ⓓ	14. Ⓐ Ⓑ Ⓒ Ⓓ	24. Ⓐ Ⓑ Ⓒ Ⓓ	34. Ⓐ Ⓑ Ⓒ Ⓓ
5. Ⓐ Ⓑ Ⓒ Ⓓ	15. Ⓐ Ⓑ Ⓒ Ⓓ	25. Ⓐ Ⓑ Ⓒ Ⓓ	35. Ⓐ Ⓑ Ⓒ Ⓓ
6. Ⓐ Ⓑ Ⓒ Ⓓ	16. Ⓐ Ⓑ Ⓒ Ⓓ	26. Ⓐ Ⓑ Ⓒ Ⓓ	36. Ⓐ Ⓑ Ⓒ Ⓓ
7. Ⓐ Ⓑ Ⓒ Ⓓ	17. Ⓐ Ⓑ Ⓒ Ⓓ	27. Ⓐ Ⓑ Ⓒ Ⓓ	37. Ⓐ Ⓑ Ⓒ Ⓓ
8. Ⓐ Ⓑ Ⓒ Ⓓ	18. Ⓐ Ⓑ Ⓒ Ⓓ	28. Ⓐ Ⓑ Ⓒ Ⓓ	38. Ⓐ Ⓑ Ⓒ Ⓓ
9. Ⓐ Ⓑ Ⓒ Ⓓ	19. Ⓐ Ⓑ Ⓒ Ⓓ	29. Ⓐ Ⓑ Ⓒ Ⓓ	39. Ⓐ Ⓑ Ⓒ Ⓓ
10. Ⓐ Ⓑ Ⓒ Ⓓ	20. Ⓐ Ⓑ Ⓒ Ⓓ	30. Ⓐ Ⓑ Ⓒ Ⓓ	40. Ⓐ Ⓑ Ⓒ Ⓓ

TEST TWO

41. Ⓐ Ⓑ Ⓒ Ⓓ	51. Ⓐ Ⓑ Ⓒ Ⓓ	61. Ⓐ Ⓑ Ⓒ Ⓓ	71. Ⓐ Ⓑ Ⓒ Ⓓ
42. Ⓐ Ⓑ Ⓒ Ⓓ	52. Ⓐ Ⓑ Ⓒ Ⓓ	62. Ⓐ Ⓑ Ⓒ Ⓓ	72. Ⓐ Ⓑ Ⓒ Ⓓ
43. Ⓐ Ⓑ Ⓒ Ⓓ	53. Ⓐ Ⓑ Ⓒ Ⓓ	63. Ⓐ Ⓑ Ⓒ Ⓓ	73. Ⓐ Ⓑ Ⓒ Ⓓ
44. Ⓐ Ⓑ Ⓒ Ⓓ	54. Ⓐ Ⓑ Ⓒ Ⓓ	64. Ⓐ Ⓑ Ⓒ Ⓓ	74. Ⓐ Ⓑ Ⓒ Ⓓ
45. Ⓐ Ⓑ Ⓒ Ⓓ	55. Ⓐ Ⓑ Ⓒ Ⓓ	65. Ⓐ Ⓑ Ⓒ Ⓓ	75. Ⓐ Ⓑ Ⓒ Ⓓ
46. Ⓐ Ⓑ Ⓒ Ⓓ	56. Ⓐ Ⓑ Ⓒ Ⓓ	66. Ⓐ Ⓑ Ⓒ Ⓓ	76. Ⓐ Ⓑ Ⓒ Ⓓ
47. Ⓐ Ⓑ Ⓒ Ⓓ	57. Ⓐ Ⓑ Ⓒ Ⓓ	67. Ⓐ Ⓑ Ⓒ Ⓓ	77. Ⓐ Ⓑ Ⓒ Ⓓ
48. Ⓐ Ⓑ Ⓒ Ⓓ	58. Ⓐ Ⓑ Ⓒ Ⓓ	68. Ⓐ Ⓑ Ⓒ Ⓓ	78. Ⓐ Ⓑ Ⓒ Ⓓ
49. Ⓐ Ⓑ Ⓒ Ⓓ	59. Ⓐ Ⓑ Ⓒ Ⓓ	69. Ⓐ Ⓑ Ⓒ Ⓓ	79. Ⓐ Ⓑ Ⓒ Ⓓ
50. Ⓐ Ⓑ Ⓒ Ⓓ	60. Ⓐ Ⓑ Ⓒ Ⓓ	70. Ⓐ Ⓑ Ⓒ Ⓓ	80. Ⓐ Ⓑ Ⓒ Ⓓ

TEST THREE

81. Ⓐ Ⓑ Ⓒ Ⓓ	91. Ⓐ Ⓑ Ⓒ Ⓓ	101. Ⓐ Ⓑ Ⓒ Ⓓ	111. Ⓐ Ⓑ Ⓒ Ⓓ
82. Ⓐ Ⓑ Ⓒ Ⓓ	92. Ⓐ Ⓑ Ⓒ Ⓓ	102. Ⓐ Ⓑ Ⓒ Ⓓ	112. Ⓐ Ⓑ Ⓒ Ⓓ
83. Ⓐ Ⓑ Ⓒ Ⓓ	93. Ⓐ Ⓑ Ⓒ Ⓓ	103. Ⓐ Ⓑ Ⓒ Ⓓ	113. Ⓐ Ⓑ Ⓒ Ⓓ
84. Ⓐ Ⓑ Ⓒ Ⓓ	94. Ⓐ Ⓑ Ⓒ Ⓓ	104. Ⓐ Ⓑ Ⓒ Ⓓ	114. Ⓐ Ⓑ Ⓒ Ⓓ
85. Ⓐ Ⓑ Ⓒ Ⓓ	95. Ⓐ Ⓑ Ⓒ Ⓓ	105. Ⓐ Ⓑ Ⓒ Ⓓ	115. Ⓐ Ⓑ Ⓒ Ⓓ
86. Ⓐ Ⓑ Ⓒ Ⓓ	96. Ⓐ Ⓑ Ⓒ Ⓓ	106. Ⓐ Ⓑ Ⓒ Ⓓ	116. Ⓐ Ⓑ Ⓒ Ⓓ
87. Ⓐ Ⓑ Ⓒ Ⓓ	97. Ⓐ Ⓑ Ⓒ Ⓓ	107. Ⓐ Ⓑ Ⓒ Ⓓ	117. Ⓐ Ⓑ Ⓒ Ⓓ
88. Ⓐ Ⓑ Ⓒ Ⓓ	98. Ⓐ Ⓑ Ⓒ Ⓓ	108. Ⓐ Ⓑ Ⓒ Ⓓ	118. Ⓐ Ⓑ Ⓒ Ⓓ
89. Ⓐ Ⓑ Ⓒ Ⓓ	99. Ⓐ Ⓑ Ⓒ Ⓓ	109. Ⓐ Ⓑ Ⓒ Ⓓ	119. Ⓐ Ⓑ Ⓒ Ⓓ
90. Ⓐ Ⓑ Ⓒ Ⓓ	100. Ⓐ Ⓑ Ⓒ Ⓓ	110. Ⓐ Ⓑ Ⓒ Ⓓ	120. Ⓐ Ⓑ Ⓒ Ⓓ

TEST FOUR

121. Ⓐ Ⓑ Ⓒ Ⓓ
122. Ⓐ Ⓑ Ⓒ Ⓓ
123. Ⓐ Ⓑ Ⓒ Ⓓ
124. Ⓐ Ⓑ Ⓒ Ⓓ
125. Ⓐ Ⓑ Ⓒ Ⓓ
126. Ⓐ Ⓑ Ⓒ Ⓓ
127. Ⓐ Ⓑ Ⓒ Ⓓ
128. Ⓐ Ⓑ Ⓒ Ⓓ
129. Ⓐ Ⓑ Ⓒ Ⓓ
130. Ⓐ Ⓑ Ⓒ Ⓓ
131. Ⓐ Ⓑ Ⓒ Ⓓ
132. Ⓐ Ⓑ Ⓒ Ⓓ
133. Ⓐ Ⓑ Ⓒ Ⓓ
134. Ⓐ Ⓑ Ⓒ Ⓓ
135. Ⓐ Ⓑ Ⓒ Ⓓ
136. Ⓐ Ⓑ Ⓒ Ⓓ
137. Ⓐ Ⓑ Ⓒ Ⓓ
138. Ⓐ Ⓑ Ⓒ Ⓓ
139. Ⓐ Ⓑ Ⓒ Ⓓ
140. Ⓐ Ⓑ Ⓒ Ⓓ
141. Ⓐ Ⓑ Ⓒ Ⓓ
142. Ⓐ Ⓑ Ⓒ Ⓓ
143. Ⓐ Ⓑ Ⓒ Ⓓ
144. Ⓐ Ⓑ Ⓒ Ⓓ
145. Ⓐ Ⓑ Ⓒ Ⓓ
146. Ⓐ Ⓑ Ⓒ Ⓓ
147. Ⓐ Ⓑ Ⓒ Ⓓ
148. Ⓐ Ⓑ Ⓒ Ⓓ
149. Ⓐ Ⓑ Ⓒ Ⓓ
150. Ⓐ Ⓑ Ⓒ Ⓓ
151. Ⓐ Ⓑ Ⓒ Ⓓ
152. Ⓐ Ⓑ Ⓒ Ⓓ
153. Ⓐ Ⓑ Ⓒ Ⓓ
154. Ⓐ Ⓑ Ⓒ Ⓓ
155. Ⓐ Ⓑ Ⓒ Ⓓ
156. Ⓐ Ⓑ Ⓒ Ⓓ
157. Ⓐ Ⓑ Ⓒ Ⓓ
158. Ⓐ Ⓑ Ⓒ Ⓓ
159. Ⓐ Ⓑ Ⓒ Ⓓ
160. Ⓐ Ⓑ Ⓒ Ⓓ
161. Ⓐ Ⓑ Ⓒ Ⓓ
162. Ⓐ Ⓑ Ⓒ Ⓓ
163. Ⓐ Ⓑ Ⓒ Ⓓ
164. Ⓐ Ⓑ Ⓒ Ⓓ
165. Ⓐ Ⓑ Ⓒ Ⓓ
166. Ⓐ Ⓑ Ⓒ Ⓓ
167. Ⓐ Ⓑ Ⓒ Ⓓ
168. Ⓐ Ⓑ Ⓒ Ⓓ
169. Ⓐ Ⓑ Ⓒ Ⓓ
170. Ⓐ Ⓑ Ⓒ Ⓓ

Independent School Entrance Examination (ISEE)—Middle and Upper Levels

Overview

Total Time

Approximately 3 hours.

Type of Questions

The first 170 questions are multiple choice, with answers to be indicated on a machine-scored Answer Sheet.

The last part of the test consists of an essay question for which students are given 30 minutes in which to read the directions, plan the contents and organization, write the essay, and proofread it.

Pacing

Students taking either the Upper Level or the Middle Level are not expected to complete all items. They are expected to work as fast as possible while maintaining accuracy. The general rule is this: Do not linger over questions you find too difficult. You may return to omitted questions if time permits.

Guessing

A blank answer receives no credit. You will *not* be penalized for guessing. However, if you have no idea which answer is the right one, your chances of guessing the correct answer are only one in four (25 percent). Your chances of being right rise if you can eliminate one or more incorrect answers; eliminating two choices gives you a 50 percent chance of being right—far better than a wild guess. Follow these guidelines:

1. If you can eliminate two answers, guess at the better of the remaining choices and mark your answer.
2. If you have no idea of the right answer, go on to the next question. Do not spend time puzzling over any one question.
3. If you have time remaining at the end of the test, return to the unanswered questions and make your best guess for each one.

Rating Results

ISEE scores compare each student's test performance only with the performances of other students in the same grade level.

Test Content

The following chart is a summary of the topics and time limits at both levels.

TEST ONE: Verbal Ability
(40 questions, 20 minutes)
- Synonyms
- Sentence Completion

TEST TWO: Quantitative Ability
(40 questions, 35 minutes)
- Concepts/Understanding
- Application

TEST THREE: Reading Comprehension
(40 questions, 35 minutes)
- Science Passages
- Social Studies Passages

TEST FOUR: Mathematics Achievement
(50 questions, 40 minutes)
- Middle Level
  - Computation
  - Application
- Upper Level
  - Arithmetic Concepts
  - Algebraic Concepts
  - Geometric Concepts

Essay *(30 minutes)*

Practice Independent School Entrance Examination 1

TEST ONE VERBAL ABILITY

Time limit: 20 minutes *Number of questions: 40*

The Verbal Ability Section consists of two types of questions. There are separate directions for each type.

DIRECTIONS: Each question consists of a word in capital letters followed by four choices. Select the one word that is most nearly the same in meaning as the word in capital letters. On the Answer Sheet, fill in the circle that has the same letter as your answer choice.

1. ABRIDGE:
(A) quarrel (B) cross (C) play
(D) shorten

2. CHEF:
(A) dishwasher (B) chief cook
(C) busboy (D) manager

3. COMPACT:
(A) powder (B) compress (C) destroy
(D) sign

4. CORRAL:
(A) ornament (B) enclosure (C) gem
(D) necklace

5. INSOLENT:
(A) penniless (B) safe (C) shoeless
(D) impudent

6. PEEVISH:
(A) irritable (B) tall (C) dangerous
(D) contagious

7. SODDEN:
(A) dirty (B) unhappy (C) soaked
(D) abrupt

8. TOLERANT:
(A) unprejudiced (B) exaggerated
(C) tricked (D) lazy

9. CACHE:
(A) trick (B) hide (C) perfume
(D) extol

10. BOGUS:
(A) monstrous (B) false (C) historic
(D) tricky

11. ARDUOUS:
(A) lighthearted (B) high (C) twisted
(D) difficult

12. DORMANT:
(A) silent (B) notorious (C) inactive
(D) volcanic

13. GRAPHIC:
(A) ashen (B) brief (C) vivid
(D) painful

14. STAMINA:
(A) stem (B) stubbornness
(C) endurance (D) pressure

15. METHODICAL:
(A) orderly (B) quick (C) creative
(D) forgetful

16. MINIATURE:
(A) mighty (B) tiny (C) religious
(D) threatening

17. NOTABLE:
(A) copied (B) outstanding (C) artistic
(D) anonymous

18. BOUNTIFUL:
(A) seaworthy (B) wavelike
(C) abundant (D) intelligent

19. PINNACLE:
(A) flag (B) signal (C) peak
(D) feather

20. WHEEDLE:
(A) steer (B) attack (C) browbeat
(D) coax

DIRECTIONS: Each question below consists of a sentence with one or two blanks. A single blank indicates the omission of one word; two blanks mean that two words are omitted. For each sentence, choose the word or words that will best complete the meaning of the sentence as a whole. On the Answer Sheet, fill in the circle that has the same letter as your answer choice.

21. Only after months of practice climbing was the team ready to __________ the high, rugged peaks of the Alps.
(A) encompass (B) reconstruct
(C) ascend (D) describe

22. Unless she is __________, an investor in the stock market can quickly lose all her life's savings.
(A) conceited (B) cautious
(C) imprudent (D) overconfident

23. The persistent questioning by the police forced the driver to __________ that he may have turned the corner too fast.
(A) reminisce (B) complain (C) foretell
(D) concede

24. Only when a struck match __________ will it become a deadly instrument in the hands of a child.
(A) glows (B) ignites (C) smolders
(D) cools

25. Honorable people __________ trickery and deception.
(A) loathe (B) admire (C) exemplify
(D) practice

26. The hiker used the heavy branch as a __________ to fight off the attack dog.
(A) baton (B) pellet (C) bludgeon
(D) trick

27. The __________ message consisting of ten small words destroyed the hopes of a lifetime.
(A) lengthy (B) terse (C) repetitious
(D) welcome

28. The claims of the __________ heirs were quickly disproved by the skillful lawyers.
(A) legitimate (B) wealthy (C) spurious
(D) ingenious

29. Twelve o'clock is the time of the day when the sun reaches its __________.
(A) schedule (B) horoscope (C) horizon
(D) zenith

30. After years of research, the test tubes of the laboratory produced __________ fibers superior to cotton and silk.
(A) natural (B) needless (C) flimsy
(D) synthetic

31. What __________ can medals give the __________ parents of a fallen hero?
(A) zeal ... mourning
(B) comfort ... vigilant
(C) solace ... grieving
(D) insight ... admirable

32. The __________ in the Far East was __________; war could break out any day.
(A) puzzle ... imminent
(B) solution ... instantaneous
(C) situation ... serious
(D) conflict ... postponed

33. I asked Lucy to act as my __________ at the next meeting since I shall be __________ to attend.
(A) substitute ... willing
(B) confidante ... required
(C) proxy ... unable
(D) representative ... compelled

34. There is no __________ attached to recognizing a bad decision in time to __________ a better one.
(A) shame ... disregard
(B) complexity ... renew
(C) honor ... reject
(D) stigma ... substitute

35. To read without __________ is like eating without digesting.
(A) reflecting (B) variety
(C) compassion (D) competence

36. Coolidge's Second Law of Perversity is that a ____________ article ____________ shows up after you replace it.
(A) worthless ... never
(B) misplaced ... invariably
(C) valuable ... rarely
(D) newsworthy ... seldom

37. Racism is humanity's ____________ threat to humanity—the maximum of hatred for the minimum of ____________.
(A) inevitable ... emotion
(B) most trivial ... turmoil
(C) least rewarding ... effect
(D) gravest ... reason

38. When the people in a democratic nation are divided in their opinion, the decision of the majority must ____________.
(A) change (B) vanish (C) prevail
(D) concede

39. The winds and the rain have ____________ the names of those for whom these monuments were erected.
(A) enscribed (B) clarified
(C) translated (D) effaced

40. People can follow a comic strip story by looking at the ____________ and never reading the ____________.
(A) illustrations ... captions
(B) copyright ... acknowledgments
(C) dialogue ... grimaces
(D) action ... headlines

TEST TWO QUANTITATIVE ABILITY

Time limit: 35 minutes *Number of questions: 40*

GENERAL DIRECTIONS: You may assume that any figures given in connection with questions are drawn as accurately as possible *except* when it is stated that a particular figure is not drawn to scale. Letters such as *x*, *y*, and *n* stand for real numbers.

For questions 41–60, select the correct answer to each problem and fill in the corresponding circle on the Answer Sheet. You may work mentally or use blank space on the test pages.

41. What is the best common denominator for the fractions $\frac{1}{3}$, $\frac{3}{8}$, and $\frac{5}{6}$?
(A) 18 (B) 12 (C) 24 (D) 48

42. If $5 < x < 9$ and $3 < x < 7$, what is the value of x?
(A) 6 (B) 5 (C) 9 (D) 4

43. Triangle *ABC* and triangle *DEF* are equal in area. If the base of $\triangle ABC$ measures 12 inches, the base of $\triangle DEF$ measures 9 inches, and the altitude of $\triangle ABC$ measures 6 inches, what is the measure of the corresponding altitude of $\triangle DEF$?
(A) 72 inches (B) 10 inches (C) 9 inches (D) 8 inches

44. A centimeter is equal to
(A) 100 meters (B) 10 kilometers (C) $\frac{1}{100}$ meter (D) 1 milligram

45. If $(4 \times 10^3) + (5 \times 10^2) + 7$ is subtracted from $(6 \times 10^3) + (7 \times 10^2) + (2 \times 10) + 4$, the result is
(A) 2270 (B) 2217 (C) 1217 (D) 2127

46. In the product shown below, what digit does $\square$ represent?
$(3 \square 6)(4) = 432$
(A) 4 (B) 5 (C) 6 (D) 8

47. Which of the following numbers is equal to $\frac{3}{5}$?
(A) 0.06 (B) $\frac{3}{5}\%$ (C) 60% (D) $5 \div 3$

48. If each side of a square is doubled in length, then
(A) the area of the square is doubled
(B) the area of the square is increased by 50%
(C) the area of the square is multiplied by 4
(D) the area of the square is not changed

49. Mr. Hart bought a sport jacket and paid a sales tax of \$4.50. If the rate of the sales tax was 6%, what was the price of the jacket before the tax?
(A) \$27.00 (B) \$75.00 (C) \$120.00 (D) \$85.00

50. When a number is divided by 7, the quotient is 19 and the remainder is 3. The number is
(A) 133 (B) 136 (C) 130 (D) 140

51. $6 \times 7 \times 8 \times \square = 48 \times 63$. The value of $\square$ is
(A) 8 (B) 9 (C) 12 (D) 6

52. If $x + 6 = y + 4$, then
(A) $x > y$ (B) $x - y = 2$ (C) $y > x$ (D) $x + y = 10$

53. 7% is equal to
(A) 7 (B) 0.7 (C) 700 (D) 0.07

54. At a sale of TV sets $\frac{2}{3}$ of the sets were sold the first day and $\frac{1}{2}$ of the remainder were sold the second day. If 15 sets were left unsold, how many sets were put on sale the first day?
(A) 80 (B) 90 (C) 100 (D) 75

55. The diagram represents a doorway that is a rectangle topped by a semicircle. If the width of the doorway is 12 feet and the height of the rectangular section of the doorway is 9 feet, what is the total area, in feet, of the doorway?

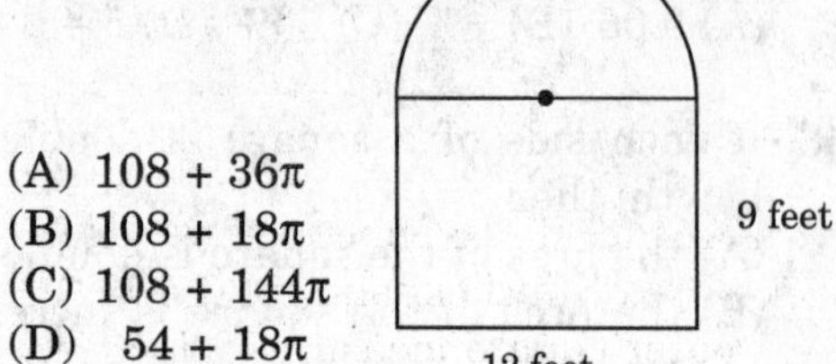

(A) $108 + 36\pi$
(B) $108 + 18\pi$
(C) $108 + 144\pi$
(D) $54 + 18\pi$

56. If $5 > x > 3$, and x is a positive integer, then $x^2 =$
(A) 25 (B) 9 (C) 4 (D) 16

57. In an isosceles right triangle, the measure of each acute angle is
(A) 50° (B) 45° (C) 90° (D) 40°

58. When written in expanded form, the number 5618 is
(A) $(5 \times 10^2) + (6 \times 10) + 18$
(B) $(5 \times 10^3) + (6 \times 10^2) + (8 \times 10) + 1$
(C) $(5 \times 10^3) + (6 \times 10^2) + (1 \times 10) + 8$
(D) $(5 \times 10^3) + (6 \times 10^2) + (1 \times 8)$

59. $\dfrac{5}{\frac{3}{7}} =$
(A) $\frac{35}{3}$ (B) $5 \div \frac{7}{3}$ (C) $\frac{5\times3}{7}$ (D) $5 \times \frac{3}{7}$

60. According to the following number line:

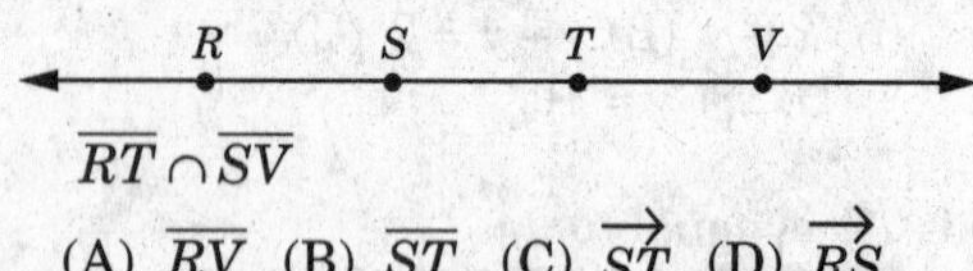

$\overline{RT} \cap \overline{SV}$
(A) $\overline{RV}$ (B) $\overline{ST}$ (C) $\overrightarrow{ST}$ (D) $\overrightarrow{RS}$

DIRECTIONS: For questions 61–80, two quantities are given, one in Column A and the other in Column B. In some cases, additional information concerning the quantities to be compared is centered above the entries in the two columns. After noting all the information given, compare the quantities in Columns A and B and fill in the circles on the Answer Sheet as follows:
(A) if the quantity in Column A is greater
(B) if the quantity in Column B is greater
(C) if the quantities in Columns A and B are equal
(D) if the information given is not sufficient to determine which quantity is greater

	Column A	**Column B**
61.	$\frac{1}{4} + \frac{5}{6}$	$1\frac{3}{8} - \frac{1}{2}$

m $\angle C = 90°$
m $\angle B = 42°$

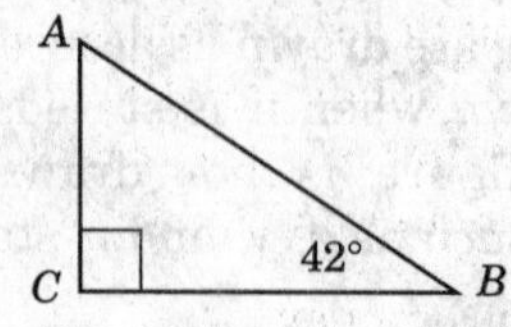

62.	AC	CB

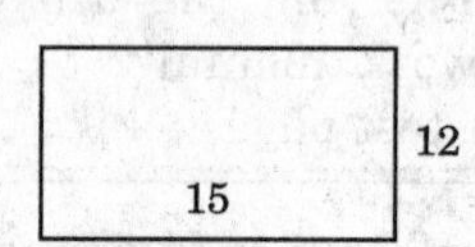

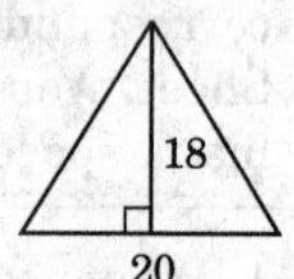

63.	Area of this rectangle	Area of this triangle

x and y are integers.
$x > y$

64.	$\frac{1}{x}$	$\frac{1}{y}$

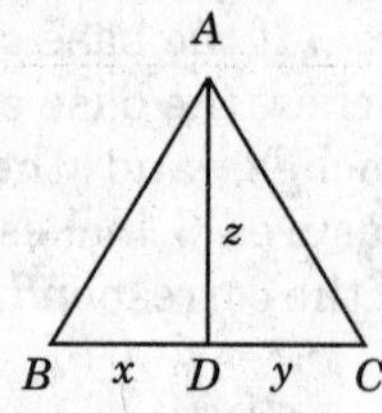

m $\angle B = 55°$
m $\angle C = 45°$
$\overline{AD}$ bisects $\angle BAC$

65.	$x + y$	$2z$

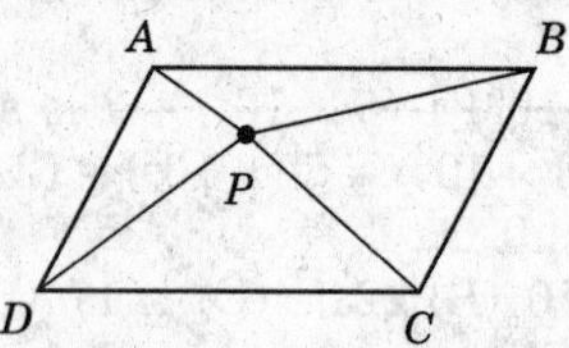

$ABCD$ is a parallelogram.

66.	Area of $\triangle APB$	Area of $\triangle APD$

$a = 3$,
$b = -1$

67.	$7 - a(b + 5)$	$b^2 - 2a$

Column A		Column B

a and b are positive integers with $a > b$.

68. $\frac{a}{b}$ | $\frac{b}{a}$

The ratio of Arthur's money to Ben's money is 4:3. If Arthur gives Ben \$5, the two boys will have equal amounts.

69. Arthur's money | \$25

$2x + y = 11$
$2x - y = 5$

70. x | y

71. $\frac{\frac{7}{8}-\frac{1}{4}}{\frac{5}{6}}$ | $\frac{\frac{1}{6}+\frac{5}{12}}{\frac{1}{9}}$

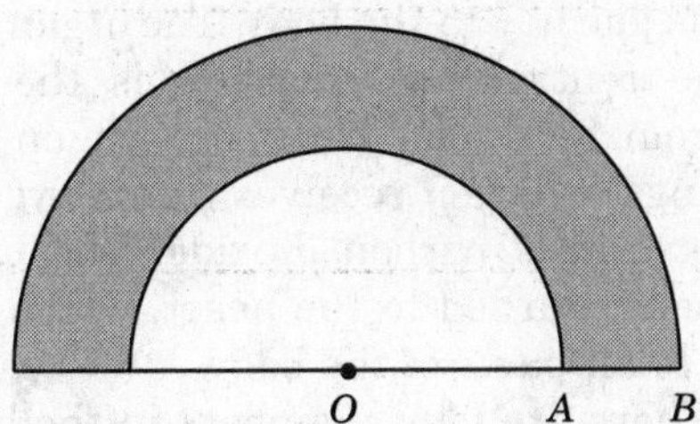

O is the center of both circles.
$OA = 6$,
$AB = 4$

72. Area of shaded semicircle | Area of smaller portion

$a > b > c$,
a, b, and c are positive integers

73. b^2 | ac

$x + \frac{1}{3}$,
$y = \frac{1}{5}$

74. $\frac{1}{x} + \frac{1}{y}$ | $\frac{x+y}{xy}$

Column A		Column B

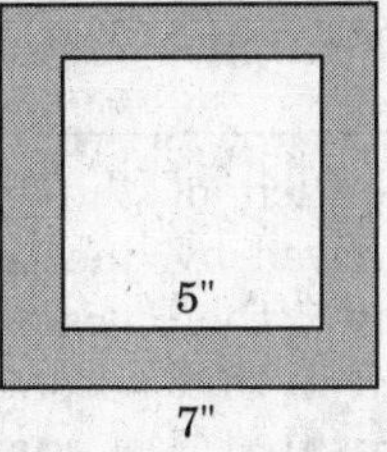

A side of the inner square measures 5 inches, and a side of the outer square measures 7 inches.

75. Area of inner square | Area of shaded portion

$3x - 1 = 15$
$2y + 5 = 12$

76. x | y

$\frac{x}{5} = 2 + \frac{4}{5}$
$\frac{y}{7} = 6 + \frac{3}{7}$

77. x | y

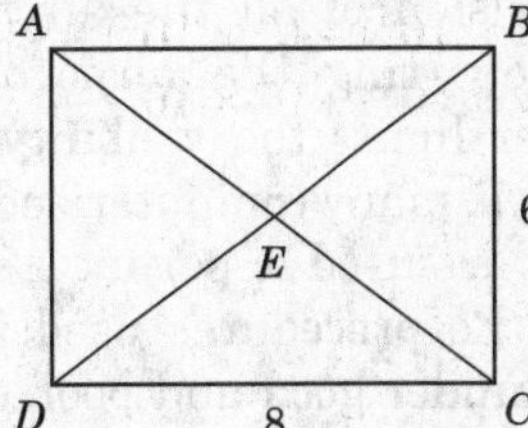

$ABCD$ is a rectangle
$BC = 6$,
$DC = 8$

78. DE | 5

$x = 5$,
$y = -3$

79. $x^2 + y^2$ | $(x + y)^2$

Mr. Ames drives a distance of 180 miles in 5 hours. The return trip over the same distance takes him 4 hours.

80. Mr. Ames's average speed | 40 miles per hour

TEST THREE READING COMPREHENSION

Time limit: 35 minutes *Number of questions: 40*

DIRECTIONS: Each of the nine passages below is followed by questions based on its contents. On the basis of what is *stated* or *implied* in that passage, choose the word or words that best answer the question. On the Answer Sheet, fill in the circle that has the same letter as your answer choice.

In a large metropolitan airport, that is, an air terminal at the edge of a major city, it is not unusual to have many landings and take-offs during a 24-hour period. The heavy air traffic is under the control of a group of people known as air traffic controllers, who direct the flow of air traffic into and out of the airport. The air traffic control group works in the control tower, which is located at the highest point in the airport terminal complex, permitting the controllers to have maximum vision of all the aircraft arriving and departing the airport. When the weather limits the visibility around the runways, many computerized navigational aids are used to permit a safe landing. All of the procedures used for handling traffic under good and poor weather conditions are established by the Federal Aviation Administration, known as the FAA.

81. Under poor weather conditions an airport will
    (A) postpone all flights
    (B) substitute the judgment of machines for that of men and women
    (C) plan emergency landings only
    (D) divert all flights

82. The word "metropolitan" in line 1 most nearly means
    (A) international and domestic
    (B) restricted to the military
    (C) serving a major city
    (D) used largely for cargo

83. The tone of this selection is best described as
    (A) argumentative
    (B) biased
    (C) emotional
    (D) factual

84. We can infer from the passage that air traffic controllers
    (A) lead lives filled with danger
    (B) must be skilled mechanics
    (C) must be trained pilots
    (D) go through a rigorous training period

The network of capillaries, veins, and arteries make up the intricate routes that the blood travels through in its continuous journey in the body. The organ that is the central headquarters is the heart. From here, the blood is sent on to the lungs, where it receives fresh oxygen and gets rid of carbon dioxide. The blood is then returned to the heart, which routes it to all parts of the body.

There are four chambers in the heart—the auricles on top and the ventricles below. The blood enters the heart from all parts of the body, coming into the right auricle. From the right auricle the blood passes into the right ventricle, which sends the blood to the lungs. The blood returns to the left auricle and then passes through the left ventricle. The left ventricle acts as a pump, pushing the blood out through the aorta to all parts of the body.

85. Blood returning from the lungs enters the
    (A) left ventricle
    (B) left auricle
    (C) right auricle
    (D) right ventricle

86. The heart acts as
    (A) a pump for the entire blood system
    (B) a disposal mechanism to get rid of waste products
    (C) an extractor to provide fresh oxygen
    (D) a reservoir for supplying new red blood corpuscles

87. Which of the following statements expresses the main idea of the selection?
(A) The lungs are an important part of the blood distribution system.
(B) The heart is a tireless pump.
(C) The heart regulates the constant flow of blood through the body.
(D) Blood pressure is kept at a constant level by the heart.

88. Which of the following best describes the tone of the passage?
(A) objective
(B) skeptical
(C) persuasive
(D) moral

89. As used in line 2, the word "routes" means
(A) circuit
(B) stations
(C) vessels
(D) organs

The role of the Supreme Court in America is a very debatable one. The Court and its area of control, its jurisdiction, are established in Article III of the Constitution. This document does not state, however, that the Supreme Court shall have the power of "judicial review," that is, the right to pass judgment on the constitutionality of Congressional and Presidential acts. This power is implied by a reading and interpretation of other articles of the Constitution, such as Article VI, section 2, which states that the Constitution is the "supreme law of the land." In the famous case of *Marbury* v. *Madison* (1803) the Supreme Court declared it had the power of "judicial review." Since that time many court decisions based on the power of "judicial review" have angered Americans. Varying alternatives have been suggested, but it would appear that this power will never be taken from the Court.

90. An implied power is one that is
(A) unquestioned
(B) found in many articles of the Constitution
(C) based on interpretation of the Constitution
(D) derived from the Bill of Rights

91. As used in line 7, the term "judicial review" means
(A) the power to abolish state judicial systems
(B) the power to declare legislative or presidential acts illegal
(C) the right to enact laws
(D) the right to advise Congress and the President

92. The author suggests that the Supreme Court's power of judicial review is
(A) used only to anger people
(B) not debatable
(C) not likely to disappear
(D) too unimportant to warrant controversy

93. The word "jurisdiction" in line 3 means most nearly
(A) the limits within which authority may be exercised
(B) personnel
(C) branches throughout the country
(D) special privileges

The Oregon trail followed a route first used by early explorers and fur traders in the Northwest. By the 1840s it had become a well-known highway, although travel was not heavy over its 2000-mile length. Travel on the trail was rough. There were many dangers, such as Indian attacks and grizzly bears, and the weather could be unkind with wind, rain, and snow at unexpected seasons. Illness, death, and the dark night were ever-present fears. In the great migration led by Marcus Williams in 1843, the distance traveled by the ox-drawn covered wagons on an easy, good day was twenty-five miles; they averaged two miles an hour. On bad days the wagons often made no more than five miles. People traveled the trail in groups with elected leaders for the train. The nightly wagon circle, with the men on the outside and the women, children, and cattle on the inside, is a familiar part of American folklore.

94. Among the dangers encountered on the Oregon Trail were
(A) drought and dry winds
(B) stampedes
(C) Indian attacks
(D) extremely high temperatures

95. By which of the following was the Oregon Trail first used?
(A) Indians
(B) early explorers
(C) oxen
(D) prospectors for gold

96. The reader can infer that the migration of 1843 led to
(A) the discovery of gold
(B) much disease and famine
(C) the killing of many Native Americans
(D) the building of many settlements

97. The author suggests that American folklore contains stories of
(A) the nightly wagon circle
(B) grizzly bear attacks
(C) humorous experiences on the trails
(D) the elation at the end of the 2000-mile trip

98. From this passage it can be inferred that Marcus Williams was
(A) an experienced explorer
(B) a member of Congress
(C) a Native American
(D) a wagon train leader

There is an interesting characteristic of the higher forms of animals, in comparison to animals lower on the ladder of the Animal Kingdom. Higher forms of animal life have a variety of systems within their bodies that are used for special functions: a circulatory system for blood, the food supplier; a digestive system for converting food into energy and body tissue; a nervous system; a respiratory system; and others. We describe this organization of systems as specialization of structure and function, typical of the higher forms of life. In a single-celled organism, the cell must carry out all of the life functions without benefit of these special systems. Thus the paramecium, a single-celled animal, uses the protoplasm and its contents as a circulatory system and a respiratory system and for life functions as well.

99. The definition that applies to "converting" in line 9 of this passage is
(A) making a goal after receiving a pass
(B) exchanging for an equivalent
(C) altering the physical or chemical nature
(D) diverting from one destination to another

100. The system for carrying supplies of nutrients to the various organs is called the
(A) circulatory system
(B) digestive system
(C) respiratory system
(D) nervous system

101. Bones are an example of specialization of
(A) circulation
(B) structure
(C) digestion
(D) function

102. According to this selection, which of the following is true of the single-celled paramecium?
(A) It is an example of a higher form of animal.
(B) It has life functions similar to ours.
(C) It lacks the ability to circulate.
(D) It lacks life functions.

103. Which of the following best describes the author's attitude toward paramecia and other lower forms of life?
(A) contemptuous
(B) compassionate
(C) admiring
(D) impersonal

Ramses II was one of the greatest military leaders of New Kingdom Egypt, according to the battles portrayed on the walls of the great temple of Amon at Karnak. His "victory" over the Hittites at the Battle of Kadesh in 1288 B.C. is reported in detail. The personal bravery of Ramses is recorded by an incident in which he rallied his army by leading it for a great attack. If the temple reports were all we knew of the battle, all books would carry it as the "victory" Ramses claimed it to be. Actually, archaeologists have found Hittite records that claim the battle as a victory for their King Hattushil. Such a discrepancy in reporting is hard to understand unless we realize that the records were propaganda to glorify each king. Further archaeological evidence indicates that the battle was, in fact, a draw and that there were periodic minor skirmishes between Egypt and the Hittites for twenty-five years after the Battle of Kadesh. Finally the two powers signed a treaty that indicated the area of influence and power for each in the Near East. To seal the treaty, Ramses II married a daughter of the King Hattushil. The treaty brought peace to the Near East and clearly indicates that Ramses was not as powerful as he claimed.

104. The conflict between the Hittites and the New Kingdom ended in
(A) the Battle of Kadesh
(B) a treaty sealed by a marriage
(C) the victory of King Hattushil
(D) the victory of Ramses II

105. The Hittite reports of the Battle of Kadesh are contradicted by the
(A) personal bravery of Ramses II
(B) portrayal of the battle on the walls of the temple of Amon
(C) records found by modern researchers in the area
(D) treaty with King Hattushil

106. The word "rallied" in line 9 most nearly means
(A) roused to action
(B) summoned up strength
(C) shot in a series of volleys
(D) trained thoroughly

107. The two contradictory versions of the Battle of Kadesh
(A) were unintentionally inaccurate
(B) proved that King Hattushil was really the victor
(C) showed that the Egyptian version was more truthful
(D) were deliberate exaggerations of the truth

There are several important applications of the principle of expansion of solids due to heating the solid. One application is found in the type of thermometer called a thermocouple. If a strip of metal is heated, it will expand. Some metals will expand more than others for the same amount of heat; each metal has a definite expansion for a specific amount of heat. Therefore, if two different metal strips are bound together and heated, the single strip of metals will tend to assume a curved position because of the greater expansion of one metal as compared to the other. This curvature can make contact with an electrical circuit, starting an electric motor or operating some other electromechanical device. In the home a thermocouple stops or starts the oil burner in accordance with the room temperature. The temperature of a gasoline engine can be measured with a device similar to a thermocouple.

108. When solids are heated, they expand
(A) at the same rate
(B) at different rates
(C) indefinitely
(D) only when heated above 100 degrees centigrade

109. A thermocouple
(A) creates heat
(B) creates electricity
(C) makes or breaks a contact
(D) cannot work automatically

110. The reader can infer that a thermocouple will NOT work when
(A) the two metals are very long
(B) both metals are four inches thick and one inch long
(C) one metal is thicker than the other
(D) the two metals are of different lengths

111. A thermocouple for a home oil burner depends on
(A) the temperature of the surrounding air
(B) the pressing of a button each time it is used
(C) the height from the floor
(D) the distance from a window

In colonial days there were few newspapers. People read them with care as they were almost the only source of news. Colonial governors realized how important the newspapers were in forming opinions and often wished to suppress or prevent stories from appearing. The governors did not like to be criticized, but such criticism is essential to democracy.

One governor who tried to control the press was Governor Cosby in New York. When John Peter Zenger published criticism of the Governor in his paper, *The Weekly Journal,* Zenger was arrested. The Governor stated that Zenger was printing lies. At the trial in 1735, Zenger's lawyer, Alexander Hamilton, proved to the jury's satisfaction that Zenger was speaking and writing the truth. The spectators at the trial cheered this decision, which is the basic decision establishing freedom of the press in our country.

112. John Peter Zenger was arrested for
 (A) committing a criminal act
 (B) writing stories about New York
 (C) publishing what he thought of the governor's actions
 (D) printing *The Weekly Journal*

113. The author of this passage believes that
 (A) Zenger was wrong in being critical
 (B) citizens have the obligation to fault an official
 (C) newspapers can print anything they wish
 (D) the governor was right in protecting himself

114. The trial of Zenger established the
 (A) reputation of Alexander Hamilton
 (B) reputation of *The Weekly Journal*
 (C) basis of freedom of the press in America
 (D) role of juries in trials

115. The trial of Zenger proved that
 (A) U.S. newspapers print the truth
 (B) colonial governors controlled the press
 (C) U.S. newspapers cannot be stopped from printing the truth
 (D) U.S. publishers cannot be punished for what they print

In the Middle Ages, from the middle of the fifth to the sixteenth century, the regular unit of European life was not the city or the open farmstead. It was the feudal castle—a fortification situated if possible upon a lofty hill, and often having a little village of crude huts of the lord's peasants clustered close beside it. During the feudal, or medieval, period the castle in most cases was simply a single huge tower, round or square, with merely a crude palisade and a ditch for outworks. The height would baffle any scaling-ladder. There was no opening in the blank masonry until a considerable distance from the ground. Then the narrow door could be entered only by a flimsy, narrow bridge, easy to demolish, or by a frail ladder, drawn up every night. Inside the tower was a series of dark, cavernous rooms, one above another, communicating by means of ladders. The sole purpose of such a comfortless castle was defense, and that defense by mere height and mass, not by any skill in arranging the various parts. The best kind of medieval castle needed only a very small number of soldiers. From behind its walls even an inferior baron could protect himself from a kingly army of knights in full battle array.

116. A word that the author uses to mean the same as "medieval" is
 (A) crude
 (B) cavernous
 (C) feudal
 (D) kingly

117. "Middle Ages" in line 1 means
 (A) ages 40 to 55
 (B) ages 19 to 40
 (C) from A.D. 500 to 1500
 (D) from A.D. 1700 to 1900

118. The chief value of the castle was to provide
 (A) ample living quarters for many soldiers
 (B) adequate protection from enemy attack
 (C) a means of counterattack
 (D) warmth and comfort in all kinds of weather

119. As used in line 13, the word "baffle" most nearly means
(A) foil
(B) confuse
(C) control
(D) destroy

120. The fact that the castle was the focal point of life in the Middle Ages reflects
(A) the bravery of the nobility
(B) the immense wealth of the barons
(C) the power of kings
(D) the lawlessness of the times

TEST FOUR MATHEMATICS ACHIEVEMENT

Time limit: 40 minutes *Number of questions: 50*

DIRECTIONS: Each question is followed by four answer choices. Choose the correct answer to each question, and fill in the corresponding circle on the Answer Sheet.

121. $(7 \times 10^3) + (4 \times 10^2) + 5 =$
(A) 7450 (B) 7405 (C) 745 (D) 7540

122. What is the area of a triangle whose base measures 8 inches and whose altitude measures 9 inches?
(A) 72 square inches
(B) 32 square inches
(C) 18 square inches
(D) 36 square inches

123. A plane travels 1260 miles in $3\frac{1}{2}$ hours. What is the average rate of speed of the plane?
(A) 350 miles per hour
(B) 300 miles per hour
(C) 320 miles per hour
(D) 360 miles per hour

124. Which of the following is a root of the equation $6 + x^2 = 70$?
(A) 8 (B) 7 (C) 6 (D) 5

125. Mr. Burns made a down payment of \$57 on the purchase of a new TV set. If this was 15% of the full price of the set, how much more remained for Mr. Burns to pay?
(A) \$323 (B) \$380 (C) \$350 (D) \$313

126. The scale on a map is $\frac{1}{2}''$ = 80 miles. If the distance between two cities measures $3\frac{1}{4}''$ on the map, how far apart are the two cities?
(A) 500 miles (B) 520 miles (C) 585 miles (D) 560 miles

127. At a theater the cost of seats in the orchestra was twice the cost of seats in the balcony. At one performance \$7000 was taken in on ticket sales of 880. If 520 orchestra seats were sold at \$10 each, how many balcony seats were sold?
(A) 360 (B) 320 (C) 440 (D) 560

128. A rectangle and a square have equal areas. If the length of the rectangle measures 20 feet and its width measures 5 feet, then the measure of a side of the square is
(A) 20 feet (B) 15 feet (C) 10 feet (D) 12 feet

129. A saleswoman is paid \$40 per week plus 8% of the sales that exceed \$2000 per week. What is the saleswoman's pay for a week when her sales amounted to \$7850?
(A) \$485 (B) \$508 (C) \$468 (D) \$540

130. The freshman class at Lincoln High School numbers 320 students. There are 18 more boys than girls in the class. Which of the following equations may be solved to find the number of girls in the class?
(A) $x + 18 = 320$
(B) $x + x + 18 = 320$
(C) $x + y = 320$
(D) $x + 320 = x + 18$

131. A man has 8 white shirts and 3 blue shirts in his wardrobe. If he selects a shirt at random, what is the probability that his choice is a white shirt?
(A) $\frac{3}{8}$ (B) $\frac{3}{11}$ (C) $\frac{3}{5}$ (D) $\frac{8}{11}$

132. If $3x + y = 14$ and $3x - y = 10$, then $y =$
(A) 4 (B) 2 (C) 3 (D) 1

133. The length of a rectangle is 8 inches, and its diagonal measures 10 inches. The area of the rectangle is
(A) 48 square inches
(B) 60 square inches
(C) 80 square inches
(D) 24 square inches

134. It takes a work crew 12 hours to complete $\frac{3}{4}$ of a job. How many more hours will the crew need to finish the job?
(A) 8 (B) 10 (C) 6 (D) 4

135. The area of a semicircle is 39.25 square inches. Find the radius of the semicircle. (Let $\pi = 3.14$.)
(A) 5 inches (B) 6 inches (C) 10 inches (D) 8 inches

136. Two cars start from the same point and travel in opposite directions at rates differing by 10 miles per hour. If the cars are 240 miles apart after 3 hours, how fast is the slower car traveling?
(A) 45 miles per hour
(B) 40 miles per hour
(C) 35 miles per hour
(D) 43 miles per hour

137. A piece of beef weighs 3 pounds 6 ounces. At $3.12 per pound, what is the cost of this piece of beef?
(A) $10.40 (B) $9.78 (C) $10.53 (D) $10.43

138. A tank holds 50 gallons of a mixture of acid and water that is 30% acid. If 20 gallons of acid are added to the mixture, what is the percent of acid in the new mixture?
(A) 35% (B) 30% (C) 50% (D) 40%

139. Eight men earn $2880 for 6 days of work. At the same rate how much will 12 men earn for 5 days of work?
(A) $3600 (B) $3200 (C) $4800 (D) $4320

140. A garden plot is 180 feet long and 60 feet wide. A gardener wishes to divide this plot into squares that measure 20 feet on a side. How many squares will he obtain?
(A) 18 (B) 20 (C) 27 (D) 25

141. If on the number line below $AC = 30$, $BD = 40$, and $BC = 12$, then $AD =$

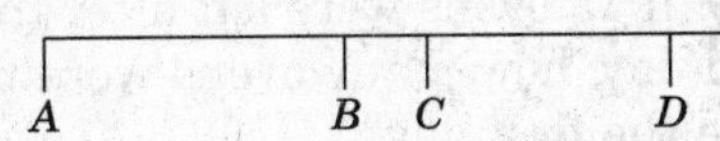

(A) 70 (B) 58 (C) 48 (D) 52

142. If $xy + 12 = 40$ and $y = 4$, the value of $x + y =$
(A) 12 (B) 15 (C) 14 (D) 11

143. If n is an even number, which of the following is an odd number?
(A) $2n$ (B) $3n$ (C) $2n + 1$ (D) $n + 4$

144. Mr. Harris left home at 8:40 A.M. to take a trip to a distant city. His driving time was 5 hours and 30 minutes. In addition, he stopped for 15 minutes to buy gas and 50 minutes for lunch. At what time did Mr. Harris reach his destination?
(A) 2:30 P.M. (B) 2:45 P.M. (C) 3:10 P.M. (D) 3:15 P.M.

145. If $a = \frac{1}{3}$ and $b = \frac{1}{2}$, what is the value of $a^2 + ab + b^2$?
(A) $\frac{7}{18}$ (B) $\frac{19}{36}$ (C) $1\frac{4}{9}$ (D) $\frac{17}{36}$

146. The diagram below shows the number of students enrolled in three major sports at Martin Luther King High School. How many students play both football and baseball?

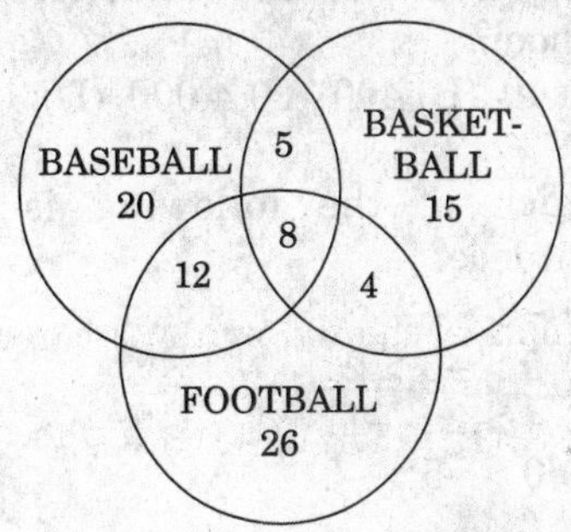

(A) 20 (B) 28 (C) 46 (D) 26

147. How long does it take to cover a mile at a speed of 50 miles per hour?
(A) $1\frac{1}{3}$ minutes (B) $1\frac{1}{2}$ minutes (C) $1\frac{1}{10}$ minutes (D) $1\frac{1}{5}$ minutes

148. If a motorist pays $10.48 for 8 gallons of gas how much would he pay for 12 gallons of gas at the same rate?
(A) $13.10 (B) $15.72 (C) $14.96 (D) $ 15.24

149. If $x + 5 = y + 3$, then which of the following is true?
(A) $x = y$ (B) $x > y$ (C) $y > x$ (D) $x - y = 2$

150. If $0.47 \times 69.8 = 47 \times \square$, then $\square =$
(A) 0.698 (B) 6.98 (C) 698 (D) 6,980

151. A team has won 30 games and lost 10 games. If the team wins one-half of the next 10 games it plays, what percent of games played will it have won?
(A) 70% (B) 50% (C) 75% (D) 80%

152. A garden plot in the form of a rectangle has a length of $4x + 5$ feet and width of $x + 10$ feet. What is the perimeter of the plot?
(A) $(4x + 5)(x + 10)$ feet
(B) $5x + 15$ feet
(C) $10x + 30$ feet
(D) $5x + 10$ feet

153. If $s = 16t^2$, what is the value of s when $t = \frac{1}{4}$?
(A) 32 (B) 1 (C) 256 (D) 4

154. The freshman class at Jefferson High School numbers 120 students. If this is 30% of the total enrollment, how many students attend Jefferson High School?
(A) 40 (B) 400 (C) 4,000 (D) 3,600

155. Which of the following is a true sentence?
(A) $-6 > -2$
(B) $5 > -3 > 2$
(C) $4 > 2 > -1$
(D) $0 > -5 > -3$

156. If the circumference of a circle is 12π, what is the area of the circle?
(A) 36π (B) 18π (C) 144π (D) 72π

157. John and Bill earn a total of $170 per day for an 8-hour work day. John earns $3 per hour more than Bill. Which of the following equations can be used to find Bill's hourly pay?
(A) $8x + 8x + 3 = 170$
(B) $8x + x + 24 = 170$
(C) $8x + 8(x + 3) = 170$
(D) $x + 8(x + 3) = 170$

158. 3 yards 2 feet 5 inches
<u>– 1 yard 1 foot 7 inches =</u>

(A) 2 yards 1 foot 8 inches
(B) 1 yard 1 foot 10 inches
(C) 2 yards 10 inches
(D) 2 yards 8 inches

159. A house is assessed for $80,000 and is insured for 75% of its assessed valuation. What is the yearly premium if it is based on $0.55 per hundred dollars of assessed valuation?
(A) $330 (B) $3300 (C) $303 (D) $350

160. $\frac{1}{2}\left(\frac{1}{3}+\frac{1}{4}\right) =$
(A) $\frac{1}{14}$ (B) $\frac{7}{24}$ (C) $\frac{1}{7}$ (D) $\frac{1}{24}$

161. If $2x + 3 = 11$, then $10 - x =$
(A) 5 (B) 3 (C) 0 (D) 6

162. Mr. Evans plans to take a trip of 210 miles, driving at an average speed of 42 miles per hour. How many hours does the trip take?
(A) $5\frac{1}{2}$ (B) 4 (C) 5 (D) $4\frac{1}{2}$

163. Ms. Hernandez rents a car while on a business trip. She pays $37 per day and $0.18 per mile for every mile above 100. If she drives 142 miles, what is her rental fee for 1 day?
(A) $62.56 (B) $44.56 (C) $55.00 (D) $46.50

164. If $BC = 8''$, $CD = 6''$, and $DE = 5''$, find the area of the figure below

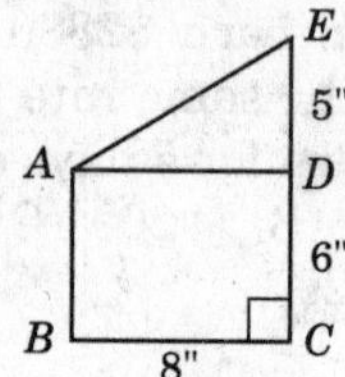

(A) 60 square inches
(B) 68 square inches
(C) 65 square inches
(D) 64 square inches

165. At a sale of microwave ovens, $\frac{5}{8}$ of the ovens were sold the first day and $\frac{2}{3}$ of the remainder were sold the second day. If 15 ovens were left after the second day, how many ovens were put on sale the first day?
(A) 100 (B) 120 (C) 112 (D) 150

166. If $3x - 2 = 16$, then 5 more than twice $x =$
(A) 12 (B) 17 (C) 15 (D) 19

167. If the sum of two numbers is y and one of the numbers is 5, then three times the other number is
(A) $3(5 - y)$ (B) $3 \times 5 - y$
(C) $3(y - 5)$ (D) $3xy - 5$

168. 30% of what number is 12?
(A) 4 (B) 4.8 (C) 48 (D) 40

169. A recipe calls for 4 ounces of butter and $1\frac{1}{2}$ ounces of sugar. If 6 ounces of butter are used, how many ounces of sugar should be used?
(A) $2\frac{1}{4}$ (B) $2\frac{1}{2}$ (C) 2 (D) $2\frac{3}{4}$

170. If $\frac{1}{4}x = 20$, then $\frac{3}{8}x =$
(A) 20 (B) 30 (C) 60 (D) 50

TEST FIVE WRITING THE ESSAY

Time limit: 30 minutes

The essay is assigned to give you an opportunity to show how well you can write. You should, therefore, take care to express your thoughts on the topic clearly and effectively. How well you write is much more important than how much you write, but to cover the topic adequately you will want to write more than one paragraph.

Write your essay on the sheets of paper provided or use some of your own. Do any scratch-work planning on this page.

It is important to remember that what you write will be read by someone who is not familiar with your handwriting. Write or print so that your essay is legible.

DIRECTIONS: Using two sheets of lined theme paper, plan and write an essay on the topic assigned below. DO NOT WRITE ON ANOTHER TOPIC. AN ESSAY ON ANOTHER TOPIC IS NOT ACCEPTABLE. You have 30 minutes for this section of the test.

Public pressure has finally resulted in network broadcasting of televised courtroom trials for criminal offenses. Not all localities and not all states have authorized such presentations.

Prompt: Write an essay discussing whether such broadcasts should be legalized throughout the country. Support your opinion with specific examples from history, current affairs, or personal observations.

Answers to Practice ISEE 1

TEST ONE VERBAL ABILITY

1. D	5. D	9. B	13. C	17. B
2. B	6. A	10. B	14. C	18. C
3. B	7. C	11. D	15. A	19. C
4. B	8. A	12. C	16. B	20. D

Rating Your Results

Middle Level

Superior	16–20 correct
Average	12–15 correct
Below Average	11 or fewer correct

Upper Level

Superior	17–20 correct
Average	14–16 correct
Below Average	13 or fewer correct

Material to Review: Chapter 4

21. C	25. A	29. D	33. C	37. D
22. B	26. C	30. D	34. D	38. C
23. D	27. B	31. C	35. A	39. D
24. B	28. C	32. C	36. B	40. A

Rating Your Results

Middle Level

Superior	15–20 correct
Average	11–14 correct
Below Average	10 or fewer correct

Upper Level

Superior	16–20 correct
Average	12–15 correct
Below Average	11 or fewer correct

Material to Review: Chapter 4

TEST TWO QUANTITATIVE ABILITY

41. C	49. B	57. B	65. B	73. D
42. A	50. B	58. C	66. C	74. C
43. D	51. B	59. A	67. C	75. A
44. C	52. C	60. B	68. A	76. A
45. B	53. D	61. A	69. A	77. B
46. C	54. B	62. B	70. A	78. C
47. C	55. B	63. C	71. B	79. A
48. C	56. D	64. D	72. A	80. C

Rating Your Results

Superior	34–40 correct
Average	26–33 correct
Below Average	25 or fewer correct

Material to Review: Chapters 8–14

TEST THREE READING COMPREHENSION

81. B	89. A	97. A	105. B	113. B
82. C	90. C	98. D	106. A	114. C
83. D	91. B	99. C	107. D	115. C
84. D	92. C	100. A	108. B	116. C
85. B	93. A	101. B	109. C	117. C
86. A	94. C	102. B	110. B	118. B
87. C	95. B	103. D	111. A	119. A
88. A	96. D	104. B	112. C	120. D

Rating Your Results

Middle Level

Superior	34–40 correct
Average	26–33 correct
Below Average	25 or fewer correct

Upper Level

Superior	36–40 correct
Average	28–35 correct
Below Average	27 or fewer correct

Material to Review: Chapter 5

TEST FOUR MATHEMATICS ACHIEVEMENT

121. B	131. D	141. B	151. A	161. D
122. D	132. B	142. D	152. C	162. C
123. D	133. A	143. C	153. B	163. B
124. A	134. D	144. D	154. B	164. B
125. A	135. A	145. B	155. C	165. B
126. B	136. C	146. A	156. A	166. B
127. A	137. C	147. D	157. C	167. C
128. C	138. C	148. B	158. C	168. D
129. B	139. A	149. C	159. A	169. A
130. B	140. C	150. A	160. B	170. B

Rating Your Results

Superior	42–50 correct
Average	32–41 correct
Below Average	31 or fewer correct

Material to Review: Chapters 8–14

Explanations

TEST ONE

21. (**C**) Key words: months, practice climbing, team, rugged high peaks. *Ascend* stresses upward direction.

22. (**B**) Key words: unless, investor, stock market, quickly lose. To avoid loss, one must be *cautious.*

23. (**D**) Key words: persistent questioning, forced driver, too fast. The pressure caused the driver to *concede* that he or she was at fault.

24. (**B**) Key words: struck match, deadly instrument. When the match *ignites,* it can easily become deadly.

25. (**A**) Key words: honorable people, trickery, deception. If one is honorable, he or she *loathes* unfair tactics.

26. (**C**) Key words: heavy branch, fight off, attack dog. A *bludgeon* is a heavy club, that is, a weapon to fight off attack.

27. (**B**) Key words: message, ten words, destroyed, hopes. *Terse* means brief, containing very few words; "destroyed the hopes" tells you that the message was not welcome.

28. (**C**) Key words: claims, heirs, quickly disproved. The only negative choice to agree with "disproved" is *spurious,* meaning false.

29. (**D**) Key words: twelve o'clock, time, sun, reaches. *Zenith* is the only choice that refers to position in the heavens.

30. (**D**) Key words: research, test tubes, fibers. The fibers were made in the laboratory; they were therefore *synthetic.*

31. (**C**) Key words: medals, parents, fallen hero. Medals can give little *solace* to the *grieving* parents of a son who has died.

32. (**C**) Key words: war, break out, any day. If war appeared imminent, the *situation* was indeed *serious.*

33. (**C**) Key words: act, next meeting, I, attend. I asked Lucy to act as my *proxy* (substitute) since I shall be *unable* to attend.

34. (**D**) Key words: No, recognizing, bad decision, better one. No *stigma* (discredit) results when a good decision is *substituted* for a bad one.

35. (**A**) Key words: read, without eating, without digesting. To absorb what we read, we must think about what the author tells us, that is, *reflect* on the content.

36. (**B**) Key words: Law, Perversity, article, shows up, after, replace. Something *misplaced invariably* shows up only after you buy a replacement; this is an example of perversity (that which is unexpected or unreasonable) at work.

37. (**D**) Key words: racism, threat, maximum of hatred, minimum. Racism, racial prejudice, is humanity's *gravest* (most serious) threat to human values since it causes violent hatred toward an individual for the least *reason.*

38. (**C**) Key words: people, democratic nation divided, decision, majority. In a democracy, the will of the majority *prevails.*

39. (**D**) Key words: winds, rain, names, monuments. Weathering wipes out *(effaces)* the names on tombstones and monuments.

40. (**A**) Key words: People, comic strip story, looking, never reading. Many people claim that they can understand the comics by looking at the pictures (*illustrations),* without reading the *captions* (titles and explanatory comments).

TEST TWO

41. **(C)** We may find the least common denominator by writing the multiples of the denominators, as follows:

    For $\frac{1}{3}$: 3, 6, 9, 12, 15, 18, 21, (24)

    For $\frac{3}{8}$: 8, 16, (24)

    For $\frac{5}{6}$: 6, 12, 18, (24)

    The first number that appears in all three multiples of the denominators is the least common denominator. In this case, the least common denominator is 24.

42. **(A)** $5 < x < 9$ means that $x > 5$ and $x < 9$, or x is 6, 7, or 8.

    $3 < x < 7$ means that $x > 3$ and $x < 7$ or x is 4, 5, or 6.

    To satisfy both inequalities, x must be 6. Note that, as the choices indicate, x is an integer.

43. **(D)** Area of $\triangle ABC = \frac{1}{2}(12)(6) = 36$ square inches

    Area of $\triangle DEF = \frac{1}{2}(9)x = \frac{9}{2}x$

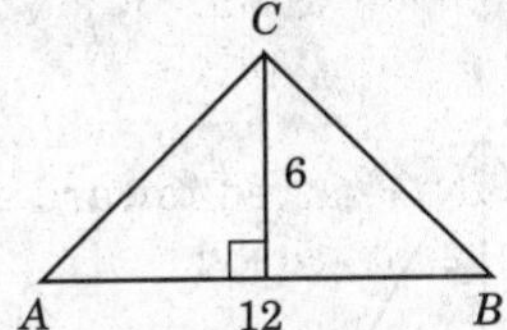

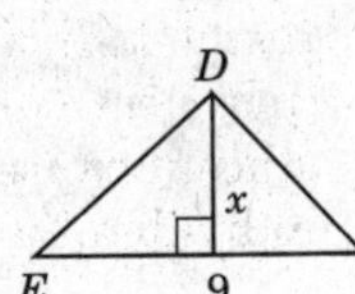

Since the areas are equal, we have

$\frac{9}{2}x = 36$

$9x = 72$

$x = 8$

44. **(C)** By definition a centimeter is equal to one hundredth ($\frac{1}{100}$) of a meter.

45. **(B)** $(4 \times 10^3) + 5(10^2) + 7 = 4507$

    $(6 \times 10^3) + (7 \times 10^2) + (2 \times 10) + 4 = 6724$

    $6724 - 4507 = 2217$

46. **(C)** $(3 \square 6)(4) = 432$

    $72 \square = 432$

    $\square = \frac{432}{72} = 6$

47. **(C)** Written as a decimal, $\frac{3}{5} = 0.60$ and $0.60 = 60\%$

48. **(C)** See the diagram. If we call the original square S and we double each side, we obtain an enlarged square having an area exactly 4 times the area of S.

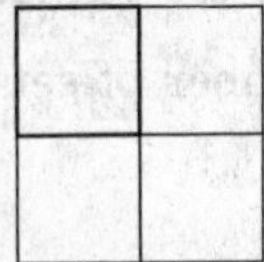

ALTERNATE METHOD

Let each side of $S = 5$ inches.

Then the area of $S = 25$ square inches.

When we double each side of S, the original square, we have 10 inches on a side. Then the area of the new square $= 10 \times 10 = 100$ square inches. To go from 25 square inches to 100 square inches is to multiply by 4.

49. **(B)** Let x = cost of jacket

    Then $0.06x = 4.50$

    $x = \frac{4.50}{0.06} = \frac{450}{6} = 75$

50. **(B)** Let x = the number

    Then $\frac{x}{7} = 19 + \frac{3}{7}$

    After we multiply both sides of the equation by 7, we have

    $x = 7(19) + 3$

    $x = 133 + 3 = 136$

51. **(B)** $6 \times 7 \times 8 \times \square = 48 \times 63$

    Since $6 \times 8 = 48$, we have

    $48 \times 7 \times \square = 48 \times 63$

    or $7 \times \square = 63$

    $\square = \frac{63}{7}$

52. **(C)** $x + 6 = y + 4$

    If we subtract 6 from both sides of the equation, we have $x = y - 2$. This means that x is 2 less than y, or $y > x$.

53. **(D)** 7% means 7 hundredths, which can be written as 0.07.

54. **(B)** After $\frac{2}{3}$ of the sets were sold the first day, $\frac{1}{3}$ of the sets were left.

$\frac{1}{2}$ of the remainder = $\frac{1}{2} \times \frac{1}{3} = \frac{1}{6}$

Thus, $(\frac{2}{3} + \frac{1}{6})$ of the sets were sold the first 2 days:

$\frac{2}{3} + \frac{1}{6} = \frac{4}{6} + \frac{1}{6} = \frac{5}{6}$, leaving $\frac{1}{6}$ unsold

Let x = number of sets put on sale the first day

$\frac{1}{6}x = 15$

$x = 90$

55. **(B)** The area of the rectangular part of the doorway = 12 × 9 = 108. The radius of the circular part of the doorway is 6. The area of this circle is 36π, and the area of the semicircle is 18π. The total area of the doorway is 108 + 18π.

56. **(D)** $5 > x > 3$ means that x is greater than 3 but less than 5. Since x is a positive integer, $x = 4$.

$x^2 = 4 \times 4 = 16$

57. **(B)** The sum of the measures of the angles of a triangle is 180°. If one angle is a right angle, the sum of the measures of the other two angles is 90°. In an isosceles right triangle the sum of the measures of the acute angles is 90°, and the measures of the acute angles are equal. Thus, the measure of each acute angle is 45°.

58. **(C)** 5000 in expanded form = (5×10^3)
600 in expanded form = (6×10^2)
10 in expanded form = (1×10)
5618 in expanded form = $(5 \times 10^3) + (6 \times 10^2) + (1 \times 10) + 8$

59. **(A)** $\frac{5}{\frac{3}{7}} = 5 \div \frac{3}{7} = 5 \times \frac{7}{3} = \frac{35}{3}$

60. **(B)** The ∩ symbol means "intersection."

$\overline{RT} = \overline{RS} + \overline{ST}$, $\overline{SV} = \overline{ST} + \overline{TV}$

The intersection of $\overline{RT}$ and $\overline{SV}$ is $\overline{ST}$.

61. **(A)** For Column A, $\frac{1}{4} + \frac{5}{6} = \frac{3}{12} + \frac{10}{12} = \frac{13}{12}$
For Column B, $1\frac{3}{8} - \frac{1}{2} = \frac{11}{8} - \frac{4}{8} = \frac{7}{8}$

The quantity in Column A is greater than the quantity in Column B.

62. **(B)** Since m $\angle C = 90°$ and m $\angle B = 42°$, m $\angle A = 180° - (90 + 42) = 48°$. Therefore, $AC < CB$ since the smaller side of the triangle lies opposite the smaller angle. The quantity in Column B is greater than the quantity in Column A.

63. **(C)** Area of rectangle = 15 × 12 = 180

Area of triangle = $\frac{20 \times 18}{2} = 180$

The quantity in Column A is equal to the quantity in Column B.

64. **(D)** x is an integer and y is an integer, with $x > y$.

If $x = 5$, $\frac{1}{x} = 5$. If $y = 2$, $\frac{1}{y} = \frac{1}{2}$.

In this case, $\frac{1}{y} > \frac{1}{x}$.

If $x = -5$, $\frac{1}{x} = 5$. If $y = -2$, $\frac{1}{y} = \frac{1}{2}$.

In this case, $\frac{1}{x} > \frac{1}{y}$.

Since x and y are integers which may have any value, we cannot decide whether $\frac{1}{x} > \frac{1}{y}$ or $\frac{1}{x} < \frac{1}{y}$. The relationship depends upon the values taken for x and y and cannot be determined from the information given.

65. **(B)** m $\angle BAC = 180° - (55° + 45°) = 80°$
m $\angle BAD = \frac{1}{2}(80) = 40°$

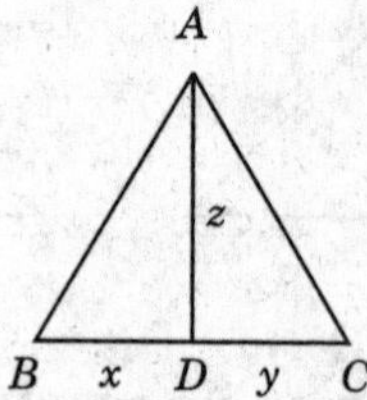

In △ABD, $z > x$ because, in a triangle, the greater side lies opposite the greater angle. In △ADC, $z > y$ because, in a triangle, the greater side lies opposite the greater angle. Therefore, $2z > x + y$. The quantity in Column B is greater than the quantity in Column A.

66. **(C)** △ADC = △ABC (in area) since a diagonal of a parallelogram divides the parallelogram into two triangles that have equal areas.

The altitude of △ADC = the altitude of △ABC because those triangles are equal in area and have the same base.

The altitude of $\triangle ADP$ = the altitude of $\triangle APB$ and those triangles have the same base ($\overline{AP}$).

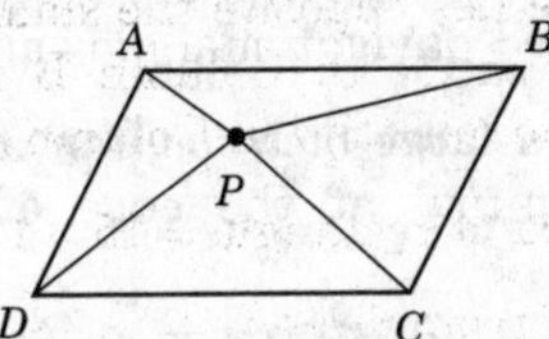

Thus, $\triangle APB = \triangle APD$ in area. The quantity in Column A is equal to the quantity in Column B.

67. (**C**) $a = 3$, $b = -1$
For Column A, $7 - a(b + 5) = 7 - 3(-1 + 5) = 7 - 3(4) = 7 - 12 = -5$
For Column B, $b^2 - 2a = (-1)2 - 2(3) = 1 - 6 = -5$
The quantity in Column A is equal to the quantity in Column B.

68. (**A**) Let $a = 10$ and $b = 3$.
Then $\frac{a}{b} = \frac{10}{3}$, and $\frac{b}{a} = \frac{3}{10}$.
In general, if $a > b$, then $\frac{a}{b} > 1$ and $\frac{b}{a} < 1$
Thus, $\frac{a}{b}$ (Column A) will always be greater than $\frac{b}{a}$ (Column B).
The quantity in Column A is greater than the quantity in Column B.

69. (**A**) Let $4x$ = Arthur's money
And $3x$ = Ben's money
$4x - 5$ = Arthur's money after Arthur gives Ben \$5
$3x + 5$ = Ben's money after Arthur gives Ben \$5
$4x - 5 = 3x + 5$
$4x - 3x = 5 + 5$
$x = 10$
Arthur's money before giving Ben \$5 = $4x$ = \$40, which is greater than \$25 (Column B). The quantity in Column A is greater than the quantity in Column B.

70. (**A**) $2x + y = 11$
$2x - y = 5$
If we add, we have
$4x = 16$
$x = 4$
Since $2x + y = 11$,
$2(4) + y = 11$
$8 + y = 11$
$y = 11 - 8 = 3$
The quantity in Column A is greater than the quantity in Column B.

71. (**B**) For Column A, $\frac{7}{8} - \frac{1}{4} = \frac{7}{8} - \frac{2}{8} = \frac{5}{8}$
$\frac{5}{8} \div \frac{5}{6} = \frac{5}{8} \times \frac{6}{5} = \frac{3}{4}$
For Column B, $\frac{1}{6} + \frac{5}{12} = \frac{2}{12} + \frac{5}{12} = \frac{7}{12}$
$\frac{7}{12} \div \frac{1}{9} = \frac{7}{12} \times \frac{9}{1} = \frac{63}{12} = \frac{21}{4}$
The quantity in Column B $\left(\frac{21}{4}\right)$ is greater than the quantity in Column A $\left(\frac{3}{4}\right)$.

72. (**A**) The radius of the larger semicircle is 10. The area of the larger semicircle is $10 \times 10\pi = 100\pi \div 2 = 50\pi$. The radius of the smaller semicircle is 6. The area of the smaller semicircle is $6 \times 6\pi = 36\pi \div 2 = 18\pi$. The area of the shaded portion is $50\pi - 18\pi = 32\pi$. The quantity in Column A (32π, the area of the shaded portion) is greater than the quantity in Column B (18π, the area of the smaller semicircle).

73. (**D**) $a > b > c$
Let $a = 50$, $b = 2$, $c = 1$
Then $b^2 = 4$, $ac = 50 \times 1 = 50$
Let $a = 10$, $b = 8$, $c = 2$
Then $b^2 = 64$, $ac = 10 \times 2 = 20$
In the first case, $b^2 < ac$. In the second case, $b^2 > ac$. Thus, we cannot tell whether $b^2 > ac$ or $b^2 < ac$. The relationship cannot be determined from the information given.

74. (**C**) $x = \frac{1}{3}$, $y = \frac{1}{5}$
$\frac{1}{x} = 3$, $\frac{1}{y} = 5$
For Column A, $\frac{1}{x} + \frac{1}{y} = 3 + 5 = 8$
For Column B, $x + y = \frac{1}{3} + \frac{1}{5} = \frac{5}{15} + \frac{3}{15} = \frac{8}{15}$
$xy = \frac{1}{3} \times \frac{1}{5} = \frac{1}{15}$
$\frac{x+y}{xy} = \frac{\frac{8}{15}}{\frac{1}{15}} = 8$
Thus, $\frac{1}{x} + \frac{1}{y} = 8$ and $\frac{x+y}{xy} = 8$. The quantity in Column A is equal to the quantity in Column B.

75. (**A**) Area of inner square $= 5 \times 5 = 25$ square inches. Area of outer square $7 \times 7 = 49$ square inches. Area of shaded portion $= 49 - 25 = 24$ square inches.
Since $25 > 24$, the quantity in Column A is greater than the quantity in Column B.

76. **(A)** $3x - 1 = 15$, $2y + 5 = 12$

For Column A, $3x = 15 + 1 = 16$

$x = \frac{16}{3} = 5\frac{1}{3}$

For Column B, $2y = 12 - 5 = 7$

$y = \frac{7}{2} = 3\frac{1}{2}$

Thus, $x > y$. The quantity in Column A is greater than the quantity in Column B.

77. **(B)** $\frac{x}{5} = 2 + \frac{4}{5}$, $\frac{y}{7} = 6 + \frac{3}{7}$

For Column A, if we multiply both sides of the equation by 5, we have
$x = 5(2) + 4$
$x = 10 + 4 = 14$

For Column B, if we multiply by both sides of the equation by 7, we have
$y = 6(7) + 3$
$y = 42 + 3 = 45$

Thus $y > x$. The quantity in Column B is greater than the quantity in Column A.

78. **(C)** Triangle *BCD* is a right triangle. Therefore,

$(BD)^2 = 6^2 + 8^2$
$(BD)^2 = 36 + 64 = 100$
$BD = 10$
$DE = \frac{1}{2}(BD)$
$DE = \frac{1}{2}(10) = 5$

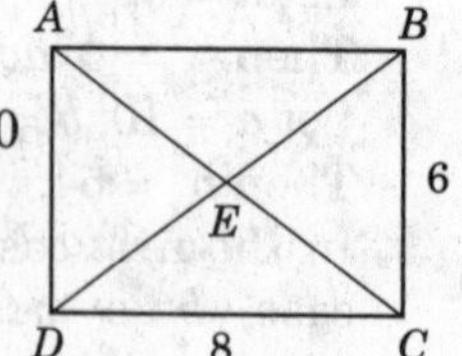

The quantity in Column A is equal to the quantity in Column B.

79. **(A)** $x = 5$, $y = -3$

$x^2 = 25$, $y^2 = 9$

For Column A, $x^2 + y^2 = 25 + 9 = 34$

For Column B, $(x + y)^2 = [5 + (-3)]^2$
$= (2)^2 = 4$

Thus, $x^2 + y^2 > (x + y)^2$, The quantity in Column A is greater than the quantity in Column B.

80. **(C)** Total mileage = 180 + 180 = 360 miles. Total traveling time = 5 + 4 = 9 hours

Average speed = $\frac{360}{9}$ = 40 miles per hour

The quantity in Column A is equal to the quantity in Column B.

TEST THREE

81. **(B)** "When the weather limits ... computerized navigational aids are used.. ."

82. **(C)** "... a large *metropolitan* airport, an air terminal at the edge of a *major city*...."

83. **(D)** The author lists facts and their consequences, making the tone factual.

84. **(D)** Inferential answer based on entire selection.

85. **(B)** "... sends the blood to the lungs. The blood returns to the left auricle...."

86. **(A)** "... central headquarters is the heart."

87. **(C)** The article describes the function of the heart in the blood circulation system.

88. **(A)** The tone of the passage is objective and unemotional.

89. **(A)** *Routes* means paths; a circuit is a circular path.

90. **(C)** "This power [of judicial review] is implied by a reading and interpretation...."

91. **(B)** See lines 7–9.

92. **(C)** "... this power will never be taken from the Court."

93. **(A)** See lines 2 and 3.

94. **(C)** "There were many dangers, such as Indian attacks...."

95. **(B)** "The Oregon trail followed a route first used by early explorers...."

96. **(D)** Inference based on section beginning with "In the great migration...." Women, children, and cattle suggest settlements.

97. **(A)** "The nightly wagon circle ... is a familiar part of American folklore."

98. **(D)** Inferred from Whitman's leading the great migration and the statement that "People traveled ... with elected leaders...."

99. **(C)** ... "digestive system for converting *food into energy and body tissue ...,*" that is, altering the physical and chemical nature of food.

100. **(A)** "... a circulatory system for blood, the food supplier."

101. **(B)** Inference based on "We describe this organization of systems as specialization of structure and function."

102. **(B)** "In a single-celled organism, the cell must carry out all of the life functions...."

103. **(D)** The author's attitude is factual and impersonal toward both the higher and lower forms of life.

104. **(B)** "To seal the treaty, Ramses II married a daughter of King Hattushil."

105. **(B)** Ramses's "'victory' ... is reported in detail."

106. **(A)** "... he rallied his army [roused it to action] by leading it for a great attack."

107. **(D)** "... The records were propaganda to glorify each king."

108. **(B)** "Each metal has a definite expansion for a specific amount of heat."

109. **(C)** "This curvature can make contact with an electrical circuit..."

110. **(B)** Two pieces of metal so thick and so short would not blend sufficiently to activate the thermocouple.

111. **(A)** The temperature in the thermocouple for the home oil burner is determined by the air surrounding the burner.

112. **(C)** "When ... Zenger published criticism of the Governor ... Zenger was arrested."

113. **(B)** "... such criticism is essential to democracy."

114. **(C)** "... the basic decision establishing freedom of the press in our country."

115. **(C)** "... proved that Zenger was speaking and writing the truth."

116. **(C)** "During the feudal, or medieval, period ..." (line 9).

117. **(C)** "Middle Ages" is defined in lines 1 and 2.

118. **(B)** The entire selection indicates this conclusion.

119. **(A)** The meaning of "baffle" can be inferred from clues in the passage ("a 'huge tower,'" "a considerable distance from the ground") and by eliminating the other choices.

120. **(D)** Inference based on complete selection.

TEST FOUR

121. **(B)** $(7 \times 10^3) = 7000$

$(4 \times 10^2) = 400$

$5 = 5$

$7000 + 400 + 5 = 7405$

122. **(D)** The area of a triangle is equal to one-half the product of the length of the base and the length of the altitude, or $A = \frac{1}{2}bh$.
In this case, $b = 8$ and $h = 9$
Area $= \frac{1}{2}(8)(9) = 36$ square inches

123. **(D)** To find the average rate of speed we divide the distance covered by the time consumed.

$1260 \div 3\frac{1}{2} = 1260 \div \frac{7}{2}$

$1260 \div \frac{7}{2} = 1260 \times \frac{2}{7} = 360$ miles per hour

124. **(A)** $6 + x^2 = 70$

$x^2 = 70 - 6 = 64$

$x = 8$

125. **(A)** Let x = cost of TV set

$0.15x = 57$

$x = \frac{57}{0.15} = \frac{5700}{15} = \$380$

$380 - 57 = \$323$

126. **(B)** $\frac{1}{2}'' = 80$ miles

$1'' = 2(80) = 160$ miles

$3\frac{1}{4}'' = \frac{13}{4}(160) = 520$ miles

127. **(A)** $520 \times 10 = \$5200$ for orchestra seats. $7000 - 5200 = \$1800$ for balcony seats

Since each balcony seat sold for $5, the number of balcony seats sold was $1800 \div 5 = 360$.

128. **(C)** Area of the rectangle = $20 \times 5 = 100$ square feet
Let x = measure of a side of the square
Then $x^2 = 100$
$x = 10$ feet

129. **(B)** $7850 - 2000 = \$5850$
8% of $5800 = 0.08 \times 5850 = 468$
$468 + 40 = \$508$

130. **(B)** Let x = number of girls in the class
And $x + 18$ = number of boys in the class
Number of girls + number of boys = 320
The equation is $x + x + 18 = 320$.

131. **(D)** Probability of selecting a white shirt
$= \frac{\text{number of white shirts}}{\text{total number of shirts}} = \frac{8}{8+3} = \frac{8}{11}$

132. **(B)** $3x + y = 14$
$3x - y = 10$
Adding, we have $6x = 24$, $x = 4$.
Since $3x + y = 14$, we have
$3(4) + y = 14$
$12 + y = 14$
$y = 14 - 12 = 2$

133. **(A)** In the right triangle ABC

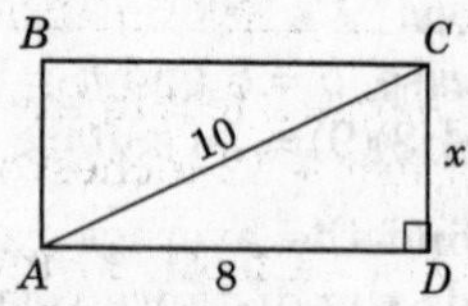

we have $x^2 + 8^2 = 10^2$
$x^2 + 64 = 100$
$x^2 = 100 - 64 = 36$
$x = 6$
Area = $6 \times 8 = 48$ square inches.

134. **(D)** $\frac{3}{4}$ of the job takes 12 hours.
$\frac{1}{4}$ of the job takes $12 \div 3 = 4$ hours.
$\frac{4}{4}$, or the whole job, takes $4 \times 4 = 16$ hours.
$16 - 12 = 4$ more hours needed to finish the job.

135. **(A)** Area of circle = πr^2
Area of semicircle = $\frac{1}{2}\pi r^2$
$39.25 = \frac{1}{2}(3.14)r^2 = 1.5\pi r^2$
$r^2 = 39.25 = 1.57$
$r^2 = 25$
$r = 5$ inches

136. **(C)** Let x = rate of slower car
And $x + 10$ = rate of faster car
$3x$ = distance covered by slower car in 3 hours
$3(x + 10)$ = distance covered by faster car in 3 hours
Sum of distances = $3x + 3(x + 10)$
$3x + 3(x + 10) = 240$
$3x + 3x + 30 = 240$
$6x = 240 - 30 = 210$
$x = 35$ miles per hour

137. **(C)** 3 pounds 6 ounces = $3\frac{6}{16}$ pounds, or $3\frac{3}{8}$ pounds
$3\frac{3}{8} = \frac{27}{8}$
$\frac{27}{8} \times 3.12 = \$10.53$

138. **(C)** 30% of $50 = 0.3 \times 50 = 15$ gallons of acid in original mixture
Amount of acid in new mixture = $15 + 20 = 35$ gallons
Amount of new mixture = $50 + 20 = 70$ gallons
$\frac{35}{70} = \frac{1}{2} = 50\%$ acid in new mixture

139. **(A)** \$2880 is earned in $6 \times 8 = 48$ man-days of work
$\$2880 \div 48 = \$60$ = amount earned by 1 man in 1 day
12 men will earn $5 \times 12 = 60(60) = \$3600$ in 5 days

140. **(C)** Area of garden plot = $180 \times 60 = 10{,}800$ square feet
Area of each square is $20 \times 20 = 400$ square feet
$10{,}800 \div 400 = 27$

141. **(B)**
$AB = AC - BC$
$AB = 30 - 12 = 18$
$CD = BD - BC$
$CD = 40 - 12 = 28$
$AD = AB + BC + CD$
$AD = 18 + 12 + 28 = 58$

142. **(D)** $xy + 12 = 40$
Since $y = 4$, we have
$4x + 12 = 40$
$4x = 40 - 12 = 28$
$x = 7$
$x + y = 7 + 4 = 11$

143. (**C**) Let $n = 4$
(A) $2n = 8$ (incorrect)
(B) $3n = 12$ (incorrect)
(C) $2n + 1 = 9$ (correct)
(D) $n + 4 = 8$ (incorrect)

144. (**D**) 8:40 + 5:30 = 13:70 = 14:10 or 2:10 P.M.
14:10 + 0:15 = 14:25 or 2:25 P.M.
14:25 + 0:50 = 14:75
= 15:15 or 3:15 P.M.

145. (**B**) $a^2 = \left(\frac{1}{3}\right)^2 = \frac{1}{9}$
$b^2 = \left(\frac{1}{2}\right)^2 = \frac{1}{4}$
$ab = \frac{1}{3} \times \frac{1}{2} = \frac{1}{6}$
$\frac{1}{9} + \frac{1}{6} + \frac{1}{4} = \frac{4+6+9}{36} = \frac{19}{36}$

146. (**A**) The football circle and the baseball circle intersect so that the numbers 12 and 8 appear in both circles.
$12 + 8 = 20$

147. (**D**) 50 miles in 60 minutes
1 mile in $\frac{60}{50}$ minutes = $\frac{1}{5}$ minutes

148. (**B**) \$10.48 for 8 gallons
10.48 ÷ 8 = \$1.31 per gallon
1.31 × 12 = \$15.72

149. (**C**) $x + 5 = y + 3$
$x - y = 3 - 5 = -2$
Multiplying both sides of the equation by –1, we have
$-x + y = 2$, or $y - x = 2$
$y = x + 2$
This equation indicates that y is 2 units greater than x.

150. (**A**) $0.47 \times 69.8 = 47 \times \square$
$\square = \frac{0.47 \times 69.8}{47}$
$47 = 100(0.47)$
Therefore, $\square = \frac{69.8}{100} = 0.698$

151. (**A**) Total games won = $30 + \frac{1}{2}(10) = 30 + 5 = 35$
Total games played = $30 + 10 + 10 = 50$
$\frac{35}{50} = \frac{70}{100} = 70\%$

152. (**C**) Perimeter = $2l + 2w$
where l = length and w = width
Perimeter = $2(4x + 5) + 2(x + 10)$
Perimeter = $8x + 10 + 2x + 20$
Perimeter = $10x + 30$ feet

153. (**B**) $s = 16t^2$
$s = 16\left(\frac{1}{4}\right)\left(\frac{1}{4}\right)$
$s = 16\left(\frac{1}{16}\right) = 1$

154. (**B**) Let x = total enrollment
$0.30x = 120$
$x = \frac{120}{0.3} = \frac{1200}{3} = 400$

155. (**C**) (A) $-6 > -2$ (false)
(B) $5 > -3 > 2$ (false since –3 is not greater than 2)
(C) $4 > 2 > -1$ (true since $4 > 2$ and $2 > -1$)

156. (**A**) $C = 2\pi r$. In this case,
$12\pi = 2\pi r$ and $r = 6$
Area = πr^2. In this case,
Area = $\pi \times 6 \times 6 = 36\pi$

157. (**C**) Let x = Bill's hourly pay
And $x + 3$ = John's hourly pay
Then $8x$ = Bill's daily pay
And $8(x + 3)$ = John's daily pay
$8x + 8(x + 3) = 170$

158. (**C**)

3 yards	2 feet	5 inches
– 1 yard	1 foot	7 inches

If we exchange 2 feet in the upper measure to 1 foot + 12 inches, we have

3 yards	1 foot	17 inches
– 1 yard	1 foot	7 inches

Now we subtract to obtain
2 yards 10 inches

159. (**A**) 75% of 80,000 = 60,000
= 600 hundreds
600(0.55) = \$330

160. (**B**) $\frac{1}{2}\left(\frac{1}{3}+\frac{1}{4}\right) = \frac{1}{6} + \frac{1}{8}$
The least common denominator is 24.
$\frac{1}{6} + \frac{4}{24}$, $\frac{1}{8} = \frac{3}{24}$
$\frac{1}{6} + \frac{1}{8} = \frac{7}{24}$

161. (**D**) $2x + 3 = 11$
$2x = 11 - 3 = 8$
$x = 4$
$10 - x = 10 - 4 = 6$

162. (**C**) $\frac{210}{42} = 5$ hours

163. (**B**) 142 – 100 = 42 miles to be paid for
42(0.18) = \$7.56
37 + 7.56 = \$44.56

164. **(B)** Area of rectangle $ABCD$ = 48 square inches
Area of triangle $ADE = \frac{1}{2}(8 \times 5) = 20$ square inches

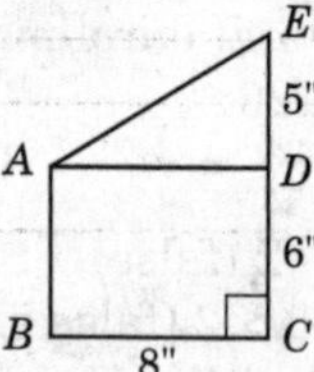

Area of entire figure = 48 + 20 = 68 square inches

165. **(B)** $\frac{5}{8}$ of the ovens were sold the first day
$\frac{3}{8}$ of the ovens were left
$\frac{2}{3} \times \frac{3}{8} = \frac{1}{4}$ of the ovens were sold the second day
$\frac{5}{8} + \frac{1}{4} = \frac{5}{8} + \frac{2}{8} = \frac{7}{8}$ of the ovens were sold the first two days, and $\frac{1}{8}$ of the ovens were left unsold.
Let x = number of ovens put on sale.
$\frac{1}{8}x = 15$
$x = 8(145) = 120$

166. **(B)** $3x - 2 = 16$
$3x = 16 + 2 = 18$
$x = 6$
Then $2x + 5 = 2(6) + 5 = 17$

167. **(C)** If the sum of two numbers is y and one of the numbers is 5, the other number is $y - 5$. Three times the other number is $3(y - 5)$.

168. **(D)** Let x = the number
$30\% = 0.3$
$0.3x = 12$
$3x = 120$
$x = 40$

169. **(A)** Let x = amount of sugar to be used
We make the proportion
$\frac{4}{6} = \frac{1\frac{1}{2}}{x}$
$4x = 6\left(1\frac{1}{2}\right)$
$4x = 9$
$x = \frac{9}{4} = 2\frac{1}{4}$

170. **(B)** $\frac{1}{4}x = 20$
$x = 80$
$\frac{3}{8}x = \frac{3}{8}(80) = 30$

TEST FIVE

Ideally, your essay should be evaluated by an experienced reader. Instead, you will find below a series of essays to which yours can be compared. This evaluation will give you a rough estimate of its standing in comparison with those written by other students. The ratings of the student essays are based solely on organization and content. You will have to have an experienced reader (perhaps a teacher) proofread your essay for technical errors.

Essay 1

In these troubled times teenagers are beset by many crucial problems that they must face upon reaching beyond the school age. In order for them to get along with others, they have to reach decisions on whether they will take drugs, quit school, leave home, read pornography, and on many many other issues. Their fate as human beings depends upon their reaching the right decisions.

I know that as far as I am concerned I have made the right decisions. Even though I have not had much experience in the outside world, I am thankful that my parents have given me good advice based on what they have seen and done. In later years I will be most grateful for their frank opinions and persuasive arguments.

Not all children are as fortunate as I have been. They make mistakes and sometimes the mistakes are so serious that they have to face a judge in criminal court. Yet, one person's loss can be someone else's gain. A teenager watching an actual court trial can learn much of what not to do.

I therefore feel that courtroom proceedings should be on home TVs to teach others the rewards and punishments we face for our deeds in the everyday world.

ANALYSIS: ______________________________

____

____

RATING: ______________________________

Essay 2

There is a saying that is most appropriate for the given topic: "Fools must learn from their own experience; the wise learn from the experience of others." What could be more instructive than seeing the sad plight of a person who went outside the law or who broke the moral code!

The contrast between the viewer's safe haven at home and watching the unfolding of a live trial and the cold objective atmosphere of the court in which the accused is seen creates an emotional jolt that could shake dangerous inclinations out of the mind of almost all teenagers.

Of course, truth can sometimes be ugly. The courtroom scenes might be too sordid or too ugly. But prudishness should not be used to prevent the viewing of reality. I think that judiciously chosen court trials should be brought into the homes of all teenagers in search of an adult way of life to follow in the years ahead. I enthusiastically favor the televising of such trials throughout our country.

ANALYSIS: ______________________________

RATING: ______________________________

Essay 3

Public pressure has finally resulted in network broadcasting of televised courtroom trials for criminal offenses. Should such broadcasts be legalized throughout the country?

This is a question that sharply divides the country. Our country is filled with mature people who differ on what is the right thing to do. Some people are for legalization. Others are just as strongly opposed. Those in favor have their arguments. Those opposed are just as willing to voice just as effective arguments.

Yet, despite the fact that we do not all agree on this topic, we should go ahead with the debate until someone finds an argument so compelling that it will convince all.

Therefore, in summary, I am firmly convinced that we must put our heads together and solve this problem. I hope that the decision results in such programs being broadcast everywhere.

ANALYSIS: ______________________________

RATING: ______________________________

Essay 4

Our judicial system seems to be breaking down. Our jails are overflowing. The headlines and news broadcasts warn us that the use of illegal drugs is increasing. The number of serious crimes is spiraling upward. The court calendars are clogged with a record number of impending cases. Could the legalization of televised court trials help to stem the tide?

It is true that the sensationalism built into such TV programs would appeal to some in the audience just for the emotional kicks they would get from such viewing. There may even be some who would be motivated to step outside the law in order to enjoy the spotlight the courtroom procedure provides. Some may even try to succeed where the accused failed. Then there are those who would see so many "live" trials that they would assume that those involved were the norm to be imitated.

As you can see, I find too many negatives in this issue. I firmly vote that such programs not be shown to the public.

ANALYSIS: ______________________________

RATING: ______________________________

Essay 5

I don't think that criminal trials should be broadcast. TV programs are for relaxation. When I get home after a hard day in school, I don't want to see serious programs. The programs should be light and humorous. The humorous programs about teenagers are the ones that I enjoy best. The best programs don't stress crimes like robbery and kidnapping. Kidnapping is one of the most horrible crimes. There are others which are almost as bad. But the worst is kidnapping. The abductors take innocent children from their homes and hold them prisoners until the parents meet their demands. Sometimes the parents have to go into heavy debt for many years in order to pay these criminals off. If these criminals would only think of the torture they put these families through they would think twice before trying to make money in this way. If I had my way, I would make kidnapping a capital offense with a mandatory life imprisonment for those committing this offense.

In conclusion, I repeat, criminal trials should not be broadcast into the living rooms where people want relaxation and not reminders of the evils in our world.

ANALYSIS: ________________________

RATING: ________________________

Essay 6

Television is a member of a unique group. It is given a special privilege. With the pressing of a button, it is invited to come into our living rooms. In return it floods our home with sports, news, and endless dramas of all varieties. Should it also bring into homes throughout our country "live" courtroom trials for criminal offenses?

Some people say that such programs should not be shown. They could give teenagers wrong ideas. They could show some school children how to do what they should not do. They stress the negative side of life. What we need are more positive programs showing us the right way rather than the wrong way.

On the other hand, there are many who feel that TV does not stress positives in much of what it has to offer. It floods our homes with stories of murder, war, stealing, etc. But there is a big difference between these programs and "live" criminal trials. The trials have a strong moral tag attached. They show the penalty for wrong doing.

As you can see, I feel strongly that such programs should be broadcast nationwide. They have a message that needs to be sent into every home: CRIME DOES NOT PAY!

ANALYSIS: ________________________

RATING: ________________________

Evaluation of Other Students' Essays

Essay 1. The essay is organized into four paragraphs. The vocabulary level is average. However, the first two paragraphs stray too far afield from the given topic. They almost seem to be a memorized introduction that could fit any topic. Only in the last two paragraphs does the essay focus on the topic. These paragraphs save the day.
Rating: Average

Essay 2. The essay is well organized, and the vocabulary level is superior. The thought content flows in a logical pattern. Although the essay is brief, the reasoning is clear and compelling.
Rating: Superior

Essay 3. The essay is well organized into four paragraphs. The first paragraph ends with a logical rhetorical question that leads into the rest of the essay but does not connect logically with the first sentence, which is a questionable use of the given topic without quotation marks. However, the essay does not follow the prompts which was to give a yes or no opinion, not state that the reader should make the decision.
Rating: Below average

Essay 4. The essay is well organized into three paragraphs. The first paragraph logically ends in an appropriate rhetorical question that leads smoothly into the rest of the essay. The second paragraph begins awkwardly, without tying directly to the flow of thought in the preceding one. Although the arguments that follow may seem a bit far fetched to some, they are clearly stated. The conclusion is a logical summary.
Rating: Superior

Essay 5. The essay begins abruptly, but the initial sentence is relevant to the topic. What follows in one overlong paragraph,

however, is not tied into the topic. The conclusion returns to the prompt too late to salvage the essay.
Rating: Below average

Essay 6. The essay is logically organized into four paragraphs. The vocabulary level is average. The rhetorical question at the end of the first paragraph leads logically to the thought content that follows. The third paragraph repeats much of what is said in the second before the arguments are clinched in the direction preferred by the writer.
Rating: Average

Evaluation of Your Own Essay

Weaknesses ____________________

Strengths ____________________

It is closest to number ________ of the student essays because ____________________

I would rate it ____________________

I could have improved it by ____________________

____

____

Answer Sheet
Practice Independent School Entrance Examination 2

TEST ONE

1. Ⓐ Ⓑ Ⓒ Ⓓ	**11.** Ⓐ Ⓑ Ⓒ Ⓓ	**21.** Ⓐ Ⓑ Ⓒ Ⓓ	**31.** Ⓐ Ⓑ Ⓒ Ⓓ
2. Ⓐ Ⓑ Ⓒ Ⓓ	**12.** Ⓐ Ⓑ Ⓒ Ⓓ	**22.** Ⓐ Ⓑ Ⓒ Ⓓ	**32.** Ⓐ Ⓑ Ⓒ Ⓓ
3. Ⓐ Ⓑ Ⓒ Ⓓ	**13.** Ⓐ Ⓑ Ⓒ Ⓓ	**23.** Ⓐ Ⓑ Ⓒ Ⓓ	**33.** Ⓐ Ⓑ Ⓒ Ⓓ
4. Ⓐ Ⓑ Ⓒ Ⓓ	**14.** Ⓐ Ⓑ Ⓒ Ⓓ	**24.** Ⓐ Ⓑ Ⓒ Ⓓ	**34.** Ⓐ Ⓑ Ⓒ Ⓓ
5. Ⓐ Ⓑ Ⓒ Ⓓ	**15.** Ⓐ Ⓑ Ⓒ Ⓓ	**25.** Ⓐ Ⓑ Ⓒ Ⓓ	**35.** Ⓐ Ⓑ Ⓒ Ⓓ
6. Ⓐ Ⓑ Ⓒ Ⓓ	**16.** Ⓐ Ⓑ Ⓒ Ⓓ	**26.** Ⓐ Ⓑ Ⓒ Ⓓ	**36.** Ⓐ Ⓑ Ⓒ Ⓓ
7. Ⓐ Ⓑ Ⓒ Ⓓ	**17.** Ⓐ Ⓑ Ⓒ Ⓓ	**27.** Ⓐ Ⓑ Ⓒ Ⓓ	**37.** Ⓐ Ⓑ Ⓒ Ⓓ
8. Ⓐ Ⓑ Ⓒ Ⓓ	**18.** Ⓐ Ⓑ Ⓒ Ⓓ	**28.** Ⓐ Ⓑ Ⓒ Ⓓ	**38.** Ⓐ Ⓑ Ⓒ Ⓓ
9. Ⓐ Ⓑ Ⓒ Ⓓ	**19.** Ⓐ Ⓑ Ⓒ Ⓓ	**29.** Ⓐ Ⓑ Ⓒ Ⓓ	**39.** Ⓐ Ⓑ Ⓒ Ⓓ
10. Ⓐ Ⓑ Ⓒ Ⓓ	**20.** Ⓐ Ⓑ Ⓒ Ⓓ	**30.** Ⓐ Ⓑ Ⓒ Ⓓ	**40.** Ⓐ Ⓑ Ⓒ Ⓓ

TEST TWO

41. Ⓐ Ⓑ Ⓒ Ⓓ	**51.** Ⓐ Ⓑ Ⓒ Ⓓ	**61.** Ⓐ Ⓑ Ⓒ Ⓓ	**71.** Ⓐ Ⓑ Ⓒ Ⓓ
42. Ⓐ Ⓑ Ⓒ Ⓓ	**52.** Ⓐ Ⓑ Ⓒ Ⓓ	**62.** Ⓐ Ⓑ Ⓒ Ⓓ	**72.** Ⓐ Ⓑ Ⓒ Ⓓ
43. Ⓐ Ⓑ Ⓒ Ⓓ	**53.** Ⓐ Ⓑ Ⓒ Ⓓ	**63.** Ⓐ Ⓑ Ⓒ Ⓓ	**73.** Ⓐ Ⓑ Ⓒ Ⓓ
44. Ⓐ Ⓑ Ⓒ Ⓓ	**54.** Ⓐ Ⓑ Ⓒ Ⓓ	**64.** Ⓐ Ⓑ Ⓒ Ⓓ	**74.** Ⓐ Ⓑ Ⓒ Ⓓ
45. Ⓐ Ⓑ Ⓒ Ⓓ	**55.** Ⓐ Ⓑ Ⓒ Ⓓ	**65.** Ⓐ Ⓑ Ⓒ Ⓓ	**75.** Ⓐ Ⓑ Ⓒ Ⓓ
46. Ⓐ Ⓑ Ⓒ Ⓓ	**56.** Ⓐ Ⓑ Ⓒ Ⓓ	**66.** Ⓐ Ⓑ Ⓒ Ⓓ	**76.** Ⓐ Ⓑ Ⓒ Ⓓ
47. Ⓐ Ⓑ Ⓒ Ⓓ	**57.** Ⓐ Ⓑ Ⓒ Ⓓ	**67.** Ⓐ Ⓑ Ⓒ Ⓓ	**77.** Ⓐ Ⓑ Ⓒ Ⓓ
48. Ⓐ Ⓑ Ⓒ Ⓓ	**58.** Ⓐ Ⓑ Ⓒ Ⓓ	**68.** Ⓐ Ⓑ Ⓒ Ⓓ	**78.** Ⓐ Ⓑ Ⓒ Ⓓ
49. Ⓐ Ⓑ Ⓒ Ⓓ	**59.** Ⓐ Ⓑ Ⓒ Ⓓ	**69.** Ⓐ Ⓑ Ⓒ Ⓓ	**79.** Ⓐ Ⓑ Ⓒ Ⓓ
50. Ⓐ Ⓑ Ⓒ Ⓓ	**60.** Ⓐ Ⓑ Ⓒ Ⓓ	**70.** Ⓐ Ⓑ Ⓒ Ⓓ	**80.** Ⓐ Ⓑ Ⓒ Ⓓ

TEST THREE

81. Ⓐ Ⓑ Ⓒ Ⓓ	**91.** Ⓐ Ⓑ Ⓒ Ⓓ	**101.** Ⓐ Ⓑ Ⓒ Ⓓ	**111.** Ⓐ Ⓑ Ⓒ Ⓓ
82. Ⓐ Ⓑ Ⓒ Ⓓ	**92.** Ⓐ Ⓑ Ⓒ Ⓓ	**102.** Ⓐ Ⓑ Ⓒ Ⓓ	**112.** Ⓐ Ⓑ Ⓒ Ⓓ
83. Ⓐ Ⓑ Ⓒ Ⓓ	**93.** Ⓐ Ⓑ Ⓒ Ⓓ	**103.** Ⓐ Ⓑ Ⓒ Ⓓ	**113.** Ⓐ Ⓑ Ⓒ Ⓓ
84. Ⓐ Ⓑ Ⓒ Ⓓ	**94.** Ⓐ Ⓑ Ⓒ Ⓓ	**104.** Ⓐ Ⓑ Ⓒ Ⓓ	**114.** Ⓐ Ⓑ Ⓒ Ⓓ
85. Ⓐ Ⓑ Ⓒ Ⓓ	**95.** Ⓐ Ⓑ Ⓒ Ⓓ	**105.** Ⓐ Ⓑ Ⓒ Ⓓ	**115.** Ⓐ Ⓑ Ⓒ Ⓓ
86. Ⓐ Ⓑ Ⓒ Ⓓ	**96.** Ⓐ Ⓑ Ⓒ Ⓓ	**106.** Ⓐ Ⓑ Ⓒ Ⓓ	**116.** Ⓐ Ⓑ Ⓒ Ⓓ
87. Ⓐ Ⓑ Ⓒ Ⓓ	**97.** Ⓐ Ⓑ Ⓒ Ⓓ	**107.** Ⓐ Ⓑ Ⓒ Ⓓ	**117.** Ⓐ Ⓑ Ⓒ Ⓓ
88. Ⓐ Ⓑ Ⓒ Ⓓ	**98.** Ⓐ Ⓑ Ⓒ Ⓓ	**108.** Ⓐ Ⓑ Ⓒ Ⓓ	**118.** Ⓐ Ⓑ Ⓒ Ⓓ
89. Ⓐ Ⓑ Ⓒ Ⓓ	**99.** Ⓐ Ⓑ Ⓒ Ⓓ	**109.** Ⓐ Ⓑ Ⓒ Ⓓ	**119.** Ⓐ Ⓑ Ⓒ Ⓓ
90. Ⓐ Ⓑ Ⓒ Ⓓ	**100.** Ⓐ Ⓑ Ⓒ Ⓓ	**110.** Ⓐ Ⓑ Ⓒ Ⓓ	**120.** Ⓐ Ⓑ Ⓒ Ⓓ

TEST FOUR

121. Ⓐ Ⓑ Ⓒ Ⓓ
122. Ⓐ Ⓑ Ⓒ Ⓓ
123. Ⓐ Ⓑ Ⓒ Ⓓ
124. Ⓐ Ⓑ Ⓒ Ⓓ
125. Ⓐ Ⓑ Ⓒ Ⓓ
126. Ⓐ Ⓑ Ⓒ Ⓓ
127. Ⓐ Ⓑ Ⓒ Ⓓ
128. Ⓐ Ⓑ Ⓒ Ⓓ
129. Ⓐ Ⓑ Ⓒ Ⓓ
130. Ⓐ Ⓑ Ⓒ Ⓓ
131. Ⓐ Ⓑ Ⓒ Ⓓ
132. Ⓐ Ⓑ Ⓒ Ⓓ
133. Ⓐ Ⓑ Ⓒ Ⓓ
134. Ⓐ Ⓑ Ⓒ Ⓓ
135. Ⓐ Ⓑ Ⓒ Ⓓ
136. Ⓐ Ⓑ Ⓒ Ⓓ
137. Ⓐ Ⓑ Ⓒ Ⓓ
138. Ⓐ Ⓑ Ⓒ Ⓓ
139. Ⓐ Ⓑ Ⓒ Ⓓ
140. Ⓐ Ⓑ Ⓒ Ⓓ
141. Ⓐ Ⓑ Ⓒ Ⓓ
142. Ⓐ Ⓑ Ⓒ Ⓓ
143. Ⓐ Ⓑ Ⓒ Ⓓ
144. Ⓐ Ⓑ Ⓒ Ⓓ
145. Ⓐ Ⓑ Ⓒ Ⓓ
146. Ⓐ Ⓑ Ⓒ Ⓓ
147. Ⓐ Ⓑ Ⓒ Ⓓ
148. Ⓐ Ⓑ Ⓒ Ⓓ
149. Ⓐ Ⓑ Ⓒ Ⓓ
150. Ⓐ Ⓑ Ⓒ Ⓓ
151. Ⓐ Ⓑ Ⓒ Ⓓ
152. Ⓐ Ⓑ Ⓒ Ⓓ
153. Ⓐ Ⓑ Ⓒ Ⓓ
154. Ⓐ Ⓑ Ⓒ Ⓓ
155. Ⓐ Ⓑ Ⓒ Ⓓ
156. Ⓐ Ⓑ Ⓒ Ⓓ
157. Ⓐ Ⓑ Ⓒ Ⓓ
158. Ⓐ Ⓑ Ⓒ Ⓓ
159. Ⓐ Ⓑ Ⓒ Ⓓ
160. Ⓐ Ⓑ Ⓒ Ⓓ
161. Ⓐ Ⓑ Ⓒ Ⓓ
162. Ⓐ Ⓑ Ⓒ Ⓓ
163. Ⓐ Ⓑ Ⓒ Ⓓ
164. Ⓐ Ⓑ Ⓒ Ⓓ
165. Ⓐ Ⓑ Ⓒ Ⓓ
166. Ⓐ Ⓑ Ⓒ Ⓓ
167. Ⓐ Ⓑ Ⓒ Ⓓ
168. Ⓐ Ⓑ Ⓒ Ⓓ
169. Ⓐ Ⓑ Ⓒ Ⓓ
170. Ⓐ Ⓑ Ⓒ Ⓓ

Practice Independent School Entrance Examination 2

TEST ONE VERBAL ABILITY

Time limit: 20 minutes *Number of questions: 40*

The Verbal Ability Section consists of two types of questions. There are separate directions for each type.

DIRECTIONS: Each question consists of a word in capital letters followed by four choices. Select the one word that is most nearly the same in meaning as the word in capital letters. On the Answer Sheet, fill in the circle that has the same letter as your answer choice.

1. ADJACENT:
(A) beneath (B) opposite
(C) approaching (D) neighboring

2. ABUSIVE:
(A) beneficial (B) deadly
(C) injurious (D) courteous

3. ACCELERATE:
(A) race (B) quicken
(C) brake (D) slash

4. APPROXIMATE:
(A) mistake (B) exaggerate
(C) estimate (D) oppose

5. BLUNDER:
(A) stumble (B) shoot
(C) rob (D) succeed

6. AUDACIOUS:
(A) hoarse (B) bold
(C) snappy (D) polite

7. LIVELONG:
(A) lively (B) elderly
(C) peaceful (D) entire

8. LAMENT:
(A) soothe (B) compose
(C) deplore (D) praise

9. PREMIERE:
(A) statesman (B) general
(C) debut (D) drama

10. RECOLLECT:
(A) recall (B) record
(C) expend (D) justify

11. SUBSIDE:
(A) support (B) overcome
(C) wane (D) revive

12. DIGRESS:
(A) retreat (B) stray
(C) lecture (D) examine

13. COMPATIBLE:
(A) harmonious (B) uninterested
(C) different (D) resourceful

14. DOGGED:
(A) fuzzy (B) playful
(C) faithful (D) persistent

15. THERAPEUTIC:
(A) curative (B) medicinal
(C) harmful (D) prescriptive

16. REVERT:
(A) retell (B) rejuvenate
(C) relapse (D) refurnish

17. IMBIBE:
(A) bribe (B) swallow
(C) capture (D) publish

18. JEOPARDIZE:
(A) guess (B) compete
(C) win (D) imperil

19. MENDICANT:
(A) thief (B) liar
(C) beggar (D) sheriff

20. RECTIFY:
(A) right (B) diagnose
(C) compensate (D) damage

DIRECTIONS: Each question below consists of a sentence with one or two blanks. A single blank indicates the omission of one word; two blanks mean that two words are omitted. Choose the word or words that will best complete the meaning of the sentence as a whole. Fill in the circle that has the same letter as your answer choice.

21. The lunchroom guard warned the _____ that he would have to eat alone if he started any more fights.
(A) victim (B) peacemaker
(C) aggressor (D) speculator

22. A fielder's glove is an _________ gift for a ten-year-old member of a Little League team.
(A) unusual (B) appropriate
(C) expensive (D) inconsiderate

23. The five-year-olds were _________ by the many strange sights and sounds of the carnival.
(A) bewildered (B) horrified
(C) disgusted (D) unaffected

24. The reward for this careful planning was that our troops suffered few _______ during the first days of the war.
(A) maneuvers (B) triumphs
(C) casualties (D) advantages

25. She has a ________ temper that erupts at the slightest provocation.
(A) fiery (B) placid
(C) controlled (D) low-key

26. The juggler was so _________ that he was able to keep eight balls in the air at the same time while he poured himself a cup of tea.
(A) awkward (B) absentminded
(C) mediocre (D) adept

27. After the severe rains the tractor was stuck in the _________ up to the driver's seat.
(A) mire (B) hay (C) snow (D) hawser

28. As the speaker stumbled along, it was ________ to everyone that she had not prepared her speech.
(A) obvious (B) uncertain
(C) significant (D) interesting

29. His need to be the center of attention on every occasion ______________ all of his friends.
(A) pleased (B) alienated
(C) extended (D) excited

30. The ________ loggers handled the heavy logs as though they were twigs.
(A) incompetent (B) elderly
(C) frail (D) burly

31. The invaders made _________ deep into the countryside in their search for ____.
(A) strolls ... antiques
(B) flurries ... scenic wonders
(C) orations ... truth
(D) forays ... booty

32. The leader of the rescue party was the _____________ of many gifts from the _________ parents.
(A) beneficiary ... irascible
(B) recipient ... grateful
(C) purchaser ... irate
(D) receptionist ... thoughtful

33. It is a(n) _________ story of a family that placed their faith and fortune in the hands of a(n) _________ scoundrel.
(A) delightful ... base
(B) uplifting ... noted
(C) sad ... unscrupulous
(D) unusual ... righteous

34. Our community _____________ offered _________ for sale at low prices.
(A) bazaar ... merchandise
(B) leader ... votes
(C) school ... prizes
(D) factory ... money

35. After weeks of searching in _________ for more than scraps of food, the pack of _________ dogs was ready to attack any living object, even human beings.
(A) earnest ... disciplined
(B) alleys ... timid
(C) campsites ... obese
(D) vain ... gaunt

36. With __________ interest we listened to the speaker __________ on and on.
(A) flagging ... drone
(B) unabated ... lecture
(C) consuming ... sermonize
(D) increasing... argue

37. I __________ her statement in which she __________ selfish motives as the basis of my decision.
(A) admire ... mentioned
(B) resent ... imputed
(C) reject ... refuted
(D) uphold ... cited

38. Her __________ ignorance of modern business methods brought the company to __________ in a short time.
(A) abysmal ... failure
(B) forgivable ... ruin
(C) unexpected ... success
(D) complete ... prosperity

39. Bess insisted on telling the __________ details of the __________ accident that had claimed twelve lives in the orphanage.
(A) bloody ... exciting
(B) lurid ... horrifying
(C) sensational ... trivial
(D) uninteresting ... fascinating

40. She __________ a(n) __________ device that selects the food from the freezer, puts it into the microwave, cooks it to perfection, and then serves it.
(A) concocted ... disastrous
(B) contemplated... self-destructing
(C) perfected ... ingenious
(D) rejected ... implausible

TEST TWO QUANTITATIVE ABILITY

Time limit: 35 minutes *Number of questions: 40*

GENERAL DIRECTIONS: You may assume that any figures given in connection with questions are drawn as accurately as possible *except* when it is stated that a particular figure is not drawn to scale. Letters such as *x, y,* and *n* stand for real numbers.

For questions 41–60 select the correct answer for each problem and fill in the corresponding circle on the Answer Sheet. You may work mentally or use blank spaces on the test pages.

41. A number equal to $\frac{1}{200}$ is
(A) 5% (B) 0.05 (C) 0.005 (D) $\left(\frac{1}{2}\right)^5$

42. The difference between the product of 12 and 11 and the product of 8 and 9 is
(A) 6 (B) 60 (C) 40 (D) 50

43. Each leg of an isosceles right triangle measures 8 inches. What is the area of the triangle?
(A) 64 square inches
(B) 48 square inches
(C) 20 square inches
(D) 32 square inches

44. On a map the cities of Fulton and Clinton are $4\frac{1}{4}$ miles apart. If the scale on the map is 1 inch = 300 miles how many miles apart are the two cities?
(A) 1350 (B) 2700 (C) 1200 (D) 1300

45. If $(3 \times 10^3) + (2 \times 10^2) + 5$ is added to $(4 \times 10^3) + (2 \times 10^2) + (7 \times 10)$, the result is
(A) 7450 (B) 8520 (C) 7475 (D) 7412

46. Mrs. Lane buys a table and pays a sales tax of of $8.75. If the sales tax is 5% of the purchase price, what is the purchase price of the table?
(A) $175.00 (B) $17.50
(C) 1750 (D) 43.75

47. 1 kilogram =
(A) 1000 grams
(B) 100 grams
(C) 0.1 gram
(D) 5 liters

48. If $4x - 3 = 21$, then the value of $x^2 + x =$
(A) 40 (B) 13 (C) 18 (D) 42

49. At a movie showing the theater is $\frac{2}{3}$ full. To fill the theater 200 more seats would have to be occupied. How many seats does the theater have?
(A) 500 (B) 1000 (C) 600 (D) 900

50. A school has 60 classes with 32 students in each class. To reduce class size to 30, how many new classes must be formed?
(A) 4 (B) 2 (C) 5 (D) 6

51. At $0.88 per pound what is the cost of a chicken weighing 3 pounds 6 ounces?
(A) $2.97 (B) $2.87 (C) $3.07 (D) $3.17

52. It takes 18 men 20 hours to complete a job. How many hours would 15 men need to complete the same job?
(A) $16\frac{2}{3}$ (B) 32 (C) 24 (D) 16

53. The least common denominator of the fractions $\frac{5}{12}$, $\frac{4}{9}$, and $\frac{3}{4}$ is
(A) 72 (B) 36 (C) 24 (D) 180

54. $96 \div 6 - 2 \times 7 =$
(A) 2 (B) 224 (C) 7 (D) 0

55. The sum of the measures of a right angle and an acute angle is equal to
(A) the measure of an acute angle
(B) the measure of a reflex angle
(C) the measure of an obtuse angle
(D) the measure of a straight angle

56. According to the following number line:

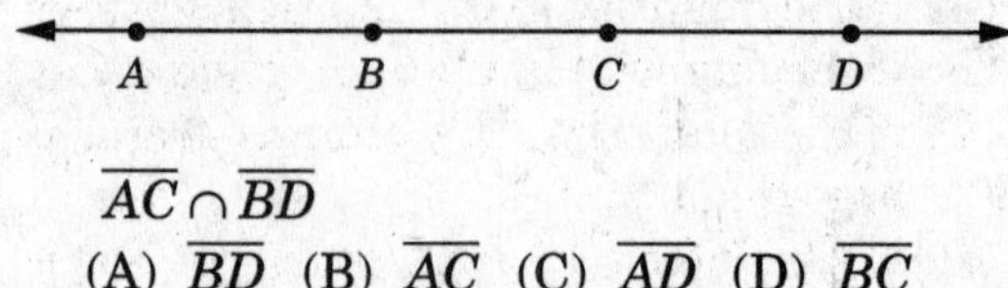

$\overline{AC} \cap \overline{BD}$
(A) $\overline{BD}$ (B) $\overline{AC}$ (C) $\overline{AD}$ (D) $\overline{BC}$

57. If a die is rolled, what is the probability that it will come up with a 2?
(A) $\frac{2}{6}$ (B) $\frac{3}{6}$ (C) $\frac{1}{6}$ (D) $\frac{5}{6}$

58. Joan buys a coat for x dollars and two sweaters for y dollars each. How much did she spend?
(A) $x + y$ dollars
(B) $(x + 2)y$ dollars
(C) $2x + y$ dollars
(D) $x + 2y$ dollars

59. *ABCD* is a square. Each side of the square measures 8 units. The area of the shaded region is

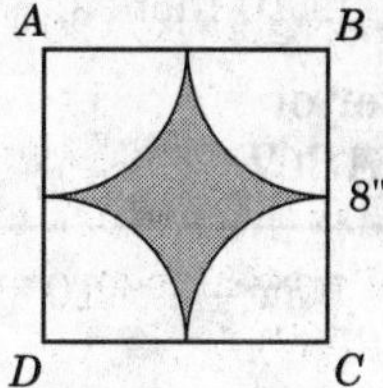

(A) $(64 - 64\pi)$ square units
(B) $(64 - 16\pi)$ square units
(C) $(64\pi - 64)$ square units
(D) $(64\pi - 16)$ square units

60. A bell rings every 30 minutes, a second bell rings every 40 minutes, and a third bell rings every 60 minutes. If all three bells ring at noon, at what time will all three bells ring together again?
(A) 2:00 P.M. (B) 2:30 P.M. (C) 3:00 P.M. (D) 3:30 P.M.

DIRECTIONS: For questions 61–80, two quantities are given, one in Column A and the other in Column B. In some cases, additional information concerning the quantities to be compared is centered above the entries in the two columns. After noting all the information given, compare the quantities in Columns A and B and fill in the ovals on the Answer Sheet as follows:
(A) if the quantity in Column A is greater
(B) if the quantity in Column B is greater
(C) if the quantities in Columns A and B are equal
(D) if the information given is not sufficient to determine which quantity is greater

Column A | **Column B**

$a = -3$,
$b = 2$

61. $a^2 + ab$ | $b^2 + ab$

62. $36 \div 4 - 7$ | $25 - 6 \div 3$

63. $3x - 2 = 10$ | $5y + 1 = 21$
x | y

x and y are integers

64. $x + y$ | $x - y$

65. $A + B$ | $B + C$

ABCD is a parallelogram.

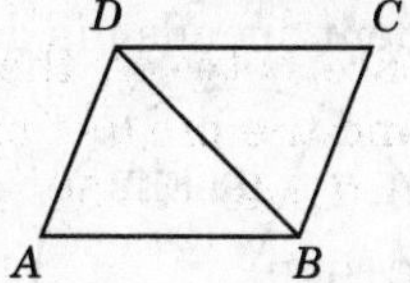

66. $DA + DB$ | DC

On six science tests John received grades of 85, 75, 50, 70, 90, and 65. On the same series of tests Roberto received grades of 90, 90, 65, 45, 80, and 75.

67. John's average on the six tests | Roberto's average on the six tests

68. $(8 \times 7) - 4(6 \div 1)$ | 2^5

x and y are positive integers.
$x - y = 3$
$2x + y = 9$

69. x | y

y is a real number.

70. $y - 7$ | $7 - y$

	Column A	Column B
	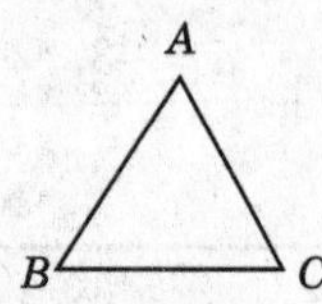 $AB > BC > CA$	
71.	$\angle A$	$\angle C$
72.	The difference between $\frac{1}{2}$ of a number and $\frac{1}{3}$ of the same number	$\frac{1}{6}$ of the same number
	$3 > y > -2$	
73.	$\frac{y}{2}$	$\frac{2}{y}$
	The circle graph shows how a student spends his day. 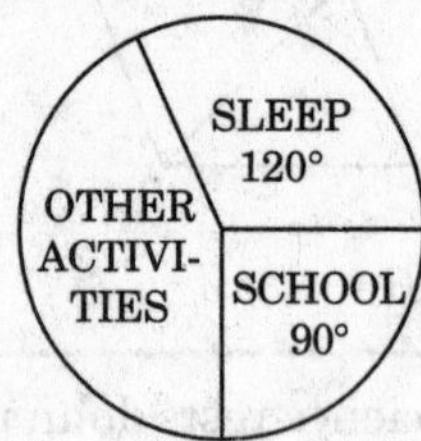	
74.	The ratio of the number of hours of sleep to the number of hours of school	4:3
75.	$2^6 \div 2^2$	8

	Column A	Column B
	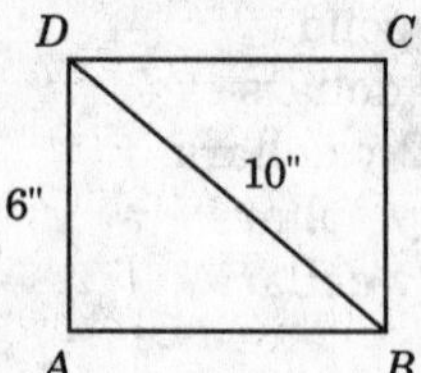 The width of rectangle *ABCD* is 6 inches and the length of its diagonal *DB*, is 10 inches.	
76.	Perimeter of rectangle *ABCD*	32 inches
	$3x - 2 > 10$	
77.	$5x^2$	100
	$\frac{x}{6} = \frac{1}{2}$ $\frac{x+3}{3} = \frac{y}{2}$	
78.	y	5
	After driving 145 miles, a motorist had completed $\frac{5}{8}$ of her trip.	
79.	Complete trip	230 miles
	A recipe calls for 8 ounces of butter and 2 ounces of sugar. Only 6 ounces of butter are used.	
80.	Proportionate amount of sugar to be used	$1\frac{1}{2}$ ounces of sugar

TEST THREE READING COMPREHENSION

Time limit: 35 minutes *Number of questions: 40*

DIRECTIONS: Each of the nine passages below is followed by questions based on its contents. On the basis of what is *stated* or *implied* in that passage, select the word or words that best answer the question. On the Answer Sheet, fill in the circle that has the same letter as your answer choice.

The internal combustion engine is used extensively in automobiles, buses and trucks. In order to produce mechanical energy to propel the vehicle, the engine must burn fuel. To accomplish this combustion the engine has a carburetor, which mixes the gasoline with air, and this mixture is then fed into the cylinder. Each cylinder is served with a spark plug that will produce a spark to ignite the fuel-air mixture. The rapid combustion produces a great amount of force, pushing down the piston within the cylinder. The piston is connected to a crankshaft by a piston rod. The turning crankshaft transmits its power through the transmission to the rear or front axle. The axle is connected to the wheels.

81. Which of the following statements expresses most appropriately the main idea of this selection?
    (A) Automobile engines have many key parts.
    (B) The carburetor mixes gasoline and air.
    (C) The automobile engine converts gasoline and air into mechanical energy.
    (D) The axle connects the engine and the wheels.

82. To be effective, all internal combustion engines require two materials, which are
    (A) air and water
    (B) air and fuel
    (C) oil and air
    (D) air and power

83. Which device transfers to the axle the power produced in the engine?
    (A) spark plug
    (B) differential
    (C) transmission
    (D) the intake manifold

84. The internal combustion engine converts
    (A) spark into ignition
    (B) fuel into energy
    (C) crankshaft into transmission
    (D) force into air

85. The word "combustion" in line 11 most nearly means
    (A) spark
    (B) transmission
    (C) burning
    (D) mixture

Two major theories exist as to the homeland of the Indo-European-speaking peoples. One theory sets the homeland in the Caucasus Mountains of southern Russia between the Caspian and Black seas. It assumes that from here some people speaking this basic language spread out to Anatolia and on to India while others crossed southern Russia to Poland, Rumania, the Balkans, and western Europe. This theory easily explains how the Indo-European language was spread from England to India. It does not account, however, for the origin of words for beech tree and salmon, which appear in the basic Indo-European vocabulary. Since salmon and beech trees are found only in the area of modern Poland along the Baltic Sea, a second theory suggests Poland as the homeland. It goes on to suggest that the tribes moved out from here to western Europe, the Balkans, Anatolia, and India. Each theory has its advocates and it is hard to determine which is more valid.

86. The two possible homelands of the Indo-European-speaking peoples suggested in this selection are
    (A) the Caspian and Black Sea areas
    (B) the region along the Baltic Sea and Poland
    (C) England and India
    (D) Poland and the Caucasus Mountains

87. What is the crucial basis of the second theory?
    (A) the location of salmon and beech trees in Europe
    (B) the wide spread range of languages based on the Indo-European vocabulary
    (C) the failure of the first theory to account for differences in local dialects
    (D) the distance between India and Poland

88. The author believes that the first theory is
    (A) invalid
    (B) not clear enough
    (C) as good as the second theory
    (D) less complicated than the second theory

89. As used in line 21 the word "advocates" most nearly means
    (A) lawyers
    (B) supporters
    (C) creators
    (D) truth-seekers

90. Anatolia (line 8) is most likely
    (A) an ancient city in Greece
    (B) an area of Africa
    (C) an area between southern Russia and India
    (D) part of India

The palace of Versailles and the royal town around it built by King Louis XIV of France symbolize his power, which political scientists refer to as absolutism. The palace was built fifteen miles from Paris, and the King withdrew there away from the noise and the crowds of the city. The building was huge, and at its very center Louis placed his bedroom. From this spot he overlooked the great parade ground where his armies could drill in front of the palace. On the other side magnificent gardens were planted. These contained statues and fountains and were laid out in an orderly plan. Each tree was shaped and pruned for the special effects the King desired. Looking at the palace from the air you can see that great vistas lead out from the palace like spokes or rays. The effect is like a wheel, with the palace as the hub, or like a sun. This was planned deliberately by Louis XIV as he considered himself the Sun-King and wanted his whole palace to symbolize this concept. In fact, the entire palace and town served as a great stage upon which Louis XIV could act out his role as absolute ruler of France.

91. Versailles was
    (A) a palace
    (B) a symbol of the King's power
    (C) a stage
    (D) all of the above

92. According to this selection, one reason why Louis XIV built Versailles was that he
    (A) loved crowds
    (B) wanted to get away from the sounds of Paris
    (C) shunned the sun
    (D) sought a simple life in the countryside

93. The attitude of the writer toward King Louis XIV is
    (A) approving
    (B) respectful
    (C) objective
    (D) condemnatory

94. Political scientists (lines 3–4) are
    (A) students of government and governmental institutions
    (B) governmental leads opposed to monarchies
    (C) people who run for office
    (D) politicians who criticize their opponents

There are three basic ways in which heat is transferred from one place to another: conduction, convection and radiation. In conduction, the transfer takes place when moving molecules actually impart their motion to other molecules that are next to them. This is illustrated by placing a pan on the stove. The heat from the stove causes the molecules of the metal pan to move rapidly and, by doing so, impart the heat to the pan. When the pan is filled with water, the molecules of water near the bottom of the pan will heat up first. After the bottom layer is heated, the warm water will rise because it is lighter than the cool water above it, and the cool water will move down to replace the warmer water. This circulatory motion is known as convection. Similar convection currents take place in heating systems in a home and in large bodies of water found in the oceans. When we hold our hand below a lamp we can feel the heat from the lamp. In this case the heat is transmitted by radiation through the air. The heat from the sun reaches the earth by radiation.

95. The transfer of heat in large quantities of liquid usually takes place by
(A) conduction
(B) convection
(C) ionization
(D) radiation

96. The basic concept involved in heat transfer in conduction and convection is based on the
(A) sun's heat
(B) movement of molecules when heated
(C) insulators and conductors
(D) coefficient of expansion

97. The word "impart" in lines 5 and 10 means
(A) separate
(B) remove
(C) relate
(D) convey

98. How does the heat from the sun reach the skin of sunbathers?
(A) by convection
(B) by condensation
(C) by radiation
(D) by conduction

Two acts passed by Congress in the early 1860s were the keys to the rapid settlement of the West. The first was the Pacific Railway Act, which authorized the building of a transcontinental railroad. The route completed in 1869 provided rapid and easy transportation westward for many settlers. The second act, the Homestead Act, had to do with public lands, that is, lands that belonged to the federal government. Before this act, land was sold to settlers for as little as $1.25 per acre but each settler had to buy many acres. Thus, many poor families could not afford to settle in the West. The new act stated that any head of a family could become the owner of a farm or homestead of 160 acres if he lived on it and worked the land for five years. The act made it possible for many Civil War veterans to move west and settle on their own land. Together with the Pacific Railway Act, the Homestead Act made certain that the West would be settled quickly.

99. Before the Homestead Act, a settler could not
(A) buy any public land
(B) buy a large number of acres of land
(C) travel by railroad to the West
(D) acquire land by working it

100. Which of the following describes the tone of this passage?
(A) argumentative
(B) factual
(C) emotional
(D) sarcastic

101. Public lands are
(A) lands owned by individuals
(B) lands used temporarily by the government
(C) lands owned by the federal government
(D) lands owned by Native Americans

102. Which of the following best states the main idea of the passage?
(A) The building of the transcontinental railroads led to the settling of the West.
(B) Civil War veterans claimed much of the western farmland.
(C) Convenient transportation and free land led to the populating of our western states.
(D) Before the Homestead Act, low prices failed to make land available to poor families.

The National Aeronautics and Space Administration is responsible for research and development of many areas concerned with aeronautics and space exploration. Shuttles are launched with increasing frequency to propel artificial satellites into space, mainly from Cape Kennedy in Florida. Some of the satellites provide ground stations with information that provides data on weather and conditions of the Earth's surface. Information about water pollution, crops, and ocean currents is received from the satellites. Space probes began the Age of Space Exploration and provided sensational data about our moon and the other members of our solar system. In order to have a continuous flow of information it was necessary to establish tracking stations in several strategic locations around the world. Through a computerized communication system this information is gathered for interpretation and publication by the Goddard Flight Center in Greenbelt, Maryland.

103. In order to have continuous information from space probes it is necessary to have tracking stations in
(A) many locations in the Eastern Hemisphere
(B) many locations in the polar areas
(C) many locations around the world
(D) a highly sensitive receiving station in Washington, D.C.

104. Shuttles are used
(A) as computerized communication systems
(B) as launching pads
(C) as tracking stations
(D) as ground stations

105. Data that the satellites send back to Earth
(A) are stored in the satellites
(B) are gathered by the satellites
(C) are sent back to the tracking stations in space
(D) reveal facts and conditions regarding the Earth

106. The name *satellites* was given to the space craft because
(A) they circle around the Earth
(B) they resemble the sun and stars
(C) they float in space
(D) they reflect sunlight back to Earth

Human beings have devised several basic machines to aid them in doing work. The pulley, lever, inclined plane, and screw are examples of these simple machines. In all cases people use these devices to multiply the force necessary, and therefore to make it easier, to move a body. A set of pulleys can be used to lift a heavy body to a desired height with a relatively small force. By using an inclined plane we can move a heavy body to a desired height with a minimum of force. If a set of pulleys makes it possible to lift a weight of 100 pounds with a force of 25 pounds, we say the machine (pulleys) have a mechanical advantage of four.

107. Several examples of simple machines are
(A) automobile, bus, and train
(B) monoplane, biplane, triplane
(C) pry bar, bolt, block and tackle
(D) bicycle, tricycle, unicycle

108. Which of the following would you probably use to lift a heavy trunk from the ground to the inside of a station wagon?
(A) a set of pulleys
(B) a jack
(C) several screws
(D) a wheel and axle

109. To lift a weight of 60 pounds with a force of 20 pounds, a pulley would have to have a mechanical advantage of
(A) three
(B) four
(C) two
(D) ten

110. The word "machine" as used in this selection means
(A) political party
(B) electronic device
(C) device to make work easier
(D) vehicle for transportation

111. The word "devised" in line 1 most nearly means
    (A) misused
    (B) condemned
    (C) invented
    (D) abandoned

The emperors of the Ming Dynasty ruled China from 1368 to 1644. Three very important events that greatly affected Chinese history occurred during their reign. First, the Ming emperors were successful in making themselves supreme over most of China. The size of the country made complete control impossible, but the Ming emperors came closer than any other government until 1949, when the communists seized power. Second, an influx of silver brought by western traders gave great wealth to the emperors. Third, cotton was introduced. It soon became the chief money crop of China and took its place with traditional food crops of millet, sorghum, and rice. With the influx of wealth and foreign trade, Chinese cotton products and porcelain vases reached the trading centers of Europe, while the arts, especially novel writing and drama flourished at home.

112. We can infer that one result of the unification of China during the Ming Dynasty was that
    (A) prices of food products rose sharply
    (B) the number of traders increased greatly in China
    (C) education improved for the peasants
    (D) porcelain vases became cheaper

113. The word "influx" in line 18 most nearly means
    (A) decrease
    (B) excess
    (C) coming in
    (D) disappearance

114. What did European traders give in exchange for Chinese products?
    (A) cotton
    (B) rice
    (C) porcelain
    (D) silver

115. The Ming Dynasty brought all of the following types of benefits to China EXCEPT
    (A) economic
    (B) spiritual
    (C) agricultural
    (D) artistic

Inuit settlements are scattered along the northern coast of North America from Labrador to Alaska's Panhandle. On Baffin Island and on other large islands there are Inuit villages. The Inuit spend most of their time near the sea and get much of their living from it. However, one tribe, the Caribou Inuit, lives inland west of Hudson Bay. Some Caribous have never seen the sea. Although life in one village is in many ways very much like life in another, there are some differences. The reason is that the Inuit must use what they find in the particular region where they live. The Copper Inuit, who live beside Coronation Gulf, build thick-walled winter houses of snow blocks. Alaskan Inuit do not use such houses, and most of them have never even seen one. Their winter homes are made of turf and mud. The Inuit of southern Greenland are expert in handling a kayak or Inuit canoe. They fish in the open water of the sea. The Inuit of northern Greenland, however, have little chance to use kayaks because the water along the coast is frozen almost all year. All tribes, however, have one thing in common: they are primarily fishermen and hunters.

116. Most Inuit live
    (A) on the plains
    (B) near the water
    (C) inland
    (D) on islands

117. The Caribou Inuit
    (A) live on the west shore of Hudson Bay
    (B) live beside Coronation Gulf
    (C) are not coastal people
    (D) are scattered along the eastern coast of North America

118. A comparison of different Inuit villages shows that the way of life in each
   (A) is quite similar to that in any other
   (B) is very unlike that in any other
   (C) is much like our own way of life
   (D) is unaffected by the location of the village

119. A kayak is a kind of
   (A) sled
   (B) temporary house
   (C) spear
   (D) boat

120. Alaskan Inuit make their winter homes of
   (A) snow blocks
   (B) wood
   (C) skins and fur
   (D) sod and wet earth

TEST FOUR MATHEMATICS ACHIEVEMENT

Time limit: 40 minutes *Number of questions: 50*

DIRECTIONS: Each question is followed by four answer choices. Choose the correct answer to each question, and fill in the corresponding circle on the Answer Sheet.

121. The value of $3 \times 1 \times 5 \times 0 =$
(A) 15 (B) 150 (C) 0 (D) 315

122. A restaurant cook has 62 pounds 10 ounces of steak. How many 6 ounce-servings can the cook prepare?
(A) 160 (B) 167 (C) 170 (D) 165

123. The scale on a blueprint is $1'' = 6'$. A living room is $30'$ long. How many inches will this length be on the blueprint?
(A) 5 (B) 10 (C) 7 (D) 8

124. The number of eighths in $3\frac{1}{4}$ is
(A) 13 (B) $11\frac{1}{4}$ (C) 20 (D) 26

125. At a price of \$0.84 per pound what is the cost of a chicken weighing 3 pounds 12 ounces?
(A) \$3.15 (B) \$2.80 (C) \$3.05 (D) \$3.25

126. In a school with a registration of 1090 students 37 classes are formed. If the classes are equal in size, as far as possible, how many classes are larger than most of the others?
(A) 17 (B) 29 (C) 15 (D) 30

127. The difference between two numbers is 8. If $\frac{1}{3}$ of the larger number is 5, the smaller number is
(A) 8 (B) 7 (C) 6 (D) 9

128. A dealer bought a chair for \$80 and sold it at an increase of 45%. What was the selling price of the chair?
(A) \$116 (B) \$125 (C) \$120 (D) \$130

129. The sum of two numbers is 57, and twice the smaller number is 3 more than the larger number. Which of the following equations may be used to find the smaller number?
(A) $57 - x + 2 = 3 + x$
(B) $2x = 57 - x - 3$
(C) $2(57 - x) = x + 3$
(D) $2(57) - x = x + 3$

130. A square and a triangle have the same area. A side of the square measures 9 inches. If the base of the triangle measures 6 inches, what is the measure of the altitude of the triangle?
(A) 12 inches (B) 27 inches (C) 9 inches (D) 18 inches

131. If, in the diagram below, m $\angle BDC$ = 140° and m $\angle BDA$ = m $\angle CDA$, then m $\angle BDA$ =

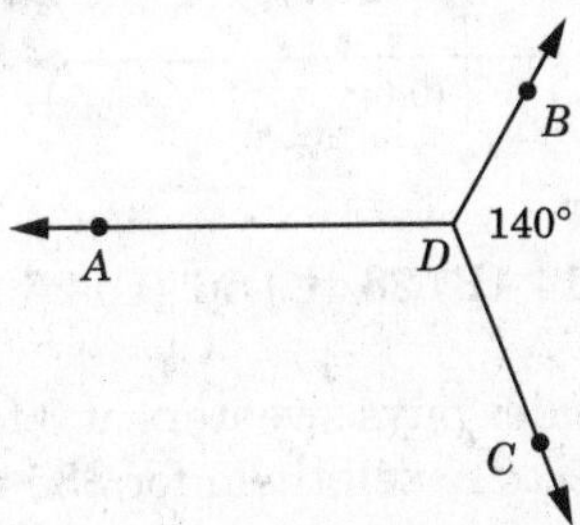

(A) 140° (B) 130° (C) 120° (D) 110°

132. If x is a positive integer and $3 + 2x < 9$, then the solution set of the inequality is
(A) {1, 2 3} (B) {0, 1, 2} (C) {1, 2} (D) {0, 1, 2, 3}

133. The ratio of Edna's money to Jill's money is 5:3. If Edna gives Jill \$5, each of the two girls will have
(A) \$5 (B) \$10 (C) \$20 (D) \$25

134. A man accepts a new job at a decrease in salary of 10%. If a year later he gets an increase of 25% in his new job, what is the net effect in comparison to his salary on the old job?
(A) an increase of $12\frac{1}{2}$%
(B) an increase of 15%
(C) an increase of 20%
(D) an increase of 8%

135. Take any two-digit number. If the number with the digits reversed is added to the original number, the sum is always divisible by
(A) 15 (B) 7 (C) 17 (D) 11

136. In the diagram below, the coordinates of $\triangle ABC$ are $A(2,3)$, $B(9,3)$, and $C(9,11)$. The area of $\triangle ABC$ in the square graph units is

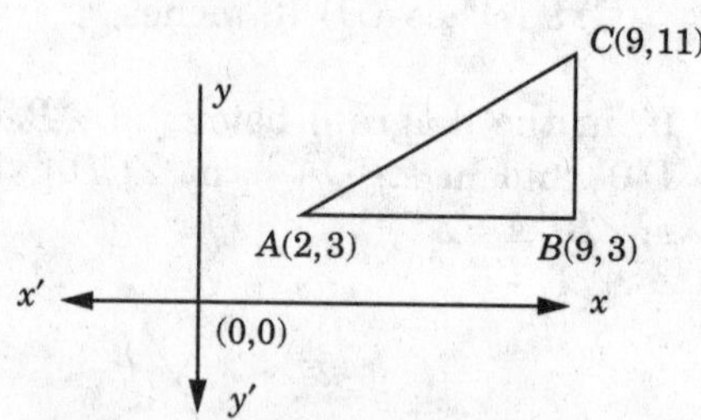

(A) 14 (B) 28 (C) 56 (D) 26

137. A dealer buys sweaters at 3 for $65 and expects to sell them for $35 each. How many sweaters must he sell to make a net profit of $600?
(A) 50 (B) 65 (C) 45 (D) 70

138. An auditorium has 1200 seats. When the auditorium is 85% full, how many seats are unoccupied?
(A) 18 (B) 1020 (C) 180 (D) 120

139. What are the prime factors of 165?
(A) 1, 3, 5, 11 (B) 1, 15, 11
(C) 3, 5, 11 (D) 1, 3, 11

140. 1 meter =
(A) approximately 35 inches
(B) approximately 39 inches
(C) approximately 43 inches
(D) approximately 47 inches

141. A storage room is 18 feet long, 12 feet wide, and 9 feet high. How many boxes in the form of rectangular solids may be stored in this room if each box measures 1 foot in length, 1 foot in width, and 1 foot in height?
(A) 39 (B) 108 (C) 162 (D) 1,944

142. Which of the following sentences is true?
(A) $3 < -5$ (B) $-9 > -7$
(C) $-6 < -4$ (D) $-8 > 0$

143. If the sum of $\frac{1}{4}$ and $\frac{5}{12}$ of a number is subtracted from that number, the result is
(A) $\frac{2}{3}$ of the number
(B) $\frac{1}{3}$ of the number
(C) $\frac{5}{6}$ of the number
(D) $\frac{3}{4}$ of the number

144. A chemist has a solution of 20 pints of acid and water that is 15% pure acid. If the chemist adds 14 pints of pure acid to the solution, what percent of the new solution is acid?
(A) 40% (B) 30% (C) 45% (D) 50%

145. Mr. Jabal earns $16.50 per hour. If he works 8 hours and 20 minutes, he earns
(A) $137.50 (B) $127.50 (C) $98.50
(D) $76.50

146. The measures of the acute angles of a right triangle are in the ratio 3:2. What is the measure of the smaller acute angle?
(A) 36° (B) 45° (C) 54° (D) 45°

147. If a number is divisible by 6 and 4, it is also divisible by
(A) 9 (B) 18 (C) 16 (D) 12

148. The coordinates of a point equidistant from points $A(3,4)$ and $B(3,14)$ are
(A) (3,9) (B) (3,10) (C) (3,7) (D) (9,3)

149. Ms. Lucas's home is assessed at $85,000. Her real estate tax at the rate of 2.1% is
(A) $1700 (B) $1785 (C) $178.50
(D) $17,850

150. The difference between $\frac{1}{3}$ of a number and $\frac{1}{4}$ of the same number is 6. What is the number?
(A) 60 (B) 84 (C) 72 (D) 80

151. A man buys a car for $15,000. He makes a down payment of $5400 and arranges to pay the balance in 24 equal monthly installments. How much is each monthly installment?
(A) $450 (B) $400 (C) $500 (D) $475

152. The length of a diagonal of rectangle *ABCD* is 20 feet, and the length of a side of the rectangle is 12 feet.

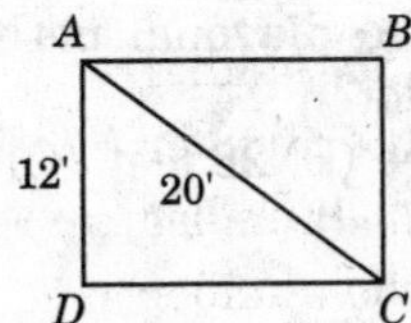

The area of the rectangle is
(A) 240 square feet
(B) 320 square feet
(C) 192 square feet
(D) 48 square feet

153. If 3 times a number is subtracted from 48, the result is 33. What is the number?
(A) 27 (B) 5 (C) 15 (D) 25

154. The Palace Movie Theater seats 960 people and charges $6 per seat except for senior citizens, who pay $4 per seat. At one performance $\frac{7}{8}$ of the seats were occupied. Of the occupied seats $\frac{1}{6}$ were taken by senior citizens. What were the total receipts for this performance?
(A) $4760 (B) $4200 (C) $5760
(D) $4800

155. The average of $\frac{1}{4}$ and $\frac{1}{6}$ is
(A) $\frac{5}{12}$ (B) $\frac{5}{24}$ (C) $\frac{5}{16}$ (D) $\frac{5}{6}$

156. A square and equilateral triangle have equal perimeters. Which of the following is true?
(A) A side of the square is larger than a side of the triangle.
(B) A side of the triangle is larger than a side of the square.
(C) The area of the square is greater than the area of the triangle.
(D) The square and the triangle have equal areas.

157. The Graham family spends 30% of its budget on rent. On a circle graph the measure of the angle at the center of the circle used to show the rent portion of Graham's budget would be
(A) 30° (B) 60° (C) 100° (D) 108°

158. Which one of the following is correct?
(A) $\frac{5}{8} > \frac{2}{3} > \frac{4}{7}$
(B) $\frac{2}{3} > \frac{5}{8} > \frac{4}{7}$
(C) $\frac{4}{7} > \frac{5}{8} > \frac{2}{3}$
(D) $\frac{2}{3} > \frac{4}{7} > \frac{5}{8}$

159. $(2^4 + 9) \div 5 =$
(A) 5 (B) 1 (C) 16 (D) 15

160 If 40% of a number is 12, find 150% of the number
(A) 30 (B) 50 (C) 45 (D) 60

161. If 15 is subtracted from twice a number, the result is 7. What is the number?
(A) 4 (B) 11 (C) 22 (D) 30

162. In an isosceles triangle, the ratio of the measure of the vertex angle to the measure of one of the equal base angles is 4:3. What is the measure of the vertex angle?
(A) 54° (B) 36° (C) 72° (D) 80°

163. The circumference of a circle whose area is 25π square inches is
(A) 5 inches (B) 10π inches
(C) 5π inches (D) 20π inches

164. Which of the following is the root of the equation $x - (9 - 2x) = 6$?
(A) 10 (B) 4 (C) 3 (D) 5

165. To pay for house repairs, Mr. Bond borrows $6000 from his bank for one year. If his interest rate is 12% simple interest, how much does Mr. Bond have to repay the bank at the end of the year?
(A) $720 (B) $6000 (C) $6500 (D) $6720

166. A chemist has 20 pints of acid that is 50% pure. How much water must he add to make the mixture 40% pure?
(A) 5 pints (B) 10 pints (C) 8 pints (D) 15 pints

167. A motorist driving a compact car gets 36 miles to a gallon of gas on the road and 22 miles to a gallon in city driving. How many gallons of gas does this motorist use in driving 234 miles on the road and 176 miles in the city?
(A) $6\frac{1}{2}$ (B) 12 (C) $14\frac{1}{2}$ (D) $16\frac{1}{2}$

168. Barbara has 7 white blouses and 3 blue blouses hanging in her closet. If she selects a blouse at random, what is the probability that her choice is a blue blouse?
(A) $\frac{3}{10}$ (B) $\frac{3}{7}$ (C) $\frac{4}{10}$ (D) $\frac{4}{7}$

169. Mr. Diego wishes to buy curtain material for 6 windows. Each window requires 4 yards and 2 feet of material. How much material should he buy?
(A) 26 yards (B) 25 yards 2 feet (C) 28 yard (D) 24 yards 1 foot

170. A rectangular garden plot is 24 feet long and 18 feet wide. What is the length of a diagonal path across this garden plot?
(A) 25 feet (B) 28 feet (C) 30 feet (D) 32 feet

TEST FIVE WRITING THE ESSAY

Time limit: 30 minutes

The essay is assigned to give you an opportunity to show how well you can write. You should, therefore, take care to express your thoughts on the topic clearly and effectively. How well you write is much more important than how much you write, but to cover the topic adequately you will want to write more than one paragraph.

Write your essay on the sheets of paper provided or use some of your own. Do any scratch-work planning on this page.

It is important to remember that what you write will be read by someone who is not familiar with your handwriting. Write or print so that your essay is legible.

DIRECTIONS: Using two sheets of lined theme paper, plan and write an essay on the topic assigned below. DO NOT WRITE ON ANOTHER TOPIC. AN ESSAY ON ANOTHER TOPIC IS NOT ACCEPTABLE. You have 30 minutes for this section of the test.

One of the most critical decisions to be faced by teenagers can be summarized by two conflicting statements.

Grasshopper: "You're young only once. Enjoy yourself now. Who knows what tomorrow may bring?"

Ant: "Plan ahead. Do your best in your school work. Study! Without a good education, you will be handicapped for the rest of your life. There will always be time for fun—later. You can't both have your cake and eat it."

Prompt: Write an essay stating the advice you would give to teenagers of today on these two points of view. Support your opinion with specific examples from history, current affairs, or personal observations.

Answers to Practice ISEE 2

TEST ONE VERBAL ABILITY

1. **D**	5. **A**	9. **C**	13. **A**	17. **B**
2. **C**	6. **B**	10. **A**	14. **D**	18. **D**
3. **B**	7. **D**	11. **C**	15. **A**	19. **C**
4. **C**	8. **C**	12. **B**	16. **C**	20. **A**

Rating Your Results

Middle Level

Superior	16–20 correct
Average	12–15 correct
Below Average	11 or fewer correct

Upper Level

Superior	17–20 correct
Average	13–16 correct
Below Average	12 or fewer correct

Material to Review: Chapter 4

21. **C**	25. **A**	29. **B**	33. **C**	37. **B**
22. **B**	26. **D**	30. **D**	34. **A**	38. **A**
23. **A**	27. **A**	31. **D**	35. **D**	39. **B**
24. **C**	28. **A**	32. **B**	36. **A**	40. **C**

Rating Your Results

Middle Level

Superior	15–20 correct
Average	11–14 correct
Below Average	10 or fewer correct

Upper Level

Superior	16–20 correct
Average	12–15 correct
Below Average	11 or fewer correct

Material to Review: Chapter 4

TEST TWO QUANTITATIVE ABILITY

41. **C**	49. **C**	57. **C**	65. **B**	73. **D**
42. **B**	50. **A**	58. **D**	66. **A**	74. **C**
43. **D**	51. **A**	59. **B**	67. **B**	75. **A**
44. **A**	52. **C**	60. **A**	68. **C**	76. **B**
45. **C**	53. **B**	61. **A**	69. **A**	77. **D**
46. **A**	54. **A**	62. **B**	70. **D**	78. **B**
47. **A**	55. **C**	63. **C**	71. **A**	79. **A**
48. **D**	56. **D**	64. **D**	72. **C**	80. **C**

Rating Your Results

Superior	34–40 correct
Average	26–33 correct
Below Average	25 or fewer correct

Material to Review: Chapters 8–14

TEST THREE READING COMPREHENSION

81. **C**	89. **B**	97. **D**	105. **D**	113. **C**
82. **B**	90. **C**	98. **C**	106. **A**	114. **D**
83. **C**	91. **D**	99. **D**	107. **C**	115. **B**
84. **B**	92. **B**	100. **B**	108. **A**	116. **B**
85. **C**	93. **C**	101. **C**	109. **A**	117. **C**
86. **D**	94. **A**	102. **C**	110. **C**	118. **A**
87. **A**	95. **B**	103. **C**	111. **C**	119. **D**
88. **C**	96. **B**	104. **B**	112. **B**	120. **D**

Rating Your Results

Middle Level

Superior	35–40 correct
Average	27–33 correct
Below Average	26 or fewer correct

Upper Level

Superior	36–40 correct
Average	28–35 correct
Below Average	27 or fewer correct

Material to Review: Chapter 5

TEST FOUR MATHEMATICS ACHIEVEMENT

121. **C**	131. **D**	141. **D**	151. **B**	161. **B**
122. **B**	132. **C**	142. **C**	152. **C**	162. **C**
123. **A**	133. **C**	143. **B**	153. **B**	163. **B**
124. **D**	134. **A**	144. **D**	154. **A**	164. **D**
125. **A**	135. **D**	145. **A**	155. **B**	165. **D**
126. **A**	136. **B**	146. **A**	156. **B**	166. **A**
127. **B**	137. **C**	147. **D**	157. **D**	167. **C**
128. **A**	138. **C**	148. **A**	158. **B**	168. **A**
129. **C**	139. **C**	149. **B**	159. **A**	169. **C**
130. **B**	140. **B**	150. **C**	160. **C**	170. **C**

Rating Your Results

Superior	42–50 correct
Average	32–41 correct
Below Average	31 or fewer correct

Material to Review: Chapters 8–14

Explanations

TEST ONE

21. (**C**) Key words: guard, warned, alone, fights. An *aggressor* is one who starts trouble.
22. (**B**) Key words: glove, gift, member, Little League. An *appropriate* gift is one that is suitable, as is a glove for a ballplayer.
23. (**A**) Key words: five-year-olds, strange sights and sounds, carnival. A *bewildered* child is puzzled and confused.
24. (**C**) Key words: reward, careful planning, troops, suffered war. Careful planning reduces the *casualties,* that is, the dead and wounded.
25. (**A**) Key words: temper, erupts, slightest provocation. A *fiery* temper erupts with slight cause.
26. (**D**) Key words: juggler, keep eight balls in the air. A person who is *adept* shows great skill.
27. (**A**) Key words: severe rains, tractor, stuck. *Mire* is soft, deep mud, which is frequently encountered after heavy downpours.
28. (**A**) Key words: speaker, stumbled along, not prepared. The lack of preparation was clear *(obvious)* from the speaker's poor performance.
29. (**B**) Key words: need, attention, every occasion. The friends were turned off *(alienated)* by the attention-seeking behavior.
30. (**D**) Key words: loggers, heavy logs, twigs. The loggers were big and strong, that is, *burly.*
31. (**D**) Key words: invaders, countryside, search. *Forays* are raids; *booty* is plunder, things stolen. None of the other pairs makes sense in the context.
32. (**B**) Key words: leader, rescue party, parents. The reader received (was the *recipient* of) gifts from the *grateful* parents of the rescued children.
33. (**C**) Key words: story, faith and fortune, scoundrel. The *sad* story tells of a family cheated by a crooked (*unscrupulous*) villain.
34. (**A**) Key words: community, for sale. *Merchandise* was for sale at the community fair *(bazaar).*
35. (**D**) Key words: weeks of searching, scraps of food, dogs, attack. The *gaunt* starving dogs had forayed in *vain* for sufficient food.
36. (**A**) Key words: interest speaker, on and on. The audience's interest *flagged* as the speaker continued too long in a monotonous voice *(droned).*
37. (**B**) Key words: statement, selfish motives, decision. He felt injured and angry (*resentful*) when she implied that he was interested in no one but himself (*imputed* selfish motives).
38. (**A**) Key words: ignorance, modern business methods. She was *abysmally* (profoundly) ignorant about how to run a business and *ruined* the company.
39. (**B**) Key words: insisted, details, accident, twelve lives. An accident that claims twelve lives is *horrifying,* and the details are likely to be *lurid* (gruesome).
40. (**C**) Key words: device, selects, cooks, serves. She had succeeded in producing a device that worked (had *perfected* it) and that performed astonishing feats (was *ingenious).*

TEST TWO

41. **(C)**
$$\begin{array}{r} 0.005 \\ 200\overline{)1.000} \\ \underline{1000} \end{array}$$
$\frac{1}{200} = 0.005$

42. **(B)** The product of 12 and 11 = $12 \times 11 = 132$.
The product of 8 and 9 = $8 \times 9 = 72$
$132 - 72 = 60$

43. **(D)** In $\triangle ABC$ we may regard $\overline{AC}$ as the base and $\overline{BC}$ as the altitude.

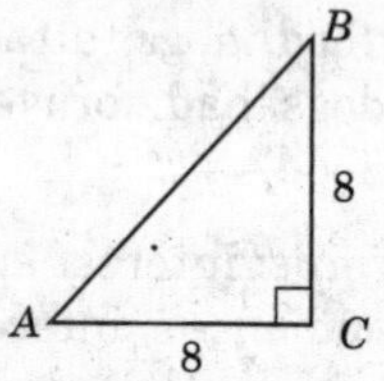

Area of $\triangle ABC = \frac{1}{2}(8)(8) = 32$ square inches

44. **(A)** Each inch on the map represents 300 miles.
$300 \times 4\frac{1}{2} = 300 \times \frac{9}{2} = 1350$ miles

45. **(C)** $(3 \times 10^3) + (2 \times 10^2) + 5 = 3205$
$(4 \times 10^3) + (2 \times 10^2) + (7 \times 10) = 4270$
$3205 + 4270 = 7475$

46. **(A)** Let x = cost of table
$0.05x = 8.75$
$5x = 875$
$x = \$175$

47. **(A)** By definition 1 kilogram = 1000 grams.

48. **(D)** $4x - 3 = 21$
$4x = 21 + 3 = 24$
$x = 6$
$x^2 + x = (6)^2 + 6$
$x^2 + x = 36 + 6$
$x^2 + x = 42$

49. **(C)** Let x = number of seats in the theater
Then $\frac{1}{3}x = 200$
$x = 600$

50. **(A)** $60 \times 32 = 1920$ students in the school
$1920 \div 30$ = number of classes needed with reduced size
$1920 \div 30 = 64$
Therefore, $64 - 60 = 4$ new classes needed

51. **(A)** 3 pounds 6 ounces = $3\frac{6}{16}$ pounds = $3\frac{3}{8}$ pounds
$3\frac{3}{8} = \frac{27}{8}$
$\frac{27}{8} \times 0.88 = \$2.97$

52. **(C)** $18 \times 20 = 360$ man-hours needed to complete the job
Let x = number of hours needed for 15 men to complete the job
$15x = 360$
$x = 360 \div 15$
$x = 24$

53. **(B)** $\frac{5}{12}, \frac{4}{9}, \frac{3}{4}$
Multiples of 12 are 12, 24, (36), 48 ....
Multiples of 9 are 9, 18, 27, (36), 45 ....
Multiples of 4 are 4, 8, 12, 16, 20, 24, 28, 32, (36).
Since 36 is the first number that appears in all three set of multiples, the L.C.D. is 36.

54. **(A)** $96 \div 6 - 2 \times 7$
We first divide ($96 \div 6 = 16$) and then multiply ($2 \times 7 = 14$) to obtain $16 - 14 = 2$.

55. **(C)** The measure of a right angle is 90°. The measure of an acute angle is between 0° and 90°.
The sum of the measures of a right angle and an acute angle is between 90° and 180°. This sum is the measure of an obtuse angle.

56. **(D)**

$\overline{AC} = \overline{AB} + \overline{BC}$
$\overline{BD} = \overline{BC} + \overline{CD}$
The intersection of $\overline{AC}$ and $\overline{BD}$ is $\overline{BC}$.

57. **(C)** If a die is rolled, there are 6 ways that it can turn up: 1, 2, 3 4, 5, 6.
Since 2 is one of the 6 ways, the probability of obtaining a 2 is $\frac{1}{6}$.

58. **(D)** Let x = dollars spent for coat
And $2y$ = dollars spent for sweaters
Then $x + 2y$ = total dollars spent

59. **(B)** The shaded portion is equal to the difference between the area of the square and the areas of the four quarter circles at the corners.

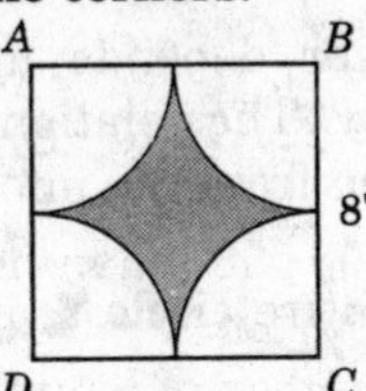

Area of square = $(8)^2 = 64$ square inches
The four quarter circles add up to one circle of radius 4.
Area of this circle = 16π
Area of shaded portion = $64 - 16\pi$

60. **(A)** We list the times that the three bells ring starting with noon.
First bell: 12, 12:30, 1:00, 1:30, 2:00, 2:30, 3:00,...
Second bell: 12, 12:40, 1:20, 2:00, 2:40,...
Third bell: 12, 1:00, 2:00,...
We see that all three bells ring again at 2:00 P.M.

61. **(A)** $a^2 + ab = (-3)^2 + (-3)(2) = 9 - 6 = 3$
$b^2 + ab = 2^2 + (-3)(2) = 4 - 6 = -2$
The quantity in Column A is larger than the quantity in Column B.

62. **(B)** $36 \div 4 - 7 = 9 - 7 = 2$
$25 - 6 \div 3 = 25 - 2 = 23$
The quantity in Column B is larger than the quantity in Column A.

63. **(C)** $3x - 2 = 10$
$3x = 10 + 2 = 12$
$x = 4$
$5y + 1 = 21$
$5y = 21 - 1 = 20$
$y = 4$
The quantities in Column A and Column B are equal.

64. **(D)** Let $x = 10$ and $y = 2$
Then $x + y = 12$ and $x - y = 8$
In this case, $(x + y) > x - y$.
Let $x = 5$ and $y = -3$
Then $x + y = 5 + (-3) = 2$ and
$x - y = 5 - (-3) = 5 + 3 = 8$
In this case, $(x - y) > (x + y)$.
We see that, for some values of x and y, $(x + y) > (x - y)$.
For other values of x and y, $(x - y) > (x + y)$.
The relationship cannot be determined from the information given.

65. **(B)** 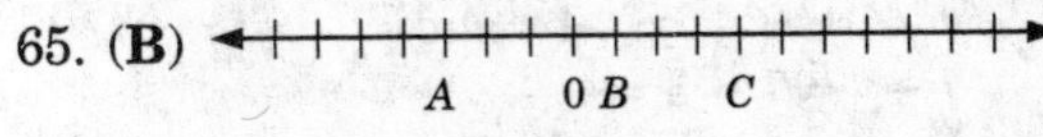

A is paired with –4.
B is paired with +1.
C is paired with +4.
$A + B = -4 + 1 = -3$
$B + C = +1 + 4 = +5$
Thus $(B + C) > (A + B)$
The quantity in Column B is greater than the quantity in Column A.

66. **(A)** $DA + DB > AB$. The sum of the measures of two sides of a triangle is greater than the measure of the third side.

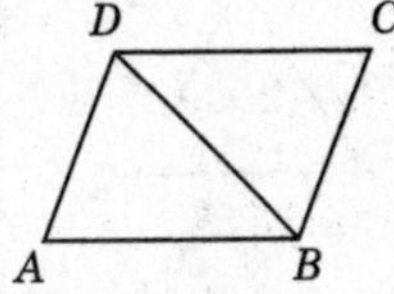

$AB = DC$
Therefore, $DA + DB > DC$
The quantity in Column A is greater than the quantity in Column B.

67. **(B)** John's average = $\frac{85+75+50+70+90+65}{6}$
$= 72\frac{1}{2}$
Roberto's average = $\frac{90+90+65+45+80+75}{6}$
$= 74\frac{1}{6}$
The quantity in Column B is greater than the quantity in Column A.

68. **(C)** For Column A, $8 \times 7 = 56$
$4(6 \div 1) = 4 \times 6 = 24$
$56 - 24 = 32$
For Column B, $2^5 = 2 \times 2 \times 2 \times 2 \times 2 = 32$
The quantity in Column A is equal to the quantity in Column B.

69. **(A)** $x - y = 3$
$2x + y = 9$
If we add these two equations, we have
$3x = 12$
$x = 4$
Substituting 4 for x in the first equation gives $4 - y = 3$ and $y = 1$. The quantity in Column A is greater than the quantity in Column B.

70. **(D)** If $y = 10$, then
$y - 7 = 10 - 7 = 3$ and $7 - y - 10 = -3$
In this case, $y - 7 > 7 - y$.
If $y = 3$, then
$y - 7 = 3 - 7 = -4$ and
$7 - y = 7 - 3 = 4$
In this case, $y - 7 < 7 - y$.
Thus, in some cases $y - 7 > 7 - y$, and in other cases $7 - y > y - 7$.
The relationship cannot be determined from the information given.

71. **(A)** Since $AB = AC$, m $\angle B$ = m $\angle C$.
Since $BC > AB$, m $\angle A$ > m $\angle C$.
Therefore, m $\angle C$ > m $\angle A$. In a triangle, the greater angle lies opposite the greater side.

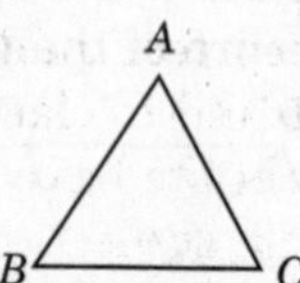

The quantity in Column A is greater than the quantity in Column B.

72. **(C)** Let x = the number
Quantity in Column A = $\frac{x}{2} - \frac{x}{3}$
Quantity in Column B = $\frac{x}{6}$
The L.C.D. = 6
$\frac{x}{2} = \frac{3x}{6}$ and $\frac{x}{3} = \frac{2x}{6}$
$\frac{x}{2} - \frac{x}{3} = \frac{3x}{6} - \frac{2x}{6} = \frac{x}{6}$, or $\frac{1}{6}$ of the number, or $\frac{x}{6}$
The quantity in Column A is equal to the Column B.

73. **(D)** $3 > y > -2$; that is, $y > -2$ and less than 3.
If we let $y = 1$, then $\frac{y}{2} = \frac{1}{2}$ and $\frac{2}{y} = 2$
In this case, $\frac{2}{y} > \frac{y}{2}$
If we let $y = -1$, then $\frac{y}{2} = \frac{-1}{2}$ and $\frac{2}{y} = -2$.
In this case, $\frac{y}{2} > \frac{2}{y}$
Thus, we cannot tell whether $\frac{y}{2}$ or $\frac{2}{y}$ is greater.
The answer depends upon the value taken for y. The relationship cannot be determined from the information given.

74. **(C)** The entire circle represents a rotation of 360°.

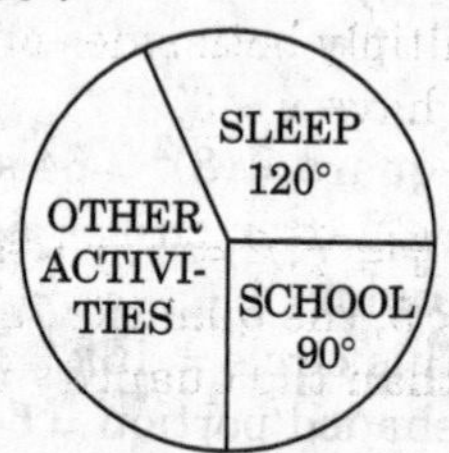

$\frac{120}{360}$ represents sleep time.
$\frac{120}{360} = \frac{1}{3}$, $\frac{1}{3}$ of 24 hours = 8 hours
$\frac{90}{360}$ represents school time.
$\frac{90}{360} = \frac{1}{4}$, $\frac{1}{4}$ of 24 hours = 6 hours
Ratio of sleep time to school time = 8:6, or 4:3
The quantity in Column A is equal to the quantity in Column B.

75. **(A)** $2^6 \div 2 = 2^{6-2} = 2^4$
$2^4 = 16$
The quantity in Column A ($2^6 \div 2^2 = 16$) is greater than the quantity in Column B (8).

76. **(B)** In right triangle DAB,
$(AB)^2 + (AD)^2 = (DB)^2$
$(AB)^2 + 6^2 = 10^2$
$(AB)^2 + 36 = 100$
$(AB)^2 = 100 - 36 = 64$
$AB = 8$

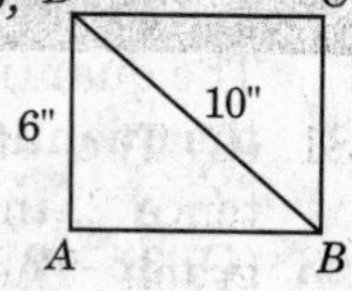

Perimeter of rectangle $ABCD$ = 6 + 8 + 8 + 8 = 28 inches
The quantity in Column B is greater than the quantity in Column A.

77. **(D)** $3x - 2 > 10$
$3x > 10 + 2$
$3x > 12$
$x > 4$
If $x = 4.1$, then $5x^2 = 84.05$
In this case, $5x^2 < 100$.
If $x = 6$, then $5x^2 - 180$.
In this case, $5x^2 > 100$.
Thus we cannot tell which answer depends upon the value of x.
The relationship cannot be determined from the information given.

78. **(B)** $\frac{x}{6} = \frac{1}{2}$
If we multiply both sides of the equation by 6, we have $x = 3$.
$\frac{x+3}{3} = \frac{y}{2}$
$\frac{3+3}{3} = \frac{y}{2}, \frac{6}{3} = \frac{y}{2}, 2 = \frac{y}{2}, y = 4$
Since $4 < 5$, the quantity in Column B is greater than the quantity in Column A.

79. **(A)** Let x = number of miles in complete trip
$\frac{5}{8}x = 145$
$x = 145 \div \frac{5}{8} = 145 \times \frac{8}{5} = 232$ miles
Since $232 > 230$, the quantity in Column A is greater than the quantity in Column B.

80. **(C)** Let x = amount of sugar to be used
We make the proportion: $\frac{8}{6} = \frac{2}{x}$
$8x = 2 \times 6 = 12$
$x = \frac{12}{8} = 1\frac{1}{2}$ ounces of sugar
The quantity in Column A is equal to the quantity in Column B.

TEST THREE

81. **(C)** The statement paraphrases sentence 2, the topic sentence of the paragraph. The other choices express only minor ideas.

82. **(B)** "the engine has a carburetor, which mixes the gasoline with air...."

83. **(C)** "... transmits its power through the transmission to the ... axle."

84. **(B)** "In order to produce mechanical energy .... the engine must burn fuel."

85. **(C)** Note "ignite the air-fuel mixture" in lines 8 and 9.

86. **(D)** "One theory ... in the Caucasus Mountains." A second theory "suggests Poland as the homeland."

87. **(A)** "...salmon and beech trees are found only in the area of modern Poland...."

88. **(C)** "... it is hard to determine which [theory] is more valid."

89. **(B)** Although "advocates" may sometimes have a legal connotation, nothing in this passage supports this interpretation of the word. None of the other choices makes sense.

90. **(C)** Caucacus Mountains to Anatolia to India is the route given in theory one.

91. **(D)** All three choices are mentioned in the passage.

92. **(B)** "... the King withdrew there away from the noise ... of the city."

93. **(C)** The attitude of the writer toward King Louis XIV is objective; he is not markedly approving, respectful, or condemnatory.

94. **(A)** Since they feel qualified to evaluate the king and to classify his power, political scientists have to be students of the political scene.

95. **(B)** Note "Similar convection currents take place ... in large bodies of water" (lines 19–21).

96. **(B)** "moving molecules actually impart their motion to other molecules...."

97. **(D)** The word *impart* means to pass on, to convey. The molecules pass on their motion to other molecules, and so forth.

98. **(C)** "The heat from the sun reaches the earth by radiation."

99. **(D)** "The new act ... any head of a family could become the owner ... if he worked the land for five years."

100. **(B)** The tone is factual; this passage consists of various items of information presented objectively.

101. **(C)** "Public lands" is defined in lines 9–11.

102. **(C)** "Together with the Pacific Railway Act [convenient transportation] the Homestead Act [free land] made certain that the West would be settled quickly."

103. **(C)** "... it was necessary to establish tracking stations in several strategic locations around the world."

104. **(B)** "Shuttles are launched ... to propel artificial satellites into space...."

105. **(D)** "Some of the satellites provide ... data on weather and conditions of the earth's surface."

106. **(A)** Natural satellites like our moon circle around planets.

107. **(C)** Pry bar = lever; bolt = screw; block and tackle = set of pulleys. Alternatively, the other choices can be eliminated because they involve complex, not simple, machines.

108. **(A)** Since the trunk would have to be raised considerably above ground level, a set of pulleys is the logical choice (see lines 8 and 10).

109. **(A)** Using the example given in the selection, divide the 60 pounds of weight by the 20 pounds of force. A mechanical advantage of three is needed to lift the 20-pound weight.

110. **(C)** Note sentence 2.

111. **(C)** The meaning can be inferred from sentence 1 or, alternatively, by eliminating the other choices as making no sense.

112. **(B)** With the increase of commerce in many different types of commodities, we can infer an increase in traders.

113. **(C)** "Influx" means flowing in. With all the wealth and trade *flowing into* China, Chinese products spread out into European markets thousands of miles away.

114. **(D)** "Second, an influx of silver brought by western traders gave great wealth...."

115. **(B)** The other three benefits are specifically mentioned in the passage.

116. **(B)** "The Inuit spend most of their time near the sea...."

117. **(C)** "one tribe, the Caribou Inuit, lives inland..."

118. **(A)** "... life in one village is, in many ways, very much like life in another...."

119. **(D)** "... expert in handling a kayak, or Inuit canoe."

120. **(D)** "Alaskan Inuit ... winter homes of turf and mud."

TEST FOUR

121. **(C)** The product of any real number and 0 is 0. Therefore, the given product is equal to 0.

122. **(B)** 62 pounds = 62×16 ounces = 992 ounces
The cook has $992 + 10 = 1002$ ounces of steak
$1002 \div 6 = 67$ servings

123. **(A)** $1'' = 6$ feet
$5'' = 30$ feet

124. **(D)** $3\frac{1}{4} = \frac{13}{4}$
$\frac{13}{4} \div \frac{1}{8} = \frac{13}{4} \times 8 = 26$

125. **(A)** 12 ounce = $\frac{12}{16}$ pound = $\frac{3}{4}$ pound
The chicken weighs $3\frac{3}{4}$ pounds = $\frac{15}{4}$ pounds.
$\frac{15}{4} \times 0.84 = \$3.15$

126. **(A)**

$$\begin{array}{r} 29 \\ 37\overline{)1090} \\ \underline{74} \\ 350 \\ \underline{333} \\ 17 \end{array}$$

The school has 37 classes with 29 in a class, but 17 students must be distributed in these classes. Thus, 17 classes must have 30 students each.

127. **(B)** If $\frac{1}{3}$ of the larger number is 5, then the larger number is $3 \times 5 = 15$.
The smaller number is 8 less than the larger number. Thus, the smaller number is $15 - 8 = 7$.

128. **(A)** 45% of 80 = $0.45 \times 80 = 36$
The selling price of the chair is $80 + 36$ = \$116.

129. **(C)** Let x = larger number
Then $57 - x$ = smaller number
Twice the smaller number = $2(57 - x)$
Three more than the larger number = $x + 3$
Thus, we have the equation
$2(57 - x) = x + 3$

130. **(B)** Let x = measure of the altitude of the triangle
Then area of triangle = $\frac{1}{2}(6)(x) = 3x$
Area of the square = $9 \times 9 = 81$ square inches
Since the two areas are equal, we have
$3x = 81$
$x = \frac{81}{3}$
$x = 27$

131. **(D)** m $\angle ADC$ + m $\angle CDB$ + $\angle BDA = 360°$ since the sum of the measure of the angles about a point in a plane = 360°.
Let m $\angle BDA = x$
Then m $\angle ADC = x$
Thus, $x + x + 140 = 360$
$2x + 140 = 360$
$2x = 360 - 140 = 220$
$x = 110$
The measure of $\angle BDA = 110°$

132. **(C)** $3 + 2x < 9$
$2x < 9 - 3$
$2x < 6$
$x < 3$
If x is a positive integer, $x = 1$ or 2.

133. **(C)** Let $5x$ = Edna's money
And $3x$ = Jill's money
Then $5x - 5 = 3x + 5$
$5x - 3x = 5 + 5$
$2x = 10$
$x = 5$
For Edna: $5x - 5 = 25 - 5 = \$20$
For Jill: $3x + 5 = 15 + 5 = \$20$

134. **(A)** New-job salary = 90% of old job salary
After 1 year
new-job salary = 90% + (25% of 90%)
new-job salary = 90% + $22\frac{1}{2}$% = $112\frac{1}{2}$%
The net result is an increase of $12\frac{1}{2}$% over old salary.

135. **(D)** Take, for example, the two-digit number 53.
That number with the digits reversed is 35.
$53 + 35 = 88$
88 is divisible by 11.

136. **(B)** $AB = 9 - 2 = 7$ units
$BC = 11 - 3 = 8$ units

C(9,11)
y
A(2,3) B(9,3)
x′ x
(0,0)
y′

Area of $\triangle ABC = \frac{1}{2}(8)(7) = 28$ square graph units

137. **(C)** The dealer bought 3 sweaters for \$65. He expects to sell the sweaters for \$35 each, or 3 for \$105.
Thus, for each 3 sweaters he sells, the dealer makes a profit of $105 - 65 = \$40$.
To make a profit of \$600, he must sell $600 \div 40$, or 15 sets, with 3 sweaters in each set.
In other words, he must sell $15 \times 3 = 45$ sweaters.

138. **(C)** If 85% of the seats are occupied, then 15% are unoccupied.
15% of 1200 = $0.15 \times 1200 = 180$

139. **(C)**
$3\overline{)165}$ = 55, $55 = 5 \times 11$
The prime factors of 165 are 3, 5, and 11.

140. **(B)** One meter, slightly larger than 1 yard, is equal to about 39.37 inches.

141. **(D)** The volume of the storage room is the product of the length, the width, and the height of the room:
$V = l \times w \times h$
In this case, $l = 18$, $w = 12$, and $h = 9$
Thus, $V = 1944$ cubic feet
The volume of each box = $1 \times 1 \times 1 = 1$ cube foot
$1944 \div 1 = 1944$ boxes may be stored in the room.

142. **(C)** We draw a diagram of the number line and locate –4 and –6 on it.

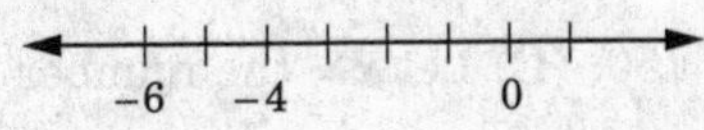

We see that –6 is located to the left of –4. Therefore, $-6 < -4$ is a true sentence. Of the other choices, $3 > -5$, $-9 < -7$, and $-8 < 0$.

143. **(B)** $\frac{1}{4}+\frac{5}{12}=\frac{3}{12}+\frac{5}{12}=\frac{8}{12}$

$1=\frac{12}{12}$, $\frac{12}{12}-\frac{8}{12}=\frac{4}{12}$

$\frac{4}{12}=\frac{1}{3}$

144. **(D)** 15% of 20 = $0.15 \times 20 = 3$ pints of acid in original mixture

$\frac{\text{Amount of acid in new mixture}}{\text{Total amount of new mixture}} = \frac{3+14}{20+14} = \frac{17}{34}$

$\frac{17}{34} = \frac{1}{2}$, or 50%

145. **(A)** 20 minutes = $\frac{20}{60} = \frac{1}{3}$ hour

$8\frac{1}{3} = \frac{25}{3}$ hours worked

$\frac{25}{3} \times 16.50 = \$137.50$

146. **(A)** Let $3x$= measure of larger angle
And $2x$ = measure of smaller angle

$3x + 2x = 90$
$5x = 90$
$x = 18$
$2x = 2(18) = 36°$

147. **(D)** If a number is divisible by 6, the number must be a multiple of 6: 6, 12, 18, 24,...
If a number is divisible by 4, it must be a multiple of 4: 4, 8, 12, 16,...
A number that is divisible by both 6 and 4 is 12.

148. **(A)** A point that is equidistant from points A and B is the midpoint of $\overline{AB}$ or C.

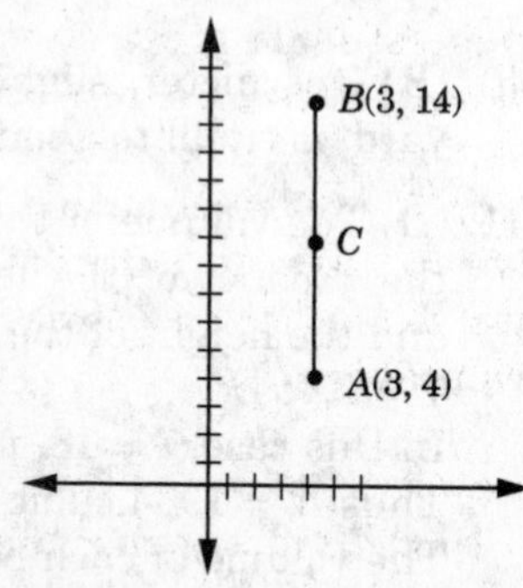

The distance from A or B along $\overline{AB}$ is $14 - 4 = 10$. Half this distance is 5.
$4 + 5 = 9$
The coordinates of point C are (3,9).

149. **(B)** $0.021 \times 85{,}000 = \$1785$

150. **(C)** Let x = the number

$\frac{x}{3} - \frac{x}{4} = 6$

If we multiply both sides of the equation by 12, we have

$4x - 3x = 72$
$x = 72$

151. **(B)** $15,000 − 5400 = $9600 balance on car
$9600 \div 24 = \$400$

152. **(C)** In right triangle ADC

$x^2 + (12)^2 = (20)^2$
$x^2 + 144 = 400$
$x^2 = 400 - 144 = 256$
$x = 16$

A B
12' 20'
D C

Area of rectangle = $12 \times 16 = 192$ square feet

153. **(B)** Let x = the number

$48 - 3x = 33$
$28 - 33 = 3x$
$3x = 15$
$x = 16$

154. **(A)** $960 \times \frac{7}{8} = 840$ seats occupied

$\frac{1}{6} \times 840 = 140$ seats occupied by senior citizens
$840 - 140 = 700$ seats occupied by others
$140 \times 4 = \$560$ receipts from seniors
$700 \times 6 = \$4200$ receipts from others
$560 + 4200 = \$4760$ total receipts

155. **(B)** $\frac{1}{4} + \frac{1}{6} = \frac{3}{12} + \frac{2}{12} = \frac{5}{12}$

$\frac{1}{2} \times \frac{5}{12} = \frac{5}{24}$

156. **(B)** Let the perimeter of the square and the perimeter of the equilateral triangle be 36 inches each. Then each side of the square will measure $36 \div 4 = 9$ inches, and each side of the equilateral triangle will measure $36 \div 3 = 12$ inches. Since $12 > 9$, a side of the triangle is larger than a side of the square. In general, if we let each perimeter be x inches, then each side of the square will measure $\frac{x}{4}$ inches and each side of the equilateral triangle will measure $\frac{x}{3}$ inches.

$\frac{x}{3}$ inches will always be greater than $\frac{x}{4}$ inches.

157. **(D)** A complete revolution around the center of a circle graph is 360°. To represent 30% of this, we have $0.3 \times 360 = 108°$.

158. **(B)** To compare the three fractions, we write them as decimals:
$\frac{5}{8} = 0.625$, $\frac{2}{3} = 0.66\frac{2}{3}$, $\frac{4}{7} = 0.57\frac{1}{7}$
We see that $\frac{2}{3}$ is the greatest, followed by $\frac{5}{8}$, and $\frac{4}{7}$ is the smallest. The correct sentence is $\frac{2}{3} > \frac{5}{8} > \frac{4}{7}$.

159. **(A)** $2^4 = 2 \times 2 \times 2 \times 2 = 16$
$16 + 9 = 25$
$25 \div 5 = 5$

160. **(C)** Let x = the number
Then $0.4x = 12$
$4x = 120$
$x = 30$
150% of $30 = 1.5 \times 30 = 45$

161. **(B)** Let x = the number
Then $2x - 15 = 7$
$2x = 7 + 15 = 22$
$x = 11$

162. **(C)** Let $4x$ = measure of the vertex angle
And $3x$ = measure of each base angle
$4x + 3x + 3x = 180$
$10x = 180$
$x = 18$
$4x = 72°$

163. **(B)** The formula for the area of a circle is $A = \pi r^2$.
In this case, $\pi r^2 = 25\pi$.
$r^2 = 25$
$r = 5$ inches
The formula for the circumference of a circle is $c = \pi r$.
$C = 2\pi \times 5 = 10\pi$ inches

164. **(D)** $x - (9 - 2x) = 6$
$x - 9 + 2x = 6$
$x + 2x = 6 + 9$
$3x = 15$
$x = 5$

165. **(D)** $6000 \times 0.12 = \$720.00$ simple interest
$6000 + 720 = \$6720$ repayment

166. **(A)** Amount of acid in mixture $= 20 \times \frac{1}{2}$ $= 10$ pints
Let x = amount of water added
$\frac{10}{20+x} = 40\% = \frac{4}{10}$
$4(20 + x) = 10 \times 10$
$80 + 4x = 100$
$4x = 100 - 80 = 20$
$x = 5$ pints

167. **(C)** On the road, gas used $= 234 \div 36 =$ 6.5 gallons
For city driving, gas used $= 176 \div 22 =$ 8 gallons
$6.5 + 8 = 14.5$ total gallons used

168. **(A)** Total number of blouses $= 7 + 3 = 10$
Number of blue blouses $= 3$
Probability of selecting a blue blouse $= \frac{3}{10}$

169. **(C)** There are 3 feet in 1 yard.
Each window requires $4\frac{2}{3}$ yards.
For 6 windows $6\left(4\frac{2}{3}\right)$ yards are needed.
$4\frac{2}{3} = \frac{14}{3}$
$6\left(\frac{14}{3}\right) = 28$ yards

170. **(C)** Let x = length of diagonal path.
In right triangle *BAD,*
$x^2 = (18)^2 + (24)^2$
$x^2 = 324 + 576$
$x^2 = 900$
$x = 30$
The path is 30 feet long.

TEST FIVE

Ideally, your essay should be evaluated by an experienced reader. Instead, you will find below a series of essays to which yours can be compared. This evaluation will give you a rough estimate of its standing in comparison with those written by other students. The ratings of the student essays are based solely on organization and content. You will have to have an experienced reader (perhaps a teacher) proofread your essay for technical errors.

Essay 1

I am tired of being told by my parents and relatives that I have to study. Where did study get them? They always tell the story of my grandfather, my mother's father. He grew up in the Great Depression. The family had to go on public assistance in order to pay the rent and put food on the table. The children never had the joy of wearing new clothes. All they got—and they were fortunate enough to get them—were hand-me-downs from sympathetic friends and relatives.

Anyway, most of the children had to leave school even before graduating from high school and get jobs so that they could help support the family. None of my aunts had a chance to go to college. Of my uncles only one, the youngest, went on to get a degree and become an engineer.

Despite all of these hardships, the family did well. They were all able to get good jobs and learn a trade that made them most comfortable. In fact, my uncle, the engineer, made most of his money after he quit his job and went to work with one of his brothers. This is why we should realize that we don't live for tomorrow. We live for today!

ANALYSIS: ____________________

RATING: ____________________

Essay 2

I don't know whether I am an ant or a grasshopper. I really think that I am a little of each, and I think that my solution is the one that could benefit every teenager who accepted it.

I learned early in life that most danger lies in going to an extreme. My motto is: Moderation in all things. Let's take education as an example. I know that all work and no play can make me a dull boy indeed. I know that too much relaxation and pleasure-seeking can make both my mind and body flabby. So I worked out a solution.

What is my solution? I am a budget bug. I try to plan my time in big units, and I give each unit an approximate amount of time. I make a list of things I have to do in, for example, the next few days. I then allot so much of my afterschool hours to each. If I have forgotten something, or something comes up, I rearrange but I do not omit.

If budgeting leaves too many hard choices, I discuss the timing with my parents, and they help me think my way to a practical solution. I get the joy of being able to do all the things I must do, and almost all the things that I enjoy doing.

ANALYSIS: ____________________

RATING: ____________________

Essay 3

Wherever teenagers turn today, they find discouraging signals that point to a bleak future. The fear of an accidental or planned setting-off of nuclear bombs that could blow up the Earth is ever-present. The world is being changed so rapidly by new technologies that any education we receive today will be useless tomorrow. If the dangers are so great and time spent in educating ourselves is futile, then why should we plan for the future?

This question is not unrealistic, especially since the world of pleasure has so much to offer. We could spend these years as couch potatoes glued to the seat facing the one-eyed monster, the TV set. We could spend our time with our friends experimenting with the offerings of the drug world. We could hitchhike and see the world. We could...

However, let us allow sanity into the picture. Education does not mean the facts we forget so easily. It does mean an attitude and a process. By studying we learn to use our minds and we learn to look ahead and enjoy the unfolding world; we join the civilized human race. And as for the nuclear threat, as real as it is, war has always been with us. We must live on faith that sanity will prevail.

This last paragraph offers a much more promising prescription than the one that advocates not even trying to know who we are and what the world is all about. As you can see, I am all for doing what youth must do: prepare for the future as best as we can.

ANALYSIS: ____________________

RATING: ____________________

Essay 4

The problem that we are discussing today is not a new one. Youth through the ages have had to decide whether they should spend their time in enjoying the pleasures of life or should put the acquiring of skills and knowledge as their top priority so that they will be better adapted to the obligations of coming adulthood. What advice would you give to the teenagers of today?

People who believe in the implications of the saying that you are young only once sound sensible when the advice is given to the young. But when the once-young reach their twenties and early maturity, they are severely handicapped by the lack of education and skills they should have learned. "Why didn't our parents and teachers warn us about the many doors closed to us!" they moan.

Youth is the time for learning how best you can fit into the world of work and into the social structure of the community in which you live. A second opportunity may come, but at an even greater cost.

My advice is loud and clear. Prepare when you are young for your future, and your future will contain enough satisfactions and pleasures to more than compensate for the time spent in preparing for responsible adulthood.

ANALYSIS: ______________________

____

____

RATING: ______________________

Essay 5

Some people feel that teenagers, with all their energy and enthusiasms, should spend their time seeking pleasure: going in for sports, socializing, traveling, developing hobbies, learning how to live with their peers. They will have time later on to adjust to the responsibilities of adulthood.

Other people feel that the teen years should be spent in formal learning. To them it is the time to learn who you are. It is the time to plan for career selection and to learn about the adult world ahead. Pleasure-seeking should not be a serious consideration.

What advice would I give? I feel that the youth who are motivated only by self-pleasuring have been dealt a bad deal. Too many of them have turned to drugs, pornography, and cynicism. Too many of them have very early ruined the physical body that is their only admission card to life ahead. Too many of them lack the skills and knowledge needed in adult life.

My advice is simple: School is for learning who you are and preparing for who you will be. Take full advantage now!

ANALYSIS: ______________________

____

____

RATING: ______________________

Essay 6

I have always thought that the story of the ant and the grasshopper had an element of truth in it. But I think that it can lead us into a dangerous position if we accept either one of these extremes as role models.

Most of us know that spending all of our time watching TV, socializing with fellow club members, and avoiding as much schoolwork as possible is a sure path to difficulty and failure. Most of us know also that spending all of our time in studying and in reading may lead to academic honors, but the lack of contact with our peers will result in agonizing loneliness.

The formula for success in high school and for the satisfaction that such success can give us lies somewhere between these two extremes. *Where* is different for each of us.

Your parents, teachers, friends, and you yourself let you know continually whether you are spending too much time in your pursuit of fun or of study. If you don't believe me, just listen! Of course, the final decision is yours; but these voices are there trying to direct you. Listen to them!

ANALYSIS: ______________________

____

____

RATING: ______________________

Evaluation of Other Students' Essays

Essay 1. The essay is divided into three paragraphs. Except for the last two sentences, the contents of the essay are not related to the given topic. Possibly the writer was too ambitious and hoped to write a much longer essay for which the present material would be the foundation.
Rating: Below average

Essay 2. The ideas flow logically through the four paragraphs. The contents, however, are mainly generalizations. The writer never connects the "I" doing the writing

with the "you" [teenagers of today] required by the prompt. The essay centers around the advantages of budgeting to the writer and only implies the advice that should be explicitly stated.
Rating: Average

Essay 3. The essay consists of four well-developed and clearly connected paragraphs. The sentences show excellent variety, and the vocabulary is mature. The writer does not allude to grasshoppers and ants, but ends with an appropriate thesis.
Rating: Excellent

Essay 4. This essay almost sounds like a sermon. The four paragraphs are clearly connected. They lead to a definite thesis. There are many generalizations, but they are forcibly expressed. The assignment is clearly handled. The reader must realize that this essay was planned and written in 30 minutes.
Rating: Excellent

Essay 5. The essay shows that the writer had a full awareness of what was required by the topic. The paragraphing and the choice of words are excellent. The length is considerably shorter than many others. This is a good example that some people can say much more in few words!
Rating: Superior

Essay 6. This essay bears the stamp of originality from the first sentence to its most unusual conclusion. The choice of language and the sentence structure reveal a student with rare potential.
Rating: Excellent

Evaluation of Your Own Essay

Weaknesses ______________________

Strengths ______________________

It is closest to number ________ of the student essays because ______________________

I would rate it ______________________

I could have improved it by ____________
____
____

MAXIMIZE YOUR MATH SKILLS!

BARRON'S EASY WAY SERIES

Specially structured to maximize learning with a minimum of time and effort, these books promote fast skill building through lively cartoons and other fun features.

ALGEBRA THE EASY WAY
Fourth Edition
Douglas Downing, Ph.D.
In this one-of-a-kind algebra text, all the fundamentals are covered in a delightfully illustrated adventure story. Equations, exponents, polynomials, and more are explained. 320 pp. (0-7641-1972-9)
$14.95, Can. $21.95

CALCULUS THE EASY WAY
Third Edition
Douglas Downing, Ph.D.
Here, a journey through a fantasy land leads to calculus mastery. All principles are taught in an easy-to-follow adventure tale. Included are numerous exercises, diagrams, and cartoons which aid comprehension. 228 pp. (0-8120-9141-8)
$14.95, Can. $21.95

GEOMETRY THE EASY WAY
Third Edition
Lawrence Leff
While other geometry books simply summarize basic principles, this book focuses on the "why" of geometry: why you should approach a problem a certain way, and why the method works. Each chapter concludes with review exercises. 288 pp. (0-7641-0110-2)
$14.95, Can. $21.00

TRIGONOMETRY THE EASY WAY
Third Edition
Douglas Downing, Ph.D.
In this adventure story, the inhabitants of a faraway kingdom use trigonometry to solve their problems. Covered is all the material studied in high school or first-year college classes. Practice exercises, explained answers, and illustrations enhance understanding. 288 pp. (0-7641-1360-7)
$14.95, Can. $21.00

BARRON'S MATHEMATICS STUDY DICTIONARY
Frank Tapson, with consulting author, Robert A. Atkins
A valuable homework helper and classroom supplement for middle school and high school students. Presented here are more than 1,000 math definitions, along with worked-out examples. Illustrative charts and diagrams cover everything from geometry to statistics to charting vectors. 128 pp. (0-7641-0303-2) $11.95, Not Available in Canada

ESSENTIAL MATH
Second Edition
Edward Williams and Robert A. Atkins
Basic math principles everyone should know are made easy by being put into the context of real-life situations. Games and puzzles help make math interesting. Practice exercises appear at the end of every chapter. 384 pp. (0-8120-1337-9)
$14.95, Can. $21.00

Books may be purchased at your bookstore, or by mail from Barron's. Enclose check or money order for total amount plus sales tax where applicable and 18% for postage (minimum charge $5.95). NY State, Michigan, and California residents add sales tax. All books are paperback editions. Prices subject to change without notice.

Barron's Educational Series, Inc. (#44) R 8/04
250 Wireless Boulevard
Hauppauge, New York 11788
In Canada: Georgetown Book Warehouse
34 Armstrong Avenue • Georgetown, Ontario L7G 4R9
Visit our web site at: www.barronseduc.com